ISBN 978-1-5278-1746-3
PIBN 10894313

For support please visit www.forgottenbooks.com

1 MONTH OF
FREE
READING

at

www.ForgottenBooks.com

By purchasing this book you are eligible for one month membership to ForgottenBooks.com, giving you unlimited access to our entire collection of over 1,000,000 titles via our web site and mobile apps.

To claim your free month visit:

www.forgottenbooks.com/free894313

English
Français
Deutsche
Italiano
Español
Português

www.forgottenbooks.com

Mythology Photography **Fiction**
Fishing Christianity **Art** Cooking
Essays Buddhism Freemasonry
Medicine **Biology** Music **Ancient
Egypt** Evolution Carpentry Physics
Dance Geology **Mathematics** Fitness
Shakespeare **Folklore** Yoga Marketing
Confidence Immortality Biographies
Poetry **Psychology** Witchcraft
Electronics Chemistry History **Law**
Accounting **Philosophy** Anthropology
Alchemy Drama Quantum Mechanics
Atheism Sexual Health **Ancient History**
Entrepreneurship Languages Sport
Paleontology Needlework Islam
Metaphysics Investment Archaeology
Parenting Statistics Criminology
Motivational

U. S. DEPARTMENT OF AGRICULTURE.

Department Bulletins

Nos. 901-925.

b3 06(9

WITH CONTENTS AND INDEX,

PREPARED UNDER THE SUPERVISION OF

JOHN L. COBBS, Jr.

CHIEF, DIVISION OF PUBLICATIONS

WASHINGTON:
GOVERNMENT PRINTING OFFICE
1922.

CONTENTS.

DEPARTMENT BULLETIN· No. 901.—GRAPEVINE FLEA–BEETLES: Page.
Introduction...   1
History..   2
The grapevine flea-beetle...   4
The lesser grapevine flea-beetle.. 11
Economic importance.. 20
Predatory enemies.. 22
Methods of control... 23
General summary.. 24
Literature cited... 26

DEPARTMENT BULLETIN. No. 902.—THE WESTERN CABBAGE FLEA–BEETLE:
Nature of injury...   1
Description..   2
Distribution...   3
Reports of injury..   4
Food plants..   7
Seasonal history...   8
Life history and habits..   9
History and literature... 13
Natural enemies.. 13
Control measures... 14
Recommendations.. 17
Summary.. 20
Literature cited... 21

DEPARTMENT BULLETIN No. 903.—THE GRAPE PHYLLOXERA IN CALIFORNIA:
California history..   1
Accidental and natural spread..   7
Distribution of phylloxera in California................................... 11
Vineyard destruction... 15
Nomenclature and synonymy of the grape phylloxera.......................... 26
Biology of the grape phylloxera in California.............................. 27
The radicicole... 44
The nymph and winged form.. 73
Hymphicals or intermediate forms... 82
The sexual forms... 90
The gallicole and its relation to California conditions.................... 95
Effects of water and heat on phylloxera.................................... 98
Diffusion of phylloxera.. 100
Summary.. 122
Literature cited... 127

DEPARTMENT BULLETIN No. 904.—THE PRODUCTION AND UTILIZATION OF CORN
OIL IN THE UNITED STATES:
Origin of the corn-oil industry..   1
Degerminating corn...   1
Methods of degermination used..   2
Expelling the oil from corn germs..   8
Handling and disposing of the crude oil.................................... 11
Handling and disposing of the oil cake..................................... 12
Buying and shipping corn germs... 13
Utilization of corn oil.. 13
Effect of color and condition of the corn on the yield and character of the
  oil.. 15
Comparison of the oil-production operation in different mills.............. 16
Economics of corn-oil production... 17
Cost of expelling corn oil... 17
Production of edible oil... 20
The future of corn oil... 22

DEPARTMENT BULLETIN NO. 905.—PRINCIPLES OF LIVE STOCK BREEDING: Page.

Evolution of animal breeding.. 1
Reproduction.. 2
The reproduction cells in relation to heredity........................... 11
Details of heredity transmission....................................... 15
The determination of sex.. 23
Mendelian heredity in live stock...................................... 30
Heredity of form and function in live stock............................ 34
The system of breeding.. 42
Methods of selection.. 47
The value of purebreds.. 54
Summary.. 65

DEPARTMENT BULLETIN NO. 906.—THE USE OF CONCRETE PIPE IN IRRIGATION:

Introduction.. 1
The use of pipe in irrigation.. 2
Incasing old pipes of metal and wood with concrete.................... 4
Concrete pipe... 4
Reinforced concrete pipe.. 6
Manufacture of plain concrete pipe.................................... 8
Quality of concrete pipe.. 9
Cost of unreinforced pipe... 12
Laying concrete pipe.. 13
Causes of failure in concrete pipe.................................... 15
Pipe systems for irrigation... 23
Settling basins and screens... 27
Air vents... 29
Relief stands... 30
Measuring devices for pipe irrigation systems......................... 31
Distributing hydrants... 44

DEPARTMENT BULLETIN NO. 907.—FUMIGATION OF CITRUS PLANTS WITH HYDRO-
CYANIC ACID: CONDITIONS INFLUENCING INJURY:

Introduction.. 1
The effect of hydrocyanic acid on plants.............................. 2
Details of experiments.. 3
The effect on plant injury of temperature, light, and moisture before fumi-
    gation.. 4
The effect on plant injury of temperature, light, and moisture after fumi-
    gation.. 10
The effect on plant injury of temperature, light, and moisture during fumi-
    gation.. 22
General discussion of factors which influence fumigation injury......... 27
The concentration of the gas.. 28
The length of exposure.. 29
The physiological condition of the plant.............................. 30
Atmospheric and light conditions...................................... 33
Summary.. 41
Literature cited.. 42

DEPARTMENT BULLETIN NO. 908.—THE MAINE SARDINE INDUSTRY.

Introduction:
    The sardine... 1
    The Maine sardine industry.. 3
    The Maine sardine... 4
    Food value of the canned sardine.................................. 5
    Purpose of investigation.. 6
Methods employed in packing sardines.................................. 6
Experimental work:
    Methods of analysis... 12
    Composition of the sea herring.................................... 15
    Food of the sea herring... 17
    Swells.. 20
    Transportation of the fish.. 26
    Pickling and salting the fish..................................... 34
    Flaking the fish.. 50
    Drying the fish... 51
    Packing the fish.. 58

DEPARTMENT BULLETIN No. 908.—THE MAINE SARDINE INDUSTRY—Contd.

Experimental work—Continued. Page.
Adding the oil... 60
Processing the sardines... 69
Storing the sardines.. 70
Decomposition of the fish.. 86
Grading the fish.. 93
Standardization of the sardine pack.................................... 96
Sanitary precautions in packing sardines............................... 98
Waste in packing sardines:
Elimination of unnecessary waste.................................... 102
Utilization of unavoidable waste.................................... 109
Economic considerations.. 115
Summary.. 121
Bibliography... 125

DEPARTMENT BULLETIN No. 909.—UTILIZATION OF BLACK WALNUT:

Introduction.. 1
Properties of the wood.. 2
Insect and fungus attack.. 6
Supply.. 7
Demand... 21
Utilization by industries.. 22
Lumber.. 22
Veneer.. 44
Ties.. 58
Posts... 59
Furniture... 61
Musical instruments... 66
Planing-mill products... 67
Sewing machines... 68
Firearms.. 68
Export... 74
War-time utilization... 76
Summary of general market conditions................................... 79
Marketing walnut timber.. 80
Summary and conclusions.. 85
Appendix: Detailed list of uses.. 88

DEPARTMENT BULLETIN No. 910.—EXPERIENCE OF EASTERN FARMERS WITH MOTOR TRUCKS:

Summary... 1
Method of study... 3
Location of farms and types of farming.................................. 3
Distance to market.. 4
Size of truck... 6
Age of trucks... 7
Are these trucks profitable investments?................................ 7
The best size... 7
Advantages and disadvantages.. 9
Road hauling with trucks... 10
Road hauling for which trucks are not used............................. 13
Hauling on the farm with trucks.. 15
Custom hauling... 17
Effect of different kinds of roads on use of trucks.................... 17
Change of market... 19
Annual use of trucks... 21
Life and depreciation of trucks.. 23
Repairs.. 24
Gasoline and oil... 26
Tires.. 27
Reliability.. 29
Cost of operation.. 32
Cost of hauling with trucks.. 33
Saving of hired help... 34
Displacement of horses... 35
Farms on which tractors are owned...................................... 36

ısurance..

cs of the hail insurance contract...........................

ems in hail insurance..

ʟʟᴇᴛɪɴ No. 913.—Tʜᴇ Wᴇsᴛᴇʀɴ Fᴀʀᴍᴇʀ's Wᴀᴛᴇʀ Rɪɢʜᴛ

right is..

acteristics of water rights......................................

of rights..

title to rights to water from streams........................

lerground waters..

er from canals...

of water..

ʟʟᴇᴛɪɴ No. 914.—Tʜᴇ Rᴇᴅ-ʙᴀɴᴅᴇᴅ Lᴇᴀғ-ʀᴏʟʟᴇʀ:

....

....

occurrences...

s...

e species..

....

ɪies...

....

....

ʒed...

ʟʟᴇᴛɪɴ No. 915.—Tᴏxɪᴄɪᴛʏ ᴏғ Bᴀʀɪᴜᴍ Cᴀʀʙᴏɴᴀᴛᴇ ᴛᴏ Rᴀᴛ

vestigation...

estigations..

l procedure...

perimental work...

icient concentration of barium carbonate....................

xperimental work on other barium compounds.............

arium carbonate to animals other than rats...............

....

....

ʟʟᴇᴛɪɴ No. 916.—Fʀᴇᴇᴢɪɴɢ Iɴᴊᴜʀʏ ᴛᴏ Pᴏᴛᴀᴛᴏᴇs Wɪ

investigations...

f the freezing process..

ork...

f undercooled potatoes...

DEPARTMENT BULLETIN No. 917.—FARM PRACTICE IN GROWING FIELD CROPS IN THE SUGAR-BEET DISTRICTS OF COLORADO—Continued. Page.

Preparation of the seed bed... 12
Planting... 19
Manurial practice... 21
Cultivation... 24
Irrigation.. 27
Harvesting.. 33
Marketing... 40
Cost of production.. 41
Summary.. 52

DEPARTMENT BULLETIN No. 918.—REPORT ON INVESTIGATIONS OF THE PINK BOLLWORM OF COTTON IN MEXICO:

The Laguna District... 1
Distribution of the pink bollworm..................................... 4
Life history.. 5
Seasonal history.. 19
Feeding habits of larvæ... 21
Damage caused by the pink bollworm.................................... 24
Food plants... 32
Dispersal... 35
Natural control... 38
Repression.. 47
Summary.. 56
Literature cited.. 57
Appendix.. 58

DEPARTMENT BULLETIN No. 919.—UNIT REQUIREMENTS FOR PRODUCING MILK IN WESTERN WASHINGTON:

Character and scope of the work....................................... 1
Methods used in obtaining the data.................................... 2
    Comparison of winter and summer results.......................... 3
Description of herds.. 3
Requirements for producing 100 pounds of milk........................ 4
Requirements for keeping a cow one year.............................. 6
    Credit for manure.. 7
    Credit for calves.. 9
Requirements for keeping a bull...................................... 9
Factors involved in production of milk............................... 10
    Feed... 10
    Pasture.. 11
    Labor.. 12
    Other costs.. 13
Per cent comparison of factors involved in milk production........... 15
Average compared with "bulk-line" costs.............................. 16
Monthly distribution of factors in milk production................... 17
Summary.. 19

DEPARTMENT BULLETIN No. 920.—FARM PROFITS: FIGURES FROM THE SAME FARMS FOR A SERIES OF YEARS:

Introduction... 1
Sources and character of data.. 3
Summary.. 5
The Ohio area.. 7
The Indiana area... 22
The Wisconsin area... 41
Good management increases profits.................................... 55

DEPARTMENT BULLETIN No. 921.—SUGAR-CANE JUICE CLARIFICATION FOR SIRUP MANUFACTURE:

Two methods in general use... 1
    Disadvantages.. 2
New method of clarification... 2
Vacuum evaporation in making cane sirup.............................. 12
Use of vegetable decolorizing carbons in connection with infusorial earth clarification... 14
Infusorial earth clarification for sugar manufacture................. 14
Summary.. 15

DEPARTMENT BULLETIN NO. 922.—CLOVER-LEAF WEEVIL: Page.

Introductory... 1
Distribution... 1
Description.. 2
Food plants and injury... 6
Life history... 6
Habits.. 12
Feeding experiments... 12
Natural enemies... 16
Control... 18
Literature cited... 18

DEPARTMENT BULLETIN NO. 923.—UNIT REQUIREMENTS FOR PRODUCING MARKET MILK IN VERMONT:

Character and scope of the work.. 1
Methods used in obtaining the data... 2
Winter and summer feeding... 3
Description of the herds... 3
Requirements for producing 100 pounds of milk.............................. 4
Requirements for keeping a cow one year.................................... 5
Credit for calves and manure.. 7
Requirements for keeping a bull... 8
Factors involved in the production of milk................................. 9
    Feed... 9
    Pasture... 10
    Labor... 10
    Other costs... 11
Per cent comparisons of factors involved in cost of milk production........ 13
Determination of the bulk line of production.............................. 14
Monthly distribution of factors in milk production........................ 14
Summary.. 17

DEPARTMENT BULLETIN NO. 924.—TEAR-STAIN OF CITRUS FRUITS:

Description of the disease... 1
Review of the literature.. 2
Spraying experiments.. 3
Cultural work... 5
Histological examination.. 9
Inoculation experiments... 9
Conclusions... 11
Summary.. 11
Literature cited.. 12

DEPARTMENT BULLETIN NO. 925.—A BRACHYTIC VARIATION IN MAIZE:

Definition of brachysm.. 1
Review of the literature.. 2
Origin and description of the variation................................... 2
Inheritence of other brachytic variations................................. 6
Morphological significance.. 8
Associated changes.. 9
Agricultural advantages... 11
Inheritance of brachysm in hybrids with commercial varieties.............. 14
    Brachytic × Boone... 14
    Teratological variations.. 19
    Ears ending in staminate spikes....................................... 20
    Brachytic × Hopi.. 23
Conclusions... 26
Literature cited.. 28

INDEX.

	Bulletin No.	Page.
Airplanes, construction, use of black walnut	909	73–74, 76–79
Alabama, walnut, stand and quality	909	9, 10, 17, 21
Alfalfa, growing in Colorado—		
farm practices (with other crops)	917	11–40
labor distribution and cost	917	8, 9, 10, 11, 12, 45
Alkali, soil, effect on concrete pipes	906	20–21
Altica chalybea—		
synonym	901	2
See also Flea-beetle, grapevine.		
Amines—		
formation in sardines during storage	908	70–78, 85
presence in fish, fresh and decomposed	908	86–93
Ammonia—		
formation in sardines during storage	908	70–78, 85
presence in fish, fresh and decomposed	908	86–93
Anchovies, preparation, elimination of undigested food	908	19
Animal—		
reproduction—		
cell theory	905	2–11
discussion	905	2–11
unit, meaning	920	3
Animals—		
selection for breeding purposes	905	47–50
sex determination in breeding, discussion	905	23–29
"Appetitsild," source of fish, and requirements	908	19
Apples, freezing by handling	916	4
APPLETON, H., report on grapes in California, citation on phylloxera	903	4
Arizona, water rights, officials, location	913	3
Arkansas, walnut, stand and quality	909	9, 10, 14, 20, 21
Arsenate, lead. *See* Lead arsenate.		
Arsenates, use against flea beetles	901	23
Atmosphere, condition of, relation to fumigation	907	33
Bacillus—		
B., occurrence in food of herring, laboratory studies	908	21, 24–25, 121
Walfischrauschbrand, occurrence in herring feed, studies	908	21, 24–25, 121
BAIN, J. B.—		
and G. E. BRAUN, bulletin on "Unit requirements for producing milk in western Washington"	919	1–19
R. J. POSSON and RALPH P. HOTIS, bulletin on "Unit requirements for producing market milk in Vermont"	923	1–18
BAKEWELL, ROBERT, pioneer in animal breeding, note	905	2
Barium—		
carbonate, toxicity to rats, bulletin by Erich W. Schwartze	915	1–11
chlorid—		
dose fatal to man	915	2
toxicity to rats and other animals	915	2, 9
compounds, toxicity to rats, experimental work	915	9
salts, poisonous dose for man and lower animals	915	2, 9
Barley, growing in Colorado—		
farm practices (with other crops)	917	11–40
labor distribution and cost	917	10, 11, 45
Basins, settling in irrigation systems	906	27–29

	Bulletin No.	Page.
Beans—		
growing in Colorado—		
farm practices (with other crops)......................	917	11–40
labor distribution and cost...........................	917{	6, 9, 10, 11, 12, 45
injury by western cabbage flea-beetle....................	902	5
Beef, food value, comparison with sardines...............	908	5
Beets—		
injury by western cabbage flea-beetle...................	902	5, 6.
sugar—		
growing in Colorado, farm practices (with other crops)...	917	11–40
growing in Colorado, labor distribution and cost.........	917{	7, 9, 10, 11, 12, 45
marketing in Colorado.............................	917	40–41
Bibliography, truck-crop insects........................	902	21
Bioletti, F. T., statement on origin of Mission grape...........	903	2
Birch, comparison with black walnut, and prices............	909	5, 41–69
Birds, enemies of—		
cabbage flea-beetle..............................	902	14
clover-leaf weevil, list............................	922	17
Blanchard, G. G., report on viticulture, California, citation....	903	7
Boats, sardine, sanitation...........................	908	99
Bollworm, pink—		
control—		
by parasites and other enemies.....................	918	38–47
methods.......................................	918	47–56
distribution..	918	4–5
in Mexico, report on investigations, bulletin by U. C. Loftin and others....................................	918	1–64
injury to cotton crop................................	918	24–32
introduction into Mexico and present distribution...........	918	4–5
larvæ mortality, studies.............................	918	38–46
life history...	918	5–19
of cotton, report on investigations in Mexico, bulletin by U. C. Loftin, K. B. McKinney, and W. K. Hanson...........	918	1–64
seasonal history and feeding habits......................	918	19–24
spread...	918	35–38
Bollworm, pink, description, generic and specific, by A. Busch....	918	58–64
Bordeaux mixture, application to plants before fumigation, cause of burning...	907	31
Boxes, construction, black walnut utilization..................	909	60, 73, 88
Brachysm—		
corn plants, advantages.............................	925	11–14, 26
use of term, occurrence on corn plant, study..................	925	1–27
variation in maize, bulletin by J. H. Kempton................	925	1–28
Braun, G. E., and J. B. Bain, bulletin on ''Unit requirements for producing milk in western Washington''....................	919	1–19
Breeding—		
corn, brachytic variation, investigations....................	925	2–27
live stock, principles, bulletin by Sewall Wright.............	905	1–67
seasons for live stock...............................	905	6–7
Britt, unfitness for sardines.............................	908	94
Brush, Warren D., bulletin on ''Utilization of black walnut''..	909	1–89
Buena Vista vineyard, California, historical notes..............	903	4–6
Buildings, dairy herd, requirements per 100 pounds of milk produced...	919	5, 6, 13–14
Bull—		
keeping requirements—		
and cost.....................................	923	8–9
and credits...................................	919	9–10
service, credit on dairy account.....................	919	10
Busch, A., citation on description of Pectinophora gossypiella.....	918	58–64
Cabbage—		
flea-beetle, western, bulletin by F. H. Chittenden and H. O. Marsh..	902	1–21
injury by western cabbage flea-beetle.....................	902	5, 6, 7
worm, control by fungous disease......................	922	17
Cabinetwork, black walnut utilization and reported consumption.	909	59–67, 88–89

	Bulletin No.	Page.
Cake, press, from filtered sugar-cane juice, description, etc., notes	921	4–7, 10, 11, 15
Calcium arsenate dust, pink bollworm control, experiments	918	51–52
California—		
cabbage flea-beetle, occurrence and injuries to crops	902	4, 6, 7
early history, notes	903	1–7
grape phylloxera, bulletin by W. M. Davidson and R. L. Nougaret	903	1–128
grapes, planting in different periods, by counties	903	13
Napa County, center of phylloxera infestation	903	6, 7, 9
phylloxera—		
infestation progress, map	903	12
introduction	903	4–7
spread and distribution	903	115, 122, 126
Santa Clara Valley, grape growing, changes	903	14
Sonoma Creek district, phylloxera source	903	4, 7, 10
vineyards, planting, historical notes	903	4–7, 122
water rights, laws, officials, etc	913	2, 3
Calves—		
credit in profits from dairy herds	923	7, 18
production, credit on dairy account	919	9
Canals, water rights, and distribution methods	913	9–14
Cane—		
juice, clarification, methods	921	1–14
sugar, juice clarification for sirup manufacture, bulletin by J. K. Dale and C. S. Hudson	921	1–15
Canneries, sardine, capacity	908	116–117
Cans, sardine—		
description, sizes, and types	908	11–12, 103–105
detinning, causes	908	80–86, 123
handling, sanitary precautions	908	100–101, 124
Cantaloupes—		
growing in Colorado—		
farm practices (with other crops)	917	11–40
labor distribution and cost	917	8, 9, 10, 12, 45
harvesting in Colorado	917	38, 42
marketing in Colorado	917	38, 42
Carbon disulphid, control of pink bollworm, experiments	918	48–50, 55
Carbons, decolorizing, use in sugar-cane juice clarification	921	14
"Carey Act," water rights of individuals under	913	11–12
Cartons, sardine, standard grade	908	
Caskets, manufacture from black walnut, demands and use	909	71, 88
Catawba grape, introduction into California	903	5
Cattle—		
beef, improvement in meat quality and quantity	905	57–59
color, heredity	905	30–31
poll, heredity	905	30
Cauliflower, injury by western cabbage flea-beetle, note	902	7
Cheese, food value, comparison with sardines	908	5
Chemistry Bureau, sardine investigations	908	6
Chickens, comb heredity	905	33
Children, poisoning by barium carbonate, danger	915	2, 9
CHITTENDEN, F. H.—		
and H. O. MARSH, bulletin on "The western cabbage flea-beetle"	902	1–21
bulletin on "The red-banded leaf-roller"	914	1–14
Chizopods, food of herring, note	908	17
Chromosomes nature, kinds, and relation to heredity	905	20
Chrysopa rufilabris, enemy of pink bollworm	918	47
CHURCH, L. M., and H. R. TOLLEY, bulletin on "Experiments of eastern farmers with motor trucks"	910	1–37
Citrus—		
fruit, injury by fumigation, conditions affecting	907	4–29
fruits, tear-stain, bulletin by John R. Winston	924	1–12

	Bulletin No.	Page.
Citrus—Continued.		
fumigation, gas concentration and length of exposure, effects. plants—	907	28–29
fumigation injury, relation of sunlight....................	907	34–37
fumigation with hydrocyanic acid, bulletin by R. S. Woglum................................	907	1–43
injury by fumigation, conditions influencing.............	907	1–43
moisture content, relation to damage by fumigation......	907	4–27, 40
Climate, Colorado, sugar-beet districts..........................	917	4–6
Clover—		
cultural control of leaf weevil............................	922	18
injuries by leaf-weevil.................................	922	6, 7, 9, 12, 13, 14
Clover-leaf weevil—		
bulletin by D. G. Tower and F. A. Fenton...................	922	1–18
See also Weevil, Clover-leaf.		
Clupea spp. See Sardines.		
Coffins, manufacture, black walnut, use.........................	909	71, 88
Colletotrichum gloeosporioides, relation to wither-tip tear-stain of citrus..	924	1–3, 5–11
Colorado—		
cabbage flea-beetle, occurrence and injuries to crops.........	902	4, 5, 6, 7
Fort Morgan district—		
field crops, labor, cost, etc..............................	917	2, 6–51
soils, climate, and farm practices.......................	917	3–51
Greeley district—		
field crops, labor, cost, etc..............................	917	2, 6–51
soils, climate, and farm practices.......................	917	3–51
growing field crops in sugar-beet districts, practices, bulletin by Samuel B. Nuckols and Thomas H. Summers..........	917	1–51
Rock Ford district—		
field crops, labor cost, etc...............................	917	2, 6–51
soils, climate, and farm practices.......................	917	3–51
sugar-beet districts, soil and climate..........................	917	3–6
water rights, laws, officials, etc............................	913	3, 4–5
Concrete pipe, use in irrigation, bulletin by F. W. Stanley and Samuel Fortier...	906	1–54
Connecticut, farmers' experience with motor trucks (with other Eastern States), bulletin by H. R. Tolley and L. M. Church....	910	1–37
Copepods, food of sea herring, description, and effect on fish......	908	17–18, 22–23
Corn—		
Boone, hybrids, brachytic characters.......................	925	10–11, 14–23
Chinese waxy varieties, hybrids, brachytic characters.......	925	2–7, 24–26
color and condition, effect on oil yield and character.........	904	15–16
degermination, methods and advantages....................	904	1–8
germs—		
buying and shipping..................................	904	13
demand and shipping.................................	904	18
oil extraction, method and machines used...............	904	8–11
Hopi, hybrids, brachytic characters.......................	925	23–26
injury by western cabbage flea-beetle.....................	902	5, 7
oil—		
production and utilization, bulletin by A. F. Sievers....	904	1–23
use in sardine packing, tests, etc......................	908	66–68, 119
See also Oil, corn.		
plant, brachytic variation, bulletin by J. H. Kempton.......	925	1–28
yields, North Central States, seven-year period.............	920	11, 26, 41
Corn-oil—		
cake, feed value and use..................................	904	12
industry, origin, demand, etc.............................	904	1
Cotton—		
bolls—		
destruction for control of pink bollworm.................	918	53–54
injury by pink bollworm...............................	918	22–24, 27
proliferation as causes of injury......................	918	24
fields, pasturing for pink-bollworm control................	918	54
losses from pink bollworm in Mexico......................	918	28–32

	Bulletin No.	Page.
Cotton—Continued.		
pink bollworm, report on investigations in Mexico, bulletin by U. C. Loftin and others	918	1–64
See also Bollworm, pink.		
poisoning in field for pink-bollworm control	918	51–52
production in Mexico, Laguna district	918	4
stalks and bolls, destruction for pink-bollworm control	918	53–54
Cottonseed oil, use in sardine packing	908	4, 66–68, 119
Cow—		
keeping requirements—		
and cost for one year	923	5–6
per year, and credits	919	6–9
pasture requirements, and cost	923	6
Cows—		
breeding and gestation periods	905	6, 7, 8
dairy—		
feed requirements	923	5–6
improvement by grading up	905	54–57
Cranberry worm. See Leaf-roller, red-banded.		
Crops—		
acreage, by States, 1910, chart	912	11, 12
farm, hail insurance, bulletin by V. N. Valgren	912	1–32
field—		
cost of materials used in producing in Colorado	917	46
growing in sugar-beet districts of Colorado, practices, bulletin by Samuel B. Nuckols and Thomas H. Summers	917	1–52
production costs in Colorado, sugar-beet districts	917	42–50
profits in Colorado, distribution of credits	917	50–51
yields in North Central States, 1912–1918, on 185 farms	920	8, 11, 23, 26, 40, 41, 42
Crossbreeding, live stock, results	905	42, 44, 62
Cucumbers, growing in Colorado—		
farm practices (with other crops)	917	11–40
labor distribution and cost	917	9, 10, 12, 45
CUTTER, E., work with grapes in California	903	4
Cuttings, grape, phylloxera spread	903	8, 120–121
DALE, J. K., and C. S. HUDSON, bulletin on "Sugar-cane juice clarification for sirup manufacture"	921	1–15
DAVIDSON, W. H., and R. L. NOUGARET, bulletin on "The grape phylloxera in California"	903	1–128
Degermination, corn, methods and advantages	904	1–8
Delaware—		
farmers' experience with motor trucks (with other Eastern States), bulletin by H. R. Tolley and L. M. Church	910	1–37
walnut, stand and quality	909	9, 10, 16–17, 19, 21
Diatomaceous earth. See Infusorial earth.		
Disease, fungous, value in control of clover-leaf weevil and other insects	922	16–17
Disking, practices, Colorado sugar-beet districts	917	15
Diversion boxes, in irrigation	906	41–44
DIXON, H. M., and H. W. HAWTHORNE, bulletin on "Farm profits: Figures from the same farms for a series of years"	920	1–56
Drying, fish, in sardine industry	908	9, 51–58, 122
Dusting—		
cabbage flea-beetle, experiments with zinc arsenite and tobacco	902	17, 18
cotton, for pink-bollworm control, experiments	918	51–52
Dwarfism. See Brachysm.		
Earth—		
flea. See Flea-beetle, western cabbage.		
infusorial. See Infusorial earth.		
Empusa sphaerosperma, enemy of clover-leaf weevil and other insects	922	16–17

Family, supplies from farms, in North Central States............. 920 { 5, 8, 17, 23, 32, 49

Farm—
    business, North Central States, 185 farms, seven-year period.. 920   8, 23, 42
    capital, use of term.................................... 920   2
    crops. hail insurance. bulletin by V. N. Valgren............. 912   1–32
    expenses, use of words.................................. 920   2
    income, use of term.................................... 920   2
    incomes on Ohio farms. 1912–1918, and factors concerning.... 920   5, 8, 13, 16
    profits. figures from the same farms for a series of years, bulletin
      by H. M. Dixon and H. W. Hawthorne................... 920   1–56
    receipts, use of words.................................. 920   2
Farmer, water rights in West, bulletin by R. P. Teele........... 913   1–14
Farmers—
    eastern, experience with motor trucks, bulletin by H. R.
      Tolley and L. M. Church............................... 910   1–37
    hauling with trucks, on road and farm, Eastern States....... 910 10–13, 15–16
    manufacture of sirup from sugar-cane juice.................... 921   1, 2, 7
    truck-owners. reports from 753 in Eastern States, bulletin by
      H. R. Tolley and L. M. Church.......................... 910   1–37
Farming—
    losses, causes.. 920   20–21
    practices in growing field crops in sugar-beet districts of
      Colorado, bulletin by Samuel B. Nuckols and Thomas H.
      Summers... 917   1–52
    profits in North Central States............................ 920   3–56
Farms—
    acreage, in North Central States, distribution of crop areas, etc. 920 { 8, 9–11, 23, 24–26, 42, 43–44
    capital on 185 farms in North Central States.............. 920 { 8, 11, 23, 27, 42, 45
    incomes—
      on Indiana farms, 1913–1918, and farm business......... 920 5, 23, 30–32
      on Wisconsin farms, 1913–1917, and farm business....... 920 { 5, 42, 45, 46, 49
    Indiana, Clinton County, profits and losses.................. 920 3, 5, 122–4
    North Central States, acreage, distribution of crop areas, etc.. 920 { 8, 9–11, 24–26, 42, 43–44
    Ohio, Washington County, profits and losses................. 920 3, 5, 7–22
    products, prices in North Central States, 1912–1918......... 920 { 5, 8, 15, 17, 23, 33, 42, 49
    trucks owned in Eastern States, relation to acreage........... 910 36–37
    Wisconsin, Dane County, profits and losses.................. 920 3, 5, 41–55
Fecundity, breeding animals, factors and conditions affecting.... 905 8–11
Feed—
    bull, requirements and cost................................ 923 8–9
    cow, requirements for producing 100 pounds of milk.......... 923 4
    dairy cows, kinds, cost, and relation to milk production..... 923 { 9–10, 13, 14–17, 18
    stock. corn oil cake.................................... 904 12
    use of fish meal, value for live stock..................... 908 111–115
Feeds, dairy, description, and requirements for 100 pounds of milk. 919 { 4, 5, 10–11, 15, 17, 18
Fenton, F. A., and D. G. Tower. on "Clover-leaf
    weevil".. 922 1–18
Fertilizer, fish waste, utilization.......................... 908 111

	Bulletin No.	Page.
Field crops. *See* Crops.		
Filter presses, clarifying for sugar-cane juice, description and cost.	921	2, 3, 6, 8–11
Filtration, sugar-cane juice, new method, materials and cost......	921	2–12
Firearms, manufacture, demands and uses of black walnut........	909 {	59, 60, 68–70, 76–79, 80
Fish—		
belly-blown, cause...	908	18, 25
buying for sardine canneries...................................	908	115
canning, bibliography.......................................	908	125–127
composition, changes during transportation...................	908	30–32, 121
cutting and eviscerating for sardines.........................	908 {	10, 47–49, 95–96
decomposed, experimental packs.............................	908	89–93
decomposition, indices.......................................	908	86–93, 123
drying, in sardine industry...................................	908	9, 51–58, 122
"feedy," unfitness for use in sardine packing.................	908	18–20, 93
flaking in sardine industry...................................	908	9, 50–51, 100
grading in sardine industry...................................	908	93–96
meat meal—		
Value as stock feed, yield and composition...............	908	111–115
yield and composition, experimental lots...............	908	113
number of various sizes per hogshead.......................	908	115–116
pickling in sardine industry................................	908	8, 34–50, 122
salting—		
during transportation.....................................	908	28–32, 121
in sardine industry.....................................	908	8, 34–50, 122
sardines, changes in pickle and in dry salt...................	908	36–46
transportation, in sardine industry, methods and details......	908	8, 26–34, 121
waste, in sardine canneries, utilization methods.............	908	102–115
Fishing, sea herring, for Maine sardines, methods and suggestions.	908	7, 19, 94
Flaking, fish, in sardine industry.................................	908	9, 50–51, 100
Flea-beetle—		
cabbage, western—		
bulletin by F. H. Chittenden and H. O. Marsh..........	902	1–21
distribution...	901	3–4
food plants...	902	7–8
repellents...	902	17–18
grapevine, description, life history, and habits..............	901	4–20, 24–25
Flea-beetles, grapevine—		
bulletin by Dwight Isley.....................................	901	1–27
economic importance and outbreaks..........................	901	20–21
hand picking for control....................................	901	23
history and literature regarding.............................	901	2–4, 26–27
Flies, control by fungous disease, note..........................	922	17
Fly, lacewing, enemy of pink bollworm..........................	918	47
Foliage, citrus, injury by fumigation, conditions affecting........	907	27–29
Food, corn oil..	904	14, 20–22
FORTIER, SAMUEL, and F. W. STANLEY, bulletin on "The use of concrete pipe in irrigation"...................................	906	1–54
Fowls, incubation periods.......................................	905	7–8
France, sardine exports to United States, 1910–1916.............	908	117, 118
Freezing, potatoes, when undercooled, injury, bulletin by R. C. Wright and George F. Taylor..................................	916	1–15
Frost, necrosis in potato tubers, studies of physiology, review of literature...	916	2–4
Fruits, citrus, injury by fumigation, conditions affecting.........	907	27–29
Fumigation—		
citrus—		
orchard, with hydrocyanic acid, night work, advantages.	906	1
plants, night work, advantages........................	906	1
plants, with hydrocyanic acid, bulletin by R. S. Woglum.	907	1–43
house, for cotton seed, description..........................	918	55–56
hydrocyanic acid, injury to citrus plants, relation to light, heat, and moisture.......................................	907	4–27
seed cotton, for control of pink bollworm....................	918 {	47–51, 55–56, 57

	Bulletin No.	Page.
Fungus, *Empusa sphaerosperma*, disease of clover-leaf weevil	922	16–17
Furniture, walnut, demand and uses	909	61–67, 88–89
"Gabelbissen," preparation, and requirements	908	19
Gall louse, grape, in California, notes	903	8, 29, 96
Gallicole, grape phylloxera—		
life history, and habits	903	95–98, 115
scarcity in California	903	8, 29, 98
Gas, concentration, injury to citrus fruits	907	28–29
Gasoline—		
motor truck, mileage cost	910	26–27
requirements for motor trucks of different sizes	910	27
Gelechia gossypiella. *See* Bollworm, pink.		
Georgia, walnut, stand and quality	909	9, 17
Gestation, periods in animals	905	7–8
Gins, cleaning for pink-bollworm control	918	55, 57
GONZALES Y FARINA, DON C., aid in pink-bollworm investigations	918	1, 26
Grades, walnut lumber, and prices	909	35–41
Grading—		
fish, in sardine industry	908	93–96
up, live stock, for improvement	905	46, 56, 60–61
Grain, seeding depth, dates and rates, Colorado	917	20, 21
Grains, marketing in Colorado	917	40
Grape—		
Catawba, introduction into California	903	5
cuttings—		
and roots, disinfection for phylloxera control	903	11
phylloxera spread, possibility	903	8, 120–121
fruit—		
inoculation with cultures of *Collectotrichum gloeosporioides*	924	9–10
tear-stain control, spraying experiments	924	1, 3–11
industry, California, growth and magnitude	903	13–14
Mission—		
description, history, and relation to spread of phylloxera	903	2–4
origin and value	903	2–3
phylloxera—		
in California, bulletin by W. M. Davidson and R. L. Nougaret	903	1–128
spread	903	8, 120–121
See also Phylloxera, grape.		
Grapeleaf, gall louse, scarcity in California	903	8, 29, 98
Grapes—		
Anaheim disease, ravages in California	903	3, 14
berry moth, life history studies in Northern Ohio, bulletin by H. G. Ingerson	911	1–38
eastern varieties, introduction into California	903	5–7
growing in California, history	903	1–7
introduction into California	903	1–4
native, resistance to phylloxera	903	2
picking boxes, source of phylloxera infestation	903	9–11, 116–117
spraying for control of grape-berry moth	911	14, 33, 38
varieties in California prior to 1875	903	7
Grapevine flea-beetles, bulletin by Dwight Isley	901	1–27
Grapevines—		
injury by flea-beetles	901	1, 3, 20–21, 23
planting in California, 1856–1910, by counties	903	13
remarkable specimens in California, description	903	3
root lesions from phylloxera, description, and results	903	22–26
spraying for control of flea-beetles	901	23–24
tuberosities, cause and description	903	22–24; 26, 53
"Ground flea." *See* Flea-beetle, cabbage, western.		
Guinea pigs, heredity studies	905	16–18
Gunstocks, manufacture from black walnut, demands and value	909	59, 60, 68–70, 76–79, 88

	Bulletin No.	Page.
Hail—		
insurance—		
companies, origin, development, and number	912	2–11
contract, characteristics, comparison with fire insurance	912	20–24
cost	912	16–20
on farm crops in the United States, bulletin by V. N. Valgren	912	1–32
State laws	912	6–10
risks, amount and distribution in various States	912	11–16, 25–29
HANSON, W. K., U. C. LOFTIN, and K. B. McKINNEY, bulletin on "Report on investigations of the pink bollworm of cotton in Mexico"	918	1–64
HARASZTHY, A. F., work with grapes in California	903	4, 6
Harrowing, practices in Colorado, sugar-beet districts, various crops	917	15–17
Harvesting, practices in Colorado, sugar-beet districts, various crops	917	33–40
Hauling, motor truck, by eastern farmers, amount and cost	910	10–13,15–16, 33
HAWTHORNE, H. W., and H. M. DIXON, bulletin on "Farm profits, figures from the same farms for a series of years"	920	1–56
Hay—		
alfalfa, harvesting practices in Colorado	917	35–37
yields, North Central States, seven-year period	920	11, 26, 41
Herd, dairy, requirements and cost in milk production	923	5–6, 8–13, 17, 18
Heredity—		
fixation in animal breeding, methods	905	37–39
live stock, Mendelian theory	905	30–33
principles, details in regard to live-stock breeding	905	11–23
Herring—		
food of, bacteriological studies	908	21, 24–25
kippered, preparation directions	908	105–106
rollmops and other German preparations	908	107
sea—		
composition, variations	908	15–17, 121
feed, description and composition	908	17–20,22–24, 121
use as sardine, identification, food value, etc	908	2–3, 5
spiced, preparation	908	106, 107
Hibiscus spp., susceptibility to pink bollworm attack	918	32–34
HILGARD, E. W., citation on spread, of phylloxera	903	9
Hillside, irrigation systems, water distribution	906	47, 50
Hogs, color heredity	905	32
Hogshead, fish, number of various sizes (1,000 pounds)	908	115–116
Hominy mills, corn oil production, operations and cost	904	16, 19
Horse, labor, seasonal distribution and costs in Colorado, diagrams and notes	917	6–42, 44–45
Horse-radish, injury by western cabbage flea-beetle	902	5
Horses—		
color heredity	905	31–32
displacement by motor trucks, eastern farms	910	35–36
HOTIS, RALPH P., J. B., and R. J. POSSON, bulletin on "Unit requirements for producing market milk in Vermont"	923	1–18
HOUGHTON, H. W., F. C. WEBER, and J. B. WILSON, bulletin on "The Maine sardine industry"	908	1–127
HUDSON, C. S., and J. K. DALE, bulletin on "Sugar-cane juice clarification for sirup manufacture"	921	1–15
Hybrids, animals, fertility	905	10–11
Hydrants, distributing in irrigation system	906	44–54
Hydrocyanic acid—		
fumigation of citrus fruits, conditions influencing injury, bulletin by R. E. Woglum	907	1–43
gas, control of pink bollworm, experiments	918	50–51
Hypera punctata. See Weevil, clover-leaf.		
Idaho—		
cabbage flea-beetle, occurrence and injuries to crops	902	4, 6
water rights, laws, officials, etc	913	3, 6

s, walnut, stand and quality...............................

nents, vineyards, source of phylloxera infestation.........
ts, sardines, 1910–1916..
ding, live stock, purpose and effects on offspring..........
·oxes, miner's, description and use...:.....................
ition, periods for fowls' eggs...............................
a—
inton County, farm profits, 100 farms, 1910, 1913–1918.....

ilnut, stand and quality.................................

rial earth—
e in clarification of sugar-cane juice.......................
e with vegetable decolorizing carbons in sirup making.....
son, H. G., bulletin on "Life history of the grape-berry moth
orthern Ohio"...
ation—
:rus fruits with cultures of *Colletotrichum gloeosporioides*....
ist necrosis in potatoes, use of term.......................
s, collection, bottle device...............................
nce, hail—

st...
.farm crops, in the United States, bulletin by V. N. Valgren.

il insurance companies and amount of risks...............

ilnut, stand and quality...................................

ion—
tes and valves, types and cost............................
easuring devices...:.......................................
pe systems, design.....:...................................
actices in Colorado, sugar-beet districts..................
e of concrete pipe, bulletin by F. W. Stanley and Samuel
Fortier...
iter rights of farmer in West, bulletin by R. P. Teele.......
Dwight, bulletin on "Grapevine flea-beetles"...........

sugar-cane, clarification for sirup manufacture, bulletin by
. Dale and C. S. Hudson.................................

s—
bbage flea-beetle, occurrence and injuries to crops.........
il insurance companies and amount of risks................
ilnut, stand and quality...................................
iter rights, officials.......................................
·on, J. H., bulletin on "A brachytic variation in maize"..

cky, walnut, stand and quality............................

;uhr. *See* Infusorial earth.

—
sts in growing various crops, Colorado.....................
come, use of term...
comes of farmers—
    in Indiana, 1913–1918...................................
    in Ohio, 1912–1918.....................................
    in Wisconsin, 1913–1918...............................
ilk-production—
    cost...

    requirements per 100 pounds.........................

	Bulletin No.	Page.
Labor—Continued.		
requirements on farms in North Central States, on 195 farms..	920	11, 27, 45
saving, by use of motor trucks	910	34–35
seasonal distribution in crops, Colorado, diagrams and notes.,	917	6–42
Laboratory, chemical, Eastport, Me., sardine investigation	908	6
Laborers, Mexican, pink bollworm spread	918	35
Laguna district, Mexico, research station for study of pink boll worm	918	1–4
Laws—		
fishing, suggestions for sardine catching	908	94
hail insurance, various States	912	6–10
Lead arsenate, sprays—		
use in control of Western cabbage flea-beetle	902	15–17, 20
use in leaf-roller control	914	12
Leaf-hoppers, control by fungous disease, note	922	17
Leaf-roller, red-banded—		
bulletin by F. H. Chittenden	914	1–14
description, distribution, life history, and control	914	2–12
enemies, list and description	914	10–12
Lettuce, injury by western cabbage flea-beetle	902	5, 6
Leveling, fields, practice, Colorado, sugar-beet districts	917	17–18
Linkage, heredity, theory and experiments	905	19–23
Live stock—		
animal units on 25 farms, Washington County, Ohio	920	11
breeding—		
effect on dam's condition on young	905	15
evolution	905	1–2
principles, bulletin by Sewall Wright	905	1–67
seasons	905	6–7
system, purpose, and results	905	42–46
crossbreeding, results	905	42, 44, 62
farm, relation to profit and loss	920	11, 13, 21, 26, 38, 40, 43, 45, 54,
feed, fish meal, use and value	908	111–115
fertility, importance, heredity, etc	905	8–10
hereditary transmissions to young	905	15
heredity—		
Mendelian theory	905	30–33
of form and function	905	34–42
inbreeding, purpose and effects on offspring	905	37–42
pedigree writing, directions	905	50–54
LOFTIN, U. C., K. B. McKINNEY, and W. K. HANSON, bulletin on "Report on investigations of the pink bollworm of cotton in Mexico"	918	1–64
Logging, walnut, methods and cost	909	41–42, 81–85
Logs, walnut—		
grades and prices	909	35, 37 55–56 81–85
measurement, lumber yields and weights	909	83–85
Louisiana, sirup manufacture from sugar-cane juice, method	921	1–3, 8, 11
Louse—		
gall, of grape, notes	903	8, 29, 96
root. See Radicicole.		
Lubricants, preparation, use of corn oil, caution	904	13
Lumber, walnut—		
prices	909	39–41
production, manufacture, and costs	909	22–44, 79
Machinery, corn degerminators, description and operation	904	5–6
Machines, concrete pipe making, description, types	906	8–9
Maine—		
farmers' experience with motor trucks (with other Eastern States), bulletin by H. R. Tolley and L. M. Church	910	1–37
sardine industry, bulletin by F. C. Weber, H. W. Houghton, and J. B. Wilson	908	1–12

	Bulletin No.	Page.
Maize, brachytic variation, bulletin by J. H. Kempton	925	1–28
See also Corn.		
Manure—		
barnyard, credit on dairy account	919	7–9
credit in profits from dairy herd	923	7–8, 18
production per cow	919	7–9
use on crops, practices in Colorado, sugar-beet districts	917	21–23
Mares, breeding and gestation periods	905	6, 7, 8
Market—		
changes by farmers, relation of motor trucks	910	2, 19–21
milk, production, unit requirements, bulletin by J. B. Bain, R. J. Posson, and Ralph P. Hotis	923	1–18
Marketing—		
crops in Colorado, sugar-beet districts	917	40–42
walnut timber	909	80–85
Marsh, H. O., and F. H. Chittenden, bulletin on "The western cabbage flea-beetle"	902	1–21
Maryland—		
farmers' experience with motor trucks (with other Eastern States), bulletin by H. R. Tolley and L. M. Church	910	1–37
walnut, stand and quality	909	9, 10, 16–17, 19, 21
Massachusetts, farmers' experience with motor trucks (with other Eastern States, bulletin by H. R. Tolley and L. M. Church	910	1–37
Mätjeshering, preparation	908	106
McKinney, K. B., U. C. Loftin, and W. K. Hanson, bulletin on "Report on investigations of the pink bollworm of cotton in Mexico"	918	1–64
Meal, fish, value as stock feed, yield and composition	908	111–115
Measuring, devices for pipe in irrigation systems	906	31–41
Mendelian theory, inheritance, explanation	905	18–20, 30–33
Mexico, pink bollworm of cotton, report, bulletin by U. C. Loftin, K. B. McKinney, and W. K. Hanson	918	1–64
Michigan, walnut, stand and quality	909	9, 10, 17, 21
Milk—		
hauling—		
cost per 100 pounds	919	5–6
in motor trucks, cost and practices	919	5–6
market, unit requirements for production, bulletin by J. B. Bain, R. J. Posson, and Ralph P. Hotis	923	1–18
production—		
cost and quantity, winter and summer	919	16–17
factors, monthly distribution	919	17–19
requirements for 100 pounds, feed, etc	923	4–5
requirements in feed, labor, and other costs	919	4–6
unit requirements in western Washington, bulletin by J. B. Bain and G. E. Braun	919	1–19
Mills—		
cottonseed oil, cleaning for pink bollworm control	918	55, 57
hominy, corn oil production, operations and cost	904	16, 19
lumber, reporting manufacture of walnut lumber, 1907–1918	909	31
Millwork, walnut, demands and uses	909	67–68, 89
Minnesota, hail insurance companies, and amount of risks	912	6, 14
Mission grape, origin and value	903	2–3
Missions, California, early history notes	903	2–3
Missouri, walnut, stand and quality	909	9, 10, 11, 20, 21, 23
Mites, rust—		
control by spraying	924	3–5
relation to tear-stain of citrus fruits	924	1–5, 11
Montana—		
hail insurance law, enactment and operation	912	7, 8, 9
law on purchase of water right	913	12–13
water rights, laws, officials, etc	913	3, 12–13
Mortar, formula for laying concrete pipe	906	14–15
Mosquitoes, control by fungous disease, note	922	17

	Bulletin No.	Page.
Moth—		
grape-berry—		
life history studies in northern Ohio, bulletin by H. G. Ingerson...	911	1–38
rearing for seasonal history studies.....................	911	1–2
pink bollworm, factor in spread...........................	918	35–36
red-banded—		
leaf-hopper, description, life history, distribution, etc...	914	2–11
leaf-roller, injury to crops, control, etc...................	914	5–12
Moths, grape-berry—		
resistance to low temperature...........................	911	35–36
seasonal history, studies, 1916, 1917, 1918, in Ohio..........	911	2–32
Motor trucks, use by farmers of Eastern States, bulletin by H. R. Tolley and L. M. Church.................................	910	1–37
See also Trucks.		
Musical instruments, manufacture from black walnut.............	909	60, 66–67, 88
Mustard—		
injury by western cabbage flea-beetle.....................	902	6, 7
sauce, use in sardine packing, composition..................	908	68–69
Nanism. See Brachysm.		
Nasturtium, injury by western cabbage flea-beetle, note.........	902	5
Nebraska—		
hail insurance—		
companies and amount of risks...........................	912	6, 14, 29
law, enactment and operation............................	912	7–8, 9
walnut, stand and quality...............................	909	9, 10, 16, 21
water rights, laws, officials, etc............................	913	2, 3
Necrosis, potatoes, caused by frost, studies...................	916	2–4
Nematodes, enemies of cabbage flea-beetle...................	902	14
Nevada, water rights, officials................................	913	3
New Hampshire, farmers' experience with motor trucks (with other Eastern States), bulletin by H. R. Tolley and L. M. Church	910	1–37
New Jersey—		
farmers experience with motor trucks (with other Eastern States), bulletin by H. R. Tolley and L. M. Church........	910	1–37
walnut, stand and quality................................	909	9, 10, 16–17, 19, 21
New Mexico—		
cabbage flea-beetle, occurrence and injuries to crops.........	902	4, 5, 6, 7
water rights, officials....................................	913	3
New York—		
farmers' experience with motor trucks (with other Eastern States), bulletin by H. R. Tolley and L. M. Church.........	910	1–37
walnut, stand and quality................................	909	9, 10, 16, 21
Nodosities, grapevine, cause and description..................	903	22, 25, 53
North Carolina, walnut stand and quality.....................	909	10, 11, 19, 21
North Dakota—		
hail insurance—		
companies, and amount of risks..........................	912	6, 14, 15, 26, 28, 29
law, provisions, etc.....................................	912	6, 7, 8
water rights, officials...................................	913	3
Norway, sardine exports to United States, 1910–1916...........	908	117, 118
NOUGARET, R. L., and W. M. DAVIDSON, bulletin on "The grape phylloxera in California"............................	903	1–128
NUCKOLS, SAMUEL B., and THOMAS H. SUMMERS, bulletin on "Farm practice in growing field crops in three sugar-beet districts of Colorado"..	917	1–52
Oats—		
growing in Colorado, farm practices (with other crops)......	917	11–40
yields, North Central States, seven-year period..............	920	26, 41
Ohio—		
northern, grape-berry moth, life history, bulletin by H. G. Ingerson..	911	1–38
walnut, stand and quality................................	909	9, 10, 13, 18, 19, 21, 23

	Bulletin No.	Page.
Ohio—Continued.		
Washington County—		
farm profits, 25 farms, 1912–1918	920	3, 5, 7–33
farming, profits and losses	920	3, 5, 7–22
Oil—		
corn—		
chemical properties, and utilization	904	13–14
crude, filtering, buying and selling	904	11–12
expelling from germs, method, and machines used	904	8–11
production and utilization, bulletin by A. F. Sievers	904	1–23
production cost	904	17–20
production operation in different mills, comparison	904	16
refining for food use	904	20–22
sardine packing, tests	908	66–68
cottonseed, losses in quantity and quality	918	30–31
lubricating, requirement for motor trucks of different sizes	910	27
use in sardine packing, food value, quantity, and kinds	908	4–5, 10, 60–68, 119
Oklahoma—		
cabbage flea-beetle, occurrence and injuries to crops	902	4, 5
hail insurance—		
companies, and amount of risks	912	6, 14, 26, 28, 29
law enactment and provisions	912	8, 9
walnut, stand and quality	909	9, 10, 14, 20, 21
water rights, officials	913	3
Okra, infestation with pink bollworm	918	33
Olive oil, use in sardine packing	908	119
Onions, freezing, effect of handling	916	4
Oranges, tear-stain, investigations, and cultural work	924	1, 5–11
Orchards, irrigation from distributing hydrants	906	46, 50, 51, 52, 53, 54
Oregon, water rights, officials	913	2, 3
Orleans Hill Vineyard, California, historical notes	903	6
Packing, sardines—		
in cans, details	908	10, 58–69, 122
methods and precautions	908	6–12, 98–101, 103–105, 124
Parasites, leaf-folder, list	914	10–12
Pasture—		
dairy cows, requirements and cost in milk production	923	4, 6, 9, 10, 13, 17, 18
requirements for dairy herd, per 100 pounds of milk produced	919	4, 6, 10, 11–12, 15, 19
Pasturing, cotton fields for bollworm control	918	54
Peas, injury by western cabbage flea-beetle	902	5, 6
Pediculoides ventricosus, occurrence on larvæ of pink bollworm	918	47
Pedigree, live stock, consideration in selection of breeding-animals.	905	50–54
Pennsylvania—		
farmers experiecne with motor trucks (with other Eastern States), bulletin by H. R. Tolley and L. M. Church	910	1–37
walnut, stand and quality	909	9, 10, 16–17, 19, 21
Pepper-grass, injury by western cabbage flea-beetle	902	6
Phylloxera—		
grape—		
biology in California	903	27–44, 98, 124–126
biology in Eastern United States and Mediterranean region	903	28, 95–98, 124

	Bulletin No.	Page.
Phylloxera—Continued.		
grape—continued.		
control by water and heat, experiments	903	98–100
diffusion means	903	100–122, 123
in California, bulletin by W. M. Davidson and R. L. Nougaret	903	1–128
in California, discovery	903	4
indications in vineyards	903	15, 18–22
infestation progress in California, map indicating	903	12
life history, hibernation, forms, and habits	903	31–98, 124–126
nomenclature and synonymy	903	26–27
rearing experiments, California, methods	903	52–53
spread, accidental and natural, in California	903	7–11
vineyards destruction, details	903	15–18, 123–124
wandering radicicole larvæ, factor of spread	903	9, 10, 72–73, 102–115, 117
winged, development, description, and habits	903	73–82
winged, factor in spread, discussion	903	8–9, 100–102
vitifoliæ. See Phylloxera, grape.		
Pickling, fish, in sardine industry	908	8, 34–50, 122
Pilchard, French sardine, identification and advantages	908	2–3, 118–119
Pink bollworm, cotton, report on investigations in Mexico	918	1–64
See also Bollworm, pink.		
Pipe—		
concrete—		
carrying capacities in miner's inches, table, etc	906	24–25, 37
description, cost, laying, and causes of failure	906	4–23
reinforced, description and cost	906	6–8
use in irrigation, bulletin by F. W. Stanley and Samuel Fortier	906	1–54
irrigation systems, design	906	23–54
Pipes—		
concrete, failure, causes	906	15–23
irrigation, types and materials, description	906	2–4
laying in irrigation work, trenching, back filling, and jointing	906	13–15
metal, description, and use in irrigation	906	2–3, 4
steel, description, surfacing, or inclosing with concrete	906	2–3, 4
vitrified, clay, use in irrigation	906	3–4
wood, use in irrigation, incasing with concrete	906	3, 4
Planing mill, products from black walnut, demands and uses	909	60, 67–68, 89
Planting, practices in Colorado, depth, dates, and rates	917	19–21
Plants—		
dormant, resistant to fumigation injury	907	33
malvaceous, infestation with pink bollworm	918	32–34
resistance to gas injury, physiological conditions causing	907	30–33
Plowing, practices, Colorado, sugar-beet districts	917	13–15
Poison, barium carbonate, toxicity to rats, bulletin by Erich W. Schwartze	915	1–11
Poisoning—		
pink bollworm, experiments	918	51–52
rats, with barium carbonate, experiments	915	2–11
Polychrosis viteana. See Moth, grape-berry.		
Pop corn, hybrid, brachytic characters	925	2–7, 10
Posson, R. J., J. B. Bain, and Ralph P. Hotis, bulletin on "Unit requirements for producing market milk in Vermont"	923	1–18
Posts, walnut, utilization of small and defective logs	909	59, 81
Potatoes—		
freezing—		
injury when undercooled, bulletin by R. C. Wright and George F. Taylor	916	1–15
points of seven varieties, studies	916	4–7
frost—		
injuries, classes	916	1
necrosis, physiology, studies, review of literature on	916	2–4

	Bulletin No.	Page.
Potatoes—Continued.		
growing in Colorado—		
farm practices (with other crops)	917	11–40
labor distribution and cost	917{	7, 9, 10, 11, 45
handling, cause of freezing when undercooled	916	3, 5–14
inoculation with frost necrosis, experiments	916	7–14
marketing in Colorado	917	41–42
Poultry—		
color heredity	905	33
comb heredity	905	33
enemies of clover-leaf weevil	922	17
feed, fish meal, use and value, note	908	111
Prepotency, animal breeding	905	34–36
Propeller, airplane, walnut stock, prices and consumption	909	74, 77–79
Purebreds, live stock, value in grading-up	905	54–63
Radicicole—		
grape phylloxera, description and life history	903	44–73
wandering, of grape phylloxera, factor in spread	903{	9, 10, 72–73, 102–115, 117
Radishes, injury by western cabbage flea-beetle	902	4, 5, 6, 7
Rats—		
destruction, bibliography	915	10–11
heredity studies	905	20–23
poisoning, toxicity of barium carbonate	915	1–11
Reclamation, Federal, water rights of individuals	913	11
Rhode Island, farmers' experience with motor trucks (with other Eastern States), bulletin by H. R. Tolley and L. M. Church	910	1–37
Roads, type, effect on motor trucks	910	17–19
Roller, leaf. See Leaf-roller.		
Root louse. See Radicicole.		
Roots—		
grape, phylloxera spread	903	8, 120–121
grapevines, lesions from phylloxera, description and results	903	22–26
Rust mites. See Mites.		
Rutabaga, injury by western cabbage flea-beetle	902	6
Salt, dry, effect on sardines	908	42–46
Salting, fish, in sardine industry	908	8, 34–50, 122
Sanitation, sardine packing	908	98–101, 124
Sardine—		
industry, Maine, bulletin by F. C. Weber, H. W. Houghton, and J. B. Wilson	908	1–127
pack, standardization	908	96–98, 124
paste, preparation	908	109
Sardines—		
analysis methods	908	12–14
cannery, sanitation	908	98–101, 124
cans, description, sizes, and types	908	11–12
deviled, preparation	908	110–111
fish species used for	908	1–3
food value, comparison with other foods	908	5
freezing and thawing during storage, effects	908	78–80
imports, 1910–1916	908	117–118
industry in United States, history of development	908	3–4
packing—		
in cans with oil, mustard, etc	908{	10, 58–59, 122
methods and sanitary precautions	908{	6–12, 98–101, 103–105, 124
sanitation of equipment	908	98–101
pickling and salting, details, and changes occurring	908	34–50, 122
processing	908	10, 69–70
Russian, preparation	908	106
storing, and changes during storage	908{	10–11, 70–80, 122
stuffed, preparation	908	108
waste, utilization in canneries	908	102–115

	Bulletin No.	Page.
SCHWARTZE, ERICH W., bulletin on "Toxicity of varium carbonate to rats"....	915	1–11
Screens, use in irrigation systems................................	906	27–29
Sea herring. *See* Herring, sea.		
Sealing, cans of sardines, methods, machines, and precautions....	908	10, 101
Seed—		
alfalfa, planting depth, dates and rate.....................	917	20, 21
barley, planting dates and rate, Colorado...................	917	21
beans, planting depth, dates and rate.....................	917	20, 21
bed, preparation for crops, Colorado sugar-beet districts......	917	12–19
cantaloupe—		
harvesting..	917	38
planting depth, dates and rate.........................	917	20, 21
cotton—		
fumigation for pink bollworm control...................	918 {	47–51, 55–56, 57
losses in weight and oil, from pink bollworm............	918	28–31
spread of pink bollworm..............................	918	35
cucumber—		
harvesting..	917	37
planting depth, dates, rates, and spacing...............	917	20, 21
grain, planting depth, dates and rates of seeding............	917	20, 21
oats, planting dates, and rate, Colorado.....................	917	21
planting depths, dates and rates, for various crops..........	917	20–21
potatoes, planting depth, dates and rates, Colorado..........	917	20, 21
sugar beets, planting depth, dates and rate.................	917	20, 21
wheat, planting dates and rate, Colorado...................	917	21
Selection, breeding animals, methods.......................	905	47–50
Sewing machines, black walnut uses for.....................	909	68, 89
Sex, determination in animal breeding, discussion.............	905	23–29
Sheep, color heredity....................................	905	33
Shrimps, food of sea herring, description, and effect on fish......	908 {	17, 18, 22–23, 121
SIEVERS, A. F., bulletin on "The production and utilization of corn oil in the United States"....................................	904	1–23
Sirup—		
making—		
calrification agents, use................................	921	2–5
from cane, vacuum evaporation.......................	921	12–13
methods, new and old, comparison, costs and results.....	921	7–12
vacuum evaporation of cane juice.....................	921	12–13
manufacture from cane, clarification of juice, bulletin by J. K. Dale and C. S. Hudson..................................	921	1–15
Soap, making with corn oil..............................	904	13
Soil—		
conditions, relation to citrus fruit injury by fumigation......	907	30–32
infested, source of phylloxera infestation..................	903	121–122
Soils, Colorado, sugar-beet districts, description.............	917	3–4
South America—		
market for Maine sardines, possibilities....................	908	119–120
sardine imports into various countries, value..............	908	120
South Carolina, walnut, stand and quality..................	909	9, 10, 17
South Dakota—		
hail insurance law, enactment and operation................	912	8, 9
water rights, officials..................................	913	3
Sows, breeding and gestation periods.......................	905	6, 7, 8
Specifications, standards for sardine pack..................	908	96–98
Spray, arsenical, use in leaf-roller control..................	914	12
Spraying—		
cabbage flea-beetle, experiments and directions.............	902	14–18, 20
grapefruit for wither-tip tear-stain, results................	924	3–5
grapes, for control of grape-berry moth...................	911	14, 33, 38
Sprays, cabbage flea-beetle, formulas and directions for use......	902	14–18, 20
Standardization, sardine pack, specifications, suggestions........	908	96–98, 124
Standpipes, irrigation systems, description and use.............	906	21–22, 29–30

	Bulletin No.	Page.
STANLEY, F. W., and SAMUEL FORTIER, bulletin on "The use of concrete pipe in irrigation"	906	1–54
Steaming, walnut lumber	909	33
Storage, sardines, and changes	908	10–11,70–80, 123
Streams, water rights, titles, and water distribution methods	913	4–8, 13
Sugar—		
losses in clarification of sugar-cane juice, control	921	10, 11, 12
manufacture from juice clarified by infusorial earth	921	14
Sugar-beet districts, Colorado, growing field crops, farm practices, bulletin by Samuel B. Nuckols and Thomas Summers	917	1–52
Sugar-cane juice, clarification for sirup manufacture, bulletin by J. K. Dale and C. S. Hudson	921	1–15
SUMMERS, THOMAS H., and SAMUEL B. NUCKOLS, bulletin on "Farm practice in growing field crops in three sugar-beet districts of Colorado"	917	1–52
"Swells," canned sardines, causes, studies, and disposal	908	20–26, 99, 121
Tanks, sardine, sanitation	908	99–100
Tariff, olive oil, suggestions	908	119
"Tassel-ear," corn plant, note	925	2
TAYLOR, GEORGE F., and R. C. WRIGHT, bulletin on "Freezing injury to potatoes when undercooled"	916	1–15
Tear-stain—		
citrus fruits, bulletin by John R. Winston	924	1–12
wither-tip—		
cultural work with oranges and grape fruit	924	5–8
of citrus fruits, description, occurrence, and importance	924	1–2
TEELE, R. P., bulletin on "The Western farmer's water right"	913	1–14
Telegony, theory, discussion	905	14
Temperature, effect on plant injury by fumigation	907	4–27, 37–40
Tennessee, walnut, stand and quality	909	9, 10, 11, 12, 13, 18, 19, 21, 23
Texas—		
cabbage flea-beetle, occurrence and injuries to crops	902	4, 5, 6, 7
walnut, stand and quality	909	9, 14, 20, 21
water rights, laws, officials, etc	913	2, 3
Thrashing beans, practices in Colorado	917	35
Ties, walnut, production and prices	909	58–59
Tin, determination in sardines	908	82–85
Tires, motor truck, mileage costs, and kinds recommended	910	27–29
Tlahualilo Co., aid in pink bollworm investigations	918	1, 26
TOLLEY, H. R., and L. M. CHURCH, bulletin on "Experience of Eastern farmers with motor trucks"	910	1–37
Tomato—		
injury by western cabbage flea-beetle	902	7
sauce, use in sardine packing	908	68
TOWER, D. G., and F. A. FENTON, bulletin on "Clover-leaf weevil"	922	1–18
Transportation, fish, in sardine industry, methods and details	908	8, 26–34, 121
Trap crops, use for control of cabbage flea-beetles	902	19
Traps—		
mechanical, use in control of western cabbage flea-beetle	902	19
pink bollworm, control experiments	918	52–53
Trash, removal from fields, farm practices in Colorado	917	12–13
Tree roots, aid in spread of phylloxera	903	117
Trenching, concrete pipe, methods and costs	906	13–15
Trichogramma minutum, enemy of pink bollworm	918	47
Truck crops, injury by—		
red-banded leaf-roller	914	1, 5, 6, 7, 9, 10, 12
western cabbage flea-beetle	902	1–2, 4–8, 20
Trucks, motor—		
cost depreciation, and cost of operating	910	23, 32–34
displacement of horses on farms in eastern States	910	35–36
gas and oil requirements per mile, various sizes	910	26–27

	Bulletin No.	Page.
Trucks, motor—Continued.		
life and depreciation on eastern farms	910	23–24
reliability, experience of eastern farmers	910	29–32
saving of time, comparison with horse wagons	910	11–13
use by farmers, advantages and objections	910	9–10
use by farmers of eastern States, bulletin by H. R. Tolley and L. M. Church	910	1–37
use in milk marketing, practices and value	919	5
Turnips, injury by western cabbage flea-beetle	902	4, 5, 6, 7
Utah, water rights, officials	913	3
Vacuum evaporation, cane-sirup manufacture	921	12–13
VALGREN, V. N., bulletin on "Hail insurance on farm crops in the United States"	912	1–32
Valves, irrigation, types and cost	906	53–54
Vegetables—		
cruciferous, injury by western cabbage flea-beetle	902	1–2, 4–7, 20
injury by red-banded leaf-roller	914	1–2, 10
Vehicles, manufacture, use of black walnut	909	71–72, 89
Veneer, black walnut, production manufacture, grades, and prices	909	44–58, 79
Venturi meters, for irrigation water, description	906	32
Vermont—		
farmers' experience with motor trucks (with other Eastern States), bulletins by H. R. Tolley and L. M. Church	910	1–37
market milk production, unit requirements, bulletin by J. B. Bain, R. J. Posson, and Ralph P. Hotis	923	1–18
Vineyard, material and implements; spread of phylloxera	903	9–11, 115–117
Vineyards—		
destruction by phylloxera, details	903	15–18, 123–124
early planting in California, and phylloxera introduction	903	4–7
pest, grapevine flea-beetle, bulletin by Dwight Isley	901	1–27
phylloxera indications	903	15, 18–22
Virginia, walnut, stand and quality	909	9, 10, 15, 19, 21
Viticulture, growth and magnitude, California	903	13–14
Vitis—		
californica, grafting stock, objections	903	2
spp., native, resistance to phylloxera	903	2
Walnut—		
airplane, propeller stock, prices and consumption	909	74, 77–79
demand for	909	21–22
description and physical properties of wood	909	2–6
exports, amounts and value, 1912–1917	909	74–76
firearms manufacture, demands and value	909	60, 68–70, 76–79
logging methods and costs	909	41–42, 81–85
lumber manufacture details, grades and prices	909	32–41
market conditions and marketing	909	79–85
supply, growth range, and quality from various sections	909	9–21
uses, detailed list	909	88–89
utilization—		
bulletin by Warren D. Brush	909	1–89
by industries	909	22–74
war-time demands and consumption	909	69, 76–79
War material, walnut, demands and use	909	76–79
Warehouses, cotton seed, cleaning, for pink bollworm control	918	55, 57
Washington—		
water rights, laws, officials, etc	913	3
western, milk production, unit requirements, bulletin by J. B. Bain and G. E. Braun	919	1–19
Waste—		
cotton, part in pink bollworm spread	918	35, 55

	Bulletin No.	Page.
Waste—Continued.		
sardine—		
canneries, utilization	908	109–115
packing, elimination, suggestions	908	102–115
Water—		
distribution to farmers from streams or canals, methods in use in West	913	13–14
flowing, part in pink bollworm spread	918	36–38
recording devices	906	40–41
registers, description and use	906	39–40
rights—		
meaning and general charactersistics, and requirements	913	1–4
officials in charge in Western States	913	3
purchase of commercial companies	913	12–13
stream, evidences of title	913	4–8
title, evidences	913	4–8
western farmer, bulletin by R. P. Teele	913	1–14
supply, sardine canneries, bacteriological examination	908	98–99
underground, rights of western farmers	913	8–9
Water-cress, injury by western cabbage flea-beetle	902	6
WEBER, F. C., H. W. HOUGHTON, and J. B. WILSON, bulletin on "The Maine sardine industry"	908	1–127
Weevil, clover leaf—		
bulletin by D. G. Tower and F. A. Fenton	922	1–18
distribution, description, and life history	922	1–12
enemies and control	922	16–18
Weirs—		
irrigation, dimensions and discharge tables	906	32–37
use in catching sea herring for sardines	908	7, 19
West Virginia, walnut, stand and quality	909	9, 10, 15, 19, 21
West, water rights of farmer, bulletin by R. P. Teele	913	1–14
Western cabbage flea-beetle, bulletin by F. H. Chittenden and H. O. Marsh	902	1–21
Wheat—		
growing in Colorado—		
farm practices (with other crops)	917	17–40
labor distribution and cost	917	10, 11, 12, 45
yields, North Central States, seven-year period	920	11, 26, 41
WILSON, J. B., F. C. WEBER, and H. W. HOUGHTON, bulletin on "The Maine sardine industry"	908	1–127
WINSTON, JOHN R., bulletin on "Tear-stain of citrus fruit"	924	1–12
Wisconsin—		
Dane County, farm profits, 60 farms, 1913–1917	920	3, 5, 41–55
walnut, stand and quality	909	9, 10, 17–18
Wither-tip, tear-stain, citrus fruits, bulletin by John R. Winston. See also Tear-stain.	924	1–12
WOGLUM, R. S., bulletin on "Fumigation of citrus plants with hydrocyanic acid: Conditions influencing injury"	907	1–43
Wood, walnut, properties	909	2–6
WRIGHT—		
R. C., and GEORGE F. TAYLOR, bulletin on "Freezing injury to potatoes when undercooled"	916	1–15
SEWALL, bulletin on "Principles of livestock breeding"	905	1–67
Wyoming—		
cabbage flea-beetle, occurrence and injuries to crops	902	4
water rights, officials	913	3

UNITED STATES DEPARTMENT OF AGRICULTURE

BULLETIN No. 901

Contribution from the Bureau of Entomology
L. O. HOWARD, Chief

Washington, D. C.   PROFESSIONAL PAPER   December 13, 1920

GRAPEVINE FLEA-BEETLES.

By Dwight Isely,

Scientific Assistant, Deciduous-Fruit Insect Investigations.

CONTENTS.

	Page.		Page.
Introduction	1	The lesser grapevine flea-beetle—Continued.	
History	2	Distribution	13
The grapevine flea-beetle	4	Food plants	13
Description of stages	4	Habits	13
Distribution	6	Life history	14
Food plants	6	Economic importance	20
Habits	7	Predatory enemies	22
Life history	7	Methods of control	23
The lesser grapevine flea-beetle	11	General summary	24
Description of stages	11	Literature cited	26

INTRODUCTION.

The grapevine flea-beetle (*Altica chalybea* Ill.) is a grape pest which, in the period of its most destructive activity in early spring, eats out the swelling buds, causing severe injury in restricted localities. It is one of the best known and most widely distributed of the insect enemies of the grape. No other is the source of so many complaints to the Bureau of Entomology, and American entomological literature is full of references to it. In general its life history is well known, yet, in spite of this, occasional discrepancies occur in accounts of its life history that have never been reconciled with the usually recorded observations. These discrepancies are usually disposed of by attributing them to the variation of individual beetles.

A study of the life history of the grapevine flea-beetle was undertaken by the writer during the season of 1916 for the purpose of comparison with that of a smaller flea-beetle also attacking grape. A close similarity between the smaller beetle and the typical species was noted, but the differences, particularly in seasonal history and habits, were so well marked and so constant that the writer was surprised when the smaller beetle was determined as "*Altica chalybea* Ill., small form." When it was noted that the seasonal history and habits of the typical flea-beetle conformed quite closely with those usually ascribed to it, particularly by Slingerland (*19*)[1] and Hartzell (*23, 24*), and that those of the "small form" coincided with the discrepancies mentioned above, the writer became of the opinion that two economic species had been masquerading under a single name. The existence of two species instead of one had long been suspected by Mr. E. A. Schwarz, who determined the reared material, but in the absence of biological data which would differentiate them he had not previously thought it advisable to erect a new species.

It is obvious that the confusion of two pests that are similar but have different seasonal histories may lead to a serious confusion in the application of remedial measures. It is, therefore, the purpose of this paper in the account of these two species, *Altica chalybea* Ill. and *A. woodsi*, herein described as new, to give particular attention to structure and habits by which they may be distinguished. Where each species must be treated separately, the typical grapevine flea-beetle, being the one generally known, is first considered, and the "small form" is then compared with it. The data presented are based on rearing records and field observations made at North East. Pa., during the seasons of 1916 and 1917 and miscellaneous field observations during the two seasons previous.[2]

HISTORY.

There are over 135 references to the grapevine flea-beetle in the literature of American economic entomology, a larger number of references than to any other American grape insect except the grapevine rootworm (*Fidia viticida* Walsh). Since 1859 there has been at least one reference to it each year except during the years 1866, 1873, and 1875. Most of these references no doubt apply to the typical form.

The grapevine flea-beetle was first described in 1807 by Illiger (*1*), who named it *Haltica chalybea*. It was again described by Le Conte (*2*) as *Galeruca janthina* and later by Thomas (*3*) as *Chrysomela vitivora*. Harris (*5*) in 1835 placed *C. vitivora* Thomas as a synonym of *H. chalybea* Ill., and the same year Herrick (*4*) showed that *G. janthina* Lec. was a synonym of the same species. In most of the recent literature relating to this insect it has been designated under the generic name Haltica. Woods (*25*) has recently shown that the original spelling *Altica* should be used instead of the amended form *Haltica*.

---

[1] Reference is made by number (italics) to "Literature cited," p. 26.

[2] During the season of 1916 the writer was assisted by Mr. James K. Primm. The writer is further indebted to Mr. J. H. Paine for the photographs used in Plates II and III and to Mr. H. K. Plank for the photograph used in Plate IV.

In the first account of the habits of the grapevine flea-beetle, Thomas recorded the destructiveness to grape buds by the adult, the feeding upon leaves by the larvæ, and the transformation through the pupal stage in the soil. Regarding these habits there has been practically no disagreement by succeeding authors. Conflicting statements have been frequently made, however, regarding the number of generations a year, the place of oviposition, and food plants.

Harris (6) outlined the seasonal history as follows: The emergence of adults from hibernation in April, followed by the development of immature stages, gives rise to another brood in July that are to pass through the ensuing winter. Harris called the brood of adults emerging in July a "second" brood, but he clearly meant that only one brood was produced annually. Harris's observations have been upheld by subsequent investigations, notably those of Slingerland (19) and Hartzell (23, 24), who have made the most thorough studies of the insect. Kirkpatrick (9), however, says that there are several generations annually, and the statement that there are two or more broods has been frequently made by subsequent writers. Lowe (20) states that there is a partial second brood in New York. Slingerland (19) offered a reason for inferring the existence of a second brood by quoting correspondence with Lowe in which the latter stated that he had found a beetle of this species ovipositing as late as July 15. At that time many newly transformed beetles were emerging while the overwintering beetles had disappeared before the last of June. Slingerland explained this unusual record of Lowe's as a record of an exceptionally late emergence of a tardy individual.

Riley (10) first stated that the eggs were deposited upon the leaves, and for nearly 30 years this was the generally accepted belief and was frequently copied by subsequent writers. Accompanying his statement of the place of oviposition he describes the eggs as "orange" and "like those of the potato beetle," making it seem probable that he had observed the eggs of some other insect. Comstock (12), in the most complete account of the insect up to that time, also stated that the eggs were found upon the leaves, either on the upper or lower side, and gave authority to his statement by accompanying it with an accurate description of the general appearance of the egg, and stated that it was "straw colored" and averaged 0.65 mm. in length. Marlatt (18) also referred to them as occurring on the leaves, but on the undersides only. Slingerland (19) stated that the eggs were usually found in groups under bud scales and strips of bark; and this observation was confirmed by Hartzell (23). Both investigators state that eggs may occasionally be found on the leaves. Hartzell describes the eggs as orange or saffron colored and with an average length of 1.03 mm.

The grapevine flea-beetle has been recorded as feeding on various plants, including the following: Grape (Thomas, *3*), black alder (Harris, *7*), plum and elm (Fitch, *8*); Virginia creeper (Saunders, *11*), apple and quince (MacMillan, *14*), peach (Neal, *16*), and blue beech (Schwarz, *17*).

Of these food plants only three have been frequently listed, viz, the grape, the Virginia creeper, and the black alder. It was suggested by Lintner (*13*) that records of feeding upon black alder were probably due to a confusion of this species with *A. bimarginata*, the alder flea-beetle, which closely resembles *A. chalybea*. This view was confirmed, at least so far as Harris was concerned, by Slingerland (*19*), who found in Harris's entomological correspondence evidence that Harris's later studies convinced him that the alder flea-beetle and the grapevine flea-beetle are separate species. Hartzell (*24*) lists only cultivated grape of the Concord variety and the wild grape (*Vitis bicolor*) as food plants.

Slingerland (*19*) records a difference of opinion among growers as to what varieties of grapes are most seriously attacked by the grapevine flea-beetle, some correspondents stating that the flea-beetle preferred Concord foliage and others that it preferred the thin-leaved varieties.

In addition to the references designating the grapevine flea-beetle as *A. chalybea* Ill., Lugger (*21*) describes the habits of an insect which he calls "the lesser grapevine flea-beetle," and believed to be *A. ignita* Ill., the strawberry flea-beetle. He describes the habits as similar to those of *A. chalybea*, the only difference noted being that the former was little more than half the size of *A. chalybea*. It is quite possible that the insect referred to was the "small form" of the grapevine flea-beetle.

In discussing the "*ignita group*" of the genus Altica, Woods (*26*) mentions a beetle believed to be a new species collected on woodbine both in 1917 and in 1918, which is probably the lesser grapevine flea-beetle. He describes the salient characteristics of the adult and mentions that the eggs are deposited singly or by twos on the under surface of the leaves.

THE GRAPEVINE FLEA-BEETLE.

DESCRIPTION OF STAGES.

THE ADULT.

Pl. II, fig. 3.

The following is a copy of Horn's (*15*) description of the beetle:

H. chalybea Illig.

Oval, of moderately robust facies, color usually metallic shining blue, rarely cupreous or greenish. Antennæ half as long as the body, piceous, the basal half with metallic lustre, joints 2-3-4 gradually longer. Head smooth, slightly rough-

PLATE I.

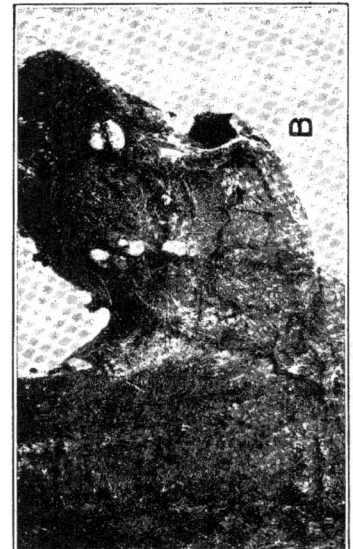

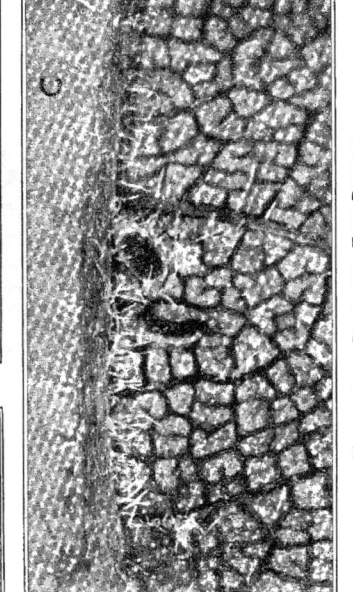

EGGS OF THE GRAPEVINE FLEA-BEETLES.

A, Eggs of *Altica chalybea* on grape cane under bark strip. B, Eggs of *Altica chalybea* on grape cane. C, Eggs of *Altica chalybea* on grape

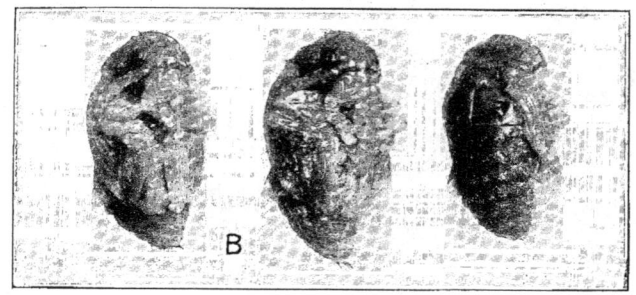

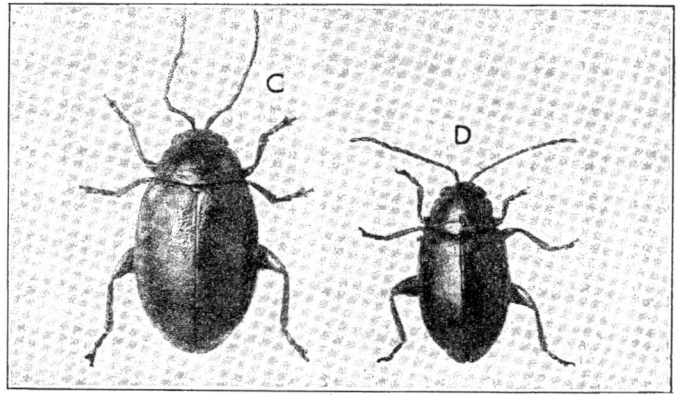

STAGES OF THE GRAPEVINE FLEA-BEETLES.

A, Mature larvæ of *Altica woodsi.*   B, Pupæ of *Altica woodsi.*   C, Adult of *Altica chalybea.*
D, Adult of *Altica woodsi.*

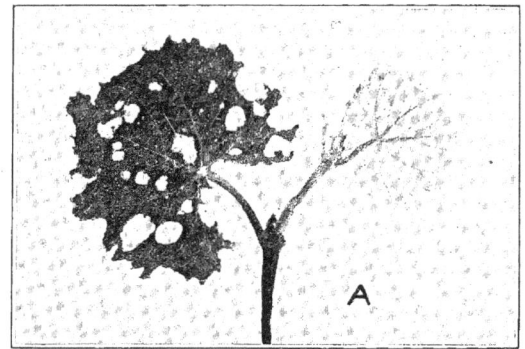

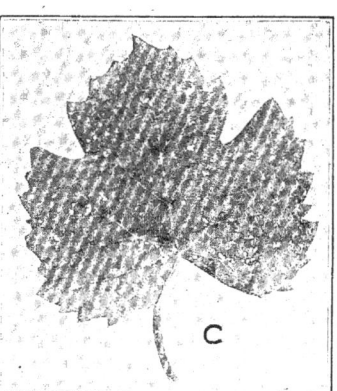

WORK OF GRAPEVINE FLEA-BEETLES.

A, Feeding marks of adult beetle of *Altica chalybea* on leaf of Concord grape.　*B*, Larvæ and feeding marks of *Altica chalybea* on upper surface of grape leaf (thick-leaved variety).　*C*, Feeding marks of adult beetle of *Altica chalybea* on grape leaf (thick-leaved variety).

WORK OF LESSER GRAPEVINE FLEA-BEETLE.

Feeding marks of larvæ and adults on grape (thin-leaved variety).

ened near the eyes, frontal carina rather acute, the tubercles small, oblique. Thorax a little more than half wider than long, narrowed in front, sides arcuate, margin narrow, slightly thickened in front, disc convex, the ante-basal impressed line rather deep and extending from margin to margin, surface with extremely minute scattered punctures. Elytra scarcely wider at base than the thorax, humeri rounded, umbone moderately prominent, smooth, limited within by a slight depression, surface sparsely punctate, nearly smooth near apex. Body beneath and legs blue-black, moderately shining, abdomen sparsely punctate. Length .16–.20 inch; 4–5 mm.

THE EGG.

Pl. I, A, B.

In general shape the egg is subcylindrical, with the ends rounded. The surface is roughly pitted, and on the surface opposite to the side of attachment is a twisted brownish strand about one-third the length of the egg. The color varies from a deep yellow to orange. Length 1.10 mm.; diameter 0.42 mm.

The size and color agree with the description by Hartzell (*23*) but differ from that of Comstock (*12*).

THE LARVA.

Similar to larva of *Altica woodsi*, Pl. II, A.

The larva is short and stout, convex dorsally and flattened ventrally, and is further characterized by a nearly hemispherical head, by short stout legs, and by an anus which functions as a locomotor organ. Each body segment is marked by a double series of chitinized plates or tubercles and the skin between these plates is dotted with minute wartlike excrescences. When the larva is newly hatched or molted it is yellow in color. Upon exposure to the air, however, the chitinized areas become shining black and as they fit closely together the larva itself becomes shining black. With growth the skin between the chitinized areas begins to show and when the larva is full grown the skin is so distended that a brownish yellow is the dominant color, the black being confined to the chitinized areas. The spiracles are located on the meso-thoracic and first eight abdominal segments. The head and body plates are furnished with sparse, long setæ.

The arrangement of the body plates and setæ on the first seven abdominal segments is as follows: Dorsally each segment is furnished with two transverse rows of setiferous plates. The mid-dorsal plates are transversely elongate, the anterior one being slightly the longer, and are furnished with a seta on either side of the median line; on either side of each of these plates and above the spiracle are two smaller circular plates each bearing a single seta; below the spiracle is a prominent, longitudinal, compound tubercle, which roughly divides the dorsal and ventral aspects, bearing a pair of setæ, and below this is another tubercle also bearing two setæ; ventrally, near the anterior margin of the segment, there is one elongate, transverse plate crossing the median line and bearing one seta on either side; on the posterior half of the segment and at either side of the median plate is a small oval plate bearing two setæ.

On the first thoracic segment all dorsal plates are fused into one large plate, the prothoracic shield, which bears five pairs of setæ along the anterior margin, and three pairs in a row on the posterior margin; laterally there is one small tubercle bearing a single seta, and at the base of each coxa is a pair of tubercles each bearing a single seta; ventrally there is one large rectangular plate bearing an anterior and a posterior pair of setæ.

The second thoracic segment resembles the abdominal segments closely. The mid-dorsal plates are not continuous but are divided at the median line; on each side of the mid-dorsal plates is a single outer dorsal plate, the anterior one being quite small and non-setiferous, the posterior one quite large and bearing two setæ; on each side below the outer dorsal plates is the laterally prominent compound tubercle which bears three setæ instead of two as on the abdominal segments; below the compound tubercle are two plates each bearing a single seta, the anterior one also bearing the mesothoracic spiracle; there is a pair of tubercles above each coxa, the posterior one of which bears a single seta; ventrally the arrangment of plates is similar to that of the first abdominal segment except that the posterior pair of plates bear only one seta each.

The third thoracic segment is like the second but without the spiracle.

The eighth abdominal segment is like the second, but with only one small dorsal plate on each side of the posterior mid-dorsal plate.

On the ninth thoracic segment the dorsal plates are fused into a single large one, the anal shield, which bears five pairs of setæ; ventrally there is a single elongate plate bearing two pairs of setæ.

The tenth abdominal segment is without plates or setæ.

Measurements: Width of head: First instar 0.32 mm.; second instar 0.51 mm.· third instar 0.74 mm. Average length of full grown larva 7.5 mm.

THE PUPA.

Similar to pupa of *Altica woodsi*, Pl. II, B.

In general appearance this pupa is similar to the pupa of other chrysomelid beetles, the dorsal line being strongly arcuate, the legs folded ventrally, bent so that the femora are directed away from the median line and the tibiæ toward it, the prothoracic and mesothoracic legs over the wings and the metathoracic legs under them.

Color bright yellow, appendages lighter. Antennal joints with a circlet of projections at the distal ends (four projections visible on each joint), especially conspicuous on the distal segments; elytra reaching the fifth abdominal segment, wings the sixth; spiracles borne on the mesothoracic and the first six abdominal segments; arrangement of setæ as follows: 3 pairs on head, 1 above clypeus, 1 on inner margin of the eyes, and 1 slightly above and between the eyes; on prothorax, 8 pairs; on mesothorax and metathorax, 2 pairs; on abdominal segments 1 to 8, 4 pairs in a row near the posterior dorsal margin; and on segment 9, 4 pairs around the anal hooks; 3 setæ on the distal end of each femur. Length 5 mm.

DISTRIBUTION.

The grapevine flea-beetle is found in the eastern half of the United States and in the Canadian Province of Ontario. In entomological literature and in the files of the Bureau of Entomology it has been recorded from the District of Columbia and from the following States: Massachusetts, Vermont, Connecticut, New York, Pennsylvania, New Jersey, Delaware, Maryland, Virginia, West Virginia, North Carolina, Georgia, Florida, Ohio, Indiana, Illinois, Michigan, Wisconsin, Minnesota, Iowa, Missouri, Arkansas, Texas, Kansas, Nebraska, Colorado, and New Mexico. Some of these records may refer to the "small form."

FOOD PLANTS.

A list of food plants recorded in the literature of the species is given under history. The writer has collected it only on cultivated grapes (*Vitis* spp.), on various species of the wild grape (*Vitis* spp.), and on Virginia creeper (*Parthenocissus quinquefolia*).

HABITS.

The beetle emerges from hibernation in the spring at the time of the swelling of the grape buds, which it attacks voraciously, boring into the sides of the buds and eating out the tender parts. (Pl. I, B.) When the shoots begin to expand it eats large holes in the leaves (Pl. III, A), and often attacks the tender stems. The beetle is most voracious when newly emerged from hibernation and at that time can do an immense amount of damage.

Eggs are usually deposited on their sides, in groups, under bud scales or strips of bark, as described by Slingerland (*19*) and Hartzell (*23* and *24*). Occasionally they are placed on leaves on either the upper or the lower side.

The larvæ feed on either the upper or lower surface of thin-leaved varieties of cultivated and wild grapes, eating out large irregular holes, and often stripping out all of the leaf tissue except the leaf veins. On Concord or similar types of leaves they feed on the upper surface, leaving as feeding marks long, chain-like, whitish patches (Pl. III, B).

During the feeding period the larva molts twice. Upon becoming fully fed it burrows into the ground and forms a pupal cell a fraction of an inch below the surface. A few days are passed in the pupal cell, the prepupal period, preparatory for pupation. At the close of the pupal stage, after eclosion, the adult does not emerge at once, but remains in the cell until it is hardened and fully colored. Following emergence the beetle feeds sparingly until it goes into winter quarters. None of the specimens under observation during either season showed any tendency to copulate or oviposit during the period between transformation to the adult stage and hibernation.[1]

All stages of the beetles' activity are greatly influenced by changes in temperature. Both adults and larvæ feed more voraciously on warm days than in cold weather and on the cold days of early spring the beetles even appear to return to winter quarters. Hatching of eggs and molting of larvæ occur in the greatest numbers during the warmest part of the day.

LIFE HISTORY.

REARING METHODS.

The rearing methods used for the two species of flea-beetles were practically identical. Oviposition was secured from adults kept in battery jars or sleeve cages on grape shoots. Larvæ were reared in

---

[1] In addition to the insects native to the Erie-Chautauqua grape belt, upon which the foregoing account of habits and seasonal history and the following of life history are based, the writer received beetles from French Creek, W. Va., collected by Mr. Fred E. Brooks, and from Arlington, Va., collected by Mr. E. R. Selkregg, during the spring of 1917. These beetles and their offspring were reared in the insectary at North East, Pa., and their habits, seasonal history, and transformations agreed in detail with those of the native insects recorded herein.

1 by 4 inch vials. Transformations from the prepupal and pupal stages to the adult were passed in vials of the same size partially filled with earth. To determine the duration of each of these periods in the ground two methods were employed, as follows:

The first was to place a vial five-eighths of an inch in diameter inside of a vial 1 inch in diameter, filling the space between the two with earth. In this narrow space mature larvæ were placed and most of them were forced to form their pupal cells next to the glass surface, where their transformations could be observed readily. The outer vial was covered with black paper, which was removed only when observations were being made. For convenience of identification each cell was marked with a wax pencil. This method was faulty, because of the difficulty of maintaining the normal soil moisture in so thin a layer.

It was later learned that by pressing the earth in the middle of the vial, leaving the earth at the sides comparatively loose, about half of the larvæ would form pupal cells along the sides of the glass. It was necessary, of course, for success with this method, as with the former, that the vials be wrapped with black paper. This method was most used in 1917.

TABLE I.—*Feeding period of third larval stage of A. chalybea, North East, Pa., 1916.*

Number of larvæ.	Duration of period.
	Days.
18	6
29	7
17	8
15	9
6	10
2	11
2	13
[1]89	[2]7.75

[1] Total.   [2] Weighted average.

These methods of observing transformation in the ground were developed in the latter part of 1916 and the data on these transformations secured during that season are very meager. Hence records for the prepupal, pupal, and callow adult stages of both species are given only for 1917.

Detailed life-history studies of the typical grapevine flea-beetle did not begin in 1916 until the majority of the larvæ were at least half grown, since they were undertaken for comparison with the more common "small form." Accordingly rearing records cited below begin with the third larval stage in 1916.

DURATION OF FEEDING PERIOD OF THIRD STAGE IN 1916.

The duration of the feeding period of the third larval stage varied from 6 to 13 days, with an average of 7.75 days, as shown in Table I. The period covered by these records extended from June 12 to July 8.

DURATION OF PERIOD IN GROUND.

The duration of the period in the ground of 87 individuals reared varied from 15 to 24 days, with an average of 20.71 days.

The period covered by records of larvæ in the soil extended from June 19, when the first larvæ entered the ground, to July 27, when the latest adults emerged. The variation in duration of this period is shown in Table II.

EMERGENCE FROM HIBERNATION AND OVIPOSITION IN 1917.

The earliest record of adult emergence is May 11, at which time grape buds were swelling. Eggs were first found May 18. Adult beetles were found on grapevines until the latter part of June, when they disappeared altogether.

TABLE II.—*Period in ground of A. chalybea, North East, Pa., 1916.*

Number of individuals.	Duration of period.
	Days.
2	15
1	16
4	17
7	18
10	19
16	20
8	21
20	22
12	23
7	24
[1] 87	[2] 20.71

[1] Total.   [2] Weighted average.

INCUBATION PERIOD IN 1917.

The duration of the incubation period in 1917 (see Table III) varied from 13 to 21 days, with an average of 15.18 days, as shown in Table III. The period covered by records on the incubation period extended from May 26 to June 28.

LARVAL FEEDING PERIOD.

The duration of the larval feeding period of 46 individuals of *Altica chalybea* reared to adults varied from 19 to 33 days with an average of 24.26 days. The period covered by records of feeding larvae extended from June 4, the earliest date of hatching, to July 20, the latest date, when larvæ entered the ground. Complete data on the larval feeding period are given in Table IV.

TABLE III.—*Incubation period of A. chalybea, North East, Pa., 1917.*

Date of oviposition.	Date of hatching.	Number of eggs.	Duration of period.	Date of oviposition.	Date of hatching.	Number of eggs.	Duration of period.
			Days.				*Days.*
May 26	June 14	6	19	June 2	June 15	10	13
26	16	6	21	2	16	4	14
29	12	1	14	2	17	5	15
31	13	4	13	2	18	2	16
31	14	4	14	2	19	2	17
31	15	2	15	4	19	25	15
31	16	2	16	4	20	17	16
June 1	14	12	13	13	28	1	15
1	15	4	14				
1	16	1	15			[1] 108	[2] 15.18

[1] Total.   [2] Weighted average.

DURATION OF FIRST LARVAL STAGE.

The duration of the first stage, of 68 larvæ reared, varied from 4 to 14 days with an average of 8.74 days, as is shown in Table V. The total period covered by records on larvæ in this stage extended from June 4 to July 2.

Date of hatching.	Date of entering ground.	Number of larvæ.	Duration of period.	Date of hatching.	Date of entering ground.
			Days.		
June 4	June 28	2	24	June 17	July 8
12	July 1	1	19	17	10
13	4	2	21	17	11
13	5	1	22	19	10
13	8	4	25	19	11
14	7	1	23	19	13
14	8	2	24	19	14
14	9	2	25	19	20
14	17	1	33	20	15
15	11	2	26	20	17
15	13	2	28	20	20
16	8	1	22		
16	10	1	24		

¹ Total. ² Weighted aver

DURATION OF SECOND LARVAL STAGE.

The duration of the second stage, of 60 larvæ rei
5 to 11 days with an average of 6.95 days, as sho

TABLE V.—*First larval stage of A. chalybea, North East, Pa., 1917.*

The total period covere
larvæ of this stage exte:
to July 8.

Number of larvæ.	Duration of stage.
	Days.
1	4
2	5
1	6
8	7
26	8
9	9
8	10
10	11
1	12
1	13
1	14
¹ 68	² 8.74

¹ Total. ² Weighted average.

DURATION OF FEEDING PERIO
STAGE.

The duration of the i
the third stage, of 47 lar
from 5 to 13 days wit
8.53 days, as is shown in
total period covered by
of this stage extended
July 20.

DURATION OF PERIOD

The duration of the pe
varied from 15 to 25 days with an average of 19.24
period covered by records on the immature stages ii
emergence are given in full in Table VIII.

DURATION OF PREPUPAL PERIOD.

The duration of the prepupal period, of 23 indi·
varied from 7 to 13 days with an average of 9.17 d
Table IX. The period covered by records on pi
from June 28, when the first larvæ entered the grc
when the latest transformed to pupæ.

DURATION OF CALLOW PERIOD.

The duration of the callow period of the adult stage varied from 1 to 4 days with an average of 2 days. The records are summarized in Table XI. Records on this period extended from July 24 to August 4.

SUMMARY.

There is only one generation annually, winter being passed in the adult stage. Beetles emerge from hibernation when the grape buds are swelling and oviposition begins soon after and continues until about the middle of June, a few days before the latest adults disappear.

TABLE VI.—*Second larval stage of A. chalybea, North East, Pa., 1917.*

Number of larvæ.	Duration of stage.
	Days.
3	5
18	6
26	7
8	8
3	9
1	10
1	11
[1] 60	[2] 6.95

[1] Total.
[2] Weighted average.

The average duration of the incubation period in 1917 was 15.18 days.

The larval feeding period averaged 24.26 days in 1917. Records of feeding larvæ began June 4 and continued until July 20. The duration of the different larval stages was as follows: First stage, 8.74 days in 1917; second stage, 6.95 days in 1917; third stage, 7.75 days in 1916 and 8.53 days in 1917.

The duration of the period in the ground averaged 20.71 days in 1916 and 19.24 days in 1917. Records taken during the two years on the transformations of this beetle while in the ground extended from June 22 to August 4. The duration of the different stages in the ground in 1917 was as follows: Prepupa 9.17 days, pupa 8.47 days, callow adult 2 days.

TABLE VII.—*Feeding period of third larval stage, A. chalybea, North East, Pa., 1917.*

Number of larvæ.	Duration of stage.
	Days.
1	5
6	6
10	7
5	8
10	9
11	10
2	12
2	13
[1] 47	[2] 8.53

[1] Total.
[2] Weighted average.

THE LESSER GRAPEVINE FLEA-BEETLE.

(*Altica woodsi* n. sp.)

The specific name *A. woodsi* is given in recognition of Mr. Woods's recent systematic and biological studies of members of the genus Altica (*25, 26*), and because he is the first to record what is probably this insect as a new species.

DESCRIPTION OF STAGES.

THE ADULT.

Pl. II, D.

This beetle is similar to *Altica chalybea*, from which it may be distinguished as follows: Color metallic green, rarely with purple or olivacious reflections; antennal joint 3 equal in length to joint 4; average length 3.05 mm., varying from 2.43 to 3.05 mm.

VIII.—*Time and duration of period in ground of A. cha.*
1917.

te of ;ring ind.	Date of emergence.	Number of indi- viduals.	Duration of period.	Date of entering ground.	Date of emergence.
			Days.		
e 28	July 23	1	25	July 11	July 30
7 2	27	3	25	11	Aug. 1
4	26	2	22	13	July 31
5	26	1	21	13	Aug. 2
7	27	1	20	14	2
8	27	4	19	15	July 31
8	28	3	18	15	Aug. 1
9	30	1	21	15	3
10	28	1	18	17	1
10	29	1	19	17	4
10	30	3	20		
11	28	4	17		

¹ Total.   ² Weighted avera

ribed from a large series of beetles reared at North East, l
27.
.—Cat. No. 22290, U. S. National Museum.

THE EGG.
Pl. I, C.

lar to that of *Altica chalybea.* Length 0.75 mm., width 0.
straw yellow. Brownish strand much larger proportion
"large form," about one-half
IX.—*Prepupal period of*   The size and color are as descri
alybea, North East, Pa.,

THE LARV
Pl. II, A.

Number of prepupæ.	Duration of period.
	Days.
2	7
2	8
11	9
4	10
4	13
¹ 23	² 9.17

¹ Total.
² Weighted average.

Similar to the larva of the "
bea) but much smaller. Th
smaller proportionately and
distinctly yellow without th
ment. The setæ on the ve
ment are wanting. Width of l
0.292 to 0.312 mm., average 0.
from 0.435 to 0.458 mm., ave
instar 0.577 to 0.624 mm.,
Average length of full grown

THE PUPA.
Pl. II, B.

writer knows of no characteristic by which this pupa l
at of its larger relative except that of size. The average

ble X.—*Pupal stage of A. chaly-.*   TABLE XI.—*Callo*
bea, North East, Pa., 1917.   *stage of A. chaly*
Pa., 1917.

DISTRIBUTION.

The writer has collected this species in the vicinity of North East and Moorheadville, Pa., and has observed it at Niagara Falls, N. Y.

FOOD PLANTS.

The grape (*Vitis* spp.), both wild and cultivated, and the Virginia creeper (*Parthenocissus quinquefolia*) are food plants of both the larva and the adult of this beetle. Of the cultivated grapes the larva flourishes on thin-leaved varieties like the Delaware but does not favor thick-leaved sorts like the Concord. Larvæ were frequently found on Concord grapes in the field but the majority of the newly hatched larvæ placed on Concord leaves in cages failed to pass the first instar. After this instar was passed little difficulty was experienced in carrying them to the adult stage.

Grape growers, mentioned by Slingerland (*19*), who stated that thin-leaved varieties of. grapes were preferred by the grapevine flea-beetle probably had this insect to deal with instead of the typical species.

HABITS.

When the adult emerges from hibernation in the spring it attacks grape leaves which are already expanded. On the leaves of favored hosts it feeds on the lower sides, riddling them with holes. (Pl. IV.) On Concord and other similar varieties it feeds on the upper surface, pitting it with short irregular feeding marks but not eating through the leaf. (Pl. III, C.) Like the typical species it feeds much more voraciously at this time than later. It also has the same habit of feigning death when alarmed.

Eggs are usually placed singly on the underside of grape leaves, along the veins. (Pl. I, C.) Occasionally two or three are together and very rarely they are on the upper surface of the leaves. This is strikingly different from the place of oviposition and arrangement of eggs described by Slingerland (*19*) and Hartzell (*24*), but agrees with the records of Comstock (*12*), Marlatt (*18*), and others.

Like the adult the larva usually feeds on the underside of thin-leaved varieties of grapes and the Virginia creeper. A newly hatched larva usually begins at the side of a leaf vein and bores upward. When leaves are first attacked a series of small holes appears along the leaf veins, producing a characteristic marking which need not be mistaken for the feeding injury of any other insect. (Pl. IV.) After feeding has progressed for some time the holes are larger and are scattered over the leaf, which may become entirely skeletonized. The larvæ do not move readily from one leaf to another and consequently the leaves on one part of the vine may be completely riddled while those near by are untouched.

On leaves of the Concord grape and similar varieties the larva feeds on the upper surface, leaving narrow, irregular, chainlike feeding marks, much narrower and less continuous than those of the larger species. On these varieties there is also a great tendency for the larva to feed on leaf veins and in the flower cluster.

Its manner of passing the pupal period and its relation to temperature are very similar to those of the larger species.

TABLE XII.—*Incubation period of A. woodsi, North East, Pa., 1916.*

Date of oviposition.	Date of hatching.	Number of eggs.	Duration of period.
			Days.
June 10	June 23	2	13
10	25	4	15
10	26	2	16
10	27	1	17
15	27	2	12
15	28	3	13
15	30	5	15
25	July 7	9	12
26	7	12	11
		[1] 40	[2] 12.82

[1] Total.   [2] Weighted average.

LIFE HISTORY.

EMERGENCE FROM HIBERNATION AND OVIPOSITION IN 1916.

Adults were first noted in 1916 on May 29 and appeared in abundance at that time. Beetles were copulating on the day when first observed and this was continued intermittently as long as beetles of this generation were found on the vines. Oviposition was first noted on June 6 and continued until after the middle of July.

INCUBATION.

The incubation of eggs recorded in 1916 required from 11 to 17 days with an average of 12.82 days, as shown in Table XII.

TIME AND DURATION OF THE LARVAL FEEDING PERIOD OF ALTICA WOODSI, NORTH EAST, PA., 1916.

Forty-one larvæ were carried through the larval feeding period from the date of their hatching to the date of their entering the ground. The duration of this period varied from 13 to 27 days, with an average of 18.71 days. The period covered by records on feeding larvæ extended from June 18 to July 26. Complete data on the time and duration of this period are given in Table XIII.

TABLE XIII.—*Time and duration of larval feeding period of A. woodsi, North East, Pa., 1916.*

Date of hatching.	Date of entering ground.	Number of larvæ.	Duration of period.	Date of hatching.	Date of entering ground.	Number of larvæ.	Duration of period.
			Days.				*Days.*
June 18	July 7	1	19	June 26	July 15	1	19
18	10	1	22	28	21	2	23
20	10	2	20	29	15	4	16
21	10	1	19	30	18	1	18
22	19	1	27	30	24	1	24
23	10	5	17	July 1	24	1	23
23	12	1	19	4	17	1	13
24	10	3	16	4	21	4	17
24	12	1	18	8	21	2	13
25	17	5	22	8	26	1	18
25	18	1	23				
26	14	1	18			[1] 41	[2] 18.71

[1] Total.   [2] Weighted average.

DURATION OF FIRST LARVAL STAGE.

The duration of the first stage, of 74 larvæ reared, varied from 3 to 9 days with an average of 6.16 days, as shown in Table XIV.

TABLE XIV.—*First larval stage of A. woodsi, North East, Pa., 1916.*

Number of larvæ.	Duration of stage.
	Days.
1	3
1	4
17	5
32	6
16	7
3	8
4	9
[1] 74	[2] 6.16

[1] Total.
[2] Weighted average.

TABLE XV.—*Second larval stage of A. woodsi, North East, Pa., 1916.*

Number of larvæ.	Duration of stage.
	Days.
4	4
18	5
15	6
11	7
14	8
2	10
1	15
[1] 65	[2] 6.46

[1] Total.
[2] Weighted average.

The records in this stage cover a period from June 18, the earliest recorded date of hatching, to July 15, the latest recorded date of passing the first molt.

DURATION OF THE SECOND LARVAL STAGE.

The duration of the second larval stage varied from 4 to 15 days with an average of 6.46 days, as shown in Table XV. The total period covered by records on larvæ of this stage extended from June 25 to July 21.

TABLE XVI.—*Feeding period of third larval stage of A. woodsi, North East, Pa., 1916.*

Number of larvæ.	Duration of period.
	Days.
2	3
2	4
9	5
12	6
7	7
1	8
4	9
3	10
1	13
[1] 41	[2] 6.51

[1] Total.
[2] Weighted average.

DURATION OF FEEDING PERIOD OF THIRD LARVAL STAGE, NORTH EAST, PA., 1916.

The duration of the feeding period of the third stage of 41 larvæ varied from 3 to 13 days, with an average of 6.51 days, as shown in Table XVI. The total period covered by records of larvæ in this stage extended from July 1 to 26.

DURATION OF PERIOD IN GROUND.

The period in the ground includes the prepupal period, which is the latter part of the third stage, the pupal period, and the early part of the adult stage before emergence from the pupal cell. Fifty-three individuals were carried through this period. The minimum time required was 14 days, the maximum 21 days, and the average of 16.15 days. The period covered by these records extended from July 7, when the first larva entered the ground, until August 29, when the last adult emerged. These data are given in full in Table XVII.

TABLE XVII.—*Time and duration of immature stages in the ground of Altica woodsi, North East, Pa., 1916.*

Date of entering ground.	Date of emergence.	Number of individuals.	Duration of period.	Date of entering ground.	Date of emergence.	Number of individuals.	Duration of period.
			Days.				*Days.*
July 7	July 24	1	17	July 21	Aug. 7	1	17
10	24	7	14	Aug. 1	7	1	14
10	25	2	15	1	16	1	15
10	26	1	16	1	17	1	16
15	29	3	14	3	19	3	16
16	Aug. 5	3	20	6	21	3	15
17	July 31	2	14	6	25	1	19
17	Aug. 2	1	16	8	25	1	17
18	2	1	15	8	26	1	18
18	6	7	19	8	29	1	21
19	2	1	14				
21	5	3	15			1 53	2 16.15
21	6	7	16				

1 Total.   2 Weighted average.

EMERGENCE FROM HIBERNATION, 1917.

A few beetles emerged from hibernation in the latter part of May, but they were not abundant until the early part of June. The first specimens were collected May 19 on wild grape, when Concord grape shoots were about 8 inches long and the flower buds were showing. None were collected on cultivated grapes until June 3, when they were common. They increased in numbers until about June 9.

TABLE XVIII.—*Incubation period of A. woodsi, North East, Pa . 1917.*

Date of oviposition.	Date of hatching.	Number of eggs.	Duration of period.
			Days.
July 19	July 2	16	13
19	3	8	14
20	3	6	13
20	4	17	14
21	5	2	14
21	6	2	15
22	6	12	14
23	7	8	14
		1 71	2 13.72

1 Total.   2 Weighted average.

OVIPOSITION.

Oviposition began about 18 days after the emergence of the earliest adults and continued until the latter part of July. The latest recorded date of oviposition was July 26. The longest recorded period of oviposition for a single female was 41 days, from June 12 to July 23; this beetle deposited eggs on 17 days during that period. The number of eggs deposited by four isolated females varied from 37 to 181, with an average of 102.5 eggs each. Thirty-one eggs is the largest number deposited on a single day.

INCUBATION.

The duration of the incubation period of 71 eggs varied from 13 to 15 days, with an average of 13.72 days, as shown in Table XVIII

TIME AND DURATION OF THE LARVAL FEEDING PERIOD.

The duration of the feeding period of 190 larvæ varied from 15 to 23 days with an average of 18.59 days. The period covered by records on feeding larvæ extended from June 26 to July 26. Complete data on time and duration of this period are given in Table XIX.

TABLE XIX:—*Time and duration of larval feeding period of A. woodsi, North East, Pa., 1917.*

Date of hatching.	Date of entering ground.	Number of larvæ.	Duration of period.	Date of hatching.	Date of entering ground.	Number of larvæ.	Duration of period.
			Days.				*Days.*
June 26	July 14	5	18	July 4	July 25	2	21
26	15	6	19	5	22	26	17
26	16	1	20	5	23	7	18
26	17	11	21	5	24	2	19
July 2	20	6	18	5	25	4	20
2	21	7	19	6	23	3	17
3	21	9	18	6	25	7	19
3	22	15	19	7	23	6	16
3	23	9	20	7	24	3	17
3	24	3	21	7	25	1	18
3	25	1	22	9	24	2	15
3	26	1	23	9	25	4	17
4	22	9	18	9	26	1	18
4	23	34	19				
4	24	5	20			[1]190	[2]18.59

[1] Total. [2] Weighted average.

DURATION OF THE FIRST LARVAL STAGE.

The duration of the first larval stage was from 4 to 11 days with an average of 6.35 days, as shown in Table XX. The period covered by records on larvæ of this stage extended from June 26, the earliest recorded date of hatching, to July 15, the latest recorded date of passing the first molt.

TABLE XX.—*First larval stage of A. woodsi, North East, Pa., 1916.*

Number of larvæ.	Duration of stage.
	Days.
2	4
29	5
85	6
74	7
39	8
4	9
3	10
1	11
[1]237	[2]6.35

[1] Total.
[2] Weighted average.

DURATION OF SECOND LARVAL STAGE.

The duration of the second stage of 209 larvæ was from 4 to 9 days with an average of 6 days, as shown in Table XXI. The total period covered by records on larvæ of this stage extended from July 1 to July 21.

DURATION OF FEEDING PERIOD OF THIRD LARVAL STAGE.

The duration of the feeding period of the third larval stage of 189 larvæ varied from 4 to 9 days with an average of 6.62 days, as shown in Table XXII. The total period covered by records of larvæ in this stage is from July 6 to July 26.

The duration of the period in the grour
varied from 12 .to 17´ days with an av(
period is covered by records extending fi
The data on time and duration of this
Table XXIII.

TABLE XXI.—*Second larval
stage of A. woodsi, North East,
Pa., 1918.*

Number of larvæ.	Duration of stage.
	Days.
6	4
41	5
113	6
45	7
3	8
1	9
[1] 209	[2] 6.00

[1] Total.   [2] Weighted average.

TABL]
of t
· wooi

[1] Toi

The prepupal period of 57 larvæ recorde
with an average of 4.68 days, as shown b
period covered by records on the prepupa
August 1.

TABLE XXIII.—*Time and duration of period in grou
1917.*

Date of entering ground.	Date of emergence.	Number of individuals.	Duration of period.	Date of entering ground.
			Days.	
July 14	July 29	1	15	July 22

DURATION OF CALLOW PERIOD.

The duration of the callow period of the adult stage, or the period after transformation of the pupa to adult and before its emergence from the ground, was recorded for 48 individuals. It varied from 1 to 4 days, with an average of 2.19 days, as shown in Table XXVI. The period covered by these records extended from July 28 to August 11.

TABLE XXIV.—*Prepupal stage of A. woodsi, North East, Pa., 1917.*

Number of individuals.	Duration of period.
	Days.
29	4
19	5
7	6
2	7
[1] 57	[2] 4.68

[1] Total.
[2] Weighted average.

SUMMARY.

The seasonal history of the lesser grapevine flea-beetle is similar in general to that of the larger species, but it is later throughout. There is a single generation annually, winter being passed in the adult stage. Beetles emerge from hibernation in the latter part of May or early June, some time after the grape shoots have expanded, or about three weeks later than the typical species. Oviposition begins early in June and continues until the latter part of July, when the last adults disappear.

The average duration of the incubation period was 12.82 days in 1916 and 13.72 days in 1917, slightly less than that of the larger species, but this difference may be accounted for by the fact that these incubation records were taken later in the season, when the temperature was higher.

TABLE XXV.—*Duration of pupal stage of A. woodsi, North East, Pa., 1917.*

Number of pupæ.	Duration of stage.
	Days.
10	6
16	7
17	8
2	9
[1] 45	[2] 7.24

[1] Total. [2] Weighted average.

TABLE XXVI.—*Callow period of adult stage of A. woodsi, North East, Pa., 1917.*

Number of individuals.	Duration of period.
	Days.
12	1
19	2
13	3
4	4
[1] 48	[2] 2.19

[1] Total. [2] Weighted average.

Larvæ are found on the vines in midsummer, the records of collection extending from June 18 to August 8. The average duration of the larval feeding period was 18.71 days in 1916 and 18.59 days in 1917, or about one-fourth shorter than that of the "large form." The duration of the three larval stages was as follows: First stage, 6.16 days in 1916 and 6.35 days in 1917; second stage, 6.46 days in 1916 and 6 days in 1917; third stage, 6.51 days in 1916 and 6.62 days in 1917.

The maximum limits of records of individuals transforming in the ground were from July 7 to August 29. The duration of this period of transformation averaged 16.15 days in 1916 and 14.50 days in 1917, or about 5 days less in each season than those required for the "large form." The average duration of the different stages in the ground was as follows: Prepupa 4.68 days, pupa 7.24 days, callow adult 2.19 days.

After emergence from the ground the beetles feed until late in autumn and then go into hibernation. A comparison of the foregoing with the seasonal history of the typical grapevine flea-beetle shows that the lesser species appears in the vineyard about three weeks later than the other and continues later throughout the season. The typical species disappeared from vineyards at the season indicated by Slingerland (19), while the "small form" was present at the time that the "tardy individual," referred to by him, was found ovipositing, some time after the overwintering adults of the typical species had disappeared. Following Slingerland's suggestion a little further, it seems probable to the writer that the collection of beetles of the "small form," if confused with the typical species, could easily give rise to the two-brood hypothesis.

This comparison also shows that the lesser grapevine flea-beetle is more rapid in its development, particularly in the larval and prepupal stages. This more rapid development can not be attributed to any extent to the fact that the larvæ appear later in the season, for even late individuals of the "large form" reared at the same time as the early individuals of the "small form" required more time for their metamorphosis.

ECONOMIC IMPORTANCE.

The grapevine flea-beetle, according to all accounts, has been one of the most destructive of insects to the grape industry. Slingerland (19) wrote in 1898 that for several years previous it had done more damage to vineyards in New York than all other grape insects combined. Emerging from hibernation at the time when the grape buds are swelling, a single beetle, by eating out comparatively few buds, destroys as many shoots and a much larger number of clusters. If the injury is repeated, according to Quaintance and Shear (22), the vines themselves may be weakened or killed. Feeding after the grapes come into leaf, either by the adults or by the larvæ, is less destructive.

Compared with its larger relative, the lesser grapevine flea-beetle is greatly limited in its possibilities for destructiveness, because the adult does not emerge from hibernation early enough to attack the buds, but, like the larva, is strictly a leaf feeder. In spite of this limitation, however, where it occurs in large numbers it can cause considerable damage by its skeletonizing of the foliage. In one instance the writer has noted the killing of 1-year-old vines of the Delaware variety by repeated defoliation. Not the least important economic consideration with regard to this beetle is the possibility of its being mistaken for the larger form and the consequent confusion of remedial measures.

In spite of their potential ability to injure the grape industry, during the years of the writer's residence in the Erie-Chautauqua grape belt (1914–1917) both of these insects were of minor importance. Such infestations as were observed were confined to vines on the borders of vineyards adjacent to woodlands in which there were heavy growths of wild grapes.

The grapevine flea-beetle, like a number of related insects, is given to sporadic outbreaks of destructiveness followed by periods of comparatively little economic importance. This is well illustrated by the periodic receipt of complaints by the Bureau of Entomology. Based on this source of information, it appears that there have been three distinct extensive outbreaks in recent years: One in 1892 in Michigan, Missouri, Iowa, and Kansas, one during 1894 and 1895 in New York, and one in 1911 in Maryland, Virginia, and the District of Columbia. Requests for information regarding this insect have been received in practically all of the intervening years, but they have been comparatively few in number and much more local. Slingerland (19), writing in 1898, also records a serious period of destructiveness in New York for several years previous. On the other hand, 17 years later Hartzell (24) estimated that in the Erie-Chautauqua grape region less than 1 per cent of the area was infested.

It is probable that the period when the writer's observations were made represented a low tide in the abundance of these beetles, due to natural checks, as they were totally absent not only in vineyards where measures to destroy them might be taken, but also from the majority of neglected vineyards and from most growths of wild grapes. But aside from the natural causes there are two other factors which have contributed to a permanent change in the economic status of this pest. Poison sprays, applied primarily to destroy the grapevine rootworm (*Fidia viticida* Walsh) and the grape-berry moth (*Polychrosis viteana* Clem.), readily destroy the flea-beetle larvæ feeding on the leaves at that time and may destroy many of the adults of the lesser flea-beetle which are also still in the vineyards. Up-to-date methods of tillage under vines, which break open the pupal cells, are also a contributing factor. These two factors make it difficult for beetles to reproduce in well-cared-for vineyards and limit them to neglected vineyards and wild vines. Sporadic outbreaks may nevertheless be expected in vineyards adjacent to favorable breeding places, and these may be very severe locally.

PREDATORY ENEMIES.

The natural causes responsible for the periods of com
importance of the flea-beetles at the time they were under
n were undetermined. Three species of carabid beetles
ants were found predatory on both flea-beetles, although
e carabids was found in large numbers. No species of
s been reared by the writer.

Lebia viridis Say,[1] the most common carabid, was clos
ted with both species of flea-beetles. It feeds upon t
væ, and pupæ of both species. This Lebia, although clas
und-beetle, is largely arboreal. It was found in leaf mo
ld grapevines, where flea-beetles were pupating in large r
t more frequently on grape leaves, both in vineyards and
es. One specimen was taken on a wild grapevine ove
ove the ground. In spite of their individual voracity,
etles always occurred singly and were never found in large r
ey were not regarded as of sufficient importance to hold th
e flea-beetles in check.

The earliest recorded collection of *Lebia viridis* was May 22,
is beetle was found feeding upon eggs under strips of bark
es. No more were found until June 22, when larvæ of th
a-beetle were quite common on the vines. After this ti
e first of August *Lebia viridis* was fairly numerous. Tl
ord of collection was September 11, in 1916, after all of th

Philadelphia vireo (*Vireosylva philadelphica*), Carolina wren (*Thryothorus ludovicianus*), and bluebird (*Sialia sialis*).

METHODS OF CONTROL.

As previously stated, no extensive infestation of either species of flea-beetle came under the writer's observation in the Erie-Chautauqua grape belt, and those infestations that did occur were confined to vines at the ends of rows or the edges of vineyards.[1] In such situations hand-picking the beetles was the best means of control. The effect of this method is immediate, which is very desirable against so voracious an insect, against which arsenical sprays act comparatively slowly. On small areas in a corner or at the edge it is also cheaper than the employment of a power sprayer, which must be drawn the entire length of each row, of which only a small part may be infested. Had an extensive infestation occurred, spraying would have been resorted to, but as none was present no spraying experiments were conducted.

The application of a spray mixture containing 3 pounds of arsenate of lead paste (1½ pounds, powdered) to 50 gallons of Bordeaux mixture is usually recommended for the control of the typical species. One of the recent investigators, Hartzell (*24*), states that this mixture protects the vines from severe injury because it is repellent to the beetles and disperses them over the vineyard, but that it does not kill them. To kill the beetles he has found that a high dosage of arsenate of lead, not less than 4 pounds paste (2 pounds, powdered) to 50 gallons of water, is most effective. This high dosage is necessary to kill the beetles quickly before much damage is done, because of their voracity and resistance to poison. He also states that the effectiveness of the poison is much increased by the addition of one-half gallon of molasses to the foregoing mixture. The addition of molasses because of its solubility has the disadvantage, however, of making the poison likely to be washed off by rains. Owing to the frequency of rains at this season of the year this is a very serious disadvantage. *Molasses should not be added to a spray solution containing Bordeaux mixture, or burning of the foliage is apt to result.* The time of application should be on the first warm day when the grape buds are swelling, or as soon as the beetles appear.

The difficulty of destroying the adults makes it important that these pests be not allowed to reproduce in a vineyard. The

---

[1] After this paper had gone to press, in the spring of 1920, the writer's attention was called to extensive destructiveness by *A. chalybea* at Neosho, Mo., by Mr. F. W. Faurot, director of the Missouri State Fruit Experiment Station at Mountain Grove, Mo. It was stated that the greater part of the crop in a number of vineyards had been destroyed by the activities of this beetle during the previous season. In 1920 it was apparently much the most destructive grape insect of the region. Spraying experiments for the control of beetles emerging from hibernation were conducted by Mr. A. J. Ackerman and the writer, in cooperation with the Missouri Fruit Experiment Station. Arsenate of lead at the rate of 3 pounds (powdered) to 50 gallons of water gave fair control, and this dosage was much more effective than one of 2 pounds to 50 gallons of water.

immature stages are very susceptible to remedial measures, and their destruction incidental to good tillage and to spraying for the control of other pests has been referred to under the discussion of economic importance (p. 20–21). The regular spray applications for the control of the grapevine rootworm and the grape-berry moth are so timed that they are entirely effective against the larvæ of *Altica woodsi* but can not be relied upon to destroy all of the larvæ of *A. chalybea.* During both 1916 and 1917 the earliest larvæ of the latter species began entering the soil about 10 days before the first regular spray application was made. In case of a heavy infestation of larvæ of this species on the grape foliage an application made just before the grapes bloom is advisable to prevent a heavy infestation of beetles the following spring. This extra application, however, probably will be rarely necessary.

GENERAL SUMMARY.

The grapevine flea-beetle (*Altica chalybea* Ill.) is a grape pest which eats out the swelling buds in early spring, thus destroying the embryonic shoots and fruit clusters. Later both the beetles and the larvæ feed upon leaves of the grape. It is single brooded. Winter is passed in the adult stage. Eggs are deposited in groups under bud scales or strips of bark; the larvæ migrate to the leaves to feed and enter the soil to pupate; and the pupæ transform to the adult stage by early summer. This is in agreement with the habits and seasonal history as usually described in the literature of the species.

Statements that the eggs are deposited on leaves, that the insect is two-brooded, and that it prefers thin-leaved varieties of grapes as hosts rather than the Concord variety, are due to a confusion with a closely allied species, the lesser grapevine flea-beetle (*Altica woodsi* n. sp.), hitherto usually determined as "*A. chalybea,* small form." This insect is also single brooded but emerges from hibernation enough later in the season to appear as a second brood of the typical species. Eggs are deposited singly, or sometimes in a cluster of two or three on the underside of the leaf upon which they feed. As in the case of the first-named species, transformations are passed in the ground and winter is passed in the adult stage.

In addition to the above-mentioned characteristics, the lesser grapevine flea-beetle may be distinguished from its larger ally by its distinctly smaller size in all stages, by the green color of the adult instead of blue, the pale yellow of the egg instead of a deep yellow or orange, the yellow body color of the larva instead of a brownish yellow, and the absence of setæ on the ventral prothoracic plate of the larva. The feeding marks of both larva and adult are also a ready means of identification. Both the adult and the larva of the lesser species merely pit the upper surface of thick-leaved varieties of grapes, and eat small holes in the foliage of thin-leaved varieties. Both stages of its larger ally strip the leaf tissue of varieties like the Delaware, while on leaves of varieties like the Concord the larva makes large whitish patches on the upper surface, and the adult, also feeding on the upper surface of the leaves, eats large holes in them.

Almost no other insect can cause as severe injury to the grape crop, in restricted areas, as that of which the grapevine flea-beetle is capable when the grape buds are swelling. The lesser species, which emerges later, is less destructive. Both species are sporadic in their occurrence from season to season and they are now restricted in their distribution largely to vineyards adjacent to wild grape arbors. A number of predatory enemies, of which *Lebia viridis* Say is the most important, contribute to its natural control.

Where vineyards are liable to injury from this pest, vigilance in early spring is essential to safety. When the beetles do appear their voracity makes prompt action necessary. If, as is usually the case, the infestation covers only a small area, hand-picking the beetles will probably be the most effective as well as the cheapest means of control, while if a large area is infested, spraying with arsenate of lead will probably be necessary. A spray application of 3 pounds of arsenate of lead paste (1½ pounds powdered) is ordinarily recommended, but if the infestation is severe and rains can be avoided, a dosage of not less than 6 pounds of arsenate of lead paste (or 3 pounds powdered) to 50 gallons of water may be used. The larvæ of the lesser species and most of those of the larger species may be readily destroyed by the usual spray applications for the grape-berry moth and the grapevine rootworm, and these measures, together with up-to-date vineyard tillage, make it practically impossible for these pests to reproduce in a vineyard and limit them to wild vines. Very rarely a spray application before the grapes bloom will be advisable to destroy the earliest larvæ of *A. chalybea*. These measures have probably been the cause for the change in the economic status of the grapevine flea-beetle from apparently a first-rate pest of 20 years ago to one of second-rate importance at present.

TION. V. 1. 459 p.
ages 104–106: *H. chalybea.*

REPORT ON INSECTS AND DISEASES INJURIOUS TO VEGETATI
Boston: Press of the Franklin Printing House.
A.
HIRD REPORT ON NOXIOUS AND OTHER INSECTS OF THE STATI
YORK. *In* Trans. N. Y. Sta. Agr. Soc., v. 16, for 1856, p. 3
ages 362 and 402: *H. chalybea.*
ICK, J.
IE GRAPE-VINE FLEA-BEETLE. *In* Practical Entomologist, v
V.
NSECTS INJURIOUS TO THE GRAPE-VINE. No. 12. THE GI
FLEA-BEETLE. *In* American Entomologist, v. 2, p. 327-
204–205.
, WM.
SECTS INJURIOUS TO THE GRAPE. *In* Rept. Ent. Soc. C
p. 17–20, figs. 8–18,
age 19, fig. 14: *H. chalybea.*
, J. H.
EPORT OF THE ENTOMOLOGIST. *In* Am. Rpt. [U. S.] Comn
1880, p. 185–347, 6 pl.
ages 213–216: *Graptodera chalybea.*
J. A.
OURTH REPORT ON INJURIOUS AND OTHER INSECTS OF THE
NEW YORK. *In* 41st Rept. N. Y. Sta. Mus. Nat. Hist. 238 j
ages 96 and 101: *H. chalybea.*
, CONWAY.
VENTY-TWO COMMON INSECTS OF NEBRASKA. Neb. Agr. I
Bul. 2. 101 p., 40 figs.
ages 42–44: *Graptodera chalybea.*
H.
SYNOPSIS OF THE HALTICINI OF BOREAL AMERCIA. *In* Tra
Ent. Soc., v. 16, p. 163–320.
age 220: *H. chalybea.*
ES C.
ITOMOLOGICAL NOTES. Fla. Agr. Exp. Sta. Bul. 9. 16 p.

(17) SCHWARZ, E. A.
  1891. NOTE ON THE FOOD-HABITS OF SOME HALTICIDS. *In* Proc. Ent. Soc.
      Wash., v. 2, p. 182–184.
(18) MARLATT, C. L.
  1896. THE PRINCIPAL INSECT ENEMIES OF THE GRAPE. *In* Ybk. U. S. Dept.
      Agr. 1895, p. 385–404, figs. 94–105.
(19) SLINGERLAND, M. V.
  1898. THE GRAPE-VINE FLEA-BEETLE. N. Y. (Cornell) Agr. Exp. Sta. Bul. 157.
(20) LOWE, V. H.
  1899. PRELIMINARY NOTES ON THE GRAPE-VINE FLEA-BEETLE. N. Y. (Geneva)
      Agr. Exp. Sta. Bul. 150. pt. 2, p. 263–265.
(21) [LUGGER, OTTO.]
  1899. BEETLES INJURIOUS TO OUR FRUIT-PRODUCING PLANTS. Minn. Agr. Exp.
      Sta. Bul. 66. p. 85–332, illus.
      Pages 241–243: *H. ignita.*
(22) QUAINTANCE, A. L., and SHEAR, C. L.
  1907. INSECT AND FUNGOUS ENEMIES OF THE GRAPE EAST OF THE ROCKY
      MOUNTAINS. U. S. Dept. Agr. Farmers' Bul. 284. 48 p., figs.
      Pages 23–24: *H. chalybea.*
(23) HARTZELL, F. Z.
  1910. PRELIMINARY REPORT ON GRAPE INSECTS. N. Y. (Geneva) Agr. Exp.
      Sta. Bul. 331, p. 485–591.
      Pages 494–514: *H. chalybea.*
(24) ——
  1915. THE GRAPE-VINE FLEA-BEETLE. *In* Official Report International Congress
      of Viticulture, p. 201–209, 3 figs.
(25) WOODS, W. C.
  1917. THE BIOLOGY OF THE ALDER FLEA-BEETLE. Me. Agr. Exp. Sta. Bul.
      265, p. 249–284, Pl.
      Pages 274–279: Synonymy of genus *Altica* Geoffroy.
(26) ——
  1918. THE BIOLOGY OF MAINE SPECIES OF ALTICA. Me. Agr. Exp. Sta. Bul.
      273, p. 149–204.
      Pages 150–151: Species in the *ignita* group.

UNITED STATES DEPARTMENT OF AGRICULTURE

BULLETIN No. 902

Contribution from the Bureau of Entomology
L. O. HOWARD, Chief

Washington, D. C.   PROFESSIONAL PAPER   October 22, 1920

THE WESTERN CABBAGE FLEA-BEETLE.[1]

By F. H. CHITTENDEN and H. O. MARSH,
Truck-Crop Insect Investigations.

CONTENTS.

	Page.		Page.
Nature of injury	1	History and literature	13
Description	2	Natural enemies	13
Distribution	3	Control	14
Reports of injury	4	Recommendations	17
Food plants	7	Summary	20
Seasonal history	8	Literature cited	21
Life history and habits	9		

NATURE OF INJURY.

An insect enemy of cabbage, turnip, and other cruciferous crops, known as the western cabbage flea-beetle, ranks as a most troublesome pest in the region which it inhabits.[2]

It is primarily an enemy of gardens, but quite too frequently becomes a pest in large commercial plantings. The chief injury is done by the overwintered beetles attacking turnip, radish, and other cruciferous vegetables just as they are coming through the ground, and by the beetles of the first generation, which are usually at the maximum of their destructiveness during June and July. The beetles appear suddenly, and frequently in incalculable numbers, and large areas are completely devastated before the grower becomes aware of their presence.

Although the larvæ feed on the roots of cruciferous vegetables, they cause little appreciable damage.

The beetles are by no means confined in their injurious attacks to cabbage and other cole crops, since when they occur in unusual abundance they attack most forms of vegetable crops, including beans, peas, table and sugar beets, mustard, kale, and rape. As with

---

[1] *Phyllotreta pusilla* Horn; family Chrysomelidae, order Coleoptera.
[2] This insect was under observation by the junior author (deceased) from 1909 until 1917, at Rocky Ford, Colo.

the majority of flea-beetles, this species does most harm to young plants, and, as an instance of its destructiveness, it has been reported to come in swarms, like black clouds, completely covering the plants.

This species is not a periodical pest, like army worms and others, but it is more or less injurious year after year in the regions which it inhabits. It is, however, like most other flea-beetles, subject to considerable fluctuation in numbers for reasons which have not yet been entirely explained, but which are doubtless due to atmospheric conditions either at the time that the insect is breeding or when it is in hibernation.

DESCRIPTION.

BEETLE.

The adult of the western cabbage flea-beetle (fig. 1) is shining metallic copper in color, measuring one-sixteenth of an inch or a little

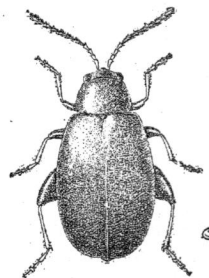

FIG. 1.—The western cabbage flea-beatle (*Phyllotreta pusilla*):Adult, highly magnified.

more in length. The body is elongate oval, much flattened. The antennæ are slender and the same in both sexes. The thighs of the hind legs are strongly developed, fitting the insect for jumping, whence its common name of "flea" or flea-beetle.

Following is the original description of *Phyllotreta pusilla (3,[1] p. 302):*

Form narrow, elongate, depressed, piceous, surface with distinct æneous lustre. Antennæ slender, half as long as the body, piceous, joints 2–3 paler. Head scarcely visibly punctate. Thorax less than twice as wide as long, widest at middle, sides arcuate, apex slightly narrower than base, disc convex, surface shining, the punctures moderate, closely placed, but not convex. Elytra wider than the thorax, humeri obtuse, punctation coarser than that of the thorax, closely placed, very little finer near the apex, but less dense, surface shining. Body beneath and legs piceous, abdomen sparsely punctate. Length .06—.08 inch; 1.5–2 mm.

Male.—Last ventral [segment] with a feeble triangular impression in the apex.

Female.—Last ventral simple.

The antennæ are alike in both sexes and the joints 3 to 10 vary little in length, although slightly broader externally.

This species is very easily confounded with related forms of similar habits. Prominent among these is *Phyllotreta albionica* Lec., which it resembles so nearly in form, size, and color that the females can scarcely be separated. It is, however, more shining, the head is nearly smooth, and the thorax and elytra are less densely punctate. Moreover, *Ph. albionica* may easily be separated by the male antennæ which have the fifth joint dilated. The female antennæ of the two species are almost identical. The color of *pusilla* is sometimes olive brown and inclined to black, but examination of a large series of properly preserved specimens does not show any material variation,

---

[1] Reference is made by number (italic) to "Literature cited," p. 21.

except in a few darker individuals from northern Colorado, the normal color being almost uniformly cupreous or copper-colored. The species is also apt to be confused with *Ph. aeneicollis* Cr., but the latter may be readily distinguished, inasmuch as it is more convex, more shining, and distinctly larger.

EGG.

The egg is light yellow, glistening, of oval form, and about 1/50 of an inch in length.

In confinement eggs were deposited in cracks in the soil about the roots of the cruciferous plants on which the larva subsists and there is good reason to believe that this is the usual habit under field conditions.

LARVA.

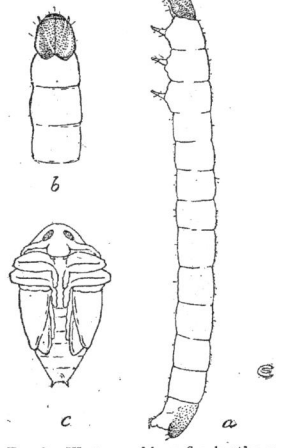

The larva (fig. 2, *a*, *b*) is thread-like in appearance, uniformly white, except for the head sclerites, the legs, and a chitinized area on the caudal abdominal segment, which are pale chestnut brown. The mature larva is about 5 mm. in length and from 0.5 to 0.65 mm. in width, or approximately 10 times as long as wide.

The larvæ feed normally on the roots of cruciferous plants and remain concealed in the soil throughout their life.

PUPA.

On reaching maturity the larva selects a suitable place for transformation and then wriggles about until it has formed a compact, well-defined cell in the soil,

Fig. 2.—Western cabbage flea-beetle: *a*, Outline of larva, lateral view; *b*, head and thoracic segments of same, dorsal view; *c*, pupa. Enlarged.

in the vicinity of the roots on which it fed. After the cell is formed the larva shortens and in about two days changes to pupa.

The pupa (fig. 2, *c*) is approximately of the same size as the adult and is entirely white. The arrangement of the antennæ, legs, and wings is the same as that of the average halticine pupa.[3]

DISTRIBUTION.

The range of the western cabbage flea-beetle, accorded by Horn and others, is from the Dakotas to Mexico and central and southern California.

[3] Detailed descriptions of the immature stages are omitted from this paper because fresh material is not available and it is, moreover, desirable to compare all of these stages with those of related species and illustrate the same.

It is widely distributed in the Rocky Mountain region of Colorado and New Mexico, and is known to occur in more isolated localities in Arizona, Wyoming, Nebraska, Oklahoma, and Kansas. It is also abundant in some portions of Texas, ranging southward to Brownsville and undoubtedly into Mexico, although only doubtfully recorded from that country. The known distribution is shown in the map (fig. 3). This species is to be found quite frequently at very high elevations and is also evidently a permanent inhabitant of lower areas, as, for example, Brownsville, Tex. It is evidently a Sonoran form and common to both the Upper and Lower Sonoran Life Zones,[4] but in some States it has been observed in the Semitropical, Transition, and Boreal Zones.

Undoubtedly the species has a wider distribution than is indicated by the map, comprising an area considerably larger in extent than one-third of the United States. It probably occurs in southern

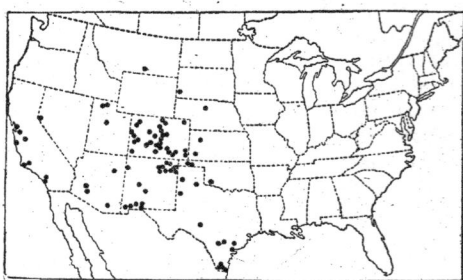

Idaho, and without doubt is more widely distributed in the States of Nebraska, Wyoming, Montana, Utah, Arizona, and Texas than is at present known. While it does not approach the border lines of several other States known to be inhabited, nevertheless a lookout should be kept in the future for invasions in southwestern Louisiana, southeastern Idaho, and Nevada.

FIG. 3.—Map showing distribution of western cabbage flea-beetle.

REPORTS OF INJURY.

Our record of injury positively attributable to the western cabbage flea-beetle begins in 1889, the year when the species was described as new to science. That year, May 25, Prof. T. D. A. Cockerell sent specimens to the Department of Agriculture with the report that the insect did great damage to the leaves of turnip at Westcliffe, Colo. Injuries were reported at intervals in 1893, 1897, 1904, and 1906. In 1908 and 1909 there were several outbreaks over considerable territory, and a somewhat smaller outbreak occurred also over a large territory in 1913.

In 1893 Prof. R. Y. Croydon sent specimens from Laramie, Wyo., that were damaging turnips and radishes.

---

[4] The species came under the observation of the junior writer at Rocky Ford, Manzanola, Fowler, Las Animas, Loma, Holly, Pueblo, Colorado Springs, Fort Collins, and Greeley, Colo.; Garden City, Kans.; Maxwell and French, N. Mex.; Sanibel and Mercedes, Tex.; Phoenix, Ariz.; and Thermal, Calif.

In 1897 specimens were received, July 10, from Mr. D. A. Pierce, Kennedy, Nebr., with the statement that the species had destroyed between 10 and 20 acres of corn in 24 hours. They were said to destroy everything in gardens. They came in swarms of black clouds and covered the plants. Later in the month Mr. Benj. F. Henry, Hill City, S. Dak., complained of a "flea"—a name commonly applied by farmers to flea-beetles—that was troublesome on cabbage and other cruciferous crops in his vicinity. Only a single grower in his neighborhood had saved any cabbage, all others having given up the fight against this flea-beetle. In addition to cabbage this species was injurious to radish, horse-radish, and turnip, and was stated also to injure peas. On the last-mentioned plant it ate the lower leaves or lower part of the stalk. Out of 1,000 good cabbage plants our correspondent saved only a hundred. The beetles seemed to prefer the younger plants, but thrived also upon the older ones. A neighbor of our correspondent reported that he had not raised a turnip for seven years on account of this insect. It was prevalent in injurious abundance throughout the region of the Black Hills. The beetles were first noticed the last week of June, and seemed to disappear toward the end of July.

In 1904, during the first week of June, this species was observed by Prof. E. G. Titus, at Paonia, Fort Collins, and Longmont, Colo., and at Blackfoot, Idaho, June 22, attacking sugar beet. May 19, 25 acres of sugar beets were reported destroyed to date by this beetle at Grand Junction, Colo.

In 1906, Miss Hannah Carr, Mineral Hill, N. Mex., wrote January 11 of this insect destroying crops in that locality, particularly turnips, beans, and cabbage. From an acre of turnips only a few pounds of the vegetable were obtained. The same year complaints of injury to cabbage, radish, and nasturtium were received from Mr. Nathan Hall, Socorro, N. Mex.

The year 1908 witnessed severe outbreaks of this pest. April 24 Miss Margaret Botchleott, Grady, N. Mex., sent specimens with complaint of injury to garden plants. At Chico, N. Mex., it was injurious to cabbage. January 22, Mr. D. K. McMillan observed many beetles on turnip at Corpus Christi, Tex. The same year the species was received April 27, and later, from Mr. C. A. Pugh, Verne, Okla., where the beetle was reported to be injuring garden truck generally. June 4 Mrs. Frank Perron, Hurley, Tex., sent specimens with report that the beetles were entirely destroying radish and cabbage crops in the Coldun Tract in the panhandle of Texas. Mr. A. Olson, Blacktower, Roosevelt Co., N. Mex., October 25, writing of this species as the "garden flea" stated that it was generally found on radish, beet, lettuce, and in fact on almost all kinds of plants when they first come up. The insect perforates the small plants with holes and eats the substance until they die. The beetles were very hard to catch and did great damage. The same year injuries were also reported to gardens in Verne, Okla., in April and May, and an invasion occurred at Brownsville and at Harlingen, Tex., on turnip and cabbage, in November. According to reports by Mr. McMillan, the beetles were to be found continuously through the month of November in south Texas.

In 1909 Mr. H. J. Kelley, Springton, Idaho, complained of this species, June 18. It was observed by Mr. M. M. High attacking potato at Lyford, Tex., March 2, and turnips and radish at Brownsville, Tex., March 26. July 25, of the same year, complaint by Mr. R. E. Chevick was made in regard to the same insect, on beans, cabbage, sugar beet, garden beet, and mangels. During July also, Mr. G. E. Thompson reported it at Akron, Colo., on kale and rape, and a heavy infestation at Fort Collins, stating that farmers complained of serious injury in their gardens, especially to cabbage, radish, and peas. November 7, H. M. Russell found the beetle at Compton, Calif., feeding on wild mustard.

In 1910 beetles were observed by Mr. High at Brownsville, Tex., in January, February, and March in large numbers on turnip, radish, and lettuce, doing great damage to young plants, the underside of the leaves being covered with excavations made by them. He wrote "in time this greatly devitalizes the growth of the plants and if the present number remains long enough, many of the leaves will wilt and die." March 2 the species was observed in numbers on young Irish potatoes at Lyford, Tex., by Mr. A. Steller.

During 1911, Mr. McMillan stated that in January and February this flea-beetle had been numerous at Brownsville, Tex., on wild water-cress (*Roripa sphaerocarpa*), wild pepper-grass (*Lepidium virginicum*), and on young turnip, mustard, and rutabaga. The beetles pass through partial hibernation, but their wild hosts were only slightly injured. July 2, this species was the subject of complaint at Goodwell, Okla., by Mr. Gus Shubert, who stated that in spite of different plantings the insect, locally known as the "earth flea," damaged radish, turnip, and cabbage. Serious infestation was reported the following day at Akron, Colo., to cabbage, lettuce, radish, and peas, and on July 25, to beans, cabbage, and sugar beets at Dulce, N. Mex.

June 10, 1912, injury was reported at Moses, N. Mex., to cabbage, radish, and turnip.

In 1913 this flea-beetle was observed in large numbers, January 27, at Brownsville, Tex., by Mr. High, attacking radish and turnip. The leaves were full of small holes made by the beetles. Injury was less noticeable on spinach and table beets. May 17, it was quite abundant on cabbage. Small excavations had been made on the underside of the leaves but were not yet entirely through the upper covering. During the same year further injuries were reported to turnip, mustard, and radish at Amarillo, Tex.; to radish at Sheridan Lake, Colo., and to radish and turnip at Albert, Union Co., N. Mex. Of the last occurrence our correspondent wrote, "we can not raise these crops for the flea eats them as soon as they come through the soil." It was also injurious to cabbage, turnip, mustard, and radish at Tucumcari, N. Mex., and to radish at Thermal, Calif.

During 1914 Mr. F. B. Milliken reported this species attacking *Lepidium pubecarpum* at Garden City, Kans. He also observed larvæ from which the beetle was reared, May 17.

During 1915 this species was reported injurious to cabbage at Chico, N. Mex.; in 1916 to radish and cabbage at Fort Stanton, N. Mex.; and in 1917 to turnip, radish, and tomato at Golden, Colo.

During 1919 this species was apparently rare, having been reported in only four localities. At Brownsville, Tex., Mr. High found it attacking crucifers, and Mr. C. F. Stahl, Bureau of Entomology, collected specimens at Riverside, Calif., June 10 and July 14 on corn leaves. During July it made its appearance in injurious numbers at Lake Valley, N. Mex., where it was reported by Mr. John Avirette, attacking mustard, radish, and cabbage in the order named. He stated that without constant spraying with arsenicals these crops would all be ruined. August 26 of the same year Mr. A. E. Mallory, Bureau of Entomology, observed this species in moderate number on turnip.

July 16, 1920, Mr. D. J. Balagna, a grower and shipper of vegetables, Florence, Colo., wrote that this beetle was "destroying the entire valley," and unless something was done promptly, cabbage, cauliflower, and all related vegetables would be destroyed. Our correspondent had tried nicotine sulphate, coal oil and soap, arsenate of lead, salt water, lime, and Paris green, but found nothing that would kill it.

FOOD PLANTS.

The western cabbage flea-beetle, although normally an enemy of cruciferous plants, frequently does much injury to sugar beets and other vegetable crops. Turnip (*Brassica rapa*), mustard (*B.* spp.), and radish (*Raphanus* spp.) are decidedly the favorite food plants. The beetles also attack horse-radish (*Radicula armoracia*), rape (*Brassica napus*), cabbage (*Brassica oleracea*), cauliflower (*B. oleracea* var. *botrytis*), water cress (*Radicula nasturtium-aquaticum, Roripa nasturtium*), Chinese mustard or pe-tsai (*Brassica juncea*), nasturtium, bee-plant (*Cleome serrulata*), sweet alyssum (*Alyssum maritimum*), candytuft (*Iberis* spp.), wild peppergrass (*Lepidium pubecarpum, L. virginicum, et al.*), hedge mustard (*Sisymbrium* spp.), wild water cress (*Roripa sinuata* and *R. sphaerocarpa*), and tansy mustard (*Sophia pinnata*). All of these are normal food plants.

When the beetles occur in great abundance they injure also sugar
beets and table beets (*Beta* spp.), mangel-wurzel (*B. vulgaris* var.
macrorhiza), lettuce (*Lactuca sativa*), beans (*Phaseolus* spp.), peas
(*Pisum sativum*), carrots (*Daucus carota*), tomato (*Lycopersicum
esculentum*), potato (*Solanum tuberosum*), and corn (*Zea* spp.).

Injury is due to the beetles eating pitlike holes in the leaves
of young plants, usually selecting the lower surface. Radish is so
seriously attacked practically everywhere within the destructive
range of this pest that it is almost impossible in such regions to grow
this vegetable unless strenuous efforts are made to prevent the inroads
of the flea-beetle. Turnip and mustard are about equally attractive
to the beetles and unprotected beds are frequently destroyed. Important injury to cabbage is confined to young plants in seedbeds or to
plants soon after they have been transplanted in the field. Horse-
radish is readily attacked and the foliage is often so completely
riddled that it has the appearance of a sieve when held up to the
light. This plant, however, is very resistant and the roots attain a
good growth in spite of severe attack to the leafage

The larvæ have been observed on radish, Cleome, and *Lepidium
pubecarpum* only, but doubtless live on the roots of many other
cruciferous and related capparidaceous plants. The injury done
by the larvæ is negligible, so far as our observations go, in which
respect this species differs from the related striped cabbage flea-
beetle and horse-radish flea-beetle.[5]

SEASONAL HISTORY.

In its more northern range the beetle passes the winter months
in hibernation under clods of earth, or under heaps of weeds, dead
leaves, or other rubbish, whence it comes forth with the first warm
days of spring. In the extreme South the beetles are active throughout the year but reproduction does not occur during the winter.
In the Arkansas Valley the beetles issue from their winter quarters
during the latter part of March or early April. At first the foliage
of *Sophia pinnata* and horse-radish supply them with food. From
these plants they go to early mustard and radish, and throughout
the season or until severe freezes have occurred the beetles are to be
found on various cruciferous vegetables and weeds. In south Texas
beetles occur afield from February until December, being found, with
the exception of two months, practically throughout the year.

There are apparently three generations annually in Otero County,
Colo. Egg laying begins within a few days after the beetles leave their
winter quarters—as early as April 14—and continues until early
September.

---

[5] *Phyllotreta vittata* Fab. and *Ph. armoraciae* Koch, respectively.

LIFE HISTORY AND HABITS.

OVIPOSITION.

Opportunity was afforded for observing the female of this flea-beetle in the act of laying her eggs, beginning June 18, 1915, at Rocky Ford, Colo. In a period of 12 minutes 17 eggs were deposited. When fully extruded, the ovipositor is from one-third to one-half the length of the abdomen. The total time taken in laying an egg varied from 2 to 5 seconds, 3 seconds being the average. During the laying there is a contracting movement of the abdomen, the ovipositor is extruded—not always to its full length—and an egg is forced through the opening. If, when the egg is forced out, it does not strike a surface and adhere to it the female twists the ovipositor about until the egg comes into contact with a surface to which it adheres. After an egg was laid the female generally ran about for a few seconds, then stopped and remained quiet for a few more seconds before laying another egg. Three different times the succeeding egg was laid at the same place within 3 or 4 seconds of the preceding one. As far as could be determined the eggs were not deposited in any particular order or arrangement, but were distributed quite promiscuously over the surface of the glass in the rearing cage. After having laid the last egg, the female ran down on the stem of a turnip leaf, which was in the cage, and commenced to eat. No further egg laying was observed, but as four other eggs were found it is presumed that they were laid before these observations began, which would give a total of about 21 eggs laid at this time.

Subsequently eggs were found in various other locations, one mass of 20 being laid on the soil, another of similar number on the lower surface of a turnip leaf, while others were scattered in small masses about the crowns of the plants.

The number of eggs that might be deposited by a single beetle was very difficult to ascertain and although attempts were made only two records of egg laying were obtained.

September 6, 1915, three beetles, two females and a male, developed in the cages at Rocky Ford, Colo. They lived through the winter under bits of earth in a rearing jar, and March 29, 1916, the male mated with one of the females. This pair was isolated in another cage and the record of the eggs deposited is given in Table I.

TABLE I.—*Egg-laying record of a single female of Phyllotreta pusilla.*

Date.	Number of eggs deposited.	Date.	Number of eggs deposited.
1916.		1916.	
April 3	21	May 21	19
12	27	25	32
21	23	29	27
29	23	June 6	21
May 6	16	13	20
9	15	Total	244

The female died June 20, and the male July 31.

The second female, which developed September 6, 1915, deposited 193 eggs beginning March 26 and ending July 26, 1916. She died July 30.

Females collected in the field and confined deposited from 27 to 163 eggs each, indicating that many of their eggs had been deposited before they were confined.

HABITS AND BEHAVIOR.

It was noticed in the occurrence of this insect in Otero County, Colo:, that the beetles could best be collected during the middle of the day, the time when they were most active and were out on the plants in larger numbers. Earlier or later in the day they were usually found lower down on the plants around the crown or in cracks in the ground.

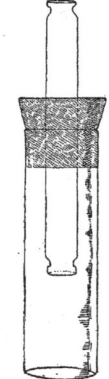

In order to collect them in numbers, a collecting bottle fixed somewhat as follows was used and found satisfactory: The bottoms of two small vials are broken out and then put end to end through the cork of the larger bottle (fig. 4). Upon inserting the neck of the outer vial over a beetle, it will invariably jump up into the vial. The neck is useful in that the beetle has a support to fall on if it does not secure a footing on the side of the vial. Hundreds of beetles can be collected in a bottle of this kind with small possibilities of any escaping. This form of bottle has been successfully used for the capture of other species of flea-beetles.

FIG. 4.—Device for collecting flea-beetles for study.

Adults mated from the middle of June to the middle of July, and were sufficiently abundant to do noticeable damage to small plants. Small radish plants were very much injured by the beetles eating into the stalk at the top or just below the surface of the ground, causing the plants to wilt and die.

In rearing experiments considerable care is required to see that the soil, or whatever the insects are in, does not become too wet or too dry. If the eggs are allowed to become too wet, they do not hatch; if not moist enough, they shrivel and dry up. In general, eggs require soil that is moderately moist.

The greatest difficulty in life-history studies was encountered in the larval stage. The larvæ were easily killed by excessive moisture, especially when accompanied by heat. Probably several thousand larvæ hatched but only a few lived to be adults. The most susceptible period is just after the larvæ have hatched. The laboratory temperature varied from 65° to 80° F. or above, with the maximum temperature for the larvæ about 70° F. This approximated more nearly the soil temperature in the field. Much below this the larvæ did not develop well and above 80° there was a considerable increase noticeable in the death rate. If too much moisture accumulates in rearing jars or "cages", the air becomes saturated during the day and at night cools off and condenses. This is detrimental to the larvæ, as they often become submerged in drops of water.

The young larvæ feed on the hair roots of their food plants and the older ones feed also on the main stalk and branches.

It was necessary to supply fresh roots every two or three days as decay is apt to set in. Parts of the crown of small turnips were supplied to the larvæ as food and they fed on this readily but did not seem to do as well as on fresh radish roots.

Upon reaching maturity the larvæ cease feeding and crawl restlessly around for a day or so before entering the soil. They make a distinct pupal cell with the inside compact and tightly cemented. Larvæ were observed in these cells, in a number of cases, for several days before they began to shorten. The contracted prepupal period ordinarily lasts 4 or 5 days.

Several times soil was secured in the field and brought to the laboratory and examined for larvæ or pupæ of this flea-beetle. In no instance was any larva or pupa observed. A number of examinations for larvæ and pupæ were made by digging around the roots of growing turnips and radishes. but neither was ever found in the field.

Since the eggs and larvæ in the laboratory seemed to be so susceptible to excessive moisture, the opinion was reached that it might be possible to control the species in the egg, larval, and pupal stages in the field by the practice of irrigation. Whenever the plants are irrigated, the soil around the roots is quite thoroughly soaked and it seems likely that the eggs, larvæ, and pupæ may not be able to withstand this.

LIFE CYCLE.

In working out the life history of the western cabbage flea-beetle adults were captured in the field and confined in cages consisting of battery jars and glass-covered boxes. The lid of a small tin salve box, filled with moistened earth, was placed in each cage, and in this earth the beetles deposited their eggs. The lids containing the earth were removed daily or at intervals of two or three days and placed in larger salve boxes. Food was supplied the larvæ by placing sprouted radish seed on the surface of the earth in the boxes. As the larvæ neared maturity most of the earth was removed from the lids in order to enable a close observation of the pupæ.

Owing to the extreme delicacy of the larvæ, it was impossible to rear large numbers at any one time. The small numbers of beetles which developed showed little disposition to breed and it was not possible to determine the number of generations occurring annually from any given "stock," or lot of specimens. The rearing records obtained, however, indicate the probability of three generations occurring annually in Otero County, Colo.

In Tables II, III, and IV records of the observed generations of the western cabbage flea-beetle in 1916 are given:

TABLE II.—*First generation of western cabbage flea-beetle.*

Item.	First generation.
	1916.
Adults captured and confined	Apr. 10
First eggs deposited	14
First eggs hatched	24
First larvæ pupated	May 23
First adults developed	June 3
	Days.
Egg stage	10
Larval stage	29
Pupal stage	11
Total duration	50

TABLE III.—*Second generation of the western cabbage flea-beetle.*

Item.	Second generation.
	1916.
Beetles confined	June 24
First eggs deposited	26
First eggs hatched	July 1
First larvæ pupated	19
First adults developed	25
	Days.
Egg stage	5
Larval stage	18
Pupal stage	6
Total duration	29

TABLE IV.—*Third generation of the western cabbage flea-beetle.*

Item.	Third generation.
	1916.
Beetles confined	Aug. 8
First eggs deposited	12
First eggs hatched	19
First larvæ pupated	Sept. 10
First adults developed	20
	Days.
Egg stage	7
Larval stage	22
Pupal stage	10
Total duration	39

HISTORY AND LITERATURE.

An account of this species, mentioned under the name of the Colorado cabbage flea-beetle (*Phyllotreta albionica* Lec.), was published by Riley in his 1884 report (*1, p. 308*),[7] in which he stated that it was injurious to cabbage and other cruciferous plants in June and July throughout the Rocky Mountain region of Colorado, having been found in great numbers at the very highest elevations.

In 1889 Prof. T. D. A. Cockerell (*2*) mentioned this species under the same name, quoting from Riley's report. In a footnote, written by hand in a copy of his paper, appears "Dr. Horn says this is *pusilla* Horn and not the true *albionica* Lec." The same year Dr. Horn (*3, p. 302*) published the original description of the species.

In 1898 an editorial account of this species was given by Dr. L. O. Howard (*4*), citing injury at Kennedy, Nebr., and Hill City, S. Dak., previously considered in this bulletin under the heading "Reports of injury," p. 4.

In 1900 Messrs. Forbes and Hart (*5, p. 471*) published an account of this species under the title "The western cabbage flea-beetle, *Phyllotreta albionica* Lec.," stating that it was reported by Bruner as injuring sugar beets in Nebraska, and by Gillette as infesting cauliflower and other cruciferous plants and the bee-plant (*Cleome integrifolia*).

In 1903 the writer published a brief account of this species under its proper name, stating that it was observed doing considerable damage to sugar beet in portions of Colorado during 1901, preferring the younger plants (*6, p. 18*).[8]

In 1909 this species was recorded (*8, p. 572*) in brief as having been very destructive to radish, turnip, cabbage, and some other truck crops in Oklahoma, Texas, and New Mexico, in 1908.

NATURAL ENEMIES.

The western cabbage flea-beetle is singularly free from natural enemies. The three species, other than birds, which have come under observation are all internal parasites.

A BRACONID PARASITE.

Perilitus epitricis Viereck, a braconid ichneumon-fly parasite of the adult beetle, was found during practically all the three summer months. It was most abundant from the latter part of June to the latter part of July. Two adults emerged September 13, and one larva was found the same date. The larva probably emerges through the abdomen and under the elytra, although this point was not

---

[7] Figures (italic) in parentheses refer to "Literature cited," p. 21.

[8] Remarks made by Prof. R. A. Cooley (*7, p. 260*) that he believes this species to be the cause of complaints of injury to turnip and cabbage in the Yellowstone Valley, Mont., may refer to the related *Ph. albionica* Lec., although *Ph. pusilla* is known to occur in that part of the State.

proved. The larva spins a light gray cocoon in which it transforms to pupa, and the adult parasite emerges through a small hole which it eats out of the end of the cocoon. The greatest percentage of parasitized beetles observed at any one time was 16.

Just what influence this parasite has in holding the beetles in check has not been determined. It is sometimes an important enemy of the related striped cabbage flea-beetle (*Phyllotreta vittata* Fab.)

A NEMATODE PARASITE.

Nematodes infest the adult beetles: As generally observed these nematodes were young and small, about 1/40 of an inch in length. From 200 to 500 were counted in a single beetle. In several instances adult female nematodes were observed which had the body sack filled with newly developed nematode young that had not yet escaped.

As nearly as could be determined the nematodes were not confined to the digestive tract but appeared to be in the body cavity. In a number of cases eggs laid by the beetles were found to be infested externally with the nematodes. The eggs had an unhealthy appearance and in no instance were infested eggs observed to hatch. Just what effect the nematodes have on the beetles would be an interesting problem to work out.

A GREGARINE PARASITE (GREGARINA).

Gregarine worms [9] occur in the intestines of the adult beetles, infestation averaging as high as 40 to 50 per cent, but it could not be determined whether these had any detrimental effect upon the host. They occur in almost all forms of insects and as far as known have no serious effect on them.

BIRD ENEMIES.

Mr. W. L. McAtee of the Biological Survey reports having found the western cabbage flea-beetle in the stomachs of three species of birds, and other beetles of the same genus in the stomachs of 12 kinds of birds. The land birds include among enemies of these beetles the common and Texas nighthawks (*Chordeiles virginianus* and *C. acutipennis texensis*), white-throated swift (*Aeronautes melanoleucus*), horned lark (*Otocoris alpestris*), starling (*Sturnus vulgaris*), song sparrow (*Melospiza melodia*), chipping sparrow (*Spizella passerina*), tree swallow (*Iridoprocne bicolor*), and marsh wren (*Telmatodytes palustris*).

CONTROL MEASURES.

EXPERIMENTS WITH INSECTICIDES AND DETERRENTS.

Ten experiments with arsenicals and one with nicotine sulphate were made in Otero County, Colo., by the junior author, and may be summarized as follows:

---

[9] Identified by the junior author.

Experiment No. 1.—August 19, 1911.

Nicotine sulphate, paste...................................ounces.. 3

Fish-oil soap...do. ... 8

Water..gallons.. 10

It was noted that when the beetles were thoroughly wet with this spray they appeared to be soon killed. Later experiments, however, demonstrated that the beetles afterward came to life. Nevertheless, the single application showed considerable value, and if additional applications had been made to the same planting, the efficiency of this deterrent could have been demonstrated. Naturally no harm was done to the plants.

Experiment No. 2.—June 3, 1911.

Arsenate of lead was used with an equal amount of soap at the rate of about 6 pounds to 50 gallons of water, on radish, cabbage, and mustard, but as only one application was made the plants became reinfested.

Experiment No. 3.—June 22, 1911.

Arsenate of lead, paste...................................pounds.. 6

Soap, common laundry....................................do.... 6

Water..gallons.. 50

In this experiment young cabbage was sprayed on both the upper and lower surfaces and the plants were heavily coated, almost whitewashed, the spray adhering well. This had the effect of deterring most of the beetles and although no dead ones could be found it was evident that the spray acted as a powerful repellent.

Experiment No. 4.—July 22, 1911.

Arsenate of lead, paste...................................pound.. 1

Whale-oil soap..do..... 1

Water..gallons.. 10

This was applied to radish and cabbage, the leaves of the latter being badly pitted. Every portion of the plants was wet on both the upper and lower surfaces. As in the previous experiments no dead beetles could be found and, although rainfall washed away much of the arsenate, in four days the plants had improved wonderfully and made excellent growth. As the rain left the plants practically unprotected a second spraying was made of the same mixture two days later. Nine days afterwards the cabbage was in excellent condition and practically free from insect pests, only an occasional beetle being found.

Experiment No. 5.—September 5, 1911.

Nicotine sulphate, paste...................................ounces.. 4

Whale-oil soap..do.... 8

Water..gallons.. 10

After the application of this spray it was noted that the beetles which came in contact with the treated leaves jumped wildly and and after a brief struggle apparently died, but revived within half an hour. The plants showed no injury from the spraying.

Experiment No. 6.—April 29, 1912.

Arsenate of lead, paste	pound	1
Whale-oil soap	do	1
Nicotine sulphate	ounces	5
Water	gallons	10

This was applied to young mustard plants which were so small that only the upper side was treated. In this case the beetles were apparently dead but after being confined in a cage revived within an hour. The following day the plants showed an even coating of arsenate on the upper surface and were almost entirely free from the beetles. Some of the worse pitted leaves had died, became very dry, and crumbled when touched, but this was due to the attack of the beetles and not to the insecticides. This plat was examined at intervals, and a week later the plants were growing excellently. As the beetles began increasing in numbers an additional spraying was necessary.

Experiment No. 7.—April 29, 1912.

Arsenate of lead, paste	pound	1
Whale-oil soap	do	1
Water	gallons	10

As in the previous experiment, the upper surface only was sprayed, radish and mustard being the plants treated. In this instance the infestation was so severe that many of the plants were so nearly destroyed that they failed to recover, partly because of hot, dry, and windy weather. It was only where the leaves were almost entirely consumed by the beetles that the plants died. The coating of arsenate was excellent and four days later the plants were growing well and were almost free from flea-beetles.

Experiment No. 8.—May 9, 1912.

The same formula as No. 7, applied to the same plants. Rain intervened for several days but nine days later the plants were described as growing beautifully and only moderately infested by flea-beetles, being beyond danger of injury. Although no dead beetles were found, the experiment was a success and the radishes were being sold at the time.

Experiment No. 9.—April 29, 1912.

A badly infested plat of mustard was dusted with dry Paris green inclosed in a cheesecloth sack, but there was a moderate wind and a considerable portion of the poison was blown away. The next day, however, although the plants were free from beetles they were nearly dead. Those which remained alive and were growing were practically free from flea-beetle attack.

Experiment No. 10.—May 2, 1912.

Arsenate of lead, paste	pound	1
Whale-oil soap	do	1
Water	gallons	10

FIG. I.—SPRAYING BEET FIELDS IN CALIFORNIA.

FIG. 2.—DUSTING CABBAGE WITH LEAD ARSENATE BY MEANS OF A TRACTION DUSTER.

THE WESTERN CABBAGE FLEA-BEETLE.

In this experiment radishes were sprayed and only the upper side was treated. A good quantity of the poison remained, no injury resulting from the spray, but no dead beetles could be found. Nine days later a rain fell, leaving many leaves unprotected, the beetles becoming abundant.

Experiment No. 11.—April 29, 1912.

A badly infested planting of mustard was dusted with undiluted arsenite of zinc. As in the foregoing experiment a moderate wind was blowing at the time and carried much of the poison away. The result, however, was practically the same, some of the poison remaining on the leaves, and although no dead beetles were found the plants were comparatively free from flea-beetle attack a week later.

It should be remarked that the plants at this time needed water but the irrigating ditch was dry.

RECOMMENDATIONS.

It appears to be practically impossible to kill an appreciable number of the western cabbage flea-beetles by spraying with arsenicals. Repeated experiments have shown that whatever application may be made does not kill the insects but drives them away. In other words, this insect can not be controlled by poisons, but by repellents and deterrents. The beetles are dainty in their feeding habits, carefully avoid foliage which has been sprayed, and attack either unsprayed portions or fly to other plants. Repellents such as tobacco dust are the most efficient of those which have been tested, and of the arsenicals, heavy applications of arsenate of lead have given the most satisfactory results.

LEAD ARSENATE.

In large plantings, and especially where cabbage is infested, spraying heavily with arsenate of lead is advised (Pl. I, fig. 1). The following formula has given excellent results:

```
Arsenate of lead, paste.....................................pound..  1
Fish-oil soap (as a sticker).................................do....  1
Water.....................................................gallons.. 10
```

This is at the rate of 5 pounds of lead arsenate to 50 gallons of water, or a trifle stronger than the standard formula of 4 to 50. One-half this weight of powdered lead arsenate, or 2 pounds in 50 gallons of water, is equally effective, with a corresponding quantity of soap to act as an adhesive or "sticker." It should be applied with a sprayer fitted with elbow extension, and a special effort should be made to coat thoroughly the under surface of the leaves. Two or three applications at 5 to 8 day intervals are sufficient even in case of severe infestation, provided the first application is made promptly on the first appearance of the insects.

BORDEAUX MIXTURE.

It has been known for many years that Bordeaux mixture is an almost perfect deterrent against flea-beetles. There is something extremely distasteful in it to this class of pests but unfortunately it has not been tested thoroughly either alone or in combination with arsenicals. It is recommended that tests be made both alone and in combination with arsenate of lead, arsenite of zinc, and calcium arsenate against this species. The standard Bordeaux formula 4–4–50 should be employed.

NICOTINE SULPHATE.

Experiments were made with nicotine sulphate at the rate of 3 ounces with whale-oil soap, 8 ounces, in 8 gallons of water, with the result that the beetles were stupefied although not killed. In these instances there is abundant proof that the flea-beetles were strongly repelled but further experiment is desirable to determine how often this preparation should be used, that is, at what intervals. Naturally since tobacco dust has been found successful, nicotine sulphate should be nearly as useful if not equally so.

INEFFECTIVE DETERRENTS.

In some regions where the western cabbage flea-beetle is destructive, growers dust the infested plants with air-slaked lime, ashes, insect powders, soot, or Paris green, but experiments made in Colorado have demonstrated that beneficial results from these substances, which also act as repellents, are of short duration in that State. The dry, high winds which prevail there render it difficult to apply an even coating of any form of dust or powder or to make such material adhere to the lower surface of the leaves where it is usually most needed.

A better coating, however, may be applied to the rough-leaved foliage of turnip, radish, and mustard than to the smooth-leaved cabbage, and some growers claim that the former class of crops may be efficiently protected by dusting with lime.

TOBACCO DUST.

A liberal application of finely ground tobacco dusted on the infested plants at 3 or 4 day intervals can be depended upon to protect radish, turnip, mustard, and similar vegetables from the beetles and for use on small areas is one of the most satisfactory control measures that can be recommended.

The accompanying illustration (Pl. I, fig. 2) shows a method of dusting with an arsenical or deterrent by means of a traction sprayer.

MAINTENANCE OF THRIFTY GROWTH.

In regions where the western cabbage flea-beetle is a dangerous pest the farmer is advised to keep the plants in vigorous condition by frequent cultivation and heavy manuring in order to stimulate the growth of the plant and enable it to recuperate from insect attack. The irrigation system should be so installed that it may be kept constantly in working order, that the plants may not suffer at any time for lack of moisture. It should be unnecessary to add that the crops be kept free from other insects and from disease.

IRRIGATION.

Irrigation has been suggested as a remedy for the hop flea-beetle in its occurrence on sugar beets and should be of value where irrigation is practiced on other crops. Its effectiveness could be increased by brushing the plants, causing the beetles to jump into the water and be carried away or drowned.

MECHANICAL TRAPS.

The use of sticky shields and tarred boards, which have proved effective in the control of the hop flea-beetle in hop yards, might be used against this pest when it occurs in its greatest numbers. The conditions, naturally, are different, but there might be some cases where either would prove effective.

In 1914 Prof. H. M. Lefroy (9) made use of what he calls the Wisley turnip-fly trap against two allied species of flea-beetles [10] in their occurrence on turnip with what he describes as amazing results, due apparently solely to the growth the seedlings make when their leaf surface is entirely unharmed. This trap is made of two boards set at a slope on a pair of runners like those of a sledge with a space between. The trap is drawn along the rows so that the plants pass through the space in the middle. In order to disturb the beetles a loop hangs from a crossbar and brushes the plants. The boards are smeared with a sticky substance, which captures the beetles as they fly up. The illustrations furnished of the trap show that it can be easily made and should prove quite successful where radish, turnip, and similar crops are planted in rows, but, of course, would not be of service where the seed is sown broadcast.

TRAP CROPS.

The fondness of this, as well as other cabbage flea-beetles, for radish, mustard, and turnip suggests the employment of these as early trap crops to attract the beetles from the later-appearing main crops of cabbage, sugar beet, and others. The beetles may be swept up from these trap crops by means of a bag sweep net of the type used by entomologists to collect beetles and similar insects. This should afford protection for the main crop.

---

[10] *Phyllotreta consobrina* Curt., and *Ph. undulata* Kutsch.

CLEAN CULTURE.

The habitual appearance of this species in great abundance on young plants is a factor which prohibits the use of anything except immediate application of poisonous substances like the arsenicals or repellents, but there is little doubt that in the course of time this pest will lessen in numbers, provided concerted action is taken to control it. Among the best remedies to be employed is the establishment of clean culture throughout the year from early spring until the crop is off and even thereafter. To accomplish this all cruciferous and related weeds on which the insects normally feed and breed should be kept down. It is desirable, therefore that the grower become familiar with all of these plants, or else it will be necessary to destroy all weeds and keep the fields free from them at all times. This may be accomplished by the ordinary process of weeding and by burning over after the crop is off and again before the crop is planted. Plowing over may be sufficient at either time.

SUMMARY.

Cabbage, turnips and other cole crops, sugar beets, other vegetables, and garden plants, are severely injured in the Western States by a minute flea-like beetle known as the western cabbage flea-beetle. Injury is chiefly due to the overwintered beetles during June and July, but the beetles accomplish more or less injury during the growing season. This flea-beetle develops on the roots of wild and cultivated cruciferous plants. The beetles frequently appear in great numbers, eat minute pitlike holes in the leaves of young plants, and often cause considerable injury in seed beds.

The entire life cycle from egg to adult may be passed in about 30 days in June and July and there are at least three generations produced annually.

Crops may be protected by means of a spray of arsenate of lead, applied at the rate of 2 pounds, powder, to 50 gallons of water, or by Bordeaux mixture, 4–4–50 formula, these sprays acting as repellents. It can also be controlled by nicotine sulphate, ½ pint 40 per cent solution in 50 gallons of water with 2 pounds of soap added, and by tobacco dust, which are deterrents. It is not possible, however, to control this insect entirely when it occurs in its greatest abundance.

In addition, it is desirable to keep the plants thrifty and well watered; mechanical and trap crops can be used with advantage, and clean culture is always advisable, especially the destruction of weeds in and near cultivated fields.

LITERATURE CITED.

(1) RILEY, C. V.

    1884. REPORT OF THE ENTOMOLOGIST. *In* Rept. U. S. Dept. Agr. 1884, p. 285–418, 10 pl.

(2) COCKERELL, T. D. A.

    1889. INJURIOUS INSECTS OF CUSTER COUNTY. *In* Fifth Rept. Colo. Biol. Ass., Jan. 9.

(3) HORN, GEORGE H.

    1889. A SYNOPSIS OF THE HALTICINI OF BOREAL AMERICA. *In* Trans. Am. Ent. Soc., v. 16, p. 163–320, 7 pl.

(4) HOWARD, L. O.

    1898. INJURY BY THE WESTERN FLEA-BEETLE, PHYLLOTRETA PUSILLA HORN. *In* U. S. Dept. Agr. Div. Ent. Bul. 10 (n. s.), p. 92–93.

(5) FORBES, S. A., and HART, C. A.

    1900. THE ECONOMIC ENTOMOLOGY OF THE SUGAR BEET. Univ. Ill. Agr. Exp. Sta. Bul. 60, p. 397–532. 11 pl., 97 figs.

(6) CHITTENDEN, F. H.

    1903. A BRIEF ACCOUNT OF THE PRINCIPAL INSECT ENEMIES OF THE SUGAR BEET. U. S. Dept. Agr. Div. Ent. Bul. 43. 71 p., 65 figs.

(7) COOLEY, R. A.

    1906. BIOLOGICAL DEPARTMENT. *In* 12th Ann. Rept. Mont. Agr. Coll., 1905, p. 255–273.

(8) [CHITTENDEN, F. H.]

    1909. INSECTS INJURIOUS TO TRUCK CROPS. *In* U. S. Dept. Agr. Ybk. 1908, p. 570–574.

(9) LEFROY, H. M.

    1914. CONTRIBUTIONS FROM THE WISLEY LABORATORY. XXIII.—A TRAP FOR TURNIP-FLY. *In* Journ. Roy. Hort. Soc. Engl, v. 40, pt. 2, p. 269–271.

UNITED STATES DEPARTMENT OF AGRICULTURE

BULLETIN No. 903

Contribution from the Bureau of Entomology
L. O. HOWARD, Chief

Washington, D. C. PROFESSIONAL PAPER April 22, 1921

THE GRAPE PHYLLOXERA [1] IN CALIFORNIA.

By W. M. DAVIDSON, *Scientific Assistant*, and R. L. NOUGARET, [2] *Entomological Assistant, Deciduous Fruit Insect Investigations.*

CONTENTS.

	Page.		Page.
California history	1	The nymph and winged form	73
Accidental and natural spread	7	Nymphicals or intermediate forms	82
Distribution of phylloxera in California	11	The sexual forms	90
Vineyard destruction	15	The gallicole and its relation to California conditions	95
Nomenclature and synonymy of the grape phylloxera	26	Effects of water and heat on phylloxera	98
Biology of the grape phylloxera in California	27	Diffusion of phylloxera	100
		Summary	122
The radicicole	44	Literature cited	127

CALIFORNIA HISTORY.

EARLY VINE PLANTING IN CALIFORNIA.

The grape phylloxera is not native to California. It has long been recognized as originating in North America, but its native habitat is east of the Rocky Mountains. The insect has not established itself upon the native vine of California (*Vitis californica*) in the wild state, whereas in Arizona it is established on native vines.

---

[1] *Phylloxera vitifoliae* (Fitch).

[2] Now in charge, Viticulture Service, California Department of Agriculture, Sacramento, Calif.

NOTE.—In connection with other work in California, the office of Deciduous Fruit Insect Investigations, Bureau of Entomology, in cooperation with the Bureau of Plant Industry, has been engaged in an investigation of the grape phylloxera during several years past, with principal headquarters for the work at Walnut Creek. The work was inaugurated by E. L. Jenne, upon his death was taken over by S. W. Foster, assisted by R. L. Nougaret. Upon Mr. Foster's leaving the service, the investigation was continued by Messrs. Nougaret and Davidson, the latter giving especial attention to biological and life-history studies and the former to investigations in the field and to remedial operations. The present report deals with the history, injuries, and life history of the insect in California. Remedial measures will be made the subject of another publication. It has been necessary to omit an extended bibliography of the subject.—A. L. QUAINTANCE, *Entomologist in Charge of Deciduous Fruit Insect Investigations.*

1900°—21——1

More specifically, the insect is a native of the Mississippi Valley, where the vines have developed a resistance to phylloxera, and such species as *Vitis riparia*, *V. rupestris*, *V. aestivalis*, etc., thrive, notwithstanding the presence of the insect. These wild species possess varying degrees of immunity and through scientific selection and hybridization have yielded types of vines possessing inherent degrees of immunity, known to viticulture as resistant vines, or resistant stocks when designated as a root upon which to graft commercial varieties of grapes in order to circumvent the ravages of phylloxera.

Vitis californica is a wild species of vine found not only in California but throughout the Pacific coast. Because normally found free of phylloxera in its wild state, it was at one time tried out as a resistant stock upon which to graft commercial varieties, but proved a complete failure in all but one or two instances. Even under normal conditions and environment, when once attacked it succumbs to the injury by the insect.[3]

The Mission grape is a cultivated variety of *Vitis vinifera*, and although of European origin, its introduction to the Pacific coast is so intimately related with the first settlement of California under Spanish rule that it well deserves the oft-attributed title of " California grape " (7)[4]. The Mission grape was introduced into California by the Padres of the Roman Catholic missions. As early as 1524 (18, p. 17), while Cortez was governor of Mexico, then called New Spain, seeds and plants were most often part of the cargo of vessels plying between the mother country and her colonies. Grapes and olives are plants mentioned as being among these. It is to be assumed that about that time *Vitis vinifera* varieties were introduced into Mexico from Spain[5] through both cuttings and seeds (1, v. 2, p. 131–133; v. 3, p. 613).

---

[3] In the Annual Report of the California Board of State Viticultural Commissioners for 1887, published in 1888, pages 47–48, may be found the following : " While visiting Mr. Hagan's vineyard, we were led to examine an old vine—*V. californica*—which appeared like one infested with phylloxera. This surmise proved correct * * *.

[4] The commission has often sought for evidences of phylloxera on our wild vines in their native state, but up to this time none has been found, this being the first case of the kind discovered." (See " Literature cited (5)," p. 127.)

[4] Numbers in parentheses refer to " Literature cited," p. 127.

[5] In this connection F. T. Bioletti, professor of viticulture at the University of California, writes as follows : " No one has yet been able to trace the Mission grape with certainty to any European variety. It is a remarkable coincidence, if nothing else, that a Sardinian grape known as the Monica resembles the Mission very closely The Monica is said to be a favorite grape of the monks in Sardinia, and it seems probable that the missionary monks of Mexico, finding it difficult to transport cuttings from their original homes, obtained seeds of the grape which they liked the best and that from the seedlings grown they chose the one which most resembled the grape they were looking for. If this is in accordance with the facts, the Mission is simply a seedling of the Monica."

He further advances the suggestion that the Mission might be a seedling of the Monica, as published in. a report (2) of the viticultural work of the agricultural experiment station of the University of California * * * 1887–1893.

Later, in the early part of the eighteenth century, a long line of missions was established throughout the peninsula of Lower California, the Mission of Loreto being the first, in 1697. These missions all grew grapes. The vines were furnished to them originally by the colonies of Mexico. As missions were founded, products and plants were furnished to the new one by the older established ones, and grapes are almost always mentioned as being cultivated by the Padres.

The Mission of San Diego was the first to be founded in upper California, and the vines planted there were brought from the missions of Lower California. As no other variety but the Mission grape is known to have been cultivated by the different missions which were founded in after years, it is to be presumed that it was introduced into this State with the founding of the Mission of San Diego, 1769.

The Mission is a long-lived, vigorous, and thrifty vine, as is attested by two remarkable specimens. · The one planted in 1775, and still living, is on the property of the San Gabriel Mission in Los Angeles County, is trained on an arbor, covers 9,000 square feet, and its trunk just below the surface of the soil has a circumference of 9 feet. The other, planted in 1842 near Carpenteria, died in 1915, presumably of the "Anaheim disease." It measured at its base $8\frac{1}{2}$ feet in circumference; at a height of $6\frac{1}{2}$ feet it divided into three branches, one of which measured $3\frac{1}{2}$ feet in circumference. As an arbor it covered one-fourth acre, and in 1895 yielded its maximum crop of 10 tons, its average crop being estimated at 5 tons.[6]

The Mission grape in early days was planted by the Padres around the missions and was used both as a table grape and especially for making wine. Gen. Vallejo (7) is authority for the statement that the Mission grapes grown at the Sonoma' Mission, were of a better quality than those grown at the other missions in California, and that a recognized superior quality of wine was made from them.

It was probably because of this reputation that the first commercial vineyards of wine grapes were established in the vicinity of the town of Sonoma. In this district the grape phylloxera was first discovered, and the dying of the vines, which for some time had puzzled the viticulturists, was finally determined to be the result of this insect's attack. An importation of vines from Europe of unparalleled importance up to that time for California, and one which may adequately be termed a "pioneer importation," occurred at about this time and very shortly prior to the discovery in France of the phylloxera, thereby furnishing grounds for the subsequent report, more or less widely spread throughout the State and which persists

---

[6] Details of its history can be obtained from the secretary of the Carpenteria Chamber of Commerce.

even at this late date, though refuted at different times by investigators, that this importation of European vines was responsible for the introduction of phylloxera into California. This is a mistaken idea. The history of the grape industry virtually proves that the insect was imported with American species or varieties of grapes from east of the Rocky Mountains.

FIRST DISCOVERY OF GRAPE PHYLLOXERA IN CALIFORNIA.

The first evidence of phylloxera infestation in California dates as far back as 1858. The dissemination of phylloxera continued for years in California before the existence of the pest was known, although its destructive work was observed, commented on, and designated a disease of vines from unknown causes. Reference to the first discovery and determination of the insect in California is to be found in a report (4, p. 108–111) dated August 28, 1880, and submitted by H. Appleton. In his report the first ravages witnessed in California are discussed, and from them is inferred the date of introduction of the insect. Extracts from this report follow:

On the nineteenth of August, 1873, an insect was found on the roots of grapevines by H. Appleton and O. W. Craig, in the vineyard of the latter, situated two miles north from Sonoma Town, on the west side of Sonoma Creek. An investigation was ordered at the time, for though the insect was identified as "the insect, or louse, known in Europe by the title of phylloxera-vastatrix, and in the United States as pemphygus vitifoliae," there existed a doubt in the minds of the investigators, because the injury was confined wholly to the roots of the vine, and no symptoms of injury such as recorded in Europe and in Eastern North America could be detected on the leaves.

From information received from Mr. A. F. Haraszthy and Captain E. Cutter, Superintendent of the Buena Vista Company's vineyards, I am able to give the following facts in regard to their large vineyards:

A vineyard of about one thousand vines was planted in 1834–35, and was watered every year. In 1850 and 1852 the vineyard was largely increased, and the system of irrigation was stopped. In 1857 about two hundred thousand vines were set out, and in 1858 one hundred acres were put in vines (six hundred and eighty vines to the acre). Again, in 1860, fifty acres were laid out. In 1862, Colonel A. Haraszthy planted 70,000 European vines, and it was among these vines the disease increased most rapidly.

In the Spring of 1863 the Buena Vista Company was incorporated, and in the Spring of 1864 that company planted 100,000 vines.

As early as 1860 decayed and dying vines were noticed in the vineyard, and they were taken up and others planted in their places. An examination was made to discover the cause of the disease in these vines, and it was attributed to alkali water, which was found a few feet underground. The roots were decayed. No examination by microscope of these roots was made. Vines died from time to time, showing short growth, small and colorless grapes, early yellow leaves—in fact, all the symptoms were observed of vines dying from the vine pest.

In 1868 about 3 acres of diseased vines were taken up (planted in 1850) on the north side of the dwelling house, and new vines planted, which grew well, showing little signs of decay till they were four years old, at which time (1873) the Phylloxera Committee, of the Viticultural Club, found the phylloxera on several vines.

The facts of this statement are significant and by no means ambiguous if considered in the light of the knowledge possessed to-day of the life history and habits of phylloxera, the nature of its injury, and the progress of its ravages.

This report also indicates how and when the first impulse was given to the development of the grape and wine industries of the State, then in their infancy. As interest grew in this direction, better varieties of grapes than the Mission would naturally be sought and given a trial. This was the case with the eastern variety of grape, the Catawba, a vine susceptible to the attack of phylloxera because of its fleshy roots and successfully grown at that time in the East as a wine grape. A weekly agricultural paper, the California Farmer (6), under date of Thursday, January 23, 1855, in an editorial article entitled " The Catawba Grape," says:

> We sincerely esteem the Catawba grape, one of the very best varieties for cultivation in California. Longworth of Ohio, whose famous Catawba Champagne is now esteemed equal to any wine imported, says it is the very finest wine grape known. Will be found far superior to our California Grape [Mission]. We earnestly urge our cultivators to give the Catawba a careful trial.

The same agricultural periodical from time to time that same year published other articles[7] eulogizing not only the Catawba but also other vines of eastern varieties and quoting fabulous yields in wine and profits.

Articles such as these undoubtedly influenced the planting of eastern varieties, if only as an experiment. Can it be doubted that many vines were brought from the East to California and the phylloxera introduced with them?

The variety of grape planted in 1850–1852 in the Buena Vista vineyard is not mentioned. It is more than likely that the major part of the planting was of Mission. If these vines were inoculated with phylloxera shortly afterwards by means of a few eastern grapevines planted near by, the vineyard would have experienced a spread of invasion as related above by Appleton. Evidence of the insects' injury would be apparent as affecting only a few vines during a few years or up to about 1860, and eight years later the vines, covering an area of 3 acres, would have become so dwarfed and nonproductive, with perhaps a few dead, that it would be necessary to grub them up. That this vineyard trouble was due to phylloxera is emphasized by the further statement that the 3 acres were again replanted with new vines, and during the four following years (1869–1872) the vines were again affected in a similar manner, but to a slighter degree, just as a recurrence of infestation would act if vines were planted in infested soil. Finally, in 1873, just five years

---

[7] E. g., " What are the best grapes ; " " Extracts of the Cincinnati Gazette."

after the replanting of the 3 acres, the committee of the Viticultu₁
Club discovered the phylloxera on the roots of several of the replan

The history of this vineyard proves conclusively by direct and c
cumstantial evidence that the trouble was due to phylloxera.
localizes the infestation, describes the progress and spread of t
injury, and, by fixing dates, determines the period of time the pro
ress covered. Finally, the presence of the insect is discovered a
its identity determined.

In 1861 Gov. Downey, of California, appointed three comm
sioners to work in the interests of the grape industry, two of t
members of this commission being Don Juan Warner and A. H
raszthy. The latter was sent to Europe to purchase for the Sta
for distribution different varieties of grapes, and the result was t
importation of 200,000 cuttings and rooted vines, comprising 1,4
different varieties of grapes from all the vine-growing countries
Europe and also from Asia Minor. It may be that some of these i
ported rooted vines harbored phylloxera, which already had caus
considerable damage to vines in France, although the insect was on
discovered in that country the following year (1862). It is qu
likely that a good portion of the 70,000 vines planted out on t
Buena Vista vineyard in 1862 and referred to in Appleton's rep
were propagated from this importation and that the pest may ha
been introduced simultaneously with the planting of the vines. T
rapid destruction of the vineyard, as stated, however, could have be
brought about in the case of the young vines just as well by infes
tion communicated by the old vineyard.

The history of the Orleans Hill vineyard furnishes an insight in
the methods of establishing vineyards with varieties of grapes i
ported from Europe in the early days of grape culture in Californ
and helps to give grounds for the belief that the earliest and origi
introduction of phylloxera into this State was due to eastern variet
of grapes only.

Data of this history are contained in a report, dated 1880, submitt
by the owner of the vineyard (4, p. 112). In 1853 the owner i
ported from Nassau on the Rhine, in Germany, 15 varieties of gra

The date when these replants were procured is not specified, but was probably about 1864 or 1865. Before the date of replanting the phylloxera had infested the Sonoma Creek district and had spread to Napa County.

In 1859 a horticultural exhibit was held in the agricultural hall just completed that year at Sacramento, and the records of the State Agricultural Society mention exceptionally good exhibits of grapes by progressive fruit growers. The eastern grape Catawba is twice mentioned.

From another report (4, p. 29–30) we learn to what extent the eastern varieties of grapes were grown prior to 1875 in El Dorado County. No mention is made of earlier dates, but it is more than probable that the European grapes were already supplanting the eastern ones, judging by the few of the latter type which were planted in later years and which to-day are found only in family vineyards and gardens. This report, written by Mr. G. G. Blanchard, commissioner of the State board of viticulture, further stated that what was true of El Dorado County could also be said of Nevada, Placer, Amador, Calaveras, Tuolumne, and Mariposa Counties. A passage reads:

The proportions and kinds (grapes) growing, taking one hundred as the sum, are as follows: Mission, or native grapes, sixty-eight; Catawba and Isabella, ten; White Muscat, Muscatella, Malaga, six; Tokay, Black Morocco, Malvoisies, one; Zinfandel, Riesling, two. The other thirteen are made up of numerous other varieties, such as Sweet Water, Black July, Hartford Prolific, Cloantha, and Concord, and some others.

In this enumeration eastern grapes would represent approximately 23 per cent of the varieties grown. We thus see the important part played by eastern varieties of grapes in the earliest plantings and can conceive how the pest was introduced directly from its natural habitat.

ACCIDENTAL AND NATURAL SPREAD.

Centers of infestation, when compared according to the modes of dissemination which they engender, are of two kinds: Accidental and natural. An accidental distribution center would be a nursery which imported, unwittingly, phylloxera-infested grapes, propagated the vines, and by so doing bred the insect and disseminated it with the sale and shipment of these vines. The same is true when vines are procured from phylloxera-infested districts. For new plantings or replants, such a center would be the infested locality in Napa, from which the Zinfandel vines were the means of introducing the pest into a locality as yet free from it. In turn, the Orleans Hill vineyard became a natural distributing center because the insect by its natural increase and habit spread to other parts of the same vineyard or even to other vineyards of the district.

Infestation from accidental distributing centers may be avoided by strictly enforced quarantine measures.

Accidental spread has been the main cause of most of the phylloxera infestation throughout the vineyards of California because of its being an initial inoculation, developing later into a center of natural dissemination.

A general survey of the growth of the grape industry, which at times, as in the late eighties and early nineties, attained the proportion of a boom, furnishes an indication of the accidental spread which took place concurrently.

Cuttings were used almost exclusively for planting vineyards in preference to rooted vines, the latter being used for replanting "misses," and even then not commonly used. As will be shown later, there is little, if any, danger in disseminating the phylloxera from cuttings, unless these are heeled in in infested soil while awaiting shipment. It is for this reason that the accidental diffusion was greatly restricted. If rooted vines had been commonly used, originating from the same district as the cuttings, the accidental diffusion would have been so general as perhaps to have precluded before long the growing of vinifera vines on their own roots.

THE WINGED MIGRANT NOT A FACTOR IN SPREAD UNDER CALIFORNIA CONDITIONS.

Profiting by the investigations and experiments that were being carried on in France, the University of California in conjunction with the State Board of Viticulture made extensive efforts to arrest the ravages of the phylloxera, and made investigations pertaining to its life history and habits. These deserve special mention in this report.

Dr. F. W. Morse (16) of Oakland, Calif., during the period 1881–1886, as an assistant in the General Agricultural Laboratory, discovered in the course of his investigations on August 26, 1884, specimens of the gall louse or leaf-inhabiting form of the phylloxera. As is noted under the heading "The gallicole and its relation to California conditions" (p. 95), this is the only recorded instance of the finding in California of the leaf galls. In this connection it may be said that in the experimental vineyards of the Bureau of Plant Industry, United States Department of Agriculture, in which are collected many varieties and hybrids of species of American vines, not a few of which are susceptible to leaf galls when cultivated in the Eastern or Middle States, an exceptionally good field for observation is offered. Mr. G. C. Husmann, under whose direction these vineyards are conducted, states that the leaf gall, to his knowledge, has never been found in them. Extensive correspondence with entomologists and prominent viticulturists in California elicited the same information.

Laboratory experiments, conducted under favorable conditions to obtain winter eggs with the existing strain of phylloxera in California, have failed to go beyond the production of the winged form in specially devised cages, although in other laboratory experiments the sexed forms were produced and the discovery in the natural state of a single winter egg must be mentioned.

A study of the life history has corroborated the observations of Dr. Morse relating to the sterility of a portion of the winged migrants and to the sterility of some and the debility of the remainder of their progeny. The writers' observations demonstrate that the normal life cycle of the insect in California is wholly parthenogenetic and that the natural spread, or diffusion, is due entirely to young radicicole larvæ possessing migratory instincts, at least during July, August, and September, and to which has been given the name of "wanderers" to distinguish them from "migrants," a term which commonly is applied to winged forms of the Aphididae.

The conclusions of the investigations of Dr. Morse point to the possibility of such a condition, though not affirming that the winged migrant is not responsible for the diffusion of the species in California. The late Prof. E. W. Hilgard (14) shared this view, which he expounded in his report, in which he indicates the discovery by him of one of the first phylloxera spots in Napa Valley, as follows:

The first phylloxerated "spot" within the Napa Valley was observed by me in 1377, close to the stage road and public highway leading directly from the worst-infested portion of Sonoma, and on which vineyard material was, and is, constantly being hauled back and forth. It is plainly from this highway and its infested wagonloads that the insect has spread in the Napa Valley.

The "spot" alluded to is believed by the writers to have been either in the old Squibb vineyard (10 acres), in the old McClure vineyard adjoining, or in the Callan vineyard (50 acres). All these were located close together. They have long since been pulled up, the land is now pasture, and only a very few of the old original vines still exist, although browsed down by the stock. These vines date back to 1866.

From present knowledge of the biology of the phylloxera, it is believed by the writers that the vineyard material referred to by Prof. Hilgard was responsible for the spread of the pest to this location, but the inoculation was due to the wandering young radicicole larvæ rather than to the winged form.

PHYLLOXERA SPREAD BY PICKING BOXES.

"Vineyard material" may imply many sources of infestation. Besides rooted vines, grape-picking boxes are very likely to transport the insect from one district to another. At times grapes are delivered to the wineries in greater quantities than can be handled, and boxes of grapes are unloaded and left at the winery instead of their contents being emptied into the elevators and the empty boxes returned to the same wagon. Boxes are exchanged, and some from infested districts find their way to uninfested vineyards. Wandering larvæ (wanderers) easily shelter themselves in cracks and joints of boxes while these remain strewn throughout the vineyard waiting to be filled with grapes, and when the boxes are transferred to other vineyards, after having been emptied at the winery, the insects may be released by the shock of the empty box against the ground in the process of unloading.

In their practical experience, certain grape growers have noticed that the first signs of phylloxera in their vineyards appear at places where they have been in the habit of dumping boxes for the convenience of grape pickers.

There were a number of wineries, reputed for the excellence of their wines, in the early-infested district around Glen Ellen, Sonoma, and Los Guillicos, and grapes were hauled to them from afar at about the time vines were dying rapidly in their vicinity. This accounts, no doubt, for the several early centers of infestation which appeared in a short period of time in Napa County.

The pest spread into Napa County from Sonoma County not only along the highway to and beyond the vineyards cited in Prof. Hilgard's report, but also over the ranges of hills referred to in the same report by means of a mountain road which ran over the divide from Sonoma and descended into a long narrow valley (Brown Valley), which itself opened out into Napa Valley quite close to the city of Napa. At the head of Brown Valley and almost on the county boundary line is the Dell vineyard. From the owner, Mr. C. Dell, the following information was obtained: In 1867, 20 acres of Mission grapes were planted with cuttings obtained from the Wing vineyard (then owned by Buhman Bros.), material for which formerly had been secured from the Buena Vista district at Sonoma. After seven years the Dell vineyard began to show signs of phylloxera in small patches, but bore good crops for four years. The Wing vineyard, located close by, began to die at the same time.

The phylloxera was introduced in this case probably by means of picking boxes, or else by rooted vines planted to fill out places where the cuttings had failed. If the dates are correct, the infestation would have been noticed, without the cause being known, in 1874, or about the time it was discovered along the Sonoma highway.

The above data are recorded to indicate how important a rôle this Sonoma Creek district played in the first introduction of the insect into California and how the spread occurred through different channels. For this reason the early plantings give an idea of how the insect could have been spread before its presence was suspected.

PRACTICAL METHODS EMPLOYED TO ARREST THE SPREAD OF THE PEST.

When the discovery of phylloxera in California was first made known, the grape growers were already acquainted more or less with the havoc it had produced in the vineyards of France, and a panic spread throughout the different grape districts. It soon subsided, however, when the vineyards were not being rapidly destroyed, and even precautionary measures were overlooked.

Of all the grape-growing counties, that portion of Alameda County known as the Livermore Valley district evolved the best organized system of quarantine measures, the aim of which was not to prohibit the importation of vines into the county, but to have cuttings, as well as rooted vines, thoroughly disinfected before they were permitted to be planted.[8]

The disinfectant used was a commercial soluble phenol. Vines were immersed for one-half hour in a solution of 1 part phenol to 60 parts water. Notwithstanding these precautions, vines were introduced without the knowledge of the quarantine commission, and there occurred three distinct centers of infestation from which the pest was remarked to spread with the prevailing summer winds. Two of these centers were planted originally with material from San Jose, and the third with vines from St. Helena, in Napa County.

DISTRIBUTION OF PHYLLOXERA IN CALIFORNIA.

As far as has been observed, Stanislaus, Merced, Kings, and Madera Counties, north of Tehachapi Pass, are free from phylloxera. South of Tehachapi Pass it has not been found so far. Most of the counties named have either enacted ordinances establishing prohibitive quarantine against the importation of grapevines or protective measures subjecting vines to strict inspection and fumigation.

The absence of infestation is without doubt not wholly due to quarantine measures, which were enacted years after the pest had many opportunities to be introduced, but more likely is due to the combined conditions of climate and soil in these counties.

The writers have made a personal investigation of the present status of phylloxera infestation, and have tried to ascertain and estimate approximately the damage caused to the viticultural interests. At this late date, however, there is much difficulty in obtaining information on which to base the estimate. Quite a number of vineyards have been replanted, some as many as three times; property has changed hands, and the history of vineyards has been forgotten. Again,

---

[8] Data personally contributed by Charles A. Wetmore, formerly chief executive of the State board of viticultural commissioners.

no traces exist of large vineyards pulled up but not replanted, and thus accurate data are unobtainable. Therefore a summarized statement based upon data to be found in the various reports of

FIG. 1.—Map indicating progress of phylloxera infestation in California. The map does not show the severity or degree of infestation. Counties having less than 250 acres of vineyards were not inspected. In those counties marked doubtfully infested inspection took place at a time of year when the insect was difficult to detect; none were found but the aerial growth of the vines suggested phylloxeration. In the counties of Kings, San Benito, Merced, Stanislaus, Calaveras, Amador, and Tehama no phylloxera was found at the time of inspection, but they should not be deemed to a certainty free of the insect.

the State Board of Viticultural Commissioners and other agricultural and horticultural reports is presented. This, with the aid of a map of California (fig. 1) to indicate infested counties in shadings to correspond to a period of years within certain dates, will enable one at a glance to conceive the degree of injury produced and the loss sustained by the viticultural interests.

A general idea can be formed of the growth of the viticultural interests of California and correlatively of the economic importance of the grape phylloxera by comparing the report on grape production of the State statistician for the year 1914 with the report of a similar nature for the period 1856–1866 (Table I).

TABLE I.—*Planting of vines in California in different perods.*

County.	Vines planted in—			Total vines existing in 1865.	Total bearing vines existing in 1866.	Total vines existing in 1910.
	1856	1857	1858			
Alameda	48,000	125,000	175,000	1,575,000	155,070	2,390,959
Amador	9,000	8,000	20,000	180,000	757,773	314,604
Butte	15,000	45,773	80,707	726,363	369,785	258,742
Calaveras		6,465	24,187	217,665	515,049	212,300
Colusa	10,000	3,120	4,285	36,000	47,800	482,417
Contra Costa	75,000	34,468	42,640	383,760	201,518	2,972,130
Del Norte			1,056	9,450	120	
Eldorado	6,390	26,400	77,472	697,248	1,441,039	581,342
Fresno	2,000	1,000	3,000	27,000		40,687,207
Humboldt	800	500	915	8,235	839	4,095
Inyo					252	39,478
Klamath		1,000	2,000	18,000	2,917	
Lake					11,000	296,752
Lassen					200	31
Los Angeles	726,000	600,000	1,650,000	14,850,000	3,000,000	4,923,877
Marin		500	600	5,400	11,542	115,198
Mariposa	1,000	15,227	15,000	135,000	51,783	28,647
Merced	10,000	15,000	15,000	135,000	100,740	1,281,342
Monterey	10,000	11,650	50,000	50,000	84,839	79,935
Napa	22,700	55,000	90,000	810,000	1,166,935	8,595,338
Nevada		6,000	8,000	72,000	124,000	94,338
Placer	2,702	5,742	5,000	45,000	397,101	1,340,132
Plumas		800	400	3,600	1,616	
Sacramento	52,200	119,500	327,900	2,951,000	951,315	7,627,510
San Bernardino	80,000	38,000	75,000	675,000	312,562	987,127
San Diego	4,000	4,000	50,000	450,000	1,915	1,228,858
San Francisco		1,200	1,000	9,000	75	3,000
San Joaquin	13,467	28,640	40,000	4,112,792	493,387	13,371,794
San Luis Obispo	1,500	2,000	10,000	90,000	18,263	265,481
San Mateo	5,000	40,000	40,000	360,000	16,000	124,990
Santa Barbara	15,000	70,000	90,000	810,000	220,000	208,595
Santa Clara	150,000	500,000	513,000	4,617,000	2,000,000	5,584,480
Santa Cruz	5,000	6,179	20,000	56,000	218,100	1,365,418
Shasta	5,348	6,100	25,000	225,000	1,534,520	117,481
Sierra		1,900	3,500	31,500	4,737	
Siskiyou	1,000	1,000	2,000	180,000	8,469	2,473
Solano	56,178	50,000	52,869	554,178	950,600	1,213,265
Sonoma and Mendocino	61,590	170,568	187,621	2,000,000	2,830,195	18,864,163
Stanislaus	4,420	3,020	1,800	162,000	112,310	1,932,302
Sutter	45,123	135,369	50,000	450,000	163,663	1,249,923
Tehama		2,000	5,500	49,500	145,883	1,307,218
Trinity	150	1,717	1,151	10,359	19,066	2,842
Tulare		400	30,000	270,000	100,950	7,227,491
Tuolumne	9,858	29,891	57,520	517,734	505,250	95,811
Yolo	26,902	61,903	155,425	1,398,825	157,434	2,568,019
Yuba	28,000	30,000	50,000	450,000	494,472	162,751
Alpine						9,000
Glenn						20,416
Imperial						298,813
Kern						419,582
Kings						4,538,732
Madera						795
Modoc						2,000
Mono						282,682
Orange						1,570,794
Riverside						177,976
San Benito						1,530,630
Ventura						36,398
Total number of vines	1,540,134	2,265,062	3,854,548	40,172,654	19,695,814	139,099,560
Total acres			11,411	59,077	28,966	

At this earlier period the pioneer growers of grapes were beginning to realize the possibilities of success due to the advantage of the peculiar suitabilities of climate and soil in California for the culture of European varieties of *Vitis vinifera*.

Within the period of 48 years (1866–1914) there had been an increase of nearly 90,000,000 vines. Within this lapse of time, so comparatively short for such a prominent industry of the State, many changes occurred in the different viticultural districts with which phylloxera had little or nothing to do, and the gradual damage and loss caused by the insect could not be compared with the acutely sinister influence of extreme fluctuations in the market values of grapes, whether for wine, raisin, or table use, which swayed the industry at different times from opulence to ruin and vice versa for the growers; yet when looking backward over the years, the phylloxera stands out preeminent and is considered as the main single factor in the loss and damage sustained by California viticulture.

In the early period the counties south of the San Bernardino boundary line were in the lead for the acreage in vines and for the production of wine. To-day in these counties viticulture is of secondary importance, yet phylloxera has never been discovered there. The Anaheim disease was one of the causes of this decline, but the change to the more lucrative investments in citrus culture, which no doubt appealed more to the tastes of the many eastern settlers who largely populated that portion of the State, is mainly responsible for the falling off in acreage of grapes and lack of interest in the industry.

Another viticultural district which underwent a great change was that of the Santa Clara Valley. There grape growing increased rapidly from 1885 to 1895, when the acreage of vineyards was the greatest and the county of Santa Clara produced almost one-third of the dry wines of the State. From 1893, when the vines began to die, the decline in acreage was much more rapid than had been its growth.

It was commonly believed at the time that the Anaheim disease, which had caused such great ravages in the southern part of the State, was also responsible for the sudden dying off of the vines in the Santa Clara Valley. The damage caused to the vineyards was so extensive that an investigation was instituted by the College of Agriculture of the University of California to determine the cause (3). The general conclusions arrived at were the following:

First, that the dying vines exhibit symptoms differing materially from those shown by the vines in Southern California which were destroyed by the Anaheim disease; and, second, that whether or not there be some "unknown influence" at work, as suggested by Mr. Newton B. Pierce, the real, determining factor is the deficiency of rainfall during the years 1897–1900.

At this time the phylloxera was known to exist more or less throughout the valley, and had been identified in different vineyards, but as yet its injury had not reached the advanced stage of noticeable characteristic phylloxera spots, was therefore little in evidence, and was not considered a prominent factor in connection with the destruction of the vineyards.

The following facts were brought out during the writers' investigations and have a direct bearing upon existing conditions in the Santa Clara Valley at that time:

Extensive areas of a vineyard may be infested by phylloxera before characteristic spots are noticeable; a lighter crop and a slight decline in vigor of growth are for some time the only apparent signs of injury.

Infested vines change suddenly for the worse, becoming rapidly stunted in growth, or even dying, when influenced by unusual conditions either from lack or excess of moisture.

Injured roots, functioning poorly under normal conditions of moisture, reproduce with difficulty fibrous roots, or feeders, to replace those which have been destroyed by the insect, and when subjected to drought they starve the vine.

Excessive moisture, instead of benefiting injured roots, causes them to rot and hastens the death of the vine.

For these reasons it is believed that the phylloxera was responsible for a far greater share of the destruction of the Santa Clara Valley vineyards than has been ascribed to it.

While Santa Clara and the southern counties have lost in acreage, a larger gain has been made at about the same period and later in other counties, especially those of Sutter, San Joaquin, and Fresno. Many vines throughout the State have been killed by phylloxera and not replanted; more have been grubbed out and replanted, sometimes more than once, and it is estimated that the loss in these respects has been very considerable.

Mr. George C. Husmann, pomologist in charge of viticultural investigations, Bureau of Plant Industry, United States Department of Agriculture, estimates the loss at 75,000 acres; Prof. F. T. Bioletti, of the viticultural department of the University of California, makes a similar estimate; and Charles C. Wetmore, for many years identified with the board of State viticultural commissioners, considers this estimate conservative.

VINEYARD DESTRUCTION.

PROGRESS OF THE DESTRUCTION OF A VINIFERA VINE.

According to conditions there is a great variation in the number of months or years that elapse between its original infestation by phylloxera and the actual death of the vine. The following points have important bearing on this:

Soil conditions and drainage.—From a survey made throughout the different districts of California, the following general statements can be made in regard to the destruction of vineyards when the vines are 8 to 10 years of age or older before becoming infested:

Vines live longer in rich, deep, well-drained soils. Under such conditions, vineyards known to have been infested for 20 years and longer still bear crops, have only a few vines actually dead, and but a small percentage bearing little or no crop.

Vines die sooner and the crop of the vineyard is more rapidly diminished in quantity and quality when established on rich soil only a few feet deep and with poor drainage, or on side-hill soils lacking moisture.

Vines are still more rapidly affected in heavy soils, more or less shallow, with compact clay subsoil. In such types of soil, the vines, more or less stunted and enfeebled, may live a number of years. After a winter of unusually heavy rainfall they may show a very rapid serious decline or even a majority of them may die within a year.

Vines growing in a well-drained, very loose, and friable sandy soil, or one with a surface of blow sand several inches in depth, seem to be almost immune to the attack of phylloxera.

As a sandy soil becomes heavier in texture and of poorer drainage, so the vine succumbs more readily to the attack of the insect.

Age of vine at infestation.—Young vines are destroyed more readily during the first three years, before they have established a fairly good root system. When vines are 8 or 10 years old the quality and texture of the soil become main factors, and the more or less rapid destruction of the vineyard depends on the adaptation of the vine to the soil and the advantages of prolification and diffusion for the insect. The general experience has been as follows:

Cuttings infested in their early growth rarely survive the first year.

Rooted vines, infested from the time of planting, produce from the start a very poor vineyard, which rarely lasts more than three or four years, the individual infested vines living after infestation hardly more than two years. If vines become infested during the second or third year from planting, they may last longer if they have a good root system, and in this case the vineyard may produce one or two crops smaller than normal and perhaps last five or six years. When a vine is three years old or more before infestation, its longevity depends somewhat on variety, much more on age, and especially on soil conditions.

Too few American varieties, either nonresistant or resistant, are grown in the State of California at this time to have been considered in this investigation.

Intrinsic vigor of vines.—Vines of great intrinsic vigor always resist phylloxera attack better than naturally weak plants.

Varieties of vines.—Amongst vinifera varieties grown in California, a few have shown certain resistance when inoculations have taken place several years after planting. Such are, in order, Flame, Tokay, Mission, and Muscat (Fresno district), and in a lesser degree Grenache, Chasselas, and Burger. Laboratory tests with certain varieties in which phylloxera lesions rotted rapidly have shown that Zinfandel, Thompson's Seedless, Carignan, Burger, and Muscat succumbed more rapidly and Tokay and Grenache less rapidly.

Destruction of a highly susceptible vine.—Under favorable conditions for rapid phylloxeration, the hypothetical progress of destruction of a highly susceptible vine, as Zinfandel, with established roots may be set down as follows: During summer and fall a few larvæ settle on a part of the root system; the following year infestation spreads to the surface fibrous and fleshy roots, and to a certain extent to the large roots near the crown, and nodosities and tuberosities are formed. The third year the subterranean infestation spreads pretty well throughout the root system, although it is rare to find year-old wood much attacked, for it appears that the habit of roots of this age to slough the outer layer of bark prevents the phylloxeræ from retaining a hold, and compels those already settled to move to other more hospitable portions of the root system. In this year some of the larger roots decay under combination of phylloxera attack and excessive moisture in the subsoil or become dried out from phylloxeration combined with too great drought, and thus the flow of sap between the feeding rootlets and the aerial portion of the vine is more or less cut off. This results in a shortening of cane growth and sometimes in an abnormally large crop of grapes. During this third summer as the larger roots die an emigration of young larvæ takes place. Many winged forms also may be developed. The fourth year finds the larger roots in great part destroyed, the cane growth correspondingly reduced, and a large number of fibrous and fleshy rootlets sent out from the trunk just below the soil surface. The phylloxeræ colonize these rootlets in spring, but leave them in summer, when they decay. There is also a heavy migration from the decaying roots farther down in the soil. In the autumn it is hard to find phylloxera on such a vine, and this explains the maxim that the best type of phylloxerated vine on which to look for the insect is not one badly stunted, but rather one with slight stunting of the canes; in fact, one in the second or third year of phylloxeration. Such a vine as has been portrayed generally dies in the fifth or sixth year from the initial attack.

As has been pointed out above, the decline of a vine is influenced by many conditions, and the hypothetical case given shows the minimum longevity of an established susceptible vine after phylloxeration. Under favorable conditions infested vines live much longer, and in extreme cases their length of life seems hardly affected by the continued presence of the insect on their roots, a slight decrease in the size of the crop being the only evidence of injury.

HOW THE PRESENCE OF PHYLLOXERA IS INDICATED.

The existence of the phylloxera in a vineyard is indicated by the well-known areas or "oil spots," so termed because of their manner of spreading. A "spot" appears first in the form of one or two vines showing a slight shortening of the canes and a premature seasonal yellowing of the leaves, although the latter symptom may be caused by the red spider (*Tetranychus bimaculatus* Harvey), or by alkali in the soil. The year following this indication the vines originally infested exhibit a more noticeably stunted appearance, while other vines surrounding them show slight shortening of canes and premature discoloration of foliage. After this the "spot" increases in size, in course of time the vines in its center die, and finally the vineyard may become totally destroyed. The writers have never observed the "spots" to increase as rapidly in California as they are reported to have done in the vineyards of France after the time the insect first reached that country, when 2,500,000 acres were destroyed in 25 years, and vineyards frequently have been observed in California which had phylloxera "spots" of more than 20 years' standing to have vines still living.

The "oil spot" generally is circular in shape, but sometimes it assumes other forms. At times it is oval or narrowly elongate, the latter form occurring on hillside vineyards through which water rills run in the spring. In such cases spread of the "spot" is often rapid in a downward direction, indicating that running water is an extra factor in the spread of infestation. The writers have demonstrated by experiment (see "Diffusion of phylloxera," p. 100) that the phylloxeræ can be carried in water from one vine to another, and when the rains of March and April occur there are plenty of active phylloxeræ on the roots. In other cases the spread of a "spot" follows the direction of the prevailing winds and it appears that this spread is caused by wind agency in the transportation of wandering larvæ in summer and autumn. In vineyards where vines are planted rectangularly (i. e., 8 by 12 feet), instead of square, the infestation very frequently spreads along the shorter 8-foot rows, indicating that the insects traverse more easily the shorter than the longer distances. Aerial and subterranean migrations of wandering larvæ play an important part in the enlargement of phylloxera "spots." Only an infinitesimal percentage of the thousands of wandering larvæ succeed in reaching their goal, but, as they are parthenogenetic radicicoles, a single larva can cause a new infestation or start a new "spot" at quite a distance from the original one, either in the same or in another vineyard.

The estimation of root injury from external appearance usually can be made with considerable accuracy, and the degree of infestation of a vineyard computed by the number of "spots," their size, and the stunted condition of the vines composing them.

The diagrams (figs. 2 and 3) indicate a phylloxera "spot" charted, respectively, in the years 1914 and 1915. This "spot" occurred on a heavy black clay soil on a hillside of moderate slope. It appeared that the "spot" started about the year 1907 when the vines were 3 years old, and that the first vines died about 1911. Surveys of the "spot" were made October 13, 1914, and November 5, 1915, and the vines were designated in the following manner: Ten was given to vines which showed no external evidences of phylloxeration; 9 to those which showed very slight evidence, such as premature yellowing of foliage and slight shortening of canes; 8 to those showing more advanced symptoms of phylloxeration, and so on down to 1, which was given to vines which showed only the most feeble vegetative growth. In order to portray the "spot" more vividly, symbols have been utilized as follows: Healthy vines, H; vines designated 9 and 8, S; vines designated 7 and 6, I; vines designated 5 and 4, U; vines designated 3, 2, and 1, D; vines killed by phylloxera, solid dot. In this vineyard every fourth vine had been replaced by a walnut tree, and these places where vines have been pulled out and not replaced are left blank in the diagrams.

In the diagrams not all the "spot" is shown, for it has extensions, the principal one being on the north side across a 24-foot avenue and continuing down a swale for some 60 feet. Enough of the "spot" is shown to indicate its general form. Between 1914 and 1915 there occurred an unusually wet winter and the "spot" grew considerably in the 12 months between the surveys. Although the number of dead vines increased only from 43 to 49, and among the badly stunted types not much increase was shown, there was a marked increase in the number of vines showing recent phylloxeration.

When more than one variety of vine is included in a "spot," a good index of the resisting power of the several vinifera varieties frequently is observable. Among the dead or moribund vines of

oxera " spot " in Zinfandel vineyard, charted in 1914. (See text.)

revious to showing a marked decline, vines freque
ally abundant crop of grapes, and stunted vines s
larger amount of grapes in comparison to the siz

FIG. 1.—Young raisin vineyard uninfested by Phylloxera.

FIG. 2.—Old vinifera vineyard infested throughout with Phylloxera and showing empty spaces where vines have been killed; vine in foreground shows less infestation by Phylloxera than others near by, and would be rated at 7, but the canes show obvious stunting.

THE GRAPE PHYLLOXERA IN CALIFORNIA.

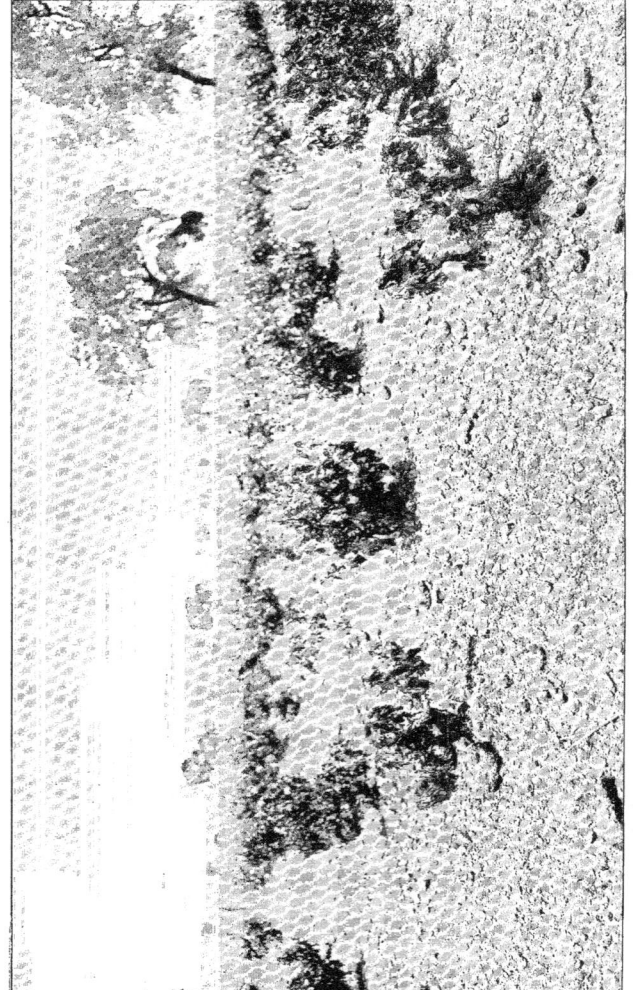

THE GRAPE PHYLLOXERA IN CALIFORNIA.

Old Tokay vineyard with Phylloxera infested "spot" in foreground; vine in central foreground to be rated at 6; the two vines on sides in foreground to be rated at 3 on the scale of Phylloxera injury.

THE GRAPE PHYLLOXERA IN CALIFORNIA.

Old vinifera vineyard infested throughout with Phylloxera, and showing many empty spaces where vines have been killed.   None of the vines in the foreground is to be rated above 3 on the scale of injury from 1 to 10.

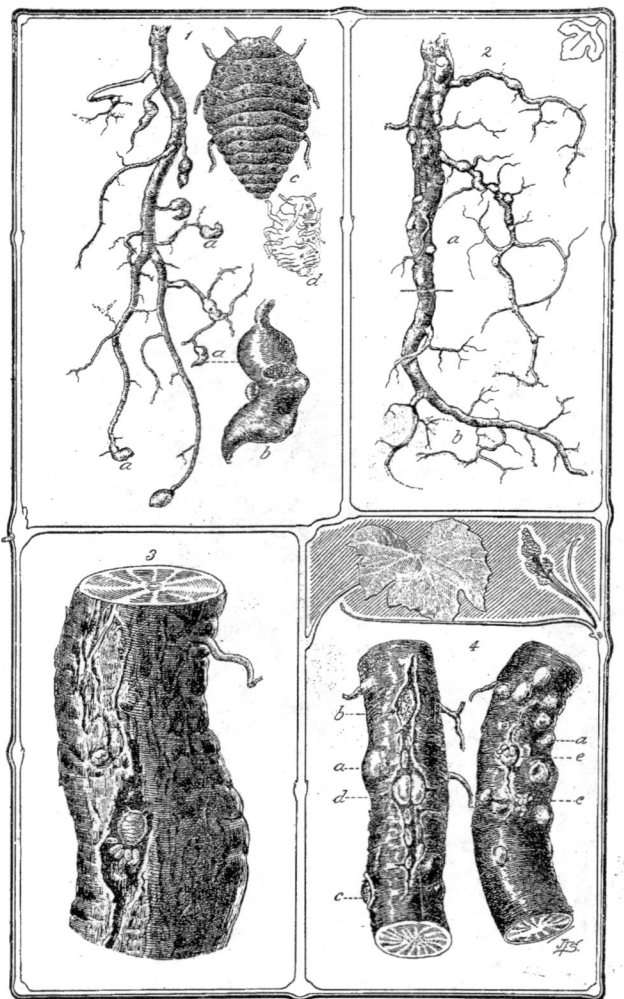

THE GRAPE PHYLLOXERA IN CALIFORNIA.

Phylloxera vitifoliae: Fig. 1.—Phylloxera nodosities shown on Zinfandel grapevine: *a*, Nodosities on terminal rootlets; *b*, nodosity showing Phylloxera feeding; *c*, adult louse; *d*, molted skin of same. Fig. 2.—Phylloxera tuberosities on smaller root: *a*, Infested portion of root; *b*, normal portion of root. Fig. 3.—Section of grapevine root showing adult louse with eggs *in situ*. Fig. 4.—Sections of root infested: *a*, Newly formed tuberosity; *b*, advanced stage of tuberosity; *c*, side view of older form of tuberosity; *d*, tuberosity causing the cracked condition of bark; *e*, young colony of insects as found on roots.

their wood growth than do healthy ones. Such grapes mature, however, without attaining a good size or their normal saccharine con-

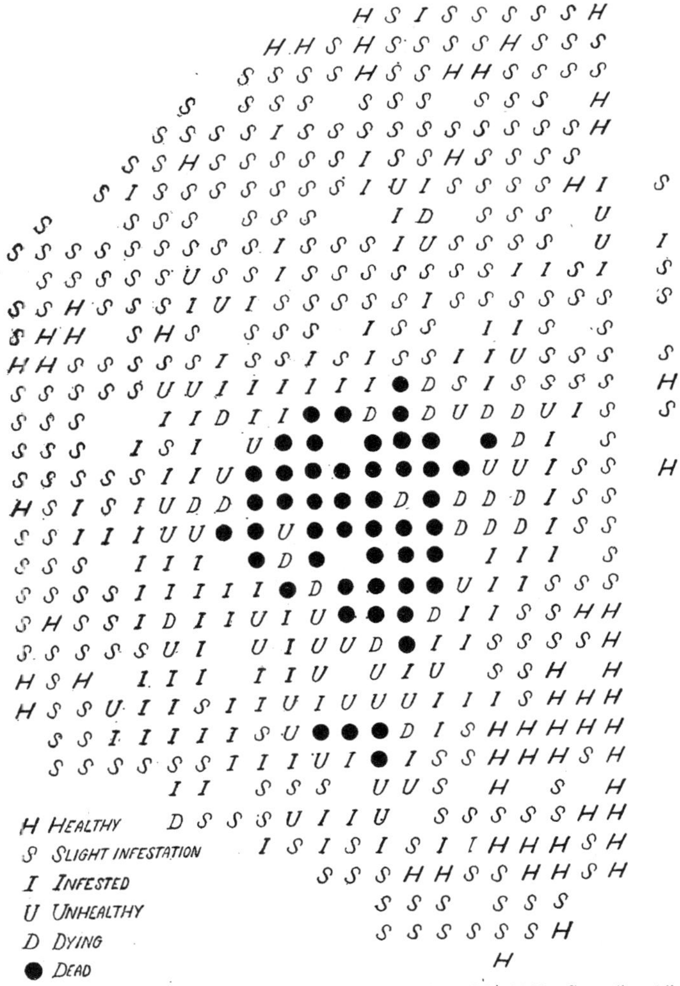

H Healthy
S Slight infestation
I Infested
U Unhealthy
D Dying
● Dead

Fig. 3.—Phylloxera "spot" in Zinfandel vineyard, charted in 1915. Same "spot"
as shown in figure 2. (For description see text.)

tent. Stunted vines produce leaves of a more uniform size than
healthy vines, and because the internodes of the canes are shorter,
the leaves appear more closely grouped, giving the "cabbage-head"

of Plate III is obviously stunted, althou

Root lesions are swellings on grape r
of the phylloxera beak. They are of tv
(2) tuberosities.

The nodosity.—Nodosities (Pl. IV, i
swellings on the white fleshy feeding r
a characteristic greenish-yellow color, a
the phylloxeræ responsible for their ir
come to lie in a depression (Pl. IV, fig.
come as much as six times the diameter c
when several insects have settled upon
ameter for a single occupant. Throug
the nodosity is very conspicuous in com
manifest proof of the presence of the ph

In most cases the formation of a nodos
rootlet. At times the rootlet grows one
and occasionally the puncture of the pl
rootlet in its growth, the subsequent s'
character and becoming a tuberosity. N
lived, lasting about a month. Excess n
lack of moisture dries them up, but a l
them to last longer.

The foregoing also applies to the Ame
nonresistant. On the rootlets of the r
phylloxeræ frequently fail to cause swe
are produced they are smaller, less flesl

also occur on the trunk of the vine, both above and below the soil surface. They are less commonly formed on roots of one year's growth than on older wood. On resistant vines tuberous swellings are normally quite unusual, but they may be formed on the healing growth of the cambium layer about an abrasion. On most American vines of nonresistant type, tuberosities are abundantly formed. On vinifera×resistant hybrids the more the resistant strain predominates the scarcer are the tuberosities.

Tuberosities are formed at any time between March and October, most abundantly during the summer months. They are formed more readily on vigorous roots than on those somewhat dried or decayed. Hibernants often choose tuberosities upon which to pass the winter, besides inducing their growth at points as yet sound and uninfested, the mere insertion of the beak being sufficient to stimulate growth. Tuberosities vary considerably in their general appearance, even on the same vine. Some are minute papillæ on the surface of the root. Others are large, fleshy, rapidly growing, globular outgrowths, as much as half an inch in diameter, and this type is found chiefly on the smaller roots. Others are enlargements of the girth of the root at intervals, a type also confined to small roots. Others consist of more or less uniformly rounded swellings of one-sixth to one-fourth inch diameter on the root surface, and these are the ones most commonly found on larger roots. Such tuberosities by their growth generally split the epidermis of the root longitudinally, and as the split tends to lengthen at both ends, the tuberosity assumes an oval or elongate shape. Later, when the split enlarges, fresh tuberosities are formed by aphids on the inner layer of bark exposed by the split, and shortly a chain of lesions occurs along the crack. These cracks lengthen and often involve a length of more than 6 inches. On roots growing horizontally or almost parallel to the soil surface, the majority of the tuberosities will occur on the lower side, the insects apparently settling there because of the greater moisture. On vertical or sloping roots tuberosities occur more or less uniformly all around. As long as they remain fresh, tuberosities provide an excellent quality of food for the aphids. This condition should be distinguished from the rapid development observed in the case of aphids settled on root callus, which forms at the point of severance and is caused by the action of the healing cells of the cambium layer becoming greatly enlarged and very fleshy, furnishing excellent food for the aphids, through the natural function of the wounded root.

Many factors influence the length of existence of tuberosities. In general, it is found that those formed in the autumn will last until the rainy season, and commence to decay immediately afterwards.

Their decay is expedited by a heavy rainfall and a high-water table. Those formed during the spring and summer in a moist environment rarely persist fresh beyond two months, and most of them decay about one month after they arise. It has been repeatedly observed how quickly a fresh tuberosity decays when it is placed against wet sand, and if a stream of water finds its way down a root the tuberosities thereon start to decay immediately. On the other hand, they are more capable of withstanding dry soil conditions than are the nodosities, and under conditions approaching drought, which sometimes occur in late summer and autumn, may last for a considerable time and even lignify, the dry environment having caused the insects settled on them to seek more favorable conditions of moisture and at the same time having kept in check decomposition. Tuberosities withstand a considerably greater range in temperature than do nodosities, and they are not affected by sudden changes in temperature in the same manner as are the nodosities.

Tuberosities grow larger and more rapidly in proportion to the soundness of the roots. On roots previously uninfested the growth of the swellings is rapid and vigorous, and a root, after it has been heavily phylloxerated for several months, becomes so greatly exhausted that it can not respond to the punctures of the aphids by developing new swellings, and the phylloxeræ that are not gradually driven away to seek more nutritious food develop on the root without causing swellings. The decay of the tuberosities begins at the place first punctured by the aphids, generally at about the center of the swellings. The tuberosity forms around the insect, and decay is first evident as a small, blackened spot, sometimes exuding a liquid. The rapidity of decay of tuberosities is in proportion to the increasing moisture content of their environment, and in an unusually dry environment they frequently will lignify without causing the tissues to rot. Under moist conditions the inflated cells rapidly break down and decay usually spreads, and fungi and molds enter the tissues, especially in the case of large bulbous swellings. Decay finally drives off the aphids, but through their stimulating action they are often able to retain the freshness of a tuberosity for some time after it has been surrounded by decayed tissues, and occasionally a fresh, vigorous specimen is found on a root otherwise quite decayed. The nutritious quality of these tuberous lesions provides for the production of nymphs in great numbers.

HOW ROOT LESIONS AFFECT THE HEALTH OF VINES.

It has been shown in the foregoing pages that the nodosities are those phylloxera lesions formed at the apex of growing fibrous rootlets, whereas the tuberosities are lesions formed on all other parts of the root system. Since the vine derives its plant food through the growing rootlets that thrust their way through the soil, it is obvious that when such rootlets rot as a result of the decay of the nodosities situated on them no more sustenance can be afforded the plant through this medium. If, on the other hand, the rootlets continue to grow notwithstanding the nodosities situated on them, and if the nodosities lignify, the supply of nourishment provided by the rootlets is not cut off, and the nodosities become in effect tuberosities. This is often the case with resistant vines, and much more rarely with vinifera or nonresistant Americans. In resistants these tuberosities generally lignify and heal, but in the other types of vines they do this only if their environment is quite dry. Nodosities effectively destroy the terminal rootlets; but since the insects spread very slowly on resistants, a vine of any vigor has abundant feeders, and thus it follows that resistant vines bearing very few or no tuberosities, but having many nodosities, do not succumb to phylloxera. Resistant vines never lack the power to produce enough feeding rootlets to sustain them as long as the following conditions, which are normal to these vines, obtain: (1) When the development and spread of the phylloxerae on them are comparatively slow; (2) when a large percentage of insects that have been raised on the nodosities become nymphs and later leave the roots as winged migrants, in an endeavor to reach the surface of the ground or the aerial parts of the vines. Both of these conditions may be affected by the quality of plant food, as will be shown. Instances have been seen in which young resistant vines have been rid of their entire infestation because all of the immature phylloxerae became winged migrants in the autumn, but in the majority of cases of infested resistant vines under observation there remained in late fall a small wingless infestation, and in some instances where the vines had been growing in small pots with insufficient nourishment infestations of wingless aphids persisted, and the production of winged migrants during the autumn was proportionately small. These wingless infestations, however, were not prolific. It appears that thrifty resistant vines afford poor nourishment for phylloxerae, and they do not respond to phylloxeric irritation by producing swellings. When, however, resistant vines become weakened through a poor supply of plant food, the phylloxerae attacking them persist and the vines respond to the phylloxeric irritation and form lesions.

Although the decay of the nodosities on vinifera vines destroys the feeding rootlets, this in itself is not a potent factor in the destruction of the vines by phylloxera. Except under abnormal conditions, such as the confinement of vines in pots with impoverished soil, no case has ever been observed in which the death of a vine could be attributed solely to the decay of nodosities, whereas instances have been observed wherein vines flourished with their vitality but slightly impaired, notwithstanding a nodositous infestation extending over several years. One such instance was that of a 20-year-old vineyard of Burger and Chasselas (viniferæ) near Napa, Calif. In 1913 the vines had been phylloxerated for upward of eight years, and each year the nodosities had been extremely abundant and practically no tuberosities had been developed, yet the vines appeared quite thrifty, owing to the maintenance of a sufficient number of uninfested feeders. It is the decay of the tuberosities on the larger roots, which the vine can not replace, that causes at first the impairment of the vine's functions and later results in its death. The simultaneous decay of many tuberosities is the cause of rapid decline in the vigor of a vine and is the prelude to the vine's death. The larger roots near the crown of the vine are especially susceptible to tuberositous decay, while the decay of a root below the crown is often very slow. This lower portion under favorable conditions is able to maintain itself undecayed for months, if not years, and is capable of providing nourishment for phylloxeræ. It is frequently observable that vines retain their vigor despite a ring of decay at the crown of the roots, and do not become stunted until the major portions of the larger roots have rotted.

In a discussion of the effect of root lesions on the health of vines, emphasis should be placed upon the decay of the tuberositous lesions and upon the fact that this decay is invariably hastened by moisture and retarded by dryness. Decomposition is often hastened by the work of fungi, molds, thysanurans, and tyroglyphid mites. The most common mite so working is *Rhizoglyphus elongatus* Banks, specimens of which were determined by Mr. Nathan Banks. It is a rather large species and is very prevalent throughout the grape sections of California. It was frequently reared on decaying roots kept in the cellar of the laboratory. The mite is hyaline white, with two brown circular spots, one behind the other, on the dorsum of the abdomen.

NOMENCLATURE AND SYNONYMY OF THE GRAPE PHYLLOXERA.

The genus Phylloxera was erected in 1834 by Boyer de Fonscolombe (10). The type species is *P. quercus* de Fonscolombe. In 1856 Asa Fitch (9) described the grape-leaf gall louse as *Pemphigus vitifoliae*. The species was obviously placed in the wrong genus. In 1867 Shimer (21) erected a new family (Dactylosphaeridae) and a new genus, Dactylosphaera, for a new species of his (*globosum*) and tentatively placed *vitifoliae* Fitch in this new family and genus. In a footnote he also proposed the genus Viteus for Fitch's insect. In 1868 Planchon (20) described the grape root louse from France as *Rhyz-*

aphis vastatrix Planchon, and in the same year Signoret (22) placed the species *vastatrix* in the genus Phylloxera de Fonscolombe. The year following Westwood (23), in England, described the insect as *Peritymbia vitisana*, but in a later article the same year he placed his species in synonymy as follows: *Peritymbia vitisana* Westwood= *Pemphigus vitifoliae* Fitch, *Dactylosphaera* (?) *vitifoliae* Shimer, and *Phylloxera vastatrix* Planchon (19). Until 1900 the name generally recognized by writers had been *Phylloxera vastatrix* Planchon. In 1900 Del Guercio (12), in Italy, erected the genus Xerampelus to receive the grapevine species, which he therefore called *Xerampelus vastator*. This genus has not been recognized by all later authors. Grassi (11, p. 12) would retain Shimer's proposed genus *Viteus* as a subgenus to *Phylloxera*, and would thus name the species *Phylloxera* (*Viteus*) *vastatrix*. The present writers are inclined to retain the specific name *vitifoliae* Fitch on account of its evident priority over Planchon's more widely known *vastatrix*, and notwithstanding the objections raised by authors as to its orthographical correctness (*vitisfolii* and *vitifolii* have been preferred and written). As to the generic title, it has been decided that *Phylloxera* will be retained, the question of the subdivision of the genus being left to those who have had more opportunity to study the specific ramifications of this group.

The synonymy of the grape phylloxera as understood by the writers is therefore as follows:

'**Phylloxera vitifoliae** (Fitch).

> *Pemphigus vitifoliae* Fitch, 1855–56.
> *Dactylosphaera* (?) *vitifoliae* (Fitch) Shimer, 1867.
> *Viteus vitifoliae* (Fitch) Shimer, 1867.
> *Rhyzaphis vastatrix* Planchon, 1868.
> *Phylloxera vastatrix* (Planchon) Signoret, 1868.
> *Peritymbia vitisana* Westwood, 1869.
> *Xerampelus vastator* (Planchon) Del Guercio, 1900.
> *Viteus vastator* (Planchon) Grassi et al, 1912.

BIOLOGY OF THE GRAPE PHYLLOXERA IN CALIFORNIA.

THE LIFE CYCLE.

The complete life cycle of the grape Phylloxera under natural conditions, i. e., on the wild vines of eastern North America, is extremely complicated (fig. 4). It is not the intention of the authors to enter into all the ramifications of this cycle in the present paper, but it may be said that the following are the main forms that occur: (1) The stem mother or fundatrix, which hatches in spring from the winter egg, ascends to an early leaf, settles on the upper surface, and causes to form around her a pocketlike gall opening on the

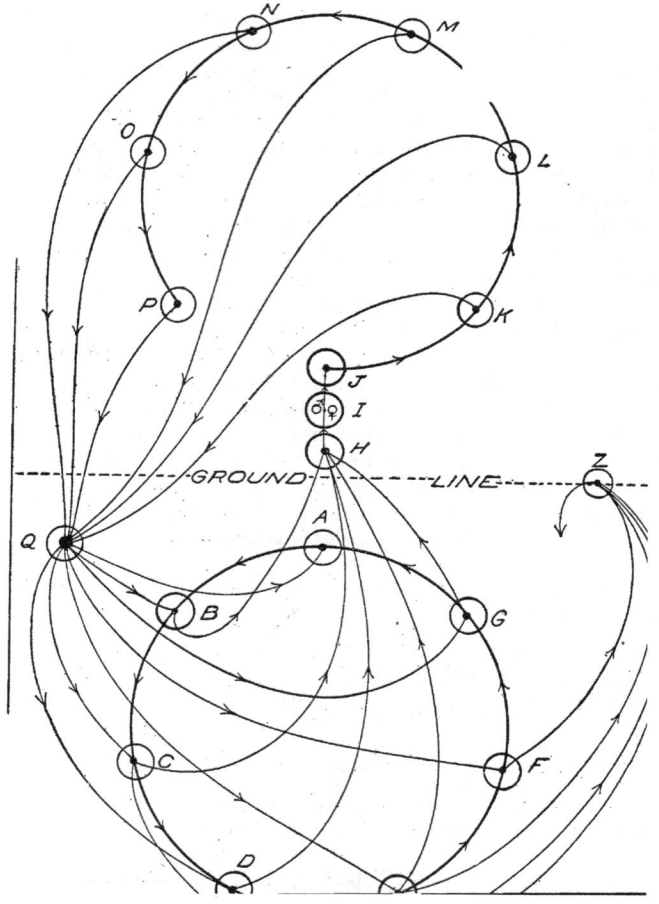

upper side of the leaf; (2) several parthenogenetic generations to which the stem mother gives rise, some of which settle on the foliage and produce new galls, as gallicoles, while others repair to the roots and settle on them as radicicoles; (3) parthenogenetic generations on the roots descended from the phylloxeræ which went from the foliage to the roots; (4) winged migratory forms, comprising a very variable percentage of the root and gall forms, produced in summer and autumn, which fly or are transported by wind to other vines and oviposit either under the bark or on the leaves; (5) the true sexes, which are wingless and beakless; (6) the winter egg, deposited under the bark by the sexed female after coition; (7) radicicoles, born on roots in the late autumn, which pass the winter thereon as small hibernants, mature the spring following, and give rise to radicicole generations which succeed one another during the summer and autumn. This, briefly, is the life cycle that occurs in parts of Europe where American vines are used for stock, and in the eastern and southern United States on the wild grapes and on varieties derived from them.

It will be observed that the winter may be passed in two forms—the winter egg and the hibernant, the former on the aerial and the latter on the subterranean or root portion of the vine. On certain wild grapes, as *Vitis riparia*, *V. rupestris*, and *V. berlandieri*, and on hybrids from these species, the former is the normal form, and hibernating larvæ are rare. On species like *Vitis labrusca*, *V. monticola*, and their derivatives, both forms may occur. On viniferæ (*Vitis vinifera*) the latter form is by far the more common. In the majority of European grape districts both forms occur, the former on American resistant vines and the latter on viniferæ, but in other localities, even where resistant vines are used, the winter egg is very scarce. These include certain regions of France and California, and it appears that in California the hibernant is normally the only form that passes the winter.

The suppression of the winter egg, and, therefore, of the succeeding gall form, brings about a modified life cycle in the California vineyard which may be briefly described as follows: (1) The hibernant radicicole passes the winter as a larva on the roots and occasionally on the trunk beneath the bark. (2) The hibernant, when mature, gives rise to generations of radicicoles, and the aphids that issue from eggs in late autumn become hibernants. (3) A certain percentage of radicicoles, varying from causes such as humidity, temperature, condition of food, and variety of vine, develop into winged migrants and issue from the ground. (4) Radicicole larvæ forsake the roots and seek to reach other vines either by way of the soil surface or through subterranean passages such as cracks.

The part of the life cycle from the sexes to the gallicoles through
the winter egg and fundatrix is either omitted or does not proceed
beyond the winter egg in California, notwithstanding the frequent

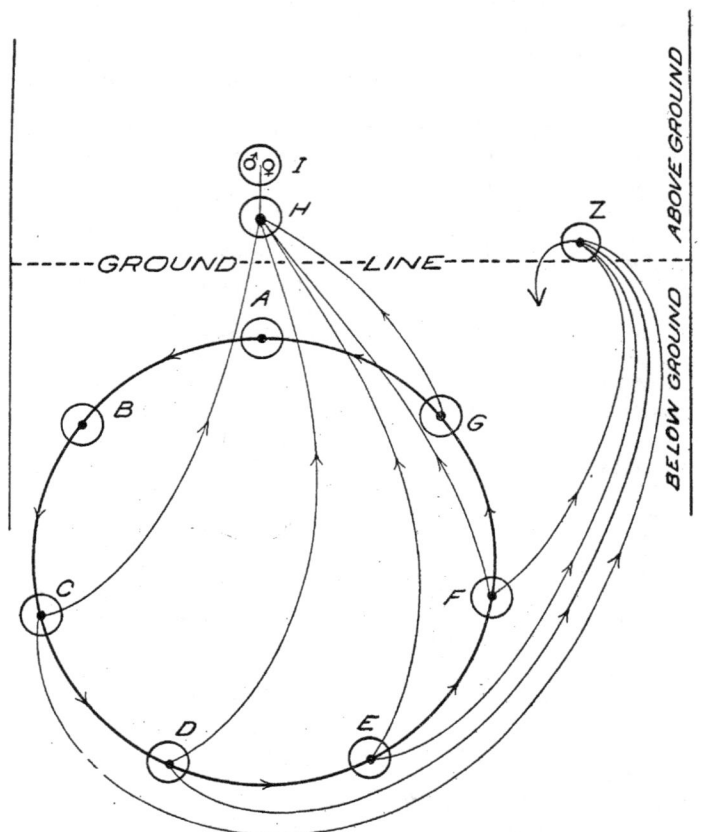

FIG. 5.—*Phylloxera vitifoliae:* Genealogical graph of the grape phylloxera in California.
A, hibernant radicicole; *B–G,* successive radicicole generations; *H,* winged sexuparous
migrant; *I,* sexes; *Z,* emergence above ground of the wandering radicicole larvæ.

abundance of resistant types of vines, types many of which normally
bear galls in other localities. The result is that the California cycle
(fig. 5) is purely parthenogenetic and is therefore greatly modified
from the original cycle (fig. 4) occurring on wild vines, the natural
hosts of the insect.

A résumé of the life history will be presented before all the dif-
·ferent stages and habits of the phylloxera in California are discussed
in detail. This résumé is confined to the biology of the insect on
viniferæ and does not consider the life history on resistant roots.

Over 99 per cent of the phylloxeræ pass the winter as small brownish unmolted larvæ, the remainder hibernating after having passed
one or two molts. All parts of the root system are used for hibernating quarters, but the majority cluster on the larger roots, following
an upward migration in the fall.

Coincident with the first sap flow in early spring is the growth of
the hibernants, but in a given vineyard the earliest individuals commence to grow fully six weeks before the most tardy ones, so that
after the foliage has opened, hibernating larvæ are still to be found
on the roots. The development of the hibernants is considerably
slower than that of the summer broods, and the former mature on
the average about five and one-half weeks after they commence their
spring growth. The development of the larvæ is at all times influenced by the quality of food and by conditions of humidity and
temperature.

Upon casting its fourth skin, the hibernant is mature and commences egg deposition. Its progeny are the first-generation phylloxeræ, and these on hatching from the eggs either settle beside the
eggshell or go in search of new food. Many aphids settle on young
growing rootlets and produce the fleshy swellings, termed "nodosities." Others settle upon older roots and produce swellings, termed
"tuberosities." Still others develop on roots without causing the
development of either perceptible swellings or lesions. Individuals
feeding upon nodosities develop more rapidly than do those on the
unswollen surface of the root. The nodosities usually decay within
a few weeks after their formation, and in most cases the destruction
of the rootlets follows. The tuberosities also usually decay in time.
The rotting of the nodosities is not very serious, as the vine can
supply new apical growth, but the decay of the tuberosities leads to
the decay of the larger roots either wholly or in part, and as a result
the vitality of the vine is greatly impaired, or the vine is killed
outright.

The first-generation individuals are mature in from four to seven
weeks after the eggs have been deposited, and they in their turn
deposit eggs, which produce further generations throughout the
summer and autumn.

Owing to the fact that, under favorable conditions, the adults
deposit eggs during an average period of 45 days, an overlapping of
generations ensues during the summer and fall. In order to avoid

confusion, it is assumed that there are five generations annually, since this number is about the average in a vineyard in which the sap moves early, although there might be, under certain conditions, from one to eight or even nine generations within a single year. The hibernant generation having matured in April, the succeeding generation matures about the time the canes have ended their first rapid growth, approximately the end of May. Succeeding generations mature on about the following average dates: Second, July 6; third, August 15; fourth, September 30; the fifth generation hibernating.

A variable percentage of the larvæ of generations 2, 3, and 4 becomes nymphs, and these later emerge from the ground as winged insects and either fly away or are borne off on the wind. Large numbers of these are caught in spider webs. Many of the newly hatched larvæ develop a wandering tendency just after they have issued from the eggshell and seek to emigrate to other vines either through the soil or over the surface of the ground. Large numbers of these migrating larvæ are also caught in spider webs on the surface, and while only a small percentage reach their destination, a single individual may start a new infestation. Those of the larvæ that succeed in fastening upon a root or rootlet develop as radicicoles. The winged forms normally occur from June to October, and the wandering larvæ are found from July to September.

During July and August, when the adult radicicoles are most prolific, incubation and development proceed most rapidly, and the phylloxera may be said then to have reached its most active stage. It is at this stage that the greatest damage is done to the roots of the vines, although the effects are not generally apparent until the fall and winter following, when the lesions formed during the summer have decayed.

At the end of September a few of the newly hatched larvæ hibernate, and throughout October successive generations become hibernants, so that by the end of the month a large majority of the phylloxera have reached this stage. During November and the first half of December, a few mature radicicoles and growing larvæ may be found, but after the middle of December, it is unusual to find any form but the hibernating larva.

Under conditions of abundant food supply, the period of egg deposition of the radicicoles averages 45 days and may reach a maximum of 110 days. This average is nearly constant throughout the season. The average number of eggs deposited is about 117, but under certain conditions the number may be increased to 486. The daily average number is about $2\frac{1}{2}+$ eggs, and as many as 23 eggs have been deposited in 24 hours by a single phylloxera.

The rate of egg deposition is usually indicated by a sharp rise shortly after commencement, followed by a gradual decline. During the period of egg laying the adult feeds, and after the last egg is laid may live for as long as three weeks.

Incubation naturally is influenced by temperature, and the duration of the incubation period may vary from five days in July to over a month in December. Very few eggs are laid in December, but in March and April, when many eggs are deposited, the maximum period of incubation is 27 days.

The larvæ mature in midsummer in about 15 days, and in April and November in about 34 days, and the hibernant generation develops in about 180 days. The winged forms mature more slowly than do the wingless individuals, since the fourth or nymphal instar is noticeably extended beyond that of the corresponding wingless stage.

In the late fall a few individuals intermediate in structure between the nymphs and radicicoles are found. These are called "nymphicals" or intermediates and, so far as is known, they deposit the same type of eggs as the radicicoles, although they are not prolific. From egg deposition to the molting of the final skin, the period covered by the sexes, which develop from eggs of two sizes laid by the winged forms, was about 12 days in confinement.

All stages of the phylloxera molt four times, and the first instar is always the longest (the adult instar excepted).

HIBERNATION.

The phenomenon of hibernation.—Throughout autumn and early winter an ever-increasing percentage of newly hatched radicicole larvæ, instead of increasing in size and maturing normally, remain as very small brown phylloxeræ (Pl. IX, *d*, p. 64). As winter progresses, the mature individuals die, leaving only the small brown larvæ and a few unhatched eggs. As soon as these late eggs hatch, the larvæ settle down, becoming brown like the others. These small larvæ are the hibernants, and as such they remain throughout the dormant period. Occasionally phylloxeræ that have passed one or two molts hibernate. This type is quite unusual, and probably consists of individuals that have reached a certain stage of development and are unable, through lack of nourishment, to mature, most of them dying before spring.

Hibernant larvæ occur on all kinds of vines—on viniferæ and on American varieties and hybrids. While this form of phylloxera occurs more or less sparingly on American resistant vines (*Vitis riparia, V. rupestris, V. berlandieri,* etc.) and on some American nonresistant $\times$ resistant hybrids, it finds its greatest development on viniferæ and on certain American nonresistant varieties of *Vitis labrusca*, *V. aestivalis*, and *V. monticola*. On the wild species of Vitis of the eastern and southern parts of North America, considered as the original hosts of the grape phylloxera, is found a complicated life cycle embracing gallicoles (gall lice), radicicoles (root lice), winged migrants, sexed forms, winter eggs, and true stem mothers. The hibernants are rarely abundant on these wild species of vines, and the winter is passed chiefly in the winter-egg stage. On vinifera (*Vitis vinifera*) this complicated life cycle is rarely completed, and a simpler one, comprising only the root forms, obtains. Therefore, in the absence of the winter egg, the winter period must be tided over by another form, which is supplied in the hibernant larva. It appears that, to the phylloxera, *Vitis vinifera* is an acquired food plant, and that the nature and construction of the Old World grapevine has changed the habits and life history of the grape phylloxera feeding on it.

On viniferæ, although hibernation takes place chiefly on the larger roots and on the subterranean portion of the trunk, it occurs also on nodosities and on smaller roots.

Hibernants are located both on lesions and on the normal surface of the roots. On the varieties of resistant vines and certain hybrids (vinifera $\times$ resistant and resistant $\times$ American nonresistant) that have been examined, it has been found that hibernation occurs chiefly on nodosities and less frequently on the normal root surface. Tuberosities rarely are formed on these vines. On American nonresistant and vinifera $\times$ nonresistant hybrids, hibernation was chiefly of the type found on the viniferæ. On Golden Champion, Agawam, Catawba, Isabella, Lenoir, and Delaware, hibernants occurred on tuberosities, nodosities, and the normal root surface. On Moore's Early they were located on nodosities and on larger roots but not on tuberosities.

Appearance of hibernants.—The hibernants (Pl. IX, *d*, *e*, *f*, p. 64) appear as little oval brown insects flatly appressed to the surface of the root, their legs folded underneath the body. The antennæ are borne at right angles to the major body axis, and hardly project beyond the maximum width of the body. The whole insect generally shows one color, but sometimes there is a darker median longitudinal line, except on the head. In those individuals which have molted before going into hibernation, a similar shade of darker brown occurs. Occasionally lighter individuals will be noted, but none is ever as pale as the growing and feeding radicicole larvæ. Hibernants located under several layers of bark, as a rule, exhibit a paler color than those living more exposed.

To secure information regarding the fixation of the beak in the root five lots of hibernants were examined on January 23, 1914. The results are given below.

TABLE II.—*Fixation of beak of hibernants of the grape phylloxera.*

Lot No.	Number of individuals.	Number with beaks fixed.	Number with beaks free.	Remarks.
1...............	25	12	13	Under 2 layers of bark on large root. .
2...............	25	24	1	Large root; insects originally under 2 layers of bark, but layers peeled off some time before experiment.
3...............	25	16	9	Small root; insects on tuberosities.
4...............	25	22	3	Do.
5...............	20	8	12	Under several layers of bark on stock of vine 3 inches below soil surface.
Total........	120	82	38	

In lots 1, 2, and 5 the individuals that had their beaks fixed in the roots were obviously the more healthy. In lots 3 and 4 all the phylloxeræ appeared equally healthy. They were on more succulent roots than those in lots 1, 2, and 5, and it may be that on such succulent food the hibernants have a habit of driving in and drawing out their beaks at will, whereas on harder roots this would not be possible. It is evident that hibernants situated on the outside bark of a root are likely to be washed off by water if their beaks are not inserted into the root. The experiment would serve to indicate that in the individuals of lots 1 and 5, wherein the hibernants were protected under layers of bark, the majority had their beaks free, while in lots 2, 3, and 4, wherein the hibernants were exposed, the majority had their beaks inserted, so that it appears that the fixation of the beak acts as an anchorage.

NOURISHMENT.

The hibernant larva partakes of nourishment very slightly, if at all, before it settles for the winter. During the period of true hibernation it apparently takes no nourishment. Therefore it is probable that the great majority of the hibernants take their first food when they arouse themselves from their lethargy in spring. Of those observed to feed before hibernating, a few pass one or rarely two molts, while the rest remain unmolted but larger in size than the true hibernating larva. The writers have observed instances in which severed pieces of roots infested by hibernants formed winter lesions, the presence of the beaks in the root affording a stimulus.

Hibernants on nodosities sometimes keep these fresh until spring by the stimulating action of their implanted beaks. Such nodosities, especially in vinifera and labrusca vines, otherwise usually fail to pass the winter in a fresh condition, as they are susceptible to rot through moisture.

DURATION OF INSTAR.

With the exception of the winter egg, the hibernant instar is the longest found in the life cycle of the phylloxera. A series of experiments undertaken in the laboratory during the winter 1911–12 showed that the average for 12 individuals was 183 days, or approximately half a year. A later series of experiments, which took place both on living vines and in the cellar on severed roots, indicated that this period may be shortened to four and one-half months and lengthened to seven and one-half months, dependent, as usual, on food, temperature, and moisture conditions, and that six months is about the average period for the development of the hibernants. This period was considered from the date in the fall on which the insect hatched from the egg to that on which the insect became mature the spring following. The actual state of dormancy is from three to six weeks shorter, and thus approximates five months. Granted that radicicoles may live for three months after reaching maturity, it is apparent that hibernating phylloxeræ might attain a total longevity of over 10 months.

MOVEMENT ON THE ROOTS.

On a sound root, the overwintered phylloxeræ rarely change their positions while they develop. If situated on tuberosities or nodosities, they cause these lesions to become enlarged, and if situated on the normal root surface they cause the formation of new lesions. Occasionally they develop without causing a lesion to appear. On decayed and decaying roots, they move away after the first or later molts and seek better food. This movement is both upward and downward, indiscriminately, and is never extensive. The individuals show only feeble inclination toward migration. This generation appears to be the lowest in vitality and the quickest to succumb to adverse conditions.

GROWTH AND MATURING OF THE HIBERNANTS.

During the true hibernation period the phylloxeræ apparently take no food, and if any be taken no increase in growth can be noted. Later a slow but appreciable growth may be observed, which indicates the termination of the true hibernation period. A growing period, varying from one to six weeks, ensues, and after this the first molt occurs. In the course of from two to six weeks after the first molt three additional molts take place, and at the conclusion of the fourth molt the phylloxera is mature. This spring growth and development, as observed in the vineyard and in cages, is extended over a period of about three and a half months, and usually occurs during the period from February 15 to April 15. The commencement of growth in phylloxera is noted to be coincident with the first movement of sap in the vine, and naturally both are influenced by prevailing meteorological conditions. Upon reaching the adult stage the hibernant immediately begins the deposition of its eggs, and in this manner the series of parthenogenetic generations destined to continue through the season is commenced.

Measurements.—During the winter of 1913–14 hibernated larvæ were measured at certain intervals to determine at what time the spring growth started. On October 27, 1913, seven individuals which had recently hibernated averaged 0.333 mm. in length and 0.202 mm. in maximum width; on January 6, 1914, four individuals which had hibernated in October, 1913, averaged 0.337 mm. in length and 0.198 mm. in maximum width; on February 23, 1914, four individuals averaged 0.410 mm. in length and 0.217 mm. in maximum width; and on March 10, 1914, five individuals averaged 0.421 mm. and 0.241 mm., respectively. Between October and January there was no difference in size, but between January 6 and February 23 there was a marked difference, both individually and collectively, showing that between these dates the hibernants had begun to feed. The measurements of the individuals taken on March 10 showed that considerable growth occurred between February 23 and that date. None of the insects measured had molted, and observations showed that perceptible growth did not begin before February 10. The average length of the beak of the newly hatched radicicole destined to hibernate is slightly over 0.2 mm., but after it has been inserted in the root it becomes somewhat telescoped and measures about 0.17 mm.

The majority of the hibernants before they start to grow are smaller than the newly hatched radicicoles, and therefore they actually shrink in size after they hatch from the egg and settle to hibernate. Those that feed before hibernating do not shrink to such a small size.

Hibernation in vineyards.—In the vineyards it has been observed that the phylloxeræ enter into hibernation as early as September 15 and as late as December 15. Prior to October 1 only a small percentage of hibernants have been found, and after November 20

only a small percentage have been observed that were not hibernar
The greater number of the aphids enter hibernation during Octol
and the first half of November; that is, a majority of the lar
hatching from eggs in this period settle down to hibernate. A f
of those hatching before October become hibernants. After Dece
ber 1 it is very unusual to find eggs. The phylloxeræ do not en
into hibernation all at one time, and even on a single given gra]
vine the entering into hibernation is protracted over several we
and often as long as two months. The causes that induce the you
larvæ to hibernate instead of proceeding with their normal grov
are three: (1) Condition of sap flow, (2) condition of food, (
temperature and humidity. Hibernation in general takes place
the time when aerial and radical growth of the vine slacken in 1
fall. If the soil temperature is high, there is a tendency to po
pone hibernating until some time after the terminal growths h:
apparently ceased. On decayed and decaying roots the phylloxe
hibernate earlier and on nodosities and sound tuberosities later th
on the surface of a normal root. Regarding the influence of te
perature, Mayet (15), in discussing the hibernant form, states tl
eggs die when the temperature falls below 10° C. He states furth

This temperature of 10° C. appears to be the minimum under which the
sects become numb, and above which they go out of their torpor * * *
Maurice Girard proved, experimentally, by means of a freezing mixture, t
the phylloxera would sustain a temperature of —8° and —10° C. without dy

attacked for years previous, it is unusual to find hibernants, except at the base of large roots or on the trunk, because the roots that were attacked the previous summer tend to rot badly when moistened by winter rains, and consequently most of the hibernants remaining thereon die, and only those higher up on sounder pieces of roots survive in abundance. The basal part of a large root is not generally badly attacked during summer, and so there are not enough tuberosities to rot it during the succeeding winter.

A very noticeable tendency is for the hibernants to congregate in masses. Such masses occur on the normal surface of the root, on tuberosities, on nodosities, and under one or more layers of bark. Perhaps in general on a grossly infested vine more masses occur on the outside bark, but this is only because the preferred sheltered places are too few and are inadequate to cover all the phylloxeræ. On younger vines a favorable location for hibernating is at the foot of the stump. On older vines this position is not so generally chosen. On vines which are only lightly infested the phylloxeræ often congregate at certain spots, while other spots, apparently as favorable, are neglected. On the heavily infested vines all the favorable spots for hibernation are utilized, the majority of the insects being forced to locate on the unsheltered outside bark of the root.

In vineyards the growth and maturing of the hibernants in spring extends over a period about as long as that covered by the entering into hibernation in the fall. The growth first becomes apparent about February 25, and proceeds until the time arrives when the most tardy individuals mature. Immature hibernants are found as late as May, but by April 15 the great majority have become mature. Just as in the case of "entering hibernation," so in the "spring development," a wide range occurs even on single given vines. The earliest individual may commence growth two months or more before the most tardy. On an average, it takes about five weeks for the hibernants to mature after they have first shown perceptible growth. On sound lesions this is shortened to as much as three weeks, and on decaying portions of roots lengthened to as much as eight weeks. Many of those on decayed roots die from ill nourishment before maturing, but the majority of such move away to seek better food.

The forces which influence the growth of the phylloxeræ in spring are a reversal of those which impel hibernation in the fall. As stated, the phylloxeræ start to grow about the time when the sap begins to flow. On dying vines in which the sap flow is either not apparent or very weak, the phylloxeræ on the more healthy roots show perceptible growth in like manner to those living on healthy vines, in which case their activity is supposedly due solely or chiefly to meteorological effect. The spring growth on unhealthy roots is curtailed and commences late. On nodosities and tuberosities which have remained fresh during winter, the succulent condition of the food induces early growth on the part of the phylloxeræ.

Hibernation under cellar conditions.—During the period 1911–1915 hibernation was observed on severed roots in the laboratory cellar. These roots were kept in glass battery jars and in petri dishes and remained in a fresh condition when systematically moistened. Good callus growth and sometimes fleshy offshoots were obtained, especially when a layer of moist sand was placed in the bottom of the dishes. The phylloxeræ caused the formation of lesions in similar manner as on roots of living vines.

Under cellar conditions hibernation was often prolonged beyond the period found to occur in the vineyards, and this prolongation resulted in a small number of phylloxeræ maturing very late. The "awakening" period in spring was not different from that found in the vineyards under equalized temperatures. Under cellar conditions a greater mortality existed among hibernants than in the vineyards. This was supposedly due to the greater range of daily temperatures, to the abnormal condition of the roots severed from the vine, and to the apparent lack of sap flow. In the cellar hibernants a greater variation in size and color existed, even in unmolted phylloxeræ, than in the vineyard on living vines. A very small percentage of hibernants were observed to pass the winter in the second and third instars. Eggs were never observed to pass the winter, since all eggs laid late in the year hatched in due course according to temperatures. No mature or fourth-instar phylloxeræ were observed to hibernate. Adult radicicoles in late autumn, as at other times, lived for some days or even weeks after they deposited their last egg, but none was found that survived until spring.

Observations on the hibernation of phylloxeræ reared on severed roots under cellar conditions may be summed up as follows: The first phylloxeræ entered hibernation as early as August, in extreme cases in July, and the percentage of hibernating individuals from that time gradually increased. By October 1, it was found that on the average about 30 per cent of the individuals were hibernants. By the last of October from 85 to 90 per cent were hibernants. All the living phylloxeræ, however, were not hibernants until the end of December, and during November and December a dwindling number of adults and unhatched eggs were observed. All larvæ hatching after November 1 settled down to hibernate, and about three-fourths of those which hatched in October did likewise, the individuals comprising the other fourth maturing toward the end of October and in November and continuing to deposit eggs up to December.

The spring growth began in the earliest individuals about January 25; by the middle of March nearly all the phylloxeræ were growing and about half were mature. Some individuals remained dormant as late as the middle of April, and the most tardy did not mature until the middle of May or even later. On very poor roots many never matured at all. The period of appreciable growth prior to the shedding of the first skin averaged two weeks and the period from first molt to maturity about three weeks. On vigorous roots the hibernants mostly developed without changing their positions, but they forsook in large numbers roots decayed or decaying. These emigrations occur both before and after molting but chiefly just following a molt.

In comparing the hibernation on severed roots as observed under cellar conditions with that on living roots as observed in the vineyards, in pots, and in special box cages, several points are to be noted. (1) The phylloxeræ on the severed roots in the cellar entered hibernation in a more irregular manner than did those on the living vines. This condition appears due to the following causes: The severed roots were cut off from a normal flow of sap, the temperature fluctuations in the cellar were greater, and in the months of July, August, and September the temperature reached a lower daily minimum than in the vineyards; (2) the phylloxeræ hibernating in the cellar matured earlier in the spring than those on living vines out of doors by reason of the higher temperature obtaining in the cellar during January and February; (3) there was a greater mortality among the hibernants in the cellar, due to the fact that the severed roots often dried up or decayed before spring; (4) numbers of the phylloxeræ occasionally hibernated after they had shown appreciable growth or even cast a skin. This phenomenon rarely has been observed on living roots. In other respects the behavior of the phylloxeræ on severed roots did not differ from that on living roots. In exceptional cases vigorous pieces of severed roots were observed to send out fleshy rootlets in early spring, indicating a modified sap flow, and on such roots the phylloxeræ moved early and appeared to be influenced by this flow of sap. The comparatively high winter temperatures obtaining in the cellar undoubtedly produced this modified sap flow, since it occurred much earlier than the corresponding flow in the vineyards.

Hibernation on vinifera vines in cages, 1913–14.—The following observations were conducted upon the roots of living vines of different varieties growing in special cages (Pls. V–VII, p. 52). The vines were young and satisfactory specimens for the experiments. The exposed portions of the roots between the upper and lower pots were about 4 inches long, one-fourth inch in diameter, and from 10 to 14 inches below the soil surface of the upper pot. Although both ends of the exposed portions of roots were surrounded by an inch of fine sand, and all inoculations were made on these exposed portions, it frequently happened that phylloxeræ found their way to the unex·posed portions, so that in the winter following the inoculations hibernants were found in both the exposed and unexposed portions.

The temperatures in the cages differed but slightly from those recorded simultaneously 2 feet below the soil surface in the laboratory vineyard. In 1913–14 in midwinter, however, the former touched a mark about 10° F. lower, besides being uniformly lower throughout December and January in both the seasons 1913–14 and 1914–15. During the period (August to November) in which the phylloxeræ entered hibernation there was no appreciable difference, and before the commencement of the spring growth of the hibernants the temperatures were again equalized. Thus, in the periods of entering into and awakening from hibernation, vineyard conditions were reproduced in the cages as far as temperature was concerned. Contemporaneous vineyard observations show that the behavior of the hibernants on living vines in the cages simulated closely the behavior of those in the vineyards in the locality, and the habit of clustering was often noted. The aphids entered into hibernation and showed spring activity much as they did in the vineyards, but in each phenomenon there was an exception. In 1914, six aphids out of a lot of nine individuals hatching between August 24 and 26 proceeded to hibernate. Such early hibernation with succulent food present is quite unusual in the field. Again, in 1914, on another vine, part of a series of hibernants cast their skins as early as February 23, indicating that growth commenced not later than February 15. In the vineyard, even upon warm soils, the first date of activity was never earlier than February 25. This early spring activity in the cages was possibly due to comparatively high temperatures in February, this being the only month during which the cage temperatures exceeded those in the soil.

Hibernation on American resistant and nonresistant vines in cages, 1914–15.—Along with the vinifera vines planted in the special cages for observing the phylloxeræ on living roots, a number of American resistant and nonresistant vines were used for similar observation. The nonresistant varieties (propagated from *Vitis labrusca* and *V. aestivalis*) were Catawba, Isabella, Lenoir, Delaware, and Champion. The Muscadine (*V. rotundifolia*) was used also. The resistant hybrids, some of which were grafted to viniferæ, comprised Mourvedre × Rupestris 1202, Solonis × Riparia 1616, Berlandieri × Riparia 157.11, Riparia × Rupestris × Aestivalis × Monticola 554.5, Aramon Rupestris Ganzin 1, Riparia Gloire de Montpelier, Rupestris St. George. These vines were planted in the spring of 1914 and inoculated thereafter.

On the Muscadine the phylloxeræ upon hatching from the eggs refused to settle or feed. The nonresistant varieties were infested throughout summer and autumn, and on their roots the phylloxeræ entered into hibernation from September 20 to the beginning of November; in the case of the Champion, they hibernated as late as December 1. On the Catawba and Champion, the most heavily infested, the aphids began hibernation earlier; on the less infested Delaware, Isabella, and Lenoir, somewhat later.

Aphids became active about the middle of February, and all hibernants were adult by April 13. This spring activity was somewhat in advance of that occurring in vineyards, but was similar to that which occurred on the caged vinifera vines. On all nonresistant varieties it was observed that the hibernants massed on tuberosities, nodosities, and the normal surface of the roots; and in cracks in a manner similar to that observed to occur on vinifera vines.

On the resistant hybrids repeated inoculations during summer and autumn failed to produce more than an extremely light infestation. The phylloxeræ settled to hibernate during October, and at the end of that month all were hibernants. They were situated on side rootlets and on the normal surface of the root, but on the Rupestris St. George hibernants occurred also on nodosities which they had caused to form shortly after they settled.

Hibernation on American vines in pots, 1912–1915.—A large series of 2-year-old vines (from cuttings) planted in 6-inch pots, originally used in resistance experiments and comprising resistant vines, were examined during the years 1912 and 1913 for hibernant observations. It was found that hibernation took place during the last half of October and first half of November and that the spring awakening proceeded from about March 10 to April 15. These vines were planted in light sandy soil. The hibernants settled chiefly on nodosities and to a smaller extent on the surface of the larger rootlets. In the spring there was a great variation in the growth of the vines. In the majority of instances the phylloxeræ on the early leafing vines molted sooner than those on the more backward plants. No temperature records were kept with this series, but it is probable that the records taken 2 feet below the soil surface (Table XII) approximated that which occurred in the pots in the winter of 1913–14.

A further series (1914) of rooted vines in 9-inch pots, comprising Agawam, Isabella, Lenoir, Delaware, Catawba, and Champion, showed that with the exception of the Delaware, which was lightly infested, hibernation proceeded from about October 1 to November 1, nearly all the insects being hibernants on the latter date. On the Delaware none of the phylloxeræ were hibernants on October 30, and the roots were on that date still running strongly in sap, while the sap flow in the other varieties was weaker. The temperature in these pots was about the same as that occurring 2 feet below the soil surface. In the spring of 1915, on the Champion, Lenoir, Catawba, and Isabella, the phylloxeræ began to grow about March 1. On the first three the bulk of the hibernants were mature April 6, but on the Isabella, which was moribund, more than half were unmolted. This vine was not retained further, but, considering the condition of its roots, it is not probable that any of the phylloxeræ would have matured. The vine was too weak to send out new rootlets, and the roots showed much decay. The abundance of phylloxeræ the summer previous had doubtless caused this weakness.

THE RADICICOLE.

EGG DEPOSITION.

The adult radicicole commences to deposit eggs within 48 hours after the final molt. Occasionally there occur abnormal individuals which delay deposition of eggs as much as two weeks, and again there are others which fail to deposit eggs but continue alive for some weeks.

Egg deposition on severed roots.—Table III gives the summarized record of the egg deposition of radicicoles under cellar conditions during the years 1911–12.

TABLE III.—*Summarized record of egg deposition of radicicoles of the grape phylloxera under cellar conditions during 1911–12, Walnut Creek, Calif.*

Gener-ation.	Num-ber of adults.	Egg-laying period for gener-ation.	Number of eggs per adult.			Days in period of deposition.			Aver-age num-ber of eggs per adult per day.
			Maxi-mum.	Mini-mum.	Aver-age.	Maxi-mum.	Mini-mum.	Aver-age.	
[1] 0	52	Apr. 21 to Oct. 1..............	347	4	84.6	110	2	55.3	1.53
1	45	May 27 to Sept. 23...........	486	10	192.0	96	5	46.3	4.1
2	57	June 29 to Nov. 6............	287	2	102.0	106	1	48.5	2.1
3	17	Aug. 4 to Dec. 7.............	266	3	141.8	96	2	44	3.2
4	[2] 11	Sept. 5 to May 15, 1912.......	119	31	67.2	83	23	41.7	1.6
[3] 5–10	27	Apr. 26 to Oct. 6.............	137	4	35.5	47	3	21.5	1.7

[1] Overwintered generation.   [2] Including 3 individuals which matured in 1912.   [3] Throughout 1912.

Neglecting the series of generations 5 to 10, the individuals of which suffered through abnormal food and other conditions, it is shown in Table III that the aphids of the second generation were the most prolific. One aphid deposited 486 eggs in 79 days, an average of 6.3 per diem. The greatest number of eggs laid within 24 hours by a single adult was 23 and the longest laying period covered 110 days. A true seasonal average of the number of eggs deposited by each aphid was 117 for 1911 and a similar average of the number of eggs per diem per aphid about 2½.

In 1913, between June 26 and November 14, a series of observations on fecundity under adverse food conditions was made. Among a large number of aphids, on two occasions only were as many as six eggs deposited in one day by a single individual. In the cellar, 431 eggs were deposited in a total of 331 days (1.3 eggs per diem per aphid), and in an electric incubator, wherein a slightly higher temperature was maintained, 787 eggs were laid in a total of 463 days (1.7 eggs per diem per aphid). These averages were considerably less than corresponding ones found to result in the 1911 series, yet the insects raised in the incubator were subjected to higher temperatures than were those in 1911, raised in the cellar.

Egg deposition on living vines.—During the years 1913, 1914, and 1915, series of generations were raised on living vines in cages. These vines were all viniferæ, and comprised the following varieties: Muscat, Zinfandel, Mission, Burger, Thompson's Seedless, and Grenache. The principal object in this work was to check up on the previous 2-year study of root cuttings under cellar conditions. The initial inoculations in 1913 were made with eggs laid by adults of the overwintered generation on Zinfandel vines in the vineyard, and thus no record of the egg production of the overwintered adults was secured in the cages. Of the first generation, records of 10 individuals were taken, but a complete record of only one was made, and this adult, between June 25 and July 14 (20 days), deposited 121 eggs, the largest number in a single day being 12. The 10 adults deposited 482 eggs in 95 days, or an average of 3.1 eggs per diem per adult.

Most of the individuals died early, and it is assumed that if they had been allowed to lay their full complement of eggs, the period of decline would have reduced this average. These adults were produced, 7 on Burger roots and 3 on Mission roots. It appeared that those on the Mission were the more prolific. On both varieties some were situated on lesions they had caused to form. These averaged better in egg production than the others situated on the normal root surface. Records for 14 adults of the second generation were taken. On a very healthy Mission root, living on lesions, 4 adults averaged 4.5 eggs per adult per diem. On two less healthy Mission roots of the same cage vine, 6 averaged 2.4 eggs per adult per diem. On a very healthy Burger root 4 averaged 3.9. The longest egg-laying period for any adult of this generation was 26 days and the maximum eggs per day 15. In all, 489 eggs were laid in 136 days, 3.6 eggs per adult per diem.

The egg-laying period of this generation ran from July 8 to August 15, with an average temperature of 68° F. Four adults of the third generation deposited 284 eggs in 88 days, at an average of 3.2 eggs per diem per adult; the longest egg-laying period was 23 days and the maximum number of eggs per diem was 8. These adults lived on a healthy Muscat root on tuberosities, their egg-laying period being from August 28 to September 26, under an average temperature of 64° F. One of them did not commence depositing eggs until the sixth day after it matured, having moved about considerably meanwhile. The fourth-generation phylloxeræ wintered on the same root upon which their immediate progenitors had oviposited and matured in the spring of 1914. Of these, 3 adults laid 79 eggs in 42 days (aggregated) or 1.9 eggs per diem per adult. The maximum number for one day for a single adult was 4 and the longest egg-laying period 24 days. In this period one adult laid 56 eggs. The egg-laying period, toward the end of which the root became lightly decayed, ran from April 6 to May 8, under a temperature averaging 58° F.

In the ensuing generations throughout 1914 and 1915, the egg-laying records were mostly incomplete. Records of the fifth generation on Muscat in the period May 28 to June 11 show an average number of eggs per diem per adult to be 2.8, the largest number deposited in a single day by a single adult being 5. The average temperature was 65° F. Records of the seventh generation on a slightly decayed Grenache root, July 29 to August 8, show an average number of eggs per diem per adult to be 5.4, and the maximum number of eggs laid in a single day to be 7. The temperature averaged 71° F. The records of these two lots are much too meager for comparisons.

In comparing the egg production on the living vines with that on root cuttings, it should be stated that during the summer and fall months the aphids on the former enjoyed higher temperatures. This advantage was somewhat counterbalanced by the greater daily fluctuations in temperature which took place on caged living vines and which frequently resulted in a daily minimum lower than that simultaneously occurring in the laboratory cellar in which the root cuttings were kept.

As a general rule the egg-depositing capacity of the adult increases rapidly after maturity, and after the zenith is reached decreases slowly, so that half the complement of eggs is deposited before one-third of the egg-laying period is completed.

The condition of the food is the chief factor in the production of eggs, but there is also a meteorological control. Frequent fluctuations in temperature and humidity adversely affect deposition.

Extrusion of the egg.—During the process of egg extrusion, which occupies from 20 to 40 minutes, the abdomen of the adult radicicole is considerably distended. It is apparent, therefore, that when an adult deposits 23 eggs within one day, extrusion will be taking place intermittently for a very considerable part of the day. During the period of egg deposition, the aphids often change their orientation by pivoting about the beak.

Time of day of oviposition.—Between April 28 and May 25, 1913, records were taken in the cellar to obtain data upon the time of day of oviposition. The maximum daily temperature occurred about 6 p. m.,[9] and the minimum about 7.30 a. m. Between 9 a. m. and 5 p. m. (8 hours), 41 eggs were deposited, and between 5 p. m. and 9 a. m. (16 hours), 52 eggs were deposited in the 27 days. Between 9 a. m. and 5 p. m., there was an average hourly temperature in excess of that occurring between 5 p. m. and 9 a. m. of about 0.02° F. It is apparent that the higher temperature of the shorter period caused a comparatively greater number of eggs to be deposited, since the 52 eggs were laid in exactly double the time in which the 41 were deposited.

Egg fertility and mortality.—A large series of experiments took place in 1911 to determine the fertility and mortality percentages of the eggs of the radicicole phylloxera. These were carried on about evenly throughout the year. One series was conducted under cellar conditions in petri dishes, and the other took place in the laboratory under a higher temperature and was exposed to subdued daylight. Table IV gives the results of these experiments:

TABLE IV.—*Fertility and mortality of the radicicole egg of the grape phylloxera, Walnut Creek, Calif., 1911.*

Generation and environment.	Total number of eggs deposited.	Number of eggs hatched.	Number of eggs that failed to hatch.	Percentage hatched.
Unknown (various)	965	772	193	80.00
1 (Cellar)	1,000	911	89	91.10
1 (Exposed to light)	490	422	68	86.12
1 (Total)	1,490	1,333	157	89.52
2 (Cellar)	1,840	1,716	124	93.26
2 (Exposed to light)	245	236	9	96.33
2 (Total)	2,085	1,952	133	93.62
3 (Cellar)	1,112	987	125	88.76
4 (Exposed to light)	524	486	38	92.75
Grand total	6,176	5,530	646	89.54

There was no appreciable difference between the fertility of those reared in the cellar and of those reared in the higher temperatures of the laboratory rooms. The results indicate that on the average almost 9 eggs out of every 10 laid will hatch. It is probable that vineyard conditions produced similar averages as no predators or other causes that might bring about a different average have been observed with the exception of the case of excessive spring moisture acting upon the eggs laid by the overwintered adults and in the case

[9] All references to clock time refer to " Standard time."

of eggs laid on rotting tuberosities. The eggs have a considerable resistance to water at ordinary temperatures and may also hatch under water. Many, probably 25 per cent, of those that are laid on rotting tuberosities fail to hatch. They seem to be so impregnated with dampness and influenced by the rotting root tissues surrounding them that they turn dark brown prematurely and finally collapse after the embryo dies. It must be considered also that very slight pressure applied to the eggshell may rupture it and kill the embryo.

INCUBATION PERIOD.

The first incubation record at Walnut Creek took place during April, 1909. Between April 9 and April 26, 24 eggs were observed in the laboratory with the results shown in Table V:

TABLE V.—*Incubation period of the eggs of the grape phylloxera, Walnut Creek, Calif., 1909.*

	Days.
Average incubation stage	13.8
Maximum incubation stage	15
Minimum incubation stage	12

No temperature records were taken. The eggs were presumably deposited by overwintered adults. During 1911 and 1912 a large series of incubation records was obtained. Table VI gives incubation records for each generation during 1911.

TABLE VI.—*Incubation records of the eggs of the grape phylloxera at Walnut Creek, Calif., 1911.*

Generation.	Environment.	Dates of period of incubation.	Average temperature.	Number of eggs laid.	Incubation period.		
					Maximum.	Minimum.	Average.
					Days.	*Days.*	*Days.*
[1] I	Cellar	Apr. 28–May 18	61	49	17	10	13.6
[2] I	....do	June 4–Aug. 19	64	889	15	8	10.8
[2] I	Laboratory shelf	June 13–Sept. 6	([3])	412	13	7	9.8
II	Cellar	June 13–Aug. 19	64.5	1,797	14	7	10.2
II	Laboratory shelf	June 5–Aug. 18	([3])	235	11	6	8.5
III	Cellar	July 7–Aug. 20	64.6	969	14	7	11.7
IV	Laboratory shelf	Aug. 9–Sept. 2	([3])	551	10	6	7.2
IV	Cellar	Aug. 18–Oct. 26	64	10	18	7	13.3

[1] Eggs deposited by overwintered adults.
[2] Later series of eggs deposited by overwintered adults.
[3] Temperature at least 5° higher than that in cellar at corresponding dates.

From Table VI it will be seen that the influence of temperature was very considerable. The records of 1912 are much more scanty and bear out the observations of 1911. Under an average temperature of 70° F. the egg stage in 1912 averaged 8.9 days, with a maximum and minimum of 10 and 7 days, respectively. The period covered was from June 19 to October 3, but the great majority of the total of 55 eggs were laid during June. A small series of 27 sixth-generation eggs, laid May 6 to 8, 1912, under an average temperature of 63° F., incubated in an average of 10.7 days.

The results shown in Table VII were obtained during 1911 and are in part a complement of those shown in Table VI:

TABLE VII.—*Incubation records of the eggs of the grape phylloxera, Walnut Creek, Calif., 1911.*

Group No.	Environment.	Average temperature.	Month of incubation.	Number of eggs.	Egg stage.		
					Average.	Maximum.	Minimum.
		° F.					
1	Exposed to light...................	57	April........	43	15.14	18	13
2	.....do..........................	60	May........	177	11.03	15	9
3	.....do..........................	65	June........	352	9.07	12	8
4	.....do..........................	52	November..	16	15.09	18	15
5	In darkness, laboratory drawer...	62	May–June...	323	10.66	14	9

The eggs of the first four groups in the preceding table were exposed to light on a shelf in the laboratory, and those of group 5 were incubated in a drawer in the laboratory. Both lots were subjected to a very abnormal fluctuation of temperature, this fluctuation in some cases reaching 20° F. daily.

In 1912, 1913, and 1915 some additional incubation records were obtained, and Table VIII indicates the relations between temperature, environment, and incubation to cover the four years, 1911, 1912, 1913, and 1915.

TABLE VIII.—*Relation between incubation, temperature, and environment in the egg deposition of the grape phylloxera, Walnut Creek, Calif., 1911–1913 and 1915.*

Lot No.	Year.	Number of eggs.	Average daily temperature.	Incubation.	Remarks on environment.
			° F.	Days.	
1	1911.............................	16	52	15.09	Exposed to light.
2	1915.............................	13	55	20.50	Cellar.
3	1913.............................	26	56.6	[1] 19.60	Do.
4	1911.............................	43	57	15.14	Exposed to light.
5	1915.............................	17	59	15.50	Cellar.
6	1911.............................	177	60	11.03	Exposed to light
7	1915.............................	16	60.5	15.40	Cellar.
8	1911.............................	49	61	13.60	Do.
9	1913.............................	38	61.3	15.50	Do.
10	1912.............................	26	63	10.70	Do.
11	1913.............................	48	63	15.50	Do.
12	1915.............................	28	63.8	11.00	Do.
13	1911.............................	889	64	10.80	Do.
14	1911.............................	10	64	13.30	Do.
15	1911.............................	1,797	64.5	10.20	Do.
16	1911.............................	969	64.6	11.70	Do.
17	1911.............................	286	65	10.29	Laboratory drawer—darkness.
18	1911.............................	352	65	9.07	Exposed to light.
19	1915.............................	13	65	9.40	Cellar.
20	1913.............................	20	67	9.65	Do.
21	1915.............................	22	67.3	8.80	Do.
22	1913.............................	22	68	9.00	Do.
23	1915.............................	62	68	[2] 7.00	Do.
24	1915.............................	21	68.5	7.60	Do.
25	1912.............................	55	70	8.90	Incubator.
26	1913.............................	61	70.3	8.40	Do.
27	1913.............................	38	72	8.70	Do.

[1] Maximum, 27 days.   [2] Minimum, 5 days.

Examination of Table VIII shows that the incubation period gradually becomes shorter as the temperature rises.

The exposure to light apparently produced abnormal rapidity in the development of the eggs. In lot 18 this influence was scarcely felt, while in lots 1, 4, and 6 it was very cogent, and it is evident that exposure to light is chiefly influential under low temperatures. The comparatively slow development of lots 25 to 27 apparently can be laid only to temperature fluctuations obtaining in the incubator. This fluctuation in the incubator sometimes consisted in the maintenance of a lower minimum for a longer period than that which obtained in the main part of the cellar. Such temperatures possibly would exert a retarding effect upon egg development that would not appear in the averaged readings of the thermometer.

Even among the lots kept in the cellar under similar conditions there were apparent exceptions to the rule that "the higher the temperature the shorter the period of incubation." One such instance is that of lots 15 and 16, in which two large series were used, yet under temperatures differing but 0.1° F. there was a difference in the average incubation periods of one and a half days.

Among the individuals enumerated in Table VIII the maximum egg stage was 27 and the minimum 5 days. The respective average temperatures influencing the two individuals were 55° F. and 68° F., and both were incubated in the cellar. It was possible only to estimate an annual average incubation stage, and this was about 11 days. It should be added that eggs have been observed in December to incubate in a period exceeding 30 days, but it is unusual to find eggs at this time of year.

Experiments conducted in the cellar demonstrated that eggs incubated as rapidly in arid as in humid surroundings, but submergence in water lengthened the incubation period, even under equal temperatures.

Incubation on living roots.—During the years 1913, 1914, and 1915 biologic records were made on the living roots of young vines of viniferæ and vinifera × American hybrids. A series of generations were conducted during these three years, and incubation was observed for each generation. In most cases immediately after deposition the eggs were removed to an unifested root, but in some they were allowed to incubate where they had been deposited. The cages containing the experimental vines were all placed together in one trench, and the temperature was alike in all of them. Table IX indicates the incubation periods with reference to temperatures and time of year. The years are not given, as in some instances single lots containing individuals incubating under the same average temperatures but belonging to more than one year have been combined.

TABLE IX.—*Incubation of the eggs of the grape phylloxera on living roots, Walnut Creek, Calif., 1913–1915.*

Lot number.	Number of eggs.	Average temperature.	Incubation.	Months or month.
		° F.	Days.	
1	19	56.8	[1] 19.0	March to April.
2	11	57	15.1	April.
3	11	58	14.8	April to May.
4	([2])	58.5	15.0	Do.
5	7	60	12.3	Do.
6	6	61.8	11.2	May to June.
7	([2])	62	9.0	Do.
8	28	63	9.0	Do.
9	([2])	64	9.7	June.
10	3	66	[3] 9.5	Do.
11	11	68	10.5	September to October.
12	23	69	[3] 8.2	June to October.
13	26	70.5	[3] 7.7	June to September.
14	21	71.5	9.4	Do.
15	11	72	8.4	August.
16	45	72.5	[3] 7.7	July to September.
17	23	73	[3] 7.0	Do.
18	8	73.2	[3] 6.4	July.

[1] Maximum, 20 days.   [2] About 20.   [3] Minimum, 6 days.

Many of the lots contained a very small number of individuals, but in the main the incubation stage became progressively shorter as the average temperature rose. Between the temperatures of 56.8° and 62° F. the incubation periods are rapidly reduced, while between 62° and 73.2° the reduction is much less rapid in proportion to the rise in temperature. This is a somewhat similar condition to that found in the cellar records.

It is evident that the stage was shortest during the months of July and August, and longest during the months of March and April. Records began as early in the year as March 31, and closed as late as October 5. Two of the individuals in lot 1 incubated in the maximum period of 20 days (Mar. 31 to Apr. 20) under an average temperature daily of 56.8° F. The minimum of six days was reached by 17 individuals in each of the months from June to September under average daily temperatures of from 66° to 73.2° F.

The condition of food had no apparent effect upon the duration of the egg stage. Eggs deposited by radicicoles which had developed from eggs deposited by gallicoles received from Virginia incubated in the same average period as those descended from radicicoles of many generations, and eggs deposited by nymphicals incubated precisely as did those laid by normal radicicoles. Individual incubation records, both of eggs reared in the laboratory cellar and of others reared on living vines, are given in connection with the development of the radicicoles under the same conditions in the section on "Development of the radicicole larva," pages 54, 55, 57, 60–62, and 63.

During 1911 and 1912 the radicicoles were reared within and without an electric incubator, in the (on which the phylloxeræ were reared were kept in petri dishes with moistened filter paper. This meth satisfactory, since it was not easy to maintain a similar to that existing under natural conditions.

In 1913, 1914, and 1915 the insects were reared ir the cages described below. The jars in the cellar v a layer of wet sand placed in the bottom. This metl cessful than in the case where moistened paper was did not decay or dry up so rapidly, and they rema ter condition through the winter.

These cages (Pls. V; VI, fig. 1; VII), construct vines, may be described as follows: A trench 3 f(wide enough to hold the cages with a space about 1 side. To prevent air passing down the cracks, sm laid across the spaces, and this resulted in a temp(cages of scarcely greater fluctuation than normall underground. The cages themselves were made (with an extra redwood bottom, and had two compar the other (Pl. VII). The upper compartment had and the lower two, detachable boards the whole le sides, and these boards were detachable to permi of the roots and the removal of the pots. The ur contained one and sometimes two pots (8 or 9 inc around the top of which was fitted the topmost boa outside measurements of which were 22 by 13 by lower compartment contained 9-inch pots in saucer

The method of planting the vines in the pots of follows: Into the middle board of the cages were f saucers having holes bored through them. A sh tubing larger inside than the diameter of the roc these holes with a cone of paraffin. Two half pots bound together by wire or tin bands to make a sin; placed to rest on the saucer. The vine was then pt of its roots being passed through the holes in the sa ing below. The upper pot was then filled with sc layer of fine sand. In the lower compartment, who or two, as the case might be, were put in place in the protruding roots planted in them, at the s(passing through about 3 inches of glass cylinder the soil in the lower pots was covered in most layer of fine sand. Fine sand was tamped into tl

THE GRAPE PHYLLOXERA IN CALIFORNIA.

General view of pit and rearing boxes employed in life-history studies of the grape Phylloxera.

FIG. 1.—Pit with rearing boxes, illustrating method of covering with quilted strips to preserve same temperature as in like depth of soil.

FIG. 2.—Galvanized tin cans used in connection with studies of the underground diffusion of Phylloxera.

THE GRAPE PHYLLOXERA IN CALIFORNIA.

THE GRAPE PHYLLOXERA IN CALIFORNIA.
Rearing box drawn up from pit; sides of box removed.

and those in the saucers above were also plugged with cotton. This procedure tended to prevent the phylloxeræ from leaving the exposed portion of the root between the saucer of the upper pot and the surface of the lower. This exposed portion of living root averaged about 4 inches in length.

Scaffolding was built above the trench and a rope and pulleys provided in order that the cages might be raised and set in place on the stand for examination of roots. Electric connections were also provided so as to enable the cages to be examined after dark.

The cages above described were designed by R. L. Nougaret.

DEVELOPMENT OF THE RADICICOLE LARVA.

The young radicicole larva (Pl. IX, *g*, *h*, p. 64), upon hatching from the egg, seeks a place on the root where it may implant its beak and settle down to feed. During the summer some of the newly hatched larvæ desert the vine and go in search of other vines, traveling either through cracks in the soil or over its surface. Newly hatched larvæ are very active at all times and, being flat, can go through very small passages. Considering only those that remain on the vine on which they were born, it is found that the length of time elapsing between the hatching and settling on the root surface varies according to conditions of food at hand. On a decaying root the insect may not find a location for several hours, but if the root is sound the larvæ mostly settle down immediately close by the eggshells.

A certain percentage of larvæ always wanders about on the roots before finally settling. Many of these make their way outward and downward to the smaller rootlets, while others (mostly of the hibernant generation) in the fall make their way up to the bases of the larger roots and even to the main trunk. Larvæ hatching on a decayed root usually leave it, but occasionally they remain and die of starvation. Observations on pieces of severed roots kept under cellar conditions indicated very little movement of the young larvæ, provided their food was in good condition and they were not too much crowded. In the summer, however, large numbers deserted the roots in a manner similar to that observed in the vineyards, and these were apparently imbued with a wandering instinct.

On vinifera vines young larvæ prefer to settle on succulent parts of roots or rootlets. When they settle on growing rootlets, they generally cause the formation of nodosities, and on the roots of one or more year's growth the formation of tuberosities. They frequently settle on lesions already formed by older phylloxeræ, and sometimes they settle and mature on the root without causing any perceptible lesion. When no lesion is formed, the insects develop slowly, and as a rule the larger and more fleshy the lesion the more rapid is the growth of the insect thereon. On resistant vines the newly hatched larva rarely fastens on any place except the apex of the rootlet or on a nodosity already formed. On American non-resistant vines the larvæ settle in the main as they do on viniferæ, but on some varieties a decided preference is given to the growing rootlets over the larger roots.

During the years 1911 and 1912 experiments were conducted to determine the growth and development of radicicoles under cellar conditions. Table X summarizes these observations.

TABLE X.—*Summarized records of incubation and development of the radicicole of the grape phylloxera under cellar conditions, during 1911 and 1912, Walnut Creek, Calif.*

Generation.	Number of individuals.	Incubation period.			Number of individuals.	Developmental period.			Number of individuals.	Generation cycle.			Average temperature during period of development.
		Maximum.	Minimum.	Average.		Maximum.	Minimum.	Average.		Maximum.	Minimum.	Average.	
		Days.	Days.	Days.		Days.	Days.	Days.		Days.	Days.	Days.	°F.
1.................	49	17	10	13.6	181	48	13	29.6	49	56	26	40.5	63
2.................	58	13	8	10.2	352	61	16	31.7	58	74	25	42.2	64
3.................	21	12	8	10.1	30	41	16	26.6	21	52	26	37.2	64½
4.................	10	18	7	13.3	8	24	17	21.9	8	38	24	34.6	64
4¹.................					13	208	125	183.0					
5–9².............	3	12	11	11.3	18	45	14	27.6	3	41	35	37.3	

[1] Hibernating individuals, maturing in 1912.
[2] In 1912 the records extend from Mar. 20 to July 22.

A summary of the observations made on the growth and development of the radicicole on severed root cuttings in the cellar in 1911 and 1912 may be given in brief. The great variation existing in the growth of individuals under the same temperatures, and even on a given piece of root, is resultant entirely from the condition of the food. An aphid living on a callus formation or tuberous lesion develops more rapidly than one living on the normal surface of the same piece of root. Individuals living on vigorous roots develop more rapidly than those on decayed or dying roots. Occasionally a decaying root will send out very fleshy lesions, and these, while they remain fresh, provide ample nourishment for the aphids and enable them to grow quickly. After a root reaches a certain point in decay or dryness the phylloxeræ can no longer develop on it and must seek better food or perish.

The growing period of the aphids recorded in Table X ranged from 13 to 61 days, hibernating individuals excluded. The grand average, hibernants not considered, was 30.57 days, practically one month. That the maximum period may be prolonged is evidenced from an observation made in the summer of 1912, in which a series of individuals lived from 90 to 105 days on a particularly innutritious piece of root without maturing.

During 1913 two series of further experiments were undertaken. One series was reared in the cellar and the other in an electric incubator, the latter under somewhat higher temperatures. Generations were followed from May to October. Table XI summarizes these observations.

TABLE XI.—*Development of radicicoles of the grape phylloxera, Walnut Creek, Calif., 1913.*

Environment.	Generation.	Number of individuals.	Average period of growth.	Average temperature.
				°F.
Cellar	1	44	27.25	65.1
Do	2	10	32.40	69.8
Incubator	1	15	35.60	65.6
Do	2	24	28.80	71.1
Do	3	3	29.70	70.3

From this table it is noticeable that temperature exerted considerable influence on the growing period of the aphids, and that warmth accelerated their development. In a series of generations reared in 1915 on very nutritious food, recorded under the heading " Maximum and minimum generations yearly " (p. 71), this temperature influence is very apparent. The greater constant warmth in the incubator induced the aphids to remain active later in the fall, after those in the cellar had hibernated. In comparing the 1913 series with those of 1911, it was found that the aphids of the former developed more slowly than did those of the latter, and this notwithstanding the fact that both the series of 1913 enjoyed higher temperatures than did the cellar series of 1911. The roots supplied in 1913 were of much poorer quality than were those supplied in 1911.

Development on living roots, 1913–1915.—During 1913, 1914, and 1915 the habits and development of the radicicoles were observed on living roots of vines growing in cages (Pls. V; VI, fig. 1; VII) kept in a trench where the temperature approximated that obtaining beneath the surface of the soil. As far as the temperature was concerned, the monthly averages ranged less than did those obtaining about 2 feet below the soil surface, but the daily fluctuations were considerably in excess of those in the soil. In the cages the roots were subjected to an average daily fluctuation of about 3° F. in summer and about 2° F. in winter. Two feet beneath the surface, the temperature never fluctuated more than 1° in any given day. As far as could be observed, this temperature fluctuation had little effect on the growth of phylloxeræ, except that it seemed to cause the nodosities to decay more rapidly than they would normally. Occasionally it was noted that some nodosities would dry up quickly after the cage had been examined and its interior subjected for a few minutes to a temperature several degrees in excess of that obtaining in the trench immediately preceding the examination.

Plate VII illustrates the details of the cages used for observing the phylloxeræ on living roots. By means of the pulley and stand the cages were hauled up and set for examination. It is obvious that only young vines could be used for this work, as 9-inch pots were the largest used. The vines were planted in early spring, certain of the longer roots, drawn through holes cut in the saucer supporting the bottomless upper pot, being planted in the lower pots. Thus about 4 inches of root between upper and lower pots were available for inoculation and observation. At the upper and lower ends of this visible portion the root passed through glass cylinders, and the intervening spaces between the root and cylinder were filled with sand and cotton (sand only was used in the lower cylinders) to prevent the escape of phylloxeræ to the invisible portions of the roots, both above and below. For the viniferæ and nonresistant American vines this, however, failed to answer the purpose in many cases. Out of 22 upper pots, which were examined several months after the exposed roots were inoculated and had suffered more or less severe infestation, 18 developed infestation on their roots, showing that phylloxeræ had found their way up to the roots in the upper pots. Out of 36 lower pots liable to infestation on their roots by reason of the fact that the exposed portions of the roots above were infested, the roots in 9 showed no infestation or indications of any previous infestation, whereas in 13 others infestation occurred which had resulted from larvæ successfully penetrating the lower glass cylinders; in the remaining 14 pots, infestation or signs of previous infestation occurred resulting from wanderers reaching the rootlets by penetrating cracks in the soil. In the case of the resistants, the cylinders of sand and cotton packed between roots and glass were effectual in preventing spread to the invisible portions of the roots. On these vines the infestation was always very slight, and the phylloxeræ exhibited very little desire to travel. On a Champini (rupestris X candicans), on which the phylloxeræ infested only the side rootlets, and which bore only a slight infestation, wandering larvæ entered the soil and infested the rootlets of one of the lower pots, but there was no penetration through the glass cylinders.

As temperature is a factor of importance in the development of the phylloxera, the following comparisons (Table XII) of temperatures are noteworthy, taken (1) inside the cages containing living vines, (2) 2 feet below the soil surface, at a point in the laboratory vineyard a few feet distant from the trench containing the cages aforesaid, and (3) in the laboratory cellar:

TABLE XII.—*Comparative monthly average temperatures; inside cages in trench, 2 feet below soil surface in laboratory vineyard, and in laboratory cellar, Walnut Creek, Calif.*

Month.	Two feet below surface.	In cages in trench.	In laboratory cellar.
1913.	° *F.*	° *F.*	° *F.*
May		[1] 59	
June		68	
July	76	71	
August	77	71	
September	77	69	68
October	70.5	65	63
November	64	56	59
December	53	49	56
1914.			
January	54	52	55
February	51	52	55
March	58	56	58
April	62	58	59
May	65.5	63	62
June	70	68	65
July	72.5	72	67
August	74	72	69
September	70.5	66	67
October	66	64	63
November	58.5	56	58
December	50.5		54
1915.			
January	49		54
February	52		55.5
March	57	56.5	57
April	62	57	58
May	63.5	59	60
June	71.5	68	65
July	75.5	73	68
August	75	73.5	69
September	71.5	69	66
October	66	64.5	62

[1] Approximate.

Examination of Table XII indicates that the cellar temperatures showed the least annual variation and that the average temperatures in the soil for every month, except February, 1914, exceeded the corresponding temperatures in the cages. It is probable, leaving other factors out of consideration, that the accumulated excess of heat in the soil over that in the cages throughout one season would produce an extra generation of phylloxeræ, besides prolonging the active development later into the autumn. The summer of 1913 was much warmer than that of the year following. This is borne out by the soil temperature comparisons, but does not appear from the cage temperatures.

To obtain life-history data, the following vines were used: Burger, Muscat, Thompson's Seedless, Mission, Champini, and Grenache. On the Champini the phylloxeræ refused to settle, except on fleshy side-rootlets, but on the others they settled at any point. On the Grenache roots, however, several of the inoculations proved unsuccessful, the young larvæ not settling. On the others, inoculations nearly always proved successful. Inoculations were made by transferring eggs from one root to another with a camel's-hair brush. Since the roots in all cases were vertical, or very nearly so, it happened occasionally that some of the eggs used in the inoculations dropped off. This was unavoidable, and when egg-laying females were under observation it frequently happened that the eggs dropped down. When more than one female was producing eggs simultaneously on a single root, there even arose doubt as to which certain of the fallen eggs should be credited. For the biological records the first season, 9 vines were used, averaging 3 separate roots each, but since 3 of these roots died, after they were planted, only 24 roots were actually used. Of these 3 were used for rearing gallicole progeny and 5 others were used for nymph production and fertilizer experiments on heavily infested vines, leaving 16 for individual records. In 1914 and 1915, only 4 vines were used each year to continue the individual series.

Many interesting habits were observed, but the behavior of the phylloxeræ in the main did not differ from that observed under cellar conditions upon severed roots. Newly hatched larvæ mostly settled close to the eggshells they had vacated, but if there were any fresh lesions near by, the young larvæ often found their way to them and settled. Occasional movements of older individuals were observed, not only at the time of molting but at any time in the instars. These movements were generally in the direction of more succulent food. Occasionally egg-laying individuals shifted their positions without apparent injury, although this was sometimes followed by a temporary halt in the production of eggs. The production of nymphs occurred from June to October, as in the vineyard. The tendency of the nymphs to crawl up the root just before transforming was noticeable. Most of them could go no farther upward than the cylinder plugged with cotton, and so perforce had to transform into migrants at this point. A small percentage transformed at points farther down the root and did not appear to have made any upward migration. On the heavily infested roots, wanderers appeared from July to October. These roamed around the inside of the compartment, and succeeded in finding their way down through cracks in the soil of the lower pots, and infested the rootlets, especially those growing against the inside of the pots. After irrigation, cracks appeared in the soil around the inside of the pot, furnishing the wandering larvæ access to the rootlets. In no case was this infestation of any great extent, although large numbers of wandering larvæ were observed in several of the cages, and only a very small percentage, presumably, found their way to a new food supply. This fact has an important bearing upon the distribution of the insect as will be noted elsewhere. Although it appeared difficult for the insects to penetrate an inch of sand in the lower glass cylinder, the occurrence of large infestations immediately below the cylinder, coupled with evidences of only slight infestations on the rootlets around the inside of the pots, showed that such a penetration had occurred. It was obvious in these instances, few though they were, that the heavy infestations could not have resulted from inoculations on rootlets from wanderers, because only a few nodosities occurred on the rootlets, showing a slight wanderer infestation, and not enough time had elapsed in the interim for the infestation present at the date of examination to be produced by so small a company of wandering larvæ. The phylloxeræ had no difficulty in finding their way through the upper cylinder to the root system of the upper pots through layers of cotton and sand each about half an inch thick. On the roots of the upper pot of cage V, Burger, there were, on November 26, 1913, upward of 1,600 hibernants disposed in large clusters on the main root. Since June of that year, the visible portions of four roots below had been well infested. Every one of those 1,600 hibernants was the progeny of phylloxeræ hatched on the visible part of the roots and which had penetrated the upper cylinders. It is obvious that a great many individuals penetrated the cylinders, as the scarcity of lesions showed that the greater part of the infestation was comparatively recent. Apparently a natural law against overcrowding comes into play, and migration was encouraged by the fact that the tuberosities on three of the four roots had become rotted and threatened to decay all the visible portions of those roots. As, on this vine, no infestation other than a few nodosities occurred below the cylinders in the lower pots, it would appear that the heavy migration had been entirely in an upward direction. As far as could be determined, there appeared no reason why the insects could not penetrate the lower cylinders just as easily as the upper ones, so the conclusion is that in most cases they did not make the attempt.

In the instances wherein phylloxeræ had undoubtedly penetrated the lower cylinders they were found to be close to the cylinder as if the packing of sand and cotton had been so loose that no effort was needed for the insect to force its way through. The sand in the upper cylinders, by reason of the weight of earth pressing upon it, always remained well packed and presented a barrier to the progress of the phylloxeræ. That they were able to surmount this barrier is shown by the large numbers present, and indicates that the upward migration was a well-defined movement. The possibility presented itself that infestations on the roots of the upper pots could have originated from wandering larvæ that had penetrated the soil of the upper pots in the same manner as they had obviously done in the lower pots of the cages. The absence of cracks except around the periphery of the soil in the pots and of nodositous infestations on the rootlets below taken in conjunction with the size of the infestations precludes this as the sole source of the inoculations of the upper pots.

Some of the lower pots of the cages were filled with quartz of mixed grades. This was done chiefly for the purpose of experimenting with liquid fertilizers as to the bearing of fertilizing substances upon the behavior of infested vines as an adjunct to similar vineyard experiments. Twelve out of 36 lower pots contained quartz. It was found that the wandering larvæ were able to descend to rootlets growing in the quartz as easily as to those growing in earth. On the other hand, the phylloxeræ were not able to exist on the larger roots in the quartz in appreciable numbers, as it appeared that they could not pass through the quartz when it was packed around the root. This is similar to the condition existing on very sandy soils, wherein the phylloxeræ are unable to travel when the sand becomes packed around the roots.

Table XIII indicates the incubation and development of the radicicoles on the roots of living vines.

TABLE XIII.—*Incubation and development of radicicole of the grape phylloxera on living vines, Walnut Creek, Calif., 1913–1915.*

FIRST GENERATION, 1913.

Individual No.	Date egg deposited.	Date egg hatched.	Incubation period.	Date insect matured.	Growing period.	Total period of development.	Variety of vine and number of cage.	Average temperature.
			Days.		*Days.*	*Days.*		° *F.*
1	Apr. 29	May 14	15	June 8	25	40	Mission VII	60
2	May 28	June 6	9	June 25	19	28	.....do.....	67
3	...do...	...do...	9	...do...	19	28	.....do.....	67
4	...do...	...do...	9	June 26	20	29	.....do.....	67
5	...do...	...do...	9	June 28	22	31	.....do.....	67
6	...do...	...do...	9	June 29	23	32	.....do.....	67
7	...do...	...do...	9	June 30	24	33	.....do.....	67
8	...do...	...do...	9	...do...	24	33	.....do.....	67
9	...do...	...do...	9	...do...	24	33	.....do.....	67
10	June 14	June 22	8	July 5	13	21	Burger VI	69
11	...do...	...do...	8	July 8	16	24	.....do.....	69
12	...do...	June 23	9	July 7	14	23	.....do.....	69
13	...do...	June 22	8	July 9	17	25	.....do.....	69
14	...do...	June 24	10	July 14	20	30	.....do.....	69
15	June 15	...do...	9	...do...	20	29	.....do.....	69
16	...do...	...do...	9	July 15	21	30	.....do.....	69
17	...do...	June 26	11	July 18	22	33	.....do.....	69
18	June 16	...do...	10	July 21	25	35	.....do.....	69
19	June 8	June 17	9	July 9	22	31	Burger V	68
20	...do...	...do...	9	...do...	22	31	.....do.....	68
21	...do...	June 19	11	July 13	24	35	.....do.....	69
22	...do...	...do...	11	...do...	24	35	.....do.....	69
23	...do...	June 20	12	July 15	25	37	.....do.....	69
24	...do...	June 17	9	July 7	20	29	.....do.....	68
25	...do...	...do...	9	July 8	21	30	.....do.....	68
26	...do...	June 18	10	July 2	14	24	.....do.....	68
27	...do...	...do...	10	...do...	14	24	.....do.....	68
28	...do...	...do...	10	...do...	14	24	.....do.....	68
29	...do...	...do...	10	July 4	16	26	.....do.....	68
30	...do...	...do...	10	July 6	18	28	.....do.....	68
31	...do...	...do...	10	...do...	18	28	.....do.....	68
32	...do...	...do...	10	...do...	18	28	.....do.....	68
33	...do...	...do...	10	July 7	19	29	.....do.....	68
34	...do...	...do...	10	...do...	19	29	.....do.....	68
35	May 25	June 4	10	June 19	15	25	.....do.....	67
36	...do...	...do...	10	June 21	17	27	.....do.....	67
37	...do...	June 5	11	June 23	18	29	.....do.....	67
38	...do...	...do...	11	June 24	19	30	.....do.....	67
39	...do...	June 6	12	June 25	19	31	.....do.....	67
40	...do...	...do...	12	...do...	19	31	.....do.....	67
41	...do...	...do...	12	June 27	21	33	.....do.....	67
42	...do...	...do...	12	...do...	21	33	.....do.....	67
43	...do...	...do...	12	June 29	23	35	.....do.....	68
44	...do...	June 8	14	July 2	24	38	.....do.....	68
45	...do...	...do...	14	July 3	25	39	.....do.....	68

TABLE XIII.—*Incubation and development of radicicole of the grape phylloxera on living vines, Walnut Creek, Calif., 1913–1915—*Continued.

SECOND GENERATION, 1913.

Individual No.	Date egg deposited.	Date egg hatched.	Incubation period.	Date insect matured.	Growing period.	Total period of development.	Variety of vine and number of cage.	Average temperature.
			Days.		*Days.*	*Days.*		*° F.*
1	June 10	June 20	10	July 8	18	28	Mission VII	68
2	June 11	June 19	8	...do....	19	27	.....do	68
3	June 12	...do....	7	...do....	19	26	.....do	68
4	...do....	June 20	8	July 11	21	29	.....do	69
5	June 30	July 6	6	July 20	14	20	.....do	70
6	...do....	July 8	8	July 22	14	22	.....do	70
7	...do....	...do....	8	July 23	15	23	.....do	70
8	...do....	...do....	8	...do....	15	23	.....do	70
9	...do....	...do....	8	July 31	23	31	.....do	71
10	...do....	July 9	9	July 24	15	24	.....do	70
11	...do....	...do....	9	July 25	16	25	.....do	70
12	...do....	...do....	9	July 31	22	31	.....do	71
13	July 1	...do....	8	Aug. 4	26	34	.....do	71
14	...do....	...do....	8	Aug. 7	29	37	.....do	71
[1] 15	...do....	...do....	8	Aug. 11	33	41	.....do	71
16	June 30	...do....	9	Aug. 8	30	39	.....do	71
17	June 26	July 3	7	July 21	18	25	Burger VI	70
18	...do....	July 4	8	July 25	21	29	.....do	70
19	...do....	...do....	8	July 26	22	30	.....do	70
20	...do....	...do....	8	...do....	22	29	.....do	70
21	...do....	...do....	8	July 28	24	32	.....do	70
22	...do....	July 5	9	July 29	24	33	.....do	70
23	...do....	...do....	9	July 31	26	35	.....do	70
[1] 24	June 27	July 4	7	July 28	24	31	.....do	70
25	...do....	July 5	8	July 31	26	34	.....do	70
26	June 30	...do....	6	Aug. 8	23	29	Burger V	71
[1] 27	...do....	July 8	6	Aug. 10	35	41	.....do	71
[1] 28	...do....	July 7	7	Aug. 12	36	43	.....do	71
[1] 29	...do....	...do....	7	...do....	36	43	.....do	71
[1] 30	July 1	July 8	7	...do....	35	42	.....do	71
[1] 31	...do....	...do....	7	Aug. 13	36	43	.....do	71
[1] 32	July 2	...do....	6	Aug. 14	37	43	.....do	71
[1] 33	...do....	July 10	8	Aug. 18	39	47	.....do	71

THIRD GENERATION, 1913.

Individual No.	Date egg deposited.	Date egg hatched.	Incubation period.	Date insect matured.	Growing period.	Total period of development.	Variety of vine and number of cage.	Average temperature.
1	July 23	July 31	8	Aug. 25	25	33	Thompson's Seedless I	71
2	July 28	Aug. 5	8	Aug. 28	23	31	Muscat IV	71
3	July 29	Aug. 7	9	Aug. 30	23	32	...do	71
4	...do....	...do....	9	Sept. 1	25	34	.....do	71
5	...do....	Aug. 8	10	Sept. 3	26	36	.....do	71

FOURTH GENERATION, 1913–14.

Individual No.	Date egg deposited.	Date egg hatched.	Incubation period.	Date insect matured.	Growing period.	Total period of development.	Variety of vine and number of cage.	Average temperature.
1	Aug. 26	Sept. 3	8	(2)	....	....	Thompson's Seedless I	[3] 71
2	Sept. 1	Sept. 8	7	Sept. 18	10	17	Champini IX	70
3	...do....	Sept. 9	8	Sept. 22	13	21	.....do	69
4	...do....	Sept. 10	9	Sept. 30	20	29	.....do	69
5	....	Sept. 23	....	Apr. 6	195	....	Muscat IV	....
6	....	...do....	....	Apr. 9	198	....	.....do	....
7	....	Sept. 24	....	Oct. 24	30	....	.....do	66
8	....	...do....	....	Apr. 6	194	....	.....do	....
9	....	...do....	....	Apr. 7	195	....	.....do	....
10	....	...do....	....	May 20	238	....	.....do	....
11	....	...do....	....	Apr. 15	203	....	.....do	....
12	....	Sept. 25	....	Apr. 24	211	....	.....do	....
13	....	...do....	....	Apr. 28	215	....	.....do	....

FIFTH GENERATION, 1914.

Individual No.	Date egg deposited.	Date egg hatched.	Incubation period.	Date insect matured.	Growing period.	Total period of development.	Variety of vine and number of cage.	Average temperature.
1	Apr. 25	May 9	14	May 28	19	33	Muscat IV	62
2	Apr. 26	...do.....	13	..do....	19	32	.....do	62
3	...do.....	...do.....	13	June 2	24	37	.....do	63
4	Apr. 27	...do.....	12	June 1	23	35	.....do	63
5	...do.....	...do.....	12	June 2	24	36	.....do	63
6	Apr. 28	...do.....	11	..do....	24	35	.....do	63
7	...do.....	...do.....	11	June 3	25	36	.....do	63

[1] Indicates winged migrants. [2] Hibernant. [3] Indicates average temperature of incubation period alone.

TABLE XIII.—*Incubation and development of radicicole of the grape phylloxera on living vines, Walnut Creek, Calif., 1913–1915*—Continued.

SIXTH GENERATION, 1914.

Individual No.	Date egg deposited.	Date egg hatched.	Incubation period.	Date insect matured.	Growing period.	Total period of development.	Variety of vine and number of cage.	Average temperature.
			Days.		*Days.*	*Days.*		° *F.*
1	May 29	June 7	9	June 24	17	26	Muscat IXA	67
2	June 2	June 8	6	July 1	23	29	Grenache IIA	68
3	June 9	June 19	10	July 10	21	31	Muscat IXA	69
4	...do	June 20	11	July 26	36	47	...do	69

SEVENTH GENERATION, 1914.

Individual No.	Date egg deposited.	Date egg hatched.	Incubation period.	Date insect matured.	Growing period.	Total period of development.	Variety of vine and number of cage.	Average temperature.
1	June 24	July 3	9	July 23	20	29	Muscat IXA	70
2	...do	July 4	10	July 29	25	35	...do	71
3	June 25	July 3	8	July 23	20	28	...do	70
4	...do	July 4	9	July 30	26	35	...do	71
5	June 26	...do	8	July 23	24	32	...do	71
6	...do	...do	8	July 30	26	34	...do	71
7	July 1	July 9	8	July 29	20	28	Grenache IIA	72
8	July 2	July 11	9	...do	18	27	...do	72
9	...do	...do	9	Aug. 1	21	30	...do	72
10	July 3	...do	8	Aug. 3	23	31	...do	72
11	...do	...do	8	...do	23	31	...do	72

EIGHTH GENERATION, 1914–15.

Individual No.	Date egg deposited.	Date egg hatched.	Incubation period.	Date insect matured.	Growing period.	Total period of development.	Variety of vine and number of cage.	Average temperature.
1	Aug. 17	Aug. 24	7	Sept. 16	23	30	Muscat XXX	70
2	...do	...do	7	...do	23	30	...do	70
3	...do	Aug. 25	8	Sept. 26	32	40	...do	69
4	...do	...do	8	Mar. 26	213	221	...do	[3]72
5	...do	...do	8	Mar. 30	217	225	...do	[3]72
6	...do	...do	8	Apr. 3	221	229	...do	[3]72
7	...do	...do	8	Apr. 4	222	230	...do	[3]72
8	...do	...do	8	(4)			...do	[3]72
9	...do	Aug. 26	9	(4)			...do	[3]72

NINTH GENERATION, 1914–15.

Individual No.	Date egg deposited.	Date egg hatched.	Incubation period.	Date insect matured.	Growing period.	Total period of development.	Variety of vine and number of cage.	Average temperature.
1	Sept. 16	Sept. 27	11	(4)			Muscat XIX	[3]72
2	...do	...do	11	Apr. 11	196	207	...do	[3]72

NINTH GENERATION, 1915.

Individual No.	Date egg deposited.	Date egg hatched.	Incubation period.	Date insect matured.	Growing period.	Total period of development.	Variety of vine and number of cage.	Average temperature.
1	Mar. 31	Apr. 19	19	May 22	33	52	Carignan XXIX	57
2	...do	...do	19	May 23	34	53	...do	57
3	...do	...do	19	May 24	35	54	...do	57
4	...do	...do	19	May 25	36	55	...do	57

TENTH GENERATION, 1915.

Individual No.	Date egg deposited.	Date egg hatched.	Incubation period.	Date insect matured.	Growing period.	Total period of development.	Variety of vine and number of cage.	Average temperature.
1	May 23	June 3	11	June 24	21	32	Carignan XXIX	66
2	May 27	June 6	10	July 1	25	35	Zinfandel XXIIIA	67

ELEVENTH GENERATION, 1915.

Individual No.	Date egg deposited.	Date egg hatched.	Incubation period.	Date insect matured.	Growing period.	Total period of development.	Variety of vine and number of cage.	Average temperature.
1	July 9	July 15	6	Aug. 10	26	32	Zinfandel XXIIIA	73
2				July 29			Carignan XXIX	
3				...do			...do	

TWELFTH GENERATION, 1915.

Individual No.	Date egg deposited.	Date egg hatched.	Incubation period.	Date insect matured.	Growing period.	Total period of development.	Variety of vine and number of cage.	Average temperature.
1	Aug. 2	Aug. 9	7	Sept. 8	30	37	Zinfandel XXXVI	72
2	...do	Aug. 10	8	Sept. 9	30	38	...do	72
3	...do	Aug. 9	7	Sept. 10	32	39	...do	72
4	Aug. 4	Aug. 11	7	...do	30	37	...do	72
5	Aug. 16	Aug. 24	8				Zinfandel XXIIIA	
6	...do	Aug. 25	9				...do	
7	Aug. 17	...do	8				...do	
8	Aug. 18	Aug. 27	9				...do	
9	Aug. 19	...do	8				...do	

[3] Indicates average temperature of incubation period alone.   [4] Died, 1915.

For the first generation, eggs deposited by adult hibernants were secured from a Zinfandel vineyard, and thereafter only eggs deposited in the cages and of known generations were used in the inoculations.

The average growing periods of the summer generations of wingless aphids varied from 34.5 to 18.25 days, but in all except two generations this period ranged between 18.25 and 24.20 days. Individuals varied between 36 and 10 days. The winged forms developed more slowly than the wingless, nine individuals averaging 34½ days. The hibernants developed in an average of 6¾ months.

Eggs were placed for the most part on roots never before infested, and tuberosities usually followed rapidly after the hatching of the larvæ. Nodosities were formed upon side rootlets. The main roots were all between one-sixth and one-third of an inch in diameter.

It was found that about 40 per cent of the larvæ remained on the exposed portions of the roots, the rest finding their way to the other portions. In spring a large percentage and in summer and autumn a smaller percentage of larvæ settled close beside the eggshells from which they had issued. In spring the larvæ did not display a tendency to roam, but in summer and autumn they wandered considerably, especially if the root had begun to decay or was drying too rapidly. Similar conditions occur in vineyards, and it is in summer and autumn that the typical wandering larvæ are found.

Excluding the winged migrants and the hibernated individuals, the summary of the growing period of all the phylloxeræ developing on living roots during the years 1913, 1914, and 1915 is recorded in Table XIV.

TABLE XIV.—*Summary of Table XIII.*

Number of individuals _____	114
Average period of growth _____days__	22.15
Maximum period of growth_____do___	36
Minimum period of growth_____do.__	10

Taking into consideration the individuals removed before they attained their full development, the average growing period is to be estimated at about 25 days. The cellar experiments with severed pieces of roots in 1911 and 1912 combined yielded an average of 30.57 days, and the experiments in the cellar and incubator combined in 1913 averaged 34.16 days. The cellar temperatures of 1911 and 1912 averaged about 1½° F. lower than the combined cage temperatures for the period 1913–1915 for the months from May to October, inclusive. The cellar temperatures for 1913 averaged about 1½° lower than the incubator temperatures for 1913 and about ½° higher than the cage temperatures for that year.

In the cellar and incubator during 1913 the phylloxeræ developed, on the average, more slowly than in the cellar during 1911 and 1912, notwithstanding higher temperatures in 1913. This resulted from the fact that the food supply was much more succulent in 1911 and 1912. Likewise the phylloxeræ developed much more rapidly in the cages in 1913–1915 than in the cellar and incubator combined in 1913, when the temperatures differed slightly (the difference in favor of the cages being about 1° daily). This also was due to the superior food of the living vines. In comparing the phylloxera development in the cellar in 1911–12 with that in the cages in 1913–1915, it would appear that both temperature and food influenced the more rapid development observed in the cages. For 1911 alone the average growing period was 29.37 days. This growth took place on succulent roots, to all appearances as succulent as the living roots upon which were reared the 1913–1915 phylloxeræ, which averaged about a 25-day period, under a temperature averaging $4\frac{1}{2}°$ in excess of that obtaining in the cellar in 1911. It would be natural to ascribe the faster growth in the cages to the higher temperatures, but in view of the discrepancies noted above in connection with the 1913 cellar and incubator observations, the writers are inclined to believe that the living roots afforded better nourishment to the phylloxeræ than did the severed roots of 1911 and that the higher temperatures of 1913 had less influence than might appear in bringing about such a difference in the growing periods.

Excepting for a few isolated instances, the phylloxeræ on living roots developed more rapidly on nodosities and tuberosities than on the normal surface of the root. On nodosities development was the most rapid, noticeably more rapid than on tuberosities, and the more fleshy the swelling the more rapid was the aphid's growth.

DESCRIPTION OF STAGES.

The egg.—When first laid, the radicicole egg (Pls. VIII, *g;* IX, *k, l*) is lemon yellow, about twice as long as wide, oval, both ends rather bluntly rounded, the micropylar end a little more abruptly so. Thirty-six eggs laid by newly matured adults August 30 and September 6, 1911, averaged 0.348 mm. in length and 0.173 mm. in width, with maxima, respectively, of 0.36 and 0.18 mm., and minima, respectively, of 0.34 and 0.17 mm. Of 25 eggs laid by overwintered radicicoles near the end of their laying period, the maximum length was 0.32 mm., the maximum width 0.18 mm., the minimum length 0.20 mm., and the minimum width 0.12 mm., the average length 0.26 mm., and the average width 0.14 mm. Thus it appears that the size of the eggs laid by individuals decreases toward the end of their egg-laying

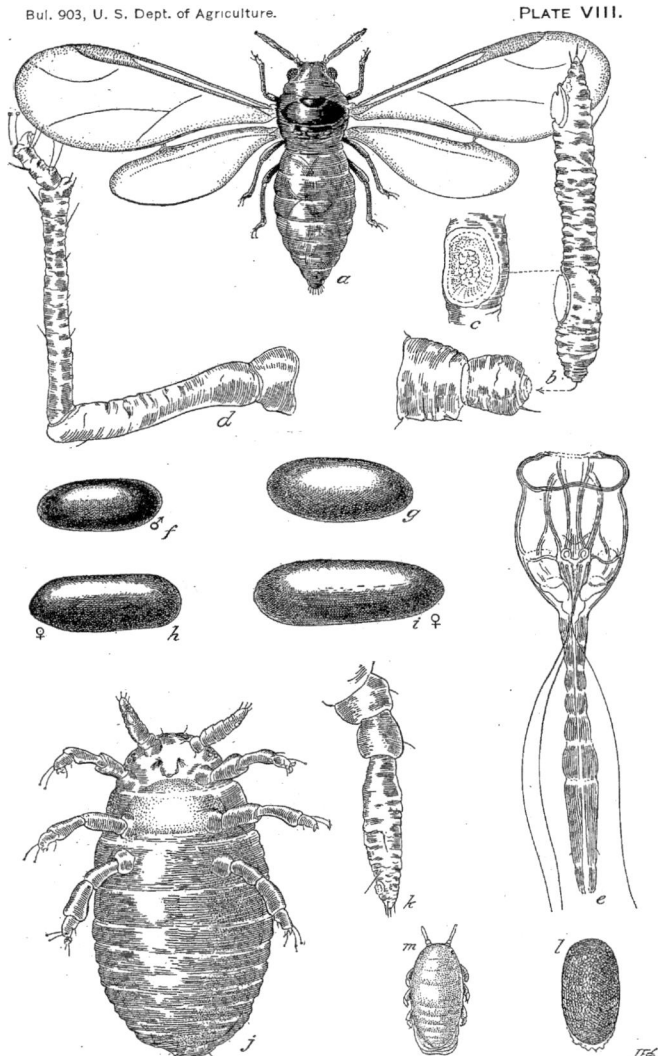

THE GRAPE PHYLLOXERA IN CALIFORNIA.

Phylloxera vitifoliae: a–e, Winged migrant; *a,* dorsal view; *b,* antenna; *c,* basal sensorium of
antennal segment III; *d,* hind leg; *e,* beak; *f,* male egg; *g,* radicicole egg; *h, i,* female eggs;
j, k, l, sexed female; *j,* enlarged ventral view showing contained winter egg; *k,* antenna;
l, newly hatched female; *m,* mature male just after casting last skin.

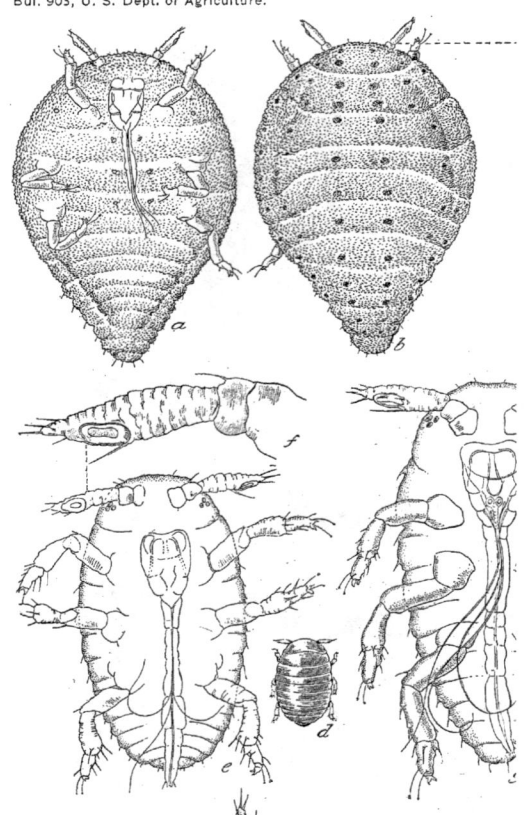

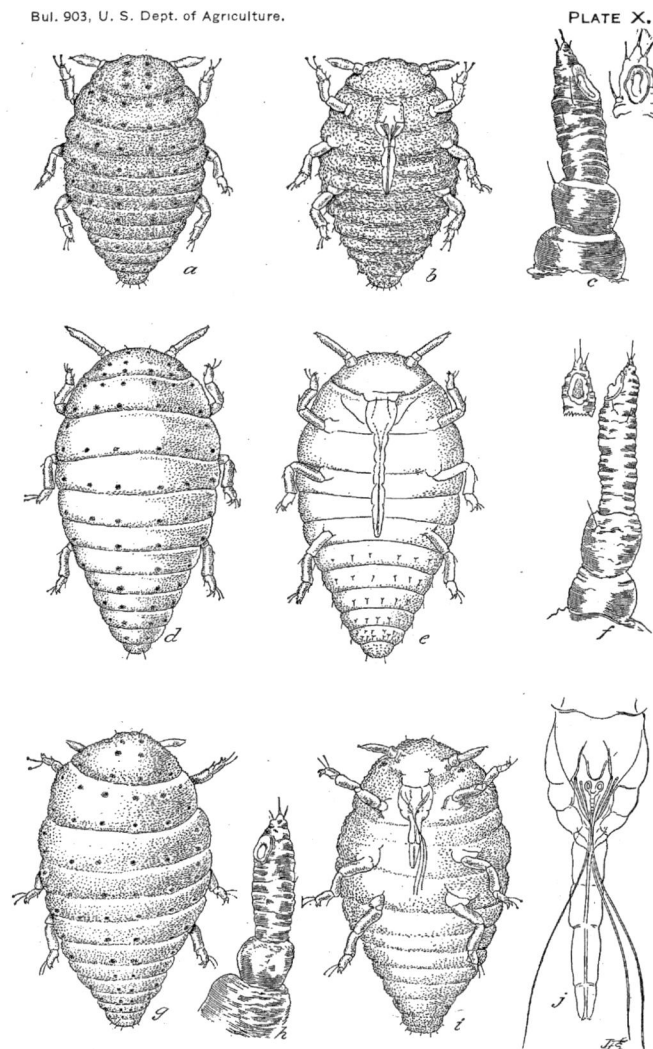

THE GRAPE PHYLLOXERA IN CALIFORNIA.

Phylloxera vitifoliae: a, b, c, Third-instar radicicole; a, dorsal view; b, ventral view; c, left antenna; d, e, f, prenymph (third instar of winged form); d, dorsal view; e, ventral view; f, left antenna; g–j, fourth-instar radicicole; g, dorsal view; h, left antenna; i, ventral view (beak shown telescoped); j, beak.

period. Toward the period of hatching the egg becomes darker and the eyespots of the embryo become visible.

The larva.—In hatching, the young larva (Pl. IX, *g*, *h*) splits the eggshell from the micropyle lengthwise to about three-fourths of its length. This splitting is more or less gradual and is caused by the thorax and head of the young phylloxera bursting the shell and then gradually enlarging the crack. The larva poises itself at an angle of 45°, with legs and antennæ appressed to the body, and slowly eases its way out. It seems to rely simply on a slow sidewise body movement to free itself of the shell. When freed, it spreads the appendages and is then able to walk off. The newly hatched larva is of a pale lemon yellow, with dark claret-colored eyes, composed each of three circular facets and placed in the form of the angles of an equilateral triangle. The body segmentation is quite distinct, more so than in later instars. The shape is oval and very flat. The antennæ, as in all forms of the grape phylloxera, are three-jointed. The terminal joint is twice as long as the two basal combined. Near the apex of the third joint occurs a circular sensorium. The beak in early generations reaches to the penultimate or antipenultimate body segment, and in later generations protrudes beyond the caudal segment of the abdomen. The legs and antennæ bear hairs. Table XV gives measurements for five newly hatched individuals.

TABLE XV.—*Measurements of newly hatched radicicoles of the grape phylloxera, Walnut Creek, Calif., Oct. 23, 1914.*

Individual No.	Length of body.	Maximum width of body.	Length of beak.	Length of hind femur.	Length of hind tibia.	Length of antennal joints.			Length of sensorium.
						1	2	3	
	Mm.	*Mm.*	*Mm.*	*Mm.*	*Mm.*	*Mm.*	*Mm.*	*Mm.*	*Mm.*
1	0.359	0.176	0.1964	0.0679	0.0571		.0161	.0705	
2	.327	.179	.2036			0.0169	.0143	.0625	
3				.0562	.0429	.0214	.0196	.0680	
4	.359	.189	.2152	.0580	.0491	.0232	.0180	.0705	
5	.341	.190	.2107	.0566	.0455	.0188	.0188	.0634	0.0231
6				.0554	.0491	.0179	.0152	.0670	.0228

The young phylloxeræ hatching in spring have shorter beaks than those which hatch in the fall, the beaks in spring averaging in length about 0.155 mm.

The first molt does not take place until more than half of the growing period is passed. The molting of the radicicoles is a procedure quite similar in detail to the hatching from the egg. After each molt the individual for about 24 hours is brighter in color than at any other time during the instar. After the first molt the phylloxera changes from oval or suboval to pyriform in shape (Pl. IX, *i*, *j*).

Table XVI gives measurements for four individuals of the second-instar radicicole.

TABLE XVI.—*Measurements of second-instar radicicoles of the grape phylloxera, Walnut Creek, Calif.*

Individual No.	Length of body.	Maximum width of body.	Length of beak.	Length of hind femur.	Length of hind tibia.	Length of antennal joints.			Length of sensorium.
						1	2	3	
	Mm.	*Mm.*	*Mm.*	*Mm.*	*Mm.*	*Mm.*	*Mm.*	*Mm.*	*Mm.*
1..................	0.419	0.234	0.154	0.0625	0.0526	0.0190	0.0204	0.0586	....
2..................	.448	....	....	.0624	.0518	.0205	.0205	.0589	....
3..................	.439	.257	1 .113	....	....	....	....	....	....
4..................	.499	.270	.168	....	....	....	....	....	0.0171

1 Telescoped.

The roughened tubercular areas on the dorsal surface are more conspicuous after the first molt, and a rapid increase in bulk is apparent during the second instar.

The second, third, and fourth molts occur at practically equidistant periods. Under highest temperatures and optimum food conditions, these instars are passed in about two days apiece. Under a temperature of 58° F. from three to eight days elapse between molts, the average being about five and one-half days.

Table XVII gives the measurements of five individuals of the third instar.

TABLE XVII.—*Measurements of third-instar radicicoles of the grape phylloxera, Walnut Creek, Calif.*

Individual No.1	Length of body.	Maximum width of body.	Length of beak.	Length of hind femur.	Length of hind tibia.	Length of antennal joints.			Length of sensorium.
						1	2	3	
	Mm.	*Mm.*	*Mm.*	*Mm.*	*Mm.*	*Mm.*	*Mm.*	*Mm.*	*Mm.*
1..................	0.592	0.303	0.178	0.0699	0.0607	0.0202	0.0321	0.0616	0.0
2..................	.524	.312	.164	....	....	.0252	.0207	.0568	.0144
3..................	.522	.332	.179	.0739	.0622	....	....	....	....
4..................	.649	.355	.155	.0732	.0687	.0241	.0205	.0634	....
				.0758	.0660	.0197	.0187	.0589	.0177
5..................	.648	.371	.145	.0741	.0692	.0206	.0194	.0598	.0186
6..................	....	....	....	....	....	....	....	....	.0190

1 Individuals 1–3, newly molted; 4, two days after molt; 5, three days after molt.

During the third instar (Pl. X, *a, b, c*) the increase in bulk continues rapidly. The dorsal tubercular areas are larger than in the previous instar, but in color and shape no differences appear.

Table XVIII indicates the measurements of seven individuals of the fourth (penultimate) instar.

TABLE XVIII.—*Measurements of fourth-instar radicicoles of the grape phylloxera, Walnut Creek, Calif.*

Individual No.[1]	Length of body.	Maximum width of body.	Length of beak.	Length of hind femur.	Length of hind tibia.	Length of antennal joints.			Length of sensorium.
						1	2	3	
	Mm.	Mm.	Mm.	Mm.	Mm.	Mm.	Mm.	Mm.	Mm.
1	0.919	0.517	....	0.0848	0.0687	0.0321	0.0259	0.0669	....
2	.851	.528	....	....	....	.0321	.0277	.0571	....
3	.824	.579	....	.0830	.0749	.0276	.0241	.0768	0.0212
4	.615	.500	0.172	....	....	.0306	.0261	.0748	.0167
5	....	....	.162	....	....	.0297	.0248	.0721	.0162
6	.753	.426	.160	.0802	.0671	....	....	....	....
7[2]	.700	....	....	....	....	....	....	....	....

[1] Individuals 1–3 were measured toward the end of the instar, and individuals 4–7 very shortly after molting.
[2] Maximum height, 0.3 mm.

A very obvious growth takes place during the fourth instar (Pl. X, *g–j*). At the end of this instar the phylloxera casts its last skin and issues therefrom as an adult. The adults, except immediately following the molt, are never as pale as the immature forms. They may be distinguished from fourth-instar individuals by two longitudinal furrows on the thorax and by the relatively larger dorsal tubercular areas. The color varies from a light green to a dark purplish brown in living specimens. This variation is to a great degree dependent on the food supply. On fresh, fleshy nodosities the insects mostly are pale green with the tubercular areas very noticeable. On tuberosities, or on the normal surface of a vigorous root, the color is yellowish green, olive green, or light brown, with the tubercular areas often less evident.

On roots of poor quality the adults are brown or orange and the tubercular areas hardly perceptible to the naked eye. After weeks of egg production old adults become brown or purplish brown. In shape the adults while not engaged in egg laying are hemispherical or short oval, about equally rounded at either extremity, but while an egg is being passed the insect assumes a pyriform shape and the caudal end is much tapered and extended.

Mature radicicole.

Pl. IX, *a, b, c.*

Color varying from pale green and pale yellow to deep purplish brown, dependent on character of food and age of individual; shape hemispherical, short oval, pyriform while passing the ova; body obscurely glabrous, often appearing to be coated on the dorsum with a very fine whitish powder; under side of abdomen paler than upper. Body about twice as long as wide, widest at middle of mesothorax; highest at about cephalic third; body flattening both cephalad and caudad from this point. Head with dusky central area; eyes dark red, each composed of three circular facets, arranged in form of an equilateral triangle; antennæ pale, not quite reaching posterior margin of head, composed of three joints, of which the two basal are subequal in length but joint 1 wider than joint 2; third joint about twice as long as the two basal combined and bearing a single oval sensorium near apex; all three joints bearing hairs. Beak pale, base and tip shining and dusky, reaching to second or third abdominal tergite; in specimens examined after they had transfixed the beak into the roots, this organ appears to be shorter, due to the telescoping of the sheath from the action of transfixing.

Mesothorax largest segment of body, twice as long as prothorax, which is next largest; mesothorax divided into two sections by transverse fold. Thoracic segments having median portions raised above lateral portions by means of two longitudinal curved folds. Metathorax very similar above to any of first five abdominal segments. Legs in pale specimens slightly darker than abdomen, coxæ dusky.

Sixth abdominal segment produced conically at each of its posterior angles and narrowed basally; caudal segment twice as long as broad, bluntly rounded, with a small central emargination and fringed with a marginal row of pale weak hairs.

The dorsum of the body bears six longitudinal rows of dusky circular tubercular areas, which under magnification appear as thickenings and roughenings of the epidermis, and each of these is surmounted by a single spine.

Table XIX gives measurements of the adult radicicole.

TABLE XIX.—*Measurements of mature radicicole of the grape phylloxera, Walnut Creek, Calif.*

Individual No.	Length of body.	Maximum width of body.	Length of beak.	Length of hind femur.	Length of hind tibia.	Length of antennal joints.			Length of sensorium.
						1	2	3	
	Mm.	*Mm.*	*Mm.*	*Mm.*	*Mm.*	*Mm.*	*Mm.*	*Mm.*	*Mm.*
1	0.854	0.502		0.0795	0.0786	0.0223	0.0251	0.0661	0.0224
				.0804	.0759	.0252	.0243	.0660	.0195
2	.878	.549	0.281	.0839	.0748	.0260	.0230	.0673	.0196
3	1.011	.584		.0875	.0768	.0197	.0230	.0705	.0265
4	.997	.558							
5	.942	.593							
6	.783	.507							
7	.778	.503							
8	.763	.455							
9	.734	.433							
10	.714	.448							
11	.712	.392							
12	.686	.408							
13	.631	.416							
14	.582	.352							

Measurements of beaks from nine adult hibernants were made March 18, 1915. Of these six, fixed in the root tissue, measured 0.276, 0.243, 0.260, 0.252, 0.198, and 0.179 mm., respectively. The other three, not fixed since casting their last skin, measured 0.329, 0.317, and 0.299 mm., respectively. The basal joints of the rostrum are telescoped when the beak is thrust into the root.

It is obvious from an inspection of Table XIX that the adult radicicoles vary greatly in size. This variation occurs whatever kind of food supply the phylloxeræ are getting, although the average size is larger on good succulent food than on that of poorer quality. Individuals 5 to 14 in Table XIX were all taken the same day (Mar. 18) from equally succulent pieces of severed roots. They show a considerable variation in dimensions, but, being hibernants, their average dimensions are less than those of the summer generations under equally favorable food-supply conditions; for among the hibernant adults there always may be found a considerable number of small-sized individuals which evidently owe their physical inferiority to the vicissitudes of the long hibernation period. Radicicoles raised on fleshy and succulent nodosities attain an average size of about 1 by 0.55 mm., those raised during the summer on other parts of the root system average slightly less, and the hibernant individuals average 0.75 by 0.50 mm.

Radicicole molts.—The radicicole, in common with other forms of the phylloxera, invariably molts four times.

In 1914 and 1915 records of molts were taken, and Tables XX and XXI indicate molting records of 20 individuals reared on severed roots in the laboratory cellar during the summer of 1914.

TABLE XX.—*Molting records of 20 radicicoles of the grape phylloxera, summer of 1914, Walnut Creek, Calif.*

Individual No.	Date egg hatched.	Date of first molt.	First instar.	Date of second molt.	Second instar.	Date of third molt.	Third instar.	Date of fourth molt.	Fourth instar.	Total growing period.	Average temperature.
			Days.		*Days.*		*Days.*		*Days.*	*Days.*	°*F.*
1	July 22	Aug. 6	15	Aug. 9	3	Aug. 11	2	Aug. 14	3	23	68
2	...do....	Aug. 7	16	...do....	2	...do....	2	...do....	3	23	68
3	July 23	Aug. 6	14	...do....	3	Aug. 13	4	Aug. 16	3	24	68
4	...do....	...do....	14								
5	July 24	Aug. 7	14	Aug. 9	2	Aug. 11	2	Aug. 14	3	21	68
6	July 25	Aug. 4	10	Aug. 6	2	Aug. 8	2	Aug. 9	1	15	68
7	...do....	...do....	10	...do....	2	...do....	2	Aug. 11	3	17	68
8	...do....	Aug. 5	11	Aug. 8	3	Aug. 9	1	...do....	2	17	68
9	...do....	...do....	11	...do....	3	Aug. 11	3	Aug. 13	2	19	68
10	...do....	...do....	11	Aug. 9	4	Aug. 12	3	Aug. 14	2	20	68
11	...do....	Aug. 6	12	Aug. 8	2	Aug. 11	3	Aug. 13	2	19	68
12	...do....	...do....	12	...do....	2	...do....	3	Aug. 14	3	20	68
13	...do....	Aug. 5	11	...do....	3	Aug. 9	1	Aug. 11	2	17	68
14	...do....	Aug. 7	13	Aug.10	3						
15	...do....	Aug. 8	14	...do....	2	Aug. 13	3	Aug. 15	2	21	68
16	...do....	...do....	14	...do....	2	Aug. 12	2	...do....	3	21	68
17	...do....	Aug. 9	15	Aug. 13	4	Aug. 15	2	Aug. 18	3	24	68
18	...do....	Aug. 11	17	Aug. 14	3	Aug. 17	3	...do....	1	24	68
19	...do....	Aug. 13	19	Aug. 20	7	Aug. 24	4	Aug. 28	4	34	68
20	...do....										

[1] Hibernant died unmolted Oct. 11.

TABLE XXI.—*Summary of Table XX.*

	Average period.	Maximum period.	Minimum period.
	Days.	*Days.*	*Days.*
First instar, 19 individuals	13.3	19	10
Second instar, 18 individuals	2.9	7	2
Third instar, 17 individuals	2.5	4	1
Fourth instar, 17 individuals	2.5	4	1
Developmental period, 17 individuals	21.2	34	15

All the individuals utilized in this experiment were reared on severed pieces of roots in a petri dish under cellar conditions. Individuals 19 and 20 lived on a much poorer root than the others, and thus is explained the relatively slow growth (34 days) of the one and the early hibernation of the other. Individuals 4 and 14 moved away after their first and second molts, respectively. It will be observed from the summary that the average period of the first instar (13.3 days) is considerably longer than is that of the three succeeding instars combined (7.9 days). The comparative periods of the instars are about constant; that is, an individual with a short first instar will have short succeeding instars and one with a long first instar will have long succeeding instars.

The records of Table XX were made in midsummer at a temperature of 68° F. In the soil at such a time of the year the temperature is higher and the development of the phylloxera more rapid, while in spring and late fall the development is correspondingly slower. The developmental period of the hibernated larvæ varies greatly, not so much from temperature as from other causes. There is an average period of two and one-half weeks from the commencement of feeding to the shedding of the first skin, and after that an average period of three weeks between the casting of the first skin and the shedding of the fourth, the second, third, and fourth instars occupying an average space of a week each. As summer progresses the development of the radicicoles becomes accelerated, as may be observed from Table XXII.

TABLE XXII.—*Molting records of radicicoles of the grape phylloxera, March to July, 1915, Walnut Creek, Calif.*

Individual No.	Date egg hatched.	Date of first molt.	First instar.	Date of second molt.	Second instar.	Date of third molt.	Third instar.	Date of fourth molt.	Fourth instar.	Total growing period.	Average temperature.	Generation.
			Days.		*Days.*		*Days.*		*Days.*	*Days.*	° *F.*	
1.....	Mar. 19	Apr. 3	15	Apr. 10	7	Apr. 16	6	Apr. 22	6	34	58.25	A.
2.....	...do....	Apr. 7	19	...do....	3	...do....	6	...do....	6	34	58.25	A.
3.....	...do....	Apr. 8	20	Apr. 13	5	Apr. 18	5	Apr. 23	5	35	58.25	A.
4.....	...do....	Apr. 10	22	Apr. 17	7	Apr. 21	4	Apr. 25	4	37	58.25	A.
5.....	May 11	May 27	16	May 30	3	June 1	2	June 5	4	25	61	B.
6.....	...do....	...do....	16	...do....	3	...do....	2	...do....	4	25	61	B.
7.....	May 23	June 7	15	June 10	3	June 13	3	June 16	3	24	63	B.
8.....	June 16	June 27	11	June 30	3	July 1	1	July 4	3	18	65	C.
9.....	...do....	June 30	14	July 2	2	July 4	2	July 9	5	23	65	C.
10....	...do....	July 3	17	July 6	3	July 9	3	July 10	1	24	65	C.

The individuals enumerated in Table XXII were reared under cellar conditions on equally succulent pieces of severed roots. Table XXII, both by itself and taken in conjunction with Tables XX and XXI, indicates the influence of temperature upon the development of the radicicole under equal food conditions. Under a temperature of 58.25° F. the period of growth averaged 35 days, under an average of 61.75° F. this period was 24.75 days, under 65° F. it was almost 22 days, and under 68° F. it was lowered to 20.3 days (individual on unthrifty root disregarded). Under the lower temperatures all the instars are correspondingly longer than under the highest midsummer temperature, but the first instar is proportionately less lengthened than are those following it, a phenomenon that becomes quite apparent in the case of the hibernants, provided their first instar be considered in a restricted sense to cover only that period between the time when they commence feeding in spring and the date of the first molt. The hibernant feeds for two and one-half weeks before and for three weeks after its first molt, while in midsummer the larva feeds for 13 days before and for 8 days after its first molt before it matures.

MAXIMUM AND MINIMUM GENERATIONS YEARLY.

In 1911 overwintered adult radicicoles matured at the end of April, throughout May and June, and as late as July 7. Eggs of the first generation were deposited from the end of April until October 1. From the earliest eggs there followed seven complete generations from hibernant to hibernant inside of the one year. No observations were taken of the hatching of the late eggs deposited by late first-generation phylloxeræ in September, but in the light of contemporary observations on individuals of later generations there is no doubt that a certain percentage of these late eggs would have hatched into hibernants, thus giving a minimum of one generation per annum. In 1915, taking advantage of a hibernant which matured exceptionally early in the spring, it was possible to secure eight complete generations within the year. Table XXIII records the development of these generations.

TABLE XXIII.—*Maximum series of generations of radicicoles of the grape phylloxera, reared under cellar conditions, Walnut Creek, Calif., 1915.*

Generation No.	Date of egg deposition.	Date of egg hatching.	Date insect matured.	Generation cycle.	Temperature (average).
				Days.	*° F.*
1[1]	— —, 1914	— —, 1914	Feb. 26, 1915		
2	Feb. 26, 1915	Mar. 19, 1915	Apr. 22, 1915	55	58.25
3	Apr. 27, 1915	May 11, 1915	June 5, 1915	39	61.20
4	June 7, 1915	June 16, 1915	July 4, 1915	27	64.50
5	July 5, 1915	July 14, 1915	July 28, 1915	23	69.50
6	July 28, 1915	Aug. 4, 1915	Aug. 23, 1915	26	68.50
7	Aug. 23, 1915	Aug. 31, 1915	Sept. 23, 1915	31	67.00
8	Sept. 25, 1915	Oct. 7, 1915	Oct. 27, 1915	32	62.50
9[1]	Oct. 27, 1915	Nov. 10, 1915	— —, 1916		

[1] Hibernant.

In this experiment the food supplied to the phylloxeræ was, as far as one could judge, of equal quality and very nourishing. The influence of temperature is noticeable.

In observations with phylloxeræ developing on living vines there were secured in a period of three years 13 generations, an average of a little over four generations a year, but had the earliest eggs of each generation been successfully utilized, and had it been possible to start the first of the three seasons with the earliest eggs procurable in the vineyards, there is no doubt that six, and possibly seven, generations could have been developed each year.

Considering that the hibernant generation occupies a period of half a year, it is apparent that if seven generations are to be produced in a year, the other six must be passed in an average maximum of one month apiece. In summer phylloxeræ have been reared from egg deposition to maturity in 21 days, but in April, May, and October the cycle rarely falls below 35 days, so that in the six-month period, April 15 to October 15, the average maximum cycle is roughly 30 days. Thus, in the vineyard, even on vines that move early in spring, it is probable that more than seven generations rarely take place in 12 months. The period, October 15 to April 15, best represents the cycle of the wintering generation, although these dates are somewhat arbitrary.

Under vineyard conditions it is always possible to find hibernant phylloxeræ as late as the beginning of June. It is also possible to find insects going into hibernation as early as September 20. Since the mature radicicoles deposit eggs for periods exceeding three months, it can be seen readily that the latest eggs of a radicicole hibernant maturing in June may develop larvæ which proceed to hibernate. A minimum of one generation a year thus may occur. Observations indicate that this minimum of one generation is not common, even on moribund vines with innutritious roots.

WANDERING RADICICOLE LARVÆ OR "WANDERERS."

By the term "wanderers" are designated those forms (almost all newly hatched larvæ) which forsake the root on which they issued from the egg and seek to reach the surface of the soil or to pass through the soil itself, with the object of finding new food. Those that strive to reach the surface exhibit in their efforts a very marked positive phototropism. It would appear that their first movement is simply one of ascending the root and that as soon as they are brought into the focus of a ray of light they immediately make it their goal, and thus finally ascend to the surface. The initial wandering movement comes irrespective of light rays, but as soon as these rays are brought to bear the activity is very pronounced. The conclusion is that the production of individuals destined to wander is due to a combination of influences more than to any single influence—the crowded condition of the phylloxeræ in summer, the decaying of the roots, especially the fleshy surface rootlets, found on

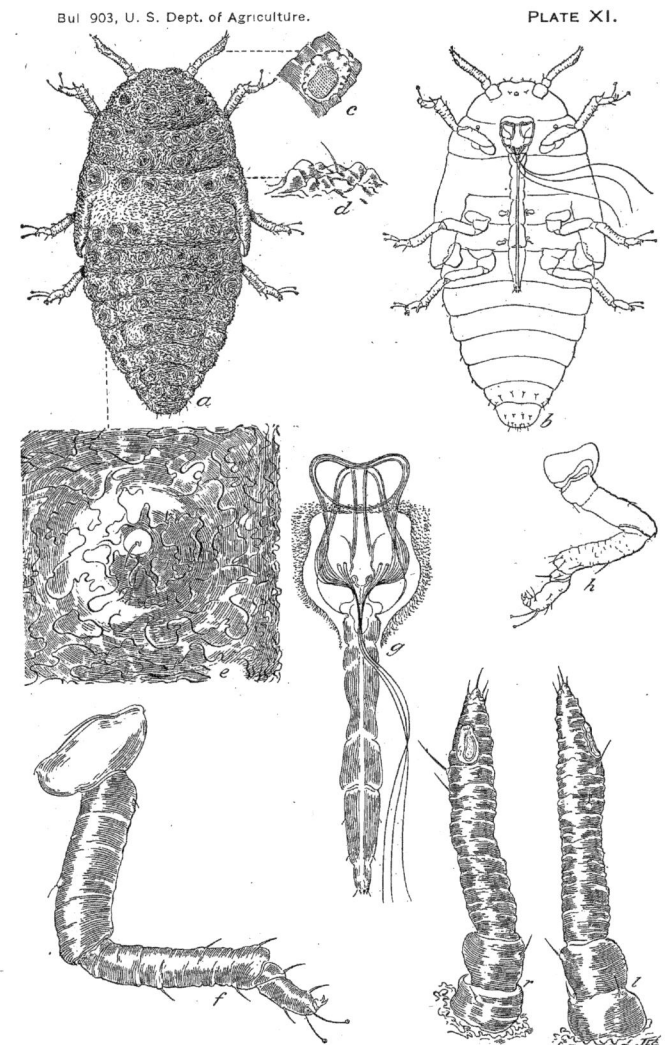

THE GRAPE PHYLLOXERA IN CALIFORNIA.

Phylloxera vitifolae: a, Nymph, dorsal view; b, outline ventral view of same; c, enlarged sensorium on antennæ; d, enlarged tubercle with spine; e, microscopic structural view of tubercle; f, hind leg; g, beak showing structure; h, middle leg; r, right antenna; l, left antenna.

phylloxerated vines, the rising temperature, and the intrinsic vigor of the vine encouraging emigration.

Apparently the young produced from the eggs deposited by over-wintered females do not become wanderers, but those of later generations may, and many wandering larvæ produced late in the autumn settle on roots and hibernate.

Wandering larvæ play an important part in the diffusion of phylloxera.

THE NYMPH AND WINGED FORM.

DEVELOPMENT.

The individuals which are destined to become winged are termed in their third instar "prenymphs" and in their fourth instar "nymphs." They are produced from eggs deposited by adult radicicoles, and until after their second molt differ in nowise from the individuals destined to remain wingless; neither is there any difference in the eggs from which the two types hatch. In their third instar the prenymphs (Pl. X, d, e, f) differ from the radicicoles of that instar in that the former have more elongate and narrower bodies and longer antennæ and legs. The prenymphs are generally pale greenish yellow, and their appendages appear quite dusky in comparison. Table XXIV gives measurements of four prenymphs.

TABLE XXIV.—*Measurements of prenymphs of the grape phylloxera, Walnut Creek, Calif.*

Individual No.[1]	Length of body.	Maximum width of body.	Length of beak.	Length of hind femur.	Length of hind tibia.	Length of antennal joints.			Length of sensorium.
						.1	2	3	
	Mm.	Mm.	Mm.	Mm.	Mm.	Mm.	Mm.	Mm.	Mm.
1.....................	0.805	0.405	0.357	0.0948	0.0821	0.0330	0.0268	0.0839	0.0196
				.0939	.0839	.0321	.0277	.0889	.0193
2.....................	.660	.325	.193	.0946	.0713	.0306	.0279	.0973	....
						.0306	.0279	.0919	....
3.....................	.541	.300	.186	....	....	....	....	....	....
4.....................	.555	.284	....	....	....	....	....	....	....

[1] Individual 1, just before molting into nymph; individuals 2 to 4, very shortly after molting into prenymphs.

The prenymph molts into the nymph or pupa. The pupa is the longest of all forms of the insect and is easily discernible on the root by the presence of wing pads, even just after it has molted from the prenymphal form, and has a greenish color. Immediately after the skin is shed, these wing pads are yellow, but very quickly they become gray or blackish. During the first few days of the nymphal instar the insect is green or greenish yellow, and the compound eyes are indiscernible, but as it grows it lengthens, becomes constricted in the region of the metathorax, and turns orange, the mesothorax, however, remaining paler than the rest of the body. The compound eyes show their red pigment and soon become prominent. Legs and antennæ are relatively long, and the femora exceed the tibiæ in length. At all times the rows of tubercular areas on the dorsum are well marked. During the nymphal instar the insect shows a very considerable growth; the newly molted individuals are quite flat, but full-grown nymphs are roughly cylindrical.

DESCRIPTION OF STAGES.

The nymph or pupa, full grown.

Pl. XI; text fig. 9, p. 85.

General color orange or orange yellow; anterior part of mesothorax and mesosternum whitish, or at least always noticeably paler than the rest of body. Antennæ pale yellow, extended but little beyond anterior margin of prothorax. Compound eyes and ocelli dark red; former composed of large number of facets. Head and abdomen bearing 4, thorax 6 longitudinal rows of dark tubercular areas (coarse roughening of epidermis), each surmounted by a spine; wing pads dark gray, grayish black, or rarely jet black; legs pale yellow, often with a dusky cast; abdomen with 7 visible segments, mesothorax apparently bisected by a transverse fold; beak very pale yellow, reaching to posterior coxæ.

Measurements of 6 individuals are given in Table XXV.

TABLE XXV.—*Measurements of nymph of the grape phylloxera, Walnut Creek, Calif.*

Individual No. [1]	Length of body.	Maximum width of body.	Length of beak.	Length of hind femur.	Length of hind tibia.	Length of antennal joints.			Length of sensorium.
						1	2	3	
	Mm.	*Mm.*	*Mm.*	*Mm.*	*Mm.*	*Mm.*	*Mm.*	*Mm.*	*Mm.*
1	1.102	....	0.3295	0.1500	0.1366	....	0.0402	0.1536	0.0223
				.1464	.1384	0.0839	.0350	.1545	.0224
2	.889	....	.3600	.1419	.1321	....	.0331	.1455	.0230
				.1438	.1304	....	.0332	.1455	.0254
3	.957	.507	.3339	.1089	.1071	.0321	.0339	.1179	.0223
						.0304	.0295	.1184	.0232
4	.851	....	....	....	....	....	....	....	....
5	.798	.511	.2695	.1389	.1252	.0315	.0309	.1577	.0198
6	.725	....	....	....	....	....	....	....	....
7	1.121	.558	....	....	....	....	....	....	....
8	1.197	.569	....	....	....	....	....	....	....

[1] Individuals 1, 7, and 8 at end of stage; 4, 5, and 6 at beginning of stage; 2 and 3 about middle of stage

Newly molted nymphs average about 0.78 mm. in length and mature nymphs about 1.1 mm. The nymphs are always more active than the immature wingless forms, wandering larvæ excepted. Their eyes are well developed, as in the winged insect, and they have the ocelli found in that form. The third joint of the antennæ bears a single sensorium corresponding to the apical one of the migrant, and as the last molt approaches the migrant antennæ show through the nymphal skin, and thus the nymphal antennæ appear to bear two sensoria.

The adult instar of the winged form shows what is probably the most highly developed form structurally of the phylloxera. The winged insect is, on the average, slightly shorter than the full-grown nymph. The antennæ are longer than those of the previous instar and bear two sensoria of about equal size. The comparatively large wings are weakly veined but necessitate strong muscles in the interior of the thorax. The legs are quite long and the tibiæ exceed the femora in length. As the migrant sheds the nymphal skin, pushing it back and moving about its appendages, the wing pads appear as little white rolls; the mesothorax is shining green, the head and abdomen bright orange. The wings unroll as the skin is being passed off the abdomen. As soon as it is entirely shed the insect moves off and then pauses while the wings assume their final shape and position, but remain whitish, hyaline, and limp. Soon, however, the wings dry and the thorax hardens and darkens until it is almost black. The head, prothorax, and abdomen remain orange, the head with a grayish luster. The molting process occupies about 50 minutes.

The adult winged form.

Pl. VIII, a–e.

General color orange or yellowish brown or gamboge yellow; head a little dusky on the anterior half, especially the cephalic margin (front); ocelli dark red; eyes brighter red than ocelli, compounded of many facets; ocular tubercle small; antennæ with three joints, not quite reaching the anterior margin of the mesothorax, pale yellow, with apical fourth of joint 3 dusky gray; third joint much the longest, considerably over twice as long as first two combined, somewhat constricted beyond the basal sensorium and at extreme base; posterior half of head, prothorax, and abdomen orange, yellowish brown, or gamboge.

Thoracic lobes, scutellar lobes, scutellum, and mesosternum dark gray or blackish; legs pale yellow, tarsi duskier; wing insertions, stigma, and veins gray (at first greenish); stigma equal in length to about one-fourth of wing.

First discoidal arising from subcosta not far from basal angle of stigma, stout, not attaining the wing margin by a space equal to one-fifth its length; second discoidal faint, arising from the first vein or discoidal a little before its center and almost reaching the wing margin at a point a little nearer to the apex of the third discoidal than to that of the first; third discoidal faint, arising from first vein close to its base and continuing with a double shallow curve almost to the wing apex (the basal half of this vein generally obsolete). Lower wings with the costal vein running parallel to the anterior margin for its whole length; cauda bluntly rounded, bearing a fringe of hairs; beak slender, pale yellow, and almost reaching to second coxæ; two longitudinal oval sensoria on the third antennal joint; basal sensorium situated at basal third of joint, apical sensorium close to apex of joint. Wings borne horizontally, apparently the positions interchangeable, the right pair sometimes overlapping the left and vice versa. Abdomen widest at second and third abdominal segments, where it is wider than the thorax, and about as long as head and thorax combined. Body about as high as wide, not at all flat.

Table XXVI gives the measurements from 8 individuals.

TABLE XXVI.—*Measurements of the winged migrant of the grape phylloxera, Walnut Creek, Calif.*

	1	2	3	4	5	6	7	8
	Mm.	Mm.	Mm.	Mm.	Mm.	Mm.	Mm.	Mm.
Length	1.101				0.906			0.900
Width (abd. seg. 3)	.428				.317			.390
Width (thorax)	.333				.309			
Antennal joints, length:								
1		0.0384	0.0375	0.0321	.0320	0.0393		
2		.0402	.0393	.0304	.0366	.0384		.033
3		.1902	.1809	.1777	.1741	.1946		.207
Antennal joint 3, base to apex of basal sensorium		.0562	.0634		.0536	.0589	0.063	
Antennal joint 3, length of basal sensorium		.0268	.0304	.0241	.0214	.0304	.0275	
Antennal joint 3, length of apical sensorium		.0286	.0289		.0250	.0277	.0297	
Hind femur, length		.1901	.1802	.1500	.1848			
Hind tibia, length		.2179	.2250	.1643	.2062			
Beak, length					.229			
Wing expanse							2.73	

The prenymphal instar is passed in three or four days, in the same time in which the corresponding instar of the wingless radicicole is passed. The nymphal instar, however, is relatively longer than the corresponding instar in the wingless form, and it is because of this fact that the migrant takes longer to mature than does the contemporaneous wingless radicicole. The nymphal or pupal instar occupies from 5 to 12 days, the average being about 8 days.

The nymphs take more food than does the corresponding wingless form, and after they have left a nodosity or tuberosity upon which they have been feeding, the lesion rapidly decays unless other individuals are settled upon it. The nymphs do not usually move much during their period of growth, but if disturbed they move quickly and display a negative phototropism when suddenly exposed to light. The newly molted nymphs, however, often wander about with apparent aimlessness. The full-grown nymphs just before molting ascend the roots, seeking the surface, and transform on the trunk or else find their way along the root until they come to a crack in the soil, and crawling up the sides of the crack transform near the surface. In glass sections cages, wherein the glass plates did not fit very tightly to the soil, the nymphs were found sometimes crawling up to within 2 or 3 inches of the surface and sometimes transforming close by the roots as much as 17 inches below the soil surface, the resultant winged aphids being compelled to find their way to the surface. It was concluded that owing to the loosely fitted glass plates of the section cages, which allowed abnormal light to penetrate below the surface of the soil, the nymphs did not wait to ascend toward the surface, but transformed below, their transformation being governed by the strength of the light rays to which they were subjected. It may be said that these section cages measured 9 by 24 inches, outside measurement, and allowed of a thickness of half an inch of soil, which was a silty loam mixed with heavier clay loam. In some half-darkened cages, containing potted vines, the nymphs were observed to ascend to the level of the soil surface to transform. On the other hand, occasional nymphs have been found to transform on the roots as much as several feet underground, and many of the resultant migrants failed to reach the surface of the soil.

HABITS OF WINGED MIGRANTS.

Occasionally it was noticed in the jars that migrants would thrust their beaks into the roots and appear to feed. While engaged thus they lower the head so as to allow the beak to penetrate the tissues of the root. This organ appears to issue from the mesosternum, because of the curvature of the sheath. The femora are kept horizontal, and the antennæ are usually in motion. While the insect is walking the antennæ are in motion. The migrants, so far as has been noted, never feed after they issue from the soil. At all times they exhibit strong positive phototropism. When placed in a room they seek to crawl toward windows, and their activity is greatly increased when placed in the direct sunlight. If placed in a petri dish in the sunlight, they travel very fast and often take to flight, and are capable of keeping up a walking gait for hours. If the surface upon which they are standing becomes heated, they quickly die. If a vine leaf or other shade-giving object is placed in the dish, the phylloxeræ will finally settle on the shady side of the object. In the vineyard most of the winged phylloxeræ were observed to issue from the soil by creeping up the stumps of the vine. On arriving at the surface many of them passed to the soil and crawled around aimlessly. Others crawled up the vine, and when they reached a point of vantage, such as the end of a cane, they spread and vibrated their wings, as though inviting the wind to bear them off. Finally they launched themselves into the air and if they struck a wind current were borne off. Often after spreading their wings once or twice they turned about and crawled down the stalk, and frequently when they launched themselves into the air no current of wind caught them, and they half fell and half flew to the ground in an oblique direction, but at other times they flew off strongly without the aid of the wind. The migrants are capable of traveling by flight and with the wind, as is evidenced by the experiments conducted with sticky papers. (See Diffusion of phylloxera, p. 100.) They have been taken on such papers at least 80 feet from the nearest infested vine, and undoubtedly they may travel much farther.

In order to ascertain whether the migrants returned to the soil by crawling down the stem of the vine, 26 migrants were placed on the upper foliage of a small American vine (9 inches in height), on

August 17, 1914. Around the base of the vin
sticky papers, and the stem was encircled with ;
kept indoors and was not exposed to wind curren
the phylloxeræ were placed on the leaves, eigl
caught on the paper. After 24 hours, 17 wing
on the paper and 3 dead on the leaves, none ha·
the circle of glue on the stem. Thus the phylloxe
or dropped down and none had descended the full
Since none of the individuals on the ·papers were
the stem it would appear that they dropped rat
the vine.

On August 22, 1914, 34 winged phylloxeræ
foliage of a riparia vine, 12 inches in height. T
and sunk in the soil and exposed to field condition
an area of sticky paper 30 by 36 inches was laid.
examination of the paper showed on the leewar·
phylloxeræ, occurring $16\frac{1}{2}$, $16\frac{1}{4}$, 16, 16, 12, 10, 6, a1
tively, from the stem, and one winged phylloxe1
side 2 inches from the stem. The remaining 25
and probably flew off or were blown beyond the 1
in which this experiment took place was subjecte
from one direction only. It is obvious that the v
the distribution of these phylloxeræ.

In the observations on the flying of the mig
that individuals would fly both in the sunlight
that very frequently they refused to launch
bright sunlight and in all varieties of wind cur1
appeared to take no definite direction in launch
a general rule, the winged ·forms fly more abu
shine than in the shade, and they are the more a

vines (mostly resistants and American nonresistants) during September and October, and some were reared in the cellar during August.

In 1913 the first nymph was observed, July 9, on the root of an American vine, and at about the same time others appeared on young resistant hybrids in pots. On the severed pieces of vinifera roots kept in jars in the cellar nymphs occurred as early as July 12, and on July 17 the first migrants appeared. This was the first year in which experiments were conducted with living vines in cages, and on these the earliest nymphs and migrants were reared on July 20 and 28, respectively. In the experimental vineyard (Zinfandel) migrants were first collected about August 1, but some nymphs were found on July 25 in a vineyard at Napa, Calif. In general, migrants continued to develop until November, but after the middle of October their production was scanty, and in the vineyard very few were found later than September.

In 1914 nymphs were first observed on June 16, both in the experimental vineyard at Walnut Creek and on roots kept in the cellar. On June 18 a migrant was reared from a nymph collected in the vineyard two days previously. On the roots of the vines growing in cages nymphs were reared June 23. Throughout July and August nymphs and migrants were abundant in the Zinfandel vineyard. In September the numbers fell off rapidly and none were found in October. In infested vines in pots migrants were secured in considerable numbers throughout August and September, but were much more scarce in October.

In 1915, in the material reared under cellar conditions, the first nymph was observed on June 14. The day following, a nymph occurred on the root of a young vine planted in a section cage. In the cages containing living vines, the first nymph was reared June 23, and in the experimental Zinfandel vineyard, nymphs were collected June 22 and evidently occurred as early as June 15. In the vineyard the production of migrants continued until the end of September, and was abundant from July 15 to the end of August. In the material in the cellar jars, abundant migrants were secured throughout the months of July, August, and September, and the production continued until November 8.

In summing up, it may be said that in California the period in which migrants are developed in vineyards extends from the middle of June until the end of October; that these forms appear in greatest abundance from the middle of July to the middle of September (the hottest time of the year); and that the production is very limited in June and October. In small vines in pots, especially if consistent irrigation is practiced, the October production of migrants was frequently large. In the case of pieces of vine roots kept in a cellar, abnormal conditions of food, temperature, and humidity frequently arose.

The conditions which affect the relative abundance of migrants are the following: Variety of vine, vigor of vine, humidity, temperature, condition of roots, character of soil.

Resistant and certain American nonresistant vines normally bear the greatest proportion of migrants. These vines are the descendants of the wild grapevines which formed, and still form, the natural food plant of the phylloxera, and which were immune from serious injury by reason of the fact that there was produced each year a large percentage of migrants, while few or no wingless forms persisted on the vines after the winged forms had departed. The wingless radicicole forms during the summer fed only upon the terminal rootlets, and when these decayed the vine was easily able to replace them without suffering injury of any consequence. The resistant vines of to-day, except in instances in which the roots have been supplied with poor or insufficient soil, as is noted below, do not support heavy and continued infestations of wingless phylloxera, and almost all the phylloxerae born in summer and autumn develop wings and become migrants. It may be said here that experimenting with resistant vines grown in pots with soil unchanged for over a year is apt to give misleading results, for as the soil becomes poorer and insufficient for the increasing root system of the vine, fibrous rootlets become scarce, and an abnormal infestation of wingless phylloxerae and a diminishing production of migrant phylloxerae ensue, thus approaching the conditions normally found on vinifera vines. On vinifera vines and on many American nonresistants, such as Isabella, Catawba, and Champion, the production of winged migrants is never proportionately as large as that which occurs on resistants. Well-nourished resistant vines have been observed to rid themselves entirely of the phylloxerae, the insects all departing as winged forms, and in all cases under normal conditions, if any wingless forms remain after the winged forms have all left, the number is very small. On vinifera vines the total nymphal production has been found to be over 33 per cent of the whole in season, although three-fourths of the individuals produced on fleshy surface rootlets and on nodosities have been observed to develop into migrants, and on succulent pieces of severed root cuttings as large a proportion has been reared.

In the vineyard the larger roots were rarely found to produce a number of migrants in excess of 25 per cent of the whole number of phylloxerae simultaneously developed, and under unfavorable conditions extremely few and sometimes no migrants were produced.

Under average conditions the proportion on the larger roots was between 5 and 10 per cent. Regarding the American vines of nonresistant type, a considerable diversity in the production of nymphs has been observed. On some, like Moore's Early, this production may be proportionately very large, while on others, like Isabella and Catawba, it may be smaller than on viniferæ, as occurred in the experiments in caged and potted vines. Vines like Agawam, Lenoir, and Delaware, vinifera crosses, bore about the same proportion of nymphs as the viniferæ, but among the labrusca types (Isabella, Moore's Early, Concord, Champion) there was considerable variation.

On resistant vines, the nymphs are developed on the nodosities, but on viniferæ and American vines of nonresistant type they are also produced on other portions of the root system. On phylloxerated viniferæ, the most abundant production of nymphs occurs on the fleshy and fibrous surface rootlets frequently observable in the vineyard. These rootlets are sent out in May and June, and often become grossly infested with phylloxeræ in June and July. Toward the end of July, they decay or dry out, and after that nymphs are produced only on the larger roots and on nodosities deeper in the soil. On the larger roots relatively few nymphs are produced before August or after September.

Among viniferæ the more vigorous vines produce the greater proportionate numbers of winged forms. Badly stunted vines showing several years of phylloxeration produce comparatively few, while the recently attacked vines around the periphery of "spots" produce large quantities. Viniferæ vines in pots produce great numbers the first year of infestation, but if the soil is unchanged in the second and third years, as the vines become weakened, they produce fewer winged forms.

As far as has been observed, all varieties of viniferæ produce the same proportion of migrants.

It has been observed frequently that a humid environment stimulates the production of migrants and a dry one precludes it. This has been especially noticeable in the cases of young vines in pots and of the severed roots kept under cellar conditions. The late appearance of the migrants in the experimental vineyard in 1913 as compared with those of 1914 and 1915 was perhaps due to lack of moisture in the soil in summer. The spring of 1913 was exceptionally dry, and the ground became very dry by June, whereas in the two years following, moisture was conserved in the top soil until July. The total migrant development of 1913, however, although at first retarded, was finally just about as large as those of the succeeding years. To hold the severed pieces of roots, glass jars and dishes were used in the cellar, and it was found that in the summer and fall

1900°—21——6

a layer of wet sand placed in the bottom of the jar was conducive to the production of migrants. When moisture was applied periodically to filter papers, the production of migrants was greater the more frequent the applications.

What effect, if any, temperature has upon the production of migrants can not be shown except that they are produced during the hottest months of the year. Contrasting the hot summer of 1913 with the cooler one of 1914, it was found that the production was about equal each year.

Migrants are produced in greater numbers in soils which retain moisture than in those which dry out rapidly. Otherwise no further influence traceable to soil conditions has been noticed. Although the general behavior of phylloxera differs considerably in relation to different types of soil, as between these different types the production of migrants does not appear to change.

In the season 1914, 12 vinifera vines were growing in cages. These were inoculated in the spring, and six of them later treated throughout the summer and autumn with fertilizers applied in liquid form periodically. These fertilizers—nitrogen, potash, phosphoric acid, and magnesium—were combined in a normal fertilizer and also used in combinations in which one element was in marked excess. The fertilized vines produced noticeably larger nymphal infestations. In 1915 other potted vines were treated likewise, except that all the fertilizer was mixed with the soil at the time of planting, and the vines were not inoculated until a month later. In this series the number of nymphs was no greater or less on the fertilized vines than on the unfertilized.

Migrants formed part of radicicole generations 2 to 5, those of the third generation being the most abundant. It was never observed that any of the first generation (direct progeny of the hibernants) became winged.

NYMPHICALS OR INTERMEDIATE FORMS.

The insects of the nymphical type are intermediate in form between the winged migrant and the wingless radicicole. In their adult stage they vary largely. Grassi (11) has figured and described several individuals which represent stages in the variation. His specimens varied from a type which differed only from the radicicole in the possession of two or three extra eye facets and in longer appendages to one which superficially resembled a nymph in that it had well-developed compound eyes and noticeable wing pads. This last type, however, upon close examination, differed from the nymph as follows: (1) The antennæ (fig. 8; compare with fig. 9, antenna of nymph) frequently bore two sensoria, as in the winged insect, but the basal sensorium was less developed than in that form; (2) the wing pads were not hard and straight and parallel to the sides of the body, but bulged out and appeared rolled up and were soft, also sometimes containing the sensory organs peculiar to the wing of the winged forms; (3) there were no wing muscles in the interior of the thorax; and (4) the structure of the vaginal segment of the abdomen was more developed than in the nymph. From this it appeared that this type of nymphical was more comparable to the winged insect notwithstanding its superficial resemblance to the nymph, and this conclusion would be the more obvious when it is considered that the nymphical is an adult insect of the fifth stage.

In Italy the intermediates are said to be quite abundant among the nymphs in the season of the year (July to October) when the latter are being produced on the vines. They were found to be especially abundant on vines of the American type but also not uncommon on viniferæ.

In California, in the year (1915) in which were carried on researches upon the intermediate forms, there was a very small available supply of infested American vines, and the observations were confined chiefly to viniferæ. On the American vines such as were examined one nymphical was found.

In looking over a series of slides made in 1914, a single nymphical was recognized; the year following, during the nymphal season (June to November), frequent examinations were made on vinifera vines, and in all 15 intermediates were secured from these. The individual from the American vine (Wyoming Red) and nine of those on viniferæ were recognized through the medium of mounting large numbers of insects and later examining them through the microscope. The remaining six were discovered on the roots through the use of a binocular microscope, and all of them had rudimentary wing pads, so that it is likely that others of the type lacking these pads were observed but not recognized as intermediates.

In the two years covering the investigation a total of 17 intermediates came under observation. None of these was found earlier in the year than the middle of September, and 12 were collected or observed between September 14 and 27, 1915, and 1 on September 10, 1914. Of the 4 remaining, 1 was observed on a piece of root October 14, 1915, and 3 others October 27, 1915, 1 of which was in the fourth stage and matured November 1. These 17 individuals differed greatly one from another and represented all the types discussed by Grassi and Foa. The types intergrade, and, in fact, no two of the examples were alike. For the sake of comparison, they may be divided into three arbitrary groups: (1) Those without vestige of wing pads; (2) those with small buttonlike wing pads not visible from above; (3) those with larger wing pads protruding (as in the nymphs, fig. 9) beyond the lateral margin of the body and therefore visible from above. In group 1 were two individuals collected on young vinifera vines. One of them greatly resembled an adult wingless radicicole, but besides the larval eyes it had two to three extra facets, and the antennæ and legs were longer than in the radicicole. The other was slender, resembling a prenymph in shape, and had about six extra eye facets, and one antenna showed two sensoria. Group 2 (fig. 6) had six representatives, all with small to very small rudimentary wing pads invisible from above. In all cases the antennæ (fig.

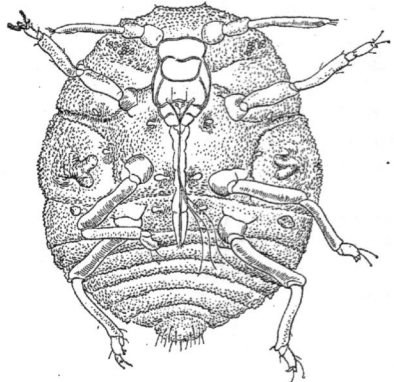

FIG. 6.—*Phylloxera vitifoliae:* Intermediate of type 2, ventral view. Much enlarged.

8) and legs were long, and one insect had two sensoria on antennal segment III. In shape the individuals resembled wingless radicicoles. One specimen (from Wyoming Red) had no extra eye facets, and the others from young viniferæ had a varying number, usually 10, although one had about 15. The remaining 9 individuals came under group 3 (fig. 7), and, because of their more pronounced nymphlike characters, these are more easily observed in life upon roots than are those of the other two groups, and 4 of the 6 individuals recognized alive on roots were of this type.

It is probable, judging from random collections, that the insects of groups 2 and 3 are about equally abundant and each somewhat more so than those of group 1. All the individuals of group 3 had rudimentary wing pads, in many cases almost as large as the wing

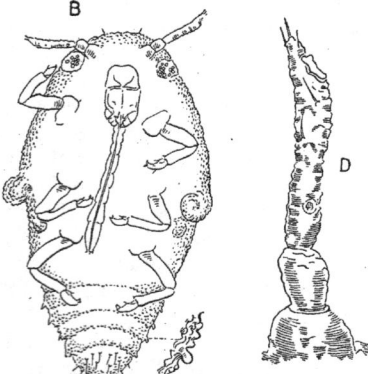

FIG. 7.—*Phylloxera vitifoliae:* Intermediate of type 3, ventral view, much enlarged; antenna at right, more enlarged.

pads of the nymphs. They bulged out from the sides of the insects, and were soft and appeared coiled (fig. 7) or curled. The compound eyes were well developed, there being from 66 to 100 per cent as many facets as in the nymphal eyes. In some cases the larval eyes were absent, and in no case were ocelli discernible. In most individuals there were two sensoria on the last antennal joint, and in one antenna there were two small basal sensoria and the usual apical sensorium, making three in all. The basal sensoria were not in any case as large as those of the winged migrant. The antennæ and legs were about as long as those of the nymph, noticeably longer on the average than those of the individuals of group 2, which in turn were longer than those of the two individuals of group 1.[10]

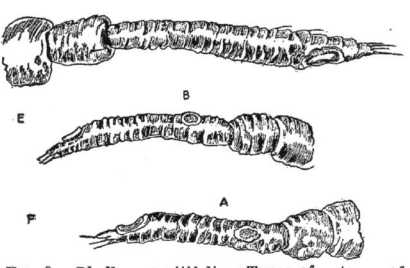

FIG. 8.—*Phylloxera vitifoliae:* Types of antennæ of intermediates. Greatly enlarged.

It would appear, therefore, that greater development of wing pads and compound eyes is complemented with a lengthening of legs and antennæ and a tendency to bear the extra sensorium of the winged forms. The femora exceed the tibiæ in length.

There is among the intermediates a tendency toward asymmetry. This was remarked in Italy and has also appeared in California.

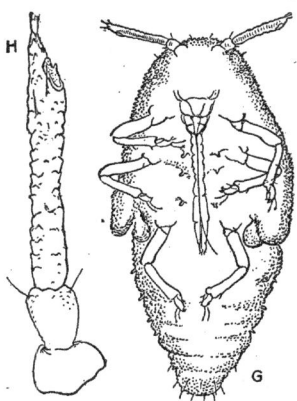

FIG. 9.—*Phylloxera vitifoliae:* Nymph and antenna of newly molted insect, for comparison with intermediates.

One eye may have more facets than the other; the lengths of antennæ and legs may differ in individuals, those of one side being longer than their counterparts, and one antenna may possess more sensoria than the other.

In two instances the fourth stage of intermediates was observed in California. In one case an individual of group 3 molted from what appeared, under the lenses of the binocular microscope, to be a true nymph. In the other case an example of the same group molted from an insect which itself resembled a nymphical; in fact, after the molt the individual did not appear to have changed its structure at all. In both fourth and fifth instars the wing pads were large and "fleshy."

From three individuals, all of group 3, eggs were obtained. These eggs could not be differentiated from eggs laid by wingless radicicoles. One nymphical deposited two eggs, which were lost. An-

---

[10] The insect depicted in figure 7 is considerably less enlarged than that represented in figure 6.

by wingless radicicoles, and two of them measured, respe
0.310 by 0.166 mm. and 0.297 by 0.168 mm. Seven eggs were
ferred for observation to another root, and three eggs hatc
from 14 to 16 days, the resultant larvæ settling down for hiber
One of these soon died, but the other two passed the winter
form, and matured in April, 1916. Both of them were
radicicoles and subsequently deposited many eggs.

In Italy Grassi and his assistants found that the great m
of the intermediates were parthenogenetic, but one individu
found to contain a sexed egg. In discussing the phenomenon
intermediates, they gave it as their opinion that the partheno
individuals were those which up to their third stage were d
to become radicicoles, but in that stage changed their devel
to that of winged migrants, while the character of their eg
been already fixed before the change and so remained parther
tic. In the case of sexuparous intermediates the change wa
in the reverse direction, the larvæ at first being destined to
migrants and, therefore, when they matured as nymphica
deposited sexed eggs.

In California the recorded eggs laid by nymphicals were a
thenogenetic, but the possibility of some of such eggs being se
not entirely excluded, in the writers' opinion.

The nymphicals do not leave the roots in the manner
winged insects, and therefore deposit their ova on the roots.
case of sexuparous nymphicals, the sexes and winter egg
presumably develop underground. Whether in California
development occurs or not can not be stated from our present
edge, but in view of the fact that for many years the leaf gal
been unknown, it appears certain that such a cycle proce
further than the winter egg.

DEPOSITION OF THE SEXUAL EGGS.

The migrants deposit eggs (Pl. VIII, f, h, i) which are
kinds, viz. male and female, and from these eggs issue the true
aphids. Sexual eggs have never been found by the writers
vineyard, either on viniferæ or on resistant vines, although,
number of vines have been examined. In laboratory experir
large number of sexed eggs have been produced. Consideral
cussion has taken place among European writers as to the

location of the sexed eggs. Taking the sum of these discussions, it appears that they are placed on the underside of the leaves and more abundantly in the bark, generally between the year-old layer and that of the current year, and are fastened to the inner side of the former. Occasionally eggs are found at the base of canes where the new wood joins the old, and rarely on the vine supports (stakes). They are laid on both viniferæ and resistant vines, but preferably on the latter.

Observations were conducted in small cages, and in a few instances on living vines in pots. In the latter instances eggs were found laid on both the foliage and bark. Many different kinds of cages were used and experiments with different degrees of light, moisture, and temperature were conducted. Vine leaves and pieces of bark were inclosed in the cages. As a rule, the migrants, though primarily attracted to light, deposited their eggs in semidarkness. They laid them on the leaves and more rarely on pieces of bark offered, but often also on the sides, lid, and floor of the cages and in cracks. In 1911 the observations tabulated in Table XXVII occurred.

TABLE XXVII.—*Sexual production of the grape phylloxera, Walnut Creek, Calif., 1911.*

Number of migrants.	Date and location of migrants.	Number of sexual eggs deposited.[1]	Date of deposition.	Date of maturing of sexes.	Number of sexes matured.[2]
25	Aug. 4-6: Riparia vine in pot....................	16	Aug. 9	....	....
52	Aug. 7-8: Vinifera vine in pot...................	0			
65	Aug. 10-12: Riparia vine in pot..................	18	Aug. 16	Aug. 26	4
				Aug. 28	1
80	Aug. 13, 14: Vinifera vine in pot................	2	Aug. 15	Aug. 30	1
		1	Aug. 20	....	0
25	Aug. 15: Riparia vine in pot.....................	2	...do.....	....	0
36	Aug. 16: Riparia vine in pot.....................	5	...do.....	....	0
30	Aug. 17: Glass tube in drawer...................	0			
83	Aug. 18, 19: Riparia leaves in petri dish........	7	Aug. 21	Sept. 6	1
		5	Aug. 22	....	0
		12	Aug. 23	....	0
1	Aug. 19: Leaves in petri dish...................	1	Aug. 19	Aug. 30	1
7	Aug. 23: Leaves in petri dish...................	7	Aug. 23	Sept. 2	1
69	Aug. 24: Riparia leaves in laboratory...........	1	Aug. 25	....	0
		1	Aug. 26	....	0
		1	Aug. 27	....	0
		8	Aug. 28	....	0
		1	Aug. 29	....	0
30	Aug. 25, 26: Riparia leaves in petri dish........	1	Aug. 27	....	0
		6	Aug. 28	....	0
		1	Aug. 30	....	0
45	Aug. 25, 28, 29: Riparia leaves in petri dish....	7	Sept. 3	....	0
103	Sept. 2-17: Vinifera vine in pot.................	30	Sept. 25	Oct. 4	1
				Oct. 5	1
				Oct. 6	2
50	Sept. 19-23: Riparia vine in pot................	6	Sept. 29	....	0
40	Sept. 25-29: Riparia vine in pot................	0	....	....	....

[1] Thirteen female and three male eggs.
[2] All maturing sexuals were females.

TABLE XXVIII.—*Summary of Table XXVII.*

Number of migrants_____ 734
Number of sexual eggs deposited_____ 171
Number of sexual eggs hatched_____ 13

Individual egg deposition by migrants, recorded for 5 individuals, was as follows: 3, 2, 1, 4, and 3; average, 2.6. Obviously the great majority of migrants died without depositing eggs. The eggs above recorded were laid in from 2 to 9 days, the majority in from 3 to 5 days, after the migrants emerged from the nymphal skin. The great majority of the migrants did not live more than 3 days after casting their final molt, confinement evidently having caused premature death.

From 100 migrants produced August 15, 1912, and placed on a small vine August 20, a single egg, which failed to develop, was deposited August 24.

In 1913 different types of cages were utilized in an effort to induce a larger percentage of eggs and mature sexuals. The results were not encouraging. From July 17 to October 17 migrants were placed in the cages. During that time in some 60 experiments, 317 migrants were used, 99 sexual eggs were secured, and 7 sexed phylloxeræ (all females) matured. The migrants in no case lived more than 6 days, the majority only 3 days, and quite a number did not move their position after having been placed in the cages. In most cases eggs were laid singly, but there was one group of 5, three groups of 4, and several of 3 and 2, laid by single phylloxeræ. In two cases eggs, presumably of separate sexes, were deposited in the same group by the same individual, but in all other cases it appeared certain that the eggs laid by individual migrants were of only the one sex. Judging from the size, about twice as many female as male eggs were laid, besides quite a number (about 20 per cent) of eggs of an intermediate size. No male or intermediate sized eggs hatched, but it was noticed that the male eggs, as they developed, assumed a darker color than did those of the female. After a certain point in the development, all the moribund eggs began noticeably to shrink and turn dark brown. None of the eggs showed signs of infertility, and within about five days of deposition hatching occurred and the eyes and body segmentation were visible, after which the moribund individuals discolored and shrank rapidly. Dead migrants were found occasionally on the roots and sides of the cellar jars, beside eggs that they had deposited. In the vineyard such a procedure was never observed, and therefore it is believed to be quite abnormal, and probably results from the inability of the migrant to escape from the cellar jar after having been overlooked in the periodical examinations for migrants.

During the summer of 1914 a further series of experiments on the production of sexual eggs took place. The temperature that year was considerably below that obtaining in the years 1911 and 1913, and this may account for the lack of sexuals maturing. In 1914 the cages utilized in 1913 and some of other types were employed.

The experiments began June 27 and terminated September 7. Three hundred and ninety-seven migrants produced a total of 143 eggs from which no sexual forms developed. Thus the proportion of deposited eggs to migrants in 1913 was 1 to 3.2, while in 1914 it was 1 to 2.75, and in 1911, 1 to 4.3. In 1914 four migrants each deposited four eggs, and three eggs were deposited in nine instances, but most of the eggs were laid singly. In no case could it be definitely said that eggs of more than one sex occurred in individual groups. About three times as many female eggs as male were deposited, and about one-fourth of the eggs were intermediate in size (probably males). The winged sexuparæ died on the average two and one-half days after they were admitted to the cages, or about four days after they had transformed from the nymphal instar.

In 1915 experiments were continued, migrants being secured from June 26 to October 27. Part of these were used in stender and petri dishes, part in small circular rubber cells ($\frac{3}{16}$ inch high, $1\frac{1}{4}$ inches in diameter) mounted on microscope slides with cover glasses for lids, and a few on a living vine (Riparia). In the dishes small pieces of vine, bark, or leaves were placed, leaves of the Champini being used mostly on account of the fact that the migrants prefer to deposit eggs on a tomentous leaf. The effect of variations in temperature and humidity was noted.

A total of 1,961 migrants deposited in all 472 eggs, and 52 sexuals matured. Thus the proportion of eggs to migrants was approximately 1 to 4.15. In the stender and petri dishes and on the living vine combined, 938 migrants deposited 167 eggs, a proportion of 5.6 to 1, of which 16 sexuals matured. In the rubber cells mounted on microscope slides, 1,023 migrants deposited 305 eggs, a proportion of 3.3 to 1, and 36 sexed forms matured. The rubber cells therefore gave a greater proportion of eggs per migrant. Part of these cells were kept in a cellar and part inside a slide box in a room of the laboratory. The egg deposition was not appreciably different in these two situations, but the sexes under the almost constant temperatures of the cellar matured better than under the fluctuating temperatures of the room. Part of the dishes also were kept in the cellar and part exposed to light in the room. Those in the latter situation averaged more eggs per migrant, but the proportion of sexes which subsequently matured was similar to that of the migrants and dissimilar to that of the eggs.

It appeared at first that exposure to light induced the migrants to deposit a greater proportion of eggs and later appeared to have prevented a large proportion from maturing. Judging from the fact that the amount of light to which these eggs were subjected during their development was not greater than occurs under natural conditions, however, it would appear that this supposition is incorrect and that the disproportionate mortality among the eggs was caused rather by the uneven temperatures prevailing in the room. The presence or absence of humidity had no apparent effect on the deposition of eggs. Eggs and sexed forms developed better in dry than in moist rubber cells, but in the dishes exposed to light the converse occurred. Part of the migrants were stimulated to fly in the sunshine before being placed in the cages, and deposited a somewhat larger average number of eggs than those which had not flown, but the flight or nonflight of the migrants did not appear to influence the subsequent development of the eggs and sexes. In July and the first half of August, when the temperatures reached a maximum, there was a higher average in egg production and in the proportion of sexuals matured, yet during the period September 16 to October 27, despite lower temperatures, a larger average proportion of eggs per migrant and of mature sexes was produced than during the intermediate period from August 16 to September 15.

On the whole, development was most successful where migrants had flown and when eggs were kept in moderate light and in a moderately humid environment.

The longevity of the migrants, the number of eggs deposited per individual, and the proportion of male and female eggs laid coincided with the results of experiments in 1914.

It is only necessary to consider the very small proportion of eggs laid per migrant (in 1915, for instance, 1 to 4.15) and the very small proportion of eggs which succeeded in developing into mature sexes (in 1915, 1 in every 9) under artificial conditions to realize how abnormal these conditions must have been. From observations made in California during 1915 the complement of migrant eggs was found to average 2.6, so that if all the migrants in the experiments in that year had deposited their full complement, ten times as many eggs as were actually deposited would have been obtained. European experimenters have had, for the most part, similar results in their study of migrants in confinement.

In not a single instance was a migrant observed to deposit other than a sexual egg, so the possibility of the occurrence in California of a parthenoparous winged form may be regarded as excluded. There occurs, however, a parthenoparous nymphical form, which has been discussed above (p. 82).

THE SEXUAL FORMS.

The sexual forms (Pl. VIII, j–m), male and female, issue from eggs deposited by the winged sexuparæ or migrants. These eggs are of two types, male (Pl. VIII, f) and female (Pl. VIII, h, i). Writers have attempted to recognize a third type intermediate in size between the larger female and the smaller male egg, but these intermediate eggs are apparently always of the male sex. Thus there is a considerable variation in the dimensions of the male eggs, as, indeed, there is in those of the mature male insects. According to Grassi (11, p. 134–135) eggs producing females vary in length from 0.384 to 0.323 mm., and in width from 0.176 to 0.164 mm.; eggs producing males, in length from 0.247 to 0.250 mm., and in width from 0.152 to 0.134 mm. He also states that eggs of the intermediate dimensions are fertile and are of the male sex, and that male and female eggs may exceed the limits in one dimension, but never in two. On the average the female eggs were slightly larger than the radicicole eggs and the male eggs slightly smaller, but intermediate eggs had measurements identical with those of the radicicoles.

Measurements of sexual eggs, made in California in 1913, indicated a range in length from 0.450 to 0.257 mm., and in width from 0.171 to 0.117 mm. A single female of these hatched (0.357 by 0.171 mm.). In the light of measurements made in 1914 and 1915 it appeared that eggs of the sexes were similar in dimensions to those recorded by Grassi for Italy, except that the range in sizes was somewhat greater.

The sexual eggs are bright shining yellow. The eggshell is very thin and membranous, quite differently formed from that of the radicicole. The egg hatches after about four or five days' incubation, the process of hatching consisting in the sloughing off of the thin shell, the emerging aphid settling at the place of hatching. The eyes and body segmentation become visible, and the undeveloped appendages are carried under the body. The insect then undergoes four successive molts, and does not move away until it is mature. During the first three instars there appears but little change, except that the body segmentation becomes more distinct. After the third molt the appendages project slightly beyond the sides of the body, but otherwise no visible change occurs. All the molted skins are contained one within another, adhering to the posterior end of the body, and when the last molt has taken place the adult moves away, leaving the "nest" of telescoped skins and eggshell behind. It sometimes happens that the adult is unable to cast off this pad of skins. The mature sexuals are capable of running actively, and, according to European investigations, they may live for some weeks, thereby facilitating a meeting of the sexes. The sexuals take no nourishment. The female is slightly larger and the male slightly smaller than the newly hatched radicicole.

DESCRIPTION.

THE SEXUAL FEMALE.

Orange or orange yellow; antennæ and legs dusky grayish; antennæ longer than those of newly hatched radicicole. Body a little longer and wider than the young radicicole. Caudal segment bluntly rounded. Eyes as in the radicicole larva. When the adult issues the single egg within is small, but within three days it becomes very evident (Pl. VIII, j) and occupies in section an area equal to about three-fourths of the entire insect.

TABLE XXIX.—*Measurements of mature sexual females of the grape phylloxera.*

	1	2
	Mm.	*Mm.*
Length of body	0.357	0.464
Maximum width of body	.200	.215
Length of "winter" egg contained	.313	....
Maximum width of "winter" egg contained	.172	....
Antennal joint 1, right, length	.017	.0200
Antennal joint 1, left, length	.016	.0179
Antennal joint 2, right, length	.013	.0205
Antennal joint 2, left, length	.013	.0188
Antennal joint 3, right, length	.054	.0580
Antennal joint 3, left, length	.053	.0553

THE MALE.

Dusky orange, darker than the sexed female; antennæ, legs, and genital segment dusky grayish; eyes of three facets each, red; beak absent. Body quite noticeably shorter, flatter, and narrower than that of the sexed female, and shorter and narrower than that of the newly hatched radicicole. Genital organ acutely conical.

TABLE XXX.—*Measurements of mature males of the grape phylloxera.*

	1	2
	Mm.	*Mm.*
Length of body	0.260	0.334
Maximum width of body	.094	.154
Antennal joint 1, length	.013	....
Antennal joint 2, length	.018	....
Antennal joint 3, length	.065	.071
Hind tibia, length	.046	....
Hind femur, length	.056	....

In confinement both sexes at first exhibit a positive phototropism, but after a day of maturity they seek shaded places. At first they are quite active, but later become sluggish. Undoubtedly they are much less active in confinement than in the natural state.

Table XXXI summarizes the development of the sexed form in the summer and fall of 1911 and 1913. All those which reached the adult state were females.

TABLE XXXI.—*Summarized record of sex development of the grape phylloxera, Walnut Creek, Calif., 1911 and 1913.*

	Number of individuals.	Days.
Average incubation period	12	5
Average postembryonic period	12	5.83
Average period of development	20	11.05

In 1915, in all, there were reared to maturity 52 sexuals, of which 9 were males, 2 of these having hatched from eggs of intermediate dimensions. These 2 males were noticeably larger than the other 7. The majority of the sexuals were reared in darkness under cellar conditions, the temperatures never averaging over 70.5° F. and in one instance falling to 61.5° F. A noticeable phenomenon was the death of a great number of sexes during the fourth instar, which appeared to be due to their inability to cast the final skin as a result of a deficiency of moisture. Tables XXXII and XXXIII show the development of the sexes in 1915.

TABLE XXXII.—*Development of sexed forms of the grape phylloxera, Walnut Creek, Calif., 1915.*

Individual No.	Date of egg deposition.	Date of maturing of sexual.	Developmental period.	Sex.	Average temperature.	Environment.
			Days.		*° F.*	
1	July 17	July 28	11	♀	70.3	
2	do	do	11	♀	70.3	
3	do	do	11	♀	70.3	}Cellar.
4	do	July 30	13	♀	70	
5	do	do	13	♀	70	
6	July 18	July 28	10	♀	....	Room of laboratory.
7	July 22	Aug. 2	11	♀	70	
8	do	Aug. 3	12	♀	70	}Cellar.
9	do	do	12	♀	70	
10	July 30	Aug. 8	9	♀	....	Room of laboratory.
11	July 31	Aug. 10	10	♀	69.8	
12	do	do	10	♀	69.8	}Cellar.
13	Aug. 1	Aug. 12	11	♀	69.7	
14	do	do	11	♀	69.7	
15	do	do	11	♀	....	
16	do	do	11	♀	....	
17	do	Aug. 13	12	♀	....	
18	do	Aug. 14	13	♀	....	
19	Aug. 3	Aug. 12	9	♂	....	}Room of laboratory.
20	do	Aug. 13	10	♂	....	
21	do	do	10	♀	....	
22	do	do	10	♀	....	
23	do	Aug. 14	11	♀	....	
24	Aug. 4	Aug. 15	11	♀	69	
25	Aug. 5	Aug. 16	11	♂	68.8	
26	do	do	11	♀	68.8	
27	do	do	11	♂	68.8	
28	do	do	11	♂	68.8	
29	do	do	11	♀	68.8	
30	do	do	11	♀	68.8	
31	do	do	11	♀	68.8	
32	Aug. 6	Aug. 17	11	♀	68.5	
33	do	Aug. 18	12	♀	68.5	
34	do	do	12	♀	68.5	}Cellar.
35	do	Aug. 19	13	♀	68.6	
36	Aug. 25	Sept. 8	14	♂	68.7	
37	do	Sept. 9	15	♂	68.7	
38	Sept. 1	Sept. 15	14	♂	66.9	
39	Sept. 22	Oct. 4	12	♀	64.9	
40	Sept. 24	Oct. 9	15	♀	64.9	
41	do	do	15	♀	64.9	
42	do	Oct. 10	16	♀	64.8	
43	Sept. 26	Oct. 12	16	♀	64.3	
44	do	Oct. 13	17	♀	64.3	
45	Oct. 6	Oct. 21	15	♀	....	}Room of laboratory.
46	do	do	15	♀	....	
47	do	Oct. 22	16	♀	....	
48	Oct. 7	Oct. 24	17	♀	62	
49	do	Oct. 25	18	♀	62	
50	Oct. 13	Nov. 1	19	♀	61.5	}Cellar.
51	do	do	19	♀	61.5	
52	do	Nov. 3	21	♀	61.7	

TABLE XXXIII.—*Summary of Table XXXII.*

	Days.
Maximum developmental period	21
Minimum developmental period	9
Average developmental period	12. 73
Average developmental period, female	12. 65
Average developmental period, male	13. 10

During the developmental period preceding September the sexes developed in an average of 11.1 days, and in the remaining period, from September 1 to November 3, in 16.1 days.

The males appeared to develop more slowly than the females, but a larger series might not indicate such a difference.

The sexes, as soon as mature, were confined in a microscope-slide cell with a piece of vine bark and some filter paper. None lived more than three days, and copulation was observed in several instances, but on the whole the sexuals showed little activity and were not much attracted to each other. Several of the females partly extruded a winter egg, but chose no especial locality for oviposition, and their action was undoubtedly abnormal.

Mating is said to occur normally on the bark of the vine, the female depositing a single egg under and between the layers of bark. The egg is attached by a curved peduncle generally to the inner surface of the 2-year-old bark, but sometimes to older layers.

The Italian investigators found that eggs were most abundant about midway between the base and head of the vine trunk, but that they might be deposited on any wood of 2 or more years of age as well as on buds. The egg at first is greenish yellow, and later becomes greenish brown, remaining so until the time for hatching in the spring following. The phylloxeræ issuing from the winter egg are said always to become the gallicole (gall-inhabiting) stem mothers.

At Walnut Creek all types of vines exposed to phylloxera infestation have been searched exhaustively without more than a single winter egg being found. Among these vines were included viniferæ taken from phylloxerated vineyards, and viniferæ and American experimental vines grown in pots and boxes. The single egg brought to light was observed in December, 1912, located under the outside layer of bark of a young potted vine (Champenal). This egg, after having been kept under observation for three weeks, died.

From all observations in California it appears that conditions are unfavorable for the successful development of the sexual phylloxeræ and, therefore, for the " winter " egg and succeeding generations of gallicoles. Since in some parts of France a similar condition in the phylloxera cycle obtains, it was concluded that some factor was lacking to insure successful development, and there was reason to believe that humidity was one of the factors until the discovery of the existence of the gallicoles in Arizona under dry climatic conditions appeared to disprove this theory. At present it is held that the phylloxera in California is undergoing, and since it was first introduced (about 60 years ago) has continuously undergone, a marked change in habits resulting from variations in the character of its food. Wherever the phylloxera is attacking vinifera vines its habits are undergoing change. In many localities the production of sexuals, winter eggs, and gallicoles proceeds simultaneously with prolific agamous radicicole infestation, and in such places speedy difusion of the species obtains by reason of the winged insects and gallicole in addition to the wanderers. In California and in certain other localities the spread of the phylloxera has been slow, primarily because the danger from the agencies of the migrants and gall inhabitants has been very slight, and this notwithstanding the presence of resistant vines, the type on which the gallicoles normally form the galls and on which the " winter " eggs develop the more successfully. Thus it appears that the phylloxera, since it has been in California, has modified its habits to suit its environment, by exchanging the complicated life cycle on its native plants (native vines of eastern North America) for the more simplified life cycle upon *Vitis vinifera*.

THE GALLICOLE AND ITS RELATION TO CALIFORNIA CONDITIONS.

In the eastern United States, in Arizona, and in the majority of the phylloxera districts in Europe the gall form or gallicole occurs. This is most prevalent in the more humid districts, and occurs chiefly on American vines and American hybrids and only rarely on *Vitis vinifera* and its hybrids. Recent research in European countries, especially in Italy by Grassi and his colleagues, has proved that the original gallicole hatches from the winter egg deposited during the previous autumn by the sexed female in a crevice in the bark. This larva hatches with the appearance of the first leaves and attaches itself to the surface of a young leaf, where its punctures produce a " pocket " formation in the leaf tissue. In this pocket it grows, matures, and deposits its eggs. Upon hatching, the resultant larvæ seek young leaves higher up on the growing cane, and, settling on the surface, cause further pocket formations. Succeeding generations follow throughout the summer, the numbers being more and more reduced by predacious enemies (Syrphidae, Agromyzidae, Coccinellidae, etc.), and also by a certain percentage of the newly hatched larvæ deserting the cane for the roots. Among the later generations the percentage of larvæ that seek subterranean existence increases, and such larvæ may be differentiated by certain characteristics, when newly hatched, from those destined to continue on the foliage. They possess relatively longer beaks and a different antennal structure, including relatively larger sensoria. To these small larvæ has been given the name *neogallicolæ-radicicolæ* (young gall lice with root louse characteristics), while to the type which merely moves from one leaf to another younger one has been given the name *neogallicolæ-gallicolæ* (young gall lice with gall louse characteristics).

On the European vine (*Vitis vinifera*), according to Grassi, winter eggs were rarely laid and galls rarely found, the majority of those found being imperfect. It was apparent also that growth was much slower than on American vine foliage. In Italy, from eggs produced by nine gallicoles that had produced galls on a European vine, a few of the progeny had radicicole characteristics. This, however, was a rare occurrence, the great majority of young larvæ hatching in galls on European vines showing the gallicole characteristics and thus not being destined for subterranean life. The Italian investigators were able to cause radicicoles to settle and produce generations of gallicoles on the leaves of a Clinton (American) vine. This succeeded after several fruitless efforts. In this connection it may be said that, at Walnut Creek, on a small Golden Champion (American) vine, radicicoles ascending the stalk and ovipositing in crotches of the stem as high as 5 inches above the surface of the soil were observed in the fall of 1914. A few of the resulting larvæ settled still higher up on petioles. Finally cold weather in November ended this aerial infestation either by killing the larvæ or compelling them to descend below ground.

On July 16, 1913, a shipment of eight leaves of an American vine well infested with gallicoles was received from Vienna, Va. The gallicoles were egg-laying females, probably of the second generation (progeny of stem mothers), newly hatched larvæ, and large numbers of eggs. Only one adult occurred in each gall. Four of these leaves were placed contiguous to foliage of three resistant vines. The varieties were Riparia × Rupestris 3309, Columbaud × Riparia, and Solonis × Riparia. The first two named, small vines in pots, each were inoculated with one infested leaf; the third vine, larger and growing in the vineyard, was inoculated with two leaves. In no case were galls developed on the foliage of the three vines inoculated. It is to be recorded that these three vines were of a different type from the infested vine, but the Riparia type is susceptible to gallicole infestation.

On September 6, 1913, a selection of foliage of a Riparia hybrid infested with gallicoles was received from Washington, D. C. The following vines growing in the vineyard were inoculated with the infested foliage in close contiguity: Riparia × Rupestris 3309, Rupestris St. George, Rupestris × Berlandieri 301 A, Berlandieri × Riparia 34 E. M., Riparia × Cordifolia × Rupestris 111–8, Riparia

Gloire de Montpellier. The infested foliage had an abundant supply of newly hatched larvæ, but in no case did the inoculation succeed. It is possible, however, that many of the larvæ of such a late generation had radicicole characteristics, and therefore none such would' settle on the leaves. Both of the foregoing series of inoculations were made under conditions of light atmospheric humidity. Recent research in Italy (11, p. 335–345) (17) shows that in that country, at least, humidity and irrigation have much influence in the production of galls on resistant vines. Both the Riparia $\times$ Rupestris 3309, and the Rupestris St. George are said by Panatelli to produce many galls in dry locations. It appears, however, that in general a greater humidity is conducive to the production of gallicoles on resistant vines and their hybrids. Thus out of 24 well-known resistant varieties enumerated by Panatelli, 21 produced many galls and 3 few galls in humid localities, while in dry locations 10 produced no galls, 5 few galls, and 9 many galls (17). In this connection, it may be added that in California resistant vines have been frequently observed growing among badly infested viniferæ and never showing any sign of gall infestation. On no occasion, indeed, have the writers ever observed phylloxera galls in California, and there is only one authenticated case in California of gallicoles, that being the discovery in August, 1884, by Dr. F. W. Morse (16), of gall-inhabiting phylloxeræ on a Canada (labrusca $\times$ riparia $\times$ vinifera) vine on the University of California grounds at Berkeley.

The two shipments of gallicoles cited above were also used in experiments to determine whether this form would live on roots. On July 16, 1913, 75 newly hatched gallicoles were placed on two pieces of severed root (Zinfandel) in a petri dish in the cellar. On a third smaller root 100 eggs from the galls were located. On August 18, on the two larger roots, five phylloxeræ with the typical radicicole characteristics matured. On September 3 there were altogether seven mature egg-laying radicicoles, of which six had matured on the two larger roots. Thus out of 100 eggs and 75 newly hatched larvæ only seven phylloxeræ matured.

On September 6 a similar experiment was begun on severed roots in the cellar. On two roots 75 eggs apiece were placed. These all turned black and none hatched, it appearing that the embryo suffered injury through fermentation that developed during the transcontinental journey. This supposed fermentation did not affect the larvæ already hatched and which were used for the foliage experiment.

A further experiment took place on roots of a living vine (Thompson's Seedless) which was inoculated July 16 with 50 eggs. Three insects from this inoculation matured August 12, 13, and 14. They were typical radicicoles and laid eggs at the rate of between two and three daily, at first exceeding that number. These eggs were typical radicicole eggs, and produced further radicicole generations. Twelve of the eggs laid August 21–24 were transferred to another root of the same vine (Thompson's Seedless) and four insects matured between September 28 and October 5, after an average egg stage of about seven and one-half days and an average growing period of 35 days. The progeny of these four became hibernants, several of which matured and oviposited the following spring. These experiments demonstrate that under California conditions it is possible for larvæ hatching in galls to mature on the roots and become typical radicicoles. No observations were noted regarding the characteristics of the newly hatched gallicoles used in the experiments. After the inoculation, July 16, of 50 eggs on the root of the living vine it was seen that most of these eggs turned dark brown and failed to hatch. The observations on the hatching of this batch of eggs indicate that those failing to hatch were the earliest deposited, and it may be that the change in conditions and environment affected the embryonic development adversely.

The present nonappearance in California of the gallicole and its work on the foliage of grapevines, a condition paralleled in certain portions of Europe, vitally affects the entire biology of the insect, since it has been ascertained that the phylloxera issuing from the winter egg can only exist on the leaf or petiole as a gallicole. The Italian investigators Grassi, Topi, Grandori, and Foa found that no larvæ hatching from winter eggs fastened on the roots and that all of this generation of stem mothers (fundatrices) had the gallicole characteristics. This is a very important biological point. It is borne out by observations in those parts of Europe where the gall form is absent and in which winter eggs are extremely rare. It is similarly borne out in the phylloxera regions of California, where similar conditions occur. During the winters of 1912–13 and 1913–14, an extensive series of vines, large and small, of all types, many of which had been infested the previous summer with winged phylloxeræ, and others which, while themselves uninfested, had been growing near such infested vines, were examined. With only one exception, no trace of winter eggs or dead sexuals was found. This exception consisted in the single winter egg noted under the preceding heading.

EFFECTS OF WATER AND HEAT ON PHYLLOXERA.

Experiments were carried out to determine (1) the resistance of hibernant larvæ and eggs to water heated to various temperatures, (2) the resistance of hibernant larvæ to submersion in water at ordinary temperatures, and (3) the resistance of eggs to the heat of the sun.

During the winter of 1913–14, two experiments were made on the resistance of hibernants to hot water. The temperatures used ranged from 116° to 137° F., and the duration of submergence ranged from one to four minutes. A temperature of 120° F. failed to destroy the aphids completely, while 125° F. with a submergence of one minute destroyed all the insects. Similar treatment of the roots of living vines resulted in no appreciable injury to dormant plants.

The same winter, between December 3 and March 17, a series of nine experiments were carried out bearing upon the resistance of hibernant larvæ to submersion in water of ordinary temperatures. Pieces of heavily infested grape roots were placed in petri dishes under about 1 inch of water. The periods of submersion ranged from 48 hours (two days) to 1,512 hours (nine weeks). It was found that with the lengthening of the submersion period the percentage of aphids succumbing increased. A submersion of six weeks, however, resulted in the destruction of only 72 per cent of the aphids, one of five weeks in 64 per cent mortality, the final test (that of nine weeks) alone destroying all the aphids. In tests of from 48 to 168 hours' submergence the temperature of the water averaged 47° F., in the final test of nine weeks it averaged 55° F., and in four intermediate tests of from three to six weeks, 53° F.

In the light of the results of this series of tests the fact that a practical vineyard submersion requires at least two months' flooding is not a cause for wonder.

An observation made during the winter of 1913–14, from December to February, showed that hibernant larvæ can withstand short intermittent submersions in water interrupted by periods of low temperatures, even passing below 32° F.

On June 9, 1914, two experiments were conducted, bearing on the resistance of eggs of the radicicole to heated water. In four of these tests the length of submersion was 90 seconds, and the temperatures ranged from 112.1° to 131° F.; in the other seven, the eggs were submerged 60 seconds under temperatures varying from 108.5° to 132° F. Results showed that a temperature of 123° F., with an exposure of 60 seconds, destroyed all eggs. For practical use it is desirable to have a temperature of at least 125° F.

In the experiments the eggs after treatment were placed on pieces of vine roots and observed for possible development. Temperatures of 123° F. or over killed the eggs immediately, but the lesser temperatures killed none or only a variable percentage. Those eggs not killed hatched normally.

During June and July, 1914, a series of tests was made with radicicole eggs exposed to atmospheric temperatures varying from 76° to 90° F. for periods varying from 5 to 60 minutes. With a shade temperature of 90° F., eggs exposed to sunlight were killed in 20 minutes. At a shade temperature of 76° F., 40 minutes' exposure to direct sunlight killed all aphids, but when placed in the shade the eggs resisted the maximum test of 60 minutes' exposure.

It is therefore apparent that eggs can resist the sun's rays to a considerable extent. The extent of their resistance to atmospheric temperatures in the shade can not be estimated, though it is of course greater than their resistance to direct sunlight. The eggs utilized in these tests were selected at random, and therefore were in various stages of embryonic development.

Experiments with the submersion in water of active newly hatched larvæ are detailed under the heading "Diffusion," which follows.

DIFFUSION OF PHYLLOXERA.

In European countries four natural means of diffusion are recognized: (1) By the winged insect; (2) by newly hatched wandering larvæ issuing from the soil; (3) by newly hatched wandering larvæ traveling through the soil; (4) by the gall-inhabiting form. To these there should be added casual means, as follows: Cultivating instruments, vine supports and picking boxes, plants between the vines, man and domestic animals, water, cuttings and rooted vines, phylloxerated land, and old stumps.

DIFFUSION BY FLIGHT.

Comparing the slower diffusion of the phylloxera in California with that of certain European vine-growing sections, it was from the first doubted that the winged form was a common diffusing agency, in spite of the fact that its production is often abundant in California vineyards on the roots of vines the second and third years after the initial infestation. This doubt became strengthened by (1) lack of leaf galls in nature and failure to discover winter eggs on a large number of vines of different varieties known to have been infested by migrants, or to have been close to vines thus infested; (2) the fact that, in confinement, during five years, thousands of migrants were utilized and only 72 sexual forms were secured, and, in turn, no normal winter eggs. On comparing the researches of European observers it is found, however, that in most cases they were unable to raise the sexual forms in confinement in any numbers, so this second point is inconclusive.

Grassi (11, p. 138–148) and his colleagues demonstrated that the insect which hatches from the winter egg always settles on the young vine leaf and becomes the gall-making stem mother (gallicole). They also found (11, p. 274–280) that there occurred a nymphlike form which deposited parthenogenetic eggs from which issued root-feeding insects. This form generally occurred on resistant vines, but also on viniferæ along with the sexuparous migrants. The individuals exhibited much diversity in development, ranging from those with large wing pads to others bearing no vestige of wing pads, but having more fully developed eyes than the typical adult radicicoles. In nearly every case their eggs were parthenogenetic, the resultant larvæ becoming root feeders. This form has been styled "intermediate," in that it is intermediate in structure between the radicicole and the winged form. Observations indicate that it occurs rather infrequently in California. It has been discussed under the heading "Nymphicals or intermediate forms" (p. 82). All the fully winged individuals observed in California which deposited eggs were sexuparous.

To sum up, it is not believed that in California there is diffusion through the winged form. It is perhaps worth while to record some observations upon the behavior of the insects of this form in the vineyard. During July and August, 1914, these occurred in a Zinfandel vineyard badly infested with phylloxera. Previously roots of many of the vines on lighter soil had been dug up, and it had been found that a large production of migrants was developing, especially on vines having the external appearance of not being badly phylloxerated. The condition of the roots on this type indicated that phylloxeration had not been in progress more than two years and the tuberosities had not reached a stage of advanced decay; but phylloxeræ were abundant, and it was evident that another year would find the vines much less thrifty. Sticky paper, tacked to boards, was placed in the vineyards, both on the surface of the ground in a horizontal position and in a vertical position. The horizontal papers were placed beside infested vines at distances varying from 6 inches to 5 feet from the trunks. The vertical boards were placed throughout the infested part and outside of the vineyard and extended from the soil surface to a height of $7\frac{1}{2}$ feet. More winged migrants were obtained on horizontal boards than on the vertical boards in proportion to a given area of paper. The majority of migrants caught on the horizontal boards were found at the edges, indicating that they reached the papers by walking rather than by flight. In some cases where individuals were found in the middle of the sticky papers it appeared that these might have fallen down from canes of the vine above, but in many instances the phylloxeræ obviously had reached the papers by flight or had been blown thither by the wind. Those on the vertical papers had either been borne by the wind or had flown voluntarily. On the vertical boards facing away from the prevailing wind no migrants were caught. Vertical boards with sticky paper were placed in the vineyard on the following dates: June 20; July 7, 10, 13, 21, 24, 31;

August 3, 7, 11, 14, 17, 20, 21, 31. Horizontal boards were placed
July 10, 13, 21, 24, 31; August 7, 11, 14, 17, 21, 25, 31; September
5, 11, 26.

On the vertical boards eight migrants were captured between July
13 and August 21, and on the horizontal boards, between July 10 and
August 17, 51 were taken. The area of paper exposed on the vertical
boards was 63,725 square inches, almost 50 square yards, while that
of the horizontal boards was 7,625 square inches, not quite 6 square
yards. The papers kept sticky for about four days on the average.
Considering the comparatively large number of migrants captured
on the limited areas of sticky paper, there must have been a
heavy infestation throughout the vineyard. Winged phylloxeræ were
observed on and about the bases of vine trunks, and many were
caught in spider webs and died. Whether the migrants deposit the
sexual eggs in the vineyard or not, the total absence of galls on
the vines (viniferæ and resistants) surely indicates that such eggs
come to nought.

From rather meager observations it appears that the sexuals require
a high temperature, coupled with considerable humidity, for their
successful development, and that the climatic conditions of California lack the requisite combination.

DIFFUSION BY NEWLY HATCHED RADICICOLES ISSUING FROM THE SOIL.

In the summer of 1868, Faucon, in France, observed young radicicoles wandering over the surface of the soil following a heavy rain,
which had caused the soil to crack open in drying. He also observed
the phylloxeræ to enter cracks and disappear. In 1872, he again
observed these phenomena between August 4 and September 30. The
year following, his observations were made from June 14 to September 13, so that he was able to see wandering larvæ during a period of
three months. In 1876, Boiteau, in France, confirmed the observations of Faucon, adding that he found that the greatest number of
wanderers issued from vines at the periphery of the phylloxera
" spot." Since then other observers have discussed the phenomenon
of "wanderer" diffusion. Grassi (11, p. 351, 138, 148) and his colleagues, working from 1907 to 1911, conducted a series of experiments
with the wandering larvæ. They found that these were strongly
attracted to light and that in walking over the soil surface they did
not go in a straight line, but deviated according to the variations of
the surface. On a piece of glass they proceeded in a straight line and
covered a distance of about 2 cm. the first minute.

As regards inoculation of vines by these wandering young, successful experiments were carried out in Europe on vines in pots, it
being found that the wanderers penetrated the cracks formed between the inside periphery of the pot and the drying soil and infested

the rootlets growing in contact with the pot. Experiments showed that when sand was dry it obstructed the wanderings of the phylloxeræ, but when moistened the phylloxeræ might be drawn through it with the water. It was also found that in sandy soils water might occupy all the interstices between the grains of sand, repelling the phylloxeræ, whereas in soils of other types air cavities existed sufficient to enable the phylloxeræ to live.

In California the wandering larvæ were first observed in glass jars in which were kept phylloxerated roots in the summer of 1913. When such jars were removed from the darkness of the cellar to a light room, young larvæ were observed wandering up the sides of the jars. In the dark cellar such wandering took place, but after light was admitted to the jar the wandering became much accentuated. Similar wandering of larvæ was observed in the cages used for observations on living roots (Pls. V, VI, fig. 1; VII).

Until 1914 no vineyard observations in this direction had been made, but in that year wanderers were observed in their normal state. For these observations, vines in a phylloxera "spot" in a Zinfandel vineyard 10 years old were selected. This "spot" was situated on light clay loam upon sloping ground, and within its confines wandering larvæ were observed during July and August. These were found in greatest numbers coming from vines near the outer edge or periphery of the "spot." Such vines had little external evidence of phylloxeration, but upon examination it developed that the roots were heavily infested and produced many migrants as well as wanderers. From vines obviously moribund a smaller number of wanderers appeared. Wanderers also were obtained on the same horizontal boards with sticky papers on which migrants were caught. These were captured close to the edge of the sticky substance and never farther from it than 6 mm., and it appeared that all those taken had crawled to the papers and that none had been borne on the wind. On vertical papers, not even when placed within 2 feet of the wanderers, and to the leeward of them, were any phylloxeræ captured. It was observed, however, that on favorable occasions wanderers are easily borne off by gusts of wind. The part of the vineyard in which wanderer activity occurred was moderately well cracked through drying. On the horizontal sticky papers wanderers were caught at points from a few inches from the vine trunk to 5 feet from the nearest vine and directly in the center of a square described with a vine at each angle. In this latter case either the phylloxeræ had ascended by the trunk of the vines, and then walked 5 feet, or else they had ascended by means of cracks nearer the paper. In either case it is obvious that the spread of a given phylloxera "spot" may result from the activities of these wanderers without the agency of wind.

Wanderers were first caught on sticky papers July 21 and first observed alive in the vineyard August 11. After August 18, no more were caught on the sticky papers, and after August 25, no more were observed alive. The weather during July and August was for the most part bright and warm. In the vineyard the wanderers were observed in by far the greatest abundance near the trunks of the vines, and it appeared that they had reached the soil surface by following up the roots. No wanderers were observed on the aerial portions of the vines themselves. They showed much activity, wandering aimlessly around over the soil. They seemed to prefer the shaded parts, but appeared also on ground surface exposed to the sun. Large numbers were found dead close to the vine trunks, and these occurred in places where the soil was very fine, indicating that the phylloxeræ were unable to progress in fine soil. Laboratory experiments bore out this supposition. Many others became caught in spider webs stretched over the soil surface. The character of the soil in the vineyard in August, 1914, was such as to enable phylloxeræ to pass from one vine to another without necessarily encountering very fine soil, as no cultivation had been practiced since May, 1914, and the vineyard had been cultivated previously only in one direction.

As regards the capture of wandering larvæ upon sticky papers, the data given in Table XXXIV are of interest:

TABLE XXXIV.—*Wandering larvæ of the grape phylloxera; diffusion in vineyard; Walnut Creek, Calif., 1914.*

Date caught on paper.	Number of wandering larvæ caught.	Distance from nearest vine trunk.	Area of sticky paper on which phylloxeræ were caught.
		Feet.	*Square inches.*
July 21–24	3	5	135
July 24–28	1	2	135
July 31–Aug. 3	20	2	135
Do	1	5	135
Aug. 7–11	2	2	135
Aug. 11–15	1	½	135
Aug. 14–18	1	2	135

During the period from July 21 to August 18 many sheets of sticky paper 135 square inches in area (9 by 15) were placed on the surface of the ground, and wanderers were caught on 7 (see above) out of 32 papers. In the majority of instances the individuals were caught on the side of the paper toward the nearest vines, which would indicate that they arrived there straight from the trunk of the vine. On sides of the paper facing vines farther away it would be natural to expect fewer wanderers when one considers how the circumference of a circle increases in proportion to its radius, and also the comparatively equal diffusion of wanderers in all radii, if the vine trunk is considered as the central point. On two occasions wanderers were caught on paper placed equidistant (5 feet) from four trunks of infested vines. Examinations showed that between one vine and another, even of apparently equal phylloxeration, a great variation in the production of wanderers took place. It also appeared that there was a tendency to produce these forms all at one time as though they had collected in a mass and then issued all together. As regards the time of day at which they were most abundant, it appeared that more might be observed between 10 a. m.[11] and 1 p. m. than at other daylight hours. European observers found that in general the wandering larvæ appeared in greatest abundance in the early afternoon, which is the hottest part of the day.

Vineyard observations were continued in 1915. The same vineyard was used, but more attention was paid to phylloxerated vines on the parts in which the soil was a heavy black clay. On this heavy soil no wanderers appeared before July 24, and none was found after July 29. The larvæ also were always very scarce, notwithstanding the fact that the soil contained numerous cracks which would enable the wanderers to reach the surface. On the lighter soil (clay loam), wandering larvæ first appeared July 14, and they continued to issue until August 18. During this period of over a month about two-thirds of the phylloxerated vines examined were producing wanderers. Between July 15 and 21 they were most abundant, as many as 20 or 30 living individuals being visible at one time beside the more heavily infested vines. In August hundreds of dead larvæ could be seen on the surface of the soil around the bases of the vine trunks, and large numbers were caught in spider webs. As in the previous year, the vines bearing the largest numbers of wanderers were those of recent phylloxeration.

In 1915, during the period of wanderer activities, the weather was for the most part quite hot and dry. Occasionally there were cool days, and on these the wanderers appeared to be as active as on the hot days.

It appeared certain that the great majority of the wandering larvæ ascended to the light by way of the main trunk of the vines, around which there occurred almost always a wide crack. More issued from Zinfandel vines than from Carignan vines equally phylloxerated, perhaps because the Zinfandel had thrown out more fleshy rootlets in May and June, and these had decayed in July while heavily infested. It would thus appear that many of the wandering larvæ are produced on these surface fleshy rootlets and leave them because they have become overcrowded or have started to decay.

In each of the years 1914 and 1915 wandering larvæ appeared in the vineyard over the same period, i. e., from the middle of July to

---

[11] All references to clock time refer to " Standard time."

the end of the third week in August. The condition of the soil was about the same in both years, moisture being somewhat higher than usual because of extra heavy precipitation each spring. The retention of moisture near the soil surface tends to produce many fleshy rootlets, and these in turn produce abundant nymphs and wandering larvæ. Thus a wet spring results in the early production of migrants and wandering larvæ.

A number of laboratory observations were made on the wandering larvæ. From these it appeared that the insects were capable of walking as much as 14 feet on a smooth surface, provided a strong light attraction was present. On fine soil their appendages became clogged very soon, and prevented further locomotion, but on hard surfaces, they progressed successfully. On warm surfaces they easily became "baked" to death, and in fact always lived the longest when least exposed to the sun, as the heating of the surface soil killed the aphids. Larvæ easily passed over wet sand and were able to make headway on dry sand, but could not penetrate sand. It was found that the larvæ could remain alive at least for three days, wandering around partly upon the soil and partly in cracks in the soil in a flowerpot subjected to an average amount of direct sunlight.

During the summer and autumn of 1914 a number of young rooted vines were planted in 9-inch pots, and these were inoculated during May and June by burying phylloxerated roots around the stalk or by transferring eggs to the larger roots. These vines included viniferæ, American nonresistants, and resistants. On the top of these pots and resting on the earth were fitted tightly circular pieces of wood with a hole in the center, through which passed the stalk of the vine. The whole aerial portion of the vine was inclosed in a muslin cage. This construction was designed to compel phylloxeræ ascending to the soil surface to make their way through the hole around the stalk; and having done so, they would be unable to escape by reason of the white muslin cage and would soon die. In October and November these cages were examined, and in some of them small numbers of dead wanderers were found, in others none, and in still others very large numbers. Those containing dead wanderers in abundance were the ones in which the vines had been fertilized with chemical fertilizers, and there was also a corresponding abundance of winged migrants from such vines. The action of the fertilizers produced many migrants and many wanderers and invigorated the vines, yet in all cases a large root infestation by wingless forms persisted through the winter following. In the cages above mentioned fertilizers, in liquid form, were applied periodically during the summer. In 1915 a similar series of vines were fertilized with solid fertilizers at the time of planting in early spring, and later observations showed that wanderers were no more abundant on fertilized than on check, unfertilized vines. On young vines in pots wanderers were often observed to ascend the vine stalks to 6 inches above the soil surface, and in one instance on an American nonresistant vine (Golden Champion) several of them fastened on the bark and matured there (1914). This vine was never exposed to the brightest light and, moreover, during 1914, within a. radius of 4 inches from its stalk was placed a glass cylinder, around the bottom of which was fastened 2 inches of black paper, so .that the stem of the vine received little light. In 1915 the glass cylinder and black paper were removed and no wanderers settled on the aerial portion, although from June 29 to September 10 a limited number of them could be seen almost daily ascending the stalk to about 6 inches as in the previous year.

During 1913 and 1914 many instances were observed of wanderers infesting the rootlets in the pots. used in the cages for observations on living vines (Pls. V–VII). In these cases the wanderers were produced on the exposed portions of the roots, and wandering off these, they found themselves on the surface of the soil in the pots. They then proceeded to pass down through the cracks around the inside periphery of the pot, where the soil had dried, and finally reached the rootlets growing against the inside of the pot. Such infestations occurred on rootlets from the surface to the total depth of 9 inches. This infestation occurred during July, August, and September, and in November, when the vines were pulled up, most of the nodosities produced by the phylloxeræ had rotted. In some cases rootlets appeared above the soil around the periphery of the pot, and these were infested easily and abundantly through the agency of wandering larvæ. In the pots in which quartz had been substituted for earth for experiments with fertilizers, the wanderers were able to find their way down to the rootlets, although the cracks in the quartz were fewer and narrower than in the earth. It may be mentioned that the earth used in the pots in 1913 was a rather heavy dark loam, mixed with sandy loam, and in 1914 only the heavy dark loam was used. A layer of gravel and sand about one-fourth inch thick was laid on the surface, but this did not prevent cracking around the inside periphery of the pot. The heavier soil of 1914 seemed to allow of easier passage for the wanderers.

In the spring and summer of 1914 three vine section cages containing cuttings were placed together in a trench. Two of these were infested with phylloxeræ throughout May and June. On July 18 it was found that a vine in the third cage was infested with two egg-laying adults, each situated on a nodosity. The vines in this section cage never had been inoculated, and it is certain that their infestation was caused by two wanderers from an adjoining cage. It was judged that this infestation must have occurred about June 20, when many eggs were hatching in the adjoining cages and many rootlets decaying, thus compelling the newly hatched larvæ to seek food elsewhere.

INOCULATIONS WITH WANDERERS.

On July 31, 1913, 30 wandering larvæ were taken from jars in the cellar and placed on pieces of sound severed roots in a petri dish. On August 13, 25 half-grown phylloxeræ found roaming around in jars were added. All the latter deserted the roots and died, but of the former, three matured August 25 to September 18. A later inoculation (Sept. 25) with 40 young wanderers resulted in none of these remaining. Another similar experiment was tried on September 29, with 40 young wanderers, but it also failed. Thus out of 135 individual wanderers only three matured.

In 1914 this experiment was repeated, and two pieces of sound severed roots were inoculated in a petri dish, one with 8, the other with 40 wanderers. In this case a layer of moist sand was placed below the roots, whereas in 1913, only filter paper had been used. Of the smaller lot 1 and of the larger lot 20 matured. Thus On August 28, 15 wanderers from jars in the cellar were placed on the living root of a Tokay, and 3 of these hibernated and developed the following spring.

In the autumn of 1913 an attempt was made to inoculate the roots of sound potted vines by means of wandering larvæ placed upon the surface of the soil in the pots. For this purpose, 35 wanderers were placed on the soil of each of four potted vines (Resistant hybrid, Sept. 18; Agawam, Sept. 23; Burger, Sept. 26; Thompson's Seedless, Oct. 6). In no case did the wanderers succeed in inoculating the roots. The soil, however, contained extremely few cracks.

The following year this phase was pursued further. Sound pieces of roots were planted 4 inches below the surface in four 9-inch pots. On July 8, 30 wanderers were placed on the soil surface of the first pot, the soil being cracked from having been watered the previous day. The root below was never infested. The soil of the second pot was watered to cause it to crack extensively. After it became well cracked about 25 wanderers were shaken on it, July 8. An examination of the root, August 25, showed it to be infested with a thriving colony of phylloxeræ. In the third pot the soil was not watered; consequently there was no cracking. On July 12, 50 wanderers were shaken out on the surface. No infestation of the root below occurred. The soil of the fourth pot was watered sparingly, and few cracks were formed. July 17, 12 wanderers were shaken onto the soil. No infestation of the root below occurred. Only one out of the four experiments resulted positively, and in that one the soil was very well cracked, affording access to the root.

Inoculation of the wanderers on living vines was attempted through the following experiments: Five lots of four vinifera vines each were planted, two on light sandy loam and three on heavy clay loam. The vines were all young rooted vines, and they were planted roughly in the form of squares during the month of June. In the center in each one of four of the groups a phylloxerated vine (potted) was put in the ground at varying distances from the four surrounding vines. In one group the four outside vines were distanced, respectively, 14 inches, 2 feet, 3 feet, 3½ feet from the central vine. In a second group they were distanced, respectively, 2, 3, 4, and 6 feet from the central vine. In the third group they were distanced, respectively, 2, 4, 6, and 8 feet from the central vine. In the fourth group they were distanced, respectively, 2, 3, 4, and 6 feet from the central vine. In the fifth group the four vines were potted, and in place of an infested central vine, infested roots were buried 1, 2, 3, and 4 feet, respectively, from the outside vines. In this last case the vines were potted to prevent possibility of underground inoculation. The four central vines remained infested throughout the summer, but it was not disclosed that they, or the buried roots, produced any wandering larvæ above the surface. The surface of the soil in the area used for these experiments was kept well cracked. In no instance did the 20 outside vines become infested.

In 1915, field experiments were conducted in a vineyard which had several large phylloxera " spots " both on light and heavy soils. The light soil might be described as a silt loam with a clay admixture, and the heavy soil was black, sticky clay. In spring a number of sound rooted vinifera vines 1 year old were procured and planted in 5-gallon kerosene cans from which one side had been cut. Different types of soil were used in these cans. The vines thus planted were kept apart until July, when they were carried out to the vineyard selected and planted level with the soil at varying distances from vineyard vines from which wandering larvæ were known to be issuing. To insure cracking of the soil, water was applied to the soil surface and also to the soil between the cans and the near-by vine. Wandering larvæ were observed in this vineyard from the middle of July to August 20. In September, after the wandering of the larvæ had ceased, the cans were dug up. Table XXXV gives the results of this experiment.

TABLE XXXV.—*Field experiments on inoculation of vines by wandering larvæ of the grape phylloxera, Walnut Creek, Calif., 1915.*

No. of vine.	Type of soil in can.	Variety of vine.	Date of planting can in vineyard.	Date of taking up can in vineyard.	Distance of vine in can from trunk of infested vine in vineyard.	Result.
					Feet.	
1 1	Silt loam	Mission	July 14	Sept. 8	2	Uninfested.
1 2	....do		..do....	Sept. 9	2	
3	....do		..do....	Sept. 17	1	
4	....do	Zinfandel	July 15	Sept. 8	1½	
5	....do		..do....	...do....	5	
6	....do		July 17	Sept. 9	2	Infested.
7	....do		..do....	Sept. 15	1½	
8	Heavy black loam, 2 parts; silt, 1 part	Carignan	..do....	Sept. 9	1	Uninfested.
1 9	....do		July 20	Sept. 15	4	
10	....do		..do....	...do....	1½	
11	Heavy black clay loam		July 21	Sept. 9	1½	Infested.
12	....do		..do....	Sept. 17	1½	
13	....do	Zinfandel	..do....	Sept. 15	5	
1 14	Sandy silt	Zinfandel	July 22	...do....	4	
15	....do		..do....	Sept. 17	2½	
1 16	....do		..do....	Sept. 15	2½	
17	Pure sand		..do....	...do....	2½	
18	Heavy black clay loam		July 24	...do....	1	
19	Sandy silt		..do....	...do....	1	
20	Heavy black loam, 2 parts; silt, 1 part	Carignan	..do....	...do....	1½	
21	Heavy black loam, 1 part; silt, 1 part		..do....	Sept. 8	8	
22	Heavy black clay loam	Zinfandel	..do....	...do....	4	
23	Sandy silt		..do....	Sept. 15	1	
24	Heavy black loam, 2 parts; silt, 1 part	Carignan	..do....	...do....	3	Uninfested.
25	....do		July 27	Sept. 17	¾	
26	Heavy black loam, 1 part; silt, 1 part		..do....	...do....	4	
27	....do		..do....	...do....	2	
1 28	Pure sand		..do....	...do....	1½	
29	Sandy loam	Zinfandel	..do....	...do....	1½	
30	....do		..do....	...do....	5	
31	Heavy black loam, 1 part; silt, 1 part		July 29	...do....	2	
32	Heavy black clay loam		..do....	...do....	2	
33	Sandy silt		..do....	...do....	2	

1 Entire vines died shortly after having been planted in vineyard, therefore can not be included in results of experiment.

Of the 27 vines which were alive when the cans were taken up, 21 had been planted in the phylloxera "spot" on light soil and 6 in phylloxera "spots" on heavy black clay. None of the latter and only 4 of the former group became infested. Vine 6 was examined September 9, and an infestation consisting of 1 adult radicicole and about 12 larvæ was found. This indicated that a single wanderer had established itself on the vine. On vine 11, on the same date, there were found 3 adults and about 20 larvæ. On vine 12 on September 17 there were 6 adults and about 200 larvæ, besides many eggs. On vine 13 on September 15 there were over 350 phylloxeræ, including some 50 adults. Vines 11, 12, and 13 were planted around the same infested vine. In the case of vine 13 the infestation was started either by a large number of wandering larvæ in August or more likely by one or two wanderers directly after the vine was planted on July 21. Since in August the phylloxera generation cycle may be passed in less than 22 days, and since each mature radicicole may average 8 eggs per diem for several weeks, it would have been possible for the infestation on vine 13 to have developed from a single wanderer. Similarly, it is possible that the infestations on vines 11 and 12 originated with one individual each.

In all of four inoculated vines the infestations were confined to the larger roots, and there was no nodositous infestation such as occurred with wanderer inoculations in potted vines at the laboratory. This is explained by the fact that the soil in the cans did not crack deeply enough to reach the rootlets (none of which came near the soil surface) while it cracked badly around the base of the stems of the vines. It is therefore most probable that the wandering larvæ passed down the vine stem. Cracks of 1 foot or more in depth were quite abundant in the vineyards in July and August, and it was possible to find rootlets such as form nodosities when punctured by phylloxeræ at a depth of 6 inches from the soil surface. At that time of year there is generally in the vineyards a wide crack about the base of the vines, and it is through these cracks that the great majority of the wandering larvæ ascend to the surface. In the vineyard a wanderer could never be kept under observation long enough to be sure that it entered a crack permanently, therefore, with the purpose of seeking a root. Wanderers readily enter any crack which they can not bridge but frequently reappear after a short period of time. In pots they have been observed to enter whatever cracks they encountered, subsequently inoculating roots buried below. In other experiments with pots the wandering larvæ have been found to crawl down the crack between the soil and the inner side of the pot and inoculate the rootlets growing around the inside of the pots. Also it has been observed that in the vineyard experiments the inoculation was probably made by the wanderers crawling down the stem, since no other available cracks were favorable. In the vineyard, therefore, it is assumed that the wanderers enter the first crack they encounter.

In the experiments of 1914 with sticky papers, wandering larvæ were captured at varying distances up to 5 feet from the nearest infested vine. The four inoculated vines the year following were 2, $1\frac{1}{2}$, $1\frac{1}{2}$, and 5 feet, respectively, from the nearest infested vines. It should be said that there was a possibility that the infestations were inoculated by wanderers coming from infested vines at a greater distance. In the instance of the three inoculated vines planted in cans around one single vineyard vine it is reasonably certain that all three became inoculated from the central vine. From this vine large numbers of wanderers were observed to issue.

No vines were planted more than $5\frac{1}{2}$ feet away from a vineyard vine, the vineyard being planted 8 by 8 feet.

The soils used in the cans were of different types, but no satisfactory conclusions were drawn from this feature. It was noted that the vines planted in lighter soils grew poorly and that the percentage that died was greater than in the case of heavy soils.

In 1914, wanderers were taken from jars in the laboratory cellar and successfully colonized on pieces of roots. It was found that they developed into the usual type of radicicole phylloxeræ. In order to ascertain definitely the future of wanderers observed in the vineyard a thrifty section of sound grape root was transported to the vineyard on July 17, 1915, and 12 larvæ, wandering upon the surface of the soil, were placed thereon. Four of these subsequently matured as wingless radicicoles between August 23 and 27, and before the advent of winter a considerable colony was established. A contemporary experiment of similar nature was carried out with a like result with larvæ taken wandering on the surface of the soil in pots containing infested vines.

In conjunction with the inoculation experiment in the vineyard four Zinfandel vines were planted in kerosene cans in the laboratory yard, and after watering to insure soil cracking they were inoculated artificially by placing the larvæ on the soil surface. These inoculations comprised, respectively, 21, 190, 300, and 625 wanderers collected during the summer. Two of the cans contained sandy silt and two heavy black clay. In no case did infestation result.

For another experiment two galvanized-iron cans, 4 by 4 inches, and 10 inches deep, were used. Sound pieces of vine root were placed in each, 7 inches below the soil surface, and the cans then filled to the top, one with sandy silt and the other with heavy black loam, after which the cans were buried, their tops at a level with the soil surface. The surfaces were watered to insure cracking of the soil. Between July 15 and August 4, several hundred wanderers were placed on the sandy silt, and between July 18 and August 4 several hundred on the black loam. On August 27 the roots in the cans were examined. Those buried in the sandy silt which had failed to crack much were uninfested, while those buried in the heavier soil bore a small infestation, indicating that one or more wanderers had penetrated to the roots.

From the results of experiments on natural and artificial inoculations of vine roots by wandering larvæ through the soil two facts stand out: (1) Notwithstanding the large numbers of wanderers available or utilized, positive results were infrequent. In the years 1913, 1914, and 1915, altogether 14 vessels containing vine roots, either living or cut into sections, were inoculated by placing wanderers on the soil surface, and only two of these gave positive results. The average number of wanderers used for each vessel was about 150. In the vineyard experiment in 1915, only 4 of 27 exposed vines became inoculated, yet all these vines were planted near vineyard vines from which wanderers were issuing. It is true that the soil surface inside the cans was a small area—126 square inches—and that the soil itself was not as thoroughly cracked as it might have been; but in many instances the cans were not more than 1 foot from the trunks of the infested vines, therefore, from the wanderers when they issued, whereas in vineyards vines are set 6 or more feet apart. (2) The presence of cracks in the soil leading directly to roots is necessary to permit the wandering larvæ to descend to roots, for the larvæ can not dig their way through the soil, and during the period when they are issuing, rain, which might provide moisture to draw them into the soil or wash them onto exposed roots, is lacking.

The writers are of the opinion that wandering larvæ are the cause of considerable local spread of phylloxera, that is, within the vineyard or district; and that they are instrumental in causing the formation of new phylloxera "spots" or foci. Under favorable conditions it has been proved that they may live for at least three days above the surface of the soil, and thus may be transported from place to place with the possibility of finally becoming located on a vine root. There is no reason why wanderers may not live for as long as two weeks on the soil surface without feeding, provided this surface is not heated by the sun. In one instance, after being placed on a piece of root, several of them wandered for as many as five days before settling down to feed. It may be said also that larvæ have been found to live in water as long as nine days without food, and it may thus be assumed that they might remain as long in the open air under average conditions of temperature and humidity. This fact would explain how the insect may be spread from one locality to another by wandering larvæ that lodge in such vine material as picking boxes (see following under "Casual agencies of diffusion," p. 115).

There are certain marked instances in California vineyard districts where phylloxeration has developed "with the prevailing winds." The only wind-borne forms of the phylloxera in California are the winged migrants and the wandering larvæ. The California biology indicates that the migrant has no bearing on the preservation of the species, and therefore such phylloxeration has resulted from wind-borne wandering larvæ.

DIFFUSION BY NEWLY HATCHED RADICICOLES TRAVELING THROUGH THE SOIL.

In 1914, experiments on subterranean diffusion were conducted. In April three Muscat rooted vines were planted in a 4-foot square box containing heavy loam covered with a 3-inch layer of fine sand. The sand was used for the purpose of preventing wandering larvæ from emerging upon the surface and reaching the sound vines. May 20, one of the vines was artificially inoculated. The second vine was 1 foot distant, and the third 2 feet distant from the first. On October 10, all three vines were dug up, and it was found that the first had a small infestation all over the root system. The second vine had a small infestation chiefly on nodosities on roots nearest those of the first vine. So far as could be observed, the roots of the two vines did not approach nearer than 2 inches at the closest point, but as some of the terminal rootlets had died during the summer and autumn it is quite possible that earlier in the season rootlets of the two vines were contiguous. The third vine was uninfested. Its roots had been separated from those of the first vine by at least 12 inches and from those of the second vine by at least 5 inches.

This experiment did not appear to show that subterranean infestation was a common mode of diffusion. The condition of the roots on the first vine when it was pulled up showed that its summer infestation had been large and that many wanderers had been produced; therefore, one would expect that some of these would have found their way to both of the other two vines. The earth at the time of planting, however, had been packed very solidly, and the layer of sand prevented cracking so that there were very few, if any, subterranean passages affording access to the phylloxeræ.

The following experiments also were made: On May 22 two young viniferæ (Feher Szagos) were planted in a galvanized tin, 8 by 8 by 10 inches. Two sides of this tin were basally produced in the shape of a cone (Pl. VI, fig. 2, p. 52), and at each apex was a hole of one-half inch diameter. The cones were then tightly fitted into wooden tubes, through the centers of which ran a square passageway of one-half inch diameter, and the junctions cemented. The cones and wooden tubes were buried 8 inches below the soil surface. At the farther ends of the two wooden tubes similar galvanized tins were connected, and in each of them was planted a single sound vine (Feher Szagos). In this experiment the tubes were, respectively, 2 and 10 feet in length. The conical projections were expected to draw the roots toward the hole, therefore toward the tubes. No earth, except for about 2 inches at the ends, was placed in the passage in the tubes. Black paper was glued on to the top of the outside of the wooden tubes so as to prevent entrance of light. Thus the phylloxeræ, if they passed through the hollow inside of the tube, would not be influenced by any light rays. On September 23 the tins and tube were pulled up and the vines examined. Both central vines inoculated in May were well infested. Their rootlets and those of the two end vines had penetrated not more than 3 inches into the hollow of the tube, but in all four cases rootlets were abundant inside the conical projections. The vine at the end of the 2-foot tube was well infested with radicicoles in all stages and with a few nymphs, indicating that the original infestation occurred at least before August 1. The vine at the end of the 10-foot tube was uninfested and showed no indications of ever having been inoculated.

On May 22 a similar experiment, with single vines (Carignan), was started, the length of the wooden tubes being 6 and 14 feet, respectively. On September 30 the vines were examined and the roots of the central vines were found to be well infested. Rootlets of all four vines had penetrated not over 3 inches into the hollow interior of the tubes. The vine 6 feet distant from the infested vines showed a good infestation, whereas the vine 14 feet away was not infested.

Thus, wandering larvæ, in two cases out of four, had found their way along the whole length of the interior of the tubes and had inoculated the roots at the farther ends of such tubes. The inoculated vines were those at the ends of the two shorter tubes (2 and 6 feet), and the sound vines those at the ends of the two longer tubes (10 and 14 feet). Thus it would appear that there is a limit to the distance over which the phylloxeræ will proceed when they have left a root, intent on finding new food. These experiments with wooden tubes demonstrated the wandering habits of the young radicicoles, and it may be readily understood how this subterranean movement may cause a phylloxera "spot" to enlarge, especially when the soil is cracked to any depth.

DIFFUSION BY YOUNG GALLICOLES.

In districts where the gall-inhabiting forms (gallicoles) are found, they may be the cause of diffusion. Either the branches of vines intertwine and the young gallicoles pass thus from one vine to another, or the young gallicoles are carried by the wind on to foliage of other vines or to the ground. Since the gall-inhabiting form is normally absent in California, this means of diffusion will not be discussed further.

CASUAL AGENCIES OF DIFFUSION.

CULTIVATING INSTRUMENTS.

During May and June badly phylloxerated vines are accustomed to put forth an abundance of short fleshy or fibrous rootlets close to the surface of the soil. Usually these are infested heavily with the progeny of the overwintered phylloxeræ. The vineyards usually are cultivated and hoed at this time, and these surface rootlets are frequently broken off and carried along by the cultivator and hoe. This possible means for spreading the insect having been considered, a series of experiments was initiated as follows: On May 30, in the vineyard, pieces of infested fleshy surface rootlets were secured, placed in earth, and the whole transported to the laboratory. Four lumps of earth and roots were partially buried in the soil of a pot containing a young sound vine (Pierce Isabella). The earth and roots exposed to the sun quickly dried up and no infestation to the vine resulted. It may be stated that the diameters of the lumps varied from one-half to 2 inches. On June 4 the experiment was repeated, but the infested fibrous rootlets were wrapped loosely in four lumps of earth with diameters 1½ to 2 inches, and half buried in the soil of a pot having a sound vine (Cornichon) growing in it. The rootlets kept in good condition and the phylloxeræ lived four days (one of which was cloudy and rainy). On September 3 it was found that the vine showed a rather scanty infestation. On July 16 many strongly infested fleshy rootlets found in the vineyard, from 4 to 8 inches below the soil surface, were inclosed in a large piece of earth, half buried in the soil of a pot in which grew a sound vine (Carignan). On September 3 the vine was found to be strongly infested, especially on its upper rootlets near the inner periphery of the pot. On July 17 the experiment of the day previous was repeated in its entirety, with a Pierce Isabella vine, and on September 3 this vine was found to be severely infested, bearing many nodosities both on the upper and lower rootlets. Thus in three out of four attempts success was obtained in securing an infestation upon sound vines by placing pieces of infested rootlets in lumps of soil half buried in the earth of the pots in which those vines were growing. In practice it would very frequently happen that such rootlets severed by a cultural instrument would be buried several inches deep after being dragged along by the instrument. It is easy to understand how the insect might be diffused in this manner.

VINE SUPPORTS AND PICKING BOXES.

Vine supports or stakes (universally used), by reason of the fact that they enter the soil contiguous to the main stem of the vine, are very likely to bear phylloxeræ upon them. Since the newly hatched larvæ can live for at least three days, and probably many more, out of the soil and when not exposed to the sun's rays, it is apparent that infested stakes could be transferred to a considerable distance and when set out in a vineyard upon their arrival could be the origin of phylloxera infestation.

Many growers have declared that in their vineyards the phylloxeræ first showed evidence of their presence at a point or points where picking boxes coming from infested vineyards had been piled. If picking boxes were scattered in an infested vineyard during the time of the aerial wanderer migration, one can readily see that the opportunity would be afforded for the phylloxeræ to climb upon them, later to be transported to other vineyards, since it is a common practice to use the same boxes many times in the picking season, and the same boxes may be used in more than one vineyard or district. In California, wine grapes are rarely picked before the middle of September, and raisin grapes are picked toward the end of August. In the experimental wine-grape vineyard, wandering larvæ were not found issuing after August 25, but in young vines in pots they were collected well into September. The fact that the wanderers were not found issuing in the wine grape vineyard at the time when picking boxes were distributed to a certain extent invalidates the theory of spread by these boxes. It is within the realm of possibility, however, that the latest issuing wanderers remained active and alive until the boxes were distributed some two weeks later. Observations on wanderers issuing from potted vines lead to the conclusion that the natural period of wanderer issuance may be considerably lengthened beyond that which was found to obtain in the experimental vineyard during the years 1914 and 1915. This longer period would include the time of picking wine as well as raisin grapes.

PLANTS BETWEEN THE VINES.

Walnut trees planted in vineyards indicate the possibility of diffusion through the agency of plants. The long roots of the walnut offer facilities for phylloxeræ to spread whenever vine roots come in contact with them or are very close to them. That phylloxeræ have been found moving on these roots would indicate that the latter often provide an underground channel of diffusion.

MAN AND DOMESTIC ANIMALS.

The possibility of the portage of phylloxeræ by man and domestic animals should not be overlooked. The winged forms and aerial wanderers may be blown on clothes or animals, and thereby spread, or they may be picked up with wet earth. This latter chance is greatly lessened under California conditions, because during the months in which wanderers and winged migrants are produced, the surface soil is dry, and the winged migrant is not a factor in diffusion.

WATER.

Recognizing the possibility of the spread of phylloxeræ through the agency of flowing water, the writers conducted the following experiments in 1914: From May 5, 11 a. m., to May 6, 11 a. m., a piece of severed root, infested by six adult overwintered phylloxeræ and about 100 eggs and larvæ, was subjected to a stream of water for the most part playing directly upon the insects and flowing 6 feet to an uninfested vine (Catáwba) so as to effect contact with some of its roots and also to stand on the surface of the soil about its stem. Examination of the piece of severed root after the experiment was concluded showed that about 40 eggs and young had been washed off. Five of the adults suffered no injury from exposure nor did most of the remaining young and eggs. On July 12 the Catawba vine was found to bear a strong nodositous infestation. On June 6, for eight hours, two pieces of severed roots bearing a total of about 200 phylloxeræ were subjected to a similar stream of water which subsequently flowed 6 feet to a sound Mission vine. On the severed roots the majority of aphids were not washed off. In this instance the roots of the living vine were not bared, and there were no cracks on the surface of the soil around it. On July 27 this vine was examined and found to be uninfested. The third experiment took place July 29. For eight hours two pieces of severed roots bearing a total of about 250 phylloxeræ were subjected to a stream of water which subsequently flowed 10 feet to a sound Feher Szagos vine growing in a pot. The surface soil in this pot had been previously watered, and thus was cracked. After the experiment was concluded, it was found that very few of the phylloxeræ had been carried off the severed roots. September 16 the vine was examined, but it proved to be quite uninfested. In each of these three experiments a fine stream of water was used and the angle of declivity was slight. In the first experiment only, wherein the roots of the living vine were actually exposed to the stream of water, did an inoculation through water agency occur. It is evident, however, that diffusion may occur by means of water-borne phylloxeræ. In the California vineyards such a condition could arise normally only between November and May, for in the other months it is very rare to have rain in any abundance. In April and May, however, when the phylloxeræ are active, heavy rains occasionally occur, and sometimes on the hillside vineyards deep waterways are formed, exposing the roots of vines to a depth of more than a foot.

In this connection some laboratory experiments were made upon the resistance of eggs and larvæ to water exposure. For this purpose small-sized glass vials and distilled water at about 64° F. were used. In one instance, in a corked vial, 9 out of 12 eggs hatched from 2 to 10 days after they were placed in the water. All those that hatched remained on the surface, while those that failed to hatch went to the bottom of the vial. In another instance eight recently deposited eggs were placed on the surface of the water in an uncorked vial. Six days later all had sunk to the bottom, but subsequently hatched. In a third experiment 11 well-advanced eggs were placed on the surface of the water in an uncorked vial. After 11 days all the eggs had hatched, six having remained on the surface and five having sunk to the bottom. In all three experiments the hatched larvæ failed to fasten to pieces of roots provided for them.

In a fourth experiment 26 eggs were placed in water in a stender dish. Two days later all but four eggs had sunk, but subsequently all eggs hatched and none of the resultant larvæ settled on the roots provided for them.

Table XXXVI indicates the results of experiments bearing on the behavior of newly hatched larvæ in water.

TABLE XXXVI.—*Behavior in water of newly hatched larvæ of the grape phylloxera, Walnut Creek, Calif.*

Date placed in water.	Number of individuals that—		Length of submersion.	Number of individuals after submersion.		Remarks.
	Sank.	Remained on surface.		Alive.	Dead.	
			Days.			
May 12	5	3	1	8	0	In stender dish without cover.
12	4	2	2	6	0	In small vial—uncorked.
27	2	0	2	2	0	Do.
15	4	2	3	2	4	In small vial—uncorked; sunk aphids dead.
19	5	1	3	1	5	Do.
June 1	4	2	4	1	5	In small vial—uncorked; sunk aphids alive.
May 24	1	1	5	1	1	Do.
June 1	0	4	6	3	1	In small vial—uncorked.
16	5	1	7	5	1	In small vial—uncorked; sunk aphids alive, but none subsequently fastened on root.
16	5	2	7	0	7	In small Vial—corked.
1	0	4	9	1	3	Do.
July 15	6	2	4	8	0	In small vial—corked; one aphid subsequently matured Aug. 12 on severed root.
15	6	2	4	8	0	In small vial—uncorked; one aphid subsequently matured Aug. 11 on severed root.

NOTE.—In all except the first experiment, distilled water was used; in the first experiment, tap water.

Prior to June 16 the phylloxeræ were not followed up after their submersion to see whether they would fasten to the pieces of roots provided for them because the experiments were made only to ascertain how many of the larvæ would be alive after submersion. It may be noted that in some cases the larvæ which sank were found to be alive when removed from the water and in others those that floated were living when removed. The phylloxeræ survived as many as nine days on the surface of the water, and as many as seven days when submerged, and at the bottom of the vial. The experiments, however, did not continue beyond nine days, and there is no reason to believe that the insects could not live in the water many days longer than that period. The fact that they did survive as long as a week was sufficient evidence of the importance of their resistance to water. The two experiments of July 15–19 demonstrated that after four days in water the young larvæ could settle on pieces of roots and later mature. In the seven-day experiment, none settled on the roots. In all except one of the vials distilled water at about 64° F. was used. The behavior of the young phylloxeræ in water was characteristic. Those on the surface were active, swimming around in circles, but those at the bottom remained almost motionless unless disturbed.

To sum up, it appears: (1) That eggs of radicicoles hatch readily in water, floating and sunken; (2) that the newly hatched larvæ may live for more than a week submerged, or on the surface film; (3) that these larvæ are capable, at least after four days of exposure. to water, of fixing upon roots and developing in a normal manner. Further proof of the ability of young phylloxeræ to live submerged occurred in an observation made from September to November, 1914. A Riparia cutting had been placed in a glass vial in the laboratory. Immediately a callus formed, and many rootlets grew around the inside of the vial. On September 15, 20 eggs of radicicoles were floated on the water surface. None of the resultant larvæ persisting, more eggs were floated October 10. October 12 the water had evaporated, and four days later two young larvæ had settled. These had hatched after the water evaporated. About 1 inch of water was then poured into the vial to cover completely all the rootlets and the two phylloxeræ. October 22, three larvæ were observed under water, one of which had been fixed since October 16. October 27, there were visible under water, besides the original larvæ of the 16th, six additional larvæ, five of which were settled. October 30 all seven observed on October 27 had settled and an eighth was visible moving over the rootlets. A small tuberosity had been set up by one of the phylloxeræ. All the unhatched eggs had died. It was noted that when the insects were exposed to sunlight they moved their appendages actively. November 2, three settled larvæ were visible. These included the individual on the tuberosity and the one which had settled October 16. All others were dead. November 10 the only survivors were the original settler and the individual on the tuberosity. Shortly after November 20 all disappeared. Thus one individual, destined apparently to hibernate, persisted more than a month fixed on a root under water, and several others lived under water from 3 to 14 days.

There also exists the possibility of infestation by seepage. On vineyards of porous soils young larvæ on the surface may be drawn into the soil in time of a storm or irrigation. Also on steep hillside vineyards in the springtime, when heavy rains may fall or when a rise and fall in the "water table" may occur, a seepage infestation may take place. Any artificial irrigation during the months June to October invites the spread of phylloxeræ because in this period phylloxeræ occur above the surface of the soil or are active on surface rootlets.

CUTTINGS AND ROOTED VINES.

In European countries where a small percentage of the winter eggs are deposited under the bark of yearling wood there is a slight danger of phylloxera infestation following the planting of a cutting from such wood. This danger does not exist in California, provided the cuttings are not "heeled in" before transportation, because the winter egg does not persist successfully. If the cuttings are "heeled in" before transportation in an infested district, the possibility of their becoming phylloxerated exists. Similarly, the possible danger from gallicoles remaining upon the foliage of canes late into autumn is nullified, because the gall-inhabiting forms do not normally occur in California.

The greatest danger of phylloxeration resides in the planting out of infested rooted vines. This is a very abundant means of distributing phylloxera. Even if only one or two out of a thousand vines are infested at planting, a "spot" or "spots" will form within a few years, and the whole acreage eventually will become infested. While the vines remain small, diffusion is slow because the roots of one vine are separated from those of its neighbors, and underground diffusion thus is rare if not impossible. Also, the relatively small number of roots coupled with the relatively small number of phylloxeræ able to flourish thereon, prevents many opportunities for aerial diffusion by wanderers. If the majority of the vines planted out contain phylloxeræ, however, the vineyard's complete phylloxeration is not long removed. In a phylloxerated district the employment of resistant roots obviates the necessity of treating the vines before planting out in the vineyard, yet danger exists in cases where grafted vines are planted too deeply and the stouter vinifera scion is enabled to send out its own roots, in many instances crowding out the roots of the resistant stock. The scion's roots, being nonresistant, decay when phylloxerated just as though no resistant stock had been employed, and the expense and trouble of the grafting process are wasted. Even though phylloxeræ live on resistant stock roots in grafted vineyards without necessarily injuring the crop or vines, there still remains the possibility that infestation will arise from these grafted vines and that nongrafted vineyards near by will become inoculated. Such a possibility is accentuated the greater the proximity of two such vine areas, and especially if the nonresistant area is to leeward of the grafted area or if water flows from the grafted to the nonresistant vineyard. It is advisable, therefore, to disinfect even resistant roots when these are to be planted in a region free from phylloxera.

PHYLLOXERATED LAND.

Experiments with potted vines have given proof that phylloxeræ may live at least 10 months on buried severed pieces of roots, and also that such pieces may remain sound for 18 months and at the termination afford acceptable food for the insect. It is evident, therefore, that the planting of vines on land from which phylloxerated vines have recently been pulled up is a dangerous procedure. It is next to impossible to pull up grapevines without leaving pieces of roots in the ground. In the case of vine nurseries, this danger is very apparent.

OLD STUMPS.

Since the phylloxeræ may live under the bark of vine stumps to several inches above the soil surface, it is apparent that these infested stumps might possibly be a means of diffusion if sound vines should be placed near them. Such stumps, however, soon decay after they have been pulled from the ground and severed from their roots. In the active season, however, any insects dwelling upon them would hasten to leave and seek other food, so that in this season it is quite possible for diffusion to occur from the stumps. In the winter the phylloxeræ would all be hibernants, and these would die as the stump decayed.

SUMMARY.

HISTORY.

The grape phylloxera was introduced into California about the year 1858, having been brought on vines imported by settlers from the East. It thus appears that the pest arrived on the Pacific coast at least as early as it reached France, where the first evidence of its activity was vaguely noted in 1862.

For many years previous to this introduction the Spanish settlers and Missions had cultivated on a moderate scale the Mission grape, and this, though a very susceptible variety, as was afterwards proved, had flourished without disease. About the time of the advent of the phylloxera grape culture was receiving a great impetus, and many European varieties were being introduced which shortly showed signs of disease in localities in which the eastern vines had been planted.

The phylloxera has since spread throughout most of the grape districts of California wherever conditions have been suited to it, but never has the pest assumed such disastrous proportions as it did during the first years of its ravages in France. It is possible that the insect has never reached such isolated vine districts as those of the southern California counties, but in many of such isolated localities the conditions are unsuited to the insect, and thus we can not be certain that it did not reach these places and fail to establish itself.

Coming upon the scene at the infancy of the commercial grape industry, the phylloxera has been present throughout the growth of that industry and, it is estimated, has in the course of some 60 years destroyed about 75,000 acres of grapes.

In many instances the insect has been distributed through the agency of infested rooted vines imported into an uninfested district or vineyard. In other cases the insect has been carried on vineyard material. In no instance has the distribution been as rapid as that which took place in the vineyard districts of France. The modified life cycle in California, i. e., sterility of the winged form, coupled with topographic barriers, consisting of mountain chains and dividing valleys, is in very great part responsible for this.

VINEYARD DESTRUCTION.

There is great variation in the rapidity of the destruction of vines and vineyards by phylloxera.

Apart from some variation in the different grape varieties, soil conditions must be considered as of great importance. In poorly drained soils the vines succumb much more rapidly than in well-drained land. Accumulation of moisture in the subsoil materially assists in the decomposition of infested roots, whereas if the subsoil is well drained, vines may flourish notwithstanding infestations extending over many years. Vines attacked when young and before their root systems have become established will succumb more rapidly than will those infested at a greater age.

The first indication of phylloxera in a vineyard occurs in the form of one or more stunted vines and a premature yellowing of the foliage. In time, adjacent vines will show similar indications, and those first infested are more noticeably stunted. Gradually more and more of the surrounding vines are affected, and those in the center become very much weakened or die outright. Thus are formed the so-called " oil spots " or foci for the distribution of the disease, which may be likened to the ever-increasing concentric circles of waves that are formed when a stone is cast into placid water.

Following the initial infestation of a vine under favorable conditions for phylloxera, the insects multiply rapidly, and within two or three years increase their range to involve the entire root system. Those which settle on the growing rootlets form fleshy lesions or swellings, which are termed nodosities. These swellings are generally somewhat curved, the insect inhabiting a depression of the inner arc. In the great majority of instances the insect stops further apical growth of the rootlet, and thus the rootlet ceases to supply nourishment to the vine. Although the percentage of rootlets thus infested is often large, a vine of vigor can easily send out more and continue to draw its nourishment from the soil. Other phylloxeræ settle on the older roots and in most cases cause swellings termed tuberosities, which vary in size, but the majority are about one-fifth of an inch in diameter. They are frequently very abundant, and two or more may coalesce. The bark of the root often cracks longitudinally, and a chain of swellings arises from phylloxera punctures. As long as these swellings remain fresh, the health of the vine is not much impaired, but as soon as they decay the vine is injured, and when they decay in numbers the roots are frequently destroyed, causing first the stunting and subsequently the death of the vine.

BIOLOGY.

The grape phylloxera was named in 1855 by Fitch in America from the gall-inhabiting form, and in 1868 by Planchon in Europe from the root-inhabiting type. In 1870 Riley and Lichtenstein proved that the two forms were two separate phases of a single species; consequently, Fitch's specific name *vitifoliae* must be conceded priority.

In its native region, eastern North America, the insect has a very complicated life cycle, which includes an aerial gall-inhabiting form. In California the gall form has been observed only once and that in the year 1884.

The California life cycle (fig. 10), as indicated by research, is much more simple than that which obtains in the East, and as far as the economy of the insect is concerned, is purely parthenogenetic.

Winter is passed in the form of the hibernant larva. Virtually all hibernants are newly hatched larvæ which settle down to hibernate immediately after hatching from the egg in the autumn, but a few hibernate in an older stage. Coincident with the first flow of sap in spring, these hibernants commence to feed, and mature on the average five and a half weeks later. The hibernant larva is light brown in color, and is about one-third millimeter long and half as wide. The mature hibernant is about 0.75 mm. long and 0.40 mm. wide, and does not differ from the adult radicicole of any other generation. On the average, it takes the hibernant six months to mature, the period ranging from four and a half to seven and a half months. The mature hibernant gives rise to a number of generations—as many as eight—of root-feeding phylloxeræ throughout the summer and autumn. Although somewhat arbitrary, April 15 to October 15 best indicates the period of the active half-year of the insect, the period October 15 to April 15 being the dormant or hibernating season.

All forms of the phylloxera are oviparous. The average number of eggs per adult radicicole is about 110 and the average egg-laying period about 45 days. Incubation varies with temperature and lasts from 5 days in midsummer to over 30 days in December. The eggs are lemon yellow and oval. Upon hatching from the egg, the bright-yellow larva seeks food. Larvæ hatching in spring mostly settle near the eggshells, but in summer and autumn a considerable percentage travel along the roots or forsake the vine altogether, either following cracks in the soil to reach neighboring vines or ascending to the surface of the soil and traversing the ground in their endeavors to reach other vines. To those that voluntarily forsake the vine has been given the term " wanderers." The larvæ molt four times, and on the

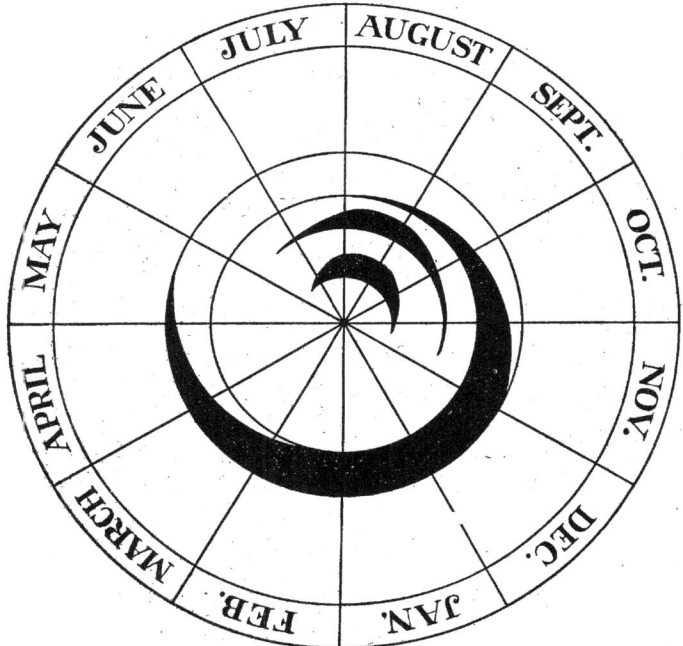

Fig. 10.—Diagram to illustrate annual life history : innermost shaded crescent, active period of wandering radicicole larvæ ; middle shaded crescent, period of development of the sexuparous migrant ; shaded portion of outer circle, hibernation period of radicicole larvæ ; unshaded portion of outer circle, period of active life on the roots.

completion of the final molt become mature insects. At first oval, they tend to become pyriform as they grow. The color, yellow, yellowish-green, or yellowish-brown, is dependent on the nature of the food. The length of the developmental period varies according to food and meteorological conditions. On succulent living roots the average period of larval development was found to be about 22 days (hibernant generation excluded), and the maximum and minimum respectively 36 and 10 days.

The winged form is produced from the middle of June until November. It is more abundant in the coastal districts than in the interior valleys. In their first two instars the larvæ of the winged form do not differ from the corresponding stages of the wingless form, but in the third and fourth stages they differ structurally, and in these stages are termed, respectively, prenymph and nymph. Both these forms are elongate in shape and are light greenish-yellow or yellowish-brown. The nymphs have two pairs of grayish-black wing pads. The winged insect is orange in color with grayish-black head and thorax and two pairs of scantily veined wings.

The nymphs transform in most instances near the surface of the soil and the winged migrants issue on the surface and fly about in the vineyard and neighboring regions.

The winged insects deposit eggs of two kinds, viz, male and female, and the insects which mature from these eggs are the true sexes. These forms are unable to take food, and under normal conditions mate upon reaching maturity and the female forthwith deposits a single egg under the bark of the vine. This egg hatches in spring and gives rise to a series of generations of gall-inhabiting and gall-making wingless aphids. A certain percentage of larvæ born in the galls, however, migrate to the roots before taking food, and in this way the species returns to the soil.

In California, under natural conditions, it is doubtful whether any sexes mature and still more doubtful whether any winter eggs hatch. Laboratory experiments indicate that the sexes mature in about 12 days.

In the late autumn, along with the nymphs are found curious forms intermediate in appearance between adult radicicoles and nymphs. These are called intermediates or nymphicals. They are not abundant and all those whose progeny have been observed were parthenogenetic.

The diffusion of the phylloxera is effected in nature by the wandering newly hatched larvæ of the radicicoles during summer and autumn. These pass from vine to vine, either on the surface of the soil or through subterranean cracks or pathways. They may also be borne by the wind or on vineyard material, such as picking boxes. Probably water is responsible for some diffusion in hilly or irrigated vineyards, and cultivating instruments by picking up pieces of infested roots may effect fresh infestations. The phylloxera is easily introduced into a vineyard or section by the practice of planting infested rooted vines to make up for cuttings which did not succeed in previous years.

LITERATURE CITED.

(1) BANCROFT, H. H.
  1883–1888. History of Mexico. 6 vols. maps. San Francisco.

(2) BIOLETTI, F. T.
  1896. Investigations of various types of grapes, their adaptability to
      different localities, and their value for wine making and other
      purposes : Made during the seasons of 1887–1894. *In* California
      Expt. Sta. Report of Viticultural Work . . . . 1887–93, p. [17]–
      372. (See p. 288.)

(3) BIOLETTI, F. T., and TWIGHT, E. H.
  1901. Report on conditions of vineyards in portions of Santa Clara Val-
      léy, California. California Univ. Agr. Expt. Sta. Bul. 134, Sept.
      23. 11 p.

(4) CALIFORNIA, BOARD OF STATE VITICULTURAL COMMISSIONERS.
  1881. First annual report. Ed. 2, rev. Sacramento.
    Pages 29–30 : Report of Mr. G. G. Blanchard, Commissioner for the El Dorado
    District.
    Pages 108–111 : Appendix C : The Phylloxera-vastatrix and its ravages in
    Sonoma Valley. By H. Appleton.
    Page 112 : Appendix D : History of the Orleans Hills vineyard and its diseases.
    By J. Knauth.

(5) CALIFORNIA, BOARD OF STATE VITICULTURAL COMMISSIONERS.
  1888. Annual report . . . for 1887. Sacramento. (See p. 47–48.)

(6) CALIFORNIA FARMER.
  1855. Catawba grape. January 23, 1855.

(7) CALIFORNIA STATE AGRICULTURAL SOCIETY.
  1859. Transactions for the year 1858. Sacramento. (See p. 312.)

(8) CALIFORNIA UNIVERSITY COLLEGE OF AGRICULTURE.
  1883. Report of the professor in charge to the president, being a part
      of the report of the regents of the University, 1882. Sacra-
      mento. (See p. 172.)

(9) FITCH, ASA.
  1856. First report on the noxious, beneficial and other insects of the
      State of New York . . . Albany. (See p. 158.)

(10) FONSCOLOMBE, BOYER DE.
  1834. Sur les genres d'hyménoptères Lithurgus et Phylloxera. *In* Soc.
      Ent. France, Annales, v. 3, p. 219–224.

(11) GRASSI, BATTISTA, ET AL.
  1912. Contributo alla conoscenza delle Fillosserine ed in particolare
      della Fillossera della vite . . . seguito da un riassunto teorico-
      pratico della Biologia della Fillossera della vite (con una
      tavola) della Dott. Anna Foà. Roma, 1912. E–L, 456, lxxv p.
      illus., pl.
      Bibliographia, p. 419–431. (See p. 12 ; 134–135 ; 335–345 ; 351 ;
      138–148 ; 274–280.)

(12) GUERCIO, GIACOMO DEL.
  1900. Prospetto dell'Afidofauna Italica. *In* Nuove Relazione R. Staz.
      Ent. Agr. di Firenze, ser. 1, no. 2, p. [1]–236.
      Page 80, Xerampelus Del Guercio.

127

(13) HILGARD, E. W.
    1883. Report of the professor in charge to the president, being a part
        of the report of the regents of the University 1882. Sacra-
        mento, 179 p. (See p. 172.)
(14) HILGARD, E. W.
    1890. Report to George J. Ainsworth, Esq., Chairman, Viticultural Con-
        . ference Committee. Report of the viticultural work during the
        season 1887–90.
(15) MAYET, VALÉRY.
    1890. Les insectes de la vigne. Montpellier and Paris. xxviii+470 p.
        5 pl.
(16) MORSE, F. W.
    1884. Observations on the Phylloxera made during 1884. California
        Univ. Agr. Expt. Sta. Bul. 19, Oct. 10. 1 p.
(17) PANTANELLI, ENRICO.
    1909. Ricerche fisiologische su le viti Americane oppresse da galle
        fillosseriche. Modena. 34 p., tab. In Le Stazioni Sperimentali
        Agrarie Italiane, v. 42, fasc. iv–vi, p. 305–336. (See p. 6.)
(18) PIERCE, N. B.
    1892. The California vine disease. U. S. Dept. Agr., Div. Vegetable
        Path., Bul. 2. 215 p., 25 pl., 1 chart.
(19) PLANCHON, J. V.
    1868. Nouvelles observations sur le puceron de la vigne (Phylloxera
        vastatrix) [nuper Rhizaphis, Planch.] In Paris. Acad. des
        Sciences, Compt. Rend., v. 67, p. 588–594.
(20) PLANCHON, J. V., and SAINT-PIERRE, CAMILLE.
    1869. Rhyzaphis vastatrix. In Société des Agriculteurs de France,
        Nov. 1, p. 113–128.
(21) SHIMER, HENRY.
    1867. On a new genus in Homoptera (Section Monomera). In Proc. ·
        Acad. Nat. Sci. Philadelphia, v. 19, p. 2–11.
(22) SOCIÉTÉ ENTOMOLOGIQUE DE FRANCE.
    1868. Annales, ser. 4, v. 8, p. xcvi.
(23) WESTWOOD, J. O.
    1869. New vine diseases. In Gardeners' Chronicle, Jan 30, p. 109.
        Mentions proposing name Peritymbia vitisana before Ashmolean Society of
        Oxford in the Spring of 1868 for Rhyzaphis vastatrix.

ADDITIONAL COPIES
OF THIS PUBLICATION MAY BE PROCURED FROM
THE SUPERINTENDENT OF DOCUMENTS
GOVERNMENT PRINTING OFFICE
WASHINGTON, D. C.
AT
30 CENTS PER COPY

UNITED STATES DEPARTMENT OF AGRICULTURE

BULLETIN No. 904

Contribution from the Bureau of Plant Industry
WM. A. TAYLOR, Chief

Washington, D. C.   PROFESSIONAL PAPER   October 29, 1920

THE PRODUCTION AND UTILIZATION OF CORN OIL IN THE UNITED STATES.

By A. F. SIEVERS,

Chemical Biologist, Drug, Poisonous, and Oil Plant Investigations.

CONTENTS.

	Page.		Page.
Origin of the corn-oil industry	1	Effect of color and condition of the corn on the	
Degerminating corn	1	yield and character of the oil	15
Methods of degermination used	3	Comparison of the oil-production operation in	
Expelling the oil from corn germs	3	different mills	16
Handling and disposing of the crude oil	11	Economics of corn-oil production	17
Handling and disposing of the oil cake	12	Cost of expelling corn oil	17
Buying and shipping corn germs	13	Production of edible oil	20
Utilization of corn oil	13	The future of corn oil	22

ORIGIN OF THE CORN-OIL INDUSTRY.

The production of corn oil from the germ of corn kernels has been practiced on a commercial scale for probably a quarter of a century. From the time the degermination of corn became an integral operation in the hominy, starch, and glucose industries, the disposition of the germ has been a decided factor in the economics of these processes. At first the general practice was to dispose of the germ material by adding it to feed products, but as the demand for vegetable oils increased, for both edible and technical uses, it was found profitable to expel the oil from the germ, and in recent years when oils have been high in price the production of corn oil has become one of the important phases of the corn-products industries.

DEGERMINATING CORN.

The germ of the corn represents approximately 10 per cent of the dry kernel and contains about 50 per cent of oil. It has been found that this amount of fat, representing about 5 per cent of the air-dried corn, has a tendency to become rancid when allowed to remain in the corn product, especially in the presence of moisture. It became desirable therefore to remove the germ in order that these manufactured products might retain their quality after leaving the mill, and this fact has led to the scientific development of the dry corn-milling process and the starch and glucose manufacturing processes.

The practice of grinding the whole kernel into meal without previously removing the germ is confined largely to the South, and the product is sometimes referred to as "water-ground" meal. There is considerable difference of opinion as to the relative nutritive value and flavor of the products from the whole and the degerminated corn, but if the products are to be shipped extensively the removal of the germ minimizes the loss from spoilage in transit and in storage.

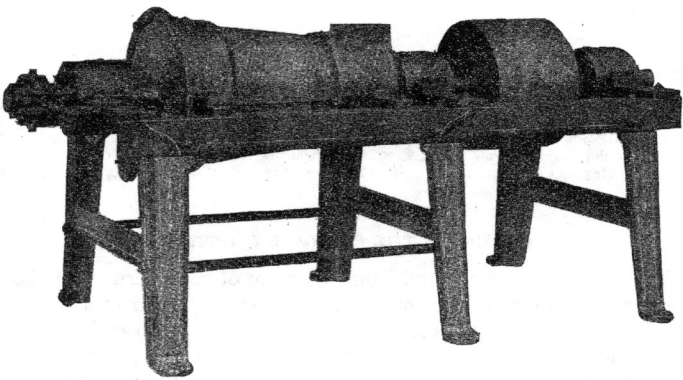

Fig. 1.—Corn huller or degerminator. This type of machine is quite generally used in the dry degerminating process.

The percentage of moisture present is of vital importance, and millers aim to reduce the moisture in their products to 12 per cent or less, in which case it is claimed that under normal conditions little difficulty is likely to be experienced in keeping the products. Cereal products are liable, of course, to infestation with weevils, and it is not probable that the removal of the germ from the corn will lessen this trouble to any considerable extent.

METHODS OF DEGERMINATION USED.

The methods of manufacturing corn products fall into two classes: The dry milling process, used for making hominy products, such as grits, flakes, meal, flour, and hominy feeds; and the wet process, used in the manufacture of starch, glucose, and related products. The methods of degerminating differ materially in these two processes, and they will therefore be considered separately.

DRY PROCESS.

After a process of cleaning to remove the dirt and foreign matter, the corn, while being agitated in a suitable container, is sprayed with water or treated with steam until it has a moisture content of about 20 per cent, after which it goes at once into the degerminating machine. (Fig. 1.) This machine consists, briefly, of a horizontal, tapering drum, which revolves on a central shaft within a casing of the same shape. The surface of the drum, or core, is covered with cone-shaped protuberances about three-fourths of an inch high, and the interior of the casing has a similar surface. A space of seven-sixteenths of an inch is allowed between the two surfaces, and the core is rotated at 700 revolutions per minute. The space between the core and the casing can readily be adjusted while the machine is in operation. The corn enters at the top and narrow end of the

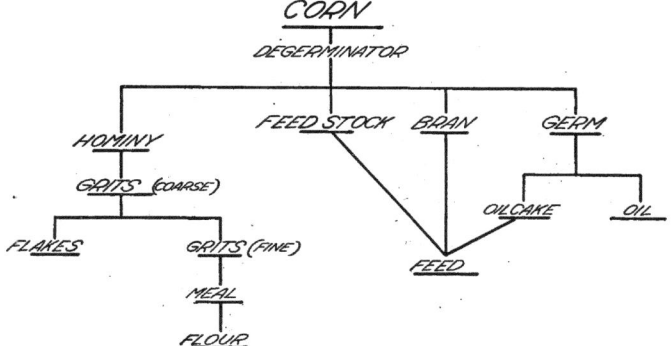

FIG. 2.—Diagram showing the various steps in the process of the dry milling of corn products in a hominy mill.

machine and is carried forward through the length of the revolving core. During its passage through the machine the kernel is torn and shredded, the husk and germ are loosened, but the starchy material is not ground to any considerable extent. The finer particles escape through perforations, while the coarse material escapes at the discharge end. The bran is partly drawn off by suction.

The germ thus separated contains some bran, husks; and meal, the quantity depending on the uniformity of the corn and the care practiced in the operation. This germ material is then run through drying machines, where the moisture is reduced to about 14 per cent, after which it is usually run through hominy reels. With the decrease of moisture more bran and feed stock (a poor grade of grayish meal containing some bran) are separated. The germ is then ready to go to the oil-expelling department. This is not the procedure followed in all mills, but the principle is the same in all. Figure 2 shows the general scheme of dry corn milling.

In most hominy mills the hominy products are the principal ones, while the feed, flour, meal, and oil are minor or by-products. Until recently the principal consumers of hominy products were the brewers, who used flakes and large quantities of grits of various sizes. These flakes are made from coarse hominy (pearl hominy), which is steamed, rolled, and dried. They are white and differ from the ordinary breakfast flakes mainly in the fact that they are not toasted. In the ordinary milling practice about 5 per cent of the corn kernel is made into flour. This amount develops incidentally during the process, owing to the breaking up in the various machines of the starchy and brittle portions of the kernel. Whenever the market demands warrant, however, the production of flour can be increased by reducing

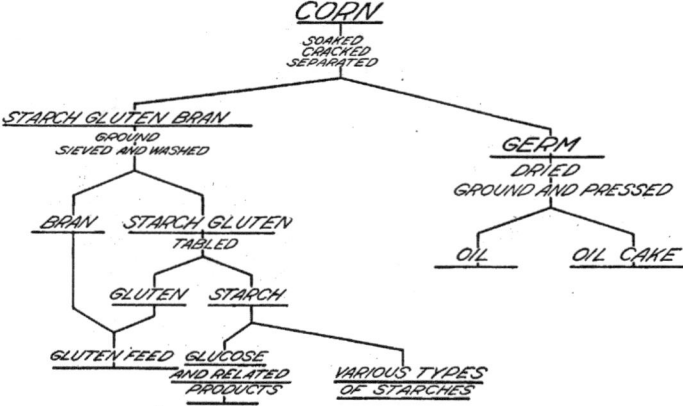

FIG. 3.—Diagram showing the various steps in the process of the manufacture of products from corn in a glucose plant.

more of the grits. During the war the demand for wheat-flour substitutes resulted in a greatly increased production of corn flour and meal.

WET PROCESS.

In starch and glucose plants the corn is degerminated by the wet process. The cleaned corn is placed in large circular wooden vats, which are filled about two-thirds full, where it is steeped or soaked in water containing 0.2 per cent of sulphurous acid. This acid is usually prepared by burning sulphur and passing the fumes of sulphur dioxid through coke towers in the presence of a spray of water. In some plants there is an arrangement to draw off the corn gradually at the bottom and to put in fresh corn at the top of the vat. The time required to prepare the corn properly for degerminating varies from 36 to 40 hours; hence in the automatic arrangement that much time should be required·for the corn to travel from the top of the vat to the outlet below.

The object of using the sulphurous acid appears to be a matter of some dispute. The following reasons have been advanced for its use: (1) It softens the corn more than plain water, and hence aids in degerminating; (2) it acts as a bleaching agent and insures a whiter starch; and (3) it acts as a preservative and prevents the starch and gluten waters from becoming sour. The acid is largely dissipated during the processes that follow, but the finished product should not contain more than a mere trace of sulphur dioxid.

Figure 3 shows in a general way the variety of products made in a plant equipped for the manufacture of glucose. In plants where

FIG. 4.—Machine for wet-degerminating. In this machine the two plates revolve in opposite directions.

only starch is made the general scheme as regards the degerminating is the same.

The soaked corn is drained and then passed through a type of attrition mill, which shreds it and separates the germ from the remainder of the kernel and also loosens the hulls from the endosperm. The type of machine generally in use consists of two vertical plates mounted on a horizontal axis and geared directly to a motor. In the early type of machine the two plates were geared to different motors and revolved in opposite directions. (Fig. 4.) In some instances they were run at different rates of speed, apparently with good results. The latest approved type, however, has one stationary plate. This eliminates one motor and greatly reduces the cost of the machine as well as the operating expense. (Fig. 5.)

The shredded corn is mixed with a large quantity of water and transferred to floating vats, which are long, narrow, metal vessels somewhat wider at the top than at the bottom. The watery mixture is slowly agitated and kept moving at the surface toward one end of the vat. Most of the germs float on the surface and over the edge of the vat at one end. The bulk of the germ material is thus removed, but in the larger plants the remaining material is put through another floating vat and additional germs are separated. The germs, together with a lot of starchy water, are then run through reels having perforated copper sides, with the perforations about 1¼ mm. in diameter. Here they are thoroughly washed to remove all starchy particles. The washings from these reels are run through a second set of reels having finer perforations, which catch the small germ fragments that passed through the first reel. The quantity of germ material thus recovered is very considerable.

The corn material, which because of its greater gravity remains in the floating vats, is ground wet, and the starchy material is reduced to a fine condition. It is then sieved and washed repeatedly. These starch washings, together with those from the germ reels, are run over long shallow tables, where the starch is allowed to settle. The process thereafter is one of drying, but in the case of boiling starches the drying is preceded by chemical treatment.

Fig. 5.—Machine for wet degerminating. In this machine one plate is stationary.

The husk and bran from which the starch has been washed are run through moisture expellers to remove part of the moisture and are then mixed or churned with the concentrated steep water from the steeping vats. This water, which contains considerable quantities of water-soluble proteins, is previously pumped into a vacuum tank and evaporated under reduced pressure. The evaporation is accomplished under a vacuum of about 26 inches, part of which is obtained by passing all the waste water of the plant through a special attachment, like a Venturi tube. The higher vacuum is secured with a power pump. As above stated, this protein water, to which is also added in some plants the gluten which tabled out at the lower end of the starch settling tables, is mixed with the feed material and the mixture pumped through filter presses. The press cakes from these filters are broken up by running them through mills. The material is then sent through driers. These driers are also used for drying the germs and will be described in that connection. After becoming partially dry the material, which has become agglutinated into small round balls, is passed through thrashers, which break up the balls, and then passed again through the driers until the moisture has been sufficiently reduced.

After all the germ material has been separated in the manner described and washed free from starch it is run through moisture expellers to take out some of the excess water. The machines used are the same as those employed for expelling moisture from the feed material. Two types are in use. One consists of two vertical plates operated separately and so attached to separate shafts that the space between the plates at the bottom is much less than at the top. The wet material is caught in this constriction and the excess water squeezed out. (Fig. 6.) The other type is constructed on lines similar to an oil expeller. It consists essentially of a worm revolving in a steel barrel through which the material travels. The pressure is adjusted by means of a steel cone at the forward end of the machine. (Fig. 7.) The quantity of water left in the germs after passing through these machines depends largely on the pressure applied. After the excess

FIG. 6.—One type of machine used for expelling moisture from wet germs and feed.

moisture has been removed, the germs are conveyed to the driers, which reduce the moisture to 5 per cent or less. These driers are also used for drying feed.

In hominy mills the germs are also dried, but apparently not to such a degree. For this purpose there is in use one main type of drier which has been revised from time to time. (Fig. 8.) The oldest form consists of a long cylinder or drum about 5 feet in diameter and 28 feet long. On the inside of this cylinder, around the circumference, are parallel steam pipes 4 inches in diameter, and the whole apparatus slowly revolves. The steam enters through an opening in the central shaft, while the material to be dried enters at one end and travels slowly down the length of the machine, as the farther end is somewhat lower than the forward end. The material rolls and tosses between the hot steam pipes, and by means of vanes on the inside of the cylinder is carried partly up the side and then tumbled back among the pipes. These driers appear to be efficient and are generally used for this purpose. Improvements have been added from time to time, but the basis of operation is the same. After being dried, the germs are ready to go to the expelling plant.

EXPELLING THE OIL FROM CORN GERMS.

While the method of handling and degerminating the corn is totally different in the dry and the wet processes, the operation involved in handling the germ material after it is dried and ready for the oil machinery is the same for both processes. At this point

Fig. 7.—A type of moisture expeller used for wet corn germs and feed.

it is logical to discuss the difference in the germ material as obtained by the two processes.

The germs separated by the dry process contain considerable portions from other parts of the corn, which on an average reduce the oil content to about 18 per cent. Approximately 6 per cent of oil remains in the cake. Dry-corn millers agree that half a pound of oil is an average yield from a bushel of corn, and if 12 per cent of oil from the germ is representative it follows that 4.17 pounds of germs are obtained from a bushel of corn.

The germs separated by the wet process are much cleaner—that is, they contain much less of the other parts of the corn, and therefore average a much higher percentage of oil, or about 45 per cent. It is not usually possible, however, to obtain a cake with as low an oil content as that obtained by the dry process. The cake usually contains about 9 per cent of oil. Assuming that 1¼ pounds of oil represent the average yield from a bushel of corn, and that 36 per cent is obtained from the germ, the germ material obtained from a bushel of corn must be about 3.47 pounds.

These figures relating to the quantity of germs and oil obtained from a bushel of corn are considered fairly representative and will be used in a later section on the economics involved in expelling the oil.

Before the oil can be expelled the germ material must be cracked or ground. The germs from the dry process are ground less fine, as a rule, than those obtained from the wet process. The former, which contains some bran and husks, can be ground in an attrition mill if necessary, but in most cases all germ material is cracked by being passed between rollers.

Without doubt the expeller is recognized as the ideal type of machine for removing the oil from corn germs and is almost univer-

FIG. 8.—Type of drier used in drying corn germs and feed.

sally used. (Fig. 9.) The dried germ is tempered with steam, which heats it and also adds moisture. It might seem that if there were less drying in the first place the subsequent addition of moisture would be unnecessary, but it is evidently a case of first removing the interior moisture and then adding surface moisture when tempering. On this point operators are agreed.

The pressure at which these machines are operated determines largely the quantity of oil left in the cake. Several factors are involved which limit the pressure that can safely be maintained. In the first place, increased pressure always involves a decrease of capacity. Furthermore, the opinion obtains generally that if the pressure is too great the oil and cake will both darken, which is very undesirable. The wear and tear on the machine is also excessive under such circumstances, and consequently, as a rule, no effort is made to reduce the oil in the cake below 5 per cent when operating on germs from the dry process and below 8. per cent when using material from the wet process.

A peculiar series of explosions often takes place in these expellers, mostly when used on germs obtained by the dry process. The cause does not appear to be well understood, but it is the general opinion that an excessive or an insufficient amount of either moisture or fiber is responsible.

The oil obtained, which in most cases is of a golden color, is next passed through filter presses which remove the fine meal. This

FIG. 9.—Complete 1-expeller oil plant.

meal is then returned to the expellers and mixed with the fresh material.

Hydraulic presses are used only to a very limited extent, having been almost entirely displaced by expellers. The question of the relative expense of operating presses and expellers is interesting, and several factors are involved. The cost of operating presses is somewhat increased at present (1920) owing to the expense of the press cloths, which cost about $2 a yard. It is estimated that the entire set of cloths must be replaced every 60 days, and since 45 yards are required for one press of 15 plates, this item amounts to $90, or $1.50

a day for each press. These figures do not include the cost of repairing the cloths, which must constantly be done in order to make the set last 60 days. In the expellers this expense is eliminated. It is estimated that the cost of repairs on an expeller amounts to about $200 a year, or about 66 cents a day. It is evident, therefore, that the replacing of parts in the expeller costs less than the press cloths for a press.

It is estimated that the presses will deliver 1,400 pounds of oil in a 24-hour run, which is the oil equivalent of about 1,000 bushels of corn when degerminated by the wet process. The expeller will deliver 3,000 to 4,000 pounds of oil in 24 hours, or the equivalent of 2,400 to 3,000 bushels of corn. The capacity of the expeller, therefore, is much greater than that of the press. However, the power required to operate the expeller is much greater, and the depreciation of the machine is also greatly in excess of that of the presses. The one great advantage of the press over the expeller is the exceedingly low upkeep and the practically indestructible character of the machine.

HANDLING AND DISPOSING OF THE CRUDE OIL.

FILTERING.

Crude corn oil as it comes from the expellers or presses is pumped through filter presses, which remove the fine meal and other sediment which has had time to settle. It is then placed in storage tanks until shipped.

BUYING AND SELLING.

Operators who do not themselves refine the oil sell it to refiners, soap makers, brokers, and in some cases to bakers. The use of crude corn oil for industrial and edible purposes will be considered later. The price obtainable depends largely on the grade of the oil, and especially on the amount of free fatty acids present. Prime crude oil is usually limited to not more than 2 per cent of free fatty acids. The next lower grade must not as a rule contain more than 3.5 per cent. Refiners protect themselves from a heavy refining loss by paying less for an oil which contains such acids in excess of the specified quantity. Under normal operating conditions with average corn the crude oil contains from 1 to 3 per cent of free fatty acids. It appears that the oil from wet-process germs has a somewhat higher percentage of free acids than that obtained from dry-process germs.

Large refiners, in order to have enough to supply the demand for their refined oil, have found it profitable to buy considerable quantities of the crude oil and refine it in addition to their own production. Producers who market their refined oil as package goods for the retail trade find this practice especially desirable in order to supply the demand created by their extensive advertising. This practice of the large refiners has furnished a valuable outlet for the crude oil of producers who for one reason or another have not installed refining equipments.

The starch and hominy plants which do not refine their oil or sell their entire output to other producers dispose of the crude oil mostly to brokers and soap makers.

HANDLING AND DISPOSING OF THE OIL CAKE.

The oil cake from corn germs has a well-recognized feeding value. As previously stated, it contains from 5 to 7 per cent of fat when obtained in hominy mills and from 8 to 12 per cent when produced in starch plants. When this cake is ground and mixed with feed products the fat content of the resulting mixture ranges from 3 to 6 per cent. Practically all the oil cake is utilized for this purpose. The bran and husks and the poorer quality of meal must be disposed of as feed and is sold by the dry millers under the name of "hominy feed." The starch makers produce a feed which they usually call "gluten feed." This gluten feed generally carries a guaranty of about 20 per cent of protein. All the feeds are marketed under a guaranty as to the content of fat. The feed stock from the hominy mills (see fig. 2) can be sold separately because it has sufficient fat, but when mixed with the bran and husks it becomes necessary to add the oil cake in order to bring the fat content up to the amount expected in feeds. It is generally stated that the value of a feed, in so far as it is reflected in the price, depends mostly on the protein content and not so much on the fat content. Thus, a feed with 6 per cent of fat would not bring an appreciably greater revenue than one containing only 5 per cent. Hence, an excessive amount of oil in the cake is carefully avoided.

The question of color is important with regard to feed. Although a dark color has no effect on the feeding value, it immediately affects the price, because buyers are accustomed to a light-colored feed. Excessive pressure in the expeller, which insures a maximum yield of oil, so darkens the cake that it is thought the reduced price obtainable for the feed because of the darker color may perhaps offset the gain in the yield of oil. At one plant where hydraulic presses are in operation the oil cake is not mixed with the feed, but is sold separately as a dairy feed.

The question of extracting the oil from the cake by means of solvents and thus removing all the oil has in recent years received considerable attention, owing largely to the high price of corn oil. It is understood that already such extracting systems are being operated by several large corn-oil producers. Just how the removal of all or nearly all the fat from the germ would affect the feed problem is a question; but since the removal of practically all the fat would concentrate the protein to some extent, it would seem, in view of what has been said regarding the relative value of protein and fat in feeds, that the feeding value would not be greatly diminished.

BUYING AND SHIPPING CORN GERMS.

Until a few years ago there was considerable trade in corn germs, but this has almost entirely disappeared because no germs are to be had. The attractive prices for oil have induced many manufacturers of corn products, who formerly disposed of the germs to others, to install expelling units and thus add a material source of profit to their business. The very fact that there was a brisk demand for the germs by oil manufacturers was convincing evidence that the expelling of the oil was a profitable operation.

Some difficulty is encountered in the shipping of corn germs because of their tendency to spoil in transit, and the loss incident to such spoilage has somewhat discouraged the practice. The germs are shipped in bags, and with rapid shipment and the proper control of moisture the spoilage can be reduced to a minimum.

UTILIZATION OF CORN OIL.

Corn oil has been used to a greater or less extent for most technical purposes for which other vegetable oils are used. One of the principal technical uses for which it has been in good demand is in the preparation of rubber substitutes, for which it seems to be well adapted. Both crude and refined oils are used for this purpose.

Corn oil is still used in considerable quantities for soap making, this being one of the principal uses for the poorer grades, which can not be refined except at a large loss. The oil is very well adapted for making soft soaps, but it is not so suitable for the harder and better quality of soaps. The foots obtained on refining the crude oil are, of course, used exclusively for soap making.

It is reported that corn oil has been used in wool spinning where a cheap noncombustible oil is demanded. The present price, however, probably makes it uneconomical for that purpose. The iodin number also would indicate that it might not be entirely safe.

In the manufacture of lubricants, corn oil has had a limited application. For this purpose it has not been used alone, but has been mixed with blown rape oil and mineral oil. However, the fact that it has a tendency to gum makes it unsuitable for this purpose, and its use in lubricants has practically ceased.

Corn oil is classed sometimes as a nondrying oil and sometimes as a semidrying oil. Its iodin value might place it in the semidrying class, but it has few drying properties and does not form a hard film. Its use in paint, therefore, has been limited to the cheap grades of barn paints, when combined with other and better drying oils. This use is also rapidly declining and will no doubt be entirely discontinued if the price of the oil remains high.

When corn oil was first produced in marketable quantities it was used exclusively for technical purposes. Gradually, however, as refining methods were improved and the demand for edible oils increased, the oil was diverted to edible purposes until at present probably 75 per cent of the total output is utilized in that way. It is in demand for practically all purposes for which cottonseed oil is used, and the producers, brokers, and refiners are confident that in time all the corn oil of good quality will be used for edible purposes.

The shortage and the high price of olive oil during recent years have served to stimulate the use of other vegetable oils for salad-oil purposes, and corn oil is being sold in increasing quantities to meet this demand. In line with this development its use in cookery has also been increased. The sale of refined corn oil for household purposes is at present limited almost entirely to a few firms.

Corn oil can be heated to a relatively high temperature without smoking or developing an odor and does not darken as readily as some other edible oils. In this connection it may be mentioned that there is a conviction that in cookery it is more economical to use liquid fats than solid fats, because there is less waste. It is easier to measure the necessary quantity when the material pours than when it is solid; consequently excess fat is more easily avoided.

There seems to be some difference of opinion among bakers regarding the adaptability of corn oil for shortening in crackers and bakery goods. The refined oil is used to some extent for this purpose and is said to give results similar to those obtained with cottonseed oil. Some bakers are inclined to believe that its use is limited because of its yellow color, such color being undesirable in the manufacture of white goods like soda crackers. For sweet goods the oil is usually used blended with other vegetable oils. In bread it is also used by some bakers when mixed with lard.

The general impression gained from interviews with large bakers is that the future of refined corn oil in the baking industries is assured. The principal reason why it is not used more generally at present is because it is not obtainable at all times in sufficient quantities. The bulk of the refined oil is marketed as package goods for the retail trade; therefore for the bakers only such quantities are available as are not needed to satisfy the retail demands. A considerable increase in the production of the refined oil could no doubt easily be absorbed in this field provided the price compared favorably with that of other oils suitable for the same purpose.

EFFECT OF COLOR AND CONDITION OF THE CORN ON THE YIELD AND CHARACTER OF THE OIL.

Both white and yellow dent corn are used in this country for the manufacture of corn products, but the white seems to be generally preferred. In hominy mills the variety used is determined largely by the kind of corn meal demanded. Certain sections of the country consume only yellow corn products, while others prefer the white. Starch and glucose makers use both kinds, most operators claiming that the products are the same. There is no indication that there is any difference in the oil from the two kinds, but it is the opinion of some that the white corn has a larger germ and hence produces more oil to the bushel. This opinion is based largely on conjecture.

The opinion seems to be quite general, especially among the dry-corn millers, that the quantity of oil obtainable decreases somewhat with the age of the corn. Their theory is that the oil "creeps" out of the germ into the starchy portion of the kernel and is thus lost in the hominy products and feed. No definite study of this question seems to have been made. It is possible, however, that with age and the drying of the kernel the germ becomes more brittle and thus chips and breaks more in the degerminators, the smaller fragments being lost in the feed. The monthly oil records for a number of years of one starch and glucose plant were carefully examined, and it was found that the quantity of oil in the corn, calculated on a moisture-free basis, was about 4.3 per cent, as determined by extraction with carbon tetrachlorid. The corn milled during the summer months was somewhat higher in oil content. While the increase was only about 0.3 per cent, it was shown by the records that this increase occurred every year. As a rule, the corn used in the summer months is the last of the previous year's crop. It would seem, therefore, that if the general assumption is true that the older corn yields less oil, it is not because there is less oil in the kernel, but because the degerminating is less efficiently performed on the older corn. In the dry process of degerminating, this is very likely to be the case.

The condition of the corn with regard to its maturity has a pronounced effect upon the character of the oil and the quantity obtainable. According to figures available at one of the glucose plants, the soft corn of 1917 had a somewhat higher oil content than well-matured corn, but the general experience with that year's crop showed a decidedly reduced yield. The explanation usually advanced is that some of the oil was distributed in the kernel outside of the germ and was lost. A most interesting feature of this oil was its high acid content. While normally the oil averages between

1 and 2 per cent of free acids, the oil from the 1917 crop averaged nearly 10 per cent and in many instances was as high as 15 to 17 per cent. It was also darker than usual and the expelling was more difficult, in some cases more than 15 per cent of the oil being left in the cake. Naturally the refining of this oil involved big losses, and consequently it brought a greatly reduced price in the crude state.

COMPARISON OF THE OIL-PRODUCTION OPERATION IN DIFFERENT MILLS.

In order to ascertain the extent to which the products from the various mills differed, determinations were made of the fat and moisture content of the germ, oil cake, and feed secured from these mills, and samples of the oils they produced were tested for free fatty acids. Table I shows the results.

TABLE I.—*Comparison of the fat, moisture, and free fatty acid content of material produced in representative corn-products mills in the United States, showing the results of the wet and dry processes of degerminating the kernels.*

Material analyzed.	Source of material, different mills (per cent).							
	1	2	3	4	5	6	7	Average of 7 mills.
SEC. A.—Hominy mills (dry process):								
Free fatty acids—								
Crude oil	1.29	0.78	0.73	0.88	2.34	1.27	0.88	1.11
Refined oil	.10							
Fat—								
Germs		13.3	14.37	15.68	22.41	16.66	24.90	17.88
Oil cake		5.80	4.19		7.90	9.38	a 12.97	6.82
Feed	5.93	6.36	6.15	5.23				5.92
Moisture—								
Germs		2.92	8.66	7.90	8.49	9.61	4.31	6.96
Oil cake		3.37	10.55		7.96	4.45	2.74	5.81
Feed	12.50	10.35	12.66	10.86	10.36			11.35
SEC. B.—Starch and glucose plants (wet process):								
Free fatty acids—								
Crude oil	1.78	b 9.17	1.39	1.65	5.34	2.14	2.05	2.39
Refined oil			.17		.11	.10		
Fat—								
Germs	51.85	c 23.78	41.99	22.35	50.14	55.96	49.20	42.23
Oil cake	8.90	8.08	7.35	9.25	a 6.04	8.35	10.30	8.70
Feed		6.85	3.63	5.20	2.85	3.36		4.38
Moisture—								
Germs	3.75	5.46	4.68	4.38	4.62	2.28	5.44	4.37
Oil cake	9.74	9.20	7.89	3.80	7.15		8.67	7.74
Feed	11.12	9.53	10.38	8.91	11.22	9.76		10.15

a Not included in average. b Immature corn of 1917, not included in average. c Immature corn of 1917.

A study of Table I shows that there is a wide variation in the character of the material produced in the various mills. While the percentage of free fatty acids in the oils is low it is evident that the oil obtained from germs separated by the dry process of degerminating is somewhat lower than that from the wet process. This might be expected from the nature of the two processes. So far as observation indicates, however, the refined oil from the two processes shows no noticeable difference. The percentages of fat in the germs and oil cake, as indicated by the averages, agree fairly well with the opinions expressed by the operators of both types. Since the moisture content may be much affected by the age of the material and the conditions under which it was shipped, figures relating to the percentage of moisture may not necessarily be indicative of actual conditions.

Attention is directed to some of the figures in section A of Table I. Mill 2 furnished germ material of exceedingly low fat content. This mill also reported a low yield of oil from a bushel of corn. It is evident, therefore, that the degerminating was not efficiently performed. Mill 7 shows an excessive percentage of fat in its oil cake, but also a germ material greatly above the average in fat content, indicating a good separation of germs, but probably less efficient handling of the expeller.

ECONOMICS OF CORN-OIL PRODUCTION.

To determine the cost of producing corn oil is exceedingly difficult, and no producer was found who had any clear idea as to just what it cost him or how to determine the cost. The difficulty lies in the fact that in the general processes of making hominy and starch the removal of the germ is a necessary factor in obtaining the best products. This cost, therefore, should be charged to those products in the manufacture of which it is a necessary process and not to the cost of producing the oil. The cost of the oil-production should be calculated only on the operations involved after the germs have been separated. Thus, in the dry process the cost charges for the oil should begin after the germs have passed through the hominy reels and the fine meal removed. In the wet process the germs must be washed several times in order to save the adhering starch, and the cost charges for the oil should therefore begin with the expelling of the moisture. If the net revenue from corn oil is to be compared with that obtainable when the germs are disposed of as feed, the cost of expelling the moisture and drying must be eliminated, since both operations are necessary in order to prepare the germs for feed. The cost, therefore, of producing corn oil in the industries here described is limited to the cost of expelling the oil and preparing it for market.

COST OF EXPELLING CORN OIL.

Among starch manufacturers the impression seems to prevail that the cost of expelling corn oil approximates half a cent per pound of oil. Since the cost per pound depends on the amount of oil obtained from a given quantity of germ material, it follows that the greater the fat content of the germ the lower the cost per pound of oil will be. Consequently, the character of the germ material as regards the presence of foreign matter is an important factor. For this reason it will cost more per pound to expel the oil from dry-process germs than from wet-process germs, because the same quantity of material yields much less oil over which to distribute an equivalent operating cost.

In an effort to determine as nearly as possible the actual cost of producing corn oil, based on the cost of equipment and of operating the same, the figures in Table II are submitted. The cost of the equipment is, of course, an estimate based on present-day prices. The cost of repairs on expellers and the items of labor, power, and productive capacity were obtained from a careful study of the operation of a 4-expeller unit in a typical hominy plant.

TABLE II.—*Itemized estimate of the cost of the process of producing corn oil.*

Itemization.	Division of cost.		
	Invest-ment.	Per year.	Per day of 24 hours.
Mill equipment, 4 expellers at $4,000	$16,000		
Depreciation and repair (12½ per cent)		$2,000	$6.66
Auxiliary equipment:			
Scales	2,000		
Storage bins	1,000		
Conveyor to expellers	1,000		
Oil conveyors	1,000		
Cake conveyor	1,000		
Pumps (2)	600		
Filter press	1,000		
Holding tanks (2)	4,000		
Total	11,600		
Depreciation (5 per cent)		580	1.93
Power, 5,312 k. w. h. per 24 hours			88.70
Labor:			
Oil miller at 50 cents per hour, $12			} 21.60
Assistant miller at 40 cents per hour, $9.60			
Total			118.89

Production.—Per machine, 3,000 pounds of oil in 24 hours, 12,000 pounds: *Cost per pound* ($118.89÷12,000), 0.99 cents.

These figures are intended to show approximately what it costs to expel corn oil in connection with hominy plants where the necessary floor space may be arranged for without the construction of an additional building. Overhead charges, such as management and selling organization, are not included. It seems probable that the installation of an expelling plant such as is here outlined would not necessitate any material addition to the pay roll except for the labor required to operate the machines. Although in making an actual cost accounting the charge for overhead expense should be included, the amount thus chargeable would be so difficult to ascertain, owing to the fact that the expelling is so involved in the other operations of the plant, that to include it here would be largely guesswork. It is evident that if an independent plant were operated exclusively for the expelling of corn oil the heavy overhead expense of management and office organization would almost certainly make the operation unprofitable.

Assuming that the foregoing estimate of approximately 1 cent is the cost to produce 1 pound of oil in the average hominy plant (dry process), it is possible to arrive at the cost for similar operations in starch or glucose plants (wet process). As previously stated, the wet-process germs yield approximately three times as much oil as the dry-process germs. The cost to produce a pound of oil in a starch plant would be, therefore, about a third of a cent. Some operators in starch plants were of the opinion that the cost would approximate half a cent a pound.

Table III gives a comparison of the revenue that may be obtained by disposing of the germ material for mixing with feed and by expelling the oil and returning the oil cake to the feed.

TABLE III.—*Comparison of the revenue obtainable from the germs from 1 bushel of corn when disposed of respectively as feed and when used for oil expelling in either starch or hominy mills.*

Items.	Wet process (starch mills).	Dry process (hominy mills).
Germs obtained from 1 bushel of corn.........................pounds..	3. 47	4. 17
Revenue from germs sold as feed, at 2.5 cents a pound.................cents..	8. 40	10. 42
Oil obtainable from germs.................................pounds a..	1. 25	.5
Revenue from oil, at 15 cents a pound.............................cents..	18. 75	7. 5
Oil cake obtainable...................................pounds b..	2. 22	3. 67
Revenue from oil cake, at 2.5 cents a pound.......................cents..	5. 55	9. 17
Total revenue from expelling operation (cake and oil).........................do....	24. 30	16. 67
Deduct cost of expelling....................................do....	c. 63	d. 5
Net revenue for expelling.................................do....	23. 67	16. 17
Balance in favor of expelling as against disposal of germs for feed stock........do....	15. 27	5. 75

a Since the percentage of oil obtainable by expelling the germs varies greatly, only the average is here used.

b The weight of oil cake obtainable is here calculated simply as the difference between the weight of the germs used and that of the oil removed. For example, 100 pounds of dry-process germs are considered as yielding 12 pounds of oil and 88 pounds of oil cake. Although not absolutely accurate, it is considered sufficiently so for the purpose here intended. However, if by actual fat determination the germs are found to contain 18 per cent of oil and the cake 6 per cent, the following formula should be used to determine the exact weights of oil and oil cake obtained, thus: $[6 (100-a) \div 100] + a = 18$ pounds (total oil present in 100 pounds of germs), in which a represents the actual number of pounds of oil which will be obtained. Upon solving this equation it is found that 12.766 pounds of oil are obtained, and 87.234 pounds of oil cake containing 6 per cent of fat.

c At one-half cent per pound.

d At 1 cent per pound.

The figures in Table III are intended to be only approximations, since several factors have not been considered which might increase slightly the cost of producing the oil. The fact that the germ material for expelling must be made more dry than that for feed purposes will add slightly to the cost. The material would also probably be reduced or ground to a greater extent than if intended for feed. These operations are not expensive, however, and since the actual cost is difficult to estimate they have been omitted from the calculations. The efficiency with which the degermination and expelling are accomplished is a determining factor. A good grade of corn and careful operation of the expellers are also necessary to obtain the margin of profit indicated. The price of corn feeds is of course dependent upon the cost of corn, and consequently the lower the price of corn and feed the greater the balance in favor of oil expelling, provided the price of the oil remains the same.

Table IV gives data comparing the respective weights of oil left in the oil cake obtained from a bushel of corn by the two types of mills.

TABLE IV.—*Comparison of oil left in the oil cake obtained from a bushel of corn when operating on dry-process and wet-process germs.*[a]

Items.	Dry process (hominy mills).	Wet process (starch and glucose plants).
Germs obtained from 1 bushel of corn..pounds..	4.17	3.47
Oil in germs...per cent..	18	45
Oil left in cake...do....	6	9
Oil obtained from 1 bushel of corn...pounds..	.532	1.372
Cake obtained...do....	3.637	2.097
Oil in the cake..do....	.2182	.1887

a The calculations in this table were made with the formula explained in footnote b of Table III.

It is evident that in expelling dry-process germs a slightly greater loss of oil results than when expelling wet-process germs, although the percentage of oil left in the cake is considerably lower.

PRODUCTION OF EDIBLE OIL.[1]

In 1919 there were 22 corn-oil producers in the United States, but early in the year several of these had suspended operations on account of adverse economic conditions. Of the 20 producers only four, so far as is known, turned out refined or edible oil, one being a hominy miller and the other three starch and glucose manufacturers. This small number of refiners, however, is no indication of the relative quantity of oil which is refined for food purposes. According to Bailey and Reuter,[2] 111,000,000 pounds of corn oil were produced in 1918, of which approximately 76,000,000 pounds, or about 70 per cent, were refined for edible purposes.

It is the practice of a few of the large operators to refine not only the oil which is produced in their own plants, but also to buy large quantities of crude oil from other producers for refining. Companies

---

[1] Since this paper deals mainly with the production of crude corn oil as a by-product in the corn-milling industry, the refining of such an oil for edible purposes, which is an industry in itself is here discussed only in a general way. A technical paper embodying the results of a detailed study of the preparation of edible corn oil may be issued later.

[2] Bailey, Herbert S., and Reuter, B. E. The production and conservation of fats and oils in the United States. U. S. Dept. of Agr. Bul. 769, sup., p. 4. 1919.

which have developed a large package trade find it necessary to do this in order to supply the demand created by their extensive advertising.

Crude corn oil as a rule is a fairly good product, especially that produced from dry-process germs, and in some cases it can be used for edible purposes without refining. The oil possesses a peculiar cereal-like odor and taste, which is not unpleasant in itself, but is undesirable when the oil is intended for salad or cooking purposes. The color is a deep yellow, which also must be removed from oil which is intended for food purposes.

The processes used for refining, bleaching, and deodorizing are in general similar to those employed for other vegetable oils. The crude oil is first treated with alkali in large refining kettles (fig. 10), the amount of alkali used depending on the quantity of free fatty acids present. This treatment almost, if not entirely, neutralizes the oil, removes albuminous matter, and lightens the color to

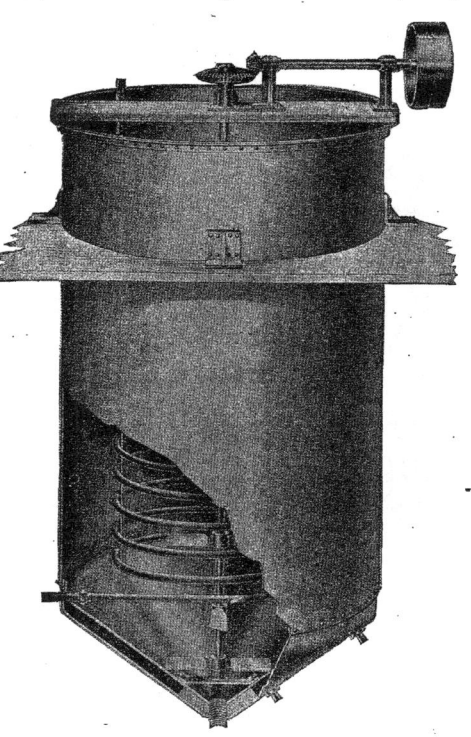

FIG. 10.—Type of tank used for refining and bleaching corn oil.

some extent. The oil is then separated from the foots, the latter being disposed of to soap makers. The neutralized oil is heated sufficiently to dehydrate it, after which it is partially bleached by the addition of about 5 or 6 per cent of fuller's earth, with constant stirring. After the oil and fuller's earth have been thoroughly mingled, the mixture is pumped through filter presses to remove the earth, and the filtered oil is pumped into the deodorizing tank. (Fig. 11.) The treatment received in this tank is of great importance. Essentially this treatment consists of heating the oil to about 400° F. under vacuum by means of steam jackets and steam coils, superheated steam being used in these coils. Through

a secondary coil with perforations, superheated steam is passed into the oil. This treatment is continued for several hours, after which the steam is turned off and the oil allowed to cool under reduced pressure to normal temperature. The oil is thus further bleached, the peculiar odor and taste are removed, and a bland, tasteless, and odorless oil is produced which varies from a pale yellow to a very light straw color, according to the efficiency of the treatment.

The process of deodorizing constitutes the most difficult part of the several processes required to produce edible corn oil, and the details of the operation vary considerably in the several refining plants. Questions of temperature and time of treatment are determined largely by experimentation and the experience of the men in charge. The character of the crude oil used is also in some cases a determining factor.

After the oil is cooled in the deodorizer it flows or is pumped into the storage tanks. While in storage it is in some cases kept at a low temperature in order to effect the separation of stearin, which, however, does not separate from corn oil to the same extent as from some other

Fig. 11c—Type of tank used for deodorizing corn oil. These tanks are also constructed with jacketed bottoms for steam heating.

vegetable oils. Finally, the oil is filtered through coarse paper or cloth to clarify and brighten it, especially when intended for the retail trade.

THE FUTURE OF CORN OIL.

So far as can be concluded from the survey of the industry, corn oil appears to have established itself as a satisfactory product for which there will be a steady demand in the trade. That the oil can always be produced is assured by virtue of the fact that it is a by-product of the manufacture of certain staple corn products, and it is only in case of an overproduction of fats and oils that it might be discontinued and the germs disposed of as feed. Such a situation seems improbable, however, and at the most would doubtless be only temporary. As to the utilization of corn oil, the consensus of opinion among those who are in position to know seems to be that within a few years the oil will be used almost entirely for edible purposes, except only that which is of such poor quality as to make its refining unprofitable. The sale of the oil in retail packages will very likely be further developed, and its use by bakers is also likely to increase. The amount of corn oil used for edible purposes in the future will be determined by the quantity available rather than by any question as to its utility. At the present time some bakers, while admitting that it is suitable for their products, use cottonseed oil because the supply of corn oil fluctuates so that it is not always obtainable in sufficient quantities. Although the supply is even now inadequate it is liable to become more so in the immediate future because of the decline in the brewing of beer. The elimination of the breweries removes one of the principal markets for hominy grits and flakes, and therefore the milling of degerminated corn is likely to decrease. As previously stated, several plants shut down in the winter of 1919. This was due in part, however, to the fact that at the close of the war there was on hand an oversupply of corn meal and flour. According to Bailey and Reuter,[1] there was a decrease in 1918 of 7,000,000 pounds of corn oil, and the 1919 production may show a further decrease. It is certain that the demand in this country for corn meal and flour is not sufficient to make a steady market for such products. In the Southern States, where the use of corn products is much more general than in other sections of the country, the supply is largely derived from mills which do not degerminate the corn and hence produce no oil. It must not be understood, however, that the elimination of the breweries entirely removes the market for brewers' grits, for in the manufacture of nonalcoholic cereal beverages the same material is required, but this market already exists, and there would need to be a great increase in the consumption of such beverages to make up for the decline resulting from the discontinuance of beer brewing. The economic situation with regard to sugar also may be an important factor. The increased demand for corn sirups and other saccharine products may result in an increased milling of degerminated corn.

---

[1] Op. cit., p. 1.

WASHINGTON : GOVERNMENT PRINTING OFFICE : 1920

UNITED STATES DEPARTMENT OF AGRICULTURE

BULLETIN No. 905

Contribution from the Bureau of Animal Industry

JOHN R. MOHLER, Chief

Washington, D. C. ▼ December 8, 1920

PRINCIPLES OF LIVESTOCK BREEDING.

By SEWALL WRIGHT,

Senior Animal Husbandman, Animal Husbandry Division.

CONTENTS.

	Page.			Page
Evolution of animal breeding	1	Mendelian heredity in livestock—Continued.		
Reproduction	2	Colors of sheep		33
The cell theory	2	Colors and comb shape of poultry		33
The reproductive cells	3	Heredity of form and function in livestock		34
Sexual maturity	4	Relations of theory to practice		34
Frequency of service	5	Equality of inheritance from the sexes		34
The breeding season and œstrous cycle	6	Prepotency		34
The gestation period	7	Variation		36
Fertility	8	Fixation of heredity by selection		37
Hybrids	10	Fixation of heredity by inbreeding		37
The reproductive cells in relation to heredity	11	Isolation of genetic differences by inbreeding		39
General considerations	11	The effect of inbreeding on vigor		40
Modification of heredity	12	Crossbreeding		42
Inheritance of acquired characteristics	13	The system of breeding		42
Telegony	14	The purposes of livestock breeding		42
Maternal impressions	15	Uniformity of type		43
Details of hereditary transmission	15	Crossbreeding for the market		44
Blending and alternative inheritance	15	Improvement		45
Hereditary units	15	Grading up		46
Color and albinism in guinea pigs	16	Methods of selection		47
Mendelian inheritance	18	General considerations		47
The chromosomes and heredity	20	Individual performance and livestock judging		49
Linkage	20	The breeding record		50
The determination of sex	23	Pedigrees		50
The normal method	23	The value of purebreds		54
Sex-linked inheritance	25	Dairy cattle		54
The sex ratio	27	Quality in meat		57
The freemartin	29	Breeding and soundness in horses		61
Mendelian heredity in livestock	30	Poultry		62
Polled cattle	30	Satisfaction from pleasing appearance		63
Colors of cattle	30	Summary		65
Colors of horses	31			
Colors of hogs	32			

EVOLUTION OF ANIMAL BREEDING.

The breeding of domestic animals dates back to remote antiquity, when the most advanced races of the Old World were still on the border line between savagery and barbarism. It far antedates any but the simplest mechanical arts. Yet, while our knowledge of the laws of nature as they apply to machines has reached very great magnitude and complexity, it is comparatively only a few years since the principles of breeding have been more than a collection of unrelated traditional beliefs. The same superstitions on which the shepherds of Asia based their practices at least 30 centuries ago are still widely current, while the one sound principle known to the ancients—selection of the best for breeding stock—is still widely neglected.

The earliest records show that the domestic animals had already become much modified from their wild ancestry. The process of change, however, had probably been exceedingly gradual and has continued so until very recently. A thoroughly self-conscious movement toward improvement of livestock dates back hardly more than a century and a half. Robert Bakewell, of Leicestershire, England, is credited with being the pioneer in this movement.

The breeders of the time of Bakewell suspected him of possessing and concealing special principles of breeding. It is often believed to-day that successful breeders have some mysterious method of which others are ignorant. Instead, the principles of the successful breeder have been exceedingly simple. He isolates and fixes a good type by careful selection and close breeding. If ambitious to take a greater step in advance, he crosses types with characteristics which seem to offer possibilities for a desirable combination and fixes the new ideal by continued selection and close breeding. He brings inferior stock up to a higher level by consistent use of prepotent sires of the same improved type. The difficulty lies not so much in knowing the principles as in applying them. Without skill in feeding and management, the possibilities of the animals can not be brought out in such way as to give a satisfactory basis for selection. Selection of breeding stock, moreover, requires the best judgment in estimating the merits of the animal's own performance, its conformation, ancestry, and previous success as a breeder, and also in giving each of these its due weight. Good judgment, industry, and persistence in following a given aim, as well as knowledge of sound principles, have been the qualities which have made successful breeders.

REPRODUCTION.

THE CELL THEORY.

There could be no clear ideas of breeding until something was known in detail of the processes through which a new individual starts on his career and develops. The most important step in this direction was the discovery that all living organisms are built up of microscopical living units, the cells, with characteristics which do not differ greatly in the most widely different plants and animals. These cells are semifluid bits of living matter, each bounded by a membrane. Each contains within itself a differentiated portion called the nucleus. The details of the structure are brought out by the use of dyes, which are seized upon by certain cell structures and not by others. Thus if an animal of plant tissue is properly preserved and stained with hematoxylin, a dye from logwood, a number of threadlike or rod-shaped bodies, called chromosomes, are made visible in the nucleus of each cell, through their taking on of a dark-blue color.

It has been found that the number of these chromosomes in the cells of each kind of animal or plant is constant, with certain qualifications, one of which will be taken up later. There are, for instance, 40 in swine, 48 in man, 8 in the fruit fly, 20 in corn, and 16 in wheat. A great deal of attention has been devoted to the chromosomes in recent years, as it has been demonstrated that they play an all-important part in heredity and the determination of sex. We shall have occasion to refer to them later.

A study of any rapidly growing part of a young animal soon reveals cells which are in the act of dividing to form two cells. New cells are formed in the body only in this way. The individual begins his career as a single cell. This divides into two, the daughter cells divide, and so on until the trillions of cells of the adult body are produced.

THE REPRODUCTIVE CELLS.

The original single cell, though barely visible to the naked eye, must somehow contain within itself all the potentialities, physical and mental, of the organism into which it is to develop. The characteristics of both the paternal and maternal lines of ancestry must be represented in it. It is, in fact, the product of the fusion between two cells, one a sperm cell furnished by the male parent, and the other an ovum, or egg cell, from the female parent.

The reproductive cells from the two sexes have very different appearances. In mammals, the ovum is a relatively large, spherical cell, just visible to the naked eye. In birds, the yolk of an egg is really a single ovum, distended to an enormous size by food material. The sperm cell is very much smaller and can be seen well only with a high-power microscope. It is something like a tadpole in shape, having a small cell body, containing little but the nucleus, and attached to this a long, whiplike process which beats rapidly while the cell is alive, enabling it to seek out and unite with the large, passive egg cell in the act of fertilization. Enormous numbers of sperm cells are produced by the male, but only one takes part in fertilization. After the first has penetrated the membrane of an egg cell, a change takes place in the latter which prevents the entrance of others.

SEXUAL MATURITY.

Animals reproduce only during the part of their lifetime following sexual maturity and preceding senescence.   During this period most of them reproduce only in a certain season of the year, the breeding season, and within this season a given female will breed during only

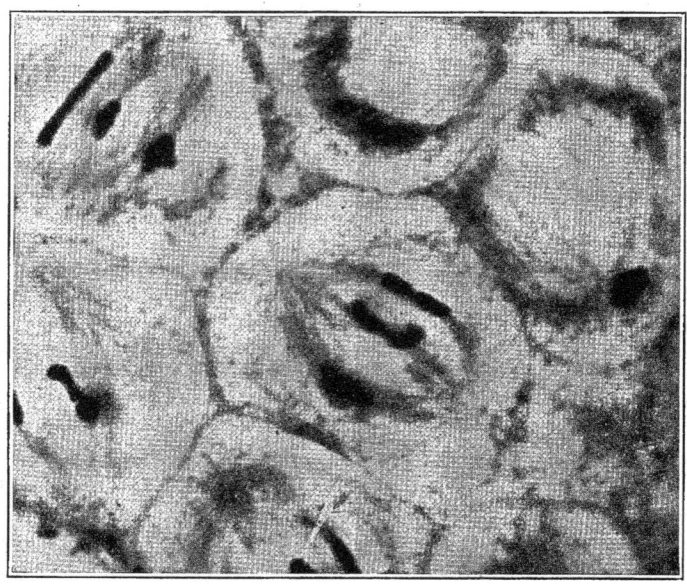

Fɪɢ. 1.—A group of dividing reproductive cells from a male grasshopper. The curious spindle-shaped figure, which is characteristic of dividing cells, is clearly brought out. In the formation of the reproductive cells, the chromosomes, which appear solid black in the illustration, come together in pairs around the equator of the spindle, separate and move to opposite poles, forming two nuclei as a preliminary to division of the cell as a whole. Each of the resulting cells has only half the original number of chromosomes. In ordinary cell divisions, each chromosome splits, the halves moving to opposite poles, each of which thus obtains the same number of chromosomes as the original cell. Only a few of the chromosomes are in focus in the picture, which was taken through a high-power microscope. (Courtesy of Dr. E. E. Carothers.)

a very brief period, the period of heat or œstrus.   In many cases the œstrous period recurs at definite intervals during the breeding season.

The age of maturity, while in a general way characteristic for a given kind of animal, depends on a great number of factors in individual cases. A warm climate, liberal feeding, and good care in general are conducive to early maturity. There are also hereditary differences. Early sexual maturity is doubtless correlated with the early maturity in growth that has been one of the characteristics for which the domestic animals have been most carefully selected.

Under favorable conditions hogs, sheep, cattle, and horses mature at remarkably early ages. Females usually become mature a little earlier than males under the same conditions, but the difference is not great. Boars and sows have been known to breed as early as 3 months, bulls and heifers at 4 months, rams and ewes at 5 months, and stallions and mares at 12 months. It is not, however, considered advisable to breed animals until some time after sexual maturity has begun; in order to avoid interference with their development. Moreover, the young will not obtain so good a start as they should unless the dam has nearly finished her own growth. It has also been asserted that the offspring of a very young sire are apt to be unthrifty, but there seems to be little evidence for this belief. Sows may usually be bred without harm at about 8 months, permitting their offspring to be born just a year from their own birth. Ewes are often bred at 7 months to lamb at a year, but under ordinary conditions a thrifty flock can not be maintained unless breeding is deferred until a year later. Heifers may usually be bred at 15 months, which means calving at 2 years of age. Most fillies can be bred at 2 years and practically all by 3 years. Limited use of males may be begun at about these same ages.

FREQUENCY OF SERVICE.

The number of females which can be served by a mature male varies greatly under different circumstances. Most care seems to be necessary with the stallion, in which fertility rapidly declines after a number of daily services. Eighty mares is about the limit of the number which should be served by one stallion in a season. With careful handling a single bull may be used with 60 or 70 cows, a single ram with even more than 100 ewes, and a single boar with 30 or 40 sows. Under range conditions the numbers are much less. One bull may run with 20 to 30 cows and one ram with 40 to 70 ewes.

The principal effect of too frequent service on a mature male seems to be temporary sterility. Daily service by a vigorous stallion was found by Lewis, of the Oklahoma experiment station, to be accompanied with a rapid decrease in both the number and vitality of the sperm cells. It is a common belief that fertilization by the weakened sperm cells, formed after excessive service, will result in unthrifty young, but the experimental evidence does not support this view. O. Lloyd-Jones and F. A. Hays, of the Iowa experiment station, made extensive experiments on rabbits to test this question. After too frequent service, they found a marked decline in the percentage of pregnancies induced and ultimately a decline in the size of litters, leading to temporary sterility. Microscopical study showed a marked decline in the motility of the sperm cells. Nevertheless, such offspring as were obtained from the late services were in every way as vigorous as those from early services.

- Artificial insemination may be mentioned at this point as a practice which is useful in extending the service of a valuable male and in overcoming certain forms of sterility. This practice is especially useful in the case of horses, but has also been used to some extent with cattle and dogs.

THE BREEDING SEASON AND ŒSTROUS CYCLE.

Wild animals generally have a fairly definite breeding season, which in most cases occurs at such a time that the young are born in the spring or summer. The smaller animals, in which the gestation period is very short and which develop rapidly, such as mice, rats, rabbits, and moles, usually have an extended breeding season from early spring through summer; wolves and foxes, with a gestation period of 2 months, breed in winter. Where the gestation period approaches half a year, the breeding season comes in the fall, as in the wild sheep and goats and the Texas armadillo. The bison and most deer, with a longer gestation period, breed late in the summer or early in the fall. There are some curious exceptions, such as bats, whose breeding season is in the fall; the ova remain unfertilized all winter and go through a development lasting 2 months in the spring.

The breeding season has become much obscured or wholly lost in most of the domestic animals. Most breeds of sheep, however, retain the definite fall breeding season and consequent spring lambing season of their wild forbears. The Dorset breed is exceptional in that the ewes will breed in the spring soon after the birth of lambs, conceived in the preceding fall. The sheep of Australia have come to breed at all seasons of the year. Mares come in heat most regularly in the spring and summer and the great majority of the foals are born in the months of April, May, and June after a gestation period of 11 months. Some are born, however, in all months of the year. About 50 per cent of all the calves and pigs are born in the months of March, April, and May. There is a secondary rise in the number of births early in the fall in both cases. Under favorable conditions sows are often bred to produce two litters a year with profit.

During the fall breeding season ewes have a number of periods of heat, each lasting 2 or 3 days and at intervals of 2 to 3 weeks. Mares come in heat normally about 9 days after foaling. The heat period lasts several days and recurs at intervals of 3 or 4 weeks. Cows come in heat from 6 to 8 weeks after calving if suckling the calf, otherwise after 3 or 4 weeks. The heat period is of very brief duration, lasting only a day or less. There is recurrence every 3 weeks. Sows come in heat 3 days after farrowing and again within a week after weaning the pigs. After this there is, as in the other cases, recurrence about every 3 weeks. Both the duration and the time of recurrence seem to vary considerably in different individuals.

THE GESTATION PERIOD.

Normally one or more ripe egg cells are released during the heat period. If fertilization takes place, there is as a rule no recurrence of heat until after the birth of the young. The average length of the gestation period is given below for a number of animals.

Gestation period in animals.

Mare	11 months (340 days).
Jennet	12 months.
Cow	9½ months (280 days).
Ewe	5 months (150 days).
Goat	5 months.
Sow	4 months (114 days).
Dog	2 months.
Cat	2 months.
Guinea pig	2¼ months (68 days).
Rabbit	1 month (30 days).
Rat	(22 days).
Mouse	(22 days).

The period of incubation in fowls corresponds to the gestation period in animals. The following periods are given for comparison:

Incubation period in fowls.

Ostrich	42 days.
Goose	30 days.
Duck	28 days.
Turkey	28 days.
Guinea fowl	27 days.
Pheasant	23 days.
Domestic fowl	21 days.
Pigeon	18 days.
Canary	13 days.

The gestation and incubation periods are both subject to considerable variation. There seem to be slight breed differences among the domestic animals. Thus, Darwin gives the average period for Southdown sheep as 144 days compared with 150 days for Merinos. The variation among individuals within a breed is, however, more important. Thus, it is about an even chance that a foal will be born between 333 and 347 days after service and there is also an even chance that it will be born outside of these limits. It is an even

) that a calf will be born within 3 or 4 days of the 280t
sows it is not quite an even chance that birth comes
114th, or 115th day. The table below gives the most
ay of birth following service on the first day of any j
ite of birth for any other day of service can easily be calc

Probable day of birth.

Date of service.	Date of birth of young.			
	Sow.	Ewe.	Cow.	Mare.
Jan. 1	Apr. 25	May 31	Oct. 8	Dec. 7
Feb. 1	May 26	July 1	Nov. 8	Jan. 7
Mar. 1	June 23	July 29	Dec. 6	Feb. 4
Apr. 1	July 24	Aug. 29	Jan. 6	Mar. 7
May 1	Aug. 23	Sept. 28	Feb. 5	Apr. 6
June 1	Sept. 23	Oct. 29	Mar. 8	May 7
July 1	Oct. 23	Nov. 28	Apr. 7	June 6
Aug. 1	Nov. 23	Dec. 29	May 8	July 7
Sept. 1	Dec. 24	Jan. 29	June 8	Aug. 7
Oct. 1	Jan. 23	Feb. 28	July 8	Sept. 6
Nov. 1	Feb. 23	Mar. 31	Aug. 8	Oct. 7
Dec. 1	Mar. 25	Apr. 30	Sept. 7	Nov. 6

FERTILITY.

re are few problems in practical breeding more importar
se in fertility. The losses to livestock farming from fai
y have been estimated as enormous. There are two
ility which must be considered—regularity of breedin
ir of young at a birth.
:attle and horses, in which twins are neither comm
ile, only the first phase is important. It is generally
wins are born in about 1 birth in 80 in cattle. Triple
arger numbers are born occasionally. The number c
in horses is generally stated as much less than in cattle
tion of 3,000 births taken at random from three recent v
General Stud Book (English Thoroughbreds) yielded 6€
rer, in 29 cases the foals were slipped, and only 12 of t
iorn alive. According to this tabulation, twins are bor

ages in heavy horses are 15 to 20 years, in cattle 10 to 15 years, in sheep 7 to 10 years, in hogs 5 to 8 years.

Examples of breeding at much greater ages can, of course, be found. A ewe is recorded as lambing at 19 years of age. As for the maximum length of life, horses are reported to have passed 40 years, cattle 30 years, sheep 20 years.

Chickens hatched early in spring usually begin to lay in from 6 to 8 months, but cases of laying at less than 5 months are on record. The best egg record is usually produced in the first full year of laying. The second and often the third years are nearly as good in the egg breeds. After this the number declines, but laying may continue to the eighth or ninth year.

That heredity is a factor in determining fertility may be seen by comparing the different breeds of hogs and sheep. Among hogs, the bacon breeds, as the Tamworth and the large Yorkshires, have considerably larger litters than the lard breeds. There are differences among the latter. In very extensive tabulations made by G. M. Rommel the average for Poland Chinas was 7.52, compared with 9.26 for Duroc-Jerseys. Averages for the other important lard breeds are intermediate. Among sheep, certain breeds, such as the Dorsets, Oxford Downs, and Shropshires, have twins more frequently than singles under favorable conditions. Southdowns are distinctly less fecund, while among Merinos twins are not common. Within a breed, the number at a birth is determined by such a variety of factors that it is not easy to demonstrate the influence of heredity. Nevertheless it has been shown for Poland China hogs (Rommel and Phillips) and for Shropshire sheep (Rietz and Roberts) that females born in large litters in the former and as twins in the latter have a slight tendency to produce more at a birth than the average.

Differences in fertility appear to be so great among individuals that breeders often look for some outer indication. It is generally believed that strong development of the masculine and feminine types in males and females, respectively, gives a special indication of fertility as well as of general vigor. It is sometimes thought that the fertility of a female is indicated by the number of mammæ. Professor Pearl has shown that this is true in a general way in a comparison of different kinds of mammals. It does not, however, seem to hold to any significant extent within a single species. Thus Alexander Graham Bell was able to increase the number of functional nipples in his flock of sheep from 2 to 6 by careful selection. This change was not accompanied to any appreciable extent by increase in the percentage of twins, although it was an advantage in those cases in which twins were born. Similarly, Pearl has shown that there is no significant correlation between the number of mammæ of a sow and the size of her litter.

The effects of inbreeding and crossbreeding on fertility are discussed later.   For the present it will suffice to say that inbreeding is very likely to lead to a reduction of fertility, both as regards regularity of breeding and number at a birth.   That this is an inevitable result is not, however, indicated by experiment.   Among a number of inbred lines, some will be found which appear to suffer little or no loss of fertility.   Experiments indicate that the fertility of a herd which has declined through inbreeding can usually be restored by an outcross even with another inbred line of reduced fertility, if the latter is not closely related.

Among factors other than heredity, a warm climate, a reasonable amount of exercise, and a condition neither fat nor thin are conducive to fertility in both males and females.   Insufficient exercise is considered to be an especially common cause of failure of stallions. Undernourishment reduces the activity of the reproductive function in both males and females.   Excessive fatness is, however, as great a cause of failure to breed in both sexes, in some cases owing to mechanical closure of ducts, in others to fatty degeneration of the sex glands, leading to permanent sterility.   Sterility from this cause is a recognized danger in fitting breeding stock for the show ring.

A gaining condition at the time of conception, following a somewhat thin condition, is considered most conducive to fertility.   This principle is much used in Great Britain in the so-called practice of flushing ewes.   Ewes which have been maintained on pasture are fed liberally for about 3 weeks before breeding, using, especially, succulent feeds. Similarly, fresh, green pasture is recommended for cows which have failed to breed.   On the other hand, certain feeds, among which sugar and molasses may be mentioned, are considered likely to lead to sterility.

There are a considerable number of pathological causes of infertility.   By far the most important is the financial loss which it occasions is contagious abortion of cattle, a germ disease.   Other causes of abortion are also sources of much loss.   A small percentage of animals are congenitally sterile.   The freemartin heifer is an example which is discussed later.   Permanent sterility which is not congenital may result from fatty degeneration, as already mentioned, or from tumors.   There are, finally, a number of conditions causing sterility, some of which can be overcome by the use of artificial insemination. The subject is too large to be more than touched on here.

HYBRIDS.

While wide crosses within the same species tend to increase fertility, crosses between different species are apt to result in offspring which are either wholly sterile or of reduced fertility in the few cases in which such crosses can be made at all.   The rather common stories of crosses between the sheep and hog may be stated confidently to have no foundation. It is even doubtful whether hybrids can be produced from two such closely related animals as the sheep and the goat, or the dog and the fox. A few possibly authentic instances have been reported, but at best a successful cross appears to be exceedingly unusual in both these cases. The European breeds of cattle cross freely with the Indian humped cattle, although the latter are considered to be of a different species. The cross with the American bison has often been made, the progeny being called cataloes. Some of the females are fertile, but the few males born alive have been sterile. Fertile males have been obtained by backcrossing with the parental species.

The most important species cross among mammals is, of course, that of the horse and ass. Both sexes of the mule, produced by a jack and a mare, and of the hinny, produced by a stallion and a jennet, are probably always sterile. There are occasional reports of fertile mare mules, but none of these seem to have been established beyond doubt. Both the horse and ass will cross with the various species of zebra, producing hybrids which so far as known are always sterile. A number of sterile hybrids have been produced in crosses between the domestic fowl, guinea fowl, peacock, pheasant, etc.

THE REPRODUCTIVE CELLS IN RELATION TO HEREDITY.

GENERAL CONSIDERATIONS.

As already noted, every individual begins his career in the union of two reproductive cells. All that is inherited from his ancestors is somehow passed on by these microscopic bits of living jelly. Any attempt to understand heredity should thus begin with a consideration of these cells and their mode of production by the parents.

At one time it was supposed that the reproductive cells were produced in some way by contributions from all parts of the body, building up, as it were, a miniature organism, ready to develop into an adult under the proper conditions. The egg and sperm cells were thus supposed to transmit the characteristics of the parents as they were at the time of their production. It was taken for granted that the powers of hereditary transmission of an individual could be changed by training, care, or even accident in such way that his subsequent offspring would show a special tendency to develop the new characteristics.

This view was first seriously questioned when it was found that the reproductive cells, like all other cells in the body, are produced only by the division of previous cells. Certain cells remain unspecialized from the beginning of development and after repeated divisions produce the reproductive cells and these only. The remaining cells undergo specialization into skin, muscle, bone, nerve cells, etc., and never give rise to reproductive cells. The two classes of cells, reproductive cells and body cells, thus have separate histories, and any influence of one group on the other must be indirect.

It will easily be seen that this leads to a very different conception of heredity from that mentioned above. The reproductive cells are not produced by the body. They are simply an unchanged bit of the same material which previously developed into the body of the parent. Heredity consists merely in their retention of the power to develop into a complete individual under the proper conditions. Thus, so far as heredity is concerned, the way in which an individual is related to his parents and more remote ancestors does not differ essentially from the kind of relationship with brothers, uncles, etc.

This view of heredity was first reached by Sir Francis Galton, in England, and August Weismann, in Germany, from a consideration of the history of the reproductive cells. Numerous experiments have also been made to test its truth. A striking illustration is given by an experiment performed by Prof. W. E. Castle and Dr. John C. Phillips, of Harvard University. They removed the ovaries of a female albino guinea pig and placed in her body the ovaries of an immature black female, aged about 3 weeks. The albino female was later mated with an albino male. Albinos, mated together, never produce any but albino young, a fact well known to all breeders of small mammals. Yet in this case, the young, six in number, were all black. These young were in three litters, born from 6 months to a year after the operation. The immature ovaries of the black female were subject to the influence of the blood of the albino for from 4 to 10 months before the egg cells attained full growth and were discharged. Through it all they retained their original hereditary potentialities unchanged.

MODIFICATION OF HEREDITY.

Although the reproductive cells are not produced by the body, the possibility must be recognized that they may be modified in some cases by substances circulating in the blood. Recent experiments have, in fact, shown that changes can be brought about in the general vigor of the offspring in this way. Dr. C. R. Stockard, of Cornell University, tested the effect of daily intoxication of guinea pigs with alcohol. The animals themselves remained vigorous throughout the treatment. Their young, however, were markedly unthrifty compared with those of an unintoxicated control stock. This was true even when an alcoholic male was mated with a normal female, indicating that the reproductive cells of the male had been damaged by the alcohol. The injury seemed to be permanent, since a second generation produced by first generation animals, which had never been treated, was likewise feeble. Prof. L. J. Cole, of the University of Wisconsin, has obtained similar results on treating male rabbits with lead. Several other experiments have been made along this general line, some of which confirm the preceding results, while others were negative. It seems clear that it is possible to injure the hereditary qualities of the reproductive cells by means of substances in the blood, but that it is not at all easy to do so.

INHERITANCE OF ACQUIRED CHARACTERISTICS.

The question whether a specific change in the sire, due to training, care, or accident, can be transmitted to the young, is quite independent of the question whether a general loss of vigor can be produced in any such way. As we have seen, the latter can be accomplished through the use of poisons, such as alcohol or lead, and the possibility exists that extreme malnutrition may sometimes have such an effect. The mechanism is at least easy to understand. This is not the case with a specific characteristic.

There is a strong negative evidence in certain cases. Weismann cut off the tails of mice for 19 generations without causing any modification of the young. Docking the tail of sheep and many similar practices have no hereditary effect. Thus it can be stated very positively that the effects of mutilation or accidental injuries are not inherited.

With regard to the functional characteristics in which livestock breeders are most interested, the evidence is not so clear cut but is still negative when of a critical character. F. R. Marshall has shown that the average age of the sires of 2.10 trotters was practically the same as that for all Standardbred horses of the same period, indicating that longer training has no effect on the speed of the progeny. F. S. Putney made an analysis of the records of the Jersey herd at the Missouri Agricultural College and found no relation between age of dam and butterfat record of the daughter.

The failure of acquired characteristics to be inherited does not mean, of course, that proper care and feeding of livestock can be neglected, even from the standpoint of breeding. It is only by testing the speed of his race horses, the butterfat record of his dairy cows, or the fattening capacity of meat animals that the breeder can determine which are likely to transmit the best heredity and so separate the desirable breeding stock from the culls. Moreover, in such a case as the development of an unsoundness in a horse, due apparently to an accident, there should be much hesitation before breeding. The development of the unsoundness is likely to indicate a hereditary weakness, and such horses will be found in general to have sired unsatisfactory colts before the accident and will continue to do so thereafter.

Thus in many respects the breeder should act much as if acquired characteristics were inherited.   On the other hand, it is important to know that it is hopeless to attempt to improve scrub stock merely by giving it the best of care for any number of generations.

Probably the strongest reason for the common belief in the inheritance of acquired characteristics is that to many it seems impossible to account for progress in any other way.   To this it may be said that while the hereditary qualities of the reproductive cells do not seem to be influenced by changes in the individual, they are not unchangeable.   Variations occur from time to time, apparently at random. By the methods discussed later these variations may be combined in desirable ways and fixed in a stock.

TELEGONY.

It was widely believed at one time that after a female has borne young, sired by a certain male, her later offspring, sired by other males, will show characteristics derived from the first—a supposed phenomenon which has been called telegony.   Such an influence could come only from a modification of the egg cells of the female by influences from the first offspring before birth, and so come under the head of the inheritance of acquired characteristics.   It is even more improbable, however, as the influence of the first male must necessarily be very indirect.   The most widely quoted example of this sort of influence was a case in which a mare was mated with a zebra, producing a hybrid, and later, after mating with a horse, produced a colt which had certain markings which resembled those of a zebra. This, however, was merely an isolated case.   A considerable number of attempts have been made to confirm it, but with no success.   The most extensive experiments were those of J. Cossar Ewart, likewise with zebras and mares.   He could find no effects which could be ascribed to telegony.   There was, indeed, one case in which a mare produced a colt with vestiges of stripes after having produced a hybrid.   It was found, however, that the sire of this colt, an Arab, produced similarly striped colts from mares which had never seen a zebra.

Similar experiments with zebra crosses, also with negative results, have been carried on by the Bureau of Animal Industry.   F. B. Mumford and C. B. Hutchinson made an investigation of the question in the mule-breeding district of Missouri.   Many cases were found in which mares bore mule and horse colts successively, but no evidence could be found for telegony.   The theory is now considered to be thoroughly discredited and is evidently one which need give the practical breeder no concern.

MATERNAL IMPRESSIONS.

There is another very ancient belief which may be mentioned in this connection. This is the belief that objects seen by a prospective mother, especially if a nervous shock is produced, have an effect on the unborn young. Such an influence appears highly improbable in the light of our present knowledge, as there is no nervous connection between mother and offspring or even a direct blood connection. The favorable evidence is all of the unsatisfactory character of anecdotes, while deliberate attempts to obtain the phenomenon have all failed. The kind of case which was formerly often explained in this way, such as the appearance of a red calf in a black Aberdeen Angus herd, is now accounted for in other ways.

DETAILS OF HEREDITARY TRANSMISSION.

BLENDING AND ALTERNATIVE INHERITANCE.

Until rather recently it was usual to consider the contributions of the two parents to the heredity of the offspring to be as inseparably mixed together as would be two liquids. This view is illustrated in the common figure of speech used in referring to the degree of heredity from a given stock. Thus the cross between a Merino and a Shropshire sheep is spoken of as half-blood Merino and half-blood Shropshire and is expected to show a blending of the two breeds in all their characteristics. Another Shropshire cross produces a three-quarter blood, which is expected to be intermediate in all respects between the half-blood and the full-blood Shropshire.

This simple formula is still as good as any in predicting the results of a cross about which nothing is known but the characteristics of the two animals which are mated, and even in a large class of cases in which a great deal more is known.

Certain cases, however, have long been known in which this fusion of characteristics does not take place. This is especially likely to be true of coat colors. Every one knows, for example, that a great variety of sharply distinct colors—black, maltese, tabby, orange, etc.—may be found within a single litter of kittens.

The gap between sharply alternative inheritance of this kind and apparent blending inheritance is bridged over by the large class of cases in which the first generation of a cross is more or less of a blend, but the second generation shows greatly increased variability, the different characteristics of the two races tending to reappear in all combinations.

HEREDITARY UNITS.

The basis for any kind of inheritance, of course, must be material contributed by the microscopic sperm and egg cells in their union. The fundamental conception of the present theory of heredity is that these contributions are composed of units which are handed on generation after generation without change. The union of sperm cell and ovum in its bearing on heredity may be compared to the mingling of two collections of solid beads instead of to a mixing of two liquids. Certain characteristics, such as coat color, depend on such a small number of these units for their development that the separate ones can easily be identified, given symbols, and followed from generation to generation. Most characteristics, including size and conformation, depend on such a large number of units for development that the effects of the separate ones can not easily be distinguished. The inheritance is naturally more or less of the blending type, but a large number of phenomena, such as prepotency and the effects of inbreeding and crossbreeding, can be understood best by the theory that the hereditary basis is composed of a limited though fairly large number of unchanging units.

The statement that these units are unchanging applies to ordinary experience. It must not be taken too literally, however, as if this were true there could be no progress. Cases have been clearly established in which a unit must have become modified so that its effect is changed or, in many cases, apparently wholly lost. Differences between individuals depend on the possession of different alternative forms of certain of the hereditary units.

It may be added that the experimental evidence indicates that there is in general equal inheritance from sire and dam with respect to all kinds of characters. With the exception of a rather unusual class of cases, which is discussed later, it appears that the sperm cell contains a full set of the hereditary units characteristic of the kind of animal and that the same is true of the egg cell. The fertilized egg cell thus receives a double set of the units.

COLOR AND ALBINISM IN GUINEA PIGS.

A concrete illustration will bring out the behavior of these hereditary units in a typical case. It has been mentioned already that albino guinea pigs always breed true. Stocks of colored guinea pigs can also be obtained which breed true in the sense that they never produce albinos. The first cross between such stocks results wholly in colored young. Color, therefore, is said to dominate over albinism, and, conversely, albinism is said to be recessive to color. If these crossbred young, whether male or female, are bred back to the albino stock, it will be found that only 50 per cent of the young are colored, the other half being albinos. These albinos, when crossed with each other, produce only albinos, and this is true of their descendants indefinitely. The power to produce color seems to have completely dropped out of their make-up. If their colored brothers or sisters are crossed with the albino stock, the result is, as before, 50 per cent colored to 50 per cent albino. These last colored young are seven-eighths blood of the albino stock, yet when crossed with albinos they again produce 50 per cent colored and 50 per cent albino. No matter how many albino top crosses are made, the colored animals continue to produce colored young in numbers which never depart to a significant extent from 50 per cent.

The animals of the original stock are supposed to have a certain hereditary unit in their make-up which we may call factor C, following the custom of representing a dominant unit by a capital letter. The albino stock have a modification of this factor, c, which is no longer able to play its normal part in the production of color. All

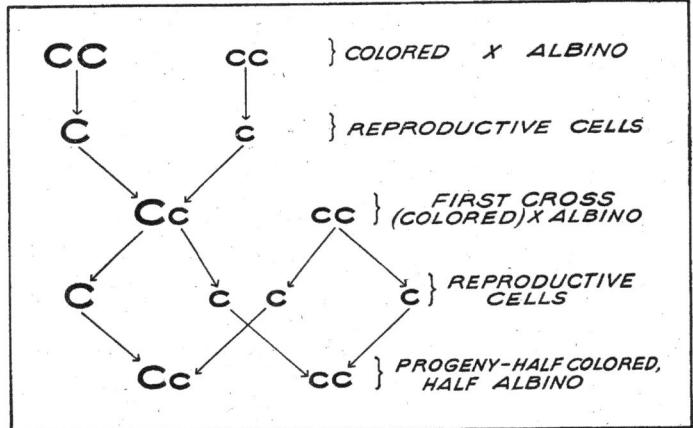

Fig. 2.—Diagram illustrating the mode of inheritance of a unit Mendelian factor. A pure colored strain of guinea pig (CC) is crossed with albinos (cc). Their progeny are all colored (Cc), but produce two kinds of reproductive cells, one transmitting color (C) and other albinism (c), as is revealed by a cross with albino stock.

the reproductive cells of the colored stock have factor C, those of the albino stock factor c. On crossing the two stocks, a fertilized egg cell is produced which must possess both. The evidence indicates, however, that the two units remain side by side in the cell, without the slightest influence on each other, and in each cell division, as the animal develops, each unit divides, with the result that every cell in the body is similar to the fertilized egg in containing both C and c. In the appropriate parts of the body—skin, eyes, and hair—factor C cooperates with other factors in the production of color, and, as a single unit appears to be sufficient in this case, the crossbred guinea pigs (Cc) are as strongly colored as the original colored stock in which factor C is received by each pig from both eggs and sperm (CC).

In the formation of the reproductive cells, it m
ne double set of units is sorted into two single s
olored guinea pigs (*Cc*) produce two kinds of r
qual numbers, those transmitting color (*C*) and
lbinism (*c*). On crossing with an albino it i
lasses of the young will be produced in equal
n whether the reproductive cells of the latter (*c*) l
cell transmitting color (*C*) or one transmitting
lbino young (*cc*) have no more tendency to tran
lbino stock, while the colored young (*Cc*), altl
lood albino, are of the same hereditary make-1
nd so breed like them.

MENDELIAN INHERITANCE.

This mode of inheritance was first worked out i
go by an Austrian monk, Gregór Johann Mende
ith a number of alternative characteristics of t.
ime principles have been found to apply to an t
1aracteristics in both plants and animals and
e true of all heredity. Most cases appear mo1
ne case of the colored and white guinea pigs, b
eristics depend on the cooperation of a large num1
lherited unit factors. Occasionally there is al
1at the same unit may have an influence on tl
umber of seemingly-independent characteristics
There are a number of technical terms which o
iscussion of heredity which it will be well to me
hich are alternatives of each other in inheritar
eing a modification of the other, are called a
ther. Thus factors *C* and *c* are allelomorphs.
ations or allelomorphs of factor *C* are known, 1

determine any particular color. It merely cooperates with other factors. One of the other factors, which we may represent by the symbol E, enables black pigment to develop. Its alternative, e, permits only red to develop. The first cross between a black stock ($CCEE$) and a red stock ($CCee$) is black ($CCEe$). Thus black is dominant over red. The first-cross animals produce reproductive cells containing E and e, respectively, in equal numbers. Since factor E and its allelomorph e are wholly independent of factor C and its allelomorphs, it is possible for a guinea pig to have any combination of the two sets. Thus an albino may transmit black only ($ccEE$) or red only ($ccee$) or both ($ccEe$). Suppose that an albino

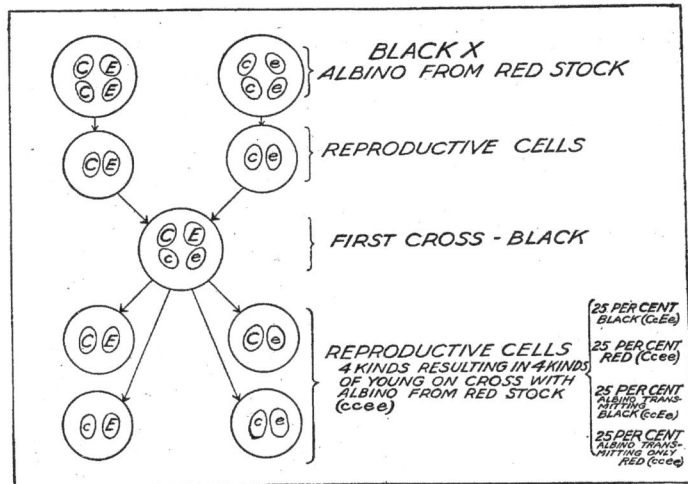

Fig. 3.—Diagram illustrating inheritance of 2 independent Mendelian factors. A pure-black strain of guinea pig ($CCEE$) is crossed with albinos from red stock ($ccee$). The young of the first cross are all black but produce four kinds of reproductive cells in equal numbers, as revealed by appropriate crosses.

of the second type ($ccee$) is crossed with a black stock which breeds true ($CCEE$); the first cross will be colored (Cc) and the color will be black (Ee). If, now, these crossbred blacks are bred with the same albino stock, we expect half the young to be colored (Cc) and half to be albino (cc). Of the colored young, half should be black ($CcEe$) and half red ($Ccee$). The albinos will be divided similarly into two classes, those which transmit black in half their reproductive cells ($ccEe$) and those which transmit only red ($ccee$). These two classes, however, will look alike. The cross thus should produce 50 per cent albinos, 25 per cent reds, and 25 per cent blacks, which it actually does.

Without going into more detail it may be said that six independent sets of allelomorphs are known in guinea pigs which cooperate to determine color. The combinations of these factors determine over a hundred distinguishable colors.

THE CHROMOSOMES AND HEREDITY.

The present theory of heredity was devised to explain the results of experiments such as those given above. Recent studies of cells under the microscope have apparently brought the mechanism under our eyes. It has already been mentioned that proper methods of staining bring out a certain definite number of rod-shaped bodies, the chromosomes, in the cells of each kind of animal or plant. The reproductive cells are found to contain just half as many as the fertilized egg and the body cells. At each ordinary cell division the chromosomes arrange themselves in a ring, each splits lengthwise; and half goes to one daughter cell, half to the other. Thus all the body cells have a double set. In the formation of the reproductive cells, on the other hand, the chromosomes do not split, but the homologous ones, derived from the sperm and egg, pair with each other and then separate, one going to each daughter cell. The reproductive cells thus get only a single set of chromosomes. It will easily be seen that if the hereditary units were located in the chromosomes the observed behavior of the latter would fully account for the laws of heredity illustrated above.

Summing up, genetic experiments prove the double nature of individuals and the single nature of their reproductive cells in regard to each set of alternative hereditary factors, while the microscope actually shows us the chromosomes in pairs in the body cells in place of the single set to be observed in the reproductive cells.

LINKAGE.

As the study of heredity has advanced, a number of complications have been found. These complications, however, have only made closer the parallelism between the facts of heredity and the observed behavior of the chromosomes. The most important of these complications is the phenomenon known as linkage. A case studied by Prof. Castle and the writer will serve as an example.

A few years ago a freak wild rat with yellow fur and red eyes was trapped on a wharf in England. Another wild rat of the same color, but with pink eyes, was trapped in another place. Two strains of yellow rats were developed which could be distinguished only by the color of the eyes. Each strain bred true. Crosses with normal wild rats showed that only one recessive unit factor was involved in each case. It may appear surprising that on crossing the two yellow strains with each other, all the young looked practically like ordinary gray rats with black eyes. This result was not, however, wholly unexpected. It is rather common to find that two variations which look alike are due to different factors, so that, on crossing, each supplies the normal factor lacking in the other, and the young appear to be normal. If we represent the wild gray rats by formula *PPRR*, the red-eyed yellows by *PPrr*, and the pink-eyed yellows by *ppRR*, we indicate that each kind of yellow is recessive and breeds true by itself, but on intercrossing produces a variety *PpRr*, which contains both of the dominant normal factors, and thus appears like a wild gray.

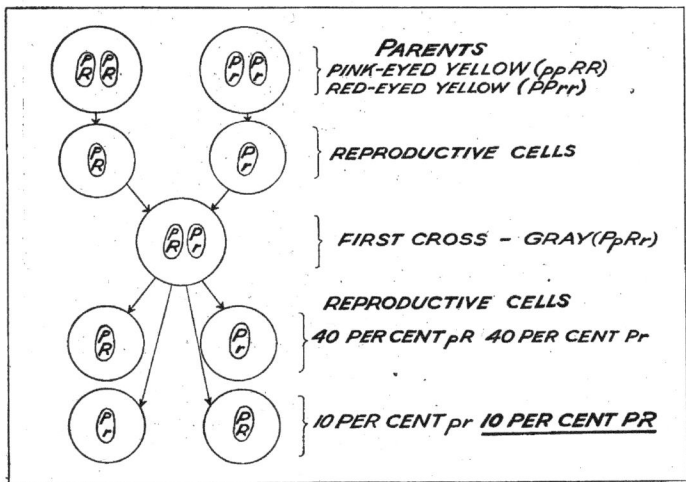

Fig. 4.—Diagram illustrating linkage. The pink-eyed and the red-eyed strains of yellow rats depend on different recessive factors. As each supplies the normal factor lacking in the other, crossing results in normal black-eyed grays. These grays produce reproductive cells in which the factors tend to be associated in the same combination as that in which they entered the cross, due, it is believed, to their transmission in the same chromosome. Only about 10 per cent of the reproductive cells are found to transmit both normal factors (*PR*).

On raising a second generation, a few pink-eyed yellows were found, which proved to transmit the red-eyed as well as the pink-eyed variation in all of their reproductive cells. Their formula would be *pprr*. On crossing this strain with ordinary gray rats (*PPRR*), we obtain gray young, which should have the same formula (*PpRr*) as the first cross between the two strains of yellows. The two kinds of first-cross grays were backcrossed with the above-mentioned double recessive pink-eyed yellow strain (*pprr*) by Prof. Castle in order to test the formulæ.

This would seem to be the same kind of cross as t]
reviously, in which black guinea pigs transmitting l
lbinism (*CcEe*) were crossed with albinos of red stoc]
hould expect half the reproductive cells of the crossbre
actor *P*, and half of these should also contain factor *R*
uarter of the young should receive both normal fact
rossbred gray parent and be gray themselves. This, :
ot the result. When grays derived from the cross
riginal two strains of yellows (*PPrr* and *ppRR*) we]
74 out of 1,714 young were gray, about 10 per cent
ray parent came from the cross between wild grays

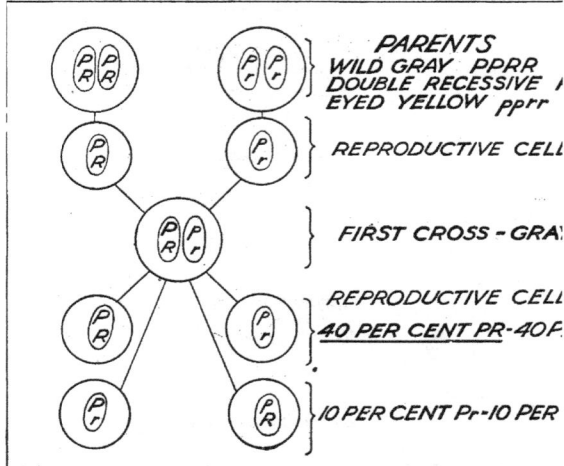

PARENTS
WILD GRAY PPRR
DOUBLE RECESSIVE /
EYED YELLOW pprr

REPRODUCTIVE CELL

FIRST CROSS - GRA^

REPRODUCTIVE CELL
40 PER CENT PR-40 F

10 PER CENT Pr-10 PER

ɪɢ. 5.—Diagram illustrating linkage. The cross between wild gray rats and double
yellows results in gray young with the same formula as in the cross between the
They breed differently, however, since in this case the two normal factors enter the c
of apart. About 40 per cent of their reproductive cells are found to transmit both r
case instead of 10 per cent.

he double recessive pink-eyed yellows (*pprr*), 1,255

stick together in the formation of the reproductive cells, according to the way in which they were combined in the production of the individual himself, is known as linkage.

A third color variation in rats, viz, albinism, has been found to be linked with both of the yellow variations. On the other hand, the other known color variations, white spotting and black, are not only inherited wholly independently of each other, but also of albinism and the two kinds of yellows.

This phenomenon of linkage has been found to be very widespread. The first case was found by Professors Bateson and Punnett, of Cambridge University, in the sweet pea. Cases are known in corn and oats, in the primrose and snapdragon, in chickens and pigeons, in mice as well as in rats, in grasshoppers, silkworms, and flies. By far the most thoroughly analyzed case is that of the fruit fly, Drosophila, in which Prof. T. H. Morgan and his coworkers, of Columbia University, have studied hundreds of Mendelian variations. They find that these variations fall into four groups, such that within each group every factor is linked more or less with every other factor, while there is never any linkage between factors in different groups. It is not merely a coincidence that in this fruit fly there are just four pairs of chromosomes.

This statement suggests the accepted explanation of linkage. Factors which are carried by the same chromosome tend to stick together. The chromosomes appear to maintain their identity through all the ordinary cell divisions. Just before the formation of the reproductive cells, the homologous chromosomes come together and twist around each other, giving a chance for an interchange of pieces. The degree of linkage between two factors is believed to measure their distance apart within the chromosome. On this basis Prof. Morgan and his coworkers have actually been able to make maps showing the location of a great number of unit factors in the different chromosomes of the fruit fly, which explain the results of crosses in a very convincing way.

The most remarkable corroboration of the chromosome theory of heredity has been the bringing of the genetic phenomenon of linkage and the visible behavior of the chromosomes into relation with the solution of the ancient problem of sex determination.

THE DETERMINATION OF SEX.

THE NORMAL METHOD.

There are few questions connected with animal breeding which have aroused so much interest from the earliest times as the determination of sex. Hundreds of theories have been advanced, and, though repeatedly disproved, keep reappearing. It is only within the twentieth century that the means by which sex is at least usually determined in the higher animals has been discovered. This mechanism, however, seems to be one that is beyond human interference.

It has been noted that a certain definite number of chromosomes can be seen under the microscope in the cells of each kind of animal. A qualification of this statement, connected with the determina-

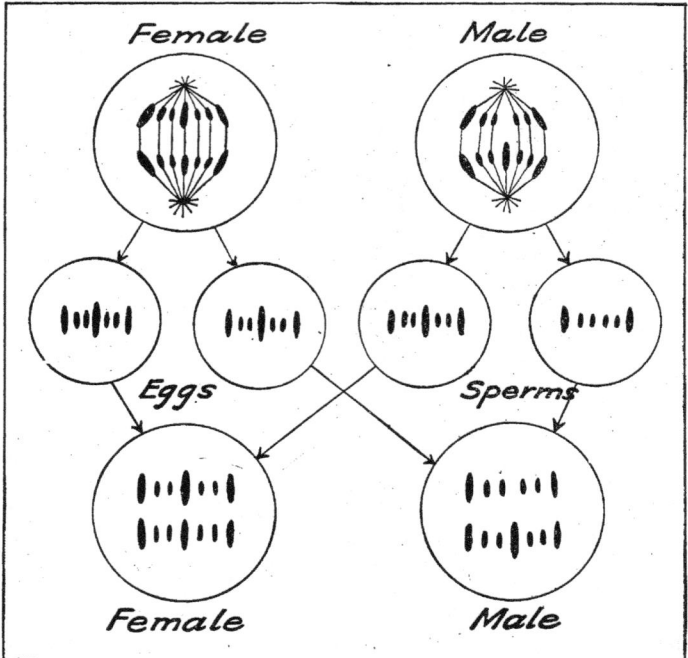

FIG. 6.—Diagram illustrating the method of sex determination in an animal with 14 chromosomes in the cells of the females, 13 in the males. All eggs have 7 chromosomes but only half the sperms have 7 chromosomes, the other half having 6. The former are female-determining sperms, the latter male determiners. Hereditary factors carried by the sex-determining chromosomes pass with it from father to daughter, never from father to son in such cases as that illustrated above.

tion of sex, was suggested in 1902 by Prof. C. E. McClung, on the basis of a study of the cells of grasshoppers. This suggestion has since been confirmed in principle by a large number of scientists working with widely different kinds of animals, ranging from worms to mammals. In most cases that have been studied carefully a difference has been found between the sexes, either in the number of the chromosomes or in the size of one pair.

As an illustration, we will consider the case of one of the grass-hoppers in which, owing to the large size of the cells and the relatively small number of chromosomes, the facts are considered to be beyond question. In this case, study of the cells from the digestive tract and muscle fibers of males shows 6 pairs of similar chromosomes and 1 odd chromosome, making 13 in all. The body cells of females contain 7 pairs of chromosomes, 6 pairs of which resemble the pairs in the male, while those in the seventh pair resemble the odd chromosome of the male. The same numbers are found in the reproductive cells before the final division which results in the functional reproductive cells. The final division is peculiar, as already noted, in that the chromosomes are sorted bodily into two groups. All the egg cells must contain 7 chromosomes, 1 from each pair. The sperm cells, on the other hand, are necessarily of two kinds, half containing 6 and half 7. The two kinds must, of course, be formed in exactly equal numbers. The inference is clear that any egg cell which happens to be fertilized by a sperm containing 6 chromosomes will develop into a grasshopper with only 13 chromosomes in the body cells, and hence a male, while fertilization by a sperm containing the odd chromosome, i. e., 7 chromosomes in all, will result in the number 14, and hence a female. From this it appears that sex is determined by chance at the moment of fertilization.

A similar mechanism has been found in a number of the mammals, including man. In the latter case, according to Von Winiwarter, there are 23 chromosomes in the male-determining sperms and 24 in those which determine the female sex.

It is naturally more difficult to establish the facts beyond question where such large numbers are involved. Fortunately, however, there is a wholly independent line of evidence which leads to the same conclusion. This is the evidence from characteristics linked with sex in inheritance.

SEX-LINKED INHERITANCE.

In the human species the mode of inheritance is best understood in the case of abnormalities which keep appearing in particular families. Most of these traits are inherited as if due to a single dominant or recessive factor. There are a number, however, including color blindness and hemophilia, which have long been known to follow a very peculiar mode of inheritance. These traits usually affect only males, yet are never transmitted from father to son, and do not reappear in the descendants of the sons. The daughters of affected males, on the other hand, though not affected themselves, are very apt to have affected sons. This rule was discovered as early as 1820 by Nasse in the case of hemophilia, a condition in

which the blood fails to clot properly, with the consequer
an affected individual may bleed to death from a slight scrat

Until recently the explanation of this kind of inheritanc
complete mystery. A little consideration, however, will sh
it is exactly what should be expected of a trait due to a factor
by the chromosome which determines sex. The evidence in
that in the human species this so-called X chromosome is s
males and paired in females. Half of the sperm cells prod
a male contain the X chromosome and hence can transmit he
traits which it contains. These are the female-determining
The other half, the male-determiners, lack the X chromoso
all that is transmitted by it. This explains why a sex-linked
teristic can not be transmitted from father to son or to an
descendants of the latter. All the daughters of an affecte
receive the abnormal factor in the X chromosome which det
their sex. They will not, however, show the abnormality thems
it is recessive, as they also in general receive a normal X chro
from their mother. Half of their ova, however, will cont
affected X chromosome. Those fertilized by sperms whi
the X chromosome are sons, and they will show the abno
as they can receive no protecting normal factor from the fs

The common yellow variation of cats is another examp
characteristic which is linked with sex in this way, except
fact that dominance is lacking. We may represent an X {
some containing the factor for yellow by X_y, and one contair
alternative factor for black by X_b. There are three kinds o
cats in this respect, yellow ($X_y X_y$), tortoise-shell ($X_y X$
black ($X_b X_b$). Males, however, having only one X chron
can be of only two kinds, yellow (X_y—) and black (X_b—).
in fact, long been known that tortoise-shell males are so ra
be classed as freaks. It should be added that there are inde
factors which may change black in either sex to maltese or th
pattern.

The female-determining sperm cells contain the extra chro

chromosomes of this insect. Microscopical study shows that sex is determined by one of these chromosomes in essentially the same way as that found in the grasshoppers and mammals in that the male produces two kinds of sperm. Parallel to this, they find that all the factors in one of the four linkage groups follow the sex-linked mode of inheritance of hemophilia and color blindness in man and the yellow color in cats.

A number of characteristics have been found in chickens, pigeons, and canaries which are linked with sex, but curiously enough the relation to sex is exactly the reverse of that described above. The barred pattern of Plymouth Rock fowls is a familiar example. When a barred male is mated with a black female all the chicks are barred. With a black male and a barred female, only the male chicks are barred, the females being black. Further tests show that the barred females in the first case have no more tendency to transmit black than pure-blood Plymouth Rocks, while in the second case the black females have no tendency to transmit barring. There is, in other words, no inheritance of either of the alternative characters from mother to daughter. The conclusion drawn from such experiments is that in birds the females produce two kinds of eggs—determining the male and female sexes, respectively—while the males produce only one kind of sperm. Prof. Raymond Pearl, of the Maine experiment station, found indications that the difference in fecundity between Plymouth Rocks and Cornish Indian Games was in part inherited in this way.

This method of sex determination is not limited to birds. It was found in a moth by Prof. Doncaster, of Cambridge University, in the first case of sex-linked inheritance to be analyzed, and has been demonstrated in the silkworm by Toyoma and Tanaka, two Japanese scientists.

THE SEX RATIO.

According to the method of determination outlined above, the sexes should be produced in equal numbers in the long run. This, in fact, is very nearly true in all the higher animals. Nevertheless, it is undoubtedly true that there is generally not exact equality. An extensive investigation in Germany by M. Wilckens gave the following numbers of males born to every 100 females: Cattle, 107.3; horses, 97.3; sheep, 97.4; swine, 111.8. The sex ratio in man varies in different countries, but always shows an excess of males, the average ratio being about 105 males to 100 females. These deviations of the sex ratio from equality are not necessarily out of harmony with the present theory of sex determination. The two kinds of sperm cells, for example, may differ in their activity or vitality.

Thus, while it appears very doubtful whether sex can ever be controlled in any exact way, the possibility of varying the sex ratio must be recognized. The results of even this very limited degree of control of sex determination, however, have been disappointing to date. Slight differences in the sex ratio among young born in different times of the year have often been published, but the results are so inconsistent that no general conclusion can be drawn. Another common theory is that a better nutritive condition of the dam favors the production of females. Great quantities of statistics have been gathered on this subject, but the evidence indicates an excess of males as often as of females under favorable conditions. Again it is believed by some that the sex of the more vigorous parent preponderates among the young, and by others the reverse is held. The two antagonistic theories seem to have just as much and as little support. The same is true of the theories which connect the relative or absolute ages of the parents with the sex of the offspring. A belief which is especially common among cattle breeders is that the time of services after the beginning of heat determines sex. The most common form of the theory is that early service tends to result in a preponderance of females, while service late in heat means more males. This theory has been most thoroughly tested by Prof. Pearl in data obtained from Maine farmers. His earlier data seemed to support the theory, but after adequate numbers had been obtained no significant differences remained.

The view that sex, or at least sex ratio, can be modified by control of such factors as those listed above has been urged most forcefully in recent years by Dr. Oscar Riddle on the basis of experiments begun by Professor C. O. Whitman with various wild species of pigeons and doves. In these experiments Whitman and Riddle found an excess of males under conditions tending toward heightened vigor and of females under the reverse conditions. In tame pigeons, Cole and Kirkpatrick have shown that the sexes of squabs of the same clutch are distributed wholly at random, indicating the lack of any external control over sex. The departures from a random distribution found by Whitman and Riddle were not very great and their significance still seems to be an open question.

A theory of sex determination which deserves mention only because of the frequency with which it is advanced is that sperm cells from one testicle produce males, from the other females. An alternative theory has it that it is one ovary which produces males, the other females. These theories are very easy to test by experiments in which one testicle or ovary is removed. Such experiments have been performed on a large scale with hogs and rats without any effect on the sex ratio.

The common belief that particular animals have a tendency to produce an excess of males or females has rather more support than the other theories mentioned above. Breeders of dairy cattle in particular often become discouraged with a bull which seems to sire largely bull calves. It must be remembered in this connection, however, that rather large departures from equality may occur simply by chance. Thus if a coin is tossed 20 times, the best expectation is 10 heads and 10 tails, but about once in 40 times a departure as great or greater than 15 heads or tails is to be looked for. Thus a large number of dairy-cattle breeders may be expected to get 15 or more bull calves out of 20 calves born. Such a result in one year would not have the slightest effect on the sex ratio in the next.

However, very extensive experiments with rats, made by Dr. Helen D. King, of the Wistar Institute, have shown that it is possible by selection, accompanied by inbreeding, to produce strains which differ considerably in sex ratio. She obtained 122 males to 100 females in the strain selected for male production and 82 males to 100 females in the strain selected in the opposite direction.

The theory that sex is normally determined by the number of chromosomes brought together by the sperm and egg at fertilization does not necessarily mean that this is the only method. There is, in fact, a certain amount of evidence which indicates that under extreme conditions the sex, as determined by the chromosomes, may be reversed. In hybridizing, especially, the normal mechanism seems likely to be upset and a great excess of males or females may be produced.

THE FREEMARTIN.

An interesting case of incomplete reversal of sex has recently been solved and may be mentioned in this connection. It has long been known that a heifer calf, born as a twin with a bull, is, in 8 or 9 cases out of 10, sterile. Such a heifer is called a "freemartin." The cause of this phenomenon has recently been worked out independently by Tandler and Keller in Germany and by Prof. F. R. Lillie, of the University of Chicago. They found that the blood systems of cattle twins usually grow together. When both twins were females or both males, no harm resulted. When a female was the twin of a male the development of the former appeared wholly normal in the few cases in which the blood systems remained separate. In all the cases in which the blood systems were connected, the female showed an abnormal development, intermediate between that of a female and a male. It appeared that the male embryo secreted some substance into the blood which tended to reverse the sexual development of the female embryo.

MENDELIAN HEREDITY 'IN LIVESTOCK.

POLLED CATTLE.

We know much less about the details of heredity in the larger animals than in a number of small ones, such as the guinea pig, rabbit, rat, mouse, and especially Prof. Morgan's fruit fly. Nevertheless unit factors have been demonstrated in a considerable number of cases. Polled and horned cattle, for example, differ by a single unit in their heredity. The factor which determines the polled condition is nearly fully dominant over its alternative in horned cattle. In a cross between the polled Aberdeen Angus and the Shorthorn, most of the calves are wholly polled, and the rest, as a rule, merely have loose scurs in the skin. These scurs are more frequent in males than females. The same factor has appeared within the Shorthorn, Hereford, and other breeds and has permitted the formation of polled subbreeds.

Polled bulls produce 100 per cent polled or nearly polled calves if they are homozygous polled like the Aberdeen Angus breed (PP). Otherwise (Pp) they produce 50 per cent polled and 50 per cent horned in crosses with horned cattle (pp). The polled animals can be crossed generation after generation with horned stock without reducing the per cent of polled calves below 50 to a significant extent. Their horned descendants, on the other hand, have no more tendency to transmit the polled condition than ordinary horned cattle. The polled character can easily be fixed if the mode of inheritance is borne in mind in making all matings. The most important point is to use exclusively bulls which have been proved to be homozygous polled (PP). Such bulls can be produced only when both parents are polled. All polled calves produced by a polled bull from a polled cow are not, however, homozygous. Unless it is known that both parents were homozygous, the most promising bull calves among those with scurs small or absent should be picked out and tested with a number of horned cows. It should be easy to find one which transmits only the polled condition.

COLORS OF CATTLE.

The black Aberdeen-Angus, Galloway, and Holstein-Friesian cattle differ in their hereditary make-up from the red breeds (Shorthorn, Hereford, Ayrshire, Devon, etc.) by a unit factor. Black is dominant over red, and thus may transmit it. The red may be handed on for generations out of sight, to appear when two blacks are mated both of which transmit it. Even to-day a red calf occasionally is born in a respectable black herd of Aberdeen-Angus cattle. In such case it is well to remember that the sire, as well as the dam, is transmitting it in half his reproductive cells and had best be replaced.

Another interesting pair of factors is found in the red and white of the Shorthorns. In this case neither is dominant. The heterozygous animals have a mixture of red and white, the familiar roan pattern. The roan is thus an unfixable color. Roan by roan produces only about 50 per cent roan calves, the rest being equally divided between red and white. Practically 100 per cent roan can be obtained by breeding a white bull with red cows, or the reverse. The factor which removes the color from the hair of roans and whites is inherited independently of the kind of color. Thus, when a white Shorthorn bull is bred with black Aberdeen-Angus or Galloway cattle, the black of the latter is dominant over the red factor which is present in white Shorthorns as well as red ones, while the white factor of the Shorthorn is imperfectly dominant over the solid color of the Aberdeen-Angus or Galloway. The result is a blue roan. When such blue roans are crossed together, blacks, blue roans, whites with black ears, reds, red roans, and whites with red ears, are all produced if enough calves are born. All but the last class were found among 21 calves produced in such an experiment at the Iowa agricultural experiment station.

Other colors in cattle have not been worked out so satisfactorily. There appears, however, to be an imperfectly dominant dilution factor which reduces black to dun color and red to fawn. The white patterns of many breeds are inherited independently of their colors and are, at least to some extent, dominant. The white face of the Hereford is thus transmitted to nearly all the calves in the first generation of a cross whether the rest of the coat is black or red, and is a useful "trade-mark" for the recognition of Hereford grades in the market. Grades of the dairy breeds are usually recognized by showing traces of the dilute color of Jerseys or Guernseys or the large, irregular, white areas of Ayrshires, Holstein-Friesian, and many Guernseys.

COLORS OF HORSES.

The colors of horses have been worked out in much detail. The power to develop black (factor H) seen in bays, blacks, duns, etc., is dominant over its absence, as seen in chestnuts (factor h). Bays (B) differ from blacks (b) by an independent factor which may or may not be transmitted by chestnuts. The dilute colored duns, creams, and mouse-colored horses differ from bays, chestnuts, and blacks, respectively, by a third dominant factor (factor D and d). Three other independent pairs of factors determine between the roan (R), gray (G), and piebald (S) patterns and their absence (r, g, and s). Since a chestnut horse is recessive in all essential factors ($hhddrrggss$), he or she can produce only one kind of reproductive cell ($hdrgs$), and two chestnuts, whatever their ancestry, can produce only chestnut foals.

It was thus very easy to fix the chestnut color in the Sussex Punch breed, but on the other hand, all other colors are dominant or, as is usually said, prepotent over it.   The degree of prepotency depends on the dominant factors which are homozygous.   A homozygous gray stallion (*GG*) will produce nothing but gray colts, however crossed.   A heterozygous gray (*Gg*) will produce 50 per cent gray and 50 per cent not gray in crosses with mares which are not gray.

Fig. 7.—The spotted coat pattern of this scrub stallion is due to a dominant hereditary unit and may be expected to appear in half of his progeny. The curby hocks and other unsoundness are also strongly transmissible.

COLORS OF HOGS.

Curiously enough we know less about the mode of inheritance of colors in hogs than in the larger animals. The results of the first crosses between the various breeds are, however, well known. The white of Yorkshires and Chesters is more or less prepotent over the red of Tamworths and Duroc–Jerseys, and, probably for a wholly different reason, over the black of Hampshires, Berkshires, and Poland Chinas. The black of Hampshires is prepotent over the red of the red breeds. Berkshires and Poland Chinas, on the other hand, when mated with the red breeds, produce pigs with a tortoise-shell mixture of black, red, and often white spots. The white belt of Hampshires, like the white patterns of many other animals, is very irregular in its heredity. It is doubtful whether a given type of belt can ever be completely fixed.

COLORS OF SHEEP.

The color of black sheep is recessive to the ordinary white color. It can thus appear only when transmitted by both ram and ewe. It is well to remember that a single black lamb in a flock indicates that the ram is transmitting the unit for black in half his sperm cells. Half of his daughters may thus be expected to transmit it.

COLORS AND COMB SHAPE OF POULTRY.

The mode of inheritance of the colors of poultry is still far from thoroughly worked out, but a few points may be mentioned. The barred pattern of Plymouth Rocks and several other color patterns are linked with sex in the way which has already been discussed.

Fig. 8.—A daughter of the stallion in figure 7. Note the inheritance of the spotted coat pattern and curby hocks.

The Blue Andalusian has a color which is inherited in a way similar to the roan of Shorthorn cattle. It is a color which can not be fixed. Blue by blue produces only 50 per cent blues, the rest being equally divided between blacks and splashed whites. It is possible, however, to produce 100 per cent blue chicks by crossing the blacks and whites with each other.

The mode of inheritance has been worked out for a number of characteristics of poultry besides color. Thus rose comb is dominant over single comb and behaves as if it differed only in one unit factor. The pea comb of Indian Games and Brahmas is also dominant over single comb but depends on a variation of a different unit factor. The combination of rose and pea comb results in the walnut comb of the Malay breeds.

HEREDITY OF FORM AND FUNCTION IN LIVESTOCK.

RELATIONS OF THEORY TO PRACTICE.

In the preceding sections we have attempted to present a brief outline of the present theory of heredity as it has been developed in the main from experiments with small animals and plants. Illustrations were given which show that these principles apply to farm livestock, at least in the case of coat color and a number of other rather superficial characteristics, such as the presence of horns in cattle and shape of comb in poultry. There is every reason for believing that these principles are of general application. and it is hardly too much to say that the normal method of inheritance is now clearly understood. Unfortunately, however, a thorough understanding does not necessarily mean easy control. The peculiarities of form and function appear to be so complex in their mode of inheritance that an understanding of the fundamental laws of heredity is at present valuable to the stock breeder largely from the light which they throw on such long-known methods of breeding as inbreeding, crossbreeding, selection, etc. In the present section most attention will accordingly be paid to these secondary principles.

EQUALITY OF INHERITANCE FROM THE SEXES.

As already noted, there is, in general, equal inheritance from the sexes with respect to all kinds of characteristics. There is, for example, no scientific foundation for such beliefs as that the dam controls the external form, the sire the constitution of the internal organs, or the reverse. The only known exceptions are the rather small class of sex-linked characteristics, which have already been discussed. For reasons other than heredity, the dam naturally has more influence in the birth weight and some other characteristics of young animals, but these effects seem to be outgrown.

The rule that there is in general equal inheritance from the sexes must not be taken as meaning that the sire or dam may not be prepotent in a particular cross on account of reasons other than sex.

PREPOTENCY.

An ideally prepotent animal is one that impresses his characteristics on all his progeny, however mated. There are many unsound beliefs connected with prepotency. It is often believed that it is a characteristic of an animal as a whole, closely related to vigor. Thus it is often held that a strongly masculine type in a male is an indication of general prepotency. This type is desirable in itself as an indication of vigor, which is of the utmost importance in all breeding, but there is no good evidence that prepotency in any other special characteristic is indicated in this way. The idea of general prepotency has also led .

to the common belief that proved prepotency in one respect, such as color, indicates prepotency in others. Experiments, however, easily prove the falsity of this claim.

A white-faced red Hereford cow with normal horns produces polled, white-faced, black calves when bred to a polled black Aberdeen-Angus bull. An Aberdeen-Angus cow produces the same kind of calf when bred to a Hereford bull. Evidently prepotency lies neither in the sex, the breed, nor the individual, but in the characteristics, polled head, black color (where there is any color besides white), and white face.

Somewhat similarly, a cross made in either way between an Aberdeen Angus and a white Shorthorn produces polled blue-roan calves. Polled head and black color are prepotent, as before, but prepotency is lacking as regards the third pair of opposed characteristics, the solid color of the Aberdeen Angus and the nearly solid white of the Shorthorn.

It is not the whole story, however, to say that certain characteristics are always prepotent. If in the case above, the polled, blue-roan Shorthorn-Angus crossbreds are bred back to a white Shorthorn, only half the calves will be polled, the rest having good horns, and only half will be black in the colored parts of the coat (that is, they will be blue-roan or white, with black ears), the rest being red roans and whites with red ears. Thus, the characters which were fully prepotent in the purebred cease to be so in the crossbred. The difficulty is that the crossbred produces more than one kind of reproductive cell. In the present case, half of the reproductive cells transmit the polled condition and half transmit horns; half transmit black and half transmit red; half transmit the tendency to develop color in the entire coat, as in the Aberdeen Angus, and half transmit the highly reduced condition of color, as in the white Shorthorn. Moreover, the representatives of the three sets of opposed characters are shuffled up and sorted out into the reproductive cells independently of one another. Some of the reproductive cells transmit the combination polled, solid color and black, others polled, solid color and red, and so on through the eight possible combinations.

In this illustration we have used characteristics which have already been discussed as examples of simple Mendelian heredity. Most characteristics probably depend on a much larger number of hereditary units, but, nevertheless, the nature of prepotency is believed to be essentially the same. So far as there is prepotency, it is a property of characteristics (or really of the hereditary units back of the characteristics), not of individuals, breeds, or sexes, and whatever the characteristic, there can be no prepotency unless the individual produces only one kind of reproductive cell so far as it is concerned.

In technical language, prepotency depends primarily on two things: The factors back of the characteristic must be dominant and each pair of factors must be homozygous. Other considerations, such as the number of factors involved and their linkage relations as well as the system of mating, play a part in determining whether the prepotency of an individual dies with him or is handed on to his descendants. Most of these elements of prepotency are beyond control and can simply be accepted thankfully when they appear. It is possible, however, to bring out such prepotency as is in a stock and preserve prepotency when it has appeared by breeding so as to fix the desired characteristics. Fixation means simply to make all the hereditary factors involved homozygous.

VARIATION.

Before discussing the methods of fixing characters it will be well to go briefly into the causes of variation. In the first place it must be recognized that a great deal of variation is not hereditary. Different characteristics are affected in very different degrees by outside conditions. Hereford cattle produce only white-faced, red calves, whether raised under the best of conditions or under the worst. These same conditions, on the other hand, may make all the difference between well-finished animals which win in the show ring and animals which would appear discreditable even to a scrub herd. The way to eliminate this kind of variation, of course, is to give all the stock uniformly favorable conditions.

Unfortunately there is in many cases variation which is neither hereditary nor due to controllable outside conditions. As already pointed out, there are hereditary differences in the average size of litter produced by different breeds of swine. There are also hereditary differences within the breeds, but their influence is so slight that Poland-China sows born in litters of 13 or more have been found to farrow less than one pig more on the average than sows born in litters of one, two, or three. Outside conditions undoubtedly play a part, but to a very large extent the size of litter produced by a sow seems to be beyond control.

Even variations in coat color, at least with respect to pattern, are not always due to heredity. Spotted guinea pigs vary all the way from nearly solid black to solid white. In a mixed stock it is easy to show that the whiter parents have on the average the whiter offspring, and vice versa, but analysis of the figures in a stock raised by the Bureau of Animal Industry indicated that most of the variation was due to chance irregularities in the course of development, and was thus beyond control.

The importance of such irregularities in development can be measured roughly by the degree of asymmetry found. Thus the patterns of hooded rats and Dutch rabbits are much less likely to be asymmetrical than that of piebald guinea pigs, and it is found that a given pattern can be fixed in them much more perfectly. The white face of Hereford cattle is usually symmetrical and has been fixed to a satisfactory extent. Whether the white belt of Hampshire swine can be so fixed seems more doubtful, owing to its frequent asymmetry.

Occasionally a variation is due to the appearance of a wholly new hereditary characteristic in a stock. The polled variation of cattle has probably appeared in this way a number of times. Such variations, or mutations, as they are called, are, however, very rare.

Most hereditary variation is due simply to recombination of the factors already present in the parent stocks. The blue roans and their varied progeny, derived from crosses between Shorthorn and Aberdeen-Angus cattle, are a good illustration of variation of this sort. It is this form of variation only which can be eliminated by methods of breeding.

FIXATION OF HEREDITY BY SELECTION.

Consistent selection toward the desired type is sometimes all that is necessary to fix a characteristic. Unfortunately, experiments have shown that what appear to be the same characteristics in two animals often depend on wholly different combinations of hereditary factors. A good example has been given in another connection in the case of two strains of light-eyed, yellow rats, each of which bred true by itself, but which produced nothing but black-eyed gray rats when crossed with each other. Thus progress by straight selection may be wholly upset at any time by an unfortunate cross of this kind. The whole breed must be lifted up at once if there is to be success by selection alone. Careful selection with breeding confined within a single herd or a few related herds, on the other hand, only requires that this small group be lifted up at once. Once success has been obtained, such a herd or group of herds becomes a powerful source of breed improvement by supplying prepotent sires. Practical experience agrees with theory in the principle that the only systematic method of fixing heredity, and so bringing out such prepotency as is in a stock, is Bakewell's old method of close breeding accompanied by careful selection.

FIXATION OF HEREDITY BY INBREEDING.

The primary effect of inbreeding is the fixation of hereditary qualities, whether good, bad, or indifferent. In other words, a sufficiently inbred animal produces only one kind of reproductive cell with respect to all hereditary characteristics (with the exception of sex and characters linked with sex in the case of male mammals

r female birds).   The closer the inbreeding, the more rapid v
his fixation of hereditary characteristics.

The reason why inbreeding fixes characteristics is easy to t
tand.   As an illustration, consider a stock of horses in which b
ays, and chestnuts are being produced.   Recalling that the
iant factor H is necessary in order that any black be present, tl
hat the horse be other than a chestnut, and that the don
actor B in the presence of H determines the bay pattern we se
he three colors may be determined by the following combin:
f factors:

Bays.......$BBHH$ $BbHH$ $BBHh$ $BbHh$
Blacks....$bbHH$ $bbHh$
Chestnuts..$BBhh$ $Bbhh$ $bbhh$

Only the first types of bay and black breed true.   Suppose,
hat the horses are mated brother with sister.   From time to
imply by chance, two animals will be mated which are homoz
n one or both of the factors.   For example, two bays of fo
$BbHH$ may thus be mated.   Neither of them transmits the
or chestnut (h) and it is evident that their descendants will
roduce chestnuts so long as they are bred only with each
Blacks, however, will frequently appear.   These blacks, being]
ygous in both factors ($bbHH$), will breed true.   If brother
natings are made among the bays, occasionally matings of the
$BBHH$ by $BBHH$ will be made by chance, in which the fact
lack is eliminated as well as that for chestnut.   The descen

one exception, however, which should be pointed out. The mating of sire with daughter is in a sense as close inbreeding as brother with sister. Yet a male may be bred successively with his daughters, granddaughters, great-granddaughters, etc., concentrating his blood to any extent, without coming any closer to fixing his type than at first if the type were not fixed in himself. This will be clear from an illustration. A bay stallion of formula *BbHh* produces four kinds of reproductive cells (*BH*, *Bh*, *bH*, and *bh*). Half of these transmit the factor for black (*b*) and half that for chestnut (*h*). It is obvious that he will sire numerous black foals and chestnut foals, no matter how much his blood is concentrated. On the other hand, if it is possible to obtain a bay stallion which is known to be of formula *BBHH*, there is no quicker way of fixing a true-breeding race of bays than by repeated crosses with his female descendants. Such a stallion is prepotent, since in crosses with blacks and chestnuts he sires only bay foals.

Speaking generally, the continued use of a sire of proved prepotency is the most rapid method of fixing his type, while the use of a sire which is not prepotent has no tendency toward fixation, but rather the reverse.

ISOLATION OF GENETIC DIFFERENCES BY INBREEDING.

It was noted in the section on variation that characteristics differ greatly in the degrees to which they are determined by heredity, outside conditions which are controllable, and by uncontrollable conditions, such as chance irregularity in development. Thus, in some characteristics, such as quality of coat color and, to a less extent, type, consistent close breeding, and uniform conditions, result in a highly uniform stock. In the case of functional characteristics, especially fertility, there remains much variation even under apparently uniform conditions and any amount of inbreeding. Color pattern is also often of this kind, as we have seen in the case of guinea pigs. The Bureau of Animal Industry has a stock of guinea pigs which is descended wholly from a single mating in the twelfth generation of brother-sister mating. Variability has been reduced only 25 per cent by this inbreeding. There is still variation from nearly solid black to solid white, but none of it is now hereditary. The progeny of the blackest parents produce progeny of the same average grade as the whitest parents. Figure 9 shows the variation in pattern in four generations of guinea pigs from this inbred family.

While inbreeding is of little use in bringing about uniformity in such cases, it does something else which, perhaps, is even more important. When there is a lot of variation which is not hereditary, straight selection is especially apt to be at fault. There can be no assured progress, since a single unfortunate mating with an animal which is good by accident, not by heredity, may at any time undo all previous work. It is only by inbreeding a number of lines and comparing them that the real hereditary differences can be recognized. This was done in the inbreeding experiment with guinea pigs referred to above. Certain inbred lines averaged 15 per cent white, others 85 per cent, while others were intermediate. It is very doubtful whether the extreme types could ever have been obtained from the original stock by straight selection without close breeding. Similarly, differences in growth, fertility, and vitality were brought to light among the different families of guinea pigs. These are discussed under the next heading.

It would be difficult to overemphasize the importance of close breeding in the past history of livestock breeding, as the agent in bringing out the real hereditary differences between different stocks, and so leading to improvement in characteristics which could not have been improved by selection alone.

Fig. 9.—Four generations of inbred guinea pigs. The young pair at the right end of the line is descended from 19 generations of matings of brother with sister. Three of these generations, the parents, grandparents, and great-grandparents are in the picture. Color and other characteristics have become fixed automatically in this family because of the inbreeding. The exact coat pattern, however, as is generally the case, is not wholly determined by heredity, and is therefore unfixable.

THE EFFECT OF INBREEDING ON VIGOR.

Along with the advantages of inbreeding, certain unfortunate effects have long been known. A general reduction in vigor, especially in fertility, has long been ascribed to inbreeding, and there can be no doubt that these are common effects. It is not, however, so certain that they are invariable effects. Dr. Helen D. King, for example, has inbred rats, brother with sister, for 25 generations without any decline in size, constitutional vigor, or fertility, but rather the reverse.

The Bureau of Animal Industry has made experiments on the subject involving more than 26,000 guinea pigs. A number of distinct families have been maintained wholly by matings of brother with sister. The fact that one of these has reached the twentieth generation without any conspicuous decline in vigor in any respect is further evidence that the evils of inbreeding are by no means as great as often pictured. Other families, however, suffered a rapid decline, and some decline is shown by the average for all families. The great differences between families confirm the suggestion that inbreeding is merely likely to lead to decline in vigor, but does not necessarily do so. This conclusion is brought out also on considering the different characteristics separately. One family lost markedly in vitality but not in size or fertility. In another the reverse was the case. In fact, nearly all combinations of favorable or unfavorable characteristics were represented by one or more families after a number of generations of inbreeding.

The results of crosses between different inbred families are interesting in this connection. The young from such crosses made distinctly better gains and a larger percentage were raised of those born alive than in their inbred cousins raised at the same time under the same conditions. The crossbred females have much larger litters and have them more frequently. More of their young are born alive and the birth weights are greater than of young born of inbred dams. The second generation, in fact, appears to be as vigorous as a control stock which has never been inbred.

These results are easily interpreted by the present theory of heredity. They confirm the view that the primary effect of inbreeding is merely the automatic fixation of hereditary factors. It seems to be the usual rule that factors favorable to vigor are dominant over unfavorable ones, and hence tend to conceal the latter under crossbreeding. Under inbreeding the unfavorable factors are as likely to become fixed as favorable ones, and hence are brought to light. One or more of the unfavorable factors affecting size, vitality, or fertility are thus very likely to become fixed in each line, especially as it is very likely to happen that some of the favorable and unfavorable factors may be linked in their heredity, which means that the attempt to fix these favorable factors involves an involuntary fixation of the unfavorable ones. It usually happens that different defects become fixed in different lines, so that on crossing each supplies the elements of vigor which the other lacks and full vigor returns.

The fixation of unfavorable characteristics can be prevented to some extent by sufficiently careful selection, but it must be remembered that fertility, vigor, etc., depend on so many factors besides heredity that even the most careful selection will often be at fault. Hereditary differences in these respects can not, in fact, be determined with certainty except by starting a large number of inbred lines and comparing them. It is the discovery of one really valuable line, out of a score or more of closely bred lines, which may be expected to make history in livestock breeding.

While the conclusions in regard to inbreeding as given above are based on experiments with higher animals, it may be well to add that extensive inbreeding of insects has given similar results and that the same is true of continued self-pollination in plants as brought out by Darwin, Shull, East, Jones, and Collins and Kempton.

Summing up, the primary effect of inbreeding is the automatic fixation of some combination of hereditary factors present in a stock. This leads to uniformity of type or function, if such uniformity is possible. When not possible, owing to variability which is not genetic, the hereditary potentialities in the lines are brought out clearly, as is possible in no other way. Decline in vigor is a common but not a necessary consequence of the fixation of heredity.

CROSSBREEDING.

As inbred animals produce only one kind of reproductive cell, it is to be expected that a cross between two inbred lines will produce only one kind of progeny so far as hereditary factors are concerned. It is, in fact, well known that the first cross between two closely bred stocks is as uniform in character as either of the parent stocks. The cross between the polled black Aberdeen-Angus breed and white Shorthorns, producing polled blue roans, has already been considered. The conformation is also uniform in the first generation. While uniform themselves, such crossbreds are anything but prepotent as breeders. When two of the above-mentioned polled blue-roan Shorthorn-Angus crosses are bred with each other, the progeny, as already mentioned, include blacks, reds, blue roans, red roans, and whites with either black or red ears. Any of the colors may be associated either with horns or polled heads. There is also increased variability in conformation.

As regards vigor and fertility, crossbreeding is likely to lead to marked improvement. As noted above, the crossing of two unrelated weakened inbred lines usually leads to a return to normal vigor.

Summing up, the first generation of a cross is as uniform in character as the parent stocks, and in general shows increased vigor. In the second generation there is increased variability, the characteristics of the grandparents being combined, as a rule, in all combinations and in all degrees.

THE SYSTEM OF BREEDING.

THE PURPOSES OF LIVESTOCK BREEDING.

Aside from mere increase in numbers, the purposes which the breeder is likely to have in mind fall under two more or less distinct heads, namely, production of a uniform product and improvement. A uniform product depends on such control over the heredity of the stock that matings can be made with the assurance that the offspring will be of a certain definite type for which there is a demand. Improvement is, of course, closely related to control over heredity, but the methods which give the greatest control are not necessarily those which lead to most rapid improvement.

UNIFORMITY OF TYPE.

The method of obtaining such uniformity of type as is possible, is, as already indicated, close breeding, accompanied by selection. This method was one of the foundations of Robert Bakewell's success in improving the Longhorn cattle and Leicestershire sheep of the eighteenth century. His example was followed in the foundation period of most of the British breeds of livestock. Injurious effects of inbreeding became apparent later in certain lines, as in the low fertility of the Bates Shorthorns. There are to-day breeders who have reached great success through inbreeding and others who have met disaster.

The degree of inbreeding which should be followed depends to a large extent on the purpose. Type, color, and utility have already been fixed to some extent in most of the pure breeds, and merely the consistent use of males of the same pure breed may be sufficiently close breeding in many cases. To fix a superior type within a breed, however, requires closer breeding. The closer the breeding, the more readily will characteristics become fixed.

The expression "line breeding" is often used for various mild forms of close breeding. Thus, continued breeding within a herd or within a few related herds, with the avoidance of close inbreeding, is a kind of line breeding. The term is perhaps most frequently used when there is an effort to concentrate the blood of an especially worthy animal by mating together animals descended from him. In either case characters are fixed more slowly than with close inbreeding. There is, in consequence, less danger of fixing undesirable qualities in the stock by accident. It may be well to add that in line breeding, as in any form of inbreeding, animals should be mated primarily on their merits, regardless of the exact degree of relationship. The attempt to follow a rigid system of mating, such as is sometimes represented on charts, usually interferes too much with selection to be a success.

The degree of inbreeding which a man can afford to follow depends in part on the size of his herd, in part on his ability in selecting the best for breeding stock, and in part on the extent to which he can take a chance. As already noted, most valuable characteristics of livestock are affected to such a large extent by feed and management and also by uncontrollable conditions, that the selection of the best individuals does not always mean selection of the best heredity. Hereditary differences can often be recognized clearly only when different inbred lines are compared with each other. Thus, among a number of inbred lines started from the same stock and maintained with equal ability, some will degenerate rapidly, the majority, perhaps, will show some unfortunate characteristic, and in only a few will the desired type become fixed in association with high vigor and fertility. Once obtained, however, the type can be kept for a long time at its high level by close breeding, and can supply prepotent males for the improvement of inferior stock.

CROSSBREEDING FOR THE MARKET.

As already noted, control over heredity, and hence uniformity, depends on the amount of close breeding back of the parents and not at all on their relationship to each other. There is no doubt, for example, that mules can be produced as true to type as any pure breed, by using closely bred jacks and mares. Experience is, of

FIG. 10.—A Poland China boar, illustrating the lard type of hog.

course, necessary to determine just what lines of jacks and mares will produce a mule of a particular size and type. It is probable that systematic crossing of breeds could be practiced to a larger extent than at present in cases in which the offspring are not to be used for breeding. An increase in vigor is to be expected. In some cases advantage can be taken of the good qualities of two breeds. The highest development of the meat type in animals is generally correlated with reduced fertility. By choosing females from a breed distinguished for its vigor and fertility, and the male from a breed of the most extreme meat type, it is possible to produce progeny of the best market type without the losses due to defective fertility.

Among hogs, Yorkshire or Tamworth sows can be used to advantage with an extreme type of Poland China or Duroc-Jersey boar. Purebred or grade Dorset ewes are useful in crosses where it is desired to produce lambs out of season. Under some circumstances dairy cows can well be bred to bulls of the beef breeds in order to produce calves which can be fattened profitably. In some cases it may even be worth while to develop races within two breeds specially designed to be complementary to each other in crosses. The danger in any system of crossbreeding is that the very excellence of the first generation will tempt the breeder to use them as breeding stock. The additional vigor due to crossing decreases after the first generation and uniformity of type is lost at once.

IMPROVEMENT.

There is a certain antagonism between control over heredity and radical improvement. Perfect control over heredity implies the absence of all variation among the progeny of a mating. A useful new type is most likely to be found where there is a maximum of variation. Thus the pioneer breeder must make wide crosses. The first generation may be expected to be about intermediate between

FIG. 11.—A group of Corriedale rams. This breed originated in Australia in the crossing of Lincoln or Leicester rams with Merino ewes. It has been developed into a true type by years of close breeding and selection.

the parents and as uniform as the uncrossed parental lines. The second generation, however, will in general show distinctly more variability. The ancestral characteristics will be found in every compatible combination and in all degrees of development if enough young are produced. Characteristics may be found which appear wholly new. If a promising new type is formed it remains to fix it by careful selection and close breeding.

There will doubtless always be room for the production of new types and from time to time even new breeds. But this work of radical improvement is not likely to occupy more than a few of the most ambitious breeders. Others will have such superior stock that they can do no better than conserve it by close breeding, making such slow improvement by selection as the limited variability of the stock permits. With a larger number, periods of close breeding must be interrupted by periods in which new blood is infused into the stock, a certain amount of uniformity being sacrificed to obtain renewed vigor and a basis for further improvement. The great body, even of the owners of purebreds, however, will own stock which is distinctly below the best of its breed. For them improvement and fixation of type can go hand in hand. The method is the consistent use of prepotent males of a given superior line.

GRADING UP.

Common stock can be improved and fixed in type by the same methods as those described last. The process in this case is known as grading up. Even two or three crosses with superior purebred

Fig. 12.—A Merino ram, an example of the fine-wool type of sheep.

males should raise the level practically to that of the average purebred, if not better, so far as individual qualities are concerned. With five or six such crosses it would doubtless be possible to produce animals better than most purebreds both in their own characteristics and in their breeding power.

It is not, however, considered practicable to permit registration of grades as purebreds, no matter how many top crosses there may be, with superior purebred males of the same breed. In all but this respect, however, a large stock of common females can be rapidly converted into a herd as good as a purebred herd by grading. It is in the grading up of the common stock of the country that scientific breeding can render its greatest service.

METHODS OF SELECTION.

GENERAL CONSIDERATIONS.

In a broad sense the whole subject of practical breeding comes under the head of selection. The considerations which should determine the general policy of mating have been discussed in the previous section.

In the present section, selection will be considered with respect to the characteristics which it is desired to improve rather than to the

FIG. 13.—A Lincoln ram, an example of the long-wool type of sheep. The Corriedale breed was developed from crosses of rams of this type with fine-wool ewes.

system of mating. The most obvious basis for such selection is the performance of the animals themselves. A dairy cow with a record of 1,000 pounds of butterfat in a year is more likely to produce a useful calf than one which produced only 200 pounds under the same circumstances. Unfortunately, the merits of most kinds of livestock can not be measured so directly. The study of conformation as an index of useful qualities has accordingly held a high place as a basis for selection of breeding stock. Livestock judging has this for its purpose. An animal of good stock is a better one to breed than one of equal individual merit but of mixed or common breeding. His

)repotency is apt to be greater. The pure breeds were
ecognition of the importance of the heredity back of the
)arents, and pedigree, though often misused, is a valu:
election, apart from its importance in following a gener:
nating. The soundest basis of all for selection of bree
3 the record of past performance as a breeder, provided tl
ufficiently extensive to give a fair test.

The selection of the male, on whatever basis, should)
vholly on the approximation to the ideal which the bre
nind, but also on the character of the females with whi
)e bred. The general rule is that the prospective sir∈

low fecundity, and excessive fatness. This show-ring type was not considered the best utility type itself, but was the best for improving the coarse, slowly maturing, common stock of that time.

INDIVIDUAL PERFORMANCE AND LIVESTOCK JUDGING.

As a general rule the most direct methods of estimating the useful qualities of animals are the most satisfactory as a basis for selection. Until relatively recently it was not practicable to make accurate tests of the milk and butterfat production of large numbers of dairy cows. The experience of dairymen with regard to the type of cow which had proved to be most productive was the best guide in selecting breeding stock. At present the records made in a cow-testing association or in attaining advanced registry in a pure breed give a direct basis for selection, and the indications from conformation are being relegated to a decidedly secondary place, although knowledge of the approved dairy conformation is still of use in picking out the more promising cows from common stock or from among untested purebreds.

Similarly, the trap-nest record is coming to be more important in finding the best egg-laying strains of poultry than the approach to a standard type. Wool production is of course judged directly. Among Standardbred trotters and pacers speed, of course, has been the all-important qualification from the first and has been fixed much better than conformation. During the longer history of the English Thoroughbred both speed and conformation have been fixed to a greater extent than in the Standardbred, but the prime basis for selection has always been success on the race course. The judging of heavy horses by conformation and action is probably as direct as is practicable. In the meat breeds of cattle, swine, sheep, and poultry study of the conformation gives the best indication of the actual quantity and quality of the meat which can be got without killing the animal and also gives indications as to early maturity. Detailed descriptions of the approved types can be found in bulletins on the various breeds of livestock.

There are constant attempts to find a short cut to correct judgment through a correlation between some easily observed characteristic and the useful qualities. The development of the so-called escutcheon of dairy cattle was at one time very widely accepted as an indication of milking capacity, although the supposed correlation appears to have no basis in fact. In the case of poultry there are a number of ways, without taking trap-nest records, of picking out the hens which have been laying consistently. In breeds with yellow shanks those with the palest color have been proved to be the better layers. This is, however, really a more direct test than it seems, since the yellow color of the yolk of the egg is the same as that in the skin. In times of heavy laying the yellow coloring matter from green feed is taken up by the eggs instead of by the skin. Other tests, such as those depending on the spread of the pelvic bones or the time of molting, are even more direct.

There is another class of indirect indications of utility which should be mentioned. There is no reason for believing that the white face of the Hereford has any physiological connection with profitable meat production. The breeders of Hereford cattle, however, fixed this characteristic at the same time that they were fixing a good beef type. As it has been fixed in no other breed of cattle, it is a valuable indication of Hereford breeding when found in common stock. Conversely, fancy points which are lost on crossing have value as indications of pure breeding.

THE BREEDING RECORD.

The most direct evidence of the value of an animal in breeding, of course, is the past record in this respect. The discovery of pre-potent animals of a desirable kind means more for breed progress than any other factor. It is only necessary to recall the influence of Hambletonian 10 and his son, George Wilkes, on the American trotter, of De Kol 2d on the Holstein-Friesian cattle of this country, and of Anxiety 4th on American Herefords. In judging the value of an animal on this basis the number of his progeny and the character of the animals with which he or she was mated must, of course, be taken into account. Uniform excellence in all of a large number of progeny outweighs a record of one champion among many culls.

This method of selection is, of course, more applicable to males than to females, since the latter seldom have offspring enough until quite old. Unfortunately, it is very common to dispose of males before their value as sires is established, largely because of fear of inbreeding. There is probably nothing which will make for progress more than a systematic recording of the breeding record of promising sires, such as we have in the advanced registry for dairy bulls, based on the performance of their daughters.

PEDIGREE.

The ancestry of an animal as a clue to his probable success as an individual and as a breeder should first be considered as a whole. It makes a great deal of difference whether he is purebred, high-grade, crossbred, half-blood, or merely scrub. If there is line breeding to some prepotent individual and the other ancestors for several genera-tions indicate consistent selection toward the same type, it is very likely both that the animal will himself develop into this type and that he will be markedly prepotent. On the other hand, an array of ancestors of varied types, even though each is among the best of its kind, indicates an animal about which little can be predicted as to his own performance and less as to his progeny.

The value of particular individuals in the pedigree depends on the degree of relationship. A noteworthy sire or dam is a very important consideration. A noteworthy great-grandsire does not mean much by himself, and the more remote ancestors hardly need be taken into account as individuals.

Attention should also be paid to collateral relatives. Each full brother or sister counts as much as a parent. Half brothers and sisters and full brothers and sisters of the parents are as closely related as grandparents. First cousins are related as closely as great-grandparents.

If the past breeding record of an individual is a better indication of his future success than his pedigree, it follows that in judging the value of a pedigree the breeding record of the sire is more important than his ancestry. The breeding record of the dam is important as

FIG. 15.—Yearling Shorthorn bull.

far as it goes, but may not be extensive enough to have much weight. The breeding record of her sire is likely to give more information. Thus, the worth and similarity in type of the progeny produced by the three or four closest top-cross males in the ancestry, in connection with their own worth and their relationship to one another, are the most important considerations in passing judgment on a pedigree. About twice as much weight should be given to the sire as to the dam's sire, and so on.

In judging the value of a pedigree, it is, of course, important to give as much weight to the inferior animals represented as to the champions. Unfortunately, it is not possible to learn much of the characteristics of any but the latter class. The rest of the pedigree consists merely of names. A knowledge of the methods and ideals of the leading breeders is of great assistance in giving substance to these names.

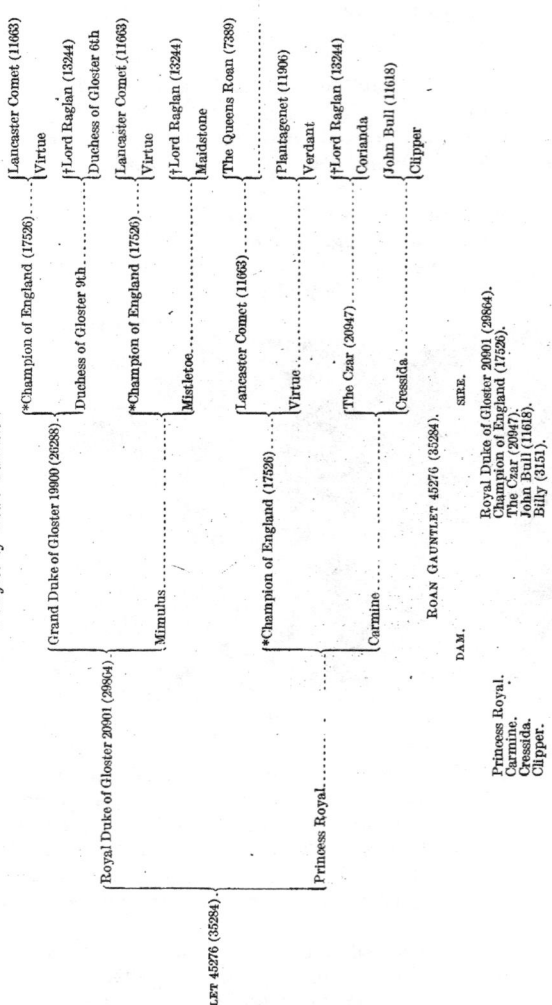

Pedigree of Roan Gauntlet.

It is evident from what has been said that it is an exceedingly difficult thing to be able to judge quickly and accurately the amount which a certain pedigree adds to or subtracts from the value of an animal as an individual. A very detailed knowledge of breed history, recent and past, is necessary, as well as good judgment. The past history can be learned in part from standard books on the breeds, while the recent history, which is more important, can be best acquired by following the results at the great shows and sales for a few years and keeping in touch with the current breed journals. The pedigree of any purebred can easily be obtained from the herd, flock, or studbook.

The best method of writing a pedigree for the purpose of study is that given for Amos Cruikshank's famous Shorthorn bull, Roan Gauntlet, in the tabulation shown. All the ancestors for a number of generations are shown in their proper relations to each other. Any line breeding in the pedigree is at once brought out. In the case of Roan Gauntlet the accompanying form shows that he traces in every line to a mating of Mr. Cruikshank's great bull, Champion of England, with a daughter or granddaughter of Lord Raglan.

The other common method of writing pedigrees is given for Roan Gauntlet below the full tabulation. The dam, her dam, and so on in the straight female line, are named in the first column. Opposite each female is written the name of her sire. It is very common in this form to add the name of the breeder after each animal, a practice which, as already noted, is often of value in giving significance to otherwise unknown names. To the breeder who is thoroughly acquainted with the leading sires in his breed, their own merit and that of their progeny, the names of the three or four males at the top of the column may be sufficient for a very satisfactory estimate of the value of the pedigree. Unfortunately, this form of pedigree is likely to lead to undue weight being placed on the female line of ancestry. Owing to their smaller numbers, the sires are in general superior to the dams both in breeding and as individuals. Thus the straight female line is apt to be the weakest in the whole pedigree. Direction of attention to this line has merely the somewhat negative justification that if it is good the whole pedigree is likely to be good.

The amount of information necessary for weighing properly the value of a pedigree is so great that a large number of men arrive at their conclusions by some short cut. The usual short cut in this case is the basing of values on family names, assigned to animals in a more or less arbitrary way. If the families really represented closely bred lines—breeds within breeds—this would be satisfactory, but that is seldom the case. In some breeds, the family name applies to all the descendants through the straight female line from some particular female. The second form of pedigree described above has the unfortunate effect of appearing to sanction this system. After a few generations such a family name may mean practically nothing as regards either type or breeding. A judgment based on a family name in the straight male line is no better. The direction of attention away from real values always means deterioration in the end. A fancy for a particular name thus tends to correct itself in the long run, but may work great harm to a breed in the meantime.

THE VALUE OF PUREBREDS.

The characteristics of our domestic animals are the result of a very gradual evolution, which has taken place in the course of centuries. Even our average scrubs are doubtless superior, in their usefulness to man, to the wild animals from which they are remotely descended. Until quite recently most of this improvement probably came about rather in spite of, than because of, the current beliefs in regard to heredity; one sound principle, the selection of the best for breeding, was, however, widely enough applied to bring about a slow progress. That our livestock are on the average still far from utilizing their feedstuffs to the greatest advantage in producing food, clothing, and work is shown by the achievements of individual animals, usually belonging to one or another of the pure breeds. These pure breeds are the tangible result of a century and a half of conscious effort at improvement. As hope for a more satisfactory livestock situation in the country depends on the further improvement of pure breeds and on the diffusion of their influence through the common stock, it will be well to consider briefly what has already been accomplished.

The value of the purebreds is clearest in those cases in which the capability of the animals is measured most directly. No one would question, for example, the supremacy of the English Thoroughbred in speed and gameness, a supremacy gained by a long period of the most direct selection. Among the farm animals, the best illustration can be found in dairy cattle, although careful yearly tests of milk and butterfat production are relatively recent affairs. The enormous differences among dairy cows when given the same opportunity have been brought out clearly in a great number of cases. Careful studies have shown that these differences are strongly inherited through both the sire and the dam. The average for purebreds and grades is also much above that for the average milk cow of the United States, which produces only about 4,000 pounds of milk and 160 pounds of butterfat in a year.

DAIRY CATTLE.

The great improvement which can be made by better feeding and by the grading up of common cows by the use of purebred sires has been demonstrated in all the many cases to which the writer has seen reference. Since, however, it is not possible in most cases to separate clearly the effects of grading up from those of better feeding and management, it may be well to refer briefly to an experiment recently reported by McCandlish, Gillette, and Kildee, of the Iowa agricultural experiment station, in which this can be done.

A number of scrub milk cows were brought to the station from a region of Arkansas in which purebred bulls had not been used. Their average milk production was not known but was doubtless much less than that which was obtained from the same cows under careful

Fig. 16.—A Guernsey bull of excellent type.

management at the station. Five of the cows were mature, 2 were 4 years old, and 7 either were very young heifers when obtained or were born at the station. These scrubs were bred to purebred bulls (Holstein, Guernsey, and Jersey), none of which were high priced. The records, all made under the same conditions, may be summarized as follows, after making the proper correction for age:

Effect of breeding scrub milk cows to purebred bulls.

Description.	Cows tested.	Lactation periods.	Average pounds milk.	Average pounds butterfat.
Scrubs—mature when obtained	5	15	3,169	154
Scrubs—4 years old when obtained	2	15	3,598	166
Scrubs—developed at station	7	28	4,086	191
One-half pure blood	13	40	5,556	253
Three-fourths pure blood	5	6	8,402	358

RESULTS OF IOWA EXPERIMENT IN GRADING UP SCRUB DAIRY STOCK.

The table indicates that a heifer which has developed under favorable conditions will produce more milk than one which did not have this advantage (increase of 27 per cent in milk, 24 per cent in butterfat). The most important thing brought out, however, is the great improvement made by one cross with purebred sires (38 per cent in milk production, 32 per cent in butterfat). The data for three-quarter bloods are rather meager, but show such a very great increase that it can be hardly doubted that a substantial increase over the first cross will be shown when larger numbers are available. When each of the grade cows is compared with her scrub dam or granddam, the improvement appears even more striking, owing to the fact that some of the dams were in the group of scrubs which were mature when brought to the station. Considerable difference was found in the value of the different bulls used. One of them produced hardly any improvement in his daughters, while others were responsible for a big increase in production.

It is important to understand the essential difference between a good and a poor producer. An investigation by C. H. Eckles, of the University of Missouri, brought out no important differences in the quantity of feed used by the cows merely in maintaining their weight when dry, nor in the amount of milk and butter produced by a given amount of additional feed. The good producer merely ate more feed in addition to the maintenance ration than the poor producer. This does not mean that a better appetite is the cause of higher production. The situation is probably the reverse. It shows, however, that the greater economy of high producers lies in the smaller percentage of their feed used for mere maintenance. The average cow, producing 160 pounds of butterfat a year, eats about 50 per cent more than if she were dry. Her milk scarcely pays for her keep. A cow which eats 100 per cent more than her maintenance requirements should produce twice as much milk as the former cow, with only one-third more feed. If the average American cow were of the latter kind, producing about 320 pounds of butterfat in a year, only half as many cows would be needed as at present and only two-thirds as much feed would be consumed in producing our present milk supply. With still more productive cows, milk can be produced still more cheaply, although it should be said that the rate of decline in feed cost decreases rapidly for production above 320 pounds. As a very considerable number of cows, including representatives of all the important breeds, have records of 900 pounds of butterfat in a year, the attainment of an average of 320 pounds is not a very ambitious undertaking.

As for the breeds of dairy cows, each has its advantages. The Jerseys and Guernseys, for example, produce richer milk than the Holstein-Friesians, but on the average less of it. The average difference in butterfat production, relative to the size of the animals and their cost of upkeep, is probably not very great. The differences between good and poor strains within each breed are much more important than differences between two breeds.

QUALITY IN MEAT.

The world-wide trend toward a falling per capita production of meat and the rising prices relative to other foods make the more economical production of meat a pressing problem. Both better methods of management and the improvement of the native stock by grading are of the greatest importance in this connection. The differences between purebred and scrub stock and the advantages to be expected by the grading up of the latter, however, are often misunderstood. The improvement is not primarily in size or even in the apparent economy of gains. The three most important breeds of beef cattle—Shorthorn, Hereford, and Aberdeen Angus—are indeed of large size, and when crossed with scrub beef cows or with milk cows which are undersized by heredity and not merely stunted by lack of proper feeding, they produce great improvement in this respect. Shorthorn and Hereford bulls have done wonders for the western range cattle in this way as well as in others. The pure breeds of swine and the larger breeds of sheep have also often been used to advantage to increase the size of native stock. There are, however, many large-sized scrubs.

The Holstein-Friesian cattle probably have the largest bony framework of all the breeds, but are not the best beef cattle. Feeding tests at experiment stations have often shown very little difference in either rate or gain or the cost per pound of gain when purebred or high-grade beef steers were compared with steers of scrub or dairy breeding. Holstein-Friesian steers, as might be expected, have shown up especially well in such tests. Similar results have been obtained in comparing purebred swine with "razorbacks" raised under the same conditions.

In the tests with cattle, however, the animals of beef type and breeding usually finished out into a class for which the market would pay considerably more than for the finished scrub or dairy steers. The per cent which the dressed weight forms of the live weight depends largely on the degree of fattening, and varies from 40 per cent in thin cows to 70 in the most highly finished steers. Under the same conditions steers of beef breeding usually dress out from 1 to 5 per cent more than common or dairy steers. There is also a slight difference in the size of the cuts from different parts of the carcass. Nature tends to develop most flesh in the muscles which do the most work. In the beef breeds of cattle, animals have been selected for breeding in which there was as much flesh as possible in the little-used muscles of the back and loin. The high-priced cuts from the back and loin, in fact, do form a slightly larger percentage of the dressed weight in beef steers than in common ones. The greater value of the meat from steers of beef breeding is largely, however, ascribed to the somewhat elusive element quality.

If the greater use of purebred bulls is merely to improve the average quality of beef and not to increase the quantity produced in the country with a given consumption of feed, it may seem to be of no very great importance. It appears, however, that in this case superior quality really means greater food value. The essential differences between a beef steer and the average scrub are probably

FIG. 17.—Aberdeen-Angus steer of excellent beef type.

brought out most thoroughly in an experiment by Dr. H. P. Armsby, and J. A. Fries (Bureau of Animal Industry Bulletin 128).

An Aberdeen-Angus steer was fed in comparison with a scrub. The utilization of the feed was investigated by the most thorough methods. In agreement with the usual results, there was little difference in gains or cost per pound of gain. The beef steer dressed out better—60 per cent compared with 54.5 per cent—and the loin formed 17.5 per cent of the dressed weight, compared with 16.4 per cent in the scrub, which had more weight in the cheaper cuts. The beef steer, though greater in height and length of body at a year of age, was reached or passed by the scrub later in those respects. The beef steer, however, greatly surpassed the scrub in girth of body. Evidently the scrub continued growing for a longer time in bone and muscle, while the purebred, after a more rapid early growth, matured earlier and turned to fattening with greater facility. There was an important difference in the amount of feed just necessary to keep the animals from losing weight, the scrub requiring about 19 per cent more feed for this purpose. The purebred, moreover, was able to consume and utilize a larger amount of concentrated feed above his maintenance requirement than the scrub, the same difference, it will be recalled, as that between a good and a poor dairy cow.

These advantages may appear impossible to reconcile with the lack of difference in gains or cost per pound of gain. The explanation is that the purebred packed more food value into a pound of gain. A pound of his meat contained a great deal more fat and

Fig. 18.—Yorkshire boar, illustrating the bacon type of hog.

practically as much protein, but very much less water. Thus a pound of meat from the purebred was not merely of higher quality, because of the superior marbling with fat, but really contained 40 per cent more food value. Thus under the same conditions a pound of meat from a properly finished purebred is no more comparable with a pound from a scrub than is a pound of rich milk with a pound of low-testing milk.

Thus the important qualities which breeders have developed in the breeds of beef cattle are the blocky conformation with the greatest development of the more valuable cuts and the smallest amount of waste; the low maintenance requirement which results from a placid disposition; the rapid but soon completed growth in bone and muscle, in which large size is combined with early maturity; and, finally, ease of fattening.

The improved breeds of hogs have a similar advantage over scrubs in conformation, disposition, early maturity, and ease of fattening, resulting in the production of a more concentrated food product at no more or at less cost per pound. The hog, however, has such an

FIG. 19.—A Piney-Woods ewe.

excessive tendency to fatten that the most improved breeds do not produce the best quality of meat. They are valuable, primarily, for the lard which they produce. The breeds with more vigorous

FIG. 20.—First cross between a Piney-Woods ewe and a purebred ram, showing improvement in type and wool.

growth and less tendency to fatten, such as the Tamworth and York-shire, produce a better quality of ham and bacon.

In parts of the Corn Belt the native hogs have been improved to such extent by crosses with purebreds that the advantages of consisteat grading to one pure breed are perhaps rather in obtaining uniformity of color and type than in efficiency of pork production. In many parts of the country, however, there is still much room for improvement in the fundamental qualities.

Sheep breeding is complicated by the simultaneous selection for wool and mutton. Each of the breeds produces its own characteristic kind of wool. Any desired fineness or length of fiber which is found in a pure breed can easily be fixed in common stock by grading up. As regards mutton, the same principles apply as in beef production. The same qualities have been fixed in the middle and long-wool breeds of sheep as in the beef breeds of cattle.

FIG. 21.—The same Piney-Woods ewe as in figure 19, showing the lack of wool on the abdomen. Total wool clip, 3 pounds.

FIG. 22.—First cross between Piney-Woods ewe and a purebred ram, showing wool on abdomen. Total clip, 8 pounds.

BREEDING AND SOUNDNESS IN HORSES.

The hereditary differences among the breeds of horses are more conspicuous than in any other kind of livestock. Differences in weight, speed, and conformation are fairly well fixed in the pure breeds, but, of course, unfixed in scrubs. The effect of a cross with a given pure breed can be predicted, at least in a rough way, but no predictions are of value in case the stallion is a scrub. Of the greatest importance for any kind of horse are good feet and legs. Scrub stallions, even if apparently sound themselves, are more likely to transmit unsoundness than stallions of the pure breeds, especially if the latter are known to come from sound stock. There is, perhaps, less excuse for scrub stallions than for scrub males of any other kind of livestock.

Whether it is advisable for a man who breeds only 1 or 2 mares a year to breed always to a stallion of the same pure breed is more often questioned. It may seem best to attempt to balance a certain defect in a grade Percheron mare by breeding to a Clydesdale stallion. The colt is practically a crossbred and should have the vigor of a crossbred with at least the general conformation and size of a draft horse. There is, however, much more uncertainty in such breeding than in consistent grading to a single pure breed. In crossbreeding,

FIG. 21.—A Percheron stallion.
Descendant of a long line of impressive ancestors and himself a sire of valuable draft horses.

one defect on which attention is fixed may be improved, but unexpected ones are likely to appear. In shifting constantly from breed to breed there can be no assured progress toward a definite ideal.

POULTRY.

The various breeds of standardbred poultry have been selected in the past largely according to type and feathers. The heavy breeds can be trusted to excel in meat production, but the situation has no been very satisfactory in regard to eggs. With the systematic taking of yearly egg records, however, it will probably not be long before reliable strains of egg producers will have become thoroughly established in all the breeds with pretensions in this direction. Great differences among breeds and strains within the breeds have been clearly demonstrated.

SATISFACTION FROM PLEASING APPEARANCE.

In this discussion, attention has been devoted in the main to the strictly practical merits of the pure breeds. It would not be fair to

FIG. 24.—A Standardbred stallion.

conclude without referring to another aspect. This is the satisfaction to be derived from a uniform stock which presents a pleasing appearance in type and color. The appeal of the beautiful or majestic in livestock has been, perhaps, the most important motive leading to their improvement. Pride in the possession of such livestock and the constant inspiration to be derived from their further improvement are considerations beyond the purely material advantages.

Fig. 25.—Typical results of grading up with poultry. A. standardbred Barred Plymouth Rock

SUMMARY.

Animals and plants are composed of microscopical units—the cells. Each cell has a specialized central portion, the nucleus, which contains a number of threadlike or rodlike bodies called chromosomes. The number of chromosomes is constant in each kind of animal or plant.

Every animal begins its career in the union of two cells—the egg cell from the dam and the sperm from the sire.

In a sense the reproductive cells are not produced by the parents but are unspecialized bits of the same material from which the parents themselves originally developed. Heredity consists merely in the retention, by the reproductive cells, of the power to develop into a complete individual under the proper conditions.

Characteristics acquired by the parents through training, care, or accident are not transmitted to their progeny. Belief in the influences of telegony and maternal impressions has no scientific foundation.

The heredity, transmitted by the reproductive cells, is composed of unit factors, each of which is handed on unchanged from generation to generation.

Hereditary differences depend on the existence of alternative forms of certain unit factors. Such alternative factors are called allelomorphs of each other.

The egg and sperm each contain, typically, a full set of the unit factors characteristic of the kind of animal. Their union results in a double set in the fertilized egg.

This double set may be composed in part of pairs of identical factors and in part of pairs of alternative factors. The individual is said to be homozygous in regard to the former, and heterozygous in regard to the latter.

It often happens that one of the alternative factors in a heterozygous individual expresses itself fully in development at the expense of the other. Such a factor is said to be dominant. The factor whose influence is suppressed is said to be recessive. The normal type of a species is usually dominant over deviations from normal.

Most characteristics depend on the combined influence of a number of pairs of factors.

The double set of factors in the individual is sorted out into single ets in the formation of the reproductive cells. Individuals produce rly one kind of reproductive cell in those respects in which they ire homozygous and two kinds in those in which they are heterozygous.

Parallel to the results of genetic experiments, the microscope reveals the chromosomes in pairs in the body cells, in place of the single set to be observed in the reproductive cells. There is convincing evidence that the chromosomes are the bearers of the hereditary factors.

In most cases two factors which come into an individual's heredity from the same parent are no more likely to go into the same reproductive cell than two factors which were derived from opposite parents.

In some cases, on the other hand, there is a tendency for factors which enter a cross together to come out together in the second generation. Such factors are said to be linked with each other in inheritance.

The hereditary factors of a species fall into groups in such a manner that those in the same group are all linked with one another, while those in different groups show no linkage. It is believed that each linkage group contains the factors which are carried by a given chromosome.

Sex is normally determined by a difference in the chromosomes. In some cases, including mammals, the male produces two kinds of sperms, male and female determining, respectively. In other cases, including birds, it is the female that is heterozygous for sex.

A number of characteristics are known which are linked with sex in inheritance in such way as to indicate that they are carried by the chromosome that determines sex.

No practical means of modifying the sex ratio is yet known, with the possible exception of inbreeding and selection.

The colors of farm livestock depend in most cases on relatively few unit factors. The same is true of a few other characteristics, such as the polled condition of cattle and the various comb shapes of poultry.

Differences in size, type, and function are believed to depend in most cases on many factors. Their inheritance can not, so far as known at present, be controlled by such direct methods as the simpler characteristics.

There is equal inheritance from the sexes.

Prepotency depends neither on breed nor on sex, nor does the prepotency of an individual in one respect indicate his prepotency in others. In part, prepotency depends on the nature of the heredity back of particular characteristics, especially on the dominance of the factors which are involved. In part, it depends on the fixation of heredity, which means the making of all pairs of factors homozygous.

Variation is composed of four elements: that due to different combinations of hereditary factors, that due to the appearance of new hereditary factors (or mutations), that due to outside conditions which can be controlled, and that due to uncontrollable conditions, such as chance irregularity in development. Some characteristics are determined to a greater degree by heredity than others.

Straight selection is sometimes effective in fixing characters, but a single unfortunate cross is likely at any time to upset much previous work.

The primary effect of inbreeding is the automatic fixation of some combination of hereditary factors present in the stock. This leads to uniformity of type or function, if such uniformity is possible. When not possible, owing to variation which is not genetic, the hereditary potentialities of different lines are at least clearly brought out. Decline in vigor is a common but not a necessary consequence of the fixation of heredity.

The first generation of a cross is as uniform in character as the parent stocks, and, in general, shows increased vigor. The type is usually, but not always, intermediate between that of the parents. In the second generation there is increased variability, the characteristics of the grandparents being combined, as a rule, in all combinations and degrees.

Aside from mere increase in numbers, the principal objects of breeding are to produce uniformity of a desired type and improvement.

Uniformity of type depends on close breeding accompanied by selection, and may either be fixed within a line or secured in the first generation of a cross.

Radical improvement depends on crossbreeding followed by close breeding and selection in order to fix the desired combination of characteristics when obtained.

Improvement of inferior types, whether scrub or purebred, depends on the consistent use of prepotent males of the same breed or line within the bred.

Selection of breeding stock requires good judgment in estimating the merits and properly weighing the claims of the animal's performance, his conformation, pedigree, and previous success as a breeder.

The most direct tests of performance are the best.

The best evidence of the value of an animal in breeding is his past record in this respect, if sufficiently extensive.

In judging the value of a pedigree, the worth and similarity in type of the progeny produced by the three or four closest top-cross males in the ancestry in connection with their own worth and their relationship to one another are the most important considerations. The sire should be given twice as much weight as the dam's sire, and so on.

The pure breeds of livestock are the successful results of past efforts at improvement and should form the basis for further progress.

UNITED STATES DEPARTMENT OF AGRICULTURE

 BULLETIN No. 906

Contribution from the Bureau of Public Roads
Thos. H. MacDonald, Chief

Washington, D. C.   ▼   March 23, 1921

THE USE OF CONCRETE PIPE IN IRRIGATION.

By F. W. STANLEY,
Senior Irrigation Engineer,
With Introductory Paragraphs by
SAMUEL FORTIER,
Chief of Irrigation Division.

CONTENTS.

	Page.		Page.
Introduction	1	Laying Concrete Pipe	13
The Use of Pipe in Irrigation	2	Causes of Failure in Concrete Pipe	15
Incasing Old Pipes of Metal and Wood		Pipe Systems for Irrigation	23
with Concrete	4	Settling Basins and Screens	27
Concrete Pipe	4	Air Vents	29
Reinforced Concrete Pipe	6	Relief Stands	30
Manufacture of Plain Concrete Pipe	8	Measuring Devices for Pipe Irriga-	
Quality of Concrete Pipe	9	tion Systems	31
Cost of Unreinforced Pipe	12	Distributing hydrants	44

INTRODUCTION.

In the more arid parts of the West, arable land possesses little value without water. The water which can be put to a beneficial use is limited to relatively small quantities, so that when it is fully utilized, only a small percentage of the total fertile and arable lands of the West can be reclaimed by irrigation. In recent years, owing to the rapid increase in the value of soil products, intensively farmed land under irrigation systems has risen in many cases to double its former, prewar value. This great advance in the value of irrigated land has placed a premium on water, and a widespread effort is being made to convey, distribute, and use the appropriated waters in such a way as to incur the least possible loss. Every gallon of water wasted by seepage and absorption in porous earthen channels or in careless use on the land, robs the farmer of so much profit, whereas every gallon saved protects fertile soil from water-logging, and results in larger yields and profits to the grower.

An experience covering a period of over a quarter of a century on the Pacific Coast, and more especially in California, has demonstrated that large quantities of water can be saved by the substitution of pipe for earthen ditches. The results of a large number of measurements made by the irrigation division of this bureau show that the transmission losses in earthen channels vary from 10 to 60 per cent, and average fully 35 per cent of the quantity of water admitted through the intake. When pipes are substituted for earthen channels, the loss of water in conveyance is usually negligible.

The use of pipe for the carriage of water and of pipe systems for its distribution to farmers, not only prevents loss of water but affords better facilities for its control, distribution, and delivery. Irrigating land by means of open channels in earth is a laborious and unpleasant task, wasteful of water, time, and effort. On the contrary it can be rendered comparatively easy and pleasant if the proper equipment is provided in the way of pipe, pipe systems with proper gates, turnouts, and other fixtures. The interest on the cost of such betterments for highly profitable crops is more than likely to be amply compensated for by the water and labor saved and a more uniform moistening of the soil.

The purpose of this bulletin is to present to the irrigation farmers and orchardists of the West information concerning pipe and pipe systems and more especially the use of concrete pipe in irrigation, with such practical suggestions regarding making and laying as may enable those engaged in this work to avoid mistakes and attain satisfactory results.

THE USE OF PIPE IN IRRIGATION.

Before proceeding to a discussion of concrete pipe as used in irrigation systems, brief references are made herewith to other kinds of piping used for the same purpose. These other kinds include metal pipe, wood pipe, and vitrified clay pipe. These, with concrete pipe, differ in strength, durability, cost, and general fitness for any particular location and use, and in planning an irrigation system where pipes are to be used in quantity, care should be exercised to select the kind of piping that will best meet the requirements of each individual case. It happens quite frequently that the same kind of piping can not be advantageously used to convey water to all parts of an irrigation enterprise.

Metal pipes, and especially riveted steel pipes, possess strength in a high degree and on this account should be used for high pressures and where excessive fluctuations in pressure occur due to water-hammer and other causes. On the other hand riveted steel pipe of the quality now manufactured is not durable when exposed to unfavorable conditions unless protected by an asphaltic or other similar coating or galvanized. The dipping of sections of riveted pipe in a bath of hot asphalt has long been practiced, but if the coating becomes brittle when cooled, it is liable to chip off and expose the metal. To guard against abrasions in the coating, roofing paper cemented to the pipe with hot tar has been successfully used on several large systems, notably those of the Terra Bella irrigation district in Tulare County and the Sweetwater Water Co. of San Diego County, Calif. In wrapping pipe, a roll of roofing paper is cut in a number of strips by means of a homemade machine. This machine winds a roll of roofing paper from one spindle to another, meanwhile drawing the paper over a series of knives; the knives can be regulated so as to cut any width of strip desired. The pipe to be wrapped is placed on a spindle which is suspended over a trough. It is then revolved by a crank by one man, while another guides the strip of roofing paper. The paper is thus wound spirally the length of the pipe. A third man pours hot tar between the roofing paper and the pipe while the winding process is going on.

For medium water pressures created by heads of 20 to 100 feet and over, wood pipe may be used. The kind of wood pipe known as continuous stave pipe may be built in sizes ranging from 1 to 15 feet in diameter. The materials of which this pipe is composed consist of wood staves, steel bands, and cast-iron clips, which are shipped to the site usually direct from the manufacturer, and the pipe is laid continuously either in a trench or on the surface of the ground along the line of the location.

So-called machine-banded wood pipe is made in the factory in shipping lengths and in sizes ranging from 2 to 52 inches. In making this pipe the staves are held together by galvanized steel wire, wound spirally and spaced according to the pressure to be sustained. After the pipe is banded and the ends are milled for couplings, each shipping length is dipped in a bath of hot asphalt and when withdrawn is rolled in sawdust or shavings. The light weight and cheapness of wood pipe and the ease with which it can be shipped and transported over mountainous and out-of-the-way places are marketable advantages. The chief objection to the use of wood pipe is the tendency of the wood to decay when in contact with the earth, exposed to the air, and alternately wet and dry. When wood pipe is kept continuously under water pressure, or covered to a depth of 2 feet or more in tight soil, it has been known to give excellent service for 30 years.

Vitrified clay pipe when well made is a suitable pipe for irrigation purposes, providing the head does not exceed 15 feet. It is easy to lay, has a smooth interior surface, and in consequence a fairly low friction factor. It is not as a rule injuriously affected by alkali. Most

Old pipe of metal and wood may be converted into
by placing a layer of concrete around their exteriors. 1
be done with the pipe in place, under pressure and in ι
the leaks are not too troublesome.

In the case of steel pipe, the pipe is uncovered and
of dirt and rust with steel brushes. The excavation :
enough to permit forms to be placed around the sides aι
bottom of the pipe. Before placing the forms triangul
forcing wire of the right width is wound spirally arc
and is kept away from the pipe by small concre
Wooden forms 12 feet in length are then put in place, ι
cient space between the forms and the exterior of the
proper thickness of concrete shell. Concrete is then ρ
the form, which is allowed to remain in place 24 hours l
ing. Recently the Sweetwater Water Co. of San Γ
Calif., incased 3,125 feet of 8-inch steel-riveted pip
cost of $1.13 per foot, which included trenching, back
etc. The same company also encased 600 feet of
for $1.39 per foot. Several years ago the Temescal ᐧ
Corona, Calif., incased with concrete 10,000 feet of
pipe, under a maximum head of 80 feet, which had b
for 30 years,[1] also shorter lengths of pipes 30 and 18
ameter. The cost inclusive of trenching, forms, backfil
$2.50 per foot for the 30-inch pipe, $1.70 for the 24-in
per foot for the 18-inch pipe. The price of labor at ι
$2.25 to $2.50 per day, while cement was worth $2.ε
The form used is shown in figure 1.

CONCRETE PIPE.

During the past 10 or 15 years the greater part of
for irrigation pipe systems has been made of concret

---

[1] See article in Engineering News-Record by H. R. Case, Sept.

cipal reasons for its extended use are its relative cheapness, durability, strength, and general adaptability to irrigation requirements. An excellent quality of cement is made in scores of factories in the West and sold at relatively low prices, while the other ingredients of sand, gravel, rock-dust, and broken rock usually are found in close proximity to where the pipe is made.

FIG. 1.—Form used in incasing riveted steel pipe with concrete.

Concrete pipe is made both reinforced and plain, the former having more or less steel embedded in the concrete shell in order to increase its tensile strength. A few years ago plain concrete pipe was placed in the same class as vitrified clay pipe as regards tensile strength and limited to less than 15 feet head. This precaution was then necessary owing to the inferior quality of the pipe made, and failures were common even under less than 10-foot heads. In recent years a marked improvement has been produced by substituting a proper concrete mixture for the cement and sand formerly used and

by adopting better methods of molding, tamping, curing, and laying.
There is to-day in successful operation a large mileage of unreinforced pipe from 6 to 24 inches in diameter under heads of 25 to 40
feet, while other lines are under heads of 40 to 100 feet. One pipe
line 16 inches in diameter is successfully operating under a head of
80 feet.

REINFORCED CONCRETE PIPE.

Reinforced concrete pipe, 12 to 72 inches in diameter, is made in
yards or temporary sites by means of collapsible forms, the larger
sizes being made frequently near the point of laying to lessen the
cost and difficulties of transportation. The forms may be of either
wood or steel, or the inside form of steel and the outside of wood.
Either wire mesh or steel hoops may be used for reinforcing material,
the size and spacing of the reinforcing depending on the head to be
exerted against the pipe. Most reinforced pipe is made by placing
a cage of reinforcing wire mesh between the inside and outside forms
and then pouring in a wet mixture of concrete. The concrete is
tamped into place. The molds are removed in about 24 hours, the
pipe being kept moistened while curing. Most manufacturers of
reinforced pipe aim to use enough steel to take all tension in the pipe,
the concrete acting as an impervious shell only. It has been found
that poured concrete has a lower tensile strength than a drier mixture
that is well tamped, but it is difficult to tamp pipe well when wire
mesh reinforcing is used.

Reinforced pipe is laid in a trench as is done with ordinary concrete
pipe. The joints are usually poured by the use of special forms for
the purpose. Some firms put out a special lock joint, which ties the
longitudinal reinforcing wires of one joint to the next. It is not
usual however, to provide enough longitudinal wires to take all
stresses due to contraction, and for this reason some pipe firms have
provided frequent expansion joints made from a thin, crimped sheet
of copper. In the latter case very few, if any, longitudinal wires
are needed.

Partially reinforced pipe may be made by dropping welded wire
rings into hand-tamped pipe while the pipe is being made. Enough
rings may be inserted to take all the tension, or two or three rings
may be used in every length, which are expected to prevent a crack
from one pipe being transmitted to another.

There are several methods of constructing continuous reinforced
pipe one of which is shown in figure 2. This is usually done by
using a collapsible inner form which is moved along the trench as the
pipe is being made. An outside form may be used on the sides and
top, or the trench may be cut so as to act as the outside form.

The Whittier Water Co., of Whittier, Calif., has laid considerable
quantities of continuous reinforced concrete pipe. One installation

is rectangular in cross section, 36 inches by 36 inches inside dimensions. Collapsible wooden forms were used, 12 feet in length, with triangular reinforcing wire mesh placed in two sections. One section of wire mesh is laid on top of the forms, with the edges turned down into the side walls, and the other section covers the bottom and extends up the sides. The sides of the earthen excavation were cut so as to leave a thickness of concrete of 6 inches. This conduit is made to stand 50 feet head. The total cost was about $2.40 per foot.

If continuous pipe is laid in cool weather and is not allowed to dry before being filled with water, there may be no trouble with contraction cracks, but this class of pipe would probably give considerable

Fig. 2.—Showing one method of building continuous reinforced-concrete pipe.

trouble if laid in the summer, especially if allowed to dry out during the winter. If possible, the pipe should be covered with at least 2 feet of earth, and if the soil is kept moist curing should take place without the concrete cracking.

One firm in Los Angeles has given the following prices at the yard, Los Angeles, under date of May, 1919, for reinforced concrete pipe:

Diameter.	Price per foot.	Diameter.	Price per foot.
12 inches	$0.86	36 inches	$3.30
16 inches	1.13	48 inches	5.15
18 inches	1.24	60 inches	7.40
20 inches	1.37	72 inches	10.12
24 inches	1.70		

cally on the ground or on a platform. Concrete i
tween the forms by one man while another tamps
is finished it is reamed off on top with a specia
side form is first removed by collapsing it and the
the proper place in the yard, where the outside forn
the pipe allowed to set. Pipe should always be
moist for at least 10 days before it is cured. I
moist enough when the pipe is tamped the outside
ripped, i. e., pulled off vertically, without loosening
so-called dry pipe is made, the forms can not be
e outside form must be loosened before lifting it off
groove ends of the pipe are made to assist in lay
e end, which is usually a simple inside taper on the
ipe, is made by dropping a cast-iron ring between
s ring is beveled to conform to the groove of the
wed to remain on the bottom of the pipe until the
sufficiently to move the pipe. (Fig. 3.) The tongue
is made when the pipe is finished, and is accom
ling the reamer over the top before the forms are
a hand-tamped pipe is made with bell and spigo
the ordinary clay sewer pipe. When pipe is made in
tside form is split so that the forms can be removed

s[2] are roughly classified as tamping machines and
ines. Some tamping machines tamp the pipe very
hand-tamping process. The mechanism of most o
causes the pipe to revolve under the tamper while
oured in between the forms. A pneumatic air tampe
tamp the pipe. The apparatus operating the ai
nded over the forms, the air tamper being guidec
l of the pipe by one man, while another feeds the
oneumatic hammer delivers about 700 blows a minute

ate Experiment Station Bulletin No. 86, by G. E. P. Smith.

ur_der heavy pressure. In other respects the pipe is made as described under hand-tamped methods.

Troweling machines make use of iron vanes that force the concrete down and against the outside form. The vane or packerhead apparatus is revolved by machinery and at the same time is lifted from bottom to top of a length of pipe while it is being made. There are a number of different types of this class of machine, many of which make pipe very rapidly. The troweling process usually makes a pipe of smooth interior finish.

FIG. 3.—Concrete-pipe yard showing forms and cast-iron rings.

It is probable that other types of concrete pipe machines will come into the market in the near future. A machine that both tamps and trowels pipe is used now. Another machine has been recently invented that compresses the concrete in the molds by squeezing in the outside form. Many other possibilities are talked of which may soon become realities.

QUALITY OF CONCRETE PIPE.

Both hand-tamped and machine-made concrete pipes are often of very inferior quality, but it is encouraging to know that the quality is constantly improving. Most pipe makers will agree to deliver a high-grade pipe if the purchaser is willing to pay for it, but as long as the latter insists on getting the cheapest pipe he is apt to get the poorest quality. Some reputable firms, however, will not make an inferior grade and do not try to compete with pipe makers who sell

pipe that is made of poor materials, poorly tamped, or th
proper proportion or kind of ingredients.

It is sometimes difficult to judge the quality of concrete
out having the necessary apparatus for testing it.   Usual
an intelligent examination with the application of a few :
will give a fair indication of its worth. . Two requiremen
sary for the best grades—strength and imperviousness.
stand high pressures and still be rather porous, but a
that is nearly impervious can be made if proper prec
taken in the choice of materials and the mixing and
troweling of the concrete.

Porosity can be tested by filling a length of pipe with
one end has been plugged. If the outside of the pipe :
after water has been in the pipe for several hours, it is p
the pipe will show very little seepage when under press
age through the shell of a concrete pipe usually shows u
pressure and does not increase proportionately with
pressures.   The porosity of pipe can be estimated by
small piece of concrete pipe before and after soakin
Dense pipe should increase very little in weight after b
for 10 minutes.

Hand-tamped pipe is often made with concrete tha
dry, for the reason that a dry mixture is easier to handle
by hand and will stand up with less tamping than a
Some of the dry mixed, poorly tamped pipe will absorb w
and become saturated throughout in a few minutes whe
water. A wet mixture is usually quite impervious, as
tamped well in order that the forms may be easily rem
that is made from a wet mixture of concrete will show a
on the outside of the pipe, while the wettest will show
coarse webbing.   This webbing or streaking shows up
the pipe is cured.   Such markings are due to moisture
outward against the outside form when the pipe is ta
mixture of water and cement is streaked vertically along
of the pipe when the form is stripped from the newly n

Wet-mixed pipe may not have the maximum strength
it can be depended upon for high-pressure work, and
durable and impervious if well cured in the yard.   Pipe
with the best known proportion of water in the mixture.

distorted pipe. Such pipe is more difficult to lay, but if care is taken in laying it should be satisfactory. Some of the pipe that presents the most attractive appearance in the yard may be of poor quality on account of having been mixed too dry.

The best grade of pipe for use against pressure should withstand a heavy blow with a hammer and should give a clear, ringing sound. The pipe should be dense when broken and be difficult to scratch with a knife. The best pipe can be thrown from a wagon to the ground without breaking, although this is not recommended except for a test.

The best grades must also be made from materials that will pass the test for any good concrete work. As much hard, broken rock or gravel containing a high proportion of hard pebbles should be used as can be incorporated. High-pressure pipe often contains as much as 50 per cent rock and is made with 1 part of cement to 3 parts of aggregate. Pipe for use under low pressures is often made of 1 part of cement to 5 parts of sand and rock. Some machines will not handle a large proportion of rock and with such more cement must be used to get the same grade of pipe. Machines are usually more reliable for compressing the concrete, and the product is liable to be more uniform. At the same time some of the most reliable pipe-making firms in the West are using hand-tamped methods, and guaranteeing their product.

Some farmers buy equipment for making hand-tamped pipe and make their own pipe. This practice is not to be encouraged as a rule, as experience is necessary if a reliable product is to be turned out. The saving in cost is small in many cases, and failures may make this method an expensive experiment. The safest thing for a farmer to do is to buy pipe from a reliable firm, have the same firm lay the pipe, and demand a guaranty that the pipe will conform to the specifications.

It is not intended to discuss the best materials required for making concrete pipe, as this subject will be taken up in another bulletin. Briefly stated, however, the sand should be clean, the rock clean, hard, and durable, and the whole aggregate well graded. If gravel is used, the materials should be clean and hard, with a minimum amount of organic matter. The presence of clay or silt free from organic matter in the gravel may not be harmful, and tends to make an impervious pipe if it is not present in too large quantities. Rock dust may be added with benefit to the pipe, while a certain proportion of lime will tend to make an impervious pipe. Soft or partially disintegrated rock or gravel is very harmful, especially if high-pressure pipe is desired. When possible, materials should be tested in the laboratory or test lengths of pipe made, which can be tested to failure in the yard. There are several types of apparatus designed by engineers of this bureau which can be used by pipe manufacturers for such purposes. In fact all pipe yards should be equipped with testing apparatus that can test pipe for an installation. A farmer should demand tests on pipe that he is ordering especially for high-pressure lines.

As regards durability, concrete pipe, if well made and laid, should last for generations. It is the improperly made pipe which causes failures and early renewal. The experience of southern California shows that the good concrete pipe installed 30 years ago is still in excellent condition, whereas some of the inferior pipe has been renewed in less than 5 years after laying.

COST OF UNREINFORCED CONCRETE PIPE.

The price of concrete pipe has increased somewhat during the last two or three years, but the increase has been less than in other types of pipe. The following prices were quoted in July, 1919, by a number of the larger manufacturers in southern California.

Inside diameter of pipe.	Price per foot at yard.	Price per foot laid in light soil.	Price per foot laid in heavy soil.	Inside diameter of pipe.	Price per foot at yard.	Price per foot laid in light soil.	Price per foot laid in heavy soil.
6 inches...........	$0.12½	$0.25	$0.28	18 inches...........	$0.46	$0.65	$0.85
8 inches...........	.14	.27	.30	20 inches...........	.70	1.00	.150
10 inches...........	.16	.30	.34	24 inches...........	.90	....	....
12 inches...........	.20	.34	.38	30 inches...........	1.60	....	....
14 inches...........	.25	.40	.44	36 inches...........	2.00	....	....
16 inches...........	.35	.52	.60				

NOTE.—Prices laid, include trenching and backfilling.

Prices quoted at the yard by the Concrete Pipe Manufacturers' Association of Northern and Central California July, 1919, are as follows:

Inside diameter of pipe.	Price per foot.	Inside diameter of pipe.	Price per foot.
6 inches.................................	$0.20	18 inches.................................	$0.72
8 inches.................................	.22	20 inches.................................	.85
10 inches.................................	.28	24 inches.................................	1.20
12 inches.................................	.35	30 inches.................................	1.90
14 inches.................................	.46	36 inches.................................	2.50
16 inches.................................	.70		

Some firms quote prices for pipe that will stand extra pressure, and guarantee the product. The cost of this pipe is about 30 per cent higher than stock pipe for 40-foot heads, and about 50 per cent higher for 50-foot heads. One firm makes pressure pipe of standard thickness from 6 to 12 inches in diameter that will stand 70 to 80 feet head, and sells it at a price 25 to 40 per cent higher than the ordinary low-pressure pipe. Pipes of 8 to 12 inches in diameter are made in stock of double thickness, which will stand heads of 150 feet and over, but the prices are about three times as high as stock pipe. Stock pipe should be safe under pressures of from 20 to 35 feet.

In connection with the above-quoted prices, it may be stated that many pipe manufacturers who operate small plants sell pipe much cheaper than the figures given.

LAYING CONCRETE PIPE.

Concrete pipe should be laid deep enough in the trench so as to reduce the range of temperature and to be safe from injury against plows, subsoilers or other farm implements. There should be at least 12 inches of earth over the top of all kinds of pipe, and high pressure pipe should have a top covering of at least 18 inches. Temperature changes in the shell of the pipe are greatly reduced when the pipe is buried deeply, and less trouble is experienced from expansion and contraction. The moisture content within the shell of the pipe is likewise kept more uniform than where the upper half is laid near the surface of the ground.

The trench should be wide enough to allow room for a man's feet when he is straddling the pipe in the act of laying the pipe. It is a mistake to make the trench too narrow, especially when large-sized pipe is laid, as there must be room to finish off the joints. Excavation in soil that is not too hard or rocky may be done with a plow and V scraper. Road scrapers and ditchers are sometimes used to start large excavations, but trenches so made are too wide as a rule. There are several makes of tile trenching machines that are used for large installations, and where there are no obstructions to interfere with the machine it may pay to use one. These may be operated over the same trench twice, thus making it of nearly double width. For the most part trenching is done with pick and shovel—handwork being necessary where pipe is laid among full-grown trees in an orchard.

Some contractors lay pipe by force account, charging a commission of 10 to 15 per cent for tools and supervision, for the reason that it is difficult to make an estimate of the cost of excavation, as trenching in hardpan, adobe, or soil full of boulders may cost several times as much as a trench in loose loam or sand. Some trenching in favorable soil has been done for 3 to 7 cents per foot for 12-inch pipe, while the actual cost of a trench for 24-inch pipe near Azusa, Calif., where bowlders were encountered, was about 35 cents per foot. Trenching for 12-inch pipe in adobe soil near Santa Ana, Calif., with a trenching machine was done for 5 cents per foot. Handwork for heavy soil often costs 15 to 20 cents per foot for 12-inch pipe.

The bottom of the trench should be laid as nearly as possible to grade, but the grade does not need to be uniform where the pipe is under pressure, although sudden changes in grade should be avoided, as such irregularities in the pipe line may collect air, which will decrease the carrying capacity of the pipe. If it is not possible to avoid alternate dips and rises, air vents should be provided for at the highest points in the line. Where the line makes a deep dip, a blow-off valve should be installed at the lowest point, so that any accumulation of sand or trash can be blown out.

Most experienced pipe layers lay small sizes of pipe by standing the joint to be laid on end and filling the groove end with mortar. The pipe is then firmly pressed against the tongue end of the pipe that is already laid in the ground, care being taken to get a good bond of mortar between the ends of the pipe. The mortar is smoothed off with a trowel on the outside, and the inside brushed smooth with a long-handled brush. The ends of the pipe are always wetted with a brush before applying the mortar.

Large-diameter pipe is usually laid by placing a batch of mortar in the bottom of the groove of the pipe that is laid and on top of the tongue end of the pipe to be laid. The tongue and groove of the two joints of pipe, respectively, are then pressed together and the joints filled in by hand, using a rubber glove or part of an automobile inner tube over the hand to protect it from the action of the cement. The inside of pipe of a diameter less than 22 inches is finished off by a long-handled brush, but larger pipe is finished or pointed off by a man who works inside of the pipe. If it is possible for a man to work inside the pipe it is best to finish the inside of the joints 24 hours or longer after the pipe has been laid. This gives the pipe time to settle, otherwise joints may crack if finished off at once. The pipe also has time to expand or contract before the inside is finished. For this reason most contractors would rather guarantee pipe against leaks when it is large enough to permit a man to work within it.

Pressure pipe and the larger sizes of ordinary pipe are usually finished with banded joints, but small pipe that is to be under low pressure is not banded as a rule. The band is formed around the joint on the outside of the pipe with a trowel. The average size of band is about one-half to three-fourths inch thick over the joint and 4 to 6 inches wide. Some pipe layers reinforce the joint of high pressure with wire mesh. The wire is tied around the joint and the band made by plastering the mortar over it.

Laying cores are made use of occasionally in assisting to make joints. The core fits inside the pipe and prevents mortar from being projected into it.

Mortar used in laying is usually made of one part of cement to one and one-half parts of fine sand. The mortar is often made by mixing the sand and cement with lime water. The addition of slaked lime makes the mortar easier to handle. One man who has had considerable experience with large sizes of pipe will not use lime in the mortar in sizes over 20 inches, as he claims mortar mixed with lime will tend to crack in the larger sizes.

Back filling should follow immediately after laying. If the earth used for back filling is moist, the mortar in the joints will cure better. Pipe laid in the trench is usually dry and a moist earth used for back filling will tend to moisten the pipe and cause a slight expansion. If the expansion takes place before the mortar in the joints is set, the pipe will conform to the new condition created by squeezing the mortar more compactly at the joints, instead of shoving the pipe ahead, which may cause failure at curves or destroy diversion boxes by crushing. The temperature in the trench after back filling is usually much lower than the air temperature, especially in the summer. A decrease in temperature causes the newly laid pipe to contract, which will probably be counteracted by the pipe absorbing moisture providing the back filling material is moist. In practice it is often difficult to procure enough water to wet the trench or back fill. In this case pipe should not be laid in the hottest weather. It sometimes happens that the pipe will expand enough when saturated after being filled with water to prevent trouble with contraction cracks. Accordingly water should be let into a newly laid pipe line as soon as possible. This subject will be discussed more fully under another heading.

After the trench is dug, and the pipe to be laid strung along the side of it, one expert pipe layer with two helpers will sometimes lay as much as 1,200 feet of 8- to 12-inch pipe in a day, but 800 feet is a good day's work for an average crew. Four men will lay the pipe and partially backfill the trench. Four men are usually needed to lay pipe from 14 to 18 inches in diameter, and will average 300 to 500 feet of this size in a day. Five to seven men will lay from 300 to 500 feet of 24-inch pipe in a day.

There is wide variation in the cost of laying pipe and the quantity of mortar used in making the joints. If heavy bands are made at the joints for high pressure lines, it often costs from 25 to 50 per cent more to lay the pipe. One pipe manufacturer estimates that one sack of cement, made into one to one and a half mortar, will lay 350 feet of 6-inch pipe, 270 feet of 8-inch, 200 feet of 10-inch, 160 feet of 12-inch, and 70 feet of 20-inch pipe. If bell-ended pipe is used, similar to the ordinary clay sewer pipe, more mortar is needed.

CAUSES OF FAILURE OF CONCRETE PIPE.

One of the most frequent causes of failure of concrete pipe is a poor grade of pipe. If the pipe is made of poor material, or a very lean mixture, it is apt to split even under low pressures. A poor grade of pipe may appear to be in good shape when first installed, but may fail after a year or more due to softening of the concrete. It is common, however, to detect causes of failure as soon as the pipe is filled with water.

More or less seepage is common to most grades of hand-tamped pipe, but if it is not too pronounced it usually disappears in time. Such materials as silt, clay, or fine sand are often used to fill up the pores and prevent seepage. As mentioned above, pipe made of a dry mixture is more subject to seepage than wet-mixed pipe, and the joints are more difficult to make in a dry, porous pipe.

If the pipe is of good quality any leaks that occur are usually at the joints. When pipe is laid by inexperienced men leaks at the joints are common, caused by poor mortar connection or by the mortar falling from the joints when the pipe is being laid. Care should be taken to see that the joints are butted against each other, and that the mortar is squeezed firmly into place. Mortar will often fall out of the joints at the top of the pipe, and the fault may be difficult to detect, particularly in the smaller sizes. When pipe is banded and under pressure it is common for water to seep out between the band and the outside shell of the pipe. Water will sometimes seep quite a distance in this manner. This may be caused by a poor union between the abutting ends, or it may be due to dry, porous pipe. Bands or joints will crack if the pipe is not properly covered with earth, and for this safeguard moist earth is preferable.

Concrete pipe should not be injured by the roots of orchard trees unless cracks appear. Large roots of shade trees may heave the pipe and cause failure, or small, fibrous roots may enter the pipe and completely clog it. Tree roots sometimes enter the pipe at the connection of orchard risers, the risers being often loosened from the pipe by being hit with plow or cultivator.

Pipe lines sometimes fill with sand or trash, where the inlet is not properly screened or settling basins provided. If velocities are high enough the pipe will be flushed out without resorting to any special means. Otherwise blowoff valves should be installed.

Adobe soil will heave and crack and rupture pipe lines very much in the same manner as it affects lined ditches. Most pipe layers are skeptical of the success of concrete pipe laid in adobe soil, and some will not guarantee work under such conditions. In some cases the trouble has been overcome by covering the bottom of the trench with 2 to 3 inches of sand. A good practice seems to be to dig the trench deeper than in sandy loam or sandy soil, and to take extra precautions in forming the joints. A minimum covering of 2 feet over the top of the pipe is sometimes specified in adobe soil.

Some soil will settle when first irrigated and this settlement will often allow the pipe line to settle also and cause cracks. If this type of soil is encountered, the bottom of the trench should be thoroughly soaked and settled before laying the pipe.

Probably the greatest trouble with breaks and leaks in concrete pipe lines is caused by expansion and contraction. It is common knowledge that concrete expands with a rise in temperature, but it is not so generally known that it also expands when saturated and contracts when becoming dry. It may surprise some to learn that a thoroughly air-dried pipe may contract as much in the process as it would under a fall of temperature of 100° F. In such cases cracks 0.18 of an inch every 25 feet or so are liable to appear. These cracks may close up when the pipe is refilled with water, or trash such as small particles of rock, sand or tree roots may enter and prevent closure.

The contraction due to pipe drying out often takes place after the pipe line has been in use for one or more seasons. For this reason it is common for a farmer to have to repair his pipe at the beginning of every irrigation season. The change of temperature in a pipe that is buried deep, especially when under the shade of large fruit trees, is very small. Usually, however, the pipe becomes thoroughly dried during the season of non-use and this drying out process is hastened when orchard distributing stands are left open.

In this connection it may be stated that a great deal of trouble is experienced where pipe is installed in desert regions. In such places the range of temperature and the drying-out process on the part of the pipe are at a maximum. A sudden contraction of 7 inches when a section of pipe was cut out is recorded. Expansion of pipe due to wetting will often crush diversion boxes or relief stands, and in extreme cases the pipe itself has crushed or telescoped. Pipe is also cracked at curves from the same cause. One manufacturer in the San Fernando Valley, Calif., has recorded a case where a 12-inch pipe laid in a straight line for a distance of 4,000 feet, expanded 18 inches through a diversion box. There are numerous cases where such stands have been crushed due to expansion of the connecting pipe line.

If the pipe can be anchored, either by concrete anchors at intervals or by reinforcing the bottoms of relief or diversion stands, failure by expansion may be guarded against; since concrete in compression should have sufficient strength to prevent the crushing of the pipe. On the other hand concrete is relatively weak in tension and the pipe is certain to crack when sufficient contraction occurs. The spacing of contraction cracks will depend upon the strength of the pipe and joints, and the force tending to hold the pipe in place. The weight of the pipe and earth pressure over it are usually the forces tending to prevent the pipe moving, therefore contraction cracks will occur when the strength of the pipe in tension is not sufficient to pull a certain length of pipe. There are a number of formulae for estimating the distance apart that contraction cracks will appear, but no records have been found where experiments were carried on in the field. It is probably safe to expect pipe of small diameters to crack about every 25 to 40 feet when laid under unfavorable conditions and subjected to sufficient contractive power. Contraction cracks usually appear at the joints, although at times the pipe is broken.

There are two methods of reducing to a minimum the trouble with expansion or contraction. The first is to lay the pipe under favorable conditions, the second is to provide expansion joints at frequent intervals.

Favorable conditions for laying concrete pipe depend upon temperature, moisture in the pipe when laid, and moisture in the ground. Pipe laid in winter, when the ground is moist from rains, seldom gives trouble, especially if the pipe is kept continually full of water after being laid. Pipe laid in sandy soil, when the ground is hot and dry, is almost certain to develop contraction cracks unless water is turned in promptly. If it is necessary to lay pipe in hot, sandy soil, the trench should be deep and the backfill kept moist until water can be turned in. As bands and joints set very rapidly, pipe can often be filled with water 24 hours after laying. Heavier soil containing moisture will protect pipe from drying out. If the pipe is dry when laid, and the soil is dry and warm, there will probably be little change in the length of the pipe until it is filled with water, but when the pipe is thoroughly soaked there is liable to be considerable expansion. This accounts for expansion troubles that are so common under desert conditions. If the movement of pipe due to expansion is prevented, no trouble may be experienced thereafter, as the elasticity of the concrete may prevent contraction when the pipe is dried out again after the first irrigation. Some engineers have advocated that the pipe be wetted before laying in desert soil, but this would not seem to be good practice because if the soil is dry the pipe would soon become dry too, causing contraction cracks, before the water was turned in. It would seem a good plan to have the pipe as cool as practicable before laying under the above conditions, as the pipe that is placed along the trench in the hot sun before being laid cools off when covered with the backfill, and this will cause contraction. It should be possible in many cases to lay pipe so that expansion due to wetting the pipe when first laid in the trench will counteract the contraction due to cooling off when covered with soil. The safest procedure to be followed in laying pipe in the desert in the summer is to do the work at night, when the temperature is low, but it is desirable that all irrigation systems in such localities be installed in the fall or winter. In any case it is best to allow the pipe to assume its permanent length in the trench before the mortar in the joints has thoroughly hardened, and to fill the pipe soon and keep it full of water continually thereafter.

There is one 8-inch stock, unreinforced concrete pipe laid in the desert soil of Antelope Valley, Calif., that is under a continual pressure of about 80-foot head. No leaks have been observed in this pipe since the water was turned in over two years ago. This pipe is always full, the water which it conveys being used for domestic purposes as well as irrigation. Other pipes in the same locality are continually giving trouble, and in most cases such trouble can be traced to the alternate wetting and drying out of the pipe.

There is little doubt that the best engineering practice to be followed in laying concrete pipe is to provide expansion joints at frequent intervals. Effective expansion joints will allow the pipe to be in longitudinal equilibrium at all times, and thus protect the pipe from stresses which may cause failure. Practically all engineers have provided expansion joints in buildings, retaining walls, concrete bridges, and other important structures, yet such joints in concrete pipe lines are comparatively unknown. Of course, temperature changes are less in buried concrete pipe than in many structures, but as has been stated, expansion due to a saturated or even moist condition may be considerable.

It is not difficult to provide expansion joints for pipe that does not carry water under pressure. One contractor has telescoped an 8-inch pipe in a 12-inch, calking part of the space between the pipe with burlap and then filling with tar or asphalt, finishing off the joint by calking with burlap. This joint will answer for low heads. Tar or roofing paper has also been used for pipes under very low heads or running less than full. The tar paper is wired to the outside of the adjoining pipes over the joint, the pipe is not butted close together, and the space filled with an asphalt mixture. A strip of galvanized sheet metal is placed under the joint inside the pipe to hold the asphalt in place. Clay pipe or concrete pipe made with a bell end is sometimes laid by pouring hot asphalt into every joint. There should be no expansion troubles with this installation if the pressure is not sufficient to force the asphalt mixture from the joints. Expansion joints have been made by painting heavy oil over one end of the abutting joints and then cementing a band of mortar over the joint, but it is doubtful if this joint will slip except under the most favorable conditions. Expansion joints have also been formed by placing an oiled thimble of galvanized sheet iron in the center of the shell of a joint of pipe after one-half of the pipe has been made and while the concrete is still in the molds, pouring asphalt over the ends of the joint after the thimble has been forced halfway down into the lower half of the pipe, as shown in figure 4. The remainder of the joint is then finished. · The concrete is expected to slide over this metal strip. Joints made in this manner· in the laboratory leaked badly when under pressure where a prepared asphalt compound was used to coat the metal strip. If oil be used, it is probable that the bond would be too strong to allow slipping.

A simple expansion joint (fig. 5) has been tried out that seems to work well under all conditions. A strip or thimble of copper or lead is welded to make a continuous ring, which is about 4 inches wide and the same diameter as the center of the shell of the pipe. This strip is then crimped and cemented into a short section of pipe. When the pipe expands or contracts the crimp in the metal gives. Such joints have been found to be water-tight under 125 feet head.

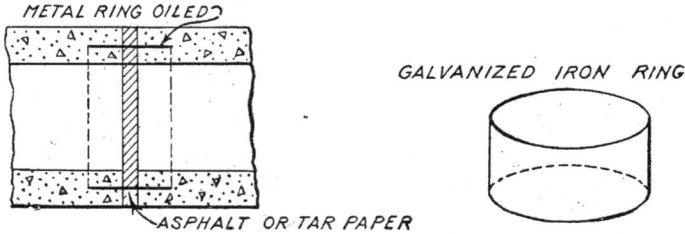

METAL RING OILED

GALVANIZED IRON RING

ASPHALT OR TAR PAPER

Fig. 4.—Expansion joints for very low pressure.

Expansion joints are made and sold by steel pipe manufacturers that are adapted to the use of steel pipe. Such joints are expensive and are not advisable except under unusual conditions. · Bolted joints fitted with rubber gaskets that are commonly used with riveted steel pipe can be used, and will be found to be much cheaper than the commercial expansion joints. Cast-iron collars that fit over the joint and are packed with oakum and asphalt, represent another type. One engineer has suggested using a short length of light weight corrugated iron pipe to be cemented at intervals in the concrete pipe line. Any expansion joint made with steel or iron is subject to corrosion, however.

Alkali will sometimes disintegrate concrete drain tile and may attack a porous, dry mixed pipe when used for irrigation. Drain tile is subjected to the most unfavorable conditions. The tile is laid where the alkali salts are continually being drained into it. The joints are not cemented and the tile is often only partly full of water. Drain tile is often made inferior to irrigation pipe, the small sizes being made of sand and cement only, with a deficiency of cement. It may not be tamped properly and is nearly always made from a very dry mixture.

Irrigation pipe if kept full of water free from alkali salts, tends to exclude ground water containing alkali, from the shell of the pipe. If the pipe is under pressure, there seems to be little chance of alkali salts entering the pores of the pipe from the outside. Then too, irrigation pipe is usually laid on the higher parts of the land that are freest from alkali. Culverts of poor grade of concrete pipe used for road crossings have been observed to be almost eaten away when exposed to water strongly saturated with alkali. On the contrary, irrigation pipe of a good grade of concrete buried in compact soils impregnated with alkali adjacent to these culverts has been found to be entirely sound.

Briefly stated, the sulphates and magnesia salts seem to be the most harmful, but dense concrete made from wet mixtures is usually very little affected. It has been suggested that drain tile laid in alkali soils be made at least of a one to three mixture of cement to aggregates. It is probable that a much leaner mixture can be used for low-pressure pipe, if care is taken to grade the sand and rock in the aggregate. Rock dust, clay, or even silt may be added to the mixture to make an impervious pipe. In any case the pipe should be made from a wet mixture and thoroughly tamped or compressed.

Another source of failure in concrete pipe is the rupture of the pipe due to sudden increases of pressure, which may be caused by water hammer. Water hammer is especially troublesome where water is pumped directly into a pipe line and where the pipe is of considerable length and runs up grade from the pump. If the pump is started and stopped gradually, the extra pressure due to water hammer will be slight, but if the pump is suddenly stopped, pressures will sometimes increase two or even three times above normal. The same thing may be caused if a valve in the discharge main from the pump is suddenly closed. Increased pressures may be recorded in any pipe that is running at full capacity under pressure, if a valve is suddenly closed.

The usual method of preventing breaks from water hammer is to provide a standpipe. The standpipe or relief stand should be high enough to allow for grade and friction in the pipe when running at full capacity and should be about the same diameter as the main, although large mains are often protected by standpipes of considerably less diameter than the main. If pressures are increased suddenly, water will rise in the standpipe and overflow, thus relieving the pressure in the line. For stands 25 feet in height and under, concrete pipe can be used. It is good practice to reinforce the first two or three joints if high stands are used, or pipe of larger diameter can be used for the first two or three joints. One standpipe near

Saugus, Calif., is 80 feet high and was built to protect a 16-inch reinforced concrete pipe that runs gradually up grade for over 2,000 feet. The standpipe is made of 12-inch riveted steel pipe, supported by a steel windmill tower.

Open boxes of concrete are built to about 15 feet in height and act as relief stands and at the same time are used as diversion boxes or for measuring water over weirs.

Where pressures are too great to permit the installation of a standpipe, it is common to use air drums to relieve back pressure. Air drums are chambers that are partly full of air, the elasticity of the air preventing excessive pressures on the pipe. Air chambers have been used successfully in some installations, but there are so many cases of the air chamber being waterlogged at a critical time that a

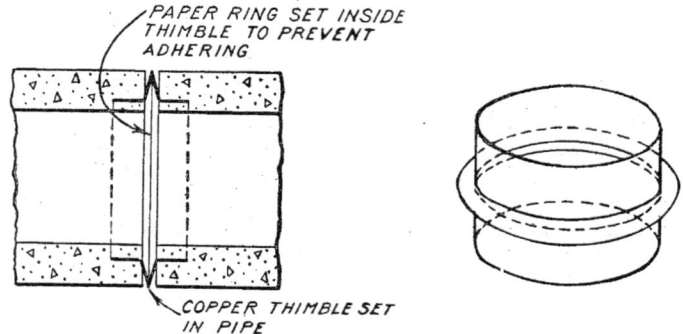

Fig. 5.—Expansion joints for high pressure.

number have been replaced by relief stands. Some air drums are equipped with an automatic air pump that keeps the chamber filled with the proper proportion of air, but as any such apparatus is liable to get out of order, the air drum may be worthless when needed the most. There are some instances on record where air pumps have delivered an excess of air which has caused large bubbles of air to collect in the main.

Relief valves have also been used. These are so adjusted that an excess of pressure will open them and let out enough water to bring down the pressure in the pipe. Relief valves are not in great favor, however, as they may stick under high pressures or blow off under small variations of pressure which occur when a pump is directly connected to a main.

Check valves have been installed at intervals along a main leading from a pump but have met with little success. Unless provision is made to allow some water to escape at the pump when it is suddenly stopped, it is not to be expected that enough water will run back to close a check valve. Water is incompressible and pressure alone may be transmitted back to the pump without any appreciable back movement of the water.

The Whittier Water Co. has equipped electric motors with heavy flywheels directly connected to centrifugal pumps, in order to reduce the water hammer. Gasoline engines have also been equipped with extra heavy flywheels, the engine being connected by gears to the pump. The function of a flywheel on an electric motor is to prevent a sudden stopping or starting of the pump, as the momentum of the flywheels will keep the pump going for about one minute after the power is turned off. Heavy flywheels on gasoline engines serve the same purpose. If a belt is used to connect engine or motor with pump, however, the flywheel would be of no use in case the power is suddenly shut off, as the belt would then slip off or break.

The engineer in charge of this work has reported excellent results from the use of flywheels, and has installed them in many of the pumping plants of the company. He has torn down standpipes as being less effective, and is of the opinion that blow-off valves and check valves are either worthless or else a never-ending source of annoyance.

When concrete pipe is directly connected to a centrifugal pump, the best practice is to eliminate any check valve and substitute a slow-closing gate valve on the discharge pipe of the pump. When the pump is started the valve can be opened slowly and thus prevent a dangerous increase of pressure on the pipe. The valve can be closed slowly when the pump is stopped and thus prevent water hammer. In case of an accidental stoppage of the power water will run down the well until the valve is closed.

DESIGN OF PIPE SYSTEMS FOR IRRIGATION.

The design of an irrigation system for a new tract where pipe is to be used differs in many respects from that where all water is carried in open ditches. The chief difference in design is due to the fact that well-made concrete pipe may be depended upon to carry water under pressure. Thus it is possible to eliminate devious routes of main ditches that must be located on grade. It is best, however, to make accurate contour surveys of large tracts that are to be irrigated by pipe. Contour maps should also be made of all possible routes of main lines and each subdivision should have contour intervals plotted close enough to enable the engineer to design economically the sizes of laterals and their location and to indicate how the individual units should be graded for effective irrigation.

Five-foot contour intervals may be close enough for estimating the location of the main pipe in hilly country, but it may be necessary to plot 1-foot or even 6-inch contour intervals on flat valley land. Furthermore the entire system should be designed before any construction work is begun.

Tracts for new colonies under the control of the Land Settlement Board of the State of California have been carefully surveyed throughout. The location of pipe lines has been determined and the sizes and location of each subdivision carefully considered. Contour intervals have been plotted accurately enough to allow all surface grading to be laid out before the farm is ready for water. The size of each subdivision is determined by the character of the soil and the methods adopted for irrigation and drainage. The location of the laterals is also determined by the prevailing grades of each unit to be watered and the kind of crops to be grown. Land for alfalfa usually has comparatively flat slopes, while orchard land may be very uneven providing pressure pipe is used.

Hilly land that has recently been subdivided for citrus orchards is frequently irrigated with little or no grading, even though the separate tracts may be very uneven. In this case pipe lines are constructed along ridges, feeding all the high knolls. Tree rows may be laid out in squares, or may be set out with respect to contours only. If contour or terrace planting is necessary it is usually possible to irrigate in two directions from one field lateral.

The sizes of pipe needed for a given tract will depend upon the acreage to be served, the grades of the pipe lines, the smoothness of the interior surface of the pipe, the water requirements of crops, the character of the soil, and the slope of the land. If the source of water is a reservoir at a considerable elevation above the lands to be irrigated, it may be possible to install pressure pipe that will carry water at a high velocity. If pressures exceed 50 feet in head it is common to install steel, reinforced concrete, or wood pipe. It is often practicable, however, to control the pressure of the main by suitable relief stands so that concrete pipe of larger diameter can be used. The latter practice is usual in recent installations. The smoothness of the interior of the pipe will also affect its carrying capacity.

The following table is compiled from data collected in the field by Fred C. Scobey, senior irrigation engineer of the Bureau of Public Roads.[3] The table is not complete but has been arranged to give approximate carrying capacities of concrete pipe under ordinary working conditions and for average pipe. Especially smooth pipe will have larger capacities and very rough pipe much lower. For average conditions small sizes should not be figured too closely. Probably pipe up to 12 inches diameter should be computed to

---

[3] "The Flow of Water in Concrete Pipe." Bulletin 852, U. S. Dept. of Agr.

carry about 20 per cent more water than shown by table, especially where there is danger of any clogging by débris, or pipe is very rough.

Table gives the carrying capacities of concrete pipe in miner's inches computed to the nearest 5 miner's inches.[1]

[Fall in feet per 100 feet.]

Diameter of pipe.	0.1	0.2	0.3	0.4	0.5	1.0	2.5	5.0
	Miner's inches.	*Miner's inches.*	*Miner's inches.*	*Miner's inches.*	*Miner's inches.*	*Miner's inches.*	*Miner's inches.*	*Miner's inches.*
6 inches	10	10	15	20	20	30	45	60
8 inches	20	25	35	40	45	60	85	140
10 inches	35	50	60	70	80	110	180	250
12 inches	60	80	110	115	120	180	275	....
14 inches	85	120	150	170	200	275	400	....
16 inches	120	170	210	235	275	400	600	....
18 inches	160	230	285	330	450	550	825	....
20 inches	225	310	380	435	500	700	1,100	....
22 inches	275	400	485	525	625	900	1,400	....
24 inches	350	500	620	710	800	1,150	....	....
30 inches	650	900	1,100	1,275	1,425	....	....	....

[1] One miner's inch is here equivalent to the one-fiftieth part of a second-foot and is nearly equal to 9 gallons per minute.

Engineers and pipe contractors will have no trouble in interpreting the above table, but for the convenience of irrigators without engineering experience, a few examples will be given to enable them to estimate sizes of pipe for various conditions.

The retarding influence to flow of water known as friction is common to all pipes, the intensity of the friction increasing with the velocity of the water and the roughness of the pipe. If the pipe is laid down grade the fall may be sufficient to overcome friction. When the water is pumped if the fall is not enough to carry the desired quantity then the water will rise in the standpipe at the entrance until there is sufficient head to force the water through. Of course if the stand is not high enough water will spill over the top. If the pipe runs up hill, when water is pumped, the delivery box or relief stand at the pump end must be high enough to overcome the difference in elevation between the entrance and outlet of the pipe, plus the head required to overcome friction in the pipe. In practice such standpipes should not be high enough to develop unsafe pressures on the pipe.

Example 1.

Assume that an irrigator has acquired the right to the use of 200 miner's inches of water and wishes to install a pipe to carry this amount to his farm, a distance of 2,000 feet. If levels show there is a total fall of 6 feet between entrance and outlet, he will have a fall of 0.3 foot per 100 feet. From the table under vertical column of 0.3 (fall per 100 feet) it is seen that a 16-inch pipe will carry 210 miner's inches. If he can fill the standpipe at entrance 4 feet deep, he will have 4 feet additional head on the pipe, or a total head of 10 feet (including fall). This gives him 0.5 foot fall per 100 feet. The table

3445°—21——4

shows that a 14-inch pipe will carry 200 inches under these conditions. (In taking levels the actual difference in elevation between the point of entrance and the point where water is discharged must be taken. If water is discharged over distributing stand, the elevation of top of the stand must be taken.)

Example 2.

Assume an orchard lateral is run down a steep grade of 5 feet per 100 feet, which is not uncommon in hillside tracts. It will be seen from the table that a 6-inch pipe will carry 60 miner's inches of water, but if a lateral is taken off this line that falls only 0.1 foot per 100 feet, the table shows that a 12-inch pipe will be needed to carry the same amount of water. If the lateral runs across a 10-acre tract or 660 feet and the delivery stand carries a head of 6 feet, we will have a total head available of 1 foot per 100 feet, requiring only an 8-inch pipe.

If grades vary, where open stands are frequent, allowing little or no pressure in the pipe, the diameters of the pipe should vary with the grade, especially where the variation is considerable. On the other hand, if the pipe is under pressure from one end to the other and there are no relief stands, the pipe should be the same diameter throughout its entire length.

Too many pipe contractors guess at the sizes of pipe to use and pay little or no attention to grades. Usually however, they are on the safe side where water runs down hill although the pipe may be several sizes larger than necessary. On the other hand, it is common for inexperienced men to install undersized pressure pipe that is used for pumping, which means that the pump must be burdened with additional lift in order to overcome the excessive frictional resistance in the small pipe. If concrete pipe is directly connected to a pump, the pipe may burst from excessive pressures, although the actual elevation between the pump and outlet may be small, the total head due to excessive friction causing failure. For example, it can be seen from the table that if 250 miner's inches are pumped into a 10-inch pipe that is laid on the level, friction will cause a head of 5 feet for every 100 feet length, or a total head at the pump of 50 feet, if the pipe is 1,000 feet long.

It is wise to keep concrete pipe under as low heads as possible and where pressure is to be applied care should be taken to get the best quality of pipe. It is often possible to control pressures on pipes especially where there is a constant down grade. If the pipe is not fitted with outlets open at the top, or other means of relieving pressure such as overflow stands, open diversion boxes and so on, the pressure on the lower end of the pipe will increase as the pipe fills, and the lower sections may fail from excessive pressure. It is a mistake to depend on valves that may be closed entirely to relieve pressures, as such valves may all be closed at one time. Safety devices will be discussed under another heading.

SETTLING BASINS AND SCREENS.

Settling basins (fig. 6) should be installed in a pipe line where vegetable or earthy material may clog the pipe. Settling basins are often necessary where water is carried from a hilly territory in an open ditch, as such conditions are favorable for picking up débris, and where the ditch terminates at the beginning of a pipe line. It is usual in this case to install the basin at the junction of the ditch and pipe line as shown in figure 7. The dimensions of the settling basin depend upon the quantity of solid material transported in the ditch or pipe line. It must be large enough in area to check the velocity of the water sufficiently to allow the solid particles to settle, and deep enough to collect sand and other trash for a considerable period, otherwise it will require cleaning at too frequent intervals. Ordinary sand is transported in a pipe or ditch at a velocity of about one-half to two-thirds foot per second and fine gravel at an average velocity of about 1 foot per second. If the grades are such that velocities suddenly become too low to carry solid particles, settling basins should be installed or the pipe is liable to become clogged. Small settling basins, such as are installed at the intake of a field lateral with a main pipe or ditch, are usually cleaned out by hand. Large basins in main ditches should be located so that the sand can be flushed out. If a ditch runs parallel to a river bed or natural drain it is usual to install basins so that the waste will flush into the river or drain. Basins are also provided at points where the pipe crosses a ravine or other waterway. In this case solid materials can be flushed out readily. In case of flat grades, however, it is necessary to clean out the collected material by hand.

Screens are often installed with settling basins for small lateral ditches that carry a large quantity of floating trash, in order to prevent orchard valves from becoming clogged. Some are placed in the basin at an angle of about 30 degrees to the vertical. In other cases multiple screens (fig. 6) are inserted in grooves. The one nearest the intake pipe may be of chicken wire having about $1\frac{1}{2}$ inch clear openings and each successive screen having a finer mesh of wire down to one-half or one-eighth of an inch. The first screen collects the larger trash such as leaves and small floating sticks, while the other screens catch the finer particles. The screens are made on frames that slide in grooves in the sides of the concrete box and can be readily removed and cleaned.

If trash is carried in large quantities it is often necessary to devise some method of greatly increasing the screened area. This may be done by building a screen completely around the outlet pipe. Some screens are built in the form of a long narrow trough which is screened on all sides, the outlet being beneath the screen. Such a screen can be set in an open ditch that is widened out a little at the pipe inlet.

Screens have also been designed that are self cleaning, reliance being placed on the velocity of the water to keep the screens open.

Care should always be taken to prevent trash entering a ditch or pipe line where water is finally distributed through orchard hydrants having small openings. It is especially necessary to take proper

Fig. 6.—Settling basin and screens.

precautions at the intake where the water is diverted from a flowing stream. For comparatively small heads of water it is sometimes possible to bury the first 20 or 30 feet of pipe under the stream bed laying the pipe with open joints and covering it with gravel. This will prevent all floating material entering the pipe and should keep out the sand. Some comparatively large mains have been protected at the intake in this manner.

Open ditches bordered by shade trees are continually gathering leaves which are particularly harmful in clogging screens, as the leaves will flatten out against a fine mesh screen and may completely obstruct the flow of water.

Where pipes are fed by open ditches and have sufficient grade so that the velocity of water will transport sand or small gravel, the entrance to the pipe is commonly protected by iron bars set on an angle in front of the pipe entrance. The bars may be spaced 6 inches or more apart. Such protection will prevent boards and large tree branches entering the pipe.

AIR VENTS.

When air is drawn into a pipe carrying water, being lighter than the water, it tends to collect at the highest points of the line. Such accumulations of air lessen the water-carrying capacity of the pipe and may obstruct it altogether. To guard against occurrences of this kind means should be provided to allow the entrapped air to escape into the atmosphere. One of the safest and best means of

Fig. 7.—Showing long screen at junction of open ditch and pipe line. Weir box and automatic register at left of picture.

doing this is by the insertion of standpipes at all points where air is liable to collect. These standpipes need not be large for the average sizes of pipe. They are not only automatic but continuous in their action. For lateral pipes a galvanized-iron pipe 1 inch in diameter and covered with a perforated cap and protected by a substantial post makes a cheap and serviceable air vent. It is also good practice to get rid of the air as soon as it enters the pipe by inserting standpipes near each intake, care being taken in all cases to extend the air pipe far enough above the pipe so that its top will be well above the hydraulic grade line, or in other words, above the head to which water will rise.

Where standpipes can not be used the confined air may be released by the use of automatic air valves which can be inserted on pipes under medium and high pressures. One of the simplest of these is a spherical rubber ball which is pressed tightly against the circular opening when the pipe is full of water, but which falls down when the water is lowered by the collection of air. Another kind operates by means of a float and lever, the lowering of the float causing the air valve to open and discharge the entrapped air.

RELIEF STANDS.

Where steel or wood pipe is used to carry irrigation water, it is not customary to make provisions for relief of pressure except in long lines that are laid on heavy grades. Concrete pipe, however, unless reinforced is only intended for low heads and provision must be taken to prevent high pressures.

FIG. 8.—Overflow and relief stand.

Where a pipe is laid down a long grade, and is large enough to carry all the water running less than full, there will be little or no head on the pipe when outlets are provided at frequent intervals with their tops always open, but as it is usual to provide shut-off gates to divert water, pressures may increase to such an extent as to break the pipe when all gates are closed unless proper precautions are taken to guard against such conditions arising.

The ordinary open diversion box is fitted with gates that divert water by closing the gate on the outlet pipe only, the gate being kept tight by water pressure against it. In this case the water can not back up in the pipe and form a dangerous head, since the water in the box will overflow, but where the pipe will withstand 20 to 30 feet head, and it is desirous to force water along a lateral that runs up hill 15 feet or more, it is not feasible to construct the ordinary diversion box, as such a box would have to be too high to be conveniently accessible. In this case, pressure gates may be provided that close the inlet pipe providing there is an open stand above the gate that will relieve the pressure. Another plan is to provide an overflow stand that will maintain a constant head at the point of diversion, the excess water spilling over into the main. Two vertical open stands made of concrete pipe cemented together may be used for this purpose. The water will rise in the pipe connected to the inlet, and flow over a crest or notch into the other pipe, and thence into the main (figs. 8 and 9). The lateral pipe leading from this stand requires no gate, as the pressure will remain constant, allowing no excessive pressures to accumulate in the lateral. If a lateral slopes down grade from an overflow stand it is usual to provide a shut-off gate where the lateral branches off from the stand. The gate may be set in a low auxiliary stand that is cemented to the side of the main relief stand. Some relief stands consist of one large standpipe of sufficient diameter to allow an overflow pipe being placed inside of it (fig. 10). Some orchard laterals have a 12-inch stand 6 to 18 feet high fitted with a 6-inch spillway pipe inside, the 6-inch pipe extending to a foot or so of the top of the 12-inch pipe. In this case water is diverted to the side lateral from the 12-inch pipe, the excess of water spilling down the 6-inch pipe into the main. There are a number of

FIG. 9.—Overflow pipe in rear and small diversion box in front.

modifications of this principle that will be taken up in detail under the subject of diversion boxes and pipe structures.

Nearly all measuring devices act as relief stands, especially weirs, miner's-inch boxes, and ordinary recording irrigation meters, as such devices are installed to allow the free flow of water over a crest in an open box.

MEASURING DEVICES FOR PIPE IRRIGATION SYSTEMS.

A number of devices are in use to measure the flow of water through pipes and laterals and from pumping plants and reservoirs. Of these the following are briefly discussed—Venturi meters, weirs, miner's-inch boxes, automatic registers, and other mechanical recording devices.

Venturi meters.

These make use of the Venturi principle by forcing water through a small throat in a pipe, thereby converting most of the static into velocity head. By keeping a continuous record of the normal static pressure and also the pressure at the throat the flow of water at any

time can be computed for a meter of a given size. Meters of this type are installed on main pipe lines when it is desired to keep a continuous record of the total q u a n t i t y of water delivered to any system. They might also be installed a d v a n t a - geously on lateral pipe lines were it not for their first cost, since they have no moving parts liable to be obstructed or c l o g g e d by sand, leaves, or other material carried by the water.

Weirs.

Fig. 10.—Twelve-inch overflow stand with 6-inch pipe inside.

The weir is the most commonly used device for measuring water in open ditches and canals. It is more difficult to adapt it to pipe systems, and when this has been attempted due consideration has seldom been given to the effects produced on the accuracy of the measurement by seemingly trivial changes from the standard specifications. One of the essential requirements of the weir is that the water shall approach the weir notch at a slow velocity and unaffected by eddies or cross-currents. These conditions are seldom fulfilled when water issues from a pipe directly above the weir.

Several years ago, a large number of experiments were conducted by V. M. Cone of this bureau at the hydraulic laboratory at Fort Collins, Colo., on the flow of water through weir notches.[4]

In figure 11 is outlined the inside dimensions of a standard weir box to measure water within 1 per cent of accuracy in accordance with the different volumes specified in Table 1. In Table 2 is given in cubic feet per second the discharge through rectangular weirs from 1 to 4 feet in length and for varying heads.

Table 3 gives the percentage of error which occurs when changes from the standard form are introduced. Thus the effect of side contractions (C in figure 11) is seen in the increase in error of a 1-foot weir and a 6-inch head from less than 1 per cent to 4 per cent when the distance of the sides from the end of the crest is reduced from 2 feet to 6 inches as shown in figure 12.

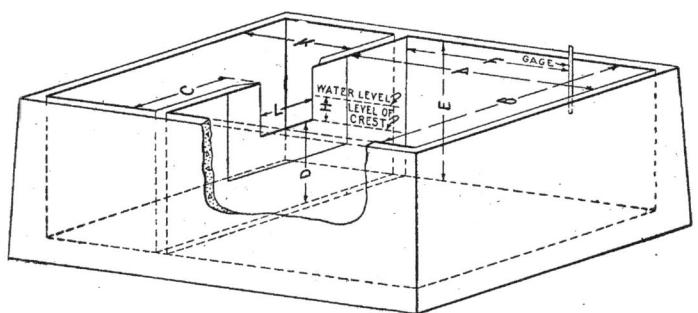

FIG. 11.—Standard 18-inch weir based on dimensions given in table.

TABLE 1.—*Weir-box dimensions for rectangular notch weirs.*

[All dimensions in feet. The letters at the heads of the columns in this table refer to figure 11.]

RECTANGULAR WEIRS.

Flow (second-feet).	H. Maximum head.	L. Length of weir crest.	A. Length of box above weir notch.	K. Length of box below weir notch.	B. Total width of box.	E.[a] Total depth of box.	C. End of crest to side.	D. Crest to bottom.	F.[b] Hook-gauge distance.	G.[c] Hook-gauge distance.
½ to 3	1.0	1	6	2	5½	3½	2¼	2	4	2
2 to 5	1.1	1½	7	3	7	4	2¼	2¼	4½	2
4 to 8	1.2	2	8	4	8½	4½	3¼	2¾	5	2½
6 to 14	1.3	3	9	5	12	5	4½	3¼	5½	3
10 to 22	1.5	4	10	6	14	5½	5	3½	6	3

[4] For further information the reader is referred to Farmers' Bulletin 813 on the Construction and Use of Farm Weirs, by V. M. Cone.
a This distance allows for about ¼ foot freeboard above highest water level in weir box.
b Equals distance from crest upstream to gauge.
c Equals distance from end of crest over to gauge.

TABLE 2.—*Discharge tables for rectangular weirs.*

Computed from the formula $Q = 3.247\, l H^{1.48} - \dfrac{0.566\, l^{1.8}}{1 + 2 l^{1.6}} H^{1.9}$

Head in feet	Head in inches	Discharge in cubic feet per second for crests of various lengths.					Head in feet	Head in inches	Discharge in cubic feet per second for crests of various lengths.				
		1 foot.	1.5feet.	2 feet.	3 feet.	4 feet.			1 foot.	1.5feet.	2 feet.	3 feet.	4 feet.
0.20	2⅜	0.291	0.439	0.588	0.887	1.19	.86	10₁₆	2.46	3.72	5.01	7.59	10.19
.21	2½	.312	.472	.632	.954	1.28	.87	10₁₆	2.50	3.79	5.10	7.72	10.36
.22	2⅝	.335	.505	.677	1.02	1.37	.88	10½	2.54	3.85	5.18	7.85	10.54
.23	2¾	.358	.539	.723	1.09	1.46	.89	10⅝	2.58	3.92	5.27	7.99	10.71
.24	2⅞	.380	.574	.769	1.16	1.55	.90	10¾	2.62	3.98	5.35	8.12	10.89
.25	3	.404	.609	.817	1 23	1.65	.91	10⅞	2.67	4.05	5.44	8.25	11.07
.26	3⅛	.428	.646	.865	1.31	1.75	.92	11₁₆	2.71	4.11	5.53	8.38	11.25
.27	3¼	.452	.682	.914	1.38	1.85	.93	11₁₆	2.75	4.18	5.62	8.52	11.43
.28	3⅜	.477	.720	.965	1.46	1.95	.94	11¼	2.79	4.24	5.71	8.65	11.61
.29	3½	.502	.758	1.02	1.53	2.05	.95	11⅜	2.84	4.31	5.80	8.79	11.79
.30	3⅝	.527	.796	1.07	1.61	2.16	.96	11½	2.88	4.37	5.89	8.93	11.98
.31	3¾	.553	.836	1.12	1.69	2.26	.97	11⅝	2.93	4.44	5.98	9.06	12.16
.32	3⅞	.580	.876	1.18	1.77	2.37	.98	11¾	2.97	4.51	6.07	9.20	12.34
.33	3¹⁵⁄₁₆	.606	.916	1.23	1.86	2.48	.99	11⅞	3.01	4.57	6.15	9.34	12.53
.34	4⅛	.634	.957	1.28	1.94	2.60	1.00	12	3.06	4.64	6.25	9.48	12.72
.35	4¼	.661	.999	1.34	2.02	2.71	1.01	12⅛	......	4.71	6.34	9.62	12.91
.36	4₁₆	.688	1.04	1.40	2.11	2.82	1.02	12¼	......	4.78	6.43	9.76	13.10
.37	4⅜	.717	1.08	1.45	2.20	2.94	1.03	12⅜	......	4.85	6.52	9.90	13.28
.38	4₁₆	.745	1.13	1.51	2.28	3.06	1.04	12½	......	4 92	6.62	10.04	13.47
.39	4½	.774	1.17	1.57	2.37	3.18	1.05	12⅝	......	4.98	6.71	10.18	13.66
.40	4⅝	.804	1.21	1.63	2.46	3.30	1.06	12¾	......	5.05	6.80	10.32	13.85
.41	4¾	.833	1.26	1.69	2.55	3.42	1.07	12⅞	......	5 12	6.90	10.46	14.04
.42	5₁₆	.863	1.30	1.75	2.65	3.54	1.08	12¹⁵⁄₁₆	......	5 20	6.99	10.61	14.24
.43	5₁₆	.893	1.35	1.81	2.74	3.67	1.09	13₁₆	......	5.26	7.09	10.75	14.43
.44	5¼	.924	1.40	1.88	2.83	3.80	1.10	13₁₆	......	5.34	7.19	10.90	14.64
.45	5⅜	.955	1.44	1.94	2.93	3.93	1.11	13₁₆	......	5.41	7.28	11.04	14.83
.46	5½	.986	1.49	2.00	3.03	4.05	1.12	13₁₆	......	5.48	7.38	11.19	15.03
.47	5⅝	1.02	1.54	2.07	3.12	4.18	1.13	13⅝	......	5 55	7.47	11.34	15.22
.48	5¾	1.05	1.59	2.13	3.22	4.32	1.14	13¾	......	5 62	7.57	11.48	15.42
.49	5⅞	1.08	1.64	2.20	3.32	4.45	1.15	13⅞	......	5 69	7.66	11.64	15.62
.50	6	1.11	1.68	2.26	3.42	4.58	1.16	13¹³⁄₁₆	......	5 77	7.76	11.79	15.82
.51	6⅛	1.15	1.73	2.33	3.52	4.72	1.17	14₁₆	......	5 84	7.86	11.94	16.02
.52	6¼	1.18	1.78	2.40	3.62	4.86	1.18	14₁₆	......	5 91	7.96	12.09	16.23
.53	6⅜	1.21	1.84	2.46	3.73	4.99	1.19	14¼	......	5 98	8.06	12.24	16.43
.54	6½	1.25	1.89	2.53	3.83	5.13	1.20	14⅜	......	6 06	8.16	12.39	16.63
.55	6⅝	1.28	1.94	2.60	3.94	5.27	1.21	14½	......	6 13	8.26	12.54	16.83
.56	6¾	1.31	1.99	2.67	4.04	5.42	1.22	14⅝	......	6 21	8.35	12.69	17.03
.57	6⅞	1 35	2.04	2.74	4.15	5.56	1.23	14¾	......	6 28	8.46	12.85	17.25
.58	6¹⁵⁄₁₆	1 38	2.09	2.81	4.26	5.70	1.24	14⅞	......	6 35	8.56	12 99	17.45
.59	7₁₆	1 42	2.15	2.88	4.36	5.85	1.25	15	......	6.43	8.66	13 14	17.65
.60	7₁₆	1.45	2.20	2.96	4.47	6.00	1.26	15⅛	......	......	......	13.30	17.87
.61	7₁₆	1.49	2.25	3.03	4.59	6.14	1.27	15¼	......	......	......	13.45	18.07
.62	7₁₆	1.52	2.31	3.10	4.69	6.29	1.28	15⅜	......	......	......	13.61	18.28
.63	7½	1 56	2.36	3.17	4.81	6.44	1.29	15½	......	......	......	13.77	18.50
.64	7⅝	1 60	2.42	3.25	4.92	6.59	1.30	15⅝	......	......	......	13.93	18.71
.65	7¾	1.63	2.47	3.32	5.03	6.75	1.31	15¾	......	......	......	14.09	18.92
.66	7⅞	1.67	2.53	3.40	5.15	6.90	1.32	15⅞	......	......	......	14.24	19.12
.67	8₁₆	1.71	2.59	3.47	5.26	7.05	1.33	15¹⁵⁄₁₆	......	......	......	14.40	19.34
.68	8₁₆	1.74	2.64	3.56	5.38	7.21	1.34	16₁₆	......	......	......	14.56	19.55
.69	8¼	1.78	2.70	3.63	5.49	7.36	1.35	16₁₆	......	......	......	14.72	19.77
.70	8⅜	1.82	2.76	3.71	5.61	7.52	1.36	16¼	......	......	......	14.88	19.98
.71	8½	1.86	2.81	3.78	5.73	7.68	1.37	16⅜	......	......	......	15 04	20.20
.72	8⅝	1.90	2.87	3.86	5.85	7.84	1.38	16½	......	......	......	15.20	20.42
.73	8¾	1.93	2.93	3.94	5.97	8.00	1.39	16⅝	......	......	......	15.36	20.64
.74	8⅞	1.97	2.99	4.02	6.09	8.17	1.40	16¾	......	......	......	15.53	20.86
.75	9	2.01	3.05	4.10	6.21	8.33	1.41	16⅞	......	......	......	15.69	21.08
.76	9⅛	2.05	3.11	4.18	6.33	8.49	1.42	17₁₆	......	......	......	15.85	21.29
.77	9¼	2.09	3.17	4.26	6.45	8.66	1.43	17₁₆	......	......	......	16.02	21.52
.78	9⅜	2.13	3.23	4.34	6.57	8.82	1.44	17¼	......	......	......	16.19	21.74
.79	9½	2.17	3.29	4.42	6.70	8.99	1.45	17⅜	......	......	......	16.34	21.96
.80	9⅝	2.21	3.35	4.51	6.83	9.16	1.46	17½	......	......	......	16.51	22.18
.81	9¾	2.25	3.41	4.59	6.95	9.33	1.47	17⅝	......	......	......	16.68	22.41
.82	9⅞	2.29	3.47	4.67	7.08	9.50	1.48	17¾	......	......	......	16.85	22.64
.83	9¹⁵⁄₁₆	2 33	3.54	4.75	7.21	9.67	1.49	17⅞	......	......	......	17.01	22.85
.84	10₁₆	2 37	3 60	4.84	7.33	9.84	1.50	18	......	......	......	17.17	23.08
.85	10₁₆	2.41	3 66	4.92	7.46	10.01							

TABLE 3.—Velocity of approach and percentage of error caused by different end and bottom contractions for rectangular weirs.

A. = Distance of sides from end of crest (Feet). B. = Distance of bottom below crest (Feet). Velocity of approach given in Ft. per sec.

B.	A.	L1 ft, Head 0.6 ft — Vel.	Per cent error	L1 ft, Head 1 ft — Vel.	Per cent error	L1.5 ft, Head 0.6 ft — Vel.	Per cent error	L1.5 ft, Head 1 ft — Vel.	Per cent error	L2 ft, Head 0.6 ft — Vel.	Per cent error	L2 ft, Head 1 ft — Vel.	Per cent error	L3 ft, Head 0.6 ft — Vel.	Per cent error	L3 ft, Head 1 ft — Vel.	Per cent error	L4 ft, Head 0.6 ft — Vel.	Per cent error	L4 ft, Head 1 ft — Vel.	Per cent error
3.0	2.5			0.132	0.77																
3.0	2.0			.157	.81			0.213	0.82			0.269	0.54			0.342	0.83			0.402	0.87
3.0	1.5			.196	.099			.260	1.08			.317	1.14			.399	1.22			.460	1.29
3.0	1.0			.260	1.40			.337	1.63			.398	1.81			.484	2.06			.543	2.22
3.0	.5			.40	2.94			.477	3.22			.540	3.44			.616	3.72			.861	3.88
2.5	2.5			.150	.74																
2.5	2.0			.178	.82			.242	.88			.302	.94			.391	1.04			.460	1.11
2.5	1.5			.224	1.05			.297	1.21			.362	1.34			.461	1.57			.528	1.69
2.5	1.0			.299	1.58			.385	1.89			.457	2.14			.553	2.50			.623	2.76
2.5	.5			.462	3.42			.549	3.73			.625	3.99			.704	4.25			.760	4.48
2.0	2.5	0.094	0.17	.175	.73																
2.0	2.0	.115	.36	.209	.84			.284	.97			.352	1.11			.458	1.30			.539	1.42
2.0	1.5	.148	.39	.261	1.13			.348	1.42			.424	1.67			.538	2.01			.620	2.28
2.0	1.0	.188	.66	.333	1.83			.450	2.28			.535	2.63			.648	3.14			.733	3.52
2.0	.5	.288	2.05	.538	4.01			.646	4.46			.728	4.80			.829	5.17			.895	5.47
1.5	2.5	.119	.17	.208	.74																
1.5	2.0	.141	.30	.252	.94			.341	1.18			.424	1.41	0.308	1.07	.539	1.71			.638	1.98
1.5	1.5	.175	.40	.314	1.31	.191	0.53	.418	1.74	0.239	0.74	.512	2.12	.363	1.44	.648	2.65	0.365	1.33	.750	3.07
1.5	1.0	.234	.76	.424	2.24	.234	.73	.544	2.87	.286	1.01	.646	3.40	.435	2.12	.790	4.14	.416	1.74	.889	4.68
1.5	.5	.355	2.26	.648	4.80	.304	1.24	.784	5.53	.361	1.62	.885	6.09	.552	3.41	1.013	6.77	.489	2.49	1.091	7.20
1.0	2.5	.154	.19	.260	.82																
1.0	2.0	.209	.36	.314	1.12			.427	1.57			.532	2.00			.694	2.69			.810	3.15
1.0	1.5	.229	.50	.385	1.59	.311	1.09	.528	2.37	.377	1.55	.645	2.99	.478	2.25	.820	3.91	.552	2.79	.952	3.60
1.0	1.0	.308	1.01	.525	2.83	.400	1.77	.688	3.86	.476	2.39	.825	4.73	.577	3.22	.999	5.87	.650	2.83	1.135	6.77
1.0	.5	.469	2.84	.822	6.00	.573	3.74	.994	7.29	.646	4.38	1.129	8.29	.735	5.15	1.298	9.55	.794	5.64	1.405	10.27
.5	2.5	.221	.25	.350	1.11																
.5	2.0	.265	.50	.417	1.45	.368	1.30	.575	2.40	.460	2.05	.720	3.27	.624	3.34	.943	4.62	.711	4.05	1.120	5.65
.5	1.5	.337	.94	.530	2.20	.453	1.94	.710	3.53	.555	2.84	.875	4.73	.705	4.17	1.119	6.50	.818	5.15	1.308	7.88
.5	1.0	.450	1.84	.716	3.83	.588	3.22	.930	5.65	.704	4.35	1.118	7.23	.862	5.92	1.380	9.40	.975	7.01	1.576	11.2
.5	.5	.695	4.63	1.120	8.25	.852	6.43	1.37	11.0	.970	7.79	1.58	13.3	1.112	9.40	1.83	16.01	1.208	10.50	2.01	18.0

TABLE 3.—*Velocity of approach and percentage of error caused by different end and bottom contractions for rectangular weirs*—Continued.

B. Distance of bottom below crest. (Feet.)	A. Distance of sides from end of crest. (Ft. ft.)	L1 ft, Head 0.6 ft — Veloc. of approach (Ft. per sec.)	L1 ft, Head 0.6 ft — Per cent error	L1 ft, Head 1 ft — Veloc. of approach	L1 ft, Head 1 ft — Per cent error	L1.5 ft, Head 0.6 ft — Veloc.	L1.5 ft, Head 0.6 ft — Per cent error	L1.5 ft, Head 1 ft — Veloc.	L1.5 ft, Head 1 ft — Per cent error	L2 ft, Head 0.6 ft — Veloc.	L2 ft, Head 0.6 ft — Per cent error	L2 ft, Head 1 ft — Veloc.	L2 ft, Head 1 ft — Per cent error	L3 ft, Head 0.6 ft — Veloc.	L3 ft, Head 0.6 ft — Per cent error	L3 ft, Head 1 ft — Veloc.	L3 ft, Head 1 ft — Per cent error	L4 ft, Head 0.5 ft — Veloc.	L4 ft, Head 0.5 ft — Per cent error	L4 ft, Head 1 ft — Veloc.	L4 ft, Head 1 ft — Per cent error
2.0	2.5			.250	1.19			.322	1.22			.386	1.24			.488	1.28			.561	1.30
2.0	2.0			.314	1.52			.397	1.70			.467	1.84			.575	2.08			.648	2.22
2.0	1.5			.422	2.40			.514	2.80			.590	3.15			.698	3.62			.769	3.92
2.0	.5			.655	6.16			.746	6.41			.813	6.61			.896	6.88			.951	7.01
1.5	2.5	0.168	0.94	.300	1.34	0.207	1.02	.388	1.49	0.251	1.21	.465	1.61	.321	1.45	.590	1.82	0.373	1.61	.680	1.98
1.5	2.0	.196	1.11	.378	1.78	.255	1.38	.477	2.10	.304	1.60	.562	2.40	.377	1.95	.693	2.85	.429	2.19	.785	3.17
1.5	1.5	.260	1.70	.508	2.89	.329	2.08	.622	2.53	.381	2.36	.714	4.06	.454	2.77	.844	4.79	.504	3.02	.937	5.31
1.5	.5	.400	3.32	.795	7.29	.469	3.83	.906	7.79	.518	4.20	.989	8.18	.580	4.66	1.094	8.64	.617	4.93	1.163	8.85
1.0	2.5	.205	.09	.374	1.60	.274	1.25	.489	2.06	.331	1.55	.586	2.44	.425	2.05	.758	3.13	.492	2.39	.864	3.55
1.0	2.0	.257	1.20	.471	2.20	.335	1.71	.601	2.92	.400	1.55	.710	3.55	.500	2.82	.888	4.53	.569	3.30	1.003	5.19
1.0	1.5	.344	1.84	.643	3.76	.434	2.60	.787	4.83	.501	3.17	.908	5.73	.607	4.06	1.083	7.07	.671	4.60	1.200	7.92
1.0	.5	.529	4.00	1.010	9.20	.622	4.92	1.159	10.28	.690	5.61	1.271	11.08	.770	6.41	1.410	12.09	.826	6.98	1.503	12.72
.5	2.5	.300	1.11	.508	2.30	.399	1.81	.660	3.64	.487	2.42	.799	4.87	.625	3.40	1.013	6.73	.725	4.09	1.202	8.39
.5	2.0	.377	1.51	.640	3.30	.492	2.55	.818	4.80	.589	3.44	.999	6.09	.737	4.79	1.210	8.08	.847	5.80	1.391	9.56
.5	1.0	.505	2.39	.864	5.40	.636	3.93	1.077	7.38	.750	5.30	1.258	9.43	.908	7.18	1.505	11.95	1.013	8.30	1.688	1.38
.5	.5	.782	6.03	1.390	11.89	.932	8.02	1.605	14.63	1.037	9.43	1.782	16.85	1.173	11.28	2.015	19.80	1.263	12.48		

When weirs are formed by the use of concrete pipe, the usual practice is to employ pipe too small in diameter in proportion to the length of the weir, thus departing at times very far from the standard weir, and introducing errors which may amount in certain cases to 5 per cent and more, a combination of this kind being shown in figures 13 and 14. If pipes are to be used for this purpose they should be of large diameter and of thin shells so as to permit the largest possible distance between the end of the weir notch and the inner surface of the pipe. According to standard dimensions and accurate measurement a weir 1 foot long would require a pipe 65 inches in diameter whereas if a 2-foot pipe is used for the same length of weir the discharge may be too large by 5 per cent.

In order that the water may approach the weir at a slow velocity and be freed from cross currents and eddies, baffle boards are frequently placed in the receiving chamber and the inlet pipe may be placed in a vertical position and at right angles to the feed pipe.

Another frequent cause of overregistering in the use of weirs is the increase in head over the weir above the normal. This may be partially overcome by having all excess water flow over spillways, the longer the spillway the greater approach to normal conditions being obtained. Another method is to keep a continuous record of the flow through the weir notch by means of an automatic register. In still other cases the head is kept constant by means of a gate regulated by a float. Apart from the long spillway perhaps the most effective way of maintaining a constant head over a weir is shown in figure 15, which is a combination of the spillway and valves. By this arrangement valve " b " in the main feed pipe when closed causes the water to rise in one chamber of the box and flow over spillway " a " into the other chamber, while valve " c " is regulated to permit the desired amount of water to flow through the weir " d " into the lateral pipe. It is thus apparent that any slight increase in the depth of water in the spillway " a " will not materially affect the measurement at " d."

Miner's Inch Boxes.

A device of this kind measures the quantity of water which flows through a rectangular orifice under a constant head (fig. 16). The dimensions of the orifice most commonly used in southern California are 4 inches deep and from 2 to 100 inches in length with a head of 4 inches of water over the center of the orifice. The quantity of water flowing through such an orifice is estimated to be 9 gallons per minute for each square inch of orifice or the one-fiftieth part of a cubic foot per second. The Azusa miner's inch box or hydrant shown in figure 17 is fitted with a cast-iron plate which contains four orifices all 4 inches deep and $2\frac{1}{4}$, $3\frac{3}{4}$, $6\frac{1}{4}$, and $12\frac{1}{2}$ inches long, respec-

FIG.' 12.—Weir box having side contractions too narrow for accurate measurement, athough the discharge over the two weirs may be proportionately accurate.

FIG. 13.—Inaccurate weir formed within concrete pipe.

FIG. 14 —Faulty rectangular weir.

tively. Under a 4-inch head over the center of these openings, they will discharge 10, 15, 25, and 50 miner's inches, respectively. When miner's inch boxes are first installed they should be checked against a standard weir in order to test their accuracy. Under constant heads, the miner's inch box measures water with fair accuracy but

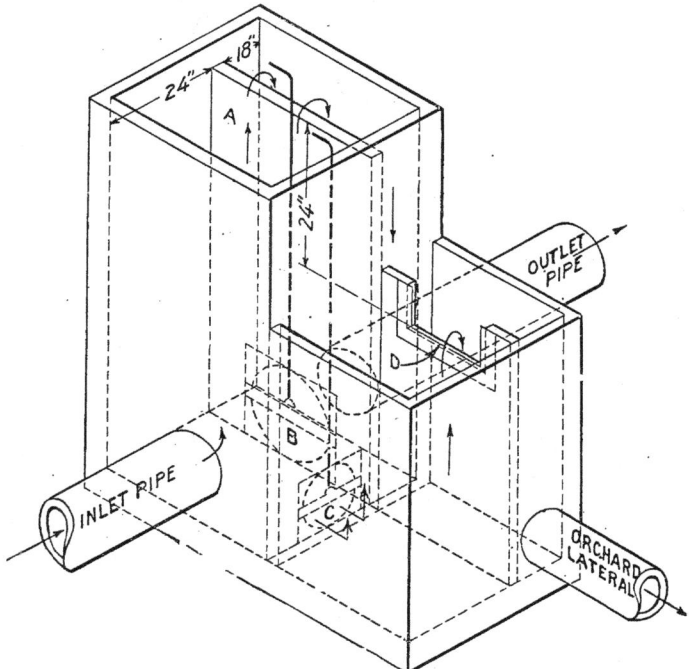

Fig. 15.—Weir box for controlling of head.

where the heads are permitted to vary errors of 100 per cent may be introduced. As in the case of weirs, spillways are used to prevent large fluctuations in heads. One of these is shown in figure 18.

Water registers.

Wherever it is desired to keep a continuous record of the amount of water passing a given point automatic registering devices known as water registers are frequently used. These consist of a drum around which the recording sheet is wrapped and both are attached to a clock which causes them to revolve once in a period of 8 days or more. The record is made on the sheet by a pen or pencil attached to

FIG. 16.—Miner's inch box with waste way.

the rod of a float. The float and its record may measure the height of water over a weir or in a rating channel.

Mechanical recording devices.

These as a rule operate by a vane or propeller revolved by the action of the water as it passes through the meter. They possess an advantage in registering a flow whose record can be readily observed.

FIG. 17.—An Azusa miner's inch box.

On the other hand, such devices may not measure water accurately particularly in reduced volumes. They are also liable to become clogged with silt, sand, moss, or other débris. Figure 19 shows the exterior of one of these meters.

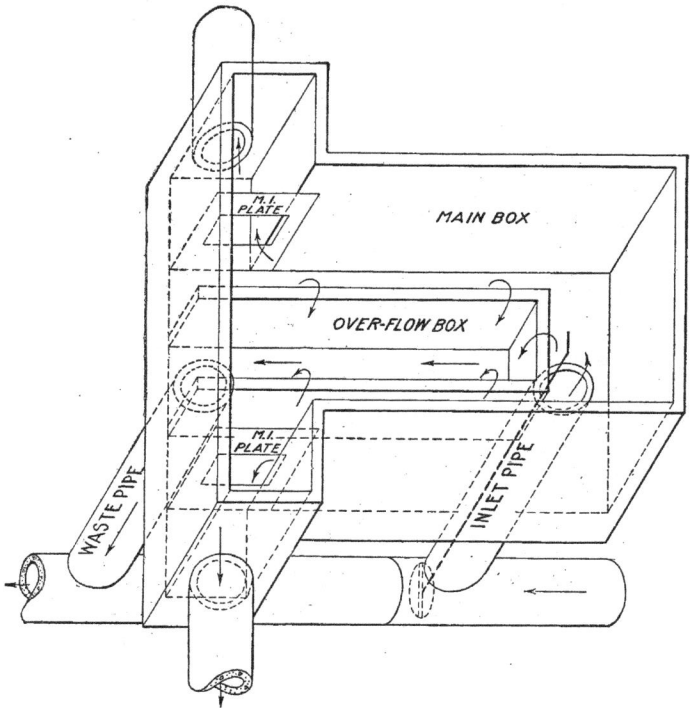

Fig. 18.—Miner's inch box fitted with long waste overflow to minimize change of head through miner's inch plates that feed lateral pipes.

DIVERSION BOXES.

As stated, weirs, miner's inch boxes, and recording devices are usually set in boxes which also act as diversion boxes. Some of the larger rectangular boxes in use have a weir or miner's inch plate on each side and divert water to three or four laterals, as illustrated in figure 20.

It is common practice to measure water at the upper end of a lateral and then install simple diversion boxes at each orchard or farm. These seldom measure water, but are designed so that all

FIG. 19.—Exterior view of recording meter.

ι. 20.—Diversion box having a weir and two miner's inch plates.

FIG. 21.—A diversion box formed partly of concrete pipe.

the water in the lateral is divided in proportion to the separate acreages to be served. The Covina Water Co. has installed diversion boxes that are fitted with galvanized sheet-iron gates. The gates are all set at the same elevation in the box and water may spill over into the orchard pipe lines on every side of the box. The gates are usually made with rectangular orifices that have several sizes of openings. As the head is the same on each gate, the correct proportion of water will be delivered to each unit, independently of the head over the orifice.

Pipe can be used to advantage for constructing diversion boxes as shown in figures 21 and 22. Where there is considerable pressure to contend with at the point of diversion, pipe structures can be built up in a single length to the required height and gates operated from the top of the stands. Overflow stands (fig. 23) can be made by building spillways and thus keeping a constant head on the mains

FIG. 22.—A diversion box formed wholly of concrete pipe having small air vents.

or laterals. Overflow stands may operate automatically, requiring no gates, or gates may be made from ordinary orchard valves that can be manipulated from the outside of the stand.

Where pressure is excessive or there is an objection to high stands, diversion boxes are sometimes built that extend only a few feet above the ground surface, and a top is provided over the stand that will withstand the pressure as shown in figure 24. Alfalfa valves are commonly used to close the top of the stand. Lateral gates may either be of the common, sliding type, or may be orchard valves that are loosened by turning on a threaded bolt.

A diversion box has been designed that will relieve high pressures without the use of high relief or overflow stands. This box makes use of an automatically controlled valve that will open the gate in the main when pressures tend to become high at the point of

FIG. 23.—Overflow stands.

diversion. The
is controlled by a
in an auxiliary s
Such an arrange
would have v ı
where high pre
pipe is laid do
steep g r a d e ,
where relief s
would have to b
cessively high to
water up to all p
of diversion. Iı
above case, watei
intended to be
for domestic 'use
some provision
necessary to keep
siderable pressu:
each diversion ı

vas not practicable to allow the entire head of water on the
ıccount of the steep grades and long length of the main, and,
ıds at frequent intervals, high enough to deliver water tı
ınd story of a house were too expensive, and at the same
ıghtly.

DISTRIBUTING HYDRANTS.

fter water has been conveyed to the field or orchard, the

FIG. 25.—A common type of distributing hydrant for orchard irrigation.

valve. The stand is connected to the underground lateral by a short riser and the water is regulated from the lateral to the stand by means of a small valve. A 6-inch concrete pipe stand usually contains two outlets, each from 1 to 2 inches in diameter; an 8-inch stand, 2 to 4 openings; a 12-inch stand, 4 to 8 openings; and a 16-inch stand contains 6 to 8 openings. The concrete risers and stands are usually connected by the pipe contractor when the orchard laterals are laid. The contractor cements the small galvanized gates into the pipe in the yard. A special mold is often used to make the concrete pipe stands, the holes that contain the gates being made when the pipe is in the mold.

FIG. 26.—Distributing hydrants on steep slopes and overflow stands.

Fig. 27.—Distributing hydrant elliptical in form.

Large elliptical, semicircular, or oval stands are used where an extra number of valves are to be connected to one hydrant These special forms (figs. 27 and 28) are also used in sandy soil, where it is desirable to space the spouts as far apart as possible. If several outlets are set in a small diameter pipe, water will wash the furrows together where they connect at the hydrant. Where the larger sized hydrants are used it is a good plan to set them against a curb or fence, otherwise they will be an obstruction to cultivation if placed in the ordinary manner. These large hydrants are sometimes used where the smaller type would answer as well, but they have their use especially in walnut orchards where a large number of furrows are required between tree rows. The oval type set with the long axis parallel to the tree rows presents the least obstruction to cultivation where the stands can not be placed against a fence or curb. There are orchard hydrants which are covered over the top, with no valve connecting stand to the underground lateral, the amount of water delivered to each furrow being regulated by means of small galvanized gates that are attached to spouts set through the sides of the stand. This type is practicable where heads are low, but where pressure is in excess of a few feet the valves are difficult to make water-tight. Leaves and trash also tend to clog this type of hydrant.

In some cases where it is not desirable to place a number of stands, the hydrants are placed a considerable distance apart, and portable pipes fitted with outlet valves are connected

Fig. 28.—Another type of distributing hydrant.

to the hydrants (fig. 29). This portable pipe is made of light-weight galvanized iron and is easily carried from one hydrant to another. This method assures even distribution to each furrow, and prevents washing at the stand. More labor during irrigation is required, however.

Where hillside land is to be irrigated, several new types of valves have been developed (figs. 30 and 31). Most of these new valves or methods of installation have been developed to assure an even flow from valves in spite of considerable variation in pressure in the orchard lateral. It is common practice in hillside irrigation systems to install the main feed lines along the upper sides of the tracts and to arrange orchard laterals to run down the steepest slope. As some of these laterals run down for several thousand feet on grades that fall from 15 to 35 feet per 100 feet, it can be seen that valves or outlets must be arranged to continually relieve the pressure in the pipe.

Fig. 29.—Distributing hydrant formed of portable pipe having small sliding gates.

There are several distinct types of distributing systems designed to control pressure. Overflow stands may be placed at stated intervals down grade (fig. 26), the stands being high enough to back water up to the next relief stand above it, distributing hydrants being placed between the relief stands. The relief stand may be made of two parallel concrete pipes set vertically, as shown in figure 32, so that water will rise in one to the required height, and overflow into the other and thence down the pipe to the next stand. The common orchard valve can be used to supply water to the furrows. The stand-pipes may consist of one pipe of small diameter set in another as described in a previous chapter.

The second plan makes use of an ordinary open stand (fig. 33) that does not stand above the ground surface over two or three feet. A pressure gate is cemented to the intake pipe which can be closed and back water up to the next box above. There is no danger of excessive pressures if this plan is followed, providing that stands are not placed too far apart or grades too steep, as water will back up to next stand and overflow it if more water is let into the pipe line than the orchard hydrants will dispose of. The disadvantage of this

FIG. 30.—A distributing hydrant to reduce water pressure on hillsides.

type is that gates must be regulated very accurately where a large number of orchard hydrants are fed simultaneously. As a rule such construction is best adapted to grades that will allow enough orchard hydrants between two successive stands to take all the water carried by the pipe line.

A third plan that is also adaptable to comparatively small pressures is to provide standpipes at intervals high enough to back water from one to another (fig. 34). The stands may be made of concrete pipe cemented together and set up vertically. A slide gate is cemented to the discharge pipe at each stand, leaving the inlet open. When the gate is closed, water will rise in the stand until it is backed up to the one above it. If an excess of water is turned in the pipe line, these stands will overflow and thus relieve the pressure. This plan is advisable where the gate can be easily manipulated from the top of the stands. If the standpipe is too high, it is possible to install a gate valve or irrigation valve that is boxed in, leaving the handle of the gate to project through a packing box in the top. Some companies have installed a short auxiliary stand immediately below the main standpipe. This stand contains

FIG. 31.—Another type of hydrant shown in Fig. 30.

a pressure gate that controls the height of water in the stand. This arrangement is applicable where there is a constant down grade.

Where excessive grades are encountered, it is usual to use overflow distributing hydrants. In this case each hydrant relieves the pres-

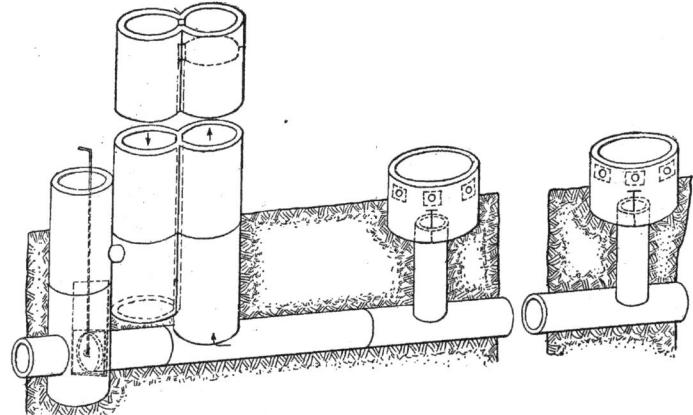

FIG. 32.—Relief stand for preventing excess pressure on concrete pipe.

sure at every tree row. It is not possible to pile up pressures that will exceed the height of the hydrants in this case, irrespective of the grade of the feed pipe. There are three general types of overflow hydrants used and each type may have several modifications

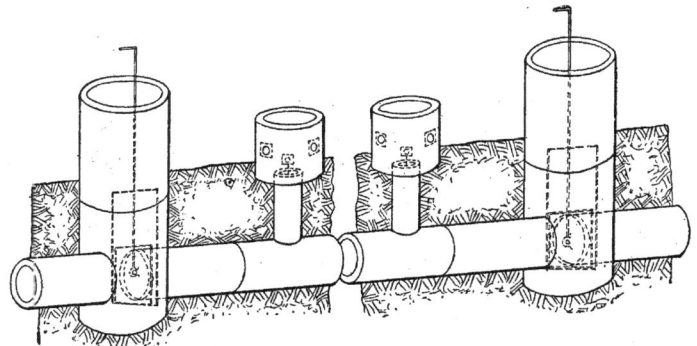

FIG. 33.—Relief of pressure accomplished by short stands with pressure gates.

The most common type consists of two lengths of concrete pipe (fig. 8) set vertically and adjacent to each other. The stand connected to the inlet pipe acts as the distributing hydrant and is fitted with valves as in the common orchard hydrant. The auxiliary pipe acts as an overflow and is cemented to the outlet pipe, permitting the excess of water to flow down the pipe line to the next hydrant. A small spillway connects the two stands, the spillway being set high enough to allo-7 a few inches head on the gates set in the upper stand (fig. 10). A modification of this hydrant is fitted with lift gates, so that all the water may flow down the pipe line and not be forced to spill over the waste-way of each valve. Others have no gates, all the water being forced to rise in each stand and overflow into the pipe line. Where the valves are set on a long lateral that runs down on a steep grade, it is usually necessary to provide gates in the pipe line so water can flow unobstructed to any set of valves.

Another type of overflow hydrant is constructed by placing a partition wall in a single length of pipe. The

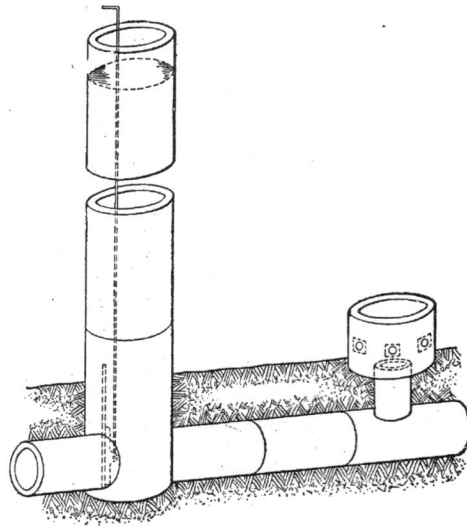

FIG. 34.—Plain relief stand. Standpipe is high enough to insure pressure on field hydrants above it. Excess pressures on pipe line impossible, as standpipe will overflow when all orchard valves above are closed.

water is forced over the partition wall when operating and spills over into the outlet to the next valve. Small outlet gates that feed the furrows are set in the inlet chamber, the pressure on the gates depending upon the height of spillway above them.

The third type is made of one large stand, consisting of one joint of concrete pipe having a pipe of smaller diameter set inside. The small pipe acts as the spillway and is connected to the outlet pipe.

When these valves are constructed properly they are nearly ideal for irrigating side-hill orchards, where only a small stream is required to each furrow. They are well adapted to contour and terrace plan of irrigation.

The greatest difficulty with overflow relief standpipes and overflow orchard hydrants is the trouble caused by entrapped air. If the sheet of water flowing into the outlet stand entirely covers the opening into the underground pipe air is carried down with the sheet of water and is not able to escape, due to the aperture being closed with water. In many cases more than three or four overflow hydrants can not be operated at one time, due to air trouble. If the hydrants or relief stands are fitted with gates at the connection to the feed pipe and the valve opening is large enough to take the full head of water, there will be little trouble with air. Such valves are sometimes difficult to adjust, however, especially where a portion of water is to be distributed through the hydrant.

The way to prevent air troubles in this type of orchard hydrant is to construct the outlet from the spillway large enough so that the entire space will not be filled with water at any time. If there is a clear space above the outlet feed pipe

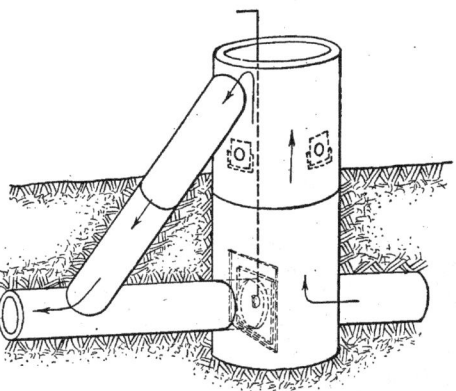

FIG. 35.—Overflow distributing hydrant. Wasteway pipe set on angle to prevent air troubles.

and the aperture from valve to feed pipe is never entirely covered with water, air will be able to escape.

The spillway pipe can also be set at an angle so that water wasting into the outlet pipe will never entirely fill it (fig. 35). If the spillway pipe is of small diameter and set inside a large diameter pipe it is necessary to have the outside pipe very much larger than the spillway pipe. The Lemon Heights Land Company near San Diego has a large number of overflow stands that are made by using the main hydrant of 20-inch pipe and the spillway of 4-inch pipe. The spillway pipe was originally set vertically, but there was so much trouble from air that all stands were changed by setting the spillway at an angle of about 45 degrees with the vertical. A notch was cut in top of the spillway pipe so that water would flow through it without entirely filling it. There has been no trouble from air since the change in design. This valve is provided with a lift gate in the bottom so that some of the water can flow to the lower hydrants without having to be forced through each valve. A much smaller pipe could be used for the main distributing hydrant if the spillway pipe was set through the lower side of the hydrant, and set on an angle to the underground pipe. Smaller spillways could also be used if this plan was followed, without danger from entrapped air.

Where sandy soil is to be irrigated, and furrows run on a gradual grade it is often best to do away with the ordinary stand that extends above the ground. An orchard valve or alfalfa valve can be

FIG. 36.—Distributing hydrant for large irrigation heads, such as are used in irrigating alfalfa.

cemented to the riser, having the riser cut off 4 inches to 6 inches below the ground surface. If the valve is set inside the first tree and in every tree row it will be no obstruction to cultivation. Where sandy soil is encountered it is often impracticable to attempt to run a number of furrows between the rows on account of the rapid percolation of water into the subsoil. It is a common sight to see sandy ground watered by using the ordinary hydrant fitted with 4 to 6 outlet gates, and either allowing all the gates to spill in one main furrow or letting the water run over the top of the stand. Where flooding or basin irrigation is practiced there is no need of a number of small outlet valves set in one hydrant.

Where flooding is resorted to for alfalfa or orchards having very flat grades and sandy soil, risers are set at convenient intervals that are capped with a special lid. This cap can be removed and a portable hood or hydrant attached to it (fig. 36). There are a number of different types on the market. The best portable hydrant can be fastened to the riser before the cap on the riser is removed or loosened. Portable pipe made from light-weight galvanized iron can also be easily attached to these portable hoods. This arrangement is often used where alfalfa is irrigated, but may be used to advantage in orchards where soil or grades will not permit of furrows.

Where steel pipe is used for distributing water, the outlet valves are usually the common hydrants or faucets used in domestic water supplies. They may be connected to concrete stands fitted with small gates or flumes and galvanized pots fitted with spouts may be used to feed the furrows. Some orchardists have utilized short lengths of standard three-quarter-inch steel pipe to distribute water to the furrows. Water is distributed through small holes bored, in the pipe, each hole feeding one furrow. In the latter case a connection is made to the iron pressure pipe at every tree row. The distributing pipes are about 8 feet long, and are fitted to the riser by pipe fittings so that the pipe may be let down on the ground when irrigating, or set up vertically out of the way of cultivation.

As regards irrigation gates and valves, it is a safe plan to install makes that have all threaded or sliding parts either of brass, bronze, or other composition metal that will resist rust. Gates whose wearing parts are cast iron throughout are liable to corrode and stick. Cast iron, however, is satisfactory for parts that do not wear, or for seats to make a water-tight connection. Most gates are constructed to work with the water pressure, the pressure tending to make them more water-tight. There are a number of pressure gates manufactured that are held against the pressure by being clamped tightly against the frame. Most gates are not built for heads over 15 to 25 feet. Special gates can be ordered for higher pressures. It is better, however, to construct boxes so that pressures will tend to hold gates in place whenever possible.

An average price for pressure gates including frames was about as follows July, 1919:

6-inch	$5.75
8-inch	8.00
10-inch	10.00
12-inch	16.00
16-inch	28.00
18-inch	36.00

These gates are fitted with a locking device that will hold the gate in any position, and are used both against and with pressure. Plain gates without the locking device sell for one-half to one-third of the above price.

Orchard valves for controlling water from pipe line to hydrant stand sell for about as follows:

6-inch	$1.25
8-inch	1.50
12-inch	4.00

Alfalfa valves without hoods cost about $4.50 for 6-inch size; $6.75 for 10-inch, and $9 for 12-inch. Portable hoods or hydrants for flooding or for use with light-weight portable galvanized-iron pipe cost about $12.50 for 6-inch hydrant and $18 for 12-inch size.

One pipe contractor in southern California quotes the following prices for standard orchard stands installed in the field fitted with 1½ inch galvanized gates:

    8-inch stands, 4 openings_____ $2. 25
    12-inch stands, 4· openings_____ 2. 50
    12-inch stands, 6 openings_____ 2. 70

Another contractor quotes the following:

    12-inch stands, with 4-hole openings_____ $3. 50
    12-inch stands, with 6-hole openings_____ 3. 75
    18-inch oval stands, with 6-hole· openings_____ 4. 00
    18-inch oval stands, with 8-hole openings_____ 4. 25

It should be borne in mind that the large majority of concrete pipe systems under operation are made of pipe of medium if not inferior grades and that the relief stands, diversion boxes, and other appliances designed to relieve water pressures have been adapted to this kind of pipe. With the introduction of a better grade of pipe capable of withstanding higher pressures the necessity will arise of modifying the present practice by using more high pressure valves and fewer standpipes, and this change should lessen the cost of pipe systems. In other words, if concrete pipe in the smaller sizes can be made to withstand with safety heads of 50 feet, it should tend to revolutionize the present costly system of reducing the pressure to 10-foot heads, particularly on steep slopes.

ADDITIONAL COPIES
OF THIS PUBLICATION MAY BE PROCURED FROM
THE SUPERINTENDENT OF DOCUMENTS
GOVERNMENT PRINTING OFFICE
WASHINGTON, D. C.
AT
20 CENTS PER COPY
▽

UNITED STATES DEPARTMENT OF AGRICULTURE

BULLETIN No. 907

Contribution from the Bureau of Entomology
L. O. HOWARD, Chief

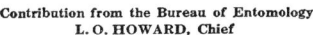

Washington, D. C.   PROFESSIONAL PAPER   October 20, 1920

FUMIGATION OF CITRUS PLANTS WITH HYDRO-CYANIC ACID: CONDITIONS INFLUENCING INJURY.

By R. S. Woglum,[1] *Entomologist, Tropical and Subtropical Fruit Insect Investigations.*

CONTENTS.

	Page.		Page
Introduction	1	General discussion of factors which influence fumigation injury	27
The effect of hydrocyanic acid on plants	2	The concentration of the gas	28
Details of experiments	3	The length of exposure	29
The effect on plant injury of temperature, light, and moisture before fumigation	4	The physiological condition of the plant	30
The effect on plant injury of temperature, light, and moisture after fumigation	10	Atmospheric and light conditions	33
The effect on plant injury of temperature, light, and moisture during fumigation	22	Summary	41
		Literature cited	42

INTRODUCTION.

The important factors long known to modify damage to the fruit and foliage of citrus trees under orchard conditions of fumigation with hydrocyanic acid include temperature, moisture, light, and physiological condition of the plant. Of these, light appears to have more completely influenced the application of this gas than any other factor and early confined fumigation to a night practice. Coquillett (3),[2] the originator of orchard fumigation with hydrocyanic acid, found early in his studies that citrus trees were less liable to injury by this gas when treated at night than in daytime, and explained that this result was due to decomposition of the gas by light and heat into other gases more injurious to the plants. Gossard (7), working with citrus trees in Florida, stated that "midday fumigation can hardly be practiced." More recently Fernald, Tower, and Hooker (5), experimenting with cucumbers and tomatoes under glass, concluded that for such tender plants day fumigation, even in cloudy weather, is unsafe.

Literature treating of the causes of fumigation injury is confined almost exclusively to the consideration of conditions, physiological

---

[1] Resigned September 11, 1920.   [2] Reference is made by number (italic) to "Literature cited," p. 42.

4533°—Bull. 907—20——1

1

as well as environmental, which prevail during the actual exposure of plants to the gas. The prefumigation and postfumigation environments have been given scant attention. The writer early in his fumigation studies observed types of injury not fully explainable by influences during the gas exposure, and subsequently it developed that certain factors must be considered, not only during but also before and after the gas treatment. Accordingly, a series of experiments was performed to determine the prefumigation and postfumigation influence, if any, of the two very important factors, heat and light. This paper presents the results of these experiments, and furthermore interprets the results in the light of field experience. In the discussion it has been found necessary to touch on other factors which also bear on the subject of fumigation injury.

THE EFFECT OF HYDROCYANIC ACID ON PLANTS.

The modification of plant injury by most external factors can be ascertained with sufficient accuracy and comprehensiveness to guide field work without attempting to determine the actual physiological action which occurs within the plant tissues when these are exposed to varying concentrations of hydrocyanic acid. Studies of the effect of this gas on plant metabolism have been made, however, and some very important papers have appeared setting forth the results of careful research on this subject. One of the earliest comprehensive papers confined to this subject was issued by Schroeder (17), in which he concluded, as the result of a long series of determinations on the effect of potassium cyanid on the fungus *Aspergillus niger*, that injury arises through paralysis of respiration, but that the reduced respiration is followed by complete recovery when the poison period does not last too long. Moore and Willaman (12), working with greenhouse plants, similarly conclude that the absorption of more or less hydrocyanic acid by plants results in a reduction of respiratory activity, and show that this inhibitory effect on respiration is due primarily to disturbance of the respiratory enzymes, oxidases, and catalase. Various other physiological effects resulting are the inhibition of photosynthesis and translocation of carbohydrates; also an increase in the permeability of the leaf septa.

Since the passage of gases takes place between the open air and the intercellular spaces of leaves through the stomata, it has been believed by most investigators of fumigation that hydrocyanic acid gains entrance into the tissues of fumigated plants through these openings. Researches by Moore (11) led to the conclusion that during fumigation hydrocyanic acid not only does enter plants through the stomata, if they are open, but also through the cuticle, depending upon its thickness and degree of cutinization. In a recent paper Clayton (1) emphasizes that the stomata seem to be the most important single factor in determining the amount of injury resulting from hydrocyanic acid fumigation, although Stone (*18*) concluded from his investigations that susceptibility to injury is due more to the condition of the tissue, whether thin and tender or resistant, than to the open or closed condition of the stomata.

It has not been uncommon in California to hear practical fumigators state that plant injury during fumigation is due to impurities in the cyanid or sulphuric acid. One writer (*23*) has attributed injury to sulphuric-acid fumes given off during the gas generation and has discussed in great detail how such action is brought about. The work of Schroeder, Moore, and others disproves any conclusion that does not mention the cyanid gas itself as the cause of plant injury, and experiments by the writer (*19*) furnish further data in disproving these theories with reference to sulphuric acid. Furthermore, the recent wide use of high-purity liquid hydrocyanic acid, a material free of sulphuric acid, has been attended by the customary fruit and foliage injury.

DETAILS OF EXPERIMENTS.

Boxed seedling orange trees, pruned to several branches and from 1 to 2 feet in height, were grown beneath a canvas shelter which afforded protection from the midday sun. The foliage was dense and for the most part consisted of heavily cutinized leaves, except for the tender growth toward the top.

The gas-tight fumigatorium (Pl. I, A) in which the experiments were performed contained 100 cubic feet of space and was equipped with two large glass windows, which permitted the regulation of light conditions. Treatment in the shade signifies that both windows were fully exposed to diffused light. The temperature of the fumigatorium for any one experiment was uniform during the exposure, unless otherwise noted. All records were made in the Fahrenheit scale. Only high-grade commercial cyanids of 96 to 99 per cent purity were used. Potassium cyanid was used according to the 1–1–3 formula, or sodium cyanid according to the 1–1½–2 formula (*19*). The foliage in all cases was dry, unless otherwise noted. Check plants were used in all experiments and failure to refer to them signifies that the checks were in no way injured. The dosages in these experiments approximate those employed in orchard treatment in California. All plants in any one experiment were fumigated at the same time. Immediately after treatment they were removed from the fumigatorium and placed in different environments of temperature and light. Final notes on results were taken five to seven days after treatment. Shade signifies protection from the sun by a canvas shelter or a wooden building. Darkness means total exclusion of light. Moisture does not include atmospheric humidity. Injury as included in this paper should be interpreted as meaning damage to or death of tissues, so that the effect is observable to the naked eye. Burned signifies severe injury amounting to the partial or total discoloration of numerous leaves, as by heat. Singed indicates slight burning, especially at the tips or edges of leaves.

Varying degrees of damage to the plants were indicated as follows in all experiments:

0—Plants entirely unaffected externally.

1—Some of the tenderest undeveloped leaves or tips of tender shoots at least slightly injured.

2—Tenderest tips with undeveloped leaves severely injured; fully grown tender leaves sometimes slightly affected; mature leaves uninjured.

3—Tender growth, including fully developed new leaves, destroyed; old leaves slightly affected.

4—Mature leaves in large numbers severely burned.

5—One-half to entire plant severely burned.

THE EFFECT ON PLANT INJURY OF TEMPERATURE, LIGHT, AND MOISTURE BEFORE FUMIGATION.

The fumigation of growing plants is usually conducted without regard to their environment prior to the gas exposure, barring the factor moisture relative to which a divergence of opinion exists. The experimental evidence presented in this paper bearing on prefumigation conditions draws attention not only to the influence of moisture but also to that of temperature and light. Data on the influence of these factors are brought out in experiments 1 to 9, inclusive, as well as in 11, 12, 14, 15, and 18, these latter experiments being discussed under the subject of postfumigation influences. Certain of these experiments, namely, 1, 2, 12, 14, 15, and 18, are of special value by reason of the number of postfumigation environments also included in each experiment.

EXPERIMENT 1.

Condition during fumigation, shade, 58°–60° F.
Dosage, 1½ ounces KCN.
Date, March 18, 1915, 8.45–9.45 a. m.
Plants in each test, 2; total, 30.
Remarks: Plants somewhat hardened.

Results.

Condition after fumigation.	Condition before fumigation.		
	Dark, 60° F.	Shade, 58° F.	Sun, 68° F.[1]
Dark, 60° F..............	1	1	3
Shade, 58° F.............	1	1	3
Dark, 86° F..............	2+	2+	5
Shade, 90° F.............	2+	2+	5
Sun, 72° F...............	3+	3+	5

[1] Plants in sunshine for 2 or 3 hours before fumigation. Maximum sun temperature for day, 77° F.

FUMIGATION OF CITRUS PLANTS WITH HYDROCYANIC ACID.

A, Fumigatorium used in experimental work, showing interior arrangement.
B, Orchard citrus tree fumigated in the daytime and immediately afterward
exposed to a hot sunshine; foliage completely destroyed. Other trees in the
same grove, fumigated at an equal temperature but free from sunshine influence,
were uninjured.

EXPERIMENT 2.

Condition during fumigation, shade, 67°–69° F.
Dosage, 1¼ ounces KCN.
Date, March 15, 1915, 9.30–10.30 a. m.
Plants in each test, 2; total, 18.
Remarks: Plants somewhat hardened.

Results.

Condition after fumigation.	Condition before fumigation.		
	Dark, 55° F.	Shade, 67° F.	Sun, 75° F.
Dark, 55° F.[1]	1	1	3
Shade, 70° F.[2]	1	1	3
Sun, 75° F.[3]	2+	2+	5

[1] Temperature 55°–57° F. throughout day.
[2] Maximum shade temperature during day, 80° F., at 1.30 p. m.
[3] Maximum sun temperature during day, 86° F., at 1.30 p. m.

EXPERIMENT 3.

Condition during fumigation, shade, 57°–58° F.
Condition after fumigation, shade, 59°–66° F., for 24-hour period.
Dosage, 1 ounce NaCN.
Date, September 28, 1915, 7.10–7.50 a. m.
Plants in each test, 5; total, 15.

Results.

Condition before fumigation.		
Shade, 56° F.[1]	Shade, 90° F.[2]	Sun, 60° F.[3]
2	2	2

[1] At cool temperature several hours before fumigation.
[2] At temperature 88°–90° F. for 1 hour before fumigation; previously at 56° F.
[3] In sun for 1½ hours before fumigation.

EXPERIMENT 4.

Condition during fumigation, shade, 63° F.
Condition after fumigation, shade, 88°–90° F.
Dosage, 1 ounce NaCN.
Date, September 28, 1915, 9–9.40 a. m.
Plants in each test, 3; total, 12.

Results.

Condition before fumigation.			
Shade, 67° F., plants wet.[1]	Shade, 67° F., plants dry.	Sun, 72° F., plants wet.[1]	Sun, 72° F. plants dry.
3	3	3	4

[1] Plants thoroughly sprinkled with tap water before fumigation.

EXPERIMENT 5.

Condition during fumigation, dark, 64°–66° F.
Condition after fumigation, dark, 60° F.
Dosage, 1¼ ounces KCN.
Date, May 17, 1916, 6.07–6.57 a. m.
Plants in each test, 7; total, 14.

Results.

Condition before fumigation.	
Dark, 64°–66° F.	Dark, 90°–102° F.[1]
2	2

[1] 5 hours before fumigation temperature raised from 70° to 90°–102° F.

EXPERIMENT 6.

Condition during fumigation, dark, 60° F.
Condition after fumigation, shade, 64° F.
Dosage, 1¼ ounces KCN.
Date, March 30, 1916, 9.37–10.27 a. m.
Plants in each test, 5; total, 15.

Results.

Condition before fumigation.		
Sun, 67° F., plants dry.	Sun, 67° F., plants wet, water temperature, 58° F.	Sun, 67° F., plants wet, water temperature, 86° F.
1	1	1

EXPERIMENT 7.

Condition during fumigation, dark, 72°–73° F.
Condition after fumigation, shade, 65° F.
Dosage, 1 ounce NaCN.
Date, October 7, 1915, 12.10–12.50 p. m.
Plants in each test, 5; total, 15.
Remarks: Plants exposed to the sunshine for several hours, then wet thoroughly immediately before fumigation.

Results.

Condition before fumigation.		
Sun, 80° F., plants dry.	Sun, 80° F., plants wet, water temperature, 64° F.	Sun, 80° F., plants wet, water temperature, 96° F.
4	3	4

All dry plants had the mature foliage quite severely burned, while only 3 of the 5 hot-water-treated plants were equally severely affected. None of the plants treated with cold water were as severely injured as where dry.

EXPERIMENT 8.

Condition during fumigation, dark, 62° F.
Condition after fumigation, shade, 67° F.
Dosage, 1¼ ounces KCN.
Date, May 17, 1916, 9.50–10.40 a. m.
Plants in each test, 5; total, 15.

Results.

Condition before fumigation.		
Shade, 65° F., plants dry.	Shade, 65° F., plants wet, water temperature, 68° F.	Shade, 65° F., plants wet, water temperature, 100° F.
2	2	2

EXPERIMENT 9.

Condition during fumigation, dark, 62° F.
Condition after fumigation, sunshine, 74° F.
Dosage, 1¼ ounces KCN.
Date, March 30, 1916, 10.57–11.47 a. m.
Plants in each test, 5; total, 10.

Results.

Condition before fumigation.	
Shade, 66° F., dry.	Shade, 66° F., wet.
4	4

DARKNESS AND SHADE.

In experiment 1 ten citrus plants in the dark at a temperature of 60° F. and ten in the shade at approximately the same temperature (58° F.) were fumigated at the same time. After treatment they were so divided that plants from each prefumigation condition were placed under five distinct postfumigation environments, each to include two plants from the darkness and two from the shade. No difference in degree of injury could be detected between the plants from prefumigation shade and those from prefumigation darkness in any of the five postfumigation conditions. Equivalent results are presented in experiment 12 between the series of plants in prefumigation shade and prefumigation darkness at 60° F. These results would appear to indicate that neither darkness nor diffused light before fumigation in any way influences the degree of injury to citrus plants from treatment with hydrocyanic acid.

The relation of temperature before fumigation to plant injury is brought out in experiments 2, 3, 5, 14, 15, and 18. In experiment 3 it is seen that plants at a shade temperature of 90° F. before fumigation were no more severely injured than others at a temperature of 56° F. Practically identical results occurred in experiment 5, where the prefumigation conditions were darkness at temperatures of 64°–66° F. and 90°–102° F., and in both cases merely the tenderest growth was slightly injured. Experiments 3 and 5 were performed at cool temperatures, and the postfumigation environment was cool. On the other hand, experiment 15, which was conducted at the high temperatures of 86°–91° F., developed no difference in injury between plants at prefumigation temperatures of 62° and 90° F.

In experiments 14 and 18 most of the plants showed no apparent difference in injury attributable to temperature before exposure. A few plants, however, did show slightly greater injury than others under similar postfumigation conditions and in these cases all the more severely injured plants were under the highest prefumigation temperatures (80° and 76° F., respectively). These two experiments were performed at comparatively high temperatures (85° to 92° F.).

It would appear from these experiments, therefore, that where plants are in shade or darkness the temperature immediately previous to fumigation has little influence on the resultant plant injury. Sometimes, however, a difference in plant injury apparently due to heat influences develops, and in such cases the greatest injury appears on those plants subject to the highest prefumigation temperatures. In the experiments in this paper the prefumigation temperatures ranged between 56° and 102° F. Within these limits there was little or no difference in injury where the fumigation and postfumigation temperatures were both below 70° F. However, slightly more increased injury did occur at the prefumigation temperatures of 76° and 80° F. than at 56° F. in two experiments in which the actual fumigation temperature was about 85° F. This would indicate the advisability of keeping plants at a cool temperature prior to fumigation in case the fumigation and postfumigation environments are hot. If the fumigation and postfumigation temperatures are cool a comparatively high prefumigation temperature appears to have little more effect on the results than a cool temperature.

The influence of sunshine on plants before fumigation is shown by the results of experiments 1 to 4, 12, 14, 15, and 18. In experiment 1 this influence previous to the gas treatment contrasts sharply with that of diffused light or darkness. Sun and shade exposed plants under cool temperature conditions were fumigated at the same time and on removal from the fumigatorium were placed under five different conditions. In each of the five conditions the prefumigation sun-exposed plants developed decidedly greater injury than those that were in shade before treatment. The results of experiment 18, in which plants were exposed to a hot sunshine (83° F.) immediately before fumigation and fumigated at a high temperature, show all sun-exposed plants killed regardless of the postfumigation conditions; yet others in the shade at approximately the same prefumigation temperature (76° F.) and placed at a temperature of 56° F. after the treatment had only the very tenderest foliage singed. The effect of prefumigation sunshine is not so conclusively brought out in the other experiments, but, with the exception of No. 3, it appears to have intensified the injury in at least a few of the trees treated. Experiment 3 alone shows no difference between plants in the shade and those in the sunshine previous to fumigation. It is noted in this case that the sunshine temperature was 60° F. and the fumigation and postfumigation conditions were equally cool, all three being ideal for exposure to cyanid gas.

A comparative study of the temperature before and after treatment shows that the effect of prefumigation sunshine is modified by the degree of heat present at these different times. For instance, in experiment 3 where the sunshine appeared not to affect the degree of injury more than the shade, all fumigation conditions, the prefumigation, postfumigation, and actual fumigation, approximated 60° F. On the other hand, experiment 2, which was performed with the same type of plants, the same dosage, and at approximately the same temperature, exhibited a decided difference in injury between the prefumigation shade and sunshine-exposed plants, the injury in the latter being greater than for experiment 3. It is noted that the sun temperature in experiment 2 was 75° F., whereas in experiment 3 it was 60° F., which shows that the degree of injury attributable to sunshine increased with the increased temperature. Thus a hot sunshine before fumigation is more to be avoided than a cool sunshine.

In conclusion it can be stated that the experimental evidence in this paper appears to show that sunshine coming in contact with citrus plants before fumigation tends to produce greater injury than where plants are in the shade or darkness; that sunshine accompanied by a high temperature is more injurious than if accompanied by a low temperature; that the degree of injury is modified by the postfumigation conditions, greater injury developing at high temperatures than at low temperatures; that the most critical environment is to subject plants exposed to a hot sunshine before fumigation to a hot sunshine after fumigation; finally, that a high temperature during fumigation probably increases the injury of prefumigation sunshine-exposed plants over that taking place at a low temperature.

MOISTURE.

The effect of moisture on fumigated citrus trees is shown in experiments 4, 6 to 9, and 11, in which varied prefumigation conditions occur. In Nos. 4, 8, 9, and 11 a number of plants in the shade at temperatures between 60° and 68° F. were drenched with water before they were placed in the fumigatorium with others having perfectly dry foliage, and were then immediately subjected to hydrocyanic-acid gas. Thirty-seven plants in all were used in these four experiments and in no case was there any apparent difference in injury between the wet and the dry plants, even though a number of the trees had some very tender foliage.

In experiments 4, 6, and 7 plants were exposed to prefumigation sunshine at temperatures ranging from 67° to 80° F. Immediately before fumigation a part was drenched with water and afterwards fumigated with others having perfectly dry foliage. Experiment 6 exhibits the same degree of injury for the wet plants as for the dry, a condition which holds true whether the water used in the treatment was 58° or 86° F. In experiment 4 the dry plants were slightly more severely injured than the wet, quite the contrary to what would be expected, and in fact to what is shown by Moore (*11*) to take place in the case of tender greenhouse plants. In experiment 7 the dry plants were likewise more severely injured than those treated with cool water, although where wet with warm water the injury was equal. While these two experiments are insufficient in themselves to prove definitely that plants subjected to a hot sunshine before fumigation are more severely injured when dry than when wet it at least indicates that the wetting of such plants can, in some cases at least, reduce the degree of injury to an extent. In this connection it should be noted that the reduction of injury to the wet plants occurred where the water used was at a temperature considerably lower than that of the sunshine. Water at a temperature equal to or higher than the sun temperature did not appear to influence the degree of injury over that normal to dry plants.

In conclusion it may be stated that water on citrus plants appears in no way to affect the degree of injury, if the plants are subjected to shade or darkness before treatment; if, however, plants are in the direct sunshine before treatment, water appears to reduce the injury slightly, at least in some cases where the temperature of the water is below that of the sunshine.

THE EFFECT ON PLANT INJURY OF TEMPERATURE, LIGHT, AND MOISTURE AFTER FUMIGATION.

Fumigation with hydrocyanic acid is usually considered completed with the separation of the treated plants from exposure to the gas. Little or no attention has been given to the postfumigation environment. That this environment may modify the degree of plant injury is shown in the following experiments, which indicate the influence of different light intensities and of different temperatures on citrus plants immediately after fumigation with hydrocyanic acid. These experiments were performed, some in darkness and some in the shade, at temperatures ranging from 60° to 91° F. All plants in each experiment were fumigated at the same time, part being placed immediately after treatment in direct sunshine, part in the shade, and, excepting Nos. 11, 13, and 19, part in darkness. An effort was made in several experiments to have the shade temperature approximate that of the sunshine, thereby eliminating consideration of the heat factor and furnishing an exact basis for determining the influence of the sun's direct rays, a factor of special consideration. Most of the experiments also contain postfumigation environments of shade or darkness at decidedly cooler temperatures than those of sunshine, and thus furnish data for study of comparative temperature influences. Four experiments, Nos. 12, 14, 15, and 18, include plants under three different prefumigation environments, each set of which was subjected to either four or five different postfumigation conditions. Such experiments offer a wide range of data on the influence of various prefumigation as well as postfumigation factors.

EXPERIMENT 10.

Condition during fumigation, dark, 64° F.
Condition before fumigation, dark, 64° F.
Dosage, 1 ounce NaCN.
Date, September 22, 1915, 7–7.40 a. m.
Plants in each test, 4; total, 20.

Results.

Condition after fumigation.				
Dark, 65° F.[1]	Shade, 65° F.[1]	Dark, 79° F.[2]	Shade, 79° F.[2]	Sun, 79° F.[2]
2	2	2	2	4

[1] At cool temperatures throughout the day.
[2] At equal temperatures throughout the day. Maximum 102° F. at 2 p. m.

EXPERIMENT 11.

Condition during fumigation, dark, 61° F.
Condition before fumigation, shade, 61° F.
Dosage, 1 ounce KCN.
Date, June 17, 1914, 8.15–9 a. m.
Plants in each test, 3; total, 12.
Remarks: Condition of plants comparatively tender. All at equal temperatures throughout the day after fumigation. Maximum 83° F. at 2 p. m. Plants wet immediately before fumigation.

Results.

	Condition after fumigation.	
	Shade, 65° F.	Sun, 65° F.
Foliage drenched with water........	2	4
Foliage dry.........................	2	4

EXPERIMENT 12.

Condition during fumigation, dark, 64°–65° F.

Dosage, 1½ ounces KCN.

Date, March 18, 1915, 10.50–11.50 a. m.

Plants in each test, 2; total, 30.

Remarks: Fumigatorium contained ice to maintain a low temperature. This absorbed much gas.

Results.

Condition before fumigation.	Condition after fumigation.				
	Dark, 60° F.	Shade, 60° F.	Dark, 90° F.[1]	Shade, 88° F.[1]	Sun, 75° F.[2]
Dark, 60° F...............	2	2	3	3	3
Shade, 60° F...............	2	2	3	3	3
Sun, 73° F...............	2	2	4	4	4

[1] Temperature maintained 4 hours after treatment.
[2] Maximum temperature for day, 77° F.

EXPERIMENT 13.

Condition during fumigation, dark 66°–68° F.

Condition before fumigation, shade, 66° F.

Dosage, 1 ounce NaCN.

Date, November 17, 1917, 9–10 a. m.

Plants in each test, 4; total, 12.

Remarks: Plant foliage tender.

Results.

Condition after fumigation.		
Shade, 68° F.	Shade, 79° F.[1]	Sun, 79° F.[1]
2	2	5

[1] At equal temperatures throughout the day. Maximum 98° F. at 2 p. m.

All foliage on plants in the sunshine was destroyed, while those in the shade exhibited injury only to the tenderest growth.

EXPERIMENT 14.

Condition during fumigation, dark, 91°–92° F.

Dosage, 1¼ ounces KCN.

Date, March 15, 1915, 1.30–2.30 p. m.

Plants in each test, 2; total, 22.

Remarks: Plants were in a somewhat resistant condition. Temperature of the fumigatorium 80° F. when plants entered, being raised immediately to 90°–91° F. before fumigation, and thus maintained throughout the exposure.

Results.

Condition before fumigation.	Condition after fumigation.			
	Dark, 56° F.[1]	Shade, 80° F.[2]	Shade, 90° F.[3]	Sun, 85° F.[4]
Dark, 56° F.........	2	3	3+	....
Shade, 80° F.........	3	3+	3+	4
Sun, 86° F.........	3	4	4	5

[1] Temperature uniform throughout day.
[2] Held at sun temperature.
[3] Temperature 85°–90° F. maintained for 3 hours after treatment.
[4] Temperature dropped to 75° F. 3 hours after exposure.

EXPERIMENT 15.

Condition during fumigation, dark, 86°–91° F.

Dosage, 1½ ounces KCN.

Date, March 18, 1915, 12.35–1.35 p. m.

Plants in each test, 2; total, 30.

Remarks: Growth as in experiment 14. Temperature of fumigatorium 73° F. when plants entered, being raised immediately to and maintained at 86°–91° F. during fumigation.

Results.

Condition before fumigation.	Condition after fumigation.				
	Dark, 63° F.[1]	Shade, 63° F.[1]	Dark, 91° F.[2]	Shade, 89° F.[2]	Sun, 77° F.[3]
Dark, 62° F..............	3	3	4	4	4
Dark, 90° F..............	3	3	4	4	4
Sun, 77° F..............	4	4	4	4	4

[1] Maximum temperature for 24 hours after treatment, 65° F.
[2] Temperature 86°–91° F. maintained for 3 hours after treatment.
[3] Temperature 3 hours after treatment, 69° F. Slight haze developed during afternoon and at 4.45 p. m. completely obliterated the sun.

EXPERIMENT 16.

Condition during fumigation, shade, 61°–63° F.

Condition before fumigation, dark, 60° F.

Dosage, 1 ounce NaCN.

Date, September 22, 1915, 6.10–6.50 a. m.

Plants in each test, 4; total, 20.

Results.

Condition after fumigation.				
Dark, 65° F.[1]	Shade, 64° F.[1]	Dark, 73° F.[2]	Shade, 70° F.[2]	Sun 73° F.[2]
2	2	2	2	4

[1] At cool temperatures throughout day.
[2] At equal temperatures throughout the day; maximum 102° F. at 2 p. m.

EXPERIMENT 17.

Condition during fumigation, shade, 60°–62° F.
Condition before fumigation, dark, 64° F.
Dosage, 1 ounce NaCN.
Date, September 21, 1915, 6.50–7.35 a. m.
Plants in each test, 5; total, 20.

Results.

Condition after fumigation.			
Dark, 64° F.[1]	Dark, 80° F.[2]	Shade, 70° F.[3]	Sun, 71° F.[3]
2	2	2	4

[1] Temperature 64°–68° F. throughout the day.
[2] Temperature 80°–91° F. during the day.
[3] Temperatures equal throughout the day; maximum 94° F. at 1 p. m.

EXPERIMENT 18.

Condition during fumigation, shade, 85°–89° F.
Dosage, 1¼ ounces KCN.
Date, March 15, 1915, 11.20–12.20 p. m.
Plants in each test, 2; total, 24.
Remarks: Growth as in experiment 14. Plants placed in fumigatorium at temperature 70°–75° F. which was immediately raised to and maintained at 85°–89° F. during fumigation.

Results.

Condition before fumigation.	Condition after fumigation.			
	Dark, 56° F.[1]	Shade, 79° F.[2]	Shade, 90° F.[3]	Sun, 85° F.[4]
Dark, 56° F........	2	3	3	4
Shade, 76° F.......	2	3	4	5
Sun, 83° F.........	5	5	5	5

[1] Temperature practically uniform for day following treatment.
[2] Maximum temperature, 80° F.
[3] Temperature, 90° F. maintained for 4 hours.
[4] Maximum temperature, 86° F. at 1.30 p. m.

EXPERIMENT 19.

Condition during fumigation, shade, 78°–80° F.
Condition before fumigation, shade, 76° F.
Dosage, 1¼ ounces NaCN.
Date, November 2, 1917, 9.20–10.20 a. m.
Plants in each test, 2; total, 6.
Remarks: Plants hardened from growth in open.

Results.

Condition after fumigation.		
Shade, 74° F.[1]	Shade, 87° F.[2]	Sun, 87° F.[2]
2	2	5

[1] Maximum temperature, 80° F. at 2 p. m.
[2] Maximum temperature, 93° F. at 1. p. m.

DARKNESS AND SHADE.

The effect on plant injury of shade and darkness after fumigation is well illustrated by experiments 10, 12, 15, and 16 which are arranged in Table I for comparison of these influences.

TABLE I.—*Comparative effects of diffused light and darkness on plants after fumigation with hydrocyanic acid.*

	Postfumigation temperatures.							
	Experiment 10.		Experiment 12.			Experiment 15.		Experiment 16.
	65° F.	79° F.	60° F.[1]	88°–90° F.[2]	63° F.[2]	89°–91° F.[1]	64°–65° F.[1]	70°–73° F.
Darkness.......	2	2	2	3	4	3	4	2	2
Shade..........	2	2	2	3	4	3	4	2	2

[1] Includes 3 fumigation conditions.
[2] Includes 2 fumigation conditions.

An examination of this table shows that in none of the several tests included is there any difference in injury between the plants placed in darkness and those placed in the shade following fumigation. This condition holds equally true at the minimum postfumigation temperature of 60° F. or the maximum of 91° F. for these experiments. Likewise this situation does not appear to be altered by the temperature of fumigation, for experiments 10, 12, and 16 were performed at 61°–64° F. while experiment 15 was carried on at 86°–91° F.

SUNSHINE.

The influence of sunshine on citrus plants immediately after fumigation is clearly developed in experiments 10 to 19. Eight of these 10 experiments show a decidedly greater injury to the plants placed in the sunshine after fumigation than to those placed in either the shade or darkness at equivalent temperatures. This condition is brought out in Table II.

TABLE II.—*Comparative degree of injury between plants placed in the sunshine and those placed in the shade or darkness following fumigation.*

	Postfumigation temperatures.										
	Exp. 10.	Exp. 11.	Exp. 13.	Exp. 14.[1]		Exp. 16.	Exp. 17.	Exp. 18.[2]			Exp. 19.
	79° F.	65° F.	79° F.	80° F.	85° F.	70°–73° F.	70°–71°F.	85°–90° F.			87° F.
Darkness..........	2					2					
Shade.............	2	2	2	3+	4	2	2	3	4	5	2
Sunshine..........	4	4	5	4	5	4	4	4	5	5	5

[1] Experiment consisting of two distinct parts.   [2] Experiment consisting of three distinct parts.

An examination of this table shows that a dosage which slightly injures merely the tenderest growth of plants placed either in the shade or darkness after fumigation may result in severe burning of even the old, resistant leaves if the treated plants are exposed to sunlight (Pl. II, A), while in extreme cases complete defoliation follows, as happened in experiments 13 and 19. Increased injury due to sunshine was apparent even at as low a sun temperature as 65° F., which was the minimum experienced (experiment 11). The plants in this case were comparatively tender, and this condition naturally invited greater injury than would have been the case with more resistant foliage. A study of the data presented in these experiments would appear to indicate that, all other conditions being the same, injury increases more or less directly with the sun temperature. The plants in experiment 11 were somewhat tender yet the degree of injury in the case of those exposed to the sunshine (65° F.) was less than to the plants in a hardened condition in experiment 19, in which the postfumigation sunshine temperature was 87° F. In this latter experiment the hardened or resistant growth of plants placed in the sunshine was almost completely destroyed, although plants placed in the shade at the same temperature merely had the tenderest growth injured (Pl. II, A). This would indicate that sunshine at such a high temperature is more injurious than sunshine at a low temperature; in short, that the toxic action of hydrocyanic acid on fumigated plants subjected to sunshine increases with the sun's intensity.

Turning to experiment 12 it is seen that the sun-exposed plants were no more injured than those in the shade at a slightly higher temperature. It so happened that in this experiment the fumigatorium contained a piece of ice which had been used to maintain a low temperature prior to the treatment. This ice absorbed gas with the result that the strength of the gas was greatly reduced at the end of the hour's exposure. A conclusion to be deduced from this experiment is that plants exposed either to a strong gas for a short period or to a dilute gas for a longer period before being placed in the sunshine are much less injured by fumigation than plants exposed to a gas which maintains its proper strength throughout the period of an hour's exposure, as in the other nine experiments. Data in support of this statement are found elsewhere in this paper and, furthermore, are supported by other experiments performed by the author but not included in this article.

The relation of the temperature of fumigation to injury to plants subsequently exposed to sunshine is not well shown by the experimental data presented. Plants in experiments 10, 11, 13, 16, and 17 were fumigated at comparatively cool temperatures (60°–68° F.), yet the injury was about as severe to those plants subsequently placed in the sunshine as to those under similar postfumigation conditions

FUMIGATION OF CITRUS PLANTS WITH HYDROCYANIC ACID.

A, Comparative effect of hot sunshine and shade, after fumigation, on citrus plants with resist-ant foliage. Immediately following the treatment two plants were placed in direct sunlight and one in the shade, at 87° F., and held at parallel temperatures throughout the remainder of the day. It is noted that leaves in the sun-exposed plants have abscissed at the base of the blade. *B*, Citrus plants with tender foliage which were exposed immediately after fumiga-tion to the sun or shade at 79° F. The plant in the shade had merely the tender tips injured. All leaves and petioles of the sun-exposed plants were completely burned and cling without abscission.

in experiments 14, 15, and 18, which were fumigated at temperatures ranging from 86° to 92° F. This would appear to indicate that the temperature of fumigation within the limits of those experiments, 60° and 92° F., has little if any modifying influence on the resulting degree of injury to plants subjected to the sunshine after treatment. It happens, however, that the prefumigation or postfumigation conditions in experiments 14, 15, and 18 were exactly comparable to those in none of the other experiments mentioned. Although section 1 of experiment 15 approximates experiment 10 as to prefumigation and postfumigation conditions, it is seen that the maximum sun temperature for the day in experiment 15 was 77° F., whereas in experiment 10 it was 102° F. Therefore, definite conclusions regarding the influence of the temperature of fumigation on plants subsequently placed in sunshine can not be drawn until there is further experimental evidence bearing on this subject.

The effect of postfumigation sunshine on plant injury appears to be modified to a certain degree by the prefumigation light condition. This is well shown by experiments 2 and 14, in which the damage to the plants under postfumigation sunshine is greater in the case of plants exposed to prefumigation sunshine than to plants in prefumigation shade at a comparable temperature. It is probable that the prefumigation temperature modifies to some degree the effect of postfumigation sunshine, but this point is not conclusively proved in this paper.

TEMPERATURE.

The importance of the temperature to which plants are subjected after fumigation as a factor bearing on plant injury is brought out by the experimental data presented in experiments 1, and 10 to 19. It is shown in experiment 12 that fumigated plants placed immediately after treatment under a shade temperature of 88° F. or a darkness temperature of 90° F. are slightly more injured than those placed at a temperature of 60° F. A like condition is presented in experiment 15 between postfumigation temperatures of 63° F. and 89° or 91° F. Experiments 1, 14, and 18 also show slightly increased injury due to higher postfumigation temperatures in the shade or darkness. On the other hand, each experiment of numbers 2, 10, 13, 16, and 17 shows the same degree of injury for plants subjected to different temperatures of shade and darkness following fumigation. An examination of the details of these experiments, however, brings out a significant difference between the two groups. In the set of experiments (2, 10, 13, 16, and 17) in which there was no apparent difference in injury due to the different postfumigation temperatures it is seen that the difference between the high and low temperatures in any one experiment varies from 9° in experiment 16 to a maximum of 16° in experiment 17; furthermore, that the maximum postfumigation temperature for these five experiments is 80° F., a maximum only a few degrees higher than the limit of optimum temperatures established for field fumigation. On the other hand, in the set of experiments (1, 12, 14, 15, and 18) which shows a difference in injury between plants submitted to high and those submitted to low postfumigation temperatures, the range is from a minimum of 23° in experiment 18 to a maximum of 34° in experiment 14. In short, the minimum range in the last set of experiments is 7° higher than the maximum range in the first set which developed no difference of injury; furthermore, the maximum postfumigation temperatures are higher, ranging from 86° to 90° F., except in experiments 14 and 18, in which they are 80° and 79° F. respectively. Another consideration of special importance is the temperature of fumigation, which in the first set of experiments ranged from 60° to 69° F., whereas in three of the five experiments of the set which developed differences in injury the fumigation temperature ranged from 85° to 92° F. Two of the experiments in this last set, namely, 1 and 12, were performed at temperatures of 60° and 64° F. In these two experiments, however, the postfumigation temperatures were very high, 86° and 90° F., and the range between the cold and hot postfumigation temperatures was from 26° to 30°.

The general conclusion to be drawn from these experiments is that the postfumigation temperature exerts an influence on the degree of injury, especially at temperatures of 80° F. or above. The effect of such high temperatures is modified by the temperature of fumigation; for instance, a high postfumigation temperature preceded by a high fumigation temperature is more destructive to plant tissue than a high postfumigation temperature preceded by a low fumigation temperature. In fact, as is well shown in experiments 10 and 15, it is possible to subject plants treated at such low temperatures as 60° to 65° F. to moderately high postfumigation temperatures (79° and 80° F.) without any more injury than at the lower temperatures of 64° or 65° F. The postfumigation temperature of shade or darkness is so closely related to the actual fumigation temperature in modifying plant injury that it is important to take cognizance of each in plant treatment. The influence of temperature on plants subjected to sunshine following treatment has been discussed under the heading "Sunshine." To avoid injury, or at least to reduce the possibility of damage to the lowest degree, the data presented in this paper appear to indicate that after fumigation plants should be placed at temperatures below 80° F. The exact number of degrees the optimum falls below 80° will depend on the prefumigation and fumigation temperatures. When these are ideal the maximum optimum apparently approximates 80° F., but if they are not the optimum is lowered a few degrees.

THE INFLUENCE OF SUNSHINE AT VARYING PERIODS AFTER FUMIGATION.

While experiments 10 to 19 clearly demonstrate the influence of sunshine on plants exposed immediately after fumigation, the following four experiments set forth the effect of this factor where plants are placed in the sunshine four hours or more after treatment.

EXPERIMENT 20.

Condition during fumigation, shade, 62°–65° F.
Condition before fumigation, shade, 66° F.
Dosage, 1 ounce NaCN.
Date, September 21, 1915, 8–8.45 a. m.
Plants in each test, 3; total, 21.

Results.

Condition after fumigation.						
Shade, 79° F.[1]	Shade, 90° F.[2]	Sun, 76° F., exposed immediately.	Sun, 79° F., exposed after 30 minutes.[3]	Sun, 80° F., exposed after 1 hour.[3]	Sun, 84° F., exposed after 2 hours.[3]	Sun, 88° F., exposed after 3 hours.[3]
2	2	5	4	4	3	2

[1] Equal to sun temperature throughout the day.
[2] Temperature held at 85°–91° F. all day.
[3] Plants removed from fumigatorium to shade (temperature approximately 70° F.) until placed in sunshine. Maximum sun temperature 94° F. at 1 p. m.

EXPERIMENT 21.

Condition during fumigation, dark, 58°–60° F.
Condition before fumigation, shade 60° F.
Dosage, 1½ ounces KCN.
Date, March 21, 1915, 8–9 a. m.
Plants in each test, 3; total, 27.
Remarks: Plants were in a somewhat resistant condition.

Results.

Condition after fumigation.								
Shade, 64° F.[1]	Shade, 90°–97° F.[2]	Sun, 77° F., exposed at once.[3]	Sun, 77° F., exposed after 5 minutes.[3]	Sun, 77° F., exposed after 15 minutes.[3]	Sun, 79° F., exposed after 30 minutes.[3]	Sun, 79° F., exposed after 1 hour.[2]	Sun, 82° F., exposed after 2 hours.[3]	Sun, 84° F., exposed after 4 hours.[3]
1	4	4	4	4	4	4	1	1

[1] Temperature 64°–70° F. all day.
[2] Temperature fluctuated 90°–97° F. all day.
[3] Plants held in shade at 61°–62° F. between time of removal from fumigatorium and placement in sunshine. Maximum sun temperature 85° F. at 1 p. m.

EXPERIMENT 22.

Condition during fumigation, shade, 58° F.
Condition before fumigation, shade, 59° F.
Dosage, 1¼ ounces KCN.
Date, March 30, 1916, 8.15–9.05 a. m.
Plants in each test, 3; total, 18.
Remarks: Plants in a slightly resistant condition. Maximum sun temperature 76° F. Plants were removed from fumigatorium to cool shade for the period elapsing before placement into sunshine.

Results.

	Condition after fumigation.					
Shade, 60° F.	Sun, 66° F., exposed at once.	Sun, 67° F., exposed after 30 minutes.	Sun, 68° F., exposed after 1 hour.	Sun, 72° F., exposed after 2 hours.	Sun, 74° F., exposed after 3 hours.	
1	4	3	3	3	2	

EXPERIMENT 23.

Condition during fumigation, shade, 65° F.
Condition before fumigation, shade, 68° F.
Dosage, 1¼ ounces KCN.
Date, March 30, 1916, 12.03–12.53 p. m.
Plants in each test, 3; total, 18.
Remarks: Plants in a slightly resistant condition. They were removed from fumigatorium to cool shade for period elapsing before placement into sunshine. Maximum sun temperature, 76° F.

Results.

	Condition after fumigation.					
Shade, 71° F.	Sun, 76° F., exposed at once.	Sun, 77° F., exposed after 30 minutes.	Sun, 76° F., exposed after 1 hour.	Sun, 74° F., exposed after 2 hours.	Sun, 71° F., exposed after 3 hours.	
1	4	3	3	2	1	

In each of these four experiments all plants were removed from the fumigatorium immediately after exposure, part being placed at once in the sun while the remainder were held in the shade. Those plants which were exposed to the sunshine at different periods following fumigation were held in the shade at a cool temperature (60° to 70° F.) between the time of their removal from the fumigatorium and placement in the sunshine. Some plants were held continuously in the shade at certain temperatures as a check on the injury attributable to direct sunshine.

It is seen by an examination of experiment 20 that the dosage used merely injured the very tenderest growth where plants were placed under shade temperatures of 79° and 90° F. immediately after the exposure, although plants exposed to the sunshine (76° F.) at the same time had almost all foliage, both tender and resistant, destroyed. Plants held in the shade for 30 minutes and one hour, respectively, after treatment and then subjected to sunshine at temperatures of 79° and 80° F. were about equally affected and this amounted to having a large part of the old resistant foliage destroyed. The injury, however, was noticeably less than where the plants had been exposed immediately after the treatment. Plants withheld for a period of two hours before placement in the direct sunshine had the tender growth destroyed and a few old leaves slightly affected, while plants held three hours before placement in the sunshine were no more

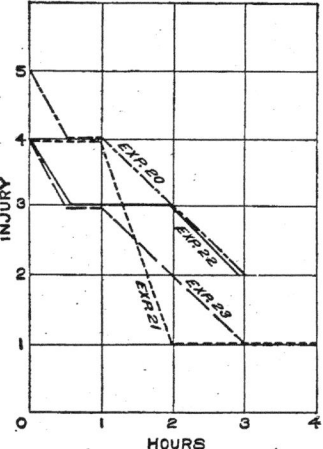

FIG. 1.—Graph showing relation of plant injury to exposure to sunshine at different periods after fumigation.

injured than those placed in the shade, only the tenderest growth being burned in either case.

The results of this experiment are fully corroborated by both experiments 22 and 23, and in part by experiment 21. In number 21, however, although the results agree with those in the other three experiments in showing that sunshine increases the toxic action of hydrocyanic-acid gas to the plant for a period of fully one hour after exposure, it differs somewhat in that the full effect of the sun is shown for one hour after which its influence quickly disappears.

The evidence presented in these four experiments shows that sunshine affects the degree of injury to fumigated citrus trees usually for a period of at least two hours after treatment where dosages equivalent to those used in these experiments are given to growing plants; that the greatest injury follows exposure to sunshine imme-

diately or within a few minutes after the fumigation; that the influence of sunshine which first reaches plants 30 minutes after treatment
is practically the same as that of sunshine which first reaches the
plants one hour after fumigation, and in all cases is severe; that the
effect when plants are withheld for three hours before exposure to
sunshine is seldom greater than where they are kept in the shade or
in darkness at equal temperatures; in short, that sunshine appears
to affect fumigated plants little or not at all at periods exceeding
three hours after treatment.

THE EFFECT ON PLANT INJURY OF TEMPERATURE, LIGHT, AND MOISTURE DURING FUMIGATION.

The effect of certain weather conditions during the period when
plants are actually exposed to hydrocyanic acid is brought out
clearly in experiments 1 to 27.

DARKNESS AND SHADE.

The comparative influence on plant injury of shade to darkness
during fumigation is shown by certain experiments, of which numbers 10 and 16 are especially representative. In these experiments
are found practically identical prefumigation and postfumigation
conditions, and the actual fumigation environments differ only in
that No. 10 was performed in the dark while No. 16 was carried on
in diffused light. The results of these experiments indicate no difference in degree of injury between plants fumigated in the shade and
those fumigated in darkness. Experiments 5 and 17 contain a series
of plants which present results corroborating those shown in experiments 10 and 16. A careful comparison of other experiments given
in this paper supports the conclusion that citrus plants are as safely
fumigated in diffused light as in total darkness.

SUNSHINE.

No experiments were performed in which plants were exposed to
sunshine during treatment, but in consideration of the results previously shown where plants exposed to the sunshine immediately
after fumigation developed very much more severe injury than
others in the shade or dark at equal temperatures, it would appear
that at least equally severe injury would develop from sunshine during the actual treatment. Factors which bring about injury from
exposure to sunshine after fumigation would appear to be present
in at least equal force in exposure to sunshine during actual
treatment. Sunshine exposure during actual treatment would be
possible only under glass, and in such cases would be accompanied
by a temperature greater than that of the outside air.

MOISTURE.

Experiments 4, 6 to 9, and 11, were performed with both dry and wet plants. A comparison of results of these experiments has been presented under the paragraph treating on prefumigation influences. It was found that moisture on plants in prefumigation shade or darkness in no way affects the results where the fumigation is performed in shade or darkness. However, where plants were in sunshine before fumigation it appeared that a wetting with cool water tended to reduce the injury below that normal to dry plants.

TEMPERATURE.

Temperature is a factor of much concern during actual fumigation, and has already been discussed in this paper. Its influence is so modified by the prefumigation and postfumigation temperature and light conditions that it is necessary to pay full attention to these two latter environments in determining the temperature of safety during actual gas exposure. The experiments included in this paper in which plants were at no time exposed to the sunshine, and in which the prefumigation and postfumigation temperatures were within the range of optimum heat conditions, exhibited very little injury where plants were fumigated at temperatures below 80° F. In some experiments in which the temperature of fumigation exceeded 80° the injury appeared to be little if any more severe than at lower temperatures of fumigation, provided the prefumigation and postfumigation temperatures were both low; in other experiments the injury appeared to be greater at the higher temperatures of treatment. When, however, either the prefumigation or more especially the postfumigation temperature was high as well as the actual fumigation temperature the injury was, in general, noticeably more severe than at cooler temperatures. This is well illustrated by a comparison of experiment 1 with either experiment 14 or 15. Unfortunately none of the experiments performed at temperatures exceeding 80° F. were held at a uniform heat throughout the exposure, but the temperature fluctuated at least several degrees after the plants were inclosed in the fumigatorium. This condition introduces a secondary factor which must be taken into consideration in drawing conclusions as to the effect of high temperatures on plant injury.

It appears from a comparative study of the experiments in this paper that severe injury is most noticeable where any two or all three of the fumigation environments, prefumigation, fumigation, and postfumigation, are at high temperatures. In short, if the actual fumigation temperature is high, a minimum of injury is likely to follow if both the other environments are cool. If, however, either the prefumigation or more especially the postfumigation temperature is also high, much more severe injury is likely to result. The evidence presented in experiments 1 to 27 appears to indicate that the greatest safety demands fumigation at temperatures below 80° F., unless the dosage is weak or the exposure short, and this condition has been corroborated by experiments in orchard treatment.

SUDDEN CHANGES IN TEMPERATURE DURING FUMIGATION.

The following four experiments, when viewed in the light of data given in the preceding experiments, show the effect of a sudden increase in temperature immediately before or during the first few minutes of exposure and followed by a fluctuation of several degrees during the remainder of the treatment. The actual temperature during the gas treatment in the first three experiments was 86° F. or above, while in experiment 27 it was cool, ranging from 61° to 70° F.

EXPERIMENT 24.

Condition during fumigation, dark, 86°–92° F.
Condition before fumigation, dark, 64° F.
Dosage, 1 ounce NaCN.
Date, September 23, 1915, 6.10–6.50 a. m.
Plants in each test, 4; total, 20.
Remarks: Temperature of fumigatorium was raised from 64° to 92° F. immediately before fumigation and held at 86°–92° F. throughout the exposure. Maximum temperature for day, 93° F. at 2 p. m.

Results.

Condition after fumigation.				
Dark, 65° F.	Shade, 67° F.	Dark, 73° F.	Shade, 73° F.	Sun, 73° F.
4	4	4	4	5

EXPERIMENT 25.

Condition during fumigation, shade, 86°–92° F.
Condition before fumigation, dark, 65° F.
Dosage, 1 ounce NaCN.
Date, September 23, 1915, 7.10–7.50 a. m.
Plants in each test, 4; total, 20.
Remarks: Temperature of fumigatorium was raised from 73° to 92° F. immediately before fumigation and held at 86° to 92° F. throughout exposure. Maximum sun temperature for day, 93° F. at 2 p. m.

Results.

Condition after fumigation.				
Dark, 65° F.	Shade, 67° F.	Dark, 75° F.	Shade, 75° F.	Sun, 75° F.
4	4	4	4	5

EXPERIMENT 26.

Condition during fumigation, shade, 86°–91° F.

Dosage, 1½ ounces KCN.

Date, March 18, 1915, 2.05–3.05 p. m.

Plants in each test, 2; total, 20.

Remarks: Temperature of fumigatorium was raised from about 75° to 91° F. immediately before fumigation and maintained at temperature of 86°–91° F. throughout the treatment.

Results.

Condition before fumigation.	Condition after fumigation.				
	Dark, 63° F.	Shade, 65° F.	Dark, 91° F.	Shade, 95° F.	Sun, 74° F.
Dark, 63° F...	4	4	4	4	4
Sun, 77° F...	4	4	4	4	5

EXPERIMENT 27.

Condition during fumigation, shade, 61°–70° F.

Condition before fumigation, shade, 54° F.

Dosage, 1¼ ounces KCN.

Date, March 30, 1916, 7.12–8.02 a. m.

Plants in each test, 6; total, 12.

Remarks: Temperature of fumigatorium was raised from 54° to 70° F. during application of gas and was held at a fluctuating temperature of 61°–70° F. during treatment. Rise in temperature was accomplished in 2 to 4 minutes.

Results.

Condition after fumigation.	
Shade, 57° F.	Sun, 61° F.
5	5

RESULTS.

The experimental evidence presented in this paper indicates that for citrus trees the safest temperatures surrounding fumigation fall below 80° F. Yet in experiment 27, in which the temperature at no time departed from this optimum, the plants were almost defoliated. Experiments 3 and 8 were conducted with equally tender plants, with the same dosage, with the same exposure in one case though a little less in the other, and at comparable prefumigation and postfumigation temperatures, yet the plants in these two experiments had merely the tender growth burned. A detailed comparison of experiments 3 and 27, however, shows a difference in temperature fluctuations during the exposure to gas, it appearing that experiment 3 was performed at a constant temperature of 57° to 58° F., whereas in experiment 27 the temperature was suddenly raised during the initial exposure to the gas from 54° to 70° F., a rise of 16°, and fluctuated within the range of 61° to 70° F. during the exposure. It would appear that the shock to the plant resulting from this sudden rise in temperature during the gas exposure accounts for the greatly increased injury in experiment 27 over that in experiment 3 or experiment 8.

The effect of a sudden rise of temperature is also shown in experiments 24, 25, and 26, all of which were performed at temperatures ranging from 86° to 92° F., which are much higher than that of experiment 27. An examination of experiment 25, in which the prefumigation temperature was 65° F. and in which part of the postfumigation conditions were equally favorable, shows that the injury is very severe irrespective of prefumigation or postfumigation environment, in all cases a large proportion of the most resistant leaves being destroyed. The degree of plant injury was much greater than that in experiments 14 and 18, which were performed at equally high temperatures with the same dosage and exposure. In experiment 25 the temperature was quickly raised 19°, from 73° to 92° F., immediately before generating the gas, and was maintained between 86° and 92° F. throughout the treatment. This sudden rise in temperature, supplemented by fluctuation during the exposure, appears to be the cause of abnormally severe plant injury. The results in experiments 24 and 26 are in full accord with that in experiment 25, and corroborate the influence of a sudden rise of temperature immediately before and during the exposure of plants to hydrocyanic-acid gas.

Experiments 14, 15, and 18 also fall within the class of tests in which the temperature was raised during the exposure of plants to the gas. The injury in these experiments is comparatively less than in Nos. 24 to 27.

An examination of the data presented in this paper shows that all experiments performed at high temperatures (above 85° F.) indicate a greater degree of injury, in general, than where plants are treated at cooler temperatures. In each of these experiments the high temperatures were attained by increasing the heat artificially during the gas exposure. These sudden increases in temperature during the fumigation exposure varied from 10° in experiment 14 to a maximum of 28° in experiment 24. Furthermore, after increase to the maximum temperature, fluctuations took place during the actual gas exposure ranging from 2° in experiment 14 to 10° in experiment 27. This condition of sudden rise in temperature, especially when accompanied by wide fluctuation during the exposure, appears to exert a highly injurious influence on the plant. Where the rise of temperature was only 10° to 14°, as in experiments 14 and 18, and was held during the exposure with slight fluctuations of 2° to 4°, the injury was not especially severe; where, however, the sudden increase was over a wider range, as in experiments 24 to 27, of from 16° to 28° and accompanied by fluctuation in temperature of 5° to 10°, the injury was most severe.

These data are of importance in showing that sudden and wide fluctuations of temperature during the gas exposure should be avoided where possible. Such fluctuations appear to be damaging to plants even where the ranges of temperatures of exposure fall below 70° F., which is considered within the range of optimum for field fumigation.

GENERAL DISCUSSION OF FACTORS WHICH INFLUENCE FUMIGATION INJURY.

Evidence has been presented in the foregoing experiments bearing on the relation of darkness, diffused light, sunshine, temperature, and moisture to foliage injury during the fumigation of citrus trees. Abundant additional data have accumulated during field and laboratory experiments to offer further corroboration of the deductions made from these experiments. The effect of hydrocyanic acid on fruit was not taken up in connection with this series of laboratory experiments, but a very large amount of data on this subject has been taken during field experimentation.

In the fumigation of citrus trees injury to fruit and injury to foliage should be considered separately. The fruit has been observed to be severely injured without the foliage being burned in the least, while on the other hand trees have been noted as defoliated although the fruit was entirely uninjured. Several different types of injury are presented in the fruit and foliage of fumigated citrus trees. These types, though somewhat related in the case of either the fruit or the foliage, are sufficiently distinct to be easily detected.

Foliage injury is properly characterized by discoloration or burning, and is usually accompanied by the shedding of leaves which vary in appearance from those completely burned to others free from defacement of tissue. The tender expanding leaves of very tender succulent stems usually show the first signs of fumigation injury, and this is not localized at any particular place, but sometimes occurs at the edge and sometimes in the body of the leaf. These affected areas are frequently confined to one surface of the leaf though more commonly the injury is equally apparent on both surfaces. As the degree of injury increases the entire tender tips are affected, this at first being evidenced by wilting and finally by death. The length of time following fumigation before tip injury appears depends upon the tenderness of the tip, the concentration of the gas, and such factors as temperature and sunshine conditions surrounding the fumigation. The tender foliage of plants placed in bright sunshine immediately after treatment with a strong dosage may start wilting or discoloration within 2 to 3 hours after the exposure. However, like plants fumigated under like conditions but placed afterwards in the shade or darkness at a cool temperature might not show injury for at least a half day. As a general rule, evidence of injury to active citrus trees unexposed to the direct sunshine for at least several hours after the treatment develops within 24 hours, though the severity of injury may not become fully apparent for 2 or 3 days. Where plants are hardened or dormant at time of fumigation a much longer period is covered before the effects of treatment are definitely exhibited.

Burning of the tender, fully expanded leaves in which the cuticular layer has not yet become fully matured requires a slightly stronger gas than to produce tip injury. As the expanded leaf matures greater resistance to the gas develops. The injury to leaves as observable by defaced tissue may be confined to small distinct areas, sometimes in the case of very tender growth not larger than the head of a pin, or in other cases may include the whole of a leaf. Severely injured leaves drop within a few days to several weeks after treatment, but the shedding of foliage having little or no defacement of tissue is indeterminable because such foliage, especially in the case of mature leaves, might be and apparently is greatly affected physiologically even when little or no superficial evidence is presented previous to the actual abscission. The abscission usually occurs at the base of the blade (Pl. IV, B, b) rather than the base of the petiole, but later this also falls.

In any examination into the causes producing plant injury from fumigation with hydrocyanic-acid gas at least four distinct conditions, each of which contributes toward modifying the result, must be considered. These are: (1) The concentration of the gas; (2) the length of exposure; (3) the physiological condition of the plant; (4) atmospheric conditions.

THE CONCENTRATION OF THE GAS.

The modifying influence of gas concentration on plant injury has already been briefly mentioned in this paper. It has been found in experimental work that under the most favorable conditions of treatment fully one-half ounce of high-grade sodium cyanid to 100 cubic feet of space in an air-tight fumigatorium is required to produce injury to normal healthy citrus plants, and dosages in excess of this amount were used in experiments 1 to 27. In orchard work fruit or foliage injury seldom results unless upward of 50 per cent strength of the full dosage schedule recommended by this department and followed in commercial fumigation in California is used. As the gas concentration increases above the strength required to produce initial injury the effect on the plant becomes increasingly severe. In extreme cases the entire plant may be killed, but this result with

·FUMIGATION OF CITRUS PLANTS WITH HYDROCYANIC ACID.

A Valencia orange tree fumigated six months after the trunk and main branches had been painted with Bordeaux paste.   All the foliage was burned and the fruit ultimately dropped.

FUMIGATION OF CITRUS PLANTS WITH HYDROCYANIC ACID.

A, B, Fumigation injury to foliage at point of infestation with purple scale (*Lepidosaphes beckii*). The injury appeared most prominent on the side of the leaf opposite the infestation. *A*, Upper side of leaf, showing purple scale. *B*, Lower side of same leaf, showing collapsed tissue opposite scale infestation. *C*, An immature Valencia orange injured by exposure to sunshine following fumigation. The uninjured area was shaded by leaves. *D*, Twig from a fumigated tree, showing how the leaves are abscissed at the base of the blade, leaving the petioles clinging to the tree.

citrus trees is seldom experienced, so extended is the range between initial injury and death.

It has been shown by the author (21) that the distribution of gas beneath the tent is modified by the method of application; that in pot-generated gas the greatest concentration is toward the top of the tree, whereas in the case of gas generated from liquid hydrocyanic acid the concentration is greatest toward the bottom of the tree. Correspondingly the injury in the case of pot or machine generated gas is most marked toward the top of citrus trees fumigated after this method; whereas, when liquid hydrocyanic acid is used, the tendency is for greater injury toward the bottom.

THE LENGTH OF EXPOSURE.

Variations in the length of exposure very naturally modify the effect of the gas on the plant, as early pointed out by Woods and Dorsett (22), and recently clearly presented by Fernald, Tower, and Hooker (5) in experiments with tomatoes and cucumbers. These latter writers performed experiments in which plants were entirely uninjured when exposed to a certain dosage for 10 minutes but when exposed to the same dosage for 2 hours the plants were killed. The writer has performed many similar experiments with citrus trees and reached the conclusion that for these plants very heavy dosages may be safely used with exposure periods up to 20 or 25 minutes' duration, but where the period of exposure approaches or exceeds 40 minutes the injury is decidedly increased.

Whereas short exposures to hydrocyanic acid have very little deleterious effect on plants, a correspondingly less destructive action to insects occurs with short exposures than with long exposures. In the commercial fumigation of citrus trees for scale insects the normal exposure ranges from 40 minutes to 1 hour. Results under shorter exposures with the dosages used have not proved entirely satisfactory from the standpoint of killing the scales. Experiments by the writer have shown that satisfactory results can be secured with shorter exposures if an increased dosage is used. If, however, the exposure with these increased dosages is greatly extended more injury results. Since commercial outfits consist of from 30 to 100 tents, their movements under all conditions within fixed periods of less than 40 minutes is scarcely practicable. At the present time it is not uncommon for large outfits operating on the basis of an hour's exposure to require 1½ hours for shifts or throws with damp tents on large trees. Thus commercial orchard fumigation appears to resolve itself into using dosages which will not injure trees even when the length of exposure slightly exceeds an hour. An outfit consisting of such a few tents that they would be operated unfailingly within short periods could undoubtedly fumigate successfully with greater dosages and shorter exposures than are now common to the practice.

THE PHYSIOLOGICAL CONDITION OF THE PLANT.

The influence of the physiological condition of the plant on injury has until recently received scant attention by writers on fumigation. It is evident that plant injury from hydrocyanic acid is influenced by the chemical condition of the cells at the time of treatment, for otherwise how could the fact, well known to every fumigator, be explained that tender growing citrus plants are less resistant to gas than those in a dormant and hardened condition, as during the winter. This is equally true with the young leaves as with the mature ones, which indicates that in becoming resistant young growth passes some sort of maturation process. In fact it appears that the condition of citrus plants which renders them hardy or resistant to frost injury likewise develops increased resistance to hydrocyanic acid.

Harvey (8) has shown that in the case of cabbage the hardening process results in an increase in the glucose and sucrose content over that present in nonhardened plants and quotes Lidforss as authority for the statement that this is a common transformation in plants generally during the cold season. Chemical changes increasing or reducing the percentage of other substances are also shown to be a result of hardening tissues. It is further stated that the hardening of plants which results in an increase in the cell-sap concentration is an accommodation brought about by low temperature. Plants can also be rendered resistant by growth in a dry soil.

Stone (18), working with cucumber plants grown under different light and soil-moisture conditions, showed that the development of tissue is influenced by these factors as well as their susceptibility to burning with hydrocyanic acid. The weaker tissue produced by inferior light or excessive moisture was decidedly more injured than that grown under full light conditions or in dry soil.

More recently Clayton (1) experimented with tomato plants and similarly observed that resistance to hydrocyanic-acid gas was modified by the conditions under which the plants were grown. Slow-growing plants with a high chlorophyll content per unit area were found to be more resistant to hydrocyanic acid than plants grown rapidly with low chlorophyll content per unit area; and his conclusions that the water supply was the underlying cause of these differences is in full accord with the prior work of Stone. Chemical examination of the two sets of plants gave results in agreement with those of Harvey (8) and others for hardened and nonhardened or actively growing plants, that the more resistant forms have greatly increased carbohydrate content, especially of the reducing sugar calculated as dextrose. Experiments conducted by this writer with plants infiltrated with dextrose showed that resistance to hydrocyanic-acid gas was developed by this procedure and the conclusion was reached that glucose in a plant acts as a protective agent against injury by cyanid.

· This important conclusion offers a possible explanation of certain features which the writer has observed in connection with orchard fumigation, namely, the greater resistance of the blossom growth than that of the leaf growth appearing at the same time on the same tree; the greater resistance of this first leaf growth in the winter or spring than that which develops during the hot summer months; the greater resistance of the ripening orange than that of immature fruit.

That chemicals in the cell sap other than reducing sugars can modify injury is strikingly brought out in the case of citrus trees sprayed with Bordeaux mixture or where trunks and main branches have been painted with Bordeaux paste a short time before fumigation with heavy dosages. This damage attributable to Bordeaux applications is evidenced by burning of the foliage and fruit. Plate III shows the severity of injury that frequently follows the fumigation of a tree whose branches and trunk were previously Bordeaux painted. Since the foliage and fruit of this tree were not touched by the Bordeaux paste, but only the branches and trunk, it is evident that certain elements of the fungicide must have been taken into the cell sap and transported to the fruit and foliage which was so severely injured. Proof of this contention has been seen in the extraction of traces of copper from the foliage of such treated trees by Mr. H. D. Young,[1] while chemist of the Citrus Experiment Station at Whittier, Calif. It would thus appear probable that the injury, at least in part, was due to reaction of the cyanid gas on the copper for which it has a great affinity.

It has been observed by the writer (20) that fruit injury from fumigation often occurs at places of weakness in the epidermis and that such a condition is sometimes the result of insect action. Plate IV, A, shows that insects can likewise influence injury to leaves by feeding. In this particular case it is of great interest to note that the injury is most apparent at the leaf surface opposite to that on which the insects rest.

It has been pointed out by different authors that the moisture conditions surrounding growing plants influence their development and their susceptibility to injury from hydrocyanic-acid gas, those growing under moist conditions being less resistant to gas than those growing under dry; in short, that dry soil induces gas-resistant plants. Studies made by the writer in the case of field-grown citrus trees appear in general to support this theory. A large lemon orchard, through which a deep, narrow swale extended, was fumigated in November, 1918. At the time of treatment the soil in this swale was moist and had been in this condition at least since the previous irrigation six weeks before. The soil on the upper slopes was very dry. The tents were pulled in a straight string which extended down the slope on

---

[1] From unpublished results.

across the swale and up on the other side. The three or four trees of each row which were in the damp soil of the swale were severely injured, whereas the trees in the dry soil of the upper slope were entirely uninjured. In another case a 16-acre orchard on heavy soil had been abundantly irrigated twice during the month prior to fumigation and was very moist at the time of fumigation. This orchard was severely injured throughout, whereas an adjacent orchard of the same soil type which had been without irrigation for so long that the soil was dry and the foliage of a hardened appearance at the time of treatment showed very little injury to any trees. Many similar instances of greater injury on damp soil have been noted.

The mere wetness of the soil does not in itself offer full explanation of plant injury due to this factor. For instance, the writer has conducted fumigation of orchard trees immediately following a heavy rain with no more injury than to trees in dry soil. Likewise fumigation frequently follows immediately after an irrigation without noticeable damage to the trees. The writer's own observation inclines him to believe that the greater injury to citrus trees in wet soil is induced especially after the plants have been subjected to a very moist condition for a sufficiently long period to set in action forces which change the general metabolism of the plant and result in foliage or fruit so constituted as to be less resistant to hydrocyanic acid. Support to this is presented by the work of Fowler and Lipman (6) on the effect of soil moisture on young lemon trees. These writers concluded that soil moisture in excess of the optimum leads to depressed growth, light colored foliage, and general lack of vigor, the visible damage being greater than if the moisture condition is below the optimum. Of further interest is the statement of Pfeffer (15) that the supply of water affects the formation of cuticle. Although a dry soil tends to slacken growth and hasten maturity of plants, thereby rendering them more resistant to hydrocyanic acid, it has been observed that protracted situation in soil so deficient in moisture that the plant suffers ultimately leads to a physiologically weakened condition. It has been stated elsewhere in this paper that plants in a state of impaired health are more susceptible to injury than normal healthy plants.

The soil type also appears so to influence the physiological condition of the tree that modified reaction to hydrocyanic acid sometimes occurs. A 30-acre lemon orchard which was fumigated experimentally in 1918 was about equally divided between two distinct soil types, one a loam designated as a "barren" soil, the other black adobe which contained about 10 per cent humus. Injury occurred throughout this orchard but the degree was noticeably greater on the loam than on the black adobe. Other instances of injury due to different soil types have been noted. Groups of trees whose growth has not kept pace with the rest of an orchard, due possibly to inferior subsoil, to hardpan, gravel, etc., are not uncommon. Trees under such adverse conditions have sometimes been noted to be more adversely affected by fumigation than healthier trees.

. The general conclusion to be drawn from this discussion is that plants best resist cyanid gas if in a hardened or dormant condition at the time of fumigation. Hardening is brought about either by cold weather or a dry soil. From the standpoint of the action of cold, plants are most matured or dormant during the winter season and at this time least injury from fumigation is to be expected. Since citrus is mostly grown in countries that practice irrigation, the dryness of the soil can be regulated by regulating irrigation. Therefore, as a general rule, fumigation should precede the run of water rather than follow, as is frequently the practice at the present time.

ATMOSPHERIC AND LIGHT CONDITIONS.

DARKNESS AND DIFFUSED LIGHT.

Experimental evidence presented in this paper has shown that diffused light before, during, or after fumigation in no way modifies the degree of injury to citrus trees. Since the active stomata of citrus plants open during the daytime and for the most part remain closed at night it is evident that the condition of the stomata does not noticeably alter the degree of injury from fumigation. Such a conclusion is not fully in accord with the statement of Clayton that "the stomata seem to be the most important single factor in determining the amount of injury resulting from hydrocyanic acid * * *. Injury closely paralleled the stomatal movement, increasing as the size of stomatal aperture increased."

These differences in results are readily explained in the light of the work of Stone (18) and Moore (11). The former states that the condition of the stomata does not appear to have anything to do with susceptibility to burning from fumigation but the injury is due rather to the development of the cuticle and texture of the tissue in general; that tender immature tissue is least resistant to fumigation injury. Moore has shown that hydrocyanic acid enters plants to a greater or less extent through the cuticle and that those with thin cuticles are far more severely injured than those with thick, strongly cutinized cuticles. Geranium, Tradescantia, and tomatoes, the plants with which Clayton worked, have very thin cuticles and were injured with a concentration of gas at the rate of approximately $\frac{1}{15}$ ounce of potassium cyanid to 100 cubic feet. The smallest dosage used in the writer's experiments with the thicker and more heavily cutinized citrus plants was 1 ounce of potassium cyanid to 100 cubic feet.

This shows the comparative resistance of the two types of leaves. Mature citrus leaves are so resistant to cyanid that it appears that the concentration needed to produce injury is so great that the gas penetrates the tissues whether the stomata are open or closed, and the amount which enters while the stomata are open over that entering while closed [1] is insufficient to modify to any great extent the degree of injury. Of particular interest in this connection are the observations of Coit and Hodgson (2) that early in the life of the leaf the stomata lose their power of opening and closing and remain for the most part practically closed thereafter. On the other hand, such tender plants as Tradescantia react to such small amounts of cyanid that the stomata seem able to exercise an influence on the passage of gas sufficient to modify the effect on the plant.

SUNSHINE.

The earliest fumigation of citrus trees was performed during the daytime and accompanied by much injury. Coquillett (3) offered as an explanation of this result that "in the daytime the light and heat decompose the gas," the assumption being that the products of decomposition are more injurious than the hydrocyanic acid gas itself. In an effort to correct the action of sunlight blackened tents were used but without marked success. The final solution was night fumigation. American writers on fumigation who have experimented with sunshine work have been unanimous in proclaiming its impracticability as a general practice.

The results of the many experiments presented in this paper show that sunshine is one of the most important factors influencing injury and that its effects are not confined solely to the period of exposure, but are also exerted immediately before and immediately after the treatment. The postfumigation influence appears to be somewhat greater than the prefumigation influence and its effects are sometimes so injurious as to discolor fruit (Pl. IV, B, a) and destroy the foliage of plants which, if protected from the direct sun, would have been but slightly affected (Pl. I, B). This action on the foliage is most conspicuous through burning which, if including the entire petiole as well as the blade, results in the destroyed foliage clinging to the tree until exfoliation takes place by mechanical means. (Pl. II, B.) This postfumigation sunshine influence in such experiments as No. 10, in which plants in the dark were fumigated in the dark and placed in the sunshine with the result of severe injury, would appear to disprove Coquillett's explanation of decomposition of the gas, for in this case the sunshine did not reach the plants until they had been removed from the fumigatorium.

---

[1] According to MacDougal (10) stomata do not close their pores so tightly that some gaseous diffusion may not take place through their diminished opening.

Temperature has a very direct relation to sunshine influence, and the degree of injury appears to be increased or decreased as the temperature of the sunshine is greater or less. Furthermore, where plants are subjected to sunshine immediately before treatment, the actual fumigation and postfumigation temperatures influence the degree of injury. Likewise in the case of plants exposed to sunshine immediately after treatment, the prefumigation and actual fumigation temperatures require consideration. The writer's own experimental evidence shows that the optimum temperatures of fumigation are below 80° F., and that work conducted at higher temperatures is performed with increased risk. The greatest injury follows the subjection of plants to both sunshine and high temperatures both before and after fumigation. The effect of this combination, sunshine and temperature, has long influenced the time of starting orchard work in California. The fumigation season begins in the summer and extends throughout the autumn into the winter. During the warmest weather work is not started until the sun has set, but with the advent of the late autumn and cooler temperatures the first row of trees is sometimes covered before sundown, and in the winter period of dormancy entire rows are treated in the sunlight. During very hot weather, when the atmosphere is clear and dry, injury to the first row fumigated at night and the last in the morning has been of frequent occurrence and in the latter case has been observed to occur even when the tents were removed from the trees before sunrise. Full explanation of this situation is presented in the results of experiments 20 to 23 which show that the postfumigation sunshine influence may extend up to three hours after exposure, although the maximum of influence is confined to the first few minutes after removal from the gas.

In spite of the fact that sunshine has from the first been considered one of the most harmful agents to plants in connection with fumigation, the greater desirability of daylight work has led to continued attempts to substitute day practice for that at night. These efforts to revolutionize accustomed practice usually were made during the winter months, and frequently successfully over short periods if the weather was moderate and the trees well hardened. Sooner or later, however, this attempt to fumigate by day without modification of dosage or exposure was followed by severe tree damage and was promptly discontinued.

It has been explained previously that cyanid injury is modified by the concentration of the gas and by the length of exposure. Therefore it is reasonable to assume that either of these factors can be so reduced as to render fumigation safe on the hottest sunshiny day. Orchard work is performed with a concentrated gas, usually as concentrated as an active tree will stand safely during cool nights. In the light of the experiments presented in this paper it is to be expected that the use of such dosages during warm sunshine would cause severe injury. Experiment 3 shows that by reducing the strength of the gas the influence of the sunshine is correspondingly reduced. One orchardist known to the writer has practiced daylight fumigation on his small lemon orchard during the growing season for several years, accomplishing his purpose through reduction of both dosage and exposure. He was observed on one occasion to fumigate lemon trees safely at a temperature of 84° to 86° F. by using a dosage calculated as less than one-half the usual dosage, with an exposure of 30 minutes. The effect on the scale was not noted.

Since liquid hydrocyanic acid has come to be used in fumigation, daylight practice is no longer considered a dangerous experiment. During the winter months outfits operate throughout the daytime in bright sunshine, in many cases with complete safety, and under conditions which in the past with pot or machine generated gas were wont to produce severe injury. Outside of possible differences in physical properties of the gas due to the method of generation and application, the one most plausible reason for the increased safety of daylight operation is the difference in diffusion throughout the tree. In pot-generated gas the greatest concentration is toward the tree top, whereas with liquid hydrocyanic acid in warm weather the greatest concentration is toward the bottom of the tree (21). The writer has determined by a series of experiments that the temperature of the tented tree rapidly rises on the sunward side after covering and that the greatest increase is toward the top of the tent. In pot-generated gas the maximum gas concentration, maximum heat, and most sudden change of temperature are exerted at the same place, the top of the tree, whereas in trees fumigated with liquid hydrocyanic acid the greatest concentration of gas at the bottom of the tree is at the coolest part of the sunward side of the tree, while at the top or point of maximum temperature the gas is most dilute. A seeming explanation is presented in the comparative appearance of damaged trees under these two methods of gas application. Sunshine-injured trees from pot-generated gas show the greatest damage on the sunward side toward the top; in the case of trees treated with liquid hydrocyanic acid the damage toward the bottom is greatly increased over that as compared with pot-fumigated trees while that toward the top is lessened.

It was stated in a previous paragraph that the open or closed condition of the stomata does not appear to affect the degree of injury to citrus plants in darkness or diffused light before, during, and after fumigation. In the case of plants subjected to sunshine either immediately before or immediately after exposure to cyanid gas, equally conclusive data bearing on this subject have not been developed. Certain experiments already presented in this paper have shown that plants in a prefumigation and fumigation environment of darkness (indicating closed stomata) were severely injured by placement in sunshine immediately after the exposure, while check plants placed in the shade at an equal temperature were little affected. In these cases the increased damage to the sun-exposed plant was brought about in spite of the fact that the stomata were apparently closed during the fumigation. Furthermore, data have been collected during daylight work, both in the morning and afternoon, showing that trees somewhat protected from the direct sun were little affected by a strength of gas that severely injured trees in the direct sunshine treated at the same time. On the other hand, the increased injury to plants in a prefumigation condition of sunshine, as previously explained, and observation that greater injury is usually apparent during morning orchard fumigation than during that performed late in the afternoon at an equal temperature, might indicate possible stomatal influence when viewed in the light of Lloyd's (9) conclusions that the morning sun may hasten stomatal opening, that this opening is at its maximum toward midday, and that closure occurs during the afternoon.

Stone, Moore, and others conclude that a strong concentration of gas tends to close the stomata. This closure of the stomata from fumigation would reduce the rapidity of the escape of gas which remained in the intercellular spaces after treatment and might thereby modify the degree of injury, especially in plants subjected to such adverse conditions as postfumigation sunshine.

The condition of the soil apparently influences cyanid injury from sunshine, as shown in the case of a 10-acre citrus orchard fumigated during a clear hot day in November, 1919. This orchard was so irrigated that the soil nearest the head of the furrows was thoroughly wet to a normal depth, whereas the soil at the lower end of the furrows was for the most part wet only for a few inches at the surface, or sometimes not at all. The trees reflected this lack of required moisture in their general less healthy appearance. The tents were strung in the direction of the irrigation furrows. Severe injury resulted from the fumigation, amounting almost to complete defoliation on the sunward side of a large part of the trees. This injury was confined almost exclusively to the trees on the dry soil, those on the moist soil being very little affected. The explanation is that the trees which had long suffered from lack of moisture were in a weakened condition at the time of fumigation, whereas the others were not.

TEMPERATURE.

It has been clearly shown by the experimental evidence presented in this paper that temperature exerts one of the most important modifying influences on injury from fumigation. Furthermore, not only must the temperature of treatment be considered, but also the temperature surrounding plants after exposure and to a much less extent that before exposure. It has been shown that high temperatures are more injurious than low, and in the case of each of the three fumigation environments, the prefumigation, actual fumigation, and postfumigation, the maximum optimum fell below 80° F. Exactly how much this maximum for any particular environment fell below 80° F. depended on the temperature of the other two; when any two were low the maximum optimum for the third approximated 80°; when they were high, however, the maximum for the third was a few degrees less than 80°. In one case it did not exceed 75°. These conclusions differ very little from the writer's experience in orchard fumigation in southern California, for which 70° is held as the maximum when a heavy dosage is used. This same maximum is recommended by Sasscer and Borden (16) for greenhouse plants. An interesting relation apparently exists between the maximum optimum temperature for fumigation and the activity of plants, for MacDougal (10) states that temperature is one of the most widely interlocking factors concerned in the activity of protoplasm, and that the temperature of greatest activity in seed plants varies from 80° to 100° F. The experimental work presented in this paper shows increasing fumigation injury as the temperature of 80° is approached or exceeded, which corresponds with the degree at which greatest protoplasmic activity commences.

It is possible to conduct fumigation at temperatures of 80° F. or above without serious injury provided the prefumigation and postfumigation conditions are ideal. A high postfumigation temperature increases the probability of damage, and especially is this true if the fumigation temperature is also above the optimum. The greatest damage follows when all three temperatures surrounding the treatment are high. A prefumigation temperature in shade and darkness, even up to 100° F., appears to alter the results very little unless the fumigation or postfumigation temperature is also high, in which case the high prefumigation temperatures are more injurious than the low. The temperature of 55° F. was the minimum at which experimental work was conducted. The little injury evidenced at this temperature showed it to be within the range of the optimum. In field work it has been stated by the writer (19) that operations are safe as low as 38° F., although fumigation below this point is not advocated.

In experiments 24 to 27 it was shown that a sudden increase in temperature immediately preceding or during the first few minutes of exposure produces very severe injury, especially if followed by sharp fluctuations of temperature. This factor offers a partial explanation for the severe injury in sunshine fumigation on the sunward side of the tree, especially toward the top, and also presents a reason for the less amount of injury in daylight fumigation with liquid hydrocyanic acid. This is shown by Table III, in which are presented data giving the increase in temperature at different parts of a 12-foot tree covered with a canvas tent, December 17, 1919.

TABLE III.—*Rise in temperature at different points within a tented citrus tree in the sunshine at varying periods following the covering. Thermometers placed from 6 to 10 inches from the canvas.*

Minutes after start.	Rise in temperature.[a]		
	Sunward side, 11 feet altitude.	Sunward side, 4 feet altitude.	Shade side, 4 feet altitude.
5	8	3	2
10	16	9	3
15	22	12	5
20	26	12	6

[a] Sun temperature at start, 75° F.; shade temperature, 69° F. Time, 10.43 a. m.

It is shown in this table that an increase of 26° occurred toward the top of the tent on the sunward side within 20 minutes after covering, whereas at the same time on the same side 4 feet from the ground the increase was only 12° and on the shaded side of the tree at the same height only 6°. Injury in daylight work has been observed to be proportionately greater at these different points in the case of pot-generated gas. The lower part of the shaded side of the tree, at which the temperature increase is very slight, is seldom injured even when very severe burning takes place on the sunward side of the tree.

The effect of the temperature is least felt in the case of thoroughly hardened trees. In fact, the extent to which sunshine fumigation can be practiced during the winter period is attributable largely to the extent of this hardened or dormant condition of the trees. This condition also offers an explanation for the safety of fumigation at very low temperatures, sometimes at the freezing point, whereas at other times, especially in the early fall, while trees are active, severe injury takes place at several degrees above the freezing point. In the Tulare County citrus belt of California the writer has noted night fumigation, with heavy dosages, carried on during the summer at temperatures as high as 85° F. without apparent injury to the plants. Fumigation in the coast region of southern California at such high temperatures would produce severe injury. He believes that this greater safety in the northern citrus region is due largely to the more resistant condition of the plants brought about by the very hot, arid climate during the summer. Duggar (4) states that green leaves exposed to sunlight show a temperature from 2° or 3° to 15° higher than the air, and according to MacDougal (10) the maximum temperature of higher plants varies from 100° to 115° F. At or above the maximum protoplasm passes into a state of immobility. Since the maximum daily temperature of the Tulare citrus belt during the summer frequently exceeds 100° F., the mean maximum for the hottest months seldom falling more than 1° to 3° below this temperature, a reason for reduced activity is presented.[2] This condition is doubtless promoted by the usual practice of withholding irrigation until after fumigation. In the more equable, damper climate of the coastal region, where the temperature very seldom attains a maximum of 100° F., but rather approaches the optimum for protoplasmic activity, dormancy during the summer is less noticeable and the physiologically active plants are more subject to fumigation injury.

MOISTURE.

Moisture, even when present in excessive amounts, appears to have no influence on injury to citrus trees either before, during, or after the treatment, under conditions of shade or darkness, and this conclusion agrees with the work of Gossard (7), Morrill (13), and others. Under conditions of exposure to hot sunshine before fumigation the application of cool water appears to reduce the degree of injury slightly. These results on the relation of moisture to the fumigation of citrus trees do not necessarily apply to tender greenhouse plants, for moisture on such plants with thin cuticles has been shown by various authors (11, 18) to produce increased injury. Clayton (1), however, in a recent paper states that some species are made more susceptible to injury by wetting the leaves while other species are not visibly affected. He places the tomato in the latter class although Moore found that wetting tomatoes as well as various other plants with thin cuticle increased their susceptibility to injury.

The influence of soil moisture has been referred to in previous discussions and may be passed with the statement that soil moisture in sufficient quantity to make plants physiologically very active and tender renders plants more susceptible to fumigation injury than where present only in such quantities as place the plants in a resistant or hardened condition.

Hydrocyanic-acid gas has a great affinity for water, and under conditions of excessive moisture sufficient gas might be absorbed to so materially reduce the concentration that less injury would be produced than otherwise, and, furthermore, its insecticidal value would be lessened. Where fumigation is conducted in gas-tight containers this condition can not be ignored, and the necessity of attention thereto has been clearly shown by Penny (14), and Sasscer and Borden (16). In orchard work under cloth tents the absorption of gas by moisture is offset by the greater gas-holding properties of the moist canvas.

---

[2] Taken from published records of the U. S. Weather Bureau, which are lower than orchard sunshine temperatures.

SUMMARY.

(1) It is necessary to consider the prefumigation and postfumigation environments of fumigated plants as well as that during the actual treatment.

(2) Sunshine is the chief prefumigation factor that increases injury and this influence is greater at high temperatures than at low. Under darkness or diffused light, temperatures upward to at least 100° F. do not appear to increase injury unless the fumigation or postfumigation temperatures exceed 80° F.

(3) The environment after fumigation approximates in importance that during the actual treatment. Of the postfumigation factors both sunshine and temperature modify the degree of injury. Sunshine, the more important, is most destructive to plants exposed immediately after fumigation, but affects them deleteriously at least two hours after the treatment. Temperatures of 80° F. or above injure plants more severely than lower temperatures.

(4) The fumigation of citrus plants is most safely performed at temperatures below 80° F.

(5) Diffused light before, during, or after fumigation exerts no more deleterious influence than darkness.

(6) Moisture on citrus plants does not increase the degree of injury. An application of cool water to plants in hot sunshine immediately prior to fumigation appears to reduce slightly the effect of the gas.

(7) Sudden changes of temperature over a wide range during exposure to hydrocyanic-acid gas tend greatly to increase plant injury.

(8) The optimum environment for safety to plants is diffused light or darkness at uniform temperatures below 80° F. before, during, and after the fumigation. The lowest temperature tried, 55° F., was within the range of the optimum.

(9) Fumigation at temperatures upward of 80° F. is safest under cool prefumigation and postfumigation environments. The maximum of injury follows high temperatures for all three environments.

(10) The physical and chemical conditions of the soil influence injury from fumigation. Trees in a wet soil tend to be more severely injured than healthy trees in a dry soil. However, trees in soils deficient in moisture for such protracted periods as to be severely weakened are more susceptible to injury than if grown under optimum moisture conditions. Irrigation should follow fumigation, not precede it.

(11) The physiological condition of plants is one of the most important factors regulating fumigation damage. A condition akin to hardiness appears to be the optimum for gas resistance and is brought about by dryness of the soil, cold weather, and possibly by continued very hot dry weather which exceeds the optimum for the plant.

(12) Sunshine fumigation can be conducted with safety by proper regulation of the dosage and length of exposure.

LITERATURE CITED.

(1) CLAYTON, E. E.
　　　 1919. HYDROGEN CYANIDE FUMIGATION. *In* Bot. Gaz., v. 67, no. 6, p. 483–500, 2 fig. (Literature cited, p. 500.)

(2) CORR, J. E., and HODGSON, R. W.
　　　 1919. AN INVESTIGATION OF THE ABNORMAL SHEDDING OF YOUNG FRUITS OF THE WASHINGTON NAVEL ORANGES. *In* Univ. Cal. Pub., Agr. Sci., v. 3, no. 11, p.283–368, 9 fig., pl. 25–42. (Literature cited, p. 368.)

(3) COQUILLETT, D. W.
　　　 1891. REPORT ON VARIOUS METHODS FOR DESTROYING SCALE INSECTS. THE GAS TREATMENT FOR THE RED SCALE. U. S. Dept. Agr. Div. Ent. Bul. 23 (o. s.), p. 20–27.

(4) DUGGAR, B. M.
　　　 1912. PLANT PHYSIOLOGY. 516 p., illus. New York.

(5) TOWER, W. V., and HOOKER, CHARLES W.
　　　 1910. FUMIGATION DOSAGE. (With introductions by H. T. Fernald.) *In* 22nd Rpt. Mass. Agr. Exp. Sta., pt. 1, p. 214–247.

(6) FOWLER, L. W., and LIPMAN, C. B.
　　　 1917. OPTIMUM MOISTURE CONDITION FOR YOUNG LEMON TREES ON A LOAM SOIL. *In* Univ. Cal. Pub., Agr. Sci., v. 3, no. 2, p. 25–36, pl. 9–11. Sept. 29.

(7) GOSSARD, H. A.
　　　 1903. WHITE FLY (ALEYRODES CITRI). Fla. Agr. Exp. Sta. Bul. 67, p. 599–666, pl. 6.

(8) HARVEY, R. B.
　　　 1918. HARDENING PROCESS IN PLANTS AND DEVELOPMENTS FROM FROST INJURY. *In* Jour. Agr. Research, v. 15, no. 2, p. 83–112, 3 fig., pl. 7–11, A. (Literature cited, p. 108–111.)

(9) LLOYD, F. E.
　　　 1908. THE PHYSIOLOGY OF STOMATA. Carn. Inst. Wash. Pub. 82, 142 p., 14 pl. (Bibliography, p. 141–142.)

(10) MACDOUGAL, D. T.
　　　 1901. PRACTICAL TEXT-BOOK OF PLANT PHYSIOLOGY. 352 p., 159 fig. New York, London, and Bombay.

(11) MOORE, WILLIAM.
　　　 1916. STUDIES IN GREENHOUSE FUMIGATION WITH HYDROCYANIC ACID: TEMPERATURE AND MOISTURE AS FACTORS INFLUENCING THE INJURY OF PLANTS DURING FUMIGATION. *In* 16th Rpt. State Ent. Minn., 1915/16, p. 93–108, fig. 23–27. (Literature cited, p. 108.)

(12) MOORE, WILLIAM, and WILLAMAN, J. J.
　　　 1917. STUDIES IN GREENHOUSE FUMIGATION WITH HYDROCYANIC ACID: PHYSIOLOGICAL EFFECTS ON THE PLANT. *In* Jour. Agr. Research, v. 11, no. 7, p. 319–338, 11 fig., pl. 34. (Literature cited, p. 336–338.)

(13) MORRILL, A. W.
　　　 1908. FUMIGATION FOR THE CITRUS WHITE FLY, AS ADAPTED TO FLORIDA CONDITIONS. U. S. Dept. Agr. Bur. Ent. Bul. 76, p. 73, 11 fig., 7 pl.

(14) PENNY, C. L.
　　　 1900. THE DIFFUSION OF HYDROCYANIC ACID VAPOR IN AN ENCLOSED SPACE. *In* Del. Agr. Exp. Sta. 12th Ann. Rpt., p. 218–235, fig. 2–4.

(15) PFEFFER, WILHELM.
　　　 1903. PHYSIOLOGY OF PLANTS. Ed. 2. Trans. and ed. by A. J. Ewart. v. 2, 296 p., illus. Oxford.

(16) SASSCER, E. R., and BORDEN, A. D.
1917. FUMIGATION OF ORNAMENTAL GREENHOUSE PLANTS WITH HYDRO-
CYANIC-ACID GAS. U. S. Dept. Agr. Bul. 513, 20 p., 3 fig.

(17) SCHROEDER, HEINRICH.
1907. ÜBER DEN EINFLUSS DES CYANKALIUMS AUF DIE ATMUNG VON ASPER-
GILLUS NIGER NEBST BEMERKUNGEN ÜBER DIE MEÇHANIK DER
BLAUSÄURE-WERKUNG. In Jahrb. Wiss. Bot., v. 44, p. 409–481.

(18) STONE, G. E.
1913. THE INFLUENCE OF VARIOUS LIGHT INTENSITIES AND SOIL MOISTURE
ON THE GROWTH OF CUCUMBERS, AND THEIR SUSCEPTIBILITY TO
BURNING FROM HYDROCYANIC-ACID GAS. In Mass. Agr. Exp. Sta.
25th Ann. Rpt., pt. 1, p. 61–72, 2 pl.

(19) WOGLUM, R. S.
1912. HYDROCYANIC-ACID GAS FUMIGATION IN CALIFORNIA: FUMIGATION OF
CITRUS TREES. In U. S. Dept. Agr. Bur. Ent. Bul. 90, pt. 1, p. 1–81,
12 fig., 8 pl.

(20) WOGLUM, R. S.
1915. FRUIT INJURY DURING THE FUMIGATION OF CITRUS FRUIT TREES. In
Proc. 45th Cal. Fr. Growers Conv., p. 190–195.

(21) WOGLUM, R. S.
1919. RECENT RESULTS IN THE FUMIGATION OF CITRUS FRUIT TREES WITH
LIQUID HYDROCYANIC ACID. In Jour. Econ. Ent., v. 12, no. 1,
p. 117–123, pl. 4.

(22) WOODS, A. F., and DORSETT, P. H.
1899. THE USE OF HYDROCYANIC-ACID GAS FOR FUMIGATING GREENHOUSES
AND COLD FRAMES. In U. S. Dept. Agr. Bur. Ent. Circ. 37, 2d ser.

(23) WOODWORTH, C. W.
1915. SCHOOL OF FUMIGATION. 184 p., 44 figs. Pomona, Cal.

ADDITIONAL COPIES
OF THIS PUBLICATION MAY BE PROCURED FROM
THE SUPERINTENDENT OF DOCUMENTS
GOVERNMENT PRINTING OFFICE
WASHINGTON, D. C.
AT
15 CENTS PER COPY
▽

UNITED STATES DEPARTMENT OF AGRICULTURE

BULLETIN No. 908

Contribution from the Bureau of Chemistry
CARL L. ALSBERG, Chief

Washington, D. C.   PROFESSIONAL PAPER   January 18, 1921

THE MAINE SARDINE INDUSTRY.

By F. C. WEBER, *Chemist in Charge*,
With the collaboration of H. W. HOUGHTON and J. B. WILSON, *Assistant Chemists*,
Animal Physiological Chemical Laboratory.

CONTENTS.

	Page.		Page.
Introduction:		Experimental work—Continued.	
The sardine	1	Packing the fish	58
The Maine sardine industry	3	Adding the oil	60
The Maine sardine	4	Processing the sardines	69
Food value of the canned sardine	5	Storing the sardines	70
Purpose of investigation	6	Decomposition of the fish	86
Methods employed in packing sardines	6	Grading the fish	93
Experimental work:		Standardization of the sardine pack	96
Methods of analysis	12	Sanitary precautions in packing sardines	98
Composition of the sea herring	15	Waste in packing sardines:	
Food of the sea herring	17	Elimination of unnecessary waste	102
Swells	20	Utilization of unavoidable waste	109
Transportation of the fish	26	Economic considerations	115
Pickling and salting the fish	34	Summary	121
Flaking the fish	50	Bibliography	125
Drying the fish	51		

INTRODUCTION.

THE SARDINE.

The sardine, popularly regarded as a particular species of fish used for canning, derives its name from the island of Sardinia, in the Mediterranean Sea, where the fish from which the sardines of that region are made abound(27).[1] The term "sardine" is now applied in this country to the small fish of the Clupea family, numerous species of which are canned as sardines in various parts of the world.[2] The pilchard (*Clupea pilchardus*) is the fish used in the French sardine industry, and the brisling or sprat (*Clupea sprattus*) in the Norwegian industry. The California sardine (*Clupea coeru-*

---

[1] The figures in parentheses refer to the bibliography at the end of this bulletin.
[2] Food Inspection Decision 64, issued by the U. S. Department of Agriculture, March 29, 1907, provides that the labels of the canned sardines shall state the country or locality from which the fish are packed, as an indication of the species.

leus), closely resembling the French species, is canned on the Pacific coast of the United States, while the immature sea herring (*Clupea harengus*) is put up on the eastern coast as the Maine sardine. .

The Bureau of Fisheries of the United States Department of Commerce states that the herring may be distinguished readily from the pilchard before it is cleaned and canned, the following points of difference being submitted:

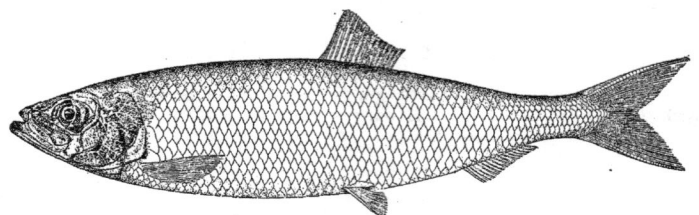

FIG. 1.—The herring.

The lower jaw of the herring (figure 1) projects a little beyond the tip of the snout when the mouth is closed; the gill covers are smooth; the fish is more or less compressed from side to side; and the belly rather sharp-edged. If the fish were cut in two, crosswise, the cross section would be somewhat egg-shaped. The fin on the back is situated nearer the base of the tail than the tip of the snout. The scales are comparatively small and have rounded edges. When the scales are removed no series of dusky spots is observable.

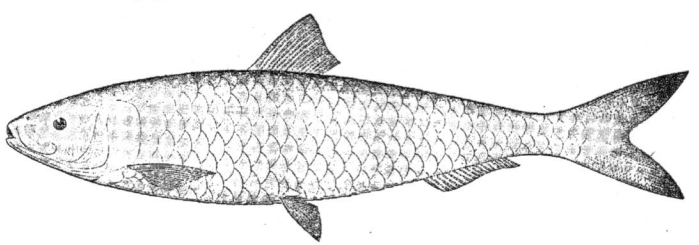

FIG. 2.—The pilchard.

The lower jaw of the pilchard (figure 2) projects but slightly, if at all, beyond the tip of the snout when the mouth is closed. Sharply-defined, fine ridges run downward and backward across the gill cover. The fish is more cylindrical than the herring, and a cross section would present a circular rather than an oval outline. The fin on the back is situated nearer the tip of the snout than the base of the tail. The scales are comparatively large, twice as large as those of the herring, and show a more or less angular outline of the edge. When the scales are removed a series of several dusky spots along the side of the front part of the body is usually plainly discernible.

To open a can of sardines of unknown origin and attempt to determine whether the fish is a herring or a pilchard presents a greater difficulty. Since the heads of both kinds are removed in the canning process, the jaw and gill cover characteristics can not be observed. The scales of both fish are easily detached and may not be present in the can. The absence of the head prevents ascertaining the position of the back fin in relation to the tip of the snout.

As the skin of the herring is thinner than that of the pilchard, it more quickly loses its silvery appearance, particularly after the loss of its scales and subjection to the cooking process. In consequence, a dull-colored, laterally flattened fish with the edge of the belly somewhat sharp-edged would suggest a herring. If the distance from the front of the base of the back fin directly to the belly, when applied twice to the distance from the rear of the base of the back fin to the middle of the base of the tail, extends beyond the base of the tail fin, it is almost positively a herring. If fine, round-edged scales are present, the diagnosis is quite positive.

On the other hand, the French sardine (pilchard), having a thick skin, has a tendency to retain much of its silvery appearance, even after being cooked, and this silveriness is more or less sharply defined from the bluish back. A silvery, plump fish with a rounded belly indicates a pilchard. If the dimension for the width of the fish, applied from the back fin to the base of the tail in the manner described, does not reach to the base of the tail, the fish is quite positively a pilchard. If conspicuous scales, with one end angular, are present, the fish positively is a pilchard; also if a series of dusky spots is observed along the side forward.

THE MAINE SARDINE INDUSTRY.

Sardines (27) have been canned in Europe since 1834, and the imported product has long been a popular article of food in this country. When the Franco-Prussian War cut off our supply of sardines from abroad, an opportunity was presented for the beginning of an American industry. It was not until 1876, however, that the first successful plant for canning sardines was established in Eastport, Me., by Julius Wolff, of the New York firm of Wolff & Reesing. Additional canneries were soon built in the vicinity of Eastport and Lubec, and at other points along the Maine coast.

In the early days of the industry it was possible to enter the business with a very small capital, as all the work was done by hand and no expensive machinery was needed. Practically the only large outlay required was for the materials used in making the cans and for oil. In many cases these supplies were advanced by the dealers in tin plate or by the commission merchants, who later accepted canned sardines in payment. Thus the packer was relieved, to a certain extent, of responsibility for the quality of his goods, and a tendency to sacrifice quality for quantity in the pack was developed. So large a number of individual canneries operated during the period from 1877 to 1899 that the business became most unprofitable. This condition resulted in an unsuccessful attempt to form a combination about 1899. A little later two large companies were organized, one of which built a factory for machine-made, machine-sealed cans, to replace the three-piece, handmade, soldered cans originally employed. These two firms soon consolidated, and two years later sold out. The general dissension which developed in the sardine industry during these two years was a factor in inducing the original packers to reenter the business on an independent basis. New factories were built and new men came into the industry.

In 1903 machine-made and machine-sealed cans, upon which experiments had been made previously, were generally substituted for the three-piece, handmade, soldered cans originally used, and an independent company undertook to supply the cans. As a result the quantity of fish packed increased markedly. In 1899, when handmade and hand-sealed cans were in use, the total pack of sardines amounted to 44,951,244 pounds, valued at $4,212,351. In 1904, just after the machine-made, machine-sealed cans had been introduced, the total quantity packed was 87,224,524 pounds worth $4,380,498. In 1909, 90,694,284 pounds, valued at $4,931,831, were put up in the sardine canneries(33). In 1914 the value of the entire pack was $6,238,933(34). It is interesting to note that while the total quantity of sardines packed in either 1904 or 1909 was approximately double that packed in 1899, the total value was practically the same for all three years.

Several factors have led those engaged in the sardine industry to strive for a large output, often with a tendency to sacrifice quality. In fact, the majority of the improvements which from time to time have been adopted have been designed to increase the quantity of the pack rather than to improve its quality. At first, the sardines canned in this country were fried and packed in olive oil, and compared favorably with the foreign article. At one time the American sardine was sold on the market as the foreign product, which deception, however, was soon detected by the trade, and the dealers were forced to sell the domestic article on its own merits. But with the increasing production and increasing competition the price which the goods commanded declined, until it became necessary to pack the sardines more cheaply, resulting in the appearance on the market of a product vastly inferior to that sold during the first few seasons of the American industry. About 1880 the practice of using cotton seed oil instead of olive oil was introduced, and some 10 years later the excellent custom of frying the fish in oil gave way to the modern method of cooking the fish in live steam. Several companies, however, still fry the fish in oil.

THE MAINE SARDINE.

As it now enters the channels of trade, the Maine sardine is packed either in oil or in mustard or some other sauce, in cans of varying sizes, known as quarter oil, high-quarter oil, half oil, quarter mustard, and three-quarter mustard (p. 11). At the close of the investigation here reported, owing to the difficulty of importing foreign sardines and the increased prices the domestic brands could command from 50,000 to 60,000 cases of sardines in olive oil were put up per annum by some 12 or 15 canneries. As a rule, cottonseed oil is used for packing sardines, the grade called prime summer yellow being most commonly employed, although several packers use the better grade known as winter-pressed oil, which they sometimes flavor with cloves, spice, or bay leaf, and a small amount of essential oil for the fancy or extra fancy grades.

Small quantities of Maine sardines are packed in tomato sauce, but a market for this article has not yet become widely established. Both the key-opening and the keyless type of cans are employed for this purpose.

FOOD VALUE OF THE CANNED SARDINE.

When well packed with a fair amount of oil, the Maine sardine constitutes an excellent food and gives the purchaser good value for the money expended. Table 1 shows the food value of sardines obtained for 5 and 10 cents as compared with that of various other common foodstuffs at the same price.

TABLE 1.—*Comparative food value of sardines and some other common foods.*

Food material.	Calories per pound.[1]	Protein.	Selling price per pound.[2]		Five cents bought[2]—			
					Total calories.		Calories from protein.	
			Oct. 15, 1915.[3]	Oct. 15, 1918.[4]	Oct. 15, 1915.	Oct. 15, 1918.	Oct. 15, 1915.	Oct. 15, 1918.
Sardines (in oil):		*Per cent.*						
Lean fish—								
1 quart of oil per case.	975	23.2	$0.25	$0.49	195	99	19	9
4 quarts of oil per case.	2,018	19.8	.25	.49	404	206	16	8
Fat fish—								
1 quart of oil per case..	1,270	22.4	.25	.49	254	130	18	9
4 quarts of oil per case.	2,309	19.1	.25	.49	426	236	15	8
Beef:								
Sirloin steak	985	16.5	.259	.41	190	120	13	8
Round (lean)	670	19.5	.233	.39	144	86	17	10
Cheese (whole milk)	1,950	25.9	.23	.385	424	253	23	13
Codfish:								
Fresh	165	8.4	.16	.23	52	36	11	7
Salt	315	19.0	.18	.25	88	63	21	15
Eggs	635	11.9	.266	.426	119	75	9	6
Ham (smoked)	1,670	14.5	.265	.52	315	161	11	6
Milk	325	3.3	.044	.074	369	220	15	9
Salmon (canned)	680	19.5	.198	.309	172	110	19	12

[1] Taken from U. S. Department of Agriculture, Office of Experiment Stations Bull. 28, except the figures for sardines.
[2] All prices are taken from U. S. Department of Labor, Bureau of Labor Statistics publications, except those for sardines and codfish.
[3] Calculated from 0.05 per 3¼-ounce can.
[4] Calculated from 0.10 per 3¼-ounce can.

It is evident that sardines packed from fat fish in the maximum amount of oil have a food value greater than that of any of the other common food materials of animal origin, considering only the amount which may be procured for 5 cents, the original price of a can of sardines. At 10 cents per can, sardines of this quality are outranked by whole milk cheese, at 39 cents a pound, in the number of calories that can be purchased for a given sum. Even as they are ordinarily packed, sardines compare very favorably with the amount of other animal foods which can be purchased for 5 cents. While the prices given in Table 1 no longer obtain, the comparative differences between them probably remain approximately unchanged.

The quantity of oil in the can is a very import
tributing to the food value of the sardine when it
packed can containing an adequate amount of e
large amount of food fuel, and, in the form of the
quantity of tissue-building food.

PURPOSE OF INVESTIGATION.

A few years before undertaking the investigatio
the Bureau of Chemistry, of the United States Depa
ture, made several studies of sardines shipped in in
from Maine, in connection with the enforcement of
and Drugs Act.   The bureau had already acquired s
such work, through its study of sardines offered fo
the United States.   These investigations of Main
that a certain portion of the pack was of unnecessari
Indeed, in some cases it constituted a flagrant vic
It seemed probable that very often the low-qualit
duced through faulty methods of handling and packi
ness, rather than to a deliberate effort to defraud th
condition seemed to offer an opportunity to render
service in assisting him to raise the standard of l
ploying better methods throughout the canning p
same time to benefit the community as a whole
important element of the country's food supply.

Accordingly, in 1913, a laboratory was establis
Me., where, during that season, as well as those
the representatives of the Department of Agricult
by the packers, studied the entire process of packi
success of this undertaking is already evident in
ment of factory conditions, in the adoption of me
efficient operation, and in the increased care show
pack from the time the fish leave the water until t
from the factory.   The majority of the canners h
selves together in an association for the bettermer
exercising its own sanitary supervision over the
in the plants of its members.   It is hoped that th
helped by the information contained in this bul
a report of the investigations on the canning of sar
of Maine, with suggestions for improving faulty
elimination of all unnecessary waste, and for the e
tion of the necessary wastes.

METHODS EMPLOYED IN PACKING SAF

The various steps in the production of canned
classified as follows: (a) Catching the fish; (b) tra
fish from the fishing grounds to the cannery; (c) pi

(d) flaking, as the process of distributing the fish upon the flakes for drying is termed; (e) steaming; (f) drying; (g) packing the fish in the cans; (h) introduction of oil into the cans; (i) sealing the cans; (j) processing or sterilization of the sealed cans; (k) testing the cans after processing; (l) shooking for shipment. In some canneries frying in oil after the fish have been dried is substituted for steaming. A brief outline of each of these steps will be first given in order that a general idea may be had of the factory operations.

FISHING.

As a rule, the small sea herring, used in the preparation of the Maine sardines, is caught in weirs, placed in comparatively shallow water along the shore. Most of the weirs are located in Canadian waters. In 1901, Bensley(1) estimated that each season between 700 and 800 weirs operated for catching these fish under licenses issued by the Dominion Government. Prince (23), in an earlier report, stated that 95 per cent of the American sardines are caught by Canadian fishermen. A weir (Pl. I) is a large circular or heart-shaped inclosure, made by driving stakes into the bottom of the sea, and intertwining brush between the stakes. Many of the oldest forms, which are known as "brush weirs," are still employed on the coast of Maine. The first "brush weir" to be constructed in this region was in use during the season of 1914. In this type, brush is placed above the surface of the water, as well as below. It is attached to posts, and extends but a few feet above the surface of the water at high tide. In many of the more recently built weirs, the brush is replaced by seine, or twine, which is removed during the winter.

The fish are directed into the weir by a lead made of brush, driven into the sea bottom, extending from the shore to the mouth of the weir. When a supply of fish has entered the weir, a net is dropped over the mouth, and the fish are seined (Pl. II, fig. 1) with a purse seine, then bailed into dories from which they are transferred to the sardine-fishing boats. Some of the weirs near Grand Manan Island are large enough to permit the entrance of the sardine boats themselves, in which case the fish are bailed or hoisted directly into the large boats (Pl. II, fig. 2).

Occasionally, when the fish remain off the shore, or for any reason do not enter the weir, the fishermen resort to seining. Fish taken in this way, however, are generally considered less desirable for packing than those from weirs, because of the large amount of feed often present in their digestive tracts. Since seined fish taken in the evening are not delivered to the cannery until the following morning, a certain amount of spoilage may occur during the night while they are held in the boat. The State of Maine has enacted laws restricting the seining of fish(17). Ordinarily the sea herring is caught while in search of food, or while actively engaged in feeding. Consequently,

weir fish also contain "feed," at times in great quantities. Su(
fish, however, free themselves of excessive feed if left long enoug
in the weir.

TRANSPORTATION.

Most of the boats which carry the fish from the fishing groun(
to the canneries are now well equipped and admirably suited to t]
purpose (Pl. III). The sailing vessels formerly used have be(
superseded by boats equipped not only with sails but also with gasoli)
engines as auxiliary power, and have a carrying capacity of from :
to 100 hogsheads [1] of fish. Each boat is provided, below decks, wi
a large tank or hold, which in the newer boats is watertight, to preve:
the entrance of bilge water. The fish are carried in these tank
The fishing fleet comprises privately owned boats, as well as tho
belonging to the various canneries. The fish are bought at the wei
by the captains of the boats, who act as agents for the canneri
employing them. In addition to the cost of the fish, the canner pa:
the boatman for transportation at a stipulated rate, usually (191
from $1.50 to $2.50 per hogshead, according to the distance the fi:
are carried.

PICKLING AND SALTING.

In early years the fish were taken in the fresh state to the canneri
(Pl. IV), where they were held in tanks of strong brine for about tv
hours, or until they "struck," a term applied by the experience
fishman in the pickling sheds to indicate the condition of the sk
and the appearance of the fish when properly salted. At prese
in order to save time during transportation, salt is sprinkled libera
throughout the mass of the fish as they are placed in the hold of t
boat, the amount varying from 1 to $2\frac{1}{2}$ sacks, of about 190 poun
each, to the hogshead, according to the length of time it takes
reach the cannery and the quality of the fish, as judged by the bo
man. Or a strong brine, made by adding the proper proportion
sea water to the fish, and salt may be used. The addition of d
salt draws out from the fish enough water to form a pickle, whi
sometimes is pumped off and at other times allowed to remain. A
rule, when the sea is rough no water is added, and the pickle form
by the addition of salt is pumped off during the voyage, so that t
fish may be carried in practically a solid bulk, thus preventi)
damage to them from the rolling of the vessel.

At the cannery the fish are hoisted from the boat (Pl. III, fig.
into long chutes down which they are conveyed by a stream of ru
ning water into tanks in the pickling room. If the fish have be
long enough in salt during the trip to the cannery, they are sim

---

[1] In practice, on the "Eastern Coast," as the shore from Jonesport eastward is termed, a hogshead is ra
as holding 10 tubs of fish, the weight of which is 1,000 pounds. The average weight of a number of t(
of fish, when taken at the weirs, has been found to be 129 pounds, thus making the weight of a hogsh
1,290 pounds. On the coast west of Jonesport, known locally as the "Western Coast," the fish are s
by the bushel, 15 bushels being considered as the equivalent of a hogshead.

PLATE I.

FIG. I.—BRUSH WEIR ON THE COAST OF MAINE.

FIG. 2.—A WEIR (LEFT) PROVIDED WITH A POUND (RIGHT).

PLATE II.

FIG. I.—SEINING THE WEIR.

Hauling the fish, by means of small dip nets, into dories, from which they are later transferred to the larger boats.

FIG. 2.—SEINING THE WEIR.

Hauling the fish directly into the sardine boats by means of a large seine.

FIG. 1.—TYPICAL SARDINE FISHING BOATS.

FIG. 2.—UNLOADING FISH AT CANNERY.

PLATE IV.

FIG. 1.—OLD TYPE OF MAINE SARDINE CANNERY.

FIG. 2.—MODERN MAINE SARDINE CANNERY.

FIG. I.—SCOOPING FISH FROM PICKLING TANK ONTO THE TAIL OF THE FLAKING
MACHINE.

FIG. 2.—FLAKING MACHINE.

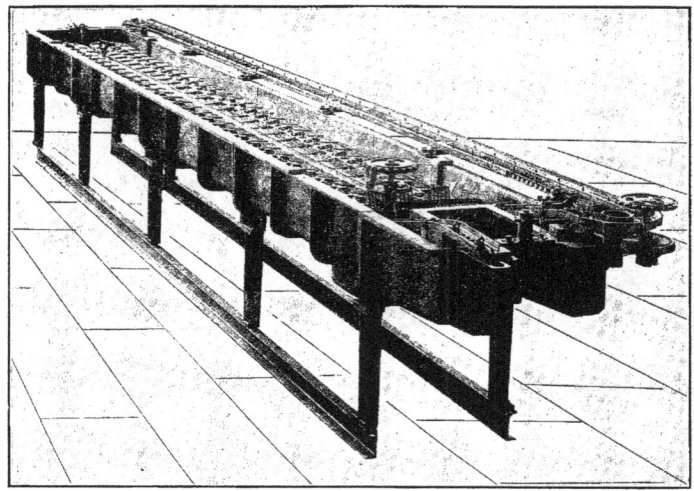

FIG. I.—MACHINE FOR FRYING FISH IN OIL.

FIG. 2.—MACHINE WHICH AUTOMATICALLY DELIVERS A DEFINITE QUANTITY
OF OIL TO PACKED CANS OF FISH.

passed through tanks containing very weak pickle. If they have not been sufficiently pickled during transportation, they are held in tanks filled with strong brine for from one to two hours .

FLAKING.

In a few canneries the fish are beheaded as soon as they are taken from the boats, but, as a rule, the whole salted fish are bailed from the pickling tank into the receiving trough of the flaking machine. The traveling apron of the machine (Pl. V, fig. 1) extends from the floor above into the pickling room below. Carried along by the traveling apron to this machine, the sardines are distributed, more or less evenly, depending upon the manner in which the machine is operated, on the flakes, square or rectangular wire frames, about 3 by 1½ feet, securely bound around the edge with a 1-inch galvanized metal band (Pl. V, fig. 2). Several of the canneries putting out a superior quality of sardines distribute, or flake, the fish by hand, thus securing a very even distribution on the flakes, a most important factor in the production of quality in the pack. The flakes carry the fish through the rest of the canning process until they are ready to be placed in the cans.

STEAMING.

From the flaking machine, the flakes are passed, on racks mounted on wheels, or, in a few cases, suspended from a track on the ceiling, to the steam chest. Here the fish are subjected to treatment with live steam for from 10 to 15 minutes.

DRYING.

The racks containing the steamed flaked fish are next taken to the drying chamber, where they are brought to the proper degree of dryness by one of several methods. Three types of driers are in use at the present time: The tunnel or "air" drier; the kiln or "oven" drier; and a combination of the kiln drier with a "Ferris wheel." In the tunnel drier, which method has practically superseded the once popular Ferris wheel device(29), as well as the old-fashioned kiln drier, the air, heated by being passed over steam coils, or by waste flue gases, is blown or drawn over the racks of fish. Where the kiln drier or Ferris wheel drier is still in use a glowing bed of anthracite coal supplies the heat.

FRYING IN OIL.

In canneries where the sardines are fried in oil, the fish, after having been flaked, either by hand or by a well-operated machine, are dried in the usual manner, without, however, having been put through the steam chest, transferred to frying baskets which are immersed in hot oil, cooked, cooled, and packed in cans (Pl. VI, fig. 1). From this point the procedure is the same as for the steamed fish.

"), or, if the sardines are small, by snipping the
("snipping"). The fish are then packed in
nneries the filled cans are placed in rectangular
of 25 cans each, the pans being then stacked ii
trucks to the sealing machine. In others th
ictly to a traveling belt which carries them to
; machines.

ADDING THE OIL.

s where the oiling device is not attached to t
ie cans are taken from the packing room to an
'l· VI, fig. 2), which can be set to deliver a defini
ch can. Twenty-five cans may be filled with oil
taining this number passes through it. Sim
ire sometimes operated by a hand lever.
· canneries, however, the oiling device is attac
chine, making it possible to accomplish these
·ation.

SEALING THE CANS.

ialing machine the covers are placed on the cans
id oil and passed through the rolls. Three diffe
is are in use for closing sardine cans. The m
·al use are equipped with rolls which travel a
edges of the can and the lid as it fits over the car
if the can and the lid together and at the same
iem (Pl. VII, fig. 1). Another type of machin
lirect compression. The can is held firmly bet
i together, crimping the lid upon the cans (Pl. \
method hermetically seals the cans by the use
aced upon the edge of the can. The lid and ca
means of a mechanical device, under heated ri

PROCESSING OR STERILIZATION.

ed cans are processed in tanks of boiling wat
fourths to two and one-fourth, sometimes twc
i, according to the individual packer's idea of
or sterilization. One or two canneries employ
1. These are cast-iron cylindrical or rectangu
tles with tightly fitting covers or doors, the c
be heated under pressure.

STORING THE CANS.

icessing the cans are removed from the tanks,·
.eaned (Pl. VIII, fig. 1) by mixing them with sa

shoveling sawdust over them. They are then sent to the storage room below and allowed to cool (Pl. VIII, fig. 2), after which each can is tested and then packed in a shipping case, or, as it is termed by the trade, "shook."

THE CANS.

As already stated, the cans used for packing sardines in oil are designated, according to their size, as quarter oil, high-quarter oil, and half oil, while those used for packing sardines in mustard sauce are called quarter mustard and three-quarter mustard. The quarter oil and the quarter mustard cans are the same size. The greater part of the sardine pack is put up in oil, in the quarter size cans, and about 25 per cent of the normal output in mustard sauce, mostly in the three-quarter size cans. Lacquered cans, made from tin coated with a preparation which prevents the action of the acid in the sauce upon the metal, are employed only for mustard sardines. A case of quarter oil or mustard sardines contains 100 cans, while a case of three-quarter size mustards contains 48 cans.

The cans used for both oils and mustards are divided into two classes, the key-opening and the keyless. Projecting from the corner of the key-opening or three-piece can, the bottom of which is soldered on, is a small lip to which the key for opening the can is attached. One objection to this type of can is that, in order to open it with the "brights" up, the fish must be packed with the belly portions against the bottom of the can. It is practically impossible to inspect properly the quality of the fish placed in such cans or the manner in which they have been packed. These cans also are more subject to small leaks than are some of the other types. The key-opening two-piece can, provided with a scored top, lacks some of the objectionable features of the three-piece can, but is less successfully opened. The keyless cans, also called drawn cans, or two-piece cans, are stamped directly from sheets of tin by means of a power press and die. Key openers for these cans are made by scoring the covers around the edges and providing a projecting lip at one corner or at the end for the key.

TABLE 2.—*Size of sardine cans.*[1]

Type of can.	Length.		Width.		Height.		Lid set in.	
	Inches.	Centimeters.	Inches.	Centimeters.	Inches.	Centimeters.	Inches.	Centimeters.
Three-quarter mustard (keyless).....	4 11/16	11.9	3 7/16	8.8	1 1/2	3.8	5/32	0.35
Half oil (key).......................	4 9/16	11.6	3 3/8	8.5	1 1/16	2.7	1/8	.3
One-quarter oil and mustard, drawn can (keyless).....................	4 3/16	10.7	2 15/16	7.5	13/16	2.0	1/8	.3
Do.............................	4 5/32	10.55	2 15/16	7.5	13/16	2.0	5/32	.35
One-quarter oil and mustard, 3-piece can (key)..........................	4 3/16	10.7	2 15/16	7.6	3/4	1.9	1/8	.3
Do.............................	4 3/16	10.6	2 15/16	7.6	11/16	1.8	1/8	.35
High-quarter.......................	4 3/16	10.6	2 15/16	7.6	1 1/8	2.9	1/8	.35

[1] Since these measurements were taken, the height of the one-quarter cans has been reduced 1/32 inch. In view of other possible changes, these dimensions may not be exactly correct to the fractions of inches or centimeters.

Table 2 gives the inside measurements, expressed in inches an
centimeters, of representative types of the cans in use. This wi
serve as a reference and give a general idea of the size of cans i
which sardines are commonly packed.

The size of the sardine cans varies from the keyless one-quarter o
and mustard drawn can, which is $4\frac{1}{8}$ inches long, $2\frac{11}{16}$ inches wide, an
$\frac{25}{32}$ inch high, with the cover set in $\frac{5}{32}$ inch, to the keyless three
quarter mustard size, which is $4\frac{21}{32}$ inches long, $3\frac{7}{16}$ inches wide, an
$1\frac{15}{32}$ inches high, with the cover set in $\frac{5}{32}$ inch. The capacity of th
low-quarter cans in use during the seasons of 1913 and 1914 varie
from 154 to 157 cc in the case of the keyless type, and from 150 t
156 cc for the key cans. With the covers on, the capacity was fror
120 to 125 cc and from 112 to 114 cc, respectively, for the two type:

At the present time, the low-quarter and three-quarter cans (P
IX) are more commonly used than the high-quarter and half size:
The number of the half-size and the high-quarter cans used, howeve:
increased greatly in 1916, and it is expected that as the quality of th
pack improves, sardines in larger cans will be more in demand. Th
quarter-size cans, designated as high-quarter and low-quarter (P.
IX, figs. 1 and 2), have the same length and width, while the heigb
of the low-quarter size is $\frac{7}{8}$ inch and that of the high-quarter can
$1\frac{1}{8}$ inches. Both types come in the form of three-piece cans, wit'
key openers, and also as the keyless, drawn cans. The same siz
cover serves for both types. The three-quarter mustard cans ar
$\frac{3}{16}$ inch higher than the half oils (Pl. IX, figs. 3 and 4); otherwis
the two varieties are of the same size. Both come with the botto:
soldered on, to permit the use of the key-opening device, but the botto:
of the keyless three-quarter can is rolled on. The same covers fit bot
types. The half oil can is the only style in that size now made, an
it is not used as extensively as its merits would seem to warrant.

The empty cans are delivered from the can factory to the canner
in the shooks or shipping cases, and are generally stored in the car
neries until they are needed. The covers are handled separately, i
large bulk, in special boxes, or crates, for containers.

EXPERIMENTAL WORK.

METHODS OF ANALYSIS.

The methods of analysis used, which were adopted after preliminar
experiments had been made with them, are as follows:

SAMPLING.

Take a quantity of fish large enough to represent fairly the entire lot. Wipe wit
a dry towel or spread out on paper for an instant, to remove the water adhering to th
surface of the fish. Behead and eviscerate, as the case requires, and thoroughly grin
and mix by passing a number of times through a meat grinder, previously drie(
Sample and transfer to a pint size, screw-cap Mason jar, provided with the usu:
rubber gasket, portions of this lot sufficient for analysis.

FIG. I.—ROLL TYPE SEALING MACHINES.

FIG. 2.—COMPRESSION TYPE SEALING MACHINES.

FIG. 1.—DEVICE FOR CLEANING CANS.

Sawdust is passed down the rotating tube with the cans.

FIG. 2.—CANS OF SARDINES AFTER THEY HAVE BEEN
PROCESSED.

It may take from 8 to 10 hours for the interior of such a pile, which is
100 feet long, 8 feet wide, and from 4 to 5 feet deep, to lose its heat.

PLATE IX.

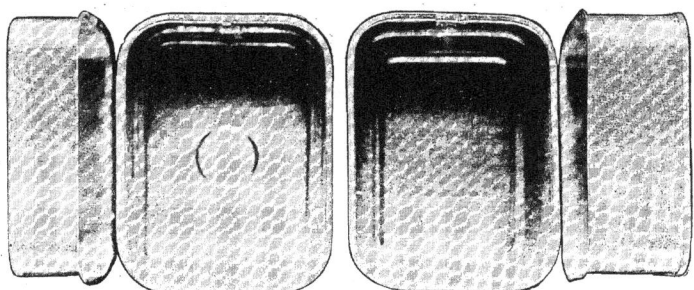

FIG. 1.—HIGH-QUARTER OIL SARDINE CAN.

FIG. 2.—ORDINARY LOW-QUARTER OIL SARDINE CAN.

FIG. 3.—ONE-HALF OIL SARDINE CAN.

FIG. 4.—THREE-QUARTER MUSTARD SARDINE CAN.

In the same way, by grinding and mixing through the meat chopper, prepare the contents of the cans. Wipe the last traces of oil from the interior of the can with the ground fish.

MOISTURE.

Spread thinly 2 or 3 grams of sample in 2½-inch lead-foil caps, and dry in vacuo (25 to 28 inches) for 5 hours at 55° C.

FAT.

Extract the dried residues from the moisture determinations for from 12 to 15 hours in a Knorr fat extraction apparatus with 50 cc of absolute ether, prepared over sodium. Evaporate the ether at as low a temperature as possible, and dry the ether extract 1 hour at 55° C. in vacuo.

ACIDITY OF FAT(9).

Dissolve the dried ether extract residues in 50 cc of benzol. Add 2 drops of phenolphthalein and determine the acidity by titrating with N/20 sodium ethylate. Calculate the acidity as cc of N/20 sodium ethylate per 1 gram of fat.

TOTAL NITROGEN.

Determine by the Gunning modification of the Kjeldahl method (A. O. A. C. Methods, 1916, p. 7).

AMMONIA NITROGEN.

Nessler(8).[1]—Weigh 3-gram samples and transfer to large test tubes, or small Kjeldahl flasks, with 20 to 25 cc of water. Add 3 cc of 10 per cent solution of potassium carbonate, 3 cc of 15 per cent solution of potassium oxalate, and a little heavy cylinder oil. Pass a strong current of ammonia-free air through this mixture for four hours. Collect the ammonia in 5 cc of N/20 sulphuric acid contained in a 100-cc volumetric flask. After aerating, dilute the contents of the flask to the 100-cc mark. Transfer a 25-cc aliquot portion to a 100-cc volumetric flask and dilute nearly to the mark. After adding 2 cc of Nessler solution and making to volume, compare the density of the color of the solution in a Duboscq colorimeter with that of a known standard.

Titration.—Weigh 3-gram samples and transfer to large test tubes, or small Kjeldahl flasks, with 20 to 25 cc of water. Add 3 cc of 10 per cent solution of potassium carbonate, 3 cc of 15 per cent solution of potassium oxalate, and a little cylinder oil. Force a strong current of ammonia-free air through this mixture for four hours. Collect the ammonia in 5 cc N/20 sulphuric acid, in a 100-cc volumetric flask. After aeration, titrate the excess acid in the flasks with N/50 alkali, using methyl red as the indicator.

TOTAL VOLATILE NITROGEN FOR THE SEPARATION OF AMMONIA AND AMINES.

Weigh thirty 3-gram samples into tubes of the Folin apparatus, or small Kjeldahl flasks, arranged for the aeration method for the determination of ammonia. To each add about 25 cc ammonia-free water, a pinch of sodium fluorid, 3 cc of 15 per cent potassium oxalate, and 3 cc of 10 per cent potassium carbonate. Aerate four hours. Collect the alkaline volatile nitrogen compounds in 5 cc of N/20 sulphuric acid. After the necessary time has elapsed, remove the flasks, and titrate back with N/50 potassium hydroxid. Use methyl red for the indicator. The acid used is equivalent to the total volatile nitrogen, that is, the sum of the ammonia and amines present.

---

[1] Although a number of determinations of ammonia by the Nessler method were made, they are reported in only a few of the tables. The term "ammonia," as used in the tables and text, represents the total volatile alkaline material (ammonia and amines) as determined by the titration method. In the decomposition studies, and the work on the formation of ammonia and amines here reported, the total volatile alkaline bases are separated into the amines and ammonia. In the work on the decomposition of the copepods (feed), and on the influence of the temperature of storage on the formation of ammonia and amines, the amines were further separated into their three classes by a method recently devised.

Unite the distillates obtained by the preceding method in a large dish, make distinctly acid, and evaporate until the volume is about 400 cc. Wash into a 500-cc graduated flask, and cool. If the total volatile nitrogen exceeds a strength equivalent to 30 cc N/10 in amount, make up to 500 cc, and transfer a portion equivalent to 20 to 30 cc of N/10 to another 500-cc flask. If the amount of total volatile nitrogen is less than the equivalent of 20 cc N/10, add enough of a standard solution of ammonia to raise the content to that point. Add to the liquid in the 500-cc graduated flask 10 cc of a solution made by mixing equal parts of 20 per cent sodium hydroxid and 30 per cent sodium carbonate. Fill to the mark with water. Now add 0.1 gram of yellow mercuric oxid for each cc of N/10 acid to which the total volatile nitrogen present in the solution is equivalent. Stopper tightly, cover with a black cloth to exclude light, and shake one hour. Allow to stand 12 hours, or overnight, to permit the oxid of mercury to settle. Separate from the mercuric oxid by forcing the liquid through a tube containing a little absorbent cotton, using a moderate blast. Discard the first 20–30 cc. Distill 200 cc of the filtrate in duplicate into standardized acid. The amount of acid required is equivalent to the nitrogen present as amines. The total volatile nitrogen minus the amine nitrogen equals ammonia nitrogen. Express the quantities as milligrams of nitrogen per 100 grams of sample.

AMINO ACID NITROGEN.

The few determinations of amino acid reported were made in Klein's (14) modification of Van Slyke's apparatus, before the latest Van Slyke method was published.

VOLATILE SULPHUR.

Weigh 100-gram samples into 800-cc Erlenmeyer flasks, to which have been added 400 cc of water and 10 cc of a 20 per cent solution of phosphoric acid. Distill 150 cc into an excess of N/20 potassium hydroxid by steam distillation in 45 minutes. Neutralize the excess of alkali by titration with N/20 hydrochloric acid. To the distillate add 25 cc of approximately N/100 iodin solution, and, after allowing it to stand from 5 to 10 minutes, titrate the unreduced iodin with N/100 thiosulphate solution. Calculate the volatile sulphur as cubic centimeters of N/100 iodin per 100 grams of fish.

CHLORIN.

Sodium chlorid (salt).—Determine by the Volhard method(31), after the samples have been ashed at a low temperature with an excess of bicarbonate of soda, free from chlorin.

TIN.

Add 50 cc of concentrated sulphuric acid to the material in a Kjeldahl flask, and add concentrated nitric acid, boiling until all organic matter is destroyed. Rinse out the flask into a 600-cc beaker with boiling water, diluting to 400 cc. Neutralize with ammonium hydroxid, and add 5 cc hydrochloric acid. Heat on hot plate to 95° C., cover with a watch glass, and pass in a slow stream of hydrogen sulphid for one hour. Digest on a hot plate for two hours. Filter, using an 11-cm S. & S. filter. Wash with three portions of a wash solution (composed of 100 cc saturated ammonium acetate, 50 cc glacial acetic acid, 850 cc water) alternated with three portions of hot water. Place filter and precipitate in a 50-cc beaker and digest with three successive portions of ammonium polysulphid, bringing to a boil each time and filtering through a 9 cm filter. Wash with hot water. Acidify with acetic acid, digest on a hot plate for one hour, and filter through a double 11-cm filter. Wash with two portions of wash solution alternated with two portions of hot water. Place filter and precipitate in weighed porcelain crucible and dry at 110° C. Ignite very gently at first, later with the full burner. Finally heat strongly with a large Meeker burner or blast lamp. Weigh as oxid of tin, and calculate percentage of milligrams of tin.

COMPOSITION OF THE SEA HERRING.

The average composition of the fresh herring, as determined from results obtained throughout the season, is given in Table 3.

TABLE 3.—*Average composition of sea herring.*

Herring.	Water.	Protein.	Fat (ether extract).[1]	Ash (mineral matter).
	Per cent.	*Per cent.*	*Per cent.*	*Per cent.*
Lean	72.5	19.5	6.5	1.5
Fat	68.5	14.3	16.0	1.2

[1] The fat content of these fish may vary from 5 to 18 per cent during the packing season.

VARIATION IN FAT AND WATER-CONTENT OF THE FISH.

Several investigators have noted the fact that the fat content of fish varies with the season, being noticeably low in the spring. Few analyses showing the difference in composition and seasonal variation in the fat content of fish have, however, been reported. According to Dr. John Hjort, director of fisheries of Norway (12), the maximum fat content, 15.52 per cent, in the Norwegian sardine (the brisling) is found in September, and the minimum amount, 4.65 per cent, in April. The amount of fat stored up in the muscular tissue and viscera of the herring during the summer is consumed during the winter. Conversely, the water content is lower during the summer than in the winter months. This fish is inferior in quality through the winter, or period of low fat content. In discussing the quality of fish used for packing sardines, Dr. Hjort stated that "The quality of all three species, herring, brisling, and pilchard, is a feature which changes with age and season."

H. Lichtenfelt (15) states that the muscular tissue of fish changes in composition at definite periods of the year, the fat content depending on the age of the fish, the food eaten, and the spawning season. During the hunger period (scarcity of food) the percentage of water increases, while that of dry matter and of protein decrease.

Milroy (18) found great differences in the composition of the muscles of fish of larger size than are commonly used for sardines, taken from the same waters in different months. The percentage of fat in fish, the ovaries of which were immature, was in the summer about the same as the average for herring. During August, September, and October the percentage of fat continued to increase. It decreased slightly in November, more in December, and most markedly during spawning, continuing at a low level until the fish began to feed again. This investigator points out the probability that the decrease in fat in the muscle tissues of the fish is accompanied by an increase in the water content.

The herring studied by Heinecke (18) contained the largest
of fat during September and October.

According to Johnstone (13), the full and unripe herrings
during the summer (June to August) are much richer in fa
than the same kind of herring caught during the fall and
(October to December). His results show also that the per
variation in the water and fat content of the fish is closely
mentary.

The monthly variations in the water and fat contents of th
herring of various sardine sizes as they were brought to the ca
are shown in Table 4. The analyses were made not on the fr
but on fish which had been held in salt or pickle for varying
The results are therefore influenced by the salt taken up by
and the amount of water and extractive material lost, and
be considered as representative of fresh fish.

TABLE 4.—*Water and fat content of sea herring by months (1913).*

Description of fish and month caught.	Number of samples.	Water.			Fa	
		Maxi-mum.	Mini-mum.	Aver-age.	Maxi-mum.	Mir mu:
July:		*P. ct.*	*P. ct.*	*P. ct.*	*P. ct.*	*P.*
Oil size—						
Not eviscerated......................	6	70.91	53.23	65.28	5.55	3.
Eviscerated.........................	2	69.68	61.54	65.61	6.06	4.
Mustard size—						
Not eviscerated......................	10	66.90	48.72	61.99	18.61	7.
Eviscerated.........................	4	64.10	52.84	60.06	14.24	9.
August:						
Oil size—						
Not eviscerated......................	10	71.28	60.62	65.32	11.25	6.
Eviscerated.........................	1	64.60	64.60	64.60	7.30	7.
Mustard size—						
Not eviscerated......................	4	65.32	58.32	61.62	15.63	11.
Eviscerated.........................	1	62.46	62.46	62.46	12.38	12.
September:						
Oil size—						
Not eviscerated......................	4	70.38	60.08	67.74	8.49	5.
Mustard size—						
Not eviscerated......................	4	64.85	59.96	62.43	15.07	8.
October:						
Oil size—						
Not eviscerated......................	8	72.16	59.13	65.10	14.25	5
Eviscerated.........................	3	71.51	64.55	69.18	9.68	7
Mustard size—						
Not eviscerated......................	3	68.13	55.54	59.81	16.00	10

The average fat content of the oil-size fish was greatest in
in the case of the uneviscerated fish, and in October in the ca
eviscerated fish. In July the fat content was comparatively
each. The mustard size, or larger, fish did not show an app
increase from one month to the next, containing approxim
per cent of fat from July until October.

The low fat content for the oil-size fish found in Septe
accounted for by the fact that a number of analyses made
obtained from Castine, Me., are included. It is said that lar
bers of these fish run into this bay, where they remain until lc
the food supply is exhausted, thus becoming very thin.

FIG. I.—COPEPOD—CALANUS FINMARCHICUS (MAGNIFIED 26 TIMES).

FIG. 2.—COPEPOD—TEMORA LONGICORNIS (MAGNIFIED 26 TIMES).

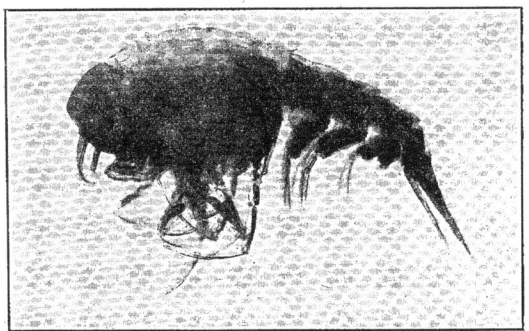

FIG. 3.—AMPHIPOD—ENTHEMISTO COMPRESSA (MAGNIFIED 3 TIMES).

THE MORE COMMON FORMS OF FEED OF THE SEA HERRING.

(Photomicrographs by E. A. Read, Microchemical Laboratory, Bureau of Chemistry.)

PLATE XI.

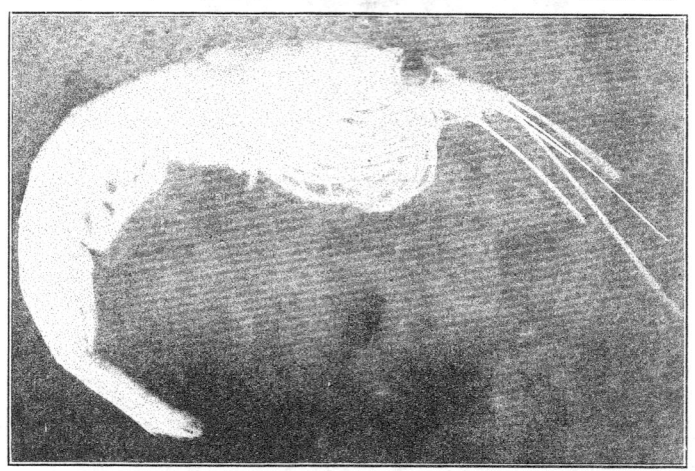

FIG. I.—SCHIZOPOD (SHRIMP). EUPHASISID—MEGANYCTIPHANES NORWEGICA (MAGNIFIED 3 TIMES).

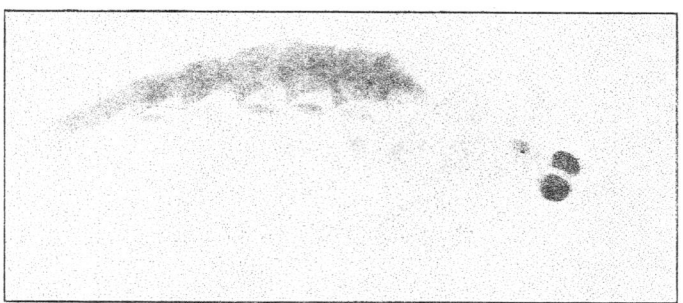

FIG. 2.—EUPHASISID—THYSANOESSA INERMIS (MAGNIFIED 6 TIMES).

THE MORE COMMON FORMS OF FEED OF THE SEA HERRING.

(Photomicrographs by E. A. Read, Microchemical Laboratory, Bureau of Chemistry.)

It is shown by these analyses that the smaller fish, of the real sardine size, contain much less fat in the early part of the packing season than later in the year.

FOOD OF THE SEA HERRING.

The sea herring, from which the Maine sardines are made, feeds upon several varieties of marine life. According to European investigators, the feed(19) consists of copepods, schizopods (shrimp-like forms), amphipods (sand fleas and their allies), the embryos of gasteropods and lamellibranchs, and young fish often of its own kind. In the examination of about 1,500 specimens at Eastport and vicinity Moore found but two kinds of food. Copepods ("red feed") appeared to constitute the sole food of the small herrings, the so-called brit, and a marked portion of that of the larger individuals from 5½ inches upward. The principal foods of the latter, however, were schizopods, crustaceans of the genus Thycanopoda, known to the fisherman as "shrimp."

Scott(26) states that of 22 species of microscopic crustaceans found in the stomachs of herrings examined by him the greater part were *Calanus finmarchicus*, *Temora longicornis*, and *Pseudocalanus elongatus*.

In an investigation on the packing of American sardines conducted by the Maine Agricultural Experiment Station, in 1911, at Eastport and Lubec(11), "red feed" was identified as the copepods *Temora longicornis*, and *Calanus finmarchicus*.

Calanus finmarchicus and *Temora longicornis* were the most numerous of the crustaceans collected in the region extending from Dochet Island to Grand Manan for the Marine Biological Station at St. Andrews, N. B.(16).

In exploring the coast water between Nova Scotia and Chesapeake Bay, July and August, 1913, Dr. Henry B. Bigelow(2) found that of the copepods the most abundant species was *Calanus finmarchicus*, the *Pseudocalanus elongatus* ranking next, while in a few regions the *Temora longicornis* was the most abundant. He considers, however, that the *Calanus finmarchicus* is the most abundant form found in the waters of the Gulf of Maine.

Apparently, therefore, the feed of the sea herring of the Passamaquoddy Bay region may be divided into two general classes:

1. The copepods[1] (Pl. X), of which *Calanus finmarchicus*, *Pseudocalanus elongatus*, and *Temora longicornis* are the species most often found, undoubtedly constitute the chief form of the "red feed." The herring consumes the copepods which, in turn, feed upon microscopic plants, such as peridinia, and diatoms. R. Ramsey Wright(40)

---

[1] Identification of specimens made by the Division of Marine Invertebrates of the U. S. National Museum.

classes copepods, which are approximately one-eighth inch lor macroscopic forms of sea life.

2. Schizopods,[1] or "shrimp" (Pl. XI), are the larger macrosc forms on which the fish feed.

FEEDY FISH.

Fish which have been feeding extensively on either of the two of food known to the fisherman as "red feed" and "shrimp" m designated as "feedy fish." While there is little difference i action of the two kinds of feed in rendering the fish unsuitab packing, fish that have been feeding upon "red feed" become b and deteriorate a little more rapidly than fish that have been fe on shrimp. Bacteriological examination of the feed showed th bacterium commonly associated with copepods grows faste produces a slightly greater amount of gas than the organism on the shrimp.

"Feedy" fish, in so far as its influence on the quality of the sa is concerned, is perhaps the most troublesome factor in the s industry. Fish more or less gorged with food deteriorate rapidly when taken from the water, while those having their dig tracts free from food remain in good condition for a compara long time thereafter. As decomposition progresses the thin portion of the fish gradually sloughs away, producing the charact ragged appearance termed "belly blown." The rate of deterio depends upon the quantity of and the stage of digestion of th material contained in the digestive tract, and the bacteria a panying it. Feed recently eaten appears to cause a greater of deterioration than that which has been partially digested. teriological studies have shown that the stomach portions digestive tract are sterile when free from feed, even when dig in the intestines is incomplete. By the time feedy fish reac cannery they have deteriorated to such an extent and are so broken that a large percentage is entirely unfit for packing.

In the French sardine industry(27), where bait is employ catching the fish, the strictest attention is given to the qual the bait in order to avoid decomposition in the fish. As late a the use of a prepared bait containing especially powdered praw shrimp was forbidden by royal decree, as it was held that it s the fish by facilitating decomposition. In this connection it is esting to note that the bacteria found associated with the feed (were capable of decomposing fish tissue. One of these orga forms spores which resist drying but are capable of growtl reproduction when conditions again become favorable. The mentioned, prepared from dried shrimp, doubtless containe

---

[1] Identification of specimens made by the Division of Marine Invertebrates of the U. S. Museum.

spores of this organism (Walfischrauschbrand) which was responsible for the decomposition of the fish.

In the preparation of anchovies, "Appetitsild," and "Gabelbissen," an extensive industry in Germany(28), the importance of using fish from which the feed has been eliminated is recognized. Practically all the fish used in the German industry are imported from Norway, where whole schools at a time are caught in powerful purse seines. The fish are kept in the seines for one to several days that they may free themselves of partly digested food, after which they are shipped to Germany in large hogsheads containing weak pickle.

The Maine sardine canners regard seined fish as inferior for packing on account of their excessively feedy condition. At times weir fish contain as much food as seined fish, but, owing to the necessity of taking fish under conditions existing at the time these investigations were made, the inferiority of such fish is overlooked and feedy weir fish are used.

ELIMINATION OF FEEDY FISH.

The solution of the difficulty experienced with feedy fish is comparatively simple. It can be accomplished by allowing the fish to remain in the water long enough to digest the feed contained in their alimentary tracts, which may vary from over one tide, 6 hours, to 12 or 18 hours, depending on the quantity of feed present. The fishermen and boatmen can readily determine when the fish are free from feed. For this purpose "pounds" or "pockets" (Pl. I, fig. 2) are attached to the weirs. A pound is practically a second weir adjoining the weir proper with a drop net between the two. The feedy fish are seined or driven into the pound, and held there for the requisite period. Doubtless a few weirs are situated where the water is so deep and the tidal currents so strong that it would be impossible to build pounds next to them. In such cases the fish may be held in the weirs. This is not, however, considered a good practice from the fisherman's point of view, as the use of the weir for holding a catch over one or two tides deprives them of the opportunity of catching fish at the succeeding tides. At most weirs, pounds can be built with the same ease as the weir itself.

A concerted demand on the part of the packers for fish free from feed will make it only a question of time before practically all of the weirs will be provided with pounds. This would improve the quality of the pack by eliminating "feedy" fish, provide a more uniform supply of fish, place the purchasing of fish and the boating on a sounder basis, and help to eliminate the taking of quantities of fish in excess of the capacity of the cannery, thus reducing one great form of waste.

Another solution of the "feedy" problem is to cut and eviscerate the fish before beginning the canning process. Thus the feed and

viscera, which harbor the bacteria producing spoilage, are rem
before an advanced stage of decomposition has been reached.

SWELLS.

During the latter part of the season of 1913 reports reachec
laboratory of trouble due to swells at a few of the canneries o1
west coast. No cause for this condition could be found by tho
charge of the canneries, and, in spite of all the precautions tak(
increased each year, until it was estimated that as much as 3(
cent of the pack of one or two factories had swelled during the se
Canners in other localities reported that they had about 1 per ce
swells in a season's pack, though more were found in some se:
than in others. As it was felt that more trouble was due to s
than the majority of the packers were willing to admit, a sp
investigation was undertaken to determine the cause.

At the close of the sardine packing season of 1913, an investig.
on the canning of clams was made at the Eastport laboratory d
which gas-producing, facultative anaerobic bacteria were foui
canned clams processed under commercial conditions.[1] A tem
ture of 240° F. was required to destroy the spores of this orga1
which suggested the possibility that this organism, or one of si
nature, might be responsible for swells in sardines.

It was first planned to carry on the experimental part of the
at local points reporting the greatest number of swells. Afte:
work was under way, however, statements from canneries alon;
whole coast indicated that the trouble was more general than at
supposed. In one case a canner reported that a large percenta
goods stored in his shipping room were "swells." Another ca
reported the finding of a large quantity of "swells" in a ship
made by boat to the Pacific coast. The reports in these cases
accompanied by samples of the "swelled" goods. Bacteriolc
examinations of cans received from these canneries, as well .
cans of swelled sardines secured from packers which would be 1
representative of the whole Maine coast, showed the presence (
anaerobic organism in pure culture. It was then decided to e1
this part of the investigation to the entire coast.

The bacteriological part of the work was begun during th(
fall of 1915 and continued during the early fall of 1916. As it
gressed it became apparent that the organism that was being st1
as a cause of swelled cans was also probably responsible fo:
decomposition of the feed of herring, and, therefore, indirectly fc
characteristic belly breaking of feedy fish. A more extensive s
including both chemical and bacteriological work, was the1
conducted during the early fall of 1916.

---

[1] Unpublished reports in the Bureau of Chemistry.

BACTERIOLOGY OF THE FEED OF HERRING AND ITS BEARING ON SWELLS IN CANNED SARDINES.

In other investigations that have been made on swelled canned sardines the relation of the bacteria associated with the feed to the swelling of canned sardines has not been considered. Thus Cathcart(5) gives the results of the bacteriological examination of swelled cans of sardines. All the cans examined emitted gas when they were opened. The contents had an extremely bad odor, but were normal in appearance. Four different organisms were isolated, one of which was found to be *Bacillus coli*. Injections made intraperitoneally into guinea pigs of cultures of the unidentified organisms proved two of them to be pathogenic, while the third, seemingly, had no effect. In a bacteriological study of swelled sardines canned in Maine and New Brunswick, Sadler isolated eight strains of gas-producing bacteria from the swells examined(25). Very complete detailed descriptions of the cultures and organisms found, including biochemical reactions and morphological and biological features, are given in Dr. Sadler's report.

A very brief summary of the bacteriological studies made during this investigation upon the feed and upon swelled cans of sardines, both native and imported, is given here.[1] No aerobic bacteria were found, but *Bacillus Walfischrauschbrand*,[2] a rapid spore former, was isolated in pure culture. This organism was traced through the gills and stomach contents of the fish to the bodies of the live schizopods, usually in the thoracic region, and to the masses of copepods. It produced gas in the dead fish by its decomposition of the feed within the digestive tract.

During the investigation another organism was isolated, first from the stomach contents of a fish ready to be packed and later traced to the massed copepods fresh from deep-sea water. This organism, designated as *Bacillus B.*, was pathogenic to mice and guinea pigs and capable of producing a chemical decomposition similar to that produced by *B. Walfischrauschbrand*. It did not form spores, however, and was therefore much less resistant to heat. The *Bacillus Walfischrauschbrand* lived through the processing of the sealed cans whenever the temperature of the bath was slightly below the boiling point and when cans floated or protruded above the surface of the water.

Samples of various portions of the bodies of many herring were cultured anaerobically and aerobically. The flesh was invariably free from bacteria when the fish were removed from the weirs.

---

[1] The bacteriological work was conducted by M. M. Obst, of the Bureau of Chemistry(21).

[2] *Bacillus Walfischrauschbrand* is the name applied by Nielsen(20) to the organism found in whales made sick by being shot with arrows previously inoculated with material from dead whales. The practice of shooting with such arrows was employed in certain whale fisheries at that time. The animal was easier to harpoon and land by this method.

The gills and digestive tract harbored bacteria as long as feed was present, but apparently as soon as all feed and waste products were eliminated these portions freed themselves of bacteria. Portions of cod, rockfish, bass, and alewives were also examined. The alewives alone were obtained with no feed present, and out of 72, 47 contained neither feed nor bacteria. *B. coli* and *B. Walfischrauschbrand* were isolated from the cod. The flesh was free from bacteria in practically every instance.

CHEMICAL COMPOSITION OF THE FEED OF HERRING.

The crustaceans, to which group of sea life the feed of the sea herring belong, differ in composition from meats and fish in having a large proportion of the carbohydrate glycogen present in the liver. This is suggestive in connection with the rapid formation of gas observed in decomposing feed, such as schizopods and copepods. Undoubtedly the composition of the feed is of such a nature as to furnish an excellent medium for the growth of gas- and nongas-producing bacteria.

In an investigation of the chemical composition of plankton, K. Brandt(4) obtained the following results on analyzing material which consisted almost entirely of copepods:

TABLE 5.—*Chemical composition of copepods (dry basis) (Brandt).*

	Per cent.
Protein	58.80
Fat	7.40
Carbohydrates (by difference)	22.88
Ash	10.92
Composition of ash:	
Silica (SiO_2)	2.31
Common salt (NaCl)	1.49
Other salts	7.12

He found the composition of the dry substance of copepods, which included varieties taken from fresh water, to be as follows:

TABLE 6.—*Average composition of copepods (dry basis) (Brandt).*

	Per cent.
Protein	59.0
Chitin	4.7
Fat	7.0
Carbohydrates	20.0
Ash	9.3

The results of the chemical analyses, made during this investigation on the feed of the sea herring, to determine the rate of decomposition are given in Table 7. The total volatile nitrogen, ammonia, and amines were determined as the indices of decomposition when the feed, copepods, and schizopods were allowed to spoil under the most favorable conditions in an incubator. The determination of the total volatile alkaline material in a catch of plankton, which consisted almost entirely of diatoms, is also given. The rate of decomposition of fresh-water herring is included for the sake of comparison with the rate of decomposition of the feed alone.

In each case as many determinations were made as were possible with the amount of material at hand, which was not often large because of the difficulty of obtaining any kind of feed unless the water was very quiet. The amount of total volatile nitrogen found before incubation was so small that it seemed unnecessary to determine amine nitrogen.

TABLE 7.—*Ammonia and amines per 100 grams in feed of sea herring.*

Feed.[1]	When taken.			Held in incubator.								
				24 hours.			48 hours.			72 hours.		
	Total.	Ammonia.	Amines.	Total.	Ammonia.	Amines.	Total.	Ammonia.	Amines.	Total.	Ammonia.	Amines.
Plankton from Woods Hole, Mass., kept at 30° C. (chiefly diatoms).........	*Mg.* 2.82	*Mg.*	*Mg.*	*Mg.*	*Mg.*	*Mg.*	*Mg.*	*Mg.*	*Mg.*	*Mg.* 4.14	*Mg.*	*Mg.*
Plankton from St. Croix River off Campobello Island (chiefly copepods)...	6.04									402.2		
Copepods from east and south of Campobello Island......	3.94			272.4	206.2	66.2	468.2	375.1	93.1			
Copepods from shallow water east of Grand Manan............				216.6	153.8	62.8						
Copepods from north end of Grand Manan in very deep water............	9.50			191.7	143.4	48.3	296.8	260.9	35.9			
Schizopods from Wilson's Beach Island, off Campobello....................	1.98									822.9	602.3	220.6
Schizopods from Wilson's Beach Island, off Campobello....................	3.95			220.4	88.2	132.2	787.6	573.7	213.9	1009.2	832.6	176.6
Feed taken from belly-blown fish at wharf, Eastport, Me..............	37.7	17.1	20.6									
Fresh-water herring from Taunton River, Taunton, Mass....................	9.94			127.0	111.6	15.4				888.3	812.6	75.7

[1] Samples were kept at incubator temperature (37.5° C.).

Both ammonia and amines in very large quantities were found in the decomposing feed, schizopods and copepods. When allowed to spoil under these conditions and to the extent that took place during a period of from 48 to 72 hours, ammonia was found in much larger amounts than amines. From the limited number of determinations it was possible to make it was apparent that little difference, if any, exists in the rate of decomposition or in materials formed between copepods and schizopods. Considering the similarity of composition of the two forms, it is quite probable that no difference in degree or kind of decomposition would be found. The examination of the feed taken from the viscera of belly-blown fish gave results

confirming those found under artificial conditions.
and amines were present in appreciable amounts,
amines in this instance being in excess of the ammon

LABORATORY EXPERIMENTS WITH BACILLUS WALFISCHRAU!
BACILLUS B.

To establish more firmly the conclusion that the d
the feed and of the fish, resulting in the condition tern
is due to the presence of *Bacillus Walfischrauschbrand*
found in great numbers in the samples of feed ai
examined, and to show that the presence of these l
cated when volatile nitrogen bases are found in b
swelled cans, etc., these bacteria were grown in pure
medium containing fish protein, and the products
their growth observed. The fish used for cultures 24
(Table 8) were fresh Boston mackerel. Fresh-caugh
were used for cultures 27, 28, 29, and 30. After ren
solid masses of meat were passed through a meat grii
with a solution of dextrose of such strength that the 1
a uniform paste consistency, contained 0.2 per ce
The whole was then sterilized under 15 pounds pres
of this paste were inoculated with 24-hour-old dextros
cultures of the bacteria, and covered with an inch la
fish broth made firm with 1.5 per cent agar and no
then incubated at $37\frac{1}{2}°$ C. until removed for analysi
sample was removed for analysis, the presence of
with which it had been inoculated was determined p

TABLE 8.—*Ammonia and amines in pure cultures of Bacillus Wal*
Bacillus B grown in the laboratory.

Bacteria and culture No.	Period of incubation.	Total volatile alkaline material			
		Nitrogen per 100 grams.			Percer of to
		Total.	Am- monia.	Am- ines.	Am- monia.
Sterile:	*Days.*	*Mg.*	*Mg.*	*Mg.*	*Per ct.*
30...............................	7	18. 5	....	....	....
B. Walfischrauschbrand:					
28...............................	2	259. 5	215. 2	44. 3	82. 9
28...............................	4				
31...............................	7	510. 1	447. 1	63. 0	87. 7
32...............................	7	334. 6	286. 2	48. 4	85. 6
Bacillus B :					
24...............................	2	146. 8	....	48. 1	76. 9
24...............................	4	208. 4	160. 3	48. 1	76. 9
25...............................	3	159. 1	127. 7	31. 4	80. 3
29...............................	2	145. 8	132. 6	13. 2	81. 0
27 [2]...............................	2	225. 2	198. 8	26. 4	88. 2
27...............................	3	....	....	....	....

[1] These determinations were made by the latest amino acid method and ap
Biol. Chem. (1913) 16:121).
[2] A few micrococci in this culture.

The results in Table 8 show that both ammonia and amines are formed when *Bacillus Walfischrauschbrand* and *Bacillus B* are grown in pure culture on fish media. Under the conditions which obtained when these experiments were made, amines are formed in smaller amounts than when the different lots of feed are decomposed at incubator temperature. It would appear that a larger proportion of amines are formed during the decomposition of the feed and the fish under natural conditions.

In the cultures of *Bacillus Walfischrauschbrand* and *Bacillus B* used for the determination of ammonia and amines, positive tests for both indol and skatol were obtained. These results confirm those shown in Table 7—that ammonia and amines are produced by these organisms during the decomposition of the feed.

CAUSE OF BELLY-BLOWN FISH.

The fact that the bacteria found with the feed and in feedy fish decompose fish tissue, elaborating the same end products of decomposition as when the viscera and contents of herring decompose, points clearly to the cause of the condition of the fish termed "belly blown." It was shown (p. 86) that when the stomach and intestinal tract of the fish are empty, or practically so, no bacteria are present. The bacteria associated with the feed are eliminated with the digested feed or destroyed during the process of digestion. Only when the stomach or intestines contain feed in an undigested or partially digested condition are these bacteria found in abundance. Their growth during these conditions, when the fish are dead, gives rise to the products of decomposition. At certain times during the prevalence of feed a large proportion of the fish on flakes just taken from the steam boxes have been seen with the belly portions ruptured in a manner suggesting an explosive bursting. Small amounts of gas often were found lodged in some portion of the digestive tract when the gas-producing organism was also present. When occurring in sufficiently large amounts, the rapid expansion of this gas during the steaming process may cause the rupturing of the partially digested and weakened tissues surrounding the viscera. From this the term "belly blown" undoubtedly originated.

As the decomposition in the viscera and contents progresses bacteria are carried into the surrounding tissues, which are rendered soft by the alkaline materials, ammonia and amines. The thin belly portion of the fish is disintegrated by the action of the bacteria, and as decomposition progresses this portion of the fish gradually sloughs away, producing the characteristic ragged appearance termed "belly blown" (Pl. XVIII). The rapidity with which this condition is brought about depends upon the extent to which the fish are gorged with feed and the kind of bacteria accompanying the feed. Several lots of fish which contained feed when taken from the water showed, on reaching the canneries, an actual loss of 85 per cent due to belly-blown fish. A 25 to 50 per cent loss is not uncommon when feedy fish are taken. It is impossible to mistake the characteristic appearance of belly-blown feedy fish before or after packing.

TRANSPORTATION OF THE FISH.

A series of experiments were made to determine, both by chemical analysis and physical examination, the rate at which the fish decompose during transportation and their fitness for packing after being transported under different conditions. As a measure of the decomposition the total volatile nitrogen (ammonia and amines) was the only determination made.

The fish were carried in the hold of a small sardine boat, in a large hogshead, approximately $3\frac{1}{2}$ feet at its greatest diameter by 4 feet deep, provided with a wire screen to serve as a well, extending from the top to the bottom, through which the water and pickle could be pumped. Samples were taken as the fish were removed from the water and at 2- to 4-hour intervals thereafter, up to 24 and 30 hours. In one case samples of fish which had stood for 50 hours were examined. The samples that were taken during transit were placed in screw-cap Mason jars, which were kept in a mixture of salt and ice. They were frozen by this method, and were thus preserved until analyzed. At the laboratory the fish were cut and eviscerated, and samples made of the flesh and of the intestines and contents. A separate analysis was made of each.

FISH CARRIED IN BULK WITHOUT SALT.

Two lots were studied to determine the effect of transporting the fish in bulk without salt. The water dipped up with them was not drained off from the first lot. It was, however, pumped off from the second lot shortly after placing the fish in the hogshead, and at regular intervals thereafter. Five tubs of small fish, 4 to 5 inches in length and weighing 625 pounds net,[1] composed the first lot.

The first four samples (Table 10), which were taken at 2-hour intervals, represent conditions while in transit, whereas the sample taken at the end of 20 hours represents conditions while the fish were lying at the wharf overnight. The temperature of the fish in the middle of the hogshead at the time the 20-hour sample was taken was 54° F. The fish of this lot seemed to be in good condition when landed after the 5-hour run. At the end of 20 hours they had begun

---

[1] This weight included about one-half of the water dipped up with the fish and not drained off. In the ordinary practice of loading the boats at weirs, the water does not completely drain from each tub of fish. The only drainage is through a number of half-inch holes in the measuring tubs while the tub is being filled.

to soften, and some water had collected. A sample of this water, weighing 2 pounds, was taken at the end of 20 hours and also at the end of 24 hours. At the end of 24 hours the fish and water had an odor of decomposition, particularly the water, which had not been pumped off during transit. Unfortunately, some of the water had leaked out of the hogshead during the night, but the amount pumped off, together with an estimate of that lost through leaking, made approximately 50 pounds of water collected from this quantity of fish standing 24 hours.

The figures in Table 10 show plainly the rate of decomposition. The viscera and contents deteriorated somewhat during the 4- to the 6-hour period. At the end of the 20-hour period the content of total volatile nitrogen was just double that found at the end of the 6-hour period. Some decomposition was also evident in the flesh of the eviscerated fish at the end of the 6-hour period, while at the end of the 20-hour period marked decomposition had occurred. In the analysis of the viscera and contents and of the flesh, samples taken from the bottom of the hogshead showed more decomposition than samples collected from the top of the hogshead. These results indicate that the viscera and contents deteriorate more rapidly than the flesh of the fish, and that no very marked deterioration in the flesh occurs during the five hours of transportation. Subsequent bacteriological studies showed that the flesh of the fish was sterile or, at most, contained but few bacteria. Bacteria were very frequently found in the contents of the viscera. Decomposition would naturally occur in the viscera and contents before penetrating to the flesh.

Five tubs of fish, weighing 628 pounds, were used in the second lot. The tubs of fish were allowed to drain thoroughly before being weighed; consequently but little water was present. After allowing the fish to stand in the hogshead for a few minutes, 1½ buckets, weighing 25 pounds, of water were pumped off. The fish were brought to the laboratory after a 2-hour run and sampled every two hours, up to and including 12 hours, during the day while lying at the wharf. A sample was also taken the next morning at the end of 24 hours. After standing for 6 hours the water was pumped off and found to weigh 24 pounds. At the end of 12 hours an additional 9½ pounds of water was pumped off. After standing over night, or at the end of 24 hours, 7½ additional pounds of water had formed. The total amount of water obtained in 24 hours was 40.6 pounds. The water pumped off during the first 6 hours had but a slight color; at the end of the next 6-hour interval it was blood red; and at the end of the next 12-hour interval it was decidedly bloody. Both the 12- and 24-hour specimens precipitated a quantity of protein from test portions.

When landed at the laboratory 2 hours after being taken the weir these fish appeared to be in as good condition as wher were taken aboard. They had settled a little in the hogshea coming more solid and compact. So far as the physical appee would indicate, they were in good condition up to and includir 6-hour period. At the end of 8 hours they had changed sli; while 2 hours later a slight odor was noticeable in the hold (boat and the fish seemed a trifle soft. After 12 hours had el this softness was more pronounced, and the bellies of some (fish were broken. At the end of 24 hours, although there w decided odor of decomposition, the fish were soft and spoile(the bellies of a number were broken. The fish on the top (load had lost their luster ("bloom") and taken on a dead w color, while those from the bottom were in worse condition, badly broken and pressed out of shape by the mass above. fish were quite unfit for packing. The temperature of th in the hogshead at the end of the 6-hour period was 51° F. temperature of the water in the bay at this time and durir time the fish lay at the wharf was 50° F.

The analyses of samples from this lot of fish show at the end 6- and the 8-hour period a sufficient increase in the amou volatile nitrogen in the viscera and contents over that found fresh fish to indicate a slight decomposition. At the end of t hour period the decomposition in the viscera and content marked, although there was no visible evidence of decomposit the flesh. At the end of the 24-hour period, however, m decomposition was shown in the flesh as well as in the inte and contents.

In this experiment the fish at the top of the load did not di amount of decomposition from those taken from the bottom pile. In this shipment the water was pumped off at int(whereas in the preceding experiment it was not. Evidentl drainage water tends to increase the rate of decomposition (fish at the bottom of the mass from which it has not been rem or, as might be expected, larger quantities of volatile nitrogen in fish standing in water drained from fish undergoing decompo;

FISH CARRIED IN BULK, SALTED AT THE RATE OF ONE-HALF SACK PER HOG

In this experiment five tubs of fish, weighing 649 pounds, employed. On being loaded, the fish were evenly salted at th of one-half sack per hogshead. The water dipped up with tl was drained off and the pickle formed during the experiment pi off at 2-hour intervals, with the exception of the 10-hour ρ This pickle was weighed, sampled, and analyzed (Table 9).

TABLE 9.—*Composition of pickle formed during transportation of fish in salt.*

Time of forming pickle.	Description.	Weight.		Specific gravity.	Salt (NaCl).	Nitrogen.
Hours.		*Pounds.*	*Grams.*		*Per cent.*	*Per cent.*
2	Very light, slight yellow color, clear......	29.5	13,409	1.155	19.93	0.072
4	Light in color, with slight reddish tinge, clear..	22.5	10,227	1.145	18.55	.134
6	Slightly reddish in color, slightly cloudy .	9.0	4,090	1.140	17.68	.178
8	Reddish, cloudy................................	4.5	2,045	1.140	17.14	.206
12	Reddish, more cloudy than that held 8 hours....................................	4.21	1,912	1.130	15.86	.245
25	.....do...	11.0	5,000	1.110	12.44	.330

Attention is directed to the decrease in the specific gravity and corresponding decrease in the percentage amount of salt, and to the increase in the percentage of nitrogen during each succeeding interval that the fish remained in salt.

At the end of the 2 hours required for the run to the laboratory all the fish had "struck," and at the end of the 4- to 6-hour period, they had begun to show the effects of salting, although still in fair condition. At the end of the 8-hour period they were hard and firm, and some showed the thin, pressed appearance characteristic of fish which have been carried too long in salt. The bellies of very few were broken at the end of 8 hours. Compared with the standard for quality obtaining at the time these experiments were made, they would at this period have been considered good fish for packing. The same can be said for them at the end of the 10-hour period, except that the shrunken and shriveled appearance had become more pronounced.

While the determination of total volatile nitrogen (ammonia and amines) is not a true criterion upon which to base decomposition changes taking place in the flesh of fish carried in salt, since the decomposition products formed, particularly ammonia and amine, pass into the brine, it is none the less interesting to note that the volatile nitrogen content of the flesh gradually diminished during the time the fish were in salt, up to and including the 12-hour period, rising noticeably after the fish had been held for 25 hours and again at the end of 50 hours. At the end of the 4-hour period the amount of ammoniacal materials in the viscera and contents of the fish carried in salt had increased appreciably.

In contrasting this experiment with the preceding experiment it is apparent that the viscera and contents of this lot decomposed a little more rapidly than those of the fish carried without salt. While this may be due, in part at least, to the difference in the quantity or quality of the food in the intestines of the fish comprising these lots, it serves to show that the salting of fish does not prevent deterioration during transportation to the extent generally supposed. In an investigation on the conservation of fish and meat products with

salt, Pettersson(22) found that anchovies and similar preparati
always contain numerous cocci, rods, and yeasts as bacterial fl
Apparently, therefore, certain forms of bacteria survive the ex
sive salting given such products. Table 10 shows that a little (
3 per cent was the maximum quantity of salt found in the fl
viscera, and contents of fish subjected to the ordinary salting
pickling process—not a sufficient amount to retard bacterial gro
In fact, a media containing 3.33 per cent salt was found to be
most favorable for the growth of bacteria common to this regio

This experiment proves also that the analysis of the viscera
contents may be taken as a very good indication of the time and
rate at which the fish deteriorate, and that the intestines and (
tents show decomposition in greater quantity at an earlier pe
than does the flesh. Another interesting point brought out in tl
experiments is the fact that decomposition extends to the flesl
fish held in salt for an excessive length of time.

FISH CARRIED IN COMPARTMENTS, SURROUNDED WITH ICE AND SALT MIXTUE

This shipment was made at the same time as the one in the
ceding experiment. Two tubs of fish, weighing 294 pounds, f
the same catch were used. The fish were equally divided among
five compartments of the box designed to carry them, and c
pletely surrounded with ice and salt mixture. They were not p
over 5 or 6 inches deep. A hole in the bottom of the hogshea
which the box was placed allowed the drainage to pass into the l
of the boat. The temperature of the iced fish in the third comp
ment from the top, after 12 hours, was 3° C. (37.4° F.). Afte
hours' standing the temperature in the third and fourth comp
ments was 1½° C. (34.7° F.), and after 30 hours the tempera
reached −1° C. (30.2° F.). Some of the ice and salt had mel
about one-fourth of the total quantity used remaining at this ti

These fish remained firm and plump, even after standing 25 ho
They did not have a leached-out appearance, but were of a brig
and better color than those which had been carried in the s
When the samples were being prepared for analysis, the iced
looked like fresh fish. At the end of 6 hours, however, a differe
was noted in the appearance of the gills which were not as brig
red as those of fresh fish. The fish retained their freshness of c
and consistency of flesh throughout the time they were kept. E
at the end of 50 hours, in spite of the fact that they had deterior
to such an extent as to be unfit for packing, they had a better
pearance than those which had been kept in salt. At the end o
hours the fish surrounded with ice were in splendid shape, still
and plump, although they had lost the stiff, rigid condition sh
previous to this time. At the end of 25 hours a few fish in both
(in salt and in ice) showed broken bellies, but one lot had no n

belly-broken fish than the other. At the end of 50 hours the iced fish were quite soft and the bellies of a few more were broken, but no more than in the case of the salted fish, which were harder and firmer in texture, though much poorer in appearance, suggesting a poor quality of salt fish.

The analyses of the samples from the lot of iced fish, which were taken at intervals of 4 hours, up to and including 12 hours, and at 25, 30, and 50 hours, indicate that the viscera and contents of the fish kept without appreciable evidence of decomposition up to and including 12 hours. At the end of 25 hours a slight decomposition was indicated, which was more noticeable at the end of 30 hours. At the end of 50 hours, decomposition of the viscera and contents was quite marked. Under the conditions of this particular experiment, practically no decomposition took place in the flesh of the eviscerated fish. It is probable that the slight evidence of decomposition obtained after 50 hours standing in excess of that found in the fresh fish represents the slight deterioration that might be expected in fish kept under these conditions.

TABLE 10.—*Changes in composition of fish when transported under varying conditions.*

Condition of fish.		Viscera and contents.				Flesh of eviscerated fish.			
Out of water.	In dry salt.	Water.	Fat.	Salt (NaCl).	Total volatile nitrogen (N) per 100 grams.	Water.	Fat.	Salt (NaCl).	Total volatile nitrogen (N) per 100 grams.
Hours.	*Hours.*	*Per cent.*	*Per cent.*	*Per cent.*	*Mg.*	*Per cent.*	*Per cent.*	*Per cent.*	*Mg.*
Lot 1 (no salt):									
Fresh		66.70	19.12	....	11.6	76.00	4.39	....	9.3
2		66.72	19.67	....	......	76.64	3.65	....	......
4		59.97	28.07	....	11.6	74.70	5.34	....	9.3
6		66.40	20.05	....	16.3	76.37	4.34	....	14.0
20		65.41	24.08	....	32.6	76.92	4.43	....	21.0
24 [1]		54.23	36.99	....	......	75.23	5.02	....	21.0
24 [2]		60.60	³28.94	....	37.3	74.86	5.38	....	28.0
Lot 2 (no salt):									
Fresh		62.40	21.75	....	12.6	74.44	4.91	....	13.0
2		60.55	19.67	....	11.7	75.68	3.42	....	13.5
4		63.53	24.14	....	14.0	76.96	3.90	....	13.8
6		63.63	23.85	....	15.0	76.78	3.92	....	14.0
8		64.73	22.91	....	17.7	76.58	3.68	....	14.0
10		62.29	26.15	....	17.7	76.42	4.03	....	10.7
12		63.41	24.65	....	22.3	77.01	3.88	....	14.5
24 [1]		65.60	21.17	....	39.1	76.65	3.30	....	24.2
24 [2]		71.82	³12.94	....	38.2	77.26	4.53	....	23.3
Lot 3 (½ sack salt per hogshead):									
	Fresh.	62.83	24.62	0.41	11.0	76.18	4.40	0.21	14.0
	2	59.45	26.62	1.22	12.1	71.26	4.99	2.41	10.8
	4	56.70	26.84	2.18	18.2	69.49	6.03	2.98	8.8
	6	56.86	27.68	1.75	18.2	70.89	5.51	2.29	8.0
	8	59.67	23.97	1.93	18.7	70.39	5.61	2.42	9.8
	10	56.21	25.16	2.76	19.1	68.93	6.29	2.93	7.9
	12	55.74	26.86	2.20	......	68.13	6.98	2.74	7.7
	25	60.14	21.20	2.94	27.6	67.22	6.14	3.69	11.5
	50	59.74	26.85	1.59	38.0	71.24	5.19	1.95	17.9
Lot 4 (kept cold with mixture of ice and salt):									
Fresh		62.33	24.62	....	11.0	76.18	4.40	....	14.0
4		57.23	37.75	....	14.9	75.99	4.35	....	12.2
8		62.02	27.66	....	17.2	74.87	3.63	....	7.9
12		56.03	36.54	....	16.3	75.86	5.33	....	9.8
25		61.20	23.71	....	18.6	76.22	4.60	....	10.3
30		62.46	26.15	....	19.6	75.64	5.04	....	11.0
50		67.84	20.10	....	33.2	76.85	3.63	....	16.3

[1] From top of load.   [2] From bottom of load.   ³ Shows effect of pressure.

These experiments show that as a means of preservation
transportation of the small sea herring, refrigeration is in
respect far superior to the use of salt. This is apparent from
parison of the physical condition of the two lots of fish at the d
intervals of time, and is confirmed by the analytical result;
same degree of decomposition in the viscera and contents of
carried under refrigerator conditions as that found for the 8-
hour period in the case of the fish in salt is not shown until
of from 25 to 30 hours.

The difference between the appearance of fish transportec
refrigeration and that of those carried an excessive length
in salt is shown in Plates XII and XIII. Kept in compa
surrounded with ice and salt they are plump and firm, and lo
fresh fish, even after they have been 30 hours out of wate
fish carried an excessive length of time in salt, in bulk, are p
appearance, and much thinner, and have been pressed out of
Each lot of fish at the time of capture varies in the amou
kind of food in the digestive tract, and also in the bacteri
tamination of the digestive tract. The keeping qualities, or t
of decomposition, of different lots of fish should therefor
directly as the contamination and quantity of feed vary.
this is true is shown by the differences in the time and ex
spoilage of the various lots of fish employed in these experim

TEMPERATURE CHANGES OCCURRING IN LOADS OF FISH DURING TRANSPO

Temperature observations were made on boatloads of fish
ported from the weirs to the canneries in pickle and in dry s;
was estimated that the fish in the three lots studied contain
ferent proportions of feed. The results are given in Table 11
temperature measurements were accurately made by mear
Leeds and Northrup potentiometer, the thermocouple of whi
inserted in the mass of fish in the boats, and readings taken
time intervals indicated. The temperature changes of the
the warmest day of the month and the changes shown fr
mean temperatures for the month in which these observatio
made are included in the table.

TABLE 11.—*Temperature changes in loads of fish during transit.*

FLOATED IN BRINE CONTAINING 150 POUNDS OF SALT PER HOGSHEAD
SLIGHT AMOUNT OF FEED PRESENT.

Time observed.	Temperature.		
	Of air.[1]		Of fish.
	Warmest day.	Mean for month.	
a. m.	° *C.*	° *C.*	° *C.*
6.30	12.7	6.9	12
7.00	....	....	13
7.30	....	....	15
8.00	13.8	8.2	16

[1] From hourly thermograph readings taken from original monthly record of observations a
Me.; for October, 1916 (courtesy of U. S. Weather Bureau).

FIG. I.—FISH CARRIED IN SMALL BULK, IN COMPARTMENTS SURROUNDED WITH ICE AND SALT.

No salt on fish.　Fish out of water 30 hours.

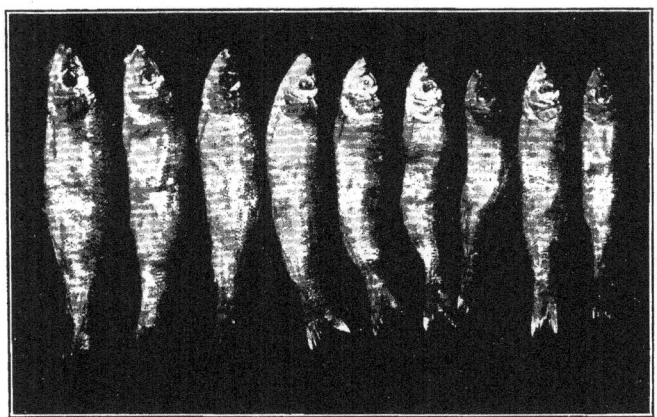

FIG. 2.—FISH CARRIED IN BULK IN SALT, ONE-HALF SACK PER HOGSHEAD.

Fish in salt 25 hours.　Note effect of excessive salting and compare with iced fish 30 hours old, with no salt.

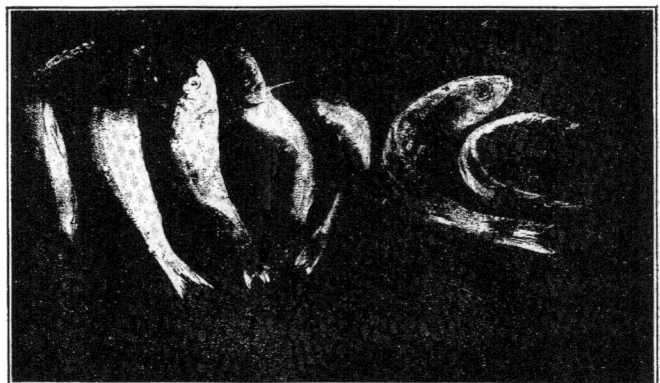

FIG. I.—FISH EXCESSIVELY SALTED AND CARRIED IN LARGE BULK.

FIG. 2.—A CAN OF SARDINES SHOWING THE EFFECT OF EXCESSIVE SALTING OF THE FISH.

Note the transverse cracks and fissures on each fish. A portion of the side of one fish has been lost.

Table 11.—*Temperature changes in loads of fish during transit*—Continued.

DRY-SALTED, 150 POUNDS OF SALT PER HOGSHEAD; FISH 2½ FEET DEEP IN BOAT; 47 PER CENT OF FEED PRESENT.

Time observed.	Temperature.		
	Of air.		Of fish.
	Warmest day.	Mean for month.	
a. m.	° *C.*	° *C.*	° *C.*
9.30	17.2	9.6	11
10.36	....	....	14
11.30	....	....	18
p. m.			
12.30	20.0	11.9	23.5

DRY-SALTED; 90 PER CENT OF FEED PRESENT.

a. m.	° *C.*	° *C.*	° *C.*	
5.56	11.7	6.7	11	
6.24	....	....	11	
9.23	....	....	12	
9.36	....	....	18.5	
10.36	....	....	22	
11.30	....	....	24.5	
p. m.				
12.30	20.0	11.9	27	
2.00	22.8	12.4	....	
4.20	20.0	11.1	37.5	

The changes of temperature in the outside air were not sufficient to account for the changes in temperature which occurred in the loads of fish. It is evident that fish heat when carried in bulk, as is now the custom, the temperature increasing in proportion to the amount of feed present. The temperature of fish which contained but a small amount of feed and were carried in pickle rose 4° during one and one-half hours. That of dry-salted fish, estimated to be 47 per cent feedy, rose 12.5° during three hours. A boatload of fish in dry salt, 90 per cent of which were estimated to contain feed, rose 11° in temperature during a run of four and one-half hours. Just before the fish on this boat were unloaded, practically 10½ hours after they had been taken from the water, the temperature of the mass, taken midway between the top and bottom, showed an increase of 26.5°.

The rise in temperature of masses of fish in bulk is caused by decomposition changes due to bacterial growth, by far the greater part of which takes place in the viscera and contents. As the temperature of the mass of fish rises and approaches the optimum temperature favorable to bacterial growth, it is evident why the decomposition of feedy fish proceeds, at times, so rapidly. It is also evident why keeping the fish in smaller bulk and at a low temperature markedly retards this decomposition.

CONCLUSIONS.

It is not necessary to salt excessively fish which are to be in transit for a reasonable length of time only. Since excessive salting does not prevent completely the decomposition of fish, salt should be used in transit with the idea of saving time in the pickling sheds rather than as a means of preserving the fish during transportation over great distances.

Fish preserved with salt should not be transported over a distance requiring more than 6 hours to cover. Sometimes 4 hours is the limit.

Where practicable it would be desirable to install some method of refrigeration on all boats used to haul the fish for long distances. Boats thus equipped not only greatly extend the fishing radius, but also bring the fish to the canneries in a condition far superior to that of fish carried in salt.

The decomposition due to "heating," which was found to occur in large masses of fish during transportation, can be retarded by shipping them in small bulk at low temperature. Small compartments, permitting the circulation of cold air, are necessary in boats equipped with refrigeration devices.

PICKLING AND SALTING THE FISH.

In earlier days all the pickling was done after the fish reached the cannery, where an expert in this work was employed in the pickling shed. As a rule, the fish were held in strong brine or pickle, usually made to a strength of 90° on the salimeter, for about two hours, although the period of holding varied with the fatness of the fish, those which were fat needing more time for the process than the lean ones. The length of time was determined by the appearance of the fish, which were said to have "struck" when they had been long enough in the salt brine.

Within the past 12 or 15 years most of the boats transporting fish have been equipped with water-tight tanks in which salt or pickle may be added to the fish as they are taken from the weirs. Thus salt came into use as a means of preserving the fish during transportation. The use of salt during the trip prevents the extreme decomposition possible under the old methods of transportation, cuts down the time required for pickling at the canneries, and permits the carrying of the fish for greater distances. While fish obtained near the canneries still are salted or pickled in the sheds, those which are to be transported far are kept in salt or pickle. When transported for great distances no attention is paid to the length of time the fish are kept in salt or pickle. This excessive salting results in an inferior pack of sardines (Pl. XIII).

The time the fish remain in pickle or salt is a most important consideration in the packing of sardines. They should be kept there long enough to acquire the proper salt flavor, but no longer. As a rule, fish are salted sufficiently or excessively during the run to the cannery and need but little or no subsequent pickling. When they have been too long in dry salt, it is customary to hold them in weak pickle for a short time after they reach the factory, to remove the excess of salt before they are started through the process. Part of the salt also is removed when they are steamed (p. 47).

According to the best practice, the fish are not allowed to remain excessively long in pickle after they have reached the cannery, overnight, for example. Held in pickle for from 6 to 10 hours, they become soft, the bellies often breaking away, and they acquire a peculiar, dull, leached appearance. Held too long in dry salt the fish, particularly those that are small and lean, become dry, hard, and brittle, with a tendency to break transversely during the steaming and drying processes, in which case they are said to be "burned by salt" (Pl. XIV, fig. 2). Fish treated in either way are very undesirable for canning.

Since it is impossible to make even a fair grade of sardines from fish which have been excessively salted or pickled, it is essential that the canner should constantly guard against excessive salting and pickling of the fish.

In order to obtain information which would be helpful in carrying out this step of the canning process, an extensive investigation of the pickling and salting of fish was undertaken.

COMPOSITION OF SALT USED.

Salt used in pickling and salting fish is said to vary in effectiveness with its calcium and magnesium content, one of a low content penetrating the tissues of the fish better than those high in these constituents. Samples of three kinds of salt used in the Maine industry during 1913 and 1914 were analyzed, with the results shown in Table 12.

TABLE 12.—*Composition of salt used in salting and pickling the fish.*

Determination.	American.	Liverpool.	Trapani.
Moisture..per cent..	1.57	4.16	3.44
Insoluble in water.......................................do....	.12	.17	.14
Calcium chlorid (CaCl₂).................................do....	.94	.46	.87
Magnesium chlorid (MgCl₂)............................do....	.09	.16	1.04
Sodium sulphate (Na₂SO₄).............................do....	1.61	.76	1.42
Potassium chlorid (KCl)...............................do....	2.22	4.03	.40
Sodium chlorid (NaCl)..................................do....	93.48	90.33	92.49
Total...do....	100.03	100.07	99.80
Sodium chlorid (NaCl) on dry basis...................do....	94.97	94.21	95.78

Each contained but a small amount of calcium and magnesium. The Liverpool salt showed the highest water content and lowest calcium and magnesium content, and the American salt the lowest water content and highest salt (NaCl) content. It had but little over 1 per cent of calcium and magnesium calculated as the chlorids. The Liverpool salt was used in the experimental work.

CHANGES OCCURRING IN FISH HELD IN PICKLE AND IN DRY SALT.

A number of experiments on a laboratory scale and on a comparatively large scale were conducted to determine what changes occur when fish remain for certain periods of time in pickle and in dry salt.

LABORATORY SCALE.

Fish about 5 inches long, said to have been out of the water only two hours, both eviscerated and uneviscerated, were used for the first series of experiments. They had been carried in pickle with a specific gravity of 1.1212 at 25°/25° C. and a salt content of 15.5 per cent.

Some of these fish, in covered porcelain evaporating dishes, were allowed to stand for some time in pickle obtained from a freshly prepared lot at an adjacent cannery. The composition of this pickle at the stated intervals is shown in Table 13.

TABLE 13.—*Composition of pickle in which fish were held.*

Condition.	From eviscerated fish.		From uneviscerated fish.	
	Specific gravity (by picnometer), 25°/25° C.	Salt (NaCl).	Specific gravity (by picnometer), 25°/25° C.	Salt (NaCl).
		Per cent.		Per cent.
Fresh	1.1279	16.49	1.1279	16.49
After 24 hours	1.1150	14.50	1.1099	13.56
After 48 hours	1.1152	14.49	1.1120	13.98
After 96 hours	1.1157	14.49	1.1132	13.97

TABLE 14.—*Composition of fish held in pickle and in dry salt (2 to 96 hours).*

Condition of fish.	Water.	Fat.	Total volatile nitrogen (ammonia and amines).	Moisture and fat free basis.		Acidity of fat (N/20 sodium ethylate per gram).
				Total volatile nitrogen (ammonia and amines).	Amino acid nitrogen.	
Eviscerated fish in pickle:	Per cent.	Per cent.	Mg.	Mg.	Mg.	Cc.
2 hours	69.68	4.36	16.3	62.8	1.53	12.3
24 hours	63.75	4.62			.96	12.6
48 hours	62.30	3.94	10.5	31.1	1.00	12.5
96 hours	67.39	3.69	7.0	24.2	1.00	10.7
Uneviscerated fish in pickle:						
2 hours	69.33	3.97	18.6	69.7	1.87	15.5
24 hours	63.22	5.86	13.9	45.0	1.68	14.6
48 hours	62.63	5.65			1.37	15.0
96 hours	68.25	3.77	12.9	46.1	1.84	16.9
Eviscerated fish in dry salt:						
24 hours	52.42	5.20	14.0	33.1	1.09	17.0
48 hours	52.68	4.85	12.8	30.1	1.00	16.7
96 hours	53.31	5.00	15.2	36.5	1.00	16.4
Uneviscerated fish in dry salt:						
24 hours	51.85	6.31	12.8	30.6	1.44	17.3
48 hours	50.58	6.01	13.9	32.0	1.03	17.1
96 hours	52.56	6.44	14.0	34.1	1.18	15.1

Other fish of the same lot, in enamel pans, were intimately mixed with salt until they were almost covered, when a final layer just covering them was sprinkled over the top. A fairly large excess of salt in proportion to the quantity of fish was used.

The changes which the fish held in pickle and in dry salt underwent at certain intervals of time are shown in Table 14.

As was to be expected, the water content of the fish decreased during the first 48 hours they remained in the salt and pickle, the loss being much greater in the case of those kept in dry salt. At the end of the 48-hour period the percentage of water lost by the eviscerated fish in pickle was practically the same as that lost by the uneviscerated fish. The uneviscerated fish in dry salt, however, showed at this period a slightly greater loss of water than did the eviscerated fish in dry salt. The water content of the fish kept in pickle and in dry salt for 96 hours increased from that shown for the 48-hour period, the increase being more marked in the case of the fish held in pickle.

There appears to be a greater loss of volatile nitrogen, as ammonia and amines, from the tissues of the fish when kept in pickle than when kept in dry salt. No change of a significant nature was found in the results obtained for the amino acid nitrogen or the acidity of the fat.

The fish used in the second experiment, brought to the laboratory during cool weather, were in good condition, having been but from 4 to 6 hours out of the water. They were oil size, packing on the average 6 fish to the can.

After a representative sample, designated as fresh fish in Table 15, had been taken from the entire portion, 500-gram lots were accurately weighed into beakers, and 350 cc of pickle reading 90° on the salimeter were added. At the expiration of the time intervals indicated in Table 15 the samples were removed and weighed, and the volume, specific gravity, and weight of the pickle determined.

Of the other fish, 500-gram portions were treated with 100 grams of salt. At the end of the stated periods the brine which had formed was poured off, and the whole mass of fish, rinsed free from adhering water and brine, was analyzed.

The results of the analyses of the fish appear in Table 15, and of those of the pickle in Table 16.

The loss in weight, 4.4 per cent of the original weight of the fish, which occurred during the first hour they were held in pickle, was almost doubled at the expiration of the 8-hour period. A gradual loss in both water and fat, corresponding to the length of time the fish remained in the pickle, occurred.

	Adde[d]	At en[d]		Wate[r]	Fat.	Total	Total (am per	Salt.	Tota
Uneviscerated fish:	Grms.	Grms.	Grms.	Per cent.	Per cent.	Per cent.	Mg.	Per cent.	P(cer
Fresh..................	......	......	......	68.51	14.18	2.54	15.2	0.16	14.
In pickle—									
1 hour..............	500	478	22	4.4	69.02	11.82	2.67	17.5	1.75	15.
2 hours.............	500	466	34	6.8	67.83	11.76	2.73	14.0	2.12	14.
4 hours.............	500	470	30	6.0	65.93	12.46	2.71	14.0	2.93	14.
6 hours.............	500	470	30	6.0	64.28	13.67	2.77	17.4	3.38	14.
8 hours.............	500	459	41	8.2	63.84	12.61	2.81	16.3	4.05	14.
Same lot dry salted: [1]									
In salt—									
14 hours...........	500	427	73	14.6	55.82	14.92	3.02	15.2	8.54	14.
18 hours...........	500	420	80	16.0	55.02	14.02	3.04	12.8	9.94	14.
Eviscerated fish:									
Fresh...............	......	......	......		71.51	9.68	2.71	14.0	......	14.
In pickle [2]—									
10 hours...........	212	195	17	8.0	69.59	10.31	2.61	13.4	......	10.
12 hours...........	237	212	25	10.6	64.25	10.31	2.71	10.5	......	10.
Same lot, uneviscerated:									
Fresh...............	......	......	......		70.79	9.81	2.63	11.6	......	13.
In pickle—									
10 hours...........	317	290	27	8.5	62.92	12.50	2.80	16.3	......	11.
12 hours...........	305	274	31	10.2	62.50	12.15	2.86	......	......	11.

[1] In 100 grams of salt. [2] 200 cc of pickle, reading 90° on the salimeter, used. [3] B

The results calculated to a water, fat, and salt free bas
an actual loss of 0.40 per cent of nitrogen, corresponding t
cent of protein during the 8 hours the fish were in pickle.
salted fish lost 14.6 per cent of their weight after remaining
14 hours and 16 per cent after being in salt for 18 hours.

Most of the loss in weight of fish held in dry salt may b
to the abstraction of water from them. The water cont
fish held in dry salt is a little less than 1.0 per cent lo
end of the 18-hour period than it was at the end of the 14-h
The total nitrogen in the fish for both periods in dry salt i
the amount found in fresh fish, and is practically the san
shown for fish held in pickle for 8 hours. The total volatil
content of the fish held in dry salt is much less than that o
the same lot which had been held in pickle.

The marked variation in the composition of the pickle in
fish were held for the different periods compared with tl
fresh pickle (Table 16) shows in an even more striking m
changes which the fish underwent.

TABLE 16.—*Composition of pickle in which fish were held (1 to 18 hours).*

Condition of pickle.[1]	Volume of pickle.		Specific gravity.	Weight.	Brine contained—			
	To which were added ·500 grams fish.	Increased after alloted time to.			Total nitrogen.	Total volatile nitrogen (ammonia and amines).	Amino acid nitrogen.	Salt.
With uneviscerated fish:	Cc.	Cc.		Grams.	Mg.	Mg.	Mg.	Per cent.
Fresh......			1.1729	410.5	(²)	0.0	4.9	22.75
After 1 hour.............	356	368	1.1487	422.5	94.41	4.1	16.9	18.98
After 2 hours.............	350	370	1.1400	421.8	144.39	5.7	22.9	18.06
After 4 hours.............	350	375	1.1306	423.9	(²)	6.3	26.7	16.86
After 6 hours.............	350	380	1.1280	428.6	262.73	8.0	31.5	16.36
After 8 hours.............	350	403	1.1212	451.8	360.36	13.5	46.5	15.47
With dry salted fish:[3]								
After 14 hours...........	(⁴)				189.97	....	53.0	....
After 18 hours...........	(⁵)				242.75	....	63.0	....
With eviscerated fish:								
Fresh...........	(⁶)		1.1841	236.8	1.5	0.0	3.2	23.31
After 10 hours...........	200	222	1.1365	252.3	244.2	7.5	46.3	17.56
After 12 hours...........	200	228	1.1227	255.9	291.8	6.9	42.9	14.95
With uneviscerated fish (same lot as last):								
After 10 hours.............	200	231	1.1200	258.7	254.1	10.7	67.9	14.89
After 12 hours.............	200	232	1.1200	259.8	290.0	....	....	14.89

[1] Pickle used with fish the analyses of which are given in Table 15.
[2] Lost.
[3] 100 grams of salt to 500 grams of fish.
[4] 125 cc brine collected made to volume of 200 cc.
[5] 130 cc brine collected made to volume of 200 cc.
[6] Volume to which first added.

The volume and weight of the pickle increased gradually and the specific gravity decreased during the time the fish remained in it. The amount of material extracted from the fish in the pickle, represented by the total nitrogen, ammonia and amines, and amino acid nitrogen, gradually increased, while the percentage of salt in the pickle gradually decreased with the length of time the fish remained in it. More nitrogenous material was extracted from the fish during the 18-hour period in salt than during the 14-hour period. The total nitrogen extracted from the fish held in salt was noticeably less than that removed during the 6 and 8 hours they remained in pickle. More of this nitrogen, in the form of amino acids, was extracted when the fish were kept in dry salt than when kept in pickle.

A supplementary experiment was made with a second lot of fish part of which were eviscerated and part of which were not. These fish, which contained about 5 per cent less fat than those used in the previous experiment, were kept in pickle for from 10 to 12 hours. Different weights of fish were added to 200 cc of pickle which read 90° on the salimeter.

The eviscerated fish and uneviscerated fish [1] showed practically the same percentage loss of weight at the end of the 10- and 12-hour

[1] These samples contained more fish to the quantity of pickle than the previous samples. The two sets of results are not, therefore, strictly comparable.

periods in pickle. The loss at the end of 12 hours in both was greater by approximately 2 per cent than that at the end of the 10-hour period. A greater loss of total nitrogen and of ammonia and amine nitrogen occurred in the eviscerated than in the uneviscerated fish. More nitrogenous material was extracted from these fish than was lost by the lot used in the previous experiment when held in either pickle or dry salt. The weight and volume and specific gravity changes were slightly greater in the case of the pickle from eviscerated fish, showing that a larger quantity of water was removed from uncut fish than from those in which the viscera had been removed. There was practically no difference in the total amount of nitrogen found in the pickle of the eviscerated and uneviscerated fish. The quantity of total volatile nitrogen, however, was slightly greater in the case of the uneviscerated fish.

It is seen from these three sets of experiments that fish lose more water when dry salted than when held in strong pickle. The amount of nitrogenous material extracted in proportion to the amount of water removed is very much less in the case of fish held in dry salt than that extracted from fish held in pickle. More nitrogenous substances are extracted from eviscerated fish than from uneviscerated fish, while a greater amount of nitrogenous extractives is removed from fish relatively poor in fat than from fairly fat fish.

LARGE SCALE.

To secure experimental conditions which would approximate as nearly as possible those of actual practice and still keep the work under control, two additional experiments were conducted on the dry salting of fish.

The first one was made on fish from Grand Manan, which had been about 8 hours out of water. The weather was decidedly cool, so that they were in good condition. The largest fish were discarded, the experiment being conducted on 70 pounds, accurately weighed to one-half ounce, of one-quarter oil and three-quarter mustard size.

The salting, which was done in a small barrel provided with a hole in the bottom, through which the pickle could be drawn off at intervals, was at the rate of one sack to a hogshead, which is approximately .180 pounds of salt to 1,000 pounds of fish, or 13 pounds to 70 pounds of fish. The brine was drawn off after the first hour and the second hour, and then at 2-hour intervals. A sample of the fish designated as fresh was taken from the lot as it was being salted. After drawing off the brine at each time interval, a sample of fish was removed, weighed, washed free from adhering salt, the heads removed, and ground thoroughly. The brine collected after each interval of time was measured, weighed, and analyzed. The results of the analyses are given in Table 17.

A gradual loss of water occurred during the entire period the fish remained in the salt until at the end of 12 hours a reduction of 11.07 per cent in moisture is noted. This loss was accompanied by an apparent gain in fat of 2.43 per cent, which, however, on being calculated to a water free basis, becomes an actual loss of 3.10 per cent. On a moisture, fat, and salt free basis 4.06 per cent of nitrogenous material was abstracted from the fish by the action of the salt and brine. The ammonia and amine nitrogen content, which fluctuated markedly, showed a general tendency to decrease in accordance with the length of time the fish remained in salt.[1] In this particular lot of fish the maximum amount of salt was absorbed during the 8-hour period.

As soon as the fish are placed in salt the formation of brine begins, and the results of analysis of the brine show that appreciable quantities of nitrogenous extractive material passed into this brine formed from water removed from the fish. The maximum amount of nitrogenous material was abstracted during the 4- and 6-hour periods of the time in salt, although the greatest quantity of brine was collected at the end of the 6-hour period. The quantity of nitrogen in the brine increased from only 206.3 mg during the first hour to 1,865 mg at the end of the second hour and was then fairly constant. The largest amount of nitrogen was obtained in the next period or at the expiration of 4 hours, during which time a total of 1,992.5 mg of nitrogen passed into the brine. During the next 2-hour period, in which the largest amount of brine was formed, the amount of nitrogen abstracted by the brine was but a few milligrams less than that found in the previous period.

The nitrogenous material extracted during the 8-, 10-, and 12-hour periods diminished noticeably, though still fairly large. The amount of ammonia and amine nitrogen per 100 cc of brine increased noticeably from the first hour on. The largest amount was found at the expiration of the 6-hour period, when a total of 90.3 mg is shown, after which a gradual decline is indicated. The greatest amount of amino acid nitrogen obtained, 435.9 mg, was found in the brine for the 4-hour period. This corresponds to the period in which the largest amount of protein material was abstracted. The total quantity of nitrogen in the brine for the entire 12-hour period was extracted at the rate of 152.4 mg per pound of fish.

The figures in Table 18 showing the loss of weight and the percentage loss of the total amount of fish and salt are interesting.

---

[1] The ammonia content of the fish in this experiment was high because the samples had begun to deteriorate before the determination could be completed, and may also have been influenced by irregularity in salting and sampling.

TABLE 17.—*Chemical changes in fish held in dry salt.*

Description.	Volume.	Weight.		Specific gravity.	Water.	Fat.	Total nitrogen (N).	Total protein (N×6.25).	Total volatile nitrogen (ammonia and amines) per 100 grams or cc.	Salt (NaCl).	Water, fat, and salt free basis.				Amino acid nitrogen per 100 cc.	Total nitrogen (N).	Total volatile nitrogen (ammonia and amines).	Amino acid nitrogen.
											Total nitrogen (N).	Total protein (N×6.25).	Total volatile nitrogen (ammonia and amines) per 100 grams.	Salt (NaCl) (water, fat free basis).				
	Cc.	*Grams.*	*Oz.*		*P. ct.*	*P. ct.*	*P. ct.*	*P. ct.*	*Mg.*	*P. ct.*	*Mg.*	*Mg.*	*Mg.*	*P. ct.*	*Mg.*	*Mg.*	*Mg.*	*Mg.*
EXPERIMENT 1.																		
Fish:																		
Fresh					69.27	10.34	2.79	17.44		0.33	13.91	86.94		1.62	±1.62	0.0	0.00	
Held in salt—																		
1 hour					66.46	11.91	2.76	17.25	21.0	1.52	13.72	85.78	104.4	7.03				
2 hours					66.98	11.72	2.90	18.13	16.3	2.84	15.71	98.21	88.2	13.35				
4 hours					63.91	12.02	2.92	18.25	17.5	3.20	13.99	87.45	83.8	13.30				
6 hours					62.67	11.02	3.05	19.06	18.2	3.69	15.01	93.89	74.8	14.35				
8 hours					63.03	10.02	3.19	19.94	18.6	4.14	14.36	89.74	83.7	15.70				
10 hours					60.08	12.22	3.14	19.63	14.0	4.01	13.60	85.02	60.6	14.79				
12 hours					58.20	12.77	3.26	20.38	21.0	4.45	13.26	82.88	85.4	15.33				
Brine:																		
Saturated salt solution (gk).	¹150	181	16.4	1.2066			0.00		0.00							0.0	0.00	
After holding fish—																		
1 hour	850	992	35.0	1.1671			.114		4.20						30.75	206.3	10.50	76.9
2 hours (b)	985	1,179	41.6	1.1969			.188		4.48						33.75	1,865.0	38.08	296.9
4 hours	1,075	1,282	45.2	1.1926			.169		6.16						44.25	1,992.5	60.67	435.9
6 hours	820	981	34.6	1.1963			.154		8.40						33.75	974.3	90.30	362.8
8 hours	755	902	31.8	1.1947			.159		6.16						38.50	1,559.8	50.51	315.7
10 hours	725	872	30.7	1.2028			.173								40.25	1,560.5		303.9
12 hours	1,610	1,917	67.6	1.1907			.173		6.64						27.75	1,508.6	46.69	201.2
20 hours																	46.69	

EXPERIMENT 2.

Fish:

	63.84	17.97	2.52	15.75	8.2	.47	14.22	88.88	46.3	2.58
Fresh	63.84	17.97	2.52	15.75	8.2	.47	14.22	88.88	46.3	2.58
Held in salt—										
1 hour	63.06	16.81	2.59	16.19	9.3	1.35	13.79	86.21	49.5	6.71
2 (M.	60.07	18.96	2.64	16.50		1.56	13.60	85.01		7.44
4 hours	59.98	18.67	2.65	16.56	14.0	2.32	13.93	87.02	73.6	10.86
6 hours	54.48	20.00	2.75	17.19	14.0	2.72	12.06	75.39	61.4	10.66
8 hours	54.89	19.45	2.81	17.56	11.6	2.97	12.38	77.39	51.1	11.57
10 hours	55.54	17.87	2.82	17.63	10.5	4.12	12.55	78.46	46.7	15.50
12 hours	52.74	19.49	2.82	17.63	5.8	4.53	12.13	75.86	24.9	16.31

Brine:

					.00				1.62			
Saturated salt solution (blank)					0.00				1.62		11.91	
After holding fish—												
1 hour	[3] 370	442	15.6	1.1954	.168		3.22		44.38	742.6	11.91	164.2
2 hours	950	1,157	40.8	1.2179	.183		2.38		46.88	2,117.3	42.36	445.4
4 hours	1,780	2,138	75.4	1.2011	.194		1.82		58.13	4,147.7	27.12	1,034.7
6 hours	1,490	1,795	63.3	1.2040	[4] .193		3.08		66.88	3,464.4	39.58	996.5
8 hours	1,285	1,546	54.3	1.2031	.188		4.34		57.50	2,906.5	51.21	738.9
10 hours	1,180	1,409	49.3	1.1941	.198		2.38		53.13	2,789.8	25.56	626.9
12 hours	1,075	1,284	45.3	1.1944	.200				52.50	2,568.0		564.4
20 hours	2,730	3,273	116.5	1.1989								

[1] Volume made to 250 cc for analysis.
[2] Saturated solution of salt.
[3] Stopcock found open, and all except that collected in the last 30 minutes of the first hour lost.
[4] Average.

The weight of the fish and salt decreased uniformly during the first 12 hours, but from the 12-hour to the 20-hour period it was small in comparison with the loss which occurred when the brine formed was drawn off at 2-hour intervals. Obviously not as much brine is formed after this period, when it is allowed to remain surrounding the fish. The greatest loss in weight occurred between the 4- and 6-hour periods, when 2.82 pounds, or 3.72 per cent, of the weight of the material at the beginning of this period was removed in the form of brine. The total loss of weight at the expiration of the 12 hours that the fish remained in salt was 17.9 pounds, which, corrected for the total weight of the samples taken (4.3 pounds), leaves 13.6 pounds, or 16.39 per cent, as the actual loss of water, salt, and protein material from the original weight of fish and salt. The total loss for the 20-hour period amounted to 18.4 pounds, or 22.17 per cent, of the original weight. In this particular lot of fish nearly one-quarter of the weight of the original fish and salt was abstracted by brine during the 20 hours in "dry salt."

TABLE 18.—*Loss in weight of fish held in dry salt.*

Condition of fish.	Weight of fish and salt.[1]		Weight of sample.	Loss in weight.			
	Total.	From which loss was obtained.		Grams.	Ounces.	Pounds.	Per cent.
EXPERIMENT 1.	*Pounds.*	*Pounds.*	*Pounds.*	*Grams.*	*Ounces.*	*Pounds.*	*Per cent.*
Fresh..............................	{ [2]70	....	....	....	....	....	....
	[3]13						
Held in salt—							
1 hour.........................	82.6	81.9	0.7	181	6.4	0.4	0.50
2 hours........................	79.7	79.1	.6	992	35.0	2.2	2.68
4 hours........................	76.5	75.9	.6	1,179	41.6	2.6	3.29
6 hours........................	73.0	72.4	.6	1,282	45.2	2.82	3.72
8 hours........................	70.2	69.6	.6	981	34.6	2.16	2.98
10 hours.......................	67.6	67.0	.6	902	31.8	2.0	2.87
12 hours.......................	65.1	64.5	.6	872	30.7	1.92	2.87
20 hours.......................	60.3	....	....	1,917	67.6	4.23	6.56
EXPERIMENT 2.							
Fresh..............................	{ [2]124	....	....	....	....	....	....
	[3]23						
Held in salt—							
1 hour.........................	146.0	145.1	.9	442	15.6	0.98	.70
2 hours........................	142.5	141.6	.9	1,157	40.8	2.6	1.79
4 hours........................	136.9	136.0	.9	2,138	75.4	4.7	3.32
6 hours........................	132.0	131.9	.9	1,795	63.3	4.0	2.94
8 hours........................	128.5	127.6	.9	1,546	54.5	3.4	2.58
10 hours.......................	124.5	123.7	.8	1,409	49.3	3.1	2.43
12 hours.......................	120.9	120.0	.9	1,284	45.3	2.8	2.26
20 hours.......................	112.8	....	....	3,273	115.5	7.2	6.00

[1] The first column gives the weight of fish and salt at the expiration of the different intervals of time at which the brine was drawn off. The second column shows the weight of fish and salt from which the brine for the succeeding interval of time was obtained. That is, the figures in the first column are corrected for the weight of the sample taken, forming the figures from which the true percentage loss for each interval was obtained.
[2] Fish.
[3] Salt.

The total volume of brine collected during the 20 hours the fish were in salt amounted to 6,970 cc, which, as a saturated salt solution, would contain 2,509 grams, or 5.5 pounds, of salt. Subtracting this amount of salt from the total actual loss during the 20-hour period gives 12.9 pounds, or 18.4 per cent, of water and protein material removed from the original quantity of fish. The same calculation applied to the results obtained for the 12-hour period indicates that 9.3 pounds, or 13.3 per cent, of water and protein material was extracted from the fish during this time.

The second experiment of this series was run on fish which had been but 3 hours out of the water, being, therefore, somewhat fresher than those used in the first experiment. They were of uniform size, about 7 inches long, and were much fatter than those of the previous lot. One hundred and twenty-four pounds of fish were treated in the same manner as the others (p. 40), using 23 pounds of salt. The results of analysis are recorded under "Experiment 2" in Table 17.

During the 12 hours they remained in salt these fish lost the same percentage of water as those in Experiment 1. A comparison of results for the two experiments shows that the fatter fish do not absorb salt quite as rapidly as the thinner ones. A more gradual absorption of salt up to, and including, the 8-hour period and a more marked increase during the 10- and 12-hour periods occurred in the fish used for Experiment 2. The percentage amount absorbed during the 12 hours, however, was practically the same for both lots of fish. The greatest quantity of ammonia and amines was found in the fish at the end of the 4-hour period.

The largest amount of brine was formed during the 2- to 4-hour interval. A decrease in the rate of formation of brine occurred when the brine was allowed to accumulate. The specific gravity of the brine was highest at the end of the 2-hour period. The greatest quantity of nitrogenous material extracted, represented by total nitrogen, was found at the end of the 4-hour period. The quantity of amino acid nitrogen was also correspondingly high for this period. In Experiment 1 the highest amount of protein material was extracted during the same interval of time, but the largest volume of brine was obtained at the end of the 6-hour period. The greatest quantity of ammonia and amines, as nitrogen, in the brine was found during the 10-hour period.

With the exception of the specific gravity of the brine and the results for ammonia and amines, the quantity of the materials determined declined gradually from the fourth period, when the maximum was reached, to the end of the 12-hour period. For the entire 12-hour period the total quantity of nitrogen in the brine was extracted at the rate of 151.1 mg. per pound of fish. None of the extractive materials was determined in the brine collected at the end of the 20-hour period.

During the first hour (Table 18) nearly 1 pound of material, or 0.7 per cent of the total weight of fish and salt at the beginning of the experiment, was lost. The greatest loss occurred at the end of the 4-hour period. After being "dry salted" for 20 hours, the total loss of material, water, salt, and protein substances amounted to 28 pounds, or 19.05 per cent of the weight of the fish and salt at the beginning of the experiment. This is 3.12 per cent less than that found in Experiment 1. The volume of the brine collected during the 20 hours amounted to 10,860 cc, which, as a saturated salt solution, would dissolve 3,910 grams, or 8.6 pounds of salt. This leaves 19.4 pounds as the actual loss of water and nitrogenous material removed from the fish during the 20 hours in salt, and is 15.65 per cent of the total weight of fish employed at the beginning of the experiment. This is 2.75 per cent less than that abstracted in Experiment 1 for the same period of time, showing that the fatter fish lose less extractive material while in salt.

Practically one-quarter and one-fifth, respectively, of the original weight of fish and salt was lost in 20 hours, the smaller loss occurring in the case of the fatter fish. An appreciable amount of nitrogenous substances was extracted from the fish during the time they remained in salt, although, as shown by the figures in Table 15, not as much as would have been removed had the fish remained in pickle for corresponding periods. This is due to the fact that a number of protein substances are rendered insoluble by salt and very strong salt solutions. As the solution grows weaker, or if very weak pickle is used, a larger proportion of these protein substances are dissolved. These substances give fresh fish the characteristics which distinguish them from salt fish. The maximum quantity of the nitrogenous material was extracted at the end of the first 4 and 6 hours, a marked increase being shown at these periods over the 2-hour period when the fish were salted at the rate of one sack per hogshead.

The results of these experiments indicate that 2 hours or less is the proper period of time for pickling or dry salting the fish, when the loss of the minimum quantity of extractive material is considered. The time allowed in the older method when the fish were pickled in the pickling sheds, usually 2 hours, permits the conservation of the maximum quantity of those extractive substances which are characteristic of fresh fish.

EFFECT OF VARIOUS STEPS IN CANNING PROCESS ON SALT CONTENT OF SARDINES.

A number of analyses were made to determine the variation of the salt content of the fish at different stages of the canning process under actual commercial practice. The results are given in Table 19.

TABLE 19.—*Variation in salt content of fish at various stages of the canning process.*

Condition of fish.	Salting and pickling period.		Chemical composition.				
	Dry salted in boat.	In pickle in factory.	On original samples.				On water and fat free basis.
			Water.	Fat.	Salt.	Ash.	Salt.
Lot 1 (oil size):	Hours.	Hours.	Per ct.	Per ct.	Per ct.	Per ct.	Per ct.
From boat	3	....	70.30	10.48	0.65	....	3.38
From pickle	3	3	72.96	7.24	1.50	....	7.57
After steaming	3	3	69.33	7.31	1.25	....	5.35
From drier (18 hours)	3	3	63.52	8.33	1.77	....	6.29
Lot 2 (oil size): [1]							
From boat	24	....	59.04	9.37	3.08	....	7.40
After steaming and drying	24	....	54.12	18.66	3.13	5.23	11.49
Packed in can, sealed, but not processed	24	....	43.54	31.74	3.52	....	14.23
Packed in can, sealed, and processed	24	....	48.23	27.92	2.70	....	11.32
Lot 3 (oil size):							
From flakes before steaming	8	....	69.63	7.15	2.22	....	9.56
From flakes after steaming and drying	8	....	61.40	9.30	2.11	....	7.20
Packed in oil and processed	8	....	50.36	24.60	2.03	....	8.11
Lot 4 (oil size):							
From boat	2	....	68.62	9.40	.75	2.92	3.41
From pickle	2	1	60.33	15.11	1.93	3.08	7.86
After steaming and drying	2	1	60.77	14.32	2.04	3.45	8.19
Packed in oil and processed	2	1	54.02	16.81	1.61	3.16	5.52
Lot 5 (mustard size):							
From boat	24	....	59.59	13.16	1.53	....	5.61
After steaming and drying	24	....	58.58	17.12	1.96	3.71	8.06
Packed in mustard sauce, sealed, and processed	24	....	67.14	16.14	2.35	3.87	14.05

[1] Salted at the rate of 1 sack per hogshead.

It is seen that the salt content is most seriously affected by the steaming process, which readily removes the salt, especially when it is present in large amounts. Further tests were therefore made to determine how much salt is lost by steaming fish under certain conditions. The results which appear in Table 20 are self-explanatory.

TABLE 20.—*Effect of steaming on salt content of the fish.*

Condition of fish.	Water.	Fat.	Salt.	Salt (water and fat free basis).	Loss.
Lot 1:	Per cent.	Per cent.	Per cent.	Per cent.	Per cent.
Out of pickle	66.61	5.93	6.66	24.25	....
Off flaking machine	64.08	6.13	6.50	21.82	2.43
Steamed 10 minutes	61.80	6.78	5.78	18.40	3.42
Steamed 15 minutes	62.71	7.07	5.57	18.43	....
Lot 2:					
Out of pickle	66.43	11.53	2.24	10.02	....
Flaked and steamed 12 minutes	65.28	10.74	1.97	8.21	1.81

EFFECT OF CUTTING AND EVISCERATING ON LENGTH OF TIME IN PICKLE.

Two large samples of eviscerated and uneviscerated fresh fish were held for varying periods of time in pickle made up to read 90° on the salimeter and containing a slight excess of salt in a solid state.

The amount of pickle used, about 1½ buckets in each case, was relatively somewhat more than would be employed in actual practice. At the end of each of the periods indicated in Table 21 samples of the fish were flaked, steamed for 10 minutes, dried, cooled, packed, oiled, and processed for 2 hours. The salt content of the fish subjected to this treatment is shown in Table 21.

TABLE 21.—*Salt content before and after packing of cut and uncut fish held for varying periods in pickle.*

Condition of fish.	Water.	Fat.-		Salt.			Gain or loss after steaming, packing, and oiling.
		Samples as taken.	Water free basis.	Samples as taken.	Water free basis.	Increase.	
	Per cent.	Per cent.	Per cent.	Per cent.	Per cent.	Per cent.	Per cent.
Cut fish taken from pickle:							
Unsalted (fresh)............	71.47	7.84	27.47	0.33	1.59	....	....
In pickle—							
30 minutes.............	67.24	10.34	....	2.16	9.64	8.05	....
1 hour.................	67.90	8.85	....	3.27	14.07	4.43	....
2 hours................	67.31	8.65	....	4.25	17.69	3.62	....
3 hours................	65.41	9.81	....	5.47	22.07	4.38	....
4 hours................	64.55	9.48	26.74	5.82	22.41	.34	....
Uncut fish taken from pickle:							
Unsalted (fresh)............	66.12	13.61	40.17	.30	1.48	....	....
In pickle—							
30 minutes.............	66.54	12.15	....	1.35	6.34	4.86	....
1 hour.................	66.35	12.46	....	1.68	7.93	1.59	....
2 hours................	65.71	10.24	....	2.85	11.85	3.92	....
3 hours................	60.58	14.77	....	3.19	12.94	1.09	....
4 hours................	59.36	14.25	35.06	3.77	14.28	1.34	....
Cut fish after steaming, packing, and processing:							
Unsalted (fresh)............	48.42	28.38	....	.42	1.81	....	+0.22
In pickle—							
30 minutes.............	48.11	29.09	....	1.92	8.41	6.60	−1.23
1 hour.................	46.87	29.49	....	2.27	9.60	1.19	−4.47
2 hours................	44.40	30.60	....	2.87	11.47	1.87	−6.22
3 hours................	35.45	35.25	....	3.98	13.58	2.11	−8.49
4 hours................	42.73	32.84	....	4.00	16.35	2.77	−6.06
Uncut fish after steaming, packing, and processing:							
Unsalted (fresh)............	51.61	25.47	....	.43	1.89	....	+ .41
In pickle—							
30 minutes.............	51.98	24.88	....	1.81	5.67	3.78	− .67
1 hour.................	46.53	30.95	....	1.79	7.95	2.28	+ .02
2 hours................	40.69	32.38	....	2.45	9.13	1.18	−2.72
3 hours................	35.12	36.17	....	3.22	11.22	2.09	−1.72
4 hours................	44.83	31.27	....	3.21	13.43	2.21	− .85

A comparison of the actual amounts of salt absorbed at the expiration of each period shows that the cut, or eviscerated, fish take it up much more readily than the uncut fish. At the end of 30 minutes the cut fish had absorbed more salt than the uncut fish at the expiration of one hour, and at the end of one hour in pickle they had absorbed practically the same amount of salt as was found in the uneviscerated fish after 4 hours in pickle. At the close of the 4-hour period in pickle, the eviscerated fish had taken up about 57 per cent more salt than the uneviscerated fish for the same period of time. At the end of the experiment after 4 hours, the pickle of both the cut and uncut fish read 85° on the salimeter. One-fourth of the time necessary for the uneviscerated fish to remain in strong pickle (90°) is sufficient for the eviscerated fish to acquire an equivalent salt content.

The effect of steaming on the salt content of the sardines packed from these two lots of fish shows the same relative differences at the various intervals of time as existed when the raw fish were taken from the pickle. The loss of salt by steaming was greater in the cut and eviscerated fish than in the uncut fish. The salt content of the packed goods prepared from fish held in pickle 30 minutes was much higher in the case of cut fish than that from uncut fish which had been in pickle one hour. The degree to which steaming removes the excessive amount of salt is well shown in the case of cut fish which had been in pickle for 2, 3, and 4 hours. Before steaming these fish contained 17.69, 22.07, and 22.41 per cent of salt, respectively. After steaming and packing they contained 11.47, 13.58 and 16.35 per cent, a loss of 6.22, 8.49 and 6.06 per cent. The pack from the uncut fish, which had been in pickle 4 hours, contained 13.43 per cent of salt, a loss of only 0.85 per cent from the amount found in the raw fish. These results show the extent to which steaming removes the salt from the fish, particularly where it is present in large amounts.

A comparison of the salt content of eviscerated with that of uneviscerated fish, at different lengths of time in pickle, points unmistakably to cutting and eviscerating as the means for obtaining the proper salt content of fish in the minimum period of time. It also follows, therefore, that cutting and eviscerating permit the proper pickling of the fish with the least loss of extractive material.

Fish that are to be fried in oil when cut and eviscerated require much less time in pickle than fish which are to be steam cooked. From 10 to 15 minutes in a 90° pickle should be sufficient for eviscerated fish which are to be fried in oil.

During the course of this experiment it was noticed that, while the bellies of the uncut fish broke out to some extent during the time they were held in pickle, the cut fish showed no signs of being belly broken.

DISTRIBUTION OF SALT IN SARDINES.

The distribution of salt in the skin and meat of the uncut fish and the loss of salt from the skin after steaming were determined. One set of samples was prepared by removing the skin from a number of fish which had been in dry salt for seven hours. Another set was prepared from the same lot of fish which had been steamed for 10 minutes. The results of the analyses of these two sets of samples are shown in Table 22.

TABLE 22.—*Distribution of salt in uncut fish.*

Contained in—	Water.	Fat.	Salt.	Salt (water and fat free basis).	Loss.
	Per cent.	Per cent.	Per cent.	Per cent.	Per cent.
Skin..	63.70	14.62	4.05	18.59	..........:
Flesh...	70.76	3.56	1.79	6.97	....
Skin:					
Before steaming..............................	56.03	21.98	4.26	19.37	....
After steaming 10 minutes....................	50.41	28.09	2.15	10.00	9.37

The skin contained four times the amount of fat or oil, and nearly two and one-half times the quantity of salt found in the flesh. The fact that one-half the amount of salt present in the skin was lost during the steaming process explains the removal of the large percentage of the salt contained in the fish shown in Table 19.

PERCENTAGE OF SALT IN SARDINES.

To obtain an idea of the length of time necessary for fish to remain in pickle to attain the proper salt flavor, a number of samples from the foregoing experiments (Table 21) were submitted to an impartial jury with no knowledge of the way the products had been prepared. Of the uneviscerated fish, the pack composed of fish which had been three hours in pickle was judged the best, while in the case of the eviscerated fish, the majority favored the packs which had been in pickle for from one to two hours.

Of the packs which were regarded favorably, the uneviscerated fish contained 3.22 per cent of salt, and the eviscerated fish 2.27 and 2.87 per cent. This discrepancy may be explained by the fact that the viscera of uncut fish which have been held in pickle or salt contain a higher percentage of salt than does the flesh which was the part tested.

While the question of the best flavor is a matter of individual taste for which no hard and fast rule may be made, an average of 3 per cent of salt may be considered the most satisfactory. At all events, an amount varying from 2.5 to 3.5 per cent in the finished product would prove satisfactory to the majority of people. It would seem wise to undersalt rather than oversalt the fish.

FLAKING THE FISH.

The purpose of flaking is to distribute the fish evenly on flakes, or wire-meshed rectangular frames, so that the drying medium can reach them all uniformly when the flakes are taken into the drying room. This purpose seemed to have been entirely forgotten in the many instances where the fish were found piled high up on the flakes, that thereby became containers of fish rather than drying racks. Figure 1, Plate XIV, shows a flake where the fish are entirely too thick, although it does not represent the maximum number of fish found upon one flake during the course of the investigation. Sometimes fish which have been flaked too thickly become glued together during the drying process (Pl. XIV, fig. 2), making it necessary to tear them apart before placing them in the cans, much to the detriment of the pack. Too thick flaking also causes uneven drying. It has been demonstrated that thin flaking of the fish results in a better degree of drying in a shorter period, facilitates packing, eliminates waste due to marred and broken fish, and produces a larger yield and a better looking can of goods.

The number of fish of various sizes that can be distributed to best advantage on the flake is shown in Table 23.

TABLE 23.—*Number of fish of various sizes per flake (hand flaked).*

Size of flakes.		Number of fish.				
Over all.	Internal.	4-inch.	5-inch.	6-inch.	7-inch.	8-inch.
Inches. 22 by 36 30 by 30	*Inches.* 19 by 33 27 by 27	106 131	87 104	53 84	49 52	48 48

Several canneries packing the higher grades of sardines flake the fish by hand, thereby securing a very even distribution and eliminating the losses from mechanical injury. Where machines are used for this purpose, the utmost care should be given to their operation to avoid a thick and uneven flaking of the fish.

DRYING THE FISH.

Drying is a very important step in the canning of sardines, particularly in the case of those which are steam cooked. Packers who fry the fish in oil realize the necessity of frying only fish which have been properly dried in order to prevent spattering and breaking when the fish are first placed in the fryer. Fish after frying in oil do not contain an excessive amount of water, one point of superiority of fried sardines over poorly dried steam cooked sardines. Fried fish contain a fairly uniform quantity of water, ranging from 60 to 64 per cent, which should be the limit for the degree of dryness to which steamed fish are brought before packing.

In the tunnel type of driers where the removal of the excess water is accomplished by drawing a current of warm air over racks of the flaked fish, a number of factors make a rigid control of drying quite difficult and at times impossible. These factors (some of which can be controlled) are the humidity of the air, the volume and temperature of the air passing through the drier, the size of the fish, the amount of water they contain, the surface exposure, and the time allowed for drying. In many instances more attention given to those controllable conditions responsible for the variations in the degree of dryness to which steamed fish are brought before being packed would insure a higher quality pack than when they are disregarded.

In the examination of a number of cans of inferior sardines during the early part of this investigation it was discovered that the conditions found could be attributed, in many cases, to insufficient drying of the fish.

The influence of some of the factors responsible for variations in the water content of the packed fish is shown in the results collected and experiments made on drying under various conditions during the course of this investigation.

EFFECT OF STEAMING AND DRYING ON COMPOSITION OF SARDINES.

Five lots of fish were steamed and dried under varying conditions, with the results shown in Table 24.

TABLE 24.—*Effect of steaming and drying on moisture and fat content of sardines.*

Stage of canning.	Water.	Fat.	Difference.	Actual loss of water.
	Per cent.	*Per cent.*	*Per cent.*	*Per cent.*
Lot 1 (large fish):				
From flakes....................................	59.90	17.61	....	....
From steam box (steamed 15 minutes)........	61.94	....	[1] 2.04	....
From drier (dried 1½ hours).................	59.10	17.00	.80	1.96
Lot 2 (three-quarter mustards):				
From steam box...........................	62.31	15.62	....	....
From drier................................	61.30	14.36	1.01	2.61
Lot 2 (one-quarter oils):				
From steam box...........................	70.12	6.99	....	....
From drier................................	60.94	....	9.18	23.50
Lot 3:				
From boat................................	66.20	....	....	....
From flaking machine.....................	64.01	12.81	2.19	6.08
Steamed 15 minutes and dried 15 minutes (kiln drier).......	59.70	....	6.50	16.13
Lot 4:				
From pickle...............................	70.31	....	....	....
Steamed..................................	68.31	....	2.00	6.31
Dried....................................	59.94	....	8.37	25.89
Lot 5:				
From pickle (in pickle 12 hours)...........	60.08	8.49	....	....
Steamed and dried........................	59.31	12.65	.77	1.89

[1] Possibly due to irregularity of sampling.

Since large fish require a longer drying period than small fish, the packer should grade his fish by size before sending them to the drying room.

EFFECT OF VARIOUS CONDITIONS OF DRYING ON SARDINES.

Experiments were conducted in certain canneries to ascertain the amount of water driven from fish under various conditions of drying and to determine the effect on the quality of the sardines of packing fish containing various quantities of water. The analytical results given in Table 25 show the water content and percentage loss of water under different conditions and periods of drying.

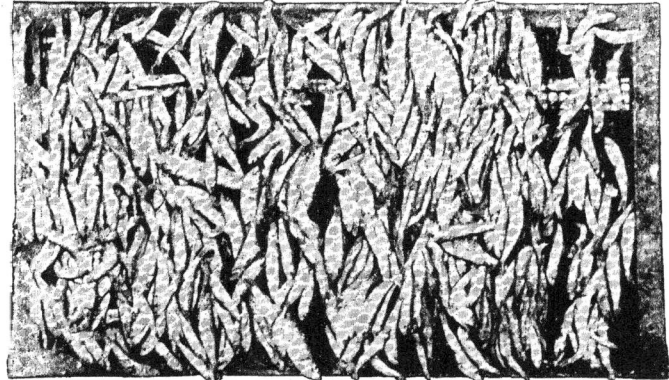

FIG. I.—FISH FAR TOO HEAVILY FLAKED.

The fish can not be properly dried when so thick, and when roughly and carelessly pulled apart
they are greatly marred and damaged as they are packed.

FIG. 2.—FISH SO THICKLY FLAKED THAT THEY BECOME GLUED TOGETHER IN
DRYING.

Entire sections of fish of this size and larger could be removed from flake. Note transverse cracks
on fish caused by excessive salting. (Castine fish.)

FIG. I.—A DIRTY FLAKE.

Note the remains of fish and débris adhering to the wires and edges.

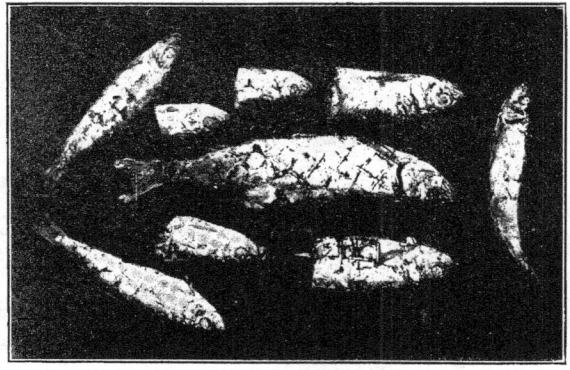

FIG. 2.— FISH MARRED BY MARKS FROM DIRTY FLAKES.

Note also the waste caused by cutting back fish of large size.

TABLE 25.—*Effect of various conditions of drying on water content of fish.*

Condition of fish.	Water content.	Difference.	Actual loss of water.
	Per cent.	*Per cent.*	*Per cent.*
Lot 1 (three-quarter mustards):			
From steam box..	63.65	....	....
Dried 2 hours at 100° F..	59.98	3.67	9.20
Dried 7 hours, left over night, and dried 1½ hours the following morning.	54.20	5.78	20.63
Lot 2 (three-quarter mustards):			
Raw fish (after salting)..	63.88	....	....
From steam box..	63.86	....	....
Dried 15 minutes, 1 revolution of wheel, coal fire, left at room tempera-			
ture for 40 hours...	55.70	8.18	18.47
Lot 3 (one-quarter oils): [1]			
Raw fish (after salting)..	65.40	....	....
From steam box, not dried...	64.70	.70	1.98
Dried 20 minutes...	62.33	2.37	8.15
Dried 40 minutes...	64.28	1.95	3.14
Dried 1 hour...	61.12	1.21	11.01
Dried 1 hour and 20 minutes...	62.67	1.55	7.31
Dried 1 hour and 40 minutes...	62.53	.14	7.43
Dried 2 hours..	60.63	1.90	12.17
Lot 4 (one-quarter oils): [2]			
Raw (after salting)...	70.38	....	....
From steam box (steamed 15 minutes)...	67.64	2.74	8.47
Dried 20 minutes [3]...	64.75	2.89	15.97
Dried 40 minutes...	61.18	3.57	23.70
Dried 1 hour...	61.18	0.00	23.70
Dried 1 hour and 20 minutes...	62.26	1.08	21.52
Dried 1 hour and 40 minutes...	58.40	3.86	28.80
Dried 2 hours..	58.05	.35	29.32

[1] Rain fell during the entire day, making the conditions most unfavorable for drying.
[2] Experiment conducted on a bright, clear, cool day, ideal for drying.
[3] Usual air (tunnel) dryer, run with a very large volume of air a little hotter than that usually found, was used.

The marked difference in the rate of drying of lot 3 and that of lot 4 is due to the presence in the air of moisture during the entire day on which the experiment with lot 3 was conducted. The effect of such unfavorable drying conditions is well shown in the small variations in the water content of the fish at different intervals of drying, an actual loss of only 12.17 per cent of water occurring during the 2 hours the fish remained in the drier.

The experiment on lot 4, consisting of fish from Castine, strongly salted and of a size packing 14 to 18 fish to the can, was conducted on a bright, clear, cool day, ideal for drying. The air (tunnel) drier was run with a large volume of air, a little hotter than is customary, the temperature in front of the steam coils ranging from 110° to 115° F. The total loss of water from these fish amounted to 29.32 per cent for the two hours they were in the drier. Under the conditions prevailing drying for a period of from 20 to 30 minutes would have been sufficient for this particular lot of fish. The fish being packed at the cannery from the same lot, however, were being dried from 40 to 45 minutes.

The physical appearance of the various packs at the different drying intervals was as follows:

Lot 1.—The mustard sauce in the cans packed with fish taken directly from the steam box was darker and somewhat thinner than the original sauce, and contained small particles of broken flesh. The flesh of the fish was dark and soft. The mustard sauce in the pack dried for 2 hours was brighter, and contained no particles of fish. The flesh of this fish was white and firm. The mustard sauce surrounding the fish which had been dried 7 hours, allowed to stand overnight, and then dried 1½ hours was bright and of about the same consistency as when put in the can, and showed no particles of fish. The flesh of this fish was very firm, although not as white as that of the fish dried for 2 hours. The contents of the cans of this last pack when opened had the best appearance of all four lots. The pack dried 2 hours differed very little in taste from that which was dried the longer time. The proper quantity of water to be driven from this particular lot of fish to be packed as mustards would seem to be 20.63 per cent.

Lot 2.—On opening the cans of raw fish from this pack a few days after they had been put up, it was found that the mustard sauce, which was of a different brand than that used in the case of lot 1, was quite thin, but retained its yellow color. The fish were soft, and had a characteristic fresh fish taste. The mustard sauce of the fish packed as they came from the steam box was of a good color and consistency, and the fish were fairly firm. The fish which had been dried and baked were, if anything, firmer than those from the steam box, but otherwise the same. The fish which had been dried, baked, and allowed to stand for an excessive length of time at room temperature were firm and hard. The mustard sauce was thick and pasty, as all the water it originally contained had been absorbed by the fish, which, however, remained hard and dry. The fish that had been packed raw differed very markedly in appearance from those packed after an excessive period of drying. In this experiment the cans with the best appearance and quality were those from the pack that had been dried for 15 minutes.

Lot 3.—The steamed fish packed without drying were soft, and the cans contained a great deal of water. Fish dried 20 minutes were much firmer, and the oil surrounding them appeared to be in good condition. The fish dried for 2 hours were the firmest of the lot, and the oil around them was the best in appearance and flavor. The physical examination of this pack was made before the determinations for water were completed. All who participated in the examination wondered at the apparent lack of improvement in the packs which were dried for the customary periods of time. The reason for this was evident when the moisture content was known (Table 25).

Lot 4.—When cans from this pack were opened and compared, it was the consensus of opinion that for both the oils and the mustards, drying for 20 minutes gave a product of very good appearance and flavor. There was not much difference between the packs after drying for 20 and for 40 minutes. It was apparent that, with this particular lot of fish, drying for a period of from 20 to 30 minutes under the conditions prevailing would have been sufficient. The fish packed after longer periods of drying were too hard, and did not make a good appearing or tasting can of sardines.

The results of these experiments show the wide divergence in the quality of sardines packed from fish containing varying amounts of water. It is true that at certain times, when the intervals of drying are short or conditions for drying the best, no very great difference in the packed goods is noticeable. The drying period should be as short as is consistent with securing the proper degree of dryness for the product.

Work still remains to be done in establishing simple tests to determine when the proper degree of dryness has been reached. It may be suggested here that the weight of a number of fish of uniform size, taken from the flakes as they enter the drier, be accurately determined. When the weight of an equal number of fish of the same size after drying is 15 per cent less than the weight of the raw fish, the proper state of dryness within the established limits will have been reached.

Oil sardines packed from fish insufficiently dried have a distinctly poor appearance. They are soft, and can not be taken readily in a whole condition from the can, while the oil surrounding them often looks milky and usually contains large drops of water. The taste is also decidedly bad, often soapy, a condition probably caused by the saponification of a small part of the oil during the sterilizing process in the presence of the excessive amount of water in the can. If dried too much, the fish become dry, hard, and brittle, and the flavor of the oil is strongly predominant. Oil sardines prepared from over-dried, hard fish lack the characteristic fish flavor.

VARIATIONS IN WATER CONTENT OF DRIED FISH TAKEN THE SAME DAY FROM DIFFERENT CANNERIES.

A series of samples were taken from several canneries at practically the same time of day, to determine how efficiently the fish were being dried, and to ascertain the variations in the degree of drying in the different canneries. Three of the canneries from which samples were taken were equipped with tunnel driers, one with the Ferris wheel oven type, and one with the old-style kiln drier. The time of drying was 60 minutes, 14 minutes, and 3 minutes, respectively, for the three types of driers.

The description of the samples, the kinds of driers, the conditions surrounding drying, and the results of this test are given in Table 26.

TABLE 26.—*Variations in water content of dried fish taken the same day from several canneries.*

Fish from—[1]	Date taken.	Weather conditions.	Cannery A, equipped with kiln drier (Ferris wheel, oven type).			Cannery B, equipped with tunnel drier (current of warm air).			Cannery C, equipped with kiln drier (oven type).			Cannery D, equipped with tunnel drier (current of warm air).			Cannery E, equipped with tunnel drier (current of warm air).		
			Time in drier.	Water.	Actual loss of water.	Time in drier.	Water.	Actual loss of water.	Time in drier.	Water.	Actual loss of water.	Time in drier.	Water.	Actual loss of water.	Time in drier.	Water.	Actual loss of water.
	1914.		Mins.	Per ct.	Per ct.	Mins.	Per ct.	Per ct.	Mins.	Per ct.	Per ct.	Mins.	Per ct.	Per ct.	Mins.	Per ct.	Per ct.
Steam box[2]	Oct. 2	Clear		70.51			65.42			70.61			68.93			68.37	
Drier	...do	...do	14	65.93	13.44	60	59.25	15.14	3	66.77	11.56	60	63.47	14.95	60	68.36	0.03
Packing tables[3]	...do	...do		63.02	20.26		65.34			65.14						67.14	
Steam box	Oct. 3	...do	14	69.78		60	[2]58.36	[2]16.76	3	[2]60.09	[2]12.65	60	69.43	[2]17.49	60	[2]66.76	1.15
Drier	...do	...do	14	66.83	8.89							780	[2]62.95	28.12			
													57.47				
Steam box	Oct. 6	...do		70.62			70.01									68.21	
Drier	...do	...do	14	69.60	3.35											66.92	3.90
Packing tables[3]	...do	...do	14	66.59	12.06	60	55.69	32.32	3	69.23	8.83	60	69.19	11.01	60		
Steam box	Oct. 9	Raining		69.01			67.79			66.25						68.47	
Packing tables[3]	...do	...do	14	65.35	10.57	60	67.64	.46					65.38		60	64.91	10.15

[1] All fish 5 inches long.   [2] From packing table.   [3] After 2 hours in packing room.

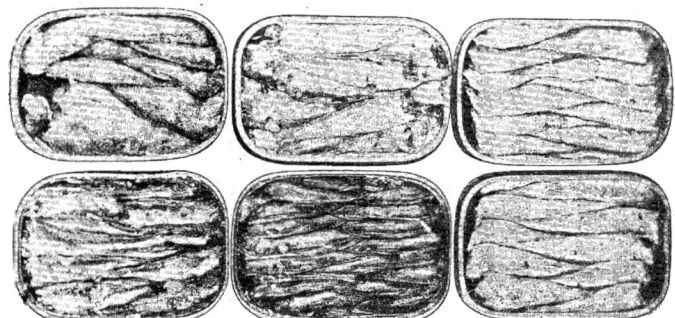

FIG. I.—TWO WELL PACKED CANS, BRIGHTS UP, CONTRASTED WITH POORLY PACKED CANS, BACKS UP, AND TWO POORLY PACKED CANS, BRIGHTS UP.

FIG. 2.—CANS OF SARDINES. FAIRLY WELL PACKED, BUT MARRED BY ROUGH HANDLING.

FIG. 1.—AN EXAMPLE OF GOOD PACKING CONTRASTED WITH POOR PACKING.

Cans taken from packing table before being oiled.   Same lot of fish, taken from the same weir on the same day, but packed by different concerns.

FIG. 2.—SARDINES FROM THE SAME LOT AS THOSE WELL PACKED IN FIG. 1, TAKEN FROM THE SHIPPING ROOM.

Note the disarrangement of the fish, due to rough handling after being processed. The mussy appearance is due to the presence of particles from the gills of snipped fish and material from the intestines.

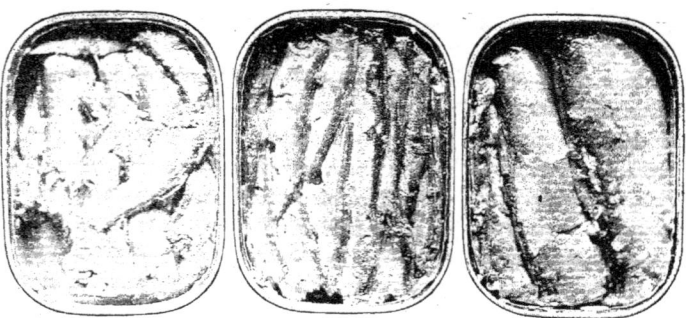

FIG. 3.—SARDINES FROM THE SAME LOT AS THOSE POORLY PACKED IN FIG. 1, TAKEN AT RANDOM FROM SHIPMENT READY FOR MARKET.

Unattractive appearance is due to slack packing and rough handling. Note the 3-fish can which shows the absence of standardization of the pack.

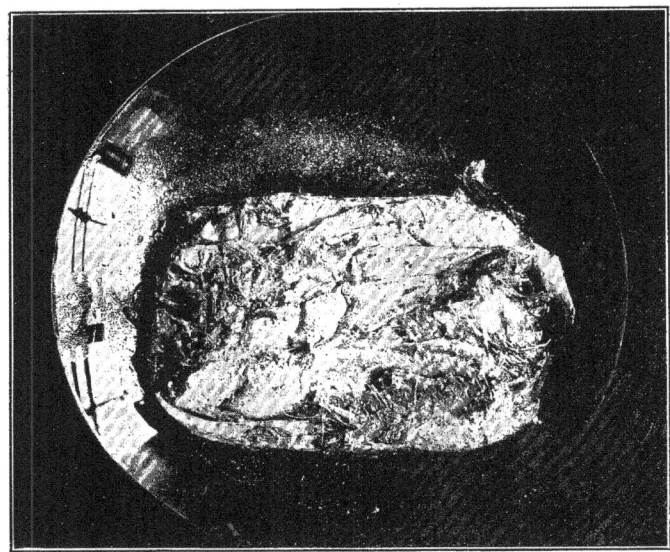

FIG. 1.—CAN OF QUARTER OIL SARDINES PACKED WITH FEEDY FISH.

It was packed backs up, thus concealing the condition shown on opening the can.

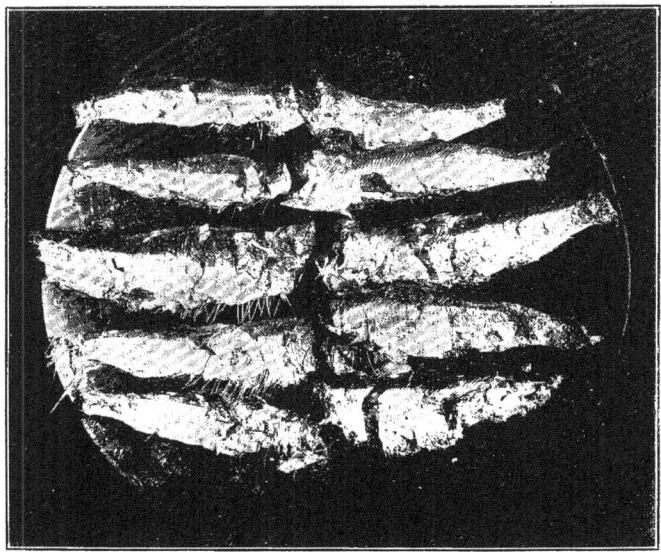

FIG. 2.—CONTENTS OF CAN OF SARDINES, SHOWING THE CHARACTERISTIC
BELLY-BLOWN FISH, RESULTING FROM FEED.

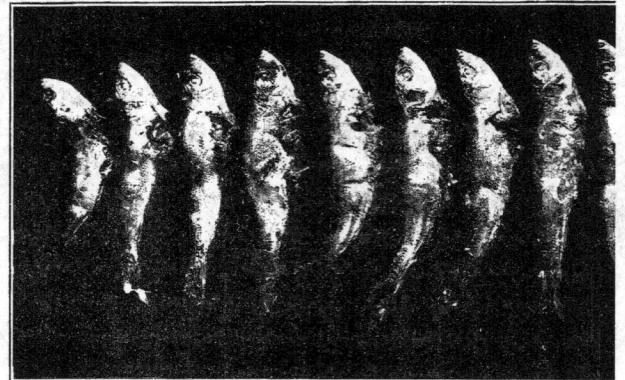

FIG. I.—EFFECT OF RED FEED.

Every fish in a boatload may be like this when excessively feedy fish are taken.

FIG. 2.—CONTENTS OF A CAN, REPRESENTING PACK OF GOODS ON A
DAY, ILLUSTRATING THE DESIRE OF SOME PACKERS TO PRODUCE C
IRRESPECTIVE OF QUALITY.

Practically all the fish were belly broken from feed, and were literally thrown into the can
tion being paid to producing a neat appearing can.

The results obtained (Table 26) show that a sufficient amount of water was abstracted from the fish in all cases except one. Less water was removed in the cannery equipped with the kiln drier than in those equipped with the air drier, and much less than in the one equipped with the Ferris wheel drier. In Cannery E, equipped with an air (tunnel) drier, practically no water was removed. Throughout the test, as the results indicate, very little attention was shown in this cannery to the important feature of drying. It is apparent that the air driers, with the exception of that in Cannery E, and the kiln drier removed a sufficient quantity of water, while the plant equipped with the Ferris wheel oven drier did not. The degree of dryness of the fish on the next day on which samples were taken varies widely. On October 9, which was a rainy day, drying was not efficient, scarcely enough in any of the canneries to remove the proper amount of water from the fish before packing.

These results indicate that a great variation in the degree of drying sardines existed among the different canneries on the same day. It is probable also that variations in the degree of dryness of the fish exist in the same factory on the same day.

INTERMITTENT DRYING.

The practice of intermittent drying, adopted by a few canneries in the preparation of mustard size fish, consists in allowing the larger fish to stand for a period of from 8 to 10 hours after the first drying, and then drying them for an additional hour or so just prior to packing. This should be done only in the case of cut and eviscerated fish and those which have been handled in a sanitary manner, because of the possibility of the development of bacteria in the viscera and contents of uncut fish (p. 86). Fish which have not been cut and eviscerated should not be permitted to stand in the driers overnight, as moist fish furnish an excellent medium for the growth of bacteria.

EFFECT OF CUTTING AND EVISCERATING THE FISH.

It was found that the drying process was aided by cutting and eviscerating the fish, particularly those of mustard size. Drying is thus facilitated by the removal of the large amount of water in and surrounding the viscera, which is particularly difficult to drive off from the uncut fish.

CONCLUSIONS.

The factors in drying which can be controlled by the canners and which are essential in obtaining a uniform degree of dryness are an even, thin flaking of the fish, the volume and temperature, within proper limits, of the air, in the tunnel type of drier, and the time of drying. Too high a temperature of the oven or of the air used in drying must be avoided on account of the resulting loss of oil from very fat fish and for fear of scorching the product. The degree of heat which may be employed in drying is therefore limited; otherwise it would be possible to overcome the difficulty of drying on excessively humid days by raising the temperature of the drying medium sufficiently to obtain the desired results regardless of the humidity. Air should be taken from a source that will not carry particles of dirt to cause contamination of the fish.

It is believed that a great deal of the difficulty experienced in packing the three-quarter mustard sardines is due to insufficient drying. Fish that are packed too wet or too "green" become soft upon standing, and the mustard sauce often becomes discolored. If the cans should happen to be packed too full, resulting in a "fat can," they are likely to be rejected, particularly if on opening (cutting) the contents are found in the condition described.

All fish for mustard sardines should be cut and eviscerated. The fact that fish of this size are packed in a sauce containing from 85 to 90 per cent of water makes it necessary to dry them a great deal more than fish packed in oil. In some cases it is the practice to allow mustard size fish to stand overnight, after a preliminary drying, and complete the operation just before packing.

It is also well to have no more than a sufficient number of racks of fish out of the drier on the packing room floor, as the fish after being dried, particularly on a rainy day, absorb enough water to make their handling very difficult. It is practically impossible to prevent breaking of the skin of fish when handling them after they have absorbed water on standing.

The fish should be separated according to their size, so that the smaller fish need not remain in the driers as long as the larger ones.

Probably 90 per cent or more of the Maine sardines are packed from fish which have been steam cooked. Attention, therefore, to drying and its better control will have a marked effect on the quality of the product.

Much still remains to be done in studying the conditions of drying sardines as packed in this region. Investigations might profitably be undertaken with the object of establishing, for example, the proper time of drying, the maximum temperature, and the requisite volume of air (in the tunnel type of drier) under varying degrees of humidity.

PACKING THE FISH.

The packing of sardines differs from that of most food products put up in cans, in that it is necessary to arrange the small fish carefully to insure an attractive looking finished product. No other foodstuff requires the same skill or technique in the matter of being placed in their containers. From the selling point of view it is most important that sardines be properly packed.

Several photographs illustrating the appearance of the contents of cans when packed with varying degrees of care and skill were taken. The cans of sardines from which these photographs were made were obtained at random from different canneries. While the illustrations of the better appearing packs must not be regarded as representative of the best packing to be found in the Maine sardine industry, they indicate the kind of packing that should be demanded in the "standard" grade of Maine sardines.

Figure 1, Plate XVI, shows two cans of well packed sardines, brights up, contrasted with poorly packed cans that were packed backs up. Carelessness in the packing process was responsible for the inferior appearance of the unattractive can. The cans in figure 2 were well packed, but the fish had been roughly handled on the flakes, causing breaking of the skin and other damage.

Plate XVII is fairly representative of well packed cans, contrasted with poorly packed cans. Figure 1 shows two cans packed the same day with fish from the same weir, but at different canneries. The cans were taken from the packing table before being oiled. The superiority of the cans at the left was typical of the entire product of the cannery at that time, and did not represent any special degree of perfection in packing. Figure 2 shows the cans taken in the shipping room from the same lot as the well packed cans shown in figure 1 after they had been oiled, sealed, and sterilized. The disarrangement of the fish in the cans was caused by rough handling received by the cans during the processing and the subsequent handling. The mussy appearance of the fish is due to the presence of particles from the gills of snipped fish and material from the stomach and intestines. Figure 3 depicts three cans from the lot of poorly packed goods shown in figure 1 after they had been taken from the shipping room. The complete disarrangement of this slack and poorly packed can is due to rough handling. One of the cans selected proved to be a 3-fish can, showing the lack of grading on the basis of the number of fish per can (p. 96). These sardines also illustrate the utter lack of standardization on a quality basis.

The kind of goods that brings the Maine sardine into disrepute is shown in figure 2, Plate XIX. Practically all of the fish used for this pack were belly-broken, from the action of feed, and were literally thrown into the cans, with no effort to secure a neat appearance. The fault here is not entirely the packer's, as there is no incentive to pack carefully when material of such inferior quality is permitted entry into the cannery.

The conditions responsible for the quality of sardines, as represented in these photographs, can be attributed to (a) lack of uniformity of opinion as to what shall constitute a fair quality of sardines, (b) lack of desire on the part of a few to produce any standard quality, and (c) a lack of control over the employees. Sardines of the poorest quality are packed in canneries where the methods are inefficient and haphazard, and where very little, if any, supervision is exercised over the labor.

ROUGH TREATMENT.

At several points in the handling of fish preparatory to packing the fish receive too rough treatment. For instance, they may be scooped from the boats after having settled in a solid mass, whereas the best practice is to float them well in the hold of the boats before bailing them out. Another source of damage is the pulling and mauling the fish receive while on the flakes, particularly when too thickly flaked.

After the fish are packed in the cans the rough treatment the cans and contents receive has a direct bearing on the final appearance of the sardines. In many cases it was found that the operators in placing the cans upon the tail of the sealing machine inserted their fingers in the packed cans, thus disarranging and marring the contents. Sometimes a few cans become crushed, or some trouble with the sealing machine causes spilling. The fish thus lost are repacked, at the close of the day's sealing, constituting an inferior product because of the careless manner in which the sealer, unskilled in packing, does the work. Other commonly found instances of rough treatment are:

Permitting the cans to fall a distance of from 2 to 3 feet from the sealing machine after the covers have been attached.

The bailing of cans from the "bath" tanks with scoopnets and forcibly throwing the cans on the floor of the cannery.

Shoveling the cans over in drying and cleaning them with sawdust.

Tumbling and rattling the cans through revolving sawdust cleaners.

Shoveling and rolling the cans down too sharply inclined chutes to the shipping rooms.

Such treatment not only disarranges the fish within a well-packed can, but it may dent the seams of the cans, causing leaks.

Those packers who maintain a definite quality and who take pains to pack the fish neatly and attractively in the cans clean the exterior of the cans, before shipping, in a careful manner to prevent disarrangement of the contents.

ADDING THE OIL.

QUANTITY OF OIL PER CASE.

A series of experiments were conducted on fish of different fat contents, packed in oil at the rate of 1 quart, 1½, 2, 2½, 3, 3½, and 4 quarts per case of 100 cans. Four packs were prepared in quarter oil size key cans. Fish of uniform size were selected from the flakes in the packing room, at the end of the steaming and drying process. The oil was run into each can from a pipette graduated to deliver the proper quantity. After allowing enough time to permit all the oil possible to soak into the fish the covers were sealed on the cans. Different types of sealing machines were used, but no provision was made to guard against leaks, such as the use of a gasket or by soldering.

In putting up the fish used for lot 4 a small patented packing device[1] was used. Some of the advantages claimed for this device, however, could not be checked in this experiment, owing to leakage of oil from the cans.

After these lots had been packed, oiled, processed, and allowed to stand for from 2 to 3 months, the contents of two representative cans from each lot were ground and thoroughly mixed. The oil was wiped out as completely as possible from the interior of the cans with the ground meat, and every effort was made to have each sample uniform. Three separate samples of the two cans from each pack were analyzed, the water, fat, and total nitrogen analyses being made in triplicate. The percentage amount of oil recovered, and the total food value per can, expressed in calories, were calculated from these results. In calculating the weight of oil added, the specific gravity of cottonseed oil was taken as 0.925. To determine the average weight of the fish per can, several lots of 100 fish each were weighed and an average taken. The results of these analyses are shown in Table 27.

The cans of lot 1 to which oil had been added at the rate of 1 and $1\frac{1}{2}$ quarts per case contained only a trace of visible oil when opened. Those to which oil had been added at the rate of 2 quarts per case were less than one-quarter full of free oil, while those having oil added at the rate of $2\frac{1}{2}$ quarts per case were less than half full. Cans to which the oil had been added at the rate of 3 quarts per case showed a reasonable amount, being about five-eighths full. At the rate of $3\frac{1}{2}$ quarts, the cans were practically seven-eighths full, while those that were packed at the rate of 4 quarts per case were found to be practically full of oil.

The figures for the recovery of the added oil vary widely, owing to loss of oil at the time of sealing full cans and to loss on standing through imperfect seams. In all instances the percentage amount of oil recovered when the sardines were oiled at the rate of 4 quarts per case was low. These figures agree with observations made at the time of sealing and with the experience of the packers that when the cans are full, or almost full, of oil a great deal of it is expelled when the lid is forced down by the chuck during the sealing operation.

---

[1] U. S. Letters Patent 1,206,977.

TABLE 27.—Composition of sardines packed in varying amounts of oil.

Amount of oil per case.	Total net weight (2 cans). Grams.	Water. Per cent.	Fat. Per cent.	Total nitrogen. Per cent.	Total protein (N×6.25). Per cent.	Oil added per can. Oz.	Oil added per can. Grams.	Total weight of oil found. Grams.	Oil recovered. Sample (2 cans). Grams.	Oil recovered. Average. Grams.	Oil recovered. Average. Per cent.	Calories per can. Total (2 cans).	Calories per can. Average per can.	Oil visible in cans on opening.
Lot 1: 8 fish per can; from flakes; not packed.	1 168.00	61.86	6.03					10.15						
Oil at rate per case of— 1 quart (25 per cent gallon).	171.00 188.00 177.00	56.94 58.79 56.90	15.79 14.00 15.72	3.60 3.52 3.58	22.50 22.00 22.37	9.50 9.50 9.50	8.79 8.79 8.79	27.00 26.32 27.92	16.85 16.17 17.77	16.93	96.3	397 402 408	201	Trace.
1½ quarts (37½ per cent gallon).	186.00 185.00 189.00	56.22 54.88 56.28	17.27 19.65 18.06	3.44 3.28 3.30	21.50 20.50 20.62	14.00 14.00 14.00	12.95 12.95 12.95	32.02 36.35 34.13	21.97 26.20 23.98	24.05	92.9	449 479 463	232	Do.
2 quarts (50 per cent gallon).	178.00 200.00 195.00	48.70 51.79 49.33	25.50 20.81 22.95	3.44 3.34 3.53	21.50 20.87 22.06	19.00 19.00 19.00	17.58 17.58 17.58	45.39 41.62 44.75	35.24 31.47 34.60	33.77	96.1	561 541 575	280	{ Less than one-fourth full.
2½ quarts (62½ per cent gallon).	191.50 195.50	47.64 47.10	26.97 29.15	3.27 3.28	20.44 20.50	23.70 23.70	21.93 21.93	51.65 56.99	41.50 46.84	44.17	100.0	621 673	324	{ Less than half full.
3 quarts (75 per cent gallon).	203.50 201.00 203.00	47.96 46.28 45.69	26.99 30.26 29.94	3.10 3.18 3.26	19.37 19.88 20.38	28.50 28.50 28.50	26.36 26.36 26.36	54.92 60.82 60.78	44.77 50.67 50.63	48.69	92.3	652 707 712	345	{ About five-eighths full.
3½ quarts (87½ per cent gallon).	201.50 211.00 202.50	42.02 43.94 45.20	35.06 32.68 30.43	3.15 3.16 3.13	19.69 19.75 19.56	33.00 33.00 33.00	30.53 30.53 30.53	70.65 68.95 61.62	60.50 58.80 51.47	56.92	93.2	794 782 753	388	{ About seven-eighths full.
4 quarts (100 per cent gallon).	218.50 229.50 215.50	42.93 43.18 43.70	32.96 33.36 32.55	3.08 3.04	19.25 19.00 19.00	38.00 38.00 38.00	35.15 35.15 35.15	72.02 76.56 70.14	61.87 66.41 59.99	62.75	89.3	816 863 795	412	{ Practically full.
Lot 2: 5 fish per can; from flakes; not packed.	2 175.60	55.54	12.94					22.72						
Oil at rate per case of— 1 quart (25 per cent gallon).	191.50 210.50 216.00	49.40 49.63 51.30	23.03 20.83 19.74	3.65 3.68 3.77	22.81 23.00 23.56	9.50 9.50 9.50	8.79 8.79 8.79	44.14 43.85 42.64	21.42 21.13 19.92	20.82	118.0	571 588 587	291	{ Less than one-fourth full.
1½ quarts (37½ per cent gallon).	201.50 198.00 226.00	50.13 51.21 49.68	22.57 21.87 22.33	3.61 3.56 3.63	22.56 22.25 22.69	14.00 14.00 14.00	12.95 12.95 12.95	45.48 43.30 50.46	22.76 20.58 27.74	23.69	91.47	591 566 666	304	{ Little over one-fourth full.

Size														Condition of oil
2 quarts (50 per cent gallon).	193.00	48.67	26.94	3.38	21.12	19.00	17.58	51.99	29.27	33.62	95.65	631	341	About half full
	219.00	46.97	27.34	3.41	21.31	19.00	17.58	59.87	37.15			725		
	204.00	46.34	28.02	3.38	21.12	19.00	17.58	57.16	34.44			687		
2½ quarts (62½ per cent gallon).	214.00	45.09	30.70	3.25	20.31	23.70	21.93	65.70	42.98	40.38	92.09	765	375	Over half full
	227.00	46.94	28.07	3.38	21.12	23.70	21.93	63.72	41.00			765		
	208.50	46.03	28.72	3.43	21.44	23.70	21.93	59.88	37.16			718		
3 quarts (75 per cent gallon).	230.50	45.22	29.78	3.45	21.56	28.50	26.36	68.64	45.92	48.15	91.32	816	410	Nearly full
	220.00	44.29	31.41	3.23	2.19	28.50	26.36	71.30	48.53			819		
	214.00	43.70	33.97	3.27	20.44	28.50	26.36	72.69	49.97			829		
3½ quarts (87½ per cent gallon).	223.00	41.92	34.01	3.26	20.37	33.00	30.53	75.84	53.12	49.95	81.82	864	419	Do.
	228.50	45.94	29.22	3.28	20.50	33.00	30.53	66.77	44.05			788		
	234.50	42.32	32.16	3.16	19.75	33.00	30.53	75.41	52.69			864		
4 quarts (100 per cent gallon).	222.50	44.15	33.62	3.02	18.87	38.00	35.15	74.80	52.08	61.93	88.05	841	469	Full
	230.00	38.69	36.63	3.04	19.00	38.00	35.15	84.25	61.53			933		
	242.50	37.22	39.14	3.07	19.19	38.00	35.15	94.91	72.19			1,040		
Lot 3: 12 lean, small fish per can; from flakes; not packed. Oil at rate per cent of—	[3] 153.80	59.13	7.94					12.21						
1 quart (25 per cent gallon).	179.00	54.45	14.56	3.75	23.44	9.50	8.79	26.05	13.84	12.96	73.72	402	194	No oil present.
	160.50	53.35	14.88	3.85	24.06	9.50	8.79	23.88	11.67			369		
	168.50	53.89	15.18	3.85	24.06	9.50	8.79	25.58	11.37			392		
1½ quarts (37½ per cent gallon).	181.50	52.44	18.29	3.66	22.87	14.00	12.95	33.19	30.98	19.06	73.59	465	221	Trace.
	168.50	51.90	16.58	3.87	24.19	14.00	12.95	27.94	15.73			414		
	169.50	50.09	19.29	3.73	23.31	14.00	12.95	32.69	20.48			452		
2 quarts (50 per cent gallon).	226.50	53.06	20.23	3.54	22.12	19.00	17.58	45.82	33.61	26.02	74.03	613	264	Do.
	166.50	44.38	22.18	4.19	26.19	19.00	17.58	36.93	24.72			507		
	177.00	48.75	18.06	3.99	24.94	19.00	17.58	31.96	19.75			464		
2¾ quarts (69¾ per cent gallon).	195.00	45.48	25.66	3.58	22.37	26.30	24.33	50.03	37.82	43.64	89.68	625	328	One-third full
	197.50	43.38	29.15	3.43	21.44	26.30	24.33	57.57	45.36			687		
	224.00	47.49	26.77					59.96	47.75					
3 quarts (75 per cent gallon).	216.00	44.91	26.73	3.27	20.44	28.50	26.36	57.73	45.52	44.18	83.79	696	343	Less than half full.
	207.50	44.65	27.26	3.49	21.81	28.50	26.36	56.56	44.35			690		
	207.00	45.62	26.51	3.45	21.56	28.50	26.36	54.87	42.66			672		
3½ quarts (87½ per cent gallon).	225.50	46.34	28.55	3.06	19.12	33.00	30.53	64.38	52.17	52.88	86.62	752	383	Half full
	230.00	41.42	28.46	3.37	21.06	33.00	30.53	65.46	53.25			783		
	208.50	41.53	31.38	3.29	20.56	33.00	30.53	65.43	53.22			760		
4 quarts (100 per cent gallon).	193.00	36.50	38.68	3.15	19.69	38.00	35.15	74.65	62.44	57.79	82.21	824	407	About three-fourths full
	205.50	39.40	34.76	3.33	20.81	38.00	35.15	71.43	59.22			814		
	185.50	34.46	38.93	3.32	20.75	38.00	35.15	72.21	51.71			804		

[1] Average weight of 16 unpacked fish.   [2] Average weight of 10 unpacked fish.   [3] Average weight of 24 unpacked fish.

TABLE 27.—*Composition of sardines packed in varying amounts of oil*—Continued.

Amount of oil per case.	Total net weight (2 cans).	Water.	Fat.	Total nitrogen.	Total protein (Nx6.25).	Oil added per can.		Total weight of oil found.	Oil recovered.			Calories per can.		Oil visible in cans on opening.
						Cc.	Grams.		Sample (2 cans).	Average.		Total (2 cans).	Average per can.	
	Grams.	*Per cent.*	*Per cent.*	*Per cent.*	*Per cent.*		*Grams.*	*Grams.*	*Grams.*	*Grams.*	*Per cent.*			
Lot 4: 6 very fat fish per can; from flakes; not packed.	¹164.60	55.76	16.00					26.34						
Oil at rate per case of— 1 quart (25 per cent gallon).	178.50 / 150.50 / 160.00	55.37 / 51.51 / 51.36	19.74 / 22.21 / 21.84	3.34 / 3.54 / 3.53	20.87 / 22.12 / 22.06	9.50 / 9.50 / 9.50	8.79 / 8.79 / 8.79	35.23 / 33.43 / 34.94	8.89 / 7.09 / 8.60	8.19	46.59	466 / 434 / 455	226	None.
1¼ quarts (37½ per cent gallon).	187.00 / 184.50 / 168.00	53.02 / 52.22 / 50.31	22.17 / 22.20 / 24.67	3.43 / 3.41 / 3.52	21.44 / 21.31 / 22.00	14.00 / 14.00 / 14.00	12.95 / 12.95 / 12.95	41.46 / 40.96 / 41.44	15.12 / 14.62 / 15.10	14.94	57.69	533 / 526 / 521	283	Trace.
2 quarts (50 per cent gallon).	176.50 / 219.50 / 191.50	45.05 / 51.62 / 46.30	31.33 / 23.84 / 29.49	3.10 / 3.26 / 3.24	19.37 / 20.37 / 20.25	19.00 / 19.00 / 19.00	17.58 / 17.58 / 17.58	55.30 / 52.33 / 56.48	28.96 / 25.99 / 30.14	28.36	80.68	634 / 650 / 663	325	Less than one-fourth full.
2½ quarts (62½ per cent gallon).	192.00 / 175.50 / 181.50	47.39 / 43.63 / 43.01	28.39 / 33.70 / 26.61	3.28 / 3.13 / 3.14	20.50 / 19.56 / 19.62	23.70 / 23.70 / 23.70	21.93 / 21.93 / 21.93	54.51 / 59.14 / 48.30	28.17 / 32.50 / 21.96	27.64	63.04	648 / 669 / 577	315	One-fourth full.
3 quarts (75 per cent gallon).	192.00 / 190.50 / 191.00	44.49 / 43.97 / 47.09	32.35 / 31.94 / 29.83	3.18 / 3.43 / 3.21	19.87 / 21.44 / 20.06	28.50 / 28.50 / 28.50	26.36 / 26.36 / 26.36	62.11 / 60.84 / 56.97	35.77 / 34.50 / 30.63	33.63	63.78	711 / 711 / 666	348	Half full.
3½ quarts (87½ per cent gallon).	201.00 / 215.50 / 226.50	41.29 / 47.63 / 46.31	35.83 / 28.88 / 28.02	3.24 / 3.16 / 3.19	20.25 / 19.75 / 19.94	33.00 / 33.00 / 33.00	30.53 / 30.53 / 30.53	72.02 / 64.39 / 63.46	45.68 / 35.05 / 37.12	40.28	65.98	811 / 750 / 752	385	Less than three-fourths full.
4 quarts (100 per cent gallon).	223.00 / 184.00 / 215.50	43.57 / 39.03 / 43.00	34.28 / 38.30 / 34.28	3.14 / 3.09 / 3.15	19.62 / 19.31 / 19.69	38.00 / 38.00 / 38.00	35.15 / 35.15 / 35.15	76.44 / 70.47 / 73.87	50.10 / 44.13 / 47.53	47.25	67.21	854 / 776 / 824	409	Three-fourths full.

¹ Average weight of 12 unpacked fish.

The influence of the increasing quantities of oil on the food value of a can of sardines is indicated in the column of Table 27 which shows the total calories per can. These figures are the average results of the analysis of six cans. The food value of the sardines composing lot 1 to which a minimum amount of oil was added was 201 calories per can, and that of those to which the maximum amount of oil was added (at the rate of 4 quarts per case) was 412 calories per can.

The fish composing lot 2 were much fatter than the Castine fish used for lot 1. The influence of the fatness of the fish on the oil present on opening the cans is shown. The cans which were oiled at the rate of 3 quarts per case were nearly full, as were also those oiled at the rate of 3½ quarts per case. The cans packed at the rate of 4 quarts of oil per case were full of oil. The percentage recovery of oil was much less when the cans were oiled at the rate of 3½ and 4 quarts than when smaller amounts of oil were added. To avoid this loss, many packers do not add enough oil to make a good showing when the can is opened. This is particularly true in cases where the pack is composed of lean fish and where the oiling device is attached to the sealing machine, allowing insufficient time for the oil to be absorbed by the fish before some of it is squeezed out of the can during the sealing operation. The resulting loss due to the method of oiling and that due to poorly sealed cans which "weep" oil after sealing are conditions which should be remedied in order to avoid waste of oil. Not only is oil lost in this way but the product also loses in food value. In this lot, at the rate of 1 quart of oil per case, the average number of calories per can was 291, while at the rate of 4 quarts per case the average was 469. The figures for the calories at the other rates of oiling increased as the amount of oil increased.

The cans of lot 3, even those containing fish which had been oiled at the rate of 4 quarts per case, were only about three-quarters full of oil. These cans were poorly sealed, and consequently lost oil during processing and while standing, as is shown by the fact that an average of only 80.52 per cent of oil was recovered for all the packs in this lot. The food value is also low as compared with that of lot 2.

The fish used in lot 4 were very fat, containing 55.76 per cent of water and 16 per cent of fat. The cans packed at the rate of 4 quarts per case were only three-quarters full of oil when opened. Considering the care taken in packing, the percentage amount of oil recovered was small. On the other hand, the food value agreed very well with that of the other packs and showed the same variations according to the quantity of oil present. That the food value was correspondingly high was due to the fatness of these fish. An inspection of the rest of the cans of this pack showed that they had leaked badly while stored in the shook. The cans were very unsightly, being covered with oil, and, in many cases, stuck together with the partially dried oil. The analyses showed that practically ⁻¹⁻ⁱⁿᵈ of the oil added had leaked through the seams of the cans.

ᴏₘ these experiments it seems fair to conclude that the proper ₜ of oil per case to add to sardines is 3 quarts (75 per cent of a gallon) for average fat fish and 3½ quarts (87.5 per cent of a gallon) for lean fish of poor quality. These quantities allow for possible unavoidable losses in oil during the sealing process. The oil in these amounts can readily be added to the standard quarter oil can without loss, if time be allowed for the absorption of oil before the cover is sealed on the can.

KIND OF OIL.

TESTS WITH CORN OIL.

As has already been stated, cottonseed oil is the oil most widely used in packing Maine sardines. During the season of 1913 the possibilities of the use of corn oil for packing sardines were investigated. The oil in corn is contained in the embryo or germ, which is separated from the rest of the kernel in the manufacture of starch, glucose, etc. The germ is heated and the oil expressed and then refined. It is a neutral, bland oil, with practically no characteristic taste. It does not, therefore, mask the flavor of the fish which are packed in it. At the time these experiments were made corn oil was cheaper than cottonseed oil. Under normal conditions, corn oil is said to sell for from 5 to 10 cents a gallon less than cottonseed oil, which should make it worthy of consideration by the sardine packers. In normal times enough refined corn oil may be had to supply the entire sardine industry.

Inquiry among the packers showed that, in previous experience, corn oil had proved generally unsatisfactory. At the time the packers had tested this oil it was the practice in all the canneries to fry the fish in oil. When the corn oil was tried out in the frying vats it gave off a disagreeable odor and foamed so badly that it boiled out of the vats. Within the last few years the process of refining has been improved, so that a fine grade of oil, much superior to that formerly marketed, can now be had. The highly refined oil was secured for the tests here reported.

BEHAVIOR ON HEATING.

Corn oil, summer yellow cottonseed oil, and winter yellow cottonseed oil, 100 to 150 cc (3 to 5 ounces) of each, were heated in beakers over the flame, stirring constantly with a thermometer, with the following results:

Corn oil did not boil at 265° C. (509° F.). An odor not disagreeable and hardly characteristic of corn appeared at about 150° C. (302° F.). At 230°–240° C. (446°–464° F.) copious fumes with a slightly irritating, pungent, penetrating odor appeared.

Summer yellow cottonseed oil did not boil at 265° C. (509° F.). A characteristic odor appeared at 165° C. (329° F.). Fumes, slight in quantity compared with corn oil, but more penetrating; appeared at 245° C. (473° F.).

Winter yellow cottonseed oil did not boil at 265° C. (509° F.). A slight characteristic odor appeared at 160° C. (320° F.). Fumes, slight in amount and with no more odor than that obtained from the oil when heated at 160° C., appeared at 250° C. (482° F.).

The results of these tests show that corn oil of the quality represented by these samples compares favorably with cottonseed oil. It does not stand heating to a high temperature quite as well as the winter yellow variety, but is equal, if not superior, to the summer yellow grade, particularly when heated at a lower temperature, around 150° to 165° C. (302° to 329° F.). Apparently corn oil breaks down a little more rapidly when heated at the higher temperatures.

When tested by the Kreis reaction for rancidity upon exposure to the air, each oil gave a negative test at first. On standing in uncovered beakers for one and two days, corn oil failed to show a test for rancidity at the expiration of 24 hours, the winter yellow cottonseed oil gave a positive test at the end of 24 hours, and the summer yellow cottonseed oil gave an intensely positive test. At the end of 48 hours the corn oil showed only a slight positive test for rancidity by this reaction, while both the winter and summer yellow oils were intensely positive. With respect to the development of rancidity on exposure to the air, corn oil appears to be far superior to cottonseed oil.

EFFECT ON FLAVOR OF SARDINES.

During the seasons of 1913 and 1914 a number of small packs using various kinds of oil—raisin, olive, peanut, winter yellow cottonseed, summer yellow cottonseed, and corn—were made. Tests with the raisin oil were at once abandoned, as its odor and sweet flavor made it entirely unsuited for use with fish. All the methods of packing in vogue at that time were employed, as well as the process of baking the fish before packing them. Samples of the packs in these oils, with the exception of raisin oil, were submitted to different people for an opinion as to the quality and taste, the samples submitted to each person or group being selected from the same pack, in which the source and treatment of the fish were identically the same, with the exception of the kind of oil used:

By all but one or two the samples packed in corn oil were pronounced superior to those packed in cottonseed oil. Some even prefer-

product by the use of corn oil.

Canneries equipped with the so-called Ferris wheel driers utilize this equipment to excellent advantage by grilling the before frying and packing them, thus attaining the very best fla

It was found also that in packing sardines in corn oil or the be grade of cottonseed oil, stearin did not settle out during cold weat Sardines packed in prime summer yellow cottonseed oil when ope in cold weather present a very unattractive appearance, due to white film or mass of stearin over the fish. It would seem wise, th fore, to pack sardines for shipment into cold climates in the win pressed variety of cottonseed oil or in corn oil and use prime sum yellow cottonseed oil for goods going to warm regions.

TOMATO SAUCE.

Sardines in tomato sauce have not been packed in Maine to great extent. During the season of 1913 an attempt was made by of the canning companies to pack a few cases in this way, but undertaking proved unsuccessful. It is understood that sev other companies are now packing a few sardines and herrings tomato sauce. In consideration of the demand for this produc is strange that herring and sardines in tomato sauce are not prep in greater quantity in Maine. That no special difficulty is enc tered in the process, and the product is very attractive, is shown the fact that packers in other localities put out a great many of this article.

MUSTARD SAUCE.

It has been estimated that 25 per cent of the season's pack of M sardines is put up in mustard sauce. A large part of the sauce for this purpose is prepared in mustard sauce mills, owned and o ated by the sardine companies. In one instance several compa operate a mustard sauce plant on a cooperative basis. Part of sauce is prepared by an independent company located in one of the principal centers of the industry, and a certain amount is furnished by a well-known sauce and spice manufacturer. The résults of the analysis of samples of the three sauces most widely used are given in Table 28.

TABLE 28.—*Composition of mustard sauce.*

Total solids.	Salt (NaCl).	Acid, as acetic.	Total nitrogen (N).	Total protein (N x 6.25).	Nitrogen in salt free solids.	Mustard and turmeric.[1]
Per cent.	*Per cent.*	*Per cent.*	*Per cent.*	*Per cent.*	*Per cent.*	*Per cent.*
11.83	3.36	3.12	0.395	2.47	4.67	6.00
12.00	4.49	1.42	.368	2.30	4.90	5.21
14.49	2.75	2.63	.523	3.27	4.46	8.47

[1] Total solids — (salt+protein).

In the preparation of the sauce represented by the second sample a smaller amount of vinegar, or one of weaker strength, was used, while in that of the sauce represented by the third sample a larger amount of mustard or turmeric was employed. These samples were also examined microscopically.[1] The first two samples contained a great deal of turmeric and more red pepper than is commonly found in a mustard sauce of this grade. The last one contained more turmeric than either of the other two and not quite as much red pepper. The amount of turmeric in this sauce is excessive, compared with that in the other two sauces.

PROCESSING THE SARDINES.

The method of processing or sterilizing the sealed packed cans by heating them in tanks of boiling water is practically universal in the Maine sardine industry. At the time these investigations were made one of the canneries employed for this purpose retorts in which the contents could be heated under pressure.

The length of time given to processing varied widely among the different canneries. The usual period was from $1\frac{3}{4}$ to $2\frac{1}{4}$ or $2\frac{1}{2}$ hours, the variation depending on the size of the cans and the canner's idea of the time necessary for sterilization. An instance was found in which the canner was giving only one hour to processing in a tank of boiling water.

To obtain data which might be helpful in determining the length of time of processing, the temperature of the inside of cans of sardines, as ordinarily processed in boiling water baths, was determined. The results, given in Table 29, show the time necessary to raise the initial temperature of the inside of the can to practically the boiling point of water.

[1] The examination was made by B. Silberberg, of the Microchemical Laboratory of the Bureau of Chemistry.

TABLE 29.—*Temperature of inside of can of sardines processed with regular lot.*

Near center of boiling tank.[1]		Near surface of water in boiling tank.[2]	
Time.	Temperature.	Time.	Temperature.
p. m.	° C.	a. m.	° C.
12.25	36	8.30	26
12.35	47	8.35	36
12.42	88	8.40	45
12.46	94.5	8.46	71
12.48	99	8.48	80
12.50	100	8.50	91
		8.52	99
		8.54	99
		8.58	99
		9.10	99.25

[1] This boiling tank was provided with a board cover which was lowered while processing the cans. The water was heated by steam passing through pipes in bottom of tank. It boiled freely during the period these temperatures were measured.
[2] Tank uncovered, heated by direct steam.

The length of time required to reach the boiling point varies with certain conditions commonly found. In this method of processing it is very important that the cans be completely submerged during the entire period. Since it was found that sardines were not always uniformly sterile, it would be safer to process for the longer periods of time.

STORING THE SARDINES.

A portion of each year's pack of sardines is stored for varying periods of time and under varying conditions before it reaches the consumer. When held by the packers the sardines are subjected to the rigid winters of Maine, as no suitable warehouse exists for storage, advantage being taken of cellars, wherever available. When shipped they are often frozen, only to be thawed out again upon coming into a warmer region, where they may be held at terminals or warehouses having relatively high temperatures. Finally, they may remain upon the retailer's shelves for some time, under varying temperature conditions.

Certain differences in the composition of canned sardines, when analyses were made directly after processing and after standing for different periods of time led to an investigation of the changes occurring in sardines kept under varying conditions of storage.

FORMATION OF AMMONIA AND AMINES.

The values for ammoniacal nitrogen in fresh and decomposed fish as determined by the Nessler method did not agree with the results obtained by the titration method. Noticeable increases in the amount of total ammoniacal material in packs of fish which had stood for a time over the amount of such material found in the same packs directly after being processed were also apparent.

Table 30 gives the results of the determinations of ammoniacal nitrogen in sardines stored for various periods of time.

TABLE 30.—*Ammoniacal nitrogen content of sardines stored for various periods.*

Condition of fish.	Period held.	Ammoniacal nitrogen per 100 grams.	
		Nessler.	Titration.
		Mg.	*Mg.*
Fresh...............	....	107.8	147.6
Do.............	24 hours.......	121.7	189.6
In pickle:			
½ hour.........	7 months......	....	203.1
1 hour.........	.....do........	....	206.1
1½ hours.........	.....do........	....	204.5
½ hour.........	19 months.....	....	271.8
1 hour.........	.....do........	....	239.4
1½ hours.......	.....do........	....	223.0

From the nature of the material, coupled with the well-known fact that amines are formed in the decomposition of fish, fish brine being a source of trimethylamine, amines were naturally looked upon as responsible for the discrepancy between the values obtained by the two methods of analysis, and possibly were partly responsible for the increase in the ammoniacal nitrogen which occurs on standing. Evidently a change occurs in canned sardines on standing, substances having an alkaline reaction (amines), determined as ammonia by the titration method, being liberated. Unfortunately, the Nessler method for determining ammonia is not reliable in the presence of amines. The difference in the values obtained by the methods employed for ammonia, while giving some indication of the amount of amines present, is not even sufficiently accurate to warrant regarding it as an approximate measure of the amine content.

The interesting fact that older packs of sardines contain larger amounts of ammoniacal material than those which have stood for only a short time was definitely proved by analyzing samples of commercially packed sardines which had stood for 2, 4, and 6 years in a cellar where the temperature was practically uniform and never reached the freezing point. In these analyses determination of the total volatile nitrogen and "ammonia" by the Nessler method, as well as the separation of ammonia and amines in the total volatile material, were made.

On opening the cans the two brands which had been packed for 2 years were found to be in very good condition. The fish were slightly colored by what appeared to be iron from the lid of the can, which was badly detinned. The cans in the 4-year-old lot looked worse than any of the other samples. A large amount of a white, soft material, probably stearin from the oil, was spread over

ɪ in the cans of the 6-year-old lot were covered
ft, white material. These cans contained only a
isible oil, and the fish adhered to the lid of the can
ɪe interior of the can was detinned to a greater
than in any of the others. The results of these
in Table 31.

ʹa and amine content of sardines after long periods of storage.

	Fat.	Total volatile nitrogen (N) per 100 grams, by—			Total volatile nitrogen (N) per 100 grams, as ʲ—			Percentage of total as—		Appearance.
		Titration.	Nessler.	Difference.	Total.	Ammonia.	Amines.	Ammonia.	Amines.	
ct.	P.ct.	Mg.	Mg.	Mg.	Mg.	Mg.	Mg.	P.ct.	P.ct.	
88	20.73	46.6	17.3	29.3	46.9	20.1	26.8	42.9	57.1	Good; slightly colored, apparently by iron; lid badly detinned.
15	21.76	40.8	17.4	23.4	46.6	15.6	31.0	33.5	66.5	
08	18.73	39.6	14.7	24.9	44.7	17.8	26.9	39.8	60.2	Particularly bright and firm.
40	20.95	43.1	18.9	24.2	37.7	5.0	32.7	13.3	86.7	
.01	33.60	33.8	14.0	19.8	37.2	5.9	31.2	15.9	84.1	Very poor; soft white material, probably stearin, spread over fish.
...	...	...	...	...	45.9	6.4	39.5	13.9	86.1	
.75	21.94	60.6	14.9	45.7	51.1	8.6	42.5	16.8	83.2	Poor, covered with white material; small amount of visible oil; fish adhered to lid; large amount of detinning.
...	...	...	...	...	69.3	...	(3)	...	...	

ʹminations and separations made on 50-gram samples.
ʹminations made on 3-gram samples.

ʳ that a change in the relative amount of ammonia
red, the degree depending on the time the fish
ge. The total amount of alkaline material was
he 2-and 4-year-old goods, but increased noticeably
ack. The quantity of ammonia, both in the actual
nd in the percentage of the total volatile nitrogen,
he amines increased directly with the age of the
ɪg one determination, which shows a very low
on the 2-year-old packs, the average percentage
ɪl was 38.7, while the three determinations on the
ɪcks showed only 15.5 per cent of the total alkaline
ɪia, with a corresponding increase of from 61.3 to
ɪectively, in nitrogen as amines.
was conducted to ascertain whether these changes
:ould be followed during shorter periods of standing
temperature. A pack of a little more than half a
ɜ was made from fish which had just been landed

at a cannery, and had been only a short time in brine. After being steamed and dried, under ordinary commercial conditions, these fish were taken to the laboratory, where the heads were removed, and the portion used for packing ground and thoroughly mixed. A representative sample was reserved for analysis and the remainder was packed in cans which were sealed and processed for 1¾ hours at 212° F. Samples taken at varying periods were analyzed, with the results shown in Table 32.

TABLE 32.—*Ammonia and amine content of sardines stored for short periods.*

Condition of fish (ground flesh).	Water.	Fat.	Total volatile nitrogen (N) per 100 grams.	Volatile nitrogen (N) per 100 grams as—			Percentage of total as—	
				Total.	Ammonia.	Amines.	Ammonia.	Amines.
	Per cent.	Per cent.	Mg.	Mg.	Mg.	Mg.	Per cent.	Per cent.
Before packing in quarter oil cans.....................	67.01	9.07	14.0	[1] 13.3	7.4	5.9	55.6	44.4
After packing and processing 1¾ hours at 212° F..........	65.75	9.13	30.3	[1] 39.7	25.3	14.4	63.6	36.4
After packing, processing, and standing—								
1 month................	65.85	9.02	42.0	[1] 46.8	27.2	19.6	58.1	41.9
2 months...............	67.00	8.72	47.8	[1] 47.3	22.6	24.7	47.8	52.2
3 months...............	66.40	8.69	52.5	[1] 53.1	24.2	28.9	45.6	54.4
4 months...............	66.64	8.18	55.0	[2] 54.3	25.9	28.4	47.7	52.3
6 months...............	66.25	9.23	55.6	[2] 55.6	19.1	36.5	34.3	65.7
18 months..............	64.79	9.93	69.0	[2] 69.0	35.8	33.2	51.9	48.1
36 months [3]...........				[2] 78.9	41.3	37.6	52.4	47.6
36 months [4]...........				[2] 82.4	44.0	38.4	53.4	46.4

[1] These determinations were made on the combined volatile alkaline nitrogen obtained from two 50-gram samples.
[2] These determinations were made on the combined volatile alkaline nitrogen obtained from thirty 3-gram samples.
[3] Normal cans.
[4] Swell cans, springers.

An increase in the amount of ammonia, with a corresponding decrease in the relative amount of amines, occurred during the processing. The actual amounts of both the ammonia and amines increased. Standing caused a gradual increase in the amount of total alkaline material obtained from the flesh, due to the formation of amines, the ammonia content remaining fairly constant, with the exception of the samples taken from the 6-months'-old pack, when a decrease in the amount of ammonia was noted.

The results expressed as percentage of the total volatile alkaline material point more clearly to a reduction in the quantity of ammonia, with a corresponding increase in the relative amount of amines, up to and including the 6-month period of standing.

The increase in total volatile material continued in the case of the cans stored for 18 and 36 months. A more marked increase over the amount found at the end of 6 months occurred during the last year and a half. The incipient swell cans contained but a slightly greater quantity of volatile alkaline material than the normal cans. The separation of ammonia and amines in the volatile alkaline material gave, in all three cases, results quite different from those obtained at the earlier periods of examination, particularly those of the 6-month period. After standing 18 and 36 months, the volatile alkaline material consisted of practically equal parts of ammonia and amines. The proportion of ammonia and amines in this pack, after the longer periods of standing, agreed closely with the results obtained on packs which were allowed to stand for an excessive length of time (Table 31).

INFLUENCE OF TIME AND TEMPERATURE OF STORAGE.

To determine the influence of the time and temperature of storage on the formation of ammonia and total amines in sardines, a number of packs were prepared from fish which had been subjected to widely diverse preliminary treatments. The fish used in the preparation of lots 1, 2, and 3 were dry salted at the rate of one-half sack of salt per hogshead of fish, when taken from the water, and were held in the salt for varying periods, as indicated in Table 33. Those composing lot 4 were surrounded with an ice and salt mixture during transportation and at no time were they in contact with salt or pickle. The fish of lot 5 were feedy fish, gorged with feed which did not look like shrimp. The fish were steam cooked, dried, packed without being eviscerated, and processed for 1¾ hours. As soon as the processed cans were cool, samples were prepared and analyzed. The rest of the packs were stored for different lengths of time at ordinary room temperature and at 33° F. When the analyses were made, the viscera of some of the fish were separated from the whole fish, so that determinations were made upon the whole fish, upon the eviscerated fish, and upon the viscera and contents. The results of these analyses are given in Table 33.

TABLE 33.—*Influence of time and temperature of storage on the formation of ammonia and amines in canned sardines.*

WHOLE FISH AS TAKEN FROM CAN.

Condition of fish.	Period held.	Period in dry salt.	Water.	Fat.	Volatile alkaline material as—							
					Nitrogen (N) per 100 grams.						Percentage of total.	
					Total.	Ammonia.	Amines.				Ammonia.	Total amines.
							Total.	Monamine.	Diamine.	Triamine.		
	Mos.	*Hrs.*	*P. ct.*	*P. ct.*	*Mg.*	*Mg.*	*Mg.*	*Mg.*	*Mg.*	*Mg.*	*P. ct.*	*P. ct.*
Lot 1:												
Packed and processed	0	4	53.07	20.87	38.2	24.8	13.4	......	......	......	64.9	35.1
Stored at room temperature.	3	4	56.94	18.19	41.5	......	......	......	......	......	......	......
Do	15	4	58.38	17.72	68.6	34.7	33.9	1.7	2.6	28.5	50.5	49.5
3 months at room temperature	15	4	52.18	22.85	50.9	26.1	24.8	3.1	2.3	18.9	51.3	48.7
12 months at 33° F												
Stored at room temperature.	32	4	......	......	79.8	43.0	36.8	0.0	6.7	26.8	53.9	46.1
Stored at 33° F	32	4	......	......	62.1	26.6	35.5	0.0	6.1	28.8	42.5	57.5
Lot 2:												
Packed and processed	0	8	48.67	26.26	34.0	24.0	10.0	......	......	......	70.6	29.4
Stored at room temperature.	3	8	48.67	27.07	39.5	......	......	......	......	......	......	......
Do	15	8	47.58	26.93	61.9	......	44.5	2.5	2.8	37.1	......	......
Do	32	8	......	......	73.2	39.3	33.9	0.0	3.3	28.1	53.7	46.3
Lot 3:												
Packed and processed	0	25	49.13	27.80	35.1	23.7	11.4	......	......	......	67.5	32.5
Stored at room temperature.	3	25	52.41	22.84	48.6	......	......	......	......	......	......	......
Do	15	25	47.05	28.70	58.3	31.7	26.6	2.2	2.0	21.9	54.4	45.6
Do	32	25	......	......	76.7	44.5	32.2	0.0	3.4	26.5	56.7	43.3
Lot 4:												
Packed and processed	0	14	59.83	19.64	32.5	22.7	9.8	......	......	......	61.0	39.0
Stored at room temperature.	2	4	60.061	18.84	40.7	......	......	......	......	......	......	......
Do	15	4	64.14	19.96	69.2	34.8	34.4	2.5	4.2	24.2	50.2	49.8
2 months at room temperature	15	4	64.49	14.78	53.4	26.0	27.4	1.1	1.4	24.7	48.7	51.3
13 months at 33° F												
Stored at room temperature.	32	4	......	......	80.1	42.8	37.3	0.0	5.1	32.3	53.4	46.6
Stored at 33° F	32	4	......	......	56.9	27.1	29.8	0.0	5.8	23.7	47.7	52.
Lot 5 (feedy fish):												
Packed and processed	0	6	58.82	23.75	25.4	15.0	10.4	......	......	......	59.1	40.9
Stored at room temperature.	2	6	50.21	28.19	38.7	......	......	......	......	......	......	......
Do	15	6	52.67	26.77	62.5	30.0	32.5	2.4	3.1	25.7	48.0	52.0
2 months at room temperature	15	6	49.96	27.80	40.7	19.2	21.5	1.7	1.5	18.5	47.2	52.8
13 months at 33° F												
Stored at room temperature.	32	6	......	......	76.4	42.4	34.0	0.0	6.7	26.5	55.5	44.5
Stored at 33° F	32	6	......	......	49.8	22.4	27.4	0.0	5.1	22.3	45.0	55.0

FISH EVISCERATED WHEN TAKEN FROM CAN.

Condition of fish.	Period held.	Period in dry salt.	Water.	Fat.	Total.	Ammonia.	Total amines.	Monamine.	Diamine.	Triamine.	Ammonia.	Total amines.
Lot 1:												
Packed and processed	0	4	57.46	16.78	40.9	27.5	13.4	......	......	......	67.2	32.8
Stored at room temperature.	3	4	59.50	25.12	44.8	......	......	......	......	......	......	......
Do	15	4	55.09	20.18	61.3	45.8(?)	15.5	1.6	1.3	12.0	74.7	25.3
3 months at room temperature	15	4	57.53	16.96	55.5	23.3	32.2	2.0	2.2	28.0	42.0	58.0
12 months at 33° F												
Stored at room temperature.	32	4	......	......	......	......	......	......	......	......	......	......
Stored at 33° F	32	4	......	......	......	......	......	......	......	......	......	......
Lot 2:												
Packed and processed	0	8	54.78	18.97	37.5	26.2	11.3	......	......	......	69.9	30.1
Stored at room temperature.	3	8	55.30	16.06	46.9	......	......	......	......	......	......	......
Do	15	8	52.00	22.16	63.7	31.3	32.4	1.9	2.2	27.6	49.1	50.9
Do	32	8	......	......	......	......	......	......	......	......	......	......
Lot 3:												
Packed and processed	0	25	52.57	21.85	37.7	27.1	10.6	......	......	......	71.8	28.2
Stored at room temperature.	3	25	56.84	16.95	49.6	......	......	......	......	......	......	......
Do	15	25	50.59	23.12	62.2	33.3	28.9	1.3	1.8	25.1	53.5	46.5
Do	32	25	......	......	......	......	......	......	......	......	......	......

[1] Surrounded with ice and salt mixture.

TABLE 33.—*Influence of time and temperature of storage on the formation of ammonia and amines in canned sardines*—Continued.

FISH EVISCERATED WHEN TAKEN FROM CAN—Continued.

Condition of fish.	Period held.	Period in dry salt.	Water.	Fat.	Volatile alkaline material as—							
					Nitrogen (N) per 100 grams.						Percentage of total.	
					Total.	Ammonia.	Amines.				Ammonia.	Total amines.
							Total.	Momamine.	Diamine.	Triamine.		
	Mos.	*Hrs.*	*P.ct.*	*P.ct.*	*Mg.*	*Mg.*	*Mg.*	*Mg.*	*Mg.*	*Mg.*	*P.ct.*	*P.ct.*
LOT 4:												
Packed and processed......	0	14	58.23	20.79	34.9	23.1	11.8	......	......	......	66.2	33.8
Stored at room temperature.	2	4	65.00	12.65	43.2	.....	.....	......	......	......	.....	.....
Do....................	15	4	51.49	16.80	62.1	30.5	31.6	0.8	1.8	26.2	49.1	50.9
2 months at room temperature. 13 months at 33° F......... }	15	4	61.70	14.75	47.5	22.2	25.3	1.9	1.3	22.5	46.7	53.3
Stored at room temperature.	32	4										
Stored at 33° F.............	32	4										
LOT 5 (FEEDY FISH):												
Packed and processed......	0	6	56.94	18.07	35.7	23.6	12.1	......	......	......	66.1	33.9
Stored at room temperature.	2	6	58.43	17.02	42.1	.....	.....	......	......	......	.....	.....
Do....................	15	6	56.48	19.03	62.9	31.4	31.5	1.1	2.2	27.9	50.0	50.0
2 months at room temperature. 13 months at 33° F......... }	15	6	53.88	22.37	40.5	19.6	20.9	1.5	1.1	18.2	48.4	51.6
Stored at room temperature.	32	6										
Stored at 33° F.............	32	6										

VISCERA AND CONTENTS.

LOT 1:												
Packed and processed......	0	4	56.78	20.01	39.9	26.2	13.7	......	......	......	65.7	34.3
Stored at room temperature.	3	4	58.81	17.35	47.0	.....	.....	......	......	......	.....	.....
Do....................	15	4	56.44	19.15	66.4	32.8	33.6	2.2	3.4	28.7	49.4	50.6
3 months at room temperature. 12 months at 33° F......... }	15	4	54.15	23.20	52.4	22.3	30.1	1.3	2.5	26.9	42.6	57.4
Stored at room temperature.	32	4										
Stored at 33° F.............	32	4										
LOT 2:												
Packed and processed......	0	8	55.61	21.59	41.2	25.9	15.3	......	......	......	62.9	37.1
Stored at room temperature.	3	8	56.10	20.41	45.6	.....	.....	......	......	......	.....	.....
Do....................	15	8	53.26	21.70	63.7	29.8	33.9	4.4	2.2	27.6	46.8	53.2
Do....................	32	8										
LOT 3:												
Packed and processed......	0	25	55.30	21.05	47.2	33.4	13.8	......	......	......	70.8	29.2
Stored at room temperature.	3	25	55.56	20.65	51.6	.....	.....	......	......	......	.....	.....
Do....................	15	25	53.52	22.25	61.2	32.8	28.4	1.4	1.1	24.4	53.6	46.4
Do....................	32	25										
LOT 4:												
Packed and processed......	0	14	61.47	18.54	36.6	25.0	11.7	......	......	......	68.3	31.7
Stored at room temperature.	2	4										
Do....................	15	4										
2 months at room temperature. 13 months at 33° F......... }	15	4	53.78	21.40	49.1	21.3	27.8	2.1	2.9	22.5	43.4	56.6
Stored at room temperature.	32	4										
Stored at 33° F.............	32	4										
LOT 5 (FEEDY FISH):												
Packed and processed......	0	6	54.68	25.66	36.6	23.4	13.3	......	......	......	63.9	36.1
Stored at room temperature.	2	6	54.02	26.84	40.5	.....	.....	......	......	......	.....	.....
Do....................	15	6	53.02	28.45	59.3	30.9	28.4	.6	9.2	16.7	52.1	47.9
2 months at room temperature. 13 months at 33° F......... }	15	6	49.39	31.98	44.8	21.9	22.9	......	......	......	48.9	51.1
Stored at room temperature.	32	6										
Stored at 33° F.............	32	6										

[1] Surrounded with ice and salt mixture.

According to these results, variations in the preliminary treatment of the fish and their condition have no effect upon the formation of ammonia or amines during storage. Only slight variations are shown in the results of the analyses of the whole fish as removed from the can, the flesh alone, and the viscera and contents, indicating that no greater changes took place in any one portion than in the others. The quantity of total volatile alkaline material gradually increased during storage at ordinary temperatures in all three of the divisions made for analysis, but when stored at a temperature of 33° F. its formation was greatly retarded.

The relative quantities of ammonia and amines composing the total volatile alkaline material changed during storage. After processing practically two-thirds of the total alkaline nitrogen consisted of ammonia and one-third of amines. After storage these proportions changed, the volatile alkaline material consisting of about equal parts of ammonia and amines. Storage at a low temperature, while causing a decrease in the total quantity of ammonia and amines, apparently does not affect the relative amounts. The quantity of ammonia and amines in the storage samples is also about equally divided.

By far the largest part of the volatile alkaline material,[1] consisting of amines, existed in the form of triamine in canned sardines stored for the lengths of time used in these tests. Apparently the separations of the canned fish had no effect on the results for triamine. No uniform increase or decrease in the amounts of triamine contained in the different portions of the fish analyzed, due to the various periods or temperatures of storage, was shown. Monamine and diamine were present in very small amounts and about equal quantities at the end of 15 and 18 months. At the end of 32 months of storage no monamine was found, while the amount of diamine had increased in some instances, being double or more than double the quantities found at the end of 15 months. The temperature of storage apparently has no influence on the quantities of monamine and diamine formed.

CONCLUSIONS.

Marked changes in the quantities and relative amounts of ammonia and total amines took place in the canned fish on standing. In the case of packs composed of ground meat, these changes could be detected at one-month intervals, amounting in the first few months to an increase of approximately 5 mg of total amines per 100 grams of the material per month. Directly after processing the volatile alkaline material contained practically two-thirds ammonia and one-

---

[1] As the method (37) for these determinations was not available at the time of the first examination of these packs, the data for the separation of the total amine fraction into its constituents are given for the longer periods of storage only.

third amines.   During storage at room temperature the pro
appeared to change slowly, until after a long period of stan
total alkaline material was about half ammonia and half a

When stored at a temperature just above freezing, the tot
tity of volatile alkaline materials was greatly reduced, as c
with that produced at ordinary temperatures.

Sardines stored just above a freezing temperature for 32
contained in most cases less volatile alkaline material tl
found when they were held at room temperature for a peri
months.   The relative amounts of ammonia and amines fo
the lower temperature of storage remain the same as the to
tile alkaline material formed while standing at room temp
The total amines composing this volatile alkaline material c
mostly of triamine (practically 80 per cent).   Monamine ar
ine also were present during the earlier period of storage (15
months), but in much smaller quantities.   At the end of
month storage period no monamine was found, but the die
some instances had increased 50 per cent or more.   The d
in the rate of formation of ammonia and of amines at a lov
perature of storage and at room temperature suggests th
changes may be caused by bacterial growth, although it
probable that this action is associated with detinning and
tion of tin by the fish protein.

When the cans of long standing commercial packs were
the fish constituting the 4- and 6-year-old goods were decide
These showed the presence of the largest amounts of amine.

The quantity of ammonia and amines in the canned sardi
has a decided bearing upon the detinning of the interior of
(p. 82).

It is planned to continue the studies on the relation of d
to the formation of ammonia and amines in canned fish.

Effect of Freezing and Thawing on Sardines.

To determine the effect of freezing and thawing upon s
cans from each of the packs put up under the drying exp
(p. 51) were frozen and thawed, after which they were c
with cans of the same goods which had not been frozen.   T
were employed.   In one the sardines were frozen and thawe
in another three times, and in the third six times.

The general appearance of the oil sardines which had bee
two, three, and six times was practically the same as that of
which had not been frozen.   On closer examination, howe
tain changes in the texture of the meat were readily recog
It was apparent that the texture of the fish which had bee
ficiently dried was partially destroyed when frozen and thaw

the meat fibers being broken and the whole fish a trifle softer. These changes were more marked in fish from the same pack which had been frozen and thawed three and six times. After having received this treatment six times, the fish were quite soft, those which had been packed too "green" being difficult to remove from the can without breaking and tearing apart. The texture of the tissues of the fish which had been dried enough or too much changed very little after the pack had been frozen twice, but slight changes were detected in the same pack which had been frozen and thawed three and six times. In the case of the fish which lost an excessive amount of moisture during the drying process, the oil taking the place of water in the tissues served to protect them during the subsequent freezing and thawing.

In nearly all cases the flavor of the fish was slightly impaired by freezing and thawing. This was not always readily determined, for these packs were put up under conditions which did not allow the best flavor and taste to be conserved. In one pack which was not properly dried the soapy taste, so often present when fish are insufficiently dried, was very pronounced in all the cans opened. In a pack put up from excessively salted fish the lack of flavor was very pronounced, particularly when the fish had been dried so long that the oil flavor predominated.

The most marked changes caused by freezing and thawing took place in the mustard sardines. In nearly all cases, particularly when frozen six times, the mustard sauce lost its homogeneous appearance, and, where the fish had not been sufficiently dried, was partially decolorized. The change in the texture of the flesh was more pronounced than in the case of oil sardines, being apparent when frozen and thawed only twice. When frozen six times, the fish were soft, even mushy in some instances, and could not be taken from the can without breaking and tearing. The texture of the flesh was destroyed, the tissues becoming granular and friable. The loss of flavor was very pronounced, much more so than in the case of the oils. The fish from Castine Bay were dry, brittle, mealy, and practically tasteless, particularly when dried too long. These fish, when excessively salted and dried, were not quite as dry or as mealy after being frozen and thawed. Packed in mustard sauce, these fish were tasteless, dry, and brittle, while packed in oil they retained some of the fish flavor and were less dry and brittle.

In conclusion it may be said that freezing and thawing have no noticeable effect on the appearance of oil sardines. The change in the texture of the meat and the impairment of taste and flavor are slight when frozen and thawed twice, but more marked after they have been frozen and thawed a greater number of times. The damage resulting to oil sardines is directly proportional to the amount of

water present in the fish and to the numbe
are frozen. Mustard sardines, however, :
by freezing and thawing, even once, part
before packing. The texture of the fles
ance injured, and the taste lost.

The desirability of storing sardines at a
demonstrated by these experiments.

DETINNING OF SARDINE

EFFECT OF SULPHUR IN SKI

More or less blackening or detinning
unlacquered sardine cans always occurs
gested by a former packer that this mig
some compound in the skin of the fish, as
fish when packed did not cause detinnir
sidered as a possible cause of the detinning
tity of sulphur in the skin of the fish an
skinned fish did not attack the tin, woul
an important factor in this phenomenon.

A small pack was made of skinned an
same source which had been the same
Part of the fish were skinned and then s
The other portion was dried and packed
Both lots were packed in oil at the rate of
and were sterilized for $1\frac{3}{4}$ hours in a boil
spects, except for the skinning of part o
sented actual commercial conditions. Re
skin and flesh of the fish composing this
the results shown in Table 34.

TABLE 34.—*Composition of skin an*

Determination.

Water
Fat
Total nitrogen (N)
Protein (N×6.25)
Salt (NaCl)
Total sulphur (S)
Total sulphur (water and fat free basis)
Total sulphur (water, fat, and salt free basis)

The amount of sulphur in the skin was
in the flesh of these fish. A marked dif
tinning between cans packed with the ski
the unskinned fish would not, then, be du
present, although it might be due to its
work, however, was done to determine

exists in the skin or flesh of the fish. Different combinations of sulphur, in the form of cystein, cystin, and keratin, are found in animal tissues. The first two occur in the true proteins or meat tissues, while the last is the principal sulphur-bearing constituent of hair, nails, skin, etc. Theoretically, if sulphur has any relation to detinning, that in skin should exert the least effect. To a certain extent this is confirmed by the results of the experiments.

The examination of a few cans from these packs three months after they had been processed showed that portions of the surface of the cans containing the unskinned fish had become blackened or detinned, usually where the skin of the fish came in contact with the can. In rolling the lid back or in taking the fish from the can pieces of skin adhered to the lid or bottom of the can. The surface immediately below this was detinned and sometimes slightly pitted, while the surface of the can not in contact with the fish remained bright. The interior surface of the cans containing the skinned fish showed black markings on both the lid and bottom, in some instances a little more marked than in the cans of the unskinned pack. In the pack of skinned fish the entire surface of the can, although not black, was tarnished or dulled. The detinning appeared to be more general over the whole surface, that is, there were no bright places on the surface, as was the case in the pack of unskinned fish. It was quite evident that more corrosion of the surface of the can occurred in the pack of skinned fish than in the pack of the unskinned fish.

After standing six months, the same markings in the interior of the cans, perhaps a little more pronounced, were found in the cans of unskinned fish. Several places where the fish had come in contact with the surface of the cans were detinned and slightly pitted. The portions of the cans not touched by the fish remained bright and untarnished. All the cans examined were attacked to about the same extent. The skin that adhered to the cans was carefully removed and added to the sample for analysis. Besides being tarnished, the surface of the cans containing the skinned fish was badly pitted, and small pieces of the fish adhered to the cans at the end of six months. This pitting and adherence of the flesh to the surface of the can had not taken place after three months' standing.

After six months' standing the interior surface of the cans containing the skinned fish had been attacked to a greater extent than had the surface of those in which the unskinned fish were packed. In both cases more corrosion was shown after six months' standing than after three months' standing, and in both instances it was more marked in the case of the unskinned fish.

The water, oil, and tin contents of samples of these two packs are shown in Table 35.

5890°—20—Bull. 908——6

TABLE 35.—*Composition of sardines (skinned and unskinned) stored in cans for 3 a1 months.*

Period held.	.Water.	Oil.	Tin.
	Per cent.	*Per cent.*	*Mg. per*
Unskinned fish:			
3 months..	52.19	18.88	
Do...	52.67	15.64	
6 months....:...	55.00	16.20	
Skinned fish:			
3 months..	56.00	14.93	
Do...	56.81	14.89	
6 months..	54.68	19.31	
Do...	56.13	17.81	

[1] Determinations made by E. L. P. Treuthardt, Food Control Laboratory, Bureau of Chemistry
[2] Least detinning in any of cans examined.
[3] Worst of lot, tarnished all over and one-half surface pitted.

The tin removed from the can varied greatly among the individ cans, but in some cases corresponded to the amount of tarnishing detinning undergone by the can. The tin content of the pack skinned fish was, on an average, higher than that of the pack unskinned fish. It was observed, incidentally, that detinning reduced to a minimum when the cans are well filled with oil, ε progresses more rapidly in cans where too little oil has been ad(or where the fish have absorbed the oil, thus removing the protect film between the fish and the can. The examination of these pa` showed that the corrosion of the interior of the can was progress and was more extensive in the packs composed of skinned fish.

Apparently sulphur is equally distributed through the flesh ε skin of the fish and is not primarily responsible for the corrosive act of the contents of the can. The blackening of the areas detinned ε the excrescences sometimes seen are due to the formation of iı sulphid. This probably is the extent to which sulphur enters into ı
. reaction in the corrosion of the tinned plate.

EFFECT OF AMMONIA AND AMINES.

That the alkaline materials, ammonia and amines, are primaı the cause of part, at least, of the detinning which occurs in sard cans was shown by the following experiments.

Ammonia and amines, found in appreciable quantities in comm cial and experimental packs of sardines, increase during stor: (p. 70). That amines have a corrosive action on tin plate when c fined in cans has been shown by experiments[1] in which monometb amine of various strengths was sealed in cans and allowed to rem for different periods of time. Bigelow and Bacon(3) attributed corrosion of the interior of tin containers used for canning shrimp monomethylamine. A. Rössing(24) found the interior of cans which sterilized lobsters and codfish had been preserved for seve

[1] Unpublished results on file in the Bureau of Chemistry.

years to be covered with a white coating composed of stannic oxid, phosphoric acid, and iron. He attributed the corrosion to the action of phosphate and ammonia contained in the codfish and lobster.

Determinations of the total amount of tin in packs of sardines in mustard sauce and of the tin content of mustard sauce, plain and fortified with acetic acid, when packed separately, showed that more tin was present in the fish and the sauce than in the sauce alone.[1] This observation is in agreement with the conclusions drawn by Goss(10) who stated that the tin which is dissolved from the can forms an insoluble compound (by adsorption) with the protein and carbohydrate (starch) elements of food. The active materials, acids or alkaline substances, responsible for the solution of the tin are then left free to dissolve more tin. This action may go on until no more tin can be taken out of solution by the food products within the can, or until detinning is complete.

It having been shown that diamine and monoamine are associated with ammonia and triamine, as constituents of the total volatile alkaline material formed in sardines (p. 75), solutions of all these amines were used to determine the extent of corrosion when present in sardine cans. The amine solutions, in approximately twentieth normal strength, prepared from Kahlbaum's highest purity 33 per cent solutions, were introduced into the ordinary quarter oil cans. The interior of the cans and the lids were thoroughly cleaned by washing with alcohol and ether. The lids were then soldered on and the solutions introduced by means of a pipette through a tap and a vent hole in the end of the cans. As soon as the cans were filled, these holes were closed by a drop of solder. The cans were next processed for one hour in boiling water. One set was opened immediately after cooling and the others placed aside for future examination. The results of the determination of tin in the solutions after being removed from the cans, and the extent to which the inner surfaces of the cans were corroded are given in Table 36.

---

[1] Unpublished results on file in the Bureau of Chemistry.

TABLE 36.—*Detinning action of weak solutions of ammonia and amines (alkylamines).*

Solution employed.	Weight of solution in can.	Titration of 10 cc of solution.		Total tin in solution.	Color and odor of solution.	Corrosion of can.
		Before canning.	After canning.			
	Grams.	*Cc N/20 H₂SO₄.* (¹)	*Cc N/20 H₂SO₄.* (¹)	*Mg.*		
Opened directly after processing:						
Distilled water	88.1	(¹)	(¹)	0.0	Very slight yellowish tinge....	Bright on opening; tarnished on exposure to air (rust). Apparently no corrosion of tin coating.
Ammonia	109.3	9.9	9.7	2.99	Ammoniacal odor; very slight yellow tinge.	Badly mottled. Corrosion of tin noticeable. Tin coating of plate dull in color. Worst attacked of lot.
Trimethylamine	115.5	9.6	9.5	3.55	Strong ammoniacal odor; slight yellow tinge.	Mottled. Interior of can, particularly cover, apparently rusted.
Dimethylamine	120.6	9.9	9.85	4.65	Slight ammoniacal odor; faint yellow tinge.	Very slightly mottled. Interior bright. No tarnish. Excluding can with water, appeared to be least attacked.
Monomethylamine	124.2	9.9	9.7	7.33	Very slight ammoniacal and aromatic odor; yellowish color.	Somewhat mottled. No tarnish; coating bright.
Equal parts ammonia and trimethylamine.	118.9	9.75	9.5	2.92	Slight ammoniacal odor; faint yellow tinge.	Badly mottled. Tin coating attacked, slightly dulled. Second in extent of corrosion.
Opened after standing 3 months:						
Ammonia	97.7	9.4	9.1	13.31	Strong ammoniacal odor on opening can; disappeared on standing; slight yellow tinge.	Noticeably mottled. Faintly tarnished. Corrosion and attacking of plate apparent at one portion of can, but interior on the whole bright.
Trimethylamine	99.4	9.4	8.6	10.24	Strong ammoniacal odor; slight yellow tinge.	Interior of can bright; scarcely mottled. Least attacked of any of cans.
Dimethylamine	70.5	10.0	9.2	58.98	Ammoniacal odor; slightly cloudy; marked yellow color.	Worst attacked can of lot. Badly tarnished and mottled. Badly corroded in places. Not as full of liquid as others. Line of corrosion at top of liquid could be determined on inside of can. Cover as badly attacked as bottom of can.
Monomethylamine	99.5	10.6	10.3	14.51	Slight ammoniacal odor; faintly cloudy; no color.	Practically no tarnish. Surface bright, but mottled.
Equal parts ammonia and trimethylamine.	87.5	9.4	8.9	17.42	Strong ammoniacal odor; yellow color, faintly cloudy.	Slightly tarnished. Interior of can dull and mottled.
Opened after standing 8 months:						
Ammonia	95.6	9.4	9.6	12.92	Ammoniacal odor; slight yellow color.	Mottled. Not badly tarnished nor deeply attacked.
Trimethylamine	99.1	9.4	9.3	7.72	Slight amount gas; slight ammoniacal odor; slight yellow...	Slightly mottled. Least attacked in appearance of any of cans of this lot.

On standing, a small amount of a white sediment containing 0.4 to 0.9 mg of tin settled out from the solutions when the contents of the cans were transferred to digestion flasks. This was undoubtedly an oxid of tin.

Of the cans opened directly after processing, those containing distilled water were not attacked. The cans containing ammonia appeared to be attacked the most. Next, in order of the apparent degree of corrosion, was the can containing equal parts of ammonia and trimethylamine, followed in order by those containing trimethylamine, monomethylamine, and dimethylamine. The apparent extent of corrosion in this series does not conform to the actual amount of tin removed. The can containing monomethylamine lost the most tin, while the least went into solution in the mixture of ammonia and trimethylamine.

In the lot which stood for three months, the cans containing dimethylamine showed the greatest effect, as well as the removal of the largest amount of tin. The fact that these cans were only partly filled may account for the greater corrosive action. Next in amount of corrosion came the cans containing ammonia and trimethylamine, with monomethylamine third. In this group the apparent extent of corrosion agrees fairly well with the actual amounts of tin determined.

Of the cans which stood for eight months, those containing ammonia and equal parts of ammonia and trimethylamine were attacked the most. Dimethylamine followed in order of severity, while the ones containing trimethylamine appeared to be the least attacked. The amount of tin in solution agreed with the observations made on this lot. Unfortunately no monomethylamine was available for comparison at this period.

The variation in the amount of tin found in these solutions at different periods may be due to variations in the quality of the tin plate of the cans. No attempt was made to obtain cans composed of the same plate, the cans used being taken from a miscellaneous lot.

These results, although limited in the number of cans tested, show that weak solutions of ammonia and amines exert a detinning action on the interior of the cans, and that this action increases on standing up to a period of at least three months.

CONCLUSIONS.

Ammonia and amines are formed in sardines stored for any length of time, the amount depending upon the period and temperature of storage. Sardines held at room temperature contain a higher percentage of ammonia and amines than when they are held just above freezing. Ammonia and amines in solution are believed to be responsible for a great part at least of the detinning which occurs in sardine cans.

The damage done to oil sardines by freezing and thawing is
gible in comparison with that done to mustard sardines.

The results of these experiments show that it is most desira
store sardines at a low, even temperature.

DECOMPOSITION OF THE FISH.

The flesh of fish differs in composition from that of anim
that it is relatively richer in gelatin-yielding material (collage
contains a smaller proportion of extractives. It is probable th
tain bacteria grow more rapidly on fish than on meat, thus expl
the greater rapidity in the decomposition of fish. The end pr
of decomposition of the flesh of fish are the alkaline subst
ammonia and amines. Fish flesh contains a small amount o
monia as a normal constituent, and the tissue juices dou
contain amines, but in such small quantities that their pr
in appreciable amounts may be considered as an evidence of d
position. This is true also of the flesh of the lobster, crab
shrimp, to which group of marine life the organisms class
feed for the sea herring belong.

INDICES OF DECOMPOSITION.

AMMONIA AND AMINES.

During the course of this investigation a number of determin
of the amount of ammonia and amines present in fresh fish a
fish at various stages of spoilage were made. Fish free from
and fish containing feed in different stages of digestion, some of
belly blown, were examined. The average of numerous deter
tions showed that the fresh fish contained from 1.5 to 2 mg of amr
and amines, as nitrogen per 100 grams of fish, or, calculated t
water and fat free basis, 11 to 12.5 mg per 100 grams of fish.

The transportation experiments (p. 26) brought out the foll
facts: In the case of small fish which contained no feed, and
kept, without the addition of salt, at 54° C., the viscera and
tents decomposed more rapidly than did the flesh. In the ca
larger fish, containing a little feed and transported without sal
ammonia and amines in the viscera and contents increased fron
mg in the fresh material to 22.3 mg per 100 grams of material a
end of 12 hours, while that in the flesh increased only from
14.5 mg during the same period. After these fish had stood f
hours, the flesh showed a decided change, with evidence of m
decomposition. In the case of fish carried in salt (1½ sack
hogshead), a noticeable increase in ammoniacal material, fro
to 18.2 mg per 100 grams, had occurred in the viscera and con
by the end of the 4-hour period of holding.

Fresh fish containing some feed, but hardly to be classed as f
after standing for certain periods of time, showed a marked inc

in the ammonia and amines in the viscera and contents, as a result of decomposition. The 11.6 mg of ammonia nitrogen per 100 grams of fish in the stomach and intestinal contents increased on standing for 6 hours to 16.3 mg, and on standing for 20 hours to 21 mg over the amount found in the fresh fish.

In still another experiment, the viscera and contents of the fresh fish contained 12.6 mg of ammoniacal material as nitrogen per 100 grams of the sample when fresh, 14 at the end of 4 hours of standing, 15 after 6 hours, 17.7 after 8 hours, and 22.3 after 12 hours.

A preliminary experiment to determine the amount of ammonia and amines formed when fish decompose showed that the greater part of these alkaline bases formed during decomposition pass into the solution when the spoiled fish are placed in pickle. These results, coupled with the condition, approximating that of salt fish, when fish for sardines are held too long in pickle or in dry salt, indicate that a transfusion of material from sound fish into the brine or pickle occurs.

Experiments were conducted to ascertain the amount of decomposition which occurs in the viscera and contents of fish kept in pickle for various periods of time. The data thus obtained are given in Table 37.

TABLE 37.—*Decomposition in viscera and contents of fish kept in pickle.*

	Before packing (raw viscera).				After packing and processing.			
In pickle.	Water.	Fat.	Salt.	Total volatile alkaline material (ammonia and amines) per 100 grams.	Water.	Fat.	Salt.	Total volatile alkaline material (ammonia and amines) per 100 grams.
Hours.	*Per cent.*	*Per cent.*	*Per cent.*	*Mg.*	*Per cent.*	*Per cent.*	*Per cent.*	*Mg.*
Lot 1:								
0	56.58	32.00	0.42	15.2	58.61	19.77	0.49	40.8
6	56.70	26.62	2.46?	16.3	43.31	28.46	3.91	46.6
12	54.40	25.96	4.53	19.8	45.76	28.16	8.69	43.7
24	57.47	27.12	4.22	28.0	47.96	27.32	4.21	42.7
Lot 2: [1]								
0	50.93	38.08	.29	13.4	56.70	23.89	.23	35.6
6	51.06	37.24	1.71	18.3	53.62	26.58	1.56	39.0
12	49.53	35.08	2.93	38.4	50.40	26.62	3.32	47.8
24	51.62	32.30	3.55	36.1	44.92	30.87	3.87	45.4

[1] Slightly feedy.

The decomposition of the raw viscera increased markedly in both lots of fish during the time they were held in pickle, lot 2, made up from slightly feedy fish, showing the greater increase. The amount of volatile alkaline material increased markedly in both lots after processing. The increase due to processing was sufficient in the case of lot 1 to mask that due to the decomposition found at any

stage.   Decomposition is indicated in the processed ?
case of the slightly feedy lot.

The amount of ammoniacal material thus far ré
section includes both ammonia and amines.   The
show the production of amines during the course of
of the flesh and the viscera and contents of fish.   ·

The flesh of eviscerated fresh fish showed the prese
of amines, in terms of nitrogen per 100 grams of sa'
portion of this lot of fish had stood for 24 hours with the
samples were prepared by eviscerating the spoiled fish
of amines had risen in the flesh to 14.53 mg per 100
fish had no pronounced odor, but the bellies of the gr
ruptured, and they were spoiled to such an extent as
packing.

The viscera from several lots of fresh fish, which co
the intestines in a state of practically complete diges
maximum of 1.60 mg and a minimum of 1.31 mg of am
as nitrogen per 100 grams of sample.   ·

The viscera of fish, the stomach portions of whic
shrimp, contained a maximum of 16.07 mg and a min
mg of amines, as nitrogen per 100 grams of sample.
fish from which the viscera were obtained were badl
while others showed only the preliminary softening
rupturing of the belly tissues.

In the special investigation conducted during th
the total volatile alkaline nitrogen determined in 1
from belly-blown fish on arrival at a cannery amoun
per 100 grams of sample.   Of this quantity 20.6 n
nitrogen, and 17.1 mg ammonia nitrogen.

Portions of the samples of the feed itself, colle
waters in the vicinity of the fishing grounds, were
compose under the most favorable conditions, at incul
tures, and samples were taken at different periods.
amines in very large quantities were found in all cas
of the decomposition.

The examination of the stomach and intestinal
number of fish which had been out of the water diffe
time showed that raw fish whose stomachs were full
shrimp gave from 10 to 15 times the quantity of a
the viscera from fish which contained material in a
stage of digestion.

VOLATILE SULPHUR.

The amount of volatile sulphur in the viscera of 1
tained feed was determined, and the results, express

cubic centimeters of N/100 iodin solution reduced per 100 grams of material, were compared with those obtained on fish containing practically no feed. In the viscera of fish containing no feed a reduction of 4.5 cc of iodin solution was obtained, against a reduction of 12.6 cc from the viscera of fish which were somewhat feedy:

EXPERIMENTAL PACKS FROM DECOMPOSED FISH.

Even in the presence of salt or pickle decomposition proceeds in the viscera of the fish, particularly when a large amount of feed is present. This fact is borne out by the experience of the fishermen and boatmen, who report that when feed is abundant, no amount of salting or any known way of treating the fish will keep them from spoiling. Decomposition begins and rapidly extends in the viscera and contents long before it is manifest in the flesh of the fish. When free from the viscera and contents (eviscerated), the fish, at the temperatures prevailing in this region, do not show evidence of decomposition for a fairly long period of time.

A series of experiments were conducted to ascertain the amount of decomposition in sardines packed under varying conditions of spoilage. Fish which would pack 6 to the can, from a lot taken without salt or pickle directly from the weir to the wharf, were flaked after they had been out of the water for three hours, and at once analyzed, to determine the water and fat content, the ammonia and amines, and the acidity of the fat.

About 1¾ buckets of these fish were placed in a barrel containing 1½ buckets of pickle, the amount usually employed for this quantity of fish. Because of a temporary lack of water at the factory where the experiment was conducted, a pickle prepared the night before, and previously used to hold 2 bushels of fish for 2 hours, was used. It registered 100° on the salimeter, however, and was but slightly colored. At intervals of 30 minutes, 1 hour, 1½ hours, and 2 hours portions of the fish were removed from the pickle, flaked, and samples analyzed. The rest of the fish were allowed to stand for 24 hours in a basket in the pickling shed, where the temperature was about 60° F. At the end of this time the same procedure was followed for the 24-hour-old fish. The results of the analyses of these fish are given in Table 38.

Although ammonia and amines were extracted from the fish by pickle, a sufficient quantity remained, at the various periods of time given, in the 24-hour-old fish to indicate an appreciable decomposition. The results obtained for the acidity of the fat suggest that this determination may also have value as a measure of decomposition. The evidence of decomposition in the fish after standing for a period of 24 hours without salt or pickle was very marked.

TABLE 38.—*Composition of fresh and 24-hour-old fish before and after being in pickle from 30 minutes to 2 hours.*

Condition of fish.	Water.	Fat.	Total volatile nitrogen per 100 grams as ammonia and amines.	Moisture and fat free basis.		Acidity of fat as N/20 sodium ethylate per gram.
				Total volatile nitrogen per 100 grams as ammonia and amines.	Amino acid nitrogen.	
	Per cent.	*Per cent.*	*Mg.*	*Mg.*	*Mg.*	*Cc.*
Fresh fish from weir:						
3 hours out of water, no pickle or salt..	69.00	8.44	21.0	93.1	2.50	7.0
In pickle—						
30 minutes..........................	67.84	7.57	21.0	85.4	....	....
1 hour.............................	67.52	8.47	18.6	77.5	....	....
1½ hours...........................	67.46	8.63	18.6	77.8	....	....
2 hours............................	67.38	6.62	18.6	71.5	2.50	9.09
Same lot 24 hours old:						
After standing 24 hours, no pickle or salt.............................	71.36	6.56	46.6	211.0	2.40	8.96
In pickle—						
30 minutes..........................	68.24	8.28	37.3	169.9	....	....
1 hour.............................	69.65	5.43	35.0	140.4	....	....
1½ hours...........................	69.40	5.42	32.6	129.5	....	....
2 hours............................	66.99	6.84	28.0	107.0	1.96	9.20

Packs of the fresh, 12-hour-old, and 24-hour-old fish were made in oil and without oil, as well as from each lot held for different lengths of time in pickle. In each pack the fish were steamed for 12 minutes, dried for three-quarters of an hour in a tunnel drier, and then packed in ordinary one-quarter cans. Oil was added to part of the pack; the rest of the cans were left dry. The cans were processed at the temperature of boiling water for 2½ hours. The fresh fish packed easily and quickly, and made a very good looking pack. At the time of packing about half of the 12-hour-old fish and nearly all of the 24-hour-old fish were belly-broken and soft.

The results of these analyses, made as soon as the sardines were allowed to cool after processing, are given in duplicate on samples of fish packed in oil from the fresh lot, and after 2 hours in pickle, and from the 24-hour-old fish, before and after they had been 2 hours in pickle (Table 39).

The evidence of decomposition was quite marked in the goods packed from the 24-hour-old fish which had not been in pickle. Holding both the fresh-fish and the 24-hour-old fish in pickle for 2 hours decreased the amount of ammonia and amines in the packs made from them. The packs made from fish which stood 24 hours showed a greater loss in alkaline material than those made from the fresh fish. The acidity of the fat of the fish packed in oil and processed increased slightly during spoilage and during the periods in pickle.

TABLE 39.—*Composition of fish packed fresh and at the end of 24 hours.*

Condition of fish.	Water.	Fat.	Total volatile nitrogen per 100 grams as ammonia and amines.			Acidity of fat as N/20 sodium ethylate per gram.	
			Original basis.	Moisture and fat free basis.			
				Total.	Average.	Total.	Average.
	Per cent.	*Per cent.*	*Mg.*	*Mg.*	*Mg.*	*Cc.*	*Cc.*
Fresh, no pickle or salt, packed in oil, and processed [1]	57.00	18.90	35.0	145.2	147.6	1.74	1.70
Do	54.12	24.13	32.6	149.9		1.65	
Fresh, 2 hours in pickle, packed in oil, and processed [1]	50.41	26.00	30.3	128.4	133.1	1.70	1.63
Do	54.00	22.35	32.6	137.8		1.55	
24 hours old, no pickle or salt, packed in oil, and processed [2]	50.06	23.48	49.0	185.2	189.6	1.90	1.83
Do	54.53	21.45	46.6	194.0		1.75	
24 hours old, 2 hours in pickle, packed in oil, and processed	47.76	25.23	39.6	146.6	154.9	2.20	2.04
Do	51.73	21.14	44.3	163.3		1.88	

[1] Same as first lot of fish given in Table 38.   [2] Same as second lot of fish given in Table 38.

Table 40 shows the results of the determination of the ammonia and amine in packs of the same fish in oil and without oil, as well as those from this same lot allowed to stand for 12 hours before being placed in pickle. The sardines on which these analyses were made stood for about 7 months under conditions of storage which would approximate those found in actual practice. The analyses were made in triplicate, but only the average results of the determination of ammonia and amines calculated to a moisture and fat free basis are tabulated. Total nitrogen was also determined on these packs, but the results showed no variation that would indicate a loss of protein material under the conditions of the experiment, for which reason they are not included in Table 40.

The cooking received during sterilizing very greatly increased the amount of ammoniacal material in the packed fish. In the case of the fresh fish, not in pickle, this increase amounted to 54.5 mg per 100 grams immediately after processing, and to practically 117 mg per 100 grams after the sardines had stood seven months. Not enough ammoniacal substances were extracted from the fresh fish during the time in pickle to cause a very noticeable decrease in the ammonia and amine content of these same fish after they had been packed and sterilized. The ammonia and amine content, however, had a tendency to decrease with the length of time the fish remained in pickle. This was more markedly shown in the case of the fish packed without oil. The ammoniacal nitrogen content was greater in the pack of fish from the 24-hour-old lot, not in pickle, than in the pack from the fresh fish without pickle. The quantity of ammoniacal material found in this pack (24-hour-old fish) decreased according to the length of time in pickle. In general, the results of the analyses of the different lots of fish packed without oil agreed very well with the results on the packs in oil, about the same quantity of ammonia being found in both cases. These results show that canned sardines contain more ammoniacal material than the fresh fish.

TABLE 40.—*Total volatile nitrogen (ammonia and amines) on water and fat free basis in packs with and without oil.*[1]

Condition of fish.	Total volatile nitrogen (ammonia and amines) on water and fat free basis per 100 grams.	
	Packed in oil.	Packed without oil.
	Mg.	*Mg.*
Fresh (3 hours out of water):[2]		
Not in pickle........	210.2	205.2
In pickle—		
30 minutes........	203.1	220.7
1 hour........	206.1	193.0
1½ hours........	204.5	224.1
2 hours........	202.8	191.3
12 hours old:		
Not in pickle........	204.0	207.0
In pickle—		
30 minutes........	204.2	194.0
1 hour........	188.8	173.0
1½ hours........	179.9	217.3
2 hours........	204.2	199.6
24 hours old:[2]		
Not in pickle........	227.2	221.0
In pickle—		
30 minutes........	209.8	206.3
1 hour........	205.4	201.0
1½ hours........	196.8	189.3
2 hours........	183.6	177.0

[1] These sardines had been packed about 7 months.   [2] Same as lot of fish given in Table 38.

In the case of fish which had undergone an excessive decomposition the results point to the possibility of detecting this degree of spoilage in the packed goods. The length of time in pickle had a more marked influence on the ammonia content when the fish were in an advanced stage of decomposition than when they were fresh.

The determination of volatile alkaline material, expressed in terms of ammonia and amines, in the canned product, therefore, becomes of doubtful value as a means for detecting decomposition of a less degree in fish which have been in salt or pickle.

The process of pickling and salting the fish is subject to extreme variations. There is no uniformity in the length of time the fish remain in pickle, in the degree of salinity of the pickle, in the amount of salt used in dry salting, in pumping off the brine formed when the fish are dry salted, or in the length of time of processing, all of which have a marked effect upon the ammonia and amine content of canned fish. In consideration of these factors it would be impossible to gage the extent of decomposition undergone by the commercial canned product from the ammoniacal substances alone. Furthermore, processing produces a quantity of ammonia and amines greatly in excess of that found normally and sufficient to mask the quantities of these substances formed during the actual spoilage of the fish in the raw state.

GRADING THE FISH.

As already stated, the fish received at the cannery vary in quality according to the season of the year and to the treatment to which they have been subjected during transportation. Obviously best results can not be obtained unless some differentiation is made in the treatment of these fish during the packing process. This investigation showed that all the fish, fat or lean, excessively salted or pickled or the reverse, were sent through the cannery together. In a majority of the canneries the fish were not sorted according to size. At one plant the best lot of oil-size fish received during the season were mixed with very inferior fish that had been in pickle over night and were soft and, in many cases, belly broken. These dull, leached-out fish should have been discarded at once, instead of which they were packed in cans with the good fish, to the detriment of the entire output from that particular cannery. It is a great economic waste for the sardine canner to adopt a routine method for treating every lot of fish brought in. Best results can be obtained only when the fish are separated at the cannery into different grades with respect to quality. Greater care should be used in handling fish of poorer quality, thus insuring better results in the finished product. The various grades should be kept together throughout the process.

FEEDY FISH.

Packing badly belly-blown fish has done more than any other one factor to bring the Maine sardine into disrepute. Excessively feedy fish should not be taken from the water (p. 18), and fish which reach the cannery in a badly belly-blown condition should be discarded (Pl. XIX). The packing of fish containing feed should not be permitted under the present methods of snipping and shearing. Small pieces from the gills and particles of partially digested food from the stomachs produce a messy appearance on the surface of the packed fish.

A reasonable limit for the amount of feed fish may contain before being rendered unfit for packing should be established. In determining such a standard, the method and time of transportation, the extent of the rupture of the belly portion of the fish, the grade of sardines into which they are to be packed, whether they are to be cut or cut and eviscerated before canning, and other factors should be taken into consideration.

SMALL FISH (BRITT).

The facilities for handling the fish and the processes
present time are not at all suited for "britt," as fisl
inches are called. With the methods now in vogue a
not be prepared from britt. In the first place, the
entirely too large quantities, 50 or 60 hogsheads o
inches long being actually landed at a cannery in one
of the canneries they are treated in exactly the same
larger fish. The waste is enormous, and the takin
which would, in from two to three months, be of s
make easy handling and packing, constitutes a grea
When the catch is composed of large and small fish, ev
separated at the cannery by running them through
loss is too great to make a sacrifice of these small fis
ties sometimes taken. If the larger fish are not sep
britt, as is the case in the majority of the canneries, t.
not discarded until they reach the packing tables. Si
thing, they can not be flaked properly, they fill up
tween the larger fish, delay drying, and increase the d
ring of the larger fish when they are separated durii

Small fish from 1½ to 2½ inches long should not be
water. Legislation should be enacted prohibiting the
this size. In the case of a mixed run, regulations
scribed as to the percentage of these small fish which :
a catch. No attempt should be made to pack fish tha
inches long, and this size should be accepted only w.
are willing to take them in small quantities and c
time and attention to their preparation to insure a fi

MARRED OR BROKEN FAT FISH.

The methods developed in packing Maine sardines, :
steaming and drying process, and others that are utili
tation and packing the fish, at the speed and in the qui
are not suited to the physical structure of the me
tender fat fish, which will not stand rough treatmen
marred and broken. Their use is not conducive to sj
with resulting quantity, which is desired in the pre
cheaper grade of sardines. For these reasons prefe
given to the thinner and firmer fish for use in this class
fish, deficient in fat, are taken during the early part of
ticularly during the spring catch or during a scarcity c
is generally conceded that sardines made from fat fis
flavor to those made from the thinner fish, they are not
among the packers because of the difficulties in hand
tissues of the fat fish are exceedingly tender, so that

marred and broken; consequently great care must be exercised to obtain a neat looking can.

To rule that all broken fat fish should be discarded would result in a great waste of good, wholesome food material. Some means should be provided for using the broken and marred fat fish, other than mixing them with, and spoiling the appearance of, packs made from undamaged fish. These fish should not be mixed with the undamaged fish, but may be utilized legitimately by packing them as mustard sardines or "backs up" in oil, with the understanding that this method of packing designates seconds or broken and marred fish.

In packing the better or fancy grade of sardines unbroken fat fish of superior quality are to be preferred. It would be desirable to select the better quality of fish, whenever they can be obtained, for packing the fancy grade of sardines and use the poorer quality of fish in the cheaper sardines.

The Norwegian sardine packers recognize the value of fish of good quality, and pack the better grades of sardines at a season when the fish are the fattest, and consequently of the best value.

CUTTING AND EVISCERATING THE FISH.

All fish used in the preparation of sardines should be cut and eviscerated. Under present conditions it would be impossible to cut all the fish. The employees are decidedly averse to hand cutting, and it would be impossible to secure a sufficient force to cut all the fish during a heavy run. Several of the canneries, however, have succeeded with hand labor in cutting fish of a certain size, while a few cut most of the large fish used for mustard sardines. Since this investigation was undertaken much progress has been made in the development of mechanical devices for doing this work. Several canneries now use mechanical means for beheading the fish. It is hoped that eventually all fish will be cut and eviscerated by machinery.

It is most desirable that fish be eviscerated as well as beheaded before starting them through the canning process. Experiments have shown that the viscera and contents are responsible for the early and rapid spoiling of the fish. Not only does cutting and eviscerating prevent such decomposition, but it also facilitates matters all along the line in the packing of sardines. It will abolish the practice of "snipping" and "shearing" the fish during packing and will practically eliminate the handling of the large amount of refuse in the packing room. It shortens the length of time in pickle after the fish reach the cannery, thus eliminating the damage and loss resulting when fish are held too long in salt and pickle. It reduces to a negligible degree the chemical changes which fish undergo in brine or pickle, causing the removal of a large part of the material which is characteristic of fresh fish and which is so largely responsible for the delicate flavor. It

greatly reduces the time required for drying, and finally an importar
reason for cutting and eviscerating the fish is that if generally adopte
it will aid materially in solving the "feedy" problem, by the remov:
of the feed and viscera before an advanced stage of decompositio1
brought about by the bacteria associated with the feed, has bee
reached.

STANDARDIZATION OF THE SARDINE PACK.

In order to satisfactorily market any commodity it is essential tht
standards should be established before sales are made.   It is then tl
duty of the manufacturer to see that his product complies with tl
standard adopted.   At present there are no uniform grades or sta1
dards for sardines upon which a satisfactory marketing and sellir
arrangement could be based.   Although several canners have sta1
dardized their pack and sell their goods on a basis of quality, the gre:
majority have in the past sold their products simply as sardine
without reference to their merit.   As a result the jobbing trade do
not look for a definite uniform quality in Maine sardines, but gover1
its purchases by price alone.   Such a condition nullifies the attem1
of those packers who have made an effort to standardize their pack
and often forces them to cast a high-grade article in with the poor
grades of those who care less for quality than for quantity.

The greater part of the Maine pack is sold under the distincti1
name "standards."   They may be very good, or they may be inferic
and often their quality is unknown to the packer.   The jobbing tra<
has become so accustomed to this class of goods that quality is not
consideration in the transaction.

Probably in no other line of goods does this lack of systematiz<
dealing between producer and distributor work more hardship on tl
consumer.   Price and the nature of the competition caused theref
rule the quality of goods produced, with the result that the who
tendency on the scale of quality is downward.

PROPOSED SPECIFICATIONS.

The following specifications, based on the division of the pack in
four subdivisions, is offered as a working basis for a standardizatic
of the pack of Maine sardines.

STANDARDS.

Cans.—Quarter size only, plain or decorated.

Fish.—Not less than 5 to a can, preferably 6.   Steamed; n
necessarily eviscerated, though this would insure a better produc
carefully packed brights up; to make a neat and attractive packag

Oil.—Prime, summer yellow cottonseed, or corn, not less than '
per cent of a gallon (3 quarts) to a case of 100 cans.

EXTRA STANDARDS.

Cans.—Quarter, high-quarter, and half sizes, plain or decorated.

Fish.—Not less than 5 to a can, preferably from 7 to 10. May be steamed, preferably fried in oil, and carefully packed brights up.

Oil.—Winter yellow cottonseed, or corn, not less than 87.5 per cent of a gallon (3½ quarts) to a case.

FANCY.

Cans,—Quarter, high-quarter, and half sizes, plain or decorated tins, brass label, or wrapped and labeled.

Fish.—Not less than 7 to a can, preferably from 10 to 15. Cut and eviscerated, fried in oil, packed brights up, carefully, neatly, and attractively.

Oil.—Winter yellow cottonseed, corn, or olive, at the rate of 87.5 per cent of a gallon (3½ quarts) to the case.

EXTRA FANCY.

Cans.—Quarter, high-quarter, and half sizes, plain or decorated tins brass label, or wrapped and labeled.

Fish.—Not less than 7, preferably 12 or more. Cut and eviscerated, fried in oil, and well packed.

Oil.—Olive, at the rate of 3½ to 4 quarts to a case.

STANDARD QUARTER OILS.

Since the grade called standards at present constitutes by far the greatest part of the pack, it may suffice at first to urge a standardization of this, the poorest grade, and allow the other grades to take care of themselves as the marketing conditions and the ideas developed by the new demands dictate. The following specifications for "standard quarter oils" are therefore suggested:

Cans.—Plain or decorated.

Fish.—Not less than 5, preferably 6; more, according to the size of the fish. Steamed and packed brights up, neatly, carefully, and attractively, to show on opening a smooth, bright, clean surface.

Oil.—Prime, summer yellow cottonseed or corn; not less than 75 per cent of a gallon (3 quarts) to a case of 100 cans.

Criticism of the number of fish to the can may be made, owing to the fact that in some seasons it would be difficult to obtain fish of proper size for packing the various grades. Two sizes only, however, are strictly specified. When fish of a more suitable size can be obtained preference is given for larger counts in the respective grades, so that these fish may be packed to better advantage by placing them in a higher class of goods than is done at present.

The too prevalent practice of packing the fish in the cans backs up undoubtedly originated in an effort on the part of the canner to con-

ceal damaged and inferior (belly-broken) fish, ε
it is still done for this purpose.   Many cases oi
have been packed brights up were found, howe
Undoubtedly a number of fish which are no
could be packed backs up to make a wholesom
nating some waste.   Such a product should be
and not in competition with better grades.   In
that may be adopted *all sardines that are paci
classed as seconds*.   A premium would then be
ing brights up and a better appearing pack ass
. A standard for the three-quarter mustard s
size of the fish, should be adopted.   Under pi
tively large fish are called herring when packe
and sardines when packed in mustard sauce in t
The sardine is generally regarded as a small fis
that the canner do nothing to prejudice the
goods by abusing this justly prevalent idea, si
dines three or four tailpieces cut from large fis

Poor quality and overproduction, two proi
fluctuation of the prices of sardines, may be
extent by the adoption of standards of quality.
may thus be utilized in several different class
in one grade, making the pack more elastic ε
establishing a better quality in the poorer grad
. It is believed that the production of a pack ι
standards of quality will in time create a dei
will always exceed the supply.   At the same ti
a better condition in the marketing of sardini
the class of staples which can be sold on meri
will buy because there is a demand for them.
eliminate the speculative feature now unfortuni
jobber waits till the price suits him before buyi

SANITARY PRECAUTIONS IN PACKIN(

THE WATER SUPPLY.

. The water supply of the canneries is obtε
through a pipe, the opening of which usually i
level of the water at low tide.   The depth to w
varies from being completely out of the water
depending upon the location of the cannery
beach.   At some canneries the intake pipe wε
close proximity to the sewer outlets or to the ς
door privies attached to the cannery.   Table 4
a bacteriological examination of representativ
plies.

TABLE 41.—*Bacteriological examination of the water supplies from representative sources around Eastport, Lubec, and North Lubec, Me. (Sept. 18, 1916).*

Source.	B. coli present in—		
	5 cc.	1 cc.	0.1 cc.
North Lubec, Me.:			
9.20 a. m., low water	+	0	0
8 feet from mouth of pipe, low water	+	0	0
Lubec, Me.	+	+	+
Very near sea wall	+	+	+
Eastport, Me.:			
Near north end of town	+	+	0
	+	+	+

DISPOSAL OF SWELLS.

Swells are caused by the activity of a specific bacterium found in and near the canneries, and associated also with the feed of the small fish. At many canneries the returned swells are dumped into the water near the cannery.

When loaded into scows the discarded fish and cuttings from the packing tables often are spilled near the wharves. If the collection of this material becomes too large before it is convenient to remove it, it may be thrown overboard below the cannery, where it furnishes an excellent medium of growth to the organisms present in the cans of swells. At low tide any contamination on the beach is gradually washed back by the receding water, and concentrated near the openings of the intake pipes. Thus the cycle of infection from the returned swells is completed when the bacteria causing them are pumped up through the intake pipe in the canneries, to contaminate the fish which will produce more swells.

Contamination of the pack in this way may be eliminated only by using fresh water free from pollution. The reprehensible practice of throwing out upon the beach near the canneries returned swells, discarded fish, and waste portions and viscera of the fish should be abandoned. Moreover, the opening of the intake pipe through which the water supply is pumped should be far enough offshore and at a sufficient distance from sewer openings to insure water free from contamination.

BOATS AND TANKS.

In some of the canneries not enough attention is given to keeping the holds of the boats and the pickling tanks clean. In order that the fish may arrive at the canneries free from any contamination from the boats, the tanks in the boats should be inspected, to see that they are thoroughly clean and sweet before the fish are put into them. These tanks should be absolutely tight to prevent any leakage into the bilge to contaminate the ballast. The bilge and ballast should always be kept clean. The sluices, pickling tanks, carriers, cutting

sheds, and benches should be thoroughly washed after each (
and no fish, parts of fish, or brine should be allowed to :
them.

FLAKING MACHINES.

After each operation the flaking machines should be wa:
a stream of water of sufficient force to cleanse them thoroi
to dislodge any fish adhering to them.

In the past the unclean condition of the flakes has been (
greatest sources of damage to the appearance of the sar(
(Pl. XV). Particles from dirty flakes and dirt and débris
to the hands of those manipulating the flakes find their wa;
cans with the fish, to the great detriment of its appearar
flakes should be thoroughly cleaned after each operation
particles of fish from the previous operation should be a
remain on them.

PANS.

The pans used for holding the packed cans should receive
care as the flakes; and should be provided with some means o1
so that when they are stacked no pan shall touch the fish in
immediately below it. Negligence of these precautions give
chance for spoiling the appearance of the packed goods by in
ing in the pack particles rubbed from the pans on the fish in
and by marring the fish with the bottoms of the pans. Th
goods should be kept covered at all times and should be
from the packing room before any sweeping or cleaning is d

PACKING.

The packers should be instructed to wash their hands in
water often enough to keep them free from bits of the fi:
unavoidably adhere to them. Roller paper towels, paper na
some other means for drying their hands should be provide(
should handle nothing but the fish and cans while packing
fish as little as possible, exercising great care that the skin o
is not broken or damaged. In cutting (shearing) the fish, w
from the flakes, the heads and tails should be kept in one
the main portion of the fish, used in packing, in another]
facilitating packing and keeping particles of refuse, heads,
and small débris from adhering to the fish and entering the
spoil the appearance of the finished product.

STORING THE EMPTY CANS.

In a majority of the canneries no special provision is .
suitable storage of the empty cans. The cans, particularly tl
are often stored in some unused portion of the cannery wl
and dirt accumulate. An improvement could be made in
lition of the cans as they sometimes leave the can facto

shooks as they are made up often contain a quantity of sawdust, a large part of which is contributed by the covers. When the covers are nailed on and during subsequent handling the sawdust is shaken into the cans, where it adheres to the thin coating of oil covering the tin plate. · When this oil dries, it is impossible to remove the adhering dust and other dirt which may have accumulated.

An effort should be made to improve these conditions. Placing the cans in the shooks upside down—that is, with the bottoms facing the cover of the shook—and keeping the shipping case in this position afterwards will prevent the sawdust from entering the can. When stored in the canneries the covered shooks should be in a dust and dirt free place, or should be kept covered with material which will prevent the entry of dust and dirt.

SEALING THE CANS.

In the course of the investigation many instances of improper sealing were found. Unless the closest attention is given to the machines of the first two types mentioned on page 10, particularly to the adjustment of the rolls and the compression jaws, the cans are but imperfectly sealed. It may be possible in the future to render cans sealed in this way tight by providing them with gaskets or with a preparation on the covers which will form a gasket, approximating the seal obtained on the hermetically sealed soldered cans. A poorly sealed can permits leakage of oil, as a result of which the product may reach the consumer in a very unsightly condition, lacking in some of the original food value, and sometimes with the contents contaminated or spoiled.

CLEANING THE CANS.

The unattractive, unclean condition of packed cans has been a point of severe criticism on the part of the wholesale and retail dealer, and has done much to bring American sardines into disrepute. It is caused by permitting the cans to leave the factories without having been properly cleaned, or, if cleaned, so poorly sealed that oil can leak over all the cans in the shook.

As a rule, the cans of sardines are cleaned by shoveling them over with sawdust or rolling them through sawdust (Pl. VIII, fig. 1). When the cans are bumped and rattled about during shoveling or when passed through revolving sawdust cleaners the fish, even if well packed, become disarranged, and leaks often occur because of dented seams. To prevent disarrangement of the contents those packers who maintain a definite quality, and who take pains to place the fish in the cans neatly, carefully clean the exterior of the cans before shipping them. Cleaning the cans may be done mechanically by passing them through a hot water bath containing soda lime and rinsing them afterwards with hot water.

WASTE IN PACKING SARDINES.

ELIMINATION OF UNNECESSARY WASTE.

Carelessness in attention to details which would eliminate waste and wasteful methods are too common in the sardine industry. For the most part, this is the result of a desire to turn out large quantities of goods and of a lack of control over labor. The owners and managers of the canneries are often so negligent in enforcing regulations governing employees that wasteful methods have developed from careless operators, and the quality of the finished product has been impaired. In regions where sardine canneries are numerous, uniform rules and conditions of labor are badly needed. The standard for discipline and the enforcement of rules can never be higher than that permitted in the plant which is the most lax in these matters. On the manufacturing side, the principal sources of loss in the industry are the waste of fish and oil, in the case of the raw material, and rough and inefficient handling of the equipment of the plants. These of course are not found to the same degree throughout the industry.

The waste of fish may be due to (a) cutting back fish of large size to pack in quarter-size cans; (b) discarding on the flakes fish that are suitable for packing; (c) using feedy fish; (d) using fish (britt) that are too small for packing by the methods employed in the industry. The waste in cutting back fish of large size to pack in small cans is very generally found. That due to negligence on the part of women packers in discarding fish that are suitable for packing can be corrected by stricter discipline.

Some concerns persistently accept feedy fish, which means that they pack a great many broken and damaged fish to the detriment of their own particular goods and of the sardine industry in general.

The lack of cooperation among the packers permits different standards in the quality of the output, and makes it difficult for a few packers to maintain a standard of quality. On a hostile, competing basis, fish that are refused at one cannery as unfit for packing are frequently accepted by a competitor, who cares little for quality, or who may have different ideas as to what constitutes a certain standard. Under such conditions the standard can never rise far above that adopted by the packer who has no consideration for the quality of his pack.

The waste of oil through spilling from the cans after the fish have been packed and oiled is found in varying degrees among the different canneries, and is directly chargeable to the lack of strict supervision of those employees whose duty it is to fill the cans with oil and of those who handle the filled cans.

Waste in Cutting Back Fish to Pack in Quarter-Size Cans.

Data were secured to show the waste occurring when fish of large size were cut in various ways to fit the can, and the use of a can of larger size to fit these fish was considered.

A high-quarter long can (Pl. XX, fig. 1), made to hold large fish without cutting away the best portions of the flesh, has the same dimensions in height and width as the ordinary high-quarter can, but is 1 inch longer. The larger fish (7 and 8 inches long), which at certain times are the only ones obtainable, can be packed more economically in this can. One of the most striking features in the preparation of sardines is the enormous waste of edible material caused by packing such fish in the common quarter oil size can (Pl. XX, fig. 2). Fish 7 and 8 inches long were cut back in different ways to properly fill the suggested higher and longer can and the ordinary low-quarter can (Pl. XXI). To fit the new type of can the 7-inch fish is cut directly back of the gills, with the tail trimmed, thus eliminating all waste of edible material. If the tail is not trimmed, a small piece of edible material is lost in cutting (Pl. XXI, fig. 1). In cutting fish of this size to fit the ordinary quarter oil can, a large amount is wasted (Pl. XXI, fig. 1, central figure). Practically half of this waste may be saved by trimming the tail of the fish when packing in the low-quarter can.

With 8-inch fish no waste occurs when the tail is trimmed and the fish cut to fit in the larger can (Pl. XXI). When the tail is not trimmed a certain amount of waste results (Pl. XXI, fig. 2). When cut according to present practice, tail untrimmed, to pack in the ordinary low-quarter oil can, practically one-half, and the best meaty portion of the fish, is discarded. By trimming the tail and cutting to pack in the ordinary quarter size can, nearly one-half of this waste can be saved. The amount thus saved is practically the same as that obtained by cutting, with the tails untrimmed, to pack in the suggested longer can. A greater saving is effected by the use of this can with the 8-inch fish than with the 7-inch fish.

The saving in material which may be obtained by the use of a can to fit the fish, rather than cutting the fish to fit the can, is strikingly shown in Plates XXII and XXIII, where the determination of the amount of waste was actually made on a number of fish 8 inches long, cut in the manner described to pack in the longer can and in the ordinary quarter oil size can. Figure 1, Plate XXII, shows the minimum waste, 19 per cent, of heads, and a portion of the tails only, of fish which had been cut and the tails trimmed to pack in the high-quarter long can. Fish cut in this manner will pack five to the can, with no waste of edible material.

The maximum waste, two-thirds of which is edible, was found to be 60 per cent in cutting 8-inch fish with the tails untrimmed, according to present practices, to pack in the ordinary low-quarter can (Pl. XXII, fig. 2). Fish of this size, cut in this manner, pack only four to the can. Tons of good food material obtained in this way (Pl. XXII, fig. 2, left-hand pan) are emptied into scows to be carried away to be made into fertilizer, or are simply thrown away.

When 8-inch fish, with the tails trimmed, are cut and packed in the ordinary can, the waste of edible material is reduced to 24 per cent, a saving of 17 per cent of edible material (Pl. XXIII, fig. 1). It makes, however, only a 4-fish can. Practically the same amount of waste of edible material, 23 per cent, is obtained when 8-inch fish, with the tails untrimmed, are cut to pack in the high-quarter long can (Pl. XXIII, fig. 2). Fish of this size, with the tails untrimmed, when packed in the longer can, make a 5-fish can, which is more desirable from all standpoints than the 4-fish can. Plate XX, figures 3 and 4, shows an ordinary low-quarter can and the suggested larger can, packed with 8-inch fish. When packed with fish of this size, the smaller can holds only four pieces, whereas the larger can holds five fish, the entire edible portion of which is utilized.

The waste thus shown is all the more deplorable when the fact is considered that the fish have already gone through the greater part of the process and need only to be placed in cans of the proper size to be entirely utilized.

From the packers' standpoint, a legitimate objection to the adoption of cans radically different in dimensions from those in ordinary use may be raised. The appliances for handling, and the machinery adapted for sealing the cans are standardized. The use of this new longer can would necessitate a refitting of the carrying table, the chuck, and headpiece of the sealing machinery, which in certain cases would be an expensive undertaking. The old type single spindle machine, which is fed by hand and would require only a chuck and headpiece in order to adapt it for use with this can, could, however, be used. In several of the canneries some of these old type closing machines are now in use; in others they are stored away. An effort to introduce sardines in these larger cans to the trade could be made to good advantage.

The fact that the objectionable 3- and 4-fish cans of domestic sardines would be eliminated should make worth while the use of the larger cans.

Other cans now in use, notably the high-quarter and the half-oil size, may be employed to effect a saving of part, at least, of the waste just discussed. There appears to be no mechanical difficulty in packing, sealing, and preparing for shipment the high-quarter and half-oil cans (Pl. IX). The high-quarter cans are a very desirable size

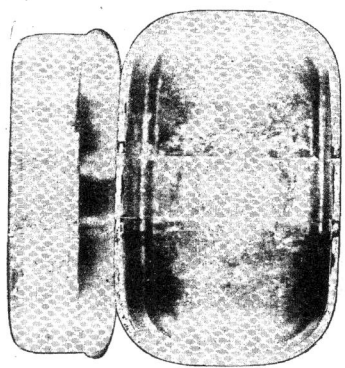

FIG. 1.—HIGH-QUARTER LONG SARDINE CAN.

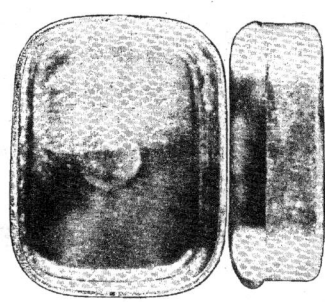

FIG. 2.—ORDINARY LOW-QUARTER OIL SARDINE CAN.

FIG. 3.—FIVE 8-INCH FISH PACKED IN A HIGH-QUARTER LONG CAN.

No waste of edible material.

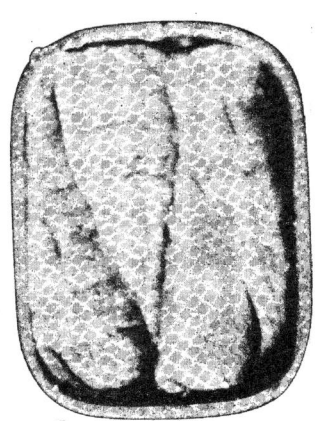

FIG. 4.—A 4-FISH CAN. ORDINARY QUARTER OIL CAN, PACKED WITH 8-INCH FISH.

Waste of edible material, 41 per cent.

FIG. 1.—CUTTING 7-INCH FISH.

Waste when packed in quarter oil cans (left), as compared with that when packed in larger cans (right).

FIG. 2.—CUTTING 8-INCH FISH.

Waste when packed in quarter oil cans (left), as compared with that when packed in larger cans (right).

MANNER OF CUTTING BACK FISH.

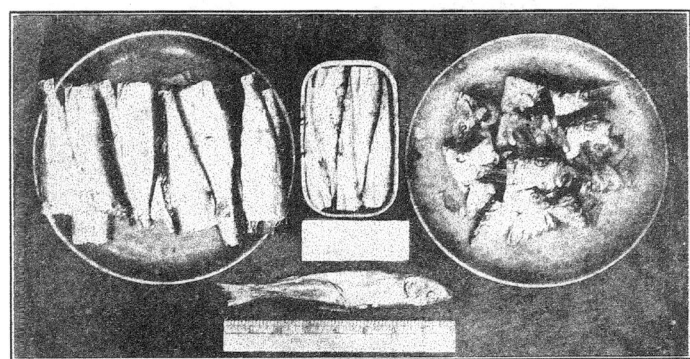

FIG. I.—MINIMUM WASTE (19%) WHEN 8-INCH FISH ARE CUT AND HAVE
TAILS TRIMMED TO PACK IN HIGH-QUARTER LONG CAN.

No waste of edible material.   Five fish to the can.

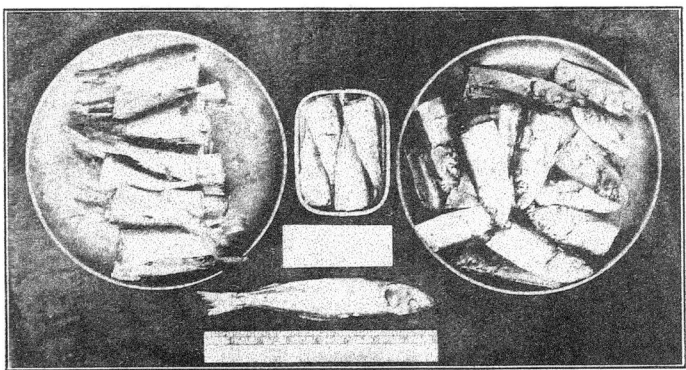

FIG. 2.—MAXIMUM WASTE (60%) OF EDIBLE MATERIAL WHEN 8-INCH FISH
ARE CUT, AS IS NOW THE CUSTOM, WITH THE TAILS UNTRIMMED, TO PACK IN
AN ORDINARY QUARTER OIL CAN.   FOUR FISH TO THE CAN.

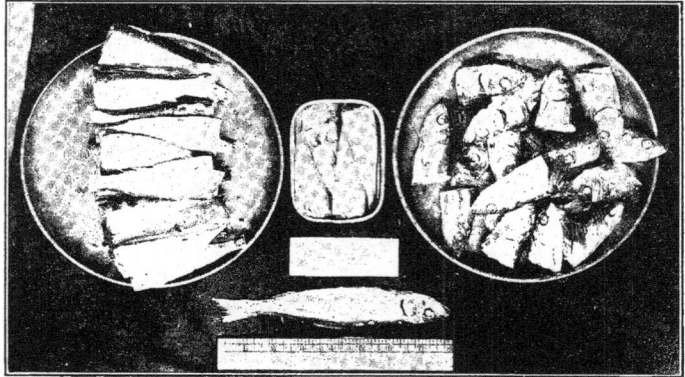

FIG. 1.—EIGHT-INCH FISH, TAILS TRIMMED, CUT TO PACK IN ORDINARY QUARTER OIL CAN (TOTAL WASTE, 43%, WASTE OF EDIBLE MATERIAL, 24%). FOUR FISH TO THE CAN.

Trimming the tails results in a saving of 17% when fish of this size are packed in quarter oil cans.

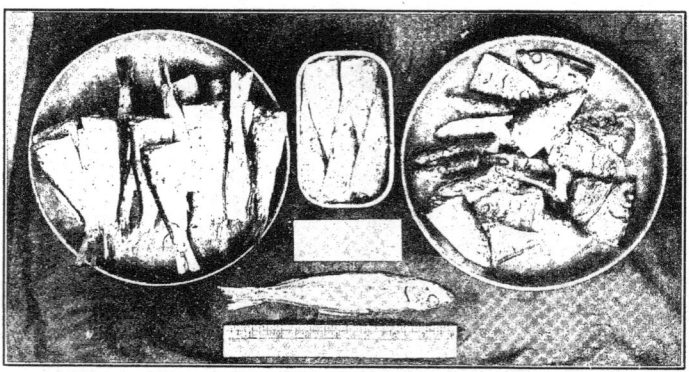

FIG. 2.—EIGHT-INCH FISH, TAILS UNTRIMMED, CUT TO PACK IN HIGH-QUARTER LONG CAN (TOTAL WASTE, 42%, WASTE OF EDIBLE MATERIAL, 23%). FIVE FISH TO THE CAN.

and furnish a quality of sardines which should be most attractive to the purchaser.

Although not quite as long, and hence not as economical in packing the larger fish, the half-oil can may well take the place of the one that has been suggested. The high-quarter cans have been successfully used by some of the canners during the past few seasons. The 1-pound and the half-pound oval cans deserve consideration for packing large fish. Oval cans are coming into use at one or two of the sardine canneries on the Maine coast. The quality of the sardines packed in them would suggest that they are being well received by the trade.

UTILIZATION OF LARGE FISH IN SPECIAL PACKS.

To do away with the waste which occurs when only fish too large for packing in the ordinary sardine can are available, various special packs may be made.

KIPPERED HERRING.

Some of the large fish which at certain seasons and in certain places are the only ones obtainable may be used to excellent advantage in the form of kippered herring. Fish that necessitate cutting back to such an extent that there is a large waste of edible material when packed in the cans at present in use, furnish the proper minimum size to use for this product.

Directions for preparing this product are given by Charles H. Stevenson(30).

Comparatively few kippered herring are prepared in the United States, the round bloaters being so much more popular. The kippered herring are split along the back from the head to the tail, like mackerel, eviscerated, washed, and salted in a manner similar to that applied to bloaters, except that they are not kept in the pickle so long. They are next hung up to dry for a few hours, then smoked for six or eight hours at a temperature of 80° or 85°, each fish being suspended by the napes to keep its abdomen open. With the exception of splitting, the cure is similar to that of bloaters. * * * Herring put up in this way are in great demand everywhere and are preferred by many to the bloater. The very best herring are required for the kippering process. * * * The fish used for kippers should be had as soon as possible after they are taken out of the water. * * * Herring put up in this way are most delicious. * * * The same materials are used for smoking kippers as are used for smoking bloaters and the same conditions apply, only that kippers, presenting a larger surface to the smoke as they do, do not require to be so long exposed to the smoke. As in the case of bloaters and red herring, the tastes of the consumers must be ascertained and the curing as to salt and smoke regulated accordingly. The manufacture of kippers is greatly on the increase in Britain. It is an important branch of the herring industry and utilizes a large proportion of the British catch of herrings.

Many of the Maine canneries are already provided with facilities for smoking fish, and those not so equipped might utilize part of the drying ovens and spaces for this purpose, making the expense of installation of suitable equipment a negligible factor. The prepara-

tion of kippered herring is comparatively simple and inexpensive,
experimental packs made during a lull in the packing of sard
showed that an excellent quality can be produced on our eas
coast. Kippered herring is one of the best products for which
herring may be utilized. It is believed that there is an excel
opportunity to prepare this food product on a larger scale than
heretofore been done in this country and that it will provide a me
for the sardine packer to utilize large fish to a better advantage t
heretofore, thus adding to his present profits.

RUSSIAN SARDINES.

In 1870 the importation of Russian sardines into the United St
amounted to 50,000 kegs a year, coming for the most part f
Hamburg. The disturbed trade conditions arising at that t
stopped the importation of this product, whereupon an attempt
made to supply the deficiency with a domestic article. That
enterprise was successful is shown by the fact that in the late nine
some 60,000 7-pound kegs, worth approximately $27,000, of Rus
sardines were prepared annually in this country. By 1900
industry had become quite important, but the next 10 years sho
a rapid decline, until in 1913 practically none of these sardines v
produced here. The imported article had taken the place of
domestic product. It is believed that many of the fish too larg
be packed as ordinary sardines now might well be put on the ma
in the form of Russian sardines.

Conditions are now similar to those which inspired the produc
of Russian sardines at Eastport in 1874. The foreign supply is a
shut off, or greatly curtailed, and an unusual opportunity is preser
to win back and hold a market in a food product which has once t
won and lost.

Stevenson has discussed the method of preparing Russian sard
(30), as well as methods for making somewhat similar products kn
as Mätjeshering and spiced herring.

MÄTJESHERING.

Fresh full herring, both spawners and melters, are well washed, and the
stomach, and intestines are removed in such a way as not to necessitate cutting
throat or abdomen, this being accomplished by pulling them through the gill
The fish are next immersed for 12 or 18 hours in a 7 per cent solution of white
vinegar, from which they must be removed before the skin becomes flabby an
wiped dry and covered with a preparation composed of 2 pounds of salt, 1 pour
powdered sugar, and a small quantity of saltpeter, this quantity being sufficien
75 herring. The fish are then packed in a barrel as upright as possible, in layers,
a sprinkling of salt over each. The following day the fish are returned with
original brine to the barrel, which is sealed. When there is not sufficient brin
fill the barrel, additional should be made of 1 part of the above mixture and 4 |
of water which has been boiled.

SPICED HERRING.

Spiced herring (Gewürzhering) are prepared in Germany in the manner above described, with the addition of spices mixed with the salt. The spices commonly used consist of 1 part of Spanish pepper, 5 parts of white pepper, 4 parts of cloves, 2½ parts of ginger, an equal quantity of mustard, and a particle of mace and of Spanish marjoram, with a few bay leaves scattered between the layers.

Some years ago one of the sardine-packing companies built up an attractive trade in spiced herring. Although the supply of fish for this product was not as uniform as could be desired, as many as 5,000 cases were prepared and sold in one season. The scarcity of fish made it difficult to supply the demands during the next season. The trade in spiced herring was finally ruined by unscrupulous canners, who packed salt herring in round cans and misbranded the product as spiced herring. It should not be difficult to create a new demand for this product.

ROLLMOPS, HERINGSROULADE, ROLLHERING, BISMARCKHERING.

These names are applied to whole or halves of herring which are rolled up with a highly seasoned filling and bound together with twine or held together by little wooden skewers, packed in wooden boxes, and a sauce poured over them. For the most part salt herring are used in their production. The methods for their preparation are given by Viktorin(35) as follows:

1. Fine, large salted herring are washed, the heads are cut off, the bodies split, the bones taken out, and the skins taken off. They are then placed in fresh water for 24 hours. The inside of the herring, now clean, is rubbed with onion sprinkled with pepper and rolled up from tail to head. These rolls (Rouladen) are then cut into two or four cross sections and laid for 8 to 14 days in vinegar which has been boiled and allowed to cool.

2. The heads, tails, and entrails of salted herring being removed, they are washed well and allowed to remain in water for 24 hours. The fish are cut along the belly, laid out back down and pressed out flat, the backbone and ribs are completely and easily removed if a hot iron or cloth dipped in hot water is laid on the backs. Upon each herring there is placed a slice of cucumber, several small onions (or a larger one cut up), some Spanish peppers, and a little piece of lemon. It is then rolled up from head to tail with the skin out and tied with a thread. Prepared in this manner the fish are placed in pure wine vinegar for two days. After the expiration of this time the rolls (Rouladen) are packed symmetrically in boxes and a sauce is poured over them made as follows: For 100 herring, the roe of three is mixed with vinegar to form a mush which is forced through a sieve. Two and one-half liters (approximately quarts) of pure wine vinegar is heated with some tarragon, lavender, bay leaves, and Spanish peppers. The mush of roe, with 100 grams of sugar, is then added, the whole thoroughly mixed, and when cold it is poured over the herring laid in the box.

The herring are put in water for 24 hours, changing the water occasionally. They are boned and prepared in the same way as "Appetitsild," except they are not skinned. The strips are laid on the table with the skin side down. The upper surface is strewn with small cubes of gherkin and onion mixed with pepper and mustard. Roll up the pieces and fasten with a skewer or thorn. As a pickle use a good vinegar, which may be treated with tarragon.

In place of onions a thick tomato sauce or grated horseradish may be used on the herring, or they may be heated and filled with finely chopped celery. In any case a little pepper, cinnamon, and mace should be sprinkled on them. Rollmops prepared in this way should be laid in vinegar which has been cooked with tomatoes, celery, or horseradish, and there may even be added some Worcestershire sauce.

STUFFED SARDINES.

In the preparation of the experimental packs, designed for use in studying the utilization of edible waste in the packing of sardines, a few packs which were classed as "stuffed sardines" were made. If the heads of the raw fish are cut off properly, the viscera can at the same time be entirely withdrawn, leaving the stomach cavity intact. As the name suggests, the interior of each fish, beheaded and entirely free from all the viscera, was filled with various ingredients, and then packed and processed. The methods employed with the small packs made to determine the practicability of preparing such a product were as follows:

After removing the heads of and eviscerating firm, plump fish, quarter oil size, they were thoroughly washed in dilute pickle, and then allowed to remain in moderately weak pickle for 5 minutes. On removal from the pickle they were rinsed for an instant in clear water. The stomach cavities were then packed with the material desired. Next the stuffed fish were placed upon flakes and grilled over a moderately hot fire by passing through a Ferris wheel oven dryer for 15 minutes. After cooling slightly the fish were packed in quarter size cans, and olive oil was added. They were processed 2¼ hours at the temperature of boiling water.

The materials used for stuffing the different packs of fish were chowchow, ground stuffed olives, sweet pickles, sour spiced gherkins, pickled onions, and pepper sauce (p. 110), respectively. These relishes were finely ground before being inserted in the fish.

Samples of these packs were submitted to a number of persons, ignorant of the method of packing and the ingredients used, for an expression of opinion as to the quality. The packs prepared with chowchow and pepper sauce were unanimously regarded as far superior to any of the others, chowchow being considered the best of all. Ground stuffed olives as a filling were also favorably received, ranking third. Samples of the packs with chowchow, submitted to the buyers of an eastern firm which handles exceptionally high-grade fancy grocery products, were pronounced very good. The buyers stated that they could place a product of this character on the market, and would be willing to give it a trial if it ever became available.

No great difficulties need be overcome to prepare and pack stuffed sardines, but the process would be somewhat tedious and the output necessarily limited. Great care in preparation and in attractive packing would be essential. A small device to aid in inserting the filling material into the interior of the fish would be necessary, the form and character of which would readily suggest itself if the project were undertaken. The only question from the packers' standpoint in regard to packing stuffed sardines is whether they can spare the time and attention required to produce them. There would be no trouble in securing a market for them.

UTILIZATION OF UNAVOIDABLE WASTE.

SARDINE PASTE AND DEVILED SARDINES.

Much of the edible portion of the large fish, now wasted in cutting them back to fit the small cans, may be made available as a wholesome food product in the form of a paste or as deviled sardines. Several experimental packs of sardine paste were put up according to a recipe taken from "Die Merresprodukte," by Heinrich Viktorin (35) with a few modifications, as follows:

Add to 1 kilogram (1,000 grams or 2.2 pounds) of ground fish meat, free from bones:
3.5 grams (0.123 ounce) white pepper
2.0 grams (0.07 ounce) ginger
2.0 grams (0.07 ounce) cloves
1.0 gram (0.035 ounce) mace
1.0 gram (0.035 ounce) cinnamon
1.0 gram (0.035 ounce) allspice
100.0 grams (3.51 ounces) butter
10.5 grams (0.37 ounce) salt
215.0 grams (7.56 ounces) olive oil

The flesh from the large middle part of the fish, cut away in packing the large sizes, was taken from the flakes as they came from the packing tables, so that it was steam cooked and dried to the same degree as sardines. After the meat had been separated from the bones, an easy matter, as the sections readily divide into two portions along the "line of cleavage" between the bones, it was passed through a meat chopper two or three times until thoroughly ground. The spices were then added and thoroughly mixed with the meat by again being passed through a meat grinder several times. The butter, in a semimolten condition, was added, then the oil, and the whole mass again passed through the meat chopper two or three times, until it was thoroughly mixed and finely ground. This made a quantity sufficient to pack 12 of the small round No. ¼ sanitary cans, having a net weight of 3½ ounces.

It is believed that by increasing the quantity of oil it would be possible to eliminate the butter in this formula without seriously affecting the quality of the product. Any of the ingredients, particularly the amount of oil, can, of course, be changed. Sardine paste, as the term implies, should be soft in texture. The product made according to the formula given was not as soft as might be desired. It did not flow, and could not be spread as readily after being processed as before. Consequently, when a softer paste is desired, it would be advisable to increase the quantity of oil for this quantity of meat.

A second lot of sardine paste was prepared according to the given formula, substituting corn oil for olive oil. Here again corn oil proved to be excellent. In the opinion of several who tasted the preparation, the corn oil was as satisfactory as olive oil in sardine paste.

The following formula was used in the p
quantity of what may be properly termed dev

Add to 1,000 grams or parts:
   500 grams or parts of olive oil
   220 grams or parts of pepper sauce
   27 grams or parts of salt

Pepper sauce.—Chop fine equal parts of green and red]
with water, bring to a boil, and then pour off. To one do:
onions, add 2 cupfuls of sugar and 4 tablespoonfuls of s
vinegar. Then boil the mixture about 1¼ hours. Larger
the same proportions.

This preparation imparted a delightful fla
fish meat was obtained and prepared in the
used in making the sardine paste.

To devise a simpler recipe for sardine paste,
small quantity of paste was made by adding
from bones and ground thoroughly, pepper a
oil to bring it to the proper consistency. The i
in the following proportions:

   1,000 grams or parts of finely ground fish meat
   5 grams or parts of white pepper
   12 grams or parts of salt
   530 grams or parts of corn or olive oil

This was well mixed and rendered fine by]
meat chopper a number of times, after which it
This product did not compare in flavor with t
of the other formulas. It would, however, se
tory cheap food product, and, if prepared att
the demand of a class of people who should be
some food of high nutritive value at a low pric

In the preparation of these pastes, it was no
of meat taken from the larger fish gave more sa
those taken from the small fish. With the id
which is so enormous when feedy fish are taker
was prepared from the ground meat taken fr
the bellies badly broken. When ground, how
dark-colored, unattractive mass. In the pre
or the deviled sardines, meat from the large i
impart the proper color and taste to the proc
to make a satisfactory food product from
have been ruined through the action of feed.

The time and temperature necessary for co
these products were not determined. Some
processed at 212° F., for from one to two hours
examined bacteriologically six months later,
during this time. The contents of cans of a

deviled sardines which had been processed at 240° F. for from one to two hours also contained bacteria. It is difficult to properly sterilize products of this nature. Before attempting to prepare them, experimental packs should be made to determine, by bacteriological control, the time and temperature necessary to insure complete sterilization. It would be unsafe to try to market a canned product unless it was sterile.

A product as easy of preparation as the deviled sardines, but superior in flavor and quality, was prepared from the square or rectangular sections of meat obtained by carefully splitting the waste pieces of the fish down the backbone, thus dividing it into two sections, and leaving the bone and a portion of the viscera. These sections were neatly packed in sanitary cans and sardine cans, and covered with a sour spiced vinegar. A sweet spiced vinegar used for a small pack was found to be unsuitable for this purpose.

The cans and contents were processed by first venting and heating for 20 minutes at 220° F., then closing the vent and again heating the cans at 220° F. for 30 minutes. Examination was not made to see if complete sterilization was effected.

FERTILIZER.

The waste residue from fish and whole inedible fish have long been used in the manufacture of pomace or fish scrap, to be incorporated in commercial fertilizers. One of the sardine packing companies at Eastport operates a reduction plant for the pressing and drying of waste from the packing houses for a fertilizer ingredient. To supply the fertilizer factory this company also purchases the raw waste material from several of the other canneries in the vicinity of Eastport and Lubec. This plant is housed in a substantial concrete structure, is well equipped, and manufactures a very good grade of fertilizer fish scrap. Prior to the season of 1915 this was the only instance along the coast where a concerted effort was made to utilize the waste as a by-product of the canning of sardines. During the two following packing seasons, however, another company was organized to produce fish scrap for fertilizer from the waste.

FISH MEAL.

Fish meal as a source of protein has been used to a large extent in foreign countries as a supplementary food for stock. It has been used to a very limited extent in this country, and then principally as the protein basis for poultry foods. The use of fish meal in feeding stock and poultry is increasing. A discussion of the use of fish meal for animal feeding and the results of feeding experiments conducted with fish meal made from the sardine waste, the preparation of which is here discussed, has already been published (36).

The waste in the sardine industry offers excellent material for the preparation of a high-grade fish-meat meal. This waste, as it comes from the packing table, has been steam cooked and partially dried, so that it can be taken after collection from the packing table directly to a plant equipped for pressing and drying. The advisability of producing fish meal in a small unit plant attached to the individual canneries or at a central plant devoted exclusively to this purpose is a question for the individual canneries to decide, and depends upon various considerations, such as the location and administration of the plant. Both methods have advantages and disadvantages. It would seem that a cooperative arrangement might be satisfactorily worked out. The prime consideration is to hasten the utilization of the total waste as a by-product for animal feeding purposes.

Looking toward the utilization of this waste material as a stock food, a quantity of fish-meat meal was prepared in an experimental way during the course of this investigation. Six different lots were made under slightly varying conditions on a small commercial scale, and the yield of the dry material and of the oil determined.

The waste material used in all these experiments was taken directly from the packing tables to a small fertilizer plant previously thoroughly cleaned, which was equipped with an iron steam cooker, a rack, and cloth No. 2 screw press capable of yielding a pressure of 120 tons, and an ordinary type rotary fertilizer drier having a capacity of 1,800 pounds of dry material. Table 42 shows the treatment given the raw material, the composition of the raw material and of samples taken during the process, the method of treatment, and the yield of fish meal and oil.

Lots 1 and 2, which were taken out of the drier much too soon and which therefore contained too much water, did not keep. Lot 1 spoiled in the course of a week and lot 2 in about four weeks' time. The meal from both these lots was discarded.

Since it was desirable to have the moisture content of the material much lower, longer drying periods were adopted in preparing the remaining lots. Drying the meal to a moisture content between 5 and 10 per cent resulted in the product keeping satisfactorily.

The dried meal composing lot 3 had a very strong odor of ammonia when drawn from the drier. This disappeared, however, on cooling and standing overnight. Lot 4 had a faint odor of ammonia when first prepared. No ammonia odor was detected in the two other lots.

The proportion of whole fish composing the waste used in these experiments varied considerably, as did also the oil content. In the case of very fat fish the oil was expressed in a pure condition, mixed with comparatively little water.

TABLE 42.—*Yield and composition of experimental lots of fish meat meal.*

Material	Water, P. ct.	Oil, P. ct.	Total nitrogen, P. ct.	Total protein (N × 6.25), P. ct.	Ash, P. ct.	Total, P. ct.	Ground or whole.	Steamed or cold.	Steam cooked, Min.	Time of pressing, Hrs.	Pressure per square inch, Tons.	Time of drying, Hrs.	Weight of raw material, Lbs.	Weight of dry material, Lbs.	Yield, P. ct.	Yield of oil, Lbs.	Gals.	P. ct.
Lot 1:																		
Raw	57.68	15.45	3.30	20.63	5.68	99.44	Whole..	Cold......		2	120	1½	2,074	[1] 1,628	[1] 30.28	165	22	8.0
After pressing	57.80	8.07	4.29	27.41	6.72	100.00												
After drying	24.94	15.39	7.34	45.88	11.62	97.83												
Composition reduced to 10 per cent.	(10.00)	(18.09)	(8.63)	(53.94)	(13.66)	(95.69)												
Lot 2:																		
Raw material—After steam cooking.	63.89	12.85	2.82	17.63	4.63	99.00	Whole..	Steam cooked.	15	1½	120	2¼	2,061	[1] 1,553	[1] 26.83	180	24	8.73
After pressing.	57.65	6.76	4.41	27.58	5.48	97.45												
After drying.	33.99	12.16	7.10	44.38	8.88	99.41												
Composition reduced to 10 per cent water.	(10.00)	(16.00)	(9.34)	(58.33)	(11.67)	(96.05)												
Lot 3:																		
Raw material—After grinding.	58.32	17.22	3.20	20.00	5.21	100.75	Ground.	Steam cooked.	25	1½	120	2½	1,567	432	27.57	120	16	7.70
After steam cooking.	61.33	13.98	3.02	18.88	5.14	99.33												
After pressing.	59.37	6.70	4.26	26.63	6.58	99.28												
After drying.	4.00	17.51	9.65	60.31	14.73	97.45												
Lot 4:																		
Raw material—After grinding.	56.51	16.49	3.26	20.38	6.19	99.59	Ground.	Cold......		2	120	3	2,197	767	34.91	187.5	25	8.53
After pressing.	57.14	7.60	3.96	24.75	7.85	97.34												
After drying.	10.83	17.14	8.52	53.25	16.20	97.42												
Lot 5:																		
Raw material—After steam cooking.	54.62	9.72	4.07	25.44	9.11	102.86	Whole..	Steam cooked.	30	1	120	2½	1,777	580	32.64	67.5	9	3.79
After pressing.	49.83	6.53	5.10	31.88	10.14	103.48												
After drying.	5.38	12.71	9.68	60.50	19.85	98.44												
Lot 6:																		
Raw material—After steam cooking.	64.99	8.54			5.93		Whole..	Steam cooked.	90	2	120	2¼-3	3,391	755	22.00			
After pressing.	56.03	5.38		12.25	12.25								13,067	3,715	[2] 28.43			
After drying.	5.16	9.69	10.53	65.81	14.99	96.65									[2] 29.04			
Average composition dried meal.	7.71	15.19	9.39	58.70	15.18	96.78												

[1] Calculated as containing 10 per cent water.　　[2] Average.

Lot 5 was made from waste obtained from small fish from 3 to 5 inches long (snippers), which would pack from 20 to 25 to a can. This waste material contained from 60 to 70 per cent of whole fish which had been discarded from the packing table because it was decomposed by feed, broken, and damaged.

The waste material used for lot 6 was composed of small fish which would pack 8 to 10 to a can. These fish were very feedy, and had been badly broken during transportation to the cannery. The waste in these fish as actually determined amounted to from 80 to 85 per cent, the largest encountered during the entire investigation. Whole flakes full were discarded at a time.

The results of the analyses made show that a large percentage of oil was removed during pressing, while the percentage amount of water was not appreciably changed. Where the material was steam cooked, the percentage of water increased, and pressing in these instances brought the percentage of water down to practically the same amount as that present in the raw waste as it came from the packing tables. The sum of the constituents—water, oil, protein, and ash—add up to practically 100 per cent in all cases in the results on the raw material, but after drying there is a shortage of undetermined matter of from $2\frac{1}{2}$ to nearly 4 per cent. This difference is in large part due to the formation of nonnitrogenous material during cooking and drying, and in part to the fact that the factor 6.25, used for calculating the total protein from the nitrogen determined, is not exact for fish protein.

The average yield of meal, ranging from 5 to 10 per cent of water, as determined in these six experiments, amounts to 29 per cent. The average would be higher than this by eliminating the last lot, in which the waste was steam cooked an excessive length of time, so that undoubtedly a great part of the protein material was lost in the water which was formed. It is safe to place the yield of material that can be obtained from this waste at 25 per cent under average commercial conditions.

In the case of the oil, cold pressing gave as good a yield as pressing the steam-cooked material. Steam cooking or heating before pressing reduces the time required for pressing. Excessive cooking should be avoided. The yield of dry meal is apparently decreased by material lost during cooking in the excess water formed by condensing steam. The small amount of oil yielded and the comparatively small amount retained in the dried meal made from small fish with a low fat content might suggest to the prospective producer of fish meal that at times in the season, when these fish are plentiful and when they are as poor in fat as those composing lots 5 and 6, it would not be necessary to press them at all before drying the waste for feeding purposes. As much of the oil as possible should be removed by efficient pressing of the raw material. In pressing there is this to be gained, that, if the material has been steam cooked, part of the water is also removed, thus making the time of drying shorter.

Based on a pack of 1,800,000 cases, and assuming that the entire amount of waste would be made into fish-meat meal, and 20 cases are obtained per hogshead, with 1¼ tons of waste for each 15 hogsheads of fish, and that the yield of meal is 25 per cent of this amount, the following amount of meal could be prepared from the waste in the sardine industry: 1,875 tons of meal, which at from $40 to $45 per ton would have an approximate value of $80,000. An estimate based on 1½ tons waste per 10 hogsheads would yield 13,500 tons of waste, which at 25 per cent yield of meal would amount to 3,375 tons. This at $40 per ton would produce a revenue of $135,000. On a basis of 15 gallons of oil per ton of waste there would be in this case 202,500 gallons of oil, which at 20 cents per gallon would be $40,500. On a basis of 10 gallons of oil per ton the revenue on the oil at 20 cents per gallon would amount to $27,000. In round numbers, it is safe to estimate that the utilization of the waste material, such as could now be obtained from the packing of sardines, would yield 3,000 tons of meal and 200,000 gallons of oil. The oil produced in this way is a very superior grade of fish oil, far superior to the ordinary grades. At the 1916 prices of fish oil the oil obtained from rendering the sardine waste should amount to a sum more than sufficient to defray the cost of manufacturing the dried meal.

As a result of this work a system has been installed in one of the canneries for utilizing the waste for fish meal for animal feeding purposes. Reports received indicate that this effort has been very successful.

ECONOMIC CONSIDERATIONS.

BUYING FISH FOR THE CANNERIES.

At present the fish are sold at auction by the owner of the weir, often creating keen competition between the various boatmen who act as the packers' agents. Within certain limits the boatmen are free to bid up the purchase price. As the packer pays the boatman a certain sum for each hogshead of fish transported, the boatman often is tempted to receive this fare without sufficient regard to the quality of the fish or the price asked for them. It would seem most advisable, therefore, to place stricter limitations upon the price the boatmen may bid for the fish, and to refuse to accept fish which are too poor to pack.

NUMBER OF FISH, OF VARIOUS SIZES, PER HOGSHEAD (1,000 POUNDS).

The unit of measure in the Maine sardine industry, the hogshead, is considered in practice to hold approximately 1,000 pounds. Ten tubs of fish of specific dimensions constitute a hogshead. It was shown that the actual weight of a number of tubs of fish, when taken at the weir, averaged more than 100 pounds each. The weight of a hogshead, therefore, should be considered as more than 1,000 pounds. Doubtless these weights vary, and for convenience the numbers of fish per hogshead are given on the basis of a hogshead weighing 1,000 pounds. The figures for the fish were determined by counting several 100-pound lots of fish of various sizes. The following results, in round numbers, were obtained:

Length of fish, inches.	Approximate number per hogshead.
4	51,000
5	33,500
6	22,300
7	9,900
8	7,200

The number of fish 4, 5, and 6 inches in length necessary to fill the quarter size can was found to be, on an average basis, 22, 11, and 8, respectively. With these figures as approximate data, it is possible to estimate the number of cases per hogshead that may be packed from a uniform lot of fish. The more efficient the operation of the factory the nearer to the theoretical the yield should approach.

CAPACITY OF THE CANNERIES.

The sardine canners along the coast of Maine are entirely at the mercy of the run of fish for their supply of raw material. Sometimes in the early spring, and usually from the summer school in August, there is an oversupply of fish, while at other times during a season there is a scarcity. The supply of fish varies during the year and also varies locally, depending upon the places where the different schools strike in.

There is an urgent need for some method to insure a more uniform supply of fish. During a period of overabundance it would be desirable to store the excess supply for use as needed rather than attempt to use all that can be taken from the water, thereby crowding the capacity of the canneries to the detriment of the quality of the finished product. This would be accomplished, to a certain extent, by the use of pounds or pockets attached to the weirs and by floating inclosures made entirely of nets in which the catch of a few weirs could be stored. Cold storage facilities would also very materially aid in solving this difficulty. It is doubtful, however, if the product could legitimately stand this added cost.

Using impounded fish only would insure a nearly constant supply of fish free from feed. Such fish could be taken at the proper time in the morning and in the desired quantity. They could be brought to each cannery in amounts governed by the capacity of the particular cannery. Under the present system the supply depends upon the irregularity of the catch, and the time of delivery is governed by the stage of tide at which the weirs can be seined. Fish beyond the capacity of the cannery are often brought in by the boatman, who is anxious to earn on each trip as large a fare as possible.

The universal application of regulations prohibiting the packing of "feedy" fish, strictly observed, will necessitate the building of pounds on a majority of the weirs. In the interest of efficiency, the elimination of waste, and the improvement of quality it would seem wise to extend the idea a little further and use nothing but impounded fish in packing sardines. Following this, it would be desirable if each cannery were on a capacity basis, taking no more fish than can be properly handled, so as to make a neat, attractive product, according to specifications adopted for the particular grade packed and which can be sealed in a working day of 10 hours.

CARTONS FOR STANDARD SARDINES.

Sardines are packed in tins with the brand name and design printed on the cover or sides, and also in plain tins. The practice of cartoning the standard grade of sardines packed in plain tins has increased rapidly in recent years. The cartons provide a place for the key in the key can goods and conceal unattractive, unclean cans. This is an expensive method of attaching the key and overcoming the difficulty of cleaning the cans. It seems a great waste of effort and material to place the so-called "standard" grade of sardines in cartons. According to present practices, all the different brands of the standards in cartons are prepared from the same grade of standard goods. Although cartoning or wrapping the fancy and extra fancy sardines may be justifiable, the margin of profit in the standard grade does not justify this additional cost on manufacture. It should be put elsewhere in the process to bring about an improvement in quality. It is hoped that the sardine canners will be able to cooperate in this feature of packing sardines, which, through competition, has developed into a wasteful and useless practice, to the end that it may be completely eliminated. This should prove particularly desirable now that labor and paper are high and scarce, and will be an advance in the direction of conservation and efficiency.

IMPORTATION AND EXPORTATION OF SARDINES (1910-1916).

Table 43, prepared from the Annual Reports on Commerce and Navigation of the United States, shows the value of the importations of sardines into the United States, for the years mentioned, from the principal sardine-producing countries. An interesting feature in the value of the sardine importations is the gradual decline in the importations of the French sardine and the increase in the value of the Norwegian product during the years 1910 to 1915. Importations from

Portugal show a slight increase during the last three years over the first three years of this period. The value of the sardines imported from Italy shows a notable increase during 1914, 1915, and 1916, while little change in the values of the fish imported from Spain is seen until 1915, when there was a decided decrease, followed in 1916 by a marked rise.

The total importations from all countries reached, in round numbers, a value of $3,000,000 during 1914 and 1915. The total value for 1915 was a little below that of 1914, owing to the great decrease in the value of the French sardines imported in 1915. During 1916 the importations of sardines fell off over $1,000,000 in value. Nearly 90 per cent of this decrease was caused by the diminished importation of Norwegian sardines. The embargo placed on the exportation of Norwegian sardines by the Government of Norway at the close of the year 1915 and the war conditions in the French sardine industry practically eliminated these goods from this country. The price of foreign sardines resulting from present conditions is practically prohibitive for the domestic market, and only small quantities are available at any price.

TABLE 43.—*Importations of fish packed in oil.*[1]

Country.	Value of imports.						
	1910	1911	1912	1913	1914	1915	1916
France	$1,317,940	$707,644	$495,903	$634,162	$700,984	$446,434	$359,701
Norway	861,944	1,034,946	947,431	1,199,850	1,427,318	1,662,609	741,697
Portugal	346,036	303,565	313,420	477,310	536,451	517,407	334,467
Italy	165,903	191,983	143,541	154,451	255,589	251,383	340,000
Spain	50,943	40,427	39,025	42,262	42,369	23,145	50,573
Total	2,742,766	2,278,585	1,939,320	2,508,035	2,982,711	2,901,978	1,826,438
Total from Europe (including all other countries)	2,982,475	2,533,218	2,079,002	2,659,074	3,178,000	2,996,596	1,911,346

[1] For the years ending June 30, 1910 to 1916. From Annual Reports on Commerce and Navigation of the United States, Bureau of Foreign and Domestic Commerce, U. S. Department of Commerce. Duties under the present tariff are levied on a class of goods packed "in oil." While it is recognized that there are a few articles, such as anchovies, etc., which would be included in the statistics gathered from this source, it is believed that by far the greater part of the values reported is due to oil sardines. The table is given for the purpose of indicating as closely as it is possible to do the business done in foreign sardines in this country.

OUTLOOK FOR THE MAINE SARDINE INDUSTRY.

The volume of foreign sardines handled (Table 43) indicates the possibility of increasing the business in grades of domestic sardines of a quality capable of giving them an entrance to this market and holding the greater portion of it now that the supply of the foreign article is practically cut off (1916). The trade and the consumer should not expect a domestic sardine of exactly the same excellence as the French article, for several factors mitigate against it.

In the first place, the pilchard, from which the French sardine is made, is generally conceded to be the most desirable in point of size, color, texture, and flavor of all the varieties of fish used in the preparation of sardines. Even if it does not possess the very fine shade of flavor characteristic of the French sardine, it is believed that a sardine satisfactory to the most fastidious may be made from the sea herring if the work is properly done. A smoked sardine packed in olive oil has been commercially prepared from the sea herring, and was considered a very superior article.

Another advantage which the French sardine has over the Maine sardine has been aptly expressed by Dr. H. M. Smith, United States Commissioner of Fisheries (27), who states that the unit of measure in the French industry is the individual fish, whereas in this country it is the hogshead. More attention to the details of the packing process on the part of the American canner will aid in eliminating this distinction.

A third point of difference between the two kinds of sardines lies in the fact that the French fish are put up in olive oil, while cottonseed is the oil commonly used in Maine. The consumer who dislikes cottonseed oil will, of course, maintain his preference for the foreign article. As already suggested (p. 66), however, the use of corn oil may improve the standing of some of the better grades of sardines. The high cost of olive oil prevents its being generally employed for this purpose in the United States. In this connection it is interesting to note a provision in the Canadian tariff laws [1] which permits the importation of olive oil, free of duty, when it is to be used in the canning of fishery products. Under this provision olive oil may be entered free under a bond stipulating that it is to be used only in the preservation of fishery products. Such an arrangement in this country might go far toward stimulating the production of an article of quality with which to bid for that portion of the domestic trade formerly occupied by the foreign sardine, and also for the South American trade.

Not only is there an excellent chance to enter the domestic field vacated by the foreign sardines, but the South American markets also offer exceptional opportunities for the introduction of sardines. There are a few features of the South American trade which packers of domestic sardines should bear in mind before attempting to enter this field. The chief consideration is that the sardines must be of good quality, as good as or better than the foreign goods of which these countries are now deprived. The grades of domestic sardines known at the present time as standards will not hold this market.

Another point to be considered is the taste of the people of the South American countries (32). They prefer fish packed in sauces

[1] Canada. The Customs Tariff, 1907, p. 31, Schedule A, Item 278. Under provisions of the Canadian war tax, oil covered by this item is now (1916) subject to a duty of 7½ per cent ad Valorem. On removal of this tax, oil under this provision will be again free.

se, highly spiced, and are also accustomed to olive
ines. Tomato sauce is a favorite and another is "esc
s made by adding vinegar, pepper, salt, and spices
h the fish have been cooked.

44 shows the import values of sardines in the differe
an countries for 1910, and, in some instances, for 1
principal exporting countries.

TABLE 44.—*Value of sardines imported into South American counti*

To—	Value.	From—
....	$1,104,898	France and Spain.
	[1] 6.80–14	Spain, Portugal, and Ita
....	[2] 1,267,575	Norway.
....	296,485	Spain.
....	48,553	Germany and Spain.
....	30,450	Germany and Great Brit
....	....	France, Spain, and Italy
....	102,871	Portugal, Spain, and Ger
....	49,546	Spain and France.
....	252,982	Spain and Germany.

[1] Value per case.   [2] Preserved fish and fish extracts.

rding to the United States Department of Comm
nd Germany lead in supplying sardines imported in
he United States furnishing only $4,427 worth of a
2. The Spanish sardine is of good quality and reas
The situation with regard to the possibility of se
rtion of this trade is well summed up by the followi
2), calling attention to the inferior quality of the
; and the necessity of producing an article appealir
the people:

it increase in exports from the United States to South America
: fish may be looked for unless the quality of the product can be
astes of the South Americans considered for fish put down in sa
tion in this line is very large and worthy of study by fish canners

publication(32) gives the rates of duty, the details
n, shipping, etc., and other valuable information p
ing goods to these countries.
appears to be no reason, other than a scarcity in th
nd an overwhelming demand from the domestic mar
erican packers of sardines should not obtain their sha
American trade. This is another irrefutable argumer
ement of quality.

SUMMARY.

The packers of Maine sardines occupy a very important position in the food industry in their ability to supply a food product which is comparatively cheap and at the same time has a high nutritive value. Careless methods on the part of some packers, due to a desire for quantity production at a sacrifice of quality and to a lack of control over the employees of the plants, have resulted in the appearance on the market of some very low-grade sardines, tending to bring the whole sardine industry into disrepute.

In an effort to assist the packer in improving the character of his output the Bureau of Chemistry conducted an extensive investigation of the packing processes, as a result of which it has been able to make various recommendations to the canners.

The salient points brought out in the course of the experimental work are as follows:

Composition of the fish.—The composition of the sea herring varies during the season, the fat content increasing from July to October. This variation is greater in the case of the smaller than of the larger fish.

Food of the sea herring.—The copepods (red feed) and schizopods (shrimp) constitute the principal food of the sea herring. When gorged with food on being taken from the water the fish are said to be feedy, in which condition they are unfit for packing. The difficulty encountered in the form of feedy fish may be overcome by holding the fish in pounds attached to weirs until they are free from feed, and by cutting and eviscerating the fish before sending them through the packing process.

Swells.—Two organisms, a bacillus apparently identical with Nielsen's *Bacillus Walfischrauschbrand* and *Bacillus B*, a nonspore-bearing pathogenic gas-producing bacterium, are associated with the feed of the small herring, the former being more frequently found with the schizopods and the latter with the copepods. During decomposition of the copepods and schizopods (feed), both ammonia and amines were produced in very large quantities. Growth of the two organisms in pure culture on fish media also produced ammonia and amines. Apparently swells are produced by the action of these organisms, also the condition of the fish known as belly blown.

Transportation of the fish.—It is unnecessary to salt excessively fish which are to be in transit for only a reasonable length of time. Such salting should be done with the idea of saving time in the pickling shed, rather than as a means of preservation, as decomposition, particularly in the viscera and contents, is not completely prevented by the presence of salt. The limit of the time to be consumed in transporting fish in salt, without refrigeration, seems to be

from four to six hours. Some method of refrigeration shou
stalled on all boats used to haul the fish over long distar
greatly extending the fishing area and bringing the fish to
neries in a condition far superior to that of fish carried in s;
boats, both the refrigerator and the ordinary type, shoulc
vided with small compartments, permitting circulation of cc
that the fish are carried in small bulk, thus preventing th
temperature which occurs when fish are carried in bulk, a
customary.

Salting and pickling the fish.—An appreciable amount
genous matter is extracted from fish held in salt, and an eve
quantity from those held in pickle.   To insure a minimum e:
of material, consistent with the proper degree of salting, unev
fish should remain in salt or pickle not more than two hou
from 15 to 20 minutes is long enough for cut and eviscerate
remain in strong pickle.   Fish which are excessively salte
kept in brine an unduly long time lose the characteristics
fish.   Sardines with a salt content of 3 per cent were recei
the most favor.   The greater part of the salt remains in th
the fish, which explains why it is so readily lost during the
process.

Drying the fish.—More attention should be paid to th
process than is now customary.   Before being packed, fro:
per cent of the water they contain should be driven from
Either too little or excessive drying ruins the appearanc
pack.   An even, thin flaking of the fish, proper control of th
and temperature of the air in the tunnel dryers, and d
exactly the requisite period are essential for securing a h
product.

Packing the fish.—Special skill and technique are nec
packing sardines.   Great care must be exercised in pla
small fish in the can and also in cleaning the cans.   Rou
ment of the filled cans not only tends to disarrange the con1
may dent the seams, causing leaks.

Oiling.—Three quarts of oil to the case should be add
fish, and 3½ quarts to the case for lean fish.   Time should b
for the absorption of this amount of oil before sealing the cai
oil appears to fulfill all the requirements for a good pac:
flavor does not mask that of the fish.   Baked fish packe
oil and fish fried in corn oil proved to be superior to fish w
steamed.

Storing the sardines.—The desirability of storing sardine
even temperatures was demonstrated by a series of experi
the freezing and thawing of sardines.   Weak solutions of

and amines were found to exert a detinning action on the interior of the cans, which increased on standing. The suggestion that detinning of cans does not occur when fish are skinned before being packed was disproved. During storage the amount of ammonia and amines in canned sardines increases, the extent of the increase depending upon the temperature. Sardines stored at room temperature showed a greater increase in these substances than sardines stored just above freezing. Triamine was found to be the chief constituent of the amine fraction.

Decomposition of fish.—A small amount of ammonia and frequently negligible amounts of amines were found as normal constituents of fresh fish. During decomposition of the fish the quantity of both ammonia and amines increased very rapidly. Greater increases were found in the viscera and contents than in the flesh of the fish. The increase in the amount of ammonia and amines in canned sardines composed of fish which have undergone excessive decomposition indicates that this degree of spoilage can be detected in the packed goods. The determination of these substances, however, is of doubtful value as a means for detecting a less degree of decomposition in fish which have been held in salt or pickle before being packed. Decomposition of the viscera and contents of fish occurs at a more rapid rate than decomposition of the flesh. Fish become belly blown as a result of the extension of the processes of decomposition from the viscera and contents to the belly portion.

Waste.—A great deal of the waste found in the canneries may be eliminated by (*a*) using cans to fit the fish instead of cutting the fish to fit the cans, or trimming the tails of the fish which are a trifle too large for the cans, and cutting the fish as close to the gills as possible, (*b*) flaking so well that 100 per cent of the edible fish on the flakes may be packed, (*c*) preventing the deliberate discarding of fish suitable for packing, and (*d*) enlarging the scope of the pack by preparing kippered herring, Russian sardines, spiced herring, and other similar products. The unavoidable waste may be utilized by (*a*) making sardine paste, deviled sardines, and similar articles from the discarded edible portions of the fish, (*b*) converting the cuttings which can not be used in this way into fish meat meal, after expressing the oil from such residues, and (*c*) converting all residues and wastes that can not be used to better advantage into fish scrap for fertilizing purposes.

Quality and appearance of sardines.—The results of the investigation indicated that the following are the chief factors responsible for low quality: Use of feedy fish rendered unfit by decomposition; excessive salting or pickling; removal of flavor by steaming process; insufficient drying; variation in composition, especially the fat content, of the fish at various times of the year; using inferior oil or oil in insufficient quantities; and permitting the packed goods to become frozen. Careless packing and rough handling at various stages of the process are responsible for poor appearance.

The following suggestions for the improvement of the pack are offered:

1. Accept feedy fish for packing only when they have been impounded for a period of from 12 to 24 hours. When this practice has been widely adopted, it will be wise to keep all fish in pounds or pockets, thus distributing the supply over a longer period and thereby aiding in placing the canneries on a capacity basis.

2. Sort the fish according to size as they reach the cannery.

3. Cut and eviscerate all fish.

4. Establish a proper period for the salting and pickling of fish, both eviscerated and uneviscerated. The salting and pickling treatment of the fish at the cannery as well as the distance they can be carried in salt will then be determined.

5. To insure the highest quality discontinue the steaming process, which causes the loss of a large amount of salt and flavor.

6. Flake the fish by hand or thinly with the flaking machine.

7. Dry the fish to the proper degree before packing them.

8. Pack the fish neatly and attractively in the cans, eliminating all slack packing. A well-packed can of sardines should be full of fish and oil.

9. Handle the packed cans carefully.

10. Establish standard grades for the sardine pack.

11. Maintain a rigid sanitary control of canneries. The law of Maine, which adequately covers this question, should be strictly enforced. The beach surrounding the canneries should be kept free from decomposing fish waste. Under no consideration should swelled cans of sardines be disposed of by being thrown out on the beach. They should be burned. The water supply of all the canneries should be investigated. Whenever a water supply giving evidence of contamination is found, requisite changes should be made.

BIBLIOGRAPHY.

(1) BENSLEY, B. A.
1901. Report on the sardine industry in relation to the Canadian fisheries. 32d Ann. Rept. Can. Dept. Marine Fisheries, Contrib. Can. Biol. 1901: 59–62.

(2) BIGELOW, H. B.
1915. Exploration of the coast water between Nova Scotia and Chesapeake Bay, 1913. Bull. M. C. Z., *59:* 151–359.

(3) BIGELOW, W. D., and BACON, R. F.
1911. Tin salts in canned foods of low acid content, with special reference to canned shrimp. J. Ind. Eng. Chem., *3:* 832–834.

(4) BRANDT, K.
1898. Beiträge zur Kenntniss der chemischen Zusammensetzung des Planktons. Wissenschaftliche Meeresuntersuchungen herausgegeben von der Kommission zur wissenschaftliche Untersuchungen der deutschen Meere in Kiel. Abt. Kiel, Bd. 3, 43–90.

(5) CATHCART, E. P.
1906. The bacterial flora of "blown" tins of preserved food. J. Hygiene, *6:* 248–250.

(6) ERDMANN, C. C.
1910. On alkylamines as products of the Kjeldahl digestion. J. Biol. Chem., *8:* 41–55.

(7) FOLIN, O., and FARMER, C. J.
1912. A new method for the determination of total nitrogen in urine. J. Biol. Chem., *11:* 493–501.

(8) ———— and MACALLUM, A. B.
1912. On the determination of ammonia in urine. J. Biol. Chem., *11:* 523–525.

(9) ———— and WENTWORTH, A. H.
1910. A new method for the determination of fat and fatty acids in feces. J. Biol. Chem., *7:* 421–426.

(10) GOSS, B. C.
1917. Adsorption of tin by proteins and its relation to the solution of tin by canned foods. J. Ind. Eng. Chem., *9:* 144–148.

(11) HANSON, H. H.
1912. The packing of American sardines. Orig. Commun., 8th Intern. Cong. Appl. Chem., *18:* 131–138.

(12) HJORT, J.
1913. Den Franske Industris kamp Mot de Norske Sardiner. (French sardines and Norwegian sardines.) Edinburgh, 1913.

(13) JOHNSTONE, J.
1915. The fat-content of Irish Sea herring. Trans. Liverpool Biol. Soc., *29:* 216–223.

(14) KLEIN, D.
1911. An improved apparatus for the determination of amino groups. J. Biol. Chem., *10:* 287–289.

(15) LICHTENFELT, H.
1904. Uber die chemische Zusammensetzung einiger Fischarten, warum und wie sie periodisch wechselt. Arch. ges. Physiol., *103:* 353–402.

125

MacDonald, D. L.
  1912. On a collection of Crustacea made at St. Andrews, N
    Biol., 1906–1910: 83–84.
Maine, State of.
  1915. Sea and shore fishery laws. Statutes for 1915.
Milroy, T. H.
  1906. The food value of the herring. Part I. 24th Ann
    Scotland, for 1905, pt. 3: 83–107. Part II. 25th Ann. R
    Scotland, for 1906, pt. 3: 197–208.
Moore, H. F.
  1898. Observations upon the herring and herring fisheri
    coast, with special reference to the vicinity of Passamaq
    U. S. Comm. Fish and Fisheries for 1896, 22: 387–442.
Nielsen, I.
  1890. Ein Stück moderner Bakteriologie aus dem 12. Ja
    Bakt. Parasiten., 7: 267–271.
Obst, M. M.
  1919. A bacteriologic study of sardines. J. Infect. Dis., 2
Pettersson, A.
  1900. Experimentelle Untersuchungen über das Conservi
    Fleisch mit Salzen. Arch. Hyg., 37: 171–238.
Prince, E. E.
  1896. The sardine-fishing industry in New Brunswick. 28
    Dept. Marine Fisheries, for 1895: xxvi–xxxiii.
Rössing, A.
  1900. Ueber Fischconserven. Z. anal. Chem., 39: 147–15;
Sadler, W.
  1918. The bacteriology of swelled canned-sardines. Am.
    216–220.
Scott, T.
  1902. Observations on the food of fishes. 20th Ann. Rep¹
    land, for 1901, pt. 3: 486–541.
Smith, H. M.
  1902. The French sardine industry. Bull. U. S. Fish Con
Stahmer, M.
  1913. Fischhandel und Fischindustrie.
Stevenson, C. H.
  1899. Preservation of fishery products by canning. Bull
    for 1898, 18: 507–540.

———.
  1899. Preservation of fishery products by smoking. Bull
    for 1898, 18: 474–506.
Sutton, F.
  1911. A systematic handbook of volumetric analysis, 10th
Thayer, E. A.
  1914. South American trade in canned goods. U. S. De
    For. Dom. Commerce, Special Agents Series 87.
United States Bureau of the Census.
  1913. Canning and preserving. 13th Census, 10: 391.

———.
  1917. Abstract of the census of manufactures, 1914: 40.
Viktorin, H.
  1906. Die Meeresprodukte.

(36) WEBER, F. C.
   1916. Fish meal: Its use as a stock and poultry food. U. S. Dept. Agr. Bull.
      378: 1-21.
(37) ——— and WILSON, J. B.
   1918. A method for the separation and quantitative determination of the lower
      alkylamines in the presence of ammonia. J. Biol. Chem., *35:* 383-410.
(38) ———.
   1919. The formation of ammonia and amines in canned sardines during storage.
      J. Ind. Eng. Chem., *11:* 121-132.
(39) ———.
   1920. The food of the small sea herring and ammonia and amines as end
      products of its decomposition. J. Am. Chem. Soc., *42:* 841-849.
(40) WRIGHT, R. R.
   1906. The plankton of eastern Nova Scotia waters.. 39th Ann. Rept. Can.
      Dept. Marine Fisheries 1906, Further Contrib. Can. Biol., 1902-1905: 1-19.

ADDITIONAL COPIES
OF THIS PUBLICATION MAY BE PROCURED FROM
THE SUPERINTENDENT OF DOCUMENTS
GOVERNMENT PRINTING OFFICE
WASHINGTON, D. C.
AT
50 CENTS PER COPY
▽

UNITED STATES DEPARTMENT OF AGRICULTURE

BULLETIN No. 909

Contribution from the Forest Service
WILLIAM B. GREELEY, Forester

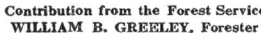

Washington, D. C. ▼ January 17, 1921

UTILIZATION OF BLACK WALNUT.

By WARREN D. BRUSH, *Scientific Assistant.*

CONTENTS.

	Page.		Page.
Introduction	1	**Utilization by industries—Continued.**	
Properties of the wood	2	Musical instruments	66
Insect and fungus attack	6	Planing-mill products	67
Supply	7	Sewing machines	68
Demand	21	Firearms	68
Utilization by industries	22	Export	74
Lumber	22	War-time utilization	76
Veneer	44	Summary of general market conditions	79
Ties	58	Marketing walnut timber	80
Posts	59	Summary and conclusions	85
Furniture	61	Appendix: Detailed list of uses	88

INTRODUCTION.

The use of American black-walnut timber for various products began in early colonial times. Probably its first extensive use was for fence rails, for which it was chosen because it was easy to split and resisted decay. Much of it was cut for fuel. Large quantities of black walnut, which prefers rich agricultural land, were wasted in clearing for cultivation. In the eighteenth century it was a favorite wood for furniture, and was one of the two native woods (wild cherry being the other) best adapted for fine cabinetwork. It was also highly valued for gunstocks. The excellent stands in the fertile valleys of eastern Pennsylvania, which furnished wood of a rich dark color that was well liked, were the main source of supplies.

During the first half of the nineteenth century there was a gradual increase in the use of walnut, which was manufactured mainly into furniture in eastern factories. In this period the region of the Ohio River basin became the chief source of supply.

From 1860 to 1880 the demand for walnut grew tremendously, because of its use for rifle stocks during the Civil War, and also because of its popularity for making furniture. The maximum walnut production was reached about 1875, when it is estimated that the

7434°—20

total cut was approximately 125,000,000 board feet. During this period a large part of the walnut timber was removed from the region east of the Mississippi River.

The past six years have seen a revival in the walnut-furniture industry, and large amounts of the wood have been called for. The greatest use of this timber recently, however, has been for rifle stocks and airplane propellers for the Great War. On account of the unprecedented demand for walnut for these uses, the sawmill cut in 1918 was about 100,000,000 board feet. The entire country was searched for available material, and even small and defective trees that had been considered unfit for lumber were taken.

Walnut has never been plentiful in the sense that large amounts of the timber were available in any one locality. Its scattered growth is the reason for this. The exhaustion of the available supply has been repeatedly announced. Nevertheless, during the war large supplies were discovered that no one thought existed, and many lots of large-sized trees were found that were equal in quality to those of the period when walnut was most popular. The annual cut of walnut timber is comparatively small, but a fairly steady supply is available because of the wide distribution of the tree.

Black walnut (*Juglans nigra* Linn.) is a very near relative of the Circassian walnut (*J. regia* Linn.) of the Old World, which is highly prized as a cabinet wood. It is also closely related to the butternut (*J. cinerea* Linn.) of eastern United States. This last wood is less valuable, however, than the black walnut. There are two other walnuts native to the United States. These are the Mexican walnut (*J. rupestris* Engelm.) and California walnut (*J. californica* Wats.). These two species grow in southwestern United States. The timber is of little importance even locally, and the trees are usually less than 12 inches in diameter, with a clear length of trunk ordinarily not more than 8 to 10 feet.

This bulletin deals with the characteristics, properties, uses, manufacture, and market values of black-walnut wood, and particularly discusses the uses for which walnut is best adapted.

PROPERTIES OF THE WOOD.

GENERAL APPEARANCE.

The heartwood of black walnut is light brown to dark brown or chocolate-brown. The sapwood is nearly white. In forest-grown trees the heartwood is generally a rich chocolate-brown. The sapwood is narrow in such trees, usually 1 inch wide or less. In open-growth trees the heartwood is lighter in color; the sapwood grows to about 3 inches in width, and is white or discolored to yellowish or purplish brown. The annual rings of growth are usually broad and are marked off from each other by the presence of many pores at the beginning and a somewhat dense growth at the end of each annual ring, as well as by a fine light-colored line between adjacent rings. This contrast between the growth rings is especially marked on tangential cuts and gives a somewhat coarse figure to the wood. The pores are compartively large and in cross sections easily visible to the naked eye; they appear as fine dark and generally short lines over the entire longitudinal surface. Figured wood is in demand for different kinds of finish. Its handsome effect is often produced by dark-colored streaks or alternate stripes of lighter and darker shades. The striped figure in quartered stock is caused by the alternate light and dark shades of the growth rings. Another kind of figure is that formed by the wavy or curly grain which is found near a knot or other defect. Abnormal or irregular growths, crooks, forks, and twists produce a special figure in the wood. Highly figured walnut, with a great variety of design, is cut from the walnut burl—an abnormal growth of wood tissue.

PHYSICAL AND MECHANICAL PROPERTIES.

Black-walnut wood is heavy, hard, strong, and stiff. It is easy to split, has good shock-resisting ability, shrinks moderately in seasoning, is susceptible of a good polish, and takes paint, stain, and other finishes exceedingly well.

The results of certain Forest Service experiments on black walnut tested green are shown in Table 1 in comparison with oak. The strength values of the green wood are considered the best basis for comparison. Walnut compares still more favorably with oak when their dry weights are taken into consideration. For instance, black walnut, which has a dry weight of 85 per cent of the dry weight of oak, has shock-resisting ability 27 per cent greater and strength in bending 14 per cent greater than that of oak. As to strength in compression parallel to the grain, walnut rates 21 per cent higher, and in stiffness 14 per cent more. The shearing strength of walnut is only slightly less than that of oak. The hardness values of walnut and oak are in the same proportion to each other as their specific gravities—85 per cent. As to strength in compression perpendicular to grain, walnut has a lower value than oak. The shrinkage of black walnut in volume is less than that of oak, which is about 16 per cent. Shrinkage in the radial direction is about the same in both woods; but in the tangential direction the shrinkage of black walnut is less than that of oak. The ratio of radial to tangential shrinkage is much less in black walnut than in oak. In weight, and likewise in dimension. walnut changes slowly with changes in atmospheric conditions.

Common and botanical name.	Locality where grown.	Weight per cubic foot.			Specific gravity, oven-dry, based on volume when green.	Shrinkage from green to oven-dry condition.		
		Green.	Air-dry.	Kiln-dry.		In volume.	Radial.	Tangent.
1	2	3	4	5	6	7	8	9
Walnut, black (*Juglans nigra*)..	Kentucky......	*Pounds.* 58	*Pounds.* 39	*Pounds.* 37	0.51	*Per cent.* 11.3	*Per cent.* 5.2	*Per cent.* 7

Common and botanical name.	Locality where grown.	Strength in compression perpendicular to grain.		Stiffness.		Hardness.	
		Fiber stress at elastic limit.	Relative strength compared with oak (oak=100).	Modulus of elasticity in bending.	Relative stiffness compared with oak (oak=100).	Load required to embed a 0.44-inch ball one-half its diameter.	Relative hardness compared with oak (oak=10).
1	2	14	15	16	17	18	19
Walnut, black (*Juglans nigra*)......	Kentucky......	*Lbs. per sq. in.* 600	72	*1,000 lbs. per sq. in.* 1,420	114	*Pounds.* 900	

CROSS SECTION OF BLACK-WALNUT WOOD MAGNIFIED 7½ DIAMETERS.

a. r., annual ring.

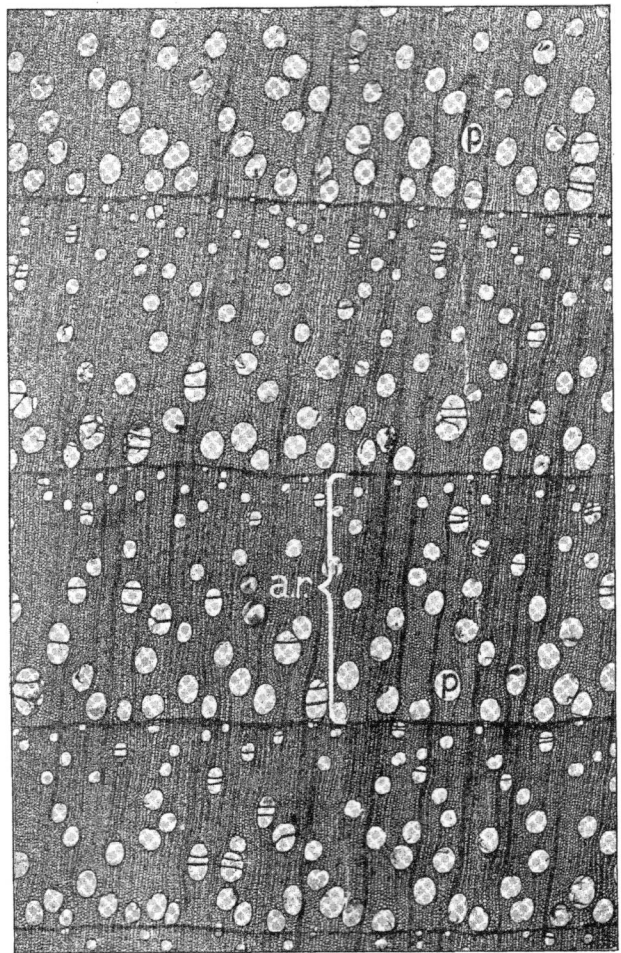

CROSS SECTION OF BLACK-WALNUT WOOD MAGNIFIED 20 DIAMETERS.

a. r , annual ring; p., pores.

PLATE III.

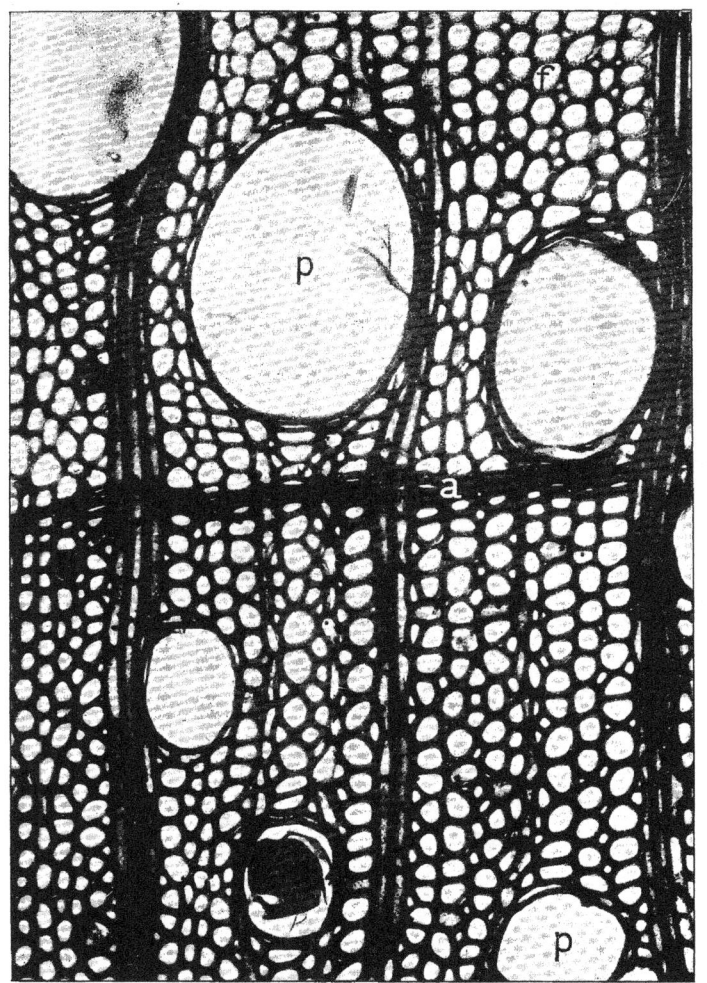

CROSS SECTION OF BLACK-WALNUT WOOD MAGNIFIED 250 DIAMETERS.

p., pores; f., wood fibers; a., end of annual ring.

Black walnut is straight-grained, easily worked with tools, is not liable to warp and check or to shrink and swell to any considerable extent after it has been seasoned, and glues well. These qualities add greatly to its value as a cabinet wood. Table 2 shows the properties of various cabinet woods in comparison with walnut as a basis. These are composite values (excepting those of weight and shrinkage), each being based on several different kinds of tests. The data show that walnut compares favorably with white and red oak in strength as a beam or post, in shock-resisting ability, and in stiffness. The hardness of walnut, however, is less than that of oak. In shock-resisting ability and stiffness birch is superior to walnut, although the two woods are about equivalent in strength. Birch is not so good in holding its shape after it is seasoned, and is also more liable than walnut to be cross-grained. Sweet birch is harder than walnut, and yellow birch is softer. Red gum ranks much lower than walnut in respect to these different properties. Oak and birch have greater dry weights than walnut, while red gum is lighter. All of the native cabinet woods listed have greater shrinkage values than walnut, with the exception of the radial shrinkage of oak and red gum. The volumetric shrinkage values of these woods are considerably greater than those of walnut. Walnut, therefore, compares very favorably with our other native cabinet woods in regard to these basic properties.

TABLE 2.—*Properties of various cabinet woods, compared with black walnut. Black walnut=100.*

	Strength as a beam or post.	Shock-resist-ing ability.	Stiff-ness.	Hard-ness.	Specific gravity, density, or weight.	Shrinkage (from green to oven-dry condition based on volume when green).		
						In vol-ume.	Radial.	Tan-gential.
White oak (*Quercus alba*)	92	98	92	125	114	141	100	127
Red oak (*Quercus rubra*)	84	99	88	111	108	127	74	117
Sweet birch (*Betula lenta*)	98	115	111	113	114	134	119	107
Yellow birch (*Betula lutea*)	99	124	109	93	107	150	140	127
Red gum (*Liquidambar styraciflua*)	76	78	84	67	86	134	98	139
True mahogany (Central America) (*Swietenia mahagoni*)	95	68	87	90	87	70	67	68

NOTE.—The relative-strength figures given in the first four columns of this table are based on composite values, each of which is a combination of several different kinds of tests.

The true mahogany of Central America, listed in the table, shows a slightly lower value than walnut in strength as a beam or post. In stiffness and hardness it is much lower. Its shock-resisting ability is far below that of walnut. The amount of shrinkage in Central American mahogany is much less than in any of the native cabinet woods listed. The relation between volumetric, radial, and tangential shrinkage is about the same as for walnut.

· STRUCTURE.

Black walnut is classed as a diffuse-porous wood, the pores being scattered throughout the annual-growth ring. These pores are comparatively large in size and easily visible to the naked eye, especially in the spring wood, and they gradually decrease in size toward the outer portion of each annual ring. Tyloses are present but do not completely fill the pores. The large pores of the spring wood sometimes give the appearance of a ring-porous arrangement. Plates I, II, and III show the structure of the wood in cross section at different magnifications. The pith rays are narrow and can not be seen without the aid of a hand lens. The structure of butternut wood closely resembles that of black walnut, but the wood of the former may be distinguished from the wood of the latter by its light chestnut-brown color.

INSECT AND FUNGUS ATTACK.

Black-walnut timber is largely free from insect and fungus attack in the tree, log, lumber, and finished product. Thrifty trees are generally sound. If the trees are very limby and are found on poor soils where growth is less vigorous, decay often gains access, through knots, to the interior of the tree trunk. A heart rot sometimes attacks the central portion of the trunk at the butt. This is called red butt rot and is most often found in the northeastern section of the area of distribution. It is especially prevalent in trees originating from sprouts, the fungus making entrance from the stump of the original tree as it rots away. Large white grubs also often gain access to the butt, and generally burrow out a small portion only. Injury from these agencies does not usually cause a loss of more than 1 to 3 feet of the merchantable length at the butt, although occasionally it may extend the entire length of the log. A more serious fungus attack than the red butt rot is a white top rot which is found mostly on the walnut of the southwestern area. This rot often extends over the greater part of the entire merchantable length of the tree, and often renders a log unsuitable for manufacture into either lumber or veneer, on account of the discoloration of the wood caused by the fungus attack.

Defective trees and logs are often attacked by small larvæ which leave what are called "pin holes." Such an attack often causes black streaks in the wood, and this damage unfits it for use on the face of veneered panels. In general, western timber suffers more than eastern timber from such attacks.

Walnut suffers little injury from fungi or insects either in the lumber or in the finished product. Green lumber or lumber partly dried is subject to fungus attack, but there is little liability of injury if ordinary care is taken.

SUPPLY.

RANGE.

The black-walnut tree grows naturally over a large area extending from southwestern New England to central Nebraska, Kansas, Oklahoma, and Texas. The limits of its distribution are shown in figure 1. Within the limits of its range, however, there are regions unfavorable to its growth where it is almost unknown. Black walnut grows best on soil that is rich, moist, and deep, but not wet. It is,

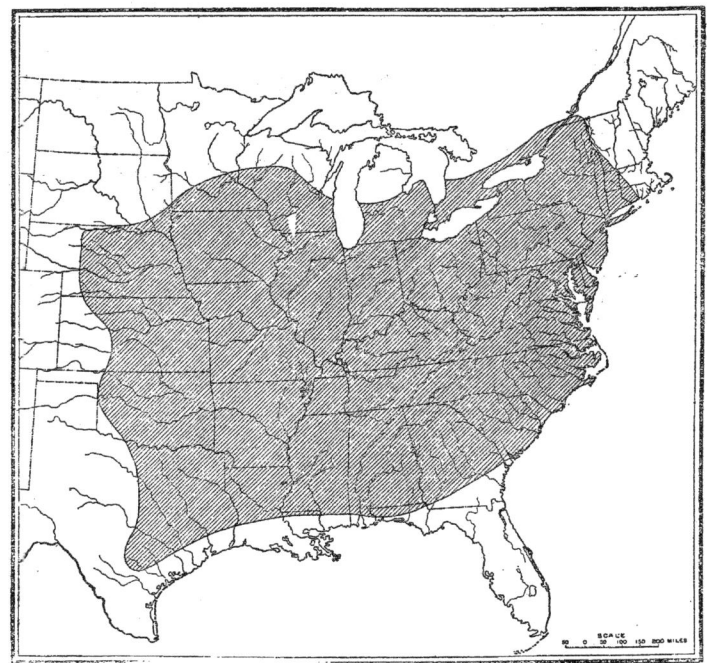

Fig. 1.—Botanical range of black walnut (*Juglans nigra*).

therefore, not generally found on the higher elevations throughout its range, nor on wet bottom lands, but in moist coves, on fertile hillsides, and on the well-drained soil of valleys and bottom lands. A limestone soil or sandy loam containing a large quantity of humus, overlying a deep subsoil of gravel, with a sufficient water supply, furnishes ideal conditions for growth. West of the Mississippi the walnut is confined generally to river valleys and moist situations.

The region throughout which black walnut is found in sufficient quantities for commercial exploitation is much more restricted (fig. 2). This region excludes the following areas embraced within its botanical range: Practically all of New York; the greater part of Pennsylvania, chiefly the mountainous and the northern portion; nearly all of New Jersey and Delaware; all but the central part of Maryland; southeastern Virginia, all but the western portion of North Carolina, and the regions of relatively high altitude in those

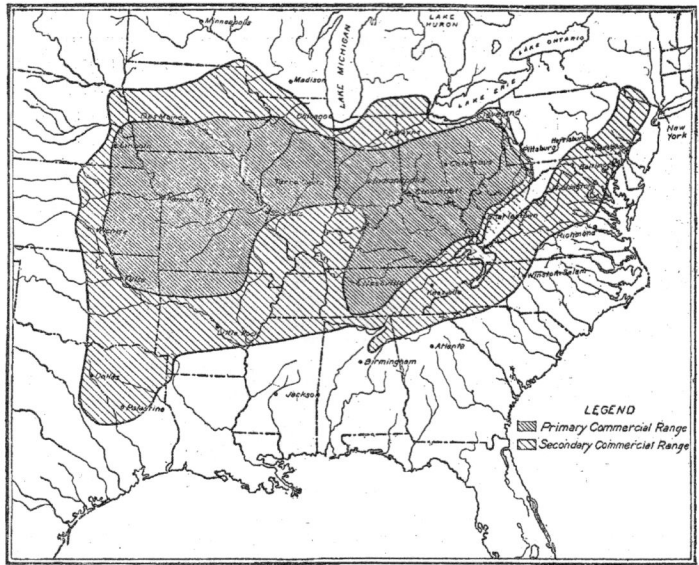

FIG. 2.—The area of primary commercial importance indicates in a general way where walnut is found in comparatively large quantities. The area of secondary commercial importance includes the region where it generally occurs in quantities large enough for commercial exploitation.

States (as also of West Virginia); practically all of the area included in the other Atlantic and Gulf States; southern Arkansas, and parts of other States on the border of its botanical range.

Throughout the commercial range indicated walnut is, of course, not everywhere found, as, for instance, on barren soils, the high ridges of Tennessee and North Carolina, and the low bottom lands. On the other hand, in the montainous sections of Virginia and West Virginia, where it is shown to be unimportant, many rich coves and fertile valleys contain profitable stands of excellent walnut timber.

The area of principal or primary commercial importance is also indicated in figure 2. This area excludes the mountainous high-altitude region of eastern United States, the region east of those mountains, Texas, Wisconsin, Michigan, and parts of States whose remaining area is within its principal commercial range.

SUPPLY OF TIMBER IN DIFFERENT REGIONS.

Table 3 gives the estimated amounts of standing black-walnut timber, by States and groups of States, for trees 12 inches and over in diameter at breast height. This estimate is based on available data from various sources, and is subject to revision as more definite data are obtained. The amount of timber available for commercial uses is, of course, considerably less than this, because many walnut logs less than 14 inches in diameter at the small end are not merchantable. Moreover, much of the timber included in the estimate is in small amounts too scattered to warrant its removal. A very large part of it is also inaccessible under present conditions; however, as conditions change, timber formerly inaccessible becomes accessible. Any statement, therefore, as to amounts available is mere conjecture.

TABLE 3.—*Estimated amounts of standing walnut, by States.*

[Trees 12 inches and over in diameter, breast high.]

State.	Amounts in millions of board feet, log scale.	Totals, by regions.	State.	Amounts in millions of board feet, log scale.	Totals, by regions.
Illinois	79		New York	2	
Missouri	107	246	Pennsylvania	26	
Iowa	60		Maryland	5	36
Kentucky	67		New Jersey	2	
Tennessee	60	141	Delaware	1	
North Carolina	14		South Carolina	7	
Ohio	63	107	Georgia	8	
Indiana	44		Alabama	6	28
Arkansas	46		Mississippi	4	
Oklahoma	18	101	Louisiana	3	
Texas	37		Michigan	15	
Virginia	29	89	Wisconsin	10	28
West Virginia	60		Minnesota	3	
Nebraska	18	45			
Kansas	27		Grand total		821

The locations from which walnut timber has been recently obtained are given in figure 3. This figure shows graphically the walnut timber that had been purchased by mills cutting gunstock blanks, and which was in the woods and at sidings at the time of the signing of the armistice.

ILLINOIS–MISSOURI–IOWA REGION.

[Estimated stand, 246 million feet.]

Estimates of standing walnut timber credit the Illinois-Missouri-Iowa region with approximately 30 per cent of the total. Large

amounts have been removed in recent years, but the supply has not
been so greatly depleted here as it has, for instance, in Ohio and

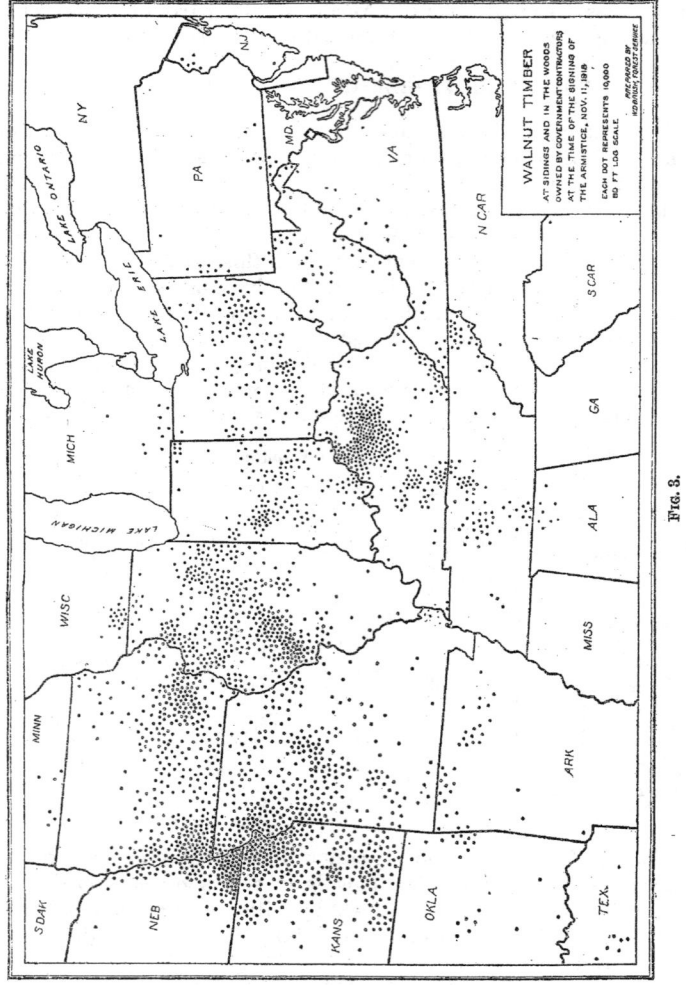

Indiana.   It seems probable that the stand of walnut in this region
was originally inferior to the Ohio and Indiana stand; but on account

of the exploitation being more recent and the timber being relatively inaccessible, the best supplies are now located in Illinois, Missouri, and Iowa. This region is, on the whole, fairly well adapted for the growth of walnut, which is quite generally distributed throughout the section, except on the poorer and drier upland soils and low, wet bottom lands. The best timber is to be found on land that has never been cleared for cultivation.

The principal walnut area in this region comprises southern Iowa and northern and central Missouri. In Iowa, walnut is found in commercial quantities principally along the streams. On the higher elevations in the northeastern part of the State merchantable trees are rarely seen. Southeastern Iowa was one of the most important sources of walnut timber during the war. There are still many valuable stands in the southern and southeastern parts of the State, chiefly on broad river bottoms where the soil is not too moist. Missouri is by far the banner State in respect to the total amount of standing walnut timber. It is said that walnut is found growing along the streams in every county. In northern Missouri, black walnut is confined principally to the alluvial soils adjacent to the streams, where the deep moist loams maintain some excellent stands. Central Missouri is also an important walnut region, especially in the western part, where there are comparatively heavy stands of walnut continuous with those of eastern Kansas. In the Ozark region of southern Missouri the walnut growth is confined to the lower elevations, principally to the deep moist soil of the stream courses. In such locations it attains large size, and in the aggregate there is a large amount of excellent walnut timber in the Ozark region, although much of the best has been removed. The low bottom lands of the southeastern portion of the State do not generally contain walnut in commercial amounts.

In northern Illinois, and particularly in the northeastern portion, there is comparatively little walnut. There is also very little on the low bottom lands of the southern portion. The principal supply is located in an east and west belt occupying the middle third of the State. Here it is confined largely to moist situations.

The walnut timber in the Illinois-Missouri-Iowa region does not, in general, grow so large as that of Ohio and Indiana. Nevertheless, as it has been culled less extensively than that farther east, the general run of the timber is probably as good as the average or better.

KENTUCKY-TENNESSEE-NORTH CAROLINA REGION.

[Estimated stand, 141 million feet.]

The presence of comparatively large supplies of walnut timber in Kentucky, Tennessee, and North Carolina is due in large part to the relative inaccessibility of the region. The best timber is now probably in the mountainous areas of eastern Kentucky and Tennessee and western North Carolina, where it grows to large size in moist coves and in the rich soil of creek bottoms and valleys. Along the streams, however, the largest timber has been taken, and the small coves are now, as a rule, the best sources. On the slopes of the ridges, where the soil is deep, moist, and loamy, particularly on the north slopes, are supplies of walnut, but the trees seldom grow to large size there. At the higher altitudes and on the ridges, where the soil is poor and lacking in moisture, the trees are small and defective. Over a large part of the mountainous region the walnut has been removed in the process of lumbering for such species as yellow poplar, with which it is generally associated in this region. In former years, because of the large size to which the trees in thrifty stands in this section generally attain, it was the practice to take only the very large timber. As a consequence many trees of good size have been found in recent years. Throughout the large timbered areas of the mountains the walnut is so scattered that it is, as a rule, impracticable to log the walnut alone. Estimates made by the United States Forest Service of mountain timber in this area show an approximate stand of 28 board feet of walnut to the acre in virgin timber and 4 feet to the acre on cut-over lands. As a rule, therefore, the walnut timber of the mountain region will become available only as it is released by general timbering operations. There are many comparatively small agricultural areas scattered throughout this mountain section in which walnut occurs as a shade or field tree or mixed with other hardwood timber. In such localities, however, the most valuable trees have usually been culled out.

Outside of the western portion of North Carolina, walnut is not of frequent occurrence in this State. Immediately to the east of the more mountainous section there was formerly much walnut timber on good soils, but this has been very largely removed as the country became populated, and merchantable trees are now infrequent.

There are considerable amounts of walnut in Kentucky and Tennessee north and west of the mountainous regions. Throughout central Tennessee there is a great deal of walnut scattered over the agricultural lands. Many of the trees are, however, small and defective, for the most desirable ones have been cut out. It is estimated that only about 16 per cent of the stand in the entire State of Kentucky is located in the western half, and this is nearly all in the west central part. There is little in the western third of the State. In central Kentucky there is a very large area in which walnut grows in quantity, principally in fertile sections of the bluegrass region in the east central part of the State. Much walnut has been obtained from this section in past years on account of its accessibility, and, although the supply has been greatly diminished, there are still stands of merchantable walnut to be had here. Probably the best available supplies in this part of the State are located in southeast central Kentucky, in localities far from the railroad, whence a haul of 15 to 20 miles or more is necessary. In eastern Kentucky, in the territory drained by the Big Sandy River, there is a good supply of walnut, but it is difficult to get it out because of lack of roads and on account of the roughness of the country. In the rugged southeastern part of the State, in fertile, moist valleys, there are supplies of good quality. On mining lands in this area, which have not been cleared, there is considerable walnut. The cost of logging in that kind of country is naturally very high. The lowlands of western Kentucky and Tennessee are not so well adapted to the growth of walnut, and only small amounts are found there.

OHIO–INDIANA REGION.

[Estimated stand, 107 million feet.]

The Ohio-Indiana region, which now stands third in importance, held first rank in lumber production for several years prior to 1914. It is remarkable that a region which has yielded so much walnut and which is so largely given over to agriculture should still contain such large amounts of this timber.

In Indiana, walnut is quite generally distributed over the entire State, but is most plentiful throughout the central portion. It is not important in the northwestern part of the State; and in the southern portion, which is somewhat rugged, it is confined to fertile valleys and slopes. Over a large part of the State, in which there are extensive areas of purely agricultural land, walnut trees, as well as other timber trees, have largely disappeared, except for a shade tree here and there, or a small patch of woodland, which the agriculturalist has spared. Along streams and in moist, fertile gullies throughout the State walnut is somewhat common. Such trees as are found, however, are more often small or otherwise not merchantable. That Indiana for a good many years continuously produced large supplies of walnut is accounted for by the fact that the species was distributed almost everywhere on good lands.

In Ohio, walnut is found generally except in the extreme northern part. The extreme western part of the State is fairly level and unbroken, and is almost entirely agricultural land similar to that in central Indiana. In consequence, the walnut and other timber has been very largely removed. The central, southern, and eastern portions, which are rougher, have the greatest amounts. Of these three sections, the central part, being the most settled, has the least. Over a large part of the extreme southern portion, the land is not suitable for the growth of walnut, but in fertile sections and valleys there is much walnut available. The eastern portion of Ohio is in general very rolling, and this area has the largest amounts. There is much nonagricultural land here among the hills and valleys. Fertile, moist slopes and valleys contain some excellent stands of the best quality of forest-growth walnut. In northeastern Ohio the walnut is scattered, is generally below the average in size, is likely to be limby, and shows a large proportion of one-log trees.

ARKANSAS–OKLAHOMA–TEXAS REGION.

[Estimated stand, 101 million feet.]

Walnut is of commercial importance in the Arkansas-Oklahoma-Texas region principally in eastern Oklahoma, northwestern Arkansas, and northeastern Texas. It is generally confined to fertile, moist locations along the streams, but avoids the low, wet bottom lands. The best walnut has been removed from this region, except in the rough, inaccessible areas, and these are chiefly in Arkansas.

The greater part of the walnut in Arkansas lies in the Ozark region north of the Arkansas River. Throughout this region there are many valleys which have a rich, moist, deep, loamy soil. In such valleys and on moist hillsides there are good stands of walnut of large size. The forest-growth walnut of this region is said to yield a higher percentage of clear material than that from farther north in Iowa and Missouri, which is largely open growth. A considerable amount of walnut is said to have been taken out of the northwest corner of Arkansas in recent years.

In Oklahoma and Texas the walnut is generally very limby and defective. In Oklahoma the best walnut is found on the fertile alluvial soils of the bottom lands, along the stream courses of the northeastern and east central parts of the State. Practically all of the desirable black walnut in the State is found east of the ninety-seventh meridian, principally along the Arkansas, Verdegris, Canadian, and Red Rivers. The black walnut west of this line is small in size, short-boled, scrubby, and very defective.

In Texas the best walnut is in the extreme northeastern part, and particularly in the Red River valley, but even this is rather poor in quality. In general, the black walnut is found north of the thirty-first parallel and east of the ninety-seventh meridian. In eastern Texas the walnut is largely confined to the better-drained, but moist, bottom lands. Along the larger rivers these bottom lands are frequently 5 miles or more in width, and the soil is rich and deep. If the soil is not too wet, walnut makes a good growth here. However, the more valuable timber has been removed from these localities. Present supplies usually stand 10 miles or more from the railroad.

Over the greater part of eastern Texas the best walnut has been taken out during the past 15 or 20 years and shipped to Europe through the Gulf ports. The level country and good railroad facilities made possible the shipment of the greater part of the best timber. South of the Trinity River and west of the ninety-seventh meridian, black walnut is replaced by Mexican walnut (*Juglans rupestris*), which is often marketed as black walnut, but is inferior in quality.

VIRGINIA–WEST VIRGINIA REGION.

[Estimated stand, 89 million feet.]

Walnut is not found at the higher elevations in the mountainous regions of southeastern West Virginia and northwestern Virginia nor in the coastal-plains region of southeastern Virginia. There are, however, many fertile valleys in the mountainous section, excluded from the commercial range on the map, in which there are small commercial stands of walnut of good quality.

In West Virginia the main walnut area occupies, roughly, the northwestern half of the State, the bulk of the timber being in the northeastern portion of this area. The largest amounts are at present in the region lying between Fairmont and Charleston. The Elk River region, exclusive of the headwaters, contains much walnut. Some excellent walnut timber is found in the southwestern part of the State, but the greater portion of the timber is difficult of access. In the territory traversed by the Great Kanawha and New Rivers the walnut has been largely cut out, and only an occasional tree remains.

During the recent war this northwest section of the State, which had not been heretofore closely worked for walnut, largely because the timber was below the average in size, was drawn upon heavily for war needs, and much suitable material was obtained. This territory is not very extensively traversed by railroads, however, and much timber remains to be cut if the demand warrants it. In the southeastern half of the State there are many broad valleys, and those whose altitude is not too great contain merchantable stands of good quality. Many of these rich, fertile valleys originally contained large amounts of excellent forest-growth walnut, the greater part of which was removed 15 to 20 years ago, the timber being hauled long distances over mountain ranges and shipped for exportation. An occasional stand of virgin walnut timber is still found in this section of the State, but is likely to be too small in amount to warrant the necessary long haul to the railroad. In southern West Virginia, because of the high altitude and the poorness of the soil, there are not many walnut trees.

In Virginia, stands of merchantable size are generally confined to fertile valleys. The Shenandoah Valley, on account of its fertility and its limestone soils, originally contained large amounts of excellent walnut timber. This timber has been very largely removed, because it was accessible to the railroad, and only an occasional tree remains. The valley is now worked largely for veneer logs, because walnut is not found in sufficient quantity to warrant its being cut for saw timber. The best walnut region extends from Winchester to Staunton, and the best supply is now being obtained from the southern part of this area. South of Staunton the land is more rugged and walnut is scarce. In extreme western Virginia walnut is seldom found, because of the high altitudes and the barren soils. East of the Blue Ridge Mountains commercial stands are generally confined to stream valleys. Scattered trees are the rule in this area.

NEBRASKA-KANSAS REGION.

[Estimated stand. 45 million feet.]

In Kansas and Nebraska, walnut is limited to the eastern parts, and the principal commercial stands are in southeastern Nebraska and eastern Kansas. It is usually found along the streams and in alluvial river bottoms, where comparatively large amounts are available, the walnut making up a large percentage of the total timber stand. The walnut timber has been exploited in this region probably less than in any other in proportion to the existing supply, and this section is one of the best sources, if not the best source, of this wood at the present time.

NEW YORK-PENNSYLVANIA-MARYLAND-NEW JERSEY-DELAWARE REGION.

[Estimated stand, 26 million feet.]

In New York, Pennsylvania, Maryland, New Jersey, and Delaware, walnut is very much scattered and the supply is small in proportion to the total area, because walnut and other species have been taken out for many years. Some good forest-growth walnut is still found in southwestern Pennsylvania, in valleys and well-drained bottom lands of agricultural areas near the Ohio and West Virginia State lines. In central Maryland, also, some walnut of good quality is obtainable. For the most part however, the walnut in these States is of the shade-tree kind. It is very limby, and the timber, consequently, is defective.

In New York State commercial stands of walnut are confined to a small area of scattered growth in the southeastern part.

In Pennsylvania commercial amounts are located only in the southeastern and southwestern parts of the State. These stands are found in rich agricultural valleys in which the soil is deep and moist, and generally in such isolated amounts that they are not worth the cost of cutting and hauling. As a shade tree, walnut is found over the entire State, with the exception of the northern and most mountainous sections. These shade trees were taken in large amounts to satisfy the great needs of the war; in normal times, however, this source of supply is unimportant.

In western Maryland the altitude is too great, and walnut is not often seen. In central Maryland, in the region of Hagerstown and Frederick, limited quantities of merchantable walnut are still available. In eastern Maryland the soil is too poor and sandy for walnut to be of importance.

Walnut is often seen throughout the States of Delaware and New Jersey, and occasionally a large tree is found; but on the barren, sandy soils the trees are limby and very defective, and little saw timber can be produced from them. In extreme northern Delaware, walnut of good quality is sometimes found; the same is true of northwestern New Jersey, where the soil is more fertile.

SOUTH CAROLINA–GEORGIA–ALABAMA–MISSISSIPPI–LOUISIANA REGION.

[Estimated stand, 28 million feet.]

The total area in the coastal region from South Carolina to Louisiana in which walnut is commercially important is very small. In South Carolina it is found in quantity only in the northwestern corner of the State, at the higher elevations and on fertile soils. In Georgia there are commercial amounts in the valleys of the northern mountainous section and especially in the valley region of northwest Georgia, where it is found in quantity in the three tiers of counties next to the northern border. In northeast Georgia it is important only in the tier of counties farthest to the north. In Alabama the only walnut of importance is in the northeastern portion in the fertile valleys of the limestone region. This timber is difficult of access, however, and it will probably not be exploited soon. In Mississippi there is no walnut area of commercial importance. In Louisiana walnut is of commercial importance only in the Red River region, in the extreme northwestern part of the State.

MICHIGAN–WISCONSIN–MINNESOTA REGION.

[Estimated stand, 28 million feet.]

Walnut is now of little commercial importance in Michigan, Wisconsin, and Minnesota. It was formerly somewhat plentiful in southern Michigan, but now it occurs only as a single tree here and there. It grows to good size, however, and is occasionally cut for commercial purposes in the extreme southern part of the State. In southwestern

QUALITY OF TIMBER FROM DIFFERENT REGIONS.

Walnut timber varies greatly in quality throughout the region of its growth. Climatic conditions have a large influence in producing this result, but the character of the soil seems to be the greatest factor. On poor, sandy, or shallow soils where there is little moisture the trees are usually undersized and defective; but on deep, rich, and moist agricultural land the timber grows to large size and is generally sound and of excellent quality.

On the agricultural lands of Ohio and Indiana walnut seems to reach its best development and is generally considered to be the best so far as the soundness and texture of the wood are concerned The logs now obtained from this section naturally run small in size but are, as a rule, sound and comparatively free from defects. A very great part of the walnut timber is now of the shade-tree kind and generally produces only one log to a tree. Unless they have suffered some injury, trees of this kind are usually sound, often of large size, and suitable for manufacture into lumber or veneer if the sapwood is not too thick for the latter use.

If forest-growth timber of good size can be obtained it is generally of the best quality, and the logs are as a rule straight and symmetrical. Each tree usually yields several logs, and the top logs are often of good quality and comparatively free from defects. The heartwood is very dark and uniformly of good color. In these logs the sapwood is thin, and this makes them very valuable for veneer Decay in trees of this kind generally occurs at the butt only and does not usually extend more than a few feet upward in the center of the log. Sawing off 2 or 3 feet from the butt log is generally sufficient to remove the worthless part.

The color of the heartwood of Ohio walnut is often ashen brown and this is well liked for veneer. Heartwood from Indiana is apt to be dark or blackish brown. In the extreme northern and southern parts of these two States, which are regions not well adapted to walnut, the trees are likely to be limby and defective.

The walnut of central and eastern Illinois on good lands does not differ appreciably from that of central Ohio and Indiana. Where conditions are not so favorable for the tree, especially in the northern and southern parts of the State, it is of inferior quality.

Throughout central Kentucky and Tennessee the timber, taken as a whole, is good in quality but somewhat more defective than that from Ohio and Indiana. It is claimed that this timber is sometimes shaky or badly worm-eaten, and these are very objectionable defects. There is a large proportion of field-growth walnut in this section. Trees of this kind of walnut often yield figured wood and are therefore in demand for veneer if they are not too defective. However, it is said that in much of this walnut the heartwood is not sufficiently dark in color to give an attractive appearance if it is used for veneer panels. Some of the peculiar brown tones are found in walnut from this section and occasionally those with a bluish cast which are well liked by the veneer manufacturer.

In the mountainous sections of the southern Appalachians, including adjacent parts of West Virginia, Virginia, Kentucky, Tennessee, North Carolina, and Georgia, the quality of the wood varies greatly, depending for the most part on whether it is grown on poor soils or in the fertile coves and valleys. The timber of the former localities is quite uniformly small and defective. In the latter sections, however, it grows to large size, and the timber is generally sound. In the rich valleys of this region on favorable sites there is excellent walnut timber, although isolated trees with spreading branches are now the rule. Even though but one log can be obtained from one of these trees, this log is generally a valuable one, because of its good form and the soundness of the wood.

In West Virginia, outside the mountain region, trees are, on the average, smaller in size than are the representative trees of Ohio and Indiana. West Virginia walnut trees generally branch nearer the ground, and the trunks are often badly shaped and defective. One-log trees are the general rule. As there is a good supply of walnut, however, much desirable timber is obtainable. The heartwood is dark in color.

In central Maryland the quality of walnut is fairly good, but the timber is generally in the form of field walnut, and is very limby. In eastern Maryland, Delaware, and New Jersey the trees have many limbs, and generally only one log is obtained from a tree, often a short log at that. Even if a log length free from limbs is obtained, it is often knotty, and the wood underneath is cross-grained and defective. Large trees are often found here, but their trunks are usually short and ill-shapen, and the wood inside is frequently cross-grained or decayed. Near the Pennsylvania State line the walnut is somewhat better in quality.

In Pennsylvania, where good walnut timber was found in the time of the early settlers, there are now generally only open-growth trees, the wood of which is defective. Good trees may still occasionally be found in the rich valleys, and there are some scattered stands of good quality in the agricultural lands near the central western border.

As a rule, however, the quality of the walnut available in the State is comparatively poor.

In general, the walnut of extreme eastern United States has many defects, including knots, decay, wormholes, and black streaks. Because of its open growth, however, the heartwood gives a figured effect when it is cut into veneer, and the different colors often produced by the eastern timber make it desirable for this use.

West of the Mississippi River the walnut timber does not on the average grow so large in size as the timber of the East, and the trees are apt to be more defective. Western timber often has a large proportion of hollow and rotten butts, and this defect may run the entire length of the butt log. Knots on the outside of the logs often indicate decay that extends to the interior. Logs cut from the upper portion of the tree are generally small and knotty. Notwithstanding the defectiveness of much western walnut, the general run of the timber is better than that of the eastern, especially in the more remote sections of the country. This is because the western timber has not been cut over so much as the eastern. Western walnut as a rule has more figure than eastern, and this makes it desirable for the manufacture of veneer. It is also said to be harder in general than eastern walnut.

The Missouri timber, except that from the southeastern part, is somewhat above the average in quality. That from low, wet locations is very defective.

The walnut of Iowa does not vary greatly in quality from that of Missouri. In the best locations for its growth in the State, along stream courses, it averages somewhat better than the Missouri walnut. The walnut of Kansas is similar in quality to that of Missouri; where the land has not been so greatly cut over the trees run larger and are less defective. The walnut of southeastern Nebraska is of very good size and quality, because the land has not been cut over to the extent to which it has in a large part of Missouri and Kansas.

The walnut of northwestern Arkansas is also said to be of a better quality than that from Missouri, the former being largely forest growth, and the latter, in a large measure, open growth. The hitherto greater inaccessibility of the Arkansas timber has contributed to produce this superiority. South of the Arkansas River the quality is more like that of the walnut of Oklahoma and Texas. Walnut from these two States is very inferior, especially that grown on the uplands. The main defects are crooked grain, windshake, sap pockets, wormholes, and large, loose knots. Logs from this region are, as a whole, not suitable for the manufacture of lumber. On account of these irregularities of growth, such logs produce a considerable amount of figure in veneer and are valued largely for this purpose. Different shades of color are often produced by the Texas walnut, purplish tones being somewhat common. In the trees grown on the heavier soils the heartwood is quite dark in color. In open-growth trees there are often light and dark stripes of brown, which make a pleasing figure. Texas logs have been in demand for many years for making veneer if highly figured stock was desired.

Computations were made on approximately 12,000,000 board feet of logs purchased near the close of the war to show the average size of logs from different States. The average number of board feet to the log is shown in Table 4. These figures indicate that in the extreme northeastern, southeastern, and southwestern portions of the range the logs run below the average in size. With the exception of Ohio, Indiana, and Missouri, the States of the central and northwestern areas are above the average in footage. The small size of logs from these States is probably the result of the extensive exploitation of the timber there, particularly in Indiana. Walnut logs from Tennessee and Kansas also have low values, particularly as compared with values in the adjacent States, Kentucky and Nebraska, respectively. In Kansas the best timber has been largely cut out in recent years. In Tennessee and Alabama the trees run smaller in size than they do farther north. The very high average shown for Michigan is doubtless occasioned by the shipment of choice lots of timber.

TABLE 4.—*Average number of board feet in walnut logs from different States.*

State.	Board feet per log.	State.	Board feet per log.	State.	Board feet per log.
Michigan	106.63	Arkansas	76.02	Pennsylvania	63.51
Illinois	79.61	North Carolina	75.12	Virginia	60.71
Iowa	79.50	Kansas	75.06	Maryland	55.10
Nebraska	79.43	Texas	73.10	Alabama	51.88
Kentucky	78.67	Indiana	70.37		
West Virginia	76.95	Tennessee	69.37	Average for all	
Ohio	76.20	Oklahoma	66.59	logs	76.38
Missouri	76.17				

DEMAND.

It is somewhat difficult to determine the total amount of walnut timber used annually, because of the fluctuation from year to year. Conditions prevailing during the war added greatly to the normal demand. The total demand for walnut is made up almost entirely of logs for export, logs for conversion into lumber and veneer, and timber for use as railway ties, posts, and fuel. On account of its high value, little walnut is used in rough building construction. Prior to the war the exportation of logs amounted to 7 to 12 million board feet, equivalent to between 8 and 15 million board feet of lumber; logs used for veneer amounted to $2\frac{1}{2}$ to 4 million board feet, equivalent to 3 to 5 million board feet of lumber; and the total lumber cut was probably between 40 and 50 million board feet. This makes a total annual use of 51 to 70 million board feet, exclusive of the wood used for ties and fuel. The years 1911 and 1912 may be taken as representative or average years. The statistics for these years show an annual demand as follows:

Logs exported from the United States (1912), 9.82 million board feet; equivalent in lumber to about 12 million board feet.

Logs manufactured into veneer in the United States (1911), 4.12 million board feet; equivalent in lumber to about 5 million board feet.

Lumber production in the United States, estimated at 50 million board feet.

Total, 67 million board feet.

Reports of wood-using factories in the United States during the years from 1909 to 1913 show a total annual use of about 24 million board feet of black-walnut lumber and veneer for the manufacture of various products. As about 55 million board feet of lumber and veneer were manufactured annually in the United States in 1911 and 1912, the difference of 31 million board feet represents exportations, which were almost altogether in the form of lumber. The amount of walnut used for ties, posts, and fuel is difficult of estimate, but is small, compared with the total for all purposes.

During the war the demand amounted to about 90 million board feet annually. In 1918 the total lumber production was about 100 million board feet, which was cut for war purposes. There was no exportation of logs, and practically no veneer was produced that year.

The home demand for walnut at present is comparatively great on account of the marked increase in its use for cabinetwork. The total future demand depends very largely on the extent to which exportations approach or exceed the amounts sent abroad before the war.

UTILIZATION BY INDUSTRIES.

PRIMARY INDUSTRIES.

LUMBER.

PRODUCTION BY STATES.

Table 5 shows by States the reported amounts of walnut lumber produced in the different years for which statistics are available. The computed annual production of walnut lumber is also given for the years 1915 to 1918. This table shows that the annual production of black-walnut lumber in the United States for the past 15 and probably 20 years did not greatly exceed 50 million board feet up to the year 1915. During the years 1915 and 1916 there was an increase of about 50 per cent over previous years. In 1917 there was a falling off in production. In 1918 there was an increase to 100 million board feet as a result of war demands. Missouri shows a marked increase in production, and Iowa a large output since 1914, because the large mills in these States obtained new supplies from a great part of the walnut region west of the Mississippi. The States of Kentucky and Tennessee have kept up a fairly steady cut of walnut lumber. Ohio, Indiana, and Illinois also have steadily furnished very large amounts from the beginning of the walnut-lumber industry.

TABLE 5.—*Reported production of walnut lumber, by States, in 1899 and from 1904 to 1918, inclusive; average value per 1,000 board feet of the product, f. o. b. mills, and total number of mills reporting.*

State	1899	1904	1905	1906	1907	1908	1909	1910	1911	1912	1913	1914	1915	1916	1917	1918
Total number of mills reporting	31,833	[1]18,277	11,666	22,398	28,850	31,231	[2]48,112	31,934	[1]28,107	[1]29,648	21,668	[1]27,506	[1]16,815	[1]17,269	[1]16,420	[1]14,753
Total number of mills cutting walnut	[2]	[2]	[2]	[2]	[4]1,803	[4]2,563	3,518	2,882	2,502	2,738	895	749	1,203	1,204	1,001	855
Average value per 1,000 board feet f. o. b. mills	$36.49	$45.64	[2]	$42.25	$43.31	$42.53	$42.79	$34.91	$31.70	[2]	[2]	[2]	$48.47	$42.38	$72.99	$77.60
Computed total cut	38,681	31,435	29,851	47,174	41,490	43,681	46,108	36,449	38,293	43,083	40,565	25,573	90,000	90,000	62,000	100,000
Total reported cut	38,681	31,435	29,851	47,174	41,490	43,681	46,108	36,449	38,293	43,083	40,565	25,573	65,144	61,167	53,676	87,305
Missouri	6,285	3,328	3,861	6,939	6,998	5,760	4,314	5,417	2,016	4,635	7,047	4,561	17,954	12,140	13,373	29,277
Indiana	10,637	8,339	8,957	12,924	9,975	8,358	7,669	5,237	9,755	6,425	10,194	4,626	11,267	10,691	7,872	11,941
Ohio	6,837	5,354	4,477	5,479	6,003	7,857	8,580	6,915	7,806	8,565	7,164	3,153	6,917	6,026	6,656	10,071
Tennessee	4,315	889	2,306	4,144	2,996	2,857	3,580	3,432	2,932	3,738	3,926	2,852	9,123	8,658	4,828	7,581
Kansas	[2]	[2]	[2]	[2]	[2]	[2]	1,114			81	81		27	27	4,010	7,507
Illinois	858	[3]3,321	4,472	5,097	4,335	4,866	5,051	4,897	4,291	5,197	3,890	1,497	7,077	3,169	2,269	6,130
Iowa	4,313	88	104	107	108	298	858	821	594	655	3,450	1,974	4,439	6,497	3,719	5,416
Kentucky	2,113	5,094	3,704	5,546	4,893	4,633	4,907	4,684	4,022	5,855	571	1,754	4,007	8,138	8,112	5,263
Virginia	296	77	51	322	660	1,423	2,308	1,761	1,415	1,123	916	263	719	1,334	450	1,686
West Virginia	150	128	377	1,004	1,626	1,430	1,968	1,849	1,666	1,597	2,064	702	1,477	2,253	887	800
Arkansas	175	66	136	4,905	58	507	544	273	342	266	305	140		205	532	335
North Carolina	100	22	88	1	114	223	267	501	798	754	2	151	249	567	230	233
Louisiana	60									2		12		1		233
Nebraska	376									[2]						222
Pennsylvania	451	[2]	[2]919	[2]342	[2]269	[2]1,249	1,762	938	1,223	2,263	25	351	504	423	255	200
Michigan	228	240	154		25	254	184	265	184	177	234	92	43	175	42	160
Oklahoma	69	1,918			807	778	302	249	197	343	31	38	187	189	71	110
New Jersey	23			15	6	44	78	56	69	79	84	51	27	40	14	85
Maryland	140	32		6	10	198	362	265	246	294	2	45	89	101	67	57
Wisconsin	141	15	20	38	413	1,828	285	85	76	68	33	7	31	45	70	46
New York	193	2,010		215			721	332	99	273	37	7	20	34	35	34
Alabama	100	6			12	141	48	99	31	82	12	82	220	51	58	25
Georgia					5	8	33	46	75	66	27		133	100	1	18
Mississippi			10		10	16	228	64	231	3	5		15	64	30	17
Massachusetts	45	145	144		15	375				8		50	21	69		17
Florida										73	70					16
Vermont								5	28	8				60		15
Connecticut	62	285			15	21	186	91	87	73	4	10	14	60		8
Texas	63	30			25	201	79	92	30	2	53	115	27	19	1	7
Rhode Island	10				16		138	11		20	40		49	39	11	6
Delaware	21			215		102	6		5	207		32		20	5	5
South Carolina			4			21	11	15	32	25		7	3		17	4
Minnesota	5					6	9	9	9	2	9	1	10	8	20	1
New Hampshire						2	28	22	6				1	2	2	1

Maine						
California	60	50	96	25		
All other States	435	67	111	57		3

[1] Mills cutting 50,000 feet and less excluded.
[2] Includes 4,543 mills cutting less than 50,000 feet; and all cooperage, veneer, millwork, box, furniture, and other factories cutting any lumber at all in 1909.
[3] Data not obtained.
[4] Mills in New York not included.
[5] Included in "All other States."

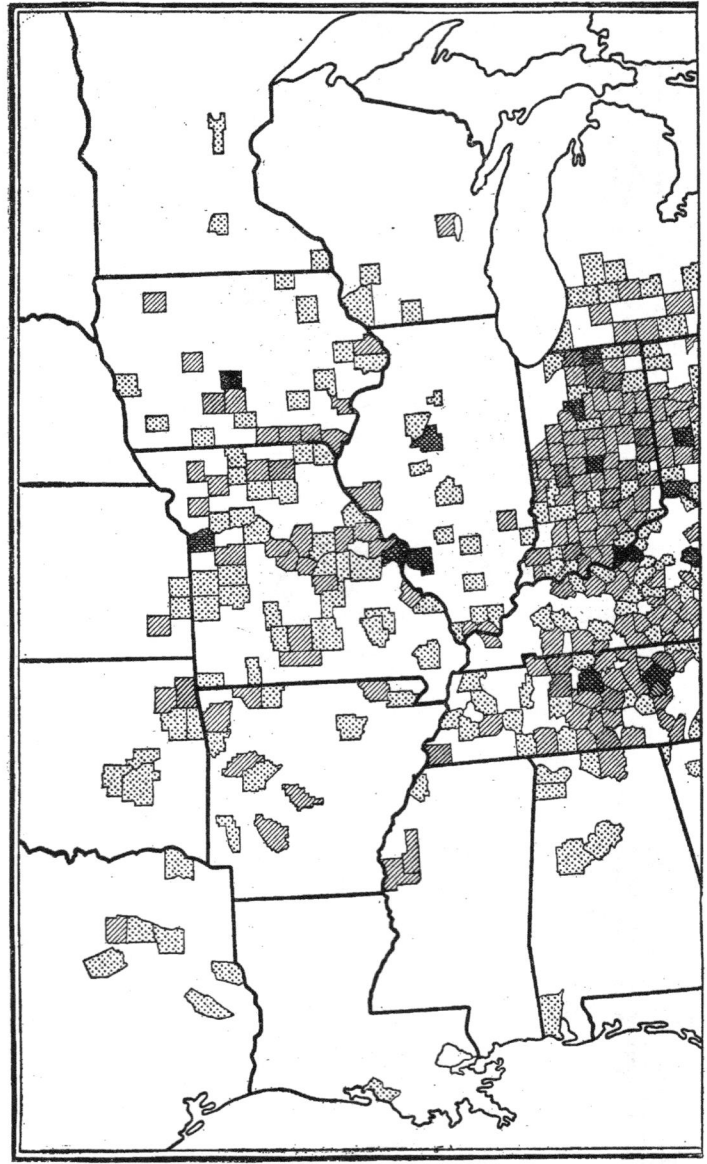

Fig. 4.—Reported production of

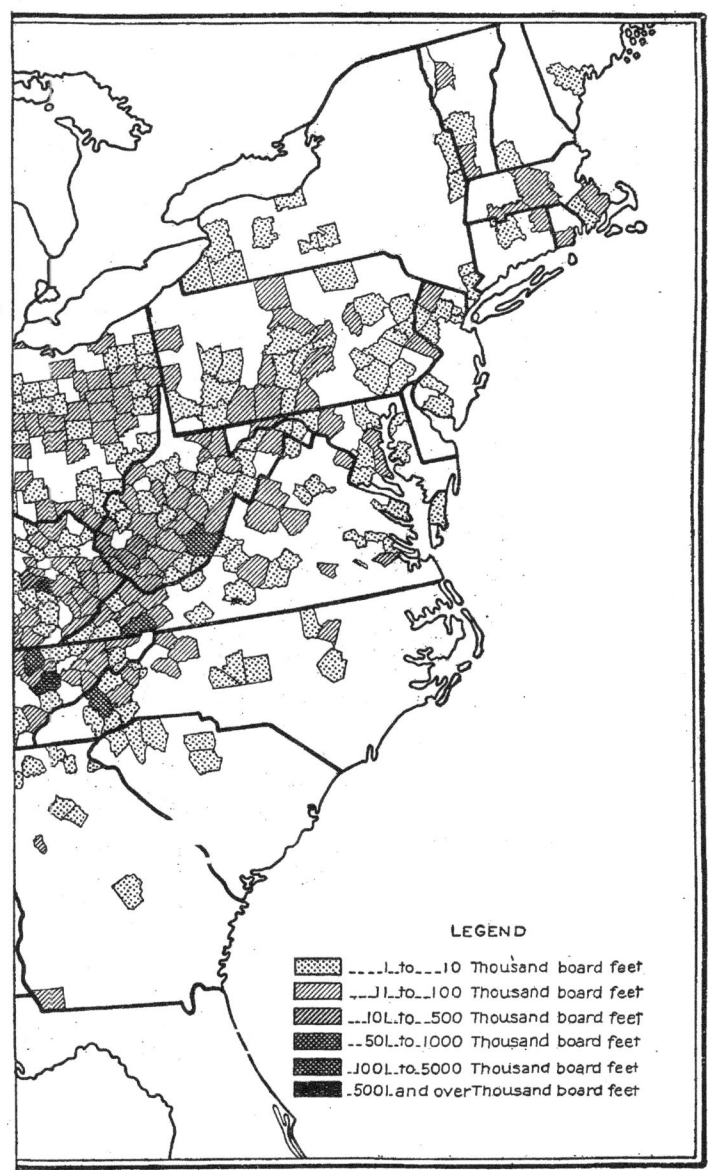

LEGEND

____l_to___10 Thousand board feet
__ll_to__100 Thousand board feet
___10l_to__500 Thousand board feet
__50l_to_1000 Thousand board feet
_100l_to_5000 Thousand board feet
_500l_and over Thousand board feet

walnut lumber in 1916, by counties.

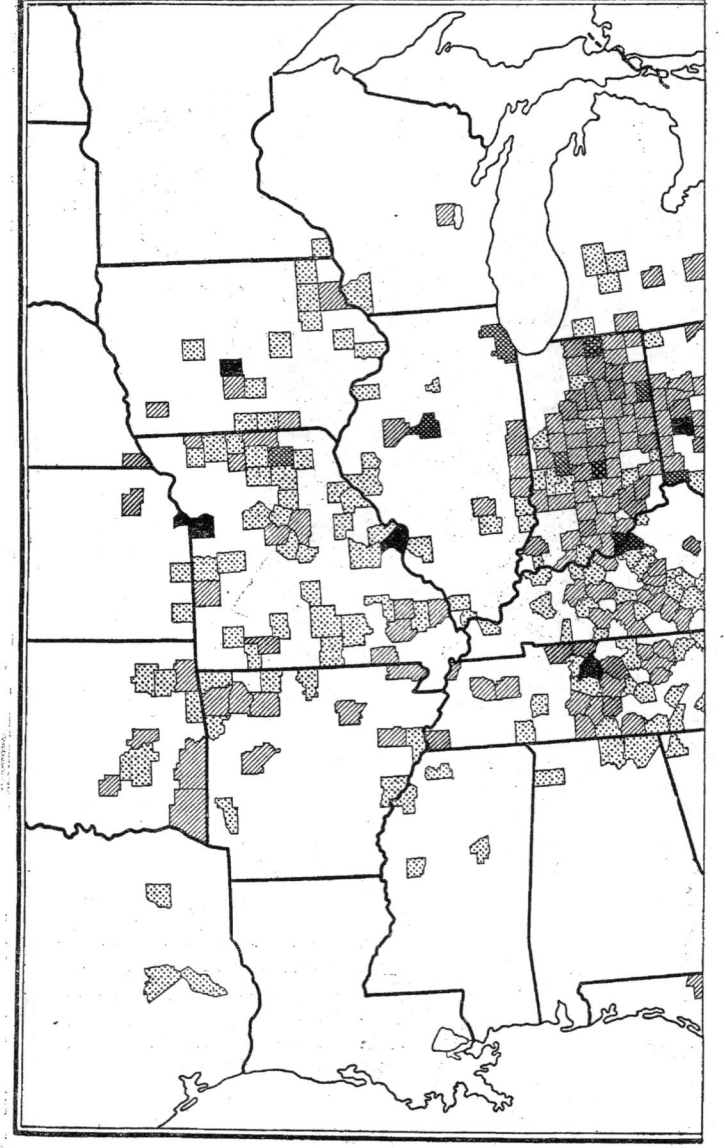

FIG. 5.—Reported production of

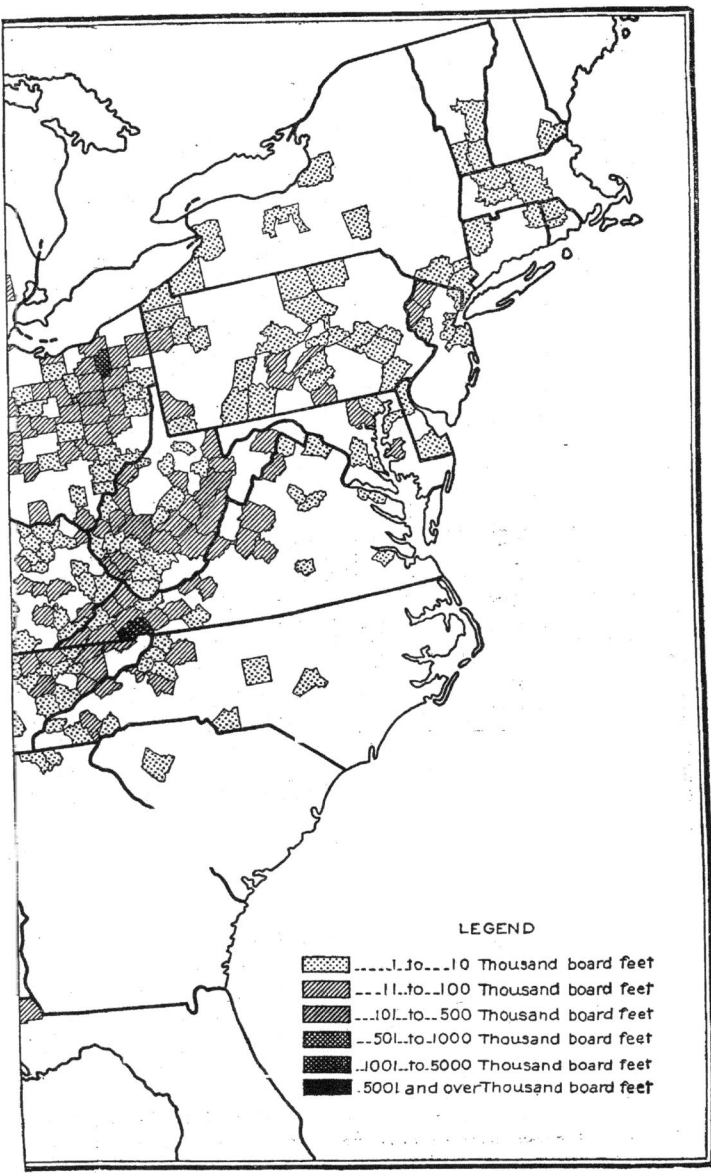

LEGEND

....1..to...10 Thousand board feet
...11..to..100 Thousand board feet
...101..to..500 Thousand board feet
..501..to..1000 Thousand board feet
.1001..to.5000 Thousand board feet
.5001 and over Thousand board feet

walnut lumber in 1918, by counties.

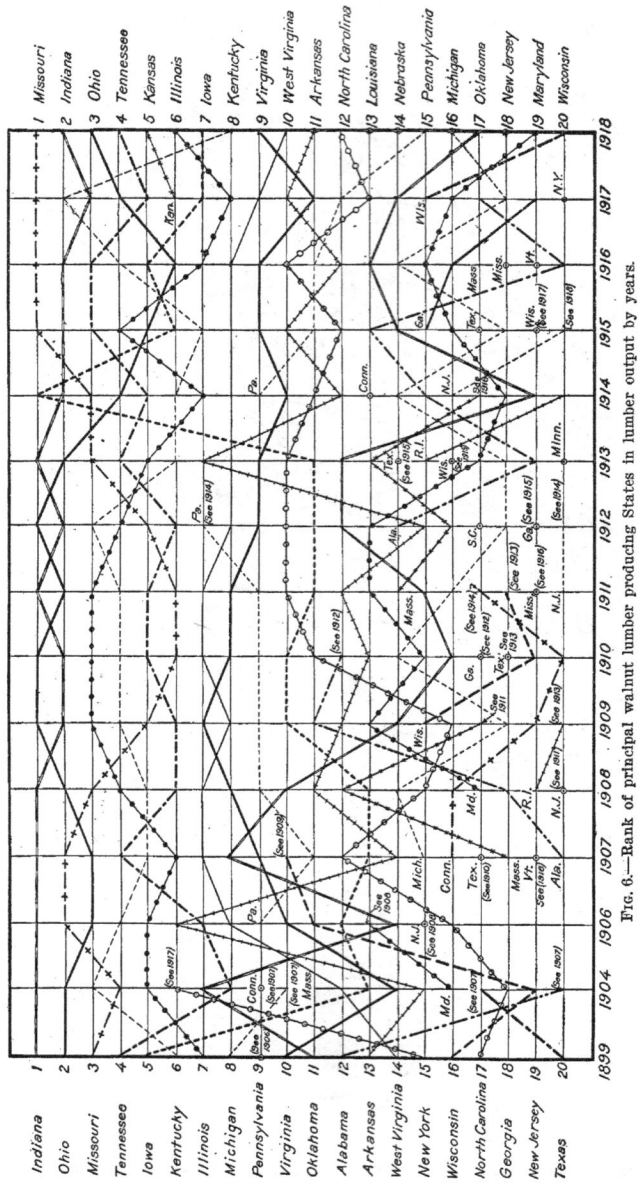

Fig. 6.—Rank of principal walnut lumber producing States in lumber output by years.

In West Virginia and Virginia the mills generally cut little walnut lumber, although these States furnish considerable saw timber. The logs are shipped very largely to mills in other States. The same is true of North Carolina and Arkansas. Pennsylvania, Michigan, and Maryland, which formerly furnished large amounts of walnut lumber, produced only small quantities during those years in which the output was recorded.

Figures 4 and 5 show graphically the reported production by counties for 1916 and 1918. These maps show a movement to the west of the Mississippi of a great part of the walnut lumber manufacturing industry.

Figure 6 shows the order in which the principal walnut-manufacturing States stood in different years in point of lumber production. It is quite remarkable that Indiana, Ohio, and Illinois, after a continuous and heavy drain upon this region for so many years, rank so high in 1918. Missouri, Tennessee, and Kentucky since 1899 have also maintained a notably steady output.

TABLE 6.—*Number of mills in the different States reporting manufacture of walnut lumber in different years, arranged in the order of lumber cut for 1918.*

State.	1907	1908	1909	1910	1911	1912	1913	1914	1915	1916	1917	1918
Total	1,803	2,563	3,518	2,882	2,502	2,738	895	749	1,293	1,204	1,001	855
Missouri	170	210	384	346	284	322	114	68	86	73	61	54
Indiana	385	478	544	421	346	413	191	176	223	203	189	149
Ohio	299	326	387	320	306	346	107	102	149	160	126	110
Tennessee	260	279	387	292	249	286	94	115	205	144	115	108
Kansas	a	3	6	3	a	5	3			3	a	4
Illinois	92	112	145	106	82	87	31	21	33	20	23	20
Iowa	a	50	114	82	82	72	27	8	45	32	31	22
Kentucky	315	348	419	367	315	320	110	77	149	153	122	96
Virginia	a	127	210	204	167	166	40	21	64	54	52	51
West Virginia	a	149	216	182	165	175	50	41	107	96	77	63
Arkansas	a	38	56	46	28	31	10	13	23	18	27	21
North Carolina	a	39	58	58	75	65	27	13	26	42	43	28
Louisiana						a		a		a		a
Nebraska						a		a				a
Pennsylvania	a	177	258	179	181	204	30	39	72	71	50	43
Michigan	a	32	46	49	40	36	9	10	9	15	9	12
Oklahoma	a	34	42	43	36	40	10	5	11	12	9	12
New Jersey	a	13	18	20	18	12	a	4	11	11	4	8
Maryland	a	34	51	45	30	38	8	7	18	17	17	8
Wisconsin	a	24	26	12	12	14	6	a	11	7	5	a
New York					a	6	5	5	6	14	8	11
Alabama	a	20	51	38	21	23	3	10	14	8	10	3
Georgia	a	10	12	11	7	16	a		5	11	4	3
Mississippi	a	8	4	8	3	5			a	3	a	4
Massachusetts	a	16	26	11	18	22	5	a	5	7	3	5
Florida						a		a				a
Vermont	a	5	a	a	3	4		4	4	4	a	3
Connecticut	a	12	18	12	10	8	a	3	3	4	4	a
Texas	a	4	7	5	3	a	4		4	4	8	a
Rhode Island		7	8	a		a	a	3		3	5	a
Delaware		a	a	a	a			a	a			a
South Carolina			10	6	9	10	a	a	5	5	a	a
Minnesota		4	8	5	4	5	a		a	3	a	a
New Hampshire		a	3	5	4	a			a	a		a
Maine											a	
All other States [1]	282	4	4	6	4	7	11	8	5	3	7	14

[1] Including those marked "a."

Table 6 gives for different years the number of mills in each State reporting the manufacture of walnut lumber. These are arranged

in order of importance for 1918. This table shows a ma:
almost universal reduction in the number of mills sawing v
the different States, particularly since the year 1912. This 1
in the number of mills cutting walnut was, of course, to be
for 1918, for during that year the manufacture of walnut
permitted only for war products. However, Missouri shows
tion from 322 mills in 1912 to 61 in 1917, and Indiana a 1
from 413 mills in 1912 to 189 in 1917. Practically every S
had a number of mills sawing walnut several years ago has
great reduction. This is largely because walnut manufactui
come in recent years a highly specialized industry, and walnu
now generally worked up at a mill specially adapted for
this kind of timber.

MANUFACTURE.

The manufacture of walnut lumber is one of the most
processes in sawmilling. The percentage of failures amon
operators is notoriously high. The problem, naturally, is
operator to get the most walnut lumber of the greatest val
the saw logs, or so to regulate his sawing that as much of t
possible will be utilized for products for which there is a
and at a price that will yield the necessary profit. Walnut
operators, therefore, do not strive for maximum lumbei
Care must be used in sawing each log, for improper mai
produces a greater proportion of less valuable stock, and tl
tion might easily result in a loss rather than a profit.

Large walnut sawmills are equipped with modern ba
which make a narrower kerf than the circular saws of sm
This gives to the large mill the advantages of faster produ(
less waste in sawdust.

As walnut saw logs are nearly always defective, the saw
be able to judge, so far as possible from the outside appear
position and character of interior defects. Walnut logs a:
be knotty toward the center, and the sawyer aims to get
wide, fairly clear lumber as possible without running into
near the center. The position of the log on the carriage, th
and thickness of the boards sawed from the log, and the ti
the log at the proper time to saw from another side have m
with getting a profit from the walnut-lumber business.

The cost of manufacture at large mills can not be easi
mined, because the veneer operations are so closely tied
lumber manufacture. At small mills the cost of sawing is
placed at $7.50 to $10 a thousand feet.

It is a general practice among walnut-lumber manufac
subject their sawed stock to a steaming process as it con

the saw. The older method was that of piling the lumber in a pit made of boards, at the bottom of which was the open end of the exhaust-steam pipe from the engine. The lumber was then covered over with sawdust and kept in the wet steam for several days. (Pl. IV, fig. 1.) The common method now is to build one or usually several large, fairly tight compartments with large doors and, after the lumber is piled in these compartments, to close them as tight as possible and turn in the steam. This method has the double effect of giving the wood, including the sapwood, a uniformly brown color, and of expediting the process of seasoning. There is usually not sufficient exhaust steam for this purpose, and live steam also must be used. Operators ordinarily steam their stock from four to five days at a temperature of 140° to 160°. If live steam is used it is difficult to regulate the temperature with the usual equipment; for when little exhaust steam is available more live steam must be used, and a higher temperature results. To regulate the moisture and temperature of the steam there is an equipment used in which the live steam is run over tanks of water; as moisture is taken up, the temperature is reduced.

Forest Service tests on walnut steamed for 10 days at a temperature of 190° and at atmospheric pressure have shown a decided loss in shock-resisting ability, or "toughness," for the steamed material. It is likely, however, that no appreciable loss in strength properties results from steaming at the usual lower temperatures. Cabinetmakers report that they find little or no difference between the properties of steamed and unsteamed walnut as it is now placed on the market.

Steaming gives a more or less uniform color to both heartwood and sapwood and makes the sapwood as valuable on the market as heartwood; for, according to the grading rules, any amount of sapwood is admitted in steamed walnut. Steaming also shortens the seasoning period. Manufacturers claim that steamed walnut, properly piled and air-seasoned, in 30 days will be as dry as unsteamed green walnut that has been in the pile for 90 days. Steamed walnut lumber 1 inch thick is considered to be "shipping dry" after being air-dried 30 days; and 1½-inch steamed walnut is so regarded after being air-dried 45 days, or one week for each quarter inch in thickness. This procedure effects a great saving in the time required for seasoning. It is also claimed that the steamed lumber is not so subject to fungus attack and discoloration when it is piled for air-drying.

The amounts of different grades of lumber produced from walnut logs are very difficult to determine, because no two manufacturers use the same general class of logs for lumber, nor do they manufacture the same kind of stock from them. The best that can be done, therefore, is to show averages derived from reports of several large representative manufacturers. These reports relate to grades of lumber produced and cover a considerable amount of material. The data are available for the years 1912 and 1919 and are as follows:

1912: First and seconds, 30 per cent; No. 1 common, 45 per cent; No. 2 common, 20 per cent; No. 3 common, 5 per cent.

1919: Firsts and seconds, 15 per cent; selects, 7 per cent; No. 1 common, 45 per cent; No. 2 common, 23 per cent; No. 3 common, 10 per cent.

From the figures covering the year 1912 the overrun of the log scale could not be determined. It is probable, however, that this overrun was greater than the average generally obtained from hardwood timber, because walnut logs usually run smaller. The high overrun during the war, amounting at many mills to about 40 per cent, was the result of sawing the thick gunstock flitches, which usually contained many defects. The small loss in saw kerf also helped to increase this overrun. For the year 1919 it is claimed that the overrun resulting from the sawing into lumber amounted to only about 10 per cent. This overrun seems remarkably low, but it is accounted for by the very poor quality of the logs remaining in the hands of the manufacturers that year, for a very large part of this timber was purchased to fill Government contracts and was intended mainly for rifle-stock blanks. Logs of that kind have many interior defects; and in most cases defects visible on the outside of the log were not scaled out, because the mill people were so desirous of obtaining the logs. Manufacturers claim that the 10 per cent overrun was entirely absorbed by the 10 per cent No. 3 common, or cull grade, which became unmerchantable, because of the very large amount of this low-grade stock on hand from the manufacture of war materials. Some walnut mills even claim an actual loss when the yield of merchantable lumber was compared with the amount of the log scale.

Under the present normal conditions, logs are scaled more closely for defects than during the war period; and, therefore, the overrun and also the proportion of firsts and seconds is greater. Furthermore, a better average grade of logs is being purchased. It is also probable that there will be a greater demand for cull or low-grade material.

The high percentage of the No. 1 common grade, as compared with that of other woods, is due, in the main, to the remanufacture of the No. 2 common grade. By resawing the widest and least defective lumber of this grade, narrower and shorter pieces are cut which will be classed as No. 1 common grade. In this way the amount of defective material is reduced.

The manufacture of walnut has become such a specialized industry that each log is generally purchased on its own merits without regard to grade. One classification used for walnut logs is grade No. 1 and grade No. 2. Grade No. 1 may have one or possibly two knots or other slight defects. Grade No. 2 includes all defective logs below grade No. 1 that are merchantable. Another classification used is Nos. 1, 2, and 3. No. 1 logs are practically clear, and generally 16 inches and over in diameter at the small end; No. 2 are of medium quality; and No. 3 of poor quality. This classification, of course, leaves much to the judgment of the log buyer. Manufacturers generally do not have any published grades. They usually purchase logs 14 inches and over in diameter at the small end, and the small sizes must be quite free from defects, particularly crook and large knots.

During the war the quality of logs was much lower than in normal times, on account of the pressing need for the timber. Small and defective logs were taken, which would not have been considered in peace times. Almost any log that would yield a clear gunstock blank was considered merchantable. The poorer class of such logs could be manufactured into lumber only at a loss.

Walnut lumber is classified by the National Hardwood Lumber Association rules according to five grades—namely, firsts and seconds, selects, No. 1 common, No. 2 common, and No. 3 common. In firsts and seconds the pieces must be at least 6 inches wide and 8 feet long. Each piece may have from one to three standard defects and a specified amount of sapwood, both depending on the size of the piece. In selects, pieces must be at least 4 inches wide and 6 feet long. In general, pieces of this grade are about equal in quality to the firsts and seconds grade on one face and to the No. 1 common grade on the other face. Specifications are given according to the size of each piece. No. 1 common must be at least 3 inches wide and 4 feet long. Each piece must be capable of yielding clear cuttings free from sapwood on one face and not over one-half sapwood on the reverse face, each cutting with at least 144 square inches, a minimum width of 3 inches, and a minimum length of 24 inches, and with a maximum waste of $33\frac{1}{3}$ per cent. Pieces in No. 2 common must yield clear cuttings free from sapwood on one face, at least 2 inches wide, and with a minimum of 72 square inches, with a maximum waste of 50 per cent. No. 3 common must be at least 3 inches wide and 4 feet long and must be capable of yielding sound cuttings at least $1\frac{1}{2}$ inches wide, and with a minimum of 36 square inches, with a maximum waste of 75 per cent. When steamed walnut is specified, restrictions as to sapwood do not apply. Standard thicknesses for walnut are as follows (in inches) : $\frac{1}{4}$, $\frac{3}{8}$, $\frac{1}{2}$, $\frac{5}{8}$, $\frac{3}{4}$, 1, 1$\frac{1}{4}$, 1$\frac{1}{2}$, 1$\frac{3}{4}$, 2, 2$\frac{1}{2}$, 3, 3$\frac{1}{2}$, 4, 4$\frac{1}{2}$, 5, 5$\frac{1}{2}$, and 6.

As walnut logs are generally not purchased according to certain specified grades, the prices for logs of different size and quality are quite indefinite. The value of each log is, as a rule, determined by the log buyer.

The representative prices of Arkansas logs, on the track at Kansas City, in 1913, based on a freight rate of 20 cents, or about $18 to $20 a thousand board feet, are shown in Table 7.

The average shipment brought about $60 a thousand feet, which is approximately the average price for 20-inch logs. Just before the war walnut logs were costing the large walnut operators between $50 and $60 a thousand board feet, on the average, at the factory.

The prices paid for several years past by one firm for three different grades of walnut logs at the factory are given in Table 8:

TABLE 7.

Diameter (inches).	Price, 1,000 board feet.
12 to 13............	$25
14 to 15............	35
16 to 17............	45
18 to 19............	57
20 to 21............	65
22 to 23............	85
24 to 25............	110
26 to 27............	145
28 and up........	210

TABLE 8.

Diameter (inches).	No. 1 (practically clear, generally 16 inches and over).	No. 2 (medium quality).	No. 3 (poor quality).
10 to 14...	$50	$35	$25
15 to 17...	55	40	30
18 to 20...	60	45	33
21 to 22...	70	50	35
23 to 24...	80	55	40
25 to 26...	90	60	45
26 to 28...	105	75	50
29 and up...	115	85	55

During the war, in order to make more timber available, higher prices were paid for walnut logs than had been paid before. The War Industries Board of the Council of National Defense drew up a schedule of fair prices for walnut logs and stumpage as shown in Table 9:

TABLE 9.

Diameter (inches).	Prices of black walnut logs, 8 feet long and over, f. o. b. cars at railroad.		Equivalent value for standing timber.	
	Minimum, 1,000 board feet.	Maximum, 1,000 board feet.	Minimum, 1,000 board feet.	Maximum, 1,000 board feet.
12 to 14....................................	$45	$55	$20	$35
15 to 16....................................	55	65	30	45
17 to 18....................................	65	75	40	50
19 to 20....................................	75	85	50	60
21 to 22....................................	85	95	60	70
23 to 24....................................	95	105	70	80
25 to 26....................................	105	115	80	90
27 to 28....................................	115	125	90	100
29 to 30....................................	125	135	100	110
31 and up....................................	135	150	110	120

Prices paid for walnut generally averaged a little higher than this, especially toward the close of the war, except for the more inaccessible and scattered timber. The average stumpage price was around $50 a thousand board feet, the price usually paid for logs 16 inches in diameter.

The cost of getting stumpage to the mill yard varies greatly, depending on the distance to mill and the extent to which trees are scattered, as well as on some other conditions. During the war the range in costs was about as given in Table 10:

TABLE 10.

Buying_____per 1,000 board feet, log scale__	$5–$10
Felling _____do____	5– 10
Hauling and loading on cars_____do____	15– 30
Freight _____do____	15– 20
Total _____	40– 70

The high cost of buying and felling is due to the widely scattered growth. If good stands of walnut are available these two items of cost should be only about half those given. If the average stumpage price of $50 is added to the sum of these costs the total cost becomes $90 to $120 a thousand at the mill yard.

For several months following the close of the war, prices paid for walnut timber ranged about the same as during the war; but a better quality of logs was purchased, and logs 14 inches and under in diameter were not taken unless they were of very good quality. Reports from walnut operators on prices paid for logs during this period show an average cost at the mill of $75 a thousand board feet, log scale, for logs 16 inches in diameter, as against a cost of $90 to $120 a thousand board feet for logs of the same size purchased during the war. The average cost for logs of all sizes was $90 a thousand board feet. This shows that the average size of logs purchased was greater than that of those purchased during the war. More recently prices paid for walnut logs have increased greatly, following much higher prices for walnut lumber and other hardwoods. These greatly increased prices are due in large part to higher logging costs.

The prices given above for large logs can not be considered as lumber-log prices, since the larger sizes, particularly if the logs are clear, are used for veneer. As lumber and veneer logs are generally purchased together, the above average for all logs does not represent average prices paid for lumber logs. It is not practicable, however, to attempt to give prices for lumber logs alone.

Table 11 shows the average value of walnut lumber at the mills, by States, for the years for which these data are available. These figures show a marked rise in price since 1911.

In Table 12 are given the average wholesale prices of ·
ber in various markets, based on actual sales for the ye
1912, inclusive, the only years for which these data ar
These figures show a steady increase in the price of firsts
grade for these years.

Table 13 gives the prices of 4/4 firsts and seconds, ·
and 8/4 No. 1 common, and of 4/4 No. 2 common, from 1
the first half of 1920, in different markets, as published k
bermen's Bureau. These figures show a general rise in
ticularly since 1915, and a marked rise since the middle

For comparison with other native cabinet woods, Table
pared from the same source. It gives prices of walnu
plain white oak, and birch, and uses 4/4 No. 1 common,
as a basis.

TABLE 11.—*Average value of walnut lumber per 1,000 board feet
by States, for different years.*

	1899	1904	1907	1908	1909	1910	1911	1915	1
United States......	$36.49	$45.64	$43.31	$42.53	$42.79	$34.91	$31.70	$48.47	$4
Missouri.............	42.59	47.60	48.30	50.73	42.39	33.39	32.39	48.78	4
Indiana.............	39.18	40.56	44.87	43.93	42.66	37.74	34.86	44.83	4
Ohio...............	42.68	50.95	47.10	46.08	55.33	38.08	32.38	48.21	4
Tennessee...........	19.27	35.27	34.62	36.39	37.37	32.88	29.37	44.28	3
Kansas..............	17.19	30.00	......	......	30.00	35.90	......	......	6
Illinois.............	33.43	72.98	51.28	54.38	54.53	36.76	33.75	62.59	4
Iowa...............	35.88	33.37	36.67	27.14	34.20	36.58	30.45	45.76	5
Kentucky...........	30.24	32.88	37.59	38.54	35.94	31.88	28.67	45.36	3
Virginia............	30.39	35.09	34.88	33.43	33.63	30.60	32.33	27.89	2
West Virginia........	25.46	31.46	32.54	31.02	29.98	32.00	31.57	31.70	3
Arkansas............	20.81	40.91	37.59	49.84	41.65	37.30	28.33	33.22	2
North Carolina.......	27.85	20.09	37.75	25.97	32.39	31.29	23.95	27.04	2
Louisiana...........	80.00	......	......	......	......	......	......	......	4
Pennsylvania........	37.28	......	39.01	37.17	36.94	30.38	21.47	36.39	3
Michigan............	47.34	61.67	42.80	40.53	36.60	38.84	36.25	35.58	4
Oklahoma...........	38.29	52.03	41.21	24.50	25.40	22.44	25.67	29.62	2
New Jersey..........	33.04	......	45.00	35.36	51.12	51.00	......	32.00	4
Maryland...........	27.65	49.50	45.40	39.76	33.45	37.59	25.00	31.47	1
Wisconsin...........	12.26	18.13	23.00	23.00	26.67	40.00	22.33	54.50	4
New York...........	36.77	40.15	......	......	......	......	......	33.70	3
Alabama............	27.31	40.00	35.83	40.19	43.57	34.47	24.86	31.75	4
Georgia.............	12.00	......	45.00	39.25	19.67	41.50	22.75	29.33	2
Mississippi..........	......	......	50.00	46.69	57.18	35.00	......	......	3
Massachusetts.......	41.67	16.21	29.33	21.26	21.37	17.00	18.67	18.33	2
Vermont............	......	......	17.00	20.00	18.00	......	......	23.00	4
Connecticut.........	25.81	28.77	30.00	20.00	20.24	24.36	23.75	20.00	2
Texas..............	16.03	33.33	40.00	25.00	30.89	......	......	50.00	2
Rhode Island........	28.00	......	......	19.52	24.85	......	......	......	2
Delaware............	60.00	......	......	55.00	27.50	......	......	25.00	
South Carolina.......	......	......	......	......	29.00	37.25	27.33	40.00	3
Minnesota...........	20.00	......	......	65.00	35.00	42.50	......	......	2
New Hampshire.......	......	......	......	21.00	20.00	19.00	......	......	2
Maine									

TABLE 12.—*Average wholesale prices of walnut lumber per 1,000 board feet, in various markets, based on actual sales made f. o. b. each market.*

	1908	1909	1910	1911	1912
Boston:					
Firsts and seconds 4/4	$105.00	$107.00	$105.00	$108.12	$112.00
No. 1 common 4/4	....	58.00	62.25	63.25	60.75
No. 2 common 4/4	....	38.00	....	40.75	37.38
Philadelphia:					
Firsts and seconds 4/4	....	110.00	....	102.50	....
No. 1 common 4/4	....	60.00	....	57.50	....
No. 2 common 4/4	....	35.00	....	33.25	....
Buffalo:					
Firsts and seconds 4/4	105.00	105.50	....	103.38	114.12
No. 1 common 4/4	63.67	61.25	....	55.38	57.88
No. 2 common 4/4	33.17	33.50	....	31.62	31.75
Cincinnati:					
First and seconds 4/4	90.25	92.25	92.17	93.33	98.50
No. 1 common 4/4	50.50	50.14	48.33	51.08	51.42
No. 2 common 4/4	28.50	27.50	25.67	26.00	30.08
Chicago:					
First and seconds 4/4	....	98.50	....	....	....
No. 1 common 4/4	....	55.50	....	....	....
No. 2 common 4/4	....	....	....	....	....
Memphis:					
Firsts and seconds 4/4	....	....	95.00	....	....
No. 1 common 4/4	....	....	50.00	....	....
No. 2 common 4/4	....	....	30.00	....	....
Minneapolis:					
Firsts and seconds 4/4	....	100.00	....	....	....
No. 1 common 4/4	....	60.00	....	....	....
No. 2 common 4/4	....	35.00	....	....	....
Denver: Firsts and seconds 4/4	....	120.00	....	....	....
San Francisco:					
Firsts and seconds 4/4	190.50	193.00	190.00	....	....
No. 1 common 4/4	147.50	140.56	140.00	. 140.00	....
Los Angeles: Firsts and seconds 4/4	150.00	160.00	....	....	....
Tucson: Firsts and seconds 4/4	....	172.50	....	....	....
Kansas City:					
Firsts and seconds 4/4	....	....	....	97.50	....
No. 1 common 4/4	....	....	....	43.50	....
No. 2 common 4/4	....	....	....	22.50	....
St. Louis:					
Firsts and seconds 4/4	....	....	....	90.25	....
No. 1 common 4/4	....	....	....	50.25	....
No. 2 common 4/4	....	....	....	27.25	....

TABLE 13.—*Average wholesale prices per 1,000 board feet of different grades and thicknesses of walnut lumber at representative markets for different years and quarter years.*

	1912	1913	1914	1915	1916	1917				1918				1919				1920	
						1st quarter	2d quarter	3d quarter	4th quarter	1st quarter	2d quarter	3d quarter	4th quarter	1st quarter	2d quarter	3d quarter	4th quarter	1st quarter	2d quarter
New York:																			
First and seconds 4/4	$116.00	$116.00	$115.40	$114.40	$122.75	$122.67	$122.67	$127.00	$147.00	$155.67	$155.17	$157.50	$157.50	$157.50	$157.50	$171.33	$188.50	$233.00	$307.50
Com. 4/4	58.55	61.00	60.40	59.00	63.75	63.33	62.00	67.00	70.33	70.67	70.17	72.50	72.50	72.50	73.17	88.67	114.67	180.33	210.83
Com. No. 1 6/4	65.14	61.50	70.90	69.50	74.25	73.67	72.00	77.00	80.33	80.67	80.17	82.50	82.50	82.50	83.17	95.00	124.67	190.33	222.50
Com. No. 1 8/4	67.14	76.50	75.90	74.50	79.25	78.67	77.00	82.00	85.33	86.33	85.17	87.50	87.50	87.50	88.17	107.17	134.67	203.67	234.17
Com. No. 2 4/4	36.00	36.00	35.40	34.00	37.75	37.67	37.00	40.00	43.33	40.67	37.17	39.50	39.50	39.50	39.50	43.17	51.33	94.33	110.83
Buffalo:																			
First and seconds 4/4	113.25	113.75	113.15	111.75	120.75	120.33	119.00	124.00	144.00	152.67	152.17	154.50	154.50	154.50	154.50	168.33	185.00	230.00	304.50
Com. 4/4	55.57	57.75	57.15	55.75	69.75	60.33	59.00	64.00	67.33	67.67	67.17	69.50	69.50	69.50	70.17	82.33	101.67	174.00	207.83
Com. No. 1 6/4	65.57	69.00	68.40	67.00	74.75	69.50	59.50	74.50	77.83	78.17	77.67	80.00	80.00	80.00	80.67	92.33	121.67	187.33	219.50
Com. No. 1 8/4	64.64	74.00	73.40	72.25	76.75	76.17	74.50	79.50	82.83	83.83	82.67	85.00	85.00	85.00	85.67	104.67	131.67	200.67	231.17
Com. No. 2 4/4	33.75	33.75	33.15	31.75	35.75	35.33	34.00	37.00	40.33	37.67	34.17	36.50	36.50	36.50	40.50	48.83	91.50	107.83
Detroit and Grand Rapids: [1]																			
First and seconds 4/4	114.25	114.25	113.40	112.00	120.75	120.33	119.00	124.00	144.00	152.17	152.17	154.50	154.50	154.50	154.50	167.00	180.50	228.50	304.50
Com. No. 1 4/4	56.07	58.18	57.57	56.00	60.75	60.33	59.00	64.00	67.33	67.67	67.17	69.50	69.50	69.50	70.17	86.00	112.17	177.50	207.83
Com. No. 1 6/4	62.89	69.18	64.40	67.00	71.75	71.00	69.00	74.00	78.33	78.17	77.67	79.50	79.50	79.50	80.17	91.67	121.17	187.17	219.17
Com. No. 1 8/4	64.89	75.55	75.00	74.00	78.75	77.33	74.00	79.00	82.33	82.17	82.17	84.50	84.50	84.50	85.17	103.83	121.17	200.50	231.17
Com. No. 2 4/4	34.25	34.18	33.40	32.00	35.75	34.00	33.33	37.00	40.33	34.17	36.50	36.50	36.50	36.50	40.50	48.83	91.50	107.83
First and seconds 4/4	113.75	113.75	113.22	112.00	120.75	119.67	117.00	122.00	142.00	150.17	150.33	153.50	153.50	153.50	153.50	167.00	183.50	228.17	302.50
No. 1 4/4	55.57	57.75	57.22	56.00	60.75	59.67	57.00	62.00	65.33	65.67	65.17	67.50	67.50	67.00	68.17	84.00	110.17	175.50	205.83
No. 1 6/4	62.64	65.00	69.00	67.00	71.75	67.00	57.00	72.00	75.33	81.33	80.17	79.50	79.50	80.50	76.17	90.00	119.67	185.33	217.50
No. 1 8/4	64.64	64.64	74.00	74.00	78.75	68.67	67.00	77.00	80.33	85.17	84.33	82.50	82.50	82.50	83.17	102.17	129.67	198.67	229.17
No. 2 4/4	33.75	33.75	33.22	32.00	35.75	34.67	34.00	35.00	38.33	38.33	34.17	34.50	34.50	33.50	34.50	46.83	89.50	105.83
First and seconds 4/4	110.00	110.00	109.40	108.00	116.75	117.00	116.33	121.00	141.00	149.67	149.00	150.50	150.50	150.50	150.50	164.33	181.00	225.75	300.00
No. 1 4/4	51.82	54.00	53.40	52.00	56.75	57.00	56.33	61.00	64.33	64.67	64.00	65.50	65.50	65.50	66.17	81.67	107.67	173.08	203.33
No. 1 6/4	58.64	65.00	64.40	62.00	59.75	67.00	66.33	71.00	74.33	74.33	74.00	75.00	75.00	75.00	76.17	88.00	117.67	183.08	215.00
No. 1 8/4	64.64	70.00	70.00	70.00	64.75	73.00	72.33	76.00	74.33	79.33	79.00	80.50	80.50	80.50	81.17	100.17	127.67	196.42	226.67
No. 2 4/4	30.00	30.00	29.40	28.00	31.75	32.00	31.00	35.00	38.33	38.50	33.50	33.50	33.50	33.50	36.50	44.33	87.08	103.33
St. Louis:																			
First and seconds 4/4	108.00	108.00	107.40	106.00	114.75	115.00	114.33	119.00	139.00	147.67	147.17	148.50	148.50	148.50	148.50	163.00	180.00	224.33	298.33
No. 1 4/4	54.59	56.50	56.35	56.00	60.75	61.00	56.33	58.00	62.33	62.67	62.17	63.50	63.50	64.17	63.17	80.33	106.67	171.67	201.83
No. 1 6/4	63.14	59.50	58.90	57.00	72.25	72.50	66.58	69.00	72.33	72.67	72.33	73.50	73.50	74.17	80.33	96.33	116.17	181.50	213.50
No. 1 8/4	64.14	73.50	72.75	71.00	75.25	79.50	71.00	74.00	77.33	73.83	73.33	78.50	78.50	79.17	98.33	126.17	194.83	225.17
No. 2 4/4	30.00	30.00	29.40	28.00	31.75	32.00	30.67	32.00	35.33	32.67	29.17	30.50	30.50	30.50	34.88	43.33	85.67	101.83
First and seconds 4/4	100.00	100.00	99.80	98.00	106.75	107.00	109.00	115.00	135.00	143.67	143.17	143.50	143.50	143.50	143.50	157.33	174.00	224.33	301.50
No. 1 4/4	48.00	49.50	48.90	47.50	52.25	52.00	50.83	55.00	58.83	58.33	58.17	58.50	58.50	58.50	59.17	74.67	100.67	171.67	204.83
No. 1 6/4	52.00	57.00	56.40	55.00	59.75	60.00	60.00	65.00	68.33	68.17	68.17	68.50	68.50	68.50	69.17	80.33	119.67	181.33	216.50
No. 1 8/4	54.00	62.00	61.40	60.00	64.75	65.00	65.00	70.00	73.33	74.33	73.33	73.50	73.50	73.50	74.17	92.50	119.67	194.67	228.17
No. 2 4/4	25.00	25.00	24.40	23.00	26.75	27.00	25.67	32.00	31.33	28.67	25.17	25.50	25.50	25.50	20.17	37.33	85.67	104.83

[1] Grand Rapids only.

FIG. 1.—STEAMING PITS FOR WALNUT LUMBER.

In the foreground the lumber is piled in one of the compartments preparatory to being covered and steamed.　The other compartments are filled with lumber, except at the extreme right in the background, where the steamed lumber has just been lifted out.

FIG. 2.—WASTE WALNUT, SUITABLE FOR MANUFACTURE INTO SMALL ARTICLES, BUT GENERALLY USED FOR FUEL.

TABLE 14.—*Average wholesale prices per 1,000 board feet of different cabinet woods for different years and quarter-years, based on 4/4-inch, No. 1 common grade at Chicago.*

Year.	Walnut.	Red gum.	Plain white oak.	Birch.
1912	$55.57	$26.18	$33.11	$25.00
1913	57.75	24.91	37.95	28.50
1914	57.22	22.40	34.60	26.70
1915	56.00	21.71	32.33	25.00
1916	60.75	26.38	35.12	27.71
1917:				
First quarter	59.67	30.00	35.67	30.67
Second quarter	57.00	33.67	37.67	37.33
Third quarter	62.00	38.00	40.33	40.67
Fourth quarter	65.33	37.67	37.00	39.33
1918:				
First quarter	65.67	39.00	40.33	36.00
Second quarter	65.17	39.67	41.83	38.50
Third quarter	67.50	42.50	46.67	40.50
Fourth quarter	67.50	41.83	46.67	40.50
1919:				
First quarter	67.50	40.67	46.67	38.50
Second quarter	68.17	45.00	51.00	37.83
Third quarter	84.00	73.00	72.33	48.50
Fourth quarter	110.17	90.50	85.67	56.33
1920:				
First quarter	175.50	157.17	133.00	115.00
Second quarter	205.83	156.33	153.:3	148.33

METHODS AND COST OF LOGGING.

Because of the scattered growth, methods of logging walnut timber differ from those employed for timber found in large quantities. Walnut is often cut by the owner and hauled to the railroad; sometimes it is cut and hauled by a local representative of the mill purchasing it or by the independent buyer with his own teams or truck. Hauling logs by large automobile trucks long distances to the railroad or mill is becoming quite a common practice. Large mills sometimes employ a regular corps of logging crews, trucks, and teams, which cover different walnut areas systematically, picking up all available walnut timber as they go. During the war some firms covered the ground very thoroughly; at first they sent out men to locate suitable timber, then they sent buyers to purchase it, and later they sent cutters, teams, and trucks to fell it and load it at the railroad or to haul it to the mill if that was not too far distant. Some firms that do their own logging have trucks specially equipped with cables and windlass, with which logs may be dragged out of steep gullies and other difficult places and loaded. Three hundred board feet of average-sized logs weigh about 2,500 pounds and are considered a large wagonload. A motor truck should carry up to four times that amount and make much more frequent trips.

As walnut splits somewhat easily it is necessary to exercise unusual care in felling the tree, especially if there is a large crotch, for the split may extend a long distance below the fork into the large trunk and cause considerable loss.

The cost of logging walnut is higher than that of logging other species, because it is often a case of picking up a few trees or only one on a farm. The cost also varies greatly with the amount of timber in any one locality. West of the Mississippi, where there are comparatively good stands and the best timber has not been removed, the trees can be felled and sawed into logs for $2 to $5 a thousand board feet, log scale. In the East, where the trees are much scattered, this cost may run as high as $8 or $10 a thousand. Digging up stumps is expensive. It generally takes a crew of five men to dig up and dress an average of two stumps a day.

The cost of hauling to the railroad varies greatly with the length of haul, the character of the country, the condition of the roads, and the equipment used. With a team and fairly good hauling conditions it generally costs $15 to $30 a thousand board feet for a 5 to 10 mile haul, or at the rate of $3 a mile. A general average would probably be about $20 a thousand for a 7 to 8 mile haul. If the timber is much scattered and the country rough, the cost will amount to $4 a thousand for a mile. A team can usually make but one trip a day, hauling about 300 board feet of logs for 10 miles over fair roads. A large automobile logging truck generally makes two round trips a day, carrying about 1,000 feet over a 20-mile haul. On this basis the truck will do 12 times as much work as one team. The cost of trucking depends to a very large extent upon the investment and expense of upkeep, and will vary greatly with the equipment used. The cost of loading logs on cars is generally figured at $2.25 to $2.50 a thousand board feet.

WASTE.

Walnut logs are utilized very closely for lumber. Material coming under the head of waste consists of saw kerf or sawdust, slabs and edgings, very low-grade and defective lumber, and relatively clear pieces of small dimension. The waste caused by the saw kerf may be reduced to a minimum by using a band saw instead of a circular saw. A timber so valuable and so scarce as walnut should not be sawed with a circular saw, and, because less waste results, small sawmills often ship their walnut logs to a large mill that has a band saw. The sawdust is generally used for fuel. It is used also, instead of hickory, to a considerable extent for smoking meats and, with the exception of hickory, is said to be the best wood available for the purpose. Large packing houses use great quantities of walnut sawdust in this way, but the demand seems to be very small in comparison with the supply available. Sawmill operators have endeavored to find other uses for walnut sawdust, such as for sweeping compounds. The dark color of walnut seems to bring it into disfavor for this use, probably because of the mistaken idea that the dark sawdust is not clean. Slabs and edgings are useful only for fuel and are generally burned in the steam boilers. At some mills located near large cities a good trade has been started up in walnut cordwood. This waste, together with pieces too low in grade or too small in size to be merchantable, is usually sold by the wagonload for about $1.25 or $1.50 a load, which is equivalent to about $3.50 a cord. Much very low-grade and defective lumber that is marketable in normal times has not been salable because of the large accumulations made during the war. This class of material may be in demand for cheap and low-grade lumber when such stocks become less plentiful. A vast quantity of small sound portions of walnut accumulated in the process of manufacturing gunstock blanks from the flitch, and from these portions many clear pieces may be cut. Some of this stock has been disposed of to manufacturers of such small novelties as air rifles, but the market is limited, and immense piles of this material must be used for fuel. (Pl. IV, fig. 2.)

Some mills convert their low-grade and small-dimension material into dimension stock. This, however, does not seem to be generally successful with walnut, on account of the large number of sizes demanded, and these can not be produced without considerable waste. Manufacturers complain that for carefully manufactured clear stock they receive much less than for No. 1 common lumber; whereas they should receive a price equal to that of the firsts and seconds grade. Factory managers claim, on the other hand, that much waste in the use of dimension stock is caused by too close cutting to the finished size, by warping and checking, and by the presence of serious defects which can not be cut out. Theoretically, the manufacture of low-grade material into dimension sizes should be a success economically, provided the sizes are made to meet factory requirements. Thus, before the war, a chair factory would purchase No. 1 common black walnut lumber for, say, $65 a thousand, kiln-dry it for approximately $6, and cut it up at a cost of $10 to $15 a thousand, making a total cost of about $83. Since the average waste in manufacture amounts to about 25 per cent, the original thousand board feet would be reduced to about 750 board feet. This would make the material cost 11 cents a board foot, or $110 a thousand, after it had been seasoned and cut up. It would seem that a good grade of dimension material should bring a price by the thousand board feet at least equal to the price which high-grade lumber would bring. As a matter of fact, managers of many furniture factories prefer to buy the lumber and cut their dimension sizes from it, for they have a large number of different designs which change from year to year, and they might suffer much waste in buying dimension sizes. Therefore, the lumber manufacturer generally cuts dimension material merely to use his low-grade lumber and get a return from stock which is difficult to market. There has been and still is a wide range in selling prices for dimension material. A price as low as $30 a thousand board feet, before the war, was reported for small clear stock cut from No. 2 common, and as high as $80 for chair stock cut from waste. Differences in price depend to a large degree on the quality of the stock. Notwithstanding the many objections to the use of dimension material, its manufacture in standard sizes in large quantity is successfully carried on. Dimension stock should be clear of defects and first class in every way. Kiln-dried or thoroughly air-dried stock is much more satisfactory than green or partially seasoned material. Low prices and lack of demand for dimension materials are, in large part, the result of the manufacture of improperly seasoned, scant, and defective stock.

Walnut-lumber manufacturers now often recut such low-grade lumber as No. 2 common, for which there is a relatively small demand, into smaller, less-defective pieces, which are classed in a higher standard lumber grade or may be sold as a special grade of stock that is narrow or short or both narrow and short. This remanufacture is generally applied to the lower grades of 4/4, 6/4, and 8/4, and to a considerable extent is taking the place of dimension manufacture. This method is advantageous in that the factories may saw their required pieces from this material, and the waste that might result from the purchase and use of dimension stock is often avoided. Some lumber manufacturers are disposing of their low-grade walnut by running factories in connection with their sawmills, in which they utilize the small sizes of material in making such products as phonograph cabinets and various kinds of boxes and novelties.

VENEER.

Because it is so easily worked with tools, walnut is an excellent wood for manufacture into veneer. The pleasing appearance due to its good color, the different figured effects and the variety of tones and patterns which can be obtained from different logs, and its excellent finishing qualities combine to make it one of the most satisfactory native woods for fine cabinet veneer. The best-growth logs are generally sound, well rounded in cross section, straight, and with little taper. Our wild cherry is also a good cabinet veneer wood, but it lacks the figure of walnut, and even the best timber generally has many small defects. Walnut, mahogany, and cherry are said to be the most satisfactory cabinet woods for making sliced veneer, because they are so easily cut with the veneer knife and make a smooth sheet without splintering. Moreover, the veneer warps very little in drying, glues very satisfactorily, and after it is made into panels does not shrink or swell excessively under varying moisture conditions.

PRODUCTION.

Data on the output of walnut in the form of veneer are available from reports of the Census Bureau for the years 1904 to 1911, inclusive. The amounts of walnut logs used in different years are given in Table 15, and also the cost of the logs per thousand board feet, log scale, where reported. Approximately 95 per cent of the total amount for the years 1906 to 1909 was used for rotary veneer. Reports for those years are given by States and are shown in Table 16.

TABLE 15.—*Walnut used in different years in the manufacture of veneer, from reports by the Bureau of the Census.*

Year.	Thousands of board feet, log scale.	Cost per 1,000 board feet.
1904	[1] 2,250	....
1905	1,725	....
1906	5,121	$67.76
1907	3,952	70.39
1908	5,176	60.53
1909	2,400	69.36
1910	2,724	....
1911	4,121	....

[1] This figure was obtained by using an average converting factor of 12 square feet of veneer to each board foot, log scale, derived from reports for the years 1905–1907, as reports for 1904 were only on veneer produced.

TABLE 16.—*Amounts of walnut logs consumed in the production of veneer, by States, for different years, in thousands of board feet, log scale.*

State.	1906	1907	1908	1909
California	....	....	3	2
Delaware	....	....	....	10
Illinois	2,329	2,590	2,813	1,492
Indiana	1,115	696	2,120	310
Kentucky	23	40	37	19
Maryland	400	200	51	51
Massachusetts	4	....	4	1
Michigan	3	6	2	20
Missouri	....	....	....	200
New Jersey	1	....	....	....
New York	35	64	12	50
Ohio	1,175	203	105	181
Pennsylvania	....	100	....	....
Tennessee	....	30	7	....
Virginia	18	13	6	6
West Virginia	18	10	16	50
Total	5,151	3,952	5,176	2,400

Recent reports obtained from practically all of the large manufacturers of walnut veneer in the United States show a consumption of 3,296,000 board feet, log scale, of logs in 1917, with a production of 64,654,000 square feet of veneer, and an estimated consumption of about 5,615,000 board feet of logs in 1919, with a production of about 111,200,000 square feet of veneer. These figures are given by States in Table 17. About 50 per cent of the total amount is straight sliced and the other 50 per cent is about equally divided between rotary proper and stay-log rotary. Of the total amount of veneer produced, approximately one-half is plain and one-half figured. During 1918 the cutting of walnut veneer, except highly figured stock from cross-grained wood, was prohibited by the War Department. Near the close of the year the cutting of walnut veneer was resumed; and the great demand that arose because of depleted stocks, together with the large supply of walnut logs on hand that had been purchased to fulfill Government war orders, accounts for the marked increase in production shown for 1919. It is also estimated that the 1920 walnut veneer production will be in excess of 100,000,000 square feet. The increase in the production of veneer in recent years is greater than the log-consumption figures indicate, for the amount of veneer obtained now is much greater from the same number of feet, log scale, largely because of the cutting of thinner veneer. For instance, in 1906, from 5,121,000 board feet of logs, 67,184,000 square feet of veneer was produced, or 13 square feet of veneer to 1 board foot of log; but in 1917 and 1919 the ratio of square feet of veneer to board feet of logs, log scale, was about 20 to 1. The estimated 1919 production was nearly double the reported production of 1906, and the estimated log consumption of 1919 was only about 9 per cent greater than the reported consumption of 1906.

TABLE 17.—*Amounts of walnut logs consumed in the production of veneer for 1917; and estimated consumption in 1919, by States.*

States.	Thousands of board feet.	
	1917	1919
Indiana	1,200	2,250
Illinois	789	650
Ohio	190	835
Michigan, West Virginia, Maryland	636	1,130
Kansas, Missouri	481	750
Toal	3,296	5,615

MANUFACTURE.

Walnut veneer is produced almost altogether by slicing, but small amounts are still sawed for special purposes. Sliced veneer is made by two processes—the rotary method in which the timber is rotated against the knife, and the straight-slice method in which the timber moves in a straight line.

Rotary-cut process.—This process has been used extensively for making veneer. It is still the method in most common use, for it has the advantage of a low cost of production.

Walnut veneer logs are sawed into the lengths required for the veneer that is to be cut. These sections are put in hot water, generally over night; hard material may require a night and a day, or even two nights and a day. Each log section is then taken out and, after the bark is removed, revolved in the rotary machine, which is constructed like a lathe. The knife is constantly advanced, the advance for each revolution of the log corresponding to the thickness of the veneer. The veneer is usually torn off where a defect occurs, often at each revolution. Logs may be sliced down to a diameter of 6 to 8 inches, depending on the machine. Some specially constructed machines cut down to a diameter as small as 4 inches. The figure in this veneer is made by the growth rings, and, since the slicing is done in the direction of these rings, a veneer with a large coarse figure is the result. Hence only the lowest grade of logs is cut in this manner. Moreover, a considerable part of the heartwood, and usually the most valuable part, is wasted in the core. If the center of the log is defective, there is some advantage in slicing by the straight rotary process.

A variation of the rotary is the half-round process, by which the log is set somewhat off the center, and veneer is cut only part way around the log. This method is most commonly used with small logs in which there is a small amount of heartwood. The veneer may be sliced from the heartwood in this way, whereas by the straight rotary process little or no veneer can be obtained from the heartwood of small logs. If they are trimmed, successive sheets may be matched up for panel work. After the slicing of two sides of the log, the rest may be straight sliced and will yield quartered stock provided the central portion of the log is not defective. If the log is not sufficiently clear for veneer, it may be made into dimension stock.

The stay-log rotary process is a development from the rotary method proper, and is now very largely used for walnut. In this process a heavy flat plate is set off center, at a distance of about 1 foot, to which the timber to be sliced is fastened. The walnut block to be sliced is in the form of a half-log, generally called a flitch, and the sapwood is largely trimmed off (Pl. V, fig. 1). Holes are then bored in this flitch to correspond with those in the plate, to which it is to be fastened with stay bolts. By this method the heartwood, which must be thrown away in the core in the straight rotary method, may be more closely utilized.

Some manufacturers cut from the "sap" side, the outside c
log (Pl. V, fig. 2), and others cut from the "heart" side or c
of the log. Those who cut by the latter method do so in ord
get wide heartwood stock that is at least partly quartered. This
to its attractiveness, particularly if there is a figure in it. Mc
the quartered stock may thus be obtained with less waste tha
the straight-slice method. It is true, as manufacturers claim wl
from the "sap" side of such flitches, that by slicing from th
heartwood side there is considerable waste in working down t
curved surface from which a continuous sheet may be obta
Moreover, since knots are more numerous near the center of w
logs, the "heart" side is more likely to be defective. On the
hand, if the center of the log is clear, considerable valuable l
wood is wasted in the "dog board" when the slicing is done
the sapwood side. Although the thickness of the sapwood mus
be trimmed off, and after that some narrow sheets of heartwoo
cut, this method makes possible the production of wider she
heartwood than are obtained by cutting from the heartwood
If the cutting is from the outside, the figure is somewhat coar
in the rotary method proper, but slicing from the "heart" sid
across the growth rings and gives a striped effect. In stay-lo
ing the flitch is sliced down to a thickness of about 3 inches, the
that is left being called the "dog board." If the veneer is cut
the heartwood side, the last sheets are nearly all sapwood.

Rotary machines are generally made to take a log as long a
10 feet. Stump or "butt" wood is sliced by the rotary sta
process, veneer being cut from the outside of the log. This ·
the reason that the figure in "butt" wood runs with the oute
face of the wood. These stumps or butts are cut in half, because
can be more conveniently handled in this form.

Straight-slice process.—In this method the timber, which is
soaked, as in the rotary method, is pushed vertically again:
knife with, however, a slightly oblique motion from end to
The log lengths are usually cut in half lengthwise and prepared
the stay-log rotary process. The cut is then made from the l
wood side. Quartered stock is, of course, obtained only ne
center of the log. The coarser figure is soon reached, particula
the middle of the sheets. The panel maker generally trims c
outside striped veneer from the central coarse figure and kee
two separate for different uses. Very large logs are sawed leng
in quarters, in order to get more of the quartered veneer stock.
quartering, logs should be at least 24 inches in diameter at the
end. Logs are also prepared for straight slicing, by squaring

FIG. 1.—WALNUT HALF LOGS, WHICH HAVE BEEN PREPARED FOR ROTARY
STAY-LOG SLICING BY TRIMMING OFF THE GREATER PART OF THE SAP-
WOOD.   At the butt end they are entirely heartwood.

FIG. 2.—A WALNUT HALF LOG BEING SLICED FROM THE SAPWOOD SIDE BY
THE ROTARY STAY-LOG PROCESS.

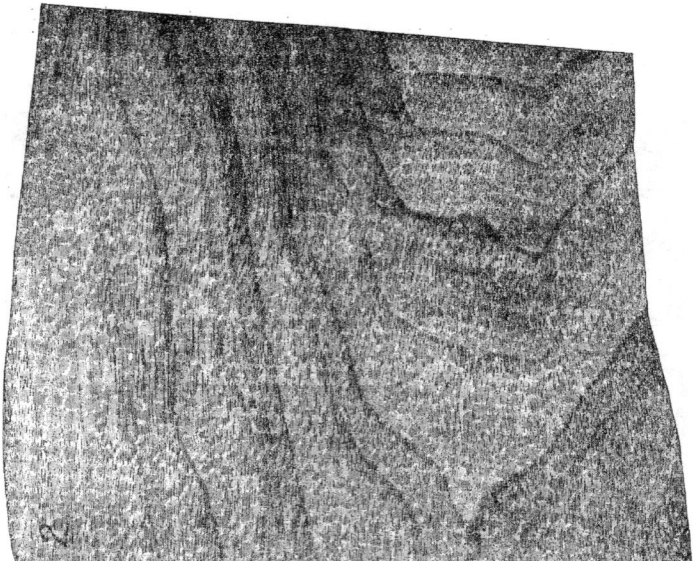

FIG. I.—A PIECE OF PLAIN WALNUT VENEER OBTAINED BY STRAIGHT SLICING
OR THE STAY-LOG ROTARY PROCESS FROM THE SAPWOOD SIDE.

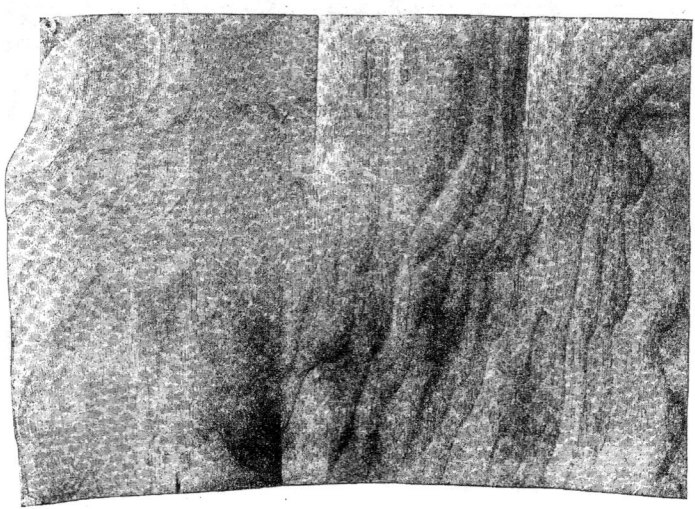

FIG. 2.—PLAIN ROTARY VENEER.

and this removes most of the sapwood. The smaller logs are handled advantageously in this way.

If there is sapwood on the edges of the veneer sheets it is trimmed off with the exception of about 1 inch. During the cutting of the sheets, the veneer from each log is piled and kept by itself, and in the same order as it came from the log. In selling this veneer, about four samples are taken from the veneer sheets from each log in different parts of the pile.

Special dimension veneer is straight sliced from clear blocks sawed from the log. These blocks are usually 4 to 6 inches thick, 1 foot wide, and $2\frac{1}{4}$ to 6 feet long, and may be sliced down to a thickness of three-fourths inch. This procedure involves much less slicing, and the sheets obtained are practically clear of defects. The method is not largely used, however, and is, on the whole, adapted to making plain veneer only, because the panel maker must choose and match his figured stock from large sheets of veneer. In the usual straight-slice process the flitch is so clamped in the machine that it may be cut down to a thickness of about 2 inches. Most slicers are made to take flitches as long as 10 to 12 feet. The longest slicer will take a flitch about 16 feet in length. These machines for cutting cabinet-wood veneers are built very heavy, in order that a smooth, clean cut of uniform thickness may be made.

Sawed veneer.—Little sawed walnut veneer is manufactured. It is claimed that the sawed veneer is of a higher grade than the sliced. In the manufacture of sawed veneer the log is squared, and long sheets, usually one-twentieth inch in thickness, are sawed from it with a fine-toothed saw. Highly figured stock, including "butt" wood, is also sawed for veneers. High-grade sawed walnut veneer is used principally in Pullman cars. The highest grade is used in private railway cars. The plain veneer is used mainly for door stiles, rail stock, and table tops. This veneer is generally about one-sixteenth to one-eighth inch thick, and is used because of the greater wear to which such stock is subjected.

Burls.—Walnut burls are made into veneer by special methods of handling that depend on the size and form of burl, the quality of wood, and the kind of figure. The burl is first cut into several pieces, as an apple is cut, and may then be made into veneer by sawing, straight slicing, or rotary slicing. The kind of product and its value depend very largely upon the way in which it is handled. To get the most out of a burl requires much care and experience.

Thickness of veneer.—The most common thickness for walnut veneer at the present time is one twenty-eighth inch. Some firms use one-thirtieth inch, and thus make more veneer from a given quantity of wood. Such highly figured pieces as burls are usually cut or thirtieth inch thick. There seems to be a tendency on the part panel makers to use thicker veneer of about one-twentieth in Although this veneer costs more, the makers figure that it is mo profitable in the end; for with the thicker veneer almost no wa results from the rejection of panels that have been sanded throuﬀ Furthermore, the panels may be sanded more rapidly, and this iﬀ particular advantage on account of the present high cost of lab One-twentieth inch was formerly the common thickness for slic veneer, but the thickness has been reduced, as walnut has become mo scarce and higher in price. Sawed walnut veneer is usually on eighth or one-sixteenth inch thick. Figured stock is usually saw one-sixteenth inch thick.

Yield by different methods.—Exact data are difficult to obtain the yield of veneer from logs of different sizes, because the differe processes are varied to suit each log. Moreover, there are wide d ferences in the quality of different logs. Average yields may calculated, however, from practically clear logs, with deductions the average amount of waste in that part of the log from which, commercial practice, merchantable veneer is produced. Table gives in terms of veneer one twenty-eighth inch thick the calculat volumes to the linear foot of logs of different diameters. Table gives the average thickness of sapwood and diameter of heartwo for logs of different diameters. In the calculations of yield, a larg allowance for sapwood is made than is shown in this table, for ﬀ reason that the sapwood is often of irregular thickness and therefﬀ a greater waste is caused than the actual thickness of sapwood dicates.

TABLE 18.—*Theoretical volumes, in terms of one twenty-eighth inch veneer, logs of different diameters, per linear foot of log.*

Diameter log (inches).	Sq. ft., $\frac{1}{28}''$ veneer.	Diameter log (inches).	Sq. ft., venee
12	264	22	
13	310	23	
14	359	24	
15	412	25	1
16	469	26	1
17	530	27	1
18	594	28	
19	662	29	1
20	733	30	1
21	808		

TABLE 19.—*Average width of sapwood and diameter of heartwood, of walnut logs of different diameters.*

Diameter inside bark.	Single width of sap.	Diameter of heart.	Diameter inside bark.	Single width of sap.	Diameter of heart.
Inches.	*Inches.*	*Inches.*	*Inches.*	*Inches.*	*Inches.*
6	0.8	4.4	19	1.6	15.8
7	.8	5.4	20	1.7	16.6
8	.9	6.2	21	1.7	17.6
9	1.0	7.0	22	1.8	18.4
10	1.0	8.0	23	1.8	19.4
11	1.1	8.8	24	1.8	20.4
12	1.2	9.6	25	1.9	21.2
13	1.2	10.6	26	1.9	22.2
14	1.3	11.4	27	1.9	23.2
15	1.4	12.2	28	2.0	24.0
16	1.4	13.2	29	2.0	25.0
17	1.5	14.0	30	2.0	26.0
18	1.5	15.0			

If the straight rotary process is employed, manufacturers generally find that there is, on the average, about 20 per cent of waste, not counting the core and the sapwood. Figuring the core at 6 inches in diameter for an average log of 18 inches in diameter, because rotary logs generally run small, and figuring 2 inches as the thickness of the sapwood, the entire log contains 359 square feet of veneer to the linear foot of log, inside the sapwood, less 66 square feet in the core, which is generally considered waste, thus leaving 293 square feet to the linear foot. If 20 per cent waste in slicing is deducted, a net yield is left of 235 square feet of veneer to the linear foot. As the original log scaled 12 feet to the linear foot, this makes a yield of about 19½ square feet of veneer to the board foot of log, log scale.

In the stay-log rotary process, a half log from a log 24 inches in diameter, which is representative for this type of veneering, will yield to the linear foot, if it is perfectly clear, about 273 square feet of one twenty-eighth-inch heartwood veneer cut from the sapwood side, and about 282 square feet cut from the heartwood side, allowing for a 3-inch "dog board" and the waste in cutting down to get a sufficiently wide sheet of heartwood veneer. Figure 7 shows the cross-sectional area from which merchantable veneer is generally cut by the two processes. Manufacturers calculate that there is a 10 per cent waste in the portion from which merchantable veneer is cut. If this 10 per cent is deducted, a balance is left of 246 and 254 square feet, respectively, in cutting from the sapwood and heartwood sides.

As there are 12½ board feet, log scale, for each foot in length in the half log referred to above, this makes a yield of approximately 20 square feet of veneer for each board foot, log scale. This figure corresponds with the general average of 20 obtained from reports of veneer manufacturers.

Because there is a somewhat greater waste in cutting from the sapwood side on account of the "dog board" being all heartwood,

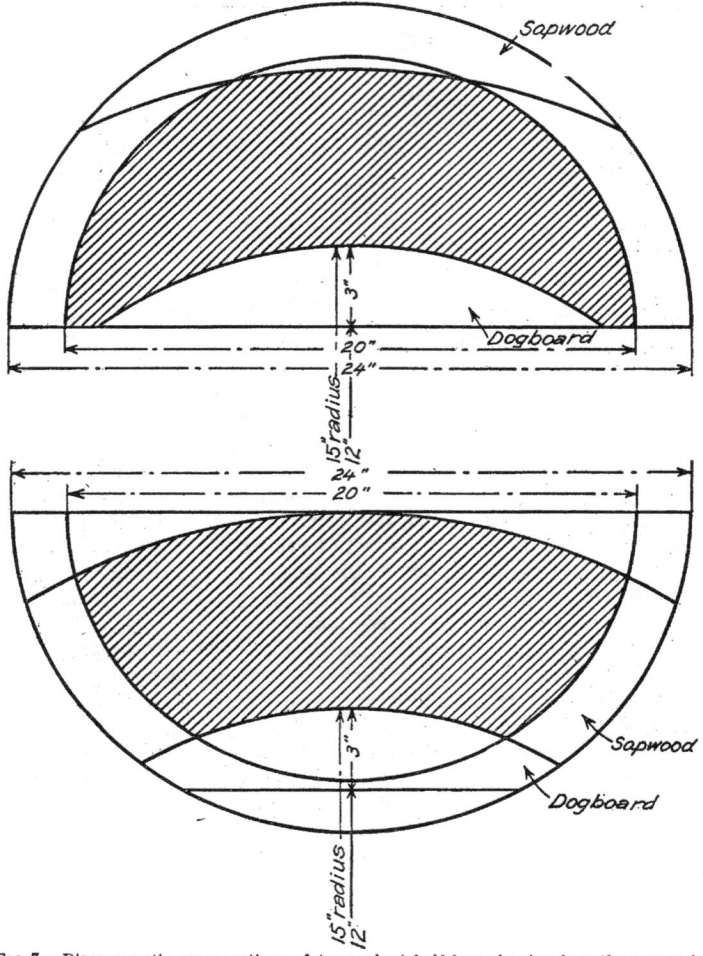

FIG. 7.—Diagrammatic cross sections of two walnut half logs showing how the veneer is sliced by the stay-log rotary process from the sapwood side (above) and heartwood side (below). In both sketches the portion above the upper curved line is trimmed off before a sheet of merchantable size is obtained. That below the lower curved line is the dog board. The part below the dog board in the lower sketch is trimmed off to secure a face for attaching the log to the veneer machine.

the yield from clear flitches will be on the average somewhat less than it is when the cutting is from the heartwood side. If the heartwood is defective the yield might be made greater by cutting from the sapwood side.

In the straight-slice process the principal waste is in squaring the log lengths and in the "dog board." A 20-inch log may be taken to illustrate the straight-slice method. Squaring this to 14 inches will remove nearly all of a 2-inch rim of "sap" and cut down to a heartwood face of about 8 inches in width. If allowance is made for a 10 per cent waste, as in stay-log rotary, a possible yield is given of 353 square feet of veneer to the linear foot of log, after a 2-inch "dog board" is deducted. As there are 16 board feet, log scale, to the linear foot in a 20-inch log, each log-scale foot will yield about 22 square feet of veneer. The figure generally given by firms that make straight-sliced veneer almost exclusively is 20 square feet to the board foot, log scale. The small amount of sapwood that was not removed in squaring the timber probably accounts for the difference in these figures.

If it is cut in halves for slicing, the log is not squared. The sapwood is largely trimmed off, and the back, or outside, of the log is trimmed down to a flat surface in order that the half log may be held in the veneer slicer. As there is a little less heartwood trimmed off by this method, the yield in veneer will be slightly greater. Although there are two "dog boards" to a log if the half log is used, each one is thinner than the "dog board" from the entire log.

The yield to the board foot of log does not, therefore, differ greatly in the three different processes—straight rotary, stay-log rotary, and straight slice—the general average of 20 square feet of veneer to each board foot of log applying very closely in each case.

If dimension walnut veneer is made from small clear pieces, only about 15 square feet of veneer is obtained to one board foot, log scale, of the logs from which the clear pieces were cut. As a matter of fact, a clear block 1 foot by 6 feet by 6 inches, containing 36 board feet, which is equivalent to about 30 board feet, log scale, will yield about 880 square feet of veneer, or 29 square feet to each board foot, log scale, in addition to a three-fourths-inch "dog board." Therefore only about one board foot of the clear piece is required to produce the same amount of veneer as may be obtained from 2 board feet calculated on the basis of the entire log; that is, only about one-half of the log is used for the small clear blocks. The remainder of the log not used in producing the clear pieces may be utilized for lumber and dimension material. Furthermore, logs of lower grade may be used than are required in making the larger-sized veneers.

Dimension veneer, cut to the size required by factories, is often obtained from veneer made by the rotary process. This plan involves much trimming of the veneer, but it makes unnecessary the shipping of a great deal of stock which would not be adapted to the needs of the purchaser.

Of sawed veneer the yield is about half what it would be in straight sliced, because the saw kerf is about the thickness of the veneer sheet. Thus, a 20-inch log with an equivalent volume to the linear foot of 524 square feet of veneer one-twentieth inch thick, after it is squared, and 10 per cent is deducted for waste in the sheets and in the " dog board," yields 126 square feet of veneer to the linear foot. This makes only about 8 square feet of veneer to the board foot of log.

Kinds of veneer.—Walnut veneer is generally termed plain, striped, or figured, although there are no hard and fast lines of distinction separating the three kinds.

Plain veneer is without stripe or figure. It is produced mainly by the rotary method, but some of it is made by straight slicing from the log in the tangential direction. (Pl. VI, fig. 1.) The veneer produced by the straight rotary process is generally plain. In forest-growth timber in which the annual rings are not very distinct the straight rotary method gives a coarse effect to the veneer, and in open-growth timber the more distinct growth rings give a still coarser effect, producing a very "wild" design. (Pl. VI, fig. 2.) Plain veneer is also produced by the stay-log rotary process. If cutting is from the sapwood side, the effect is somewhat similar to that produced by the rotary process, but some striped effect is obtained, especially toward the center of the log. If cutting is from the heartwood side, the striped effect is obtained at first, the veneer becoming plain in the middle, and entirely plain before the flitch is sliced down to the " dog board." Plain veneer is also produced by straight slicing near the outside of the log.

In striped veneer the lines caused by the growth rings are fairly straight. This effect is produced both by straight slicing and the rotary stay-log method. The veneer straight sliced from near the center of the log has the most distinctly striped effect, especially if the veneer is from an open-growth tree in which dark and light lines alternate. These stripes are sometimes so marked that the veneer resembles that made from Circassian walnut. In straight slicing the stripes become broader as the sheets are cut at a greater distance from the center and the striped effect is not so pronounced.

Striped veneer is produced by the stay-log method when the cutting is from the heartwood side. Near the center of the log a quartered effect is produced. (Pl. VII, fig. 1.) At a short distance from the center striped veneer is obtained along either edge of the strip. Slicing from the outside of the log gives a striped effect to the middle part of the sheets cut near the center of the log.

Figured veneer is cut from curly or highly figured wood. Walnut veneer cut on the quarter either by the straight-slice or stay-log rotary process shows a striped and cross-figured effect if the grain is wavy or curly. (Pl. VII, fig. 2.) This waviness of grain is not brought out so well if the cut is made tangentially. In figured stumps or "butt" wood the curl is along the surface of the trunk, and the cross-figured effect is here obtained by slicing along the surface. (Pls. VIII and IX.)

Highly figured veneer cut from burls, crotches, and stumps has a great variety of figure. (Pl. X, figs. 1 and 2.) Burls are particularly highly figured with islets and bird's-eye effects. Burls from very old trees often have a mottled appearance on a glossy dark groundwork, ranging from almost jet black to lighter shades of brown or chocolate color. This gives them an extravagant value. Such highly figured veneer is sometimes marketed under the names of "French burl" and "Circassian walnut."

Prices of veneer.—The prices given in Table 20 prevailed in the summer of 1919 for different kinds of walnut veneer. There is considerable range in price within some classes because the veneer itself differs greatly in quality and figure.

TABLE 20.

Sap and defective _____cents per square foot__	$\frac{1}{4}$ to	$\frac{3}{4}$
Plain rotary_____do____	$\frac{3}{4}$ to	1
Straight sliced, plain_____do____	1 to	$1\frac{1}{2}$
Straight sliced, cross figured_____do____	$1\frac{1}{2}$ to	$2\frac{1}{2}$
Highly figured (including stump wood) _____do____	3 to 20	
Burl wood_____do____	3 to 30	

Some manufacturers who turn out high grades of walnut veneer got an average of $2\frac{1}{2}$ cents a square foot for their product. The average value, derived from reports to the census for 1904, was $14.70 a thousand square feet, or nearly $1\frac{1}{2}$ cents a square foot.

GRADES AND PRICES OF VENEER LOGS.

Walnut is a timber so variable in quality that veneer makers find it difficult to draw up any hard-and-fast rules that will indicate the value of any particular log. They take the view that each log must be judged on its own peculiar merits, with reference to its size, the amount of sapwood, the straightness and form of log, the number, size, and position of defects, and, particularly, the kind and amount of figure in each log.

Veneer manufacturers do not generally publish any prices for their logs, for they claim that the prices depend on the quality of

each log and the general run of the lot. The company's
usually proposes a lump sum after he has gone over the log

Some veneer companies buy both plain and figured lo;
the plain ones into lumber. Others buy only figured 1
firms will take logs that are at least fairly clear and 16
over in diameter at the small end, or as small as 14 inch
is a sufficiently large portion of clear heartwood, or if
figured. They prefer logs that are 18 inches and up ar
defects. Logs having more than a 2-inch ring of sapwo
so well adapted for making veneer unless they are very l;

Merchantable stump or "butt" wood should be at leas
in diameter at the small end, and from 30 to 42 inches long
to the specifications of different buyers. Some manufa
lengths of 30 and 36 inches to correspond with the stan
sizes. Figured stumps usually bring a price of $100 to $.
sand board feet, depending on size and figure.

Veneer logs should have a minimum length of a li!
feet. Some mills buy 6-foot logs, and some accept 4½-f;
they are of exceptional size and quality. During the fi
1919 the price of walnut veneer logs ranged from $75 to $
sand board feet, log scale, depending on size and quality.

Walnut burls are very high in price, and, on accou!
irregular form, are usually sold by the pound. Before t
general range in price was 10 to 15 cents. Genuine bu!
very scarce.

Two somewhat common grades for walnut veneer logs
lows: No. 1 logs, which may have one or two sound knots
are 10 feet or over in length, but must be free from worm
pecks, and shakes; and No. 2 logs, which must have a c
of at least 43 inches.

WASTE.

The waste in the manufacture of walnut veneer is ma
form of the loss that results from trimming down the
ciently for a sheet of merchantable veneer to be cut; the "
or core, left after cutting off as much veneer as possible;
trimmed out of the veneer, including pith center and sap
in the case of dimension veneer cut from rotary stock, th
cutting to size.

The only data available on the amount of waste in difl
esses are those derived from calculating the yield of
representative logs, as given in the section on "Produc;
proportions of waste in different processes, according t;

FIG. I.—A PIECE OF STRIPED WALNUT VENEER.

Sliced on the quarter either by the straight-sliced process or by stay-log rotary cutting from the heartwood side of the half log.

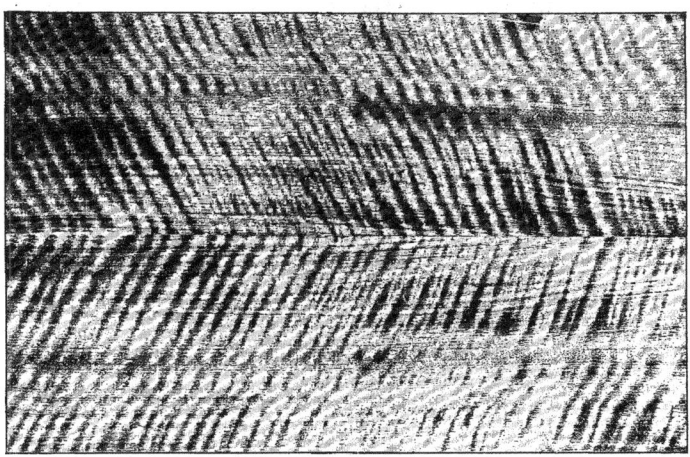

FIG. 2.—PANEL COMPOSED OF TWO MATCHED SHEETS OF CROSS-FIGURED WALNUT VENEER.

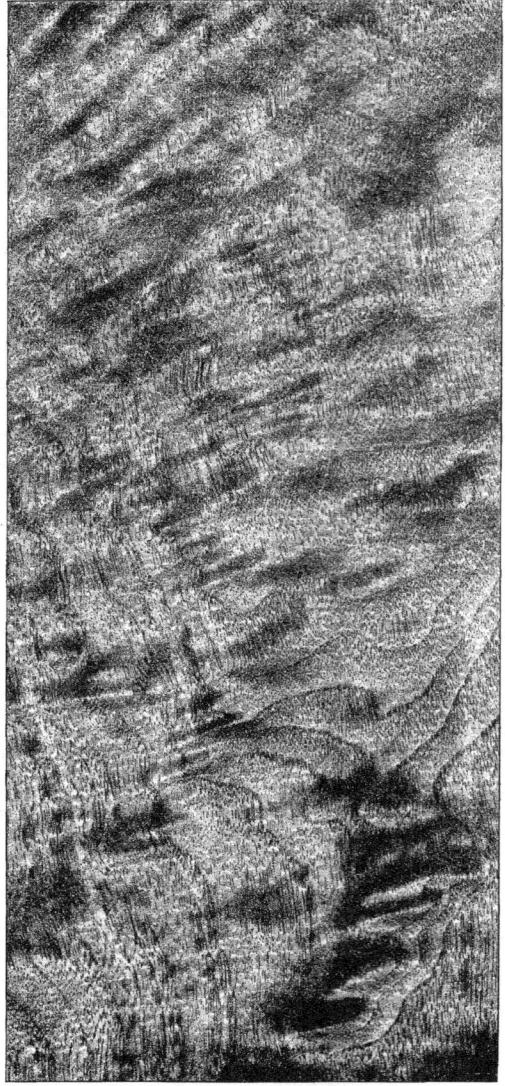

A PIECE OF FIGURED WALNUT "BUTT" WOOD VENEER.

Produced by slicing in the stay-log rotary process from the outside
of the log—that is, approximately in the direction of the annual-
growth rings.

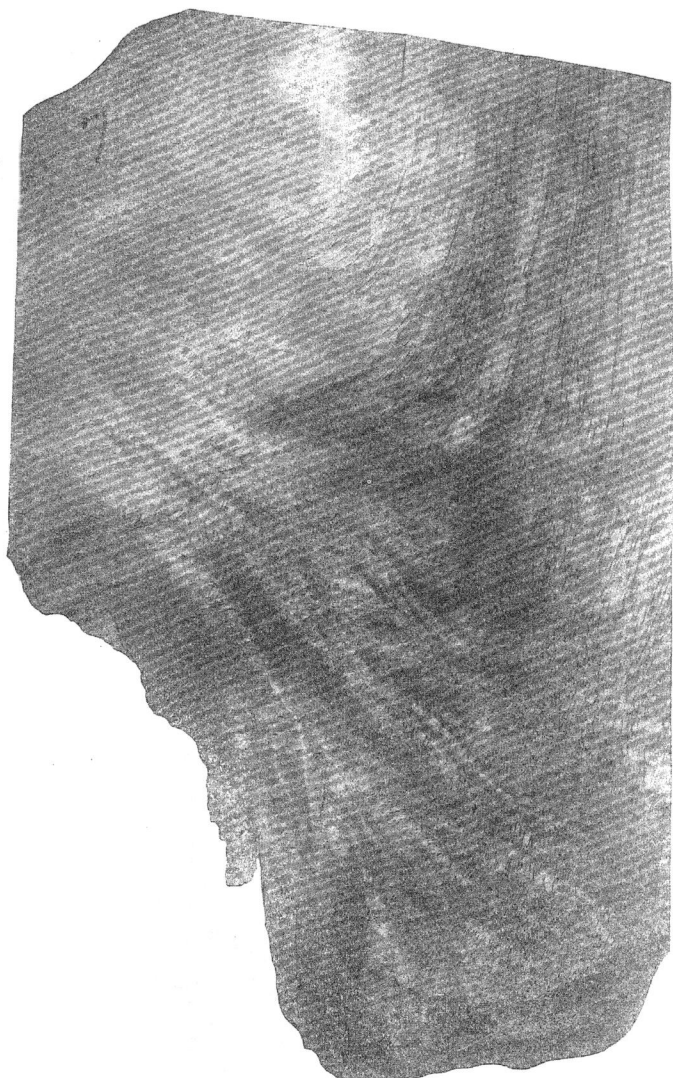

SMALL SHEET OF FIGURED "BUTT" WOOD VENEER AS IT COMES FROM
THE SLICER.

The light-colored wood is sapwood.   The figure is in that part where the rings of growth bend
out toward the root spurs.

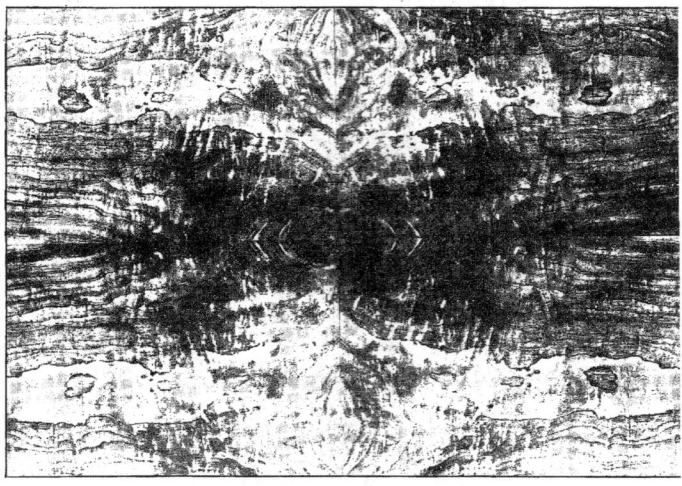

FIG. 1.—PANEL COMPOSED OF FOUR MATCHED SHEETS OF FIGURED WALNUT
VENEER.

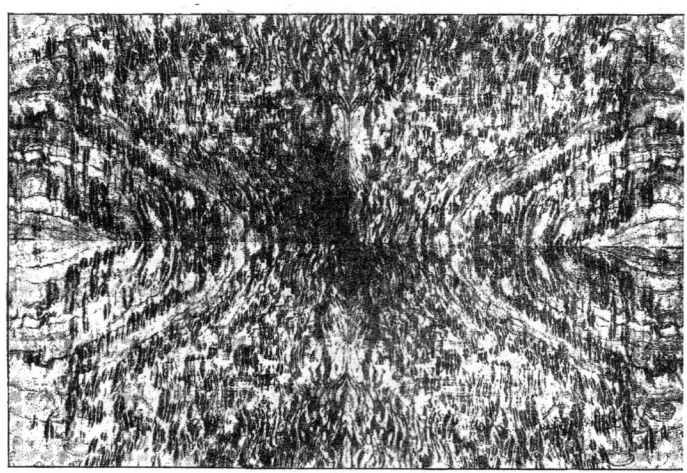

FIG. 2.—PANEL COMPOSED OF FOUR MATCHED SHEETS OF HIGHLY FIGURED
"BUTT" WOOD VENEER.

culations, are given in Table 21. The amount of waste in the industry as a whole may be approximated by converting into terms of veneer the total quantity of logs used for veneer manufacture, and comparing this amount with the actual yield according to the reports of veneer manufacturers. If the average log is assumed to be 20 inches in diameter there is about 733 square feet of veneer one twenty-eighth inch thick and 16 board feet to each linear foot of log, or approximately 46 square feet of veneer to each board foot of log. If, according to figures on the production of walnut veneer for 1917, 20 square feet of veneer is produced for each board foot of log, 43½ per cent of the log is veneer stock, and 56½ per cent is waste. As about 50 per cent of the total output of walnut veneer is straight sliced, 25 per cent straight rotary, and 25 per cent stay-log rotary, a weighted average of the percentages of waste shown in Table 21 gives a general average of 54 per cent for the industry. This corresponds closely with the general average of 56½ per cent, as determined from the manufacturers' reports.

TABLE 21.—*Calculated percentages of waste in the manufacture of walnut veneer by different methods.*

Method.	Diameter of representative log.	Entire volume of log, in terms of veneer, per linear foot of log	Amount of veneer obtained per linear foot of log.	Waste.
	Inches.	*Square feet.*	*Square feet.*	*Per cent.*
Rotary proper	18	594	235	60
Rotary, stay-log	24	[1] 528	[1] 250	52
Straight-slice	20	733	353	52
Sawed	20	524	126	76

[1] Half log.

From the standpoint of utilization there are three general classes of waste in veneer manufacture: Trimmings from logs, flitches, and veneer sheets; pieces such as "dog boards" and cores that are left after cutting the veneer; and defective material, including sapwood. The first class of waste is useful only for fuel and is generally disposed of in that way. "Dog boards" from straight-sliced veneer, if they are not too defective, are often resawed into boards; if they are figured, valuable stock may be secured from them. The "dog board" of the stay-log rotary process, on account of the stay-bolt holes, is generally useful for fuel only. Cores are usually 3 or 4 inches in diameter and are often resawed into dimension stock if they are not too defective. Such dimension material shortly after the war often sold for $50 to $80 a thousand board feet at furniture factories. Veneer cores have been used for porch pillars, but they are

usually too defective for this purpose and, moreover, t
demand for a perfectly straight and plain pillar. The
not generally suitable for rollers because the wood is toc
manufacturers use them for fuel.

Defective and sapwood veneer is often used for fue
the small demand for such stock. Some manufacturer
often they can get only one-eighth cent a square foot for
it is not profitably marketed at this price. It is used :
pianos, bureaus, and mirrors, and for drawer bottoms.
factories prefer to buy yellow poplar or some other ch
for such purposes because the use of the larger sizes in
to be had involves less work and a lower cost for the labo

Some manufacturers utilize their logs very closely
straight rotary veneer. They stop the slicing before th
small, and then either saw or straight slice it. In this
the heartwood is wasted.

USES.

Walnut veneer is used mainly in dining and bedroo
musical instruments (principally pianos and phonog
cabinetwork in general. It is used, as a rule, in the pan
smaller pieces, such as corner posts, being made solid
manufacturers may either make their own panels or buy
to size from panel manufacturers.

TIES.

Walnut makes a satisfactory tie because of its dura
used untreated by the railroads. Locust, black walnu
oak are generally considered the best tie woods and c
highest prices.

There is a considerable quantity of small and def
in the course of logging walnut, which may be conver
at a profit. Ties are usually 6 by 7, 6 by 8, 7 by 8, or '
in cross section and 8 or 8½ feet in length. A 12-inch
straight and not too defective, may be cut into a 7 by
tie. A 10-inch log will make a 6 by 8 tie if it is not
cut the log down on account of a defect. Top logs a:
the limbs of walnut are liable to be so crooked that t
waste in cutting up such material. Ties as small as ℓ
are sawed for use on sidings and on trolley lines.

The prices paid for walnut ties generally amount
same as the market value of cull walnut lumber. I
therefore, a question with the manufacturers whether it

to-turn this kind of stock into ties. There is, however, a larger percentage of overrun in sawing into ties, and for this reason the manufacture of ties is often profitable, especially if the mill is in a region where the best prices are paid. Defective ties are sometimes cut into mine caps about 6 inches thick if there is a demand for such material. Wedges to be used with the caps are also sawed out of waste walnut.

POSTS.

Close utilization may be effected by sawing small and defective walnut into fence posts. Although it is not so durable as locust and some other woods, walnut is suitable for posts and is in demand for this purpose. A common size for posts is 5 by 5 inches at the bottom and 2 by 5 inches at the top. This manner of sawing is advantageous, because the yield is greater than it would be if the posts were of the same size throughout.

SECONDARY INDUSTRIES.

Walnut is manufactured by factories mainly into three classes of products—cabinetwork in general, interior finish, and firearms. Under cabinetwork are included furniture, fixtures, chairs, cabinets and cases for musical instruments and sewing machines, and caskets. Inside finish includes products of the planing mill, doors, and panels for stores, offices, and railway cars. Gun and rifle stocks and pistol grips are the parts made for firearms. Of minor importance are such small articles as handles of various kinds and fancy boxes.

Table 22 gives the annual consumption of walnut, as reported by factories and grouped according to classes of products. These figures apply to the years 1909 to 1913 and represent the pre-war consumption. There has probably been an increase over these figures in the use of walnut for general cabinetwork, on account of the great recent demand for walnut furniture. This increase in the use of walnut for furniture has been largely offset by the greatly lessened demand for certain kinds of cabinetwork, such as sewing-machine cabinets, which were made almost entirely for supplying the foreign trade. In other classes of products lessened foreign demand is also generally more than balanced by an increased use of similar products at home. It is believed, therefore, that the figures shown in the table are somewhat representative of the importance at the present time of the different industries in walnut utilization. The figures on the cost of material are of value only for the purpose of comparison.

TABLE 22.—*Reported annual factory consumption, and cost of black walnut, by industries.*[1]

Industry.	Quantity used annually.		Average cost per 1,000 feet.	Total cost f. o. b. factory.
	Feet board measure.	Per cent.		
General cabinet work [2]	10,147,407	42.30	$80.66	$818,508.77
Instruments, musical	4,991,808	20.81	81.31	405,898.95
Planing-mill products, sash, doors, blinds, and general millwork	4,606,420	19.20	76.55	352,618.50
Firearms	1,700,135	7.09	61.53	104,601.00
Caskets and coffins	474,000	1.98	106.66	50,557.00
Machinery and apparatus, electrical	452,600	1.89	79.53	35,994.00
Vehicles and vehicle parts	390,450	1.63	91.44	35,702.00
Chairs and chair stock	263,200	1.10	76.73	20,196.00
Car construction	256,181	1.07	87.63	22,450.00
Boxes	163,250	.68	39.27	6,411.00
Frames and molding, picture	125,004	.52	117.76	14,721.00
Instruments, professional and scientific	71,200	.30	64.72	4,608.00
Clocks	58,527	.24	65.22	3,817.00
Bungs and faucets	56,000	.23	31.04	1,738.00
Sporting and athletic goods	41,000	.17	92.93	3,810.00
Woodenware, novelties, and dairymen's, poulterers', and apiarists' supplies	38,547	.16	96.29	3,711.50
Handles	29,050	.12	45.65	1,326.00
Brushes	26,700	.11	77.15	3,060.00
Patterns and flasks	21,500	.09	57.44	1,235.00
Laundry appliances	20,000	.08	90.00	1,800.00
Whips, canes, and umbrella sticks	20,000	.08	51.00	1,020.00
Machine construction	10,817	.05	40.40	437.00
Plumbers' woodwork	10,300	.04	78.64	810.00
Agricultural implements	8,000	.03	16.50	132.00
Ship and boat building	3,750	.02	120.80	453.00
Rollers, shade and map	2,000	.01	110.00	220.00
Carpet sweepers	500	(3)	200.00	100.00
Total	23,988,346	100.00	78.99	1,894,935.72

[1] Data collected by the Forest Service during the period from 1909 to 1913, inclusive.
[2] Includes furniture, fixtures, and cabinets for sewing machines.
[3] Less than one one-hundredth of 1 per cent.

Table 23 gives the same data by States. Ohio, Indiana, Illinois, and Kentucky are the States that have comparatively large amounts of walnut available and that use large amounts in manufacturing finished products. The States of New York and Michigan, which have to go farther for their raw material, also use considerable quantities in manufacturing:

TABLE 23.—*Reported annual consumption of black walnut in factories, by States.*[1]

State.	Quantity used annually, feet board measure.	State.	Quantity used annually, feet board measure.
Indiana	5,538,115	West Virginia	49,500
Illinois	4,340,350	Rhode Island	40,300
Ohio	2,920,040	Kansas	26,500
New York	2,629,128	District of Columbia	26,000
Michigan	1,473,128	Iowa	11,500
Kentucky	1,463,500	South Dakota	10,500
Massachusetts	874,250	South Carolina	10,000
Pennsylvania	782,615	New Hampshire	9,000
Connecticut	648,650	Georgia	7,000
North Carolina	594,000	Mississippi	3,000
Maryland	548,500	Maine	2,000
Tennessee	520,000	Oklahoma	2,000
New Jersey	301,850	Delaware	1,948
Virginia	277,300	Oregon	1,900
Minnesota	161,639	Nebraska	1,252
Vermont	141,042	Washington	1,000
Missouri	140,573	Louisiana	500
Texas	135,000	Montana	250
California	112,916	Colorado	100
Alabama	62,500		
Wisconsin	62,000	Total	23,988,346
Arkansas	55,000		

[1] Data collected by the Forest Service during the period from 1909 to 1913, inclusive.

FURNITURE.

The extensive use of walnut for furniture dates back to the latter part of the seventeenth century, when walnut furniture replaced oak in Europe. England was the first to appreciate the value of American walnut, and it was used there at that time and often preferred to the English or Circassian walnut of Europe. Elaborately carved pieces, often with highly figured veneer, were well liked. Exports to England reached fair proportions by the end of this period, and large shipments for that purpose have gone to European countries ever since. Walnut furniture (including chairs and chests of drawers) was made in New England in the latter part of the seventeenth century, and at about the same time it was used in Virginia. In the eighteenth century wild cherry and walnut were the principal native cabinet woods. During the first half of the eighteenth century much furniture was made of walnut in eastern Pennsylvania and New Jersey; probably the best was made in and near Philadelphia. The walnut grown in this region had a uniformly dark and rich color which was well liked. Mahogany also was much used. The "lowboy," a very low dresser with one or two drawers, and the "highboy," a dresser of six or seven drawers, were characteristic pieces of furniture at that time.

In the latter part of the eighteenth century walnut as a furniture wood went out of fashion in England. During the first half of the nineteenth century, however, walnut was utilized in large quantities for furniture in this country. The source of supply of the timber was now farther west than the region of supply during the eighteenth century, and large amounts were obtained from Ohio and Indiana for shipment to eastern factories, mainly in Philadelphia, New York, and Boston, where furniture of the better quality was produced. Veneer was much used at that time. During the third quarter of the nineteenth century heavy, cumbersome walnut furniture of grotesque and ungainly patterns came into vogue in this country. The dark stain with which the wood was generally covered gave it a uniformly dull, lifeless appearance, which, together with the unattractiveness of these styles, resulted in so discrediting the wood that by the latter part of the nineteenth century it became extremely unpopular. Its employment in large quantities during the earlier part of the nineteenth century served to reduce greatly the best of the available supply in eastern United States, and that fact in time helped to discourage its use.

During the past several years there has been a revival in the demand for walnut furniture in this country. This is mainly because of the adoption of lighter finishes and figured effects, which are in contrast with the dark, somber finishes in earlier use, and because of the obtaining of new supplies of the wood. On account of the high price of oak and the relative scarcity of mahogany that resulted from restricted imports during the war, walnut has recently displaced these woods to a large extent for furniture.

There are several reasons for the high value placed upon walnut as a cabinet wood. It has good seasoning properties, will hold its shape well, and will not deteriorate after it is properly seasoned; it has an attractive appearance, may be polished to a smooth surface, and will take stains and varnishes very well; it may be cut easily with tools, and is thus adapted to carving and veneer making; it may be glued with very satisfactory results; it possesses moderate strength and weight.

To a degree equaled by few other woods walnut possesses all the different qualities that are essential to a first-class cabinet wood. Greater strength would be of advantage, but this would involve greater weight and greater hardness, and the greater hardness would interfere with its being easily worked with tools.

The principal articles of furniture made of walnut are dining-room and bedroom suites. Dining-room tables of walnut are much in demand, because they are very serviceable and do not show to the extent to which some other woods do the hard usage to which such tables are subjected. Bookcases, desks, living-room tables, and many other pieces are commonly made of walnut. Recently, on account of its serviceability, there has been a considerable demand for office furniture of walnut.

There are three general classes of furniture—that made along plain lines and of figured wood; that characterized by elaborate design and made almost altogether of plain wood; and cheaper grades of furniture, simple in form and of plain wood.

The greatest demand now is for walnut furniture of plain lines and finished to show the natural figure of the wood. Much plain walnut furniture is made, but usually some figured wood is employed for the most conspicuous parts. Large-figured effects in walnut are not so popular now as formerly. The highest class of walnut furniture generally has stripe and cross figure, and often some crotch and burl-wood pieces. Some large, heavy walnut furniture of antique design, usually with large carvings, is also made. These pieces are for large rooms of expensively furnished houses, and are generally copied after the early-period designs of walnut furniture.

Dining-room tables of walnut are manufactured in large numbers. They are generally finished in plain wood, because the only conspicuous part is the top, and this is often kept covered. Table tops are generally made of three or five plies, with a core of solid wood and one or two sheets of veneer on either side of the core. Occasionally table tops are made with the upper ply of sawed veneer one-sixteenth or one-eighth inch thick. This will stand more wear than the thinner sliced veneer if hard usage is involved. The top may also have a small bent rim of walnut along the edge to cover the core. Table rims are usually made of three or four plies, each about one-fourth inch thick. These may be of walnut or covered over with walnut veneer.

Buffet and serving-table tops are made of three or five plies. They may be plain, but more often they have stripe and cross figure. Doors and drawer fronts of buffets and serving tables are also made of three or five plies and they generally show some figure. Small drawer fronts are often of highly figured crotch or burl. The ends of such pieces are generally of plain wood, except in very expensive stock. Doors in furniture of high grade have a ply of walnut veneer on the back and an edge of walnut.

Plain rotary-cut walnut veneer is used also for drawer sides and bottoms. China closets are usually made of plain wood. The shelves are more often made of some cheaper wood with the front edge of walnut veneer.

In bedroom furniture the same general style of finish is used. Built-up tops may be plain, but more often they have some figure. Drawer fronts and panels are made of three or five plies, and, if they are conspicuously placed, figured effects are often made use of, including stump wood and burl.

Legs, corner posts, and mirror frames are to a very large extent made of solid pieces of other woods, except in the manufacture of the most highly priced furniture. In very expensive pieces such parts as the corner posts are veneered in order to secure the desired figure. In low-priced walnut furniture the ends and other inconspicuous parts are entirely of less expensive woods.

The best panels in common use are made of five plies. The core is of some such wood as oak, quarter-sawed red gum, birch, chestnut, basswood, or yellow poplar. This should be constructed of narrow pieces to prevent warping, and the two plies on either side should be so laid that the grain in the ply next to the core is at right angles to that of the outside ply and that of the core. This method makes a strong panel and minimizes the effects of shrinking and swelling. A small piece of highly figured veneer, usually stump wood, crotch, or burl, is often placed upon the center of a large panel of plain or striped wood. This is called an "overlay" and is popular at the present time. An "overlay" of walnut burl or crotch is sometimes used on mahogany furniture. It is stained to match the mahogany panel and is regarded as adding much to the attractive appearance of the mahogany. Maple burl is sometimes used as an "overlay" panel with walnut.

e. A tendency is now observable, however, towar
carvings made of genuine wood. These carving
ade by machinery and at a lower cost than whe

are now more nearly like the natural color of th
rom light to dark brown. A medium light-brow
a figure of darker streaks is considered especiall
light and very dark brown finishes are not so pleas
ws to better advantage when rubbed to a dull finis
a high polish. These dull finishes are popular a

argest amount of walnut used for furniture is i
er, for in a very large part of this furniture th
ed) parts are of some other wood. All kinds o
e used in furniture, the highest grade largely de
tripe, cross figure (often with rippled and "fiddle
ured stump wood, crotch, and burl. A large amoun
s used. Rotary veneer that is unsuited for outsid
es used for sides and bottoms of drawers and i
e it is not conspicuous.
buy much of their walnut cut to the approximat
e finished pieces. This applies particularly to di
Common sizes purchased are 2 by 2, 2½ by 2½, an
inches long, and used largely for corner posts an
ufacturers consider that the purchase of this stoc
usand board feet, means a saving to them in bot
nery in comparison with the cost of working it u
ther manufacturers find that, if they have to dr
it is not then perfectly clear and first class in ever
effected, on account of the waste involved. One o
ctions to the purchase of dimension stock for fui
re are so many different and special sizes used, it .
able to have them cut at the sawmill. Moreove:
re change frequently and with resultant changes i
ifferent pieces.
ufacturers are, therefore, purchasing more walnt
ing it to the desired sizes. No. 1 common is tl
ound most advantageous. Some factories purchas
onds grade also, and others get No. 2 common an
ll their stock from this combination of grades. Th
cknesses used are 4/4, 5/4, 6/4, and 8/4.

Furniture factories generally buy steamed walnut lumber in order that the sapwood as well as the heartwood may be used. Some factories make a practice in manufacture of so placing squares and other solid walnut pieces that only the heartwood is exposed to the outside.

The principal waste in furniture manufacture is in the making of panels from the veneer sheets. Panel manufacturers estimate that there is about 50 per cent waste in rotary and stay-log veneer, and 60 per cent in straight sliced. If the veneer sheets are cut at the veneer mill to the approximate size of the panel, or sliced from small clear blocks to the required size, the waste in veneer is much less. In the latter case, it is figured that the waste in veneer ranges between 10 and 20 per cent, with an average of 15 per cent.

There should be less waste in solid stock if the dimension sizes are purchased than if they are cut from lumber. Waste in dimension material may come from stock that is poor because of a lack of proper or sufficient seasoning or because of improper handling. Scant sizes, as well as knots and other defects, are also the cause of waste in this material; or, loss may result from a change in the size required, after the stock has been purchased. The waste of high-grade dimension stock is, of course, a much more serious matter to the factory than the waste of a like amount of No. 1 common lumber from which it is generally sawed by the furniture makers. The use of lumber instead of dimension stock requires, of course, the shipment of defective material which would have been cut out at the mill; but this is preferable to the waste of dimension stock. The purchase of standard sizes of clear dimension material should be profitable to the furniture manufacturer. The amount of waste in the use of a certain grade of lumber depends on how advantageously the required sizes may be cut out. The greater the number of sizes to be cut, the less the amount of waste should be.

The most common substitute for walnut in furniture manufacture is red gum. It is a general practice to utilize red-gum wood finished in imitation of walnut for corner posts, legs, mirror frames, and, in fact, for practically all but the veneered parts. The reason for this has been that gum was a lower-priced wood than walnut. On account of the recent rapid rise in the price of red gum, however, there is now relatively less difference in cost. The same styles of furniture are generally made in either walnut or mahogany, and the gum may be finished in imitation of either wood. This is obviously a distinct advantage to the furniture manufacturer. Birch also is used in the same way. On account of the difference in the figure or grain, neither of these woods has the same appearance as the walnut, even when it is stained to match the color. Consequently, in making the highest class of walnut furniture, walnut wood is utilized for all outside work. Some factories finish their best pieces with walnut on the edges and backs of doors and on the inside of drawers.

The quarter-sawed plain heartwood of red gum is considered most desirable as a substitute for walnut, because it is not so liable to warp as the plain sawed, and the heartwood is nearer the natural color of walnut. The sapwood is objectionable because of the lighter color, and the figured wood is not so suitable because it does not match so well the appearance of the walnut. Wood with dark streaks is objectionable for this reason.

As a matter of fact, walnut is a suitable wood for the solid pieces in furniture, and there is no advantage other than that of lower cost to be gained by the use of another wood, and the substitution is liable to make the piece less attractive.

Black walnut is sometimes used in the form of veneer to imitate Circassian walnut. Only pieces with unusually dark, distinct streaks running through them are suitable, such wood being sometimes found in the extreme southwestern portion of its range. Some very pleasing effects are obtained from this kind of wood, but the usual plain or figured walnut is unsuitable.

Plastic material colored to resemble walnut is quite often used to imitate the carved walnut wood. These imitation carvings are pressed to shape in a mold that is usually made from the genuine wood carving and so successfully simulates the pores of the wood that a resemblance to walnut wood is produced. Such imitation carvings, on account of their uniform coloring, are apt to have a dull, lifeless appearance and do not match well the genuine wood. These composition carvings are often overdone in detail and are generally distinguishable from the wood carvings, which are considered more attractive and in better taste.

MUSICAL INSTRUMENTS.

Walnut is well suited for the manufacture of cases for musical instruments because of those characteristics that make it so valuable as a cabinet wood, namely, its good seasoning and working qualities, its adaptability to panelwork, and its fine appearance when finished.

In this industry its greatest use at the present time is for phonograph cabinets. The solid pieces used for legs, corner posts, and crosspieces are of plain walnut; panels are usually of figured veneer, the striped wood being popular. The cabinets are usually finished in a light shade, but they may also be given a dull, dark wax finish in antique style to match old walnut furniture. Lumber about 1¼ inches thick of the Nos. 1 and 2 common grades is used to a large extent for these cabinets. The lumber manufacturer sometimes finds it advantageous to make these cabinets in conjunction with the sawmill. In this way a very close utilization is effected, and much small-sized and low-grade lumber may be made use of. Mahogany and walnut are sometimes used interchangeably in the manufacture of these cabinets, a light stain being used to give a walnut finish and a dark stain to give a mahogany finish. By this method one wood may be used for the solid parts and the other for the panels, walnut being generally used for the former and mahogany veneer for the latter. A cabinet made in that way does not give so good an appearance as if all walnut or all mahogany had been used. Moreover, each wood should be given a finish particularly suited to it.

Piano cases are sometimes finished in walnut. There was formerly a good demand in Europe for walnut-finished pianos, but this business was interrupted by the late war. There has recently been a large demand from Australia, Mexico, and South America for pianos finished in walnut. Exports to these countries were, in fact, increased by the war, because the supply of German-made pianos was cut off. The United States is the largest manufacturer of pianos; before the war Germany was second, and England third. Figured walnut is now largely used for walnut piano cases. The figured "butt" or stump wood is quite generally used to form a panel for the front. The figured ends are matched together in the middle, and the figured wood generally runs out into plain wood on either side. Walnut cases are sometimes given a very light finish, resembling maple. The different streaks and shadings in the figured walnut are regarded as giving more character to the wood than the figured maple does. Walnut is sometimes used for the core wood on which the veneer is placed, because under varying moisture conditions it shrinks, swells, and warps very little.

Piano benches are made of walnut to match the finish of the piano. The seat is usually a panel of figured veneer which is veneered with walnut on the edges also, in order to give the appearance of solid walnut.

Walnut was formerly much used in the manufacture of reed organs, but very few of these instruments are now made. The proper finish of a pipe organ depends entirely upon the finish of the woodwork of the room in which it is to be placed, and the two should be in harmony.

PLANING-MILL PRODUCTS, SASH, DOORS, BLINDS, AND GENERAL MILLWORK.

Black walnut is manufactured into many products that go to make up the finish of houses, offices, and stores. A large proportion consists of planing-mill products, such as flooring, ceiling, molding, baseboards, and those other dressed and matched materials that are considered finished when they leave the planer. Walnut was formerly much used for borders and designs in floors laid mainly in other

the light-colored woods, oak and maple. Walnut
in the form of panels for inside finish, especially
c buildings where fancy figured effects are in den
and rail stock are sometimes made of plain sawed
nth to one-eighth inch thick. This thickness of ve
er wear than can be obtained from the thinner sl
loor panels are of figured sliced stock. Walnut is v
hese uses, because it polishes to a smooth, even su
s and other wood finishes well, and has a wide rang
s in the finished state. Much of this class of mate
d in former years because of the popularity of w
reign countries. The demand in this country has
er in recent years than formerly.

SEWING MACHINES.

lnut has been used in very large amounts for sew
ets on account of its good qualities as a cabinet w
of its fine appearance, which is very well liked abro
de use of very largely. The cabinet type of sewing
1 the working parts may be entirely inclosed, is mos
ed in walnut. Relatively small amounts have been u
iis purpose, because exportations have been largely
lemand for walnut-finished cabinets in this coun

FIREARMS.

ick walnut is particularly suitable for the manufac
s. The properties fitting it for this use are as fo
only in a slight degree to warp and check, and s
amount of shrinking and swelling after it has be
ied; it is easy to work with tools to its final shape;
parts with little wear; it possesses a uniformity
ness of texture which render it easily gripped and
; it has a good degree of strength without excessiv
tand considerable shock without injury; on accoun
it is attractive in appearance and is not easily soiled
s important that a wood used for gunstocks should
to insure the metal parts fitting satisfactorily.
cularly objectionable in the stock of rifles (for exa
in the Army) in which the barrel is incased in woo
y its entire length, because the warping of the wo
ring the barrel out of a straight line, and thus int
curate shooting of the rifle. Cross grain is, therefor

able, for it is said that the heating of the rifle barrel will cause sufficient warping to make the gun shoot inaccurately. Figured walnut is highly prized in the butts of sporting rifles on account of its attractive appearance. Such stocks must be finished by hand, however, because the machine tool will follow the grain of the wood, inaccurate cutting of the stock will result, and the metal parts will not fit accurately. Army-rifle stocks are manufactured by very specialized machinery. The rifle blank (Pl. XI, fig. 1) is subjected to between 40 and 50 different machine operations; it is then dipped in stain; the excess stain is rubbed off; and the metal parts are fitted to it. Sapwood is used with the heartwood without discrimination. American walnut was the standard gunstock wood in the United States during the late European war, and was also used extensively by England and other European countries.

In 1861 the subject of stocks for guns was formally discussed at a convention of gunsmiths at Atlanta, Ga. The consensus of opinion among those present was that black walnut was superior to all other woods for muskets; after walnut, maple was to be preferred, and persimmon was ranked third. It was then claimed that no artificial seasoning would suffice, and that gunstock material should be air-dried for 20 years. Walnut for gunstocks was, therefore, procured both in the North and South by taking floors, beams, and joists out of old barns and mills in which some of the walnut had been seasoning for a quarter or half of a century, and also by purchasing miles of fence rails. Modern methods of kiln drying the wood have largely taken the place of air seasoning, and with much more satisfactory results. Black-walnut stocks are now dried from the green state in special kilns in about 60 days. The modern rifle and shotgun require much less wood for the stock than was used by the old-style long musket, which was incased in wood nearly its entire length. Gunstock blanks for the United States Army rifle are clear cuttings, approximately 4 feet in length, made from $2\frac{1}{2}$-inch flitches, sawed from the log, and equivalent to a little better than the No. 2 common grade.

Although black walnut is the best wood for this use, yellow birch has been found to be an excellent substitute. Yellow birch is about equal to black walnut in weight, strength, and toughness, but is not quite so good in holding its shape, shrinks more, and is more apt to be cross-grained. It is light in color, but may be readily stained. Gunstock manufacturers report that birch, when properly seasoned, makes as good a stock as black walnut. Birch is more difficult to "machine," however; the production is slower; and there is more waste in the "machining" operation than with walnut. Birch timber is quite often wavy and cross-grained, and that kind of stock is unsuited for the manufacture of gunstocks by machine process. There is also some waste in "machining" walnut stocks, but this is, for the most part, because of internal defects that are not visible on the surface of the blank. Red gum is a suitable wood for small rifles, but not for long army rifles, on account of its tendency to warp and twist.

A considerable amount of walnut is used in the manufacture of air rifles, chiefly in Michigan. Manufacturers of air rifles do not require such thick material as is used for the military rifle. The wooden stock of the air rifle usually consists of a comparatively small piece forming only the butt. (Pl. XI, fig. 2.) Air-rifle factories can, therefore, utilize fairly low-grade material by cutting out the defects. They generally use No. 1 and No. 2 common grades, 1 inch in thickness. A special grade of "shorts" is sometimes made use of. This grade consists of pieces of good quality, the length of which is less than is allowable in the upper grades. Air-rifle manufacturers can utilize this stock very closely on account of the small sizes used. Several different models are usually made, and the maximum size of the stock is about 3 to 4 inches in width by 14 inches in length in the rough. The dark-colored heartwood of black walnut is well liked for the small rifle, and the makers must either use heartwood entirely or stain the sapwood to match. Black walnut also holds screws well and is, therefore, particularly desirable for the small gun, in which the stock is a very short piece and is attached to the metal part by a few screws. Other woods also, particularly red gum, are used for air rifles and small-cartridge rifles, and are stained to resemble walnut. There is some objection to the gum on account of its warping and because there is a tendency for the screws to become loose in it. The cartridge rifle is made from lumber $1\frac{1}{2}$ to 2 inches in thickness. A considerable quantity of walnut is used for shotgun butts also (Pl. XI, fig. 3), for which short pieces and such waste material as veneer cores may be utilized. Much high-grade walnut is used for pistol grips, although the individual revolver requires only a small piece. European walnut (Circassian walnut, which was long ago naturalized in Europe) has been used for gunstock material in European countries for many years. This is a satisfactory wood, but the lack of a sufficient supply has necessitated a large use of the American walnut in recent years.

FIXTURES.

Black walnut is utilized for bank, office, and store fixtures, in which it shows to good advantage in broad panels on account of its attractive color and figure. It is usually employed only for the exterior parts of fixtures and other cabinetwork. It is much used for showcases, for large cabinets in drug stores, for standing desks in banks, for counters, and for bars. On account of its dark color, black walnut is popular for the interior woodwork of churches and lodge rooms, and for altars, pews, and Bible stands.

CASKETS AND COFFINS.

Less than 2 per cent of the total amount of black walnut used annually was reported as being employed in the casket and coffin industry. Its value for this use consists in its rich and somber appearance, and in its relative freedom from decay and the effects of moisture. It is utilized principally for high-priced caskets, the natural wood being highly polished and attractively finished, and the most expensive cases being richly carved. Oak and mahogany are much more used, however, than walnut. By far the greater number of caskets and coffins are made of some cheap wood like low-grade chestnut and covered with cloth. Coffins are not so much employed as they were formerly. Black walnut for many years was the principal coffin wood and is still used for the better grades. Black-walnut coffins are often made by hand by cabinetmakers who supply the local trade in small towns where the wood is available. The use of black walnut at the present time for caskets and coffins is largely a matter of custom or sentiment. It is restricted for the most part to regions where there is a good supply of high-grade walnut and is dependent on a personal preference for the wood.

In 1912 Pennsylvania reported the use for burial cases of over 200,000 board feet of walnut annually, and Kentucky reported one-half this amount. Other States reported small quantities. A high grade of black walnut was used for manufacture into these products.

ELECTRICAL MACHINERY AND APPARATUS.

Black walnut constitutes a large proportion of the wooden parts of telephone outfits and of other electrical apparatus. It is much used for base blocks for electrical appliances and for boxes to hold such equipment. Its dark color and excellent working qualities adapt it for these uses. It is used also to a small extent for subscribers' telephone sets, mostly of the wall kind, where it is wanted to match the woodwork of the room. The piece that goes against the wall and the bell box are the wooden parts. Black walnut is not essential for this use, however, for other woods could be substituted with the same effect. American walnut is in demand for public telephone booths in Europe, particularly where the inside of the room is finished in walnut.

VEHICLES AND VEHICLE PARTS.

The use of walnut in this industry is confined almost entirely to automobiles. It is employed for the rims of steering wheels, for which purpose it is admirably suited. The wood has a slightly coarse texture and can be gripped well by the hand; moreover, it does not become either rough or slippery from wear. The dark color of the heartwood also precludes its presenting a soiled appearance. As they are made in sections, which are dovetailed and glued together, very strong, serviceable rims are produced. The dash or instrument board of certain makes of automobiles is covered with figured walnut veneer, which gives a pleasing appearance. For this use, waterproof glue is required, because this part of the car is frequently exposed to the weather. In general, a high grade of walnut is used for these purposes.

Battery boxes also are made of walnut. These boxes must be strong, tight, and serviceable. They are dovetailed and glued at the joints, and wooden dowels are also used to prevent their coming apart. The sides and bottoms are one-half to nine-sixteenths inch in thickness. Walnut makes a strong tight box, is not liable to warp, and is not soiled so readily as most other woods. The walnut used in the manufacture of these boxes is mostly No. 2 common and cull, five-eighths inch thick.

CHAIRS AND CHAIR STOCK.

Black walnut is used for chairs of all kinds, except very cheap ones, but it appears to best advantage in the large and ornamental kinds seen in club and lodge rooms, offices, hotel lobbies, and public waiting rooms. Its dignified and pleasing appearance makes it appropriate for such locations. It is also used to match high-grade walnut furniture, particularly dining-room chairs. It is used almost entirely in the form of lumber and dimension stock for this purpose. A small overlay of highly figured walnut veneer or burl is sometimes used to match the other pieces. Veneer is also employed to some extent for large and very expensive chairs in order to get some special figured effect.

CAR CONSTRUCTION.

About 1 per cent of the total amount of black walnut reported for factory use was utilized in the construction of railway and street cars. Practically all of it was used for the interior finish of Pullman cars, and mainly for the large panels. For such uses highly figured veneer is well adapted and largely employed on account of the beautiful effects that may be secured and because of its excellent finishing qualities. The most expensive veneers, particularly those from crotch and stump wood, are used in private cars. On the average a high grade of walnut is used in car construction.

BOXES.

The use of black walnut in the box industry is confined to making small fancy boxes for holding jewelry, silverware, and other expensive merchandise, and the box is usually sold with the article it contains. Walnut is also made into small boxes for office use. A comparatively low grade of walnut is used for making boxes; the average value of the walnut is high, however, when compared with that of all wood used in the box industry.

PICTURE FRAMES AND MOLDING.

Black walnut is an excellent wood for picture frames and molding on account of its fine appearance and its good finishing qualities, and because it holds it shape when seasoned. A very high grade of wood is required for these uses.

OTHER FACTORY USES.

Sixteen other industries reported an aggregate annual use of less than 100,000 board feet of black walnut. Some of the most important of these uses are for parts of professional and scientific instruments; for the outside finishing pieces of clocks; for bungs and faucets on account of the uniform texture of the wood, which makes them fit well; for the decorative parts of sporting and athletic goods, especially of billiard cues; for woodenware and novelties, particularly carved articles of various kinds; for fancy handles; and for brush backs. It is sometimes made into tobacco pipes to take the place of the French briar because it does not burn readily and has a very attractive grain.

There is a large range in prices reported for the smallest amounts, as shown in Table 22. The unusually high prices reported for some of these items indicate that some special stock was purchased. For instance, the 500 board feet purchased for carpet sweepers, for which a very high price for that time was paid, was doubtless figured stock. Very little walnut is now used for carpet sweepers. The 8,000 board feet used for agricultural implements at a low cost may have been purchased locally where there was little market for walnut and was probably low-grade material. That employed in ship and boat building at an unusually high cost was doubtless selected figured wood for inside-finish work.

AIRPLANES.

Black walnut is valued highly for airplane propellers chiefly because of its excellent seasoning and working properties and also because it possesses strength without excessive weight. Some authorities claim that black walnut is by far the best wood for this pur-

grade and entirely clear. Wide lumber, usually.
manded. Statistics are not available on the amou
consumed in the industry or on the average pr
was used. The United States, through the Bure
duction, paid during the war as much as $310 a t
for black-walnut propeller stock, and this was cor
price at that time.

EXPORT.

Exportation has always played an important
lumber industry. European countries early reco
the timber, particularly for cabinetwork. It is
walnut timber was shipped to Europe as early
ditions have interfered with its exportation dt
years. During the year 1918 its shipment from
in the form of the log and for any but war use:
on account of the disturbed conditions abroad,
considered below normal. However, the amount
steadily increasing.

Walnut is exported in the form of both logs an(
gives the amounts of logs and the total and ave.
ferent years, by countries. Similar data are not a
Records of walnut-lumber exports for the year
proximately 75 per cent of the total lumber outp
nut producers was exported during that year.
calculated amounts shown in the section on " Der
tion amounted to about 31 million feet, which v
about as follows: Germany, 50 per cent, 15.5
British Isles, 35 per cent, 10.85 million board f
(principally Denmark. Scandinavia, Holland, B
15 per cent, 4.65 million board feet. During th(

1919 only about 25 per cent of the total lumber output was exported, and about 95 per cent of this went to the British Isles and to parts of Denmark and Sweden. The greatest demand for both logs and lumber before this had been from Germany. There is little demand from either France or Italy. According to these data the total exportation of walnut logs and lumber in 1912 amounted to about 43 million board feet, lumber measure.

TABLE 24.—*Amounts and values of walnut logs exported from the United States during the fiscal years ending June 30, 1912 to 1917.*[1]

Country.	1912		1913		1914		1915		1916		1917	
	1,000 board feet.	Value per 1,000 board feet.	1,000 board feet.	Value per 1,000 board feet.	1,000 board feet.	Value per 1,000 board feet.	1,000 board feet.	Value per 1,000 board feet.	1,000 board feet.	Value per 1,000 board feet.	1,000 board feet.	Value per 1,000 board feet.
Total	9,816	$62.35	12,711	$54.49	6,951	$54.96	1,090	$71.87	1,083	$81.49	1,604	$104.33
Europe:												
Austria-Hungary	4	259.25										
Belgium	791	71.30	395	54.98	509	55.43	15	56.67				
Denmark	19	49.47	12	37.50								
France	77	60.39	416	87.59	672	28.47	105	67.82	22	77.45		
Germany	7,759	61.52	10,307	52.15	4,535	57.09	209	62.89				
Netherlands	140	78.64	161	72.90	144	69.74			9	66.67		
Portugal	9	133.33	11	81.82	6	80.33			5	45.00		
Spain			4	111.25	39	61.00						
Sweden									144	73.64		
United Kingdom:												
England	964	57.81	1,213	57.98	847	59.72	720	74.32	825	85.93	1,209	106.64
Scotland	41	69.15	84	67.08	120	60.33	37	94.59	19	54.79	382	97.97
Ireland	10	80.00										
North America:												
Canada	2	78.50	72	72.18	60	65.80	4	53.75	56	55.18	11	76.27
Mexico			34	60.29								
Central America: Panama									3	33.67		
Africa: British South			2	104.00	19	60.53					2	77.50

[1] None exported for the year 1918.

Data are not available on the export of walnut veneer. It is said that foreign countries generally manufacture their own veneer from the logs. On account of the extensive use of carved work thin lumber five-eighths and three-fourths inch thick largely takes the place of veneer in Europe.

Walnut logs have always been in great demand from foreign countries, especially from Germany. There is hardly any section throughout the walnut area of the United States from which the choice walnut timber has not been taken, often hauled long distances, and shipped to Germany, usually to Hamburg. Thence it was redistributed in the form of logs, veneer, or lumber, largely to Russia, Poland, Austria, and Scandinavia. This timber was used chiefly for furniture, walnut furniture being well liked in those countries. A large part of the shipments to England also was reshipped to Germany. Canada, Mexico, South America, and South Africa are promising markets for this timber.

There has always been a big foreign demand for such walnut-
finished articles as sewing machines and music cabinets. Many firms
depended upon the export trade almost entirely to take their walnut-
finished products. Formerly the dark-finished walnut of uniform
shade was in demand, but now the foreign trade prefers the more
natural color of the wood. The plain heartwood finished in a brown
natural color is now well liked.

WAR-TIME UTILIZATION.

Two products made from walnut are used in warfare—airplane
propellers and gunstocks. To obtain maximum production, both
propeller and gunstock material should be cut, so far as possible,
from the same log. High-grade stock, 1 inch in thickness, is required
for propellers; and it should be 8 inches wide and over and 8 feet
long and over, although a specified maximum proportion of the
lesser widths and lengths is allowed. The propeller grade is about
equivalent to firsts and seconds, but will include some of the large-
sized pieces of No. 1 common. Gunstock material is sawed from the
log in the form of flitches—that is, without the bark being edged
off—and low-grade flitches may be used. Any piece is of value that
will yield a gunstock blank free from all defects, including both
cross grain and pith, the latter being called "heart." The flitches
are $2\frac{1}{2}$ inches in thickness.

Small and defective logs do not usually yield propeller stock, but
are sawed entirely into flitches. Large and mostly clear logs usually
yield a high percentage of propeller lumber. Because walnut logs
are apt to be defective near the center, the propeller lumber is usually
sawed from near the outside of smooth logs; if serious defects are
encountered, gunstock flitches are cut.

Straight-grained material is particularly in demand for propeller
laminations, and is more often obtained by sawing tapered logs with
the grain—that is, in a line approximately parallel to the bark
rather than to the central axis of the log. This generally leaves a
wedge-shaped piece in the center, but does not increase the amount
of waste, as logs from which propeller stock is cut are more liable
to be defective toward the center.

Some gunstock material is obtained even from practically clear logs
in sawing on two parallel sides. By sawing from four sides of the log
a larger yield of propeller lumber may be obtained from high-grade
logs than from sawing from two parallel sides. This method, however, reduces the yield of gunstock material, increases the proportion
of waste, and makes narrower propeller stock. During the late war,
manufacturers were required by regulations of the War Department
to saw the logs with all cuts parallel, in order that the propeller

lumber might be of full width and the gunstock flitch might not be edged. This was a great advantage in cutting out the clear blanks.

Some mills found it possible to saw as much as 40 per cent of propeller stock from their logs. This was generally accomplished by sawing on four sides of the log. The small amount of gunstock flitch obtained by this method was very defective and yielded few blanks; hence the resultant waste, including low-grade lumber unsuited for war material, amounted to about 50 per cent. When the best utilization was reached in the production of war materials, the average yield was about as follows: Propeller lumber, 15 to 18 per cent; gunstock flitch, 65 to 70 per cent; waste, in the form of low-grade lumber, 15 to 18 per cent.

TABLE 25.—*Proportionate amounts of propeller stock, gunstock flitch, and low-grade lumber; and values per 1,000 board feet, sawed from walnut logs.*

TYPE 1.—FAIRLY SMOOTH LOG, 15 INCHES IN DIAMETER ("GUNSTOCK LOG").

[In cases A, B, C, and D all cuts are parallel.]

Case.	Propeller stock.			Gunstock flitch.			Low-grade lumber.			Total value per 1,000 feet.
	Per cent.	Amount.	Value ($300 per 1,000 feet).	Per cent.	Amount.	Value ($1 per gunstock blank).	Per cent.	Amount.	Value ($20 per 1,000 feet).	
		Feet.						*Feet.*		
A....				85	850 feet, at $143 per 1,000 feet (7 feet per blank).	$121.55	15	150	$3.00	$124.55
B....	10	100	$30.00	70	700 feet, at $111 per 1,000 feet (9 feet per blank).	77.70	20	200	4.00	111.70
C....	15	150	45.00	60	600 feet, at $100 per 1,000 feet (10 feet per blank).	60.00	25	250	5.00	110.00
D....	25	250	75.00	20	200 feet, at $67 per 1,000 feet (15 feet per blank).	13.40	55	550	11.00	99.40

TYPE 2.—SMOOTH LOG, 18 INCHES IN DIAMETER ("PROPELLER LOG").

[In cases E and F all cuts are parallel. In case G the log is cut on all four sides.]

Case.	Propeller stock.			Gunstock flitch.			Low-grade lumber.			Total value per 1,000 feet.
E....	50	500	$150.00	45	450 feet, at $111 per 1,000 feet (9 feet per blank).	$49.95	5	50	$1.00	$200.95
F....	60	600	180.00	30	300 feet, at $100 per 1,000 feet (10 feet per blank).	30.00	10	100	2.00	212.00
G....	75	750	225.00	10	100 feet, at $80 per 1,000 feet (12 feet per blank).	8.00	15	150	3.00	236.00

During the war period logs were divided roughly into two classes— airplane logs, which would saw out comparatively large amounts of propeller stock, and gunstock logs, which were of value chiefly for the gunstock flitch. When the best utilization was practiced smooth logs 16 inches and over in diameter at the small end were generally considered as airplane logs, and rough logs of all sizes and smooth logs under 16 inches in diameter at the small end were classed as gunstock logs. Some flitch was, of course, obtained from propeller logs, and a small percentage of propeller stock was sawed from the better grade of gunstock logs.

If a fairly smooth log 15 inches in diameter is regarded as typical of gunstock logs as a class, the manufacturer could obtain stock in about the proportions and amounts and at the values given under Type 1 in Table 25. Naturally, the smaller the proportion of propeller lumber sawed, the larger the proportion of flitch and the better its quality. The better the quality of the flitch, the smaller will be the number of board feet required to produce a gunstock blank, because of the smaller amount of waste. If a smooth log 18 inches in diameter is taken as representative of the propeller-log class, proportions and values would be those given under Type 2 in Table 20. It was, therefore, more profitable to cut a high percentage of gunstock flitch from the gunstock logs than to saw the maximum amount of high-priced propeller stock from them with the large amount of low-grade lumber that would also be produced. From propeller logs the greatest profit could be obtained by sawing the maximum amount of propeller stock, notwithstanding the greater proportion of low-grade material produced. A yield of as much as 75 per cent of propeller stock could ordinarily be obtained only by sawing on four sides of such logs.

Many small mills sawed only inch lumber from walnut logs. This lumber was generally purchased by other firms and the propeller grade sorted out. This practice resulted in much waste of war material. Mills were later required to saw gunstock flitch along with the propeller stock in order to effect better utilization.

Two types of United States Army rifle stocks were made during the war—the Enfield, which was made in by far the largest quantities, and is a modification of a new model British Army rifle; and the Springfield, which is slightly shorter and smaller than the Enfield, and is the older United States Army model. Large amounts of British Army stocks were made of American black walnut. Fortunately, the model commonly used by the British Army is a two-piece stock made up of a "butt" and a "fore end." These parts were manufactured from the pieces of flitch left after cutting out the one-piece United States Army rifle blank. Smaller pieces called "hand guards," which go over the barrel of the rifle and protect the hand from the heat of the barrel, were also made from the waste walnut.

Statistics compiled by the War Industries Board show that the following amounts of black-walnut timber were used by the United States and the Allies during the late war: For airplanes, 9.609 million board feet; for gunstocks, 94.832 million board feet; total, 104.441 million board feet. In explanation, it may be well to state that a certain portion of this material was manufactured into the finished product outside of the United States.

During the war very high prices were paid by the Bureau of Aircraft Production for propeller stock, amounting to as much as $310 a thousand board feet for walnut. The contract price for walnut gunstock blanks was about $1 a blank, amounting to about $120 a thousand board feet for the flitch material.

SUMMARY OF GENERAL MARKET CONDITIONS.

On account of the scarcity and high cost of walnut logs they are generally utilized very closely. The great bulk of the walnut is handled at large mills that are equipped for the manufacture of both lumber and veneer. Band saws, experienced sawyers, and modern kilns contribute to make a very efficient utilization. In veneer manufacture 20 square feet of veneer are obtained to each board foot, log scale, of logs, and in the making up of panel stock about one-half of this is wasted. There is a waste of about 25 per cent also in manufacturing furniture from the lumber. Allowing a 20 per cent over-run of the log scale in the manufacture of lumber, we have the yields shown in Table 26 from 100 board feet of lumber, log scale:

TABLE 26.

	Original log scale.	Total product.	Net amount used in finished product.
Lumber	100 board feet	120 square feet, 1 inch thick	90 square feet, 1 inch thick.
Veneer	do	2,000 square feet veneer, $\frac{1}{20}$ inch thick.	1,000 square feet (finished panel).

There is evidently a great economy in using veneer in place of lumber; moreover, a much better, more attractive, and more durable piece of furniture may be made by the use of veneer.

The principal problem of the walnut manufacturer is the disposal of his low-grade stock, both of lumber and veneer. It is most profitable for him to turn his large, clear, and especially his figured logs into veneer; for, although the lumber sawed from such logs may bring a high price, the veneer sliced from them will bring much more. However, if only small and defective logs are converted into lumber, only low-grade stock will be obtained, and this is difficult to market. The stocks of walnut veneer were greatly reduced because of the discontinuation of the making of veneer during the war. For this reason comparatively small amounts of the highest grades of lumber are being manufactured, and furniture factories are using more of the lower-grade stock.

Many sawmills find it profitable to cut low-grade lumber into furniture dimension stock. Many furniture factories, however, object to using dimension stock because the quality is not good enough, or the sizes are not exactly suited to their needs. They prefer to buy the lumber and cut their stock sizes from that. It is, of course, more expensive to ship the lumber than the dimension sizes cut from it. Sawmills should be able to saw the stock sizes more cheaply than the factory can; but if there is considerable waste in the use of dimension stock it is more profitable to buy the lumber. The sawmills can often recut their low-grade walnut lumber into a special grade of stock for furniture, and therefore it is not necessary for the factories to handle so much waste material. This is also more economical for the factories than cutting clear stock from very defective lumber. A large surplus of very low-grade stock and of small clear pieces accumulated from the manufacture of walnut war material is now in the hands of the large walnut operators. This stock is absorbed very slowly. Since only small dimension pieces can be made from this stock, markets for this material are very limited, and a great deal of it goes into the waste pile and is used for fuel.

The more extensive use of walnut instead of the various woods now substituted for it in making the small solid parts of walnut furniture would effect a closer utilization of the wood. These small pieces should be sawed from low-grade stock, of which there is usually a surplus in the hands of lumber manufacturers.

The small demand for low-grade walnut veneer makes the waste in veneer manufacture greater than it would otherwise be. This low-grade veneer is suitable for backings and drawer bottoms, but factories prefer large sheets from a lower-priced wood, because there is less trouble in cutting out the required sizes. Under present conditions a large part of the sapwood and defective veneer must be used for fuel.

MARKETING WALNUT TIMBER.

Owners of standing walnut timber generally dispose of their trees through a log buyer, who may be either an independent buyer or regularly employed by a walnut-manufacturing concern. Professional log buyers generally have connections or arrangements with some establishment for reselling the timber. Because, as a general thing, the occurrence of the tree is occasional, walnut is often handled by small log buyers, who may dispose of it to a larger log buyer. Small country sawmill owners often purchase walnut logs and sell them, or at least the choice ones, to a large mill or factory. As the timber passes through the hands of several men before reaching the mill, the original owner may get comparatively little for it. Some

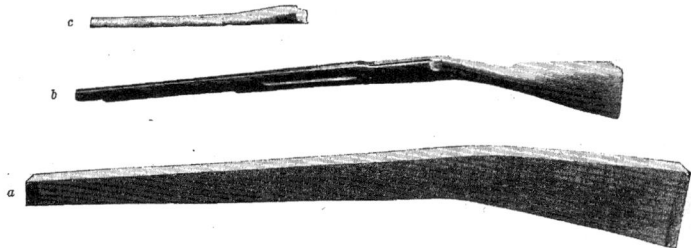

FIG. 1.—STOCK OF A UNITED STATES ARMY RIFLE.

a, blank; b, finished stock; c, front hand guard.

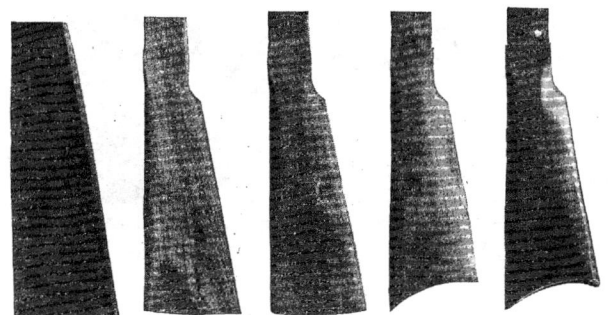

FIG. 2.—EVOLUTION OF AN AIR-RIFLE STOCK FROM THE PLAIN BLANK TO THE FINISHED STOCK.

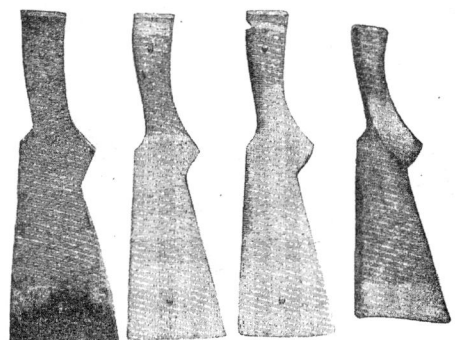

FIG. 3.—EVOLUTION OF A SHOTGUN BUTT FROM THE ROUGH BLANK TO THE FINISHED STOCK.

These butts are sometimes made from waste rotary veneer cores.

FIG. I.—WALNUT LOGS SUITABLE FOR LUMBER AND VENEER.

FIG. 2.—WALNUT VENEER LOGS OF GOOD SIZE AND QUALITY.

Well shaped, with small amounts of sapwood, and nearly clear of large defects.

FIG. I.—WALNUT STUMPS FOR SLICING INTO FIGURED "BUTT" WOOD VENEERS.

FIG. 2.—WALNUT VENEER LOGS.

The two small logs near the top, although only 13 and 14 inches in diameter, are suitable for making veneer because the rim of sapwood in each is less than one inch in thickness.

FIG. 1.—TWO WALNUT STUMPS WITH ROOTS PROPERLY TRIMMED OFF FOR
MAKING VENEER.

The longer stump is 7 feet in length, with a crotch at the top end, and is particularly valuable
for veneer.

FIG. 2.—A 12-FOOT WALNUT LOG (THE LARGE ONE IN THE FOREGROUND) THAT
SHOULD HAVE BEEN CUT TO 10 FEET IN LENGTH.

.If a portion had been sawed from each end it would have scaled as a 16-inch log, and the general
quality would have been much higher.

FIG. 3.—A VERY DEFECTIVE KNOTTY WALNUT LOG.

Scarcely worth sawing into lumber and worthless for veneer.   The defectiveness of this log is indicated by the large knots visible on the surface, which have not healed over smoothly.

manufacturers prefer to buy their walnut logs through dealers only, rather than to purchase in small lots from owners. This is particularly true of firms that make a specialty of figured walnut veneer. Other manufacturers prefer to buy from the owners of the standing timber through their salaried log buyers. A few firms buy walnut logs subject to inspection at the mill.

Walnut trees are usually converted into logs for the manufacture of either lumber or veneer, because of the comparatively high value of walnut in these forms. (Pl. XII, fig. 1.) Conversion into ties, fence posts, and fuel wood, except in regions far removed from the railroad, is confined to that part of the tree which is too small or defective for lumber or veneer. Large and figured logs may be hauled and shipped long distances at a profit. (Pl. XII, fig. 2.)

Formerly choice walnut timber for export was purchased from remote mountainous sections of the eastern United States, where a good supply was found, and hauled 25 or 30 miles over rough mountain roads to the railroad for shipment to the coast. During the war walnut timber was hauled as far as 20 miles to the railroad in sections west of the Mississippi, where there were comparatively large stands.

Walnut butts or stumps are very valuable if they are highly figured. (Pl. XIII, fig. 1.) If they are plain they do not have special value. The figured portion should be at least 28 or 30 inches in length. Burls are very rare and bring high prices at veneer plants. These burls have the appearance of a knot, and typical specimens are covered with little conical spines. They are more often found near the outer western limits of the area of distribution, where the trees are apt to be stunted and not thrifty. As a general thing, only those burls at the stump or root of the tree, called root burls, and mostly beneath the surface of the ground, are of value; those higher up on the trunk or on large limbs are generally full of cavities. A good burl should have sound, solid wood like the normal growth. The best burls are usually turnip shaped.

It is impossible to give current prices for walnut logs, both because there has been a great fluctuation in price on account of the war's demand, and because walnut mills do not generally put out a price list, the amount paid being determined by the quality of the individual logs, particularly in regard to their suitability for veneer. During the war, prices ranging from $20 to $120 a thousand board feet, log scale, were paid for standing timber, depending on size and location. This averaged about $50 a thousand. The prices for logs on board cars at the railroad ranged from $45 to $150 a thousand for diameters 12 inches and over, making in most cases a cost for all sizes of $100 to $110 a thousand at the mill. The average-sized log

7434°—20——6

measured between 15 and 16 inches, and low-grade logs were inclu
if they were not too defective. Comparatively little standing wal
timber was purchased for a short time after the close of hostili
because of the large stocks on hand at the time of the signing of
armistice.

Prices of $75 to $175 a thousand board feet at the mill were
ported soon after the close of the war, $75 representing the p
for 16-inch logs, and the average cost for logs of all sizes be
about $90 a thousand. The higher prices were for large veneer
of special value. If $50 a thousand is allowed for logging
freight costs, the variation of stumpage prices is from $25 to $
a thousand for logs 16 inches and over, or an average price of al
$40 a thousand, this average price applying to a log about 19 inc
in diameter. These prices are given only for the purpose of indi
ing the variation. They vary greatly with the quality of the t
ber and the distance from market. While the prices paid sho
after the war were slightly higher than those paid during the war
quality of the logs was much better, the prices applying to logs
were comparatively clear. War-time costs of 16-inch logs at the
amounted to about $110 a thousand on the average, while $7
thousand was paid more recently for logs of the same size and
better quality. During the first half of the year 1920 prices for
nut and other hardwoods were very high. Prices paid in Indiana
walnut logs at the mill in some cases averaged about $300 a thous
board feet, log scale, and large, high-quality veneer logs brou
about $500 a thousand board feet at the mill. Whether high pi
will prevail depends for a large part on future prices of wa!
lumber and on prices of other hardwoods. The very high cos
marketing timber is one of the main factors responsible for t
greatly increased prices at the mill. Highly figured wood, inc.
ing stumps, crotches, and burls, is worth more than the ave
veneer log, the value depending on the size and quality of log
the kind of figure. Burls are sold by weight, usually for 10 o:
cents a pound and up.

If the farmer has walnut trees which he wishes to dispose of,
generally more profitable for him to fell the timber and haul it to
railroad than to sell it on the stump. After the timber is sawed
log lengths its actual worth may be better judged than when it
the standing tree. Firms often buy standing timber by payir
lump sum for the lot. It is generally more satisfactory, howe
to sell in conformity with a scale of prices, by the thousand be
feet, according to the size of logs. The size is generally determ
by the average of two diameters taken at right angles to each o
and measured inside the bark at the small end. A 14-inch lo
usually the minimum size desired; however, 12-inch logs are take

they are straight and first class in every way. Small figured logs also are in demand. Trees should be felled by cutting as near the ground as possible if the wood is sound, in order to get the advantage of the extra length of large-sized material.

The usual merchantable lengths are 8, 10, 12, 14, and 16 feet. An allowance of at least 2 inches over these lengths should be made for trimming the lumber at the mill. Some firms allow odd lengths; some allow only certain proportions of lengths under 10 and under 12 feet. Shorter lengths than 8 feet may be allowed when it is necessary to cut the log short, if it is large and of good quality, and especially if it is a figured or otherwise high-grade veneer log. Veneer logs 6 feet or even 4½ feet in length are accepted by some mills.

Unless they are very large, logs for veneer manufacture preferably should not have more than a 1-inch rim of sapwood. (Pl. XIII, fig. 2.) Three and even 2 inches of sapwood spoils the ordinary-sized log for veneer. Open-growth timber often has much sapwood. If there is a good amount of heartwood, and if it is not too defective, this timber is often very valuable for veneer on account of the figure that is generally present.

Figured logs are now greatly in demand. Highly figured stump or " butt " wood is especially valuable. However, few stumps have the valuable wrinkle, curl, or roll figure. This figure is generally evidenced by a ridged surface under the bark. Panel lengths are 30 and 36 inches, and, if the figure extends over this entire length, the log is of much value. Stump wood, to be marketable, should be at least 20 inches in diameter at the small end and from 30 to 42 inches long. Only the solid portion of the stump can be used, and the base should be squared off by sawing. The root spurs along the side of the stump should be cut off nearly flush with the surface of the trunk. (Pl. XIV, fig. 1.) The roots are sometimes used for hatracks and coat racks, for hall trees, and for couch legs. Crotches are often of value and should be cut about the same length as stump wood.

Walnut logs are usually measured by the Doyle log rule. Table 27 gives the number of board feet in logs of different diameters and lengths. Careful attention should be given to cutting the logs into the most advantageous lengths. If it is practicable, logs should be cut at a crook, crotch, or knot, in order to get as straight and clear lengths as possible. (Pl. XIV, fig. 2.) The amount of scale obtained and the price may vary with the method of cutting. For instance, a log cut 16 feet long, having a diameter of 14 inches, and containing 100 board feet, on account of a marked taper in the upper 2 feet, might measure 16 inches at a length of 14 feet. This would give a scale of 126 board feet (over one-fourth more) at a price of, perhaps, $10 a thousand more, on account of the greater diameter. This does not mean that there is necessarily an advantage in cutting short log lengths, for some log buyers take the diameter measure of long logs at some specified distance back from the small end. If, however, there is a decided taper at the upper end of the merchantable length of the tree, it would often be a loss to the owner to leave that small-diameter material on the log. Defective parts of the bole may often be left out altogether to better the quality of the logs. (Pl. XIV, fig. 3.) After the trees are cut the logs should not be left lying for a long time on the ground or exposed to the sun. The logs should be raised from the ground and the ends should be painted. If the ends of the logs are checked at the time of felling, it is customary for the cutters to make a blunt cut with a wedge across each end of the check. This helps to prevent the check from extending to the bark and, what would often result, the log splitting open its entire width.

TABLE 27.—*Amounts of board feet, log scale, contained in logs of different lengths and diameters, measured according to the Doyle log rule.*

Diameter, small end inside bark (inches).	Length in feet.										
	6	7	8	9	10	11	12	13	14	15	16
	Board feet.										
6	1	2	2	2	2	3	3	3	3	4	4
7	3	4	4	5	5	6	7	7	8	8	9
8	6	7	8	9	10	11	12	13	14	15	16
9	9	11	12	14	16	17	19	20	22	23	25
10	13	16	18	20	22	25	27	29	31	34	36
11	18	21	24	28	31	34	37	40	43	46	49
12	24	28	32	36	40	44	48	52	56	60	64
13	30	35	40	46	51	56	61	66	71	76	81
14	37	44	50	56	62	69	75	81	87	94	100
15	45	53	60	68	76	83	91	98	106	113	121
16	54	63	72	81	90	99	108	117	126	135	144
17	63	74	84	95	106	116	127	137	148	158	169
18	73	86	98	110	122	135	147	159	171	184	196
19	84	98	112	127	141	155	169	183	197	211	225
20	96	112	128	144	160	176	192	208	224	240	256
21	108	126	144	163	181	199	217	235	253	271	289
22	121	142	162	182	202	223	243	263	283	304	324
23	135	158	180	203	226	248	271	293	316	338	361
24	150	175	200	225	250	275	300	325	350	375	400
25	165	193	220	248	276	303	331	358	386	413	441
26	181	212	242	272	302	333	363	393	423	454	484
27	198	231	264	298	331	364	397	430	463	496	529
28	216	252	288	324	360	396	432	468	504	540	576
29	234	273	312	352	391	430	469	508	547	586	625
30	253	296	338	380	422	465	507	549	591	634	676

Costs of marketing include those of buying the timber, felling the trees, cutting into lengths, hauling to the railroad, loading on cars, and transporting to market. Buying costs generally range from $5 to $10 a thousand board feet. The cost of felling is variable, depending mostly on the extent to which the timber is scattered. If the trees are frequent, the cost of felling and sawing into logs generally varies from $2 to $5 a thousand; if the growth is much scattered, and if considerable time is lost in going from one tree to another, the cost may amount to several dollars a thousand more. The cost of hauling and loading on cars varies almost directly with the distance; it usually runs from \$15 to \$30 a thousand for a 5 to 10 mile haul. The freight cost depends, of course, on the distance to the mill or factory.

Farmers owning walnut timber usually find it profitable themselves to haul their logs to the railroad, especially during the winter months, when work is comparatively slack. The timber is not so apt to deteriorate at this time of the year, and hauling may then be done more conveniently. Inspection may be made by the buyer's representative at the farm, the railroad, or the mill. If the logs are of average size and quality the mills will purchase as little as 3,000 board feet, log scale—an amount which is considered a minimum carload. Smaller shipments are often made if the logs are very high grade or figured. Owners of small lots of timber may often combine to ship a carload. Following are the shipping weights of walnut in various forms:

	Pounds.
Rough lumber, 1 inch thick, 1,000 board feet, green	[1] 4, 900
Rough lumber, 1 inch thick, 1,000 board feet, dry	[1] 3, 800
Logs, 1,000 board feet, log scale, Doyle rule:	
Diameter, inside bark at small end, 12 inches, green	11, 900
Diameter, inside bark at small end, 12 inches, dry	8, 200
Diameter, inside bark at small end, 18 inches, green	8, 300
Diameter, inside bark at small end, 18 inches, dry	5, 700
Diameter, inside bark at small end, 24 inches, green	7, 100
Diameter, inside bark at small end, 24 inches, dry	4, 900
Cordwood, bolts, butts, etc., 1 cord of 128 cubic feet, green	[2] 4, 700
Cordwood, bolts, butts, etc., 1 cord of 128 cubic feet, dry	[2] 3, 200

SUMMARY AND CONCLUSIONS.

The use of black walnut covers as long a period as that of any other native wood. It has been repeatedly predicted that the supply would soon be exhausted. The timber has never been plentiful; but, on account of its being scattered throughout a large area, there has been a fairly steady supply since colonial times. Its area of commercial distribution is, roughly, the eastern half of the United States exclusive of the coastal regions, the southern Mississippi Valley region, and the extreme northern regions. The principal supplies are now located in central Tennessee, eastern Kentucky, northwestern West Virginia, Ohio, Indiana, Illinois, southern Iowa, Missouri, southeastern Nebraska, eastern Kansas and Oklahoma, northeastern Texas, and northwestern Arkansas. Although the best quality of walnut has come from Ohio and Indiana, the general run of the timber is now better in the western part of its range, because it has not been

---

[1] Official standard weights of the National Hardwood Lumber Association.
[2] Figured on the basis of 90 cubic feet of solid wood content.

cut out to the extent to which it has in the eastern part. The stands are now west of the Mississippi River.

Before the war the annual demand amounted to about 60 mi board feet; during the war it increased to about 90 million b feet. A large part of the total is exported in normal times, pr pally to European countries.

The greatest problem of the lumber manufacturer is to dis of his lower grades, of which there was a surplus from the m facture of high-grade airplane-propeller lumber during the. The cutting of dimension stock is often impracticable, on accour the varying needs of the factories using this stock. It is no common practice among walnut-lumber manufacturers to recut grade stock in order that it may be classed in a higher grade may be sold as a special grade of small-dimension stock of a be kind.

Walnut is valued mainly for its good seasoning, working, gluing qualities, its fine appearance, and its good finishing pro ties. Its principal uses are for cabinetwork in furniture, n cal instruments, and sewing machines, for interior finish, and gunstocks. For cabinetwork and inside finish it is used very lai in the form of veneer panels. Thin lumber is used extensivel European countries for cabinetwork, instead of veneer. Other net woods—as, for instance, red gum and birch—are commonly for the solid pieces in cabinetwork. A substitution, however tracts from the appearance and general quality of the piece. P: are usually made of five plies, and the outer ply is generally o: striped walnut that is characteristic of open-growth trees, or of other highly figured walnut as, for example, cross figure, st wood, crotches, or burls.

There has been a recent revival in the popularity of black wa furniture, which is now given lighter finishes more nearly like natural color of the wood. This treatment brings out the na beauty of the grain and figure. For this reason the rapid-gro light-colored heartwood is now more in demand than is the uniformly colored. Figured wood is scarce and highly valued is cut into veneer usually one twenty-eighth inch in thickness.

Walnut veneer is cut by the straight rotary, stay-log rotar straight-slice process. Manufacturers get about 20 square fee

Walnut is a suitable wood for railway ties, fence posts, and firewood, but only small and defective material is ordinarily converted into these products.

The price of walnut lumber has increased greatly during recent years, and the same thing is true of the price of such other cabinet woods as red gum, white oak, and birch. These prices have also effected a great increase in the price of logs. During the war, on account of the unprecedented demand for walnut, much small and defective material was accepted. Logs 14 inches and over in diameter and at least fairly clear are now generally specified. The increased expense of logging and of freight has been an added factor in making the cost of logs higher than before the war.

Owners of walnut timber can dispose of their trees to best advantage to walnut lumber and veneer manufacturers, and to factories that purchase walnut in the log form. Figured walnut is more valuable than plain. Walnut firms do not, as a rule, publish a fixed scale of prices and log grades, the price generally being set by the log buyer.

Although the present very high market price of the timber may not be maintained, walnut will always be in demand, and will bring good prices because of the intrinsic value of the wood. Owners of timber tracts containing walnut will generally find it profitable to favor the young growth of this timber over that of less valuable species.

APPENDIX.

DETAILED LIST OF USES OF BLACK WALNUT REPORTED BY FACTORIES.

Boxes and crates.—Ballot boxes; lodge ballot boxes; box handles; machine boxes; seed boxes; storage battery boxes; tool boxes; tool chests.

Brooms and carpet sweepers.—Carpet sweepers.

Bungs and faucets.—Bungs.

Car construction.—Cabinetwork (electric cars); cabinetwork (passenger cars); car repairing; cars (finish); cars (interior finish); passenger cars; passenger cars (interior finish); railroad cars; switch-box covers (Pullman cars); upper berth doors (sleeping cars); grilles (Pullman cars); panel wainscoting (Pullman cars); push buttons (Pullman cars); sash (Pullman cars).

Caskets and coffins.—Casket cases; caskets; coffin cases; coffins.

Chairs.—Chair arms; chair arms (Pullman cars); chair-back posts; chair legs; chairs; desk chairs; ecclesiastical chairs; office chairs; official chairs (lodge room); rocking chairs; chairs (spindles): rockers; parlor rockers; settees; settles.

Clocks.— Clock cases; hall-clock cases; clocks.

Firearms.—Gun butts; gun forearms; fore-end blanks; gun fore ends; air-gun stocks; air-rifle stocks; gun stocks; pistol stocks; rifle stocks.

Fixtures.—Altars; church altars; lodge altars; church Bible stands; bookshelves; cellarettes; barber chairs; closet seats: commodes; counter tops; fixtures; bank fixtures; bar fixtures; church fixtures; fixtures (exterior parts); office fixtures; store fixtures; church pews; showcases.

Frames and molding, picture.—Picture frames; picture molding.

Furniture.—Beds; folding beds (exterior parts); bedsteads (exterior); benches; bookcases; bookcases (exterior); revolving bookracks; bureaus; bureaus (exterior); cabinets; drug cabinets; filing cabinets; humidor cabinets; letter-filing cabinets; magazine cabinets; music cabinets; smoker cabinets; thread cabinets; furniture carving; carvings; case work; chests; chiffoniers; chifforobes; china closets; couch legs; desks; house desks; ladies' desks; office desks; drawer handles; dressers; dressers (exterior); princess dressers (exterior); newspaper files; foot rests; footstools; frames; mirror frames; mirror frames (Pullman cars); furniture; case-goods furniture; church furniture; lodge furniture; office furniture; hall hatracks; inlaid work; knobs; cheval mirrors; bed molding; case panels; desk panels; veneered panels; chair pillars; rails (billiard tables); rails (card tables); rails (pool tables); sideboards; chafing-dish stands; stools; tables; card tables; dining tables; drop-leaf tables; extension tables; library tables; portable lunch tables (Pullman cars); parlor tables; side tables; tea tables; taborets; veneer; wallcases.

Handles.—Handles; package handles; handles (saddlers' tools).

Instruments, musical.—Accordions; phonograph cabinets; consoles; drum shells; mandolin bodies; molding (piano players); music benches; piano music shelves; orchestrions; organ actions; pipe-organ blocks; organ cases; reed-organ cases; pipe-organ casing; organ frames; organ parts; cabinet organs; interior organs; pipe organs; pipe organs (exterior); reed organs; reed organs (exterior); panels; piano actions; piano benches; piano cases; piano chairs; piano legs; piano molding; piano parts; piano players; piano seats; piano stools; veneer cores (piano cases); veneer cross-band work (pianos); veneer (piano cases).

Instruments, professional and scientific.—Carpenters' tools; dental cases; optical cases; embalming boards; heads (carpenters' squares); heads (draftsmen's T-squares); miter boxes.

Machine construction.—Cylinder heads; machinery construction; flour-mill machinery; flour-mill trim.

Machinery and apparatus, electrical.—Cabinets (electrical work); coil cases; electrical appliances; electrical appliances (bases); electrical equipment; telephone-subscriber sets; switchboards; telephones.

Patterns and flasks.—Patterns; foundry patterns.

Planing-mill products.—Finish; interior finish; flooring; parquetry flooring; flooring (parquetry borders); flooring strips; floors; interior trimming (house); molding; base molding (house); molding (caps, interior trim); house molding; quarter-round molding; spring-cove molding (house-interior trim); nosing (house-interior trim); panel strips (house-interior trim); panels, ceiling panels; window panels; partitions; dining-room plate rails; window aprons; window stools (house-interior trim).

Printing material.—Printers' materials.

Refrigerators and kitchen cabinets.—Kitchen cupboards.

Sash, doors, blinds, and general millwork.—Balusters; stairway balusters; baseboards; flat battens; dining-room ceiling beams; boards (fillers); brackets (plate rails); cabinetwork; cabinetwork (stairs); carpet strips; casing; door casing; head casing (house); window casing; doors; folding doors; mirror doors (house); doors (rails); sliding doors; dust caps (house-interior trim); fillet (house-interior trim); fret wood; grilles; grilles (house-interior trim); stairway hand rails; joiner work; millwork; exterior·millwork; screen molding; newels; pilasters; railing; sash; door screens; fire screens; window screens; stairwork; stiles (doors); wainscot rails; wainscoting; wainscoting caps; window aprons; window stops.

Sewing machines.—Cabinets (sewing-machine); sewing-machine parts.

Ship and boat building.—Boats; interior cabinets (ship); interior cabinets (yacht); pilot wheels (ship); pilot wheels (yacht); steering wheels.

Sporting and athletic goods.—Cigar wheels (wheel of chance); tennis-racket throats; tennis rackets.

Vehicles.—Automobile bodies; automobile dashboards; automobile dashboards (fillers); automobile dash frames; automobile deck rails; automobile handrails; automobiles (interior finish); dashboards (buggy); vehicles; wind shields (automobile); window frames (automobile).

Whips, canes, and umbrella sticks.—Canes; umbrella handles.

Woodenware and novelties.—Fancy boxes; gavels; novelties; rolling-pin handles; toddy sticks; jewelry trays; serving trays; woodenware.

UNITED STATES DEPARTMENT OF AGRICULTURE

BULLETIN No. 910

Contribution from the Office of Farm Management
and Farm Economics.
H. C. TAYLOR, Chief

Washington, D. C.   ▼   December 10, 1920

EXPERIENCE OF EASTERN FARMERS WITH MOTOR TRUCKS.

An Analysis of 753 Reports from Farmer Truck-Owners.

By H. R. TOLLEY, *Scientific Assistant*, and L. M. CHURCH, *Assistant in
Farm Accounting.*

CONTENTS.

	Page.		Page.
Summary	1	Effect of different kinds of roads on use of	
Method of study	3	trucks	17
Location of farms and types of farming	3	Change of market	19
Distance to market	4	Annual use of trucks	21
Size of truck	6	Life and depreciation of trucks	23
Age of trucks	7	Repairs	24
Are these trucks profitable investments?	7	Gasoline and oil	26
The best size	7	Tires	27
Advantages and disadvantages	9	Reliability	29
Road hauling with trucks	10	Cost of operation	32
Road hauling for which trucks are not used	13	Cost of hauling with trucks	33
Hauling on the farm with trucks	15	Saving of hired help	34
Custom hauling	17	Displacement of horses	35
		Farms on which tractors are owned	36

SUMMARY.

This bulletin is based on the experience with motor trucks of 753 farmers in the States of Maine, New Hampshire, Vermont, Massachusetts, Rhode Island, Connecticut, New York, New Jersey, Pennsylvania, Delaware, and Maryland who have motor trucks for use on their own farms.

These farms are of all sizes and types, and the motor trucks used on them are of all sizes from ½ ton to 5 tons. The rated capacity of very few of the trucks is over 2 tons, however, and nearly half are of the 1-ton size.

Only 18 per cent of these farms are less than 5 miles from market, and nearly one-fourth are 20 miles or more from market.

Ninety-five per cent of these men believe that their trucks will prove to be profitable investments.

One-ton trucks are preferred by more of them than prefer any other size. About half of the owners of ½- and ¾-ton trucks prefer sizes larger than they now own.

In the opinions of these men the principal advantage of a motor truck is in saving time, and the principal disadvantage is "poor roads."

As compared with horses and wagons, the trucks save from half to two-thirds of the time required for hauling materials to and from the farms.

These men have return loads for their trucks on about one-fourth of the trips.

A majority still use their horses for some road hauling.

On most of the farms all the hauling in the fields and around the buildings is done with horses and wagons.

About one-fourth of these men do some custom hauling with their trucks. The average amount received per year by those who do such work is $174.

On the average there are about eight weeks during the year when the roads are in such condition on account of mud, snow, etc., that the trucks can not be used. Three-fourths of them usually travel on roads that are all or part dirt.

About one-fourth of the men have changed their markets, for at least a part of their produce, since purchasing trucks. For those who have changed market, the average distance to the old market is 7 miles, and the average distance to the new market is 20 miles.

According to owners' estimates, each of these trucks travels an average of 3,820 miles per year and is used on 173 days per year.

The average estimated life of the trucks is between 6½ and 7 years, and, in most cases, depreciation is the largest single item of expense.

Most of the owners of the ½-ton and ¾-ton trucks prefer pneumatic tires, the owners of the 1-ton trucks are about evenly divided in their preference, but most of the owners of trucks larger than 1 ton prefer solid tires.

Over two-thirds of these trucks had not been out of commission, when needed, for a single day during the year covered by the reports, and nearly the same proportion of the owners stated that they had not lost any appreciable time on account of motor and tire trouble, breakage, etc., when using their trucks. However, about one truck in thirty had been out of commission 10 days or more.

The average cost of operation of the ½-ton trucks was about 8 cents per mile; of the ¾-ton trucks about 13 cents; of the 1-ton about 12 cents; of the 1¼-ton and 1½-ton about 19 cents, and of the 2-ton about 20 cents.

The average cost of hauling crops, including the value of the driver's time at 50 cents an hour, was about 50 cents per ton-mile with the

½-ton trucks, 34 cents with the ¾-ton, 26 cents with the 1-ton, 24 cents with the 1¼-ton and 1½-ton, and 18 cents with the 2-ton trucks.

About four-fifths of these men state that their trucks save hired help. On the average they estimate that this saving amounts to $324 per year.

About half the men have decreased the number of work stock by at least one head since purchasing their trucks. Less than one man in ten had disposed of more than two head, however.

Over half of the men whose farms contain more than 120 crop-acres own tractors. The number of work stock kept on the farms where both trucks and tractors are owned is only slightly less than the number kept on the farms of corresponding size where only trucks are owned.

METHOD OF STUDY.

In December, 1919, the crop reporters of the Bureau of Crop Estimates were asked to report the names and addresses of farmers who owned motor trucks for farm use. Nine thousand six hundred and fifty-nine names and addresses of farmers in the 11 States included in the study were received, and to each was sent a questionnaire on which to report the type and size of his farm, the use he makes of his motor truck, the cost of operating it, his idea of its profitableness, the advantages and disadvantages of a truck for farm use, and other related information. In all, 2,314, about 24 per cent of the farmers queried, replied to the questionnaire.

However, no reports from men owning second-hand trucks nor trucks made by the addition of truck units or attachments to passenger cars, were included in the study. Twenty-seven per cent of the reports were on machines of these classes. About 10 per cent of the reports were from men who had owned their trucks only six months or less, and they were also excluded. Another 30 per cent of the reports were excluded for other reasons. Some were from farmers who are using their trucks primarily for custom work, or in connection with other business, and only incidentally for farm work; some were from men who had sold their trucks; and a few of the reports were not filled out in sufficient detail to make their use worth while. The questionnaire called for information on over 150 items.

LOCATION OF FARMS AND TYPES OF FARMING.

The number of reports tabulated from each State follows:

Maine	11	New York	241
New Hampshire	11	New Jersey	92
Vermont	16	Pennsylvania	235
Massachusetts	63	Delaware	11
Rhode Island	16	Maryland	40
Connecticut	17		

These farms are of all sizes and types, varying from truck farms of only a few acres to large crop farms containing several hundred acres. The types of farming practiced have been classified into five groups, as follows:

(1) Truck farms, on which the raising of vegetables and similar produce predominates.

(2) Dairy farms, on which dairying is the principal enterprise.

(3) Fruit farms.

(4) Crop farms, on which general field crops are raised, but few or no dairy cows are kept, and no live stock is raised for sale.

(5) General farms, where no one special enterprise predominates.

In the region studied there are many more general farms than any other type. Although more reports were received from men who operate general farms than from any other class, this does not necessarily mean that the percentage of such farmers who own motor trucks is larger than that of men who follow special types of farming.

The number of farms of the different types and their average size are shown in Table I.

TABLE I.—*Number of farms of different types, and their acreages.*

Type of farm.	Number.	Average size.
		Acres.
Truck	149	64
Dairy	129	234
Fruit	113	111
Crop	48	237
General	314	210
All	753	173

DISTANCE TO MARKET.

Probably the most striking point concerning these farms is their great distance from market as compared with other farms in the same section. Only 18 per cent of these farms are less than 5 miles from market, while nearly one-fourth of them are 20 miles or more. As will appear later, some of the men who have very long hauls have changed their markets since purchasing their trucks, but the average distance from market, even before the purchase of the trucks, was a little over 10 miles. (See fig. 1.)

Seven hundred and four men reported the distance to the towns where the materials hauled by trucks are usually marketed. The exact number of farms of different types at different distances from market is as follows:

Of 143 truck farms—

    11 are less than 5 miles from market.
    32 are from 5 to 9 miles from market.
    34 are from 10 to 14 miles from market.

Of 143 truck farms—Continued.

33 are from 15 to 19 miles from market.
17 are from 20 to 24 miles from market.
9 are from 25 to 29 miles from market.
7 are 30 miles and over from market.

Of 117 dairy farms—

48 are less than 5 miles from market.
45 are from 5 to 9 miles from market.
8 are from 10 to 14 miles from market.
2 are from 15 to 19 miles from market.
7 are from 20 to 24 miles from market.
4 are from 25 to 29 miles from market.
3 are 30 miles and over from market.

FIG. 1.—If a farmer is located on an improved road, such as is illustrated here, a motor truck will enable him to reach a distant market in a short time practically any day in the year.

Of 98 fruit farms—

18 are less than 5 miles from market.
21 are from 5 to 9 miles from market.
16 are from 10 to 14 miles from market.
10 are from 15 to 19 miles from market.
9 are from 20 to 24 miles from market.
9 are from 25 to 29 miles from market.
15 are 30 miles and over from market.

Of 44 crop farms—

11 are less than 5 miles from market.
15 are from 5 to 9 miles from market.
4 are from 10 to 14 miles from market.
4 are from 15 to 19 miles from market.
4 are from 20 to 24 miles from market.
1 is from 25 to 29 miles from market.
5 are 30 miles and over from market.

Of 302 general farms—

    36 are less than 5 miles from market.
    67 are from 5 to 9 miles from market.
    68 are from 10 to 14 miles from market.
    57 are from 15 to 19 miles from market.
    22 are from 20 to 24 miles from market.
    23 are from 25 to 29 miles from market.
    29 are 30 miles and over from market.

Of all the 704 farms—

    18 per cent are less than 5 miles from market.
    25 per cent are from 5 to 9 miles from market.
    19 per cent are from 10 to 14 miles from market.
    15 per cent are from 15 to 19 miles from market.
    8 per cent are from 20 to 24 miles from market.
    7 per cent are from 25 to 29 miles from market.
    8 per cent are 30 miles and over from market.

The distances from market of more than 4,000 farmer
States, as shown by farm survey records in the Office of Farr
ment and Farm Economics, indicate that only a small]
of all the farms in this section are more than 10 miles fror
The average distance from market of 4,271 farms is 4.1 mile
number at different distances is as follows:

    2,936, or 68.7 per cent, are less than 5 miles from market.
    1,018, or 23.8 per cent, are from 5 to 9 miles from market.
    241, or 5.7 per cent, are from 10 to 14 miles from market.
    51, or 1.2 per cent, are from 15 to 19 miles from market
    25, or 0.6 per cent, are 20 miles and over from market

SIZE OF TRUCK.

The motor trucks owned on these 753 farms are of many
rated capacities running from ½ ton to 5 tons. However,
use more 1-ton trucks than any other size, and only a]
than 2 per cent of the total number are rated at more th
The number of the different sizes on the farms of differer
as follows:

On the 149 truck farms, there are—

    24 ½-ton trucks.
    18 ¾-ton trucks.
    59 1-ton trucks.
    19 1¼- and 1½-ton trucks.
    22 2-ton trucks.
    7 over 2 tons.

On the 129 dairy farms, there are—

    43 ½-ton trucks.
    14 ¾-ton trucks.
    62 1-ton trucks.
    4 1¼- and 1½-ton trucks.
    4 2-ton trucks.
    2 over 2 tons.

On the 113 fruit farms, there are—
  17 ½-ton trucks.
  17 ¾-ton trucks.
  48 1-ton trucks.
  11 1¼- and 1½-ton trucks.
  18 2-ton trucks.
  2 over 2 tons.
On the 48 crop farms, there are—
  1 ½-ton truck.
  5 ¾-ton trucks.
  19 1-ton trucks. .
  11 1¼- and 1½-ton trucks.
  11 2-ton trucks.
  1 over 2 tons.
On the 314 general farms, there are—
  65 ½-ton trucks.
  41 ¾-ton trucks.
  156 1-ton trucks.
  22 1¼- and 1½-ton trucks.
  24 2-ton trucks.
  6 over 2 tons

AGE OF TRUCKS.

The length of time the 753 trucks had been in use at the time the reports were made is as follows:

  201 had been in use 7 to 12 months.
  269 had been in use 13 to 24 months.
  164 had been in use 25 to 36 months.
  119 had been in use 37 months or over.

ARE THESE TRUCKS PROFITABLE INVESTMENTS?

No attempt was made to determine to what extent the incomes of these men had been increased through the use of the trucks, but 95 per cent of the total number stated that in their opinion their machines bid fair to be profitable investments. So far as could be determined, the size of the truck, the type of farming practiced, and length of time the machine had been owned had little to do with the owner's idea of its profitableness. Some of those who did not consider that their motor trucks had been profitable were men who had found them unreliable, as they were often out of commission when needed, or their repair bills had been exceptionally high. Others had found that they did not have enough work for the truck to justify the investment in such an expensive piece of equipment.

THE BEST SIZE.

The fact that most of these men consider their motor trucks profitable investments does not mean, however, that they are all entirely satisfied with the particular machines which they own. It is very important that the truck should be of the proper size for the hauling

which it is to do. Ordinarily both the first cost and the cost of operation of a small truck will be less than of a large one, but often the
small truck will not carry as large loads as is desired, and more trips
to haul a given amount of material will therefore be necessary than
with a larger truck. A truck which is too large, however, would
have to be operated with only a partial load a great part of the time,
and the extra cost would more than offset the advantage of being
able to carry larger loads on exceptional occasions.

Each farmer was asked to state what size he considers the best for
his conditions, regardless of the size he now owns, and 696 men
answered as follows:

Of 131 who now own ½-ton trucks—
    47 consider that the best size is ½-ton.
    14 consider that the best size is ¾-ton.
    56 consider that the best size is 1-ton.
    9 consider that the best size is 1¼- or 1½-ton.
    4 consider that the best size is 2-ton.
    1 considers that the best size is over 2-ton.
Of 83 who now own ¾-ton trucks—
    1 considers that the best size is ½-ton.
    46 consider that the best size is ¾-ton.
    28 consider that the best size is 1-ton.
    6 consider that the best size is 1¼- or 1½-ton.
    1 considers that the best size is 2-ton.
    1 considers that the best size is over 2-ton.
Of 329 who now own 1-ton trucks—
    2 consider that the best size is ¾-ton.
    242 consider that the best size is 1-ton.
    54 consider that the best size is 1¼- or 1½-ton.
    30 consider that the best size is 2-ton.
    1 considers that the best size is over 2-ton.
Of 63 who now own 1¼- and 1½-ton trucks—
    2 consider that the best size is 1-ton.
    39 consider that the best size is 1¼- or 1½-ton.
    19 consider that the best size is 2-ton.
    3 consider that the best size is over 2-ton.
Of 77 who now own 2-ton trucks—
    1 considers that the best size is 1-ton.
    5 consider that the best size is 1¼- or 1½-ton.
    59 consider that the best size is 2-ton.
    12 consider that the best size is over 2-ton.
Of 13 who now own 2½-ton and over—
    2 consider that the best size is 2-ton.
    11 consider that the best size is over 2-ton.
In all—
    48 consider that the best size is ½-ton.
    62 consider that the best size is ¾-ton.
    329 consider that the best size is 1-ton.
    113 consider that the best size is 1¼- or 1½-ton.
    115 consider that the best size is 2-ton.
    29 consider that the best size is over 2-ton.

. There has evidently been a tendency on the part of some of these men to purchase trucks which experience has shown to be too small for their needs. While 444, or 64 per cent, prefer the size they now own, only 13 of the entire number prefer smaller sizes and 239 prefer larger sizes. However, the 1-ton size is preferred by nearly three times as many men as any other size, and only about 1 man in 25 prefers a truck of over 2 tons capacity.

ADVANTAGES AND DISADVANTAGES.

There are advantages in the ownership of a motor truck, but just how great these advantages are and which should be given the greatest weight are questions unanswerable by the man who has not had experience with a truck. A summary of the answers of 638 of these truck owners to the question "What is the principal advantage of a truck for farm use?" is given in Table II.

TABLE II.—*The "principal advantage" of a motor truck as reported by 638 farmers.*

Principal advantage.	Number reporting.	Per cent of total.
Time saved	577	91
Saves horses	19	3
Better market	15	2
Convenience	13	2
Reduces expense	9	1
Other	5	1
Total	638	

More than 90 per cent of the owners believe that time saving is the principal advantage. There are other advantages, of course, but in the minds of these farmers this is the principal one. While only 15 of the men report that the principal advantage of the truck is that it enables them to go to a better market, a much larger number are going to a better market now than before the purchase of their trucks. Going to a market which is farther from their farms is simply a matter of taking more time for marketing, and part of the men who say that saving of time is the principal advantage find that the truck saves them sufficient time to enable them to go to the better market.

The fact that such a small number consider the saving of horses, the reducing of expense, and added convenience as the principal advantages of the truck, indicates that the amount of time which the motor truck will save, which may incidentally result in reaching a better market, is the item which should be given paramount importance when considering the purchase of a motor truck.

Disadvantages of the motor truck were reported by 283 men. (See Table III.) Of the remaining 470 farmers 297 did not answer the question and 173 stated that they knew of no disadvantages in owning a truck.

TABLE III.—*The "principal disadvantage" of a motor truck as reported by 283 farmers.*

Principal disadvantage.	Number reporting.	Per cent of total.
Poor roads	168	59
Cost of operation	48	17
Soft ground	25	9
First cost	15	5
Incompetent driver	14	5
Mechanical trouble	8	3
Other	5	2
Total	283	

It is seen that "poor roads" was given as the principal disadvantage by 59 per cent of those who reported on this item. A large percentage of the reports stated that there is some time during the year when the roads are in such a condition that motor trucks can not be used. (See page 18.) The men who live on unimproved roads, of course, have the greatest handicap in this respect, but even the best of roads may be impassable for a truck because of snow at certain times of the year in the region in which this study was made. After poor roads, either the cost of operation or soft ground is considered the greatest disadvantage, 17 per cent giving the cost of operation and 9 per cent soft-ground as the greatest disadvantage. First cost is next in importance, 5 per cent considering it the most serious disadvantage, and troubles due to incompetent drivers and mechanical defects are considered prime disadvantages by 8 per cent of the owners.

ROAD HAULING WITH TRUCKS.

All materials hauled to and from the farms were divided into five general classes, viz, "Crops," "Milk," "Feed," "Fertilizer" (including lime and manure), and "Other." An idea of the relative amounts of these different classes of material hauled by the trucks may be obtained from the fact that 444 farms reported hauling a total of 52,977 tons of crops during the year; 100 reported hauling a total of 10,371 tons of milk; 96 reported hauling a total of 2,847 tons of feed; 118 reported hauling 6,487 tons of fertilizer; and 159 farmers reported hauling 14,599 tons of other material. The character of the crops to be hauled depends, of course, upon the type of farming practiced. All the crops raised on the different types of farms represented in this study are included.

Each farmer reported the size of load, length of haul, and the time required for the round trip with the truck. Similar information was given for hauling with wagons before the purchase of trucks. The time required for the round trip included the time required for loading and unloading the truck or wagon.

Table IV shows a comparison of the size of load, length of haul, and time required for hauling crops with trucks of different sizes and with wagons.

TABLE IV.—*Time required to haul crops with trucks, and with wagons before purchase of trucks (567 reports).*

Size of truck.	With truck.				With wagon.			
	Size of load.	Distance.	Hours per round trip.	Hours per ton-mile.	Size of load.	Distance.	Hours per round trip.	Hours per ton-mile.
	Pounds.	*Miles.*			*Pounds.*	*Miles.*		
½-ton	960	10.4	2.5	0.50	1,505	9.0	7.2	1.06
¾-ton	1,851	12.9	3.2	.27	2,213	11.4	8.6	.68
1-ton	2,391	13.0	3.4	.22	2,582	10.4	8.3	.62
1¼- to 1½-ton	3,469	10.1	2.8	.16	3,306	9.2	7.3	.49
2-ton	4,928	13.6	3.6	.10	4,488	12.9	9.5	.34
Over 2-ton	8,125	21.1	6.0	.07	5,783	19.7	13.8	.24

Table V gives a like comparison for hauling milk, Table VI for hauling feed, and Table VII for hauling fertilizer.

TABLE V.—*Time required to haul milk with trucks, and with wagons before purchase of trucks (132 reports).*

Size of truck.	With truck.				With wagon.			
	Size of load.	Distance.	Hours per round trip.	Hours per ton-mile.	Size of load.	Distance.	Hours per round trip.	Hours per ton-mile.
	Pounds.	*Miles.*			*Pounds.*	*Miles.*		
½-ton	609	4.3	1.4	1.10	657	4.1	3.1	2.30
¾-ton	1,264	7.9	2.6	.52	1,332	8.4	5.0	.90
1-ton	1,301	5.1	1.6	.48	1,309	4.9	3.6	1.12

TABLE VI.—*Time required to haul feed with trucks, and with wagons before purchase of trucks (113 reports).*

Size of truck.	With truck.				With wagon.			
	Size of load.	Distance.	Hours per round trip.	Hours per ton-mile.	Size of load.	Distance.	Hours per round trip.	Hours per ton-mile.
	Pounds.	*Miles.*			*Pounds.*	*Miles.*		
½-ton	942	4.6	1.2	0.55	1,943	4.8	3.9	0.84
¾-ton	1,555	6.6	1.8	.35	2,331	7.4	6.7	.75
1-ton	2,407	6.8	1.9	.23	2,824	5.7	4.8	.60
1¼- to 1½-ton	3,214	5.6	1.8	.20	3,071	5.6	5.0	.59
2-ton	4,300	8.0	2.5	.14	3,300	7.8	7.0	.56

TABLE VII.—*Time required to haul fertilizer with trucks, and with wagons before purcha of trucks (121 reports).*

Size of truck.	With truck.				With wagon.			
	Size of load.	Distance.	Hours per round trip.	Hours per ton-mile.	Size of load.	Distance.	Hours per round trip.	Hours p ton-mi
	Pounds.	*Miles.*			*Pounds.*	*Miles.*		
¾-ton..............	1,917	7.5	2.0	0.28	2,444	8.9	6.9	0.
1-ton................	2,444	7.3	2.3	.27	2,962	6.8	5.7	.
1¼- to 1½-ton.........	3,840	6.2	1.8	.15	3,681	6.1	4.5	.
2-ton...............	5,281	7.2	2.2	.12	4,107	5.5	5.3	.

It will be seen that the men who are using the smaller trucl hauled comparatively small loads with their wagons; however, tl average size of loads of crops hauled with the ½-, ¾-, and 1-ton trucl is less than the average size of loads which were formerly haule with wagons. The same is true with feed and fertilizer.

Milk was hauled almost entirely with 1-ton trucks or smaller, onl 7 of 139 men who reported hauling milk having trucks larg than 1 ton. The size of load is smaller and the distance hauled shorter for milk than for the other three materials. For each si of truck the average distance crops are hauled is slightly greater tha the distance hauled with the wagons before the trucks were pu chased, this difference being due to the fact that a number of me changed their markets after buying their trucks.

The hours per ton-mile were arrived at by dividing the hours fc the round trip by the product of the distance in miles and size (load in tons. For instance, in Table IV the ½-ton truck carryir a load of 960 pounds a distance of 10.4 miles accomplishes 4.9 ton-miles of hauling. Since 2½ hours are required for making th trip the time required per ton-mile is 0.50 hour. A compariso of the hours required per ton-mile for hauling by truck with tl hours per ton-mile required for hauling by horses and wagon giv the proportion of the time saved by using the truck.

TIME SAVED BY TRUCKS.

Table VIII shows the percentage of time which the trucks of diffe ent sizes are saving their owners in hauling different materials. I nearly every case the trucks are saving more than half of the tin formerly required to haul with wagons.

TABLE VIII.—*Percentage of time which trucks of different sizes save in hauling different materials.*

Size of truck.	Time saved in hauling.			
	Crops.	Milk.	Feed.	Fertilizer.
	Per cent.	*Per cent.*	*Per cent.*	*Per cent.*
½-ton.................	53	52	35	....
¾-ton.................	60	42	53	57
1-ton.................	65	57	62	52
1¼- to 1½-ton.........	67	....	66	63
2-ton.................	71	....	75	75
Over 2-ton...........	71	....	....	....

If the men who own small trucks had hauled as large loads with wagons as the men with larger trucks did, the saving of time effected by the small trucks would have been much less. As shown in Table IV, the time per ton-mile required to haul crops with the ½-ton trucks is 0.50 hour, while the time required per ton-mile by these same men in hauling with wagons before the trucks were purchased was 1.06 hours, the trucks thus saving 53 per cent of the time. The men who now own 1¼- and 1½-ton trucks required only 0.49 hours per ton-mile for hauling with wagons before purchasing their trucks. This difference is due entirely to the fact that the men who now own ½-ton trucks formerly hauled loads with wagons which averaged 1,505 pounds, while the men owning 1¼- and 1½-ton trucks hauled loads which averaged 3,306 pounds.

RETURN LOADS.

The percentage of time which a truck is run without a load has a direct influence on the cost per unit of hauling with the truck. If a farmer can arrange to haul a load of produce to market and bring back a load of supplies to the farm on the same trip, he will reduce the time required and expense for hauling practically 50 per cent. (See fig. 2.) The reports of these men show that they have loads both ways for their trucks on an average of about 26 per cent of their trips. Thirty per cent of the men, however, stated that they never have return loads. The dairy farmers and general farmers reported return loads a considerably larger percentage of the time than did the fruit, truck, and crop farmers.

ROAD HAULING FOR WHICH TRUCKS ARE NOT USED.

A majority of these men still use their horses to supplement their trucks in hauling on the road. While 516 men reported concerning their present use of horses for road hauling, only 193, or 37 per cent, stated that they did all their road hauling during the year preceding the time of reporting with trucks. Table IX shows the reasons given by the remaining 323 of these 516 men for using their horses on the road.

Nearly one-half gave "poor roads" as the reason for using horses; that is, they found it necessary to use their horses for hauling which had to be done at times when the condition of the roads was such that their trucks could not be used. A majority of the remainder stated that they used their horses either because the truck was too light for the load which it was desired to haul, or because the body was unsuitable for carrying the material. However, no farmer with a truck larger than the 1-ton size stated that he used horses because the truck was too light. About 7 per cent of the total number said that they used their horses to help out when the truck

Fig. 2.—A market gardener hauling manure to his farm on the return trip from market.

was busy, and about an equal number said that since they must keep their horses anyway they used them for some road hauling when they were not busy at other work.

It was not possible to determine from the reports the exact proportion of the road hauling which is still done with horses on these farms. However, on a large majority of them horses were used only for road hauling which it was necessary to do at times when the trucks could not be used or for which the trucks were not suitable, and such hauling would amount to only a small percentage of the total. The size of loads and distance hauled with horses are approximately the same as given in Tables IV to VII.

TABLE IX.—*Reason for using horses for hauling on the road.*

Reason for using horses.	Number reporting.	Per cent of total.
Poor roads	146	45
Truck body unsuitable	49	15
Truck too light	47	15
Keep horses busy	24	7
Truck busy	22	7
Soft ground	5	2
Reduce expense	4	1
Other	26	8

HAULING ON THE FARM WITH TRUCKS.

Of 416 men who reported on the use of their trucks for hauling on the farm, i. e., in the fields and around the buildings, 294, or more than 70 per cent, stated that they do not use their trucks at all for

FIG. 3.—The truck can often be used to advantage for hauling fruit from the orchard to the packing house.

such work. The reasons for not using the truck for hauling on the farm were not given in every case, but a large number stated that their trucks were not suitable for such work. The smaller trucks in many cases will not carry as large loads as it is desired to haul, often the truck can not obtain traction in the fields, and sometimes the body with which it is equipped is not suitable for some of the hauling on the farm.

Many others stated that they used their horses for all hauling on the farm because there was no advantage in using the truck for such work. Most of the time required for hauling on the farm is taken up with loading and unloading, and the percentage of the total time which will be saved by the truck when used for such work is small as compared with the time it will save in road hauling.   When there are horses on the farm which would otherwise be idle, it would naturally be more profitable to use the horses and let the truck stand idle if there is no advantage in time saved or convenience in using it.

The reasons for using their trucks, as given by 122 men who reported that they did some hauling on their farms with their trucks, are summarized in Table X.   Practically all of this hauling was either crops or fertilizer, including lime and manure.   The average length of haul for 94 of these men who reported on hauling crops was 148 rods, and for 40 who reported hauling fertilizer it was 149 rods. The average size of all the farms included is only 173 acres (see Table I), and 149 rods is considerably greater than the average distance which crops and fertilizer are usually hauled on such farms.

TABLE X.—*Reason for using truck for hauling on the farm.*

Reason for using truck.	Number reporting.	Per cent of total.
Time saved	78	64
Convenience	22	18
Horses busy	13	11
Other	9	7

Sixty-four per cent of the 122 men reporting gave the saving of time as the reason for using their trucks for this work.   A truck will save some time over horses on hauls of this distance if the truck body is suitable for carrying the material to be hauled, and if there is no difficulty in obtaining traction in the fields.   It may also save time to use the truck when only one or two loads are to be hauled, and the horses and wagons are not ready for use.

Eighteen per cent reported that they used their trucks for hauling on their farms because it was more convenient than to use their horses. There is some hauling on the farms where frequent stops must be made, or where the horses or truck must be left without attention for a considerable length of time.   In such cases it may be preferable to use the truck even though the horses are allowed to remain idle and the use of the truck does not save any time.   (See fig. 3.)

The men who do use their trucks for hauling on the farm reported hauling only an average of 45 tons of crops and 37 tons of fertilizer per year (including lime and manure) with them, while the average amount of crops hauled to market per year with trucks for all farms is 119 tons, and the average amount of fertilizer hauled on the road with trucks is 55 tons per year.   Thus, even the comparatively small number of men who use their trucks for hauling on the farm still use their horses for a goodly share of such work.

CUSTOM HAULING.

While all the men whose reports are included use their trucks primarily for hauling to and from their own farms, about 28 per cent reported that they did some custom work during the year preceding the time of reporting. Of 492 farmers who reported concerning custom work 355 said that during the past year they had done none whatever. The remaining 137 had received on the average $174 for such work. The number of men who reported hauling different materials, and the price which they received per ton-mile, are given in Table XI.

TABLE XI.—*Returns for custom work.*

Material.	Number of reports.	Price per ton-mile.
Crops	60	$0.37
Milk	6	.69
Feed	6	.39
Fertilizer	6	.28
Other	71	.48

About 30 per cent of these men who had done custom work stated that it had not been profitable. Many of them stated that the main reason for doing custom work was to accommodate their neighbors, and ordinarily in such cases the price was not high enough to make the work profitable. Most of the custom work reported was done by men owning large or medium sized trucks. Only seven of the men who own half-ton trucks reported that they did any custom work, and the average amount received by the seven for the work which they did during the past year was $53.

EFFECT OF DIFFERENT KINDS OF ROADS ON USE OF TRUCKS.

It has been shown that the majority of these farmers considered poor roads the greatest disadvantage in the use of a motor truck, and that most of those who still use horses for part of their road hauling do so because of poor roads. In order to gain a more definite idea of the effect of the kind of roads on the use of motor trucks, each farmer was asked to specify the kind of roads over which his truck traveled and the number of weeks during the past year the roads had been in such condition on account of mud or snow that the truck could not be used.

All kinds of roads, from unimproved dirt roads to high-class State highways, were reported. Twenty-nine per cent of the men who reported on this point stated that their trucks ordinarily travel only on dirt roads, 46 per cent stated that the roads which they ordinarily use are part dirt and part improved, and the remainder stated that they have all improved roads, either macadam, gravel, or better.

Of course, snow may make even the best of roads impassable fo truck, and this must be remembered in interpreting these figures.

The exact number of men with different kinds of roads and number of weeks they could not use their trucks is as follows:

Of 187 men with dirt roads only—
> 17 were able to use their trucks every week in the year.
> 36 were unable to use them for 1 to 4 weeks in the year.
> 32 were unable to use them for 5 to 8 weeks in the year.
> 38 were unable to use them for 9 to 12 weeks in the year.
> 24 were unable to use them for 13 to 16 weeks in the year.
> 19 were unable to use them for 17 to 20 weeks in the year.
> 21 were unable to use them for 21 weeks and over.

Of 298 men with roads partly improved—
> 62 were able to use their trucks every week in the year.
> 68 were unable to use them for 1 to 4 weeks in the year.
> 59 were unable to use them for 5 to 8 weeks in the year.
> 43 were unable to use them for 9 to 12 weeks in the year.
> 30 were unable to use them for 13 to 16 weeks in the year.
> 20 were unable to use them for 17 to 20 weeks in the year.
> 16 were unable to use them for 21 weeks and over.

Of 159 men with improved roads only—
> 78 were able to use their trucks every week in the year.
> 38 were unable to use them for 1 to 4 weeks in the year.
> 19 were unable to use them for 5 to 8 weeks in the year.
> 16 were unable to use them for 9 to 12 weeks in the year.
> 5 were unable to use them for 13 to 16 weeks in the year.
> 1 was unable to use it for 17 to 20 weeks in the year.
> 2 were unable to use them for 21 weeks and over.

On the average, there were 10.7 weeks when the men with all-(roads could not use their trucks, 7.8 weeks when those with part-(roads could not use them, and 3.5 weeks when those with whe improved roads could not.

In all, less than 25 per cent of the men found it possible to their trucks every week in the year, and between 35 and 40 per c reported that there were more than 8 weeks during the year wl they could not use their trucks. About one-half of the men w wholly improved roads stated that they could use their trucks t time during the year, but only 9 per cent of those with all-dirt ro were able to do so, and there were more than 8 weeks during the y when 55 per cent of these men with all-dirt roads were unable to their trucks. Snow was doubtless the main factor in making roads impassable for the 81 men who have improved roads only, who found there was at least one week during the year when t were not able to use their trucks.

The kind of tires with which the trucks are equipped apparer has little to do with the amount of time which they can not be u on account of the roads. That there was no apparent relation tween the character of the roads and the different kinds of tires, ;

no great difference in the length of time during which the condition of the roads prevented use of trucks with different kinds of tires, is shown by the following:

Of 222 owners of pneumatic-tired trucks—
 69 have all-dirt roads.
 96 have part-dirt roads.
 57 have no dirt roads.
  On the average there were 7.9 weeks during the year when the condition of the roads prohibited the use of the trucks.
Of 211 owners of solid-tired trucks—
 47 have all-dirt roads.
 98 have part-dirt roads.
 66 have no dirt roads.
  On the average there were 6.4 weeks during the year when the condition of the roads prohibited the use of the trucks.
Of 211 owners of trucks with pneumatic tires in front and solid tires behind—
 71 have all-dirt roads.
 104 have part-dirt roads.
 36 have no dirt roads.
  On the average there were 8.6 weeks during the year when the condition of the roads prohibited the use of the trucks.

Seven out of 69 men whose trucks are equipped with pneumatic tires and who have dirt roads only, and 4 out of 47 whose trucks are equipped with solid tires and who have dirt roads only, stated that there was less than a week during the year in which they could not use their trucks. The time during which the pneumatic-tired trucks with all-dirt roads could not be used was practically the same as for the solid-tired trucks with dirt roads only, the average being between 10 and 11 weeks in each case.

It does not necessarily follow that horses were always used for hauling when the roads were in such a condition that the trucks could not be used, as on at least a part of these farms there was no hauling which it was necessary to do at such times.

CHANGE OF MARKET.

Each truck owner was asked to give the name of the town where his produce was usually marketed before the purchase of the truck, and its distance from the farm. He was also asked to give the name of the town where the produce hauled by the truck is usually marketed and its distance from the farm. Answers of 704 men to these questions show that about one-fourth of them have changed their markets since purchasing their trucks. The exact number of men on each type of farm who answered the questions concerning their markets, the number who changed markets, and the average distance to the new markets is given in Table XII.

TABLE XII.—*Change of market after purchase of motor trucks.*

Type of farming.	Number reporting.	Number who changed market.	Average distance to new market.
			Miles.
Truck	139	31	18
Dairy	119	18	16
Fruit	102	23	27
Crop	44	12	22
General	300	88	19
All	704	172	20

A somewhat smaller percentage of dairy farmers than of any other type changed their markets. When milk is hauled to a condensery or to a station for shipment it is not often that one market or station is enough better than another to warrant a change.

A large percentage of these men who have changed their markets stated that they did so because the new market was better than the old one. A few, however, stated that they changed for other reasons, several saying that the better roads between their farms and the markets they are now using were responsible for the change. It should be remembered that a considerable number of the men who have not changed their markets were using first-class markets before purchasing their trucks.

The fact that a man has changed his market does not necessarily mean that all his produce is hauled to the new market, or that he purchases all the material for his farm at the new market. In fact, a considerable number of these men who usually market their produce at a different place than before purchasing their trucks reported that they still haul some material either to or from the old markets.

The distances from 156 of these farms to the markets which they used before buying their trucks, and the distances to the markets which they are now using are as follows:

Of 64 men who formerly used markets 1 to 4 miles distant—
    2 now use markets 1 to 4 miles distant.
    17 now use markets 5 to 9 miles distant.
    14 now use markets 10 to 14 miles distant.
    15 now use markets 15 to 19 miles distant.
    10 now use markets 20 to 24 miles distant.
    3 now use markets 25 to 29 miles distant.
    3 now use markets 30 or more miles distant.
Of 53 men who formerly used markets 5 to 9 miles distant—
    7 now use markets 5 to 9 miles distant.
    7 now use markets 10 to 14 miles distant.
    7 now use markets 15 to 19 miles distant.
    7 now use markets 20 to 24 miles distant
    9 now use markets 25 to 29 miles distant.
    16 now use markets 30 or more miles distant.

Of 26 men who formerly used markets 10 to 14 miles distant—
  1 now uses market 5 to 9 miles distant.
  4 now use markets 10 to 14 miles distant.
  7 now use markets 15 to 19 miles distant.
  2 now use markets 20 to 24 miles distant.
  2 now use markets 25 to 29 miles distant.
  10 now use markets 30 or more miles distant.
Of 8 men who formerly used markets 15 to 19 miles distant—
  1 now uses market 5 to 9 miles distant.
  2 now use markets 15 to 19 miles distant.
  1 now uses market 20 to 24 miles distant.
  2 now use markets 25 to 29 miles distant.
  2 now use markets 30 or more miles distant.
Of 5 men who formerly used markets 20 or more miles distant—
  1 now uses market 1 to 4 miles distant.
  1 now uses market 20 to 24 miles distant.
  3 now use markets 30 or more miles distant.

Before purchasing their trucks the operators of 75 per cent of these farms used markets less than 10 miles from their farms, but now over 80 per cent of them are using markets 10 miles or more from their farms. The average distance to the old market was 7 miles, and the average distance to the new market is 20 miles.

Seventy-one of these 156 men now use markets which are 20 miles or more from the farm. Of the entire 704 men who reported concerning their markets only 164 are now using markets which are 20 or more miles from the farm (see p. 6). Thus over 40 per cent of the men who now use markets which are such a great distance from their farms have changed markets since purchasing their trucks.

ANNUAL USE OF TRUCKS.

The number of miles per year which a motor truck travels has a direct bearing upon the cost per mile run or per ton hauled. Depreciation, interest, and repair charges appear all more or less independent of the number of miles which the truck travels per year, and the greater the number of miles traveled per year, or the greater the amount of material hauled, the less will be the charge per mile or per ton hauled for these items.

Following is a summary of the estimates of 553 men as to the number of miles per year which their trucks travel:

  58, or 10 per cent, estimated the annual mileage at 1,250 or less.
  118, or 22 per cent, estimated the annual mileage at 1,251 to 2,250.
  115, or 21 per cent, estimated the annual mileage at 2,251 to 3,250.
  92, or 17 per cent, estimated the annual mileage at 3,251 to 4,250.
  66, or 12 per cent, estimated the annual mileage at 4,251 to 5,250.
  34, or 6 per cent, estimated the annual mileage at 5,251 to 6,250.
  19, or 3 per cent, estimated the annual mileage at 6,251 to 7,250.
  19, or 3 per cent, estimated the annual mileage at 7,251 to 8,250.
  7, or 1 per cent, estimated the annual mileage at 8,251 to 9,250.
  14, or 3 per cent, estimated the annual mileage at 9,251 to 10,250.
  11, or 2 per cent, estimated the annual mileage at 10,251 or more.

The average of the estimates of these 553 men is 3,8
53 per cent of the estimates were 3,250 miles or less.

The amount of material hauled from and to the
depends on the type of farming and the size of the far
load, which depends on the size of the truck; and the l
all have an influence on the distance per year which a
but for the farms under consideration these factors are
in such a way that no one of them exerts a predominat
For instance, the average of the estimates of the numbe
year traveled by the trucks on the farms of differer
follows:

108 truck farms...
 93 dairy farms...
 89 fruit farms.....:.......................................
 36 crop farms...
227 general farms..

Similarly, the size of the truck and the distance from
market show very little relation to the number of miles
year.   The average of the estimates of—

113 men who own $\frac{1}{2}$-ton trucks is 3,790 miles per year.
 80 men who own $\frac{3}{4}$-ton trucks is 4,370 miles per year.
232 men who own 1-ton trucks is 3,660 miles per year.
 . 52 men who own 1$\frac{1}{4}$- and 1$\frac{1}{2}$-ton trucks is 3,100 miles per yea
 60 men who own 2-ton trucks is 4,070 miles per year.
 16 men who own 2$\frac{1}{2}$-ton and larger trucks is 4,980 miles per y

These farmers were also asked for their estimate of t
days per year on which they used their trucks—not t
full days work per year which the truck did, but simpl
of days on which some use was made of it.   The a
estimates of the number of days per year on which son
of the trucks on farms of different types is shown in
The dairy farmers use their trucks on the most days
farmers on the fewest.   The estimates also showed that
smaller trucks were used on a somewhat greater numbe
were the larger ones.

TABLE XIII.—*Days per year on which trucks are used*

Type of farming.	Number of estimates.	Days pe year on which truck is used.
Truck.........................	133	160
Dairy.........................	109	244
Fruit.........................	99	159
Crop..........................	43	127
General.......................	255	162
All......................	639	173

LIFE AND DEPRECIATION OF TRUCKS.

The average first cost, average life, and average depreciation per year and per mile traveled for trucks of ½ to 2 tons in size are shown in Table XIV. There were so few reports on trucks over 2 tons in size that no figures for them have been included.

TABLE XIV.—*First cost, life, and depreciation charges for trucks of different sizes.*

[Italic figures in parentheses indicate number of reports for respective items.]

Size of truck.	½-ton.	¾-ton.	1-ton.	1¼ and 1½-ton.	2-ton.
First cost............................	$574 (*149*)	$1,269 (*94*)	$900 (*342*)	$1,731 (*67*)	$2,366 (*9*)
Extra equipment......................	26 (*118*)	37 (*66*)	59 (*289*)	111 (*50*)	99 (*58*)
Total cost.....................	600	1,306	959	1,842	2,465
Present age (years)...................	2.7 (*150*)	2.3 (*95*)	1.6 (*344*)	2.1 (*67*)	2.5 (*79*)
Remaining life (years)...............	3.9 (*94*)	4.8 (*56*)	4.7 (*196*)	5.1 (*40*)	5.4 (*48*)
Total life (years)...............	6.6	7.1	6.3	7.2	7.9
Annual depreciation..................	$91	$184	$152	$256	$312
Miles traveled per year..............	3,790 (*113*)	4,370 (*80*)	3,660 (*232*)	3,100 (*52*)	4,070 (*60*)
Depreciation per mile of travel.......	$0.024	$0.042	$0.041	$0.083	$0.077

The quoted price of the truck often does not include some equipment which it is necessary or desirable to have, and each man was asked to report not only the first cost of his truck, but also the cost of any extra equipment he had purchased for it. It was found that nearly 75 per cent of the men had bought some equipment which was not included in the quoted price. This extra equipment varied from minor attachments costing only $2 or $3 to bodies and cabs costing as much as $200 or $300. As shown in the table, the amount spent for this extra equipment has been added to the reported first cost to obtain the total cost.

In all, 7 men reported that they owned trailers for use with their motor trucks. However, the cost of these trailers was not included in the total cost of the trucks.

The total life of the trucks was figured by adding the present age (that is, the average number of years which the trucks had been owned) to the average of the estimates of the remaining number of years for which the trucks will give satisfactory service. The remaining life of the truck depends not only upon its present condition, but also upon the probable work it will do in the future, and the owner's idea as to when it will be cheaper to discard it and purchase a new one than to spend more time and money on it for repairs. There is quite a wide variation in the individual estimates on this item, but the average life as obtained in this manner gives the best available basis for figuring depreciation costs. The average life of all trucks as figured by this method was 6.7 years.

The annual depreciation was figured by dividing the
the life in years, the depreciation per mile of travel by
annual depreciation by the average number of miles trave
A comparison of these figures with those for the cost of
in Table XVI and for tires in Table XVII shows that i
the depreciation charge is greater than the cost of fuel
for the larger sizes it is greater than the combined cost
and tires.

REPAIRS.

Each truck owner was asked to report the amount he l
repairs since the purchase of his truck. A summary c
for trucks of different sizes is given in Table XV.

TABLE XV.—*Average repair costs of trucks of different sizes ar*

Present age (months owned). .	Size of truck.		
	½-ton.	¾-ton.	1-ton.
	Average total expense f		
12 and less	$9	$20	$14
13 to 24	36	42	49
25 to 36	52	116	65
37 and over	136	191	155

In all, 40 per cent of the men who had not owned th
months had spent nothing on them for repairs. Howev
of those who had owned their trucks for more than 12
been free from expense for repairs. The amounts whic
of the trucks of different sizes had spent are as follows:

Half-ton trucks:

    Of 20 men who had used their trucks 12 months or less—

        7 had spent nothing for repairs.

        13 had spent from $1 to $87.

    Of 30 men who had used their trucks 13 to 24 months—

        28 had spent from $1 to $87.

        2 had spent from $88 to $187.

    Of 41 men who had used their trucks 25 to 36 months—

        1 had spent nothing for repairs.

        30 had spent from $1 to $87.

        9 had spent from $88 to $187.

        1 had spent from $188 to $287.

    Of 36 men who had used their trucks 37 months or more—

        1 had spent nothing for repairs.

        21 had spent from $1 to $87.

        4 had spent from $88 to $187.

        3 had spent from $188 to $287.

        2 had spent from $288 to $387.

        5 had spent $388 or more.

Three-fourths-ton trucks:

Of 18 men who had used their trucks 12 months or less—

7 had spent nothing for repairs.

11 had spent from $1 to $87.

Of 27 men who had used their trucks 13 to 24 months—

4 had spent nothing for repairs.

19 had spent from $1 to $87.

3 had spent from $88 to $187.

1 had spent from $288 to $387.

Of 25 men who had used their trucks 25 to 36 months—

3 had spent nothing for repairs.

12 had spent from $1 to $87.

4 had spent from $88 to $187.

3 had spent from $188 to $287.

2 had spent from $288 to $387.

1 had spent $388 or more.

Of 18 men who had used their trucks 37 months or more—

1 had spent nothing for repairs.

7 had spent from $1 to $87.

2 had spent from $88 to $187.

4 had spent from $188 to $287.

2 had spent from $288 to $387.

2 had spent $388 or more.

One-ton trucks:

Of 127 men who had used their trucks 12 months or less—

50 had spent nothing for repairs.

73 had spent from $1 to $87.

4 had spent from $88 to $187.

Of 134 men who had used their trucks 13 to 24 months—

15 had spent nothing for repairs.

96 had spent from $1 to $87.

13 had spent from $88 to $187.

7 had spent from $188 to $287.

3 had spent from $288 to $387.

Of 39 men who had used their trucks 25 to 36 months—

3 had spent nothing for repairs.

26 had spent from $1 to $87.

7 had spent from $88 to $187.

2 had spent from $188 to $287.

1 had spent $388 or more.

Of 25 men who had used their trucks 37 months or more—

12 had spent from $1 to $87.

6 had spent from $88 to $187.

1 had spent from $188 to $287.

4 had spent from $288 to $387.

2 had spent $388 or more.

Trucks of 1¼ to 1½ tons:

Of 10 men who had used their trucks 12 months or less—

8 had spent nothing for repairs.

2 had spent from $1 to $87.

Of 28 men who had used their trucks 13 to 24 months—

7 had spent nothing for repairs.

18 had spent from $1 to $88.

3 had spent from $88 to $187.

Trucks of 1¼ to 1½ tons—Continued.
    Of 12 men who had used their trucks 25 to 36 months—
        2 had spent nothing for repairs.
        4 had spent from $1 to $87.
        4 had spent from $88 to $187.
        2 had spent from $188 to $287.
    Of 11 men who had used their trucks 37 months or more—
        5 had spent from $1 to $87.
        4 had spent from $88 to $187.
        1 had spent from $188 to $287.
        1 had spent $388 or more.
Two-ton trucks:
    Of 10 men who had used their trucks 12 months or less—
        4 had spent nothing for repairs.
        5 had spent from $1 to $87.
        1 had spent from $88 to $187.
    Of 23 men who had used their trucks 13 to 24 months—
        3 had spent nothing for repairs.
        13 had spent from $1 to $87.
        2 had spent from $88 to $187.
        2 had spent from $188 to $287.
        3 had spent $388 or more.
    Of 27 men who had used their trucks 25 to 36 months—
        3 had spent nothing for repairs.
        12 had spent from $1 to $87.
        6 had spent from $88 to $187.
        2 had spent from $188 to $287.
        1 had spent from $288 to $387.
        3 had spent $388 or more.
    Of 11 men who had used their trucks 37 months or more—
        3 had spent from $1 to $87.
        1 had spent from $88 to $187.
        7 had spent $388 or more.

The average age of the trucks which had been ov
or more was not far from 4 years, and on this ba
annual repair costs for the first 4 years of these tr
approximately $35 for the ½-ton trucks, $50 for th
the 1-ton, $35 for the 1¼-ton and 1½-ton, and $110 fc
is apparent that these figures are too low for the
repair cost for the entire life of the machines, but s
machines reported on were entirely worn out it i
obtain accurate figures for this item. In the abse
figures, allowances of $50 per year for the ½-ton tru
¾-ton trucks, $75 for the 1-ton trucks, $100 for the 1¼
trucks, and $150 for the 2-ton trucks, have been mad
for the average annual repair costs in figuring the c
in Table XX on page 32.

GASOLINE AND OIL.

The average number of miles obtained per gallon
per quart of cylinder oil by the men who use trucks

are shown in Table XVI. The average price which these men paid for gasoline at the time they made their reports (January and February, 1920), was 27 cents per gallon, and the average price of lubricating oil was 65 cents per gallon. The costs per mile traveled are computed from these figures. No attempt was made to learn the amount and value of the grease used, but in any case its value should be only a fraction of that of the lubricating oil.

TABLE XVI.—*Gasoline and oil requirements of trucks of different sizes.*

[Gasoline at 27 cents per gallon; lubricating oil at 65 cents per gallon.]

Size of truck.	Gasoline.			Oil.			Total cost per mile for gasoline and oil.
	Miles per gallon.	Number of reports.	Cost per mile.	Miles per quart.	Number of reports.	Cost per mile.	
½-ton	14.8	138	$0.018	.59	93	$0.003	$0.021
¾-ton	12.1	92	.022	58	71	.003	.025
1-ton	11.2	332	.024	48	281	.003	.027
1¼ and 1½-ton	9.5	64	.028	49	54	.003	.031
2-ton	8.0	75	.034	40	62	.004	.038

TIRES.

Each man was asked to state what he paid for tires and the mileage obtained. The cost per mile for tires as shown in Table XVII is figured by simply dividing the average cost per tire by the average number of miles which the tire runs, and multiplying this result by four to obtain the cost for four tires. According to the estimates of 318 men, the pneumatic tires on these trucks run an average of 4,500 miles, and according to the estimates of 206 men the solid tires run an average of 8,200 miles. Such a large percentage of the ½-ton and ¾-ton trucks used are equipped with pneumatic tires that no figures for solid tire costs for these sizes are given, and such a large percentage of the trucks over 1 ton in size are equipped with solid tires that no figures for pneumatic tire costs for them are shown.

An allowance for the mileage obtained from the tires with which a machine is equipped when purchased must be made in order to determine the net tire cost to the user, as the cost of the first set of tires is included in the purchase price of the truck.

According to the estimates of these men the percentage of the total mileage of the trucks obtained from the tires with which they are equipped when purchased is as follows:

Pneumatic tires on the ½-ton trucks run 18 per cent of the total mileage.
Pneumatic tires on the ¾-ton trucks run 17 per cent of the total mileage.
Pneumatic tires on the 1-ton trucks run 19 per cent of the total mileage.
Solid tires on the 1-ton trucks run 36 per cent of the total mileage.
Solid tires on the 1¼- and 1½-ton trucks run 40 per cent of the total mileage.
Solid tires on the 2-ton trucks run 26 per cent of the total mileage.

The cost per mile as indicated by the cost of the tires and mil ich they run has been reduced by these percentages in order tain the net cost per mile traveled. No attempt was made tain the cost of inner tubes for pneumatic tires or to obtain t: it of tire repairs separately from the entire repair costs of t: cks.

TABLE XVII.—*Tire costs.*

Size of truck.	Kind of tires.	Cost per mile.	Number of reports.	Allowance for tires on machine when bought.	Net cc per m)
1	Pneumatic	$0.020	113	$0.004	$0.
1	do	.035	47	.006	.
1	do	.020	151	.004	.
1	Solid	.020	94	.007	.
nd 1½-ton	do	.029	20	.012	.
1	do	.034	25	.009	.

KIND OF TIRES RECOMMENDED BY USERS.

These truck owners were asked what kind of tires they consid ə best for their conditions, regardless of the kind actually use e kinds of tires which 637 men with trucks of all sizes are nc ng, together with the kinds they prefer, are as follows:

Of 231 men who use pneumatic tires—
    230 prefer pneumatics.
    1 prefers pneumatics in front and solids in rear.
Of 209 men who now use solid tires—
    16 prefer pneumatics.
    192 prefer solids.
    1 prefers pneumatics in front and solids in rear.
Of 197 men who now use pneumatics in front and solids in rear—
    75 prefer pneumatics.
    67 prefer solids.
    55 prefer pneumatics in front and solids in rear.

In all, 36 per cent now use pneumatics, 33 per cent use solids, a) per cent use pneumatics in front and solids in the rear, while . ' cent prefer pneumatics, 41 per cent prefer solids, and only 9 p it prefer pneumatics in front and solids in the rear. The kind əs which a man prefers depends considerably upon the size of l ıck and the kind of tires which he now uses. Four hundred a) ʼenty-seven of these 637 men recommend the same kind of ti ıipment as they are now using, and doubtless in a majority əse cases the kind of tires now used is the same as the kind wi ich the truck was equipped when it was purchased.

A large percentage of the owners of the ½- ton and ¾-ton truc ısider pneumatics the best; the owners of the 1-ton trucks a out evenly divided in their preference, and a large percentage the owners of trucks larger than 1 ton prefer solid tires. The exact number of owners of trucks of different sizes, and their recommendations, is as follows:

Of 135 owners of ½-ton trucks—
    129 recommend pneumatics.
    5 recommend solids.
    1 recommends pneumatics in front and solids in the rear.

Of 92 owners of ¾-ton trucks—
    64 recommend pneumatics.
    25 recommend solids.
    3 recommend pneumatics in front and solids in the rear.

Of 278 owners of 1-ton trucks—
    111 recommend pneumatics.
    120 recommend solids.
    47 recommend pneumatics in front and solids in the rear.

Of 54 owners of 1¼- and 1½-ton trucks—
    8 recommend pneumatics.
    44 recommend solids.
    2 recommend pneumatics in front and solids in the rear.

Of 65 owners of 2-ton trucks—
    9 recommend pneumatics.
    52 recommend solids.
    4 recommend pneumatics in front and solids in the rear.

Of 13 owners of trucks over 2 tons in size, all recommend solids.

RELIABILITY.

The reliability of a motor truck, as that of any other machine, has a very decided effect upon its profitableness. If a truck is out of commission for several days at a time when its services are needed and when its owner is depending upon it to help him through a busy time it can scarcely be considered a profitable machine for him to own. Likewise, if a great deal of time is lost on the road on account of motor and tire trouble, breakage, and other delays, this loss and annoyance may overcome all the advantages attending its use. In order to obtain information as to the reliability of motor trucks for farm use these truck owners were asked to give both the number of days their trucks had been out of commission when needed during the past year, and the percentage of the time lost while using them. Table XVIII shows the average number of days 682 trucks of different ages were out of commission during the year preceding the time of reporting. The reports indicated that there is practically no difference in this respect among the trucks of different sizes.

TABLE XVIII.—*Days per year trucks were out of commission when needed.*

Age of trucks (months).	Total number of reports.	Average days out of commission.
12 and less	187	0.7
13 to 24	245	1.7
25 to 36	147	2.0
37 and over	103	3.2
All	682	1.7

The total number of days the trucks of different ages were out c commission is as follows:

Of the 187 which had been in use 12 months or less—
    157 were out of commission no days.
    23 were out of commission from 1 to 5 days.
    5 were out of commission from 6 to 10 days.
    2 were out of commission over 10 days.
Of the 245 which had been in use 13 to 24 months—
    173 were out of commission no days.
    44 were out of commission 1 to 5 days.
    18 were out of commission 6 to 10 days.
    10 were out of commission over 10 days.
Of the 147 which had been in use 25 to 36 months—
    93 were out of commission no days.
    39 were out of commission 1 to 5 days.
    10 were out of commission 6 to 10 days.
    5 were out of commission over 10 days.
Of the 103 which had been in use 37 months or more—
    56 were out of commission no days.
    32 were out of commission 1 to 5 days.
    9 were out of commission 6 to 10 days.
    6 were out of commission over 10 days.

Seventy-one per cent of the trucks had not been out of commissio at all when needed, 20 per cent had been out of commission 5 days c less, 6 per cent had been out of commission from 6 to 10 days, and per cent had been out of commission over 10 days. In general, th newer trucks are more reliable than the older ones. While nearly 8 per cent of the trucks which had been owned 12 months or less ha not been out of commission when needed, only a little more than on half of those which had been in use more than 3 years had not bee out of commission during the preceding year.

The average percentage of time lost on account of motor and ti trouble, breakage, etc., by 542 men owning trucks of different ages shown in Table XIX.

TABLE XIX.—*Per cent of time lost by trucks of different ages on account of motor and tire trouble, breakage, etc.*

Age of truck (months).	Number of reports.	Average per cent of time lost.
12 and less	155	0.6
13 to 24	190	1.1
25 to 36	120	1.6
37 and over	77	1.6

The estimates of the men who had used their trucks different lengths of time were as follows:

Of 155 who had used their trucks 12 months or less—
122 reported the loss of no time.
32 reported the loss of 1 to 5 per cent.
1 reported the loss of more than 10 per cent.
Of 190 who had owned their trucks 13 to 24 months—
130 reported the loss of no time.
52 reported the loss of 1 to 5 per cent.
7 reported the loss of 6 to 10 per cent.
1 reported the loss of more than 10 per cent.
Of 120 who had owned their trucks 25 to 36 months—
73 reported the loss of no time.
39 reported the loss of 1 to 5 per cent.
6 reported the loss of 6 to 10 per cent.
2 reported the loss of more than 10 per cent.
Of 77 who had owned their trucks 37 months or more—
39 reported the loss of no time.
34 reported the loss of 1 to 5 per cent.
3 reported the loss of 6 to 10 per cent.
1 reported the loss of more than 10 per cent.

The newer trucks are more reliable in this respect, just as they are in respect to the amount of time they are out of commission when needed. Eighty per cent of the men whose trucks have been in use 12 months or less stated that they lost no time, and only one-half of the men whose trucks have been in use more than 3 years stated that they had lost no time. In all, 67 per cent of the total stated that they had lost no time, and only 1 man in 26 stated that more than 5 per cent of the time was lost on this account.

The average distance crops are hauled by these men is about 10 miles, and the average time required for the round trip is not far from 3 hours (see Table IV). A loss of 5 per cent of the time on such a trip would mean a delay of about 10 minutes, and a loss of 10 per cent of the time would be a delay of about 20 minutes. Such delays, even with the trucks which give the most trouble in this respect would scarcely be as serious as the loss due to having the truck out of commission several days when it was needed.

To a certain extent the reliability of a motor truck depends upon the ability of the operator and the care which the truck is given.

Roughly, about 60 per cent of these trucks are operated by their owners, about 30 per cent by the sons of the owners, and about 10 per cent by hired men. Automobiles are owned on about three-fourths of the farms and tractors on about one-fourth of them. It is to be expected that the owner of such an expensive machine as a motor truck, or any member of his family, would give it a reasonable amount of care and operate it with a reasonable degree of intelligence, and the fact that automobiles or tractors were owned on a large percentage of these farms indicates that most of the operators were more or less skilled in the operation of gas engines. That such a large percentage of these trucks were operated without any loss of time and were always ready for work when needed is very probably partially due to these facts.

COST OF OPERATION.

The cost of operating trucks of different sizes reported by these men is shown in Table XX. The items considered in making up these costs are depreciation, repairs, interest on investment, registration and license fees, cost of gasoline and oil, and of tires.

TABLE XX.—*Cost of operating trucks of different sizes.*

	Size.				
	½-ton.	¾-ton.	1-ton.	1¼ and 1½-ton.	2-ton.
Fixed charges:					
Annual depreciation	$91	$184	$152	$256	$31?
Annual repairs	50	75	75	100	15?
Annual interest	21	45	33	63	8?
Annual registration and license fees	10	15	18	22	2?
Total fixed charges	172	319	278	441	57?
Miles traveled per year	3,790	4,370	3,660	3,100	4,07?
Fixed charges per mile	$0.045	$0.073	$0.076	$0.142	$0.14?
Gasoline and oil per mile	.021	.025	.027	.031	.03?
Tires per mile	.016	.029	.016	.017	.02?
Total cost per mile	.082	.127	.119	.190	.20?

The figures for annual depreciation are obtained from Table XIV those for annual repairs are obtained from page 26.

Interest is figured at 6 per cent on the average investment. The average investment has been found by the rule: Average invest ment $= \text{first cost} \times \dfrac{\text{years of service} + 1}{\text{years of service} \times 2}.$ This is the generally accepted method for determining the average investment in equipment where a fraction of the first cost is charged off each year for depreciation The interest charge when computed on this basis is slightly greater than when computed on one-half of the first cost.

Registration and license fees vary considerably in the different States. No attempt was made to determine the exact average of the fees paid by the different men. The amounts used as shown in the table are, however, representative of such fees for the year 1920 in the Eastern States, and include both the registration of the truck and the operator's license. In nearly every instance these amounts are within $5 of the actual fees charged in the different States.

No charge has been made for taxes, insurance, housing, or labor spent in caring for the truck. However, these items would ordinarily amount to a very small percentage of the total cost.

The number of miles traveled per year are shown on page 22. The gasoline and oil charges are obtained from Table XVI, and the tire charges from Table XVII. The tire charges for the $\frac{1}{2}$-ton, $\frac{3}{4}$-ton, and 1-ton trucks are for pneumatic tires, while for the $1\frac{1}{4}$-ton, $1\frac{1}{2}$-ton, and 2-ton trucks the tire charges are for solid tires.

COST OF HAULING WITH TRUCKS.

The cost of hauling with a motor truck is determined by the cost of operating the truck, the charge for the driver's time and labor, the size of load hauled, and the percentage of time the truck runs without a load. In Table XXI are given the cost per mile of haul, and the cost per ton-mile of hauling crops with trucks of different sizes. The cost of operating the truck is taken directly from the preceding table. The charge for the driver is obtained by allowing a rate of 50 cents per hour for his time while driving and while loading and unloading the truck. The average time required for hauling different materials as given in Tables IV to VII is 0.14 hour per mile of travel for the $\frac{1}{2}$- and $\frac{3}{4}$-ton trucks, and 0.15 hour for the 1-, $1\frac{1}{4}$-, $1\frac{1}{2}$-, and 2-ton trucks.

It is stated on page 13 that these men had return loads for their trucks about 26 per cent of the time; that is, each truck hauls loads both ways on 26 out of every 100 round trips it makes from and to the farm, and runs without a load 74 one-way trips. The cost of operating the truck and the value of the driver's time for these 74 trips with no load must be charged to the 126 trips with loads, in order to obtain the actual cost per mile of haul. That is, every 126 miles of haul must bear the expense of 200 miles of travel, or every 63 miles of haul must bear the expense of 100 miles of travel. The cost per mile of haul as given in the table is obtained by multiplying the total cost per mile traveled by 100 and dividing the product by 63.

The cost per ton-mile hauled is determined by dividing the cost per mile hauled by the weight of the load in tons. As shown in Table IV, the average weight of a load of crops hauled with $\frac{1}{2}$-ton trucks is

0.480 ton; for ¾-ton trucks the load is 0.926 ton; for the 1-ton trucks, 1.196 tons; for 1¼-ton and 1½-ton trucks, 1.734 tons; and for the 2-ton trucks, 2.464 tons. The costs per mile of haul for the trucks of different sizes divided by these figures give the costs per ton-mile.

TABLE XXI.—*Cost of hauling with trucks of different sizes.*

Size of truck.	½-ton.	¾-ton.	1-ton.	1¼- and 1½-ton.	2-ton.
Truck cost per mile run............................	$0.082	$0.127	$0.119	$0.190	$0.203
Charge for driver per mile run......................	.070	.070	.075	.075	.075
Total...	.152	.197	.194	.265	.278
Cost per mile of haul (37 per cent idle running)......	.241	.313	.308	.421	.441
Cost per ton-mile for hauling crops..................	.502	.338	.258	.242	.179

SAVING OF HIRED HELP.

The saving of time is given by these men as the greatest advantage in the use of a motor truck, but the saving of time will not be of any financial benefit to a farmer unless he uses the time thus saved on other work, or unless it enables him to reduce the expense for hired help.

These men were asked whether or not their trucks reduce the expense for hired help, either man or horse, and, if so, to estimate the amount thus saved per year. Of 711 men who answered the question as to whether the truck reduces the expense for hired help, 562, or 79 per cent, said that it does, and the remaining 149 that it does not.

Three hundred and fifty of the 562 estimated the amount thus annually saved, and the average of these estimates is $324. This figure can scarcely be taken to represent the actual amount which the labor bills of these men have been reduced since purchasing their trucks, but rather as their estimates of the amounts by which their bills would be increased if they did not now own trucks, and if they were doing the same amount of work they are now doing.

Eighty-four per cent of the operators of fruit farms think that their trucks reduce the expense for hired help. This is a slightly higher percentage than is reported for any other type of farming. The average of the estimates of those of this 84 per cent who attempted to place a value on the amount of help saved is $364.

The owners of the larger trucks make higher estimates of the amount that their trucks reduce expenses than do owners of the smaller ones. The averages of the estimates of the owners of the ½-ton, ¾-ton, and 1-ton trucks, who report that their trucks reduce the bill for hired help, were all between $250 and $300, the average of the estimates of the owners of the 1¼-ton and 1½-ton trucks was between $375 and $400, while the estimates of the owners of the 2-ton trucks and of those over 2 tons averaged more than $600. There is no great difference in the percentages of the owners of the different sizes who consider that their trucks do not reduce the expense for hired help.

DISPLACEMENT OF HORSES.

The operators of 610 farms reported the number of head of work stock they owned before purchasing their trucks and the number they had disposed of since that time. Four of these 610 farms were small ones which had been operated without horses even before trucks were purchased. The number of head of work stock kept on the other 606 farms varied from 1 or 2 on the smaller farms to 20 and more on a few of the larger ones. The total number of work stock kept on the 606 farms was 3,103. On 296 of them the number had been reduced since the trucks were purchased by a total of 586 head, an average reduction of 19 per cent for the 606 farms and an average displacement of 1.0 head per truck.

A man with only 1 or 2 horses will usually need to keep them for work on the farm even after buying a truck, and only about 1 man in 7 who owned 1 or 2 horses had sold any since buying his truck. Similarly, the purchase of a motor truck will not often enable a man who owns 3 or 4 horses, all of which he sometimes uses as a single unit, to reduce the number of his work stock. A little less than one-half of the men who had owned 3 or 4 horses before purchasing their trucks reported that they had disposed of any since that time, but nearly two-thirds of those who had owned 5 or more had disposed of at least 1 after purchasing the truck. The exact number of work stock formerly owned and the number disposed of by the different men is as follows:

Of 90 men who owned 1 or 2 head before purchasing trucks—
    77 had disposed of none.
    10 had disposed of 1.
    3 had disposed of 2.
Of 232 men who owned 3 or 4 head before purchasing trucks—
    130 had disposed of none.
    59 had disposed of 1.
    42 had disposed of 2.
    1 had disposed of 3.
Of 156 men who owned 5 or 6 head before purchasing trucks—
    66 had disposed of none.
    35 had disposed of 1.
    43 had disposed of 2.
    8 had disposed of 3.
    4 had disposed of 4.

Of 63 men who owned 7 or 8 head before purchasing trucks—
    16 had disposed of none.
     7 had disposed of 1.
    25 had disposed of 2.
     5 had disposed of 3.
    10 had disposed of 4.
Of 34 men who owned 9 or 10 head before purchasing trucks—
     8 had disposed of none.
     1 had disposed of 1.
    10 had disposed of 2.
     4 had disposed of 3.
     5 had disposed of 4.
     6 had disposed of 5 or more.
Of 31 men who owned 11 or more head before purchasing trucks—
    13 had disposed of none.
     2 had disposed of 1.
     4 had disposed of 2.
     3 had disposed of 3.
     3 had disposed of 4.
     6 had disposed of 5 or more.

This displacement of horses by motor trucks is quite comparable to the displacement by tractors in this section. A study of 252 New York farms on which tractors are owned, as reported in Farmers' Bulletin 1004, "The Gas Tractor in Eastern Farming," showed that on these farms the total work stock owned when the tractors were purchased amounted to 1,321, while the total after the purchase of tractors was 1,018, a reduction of 22 per cent, and an average displacement of 1.2 head per tractor.

FARMS ON WHICH TRACTORS ARE OWNED.

Of 675 men who reported on whether or not they own tractors, 180, or 27 per cent, stated that they own tractors. Tractors are owned on a larger percentage of the crop and fruit farms than on farms of other types. They are owned on 9 per cent of the truck farms, 33 per cent of the dairy farms, 38 per cent of the fruit farms, 42 per cent of the crop farms, and 25 per cent of the general farms. Size of the farm, however, evidently had a greater influence in this regard than did the type of farming. The number of men with farms of different sizes (*crop* acres, not *total* acres), who do and do not own tractors, is as follows:

Of 243 men with 60 or less crop-acres—
    21 own tractors.
    222 do not own tractors.
Of 227 men with 61 to 120 crop-acres—
    47 own tractors.
    180 do not own tractors.
Of 103 men with 121 to 180 crop-acres—
    42 own tractors.
    61 do not own tractors.

Of 45 men with 181 to 240 crop-acres—
  31 own tractors.
  14 do not own tractors.
Of 30 men with 241 to 300 crop-acres—
  20 own tractors.
  10 do not own tractors.
Of 27 men with 301 or more crop-acres—
  19 own tractors.
  8 do not own tractors.

Over two-thirds of the 675 farms consisted of not over 120 crop-acres. Tractors are owned on only about 15 per cent of such farms, while they are owned on 55 per cent of those with more than 120 crop-acres. In most cases the reports did not show the size of the tractor owned, but at least a part of the tractors owned on the 21 farms with 60 or less crop-acres are small ones of only one or two draw-bar horsepower, and are capable of doing the work of only about one horse.

The ownership of both motor trucks and tractors, even on the large farms, has not resulted in a very great reduction in the number of horses. The men who own both trucks and tractors and who have from 61 to 120 crop-acres still keep nearly 4 horses on the average—one horse for each 24 crop-acres—and only 6 of them are farming with fewer than 3 horses. The men who have from 121 to 180 crop-acres still keep an average of 5 horses—one for each 30 acres—and only six of them are now farming with fewer than 4 horses. The men who have over 180 crop-acres still keep an average of between 8 and 9 horses—one to each 39 crop-acres—and only 3 of them are farming with fewer than 4 horses.

The number of crop-acres per horse on the farms of different sizes where trucks are owned, but not tractors, is only about 2 acres less in each case than on the farms where tractors are owned, there being 22 crop-acres per horse on the farms with 61 to 120 crop-acres where tractors are not owned, 28 per horse on those with 121 to 180 crop-acres, and 37 per horse on those with over 180 crop-acres.

ADDITIONAL COPIES
OF THIS PUBLICATION MAY BE PROCURED FROM
THE SUPERINTENDENT OF DOCUMENTS
GOVERNMENT PRINTING OFFICE -
WASHINGTON, D. C.
AT
10 CENTS PER COPY
△

UNITED STATES DEPARTMENT OF AGRICULTURE

BULLETIN No. 911

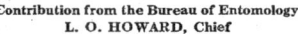

Contribution from the Bureau of Entomology
L. O. HOWARD, Chief

Washington, D. C.   PROFESSIONAL PAPER   December 13, 1920

LIFE HISTORY OF THE GRAPE-BERRY MOTH IN NORTHERN OHIO.[1]

By H. G. INGERSON, *Scientific Assistant, Deciduous Fruit Insect Investigations.*

CONTENTS.

	Page.		Page.
Method of conducting rearing work	1	Seasonal-history studies, 1918	24
Weather conditions in 1916, 1917 and 1918	2	Miscellaneous records	32
Seasonal-history studies, 1916	2	Summary	37
Seasonal-history studies, 1917	7		

METHOD OF CONDUCTING REARING WORK.

The studies reported in this paper on the grape-berry moth (*Polychrosis viteana* Clem.) began in 1916 with the collection of grapes which were infested with early hatching first-brood larvæ. These infested grapes were taken to the open-air insectary and placed in cylindrical wire baskets which held from 1 to 1½ quarts each. These baskets were placed in glass battery jars which had been supplied with about one-half inch of sand in the bottom. This sand absorbed the juice from the infested grapes and maintained a fairly constant humidity in the jars. The jars were closed with cloth covers.

Fresh grape leaves were placed in the battery jars in the space between the wire baskets and the glass surface, and the larvæ pupated

[1] The data reported in this paper were accumulated during the seasons of 1916, 1917, and 1918. The actual rearing records were secured at Sandusky, Ohio, and the field observations were made in the grape sections about Sandusky, including the Lake Erie islands, in Dover and Avon sections west of Cleveland, and in the Euclid section east of Cleveland.

Control experiments based on these life-history studies were conducted each season and the satisfactory control effected proved the value of such life-history data. The results of the control experiments are published separately as U. S. Department of Agriculture Bulletin 837.

These investigations were conducted in cooperation with the Ohio Agricultural Experiment Station.

During the season of 1916 the writer was assisted by E. R. Selkregg, then field assistant in the U. S. Bureau of Entomology. Mr. Selkregg was in direct charge of the rearing work for 1916. In the seasons of 1917 and 1918 the writer was assisted by Chester I. Bliss, field assistant in the U. S. Bureau of Entomology.

until the moths emerged. The moths were removed ea
;he records were taken. To secure oviposition records wh
;hs are confined several different methods have been tri
without satisfactory results.

ighout this work the rearing records have been checked a)
iented by extensive field observations and, except whe
epresent as nearly the actual conditions as it was possible
mate. Each table presented is to be considered complete
id not dependent on any other table. Special methods f
iring of any particular records are given with the records.

WEATHER CONDITIONS IN 1916, 1917, AND 1918.

nal-history data sufficient for accurate timing of spr:
ions were secured in 1916 and the other data secured we
al. The weather conditions in the season of 1916 we
ormal except for an unusually warm dry autumn. In 19
rds are more complete, but represent an abnormally late a)
son throughout. The fall was unusually cold and rainy a)
ably retarded the development of the second-brood larv
8 berry-moth infestation was generally light througho
a Ohio and difficulty was experienced early in the season
; sufficient material for rearing records. The season of 19
unseasonably early and remained advanced throughout.

SEASONAL-HISTORY STUDIES, 1916.

) studies began with the collection of early hatching fir:
arvæ in the vineyards. Vineyards known to have been
infested in 1915 were searched carefully on June 1, 5, 1
but not until June 20 was a larva found. At this time on
sional larva could be found and there was no general infest
the grape cluster buds. Not until July 5 were larvæ prese
vineyards in any considerable number. Collections of lar
ide frequently and regularly throughout the season, beginni
.

FIRST GENERATION.

TIME OF FIRST-BROOD LARVÆ LEAVING THE FRUIT.

il records began with the early hatching larvæ leaving t
Table I shows the dates on which the first-brood larvæ sp
coons. The earliest date is seen to be June 28 and the lat
18, with the greatest number cocooning on July 21.
vorthy of note that a very large percentage, 81.35 per ce:
d within the 12-day period from July 16 to July 27, inclusi'

Table I.—*Time of leaving grapes of first-brood larvæ of the grape-berry moth in 1916. Fruit collected at Venice, Put-in-Bay, and Kelley's Island, Ohio.*

Date of leaving fruit.	Number of larvæ.	Date of leaving fruit.	Number of larvæ.
June 28	1	July 26	142
29	1	27	139
July 2	1	28	95
4	3	29	8
5	1	30	28
6	3	31	35
7	5	Aug. 1	27
8	6	3	8
9	4	5	10
10	4	6	73
12	22	7	70
13	63	8	60
14	28	9	59
15	32	10	18
16	163	11	12
17	349	12	11
18	151	13	29
19	316	14	22
20	376	15	12
21	425	16	4
22	346	17	6
23	398	18	14
24	381		
25	164	Total	4,125

LENGTH OF TIME OF FIRST-BROOD INDIVIDUALS IN THE COCOON.

The time of cocooning and length of time in the cocoon for 38 individuals observed are shown in Table II. The maximum time is 19 days, the minimum 9 days, and the average 11.7 days.

Table II.—*Time of cocooning and the length of time in cocoon of the first brood of the grape-berry moth at Sandusky, Ohio, in 1916.*

Number of larvæ.	Larvæ left fruit.	Moths emerged.	Days in cocoon.	Total.	Larvæ collected at—
1	June 28	July 11	13	13	Put-in-Bay, Ohio.
1	...do	July 12	13	13	Do.
1	July 2	...do	10	10	Venice, Ohio.
1	July 4	July 14	10	10	Do.
2	...do	July 15	11	22	Do.
1	July 5	July 16	15	15	Do.
1	July 6	...do	10	10	Kelley's Island, Ohio.
1	...do	July 18	13	13	Do.
1	...do	July 25	19	19	Do.
1	July 7	July 17	10	10	Do.
1	...do	July 19	12	12	Venice, Ohio.
1	...do	...do	12	12	Kelley's Island, Ohio.
6	...do	July 21	14	84	Do.
5	July 12	...do	9	45	Do.
1	July 13	July 24	11	11	Do.
10	...do	...do	11	110	Venice, Ohio.
2	...do	July 25	12	24	Do.
1	...do	July 26	13	13	Do.
38		Average	11.7		
		Maximum	19		
		Minimum	9		

TIME OF EMERGENCE OF FIRST-BROOD MOTHS.

The material for securing emergence records of first-brood moths included the larvæ collected beginning June 20 and shown in Tables I and II, and pupæ collected in the field at frequent intervals. It will be seen in Table III and figure 1 that moths began to emerge July 11 and continued until August 31, with the greatest number on August 3. A large part, 63 per cent, of this emergence came within the 11-day period, July 27 to August 6.

TABLE III.—*Time of emergence of moths of the first brood of the grape-berry moth at Sandusky, Ohio, in 1916.*

Date of emergence.	Number of moths.	Date of emergence.	Number of moths.
July 11	1	Aug. 7	78
12	2	8	70
13	1	9	25
14	1	10	37
15	2	11	42
16	2	12	20
17	1	13	25
18	1	14	28
19	1	15	37
20	3	16	18
21	11	17	111
22	10	18	67
23	7	19	56
24	13	20	22
25	10	21	18
26	43	22	24
27	116	23	35
28	168	24	13
29	164	25	7
30	119	26	5
31	111	27	6
Aug. 1	78	28	4
2	118	29	1
3	194	30	2
4	109	31	1
5	190		
6	112	Total	2,340

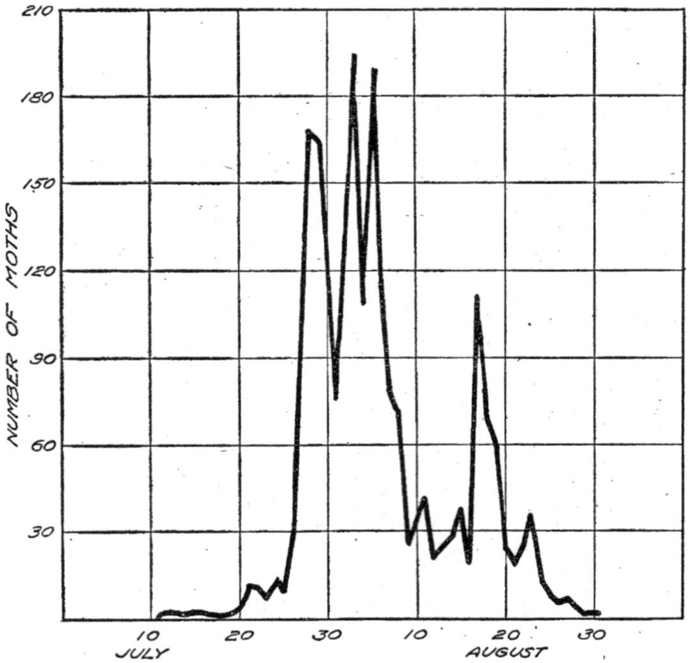

FIG. 1.—Diagram showing time of emergence of first-brood moths of the grape-berry moth (*Polychrosis viteana*) at Sandusky, Ohio, 1916.

OVIPOSITION OF FIRST-BROOD MOTHS.

The oviposition records were secured from some of the moths recorded in Table III. The oviposition of a few of these moths is shown in Table IV. No attempt was made to secure oviposition records throughout the entire oviposition period. From observations made in the vineyards during the season it was found that the heaviest oviposition was in the period from about August 1 to 10. Freshly deposited eggs were found in small numbers in the vineyards as late as August 17, and eggs were being deposited in the insectary as late as September 1.

TABLE IV.—*Oviposition by first-brood moths of the grape-berry moth in rearing jars at Sandusky, Ohio, in 1916.*

No. of jar.	Number of moths.		Date of—			Days—		
	♂	♀	Emergence.	First oviposition.	Last oviposition.	Before oviposition.	Of oviposition.	From emergence to last oviposition.
1	2	9	July 24	July 26	July 26	2	1	2
2	14	9	July 27	July 30	July 30	3	1	3
3	12	18	July 28	Aug. 3	Aug. 5	6	2	8
4	(1)	(1)	Aug. 5–6	Aug. 7–8	Aug. 11	2–2	3	6
5	3	14	Aug. 22-23	Aug. 26	Aug. 26	4	1	4
Average						3.4	1.6	4.6
Maximum						6	3	8
Minimum						2	1	2

[1] No record.

SECOND GENERATION.

TABLE V.—*Incubation period of second-brood eggs of the grape-berry moth at Sandusky, Ohio, 1916.*

Number of observation.	Date of oviposition.	Date of hatching.	Days of incubation.	Number of eggs.
1	Aug. 3	Aug. 8	5	No record.
2	Aug. 7–8	Aug. 11	4	Do.
3	Aug. 9–10	Aug. 13	4	52.
4	Aug. 11	Aug. 16	5	39.
5	Aug. 27–28	Sept. 3	7	No record.
6	Aug. 30	Sept. 5	6	Do.
7	Sept. 1	Sept. 6	5	Do.

Average length of incubation period, 5.1 days.
Maximum length of incubation period, 7 days.
Minimum length of incubation period, 4 days.

The incubation period of second-brood eggs as shown in Table V averaged 5.1 days with 7 days as the maximum time and 4 days as the minimum. It may be assumed then that the earliest second-brood larvæ began feeding about July 21, 10 days after the emergence of moths on July 11. The hatching, however, was light until about August 5, when larvæ began to be present in the vineyards in large numbers. Though some larvæ hatched in the insectary as late as September 6, in the vineyards most of the larvæ had hatched by August 25.

FEEDING PERIOD OF SECOND-BROOD LARVÆ IN REARING CAGES.

Records from the date of hatching to the date of cocooning were secured from 51 individuals as shown in Table VI.

TABLE VI.—*Feeding period of second-brood larvæ of the grape-berry moth in rearing cages, Sandusky, Ohio, 1916.*

Date of hatching.	Date of cocooning.	Number of cocoons.	Feeding period.	Total.
			Days.	*Days.*
Aug. 11	Aug. 31	2	20	40
Do	Sept. 1	5	21	105
Do	Sept. 6	4	26	104
Do	Sept. 7	1	27	27
Aug. 13	Aug. 31	1	18	18
Do	Sept. 1	2	21	42
Do	Sept. 2	1	22	22
Do	Sept. 4	4	24	96
Do	Sept. 7	4	27	108
Do	Sept. 9	2	29	58
Do	Sept. 10	1	30	30
Aug. 16	Sept. 1	3	16	48
Do	Sept. 4	5	19	95
Do	Sept. 9	3	24	72
Do	Sept. 10	3	25	75
Do	Sept. 11	3	26	78
Do	Sept. 12	3	27	81
Do	Sept. 14	1	29	29
Sept. 5	Oct. 11	1	36	36
Sept. 6	Oct. 9	1	33	33
Do	Oct. 12	1	36	36
Total		51		1,233
Average			24.18	
Maximum			36	
Minimum			16	

The average length of the feeding period for the 51 larvæ was 24.18 days, a much shorter period than has previously been recorded as the average for the second brood. This shortening was due no doubt to the unseasonably warm weather that prevailed during August, September, and early October of 1916. This figure should not be taken as representing the usual condition, but is presented here to show the influence of a warm fall on the maturing of the larvæ. The maximum length of the feeding period was 36 days and the minimum 16.

LENGTH OF THE PREPUPAL PERIOD.

The length of time between the spinning of the cocoon and pupation was recorded for 13 individuals as shown in Table VII.

TABLE VII.—*Length of the prepupal period of 13 individuals of the second brood of the grape-berry moth, Sandusky, Ohio, 1916.*

Date of spinning cocoon.	Number of cocoons.	Date of pupation.	Number of days in prepupal stage.	Total number of days.
Aug. 31	1	Sept. 3	3	3
Do	1	Sept. 4	4	4
Do	1	...do....	4	4
Sept. 1	2	...do....	3	6
Do	5	Sept. 5	4	20
Do	2	Sept. 6	5	10
Do	1	Sept. 8	7	7
Total	13			54

Average length of prepupal period, 4.15 days.
Maximum length of prepupal period, 7 days.
Minimum length of prepupal period, 3 days.

The average length of the prepupal period was 4.15 days, the maximum 7 days, and the minimum 3 days.

TIME OF COCOONING OF THE SECOND-BROOD LARVÆ.

In an effort to determine the percentage of worms normally removed from the vineyards with the harvested grape crop the following records were secured:

TABLE VIII.—*Time of cocooning of the second brood of the grape-berry moth at Sandusky, Ohio, in 1916.*

Date of cocooning.	Number of co-coons.	Date of cocooning.	Number of co-coons.
Aug. 22	1	Sept. 27	244
Aug. 23	1	Sept. 28	109
Aug. 24	6	Sept. 29	46
Aug. 25	3	Sept. 30	18
Aug. 28	44	Oct. 1	33
Aug. 29	5	Oct. 2	40
Aug. 30	39	Oct. 3	64
Aug. 31	43	Oct. 4	87
Sept. 1	157	Oct. 5	119
Sept. 2	121	Oct. 6	64
Sept. 4	350	Oct. 7	51
Sept. 5	163	Oct. 8	55
Sept. 6	120	Oct. 9	16
Sept. 7	335	Oct. 10	10
Sept. 8	340	Oct. 11	15
Sept. 10	254	Oct. 12	9
Sept. 10	153	Oct. 13	15
Sept. 11	343	Oct. 14	14
Sept. 12	309	Oct. 15	9
Sept. 13	402	Oct. 17	16
Sept. 14	233	Oct. 19	8
Sept. 15	197	Oct. 21	6
Sept. 16	94	Oct. 23	5
Sept. 17	145	Oct. 25	4
Sept. 18	114	Oct. 27	6
Sept. 19	101	Oct. 29	6
Sept. 20	142	Nov. 1	6
Sept. 21	251	Nov. 3	2
Sept. 22	171	Nov. 5	4
Sept. 23	94	Nov. 7	4
Sept. 24	68		
Sept. 25	126	Total	6,138
Sept. 26	128		

Larvæ began to leave the grapes as early as August 22 and continued to leave as late as November 7. The table further shows that 77 per cent of the larvæ left the fruit previous to September 25, the date of the beginning of the Concord harvest, and that 90 per cent had left the grapes previous to the beginning of the Catawba harvest on October 3. From these data it would seem that little control is effected by the removal of the worms with the crop.

SEASONAL-HISTORY STUDIES, 1917.

The 1917 rearing records begin with the emergence of spring-brood moths from overwintered pupæ. These pupæ were kept under a leaf blanket in the insectary yard, a condition similar to that in a protected part of the vineyard. At the time when "plowing away" from the vines began in the Sandusky section May 14, the cocoons were moved from the wintering place to the insectary, placed in rearing jars, and records of moth emergence taken as shown in Table IX.

TABLE IX.—*Time of emergence and sex of moths of the spring brood of the grape-berry moth, Sandusky, Ohio, 1917.*

Date of emergence	Number of moths.				Mean daily temperature.	Date of emergence.	Number of moths.				Mean daily temperature.
	♂	♀	¹♀	Total.			♂	♀	¹♀	Total.	
June 9		2		2	62	July 10	5	35		40	65
June 10		1		1	62	July 11	2	6		8	63
June 12	2	1		3	70	July 12	10	37		47	66
June 13	2	1		3	72	July 13	1	6		7	64
June 15		1		1	51	July 14	4	20		24	70
June 16	1	1		2	54	July 15	8	22	1	31	72
June 17		3		3	60	July 16	7	20	1	28	74
June 18	5	9	3	17	69	July 17	5	27		32	72
June 19	10	16	2	28	73	July 18	1	12		13	70
June 20	1	1		2	66	July 19	4	28	2	34	71
June 21	10	6	3	19	68	July 20	3	4	3	10	76
June 22	34	46	1	81	68	July 21	5	14	2	21	76
June 23	3	6		9	72	July 22	2	11		13	76
June 24	13	51		64	62	July 23	1	7		8	78
June 25	18	82	2	102	63	July 24	1	8		9	80
June 26	17	56	3	76	78	July 25		7	1	8	78
June 27	7	31		38	69	July 26		2	1	3	80
June 28	32	90	2	124	70	July 27		1	1	1	76
June 29	13	39	1	53	68	July 28		9	1	10	72
June 30	17	79	2	98	69	July 29		2		2	86
July 1	15	36	3	54	76	July 30		2	1	3	87
July 2	10	37	2	49	69	July 31		2		2	88
July 3	6	27		33	64	Aug. 1	1	1		2	88
July 4	1	31	1	33	63	Aug. 2		1		1	74
July 5	5	32	1	38	64	Aug. 5		1		1	80
July 6	6	35		41	66	Aug. 10		1		1	66
July 7	5	46		51	74						
July 8	4	26	4	34	71	Total	305	1,116	43	1,464	
July 9	8	38		46	76						

¹ ♀ Denotes specimens the sex of which was undetermined.

SPRING BROOD.

EMERGENCE OF SPRING-BROOD MOTHS.

In addition to the time of emergence and number of moths emerging each day, the sex of the moths was determined and recorded.

Moths began to emerge June 9, but did not emerge in any considerable numbers until June 22. (Fig. 2.) From this date emergence was heavy for about 10 days and then fell off gradually until the end of the emergence period on August 10.

RELATION OF EMERGENCE OF SPRING MOTHS TO GRAPE BLOOM.

The relation between the time of emergence and the blossoming period of grapes is of interest in substantiating earlier records.

TABLE X.—*Relation between the time of emergence of the spring brood of grape-berry moths and the period of grape bloom, Sandusky, Ohio, 1917.*

Period.	Dates inclusive.	Male moths.		Female moths.		Sex undetermined moths.		Total.	
		Number.	Per cent.	Number.	Per cent.	Number.	Per cent.	Number.	Per cent.
Before grape bloom	June 9-20	21	6.88	36	3.22	5	11.63	62	4.23
During grape bloom	June 21-July 1	179	58.68	522	46.77	17	39.53	718	49.04
Ten days after bloom	July 2-11	52	17.05	313	28.04	8	18.60	373	25.47
Remainder of season	July 12-Aug. 10	53	17.38	245	21.97	13	30.24	311	21.25
Total		305		1,116		43		1,464	

The blooming period of grapes from June 21 to July 1 begins with the bloom of the Ives variety, one of the varieties grown commercially in the northern Ohio sections, and ends with the falling of bloom from the Catawba variety, also a commercial variety of importance in the sections studied. It is seen that less than 5 per cent of the total emergence occurred before the beginning of bloom, 50 per cent in the 10-day period during bloom, 25 per cent in the next 10-day period, and 21 per cent during the remainder of the season.

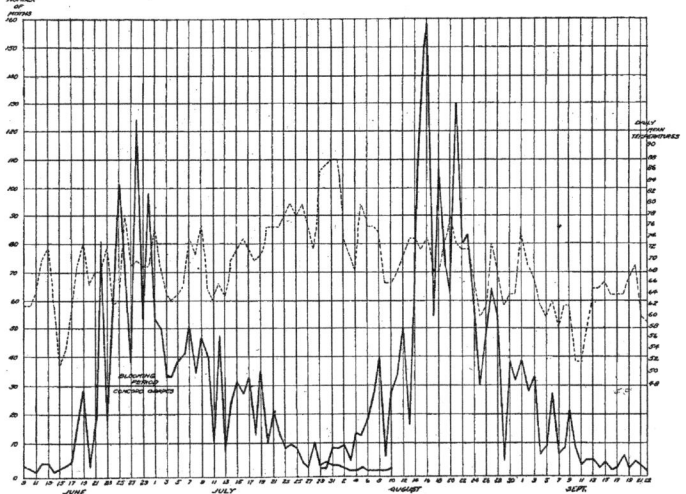

Fig. 2.—Diagram showing the time of emergence of spring-brood and first-brood moths of the grape-berry moth at Sandusky, Ohio, 1917.

A rather close correlation is evident between the rate of emergence and the daily mean temperatures.

PROPORTION OF SEXES OF SPRING-BROOD MOTHS.

TABLE XI.—*Proportion of sexes of spring moths of the grape-berry moth, Sandusky, Ohio, 1917.*

Sex of moths.	Number of moths.	Per cent of sexes.
Male	305	21.46
Female	1,116	78.54
Undetermined	43	....
Total	1,464	100.00

The high percentage of female moths, as shown in Table XI, seems to account for the frequent heavy infestation by second-brood larvæ after a comparatively light first-brood infestation.

7678°—20——2

PERCENTAGE OF EMERGENCE OF SPRING MOTHS.

TABLE XII.—*Percentage of emergence of spring moths of the grape-berry moth from hibernation under a leaf blanket in insectary yard, Sandusky, Ohio, 1917.*

Lot No.	Source of material.	Number of cocoons.	Number of moths emerged.	Emergence.
				Per cent.
1	Collected as larvæ at Venice, Ohio, 1916	2,082	780	37.46
2	Collected as larvæ at Put in Bay, Ohio, 1916	1,493	236	15.80
3	Collected as larvæ at Kelleys Island, Ohio, 1916	2,371	231	9.74
4	Collected as larvæ at Venice. Ohio, 1916	82	12	14.63
	Total	6,028	1,259	
	Average			20.88

No explanation is offered for the variations in percentages of emergence from material collected at the different places. The material was all collected as larvæ in the infested grapes at similar times and kept under identical conditions after collection. That but 20 per cent of the cocoons formed withstood the winter under a light leaf blanket indicates that the natural mortality is considerable.

TIME OF DAY OF MOTH EMERGENCE.

Records were taken as opportunity offered on the time of day of moth emergence. These records were in the period July 8 to July 17 or about in the middle of the emergence period. They indicated in a general way that emergence began in the morning as soon as the heat of the day was felt and that practically all emergence took place between 6.30 a. m. and noon.

OVIPOSITION BY THE SPRING BROOD OF MOTHS.

A few records of oviposition were secured and are shown in Table XIII. These meager records serve only as an indication of the actual conditions prevailing.

TABLE XIII.—*Oviposition of spring moths of the grape-berry moth in rearing cages, Sandusky, Ohio, 1917.*

Observation No.	Number of moths.		Date of—			Days—		
	♂	♀	Emergence of moths.	First oviposition.	Last oviposition.	Before oviposition.	Of oviposition.	From emergence to last oviposition.
1	2	4	June 18	June 21	June 24	3	4	6
2	10	10	June 27	July 2	July 2	5	1	5
3	4	10	July 18	July 21	July 23	3	3	5
4	4	12	July 20	July 22	July 26	2	5	6
5	2	11	July 23	July 24	July 28	1	5	5
Average						2.8	3.6	5.4

PLACE OF OVIPOSITION ON THE VINE.

It was found that a vine of the Clinton variety set in a row of Concords was heavily oviposited upon before the Concord berries were formed. For use in the spacing of spray nozzles for the set-nozzle method of spraying, the place of oviposition on the vine seemed important. The place of oviposition on this one vine by the spring brood of moths was recorded and the data are presented in Table XIV. The vine was trained according to the fan system of grape training which is generally used for all varieties in the northern Ohio sections. In the fan system the vine growth which is trained to an upright trellis is annually renewed to within a short distance of the ground. The vines are cut back usually to from 2 to 4 canes and as many spurs each year; the canes are spread out and tied to the trellis obliquely, giving the shape of a fan.

TABLE XIV.—*Place of oviposition on vine by spring moths of the grape-berry moth under natural conditions in vineyard, Venice, Ohio, 1917.*

Place on vine.	Dis-tances.	Num-ber of clusters.	Num-ber grapes bearing eggs.	Num-ber eggs.	Num-ber eggs per cluster.	Percentage of—	
						Depo-sition in this space.	Clusters in this space.
	Inches.						
Between ground and first wire............	21	15	82	107	7	17	33.3
Between first and second wire............	21–33	23	260	333	15	53	51.1
Between second and third wire............	33–49	7	124	190	29	30	15.5
Total...........................	....	45	466	630	....	100	100.0
Average........................	....	....	....	....	14.0	....	....

The figures in Table XIV agree with the usual observation that the clusters near the ground are less heavily infested than those higher up on the vines. Thirty per cent of the deposition occurred between the middle wire and top wire, whereas but 15 per cent of the clusters were in that space. These figures likewise agree with field observations in that the heavy infestation is generally where the clusters are well covered with foliage, a condition which prevails near the top of the trellis.

In Table XV are presented records of the length of the incubation period of eggs of the first brood. The average number of days required for incubation was 4.39, the maximum 8 days, and the minimum 3 days. These figures include both insectary material and eggs collected in the vineyard when the date of deposition was known. In obtaining the eggs from the vineyards all eggs were removed from the vines each day.

INCUBATION PERIOD OF FIRST-BROOD EGGS.

TABLE XV.—*Incubation period of first-brood eggs of the grape-berry moth, Sandusky, Ohio, 1917.*

Date of oviposition.	Date of hatching.	Number of larvæ.	Incubation period (in days).
June 21	June 28	4	7
30	July 4	28	4
30	July 5	18	5
30	July 6	8	6
30	July 8	1	8
July 1	July 5	24	4
1	July 6	6	5
1	July 7	2	6
1	July 6	18	4
1	July 7	2	5
21	July 24	1	3
22	July 25	2	3
23	July 26	1	3
23	July 28	1	5
24	July 28	2	4
24	July 30	4	6
26	July 29	2	3
26	July 30	3	4
26	July 30	27	4
27	July 31	11	4
Total		165	

Average length of incubation period, 4.39 days.
Maximum length of incubation period, 8 days.
Minimum length of incubation period, 3 days.

LENGTH OF FEEDING PERIOD OF FIRST-BROOD LARVÆ.

Records from the date of hatching until date of leaving fruit were secured on 70 larvæ in the insectary.

TABLE XVI.—*Length of feeding period of 70 first-brood larvæ of the grape-berry moth in grapes in rearing jars in the insectary, Sandusky, Ohio, 1917.*

Number of larvæ.	Larvæ hatched.	Larvæ left fruit.	Feeding period.	Number of larvæ.	Larvæ hatched.	Larvæ left fruit.	Feeding period.
			Days.				Days.
2	July 3	July 21	18	2	July 5	July 25	20
2	do	July 25	22	1		July 28	23
1	do	July 26	23	2	July 5	July 29	24
1	do	July 29	26	1	do	July 31	26
1	do	July 30	27	1	do	Aug. 1	27
1	do	Aug. 5	33	1	do	Aug. 2	28
2	July 4	July 19	15	2	do	Aug. 6	32
3	do	July 21	17	3	July 6	July 22	16
2	do	July 22	18	6	do	July 23	17
6	do	July 23	19	1	do	July 26	20
2	do	July 24	20	1	do	July 27	21
1	do	July 27	23	1	do	July 30	24
1	do	July 28	24	1	do	July 31	25
2	do	July 29	25	1	do	Aug. 1	26
1	do	Aug. 5	32	1	do	Aug. 2	27
1	July 5	July 19	14	1	do	Aug. 12	37
1	do	July 20	15	1	July 7	July 21	14
3	do	July 21	16	1		July 25	18
4	do	July 22	17	—			
3	do	July 23	18	70			
2	do	July 24	19				

Average days, 20.62.
Maximum days, 37.
Minimum days, 14.

The average length of the feeding period is seen to be 20.62 days, the maximum 37 days, and the minimum 14 days. The records extended throughout the regular hatching period, and therefore reflect vineyard conditions closely.

LENGTH OF THE PREPUPAL PERIOD OF FIRST-BROOD INDIVIDUALS.

In Table XVII are given the dates of cocooning and the length of the period from the time of spinning the cocoon until pupation for individuals some of which were supplied with sprayed foliage and others with unsprayed foliage.

TABLE XVII.—*Time of cocooning and length of prepupal period of 231 individuals of the first brood of the grape-berry moth, Sandusky, Ohio, 1917.*

Foliage unsprayed: Dates of cocooning—	Number of cocoons.
August 3	50
August 4	50
August 5	50
August 7	39
August 8	34
Foliage sprayed:	
August 7	40
August 8	24

Dates of pupation.	Number of pupæ by days.						
Aug. 4	17						
5	26	7					
6	3	28	21				
7		7	18				
8			1	21		2	
9				14	1	11	
10				1	18	7	2
11					11		5
12						3	6
13							1
Total number of pupæ	46	42	40	36	30	23	14
Dead in cocoons	4	8	10	3	4	17	10

TABLE XVIII.—*Summary of Table XVII. Length of prepupal period of 231 individuals of the first brood of the grape-berry moth, Sandusky, Ohio, 1917.*

Number individuals.		Prepupal period.
Cocooned on unsprayed foliage.	Cocooned on sprayed foliage.	
		Days.
67	2	1
104	13	2
23	12	3
	6	4
	4	5
194	37	
Average........ 1.77	2.9	
Maximum....... 3	5	
Minimum....... 1	1	

The data from Table XVII are summarized in Table XVIII. The average length of the prepupal period was 1.77 days, the maximum period 3 days, and the minimum 1 day, where unsprayed foliage was supplied. Where the cocoons were formed on sprayed foliage the average prepupal period was 2.9 days, the maximum 5 days, and the minimum 1 day. The spray material apparently had a repellent action, for in another experiment where both sprayed and unsprayed foliage were equally accessible to larvæ there were 226, or 63 per cent, of the total number of cocoons formed on unsprayed leaves and but 135, or 37 per cent, formed on sprayed leaves. Considerable mortality can be attributed to cocooning on sprayed leaves, since 194 pupæ were formed in 223 cocoons on unsprayed leaves, a mortality of 13 per cent as compared with the individuals that cocooned on sprayed leaves, where but 37 pupæ were formed in 64 cocoons, showing a mortality of 42 per cent.

TIME OF COCOONING OF FIRST-BROOD LARVÆ.

TABLE XIX.—*Time of cocooning of 2,447 larvæ of the first brood of the grape-berry moth, Sandusky, Ohio, 1917.*

Date of cocooning.	Number of cocoons.	Mean daily temperature.	Date of cocooning.	Number of cocoons.	Mean daily temperature.
		°F.			°F.
July 19	3	71	Aug. 14	51	74
July 20	2	76	Aug. 15	28	72
July 21	9	76	Aug. 16	36	74
July 22	9	76	Aug. 17	31	68
July 23	18	78	Aug. 18	58	68
July 24	10	80	Aug. 19	35	73
July 25	31	78	Aug. 20	58	78
July 26	44	80	Aug. 21	33	73
July 27	55	76	Aug. 22	33	72
July 28	73	72	Aug. 23	30	72
July 29	54	86	Aug. 24	21	66
July 30	128	87	Aug. 25	8	60
July 31	170	88	Aug. 26	9	62
Aug. 1	129	88	Aug. 27	17	73
Aug. 2	142	74	Aug. 28	5	68
Aug. 3	230	71	Aug. 29	5	62
Aug. 4	117	68	Aug. 30	1	64
Aug. 5	112	80	Aug. 31	6	64
Aug. 6	131	76	Sept. 1	4	75
Aug. 7	158	76	Sept. 2	8	69
Aug. 8	111	75	Sept. 3	1	67
Aug. 9	26	66	Sept. 6	1	66
Aug. 10	64	66	Sept. 8	1	62
Aug. 11	37	68			
Aug. 12	62	71	Total	2,447	
Aug. 13	45	74			

In Table XIX are given the complete records of cocooning for the first-brood larvæ. Cocooning began on July 19 and continued until September 8 with a distinctly high period from July 30 until August 8. The correlation with temperature is of interest, showing that as the mean temperature dropped below 70° F. there was a drop in the rate of cocooning.

LENGTH OF PUPAL STAGE OF FIRST-BROOD PUPÆ.

TABLE XX.—*Time of cocooning and length of pupal stage of 90 individuals of the first-brood pupæ of the grape-berry moth, Sandusky, Ohio, 1917.*

UNSPRAYED FOLIAGE FOR COCOONING.

Number of larvæ.				Date of pupation.	Date of moth emergence.	Days in pupal stage.		
♂	♀	♀̂	Total.			♂	♀	♀̂
....	3	....	3	Aug. 4............	Aug. 16	0	12	....
....	4	....	4	....do............	Aug. 18	....	14	....
.....2...	7	....	9	Aug. 5............	...do....	13	13	....
3	8	....	11	....do............	Aug. 19	14	14	....
1	2	....	3	Aug. 7............	Aug. 21	14	14	....
....	1	....	1	....do............	Aug. 22	....	15	....
....	1	....	1	....do............	Aug. 23	....	16	....
....	2	1	3	Aug. 8............	Aug. 20	....	12	12
1	8	....	9	....do............	Aug. 21	13	13	....
....	1	....	1	....do............	Aug. 22	....	14	....
....	4	1	5	Aug. 9............	Aug. 21	....	12	12
1	2	....	3	....do............	Aug. 22	13	13	....
.....2.	5	....	5	Aug. 10...........	...do....	....	12	....
2	5	....	7	....do............	Aug. 23	13	13	....
....	2	....	2	....do............	Aug. 24	....	14	....
....	1	....	1	Aug. 11...........	Aug. 22	....	11	....
....	2	....	2	....do............	Aug. 23	....	12	....
....	1	....	1	....do............	Aug. 27	....	16	....
10	59	2	71	Average.......	....	13.4	13.11	12

SPRAYED FOLIAGE FOR COCOONING.

Number of larvæ.				Date of pupation.	Date of moth emergence.	Days in pupal stage.		
♂	♀	♀̂	Total.			♂	♀	♀̂
....	1	....	1	Aug. 8............	Aug. 21	....	13	....
....	1	....	1	....do............	Aug. 22	....	14	....
....	3	....	3	Aug. 9............	Aug. 23	....	14	....
....	2	....	2	....do............	Aug. 24	....	15	....
....	1	....	1	....do............	Aug. 25	....	16	....
....	1	1	2	Aug. 10...........	Aug. 23	....	13	13
....	1	....	1	....do............	Aug. 24	....	14	....
....	1	....	1	Aug. 11...........	Aug. 23	....	12	....
1	....	....	1	....do............	Aug. 27	16	....	....
....	2	....	2	Aug. 12...........	Aug. 26	....	14	....
....	1	....	1	....do............	Aug. 27	....	15	....
1	1	....	2	....do............	Aug. 28	16	16	....
....	1	....	1	....do............	Aug. 30	....	18	....
2	16	1	19	Average.......	....	16	15	13

In Table XX the length of the pupal stage of 90 individuals is given. The average length of the stage was 13.4 days for males and 13.11 for females, all on unsprayed foliage. On sprayed foliage the average length of the period was 16 days for males and 15 for females.

LENGTH OF TIME SPENT IN THE COCOON BY FIRST-BROOD INDIVIDUALS.

The average length of time in the cocoon on unsprayed foliage is shown in Table XXI to be 15.52 days for males with 32 days as the maximum period and 9 days as the minimum. For females on unsprayed foliage 14.62 days was the average period, 32 days the maximum, and 6 the minimum. On sprayed foliage males were in the cocoons 16.82 days as the average with 20 days as the maximum and 16 days the minimum period. Females were in the cocoons an average of 17.06 days with 27 days as the maximum and 13 days the minimum.

TABLE XXI.—*Length of time in cocoon of 1,318 individuals of the first brood of the grape-berry moth, Sandusky, Ohio, 1917.*

Sex of moths.	Number of moths.	Number of days in cocoon.		
		Average.	Maximum.	Minimum.
Male	226	15.52	32	9
Female	1,003	14.62	32	6
Undetermined	25	14.32	20	9
Total	1,254	14.78	32	6
Cocooned on sprayed foliage:				
Male	11	16.82	20	16
Female	53	17.06	27	13
Total	64	17.01	27	13

TIME OF EMERGENCE OF FIRST-BROOD MOTHS.

TABLE XXII.—*Time of emergence and sex of the first-brood moths of the grape-berry moth, Sandusky, Ohio, 1917.*

Date of emergence.	Number of moths.				Date of emergence.	Number of moths.			
	♂	♀	⚥	Total.		♂	♀	⚥	Total.
July 29	0	1	0	1	Aug. 26	8	42	0	50
30	0	1	0	1	27	12	50	3	65
31	1	6	1	8	28	7	45	1	53
Aug. 1	2	5	1	8	29	0	3	0	3
2	4	4	1	9	30	14	23	0	37
3	0	3	1	4	31	4	27	1	32
4	1	12	0	13	Sept. 1	5	31	1	37
5	4	8	0	12	2	2	27	1	30
6	1	16	0	17	3	10	23	0	33
7	7	20	0	27	4	0	6	0	6
8	4	33	3	40	5	5	3	0	8
9	0	5	0	5	6	4	20	2	26
10	2	25	1	28	7	1	5	0	6
11	7	26	0	33	8	1	8	0	9
12	7	43	0	50	9	4	14	0	18
13	2	14	0	16	10	1	7	0	8
14	20	66	0	86	11	0	2	0	2
15	19	110	1	130	12	1	3	0	4
16	24	128	8	160	13	2	2	0	4
17	10	41	3	54	14	0	1	0	1
18	21	85	0	106	15	1	2	0	3
19	19	49	4	72	17	0	1	0	1
20	6	55	1	62	18	1	4	0	5
21	23	105	2	130	19	0	1	0	1
22	19	61	0	80	20	1	2	0	3
23	13	66	4	83	21	2	0	0	2
24	9	44	1	54	22	0	1	0	1
25	5	27	0	32	Total	316	1,412	41	1,769

First-brood moths began to emerge on July 29 and emergence continued until September 22. It will be seen in figure 2 that the emergence was high for the entire period of August 12 to 28, varying with the mean daily temperature. It is also shown that the emergence

of the first-brood moths began before the spring brood emergence
ended. This means that moths were emerging practically from
grape bloom until grape harvest; the majority of all emergence,
however, occurred in two well-defined periods, as shown graphically
in figure 2.

PROPORTION OF SEXES OF FIRST-BROOD MOTHS.

·Table XXIII.—*Proportion of sexes of first-brood moths of the grape-berry moth,*
Sandusky, Ohio, 1917.

Sex of moths.	Number of moths.	Percentage of sexes.
Male	316	18.28
Female	1,412	81.72
Undetermined	41	....
Total	1,769	100.00

The high percentage of female moths helps further to explain the
occurrence of a large second-brood of larvæ.

LIFE CYCLE OF THE FIRST GENERATION.

Table XXIV.—*Life cycle of the first generation of the grape-berry moth as determined*
from observations on the separate stages; summaries from the previous tables, Sandusky,
Ohio, 1917.

Summary from Table No.—	Stage.	Number of individuals.	Days of duration of stage.		
			Average.	Maximum.	Minimum.
XV	Egg stage	165	4.39	8	3
XVI	Length of feeding period of larvæ	70	20.62	37	14
XXI XXI	}Making of cocoon and pupal stage	1,254	14.78	32	6
	Total life cycle	....	39.79	77	23

The life cycle as here presented is seen to average 39.79 days with
77 days as the total of the maximums and 23 days as the total of the
minimums. To the average of 39.79 should be added the period
between moth emergence and oviposition, which is usually 3 days,
thus making the total life cycle 42.79 days.

SECOND GENERATION.

INCUBATION PERIOD OF SECOND-BROOD EGGS.

One record only was secured concerning the incubation period of
second-brood eggs, and that late in the season when the temperature
was comparatively low. Twenty-two eggs were deposited on September 1, the black spot was evident on September 9, and the eggs
hatched September 11, 10 days after oviposition.

TIME OF COCOONING OF SECOND-BROOD LARVÆ.

The dates on which larvæ were leaving the grapes and spinning cocoons are shown in detail in Table XXV.

TABLE XXV.—*Time of cocooning and number of cocoons of the second brood of the grape-berry moth, Sandusky, Ohio, 1917.*

Date of cocooning.	Dates of collection of larvæ.						
	August—			September—			
	30	30	30	2	3	3	6
Sept. 7		1	1	1			
8							
9		1		1		1	
10						1	
11			1				
12							
13		2	1	2			
14		1	2	1		1	
15	1	1	1	1	1	2	
16	1	1	2	2			
17		2	2	1			
18	1	1	1	1		2	
19	1	1	3	1	1		
20	1	2	9	2	1	7	
21	2	1	5	3	1	1	1
22	5	2	9	3	0	2	1
23	0		5	2	3	3	1
24	5	2	10	8	8	10	7
25	5	4	8	6	8	3	4
26	5	1	5	1	2	9	3
27	8	3	6	6	8	7	5
28	5	9	5	7	4	11	10
29	7	2	3	4	6	3	7
30	5	2	5	12	2	1	6
Oct. 1	1	4	2	2	1	2	4
2	8	2	4	3	6	2	4
3	3	4	7	10	9	4	8
4	2	1	5	6		5	6
5	6	10	6	3		2	5
6							
7	4	2	2	3	2		1
8		1		1	4	2	7
9	1			2		2	1
10		2			1		1
11	2	2			5	2	2
12					2	4	1
13				1			
15	4	7	3	9	10	6	3
16	7	6	5	5	10	3	1
17		3	1	3	1	2	3
18		5	3	2	8	4	4
19	4	3	6	5	13	5	14
20							
21					1		
22					1		
23							
24							
25							
26							
27							
28					1		
29							
30		4				2	
31							
Nov. 5							
10							
Jar discontinued	Oct. 22	Nov. 10	Nov. 10	Nov. 21	Nov. 10	Nov. 10	Nov. 10

TABLE XXV.—*Time of cocooning and number of cocoons of the second brood of the grape-berry moth, Sandusky, Ohio, 1917*—Continued.

Date of cocooning.	Dates of collection of larvæ. September—						
	6	6	9	9	9	12	12
Sept. 7		3					
8							
9							
10							
11							
12							
13		1				1	
14	1						
15	1			1	1		
16	1	1			3		
17					3	1	
18						1	
19	1	1				2	2
20	1						1
21		1			3	3	1
22	1	2		2		4	3
23	2	1				2	
24	5	2		4		3	1
25	4	1	1		4	7	
26	1	2	2	2	1	4	
27	4	3	3	3	14	7	5
28	4	5		2	11	8	4
29	4	2	1	3	14	2	1
30	4	4	3	2	4	5	2
Oct. 1	1	2		3	1	2	
2	3	1	4	1	1	1	1
3	1		6	2	4	3	4
4	7	5	1	4	4	2	4
5	8	3	3	9		1	
6							
7	12	5	2	2	4	4	1
8	4	2	1		7	2	1
9	1		1	1	2		
10	1						
11					3	1	2
12	1	4		2	4		3
13		1					
15	15	8	1	4	20	3	12
16	12	6	3	2	8	1	8
17	1	2	3	1	6		2
18	5	5		6	6	4	10
19	9	10		4	19		11
20							
21		1					
22	2						1
23	4			1			
24				1			1
25		3					
26					2		
27							
28	3			1	3	1	1
29					2		
30	4		2	2			
31							
Nov. 5							
10					13		
Jar discontinued	Nov. 21	Oct. 31	Nov. 21	Nov. 21	Nov. 10	Nov. 10	Nov. 10

TABLE XXV.—*Time of cocooning and number of cocoons of the second brood of the grape-berry moth, Sandusky, Ohio, 1917*—Continued.

Date of cocooning.	Dates of collection of larvæ.						
	September—						
	12	14	15	15	15	18	18
Sept. 7							
8							
9							
10							
11							
12							
13							
14							
15							
16							
17							
18				1			
19					1		
20	3			2	2		
21	2				2		
22	2				1		
23			1				
24	4		3	4	2		
25	2	1	3	8			1
26	1		3	2	2		
27	12		4	7	8		1
28	4	1	6	11	10		1
29	7	1	2	9	5	1	
30	5		4	4	5		1
Oct. 1	1	1	4	4	5		
2			1	2			3
3	7	4	11	13	16	1	3
4	8	3	3	8		1	1
5		3	9	14	6	2	
6							
7	7		3	9	5		
8	2		3	3	2	1	2
9					2		
10			1	2	2		
11	1		1	1	3		
12	2		1	6	2	1	
15	15		9	17	4		2
16	10		8	11	5	1	2
17	3		3	3	3		
18	12		2	10	11	4	
19	14						
20			12	27	11		
21				1	1		
22					1		
23	1	2					
24					2		
25				1			
26							
27							
28	2			9	6		
29	4			4			
30			1	3	5	2	2
31							
Nov. 5							
10							
Jar discontinued	Nov. 21	Nov. 22	Nov. 21	Nov. 26	Nov. 21	Nov. 21	Nov. 21

Table XXV.—*Time of cocooning and number of cocoons of the second brood of the grape-berry moth, Sandusky, Ohio, 1917*—Continued.

| Date of cocooning. | Dates of collection of larvæ. | | | | | | |
| | September— | | | | | | |
	18	22	22	22	29	29	29
Sept. 7							
8							
9							
10							
11							
12							
13							
14							
15							
16							
17							
18							
19							
20							
21							
22							
23							
24		2					
25							
26	1		1				
27	1	2	1	1			
28		5					
29	1	3					
30	1	3					
Oct. 1		1					
2	1		1		1		
3		3		2	3	6	
4	1	2		6	1		3
5		2	2	2		1	2
6							
7		3		1		6	4
8		7		2	2	2	3
9		3					
10		1					
11					1		
12					1		
15	1	6	3	2	2	1	1
16	1	6	1	1	1	10	9
17		1	2	1		3	5
18	1	5	5	6	3		
19							
20	3	4	7	6	4	13	7
21	1						
22				1			
23							
24						1	
25				1	1		
26							
27							
28			2				
29							
30	1			1		1	
31							
Nov. 5							
10							
Jar discontinued	Nov. 9	Nov. 9	Nov. 9	Nov. 9	Nov. 6	Nov. 9	Nov. 9

TABLE XXV.—*Time of cocooning and number of cocoons of the second brood of the grape-berry moth, Sandusky, Ohio, 1917*—Continued.

Date of cocooning.	Dates of collection of larvæ.						Total co-coons.	Mean daily tem-pera-ture.
	Oct. 2 to Nov. 4.							
Sept. 7							6	58
8							0	62
9							3	62
10							1	52
11							1	52
12							0	58
13							7	65
14							6	65
15							10	66
16							8	64
17							9	64
18							7	64
19							14	67
20							29	69
21							26	60
22							37	59
23							20	57
24							78	59
25							72	59
26							48	64
27							119	66
28							123	58
29							88	60
30							80	52
Oct. 1							42	48
2							50	52
3							134	58
4							93	54
5							99	50
6							0	44
7							82	50
8							61	45
9							16	43
10	1						15	45
11							26	45
12	1	1					36	40
13							2	38
15	1	4	1	2	1		177	55
16	1						144	50
17		1		2			55	49
18							121	64
19		3	1	1	1	1	124	47
20	2					4	100	40
21	1					1	6	43
22							7	41
23							8	40
24						1	6	42
25							6	42
26							2	44
27							0	42
28						3	32	44
29							10	48
30	3		1	1	4	7	46	31
31				1	1		1	32
Nov. 5						3	3	46
10							13	50
Jar discontinued	Nov. 21	Nov. 21	Nov. 21	Nov. 21	Nov. 21	Nov. 21	2,309	

PERCENTAGE OF COCOONING PREVIOUS TO AND DURING GRAPE HARVEST.

Table XXVI shows the time of cocooning of the larvæ that left the fruit in the fall of 1917. This does not necessarily indicate, however, that all the larvæ left the fruit before the end of grape harvest, for observation showed that a considerable part of the second brood of larvæ were only partially grown at the time of harvest and that large numbers of larvæ actually left the vineyards in the fruit. No accurate method of determining what part of the total number of larvæ were thus removed occurred to the writer, but an estimate of one-third would be conservative. This had a decided influence on the number of overwintering pupæ and subsequent infestation in 1918.

TABLE XXVI.—*Percentage of cocooning previous to and during grape harvest, Sandusky, Ohio, 1917.*

Time.	Date.	Number of cocoons.	Percentage of total.
Previous to beginning of Concord harvest.....................	To Oct. 8..........	1,291	55.91
During Concord harvest..	Oct. 8–18..........	653	28.28
Previous to end of Concord harvest............................	To Oct. 18.........	1,944	84.19
Previous to beginning of Catawba harvest.....................	To Oct. 22.........	2,174	94.16
Previous to end of Catawba harvest...........................	To Nov. 10........	2,309	100.00

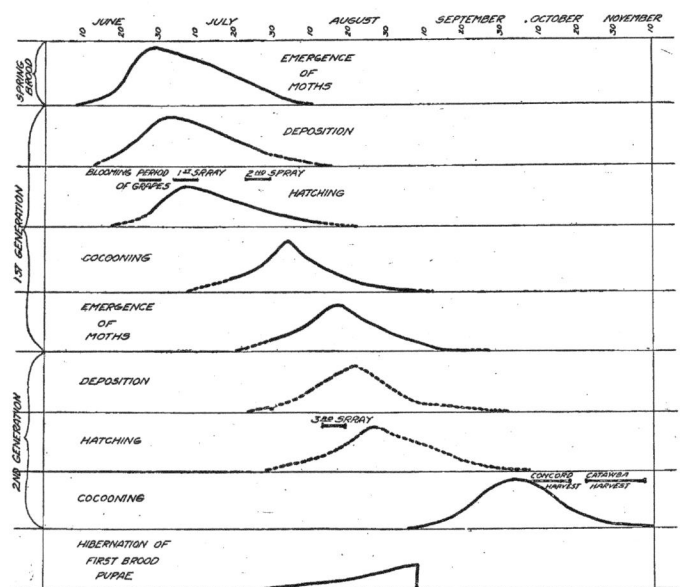

FIG. 3.—Diagram showing summary of the life-history data for 1917 of the grape-berry moth. Solid lines indicate actual records and dotted lines indicate occurrence of stages as observed in the field and computed from the average length of period.

SUMMARY OF SEASONAL-HISTORY STUDIES IN 1917.

A summary of the data presented in the preceding tables is shown graphically in figure 3.

It should be kept in mind in applying this diagram to future seasons that the season of 1917 was later than the average for northern Ohio and was unseasonably wet and cold throughout the fall.

TABLE XXVII.—*Time of emergence and sex of moths of the spring brood berry moth, Sandusky, Ohio, 1918.*

Date of emergence.	Number of moths.				Mean daily temperature.	Date of emergence.	Number of moths.			
	♂	♀	⚥	Total.			♂	♀	⚥	
May 22	1	......	......	1	74	June 17	8	26	......	
25	1	3	......	4	72	18	3	16	......	
26	0	2	2	4	78	19	2	6	1	
27	0	4	1	5	78	20	1	6	......	
28	1	2	......	3	66	21	2	14	......	
29	4	9	......	13	64	23	......	12	......	
30	3	11	2	16	72	24	1	13	1	
31	2	6	2	10	78	25	4	10	......	
June 1	12	21	3	36	81	26	......	11	1	
2	12	17	7	36	75	27	1	7	1	
3	14	26	2	42	68	28	2	8	2	
4	6	17	2	25	74	29	3	13	......	
5	9	20	......	29	67	30	......	8	......	
6	12	22	2	36	73	July 1	......	4	......	
7	4	17	......	21	66	2	......	1	......	
8	5	6	......	11	64	3	......	2	1	
9	10	25	1	36	69	4	1	2	2	
10	10	20	......	30	66	5	......	2	......	
11	5	6	1	12	70	6	......	2	1	
12	7	30	1	38	72	7	......	4	......	
13	2	12	......	14	62	9	......	1	......	
14	6	22	1	29	66	12	......	1	......	
15	3	8	......	11	64	Total...	161	482	38	
16	4	7	1	12	72					

The early opening of the season hastened the grape gr
moth emergence was correspondingly early. The first e
took place on May 22 and emergence in considerable numb
on June 1. A rather high rate of emergence prevailed fo:
two-week period and then gradually subsided. (Fig. 4.)

PROPORTION OF SEXES OF MOTHS OF THE SPRING BF

TABLE XXVIII.—*Proportion of sexes of moths of spring brood of the grap*
Sandusky, Ohio, 1918.

Sex of moths.	Num of mo
Male	
Female	
Undetermined	
Total	

The proportions as shown in Table XXVIII are compar
the figures in Table XI on the spring brood of moths in
appears that the preponderance of females is the usual cor

PERCENTAGE OF EMERGENCE OF SPRING MOTHS.

The overwintering material was collected and kept under the same conditions as that of the previous winter. The percentage of emergence was slightly higher but still indicating a high rate of mortality.

TABLE XXIX.—*Percentage of emergence of spring moths of the grape-berry moth, Sandusky, Ohio, 1918.*

Source of material.	Number of cocoons.	Number of moths emerged.	Emergence.
Collected as larvæ at Venice, Kelleys Island, Put in Bay, and Dover, Ohio.	2,544	681	*Per cent.* 26.70

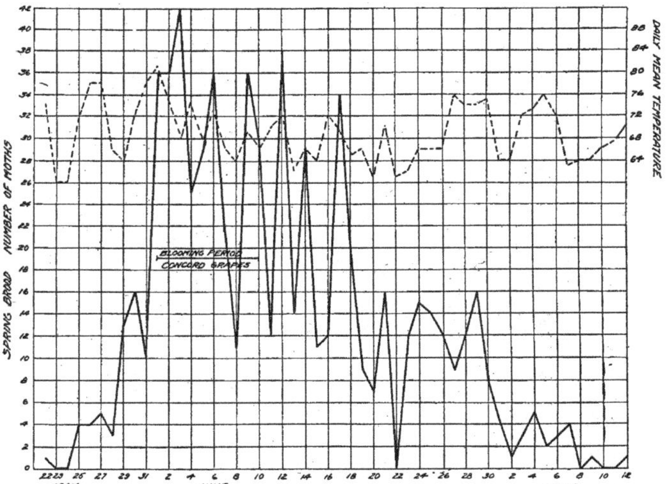

FIG. 4.—Diagram showing emergence of spring brood of moths of the grape-berry moth at Sandusky, Ohio, 1918.

The winter of 1917–18 was the most severe of 47 years on record at the Sandusky station of the United States Weather Bureau, and included intensely cold periods with little covering. This is of importance in connection with the foregoing records, for it must be concluded that the grape-berry moth pupæ are very resistant to severe winter conditions.

FIRST GENERATION.

TIME OF COCOONING AND LENGTH OF TIME IN THE COCOON OF FIRST-BROOD INDIVIDUALS.

TABLE XXX.—*Time of cocooning and length of time in cocoon of the first brood of the grape-berry moth, Sandusky, Ohio, 1918.*

Number of larvæ.	Date larvæ left fruit.	Moths emerged.	In cocoon.	Total.
1	July 7	July 23	16	16
4	July 9	...do....	14	56
1	...do.....	July 24	15	15
3	July 10	...do.....	14	42
3	July 11	...do.....	13	39
2	July 12	...do.....	12	24
3	...do.....	July 25	13	39
2	July 13	July 24	11	22
1	...do.....	July 25	12	12
2	...do.....	July 26	13	26
1	...do.....	July 27	14	14
3	July 14	July 26	12	36
2	...do.....	July 27	13	26
5	July 15	...do.....	12	60
1	...do.....	July 28	13	13
1	...do.....	July 29	14	14
2	July 16	July 27	11	22
3	...do.....	July 28	12	36
2	...do.....	July 29	13	26
1	...do.....	Aug. 2	17	17
9	July 17	July 29	12	108
2	...do.....	July 31	14	28
7	July 18	July 29	11	77
5	..do.....	July 30	12	60
11	...do.....	July 31	13	143
1	July 19	July 29	10	10
8	...do.....	July 31	12	96
3	...do.....	Aug. 1	13	39
1	...do.....	Aug. 2	14	14
1	July 20	July 30	10	10
3	...do.....	July 31	11	33
9	...do.....	Aug. 1	12	108
4	...do.....	Aug. 2	13	52
3	July 21	...do.....	12	36
9	...do.....	Aug. 3	13	117
7	...do.....	Aug. 4	14	98
16	July 22	...do.....	13	208
14	...do.....	Aug. 5	14	196
1	...do.....	Aug. 6	15	15
18	July 23	Aug. 5	13	234
11	...do.....	Aug. 6	14	154
6	July 24	...do.....	13	78
1	July 25	Aug. 7	13	13
8	...do.....	Aug. 8	14	112
1	July 26	Aug. 6	11	11
8	...do.....	Aug. 8	13	104
10	...do.....	Aug. 9	14	140
2	July 27	Aug. 8	12	24
7	...do.....	Aug. 9	13	91
3	...do.....	Aug. 10	14	42
9	July 28	...do.....	13	117
6	...do.....	Aug. 11	14	84
1	July 29	Aug. 10	12	12
6	...do.....	Aug. 11	13	78
1	July 30	Aug. 10	11	11
1	...do.....	Aug. 11	12	12
7	July 31	Aug. 12	12	84
3	...do.....	Aug. 13	13	39
1	...do.....	Aug. 14	14	14
2	Aug. 1	Aug. 12	11	22
2	...do.....	Aug. 13	12	24
1	...do.....	Aug. 14	13	13
5	Aug. 2	Aug. 13	11	55
9	...do....	Aug. 14	12	108
1	...do.....	Aug. 15	13	13
6	Aug. 3	Aug. 14	11	66
1	...do.....	Aug. 16	13	13
12	Aug. 4	Aug. 15	11	132
1	...do.....	Aug. 16	12	12
1	...do.....	Aug. 17	13	13
1	...do.....	Aug. 18	14	14
1	...do.....	Aug. 20	16	16
1	Aug. 5	Aug. 17	12	12
3	Aug. 6	Aug. 18	12	36
10	...do.....	Aug. 19	13	130
5	...do.....	Aug. 20	14	70
1	...do.....	Aug. 21	15	15
3	Aug. 7	Aug. 18	11	33
9	...do.....	Aug. 19	12	108
12	...do.....	Aug. 20	13	156
3	...do.....	Aug. 21	14	42
2	...do.....	Aug. 22	15	30
2	...do.....	Aug. 23	16	32
1	...do.....	Aug. 26	19	19
15	Aug. 8	Aug. 20	12	180
18	...do.....	Aug. 21	13	234
11	...do.....	Aug. 22	14	154
1	...do.....	Aug. 23	15	15
5	Aug. 9	Aug. 21	12	60
22	...do.....	Aug. 22	13	286
12	...do.....	Aug. 23	14	168
1	...do.....	Aug. 25	16	16
2	Aug. 10	Aug. 21	11	22
4	...do.....	Aug. 22	12	48
10	...do.....	Aug. 23	13	130
1	...do.....	Aug. 24	14	14
1	...do.....	Aug. 25	15	15
3	Aug. 11	Aug. 23	12	36
4	...do.....	Aug. 24	13	52
8	Aug. 12	...do.....	12	96
9	...do.....	Aug. 25	13	117
1	...do.....	Aug. 27	15	15
3	Aug. 13	Aug. 26	13	39
2	...do.....	Aug. 27	14	28
3	...do.....	Aug. 28	15	45
2	Aug. 14	Aug. 27	13	26
2	...do.....	Aug. 28	14	28
4	Aug. 15	...do.....	13	52
2	...do.....	Aug. 29	14	28
1	Aug. 16	Aug. 28	12	12
1	...do.....	Aug. 29	13	13
1	Aug. 17	Aug. 28	11	11
2	...do.....	Aug. 29	12	24
2	...do.....	Aug. 30	13	26
1	...do.....	Aug. 31	14	14
1	Aug. 18	...do.....	13	13
1	Aug. 19	Sept. 2	14	14
1	Aug. 20	Sept. 4	15	15
1	Aug. 21	Sept. 5	15	15
1	Aug. 22	Sept. 6	15	15
1	Aug. 23	...do....	14	14
Total, 522	....	....	....	6,731

Average days, 12.9.
Maximum days, 19.
Minimum days, 10.

It is seen in Table XXX that first-brood larvæ began to leave the fruit July 7 and continued to leave until August 23. The table does not show as well defined a high period as usually exists; the comparative dearth of rearing material is thought to account for this condition.

TIME OF EMERGENCE AND SEX OF FIRST-BROOD MOTHS.

The dates of emergence and number of moths are shown in Table XXXI and in graph in figure 5. Attention is directed to the rise in emergence on August 4 and 5 and then the sudden drop without another high point until August 20. The writer accounts for this, partly by a comparable drop in the cocooning in the period previous

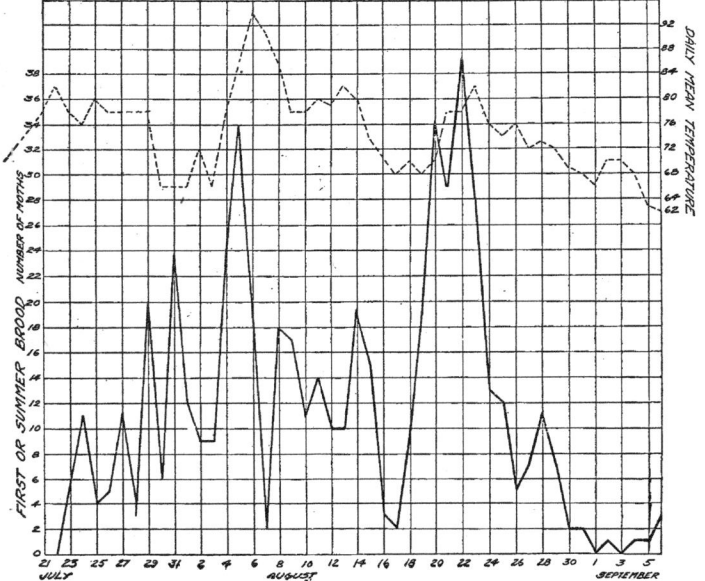

FIG. 5.—Diagram showing dates of emergence and number of moths of the grape-berry moth at Sandusky, Ohio, 1918.

and partly by an actual killing of the pupæ by excessive heat that prevailed on August 5 to 8. On August 5 the official Weather Bureau records showed a maximum temperature of 94° F., on the 6th 105°, on the 7th 100°, and on the 8th 97°. When emergence dropped off suddenly on August 6 and 7 examination of the pupæ then about to transform to moths showed considerable mortality. Extensive records could not be taken without destroying the material that was to serve for further life-history studies.

TABLE XXXI.—*Time of emergence and sex of first-brood moths of the grape-berry moth, Sandusky, Ohio, 1918.*

Date of emergence.	Number of moths.				Mean daily temperature.	Date of emergence.	Number of moths.				Mean daily temperature.
	♂	♀	⚥	Total.			♂	♀	⚥	Total.	
					°F.						°F.
July 23	....	6	....	6	78	Aug. 15	1	14	....	15	74
24	1	9	1	11	76	16	....	3	....	3	71
25	1	3	....	4	80	17	1	1	....	2	68
26	....	5	0	5	78	18	....	9	....	9	70
27	1	9	1	11	78	19	2	17	....	19	68
28	....	2	1	3	78	20	7	25	2	34	70
29	2	15	3	20	78	21	6	20	3	29	78
30	1	3	2	6	66	22	14	23	2	39	78
31	6	16	2	24	66	23	9	17	2	28	82
Aug. 1	....	9	3	12	66	24	3	9	1	13	76
2	2	7	....	9	72	25	2	9	1	12	74
3	2	7	....	9	66	26	1	4	....	5	76
4	5	18	....	23	78	27	1	6	....	7	72
5	4	26	4	34	85	28	. 1	10	....	11	73
6	4	15	....	19	94	29	2	5	....	7	72
7	1	1	....	2	91	30	....	2	....	2	69
8	8	10	....	18	86	31	....	2	....	2	68
9	6	9	2	17	78	Sept. 2	1	....	....	1	70
10	4	5	2	11	78	4	....	1	....	1	68
11	2	12	....	14	80	5	....	1	....	1	63
12	....	9	1	10	79	6	1	2	....	3	62
13	2	8	....	10	82	Total..	106	399	35	540	
14	2	15	2	19	80						

PROPORTION OF SEXES OF FIRST-BROOD MOTHS.

TABLE XXXII.—*Proportion of sexes of first-brood moths of the grape-berry moth, Sandusky, Ohio, 1918.*

Sex of moth.	Number of moths.	Percentage of sexes.
Male	106	21.00
Female	399	79.00
Undetermined	35	....
Total	540	100.00

The proportion of sexes as shown in Table **XXXII** maintains the preponderance of females that has been shown in previous tables.

OVIPOSITION BY FIRST-BROOD MOTHS.

A single record of oviposition and incubation was secured. In a jar containing 14 male moths and 12 female moths, all of which emerged on August 22, 5 eggs were deposited on August 26 and hatched on September 2. The period from emergence to oviposition was therefore 4 days and the incubation period 7 days.

NUMBER OF TRANSFORMING AND OVERWINTERING INDIVIDUALS OF FIRST BROOD.

In Table **XXXIII** are presented the data on the overwintering first-brood individuals.

It will be seen that the first larva to hibernate left the fruit on August 2 and that the number gradually increased as the season progressed.

TABLE XXXIII.—*Number of transforming and overwintering individuals of the first brood of the grape-berry moth, Sandusky, Ohio, 1918.*

Number of larvæ.	Date larvæ left fruit.	Number of—			
		Moths emerged.	Pupæ hibernating.	Larvæ parasitized.	Dead.
1	June 30				1
1	July 7	1			
5	July 9	5			
4	July 10	3			1
4	July 11	3			1
5	July 12	5			
10	July 13	6		1	3
7	July 14	5		1	1
11	July 15	7		3	1
8	July 16	7		1	
23	July 17	11		3	9
25	July 18	23		1	1
18	July 19	13			5
26	July 20	17			9
29	July 21	19			10
44	July 22	31		1	12
41	July 23	29		1	11
34	July 24	6			28
21	July 25	9			12
22	July 26	19			3
19	July 27	13		1	5
20	July 28	15			5
12	July 29	7			5
4	July 30	2			2
14	July 31	11			3
11	Aug. 1	5			6
24	Aug. 2	15	1		8
9	Aug. 3	7			2
28	Aug. 4	16			12
37	Aug. 5	1	1		35
52	Aug. 6	19			33
55	Aug. 7	32	1		22
67	Aug. 8	45	2		20
48	Aug. 9	40	2		6
27	Aug. 10	18	1		8
12	Aug. 11	7	1		4
29	Aug. 12	18	3		8
13	Aug. 13	8	1		4
11	Aug. 14	4	4		3
8	Aug. 15	6	1		1
3	Aug. 16	2			1
6	Aug. 17	6			
5	Aug. 18	2	3		
1	Aug. 19	1			
3	Aug. 20	1	2		
5	Aug. 21	1	3		1
7	Aug. 22	1	5		1
10	Aug. 23	1	7		2
6	Aug. 24		6		
9	Aug. 25		9		
Total, 894		523	53	13	305

TABLE XXXIV.—*Summary of Table XXXIII, showing number and percentage of first brood individuals of the grape-berry moth that transform.*

Observations on—	Number.	Per cent.
Number of larvæ	894	100.0
Number of moths emerged	523	58.5
Number of hibernating pupæ	53	5.9
Number of parasitized larvæ	13	1.4
Number of dead individuals	305	34.1

Table **XXXIV** summarizes the data in Table **XXXIII** and shows that but 5.9 per cent of all the recorded larvæ hibernated, that 58.5 per cent emerged as moths the same season, that 1.4 per cent of the larvæ were parasitized when collected, and that 34.1 per cent of all died.

SECOND BROOD.

TIME OF COCOONING OF SECOND-BROOD LARVÆ.

Table **XXXV** presents the cocooning data in detail.

TABLE XXXV.—*Time of cocooning and number of cocoons of the grape-berry moth; Sandusky, Ohio, 1918.*

| Date of cocooning. | Dates of collections of larvæ. | | | | | |
| | August— | | | September— | | |
	14	10	24	6	14	21
Aug. 15	2					
16	3					
17	2					
18	3					
19						
20	1	2				
21	1	3				
22		6				
23	3	7				
24	1	5				
25	7	2				
26	5	8	5			
27	3	3	1			
28	5	8	2			
29	2	8				
30	2	2	6			
31	1	4	1			
Sept. 1	1	1	2			
2	2	2	3			
3	1	3	4			
4	1	8	9			
5	1	2	2			
6		4	3			
7		5	2	1		
8		10	9	3		
9	1	3	7	9		
10	1	8	2	7		
11		6		2		
12	1	3	6	6		
13		1	2	3		
14	1	3	7	4		
15		6	10	10	2	
16		5	3	4	4	
17		1	2	8	1	
18		1	1		1	
19		1		3	1	
20			1	1		
21				1		
22		1	2	1		1
23		1	9	6	2	1
24			2	8	2	3
25		2	11	9	4	6
26				7	2	1
27				7	2	
28				6	3	5
29				5	3	4
30		1	1	3	2	1
Oct. 1				3	1	1
2				5	3	2
3			1	4	5	3
4				2	2	1
5			1	5	1	1
6			2	2	2	4
7					1	1
8				1		
9				2		
10			1			2
11						
12						2
13					1	
14						
15						
16						2
17						
18						
19						
20						
21						
22					1	
23					1	
24						
25						
26						
27						
28						
29				1		
30						
31						
Dates jars discontinued	Oct. 1	Oct. 21	Oct. 21	Nov. 1	Oct. 26	Nov. 1

TABLE XXXV.—*Time of cocooning and number of cocoons of the grape-berry moth, Sandusky, Ohio, 1918*—Continued.

Date of cocooning.	Dates of collections of larvæ.				Total cocoons.
	September—	October—			
	28	14	15	16	
Aug. 15					2
16					3
17					2
18					3
19					3
20					3
21					4
22					6
23					10
24					6
25					9
26					18
27					7
28					15
29					10
30					10
31					6
Sept 1					4
2					7
3					8
4					21
5					5
6					7
7					8
8					22
9					20
10					18
11					8
12					16
13					6
14					15
15					28
16					16
17					12
18					3
19					5
20					2
21					1
22					5
23					19
24					15
25					32
26					5
27					11
28					16
29	21				37
30	20				28
Oct. 1	9				14
2	17				29
3	11				24
4	7				12
5	34				42
6	20				30
7	3				5
8	3				4
9	9				11
10	6				9
11	4				4
12	1				3
13	3				4
14	3				3
15					0
16	2				4
17		2	4	3	9
18	10	6	7	3	26
19		3	2	2	7
20	2	2	5	5	14
21	1	4	6	4	15
22			1	1	2
23		2	1	1	4
24	3	8	6	1	18
25	1	4	4	5	14
26		1	1		2
27		1	5	2	8
28		2	1	3	6
29		2			3
30		1			1
31	1				1
Dates jars discontinued	Nov. 1	Nov. 1	Nov. 1	Nov. 1	842

Cocooning began as early as August 15 and continued until October 31.

PERCENTAGE OF COCOONING PREVIOUS TO AND DURING GRAPE HARVEST.

TABLE XXXVI.—*Percentage of cocooning previous to and during grape harvest, Sandusky, Ohio, 1918.*

Time.	Date.	Number of cocoons.	Percentage of total.
Previous to beginning of Concord harvest	To Sept. 20	343	40.73
During Concord harvest	Sept. 20–Oct. 10	342	40.62
Previous to end of Concord harvest	To Oct. 10	685	81.35
Previous to beginning of Catawba harvest	To Oct. 8	670	79.57
Previous to end of Catawba harvest	To Oct. 26	821	97.50
After Catawba harvest	To Nov. 1	21	2.50

The data in Table XXXV are summarized in Table XXXVI and emphasize similar records for the seasons of 1916 and 1917. From these records of three seasons involving a large quantity of larvæ regularly collected it must be concluded that a very large part of the second-brood larvæ leave the fruit previous to and during the early part of grape harvest.

MISCELLANEOUS RECORDS.

In the course of the life-history studies some observations were made that have a bearing on the habits of the insect and the development of the different stages.

ADULT.

The pupæ formed in the fall of 1916, from which moths emerged in the spring of 1917, were kept through the spring emergence period of 1918 to determine if any pupæ lived over and emerged the second spring. No moths emerged from this material the second year.

In an effort to approach natural conditions for moths in confinement dilute strained honey was supplied in the rearing jars. The usual observation was that the moths were not attracted to the food, but would feed if they came in contact with it. In one case when no new food had been supplied for six days, upon placing water on the sand in the bottom of the cage two moths immediately went $1\frac{1}{2}$ inches to the water and appeared to drink of it.

The adults seldom are seen in the vineyards during the day, and throughout these investigations, though the writer was in heavily infested vineyards almost daily, moths were rarely observed. In one case a moth was seen resting on a young cluster of grape buds, another was observed on the upper side of a grape leaf, and a third adult was seen in flight about the lower part of a grapevine. It alighted on a cane, ran into the angle of a small stub on the cane, and rested there, its head in the angle.

MATING.

Mating was observed but once, this in the insectary on July 19, 1917, at 2.45 p. m. The moths emerged the day previous and the jar contained 4 males and 10 females with a sprig from a grapevine bearing a grape leaf and cluster. The moths were on the bottom of the jar, not mounted, but with their bodies in opposite directions, the posterior parts touching.

OVIPOSITION.

The following observations on oviposition were made in a heavily infested part of a large vineyard on June 30, 1917. Oviposition began about sundown or 6.30 p. m. When the moths first appeared they fluttered nervously about the vines, alighting seemingly at random, generally upon clusters, though often upon stems or leaves. Upon finding a cluster a moth would walk rapidly about upon a grape berry, covering practically the entire surface. Finally becoming quiet she would flex the abdomen until its tip touched the berry. During the process the abdomen twitched or shook slightly but the tip was at no time lifted and then replaced. The deposition of the egg required less than a minute's time but was not instantaneous. Upon completion of the deposition of a single egg the moth usually flew nervously away from the cluster. The following exception occurred among four depositions observed. A moth alighted upon a grape and oviposited immediately without any preliminary inspection and upon completion walked directly onto the next grape in the same cluster and repeated the operation.

The spring brood of moths deposits a considerable percentage of the eggs near the attachment of the grape to the cluster, and the first-brood moths seem frequently to select a place on the underside of the cluster, away from the light.

Repeated observation has shown that the moths discriminate between sprayed and unsprayed grapes as places for oviposition. This was most marked in one experimental vineyard in 1916. Four rows had been left unsprayed and the adjoining rows sprayed, with the exception of the side of one row next to the checks. This row was thoroughly sprayed from one side by the trailer method and the grape clusters well covered on that side. About a third of the surface of the clusters remained unsprayed and deposition by first-brood moths was apparently as heavy on this unsprayed surface as on the adjoining check rows, whereas practically no eggs were deposited on the sprayed side of the same clusters. This observation led to continued study on the same point and it was substantiated repeatedly during the investigations. That eggs are deposited to some extent on the sprayed surface has been shown by infestation of sprayed plats.

That early blooming varieties of grapes are more heavily infested than mid-season varieties has been known generally among grape growers. During these investigations the writer has been led to believe that the moths normally prefer to deposit their eggs on the formed grapes rather than on the unopened buds. This was strikingly shown in the case of the Clinton vine on which oviposition records were taken for Table XIV. On this single Clinton vine, growing in a row of the Concord variety with the Ives variety close by, were 994 grapes bearing eggs on June 29. Subsequently 630 more eggs were recorded on this one vine. Careful search was made on adjoining vines of the other varieties and not until the grapes were well formed could eggs be found, whereas heavy oviposition continued on the Clinton vine. Repeatedly vines of the Shrides variety, the earliest of any to bloom in northern Ohio, have been heavily infested with larvæ when adjoining vines of the Concord and Catawba varieties bore no eggs and were not infested. This condition also prevailed where several rows of the Clinton or other early blooming varieties paralleled rows of the later blooming varieties. In years of heavy infestation it is advisable to spray the early blooming varieties earlier than the midseason varieties.

EGG.

A single observation was made on the issuance of the larva from the egg, on August 9, 1916. When first observed, the head of the larva was just through the eggshell and 2½ minutes more were required for the larva to free itself entirely from the shell. The larva did not consume the empty eggshell.

LARVA.

Mention is often made of the habit of the first-brood larvæ to web the young grape clusters before or during bloom. In but one instance during three seasons has the writer seen these webbed clusters in the grapes of the mid-season blooming period. Webbing frequently occurs in the Delaware variety which is in full bloom a few days after the Concords and just at the time when the spring-brood moths are emerging in large numbers, as shown in figures 2 and 4. This same condition exists with the Norton variety, which blooms very late.

The grape-berry moth larvæ occasionally feed on grape leaves in the rearing cages even when grapes are present, and in at least one case a larva developed from about one-half size to maturity by feeding in this way.

LARVÆ FEEDING ON PHYLLOXERA GALLS.

On August 25, 1916, and again on October 2, 1917, vines of the Clinton variety of grape were observed which were heavily infested by the leaf form of the grape phylloxera. Examination of the phylloxera galls showed that they had been eaten into and in some cases much of the gall actually consumed. On these same leaves with the galls were thin white silken webs containing larvæ which closely resembled the grape-berry moth larvæ. A quantity of the leaves were collected on August 25, 1916, and placed in battery jars containing no other food for the larvæ. The larvæ at the time of collection varied from less than half-grown to nearly mature specimens. The leaves dried out but the larvæ completed their feeding and cocooned in the leaves, a total of 79 cocoons being secured. Pupæ from this material were identified by August Busck of the U. S. Bureau of Entomology as *Polychrosis viteana* Clem. The pupæ were kept over winter under outdoor conditions and 12 moths emerged the following spring. In a single instance an empty eggshell was found on the under surface of the leaves close to a phylloxera gall. In the observation made on October 2, 1917, about 1 leaf in 5 had the web formed by the larvæ which were feeding on the galls. In no case could it be definitely determined whether the phylloxera in the galls were consumed with the gall tissue. No leaf feeding other than on the galls occurred with the larvæ under observation.

CANNIBALISM AMONG GRAPE-BERRY MOTH LARVÆ.

To determine if the larvæ would be cannibalistic with a restricted food supply the following experiment was conducted: From field-collected second-brood larvæ, 40 between 4 and 7 mm. in length were taken and divided into two lots of 20 each on September 14, 1917. One lot was placed in a jar with 20 grapes and the other lot was similarly placed with but 5 grapes. Grape leaves were provided in both jars for pupation of the larvæ. On November 22 the following results were recorded: In the lot where 20 grapes were provided, 15 cocoons had been formed and 2 full-grown live larvæ were present. Considerable substance remained in the grapes. Careful search for the other 3 individuals failed to locate them. In the lot where but 5 grapes were supplied, 5 cocoons had been formed, 2 dead and 2 live larvæ were present, or a total of 9 accounted for. A careful search was made for the head shields of the other 11 larvæ but they were not to be found. All the pulp from all the grapes had been consumed. From this single experiment it appears that cannibalism exists among the larvæ when the food supply is restricted and may occur even with sufficient food present for all.

LARVÆ NOT KILLED BY LOW TEMPERATURES.

The resistance of grape-berry moth pupæ to severe winter conditions has been noted. On October 30, 1917, a severe freeze occurred in northern Ohio, sufficient to freeze Concord and Catawba grapes. The lowest temperature recorded at the Sandusky station of the United States Weather Bureau on October 30 was 25° F., 26° on October 31 and November 1, and 28° on November 2. When recording the results of spraying experiments at Put-in-Bay, Ohio,

on November 5, and at Kelleys Island, Ohio, on November 7, live
larvæ were plentiful in the grapes and no case was found where the
larvæ had been killed by the freeze. In the insectary at Sandusky
after a minimum temperature of 23° F. had been recorded, larvæ continued to leave the grapes and spin cocoons. Live larvæ persisted
in the insectary on December 3, 1917, after a minimum temperature
of 17° F. had been recorded.

LARVA SPINNING ITS COCOON.

On July 9, 1916, a first-brood larva was observed making its
cocoon. When first observed the characteristic flap had been cut
in the leaf but was not folded. The process observed was the turning
over and tying down of the flap. The larva began at one end and by
rapid movements of its head from the free edge of the flap to its
place of attachment it gradually drew the flap over, the body of the
larva resting on the flap, and eventually inclosed in it. The entire
process observed occupied 35 minutes.

PARASITISM.

Considering the large numbers of individuals observed during
these investigations the total amount of parasitism was very low,
particularly among first-brood pupæ taken for the following emergence records.

That some parasitism of first-brood pupæ occurred is shown in
Table XXXVII.

TABLE XXXVII.—*Percentage of. parasitism of field collected first-brood grape-berry
moth pupæ from Venice, Ohio, 1917.*

Date of collection.	Number of co-coons col-lected.	Number of para-sites emerged.	Percent-age of para-sitism.
July 26	18	0	0
July 28	34	8	20.58
July 30	32	1	3.12
Aug. 1	41	11	26.82
Aug. 4	64	2	3.12
Aug. 6	47	8	17.02
Aug. 8	51	12	23.53
Aug. 10	35	12	34.28
Aug. 20	8	0	0
Do	31	4	12.90
Total	361	58	....
Average	....	....	16.06

The parasitism of field-collected pupæ is seen to vary from 0 to 26
per cent with an average of 16 per cent for pupæ collected between
July 26 and August 20.

In a single instance, September 8, 1916, eggs of the berry moth
were found which were parasitized to an appreciable extent. A total
of 760 eggs were collected on 11 clusters, of which 236, or 31 per cent,

were parasitized. The parasite was not determined but was thought to be the same as recorded by Johnson and Hammar[1] at North East, Pa., in 1906, *Trichogramma pretiosa* Riley.

SUMMARY.

The present account of the life history of the grape-berry moth in northern Ohio is based upon a series of studies made in 1916, 1917, and 1918.

In the course of a year the grape-berry moth in northern Ohio produces one full brood and a partial second, the second brood of larvæ being much larger and more destructive than the first.

The grape-berry moth passes the winter in the pupal stage in cocoons in old grape leaves under the grape trellis. Under a leaf blanket approximating conditions in a protected part of a vineyard the mortality among the pupæ was 80 per cent during the winter of 1916–17 and 76 per cent during the winter of 1917–18.

The first moths emerge in the spring about 10 days before grapes begin to bloom but emerge in greatest numbers during and immediately following the period of grape bloom. In 1917 but 4 per cent emerged previous to bloom, 50 per cent during grape bloom, 25 per cent in the 10-day period following bloom, and the remaining 21 per cent later in the season. Moths begin ovipositing about 4 days after emergence and the eggs hatch in from 3 to 10 days, with 5 days as the average length of the egg stage.

The first-brood larvæ feed in the young grapes for a period of from 14 to 37 days, and the average length of the feeding period was 20.6 days in 1917. At the end of the feeding period the larvæ leave the grapes and go to tender grape leaves on the vines in which they spin their cocoons. The prepupal period lasted for from 1 to 3 days and averaged 1.77 days with the first brood in 1917, and lasted for from 3 to 7 days and averaged 4.15 days with the second brood in 1916. The pupal period varied from 11 to 16 days and averaged 13 days for first-brood pupæ in 1917. The total period in the cocoon varied from 6 to 32 days with an average period of 15 days.

The life cycle of the first generation in 1917, taken as a total of the average length of the separate stages, was 39.79 days. The total of the maximums was 76 days and of the minimums 23 days.

The incubation period of second-brood eggs varied from 4 to 10 days with 5.1 days as the average period. The feeding period of second-brood larvæ was from 16 to 36 days and averaged 24.18 days in 1916. All other records have given this period as about 40 days which is probably nearer the average condition than the figures presented here.

---

[1] Johnson, Fred, and Hammar, A. G. The grape-berry moth. U. S. Dept. Agr., Bur. Ent. Bul. 116, pt. II, p. 39. 1912.

Second-brood larvæ begin to leave the fruit early in the fall, August 22, 1916, August 15, 1918, September 7, 1917, but leave in greatest numbers just previous to and during the early part of the harvest season. In 1916, 77 per cent of the larvæ left the fruit previous to the beginning of the Concord harvest and 90 per cent previous to the beginning of the Catawba harvest. In 1917 corresponding figures were 56 per cent and 94 per cent.

In each brood of moths the females occur in much larger number than the males, the proportions being 21 per cent males, 79 per cent females in the spring brood, 1917; 18 per cent males, 82 per cent females in the summer brood, 1917; 25 per cent males, 75 per cent females in the spring of 1918; and 21 per cent males and 79 per cent females in the summer brood of 1918. A small part of the first-brood larvæ do not transform to moths the same season but hibernate and emerge as moths the following spring. In 1918 this amounted to 5.9 per cent of the total number recorded. Of the same lot of larvæ but 1.4 per cent were parasitized.

Mating and egg deposition were observed during these investigations. The habit of the grape-berry moth larvæ of feeding on grape leaf galls formed by the grapevine phylloxera was noted. Extreme resistance of the larvæ to low temperature was also noted, live larvæ persisting after a minimum temperature of 17° F. had occurred. Parasitism was very low and of little consequence as a control during these investigations.

Control measures recommended are cultural methods which will leave the overwintering pupæ exposed to the elements as much as possible. Satisfactory control was effected by two spray applications by the "trailer" or hand method of spraying. The first application should be made 3 to 5 days after the young grapes set and the second when the grapes first touch in the clusters.

ADDITIONAL COPIES
OF THIS PUBLICATION MAY BE PROCURED FROM
THE SUPERINTENDENT OF DOCUMENTS
GOVERNMENT PRINTING OFFICE
WASHINGTON, D. C.
AT
10 CENTS PER COPY
▽

UNITED STATES DEPARTMENT OF AGRICULTURE

BULLETIN No. 912

Contribution from the Office of Farm Management and Farm Economics
H. C. TAYLOR, Chief

Washington, D. C. ▼ November 17, 1920

HAIL INSURANCE ON FARM CROPS IN THE UNITED STATES.

By V. N. VALGREN, *Associate Agricultural Economist.*

CONTENTS.

	Page.		Page.
Introduction	1	Characteristics of the hail insurance	
Origin and development	2	contract	20
Territorial distribution	11	Special problems in hail insurance	24
Cost of hail insurance	16		

INTRODUCTION.

The business of farming involves numerous risks. These risks may be minimized, if not wholly removed, by the application of principles of insurance. The insurance method of dealing with risks and losses is widely current among men in commercial pursuits. To the latter, insurance is now available, and very generally procured, against nearly every form of loss to which their business is subject.

The most common source of loss to the farmer is the partial or total failure of his crops. Hitherto, with negligible exceptions, the only form of crop insurance available has been that against loss by hail, and even this limited insurance coverage is of relatively recent origin. In the last few years, however, hail insurance has attained a quantitative importance that only those in close touch with the business have been in position to realize.

Hail insurance on growing crops is written in the United States by organizations representing three different groups of business institutions. These groups are: (1) Mutual hail insurance companies, which, with few exceptions, limit their business to the insurance of growing crops against hail; (2) joint-stock fire insurance companies, which write hail insurance on growing crops more or less as a side line; (3) State hail insurance boards or departments, under whose direction and control are administered State hail insurance funds.

7676°—20——1

During 1918, the latest date for which State insurance reports are available, the three groups of hail insurance organizations just mentioned had in force in the United States insurance on growing crops to a total amount of approximately $318,543,000, on which the premiums amounted to $17,631,000. The figures for 1919, as ascertained from correspondence with the companies and the State insurance commissioners, as well as from various unofficial published reports, show a remarkable increase, the total risks and premiums being approximately $559,134,000 and $30,330,000, respectively.

ORIGIN AND DEVELOPMENT.

The first organization in the United States to write hail insurance on growing crops, so far as official records reveal, was a small mutual concern organized in 1880 by the tobacco growers in Connecticut. This company, for some reason or other, dropped out of existence in 1887, but was promptly succeeded by another hail mutual organized in an adjoining county, which is still doing business. No other exclusive hail companies are revealed by official records earlier than the year 1889, in which year four mutual hail insurance companies were reported from North Dakota.

In the meantime one of the larger joint-stock fire insurance companies had begun to write hail insurance on growing crops. The first risks were written in Minnesota in 1883, while in the following year a small amount of hail insurance was also written by this company in what was then Dakota Territory, in Nebraska, and in Kansas. The State of Iowa and the Territory of Oklahoma were included in the hail insurance territory of this company in 1897, followed by Wisconsin, Texas, and Colorado in 1898.

Although many of these early mutuals proved to be short-lived experiments, by 1900 there were 37 mutual hail insurance companies in existence, located in seven different States, as follows: Connecticut 1, Wisconsin 4, Minnesota 13, Iowa 7, North Dakota 2, Nebraska 7, and Kansas 3. The total premiums and assessments collected by these companies during the year were approximately $643,000, and the losses incurred amounted to $407,000. More than one-third of the total hail insurance premiums were reported from Iowa, while Minnesota and Nebraska each reported more than one-fifth, Kansas somewhat less than one-sixth of the total, and the other three States smaller amounts.

In 1905 the total number of hail mutuals was still 37, those that had dropped out since 1900 having been replaced by new organizations. The total premiums of these companies during the year approached $800,000, and the losses were approximately one-half of the premiums collected. By this time at least one additional joint-stock fire insurance company had begun to write hail insurance. The total hail premiums reported for these two companies in 1905 were approximately equal to the amount collected by the mutual companies, or about three-fourths of a million dollars.

By 1910 the total number of mutual hail insurance companies had decreased to 28, as against 37 in 1905. The total premiums for the year, however, showed a considerable increase, being more than $1,000,000. Of the hail mutuals reported by State insurance departments in 1910, one was located in Connecticut, five in Wisconsin, four in Minnesota, nine in Iowa, one in North Dakota, two in Nebraska, three in Kansas, two in Oklahoma, and one in Montana. Two of the Minnesota hail mutuals wrote insurance in Kansas and Montana, as well as in their home States, and one of these companies wrote also in North Dakota. In later years these same Minnesota mutuals have been doing business in several States, and a few of the Iowa companies have also been admitted to neighboring States.

At least five joint-stock companies were writing hail insurance on growing crops by 1910. The total hail premiums received by this class of companies for the year, so far as these figures have been obtained, were approximately the same as those reported for the year 1905, or about $750,000, though they exceeded this amount in some of the intervening years. During this five-year period, therefore, the mutual hail insurance companies had made a material growth, while the hail business of joint-stock fire insurance companies had been approximately stationary.

In the five-year period following 1910 the hail insurance business in the United States advanced by rapid strides. The number of mutual companies increased to 39. Their total premiums in 1915 exceeded $3,336,000, and were thus more than three times as great as in 1910. Although the mutual hail insurance companies thus made a material advance in the five years from 1910 to 1915, the hail business of the joint-stock fire insurance companies showed a far greater advance. The total number of such companies in the field increased from 5 to 35, while their total hail premiums in 1915 amounted to approximately $6,400,000, as against three-fourths of a million for 1910.

The year 1915, as will be brought out later in this bulletin, was an extremely severe one from the point of view of hail losses. A number of the mutual companies, as on various previous occasions, were caught without adequate reserves or other resources and had to prorate their losses. As a result, mutual hail insurance suffered a severe setback, this being particularly true in the State of Kansas. During the season of 1916 only 35 mutual companies were in the field, and the premiums collected by the mutuals in this year amounted to only about two-thirds the total premiums collected by this group of companies in 1915. In the three years following 1916, however, the premiums of the mutuals again increased each year, reaching $4,775,-000 in 1919.

During these same years the joint-stock insurance companies showed continued and rapid progress. The number of such companies writing hail insurance continued to increase, and their total premiums in 1916. as well as in 1917, exceeded $8,000,000. In 1918 the hail premiums of joint-stock companies on their business in the United States exceeded $12,850,000, and for 1919 the corresponding figure was approximately $19,460,000.

In the early days of hail insurance but little information existed as to the nature of the hail hazard and its relative severity in different localities. Many of the early hail mutuals appear to have been patterned on the local farmers' mutual fire insurance companies, without an adequate recognition, on the part of the organizers and managers, of the radical difference between the fire hazard in relation to segregated farm buildings and the hail hazard in relation to fields of growing grain. With a reasonable number of risks in a given locality, the law of average will apply to the losses of farm buildings by fire in a way that it can not possibly apply to the losses in the case of hail insurance on growing crops. Unlike fire, a hailstorm seldom, if ever, strikes one farm only but cuts a swath through a limited territory, resembling in its effects a conflagration in the case of urban fire risks. The fact that mutual hail insurance in the West North-Central States continued to increase in volume as well as in the number of companies writing it may be credited, therefore, to the need for such insurance on the part of the farmers rather than to any general success on the part of the mutuals offering this protection.

The causes of the frequent failure among the early hail mutuals can not be charged entirely, however, to lack of knowledge of the hail hazard. In many instances the failures were due to reckless or unscrupulous promotions, the organizers taking advantage of the general inadequacy of insurance laws, which were especially lax in regard to mutual companies. In cases of this kind the permanency or soundness of the company was frequently a minor consideration with the managers, whose direct object was prompt and liberal incomes from salaries and commissions.

Mutual promotions of the speculative type have tended to discredit all hail mutuals and have constituted a serious handicap to the growth and development of companies organized by men of ability aiming at real service to their constituents. To a somewhat less extent the same has been true of hail mutuals which were promoted by men who, while honest and sincere, were lacking in knowledge of the hail hazard or in ability as managers.

As time went on the nature and severity of the hail hazard in the different States became better known. Insurance laws, as well as the administration of these laws, became in general more effective in safeguarding the interests of the policyholders, and farmers to an increasing extent became aware that it is necessary to know something about the men in charge of the mutual organizations as well as to see that the plan on which insurance is offered is a reasonably workable one. Because of these changes in conditions ill-considered and speculative promotions of hail mutuals appear in general to have passed their climax in each State a few years after the organization of the first hail mutuals in the State. Such climax in promotions was reached in the State of North Dakota in the middle nineties, in Minnesota and Nebraska during the last few years of the past century, and in Iowa during the first years of the present century. In Oklahoma the promotion period centered about the year 1903, and in Texas it occurred nearly 10 years later. The State of Kansas presents an exception to the general rule, in that the period of most rapid promotion of short-lived companies came more than two decades after the first hail mutuals were organized. The earliest hail mutual in Kansas, as already stated, began business in 1889, but the climax in the promotion of hail mutuals in that State was not reached until the five-year period following 1910.

One of the most spectacular mutual hail insurance promotions that has occurred in any State took place in Missouri in 1919, and the organization in question is now in the hands of receivers. This company did not limit itself to hail coverage, however, but included destructive storms of whatever nature, and partly for this reason the risks assumed by it have not been included in the data contained in this bulletin.

The total number of mutual hail insurance companies of which record has been found, either from insurance reports or from other sources, is 121. Of these 121 hail mutuals, only 41 companies were in existence at the date of the most recent insurance reports. The other 80 hail mutuals have ceased operations, either voluntarily for lack of patronage or under pressure applied by State insurance departments. This relatively high mortality among the mutual hail insurance companies as a class has frequently been interpreted as proof of unsoundness and instability in every mutual hail insurance company, without regard to its individual record or merit. Such a conclusion is no more justified than would be a conclusion that all joint-stock fire insurance companies are unsound because of the large percentage of such companies that, for one reason or another, have gone out of business. No reliable figures are at hand for the total number of joint-stock fire insurance companies that have been organized in the United States. According to some of the best-known

nsurance summaries which contain lists of companies that ha
ailed or retired, however, at least six joint-stock fire insurance co
ianies have gone out of business in the last 50 years for every su
ompany now in the field.

Considered by States, the number of hail mutuals organized a
he number now in existence are as follows:

North Dakota, 13 companies organized and 1 in existence; M
esota, 25 organized and 7 in existence; Iowa, 18 organized and 6
xistence; Nebraska, 16 organized and 4 in existence; Kansas,
rganized and 7 in existence; Wisconsin, 8 organized and 4 in ‹
stence; Oklahoma, 9 organized and 2 in existence; Montana, 6 ‹
anized and 2 in existence; Texas, 6 organized and 3 in existenc
South Carolina, 2 organized and both in existence; Connectic
lichigan, and New Mexico, 1 company organized in each State a
ach still in existence.

Of the hail mutuals that have ceased doing business, 11 compan
vere in existence for one year only, 38 operated more than one ye
ut under five, while 20 operated five or more years but under t

In this connection the various ages attained by the 41 hail mutu:
low in the field should be of interest. The approximate ages of th
ompanies, by five-year periods, are indicated by the following su
nary of their organization:

1885–1889	2 companies.
1890–1894	2 companies.
1895–1899	6 companies.
1900–1904	4 companies.
1905–1909	7 companies.
1910–1914	5 companies.
1915–1919	15 companies.

The year 1911 marks the entry into the hail insurance field of t
hird type of business institution above mentioned, North Dakota
his year having put into operation its first State hail insurance l
vhich provided for the writing of this form of insurance througl
State hail insurance department. During the first year of St:
ail insurance in North Dakota premiums to the amount of $26,(
vere collected, representing risks of slightly more than $1,000,0
The losses experienced during the year exceeded the premium
ome, however, by nearly 18 per cent, and the losses as adjusted h
o be prorated at 70 per cent. The business during 1912 showec
elatively marked increase; the premiums amounted to nearly $65,(
nd the risks were in excess of $2,500,000. During this year, hc
ver, the losses were nearly one and two-thirds times the tc
remiums, and for this reason had to be prorated on a basis of
er cent. These experiences discouraged the farmers from tak
ail insurance with the State department, and the total business

each of the next six years was less than one-half as great as that of 1912. During each of these years it was found necessary to prorate the losses, the percentages paid being as follows: 1913, 88 per cent; 1914, 65 per cent; 1915, 75 per cent; 1916, 38 per cent; 1917, 62 per cent; and 1918, 53 per cent.

The rather discouraging experience on the part of North Dakota with its State hail insurance department under the law as first enacted may be ascribed chiefly to two causes. In the first place, the premium charges provided for in the law were inadequate, such charges for the years 1911 and 1912 having been 20 cents per acre on $8 of insurance, making a rate of only 2½ per cent, or exactly one-fourth of the rate now charged by joint-stock companies in the State. In the spring of 1913 the law was amended so as to make the rate of premium 30 cents per acre on $8 of insurance, or 3¾ per cent, at which figure the rate remained until the complete revision of the law in the spring of 1919. The other outstanding cause of failure of the original North Dakota plan was that applications for insurance had to be made to the assessor in the early spring and the premiums for such insurance advanced at that time, before any crops were actually in existence.

In spite of this apparent failure of State hail insurance in North Dakota, the States of Montana and Nebraska enacted laws providing for State hail insurance departments in the spring of 1917. The Montana department began operations shortly after the law was passed, but no insurance was written by the Nebraska department until the season of 1918. The premiums collected by the Montana department during its first year of operation amounted to $107,000, and the losses incurred were moderate, being only $62,000. Although the law permitted a maximum assessment of 60 cents per acre, the department assessed and collected hail premiums of only 40 cents per acre on $12 of insurance, being at a rate of 3⅓ per cent. With the funds so collected the department was able to pay its losses, together with expenses of operation, the latter amounting to $4,700, and to complete the year with a surplus of $40,000. This favorable beginning of State hail insurance in Montana in 1917 was, however, followed by a very trying experience in 1918. The losses this year were extremely heavy, caused largely by a severe and unusually extensive hail storm just at the time when the wheat was ripe and ready for harvest. The losses as adjusted approximated $870,000. The maximum levy of 60 cents per acre brought only a little over $400,000, and this amount, together with the small surplus from the preceding year, was only enough to pay 46 per cent of the losses.

The Nebraska State hail insurance department during 1918, its first year of operation, collected $154,260 in premiums. The law in this case provided fixed rates which varied from 25 cents per acre for the eastern part of the State to 45 cents for the western. The amount of insurance per acre was $10. The losses during the year proved to be moderate, amounting to only $127,060, and the total cost of administration was $6,072. All losses were, therefore, paid in full and the year was closed with a balance or surplus on hand amounting to $21,128.

During the early months of 1919 the States of North Dakota, Montana, and Nebraska materially amended their hail insurance laws. During the same months the States of South Dakota and Oklahoma also enacted laws providing for State hail insurance.

The new North Dakota law and that of South Dakota provide what is frequently called " compulsory insurance," although the term " automatic " would seem more accurately to describe the plan. In each of these States every acre of crop is now, without action on the part of the owner, insured against loss or damage by hail, the amount being $7 per acre in North Dakota and $10 per acre in South Dakota. In the latter State such owner may, however, exempt his land entirely from the operation of the hail insurance law by filing an application for exemption with the county auditor before June 1 of each year. He may also, if he so desires, retain one-half of the $10 insurance per acre and be subject to one-half of the indemnity tax. In North Dakota the owner of a growing crop may exempt such crop by filing a statement with the commissioner of insurance, except that a flat acreage tax of 3 cents per acre must be paid to the hail insurance fund whether the owner retains or rejects the hail insurance provided by the State.

In both the Dakotas hail insurance premiums are now collected by the State in a manner similar to that provided for the collection of taxes. The same is true under the laws as now existing in Montana and Nebraska. In the last two States, however, the State hail insurance takes effect only upon the application for such insurance by the owner or tiller of the land. The Oklahoma law, which was not operative in 1919, is similar to the Montana and Nebraska laws in providing for strictly voluntary or optional insurance and follows the original North Dakota law in requiring premiums to be paid in advance.

The maximum hail indemnity tax that may be levied in North Dakota under the existing law is 50 cents per acre or $7\frac{1}{2}$ per cent of the insurance. The actual levy in 1919 was only 25 cents per acre, exclusive of the so-called acreage tax of 3 cents per acre. In South Dakota, where the regular amount of insurance per acre is $10, a fixed rate is applied for each of four different districts, into which the State is divided, these rates being, respectively, 35 cents, 40 cents, 42 cents, and 45 cents per acre. Such rates are not to be reduced until the department has a surplus or reserve fund of $2,500,000.

The Montana law, like the North Dakota law, provides a uniform maximum limit of assessment for hail indemnity for all parts of the State, such limit being fixed at $1.20 per acre for $12 of insurance. This maximum rate was actually applied in 1919 and proved sufficient to pay the cost of insurance and leave a small surplus.

The Nebraska law provides for three hail insurance districts in the State with fixed rates applying to each. The rates for these districts are 25 cents, 40 cents, and 60 cents per acre, respectively, when the amount of insurance carried is $10 per acre. The farmer may, however, take $15 per acre at one-and-a-half times the rate charged for $10 per acre. The hail losses in Nebraska during 1919 were heavy, and there was left but a small balance when losses and expenses were paid.

The Oklahoma law provides for the division of the State into four hail insurance districts. The insured may take any amount of insurance be desires up to $20 per acre. The rates are 3 per cent, 6 per cent, 7½ per cent, and 9 per cent of the insurance according to the district in which the crop is located. In each of the three States, where different rates for specified parts of the State are provided, the lowest rates apply to the eastern district and the highest to the western.

The total risks of the four State hail insurance departments in operation in 1919 were approximately $139,300,000; the premiums, $6,095,000; and the losses, $4,500,000. Of the total risks, North Dakota had about 62 per cent; South Dakota, 23 per cent; Nebraska, 14 per cent; and Montana, less than 1 per cent. The South Dakota department alone laid aside a material surplus or reserve from the year's business, such surplus being approximately $900,000.

As already stated, the total hail business in the United States during the summer of 1919 surpassed the already outstanding record of 1918 by a very wide margin. In fact, it is believed by many hail underwriters that the volume of this form of insurance written during the season of 1919 will not be equaled in the years immediately ahead. Certainly the record, as compared with those of earlier years, is a remarkable one.

While not all of the State insurance reports that give hail premiums and losses give also the hail risks involved, it is, of course, possible to arrive at approximate figures for the latter quantities by taking into consideration the amount of premiums and the average rates. Estimates for these missing figures have been worked out on the basis of such information as was available.

The development of the hail insurance business in the United States, as measured by the approximate amount of risks in force each year from 1890 to the present time, may be seen from figure 1. Besides showing the growth in the total hail risks, the figure also

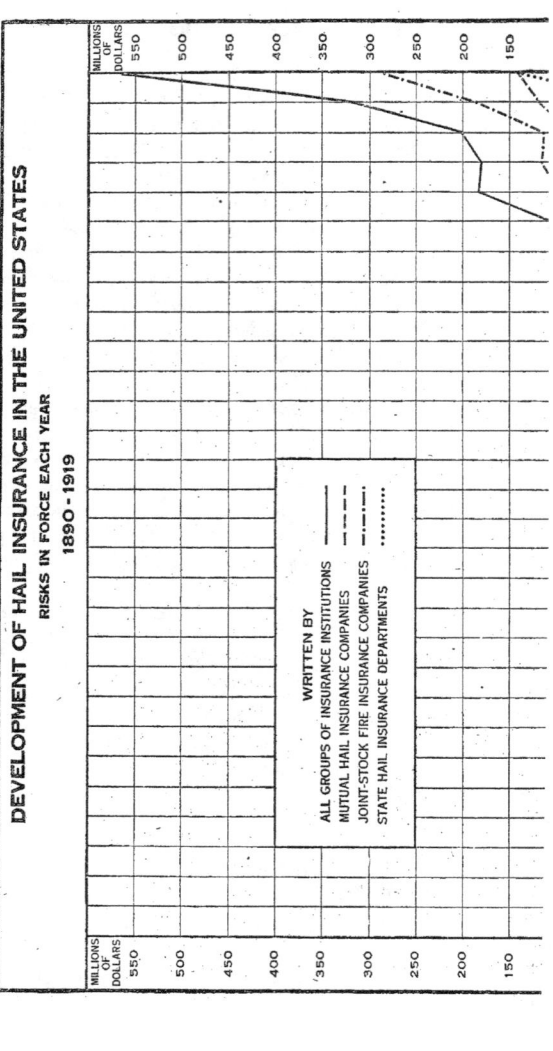

DEVELOPMENT OF HAIL INSURANCE IN THE UNITED STATES

RISKS IN FORCE EACH YEAR

1890-1919

WRITTEN BY

ALL GROUPS OF INSURANCE INSTITUTIONS ——————
MUTUAL HAIL INSURANCE COMPANIES – – – –
JOINT-STOCK FIRE INSURANCE COMPANIES –·–·–·
STATE HAIL INSURANCE DEPARTMENTS ··········

MILLIONS OF DOLLARS

550
500
450
400
350
300
250
200
150

indicates the amount of risks and the annual increase in business for each of the three groups of insurance institutions already discussed, namely, mutual hail insurance companies, joint-stock fire insurance companies, and State hail insurance departments. The fact that the risks in force by mutual companies continue to exceed those in force by joint-stock fire insurance companies until the year 1916, while the premiums received by the two groups of insurance institutions change place at a considerably earlier date, is to be explained in part by the uniformly lower rates charged by the mutuals. The prime reason, however, is to be found in the fact that a large percentage of the mutual risks occurred in States, such as Iowa, Minnesota, Wisconsin, and Michigan, where the hail hazard is less severe than in the States farther west and where the rates and premiums are on this account relatively small in proportion to the volume of risks.

The total risks shown for 1919 represent those of 41 mutual companies, 43 joint-stock companies, and 4 State hail insurance departments. Of the $559,000,000 of hail risks in force during 1919, the joint-stock companies had almost exactly one-half, while the mutuals and the State hail insurance departments each had one-fourth.

TERRITORIAL DISTRIBUTION.

The territorial distribution of the hail insurance business is determined mainly by two factors, namely, acreage in crops subject to damage and the severity of the hail hazard in relation to other hazards to which crops are exposed. In other words, hail insurance in large volume can be written only where there is a large acreage of crops to insure, and where at the same time the probability of destructive hail storms is present in such degree as to make the growers of crops conscious of the need for protection. These two factors coexist in a marked degree in the West North Central States. While from the point of view of acreage in crops subject to damage when hail does occur, a large percentage of the area of about three-fourths of the States would be insurable, the hail hazard in a considerable number of these States is relatively so slight as to preclude the taking of any special precaution against loss from this source.

The acreage in crops in the different States, according to the census of 1910 is shown in figure 2.[1] Except for a few of the Western States, where there has been a marked increase in the crop acreage, this map represents the situation as to relative crop acreage in the different States very much as it exists at the present time. Later data of an accurate character will not be at hand until the results from the 1920 census are available.

---

[1] Reproduced from Yearbook of the U. S. Department of Agriculture, 1915, p. 340.

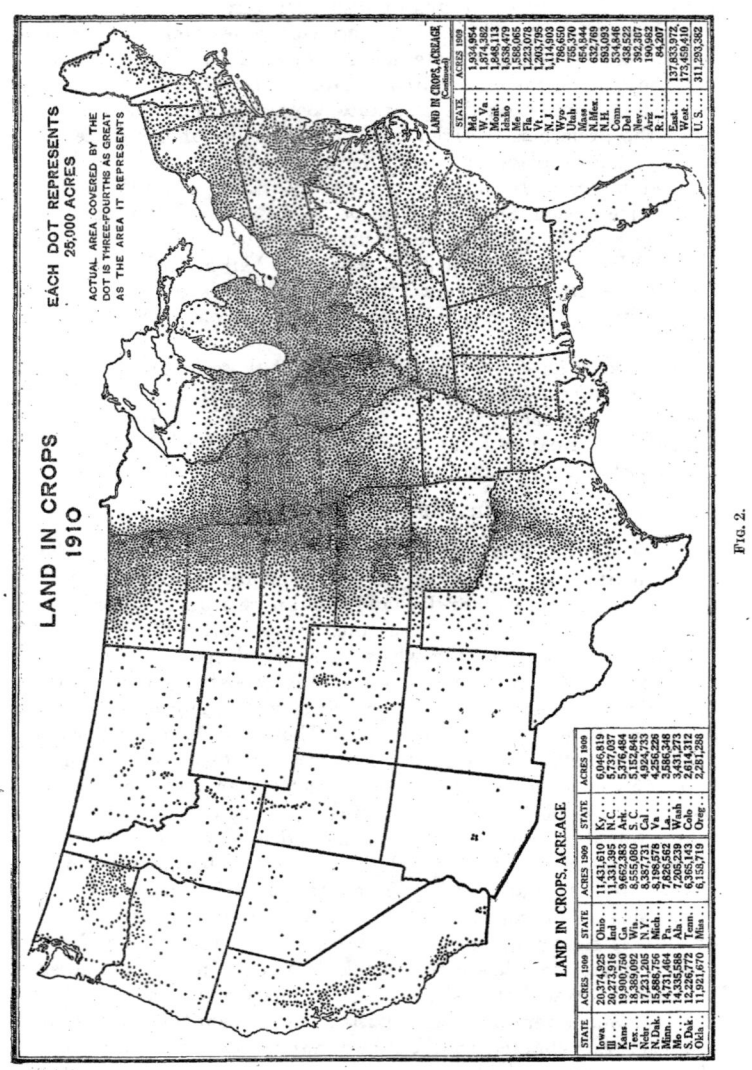

Fig. 2.

Some idea of the relative importance of the hail hazard in different parts of the country may be obtained from figure 3, which indicates in a general way the frequency of the occurrence of hail in the United States during the four months, May, June, July, and August. The data represented on this map are based on reports from the various United States Weather Bureau stations, and cover the 14-year period 1906–1919, inclusive. The map or chart in question, it should be emphasized, indicates only the average annual frequency of the occurrence of hail during the months stated, no attempt having been made to allow for differences in the severity or the destructiveness of hail storms. It should perhaps also be pointed out, as has been done by the Weather Bureau in connection with earlier published

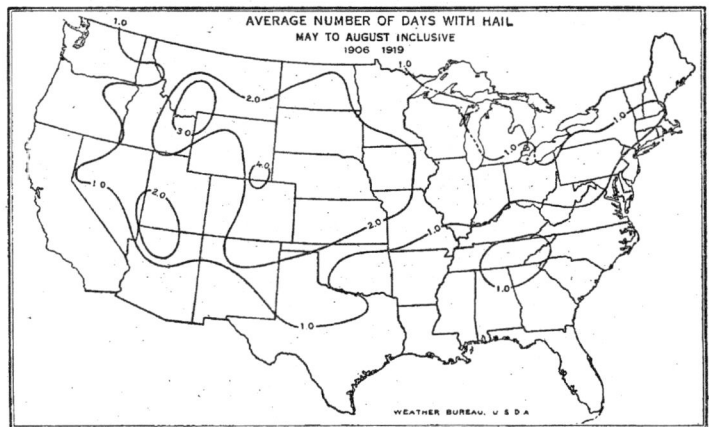

AVERAGE NUMBER OF DAYS WITH HAIL
MAY TO AUGUST INCLUSIVE
1906 1919

WEATHER BUREAU, U S D A

FIG. 3.

data on this subject,[1] that the reports on which the chart is based come from only 167 stations rather unevenly distributed throughout the United States. Since hail storms are frequently very local in character, it follows that the data as represented embody an element of chance even as to the average frequency of hail. It is probable, for example, that the total number of times at which hail occurred and, hence, also the average yearly number of such occurrences reported from a given station, may represent either more or less than the average frequency for all parts of the area for which such station is considered a center.

To a certain extent the relatively long period of time covered by the reports will, of course, tend to eliminate some of the chance elements involved in the lack of a sufficient number of reporting stations.

---

[1] See Weather Bureau Review for March, 1917, pp. 94 et seq.

It is quite probable, however, that the frequency indicated for the territory about Cheyenne, Wyo., for example, might have been equaled or even exceeded by other localities had all local areas in the relatively severe hail territory been represented. With all due allowance for these limitations, the chart doubtless indicates the prevalence of hail with a reasonable degree of accuracy.

The lines on the chart are intended to connect various points at which the average annual frequency of hail during the months mentioned and for the period indicated has been found to be equal or very nearly equal. Thus the lines marked 1:0 are intended to connect the places at which hail occurred on the average once each year during the 14-year period, while the lines marked 2.0 are intended to connect the places with an annual average of two occurrences of hail during the months considered, and so on.

The approximate distribution of hail insurance on growing crops in the United States during the year 1919 is shown in figure 4. The total of such risks in force was estimated to be $559,134,000. The circles on this map represent by their respective areas the relative amounts of hail risks in force in the various States. They also indicate by the sectors into which they are divided the group or type of insurance institution by which such insurance was carried. The sectors colored black in various circles indicate the part of the total hail insurance in a given State carried by mutual hail insurance companies; the checkered sectors indicate the part carried by joint-stock fire insurance companies; and the striped sectors, the part carried by State hail insurance departments.

As indicated by the map, the three States of Kansas, North Dakota, and Iowa, ranking in the order given, led all other States in the amount of hail risks in force. In fact, these three States together had more than one-half of the total hail risks in force in the United States. The approximate amount of risks reported from each of the three was: Kansas, $116,056,000; North Dakota, $99,603,000; and Iowa, $73,471,000. These amounts represent, respectively, 21 per cent, 17 per cent, and 13 per cent of the total risks in the United States. The States of Nebraska, South Dakota, and Minnesota follow in the order named having risks, respectively, equal to 9 per cent, 8 per cent, and 6 per cent of the total. The State of Oklahoma is seventh on the list, with risks equal to 4 per cent of the total. None of the remaining States had an amount equal to much over 2 per cent of the total, and most of them had less than 1 per cent.

With reference to the distribution of the risks between the three types of insurance institutions, it may be recalled from figure 1 that the joint-stock companies, in 1919, carried approximately one-half of the total risks, while the mutual companies and State departments carried about one-fourth each. The predominance of joint-stock hail insurance during the year in question may also be seen from figure 4.

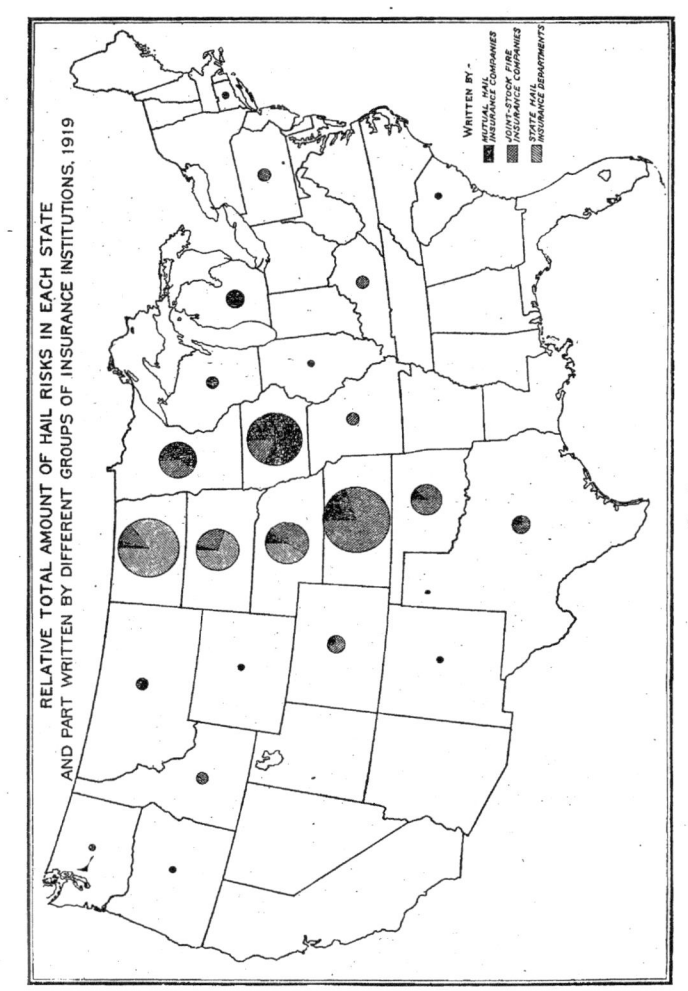

RELATIVE TOTAL AMOUNT OF HAIL RISKS IN EACH STATE AND PART WRITTEN BY DIFFERENT GROUPS OF INSURANCE INSTITUTIONS, 1919

WRITTEN BY -

MUTUAL HAIL INSURANCE COMPANIES

JOINT-STOCK FIRE INSURANCE COMPANIES

STATE HAIL INSURANCE DEPARTMENTS

FIG. 4.

In the States of Iowa and Minnesota, however, the mutuals carried the major part of the total risk, while the same was true for
the State hail insurance departments in two other of the more important States from a hail-insurance standpoint, namely, North
Dakota and South Dakota. The map further indicates that in the
State of Michigan all of the hail insurance of which record was
found was carried on the mutual plan, while in the State of Wisconsin all but one-tenth of 1 per cent was carried on the same plan.

COST OF HAIL INSURANCE.

In hail insurance as well as in fire insurance it is, of course, essential that the rates of premium or assessment yield a sufficient income to cover the losses that occur and the necessary expenses of
operation. In the case of joint-stock insurance companies, it is
naturally the intention so to adjust the rates that in addition to
losses and expenses there will be a margin of profit for the stock-
holders who have risked their money in the enterprise.

In the early days of hail insurance, as already stated, relatively
little knowledge of the hail hazard was possessed by those engaging
in the hail insurance business. It seems that a common rate of
premium was 5 per cent of the insurance written. The variation in
the severity of the hail hazard found in different States, as well as
in different sections of the same State, was soon recognized, however, and the rates were adjusted in an effort to make them reflect
these variations. Rates in Minnesota, Iowa, Missouri, and States
east and south of these were lowered until a rate of 3 per cent became fairly general for the more common cereal crops in this territory. West and south of the States named, however, rates were
gradually advanced for succeeding districts, reaching 6, 8, 10, 12, and
even higher percentages of the insurance written.

While most of the mutuals started out strictly on the assessment
plan, a few began operations on predetermined rates. Thus one of
the Kansas mutuals which is still in the field at first wrote insurance
anywhere in the State at 4 per cent. After a number of years of
experience in the business this company graduated its rates according to the losses experienced, until such rates were only 2½ per cent
for the southeastern part of the State and reached 10 per cent for
some of the western counties.

The prevailing commercial rates for the year 1919 are shown in
figure 5, the figures on this map representing dollars per hundred
of insurance for the crop season. It will also be noticed that the
relative heaviness of the shading or crosshatching on the map has
been made to represent the relative hail rates for the different States
or parts of States indicated on the map.

The rates here shown apply mainly to the more common cereal
crops, namely, wheat, oats, corn, flax, and speltz. Grasses produced

for hay or seed are, however, usually insured at the same rates as the grains just enumerated. For barley and rye the rates in most of the States are 2 per cent higher than those shown on the map, and the same is true for corn where protection is desired against damage to the leaves as well as to the ear. Tobacco is given a rate varying from about one and one-half times the rates on wheat, oats, and corn in some districts to more than two and one-half times the rates on these cereals in other localities. The rates on cotton are even less closely related to the rates on cereals. In the South Atlantic and the East South Central States the rates for cotton are in general the same as the cereal rates, and in a few instances even 1 per cent lower. In the West South Central States, on the other hand, the hail rates for cotton are from 2 to 4 per cent higher than the rates for cereals.

In the extreme eastern part of the United States, as well as in the extreme western part, the rates on fruits and on garden vegetables, including peas and beans, even when raised as ordinary field crops, are in general from one and one-half to two times the rates on cereal crops. In parts of the West South Central and Mountain States these crops may be insured at a rate 2 per cent higher than the regular rate on cereal crops in the locality in question. The latter statement holds true for the North Central States also, except that such rates for this part of the country have usually covered garden vegetables only.

It is difficult to give any definite figures for rates of premium or assessment of mutual companies, since many of these continue to operate on the assessment plan without the application of fixed rates in advance. Where such rates are actually determined in advance by mutual companies they are usually somewhat lower than the joint-stock rates, although a few mutuals adhere to the commercial rates, returning a part of the premiums in dividends or rebates when the losses and expenses together are low enough to permit of such action.

Only fragmentary data are at hand for the average expense ratio of the various companies writing hail insurance. Such figures as are available, however, point to an average expense of operation equal to about 35 per cent of the premium. This expense of operation, calculated as a percentage of the premiums, will, of course, vary to some extent with the rates on the business written. Many overhead items of expense will be approximately the same for two policies, each representing a thousand-dollar risk, even though one be written in territory where the rate is 3 per cent and the premium $30 and the other in territory where the rate is 12 per cent and the premium $120. Six dollars of overhead expense attached to each of these policies will mean 20 per cent of the premium in one instance and 5 per cent in the other. Hence, to the extent that the expenses of

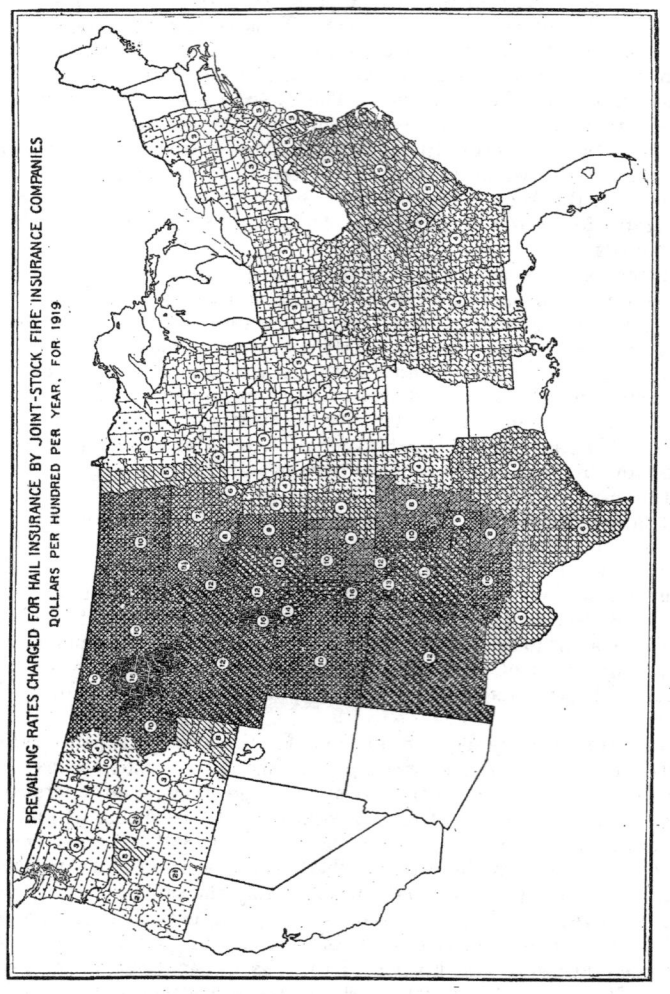

PREVAILING RATES CHARGED FOR HAIL INSURANCE BY JOINT-STOCK FIRE INSURANCE COMPANIES
DOLLARS PER HUNDRED PER YEAR, FOR 1919

FIG. 5.

operation are proportional to the number of risks rather than the premiums, the expense ratio should tend to vary inversely with the rate of premium. The biggest single item of expense in connection with an insurance policy, however, namely, the commission to the agent who solicits the business, is generally based directly on the premium collected and not on the number of risks written. While such commission in the case of hail insurance written at a predetermined rate is now very generally fixed at 15 per cent of the premium, formerly as much as 20 per cent of the premium or even more was paid for this service. Assessment mutuals pay their agents, as a rule, on the basis of risks written.

Some of the hail mutuals operating on the assessment plan limit the liability of their members and at the same time reserve to themselves the right to prorate their losses if the income from maximum assessments, together with any reserve on hand, proves insufficient to meet losses and expenses incurred. Other hail mutuals, operating, as a rule, in States where the hail hazard is less severe, write unlimited liability contracts on the plan followed by nearly three-fourths of the farmers' mutual fire insurance companies. Still other hail mutuals collect a fixed premium somewhat below the commercial rates for the territory in question, while the policy provides for a contingent liability on the part of the insured equal to the fixed premium. Under this plan the insured may in some years have rebated to him a part of the fixed premium already paid, while in severe years he may be called upon for a part of the obligation assumed under the contingent liability clause. This plan has been found desirable more particularly for territory where the hail hazard is severe and where annual advance-payment policies are the rule.

No matter which plan is used with reference to the contribution or liability to contribution by the insured, a wise and conservative management of a hail mutual demands that a reasonable reserve be provided in years when losses are relatively light against the years when relatively heavy losses will be incurred. This is, of course, the plan aimed at by the joint-stock companies, who neither reduce their charges nor give any rebate because a given year brings losses only half, or even less than half, of the average annual losses for the territory in question. No hail mutual operating on the fixed-premium plan should place its rates at so low a point that they will not amply care for an average loss experience for the territory, plus reasonable operating expenses, plus a fair contribution to the reserve fund. In a year of very light losses a part of the surplus premiums may, of course, be returned to the insured as a rebate; but before such rebate is declared a liberal addition to the reserve should be made. This plan should be adhered to until the company has on hand reserves equal to at least the average annual premium income. A hail mutual operating on the assessment plan should similarly add to its reserve fund each year in which its losses represent for its territory an average loss experience or less. This may be done, of course, by a proper addition to the rate of assessment over and above what is found necessary to meet losses and expenses of operation during the favorable year. In the States where the laws governing mutual companies do not permit assessment mutuals to follow the plan above outlined, such laws should be amended in the interest of better insurance and of a higher degree of stability among the companies.

It is encouraging to note that the hail mutuals are to an increasing extent recognizing the principle above set forth. Complete figures for the reserves of these mutuals are not available, but 10 of the older and larger hail mutuals now doing business had a total of surplus or reserves at the end of 1918 amounting to nearly $920,000.

CHARACTERISTICS OF THE HAIL INSURANCE CONTRACT.

The characteristics of the hail insurance contract are perhaps most easily brought out by a brief comparison with the more familiar fire insurance contract. While the hail policy, as well as the fire policy, is generally considered a contract of property insurance as distinguished from life or casualty, there is a fundamental difference in the nature of the property covered by the two policies as well as in the hazards against which insurance is written.

Fire insurance is written, as a rule at least, on material things of value which are already in existence, such as buildings, stocks of merchandise, household goods, live stock, and various other forms of tangible wealth. Hail insurance, on the other hand, is written on growing crops which represent goods in prospect rather than goods in existence. In fact, the latter form of insurance expires almost coincidentally with the transformation of prospects of wealth into actual wealth, consisting of useful or marketable products.

While fire insurance is generally written for a specified period of time, hail insurance covers, as already intimated, the period or stage of development of crops. Most hail policies, to be sure, stipulate that the liability of the company shall definitely cease at a specified time, which, for most of the territory in which hail insurance is written, is noon on September 15. Other stipulations in such policies, however, provide that the company ceases to be liable as soon as the grain or other crop has been "cut or picked." Since the hail contract usually takes effect 24 hours after the signing of the application by the prospective insured even though the policy may not yet be executed, and terminates with the process of harvesting, it follows that in the case of the more common field crops other than corn left to mature on the root, the term for which the insurance is in force is measured by the period elapsing between the day following the date of application for such insurance and the date of harvest. No difference in the premium charges is made, as a rule, either because of the lateness of the date at which the insurance takes effect or the early maturity and consequent early harvesting of the insured crop. One risk may remain insured twice as long as another without affecting the premium charges for such insurance.

All the joint-stock fire insurance companies, so far as known, limit themselves to a policy covering a specific crop growing on a designated piece of ground. The same is generally true of the mutuals operating west and south of Minnesota and Iowa. In the States just named, as well as in the States farther to the east, a number of the mutuals write a term policy for either three or five years and cover certain enumerated crops on a given farm. One very successful mutual, in fact, writes a perpetual policy which means, of course, that the insurance contract continues in force until canceled either by the insured or by the company.

While the disregard of the time element in the typical hail policy at first sight appears highly inconsistent, it is again, in part at least, explained by the peculiar nature of the objects insured. Even though hailstorms may be no more frequent or severe in the latter part of the season during which the hail policy is in force, the risk in the sense of probability of loss may be said in the case of most crops, at least, to increase rapidly as the time of harvest approaches. During the early stages of the growing crop the ravages of hail storms may cause a set-back merely, without materially affecting the final outcome or yield. As the crop develops, however, the possibility of such recovery becomes more and more remote and eventually disappears. Furthermore, a hailstorm occurring at the time when the crop is ready for harvest means not only that the damage wrought is irreparable, but a larger percentage of the stems of grain are actually broken, than would have been the case at an earlier stage. The heads on broken stems drop to the ground, while the heads on unbroken stems may have lost a part of their contents.

The difference between the hail policy and the fire policy, already pointed out, is based mainly on differences inherent in the objects covered by the insurance. Additional differences arise from marked dissimilarities in the hazards involved. The fire hazard originates in two kinds of underlying causes, namely, natural forces or agencies and bad or careless human actions. Of these two sources of the fire hazard the latter is beyond doubt the more important. In the case of hail insurance, on the other other hand, the hazard insured against originates entirely in natural forces over which man has no control. Most of the elaborate provisions against the so-called moral hazard, which are embodied in the fire insurance policy, therefore, have no place in the hail insurance contract.

While an individual whose crop is insured can not by his own action or lack of action bring about the occurrence of hail, he may, however, under certain circumstances increase the apparent loss due to hail by failure properly to care for a damaged crop after hail has occurred. There is also the possibility that the description of the acreage covered be made so inaccurate or misleading as to apply equally

well to more than one piece of land, or that the insured may otherwise either carelessly, or with intent to defraud, make misstatements
in regard to the insured crop or the damage suffered thereon. These
phases of the moral hazard are, therefore, guarded against in the hail
policy as well as in the fire policy.

Because, in the case of hail insurance, the insured can not himself
bring about the contingency insured against, slight consideration, as
a rule, has been given to the question of overinsurance. While a
maximum has almost invariably been fixed by each company on the
amount written per acre, concurrent insurance purchased from other
companies has until recently been given little attention. Hence, instances have occurred in which individuals have taken out insurance
in several different companies on the same crop, making the total of
such insurance greatly in excess of the value of any possible harvest
from the acreage in question. Such a practice may, of course, be
characterized as gambling in hail insurance and is no more to be
defended than gambling in any other field of human activity.

Unless the locality in question happens to be peculiarly susceptible
to hail and the premiums have not been adjusted to meet such conditions, the gambler in hail insurance is, of course, playing with a die
heavily loaded against him. With fair " luck," however, it has been
possible for individuals operating on this plan to pocket occasional
winnings. Especially was this true before cooperation in the adjustment of losses came into practice among many of the larger writers
of hail insurance.

The maximum amount of hail insurance per acre written by the individual company has been increased in recent years in response to
the higher value of farm crops. While formerly $8 or $10 were
common limits, nearly all companies operating in the Middle West,
where the bulk of the hail insurance is carried, now write a maximum
amount of $12 per acre on cereal crops grown on nonirrigated land
and $25 per acre on the same crops grown on irrigated land. In some
of the Eastern States $20 per acre is written on cereal crops by indi-
vidual companies even though such crops are grown by the ordinary
method. In the case of cotton such maximum usually ranges from
$20 to $30 per acre, and in the case of tobacco and other crops requiring a considerable amount of hand labor, it reaches $100 or more per
acre. Relatively little hail insurance has hitherto been written on
truck or orchard crops and no fixed standards as to amounts per acre,
or in many States even as to rates, appear to have been agreed upon
by the companies.

While the hail insurance companies have thus placed a limit on
the amount of insurance that they will individually write on a given
acre, which limit is well within the probable value of the crop, concurrent insurance was formerly, as above stated, permitted to any
amount desired by the insured. At present, however, most companies in the case of nonirrigated cereal crops prescribe a limit of

$40 per acre for such concurrent insurance, including the amount carried by the company in question. For similar crops on irrigated land the prevailing limit on total concurrent insurance is $75 per acre. Should the total concurrent insurance exceed these limits, each company will be liable only for its pro rata part of the maximum amount of insurance permitted.

The hail insurance contract as ordinarily written is a valued policy, the crop for adjustment purposes being literally valued at the amount of insurance carried per acre. In the case of a total loss by hail the indemnity due is the amount of insurance carried per acre, while in the case of a partial loss the indemnity due is such part of the insurance per acre as the part of the crop lost by hail is of the undamaged crop before the hailstorm occurred. Let it be assumed, for example, that an individual carries hail insurance on his grain in a given company to the amount of $12 per acre and that a hailstorm occurs and damages the crop. The problem of the adjuster under the prevailing type of hail policy is not that of ascertaining the actual amount by which the value of the crop has been reduced, but merely to ascertain the percentage of the crop which has been lost by reason of hail. If the estimated loss is equal to 50 per cent, or one-half of the crop, the insured is awarded indemnity equal to one-half of the insurance carried, or $6 per acre, while if it is found that three-fourths of the crop has been lost by hail the indemnity is $9 per acre. This holds true, no matter whether the actual value of the crop just preceding the hailstorm is estimated to have been greater or less than the amount of the insurance thereon, provided the crop was not so injured or damaged from any other cause or causes as to preclude a profit over and above the actual cost of harvesting, gathering, thrashing, and marketing. Should it happen, for instance, that one farmer whose field is insured at $12 per acre had in prospect a yield valued at $60 per acre, while the field of his neighbor, similarly insured, for one reason or another, promised a yield equal to but $6 per acre, and a hailstorm passed over the two fields, causing a 50 per cent damage, each farmer would receive $6 per acre, or one-half of the amount of insurance carried. One of these farmers would, of course, be paid only one-fifth of the actual loss suffered, or one-tenth of the value of the undamaged crop, while the other would receive twice the amount of his actual loss, or a sum equal to the entire undamaged value of his crop.

It must be admitted that the practices in hail insurance above referred to violate the frequently quoted principle of insurance, namely, that the contract involves indemnity for actual loss, and that no profit to the insured is contemplated or permitted. On the other hand, it would seem that to limit the indemnity on the basis of the reduced value of the crop preceding the occurrence of hail would give the company an unfair advantage unless provision were also made for the return of a part of the premium corresponding to the reduced liability. Such a provision would, in practice, involve considerable difficulty, and the necessary adjustments, assuming that the plan were otherwise practical, would add materially to the expense of operation.

Barring some such additional change in the contract as just indicated, there seems to be no reason why the company should have its indemnity payments reduced on the ground that adverse conditions, other than the occurrence of hail, have reduced the value of the insured crop. The premium rates are fixed on the basis of the prevalence of hail in a given locality coupled with the susceptibility of the insured crop to damage from this hazard, and not on the basis of any probability of earlier loss from other causes. From this point of view it would seem that even the provision in the hail contract which denies liability in cases of earlier damage, from causes other than hail, to such an extent that the crop is not worth harvesting, should be coupled with a provision for the return of an appropriate portion of the premium in cases where the company uses its right to deny liability under this provision.

Where mutual hail insurance companies write a term policy covering specified crops on a given farm, the amount of insurance on a given acre will naturally vary with the total acreage of crops which are enumerated in the policy. The insurance per acre is ascertained under these circumstances by dividing the total amount of insurance or the face of the policy, by the number of acres planted to the kinds of crops which are covered by the insurance contract. Companies writing term hail policies have as a rule the same provision for the adjustment of losses as is in vogue with companies writing seasonal policies applicable to specific crops on specified fields. In a few instances, however, such companies adjust losses on a plan similar to that on which fire losses are settled, paying the actual estimated loss on each acre up to the amount of the insurance carried.

Provisions in the hail policy with regard to notice of loss, proof of loss, and the payment of the indemnity due are essentially the same as in the fire policy. No liability is assumed, however, for a loss which does not equal 5 per cent or more of the insurance on a given crop, and in case the insured reports a loss representing less than such percentage of the crop he is himself liable for the cost of investigating the claim for indemnity against such loss. This provision appears to be rarely, if ever, enforced. The payment of a partial loss does not terminate the policy, but reduces the liability of the company by the amount paid on such loss.

SPECIAL PROBLEMS IN HAIL INSURANCE.

Whether the specific, one-season, hail policy is written, or the blanket term policy, certain peculiar administrative problems enter which are not present in fire insurance. The writing of the former kind of policy gives rise to a strictly seasonal activity, hail insurance rarely being purchased on this plan until after the crop is already growing and giving promise of a fair harvest. This means that, in order to secure business in any considerable volume, competent solicitors must be employed during the relatively busy summer months, while the company has no employment for them after the hail-writing season ends except to the extent that the same men are also used as adjusters. The adjustment work, however, begins shortly after the hail-writing season opens and continues but a few weeks at the most after the acquisition of business has ceased. What is true of the field work in hail insurance is true to a considerable extent also of the office work, most of which is coincident with the writing of insurance and the adjustment of losses.

This seasonal nature of the business adds materially to the problems of administration as well as to the expenses of operation, it being obviously difficult, if not impossible, to attract efficient workers under these conditions without the offer of special inducements. In the case of most mutuals writing term policies the cancellations at the end of the first season are relatively large. Even in such companies, therefore, the risks in force during a given season rest to a considerable degree on policies written after the fields were giving substantial promise of harvest.

There is, of course, a considerable economy in the expense item of an insurance company resulting from term policies, providing the policies actually remain in force for the term contemplated. As a rule, this advantage, for reasons already indicated, has been only partially realized. Certain notable exceptions are to be found, however, a few mutuals having succeeded in making their membership practically as continuous as is the general rule in the case of farmers' mutual fire insurance companies. In such cases, as might be expected, the expense item of the company has been strikingly small and the total saving to the members has been correspondingly great.

A particularly difficult problem in the administration of a hail insurance company as compared with that of a company insuring isolated buildings and other farm property against fire, is to be found in the peculiarly erratic nature of the hail hazard, and the resulting wide variation in the losses experienced. In 1914, for example, the total hail premiums collected by all classes of insurance institutions in the United States approximated $5,558,000 and the losses were only $2,677,000, or 48 per cent of the premiums. The following year, 1915, the total hail premiums received amounted to about $9,752,000, while the losses incurred were $11,833,000, or over 121 per cent of the premiums collected. The summer of 1916 was again a season of severe losses for the hail insurance companies, as well as for the farmers who carried their own risks. The years 1917 and 1919 were both years of relatively small hail losses for the country as a whole, while 1918 was what may be termed moderate or approximately an average year. During the six years above mentioned the percentages of total hail premiums paid out for losses by all classes of insurance institutions were, respectively, as follows: 1914, 48.2 per cent; 1915, 121.3 per cent; 1916, 87.3 per cent; 1917, 50.7 per cent; 1918, 63.7 per cent; and 1919, 47.8 per cent. With such variations occurring when the experience of all companies and organizations operating in a large number of different States is taken into account, including those operating on an assessment plan and whose premium income is adjusted on the basis of losses already incurred, it will be apparent that the loss ratio to be expected during any given year is highly problematical when the figures for a single company charging a fixed premium rate and operating in a severe hail district, are considered. More particularly is this the case when such company limits its field of operations to a relatively restricted area.

One of the larger mutuals operating in Kansas collected premiums during 1914 amounting to $108,459 and incurred losses of only $19,649, or a little over 18 per cent of the premiums. During the year following, 1915, the same company collected premiums amounting to $348,389 and incurred losses of $651,173, or nearly 187 per cent of the premiums collected. For the first of the two years mentioned this company was, of course, able to pay back to its members a substantial rebate, besides adding a considerable sum to its reserves. In 1915, however, only the accumulated reserve on hand, coupled with the fact that a considerable part of the risks had been reinsured, saved the company from being obliged to prorate its losses, since it collects a fixed premium without contingent liability. Most of the other Kansas hail mutuals, which also operated on a fixed-premium basis, were obliged to prorate their losses in the year last mentioned.

One of the joint-stock fire insurance companies writing hail insurance in Kansas in the year 1908 collected hail premiums amounting to $134,498 and paid losses amounting to $214,633, or 159 per cent of the premiums. In 1912, on the other hand, the same company collected hail premiums nearly as large as those of 1908, namely, $112,889, while its losses were only $39,653, or 35 per cent of the receipts. The State of Oklahoma has in recent years shown variations in hail losses quite as great as those of Kansas. In 1915, two of the joint-stock companies with a relatively large hail business in this State had loss ratios of 112 per cent and 192 per cent, respectively. In 1918 the same companies had loss ratios in the State of only 18 per cent and 30 per cent, respectively, and one other company with nearly $90,000 in premiums had a loss ratio of but 7 per cent. In 1916 one of the joint-stock companies operating in North Dakota collected premiums amounting to $206,424, and paid losses amounting to $245,767, or 119 per cent of the premiums, while in the following year the company had premiums in the same State amounting to $146,516 and paid losses of only $66,996, or 46 per cent. Even more extreme variations in loss ratio could, of course, be cited by giving the experience of companies with relatively small amounts at risk. One of the smaller hail mutuals in Kansas, with a fixed-premium rate, had a loss ratio in 1915 equal to 259 per cent of the premiums.

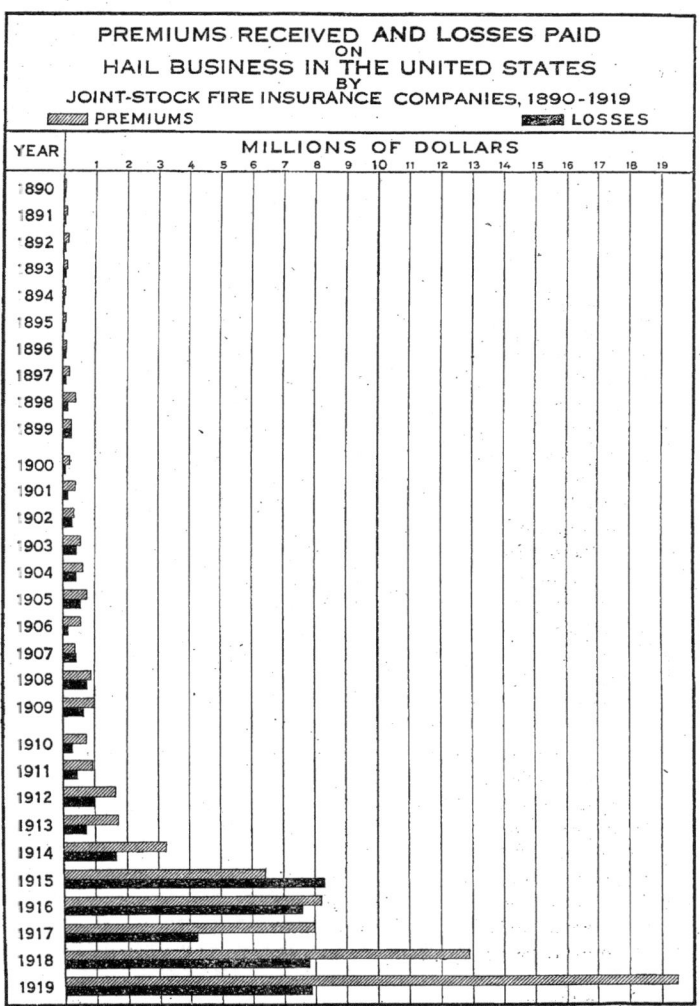

FIG. 6.

In connection with the phase of the hail business just discussed, figure 6, which shows the approximate hail premiums received and losses paid by joint-stock fire insurance companies from 1890 to 1919, inclusive, will be found of interest. As indicative of the variation in the hail hazard from year to year, the figures for premiums and losses of the joint-stock companies are, of course, more significant than the corresponding figures for mutual companies.[1] Many of the mutual companies, as already stated, operate on the assessment plan, and hence their premium or assessment income expands or contracts each year in proportion to the losses incurred. In the case of joint-stock companies, while the rates have been frequently adjusted they have, however, been fixed in advance on the basis of past experience.

Figure 6, it should be noted, compares the premium income of the companies as a group, not with the cost of the business to them, but only with the losses paid. It is doubtful if any of the companies represented in these figures have had an expense ratio much below 35 per cent of the premium income. In the case of some of them, such ratio has certainly exceeded this figure. Assuming that on an average 35 per cent of the premiums has been required to cover expenses of operation, it would follow that the companies, as a group, have lost money during each year in which the actual losses, as indicated in the diagram, have exceeded 65 per cent of the premiums, and have made a profit during each year in which the loss ratio has fallen below this figure. The net profits in the hail business taken as a whole have by no means been as large as many persons have assumed. The last four years have been highly favorable, but many of the companies showed a net loss on their hail insurance experience at the close of 1916.

The variation in the destructiveness of hail in a given State depends, of course, to some extent upon the degree to which the land is given over to one or two commercial crops. Thus, Kansas and Oklahoma, for example, with their large winter-wheat acreage in proportion to the total acreage in crops, North Dakota and Montana with their similarly large spring wheat acreage, or parts of Texas with their cotton acreage, are likely to be subject to especially great variations. One or more bad hail storms occurring at a critical period in the development of the main crop in these States may, of course, ruin a relatively large percentage of the total crops on the farms in the territory visited by such storms. Even though during the next season equally severe hail storms occur, the damage will be far less in case such storms occur either before or after the critical period of the principal crop. The variation in the annual hail losses experienced by insurance companies in States where a single com-

---

[1] The figures represented in this diagram, as well as those given in the text, are as complete and accurate as it was possible to make them. An effort to supplement as well as to check up the figures given in the various published reports, by data secured direct from the home records of the companies, was only partially successful. While a large percentage of the companies, and among these the more important pioneers in the business, generously furnished all the data requested, other companies for one reason or another failed to do so.

mercial crop predominates is further heightened by the fact that this commercial crop is very generally insured by the farmer without including his other field acreage, thus causing hail risks of the insurance companies to be concentrated in a single crop to a degree even greater than are the farmer's crop prospects taken as a whole.

In States in which considerable diversification of crops occurs there will exist at no given time this high degree of susceptibility to damage from hail. In such States farmers more generally insure more than one crop. The critical period of one or more of these crops is likely to be past before that of other crops is reached. The total hail loss in such States, as well as the part of such losses covered by insurance will, therefore, tend to vary less from year to year than is the case in States where there is little diversification. However, since the amount of hail that falls and the angle at which it falls, depending upon the intensity of the wind during the hail storm, are uncertain and variable, as well as the time at which hail occurs, it follows that considerable variations in hail damage from year to year will be found even in States having a wide diversification of crops.

It should be apparent, therefore, that no insurance company can with safety assume a large volume of hail risks in a limited territory unless it has available assets in considerable amount. While this is especially true with reference to the tier of States composed of Texas, Oklahoma, Kansas, Nebraska, and the two Dakotas, as well as for the States immediately to the west of the tier, it is essentially true for all localities where hail constitutes a hazard severe enough to merit special attention. A new company, obliged to rely for the meeting of its obligations largely or entirely upon the premiums collected during the year, should see that the risks assumed are scattered over as wide a territory as circumstances permit. A limit must be placed on the acreage that may be accepted for insurance in any one square mile of area, in any one township, and, finally, in any one county. Even with restrictions of this kind carefully provided for and applied, the small, joint-stock company without accumulated reserves takes greater or less chances of direct failure, while the mutual hail insurance company, similarly situated, takes chances of having to collect unduly large premiums if operating on the unlimited liability plan, and of having to prorate its losses if operating on the fixed premium plan.

The mutual as well as the newly organized or small joint-stock company doing a hail insurance business must use every reasonable opportunity to build up a surplus or reserve fund. In the case of mutual companies, the mutualism must, in the case of hail insurance at least, be interpreted to embrace not only the members of the company during a given year, but must be held to embrace, to a considerable extent, the membership included for a series of years. Those who join the company in a year when the hail hazard happens to be unusually light, for example, must be willing to be assessed

an amount considerably greater than that requir
for that year and to leave a part of the funds wh
tributed in the reserve fund of the company to
ment the premiums collected in years when the h
to be exceptionally severe. Unless a mutual con
plan, it is quite ·certain, assuming that it is opera
territory, to have to prorate its losses in years of l

There is, of course, no serious objection, either
the plan of prorating losses by a mutual company
members have joined with the understanding tha
be expected in case the contributions to the com
cient to meet the losses incurred together with leg
operation. The danger, however, is that the soli
representing the company, in their desire to se
and to earn commissions for themselves, will pe
courage the prospective insured to believe that t
by the company are not only sufficient to meet al
that a rebate may reasonably be expected. Mer
company with this understanding are of course
losses are prorated, that they have been the victim
tion and fraud, even though the policy specificall
will be prorated in case such action is found neces

In any case, it has been the general experienc
as well as of mutuals operating in other fields
whenever it has been necessary to prorate losses
the years following such action has materially dec
agement of the company is almost invariably blar
to settle in full, regardless of the facts in the
panies have failed to survive the prorating of loss
companies were managed by men whose integrity
among those who knew them personally.

Another problem in hail insurance which is not
extent in fire insurance may be pointed out with p
to mutual companies. This difficulty, namely, i
management and control of the company, arises f
hail mutual, as already stated, can not be operate
territory of small area. A possible exception to thi
in the case of certain districts where the hail hazar
and where the insurance covers only one or two sp
ing a minor part of the acreage of each farm.

With a fire insurance mutual operating in a lim
degree of real cooperation in management is possi
resides within a reasonable distance of the place
meeting is held, and is therefore in position to be p
his influence felt at such meeting in case he choo
mutual, on the other hand, which very properly o
State, or perhaps in several States, it is not possi

member directly to participate in the management, and hence the control of the company must of necessity be left to a relatively small group of men. Most hail mutuals, in fact, have their directors all living in the same locality, while the average member takes no part either in the annual elections or in the decision of other problems of management.

As yet another problem in hail insurance not to be met with in the same degree in fire insurance, may be cited the difficulty of determining the loss caused to a growing crop by hail. Frequently hail will occur before the crop has reached a stage at which its occurrence will result in permanent or material damage. At certain stages the entire crop above the ground may be entirely beaten down and the farmer claim a total loss, when as a matter of fact, with favorable weather conditions following the hail storm, a partial or even a complete recovery of the crop may take place. In other instances, the crops may have been partially damaged by certain plant diseases or insect pests before the hail occurred. Only an expert on these matters may be able to determine whether or not the damage pointed out by the claimant is directly due to the occurrence of hail or to the other natural agencies mentioned. When a difference arising between the company and the claimant for loss involves the extent to which a damaged crop will recover, the adjustment may be postponed until harvest by which time nature will in part have answered the question in dispute. When the difference, on the other hand, hinges upon the cause of the damage rather than the extent thereof, postponement of the settlement is likely to increase the difficulty rather than to remove it. Because of the greater uncertainty as to the amount of damage suffered by hail, it is considerably more difficult, as a rule, to satisfy the claimant for loss than is the case in fire insurance.

While unscrupulous adjusters have at times attempted to browbeat claimants and to settle for less than a fair indemnity, it is probable that in hail insurance as in fire insurance more losses have been overpaid than underpaid. Willfully unfair adjustments have at times been resorted to in order to injure or ruin a competing company and have resulted in profit to the claimant. A number of companies will, of course, carry risks in the same locality, and in the case of concurrent insurance two or more companies will be involved in a loss on the same field. A hail storm striking such a locality may cause total damage in some areas and partial damage in others. Certain companies operating in this territory will be found to have suffered a large number of heavy losses, while other companies will have suffered but few minor losses. The representative of an organization with only a few risks affected, knowing the situation in which the competing companies find themselves, may arrive on the scene promptly following the loss and make an extremely liberal adjustment with the few claimants against his company, paying perhaps three or four times the actual damage suffered. The same farmers

he has settled, or in any case their neighbors, w
d the same liberal settlement from the other
ally liberal settlements are made it will be dif
companies to secure business in this locality in
' this form of unscrupulous competition, losses in
grossly overpaid, resulting in immediate injur
affected and in needless increase in hail rates for
ceeding years. The evil just outlined has been
erable extent by an arrangement on the part o
of the joint-stock companies for a jointly mainti
ireau.

l reasonable adjustments, as well as economy in
ie business, are, in the long run, as much in the
ers of hail insurance as they are in the intere
ins engaged in this form of underwriting. Thi
whether the farmers in a given State or locality
ock companies, mutual companies, or State ha
tments. Extravagance, either in the adjustment
expenses of operation, is quite sure to be reflect
imium rates or assessments. In the case of mut
l more particularly those operated on the asses
liability plan, this relationship between expendit
y direct, and therefore apparent to every intellig
nsurance. The same may be said to be true wi
ite hail insurance departments. In the case of jc
the connection between expenditures and rates
direct and is frequently overlooked entirely by
insurance. The income from excessive rates i
i time to go to increased dividends to the stoi
e general surplus of the company, while a de
iome form of extravagance in expenditures or
actually inadequate, may be temporarily cared fi
sumulated from the business of preceding years
ier lines of business during the same year. In
rer, no company is going to continue a line of
munerative rate, nor, in the face of legal regula
tion, actual or potential, is it probable that a
collect a rate greatly out of proportion to the
business. In hail insurance, as well as in othe
ng, adequate rates of premiums or assessments a
true success. Excessive rates, on the other hand
extravagance or cupidity, tend to discourage th
ie on the part of many of those who need it, to r
business and lessen the usefulness of the insura
d to place an unfair and unjustifiable burden uj
ivide themselves with needed protection.

O

UNITED STATES DEPARTMENT OF AGRICULTURE

BULLETIN No. 913

Contribution from the Bureau of Public Roads
THOS. H. MACDONALD, Chief

| Washington, D. C. | PROFESSIONAL PAPER | September 21, 1920 |

THE WESTERN FARMER'S WATER RIGHT.

By R. P. TEELE, *Irrigation Economist.*

CONTENTS.

	Page.		Page.
What a water right is	1	Rights to underground waters	8
General characteristics of water rights	2	Rights to water from canals	9
Acquirement of rights	3	Distribution of water	13
Evidences of title to rights to water from streams	4		

WHAT A WATER RIGHT IS.

In the western part of the United States the rainfall is insufficient to supply the moisture needs of growing crops, and it is necessary to make up the deficiency by irrigation. The water used for irrigation comes principally from streams, but in part from other sources. There is not sufficient water in these sources to supply all the demands, and consequently some land is supplied with water while other land must go without. In order that arid land shall be cultivated, the farmers of that land must have assurance that they may continue to use water in the future, for without such assurance no one would engage in agriculture in arid regions on account of its uncertainty. Under these conditions there has grown up in the West a system of laws and customs controlling the use of water, under which a farmer secures a " water right," which assures, in greater or less degree, his future water supply. Without such a right arid land has very little value, while with a right such land has higher value than much of the land in the humid parts of the country.

It is probable that there is no more complicated subject in the whole field of property rights than water rights, yet the practical working of the system is comparatively simple and easily understood. It is believed that a general understanding of the subject is within the reach of all and will be of great value to every farmer in

185335°—20

the arid section of the United States and to any who may co
plate taking up farming in that region. The object of this b
is to give such a general knowledge of water rights. The b
does not discuss fundamental principles and theories, but
describes those features of water rights with which every perso
farms or intends to farm where irrigation is practiced sho
familiar.

GENERAL CHARACTERISTICS OF WATER RIGHTS.

Though the irrigation laws of the Western States differ in
respects, they agree in several particulars:

The use of streams and other surface water supplies for irri
and like purposes is subject to control by the States.

Water may be taken from streams and other sources for irri
and other beneficial uses, but only in accordance with State
This is known as the right of " appropriation."

Actual use of the water is a necessary step in the holding
right and when the use ceases the right is abandoned or for
That is, no one can acquire a right to water and hold it w
actually using the water, either immediately or within a reas
time thereafter. This is known as the doctrine of " beneficial t

Among users from the same source, the " first in time is th
in right." When there is not enough water for all, the righ
supplied, to the extent of the supply available, in the order
dates on which they were acquired. This is known as the do
of " priority." Exceptions to this rule exist in a few of the
where, in cases of unusual scarcity, the available water is a
tioned among the users either by the State officers or by the

The date of a right is fixed by the time of taking the firs
to acquire it, rather than by the time of putting the water
This is known as the doctrine of " relation," as the rights relat
to date of beginning. (See p. —.)

Some of the Western States recognize also riparian righ
riparian right is a right to use water from a stream which
through or borders the land to which the right belongs, arising
the fact that the land borders the stream, not from approp
or use and " use does not create or disuse destroy " the right.
riparian rights are recognized, each owner of riparian land
right to make any reasonable use of the water which will
terfere with a like reasonable use of it by all the others. Hen
value of a right depends very largely on other rights to th
source.

Even in those States where riparian rights are recognized
fornia, Nebraska, Oregon, Texas, and Washington), approp

rights are recognized also, and most of the irrigating is done under appropriation rights. Consequently, the subject of riparian rights will not be discussed further.

ACQUIREMENT OF RIGHTS.

In each of the arid or semiarid States, except Kansas and Montana, the acquirement of rights to water direct from surface sources is under the control of State officials, and one wishing to get such a right must follow the procedure prescribed by law. The procedure is much the same in all the States and consists in (1) making application to some State official or board on forms supplied by the State, giving full information as to plans for irrigation works and use of water; (2) carrying out of the plans as approved by the State; (3) submitting proof of completion of works and use of water; and (4) granting of certificate or license by the State, defining the right as to quantity of water, use to be made of water, and time during which it may be used.

The official or board to which application should be made in each of the States is shown herewith:

Arizona—State water commissioner, Phoenix.
California—State water commission, San Francisco.
Colorado—State engineer, Denver.
Idaho—State commissioner of reclamation, Boise.
Nebraska—State engineer, Lincoln.
Nevada—State engineer, Carson City.
New Mexico—State engineer, Santa Fe.
North Dakota—State engineer, Bismarck.
Oklahoma—State engineer, Oklahoma City.
Oregon—State engineer, Salem.
South Dakota—State engineer, Pierre.
Texas—State board of water engineers, Austin.
Utah—State engineer, Salt Lake City.
Washington—State hydraulic engineer, Olympia.
Wyoming—State engineer, Cheyenne.

In Kansas and Montana it is required that one wishing to acquire a water right shall post at the point of diversion, and record with the county clerk, a notice showing the intention to take water, the amount to be taken, and the use to be made of it. The proposed work must begin within a reasonable time and must be prosecuted diligently to completion, and the water must be put to a "beneficial use." In Montana, if a court has defined previously existing rights to water from a source from which one proposes to take water, application for a right to divert the water must be presented to the court which defined the existing rights. In each of the two States the law specifies what must be shown in the notice posted, and anyone proposing to obtain a right direct from a stream or other surface source should consult the law of the State in which the land to be irrigated is located. In the States given above, application to the State engineer, or the board named, will bring blanks and full instructions. The point to be kept in mind is that title to water is fully as important as title to land, and it should receive the same careful attention. However, very few will have occasion to acquire rights direct from streams, and the subject need not be discussed at length.

Although few farmers will have occasion to acquire rights direct from streams, many will acquire them by purchasing land served by such rights, and rights to water from canals relate back to the rights from the streams or other sources from which the water is taken, and one can judge of the value of rights from canals only by examining their rights to water from the original source. A right to water from a canal can be no better than the right under which the canal gets its supply.

EVIDENCES OF TITLE TO RIGHTS TO WATER FROM STREAMS.[1]

Rights to water direct from streams are represented by the following evidences of title: Filings in the county records; filings in State engineers' offices; certificates from courts, State engineers or boards; and permits from State engineers or boards. The force of these evidences of title as guarantees of the value of the rights represented is discussed in the following paragraphs:

The posting and filing of a notice regarding a proposed diversion of water merely gives notice of intention to take the additional steps necessary to the acquirement of a right, and its only effect is to fix the date of the right at the date of filing, rather than at the date of beginning construction. The filing itself gives no right to water, but it must be followed by the construction of works and the use of water. Construction may or may not have followed the filing of a notice, so that, taken by itself, such a filing is of little value as evidence that the party making the filing has a right to the water claimed. No one should purchase a right based on such filing without additional evidence that the right is valid and that there is sufficient water in the source from which water is claimed to supply not only the right in question but all prior rights.

In Colorado, a person wishing to divert water from a stream must file a map and plans with the State engineer, and if the map and plans are in proper form and set forth clearly what is claimed, they must be approved by the engineer and a copy showing this

---

[1] The following discussion is taken principally from Irrigation in the United States, by R. P. Teele. New York, 1915.

approval returned to the claimant. These filings, like those in county offices, are merely notices of intention to divert and use water, and the approval of the engineer conveys only the authorization to proceed with the other steps necessary to the acquirement of a right. Thus the approval of the engineer is no proof of the existence of a right. As is the case with filings in the counties, the rights represented by plans approved by the State engineer in Colorado may be good, but the approved plans alone are not conclusive evidence of that fact.

In many of the arid States rights to water are defined by the courts, and when rights have been defined certificates are issued to the holders thereof, stating the volume of water to which each is entitled, the dates of the rights, and the numbers of the rights in the order of their priority. These certificates are proof that the persons holding them had, at the time the adjudications were made, rights to the volumes of water set forth in the certificates. They do not, however, show that there is water in the stream to supply these rights. As previously explained, these rights are to be supplied in the order of their dates, and if the stream does not supply water enough for all rights those of late date receive no water. A certificate showing that a court has confirmed a right to a certain amount of water from a given stream is no evidence that the holder can get the given amount of water. The value of the right depends upon the relation between the volume of rights of earlier date and the flow of the stream. A further element of uncertainty is added by the fact that rights are forfeited by nonuse, the period of nonuse which brings about such forfeiture being fixed by law in most of the States. A right certified to by a court and good at the time may have been lost by abandonment or forfeiture, although the certificate is still in the hands of the former holder of the right.

In other arid States rights to water direct from streams are represented by certificates from the State, setting forth the dates, extent, and locations of the rights. Such a certificate is conclusive evidence that the holder had a right to the volume of water named in it for use on the land specified, but like a certificate from the court, it does not carry any guarantee that there is or will be water in the source named to supply the right for any considerable part of the season or that the right has not been lost by nonuse. There may be enough prior rights to water from the same source to use all the water in ordinary stages of the supply. As with rights represented by certificates from a court, rights represented by a certificate may be lost by abandonment or may be forfeited, without the surrender of the certificate.

Permits from State engineers to appropriate water have different effects in the various States. An approved application constitutes a permit to take water from the source named in the application if any is available. In several States the engineer has authority to refuse to approve an application if there is no unappropriated water in the source of supply, or if the approval is contrary to the public interests. In Idaho, on the other hand, the engineer is required to approve any application that is in proper form. An approved application to appropriate water in one of the first group of States referred to would be some indication, although not a guarantee, that in the opinion of the engineer there was unappropriated water in the source named in the application.

However, some State engineers take the position that the applicant is presumed to have examined the water supply and makes his investments at his own risk; that, furthermore, neither the engineer nor the applicant can predict with any assurance how much water a given stream will supply in any season, and that for these reasons he is justified in approving applications to some extent in excess of the apparent supply if the applicant wishes to take a chance on getting water. Against this practice there is one serious objection—it robs such permits of all value as evidence of the value of the rights represented. Enterprises based on permits to appropriate water which, in all probability, does not exist, are launched, and stock, bonds, lands, or water rights, or all four, are sold to individuals who assume that a permit from a State official to take a certain volume of water from a certain source is a guarantee that water is there to be taken. In this way the holder of the permit transfers the risk, which he fully understands, to parties who do not understand it.

The purchaser of irrigated land should understand that a permit to appropriate water is not a guarantee on the part of the State issuing it that the quantity of water named in the permit is available. Even if water is available, a permit, in itself, does not constitute a right to the use of water. Building works and taking and using water are necessary to the holding of the right. The permit itself fixes the time within which the works must be begun and completed and the time within which the water must be put to use, and a failure to comply with any of the conditions is fatal to the holding of the right.

The States which require applications for permits to appropriate water provide for issuing certificates that the works described in permits have been built and the water put to use. These certificates or licenses are in the same class as court decrees as evidence of rights. Rights represented by certificates or licenses can be lost by abandonment or nonuse just as any other right, but are not so likely to have been, since the laws providing for them are comparatively recent and the time for them to have been abandoned is short.

Certificates or licenses representing rights acquired in accordance with permits issued by States and as the results of adjudications made by State boards or officials and based on surveys made and testimony collected by State officials are the best documentary evidence of the possession of rights which are likely to be supplied by streams in average years, since they are based on proof submitted to a State board or official whose duty it is to protect the public and are usually issued after inspection by those officials; court decrees and certificates rank next; while permits from State boards or officials and copies of filings in county or State offices rank last.

The preceding discussion may create the impression that there are no good titles to the use of water, but that is not the case. The point is that documentary evidence alone is not sufficient to establish either the existence of a water right or its value. Documentary evidence must be backed by evidence of the existence of a water supply in excess of the demands of prior rights. This involves the study of records of stream flow and of existing use. If a stream supplied continuously a given quantity of water, and each holder of a right continuously used all the water to which he is entitled, the determination of the value of a right would be the simple matter of adding the amounts of all the prior rights and comparing the sum with the total supply of water. But neither the total supply nor the demand made on that supply is uniform. The flow of any stream varies from hour to hour, from day to day, and from season to season, while the demand made by any one user may vary in the same way, so that the probability of receiving water under any right when there is not enough water for all rights is extremely hard to determine. On the same stream there will be early rights whose holders can get water whenever they need it, rights whose holders usually get water as they need it, and other rights whose holders get water only in flood season—with all degrees between these extremes.

In States having water commissioners, these officials keep records of the dates when each ditch received water and how much it received. These records, covering a series of years, will disclose what ditches have good rights and whether there is water in any source beyond the demands of existing rights. Where such records do not exist, it is usually possible to learn from local disinterested persons what ditches receive a good supply, what ditches ordinarily are short of water, and whether, in ordinary seasons, there is more water than is demanded by existing rights. A prospective purchaser of a water right should look carefully into both the docu-

ary and the physical evidence of the value of the righ
1ased, giving, perhaps, more attention to the latter thar
2r.

RIGHTS TO UNDERGROUND WATERS.[2]

ough most farmers who settle on irrigated land obtair
gh organizations of some kind rather than direct from s
is large opportunity for individuals to obtain independe
of water from underground sources through wells.
.th relation to the nature of rights to their use, under
:s are divided into four classes: (1) Underground :
ng in known and defined channels; (2) underground
ng in unknown and undefined channels; (3) artesian wate
)ercolating waters. While these classes are distinct in la
ılways easy to tell to which class a particular supply l
ıct, water which has long been considered in one class
ı to be in another class, and thus subject to a different l
bterranean streams flowing in known and defined chanı
:ct to the same laws as surface streams—that is, in most
)propriation rights—and one may not take water fro
eam by means of wells or other means if it interferes ν
.s of prior appropriators. Ownership of the land on ν
is located does not give any right if the water is, in fact
e stream.
ıt if a well draws water from an underground stream
nel is unknown and undefined, the ownership of land
it the right to take the water. It is clear that the cha
a stream may become known as a result of investiga
h case the stream will become subject to the law of apr
and the prior users may stop the use by later appropria
tesian water—that which is under pressure within the
.at it will rise in the well to or toward the ground sur:
to belong to all the land overlying the artesian basin, a
ır of such land is permitted to make any reasonable usı
r which will not interfere with a like use by all the othı
:rs. In this respect rights to artesian waters are sin
:ian rights on streams—they are not fixed and defin
nd upon the total supply and the total demand by all
nd overlying an artesian basin. Since the water is the ı
erty of many owners, it is subject to public control, aı
e States have more or less legislation on the subject.
rcolating water—that is, water moving through the soil,
r pressure and not confined to a known and defined cl

---

is discussion is based on Kinney's " Law of Irrigation and Water Right
ı, San Francisco, 1912.

belongs to the overlying land, and the owner of the land may withdraw all he can get for use on his land.

As stated before, in many instances it is difficult to tell in which class the water found under any tract of land falls, but under the law all underground water is presumed to be percolating water until it is proved otherwise. Artesian water is easily recognized, because it rises above the level at which it is found when a well is drilled. In narrow stream valleys there is a strong presumption that the underground water is a part of a stream and that pumping from a well may be considered an appropriation from the stream. But on the plains, and in the intermountain valleys which contain no streams, there is a strong presumption that water which does not rise above the stratum in which it is found is percolating water and belongs to the landowner.

RIGHTS TO WATER FROM CANALS, ETC.

As has been stated, most farmers get water rights from canal companies or other organizations controlling enterprises which supply water to farmers. In the preceding pages the rights of these enterprises to water from streams or other sources have been discussed. In the following paragraphs the nature of rights conveyed by such enterprises to the farmers to whom they supply water is discussed.

Rights to water from canals differ from rights to water direct from streams in one very important particular—usually priority does not hold among users from the same canal. Their rights are all on the same basis, without reference to the dates when they were acquired. Each farmer is entitled to his share of the supply belonging to the canal. The companies are supposed not to dispose of water in excess of their capacity to supply it, but the relation of the total rights disposed of and the total water supply should be investigated with the same care as the water supply generally. The character of rights to water from canals and the conditions limiting them are fixed by the contracts, by-laws, and regulations of the organizations controlling the canals, and these are discussed below.

The principal agencies supplying water to farmers are cooperative or mutual stock companies, irrigation districts, the United States Reclamation Service, Carey Act companies, and commercial companies.

COOPERATIVE OR MUTUAL COMPANIES.

Cooperative or mutual stock companies serve by far the larger part of the acreage irrigated by enterprises supplying water to farmers—62 per cent of this area in 1910, according to the census reports. Water rights in such companies are represented by stock in the companies, and each share of stock entitles its holder to a share of the total supply of water belonging to the company rather than to any fixed quantity. Water is not delivered in proportion to the acreage but in proportion to the stock owned, although there is a tendency for stock to be held in proportion to acreage. The cost of operation and maintenance is raised by assessments on stock, and the laws of many of the States provide that companies may sell the stock of parties who fail to pay assessments levied on their stock. Usually the stock may be rented, and the lessee may draw the water represented by the stock. In this respect, a right represented by stock in a mutual company differs materially from rights in other companies or districts. In the latter enterprises the water may be used only on particular tracts of land and if it is not used on those tracts the owners are not permitted to draw it or dispose of it in any way.

The plans of enterprises of all the other classes mentioned, except irrigation districts, contemplate that eventually they will become joint stock companies of the type just described, or irrigation districts. This change is discussed in connection with the discussion of the other types of enterprises.

IRRIGATION DISTRICTS.

In irrigation districts a right to water is an incident to ownership of land within the boundaries of a district and goes with the land. Each acre of land in a district is entitled to its share of the water supply of the district, whatever that supply may be. Here the quantity of water which will be received depends entirely upon the relation between the quantity available and the acreage of land in the district. Thus an examination of the water right of the district itself is the only means of forming an idea of the value of the right. Every district has a nominal water supply of a certain quantity for each acre in the district, but, as pointed out, this may be only nominal. The actual supply may be much less.

In districts there is no purchase of a water right, as such, but merely the purchase of land. Districts issue bonds to obtain funds for securing a water supply, and taxes are levied to raise funds to pay the bonds and interest and the cost of operation and maintenance. These taxes, if unpaid, become a lien on the land, and the amount of bonds which must be paid off by each acre of land is in effect the price of a water right for that acre, although it may not be called that. At present (1920) there is a very strong tendency to reorganize enterprises of other types, particularly United States reclamation projects, into districts.

UNITED STATES RECLAMATION PROJECTS.

To obtain a right to water in a United States reclamation project it is necessary to acquire land within the limits of the project and make application to the Reclamation Service for water. For each project the Secretary of the Interior fixes the size of farm unit (the acreage for which one person may obtain water), the price of rights per acre, the quantity of water to be delivered per acre, and the annual charges for water. These items vary for the different projects, but full information regarding any of them can be obtained from the United States Reclamation Service, Washington, D. C. Though the Secretary of the Interior fixes for each project the quantity of water which is to be delivered to each acre of land, the water user on these projects, as under the others, is, in fact, entitled to his share of whatever water is available for the project, rather than a fixed quantity.

Originally the United States reclamation projects consisted largely of public lands, and entrymen on these lands took them subject to the water-right charges, and title to the land is not received until the charges are paid. Owners of private lands within these projects are required to apply for water and agree to make their land subject to the water-right charges. There is little public land in these projects open to entry, so that the purchase of private land or relinquishments from entrymen on public land subject to the water-right charges is about the only way to acquire rights under such projects. Before making such a purchase, one should find out from the local office of the United States Reclamation Service the exact status of the land in question with reference to payments made and to be made for water rights. Prices of land or relinquishments will be a matter of agreement between the parties.

Water-right charges are to be paid in 20 years, with no interest on deferred payments.

In 1917 and 1919 many of the States in which the United States Reclamation Service is operating amended their irrigation district laws to provide that districts may contract with the United States for a water supply. It is expected that under these laws the land in reclamation projects will be organized into irrigation districts, when the water-right charges will assume the form of a tax lien, as in other districts. If this is done, the acquirement of land within a district will carry with it a right to water.

CAREY ACT PROJECTS.

The so-called "Carey Act." (act of Aug. 18, 1894) grants public lands to the States containing arid lands on condition that the States provide for their irrigation and settlement. The States enter into contract with construction companies which build the works and sell water rights to settlers, while the States sell the lands. The States sell land only to purchasers of water rights and the companies sell rights only to purchasers of land.

Water rights are usually sold on deferred payments, and the notes given for deferred payments are made liens on the settlers' interest in the lands and each agrees to give a mortgage on the land itself as soon as he gets title.

The contracts usually provide for the delivery of a fixed quantity of water per acre per year, or for the continuous delivery of a stream of a given size for a given acreage, but they provide also that in case of shortage the supply available shall be divided among all users in proportion to the acreage. Here, as in the other types of enterprises discussed, the relation of the water supply of the company to the total acreage in the enterprise is the important consideration, and not the quantity of water named in the contracts.

Most Carey Act contracts provide that the projects shall be turned over to stock companies of the type described, when a certain proportion of the rights are sold. Purchasers of rights receive shares of stock in the new companies, so that when the rights are paid for the works belong to the water users.

COMMERCIAL COMPANIES.

Commercial companies have all sorts of plans for disposing of water rights, but their contracts have a general similarity. The laws of many of the States prohibit the sale of rights which merely allow the purchaser to get water upon the additional payment of annual charges. In consequence, almost every plan provides that the purchaser of a water right shall secure an interest in the works and rights belonging to the company. Usually the plan is the same as that followed in Carey Act enterprises—the exchange of the water-right contract for stock in the company when a certain proportion of all the rights in the company is sold. These contracts, like the others, fix the quantity of water to be delivered, the land on which the water is to be used, and the charges which are to be paid annually until the works are turned over to the contract holders. Here, again, water is to be prorated in times of scarcity.

It is seen, therefore, that under practically every type of enterprise, no matter what the nominal quantity of water to be delivered may be, the actual quantity is a share in the available supply, based, in most instances, on the acreage owned, but in mutual companies on the number of shares of stock owned.

In 1919 Montana enacted a law creating an irrigation commission, and providing that any parties wishing to sell water or water rights or to contract to supply water, shall apply to the commission for a permit. If the commission, after investigation, finds that it is likely that there will not be sufficient water, or that the proposed contracts or terms of sale are not fair, it is to refuse permits. Persons thinking of buying irrigated land in Montana should apply to this commission, at Helena, for information as to the water rights and water supply of the parties offering land for sale.

DISTRIBUTION OF WATER.

DISTRIBUTION OF WATER FROM STREAMS.

Water from streams is distributed to canals in accordance with their rights by public officials, usually called water commissioners. Each commisioner has charge of the water within a certain district. He has a list of the rights showing amounts, dates, and locations, and distributes the water accordingly. In most States commissioners control diversions only when called upon by water users. When there is water enough for all each takes it as he pleases. In the more highly developed communities commissioners are on duty most of the time. Interference with the work of a water commissioner, by changing gates set by him, is a misdemeanor in most States.

DISTRIBUTION OF WATER FROM CANALS.

The method of distributing water adopted under any canal system has much to do with the value of its rights to farmers, as it has a large influence on the economy with which they can use not only their water supply but also their time. In many instances the regulations under which water is distributed have more practical effect than the terms of contracts under which rights are acquired. Three systems of distributing water from canals are in common use: In continuous flow; in rotation; and on demand.

Contracts or agreements under which rights are purchased usually provide either for the delivery of a stream of a given size continuously throughout the irrigating season or for the delivery of a certain quantity or depth of water on the land per season; and in many instances where contracts call for continuous delivery, water is, in fact, delivered in rotation. In only a few instances is water delivered on demand.

Delivery in continuous flow is the oldest system, but is giving place to rotation. The size of the stream delivered depends on the acreage, a common ratio being 1 cubic foot per second for 80 acres. Under this system the farmer with a few acres gets a very small stream, while the one with a large acreage gets a large stream. This system has several serious disadvantages. Small streams can not be used economically. On light soils a small stream can not be distributed evenly over the fields, and, whatever the type of soil, irrigating with a small stream takes much more time than should be used for that purpose. When a farmer has a large enough acreage to give him a stream of 2 or more cubic feet per second he can use a continuous flow to better advantage, since it is a large enough stream to work with, and he can rotate the water among his own fields.

Under rotation systems the various farmers under a canal receive water in turn, and in this way each gets a larger stream than if he received a continuous stream, and he can use the water to good advantage and get through with it, leaving him more time for other work. The quantity of water received is regulated by the length of time a stream is used by each farmer, rather than by the size of the stream. This system has the disadvantage that the farmer can not always get water just when he thinks he needs it, but usually rotation schedules are arranged to fit, as nearly as possible, the needs of the crops grown, and the advantages of having large streams and doing the watering quickly more than offset any disadvantage of waiting for turns.

The ideal system is to get water on demand. In such cases a water supply is like a bank account. The farmer has a credit of his season's supply and can draw as he needs it. This system can be adopted only where storage facilities are available for holding the water until it is called for.

Usually the farmer will have no choice as to which system he will work under, except that he may choose where he will settle, and keep this point in mind in making his choice. If a farmer is acquiring land under an established irrigation system, local inquiry as to results under the system will be the best means of determining the satisfactory character of a distributing system, as well as the value of the water supply.

UNITED STATES DEPARTMENT OF AGRICULTURE

BULLETIN No. 914

Contribution from the Bureau of Entomology
L. O. HOWARD, Chief

Washington, D. C.   PROFESSIONAL PAPER   December 9, 1920

THE RED-BANDED LEAF-ROLLER.[1]

By F. H. CHITTENDEN, *Entomologist in Charge, Truck Crop Insect Investigations.*

CONTENTS.

	Page.		Page
Introduction	1	Food plants	10
Descriptive	2	Natural enemies	10
Distribution	4	Control	11
Injuries and occurrences	5	Summary	11
Biologic notes	7	Literature cited	13
History of the species	8		

INTRODUCTION.

A small greenish caterpillar, about three-fourths of an inch long when mature, and known as the red-banded leaf-roller, attacks the foliage of beans, sweet potato, asparagus, strawberry, raspberry, and various other crops, and at times attracts considerable attention. Such was the case in October, 1919, when the species was abundant in and near the District of Columbia.

October 9, 1919, the writer, in company with W. H. White, Bureau of Entomology, noted that the foliage of sweet potato at College Park, Md., showed considerable injury near the petioles or leaf-stems manifested by large, irregular, more or less elongate holes between the ribs. Some of these were made by a leaf-miner and had been cut out earlier in the season, but many were the work of this leaf-roller which had tied or joined the leaves in different manners. In some cases the leaves were folded between the midrib and the next rib, and the larva had gouged out a hole about twice this length and half the width. Where the leaves were joined the surface at one end was lined with silk. In many cases the larva joined the leaves near the middle of one side and cut out a similar hole, constructing its tent-like shelter at one end.

A very considerable proportion of the top leaves had been attacked by this species and the leaf-miner, but at the time these observations were made there were many more parasites and parasitic cocoons present on the leaves than larvæ.

---

[1] *Eulia velutinana* Walk. ; family Tortricidae, order Lepidoptera.

10299°—20

October 27, 28, and 31, 1919, Miss Marion T. Van Horn collected this leaf-roller in war gardens at Potomac Park in the District of Columbia on sweet potato and on lima and other beans. The leaf-rollers were found in particular abundance where sweet potato and bean vines grew together. Half a dozen or more larvæ were frequently found in a hill, while many rolled and webbed leaves proved that the larvæ had been quite plentiful earlier in the season.

It was noted that toward the end of October and the early days of November the larvæ rolled the leaves from the sides and from the ends, making a more substantial shelter than when they were immature, and lined it with white silk preparatory to pupation.

The fact is noteworthy that this species was more numerous on sweet potato and beans in 1919 than in previous years, the first being an unrecorded food plant. In former years this species has sometimes occurred in raspberry quite as abundantly as the strawberry leaf-roller (*Ancylis comptana* Froehl.).

DESCRIPTIVE.

THE MOTH.

The moth which produces the red-banded leaf-roller is a small, mottled brown form with the fore-wings having an expanse of between a little more than half to nearly three-fourths of an inch (13 to 19 mm.). The pattern of the fore-wings varies to a considerable extent. In the female there is a large, median, dark reddish-brown band running obliquely from the middle of the costa to the tornus, a subapical, irregular, smaller one, and a third postero-basal patch of the same color. The lighter parts of the wings are pale reddish brown, arranged in irregular bands with borders of pale yellow and silver white. The hind-wings are infuscated, with wide white borders and an inner ciliary line. The abdomen is dark gray and the tufts of the head and thorax are reddish brown.

The females are usually considerably larger than the males, with rather more distinct and larger patterns.

The female moth is shown in figure 1 with expanded wings at *a*, and in natural position, when at rest with the wings folded, at *b*. Technical descriptions have been given in so many available publications that a more complete one than here given may be dispensed with for the present purpose. The synonymy is as follows:

Eulia velutinana Walker.

> Cacoecia (?) *velutinana* Walker, 1863, List Lep. Brit. Mus., p. 314.
> Cacoecia triferana Walker, 1863, l. c., p. 314.
> Tortrix incertana Clemens, 1865, Proc. Ent. Soc. Phila., v. 5, p. 138.
> Tortrix lutosana Clemens, 1865, l. c., p. 138.
> Lophoderus triferanus Walker, Walsingham, 1879, Lep. Het. Brit. Mus., pt. IV, p. 15.
> Eulia triferana Walker.

THE EGG.

The eggs resemble those of other leaf-rolling species of Tortricidae. They are much flattened to the surface upon which they are deposited, and to which they tightly adhere, are scale-like in appearance, and overlap, are very pale dull-yellowish in color, the surface finely granulate and moderately shining. The length is about 0.8 mm. to 0.85 mm. (0.03 inch) and the width 0.7 mm.

THE LARVA.

The larva is shown in figure 1, *c*. It suggests at first glance *Epagoge sulfureana* Clem., with which it agrees in many respects. It is, however, larger and readily distinguishable by the lighter and more nearly uniform color of the head and thoracic plate; the head is perceptibly yellowish or light brownish in life but the plate can scarcely be distinguished from the general color of the body. The two lobes are closely joined at the middle, being separated by a very narrow strip of lighter color. The two lateral piliferous spots below the thoracic plate are pale. In Dichelia, on the other hand, the head and thoracic plates and lateral thoracic spots are a decided

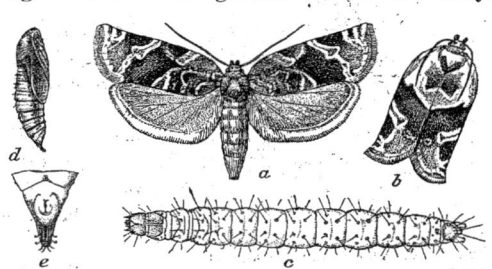

FIG. 1.—Red-banded leaf-roller (*Eulia velutinana*) : *a*, Female moth ; *b*, moth with wings folded at rest ; *c*, larva, dorsal view ; *d*, pupa, lateral view ; *e*, tip of abdomen of pupa, showing abdominal hooks. *a–d*, About three times natural size ; *e*, more enlarged.

brown, the latter well chitinized and with a darker posterior margin.

The form is elongate cylindrical, about 8 or 9 times as long as wide when extended. The piliferous tubercles are larger and more prominent, but in their arrangement as well as in the vestiture itself they are very like Epagoge.

The entire surface of the body except the head is in life a rather pale grass-green much mixed with yellow, the dorsal surface being a little lighter and the head less greenish and tinged lightly with brown. In alcohol the dorsal surface, including head and thorax, becomes pale yellow, except at the sutures, where the remaining white color of the body is visible. Partially grown larvæ (8 mm. long) are uniform pale green.

The thoracic legs are just perceptibly darker, as a rule, than the abdomen, and the apices of the tarsi are infuscated.

The form is less flattened than in Dichelia, otherwise the shape of the body and of the head, thorax, and legs is very similar. The last segment is of the appearance shown in figure 2 at c, the anal plate presenting no special characters worthy of notice, although the extreme apex is remarkable on account of the comb-like process, consisting of 6 spines, with which it is armed.

The length of the largest full-grown larva is about 0.7 inch (18 to 19 mm.); the width, 0.8 inch (2 to 2.2 mm.). Some larvæ are considerably smaller.

The head and first and second thoracic segments are shown from above, much enlarged, in figure 2, a. Figure 2, b, shows an abdominal segment with proleg from the side.

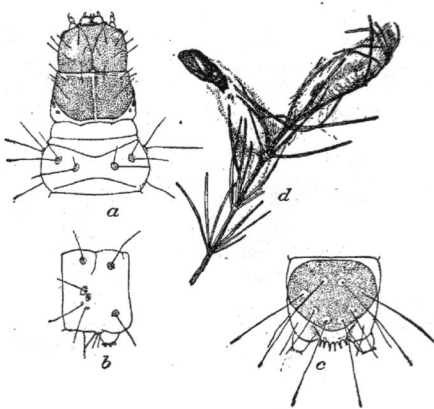

THE PUPA.

The pupa appears still more like that of *Epagoge sulfureana*. It is a little stouter on the average, the greatest width being across the wing-pads. (See fig. 1, d.) The last ventral segment, shown from below (fig. 1, e), also bears a pair of lateral and two pairs of terminal hooked processes as in Epagoge (eight in all).

Fig. 2.—Red-banded leaf-roller: a, Head and first two thoracic segments, dorsal view; b, third abdominal segment, lateral view; c, last -abdominal segment, from above, showing anal plate and comblike tip; d, sprig of asparagus showing web of larva and chrysalis working its way out of web at left. a, b, c, Much enlarged; d, somewhat enlarged.

The length is about 0.4 inch (8 to 10 mm.), the width is about 0.1 inch (2.2 to 3 mm.).

DISTRIBUTION.

Eulia velutinana is native to this country, and has been known for a considerable number of years from Maine to Texas.

It is well established in the Transition Life Zone and available records show greater abundance there and in the northern portion of the Upper Austral, although it is to be found also in the Lower Austral. Possibly it has been introduced into California through commerce with the East. (See map, fig. 3.)

INJURIES AND OCCURRENCES.

The records of the Bureau of Entomology show a wide diversity in larval food habits. The earliest are those of Dr. C. V. Riley, made at St. Louis, Mo., or in that vicinity. The rearing of this insect on grapes was noted July 28, 1870, and the issuance of the moth from larvæ found on raspberry was noted August 4, 1876.

June 11, 1879, pupæ were found rolled up in the leaves of red clover, from which the moths emerged June 13. June 23 another moth issued from larvæ feeding on clover June 10, and the following day an additional specimen issued from a larva feeding on white clover. August 11 a moth was reared from a pupa found spun up on a leaf of apple. August 7. October 12 the larva was found on aspen and the moth issued December 10.

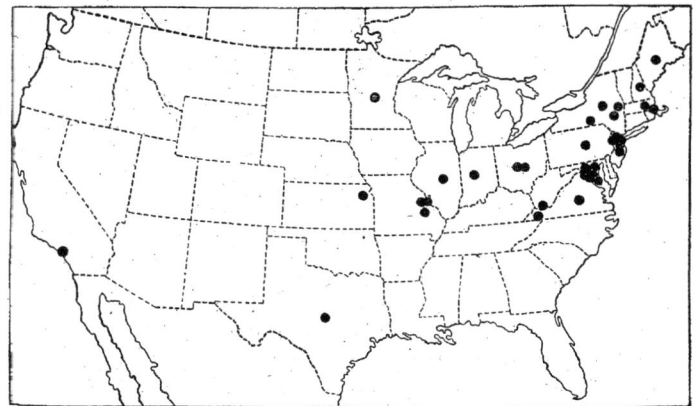

Fig. 3.—Distribution of the red-banded leaf-roller.

June 15, 1882, the moth was reared from larvæ found on apple in the District of Columbia.

Moths were reared June 7, 1885, from larvæ taken on Solidago.

June 12, 1886, the moth was reared from larvæ taken on roses, and on July 27 from others taken on privet and on willow. There is also a note on the rearing of this species June 7, 1886, from the galls of a species of Phylloxera.

This species was reared by Mr. Albert Koebele at Los Angeles County, Calif., from material found on the leaves of orange, April 24, 1888; and on July 26, 1893, specimens were received from Mr. J. G. Barlow, Cadet, Mo., with the report that the larvæ were found boring in the tips of chrysanthemums.

August 13, 1897, the moth was reared from larvæ which had been feeding on violet in the District of Columbia.

There are also three notes on specimens collected by Miss Mary E. Murtfeldt, presumably at her home at Kirkwood, Mo., recording the occurrence of the larvæ on lobelia, smartweed, and asparagus.

May 15, 1898, isolated individuals in the larval stage were observed on the twisted-up leaves contiguous to immature buds of blackberry at River View, Md., the buds having been eaten into in many cases and prevented from blooming. During July larvæ were observed in considerable abundance at Marshall Hall, Md., also on blackberry and on the webbed-up leaves of pigweed (*Amaranthus retroflexus*). Moths issued August 9 and 10.

July 14 to 25, 1899, larvæ were found at Alexandria, Va., by Mr. T. A. Keleher, Bureau of Entomology, on cabbage, raspberry, and cultivated honeysuckle. Moths began to issue July 31. September 26 the larva was received with the information that the material had been obtained from Mr. C. H. Stuart, Newark, N. Y., and that the species was infesting popcorn. Mr. Stuart made the statement that 27 per cent of the ears of popcorn were infested, and that 37 per cent of the corn on each infested ear were destroyed by this caterpillar, an unusual instance of injury.

During the latter part of May and early June the moths of this species were several times observed in the field, and June 13 the moths were seen at rest upon cabbage and rhubarb. On the former plant a deserted pupal skin was found on the under surface of the leaf directly below the point where the moth had been resting, and the midrib was found to have been eaten to the extent of 6 or 8 inches along both sides. Subsequently other cabbage plants were found to have been similarly affected, and a pupa was found in one of these from which the moth afterwards issued.

October 5 larvæ were observed on celery at Washington, D. C., and later the same species was found at work on celery and still more abundantly on asparagus at Brookland, D. C. Later it was observed on parsley, strawberry, and raspberry at Cabin John, Md., and on potted geranium at Washington, D. C. On celery and parsley the larvæ were apparently less abundant, as on these plants they are more difficult to see without close scrutiny, since they web up the leaves very neatly and in such a manner as not readily to attract attention. On asparagus, however, the webs are quite noticeable and could be seen at some little distance. In the formation of their temporary homes, the larvæ use an abundance of silk, often distorting the asparagus stems by drawing them together.

In every instance above mentioned the adults were reared from the material obtained.

In the manner of their attack the larvæ of this species do not differ markedly from those of the sulphur leaf-roller. In work upon corn the young blades are either folded lengthwise so as to form a cylindrical case or simply rolled up as are all other plants when attacked.

This moth was reared December 31, 1903, from larvæ found on cabbage by E. N. Burke, Macon, Ga. The same date the moth was reared from larvæ found on okra in the District of Columbia.

The species was found in great abundance on asparagus in the District of Columbia in the latter days of September, 1904, the larvæ at this time being full grown or nearly so. Many deserted nests were also found, as well as the usual number of spider nests, which so closely resemble those made by the leaf-roller.

Beginning March 23, 1907, the adults of this species issued from foliage of elderberry collected at Arlington, Va., September 3, 1906.

During the last week of October, 1907, Mr. C. H. Popenoe, Bureau of Entomology, observed specimens of this green larva working on species of ground-cherry (Physalis) at Arlington, Va.

The following year he observed the larvæ at Topeka, Kans., working in the tips of ripe ears of sweet corn under the husk, lining the tunnels with silk.

Most of the foregoing records were made from observations of the writer and his associates in the Bureau of Entomology, and there are also some others which need not be mentioned in detail. These include the finding of the larvæ working on zinnia, syringa, hollyhock, snowball, and magnolia. There is also record of attack to catalpa at Welch, W. Va.

BIOLOGIC NOTES.

The larvæ taken on asparagus by Miss Murtfeldt were found October, 1882, and the moths of this lot issued February 21, 1883.

In the writer's recent experience with this insect in the neighborhood of Washington, D. C., nearly all of the larvæ that were obtained in the autumn were approaching maturity during the first week of October, and some had formed their webs for pupation by the middle of that month. By the close of the month all the individuals observed had transformed to pupæ, the moths beginning to issue January 23 and continuing until March 22. In every case that came under observation pupation took place within the larval web or in another close to the place where the larva had been feeding.

The moths kept under unnatural conditions in a warm room issued in January.

A larva obtained from Newark, N. Y., previously mentioned, began forming its cocoon September 28, and the following day appeared to have finished, but further observation showed that it had not entirely completed it, since more silk was added apparently from day to day. It was noted that the larva, before transforming to pupa, cut out a round hole of about the same size or a little larger than the pupa itself. Transformation to this stage took place the first week in October, the moth issuing in January, having been kept with others in a warm room. There is a singular agreement in the times of pupation and issuance of the specimens at Washington and in Missouri, and of the one individual observed from Newark, N. Y.

In the District of Columbia, and probably elsewhere as well, hibernation takes place exclusively in the pupal state.

From the facts that larvæ have been observed in the open on May 15, that pupæ have been found as early as the second week in June, and that moths have issued during the third week, it was readily surmised that the moths which have hibernated as pupæ appear some time in April and lay eggs for the first generation. The moth was collected during the latter days of April in 1900.

The moths from the first new generation emerge for the most part during the second and third weeks of June, and of the next generation the last of July and the first two weeks of August, the third generation developing in October and early November and wintering as previously mentioned.

It seems to be fairly certain that there are at least two, and probably three generations annually in a climate like that of the District of Columbia and Missouri, and probably no more than two in a more northern latitude like that of the New England States.

From a female captured June 14, eggs were obtained in two masses of about 45 and 65 respectively upon the two following days, and the larvæ hatched in 11 days. The weather was rather cooler than seasonable during this time. A portion of the eggs were placed in a large rearing jar with growing strawberry plants, and the imago obtained July 23, the larval and pupal stages having been passed in 28 days. The weather was extremely hot (80° to 90° F. indoors) during the latter portion of this period, and the pupal stage must have been about 6 days, which would give 22 days or about 3 weeks as the larval period.

Of the larvæ which were collected in the vicinity of the District of Columbia in October, 1919, all had transformed to pupæ by the middle of November and the first moth issued April 15 of the following year, others continuing to issue for a few days thereafter. April 19 an imago was captured at light in the open.

It will thus be seen that the pupal or resting stage of this species for the District of Columbia and vicinity is an even 5 months, leaving 7 months for the active or working periods of the species.

HISTORY OF THE SPECIES.

The species was given its specific name in 1863 by Walker (*1*)[2], who described it under the name of *Cacoecia* (?) *velutinana*.

---

[2] Italic figures in parentheses refer to "Literature cited," p. 13.

C. triferana, described at the same time, is now considered a synonym, the former name having been given to the male, the latter to the female. In 1865 it was again described as new by Clemens (*2*) as *Tortrix incertana.* Four years later it was redescribed under the same name by Robinson (*3, p. 278*). With this last description illustrations of both sexes were furnished.

In 1870 our first account of the habits of this leaf-roller was published by Dr. A. S. Packard (*4, p. 40*). It is mentioned as the red-banded cranberry Tortrix or "cranberry Tortrix" and is treated in connection with insects affecting the cranberry in Massachusetts, the account including a description of the adult and a short description of the pupa. This paper was republished in later years (*5, 6*).

In Dr. C. H. Fernald's catalogue of the Tortricidæ, published in 1882–83 (*7, p. 15*), some new localities are added for the species and several new food plants, the latter on the authority of Miss Murtfeldt. Besides cranberry the list includes elm, soft maple, oak, apple, rose, beans, and *Gnaphalium polycephalum.*

It was not until 1885 that any extensive account of the insect was published. This was by Dr. S. A. Forbes (*8*) and is in connection with insects found attacking corn in Illinois. Strawberry and clover are added to the list of food plants.

In 1890, Mr. F. M. Webster (*10*) included this species in a list of insects observed at Lafayette, Ind., affecting salsify. The same year Packard (*11*) wrote again concerning this insect. The following year Prof. Lawrence Bruner (*12, p. 267*) mentioned this species briefly in an account of corn insects.

In 1893 Miss M. E. Murtfeldt (*13*) referred to this species as one which webs and curls the leaves of Osage orange. In 1898 the writer (*15*) mentioned it briefly in connection with insects that attack asparagus. There followed Dr. Otto Lugger's short description (*16*), in which it was called the apple Lophoderus.

In 1901 the writer (*17*) recorded the feeding of the larva on violet in the District of Columbia. The same year Felt (*18, p. 998*) recorded the depredations of this insect on green popcorn at Newark, N. Y.

In 1904 Slingerland (*19; 20, p. 47*) stated that this insect was observed with the grape-berry moth on clusters of blossoms and recently set fruit of grape, and was quite often found at the same destructive work. In reviewing the known food plants, he records attack to Solidago and dogbane and mentions *Urogaster canarsiae* Ashm. as a parasite.

In 1905 Forbes (*21*) again mentions this species as an enemy of Indian corn, and the year following Felt (*22*) includes it in a report on insects affecting park and woodland trees.

FOOD PLANTS.

The red-banded leaf-roller is nearly omnivorous, its food plants comprising many botanical orders. The list follows:

Asparagus, beans, sweet potato, cabbage, horse-radish, celery, parsley, rhubarb, salsify, tomato, sweet corn, pepper, okra, ground cherry (Physalis), blackberry, raspberry, and strawberry among truck crops; chrysanthemum, geranium, rose, lobelia, violet, snow-ball, syringa, hollyhock, zinnia, privet, and honeysuckle comprise the list of ornamental plants. Other plants affected are clover, field corn and popcorn, cranberry, elderberry, grape, orange, apple, plum, elm, maple, oak, laurel oak, aspen, willow, magnolia, catalpa, balsam fir, and Osage orange. The larva also attacks pigweed (*Amaranthus retroflexus*), goldenrod (*Solidago* spp.), smartweed, dogbane, *Solanum* sp., and *Gnaphalium polycephalum*.

NATURAL ENEMIES.

The red-banded leaf-roller is no exception to a somewhat general rule that larvæ which conceal themselves from view in rolled and

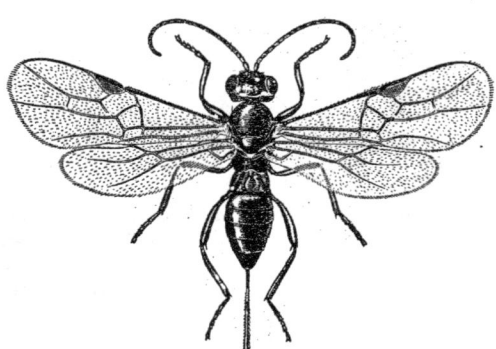

webbed leaves and similar places of shelter are the more subject to parasitic attack. The following list of parasites is in evidence:

Exochus curvator Fab., an ichneumonid, was reared by the writer August 7, 1900, from the host larva collected at Camerons Mills, Va.[3]

Fig. 4.—*Microbracon* sp., a parasite of the red-banded leaf-roller.

Epiurus indagator Walsh was reared from this leaf-roller on oak at Kirkwood, Mo., November 7, 1878.

An ichneumonid parasite allied to Pimpla was reared from material received from Cadet, Mo., in July, 1893, previously mentioned. (Dept. Agr. No. 5861°.)

Lampronota pleuralis Cress. was reared at St. Louis, Mo., November 7, 1878.

Limnerium sp. is mentioned by F. M. Webster as having been reared with this leaf-roller and two others on salsify.

---

[3] Identified by Ashmead, who also identified practically all of the other species mentioned unless otherwise noted.

Opius foersteri Gahan, a braconid, wrongly determined as *Opius mellipes* Prov., and published under that name in Insect Life (*9*), was reared from material received from Kirkwood, Mo., September 25, 1881.

Epirhyssalus atriceps Ashm., a minute yellow braconid, was reared from its host July 1, 1907, breeding on rose and collected by Mr. I. J. Condit at Pataskala, Ohio.[4]

Microbracon sp. (fig. 4) was reared from material collected by Mr. M. R. Smith at Plymouth, Ind.

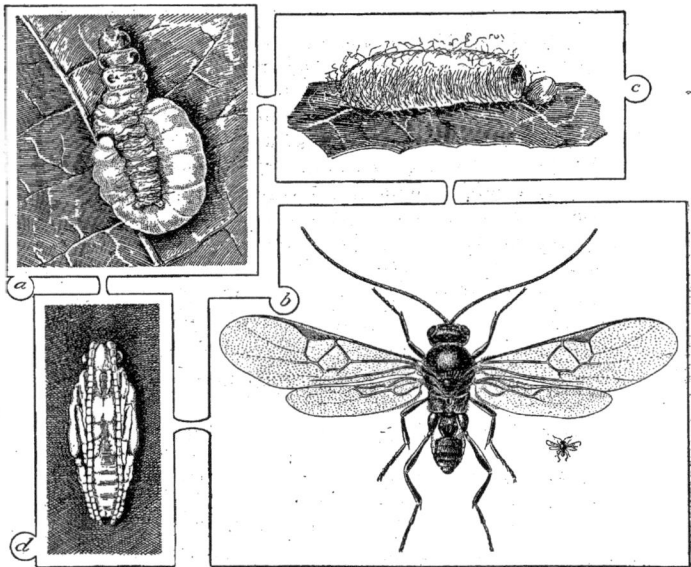

Fig. 5.—*Apanteles canarsiae*, a parasite of the red-banded leaf-roller: *a*, Larva feeding on leaf-roller larva; *b*, adult parasite; *c*, cocoon; *d*, pupa. All much enlarged. (Strauss.)

Smicra deliva Cress., a chalcidid, was reared by the writer during the last week of July and first week of August from raspberry leaves infested by this leaf-roller from Camerons Mills, Va.

Smicra torvina Cress. was reared with the foregoing.

Apanteles canarsiae Ashm. (fig. 5) was reared from this leaf-roller by Slingerland (*20*) in New York, and is somewhat better known as a parasite of the grape leaf-folder (*Desmia funeralis* Hbn.) and some other species.

---

[4] Identified by Mr. J. C. Crawford.

Phorocera parva Bigot,[5] a tachina fly, is reported as a parasite of this leaf-roller by Coquillett (*14*).

CONTROL.

The red-banded leaf-roller is seldom sufficiently abundant to warrant artificial methods for its control. Since it conceals itself in leaves, rolled or bound together, it would appear difficult to reach it with insecticides, but as it must issue from this shelter to feed on surrounding leafage it can then be reached by the application of arsenicals. The best time to apply these is soon after the eggs are laid. Arsenate of lead is the standard insecticide, used at about 2 or 3 pounds to 50 gallons of water and applied as a spray.

The webbed leaves can be readily detected after a little practice, and when infestation is not too heavy these can be clipped and burned, or they may be pinched so as to crush the larvæ within.

Early fall plowing and burning over the garden after the crop is off, either in fall or early spring, are two farming methods which, if vigorously practiced, will undoubtedly help greatly toward holding this insect in check. They should both be put into practice in case of infestation.

SUMMARY.

The foliage of beans, sweet potato, asparagus, strawberry, raspberry, and various other crops is subject to attack by a small greenish caterpillar about three-fourths of an inch long when mature, known as the red-banded leaf-roller, which rolls the leaves in various ways, according to the nature of the plant attacked, and breeds continuously throughout the growing season, from April to November.

It is native to this country, where it enjoys a wide distribution from Maine to Texas and has been found in California.

The species has been studied in the District of Columbia and vicinity. Hibernation takes place exclusively in the pupal state, which occupies a period of 5 months, leaving 7 months for the active or working stage. The ascertained period of the egg stage is 11 days, of the larva 22 days, and of the pupa a minimum of 6 days. There are at least two and probably three generations annually in the climate where observed.

Several natural enemies, mostly parasites, attack this species.

The red-banded leaf-roller is seldom sufficiently abundant to warrant artificial methods for its control, and since it conceals itself in rolled-up leaves, it is difficult to reach with insecticides. It can, however, be reached with a spray of lead arsenate, inasmuch as it issues from this shelter to feed on surrounding leafage. Clipping the webbed leaves from the affected plants, early fall plowing, and burning over affected areas after the crop is off, will help to hold the insect in check.

---

[5] Identification by Coquillett.

LITERATURE CITED.

(1) WALKER, F.

    1863. LIST OF THE SPECIMENS OF THE LEPIDOPTEROUS INSECTS IN THE COL-
        LECTION OF THE BRITISH MUSEUM. pt. xxvii, p. 314.

(2) CLEMENS, BRACKENRIDGE.

    1865. NORTH AMERICAN MICRO-LEPIDOPTERA. *In* Proc. Ent. Soc. Phila., v.
        5, p. 133–147.

(3) ROBINSON, C. T.

    1868–69. NOTES ON AMERICAN TORTRICIDAE. *In* Trans. Amer. Ent. Soc.,
        v. 2, p. 261–288.

(4) PACKARD, A. S.

    1870. NEW OR LITTLE KNOWN INJURIOUS INSECTS. *In* 17th Rept. Secy.
        Mass. Bd. Agr., 1869, p. 235–263.

(5) ——

    1878. INSECTS AFFECTING THE CRANBERRY, WITH REMARKS ON OTHER IN-
        JURIOUS INSECTS. *In* Rept. U. S. Geol. Surv. for 1876, p. 521–526.

(6) ——

    1880. INSECTS INJURIOUS TO THE CRANBERRY. *In* Trans. Wis. State Hort.
        Soc., v. 10, p. 313–322.

(7) FERNALD, C. H.

    1882–3. A SYNONYMICAL CATALOGUE OF THE DESCRIBED TORTRICIDAE OF
        NORTH AMERICA NORTH OF MEXICO. *In* Trans. Amer. Ent. Soc.,
        v. 10, p. 1–72. May, 1882.

(8) FORBES, S. A.

    1885. FOURTEENTH REPORT STATE ENT. ILL., 1885, p. 20–21.

(9) [RILEY, C. V., and HOWARD, L. O.]

    1890. SOME OF THE BRED PARASITIC HYMENOPTERA IN THE NATIONAL COL-
        LECTION. *In* U. S. Dept. Agr., Ins. Life, v. 3, no. 2, p. 59.

(10) WEBSTER, F. M.

    1890. INSECTS AFFECTING SALSIFY. *In* U. S. Dept. Agr., Ins. Life, v. 2,
        p. 255–256.

(11) PACKARD, A. S.

    1890. THE RED-BANDED LEAF-ROLLER. *In* 5th Rept. U. S. Ent. Comm.,
        p. 195–196.

(12) BRUNER, LAWRENCE.

    1891. REPORT OF THE ENTOMOLOGIST. *In* Ann. Rept. Neb. State Bd. Agr.,
        p. 240–309.

(13) MURTFELDT, M. E.

    1893. THE OSAGE ORANGE PYRALID. *In* U. S. Dept. Agr., Ins. Life, v. 5,
        p. 155–157, fig. 11.

(14) COQUILLETT, D. W.

    1897. REVISION OF THE TACHINIDAE OF AMERICA NORTH OF MEXICO. U. S.
        Dept. Agr., Div. Ent., Tech. Ser. No. 7. 154 p.

(15) CHITTENDEN, F. H.

    1898. SOME MISCELLANEOUS RESULTS OF THE WORK OF THE DIVISION OF
        ENTOMOLOGY. U. S. Dept. Agr., Div. Ent., Bul. 10, n. s. 99 p.,
        19 figs.

(16) LUGGER, OTTO.

    1899. THE RUSTY-BROWN TORTRIX. In 4th Ann. Rept. Ent. State Exp.
        Sta. Minn. 1898, p. 231–232.

(17) CHITTENDEN, F. H.

    1901. SOME INSECTS INJURIOUS TO THE VIOLET, ROSE, AND OTHER ORNA-
        MENTAL PLANTS. U. S. Dept. Agr., Div. Ent., Bul. 27, n. s. 114
        p., 4 pls., 29 figs.

(18) FELT, E. P.
    1901. SIXTEENTH REPORT . . . ON THE INJURIOUS AND OTHER INSECTS OF
        THE STATE OF NEW YORK. 1900. Bull. N. Y. State Mus., No. 36,
        v. 7, p. 951–1048.
(19) SLINGERLAND, M. V.
    1904. THE GRAPE LEAF-FOLDER. *In* Rural New Yorker, v. 63, no. 2818,
        Jan. 30, p. 68.
(20) ———
    1904. THE GRAPE-BERRY MOTH. Cornell Univ. Agr. Exp. Sta. Bul. 223.
        p. 43–60.
(21) FORBES, S. A.
    1905. THE RED-BANDED LEAF-ROLLER. *In* 23rd Rept. State. Ent. Ill., p.
        175–176.
(22) FELT, E. P.
    1906. RED-BANDED LEAF-ROLLER. *In* Rept. N. Y. State Mus., Memoir 8,
        p. 532.

UNITED STATES DEPARTMENT OF AGRICULTURE

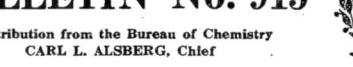

BULLETIN No. 915

· Contribution from the Bureau of Chemistry
CARL L. ALSBERG, Chief

Washington, D. C.　　　　▼　　　　November 12, 1920

TOXICITY OF BARIUM CARBONATE TO RATS.

By ERICH W. SCHWARTZE, *Junior Pharmacologist, Pharmacological Laboratory.*

CONTENTS.

	Page.		Page.
Purpose of investigation	1	Results of experimental work on other barium	
Previous investigations	1	compounds	9
Experimental procedure	3	Toxicity of barium carbonate to animals	
Results of experimental work	4	other than rats	9
Minimum efficient concentration of barium		Conclusions	9
carbonate	6	Bibliography	10

PURPOSE OF INVESTIGATION.

A series of experiments on the toxicity of various substances to rats and their suitability for poisoning these animals was undertaken, in 1918, at the request of the Bureau of Biological Survey of the United States Department of Agriculture, for the purpose of obtaining toxicological data for use in connection with the rat-extermination work in the zone of occupation of the American Expeditionary Forces. Although this incentive ceased with the signing of the armistice, the studies have been continued because of their importance to agricultural economics as well as to the public health.

PREVIOUS INVESTIGATIONS.

The literature contains no references to work dealing with the toxicity of barium carbonate to rats, in spite of the fact that many articles give directions for its use as a rat poison and discuss its toxicity to other animals. The earliest communication which is of interest here is one by Crampe (5),[1] who recommended 20 per cent barium carbonate in bait for poisoning field mice. Lantz's (9) barium carbonate formula also calls for 20 per cent of this substance. Recently White (20) has reported good results from poisoning *Mus rattus* by the use of 25 per cent of barium carbonate. This concentration, however, was ultimately diluted, as water was added to the barium carbonate bait mixture. White set out individual baits containing 3 grains (200 mg.) of barium carbonate. If entirely con-

---

[1] The figures in parentheses refer to the bibliography at the end of this bulletin.

10939°—20—Bull. 915

sumed, one such bait for a rat of average size would amount to 600 or 800 mg. of the poison per kilo. Storer (19) reported that calcium carbonate (whiting) protected rats and mice against barium carbonate as well as lead carbonate poisoning. There is, however, some uncertainty about these experiments, in the absence of definite quantitative poison and food-intake data.

An illustration of an old popular conception of the ideal rat poison which was held by some investigators is found in the following translation by Boelter (4) from Raebiger (15): "I have come to the conclusion that preparations which are really nonpoisonous are unable to kill rats, and poisons, call them what you like, if they kill rats will also kill domestic animals." Raebiger's results are in harmony with all known facts, and demonstrate the fallacy of the conception of a poison specific for rats.

As the toxicity of barium salts to other animals is of interest both to the user of barium rat baits and to the laboratory worker, a few citations (Tables 1 and 2) on this point are quoted.

TABLE 1.—*Toxicity to various animals of barium chlorid administered subcutaneously.*

Animal.	Salt.	Sublethal dose.	Lethal dose.	No. experiments.	Citation.
		Mg. per kilo.	*Mg. per kilo.*		
Rat	$BaCl_2$	35	45 to 89	Many	Table 4 (p. 4).
Do	do	40(?)	60	1	Bary (3).
Rabbit	do	20 and 46	50 to 75	5	Do.
Do	do	40 to 50	50 up	Many	Maurel (10).
Do	do		40 to 60	5	Kissner (8).
Dog	do		10 to 15		Aloy and Cournet (1).
Do	do		15 and 17	2	Schedel (17).
Do	do	6 and 10	15 to 20	5	Bary (3).
Do	do	4.5 to 14.3	9.1 and 14.3	2	Pilliet and Malbec (14).
Cat	do	15	18 to 60	5	Bary (3).
Chicken	do	40(?)	50 and 80	3	Do.
Pigeon	do	75	80 up		Maurel (10).
Do	do		60	1	Bary (3).

TABLE 2.—*Toxicity to various animals of barium salts administered per os.*

Animal.	Weight.	Barium salt.	Absolute dose.	Dose per kilo.	Result.	Citation.
	Kilo.		*Grams.*	*Grams.*		
Rat		$BaCl_2$		0.355 to 0.533	Fatal	Table 5 (p. 4).
Rabbitt	1.177	$Ba(C_2H_3O)_2$	0.200	.170	do	Crawford (6).
Do	1.630		.500	.300	do	Do.
Do	1.800	$BaCl_2$		.170	do	Bary (3).
Sheep		do	4.000		Survived	Dieckerhoff (7).
Do		do	6.000		Fatal	Do.
Cattle		do	40.000		Survived	Do.
Horse		do	8.000 to 12.000		Survived; therapeutic.	Do.
Do		do	[1] 15.000	.033	Fatal, with local effects in stomach from two boll.	Reynolds (16).
Dog	8.000 to 10.000	do	.720 to .900	.090	Fatal	Aloy and Cournet (1).
Pigeon		do		.500	Survived [2]	Maurel (10).
Chicken		$BaCO_3$	1.333		Fatal	White (20).
Man		$BaCl_2$	[3] 8.6		Fatal in 10 hours	Stern (18).
Do		do	[3] .9		Fatal	Am. Med. Assoc. (2).

[1] Dose per 1,000 pounds of horse weight.
[2] Vomited.
[3] A. P. Chadbourne (personal communication) found that the lowest fatal dose of barium chlorid for man was that reported by Stern. Approximately 8.6 grams were fatal in 10 hours. In view of the proximity of the fatal and therapeutic doses reported (2), the fatal dose therein given would seem to be rather small.

Unfortunately, in some cases, exact lethal and sublethal doses are not known, since the amounts administered have not been based upon body weight. In other instances it has been necessary to calculate some of the figures from the authors' data. It would appear, however, that rabbits, chickens, and pigeons are about equally susceptible to barium administered subcutaneously, while cats and dogs are approximately three times as sensitive. Owing to differences in the physiology of the stomachs of the different species, and presumably to the differences in the average size between species, the toxicity of barium by mouth varies markedly, the purely species characteristic becoming more or less masked. For practical purposes, however, it may be assumed that the lethal dose of barium per os per kilo tends to decrease relatively as the size of the animal increases.

EXPERIMENTAL PROCEDURE.

In the experiments here reported the brown rat (*Rattus norvegicus*) was used as often as practicable. The domesticated white strain was employed for obtaining accurate food-intake data and for testing the relative efficiency of different percentages of barium carbonate in the bait. The melanotic strain was used in only a few toxicity experiments for purposes of comparison. The substitution of the white rat for the brown strain would seem fair, since the toxicity of barium to these two strains was found to be the same. The feeding experiments were confined, as far as possible, to the laboratory phase, although at times it was necessary to consider in some detail the practical aspects. In the experiments in which the stomach tube was used, the animals were first anesthetized with ether. The lethal doses are regarded, not as the minimum amounts which might be fatal, but those amounts which will kill a large proportion of the rats.

The barium chlorid administered was the ordinary crystalized salt ($BaCl_2 \cdot 2H_2O$). The carbonate, which was of high purity and free from soluble chlorid, was always used in the form of fine powder, having been passed through a 100-mesh sieve. The molecular weight and barium content of these preparations are given in Table 3, since their relative toxicity is determined on the basis of their barium content.

TABLE 3.—*Molecular weight and barium content of barium chlorid and barium carbonate.*

Salt.	Molecular weight.	Barium.	Conversion factor of barium into salt.
		Per cent.	
$BaCl_2 \cdot 2H_2O$..	244.32	56.2	1.778
$BaCO_3$......	197.37	69.6	1.437
Ba..........	[1] 137.37	....	....

[1] Atomic weight.

RESULTS OF EXPERIMENTAL WORK.

The results from the subcutaneous and oral administration of barium chlorid are summarized in Tables 4 and 5, respectively.

TABLE 4.—*Toxicity of barium chlorid to brown rats (injected subcutaneously on the abdomen).*

Number of rats.	Barium chlorid in 0.65 per cent NaCl solution.	Barium.	Barium chlorid.	Fatalities.				
				16th hour.	24th hour.	Later.	Number.	Total per cent.
	Per cent.	*Mg.per kilo.*	*Mg.per kilo.*					
2.....	0. 45	20	35	0	0	0	0	0
7.....	.45	25	45	0	0	3	3	43
3.....	.45	35	62	1	1	0	2	67
5.....	.45	50	89	1	0	3	4	80
1.....	.45	75	133	1	0	0	1	100
9.....	.45	100	178	8	0	0	8	89

TABLE 5.—*Toxicity of barium chlorid to brown rats (injected by stomach tube after preliminary light etherization).*

Number of rats.	Barium chlorid.	Barium.	Barium.	Fatalities.					
				16th hour.	24th hour.	Later.	Number.	Total per cent.	Average per cent.
	Per cent.	*Mg. per kilo.*	*Mg. per kilo.*						
6.....	3. 5	100	178	1	0	0	1	17	17
2.....	1. 7	200	355	0	0	0	0	0	57
5.....	3. 5	200	355	4	0	0	4	80	
2.....	1. 7	250	445	0	0	0	1	50	71
5.....	3. 5	250	445	0	0	0	4	80	
2.....	1. 7	300	533	2	0	0	2	100	100
5.....	3. 5	300	533	5	0	0	5	100	

The subcutaneous lethal dose was from 45 to 89 mg. per kilo, and the oral lethal dose from 355 to 533 mg. per kilo. From this it would appear that barium chlorid is about six or seven times more toxic subcutaneously than per os.

The data obtained from the administration of barium carbonate in starch paste suspension by a stomach tube to etherized rats are given in Table 6.

TABLE 6.—*Toxicity of barium carbonate, 100 fine, suspended in starch paste (injected by tube after preliminary light etherization).*

Kind of rats.	Number of rats.	Barium carbonate in suspension.	Barium.	Barium carbonate.	Fatalities.					
					16th hour.	24th hour.	Later.	Number.	Total per cent.	Average per cent.
		P. ct.	*Mg. per kilo.*	*Mg. per kilo.*						
Brown............	16	10	350	500	3	0	0	3	19	19
Do............	7	10	400	630	5	0	1	6	86	85
White............	6	10	400	630	2	0	3	5	84	
Brown............	7	20	525	750	4	1	1	6	86	
Black............	7	20	525	750	2	2	2	6	86	90
White............	7	20	525	750	3	1	3	7	100	
Brown............	7	10	700	1,000	5	2	0	7	100	
Do............	16	10	830 to 1,400	1,200 to 2,000	14	0	1	15	94	92
Do............	17	10	1,400	2,000	15	0	0	15	88	

From 630 to 750 mg. per kilo was found to be the least amount which could be considered* efficient. On increasing the amount administered, however, there were still a few survivals, although the increased potency of the larger doses was clearly indicated by the relative increase of fatalities occurring within the first 16 hours. The occasional survival of an animal from a large dose would indicate that a 100 per cent mortality could not be expected.

Since it is possible for liquid to be forced through the pyloris under some conditions, these data have been checked against the results of feeding experiments (Table 7).

TABLE 7.—*Intake by hungry white rats of food containing 5 or 10 per cent barium carbonate.*

Weight of rat.	Amount of food eaten.	Barium carbonate in food.	Barium carbonate eaten.	Result.
Grams.	Grams.	Per cent.	Mg. per kilo.	
295	0.55	5	90	Lived.
159	.20	10	125	Do.
185	.25	10	135	Do.
184	.50	5	140	Do.
167	.25	10	150	Do.
286	.90	5	155	Do.
174	.30	10	170	Do.
198	.35	10	175	Do.
292	1.40	5	240	Dead within 48 hours.
310	1.55	5	250	Lived.
215	.55	10	255	Do.
192	1.00	5	260	Do.
245	1.40	5	285	Do.
330	2.45	5	375	Do.
206	1.55	5	375	Dead within 24 hours.
155	.65	10	420	Lived.
291	2.50	5	430	Do.
250	2.25	5	450	Dead within 40 hours.
175	.85	10	485	Dead within 48 hours.
343	3.50	5	510	Lived.
148	1.60	5	540	Do.
166	1.85	5	555	Do.
188	1.05	10	555	Do.
193	2.40	5	620	Dead within 16 hours.
160	1.00	10	625	Dead within 72 hours.
270	3.60	5	655	Dead within 40 hours.
264	3.50	5	655	Do.
215	1.45	10	665	Dead within 48 hours.
280	4.10	5	730	Dead within 40 hours.
320	4.70	5	735	Do.
170	2.60	5	765	Do.
252	3.90	5	775	Lived.
366	5.70	5	780	Dead within 40 hours.
175	1.40	10	800	Dead within 24 hours.
215	1.75	10	815	Dead within 48 hours.
205	1.70	10	830	Dead within 24 hours.
167	1.40	10	840	Do.
167	1.45	10	870	Do.
150	1.35	10	900	Do.
144	3.60	5	1,270	Dead within 20 hours.

The results of these two sets of experiments, given in the order of the barium carbonate intake per kilo, are in general agreement, the efficient lethal dose of barium carbonate being 630 mg. per kilo, or, more conservatively, 750 mg. On the basis of the barium content, this preparation of barium carbonate was from 57 to 75 per cent as potent as barium chlorid. In other words, approximately two-thirds of the carbonate was utilized in poisoning the animal. This does not mean, however, that every preparation of barium carbonate possesses an equally favorable ratio of toxicity, since both fineness and physical texture undoubtedly influence the relative ease of disintegration and rate of solution.

MINIMUM EFFICIENT CONCENTRATION OF BARIUM CARBONATE.

Since the experiments already discussed have dealt with the toxicological consideration of barium, there remained to be determined the minimum concentration of barium carbonate in the poisoned bait which would give a high percentage of relatively quick fatalities. For these tests white rats were starved 12 to 24 hours before being fed the poison, to insure an empty stomach and a sharp appetite. The rat is a nocturnal animal and under ordinary circumstances probably would not be deprived of food for longer than 12 hours. A series of 14 rats, therefore, were starved for 12 hours and fed at 9 p. m. with the poisoned bait. As there was no marked difference between the results of this series and those of the experiments carried on in the daytime, with respect to both the average food intake and the percentage of fatalities from the concentration of barium carbonate used, it was concluded that the daytime experiments were valid.

It was occasionally observed for group tests that the average food intake varied somewhat, although the experiments were tried under as closely similar conditions as possible. For this reason the experiments were performed at widely separated intervals to minimize accidental influences and to make the general averages as representative as possible. Sometimes the same rats were used over again, in which instances no evidence was obtained of their having derived any benefit from their previous experience. Because of the fact that the rats used in these tests had been living upon the concentrated type of experimental diet and had accordingly adjusted their appetite or daily food intake, the averages expressed for this type of food might be slightly less than those which would have been secured by the use of a more bulky type of food. Such a possibility, however, is of minor importance, since it would favor the probability of fatal poisoning because of the larger amount of food which might be consumed.

Several series of starved rats were for an hour offered different types of diet, such as grain, dog biscuit, and soft, mealy food. The last-named food, which consisted approximately of 70 per cent peanut meal, 10 per cent milk powder, and 20 per cent lard, was usually consumed much faster, more of it was eaten before the appetite was satisfied, and less was scattered or wasted. In addition, the rapid consumption of food would occasionally seem very important, since a few rats fairly soon gave evidence of discomfort, due presumably to the relatively quick solution of the barium carbonate by the acid of the stomach, with consequent irritation.

The results obtained from feeding both poisoned and unpoisoned food are summarized in Tables 8 and 9. The rats were divided arbitrarily into weight groups, and the food intake calculated on the per rat and the per kilo basis. The probable errors are given for individual observations as well as for each group.

TABLE 8.—*Intake of control food (rats divided into weight groups).*

Weight group.	Number rats.	Weight.		Amount eaten.		Probable error.		Amount eaten per kilo.	Probable error.	
		Total.	Average.	Total.	Average.	Single.	Series.		Single.	Series.
Grams.		*Grams.*	*Grams.*	*Grams.*	*Grams.*			*Grams.*		
140 to 199............	14	2,418	173	32.0	2.29	±0.79	±0.21	13.2	±4.6	±1.23
200 to 249............	19	4,430	233	49.35	2.59	±0.48	±0.11	11.1	±2.1	±0.49
250 to 299............	15	4,094	273	57.45	3.83	....	....	14.03	....	....
300 up..............	8	3,166	396	11.6	1.45	....	....	3.50	....	....
Total for 250 up..........	23	7,260	316	69.05	3.00	±0.78	±0.15	9.51	±2.5	±0.51
Total for all experiments	56	14,108	252	150.4	2.7	....	....	10.65	....	....

TABLE 9.—*Intake of food containing barium carbonate, all percentages (rats divided into weight groups).*

Weight group.	No. rats.	Weight.		Amount eaten.		Probable error.		Amount eaten per kilo.	Probable error.	
		Total.	Average.	Total.	Average.	Single.	Series.		Single.	Series.
Grams.		*Grams.*	*Grams.*	*Grams.*	*Grams.*			*Grams.*		
140 to 199............	22	3,791	172	56.6	2.57	±0.65	±0.15	14.9	±3.88	±0.86
200 to 249............	26	5,703	220	68.5	2.64	±1.3	±0.26	12.0	±5.92	±1.12
250 to 299............	17	4,614	271	44.65	2.62	±1.0	±0.25	9.7	±3.72	±0.90
300 up..............	14	4,795	312	35.8	2.56	±0.79	±0.21	7.5	±2.30	±0.62
Total.........	79	18,903	239	205.55	2.60	....	....	10.85	....	....

Slightly greater variations occurred in the control series, and would seem to indicate the need of caution in too strict a mathematical interpretation. The data indicate, however, that on the average the food intake was approximately one one-hundredth of the rat's weight, both for the control and the barium-carbonate-fed series, from which it was concluded that the barium carbonate added to the diet was perfectly palatable. Just why the food intake per rat for all of the groups is approximately the same, when the stomachs of larger rats have greater capacity, is not at present clear. The greater food intake per kilo for the smaller rats is, under these circumstances, without significance.

For practical purposes, however, the individual food intake is the most important (Table 7), since the rats which eat scantily are the ones which necessarily determine the percentage to be placed in the diet, because they must also ingest a lethal dose. With this object in view, different percentages of barium carbonate were fed. The results of these experiments are summarized in Table 10.

TABLE 10.—*Efficiency of different percentages of barium carbonate in the diet.*

Date.	Barium carbonate in food.	No. rats.	Type of experiment.	No. rats lived.	Fatalities.				
					16th hour.	24th hour.	48th hour.	Later.	Total.
1920.	*Per cent.*								*Per cent.*
Feb. 7.................	5	¹ 14	Individual, in very large cages.	6	0	2	6	0	......
1919.									
Mar. 24................	5	10	Individual, in very small cages.	5	0	1	1	3	......
Feb. 15................	5	10	.....do.....	6	(²)	1	2	1	......
Mar. 8.................	5	10	.....do.....	6	(²)	1	3	0	......
Total...............	5	44		23	......	5	12	4	48
1919.									
June 17................	10	3	Individual, in very small cages.	2	(²)	1	0	0	......
1920.									
Jan. 27................	10	10	Group, in very large cages.	0	5	4	1	0	......
May 5.................	10	10	.....do.....	5	(²)	1	1	3	......
Total...............	10	23		7	......	11	2	3	70
1920.									
Jan. 27................	20	15	Group, in very large cages.	0	13	2	0	0	......
Feb. 1.................	20	11	Individual, in very large cages.	1	(²)	5	3	2	......
Total...............	20	26		1	......	20	3	2	96

¹ Fed at night.   ² No observation made.

About 50 per cent of the rats succumbed when fed 5 per cent barium carbonate. Most of the fatalities occurred after the twenty-fourth hour. On a diet containing 10 per cent, about 70 per cent of the rats died, the majority succumbing within the first 24 hours. Twenty per cent barium carbonate was even more efficient, only 5 per cent surviving and a great majority of fatalities occurring within the first 16 hours.

As already stated, the average food intake at a meal for the average hungry rat is one one-hundredth of the body weight, and from 630 to 750 mg. of barium carbonate per kilo may be regarded as the fairly certain fatal dose. When 5 per cent barium carbonate is fed in the bait it would be necessary for all rats to eat 12.5 to 15 grams per kilo, or one-eightieth to one sixth-seventh of their body weight. Some of the rats will do this and die, and a few of those which eat slightly less will succumb. This explains why about 50 per cent of the rats which were fed this diet died. When a 10 per cent barium carbonate bait is fed, a rat must eat one one-hundred-and-sixtieth to one one-hundred-and-thirty-third of its body weight, or 63 to 75 per cent of a meal of average size. A 70 per cent mortality on this concentration is then readily comprehensible. In case of 20 per cent barium carbonate in the bait, it is necessary for the rats to consume only one three-hundred-and-twentieth to one two-hundred-and-sixty-sixth of their body weight, or 31 to 37 per cent of the average food intake, in order to ingest a lethal dose of barium carbonate. As a few will fail to do this and many eat much more, this concentration is efficient, as well as quickly fatal.

RESULTS OF EXPERIMENTAL WORK ON OTHER BARIUM COMPOUNDS.

Barium chromate was found to be nontoxic in doses as high as 2,000 mg. per kilo.

Barium soap, chiefly palmitate, was fairly toxic. Although not enough experiments were performed to definitely fix the lethal dose, it would seem to be approximately equal to that of barium carbonate. Its ease of hydrolysis apparently would favor the mobilization of the barium, upon which basis it would be more desirable than the carbonate. This fact, however, precludes its use in rat bait, since the hydrolysis occurring from a small amount of moisture would impart a disagreeable taste.

TOXICITY OF BARIUM CARBONATE TO ANIMALS OTHER THAN RATS.

Apparently rats are about as susceptible to barium administered subcutaneously as rabbits, chickens, and pigeons, and approximately one-third as sensitive as cats and dogs. When the barium is administered by mouth, however, the rat is comparatively the least susceptible of all the mammals cited, although the absolute amount is less, because of the small size of the rat.

If 20 per cent barium carbonate is used, it will be possible, on the basis of the recorded doses of barium chlorid, for adult animals to eat without fatal effects the following amounts of this rat bait: Sheep, one-half ounce; horses, 1½ ounces; and cattle, 5 ounces. Presumably, one and a half times this amount could be borne, since barium carbonate is less toxic than the soluble chlorid. The lethal dose of barium carbonate for chickens (20) is 20 grains, or one-fifth ounce, of rat bait containing 20 per cent of this poison. The danger to man, particularly children, is so very great that an amount of bait set for one or two rats might prove fatal.

CONCLUSIONS.

The lethal dose of barium compounds for rats is as follows: Barium chlorid, subcutaneously, 45 to 89 mg. per kilo; barium chlorid, by stomach tube, 350 to 535 mg. per kilo; barium carbonate, per os, 630 to 750 mg. per kilo. On the basis of the barium content, the carbonate is about two-thirds as active as the chlorid per os.

ınt concentration.   With this percentage a rat is ro
  one-third or three-eighths of a meal of average ؛
undred-and-twentieth to one two-hundred-and-sixt
veight, in order to secure the ingestion of a lethal a
concentration, many of the rats die within the ؛
chief factor being the consumption of an amount
inimum efficient lethal dose.

e results of both the pharmacological and the
ould not seem advisable to always expect 100 p
'rom the administration of barium carbonate, in
o rats.

BIBLIOGRAPHY.

, and COURNET, A.
ıerches toxicologiques sur le chlorure de baryum.   J. pharm
)18), *17:* 76.
N MEDICAL ASSOCIATION.
t. Council Pharm. Chem.   Council Reports (1911): 53.
.LEXANDER.
räge zur Baryumwirkung.   Inaugural Dissertation.   Dorpat, 1
t, W. R.
t problem, p. 121.   London, 1909.
  HUGO.
ährte Mittel gegen Feldmäuse.   Deut Landw. Presse (1878)
hresb. Agr. Chem. (1878) *1:* 347.
RD, ALBERT C.
um, a cause of the loco-weed disease.   U. S. Dept. Agr., B. P
9 (1908).
:HOFF, W.
er die Wirkung des Chlorbaryum bei Pferden, Rindern und
arl. tierärztl. Wochschrift.   (1895): 265.
:, G.
er Baryum-Vergiftungen u. deren Einfluss auf d. Glykogeng
eber.   Diss. Schotten (Hessen), 1896.
D. E.
  house rat: The most destructive animal in the world.   U.
ır. Yearbook (1917): 235.
, E.
ıtion des doses minima mortelles, toxiques et thérapeutiques, de
a baryum donné par la voie sous-cutanée a la grenouille, au
ı lapin.   Compt. rend. soc. biol. (1912), *72:* 182.

uence de la voie d'administration sur les doses minima mortel
s doses thérapeutiques de chlorure de baryum.   Compt. rend.
912), *72:* 250.

l'influence de la voie d'administration sur la production de la
ır le chlorure de baryum.   Compt. rend. soc. biol. (1912), *72:*

(13) MAUREL, E.
Nouvelles recherches sur la dose minima mortelle de chlorure de baryum donné au lapin par la voie hypodermique. Compt. rend. soc. biol. (1912), *72:* 360.

(14) PILLIET, A., and MALBEC, A.
Note sur les lesions histologiques du rein produites par les sels de baryte sur les animaux. Compt. rend. soc. biol. (1892), *44:* 957.

(15) RAEBIGER.
Maßznahmen zur Bekämpfung der Ratten, Mäuse und Schneckenplage. Berlin, 1907.

(16) REYNOLDS, M. H.
A study of certain cathartics. Univ. Minn. Agr. Exp. Sta. 15th Ann. Rept. (1907): xxi.

(17) SCHEDEL, H.
Beiträge zur Wirkung des Chlorbariums, besonders als Herzmittel. Mit einem Vortwort von R. Kobert. Diss. Stuttgart, 1903.

(18) STERN, E.
Vergiftung mit Chlorbaryum. Zeit. Medizinalbeamte (1896), *9:* 381.

(19) STORER, F. H.
Experiments on feeding mice with painter's-putty and with other mixtures of pigments and oil. Bull. Bussey Inst. (1884), *2*, pt. iv: 264.

(20) WHITE, F. NORMAN.
Rat destruction. British Med. J. (Nov. 15, 1919): 629.

UNITED STATES DEPARTMENT OF AGRICULTURE

BULLETIN No. 916

Contribution from the Bureau of Plant Industry
WM. A. TAYLOR, Chief

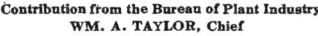

Washington, D. C. PROFESSIONAL PAPER June 13, 1921

FREEZING INJURY TO POTATOES WHEN UNDERCOOLED.[1]

By R. C. WRIGHT, *Physiologist*, and GEORGE F. TAYLOR, *Chemical Laboratorian*,
Office of Horticultural and Pomological Investigations.

CONTENTS.

	Page.		Page.
Scope of the investigations	1	Inoculation of undercooled potatoes	7
Physiology of the freezing process	2	Summary	14
Plan of the work	4	Literature cited	15

SCOPE OF THE INVESTIGATIONS.

Each year the loss to growers, shippers, and carriers of potatoes due to freezing reaches an enormous figure. This is particularly true of the late or main crop produced in the Northern States. This crop is usually in constant danger of exposure to freezing temperature from just before it is harvested until it reaches the consumer. There are two general classes of frost-injured potatoes—those frozen solid and subject to collapse immediately on thawing and those that show evidence of injury only on being cut open a few hours after being warmed. The first class of injured potatoes is easily identified by the soft, wet condition that develops on thawing. This type of injury is due to the potato being subjected to freezing at very low temperatures or to prolonged exposure at higher freezing temperatures. The second type of injury is not apparent on superficial examination. It is due to exposure to temperatures just below the freezing point or to a very low temperature for a short time. If after the potato has been thawed a few hours it is cut open, evidences of this type of freezing injury are apparent by the presence of vascular discoloration of three types or a combination of any of the three.

[1] This bulletin gives the results of a portion of the work carried on under the project " Factors affecting the storage life of vegetables."

11310°—21

PHYSIOLOGY OF THE FREEZING PROCESS.

The frost necrosis of potato tubers is described by Jones, Miller, and Bailey (4)[2] as being characterized by three types, viz, ring, net, and blotch. In the ring type only the vascular ring, an area near the surface, is discolored. In the net type threadlike areas radiating from the center are discolored. The third type is marked by irregular blotched areas. Ordinarily no further change takes place after the injured potato thaws, although in the most severe cases the tubers soon begin to break-down if kept warm.

Frost injury seems to be the result of actual ice formation within the potato tissue. Abbe (1), in his investigations of the effect of freezing upon plant tissue, considers that as the tissue cools water exudes from the cells into the intercellular spaces. After sufficient undercooling this water freezes. The concentrated sap remaining in the cells will not freeze until cooled below the freezing point of water. On thawing, this intercellular water escapes by transpiration and the plant wilts. Göppert (3) and Sachs (6) both observed the presence of ice within the cells and the intercellular spaces of plant tissue. However, Sachs found crystals of ice usually present in the intercellular spaces. Müller-Thurgau (5) was one of the first to publish (1880) upon frost injury of potatoes in his investigations upon the freezing point of plant tissue. The phenomena of undercooling were investigated by him to a considerable extent. He showed that plant tissue required undercooling below the true freezing point before actual freezing commences. He also showed that the expressed sap of the potato tuber freezes at a higher temperature than the living tissue. The ultimate freezing point of potatoes is placed at 30.21° F. by Müller-Thurgau and between 28° and 26° F. by Appleman (2). Vaughan and Miller (7) state that "actual freezing does not begin in potatoes until the temperature drops below 28° F." Jones, Miller, and Bailey (4) place the freezing point at 28.4° F.

The author of an unsigned article in the Potato Magazine (8) states that exposure at 30° F. for 9 or 10 hours or at 16° F. for 1 hour will develop signs of frost necrosis. In results published by Wright and Harvey (9) the freezing point varied from 29.67° to 28.13° F. according to variety and season. In this investigation the freezing points of 18 different varieties were determined. The freezing points varied in different varieties and according to family groups. The early and medium-early potatoes froze at a higher point than the purely late varieties. The subject of undercooling was discussed. It was stated that potatoes, since their sap consists of salts, sugar, and other soluble material, freeze at a lower temperature than pure water.

---

[2] The serial numbers in parentheses refer to "Literature cited" at the end of this bulletin.

It was shown that potatoes could be undercooled several degrees below the true freezing point without actual freezing taking place. In addition, it was shown that when once cooled below the true freezing point the process of undercooling can be terminated at any point by inoculating the tuber. The term "inoculation"[3] is used in this connection to indicate any disturbance which will start crystallization or ice formation. Following inoculation the temperature of the potato rises quickly to the true freezing point, accompanied by the formation of ice within the tissue. Inoculation is caused by some mechanical disturbance, such as a jolt or jar sufficient to cause freezing to commence. It is a well-known fact that water, for example, can be undercooled below its freezing point. After a certain amount of undercooling actual freezing will result from any slight disturbance or by the addition of a crystal of ice.

In the potato, inoculation is readily accomplished by striking or jarring the undercooled tuber. The degree of force necessary to accomplish this is determined by the extent of undercooling. It seems that a potato can be undercooled to such a point that the slightest perceptible jar will instantly inoculate it. Water on the surface or sap from a bruise will prevent a potato from reaching the degree of undercooling it would attain if dry, since this free moisture will freeze at a higher temperature than the living tissue and will in this way inoculate the entire potato. Müller-Thurgau (5) and Jones, Miller, and Bailey (4) found that a freshly cut potato will freeze more quickly; that is, it will not undercool as far as a dry potato.

Müller-Thurgau was of the opinion that the undercooling point varies with the air temperature to which potatoes are exposed. He attempted to justify this view by data. In one instance freezing occurred in two hours at an exposure of 23.9° F. and in another in five hours at an exposure varying from 15.8° to 10.7° F. Jones and his colleagues (4), commenting on these results, state that possibly the earlier freezing at the higher undercooling temperature was due to a more rapid fall in temperature in this case. Data submitted by them and also in Department Bulletin 895, heretofore cited (9), indicate that the degree of undercooling is dependent for one thing upon the rate of fall of temperature. It is also entirely possible that a sudden unnoticed jar might have caused earlier freezing where the undercooling temperature was higher. In Department Bulletin 895 (9, p. 6) a diagram is presented in which results are illustrated when two potatoes were exposed to different temperatures. One potato ex-

---

[3] It is considered that the term "inoculation" is rightly used here, as it is directly comparable to the process in physical chemistry, known by the same term, in which crystallization is started in a concentrated solution by adding a crystal of the solute or when freezing is started by adding a crystal of ice to pure water that has been undercooled.

posed to a temperature of 8.7° froze in 6 minutes when the actual internal temperature had reached 23° F. The other potato was exposed to 15.8° and froze in 12.5 minutes when the internal temperature had reached 20.2° F. The actual freezing point of both potatoes was 29.15° F. This substantiates the results obtained by Jones, Miller, and Bailey (4). They cite an instance of a tuber freezing in 80 minutes when undercooled to 24.44°, while another exposed to a slowly diminishing temperature did not freeze until 13.1° F. was reached. Another specimen froze in 40 minutes when undercooled to 26.4° while exposed to a rapidly diminishing temperature which had reached 12.2° F. They state that, in general, potatoes do not freeze until exposed to 26.6° F. or lower. To judge from the results submitted in this report it is possibly safe to state that except in the case of accidental inoculation the degree of undercooling at which freezing occurs depends upon the variety, the rapidity with which undercooling progresses, and the length of exposure to a given degree of undercooling.

PLAN OF THE WORK.

In order to apply to the handling of potatoes the knowledge of the process of undercooling and freezing already gained, a series of experiments was conducted at the Arlington cold-storage plant of the Bureau of Plant Industry. It has been noted by potato growers and shippers that sometimes one lot of potatoes while being handled or otherwise disturbed in transit will freeze when another left undisturbed at the same temperature remained uninjured. Some apple handlers are very careful not to jar or jolt frosted apples, because they say it will cause them to bruise and rot. It is a practice among some onion growers to store their onions through very severe winter weather in mows or buildings between layers of hay where they are undisturbed during the winter. These persons will often guard against loose doors or shutters which can be slammed by the wind, as this is liable to cause the onions to freeze and subsequently to rot. Numerous instances are reported where potatoes have been exposed for hours or even days to temperatures below their freezing point without injury. Müller-Thurgau reported having stored potatoes at 32° to 26.6° F. for two weeks without injury. Of course, internal frost injury may have been present without its being detected unless the potatoes were cut open and examined.

In the present work seven standard varieties of potatoes, all true to name and grown under the same conditions by the Bureau of Plant Industry at the Aroostook Farm of the Maine Agricultural Experiment Station, were used. These varieties were the Triumph, Irish Cobbler, Spaulding No. 4, American Giant, Rural New Yorker,

Russet Rural, and Green Mountain. They were all held at 40° F. previous to experimental use.

Storage tests on the seven varieties held at temperatures below the true freezing points were conducted in order to correlate, if possible, the freezing points (Table I) of these varieties as determined by the thermoelectric method described by Wright and Harvey (9) and the actual freezing of the different varieties in storage. These tests were conducted at 28° and 25° F. The higher temperature was chosen because it represented about the minimum degree of undercooling to which the potatoes could be subjected, since it was just below the freezing points of most of the varieties used. The lower temperature was chosen because it was far enough below the freezing points of all varieties to represent a definite degree of undercooling at which freezing quickly follows a very light inoculation. When the potatoes were selected for the freezing tests they were placed in small wooden baskets holding from 8 to 10 specimens, in order that they might cool down without much delay. At the conclusion of each test the potatoes were removed, to be held at ordinary room temperature for about 24 hours before being cut longitudinally for examination. If cut immediately after being removed from storage, no evidence of freezing injury will be apparent unless they have been frozen solid. Unless specially noted, all injury reported is of the vascular type, as described by Jones, Miller, and Bailey.

TABLE I.—*Freezing points of seven varieties of potatoes.*

Variety.	Freezing point.	Variety.	Freezing point.
	°F.		°F.
Triumph	29.04	Rural New Yorker	28.70
Irish Cobbler	29.66	Russet Rural	28.32
Spaulding No. 4	29.33	Green Mountain	28.50
American Giant	29.64		

Tables II and III show the results obtained from these tests at 28° and 25° F. The data presented in Table II show that potatoes did not freeze to any serious extent when exposed to 28° F. for many hours. In experiment No. 1 two specimens of each variety were held seven hours, one specimen of Rural New Yorker being injured. In experiment No. 2 twenty specimens of each variety were held 24 hours. Only two varieties showed injury. These included two specimens of Irish Cobbler and one specimen of the American Giant. In the third experiment two specimens of each variety were held 48 hours, one Rural New Yorker being injured. In experiment No. 4 half-bushel lots of Triumph, Spaulding No. 4, American Giant, and Russet Rural varieties were held in bags for 48 hours with no injury. In experiment No. 5 eleven specimens of each variety were held for 70 hours.

Serious injury was apparent in this experiment. Injury occurred to five specimens of Triumph, six of Irish Cobbler, five of Spaulding No. 4, four of American Giant, one of Rural New Yorker, two of Russet Rural, and one of Green Mountain. The most serious injury occurred in the early-maturing varieties. In experiment No. 6 six tubers of each variety were held 96 hours, with injury occurring to two specimens of Triumph, two of Irish Cobbler, two of American Giant, and one of Russet Rural. The Spaulding No. 4, Rural New Yorker, and Green Mountain varieties suffered no injury. The aggregate injury in this experiment was 17 per cent, while in experiment No. 5 the injury totaled 31 per cent.

TABLE II.—*Freezing injury to seven varieties of potatoes held at 28° F. for different lengths of time.*

Variety.	Number of experiment and duration of exposure.											
	No. 1, 7 hours.		No. 2, 24 hours.		No. 3, 48 hours.		No. 4, 48 hours.		No. 5, 70 hours.		No. 6, 96 hours.	
	Number of specimens.	Number injured.	Number of specimens.	Number injured.	Number of specimens.	Number injured.	Quantity of specimens.	Number injured.	Number of specimens.	Number injured.	Number of specimens.	Number injured.
Triumph	2	0	20	0	2	0	*Bush.* ½	0	11	5	6	2
Irish Cobbler	2	0	20	2	2	0			11	6	6	2
Spaulding No. 4	2	0	20	0	2	0	⅛	0	11	5	6	0
American Giant	2	0	20	1	2	0	⅛	0	11	4	6	2
Rural New Yorker	2	1	20	0	2	1			11	1	6	0
Russet Rural	2	0	20	0	2	0	⅛	0	11	2	6	1
Green Mountain	2	0	20	0	2	0			11	1	6	0
Total	14	1	140	3	14	1	2	0	77	24	42	7

In no case at 28° F. were the potatoes frozen solid. A superficial examination would not have revealed any evidence of freezing injury in any of these varieties. It is true that during subsequent storage, however, these internally injured specimens are the first to break down, although these potatoes do not show injury so far as their external appearance is concerned and would be as salable in the ordinary market as the uninjured ones. After a few days at ordinary room temperature they are quite unfit for food. While no serious injury occurred till the potatoes were held at least 70 hours, isolated cases of freezing injury did occur even when potatoes were held only 7 hours. It is difficult to explain these isolated cases. For some unknown reason certain individuals seem to bear much less undercooling than others of the same variety. Similarly, certain varieties bear less undercooling than other varieties. There is a certain varietal difference shown here. The Irish Cobblers seem to be the first to succumb to freezing injury, followed by the Triumph, American Giant, Spaulding No. 4, and Russet Rural varieties. The Rural New Yorker and Green Mountain varieties are the most resistant.

TABLE III.—*Freezing injury to seven varieties of potatoes held at 25° F. for different lengths of time.*

Variety.	Number of experiment and duration of exposure.							
	No. 1, 5 hours.		No. 2, 19 hours.		No. 3, 24 hours.		No. 4, 43 hours.	
	Number of specimens.	Number injured.	Number of specimens.	Number injured.	Number of specimens.	Number injured.	Number of specimens.	Number injured.
Triumph	2	0	6	0	11	5	3	a 1
Irish Cobbler	2	0	6	2	11	6	3	a 2
Spaulding No. 4	2	0	6	0	11	8	3	1
American Giant	2	0	6	2	11	6	3	3
Rural New Yorker	2	0	6	1	11	5	3	0
Russet Rural	2	0	6	1	11	2	3	b 3
Green Mountain	2	0	6	1	11	4	3	1
Total	14	0	42	7	77	36	21	11

a Frozen solid.   b Two were frozen solid.

In Table III are shown the results obtained when the different varieties were held at 25° F. In experiment No. 1 two specimens of each variety were held 5 hours with no evidence of injury. In experiment No. 2 six specimens of each variety were stored 19 hours, with injury to two Irish Cobblers, two American Giants, one Rural New Yorker, one Russet Rural, and one Green Mountain. It is worthy of note that the Triumph and Spaulding No. 4 varieties, which according to Table I have a comparatively high freezing point, did not show injury in this experiment. In experiment No. 3 eleven specimens of each were held 24 hours, with serious consequences to most of the varieties. Injury was found in five Triumphs, six Irish Cobblers, eight Spaulding No. 4, six American Giants, five Rural New Yorkers, two Russet Rurals, and four Green Mountains. The total injury was 47 per cent. In experiment No. 4 three tubers of each variety were held 43 hours, with injury to one Triumph, two Irish Cobblers, one Spaulding No. 4, three American Giants, three Russet Rurals, and one Green Mountain. Tubers of the Rural New Yorker were not injured; one specimen of Triumph, one of Irish Cobbler, and two of the Russet Rural varieties were frozen solid. The total injury in this experiment was 52 per cent.

Generally speaking, when potatoes of the seven varieties were held for varying lengths of time at 28° or 25° F. they did not freeze in any definite order or with relation to their freezing points. At 28° F. the early-maturing varieties with the higher freezing points possibly showed more freezing injury.

INOCULATION OF UNDERCOOLED POTATOES.

Attention is called to the fact that in the experiments just described the potatoes were purposely held entirely undisturbed, as it had been found that potatoes when undercooled are liable to freeze when jarred.   It is considered highly important to call the attention of growers and shippers to this point, since under some circumstances it would be entirely possible that a lot of potatoes or even other products might be undercooled considerably below the freezing point and escape injury if they remained undisturbed till their temperature was above the freezing point.   If it should be found necessary to move such a lot in order to protect them from further lowering of the temperature, this should be very carefully done, having in mind the danger of freezing as the result of jarring or jolting.   These statements seem justified and are supported by the results brought out by the following experiments, which were conducted to determine the amount and character of the disturbance necessary to cause freezing when different varieties of potatoes are held at temperatures between 28° and 25° F.   The same seven standard varieties before named were used in these experiments.

EXPERIMENT NO. 1.

Duplicate lots of potatoes, consisting of a single specimen of each variety, were held between 26° and 27° F. for 5½ hours.   Then each specimen in one lot was dropped from a distance of 4 feet to the concrete floor.   After 17 hours from the time they were dropped, both lots were removed and held at ordinary room temperature several hours before they were cut open.   In the check lot only the Irish Cobbler and the American Giant were injured.   All specimens in the treated lot were not only badly bruised, as might be expected from the rough treatment, but they were all frost injured, as was shown by extensive blackened vascular areas of the blotch type. (Pl. I.)   None of the potatoes were frozen hard enough to cause collapse of the tissues.

EXPERIMENT NO. 2.

Duplicate lots of one potato of each variety were held at 28° F. for 22 hours.   One lot was then dropped as before and left for three hours.   Both lots were then removed.   As before, at the lower temperature all the dropped potatoes were bruised and showed extreme freezing injury.   In the undisturbed check lot only the Irish Cobbler was injured.

EXPERIMENT NO. 3.

Duplicate lots of one potato of each variety were placed at 28° F. for 24 hours.   Each specimen from one lot was dropped from a distance of 2 feet, and after another 24 hours all were removed.   On the usual examination it was found that these potatoes were badly bruised and showed extensive injury, as before, except the American Giant and Spaulding No. 4 varieties, which showed no frost injury and were not bruised.

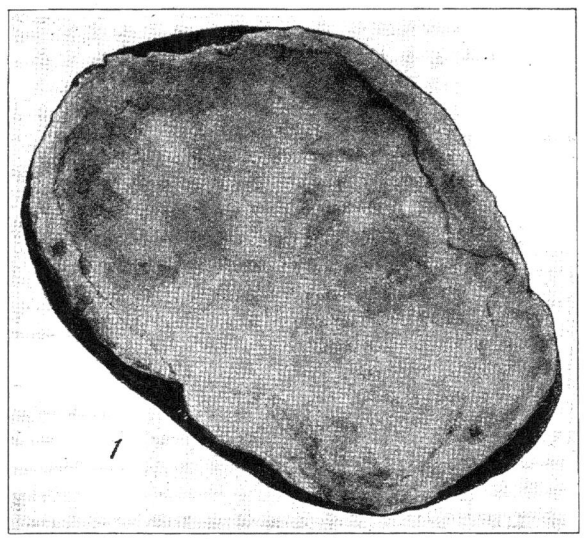

FREEZING INJURY TO POTATOES ARTIFICIALLY PRODUCED.

The potatoes were undercooled at 25° F. for 24 hours, then inoculated by dropping 6 inches. In one hour after inoculation they were removed to a warm room. One specimen (Irish Cobbler, fig. 1) shows only slight freezing injury of the ring type. The other specimen (American Giant, fig. 2) shows severe injury of the ring and blotch type.

EXPERIMENT NO. 4.

Duplicate lots of two potatoes of each variety were held at 28° F. for 24 hours, after which all of one lot were dropped 1 foot. After another 24 hours all were removed. Examination showed no bruising; however, most of the potatoes were frozen. The results are shown in Table IV.

TABLE IV.—*Freezing injury to potatoes of seven different varieties undercooled at 28° F. and dropped 1 foot.*

Variety.	Dropped.		Check.	
	Injured.	Uninjured.	Injured.	Uninjured.
Triumph	2	0	0	2
Irish Cobbler	2	0	0	2
Spaulding No. 4	0	2	0	2
American Giant	2	0	0	2
Rura. New Yorker	2	0	1	1
Russet Rural	2	0	0	2
Green Mountain	0	2	0	2
Total	10	4	1	13

EXPERIMENT NO. 5.

A total of 24 potatoes of the Rural New Yorker variety were placed at 28° F. After 24 hours 12 were dropped 12 inches. In no case was a potato bruised or even the skin broken. In 4 hours both lots were removed. Examination showed all of the lot that was dropped to be injured by freezing. None of the check lot was injured.

EXPERIMENT NO. 6.

This experiment was conducted to ascertain, if possible, the minimum distance from which an undercooled potato may fall and still succumb to freezing injury. Five lots of 12 potatoes of the Rural New Yorker variety were held at 28° F. for 18 hours. Then lots were dropped 2, 4, and 6 inches, and in one lot each individual was struck with a pencil. After seven hours all were removed. Examination showed that only the potatoes that were struck with the pencil were injured.

EXPERIMENT NO. 7.

Lots of three potatoes of each variety were dropped, as in experiment No. 6, with the exception that each potato was dropped six times instead of once. The results are shown in Table V. Practically the same amount of freezing injury was produced in all dropped potatoes without relation to the length of the fall. The injury produced was of the blotch type. It may be stated here that the potatoes used in this experiment were purposely selected and weighed, so as to have both large and small specimens in each lot, thus varying the force of the blow caused by the fall. There was apparently no relation between the weight of the potato and the freezing injury. In addition to the lots already described in this experiment, an additional lot of two of each variety was treated by striking each potato sharply with a pencil once, with the results shown in Table V. It is difficult to state why it was necessary to drop the potatoes several times from 2, 4, and 6 inch heights to produce frost injury, while one sharp blow with an ordinary pencil results in serious injury. The possible explanation is that the blow from the pencil caused a more violent concussion in a smaller area, from which the whole potato was inoculated.

TABLE V.—*Freezing injury to potatoes of seven different varieties undercooled at 28° F. and inoculated in different ways.*

Variety.	Dropped 2 inches.		Dropped 4 inches.		Dropped 6 inches.		Struck with pencil.		Check.	
	In-jured.	Unin-jured.	In-jured.	Unin-jured.	In-jured.	Unin-jured.	In-jured.	Unin-jured.	In-jured.	Unin-jured.
Triumph...........	3	0	3	0	3	0	1	1	0	3
Irish Cobbler.......	3	0	3	0	3	0	1	1	0	3
Spaulding No. 4.....	1	2	3	0	2	1	1	1	0	3
American Giant.....	3	0	3	0	3	0	2	0	1	2
Rural New Yorker..	3	0	3	0	3	0	2	0	0	3
Russet Rural........	3	0	3	0	2	1	2	0	0	3
Green Mountain....	3	0	2	1	2	1	2	0	1	2
Total.........	19	2	20	1	18	3	11	3	2	19

EXPERIMENT NO. 8.

Two lots of one specimen of each variety of potato were held at 28° F. for 24 hours, after which each potato of one lot was repeatedly bounced on the floor for about 10 seconds by dropping it from a height of not over 1 inch. After another 24-hour period all were removed. While none of the bounced specimens showed bruising or mechanical injury, they were all frost injured. The specimens of American Giant and Green Mountain froze solid, with resultant complete collapse on thawing. Of the check lot the Spaulding No. 4 and the Green Mountain varieties showed slight freezing injury.

EXPERIMENT NO. 9.

Lots of three potatoes of each variety were held at 25° F. for 18 hours, after which they were dropped once from distances of 6, 4, and 2 inches. After another hour all were removed. Examination showed that all dropped potatoes were injured, while in the check lot frost injury resulted to only one each of the Irish Cobbler, American Giant, Russet Rural, and Green Mountain varieties.

Several experiments were conducted to test the rate at which the temperature of a potato will fall when exposed to a temperature below its freezing point. Figure 1 illustrates a typical set of results.

A Triumph potato was suspended in a metal container 18 inches long by 4 inches in diameter, which was in turn immersed in a brine tank. Thermoelectric couples were located at the center and near the surface of the potato; also one was suspended in the air 1 inch from the potato. Periodical readings were made from the time the temperature of the potato was near 40° F. The temperature of the atmosphere surrounding the potato gradually fell from 27.2° to 25.6° F. The temperature of the potato at the beginning was 40.8° at the surface

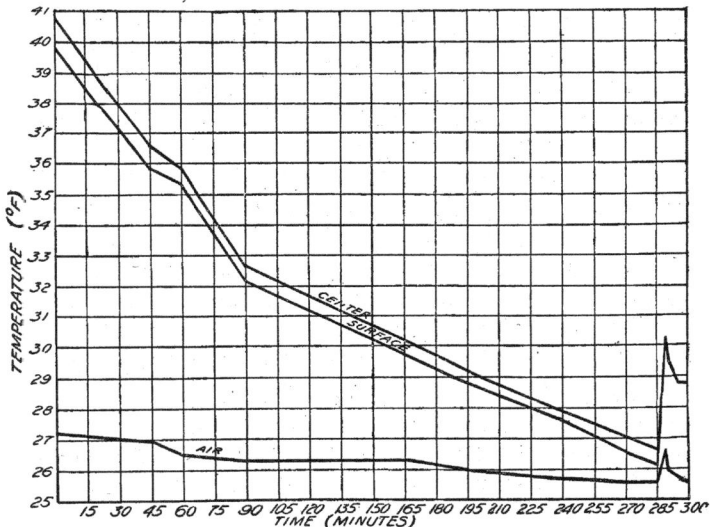

Fig. 1.—Temperatures at the center and near the surface of a Triumph potato as it undercooled to between 26° and 27° F. At this point it was inoculated by tapping it sharply with a pencil. As the potato froze, the temperature rose. When all the heat was liberated, the temperature of the potato reached 28.7° F. and remained several minutes. The temperature of the air bath to which the potato was exposed is also shown. Note the accompanying rise in the temperature of the surrounding air as the potato froze and liberated heat.

and 39.9° F. at the center. The difference in temperature at the surface and center gradually diminished until at 240 minutes there was a difference of only 0.4 of a degree. After this the difference became somewhat greater. In 285 minutes the temperature fell from 40.8° and 39.9° F. at the surface and center, respectively, to 26.7° and 26.2° F. At this point the potato was tapped sharply with a pencil, and freezing commenced. The temperature at both points began to rise as heat was liberated, due to crystallization of the water. In five minutes the temperature at the center rose to 30.2° F., and at the surface to 29.5° F. In 10 minutes the temperature at both points was practically the same, 28.7° F. This represents the freezing point.

The temperature of the air surrounding the potato at the time freezing took place rose from 25.6° to 26.6° F., due to heat liberated by the potato.

SUMMARY OF RESULTS OBTAINED BY DROPPING UNDERCOOLED POTATOES.

When undercooled at 28° F. and dropped 4 feet and 2 feet, the potatoes were severely bruised and showed extreme freezing injury of the vascular type. When dropped 1 foot, no bruising resulted, but all varieties froze except the Green Mountain and Spaulding No. 4. The type of injury was a faint blotch. When dropped 6, 4, and 2 inches once, no freezing injury resulted; but when dropped six times from these heights, severe injury followed. When bounced several times by dropping 1 inch, severe injury followed; in some cases the potatoes were frozen solid. When undercooled at 25° F., dropping once from 6, 4, and 2 inches caused injury.

Some further experiments were undertaken to determine what other forms of disturbances will inoculate undercooled potatoes. Duplicate lots of 12 specimens each of the Rural New Yorker variety were placed at 25° and 28° F. for 24 hours. At each temperature one lot was placed in the direct draft from an electric fan, while the other lot was protected from the draft to act as a check. At 25° F. 10 of the 12 potatoes in the draft showed injury; also 3 of the check lot were injured. At 28° F. no injury was found in either lot. A possible explanation for the fact that the potatoes froze when exposed at 25° F. to a strong current of air is that they undercooled much more rapidly than the lot not in the draft.

Two lots of six specimens each of Rural New Yorker were held at 28° F. for 24 hours, then wet and removed after another 24 hours. All of the lot that were wet were injured, while three of the lot that were not wet also were injured. In the next experiment two lots consisting of two of each variety were held at 28° F. for 24 hours; they were then wet and held for another 24 hours. The results obtained on examination are shown in Table VI.

TABLE VI.—*Freezing injury to potatoes of seven different varieties held at 28° F. for 24 hours and then wet while undercooled.*

Variety.	Wet.		Check.	
	Injured.	Uninjured.	Injured.	Uninjured.
Triumph	2	(a)	0	2
Irish Cobbler	2	0	0	2
Spaulding No. 4	0	2	0	2
American Giant	1	1	0	2
Rural New Yorker	2	0	1	1
Russet Rural	2	0	0	2
Green Mountain	1	1	0	2
Total	10	4	1	13

a Faint blotch.

The injury to these potatoes was not serious. All affected ones showed only a faint blotching. In the next experiment a mixed lot of 12 potatoes was held at 28° F. for 72 hours while supporting a 100-pound bag of sand. No evidence of injury was apparent.

An attempt was made to show that potatoes when undercooled are liable to be injured by ordinary handling. Duplicate half-bushel lots of potatoes representing four varieties, viz, Triumph, Russet. Rural, Spaulding No. 4, and American Giant, were put together in four bags and held at 28° F. for 24 hours. Then one lot of two bags was rolled across the floor for a distance of about 30 feet. After 24 hours all were removed. Examination showed the results presented in Table VII.

TABLE VII.—*Freezing injury to potatoes of four different varieties held at 28° F. for 24 hours and then rolled 30 feet in a bag while undercooled.*

Variety.	Rolled.	Check.
	Per cent injured.	*Per cent injured.*
Triumph	10	0
Spaulding No. 4	0	0
American Giant	20	0
Russet Rural	50	0

A similar experiment was carried out in which two lots of 12 of each of the seven varieties were placed in two bags and held at 28° F. for 24 hours. One was then rolled about 50 feet. After another period of 24 hours all were removed and held for examination. The results obtained are shown in Table VIII.

TABLE VIII.—*Freezing injury to potatoes of seven different varieties held at 28° F. for 24 hours and then rolled 50 feet in a bag while undercooled.*

Variety.	Rolled.		Check.	
	Number injured.	Number uninjured.	Number injured.	Number uninjured.
Triumph	5	7	0	12
Irish Cobbler	12	0	0	12
Spaulding No. 4	0	12	0	12
American Giant	2	10	0	12
Rural New Yorker	12	0	0	12
Russet Rural	8	4	0	12
Green Mountain	7	5	0	12
Total	46	38	0	84

A distinct varietal difference is shown here. In neither experiment did the Spaulding No. 4 variety show injury. The American Giant was also less susceptible than the rest of the varieties. The Irish Cobbler, Rural New Yorker, and Russet Rural showed the greatest percentage of injury. In these experiments the potatoes did not receive the amount of jolting or rough handling that they might be

:reeze more quickly when exposed to a rapidly dimin-
ure than when the temperature diminishes slowly.
can be undercooled several degrees below their true
nd then warmed again above the freezing point with-
ury, provided no ice formation takes place within

dercooled, jarring resulting from rough handling or
uling is liable to cause potatoes to freeze.
lercooled in a temperature of 28° F., dropping from a
caused potatoes to bruise badly and to show exten-
ury. When dropped 1 foot they did not bruise, but
ury. When dropped 6, 4, or 2 inches once no injury
ien dropped six times frost injury followed. When
resulted. Potatoes supporting a 100-pound weight
1.
dercooled at 28° F. and rolled across the floor for a
it 50 feet in bags freezing injury resulted.
idercooled at 25° F. and dropped 6, 4, and 2 inches
y was apparent.
ezing commences it is progressive. The amount of
vithin a stated time seems to depend upon the sur-
rature.
ely after inoculation the temperature of the potato
freezing point and remains for a varying length of
upon the surrounding temperature.
rieties apparently are inoculated more easily than
ugh their freezing point is higher.

LITERATURE CITED.

(1) ABBE, C.
    1894. The influence of cold on plants. A résumé. *In* Exp. Sta. Record, v. 6, no. 9, p. 777–781.

(2) APPLEMAN, CHARLES O.
    1912. Changes in Irish potatoes during storage. Md. Agr. Exp. Sta. Bul. 167' p. 327–334.

(3) GÖPPERT, H. R.
    1830. Ueber die Wärme-Entwickelung in den Pflanzen, deren Gefrieren und die Schutzmittel gegen dasselbe. xiv, 272 p. Breslau.

(4) JONES, L. R., MILLER, M., and BAILEY, E.
    1919. Frost necrosis of potato tubers. Wis. Agr. Exp. Sta. Research Bul. 46, 46 p., illus. Literature cited, p. 45–46.

(5) MÜLLER, HERMAN, *Thurgau.*
    1880–86. Ueber das Gefrieren und Erfrieren der Pflanzen. *In* Landw. Jahrb., Bd. 9, p. 133–189, 1880; Bd. 15, p. 453–610, 1886.

(6) SACHS, JULIUS.
    1860. Krystallbildungen bei dem Gefrieren und Veränderungen der Zellhäute bei dem Aufthauen saftiger Pflanzentheile. *In* Ber. Verhandl. Sächs. Gesell. Wiss. Leipzig, Math.-Phys. Cl., Bd. 12, p. 1–50.

(7) VAUGHAN, R. E., and MILLER, M.
    1919. Freezing injuries to potato tubers. Wis. Agr. Col. Ext. Serv. Circ. 120, 4 p., 3 fig.

(8) Watch potatoes in storage and transit. *In* Potato Mag., v. 2, no. 7, p. 16. 1920.

(9) WRIGHT, R. C., and HARVEY, R. B.
    1921. The freezing point of potatoes as determined by the thermoelectric method. U. S. Dept. Agr. Bul. 895, 7 p., 1 fig.

UNITED STATES DEPARTMENT OF AGRICULTURE

BULLETIN No. 917

Joint Contribution from the Bureau of Plant Industry, WM.
A. TAYLOR, Chief, and the Office of Farm Management and Farm Economics, H. C. TAYLOR, Chief.

Washington, D. C.   ▽   March 11, 1921

FARM PRACTICE IN GROWING FIELD CROPS IN THREE SUGAR-BEET DISTRICTS OF COLORADO.

By Samuel B. Nuckols, *Agriculturist, Office of Sugar-Plant Investigations, Bureau of Plant Industry*, and Thomas H. Summers, formerly *Scientific Assistant, Office of Farm Management and Farm Economics.*

CONTENTS.

	Page.		Page.
The districts studied	1	Manurial practice	21
Method used in collecting data	3	Cultivation	24
Soil types of the region	3	Irrigation	27
Climatic conditions	4	Harvesting	33
Seasonal distribution of labor	6	Marketing	40
Farm practice	11	Cost of production	42
Preparation of the seed bed	12	Summary	51
Planting	19		

THE DISTRICTS STUDIED.[1]

In 1915 and 1916 a study was made of the farm practice in growing sugar beets in three districts of Colorado. These data were published in Department Bulletin 726. In the summer of 1918 these districts were revisited and data obtained for the 1917 farm year, showing the farm practice and labor requirements in handling the crops grown in rotation or in competition with sugar beets.

It is believed that this information will show not only the comparative requirements of labor, materials, etc., for the various crops, but also how these crops fit into the rotation system in these areas.

An attempt has been made to present the comparative cost of producing these crops. Many items of cost in 1917 were abnormal, but as many of these enter into the production of all crops, the opportunity for comparison remains the same.

The data presented were worked out from 328 records. The distribution of these among the various crops is shown in Table I.

[1] Acknowledgment is due to Miss Catherine Hawley, of the Office of Farm Management and Farm Economics, for careful work in supervising the tabulations which have been used in this bulletin. Thanks are also due the farmers of these districts for their hearty cooperation in giving complete estimates concerning the man and horse labor requirements and other costs of producing the crops included in this study.

. 11311°—21—Bull. 917——1

TABLE I.—*Crop enterprise records obtained in Colorado in 1918.*

[The data collected pertain to the 1917 crop year.]

District.	Number of records obtained.[1]								
	Alfalfa.	Barley.	Wheat.	Oats.	Beans.	Corn.	Potatoes.	Cantaloupes.	Cucumbers.
Greeley............	36	33	9	15	58	5	46	....	....
Fort Morgan.......	35	22	7	12	2	2	....	....	....
Rocky Ford........	25	....	6	10	14	3	....	16	16
Total.........	96	55	22	37	74	10	46	16	16

[1] The 46 potato records which have been included in this study were obtained by the Office of Farm Management in a preliminary survey of the cost of producing potatoes during the years 1912 and 1913. These potato-enterprise records were taken in Weld County, Colo., by Mr. H. H. Clark.

The importance of the various crops is reflected to some extent in the number of records obtained in the three districts. For instance, alfalfa is an important crop in all areas, while potatoes were relatively

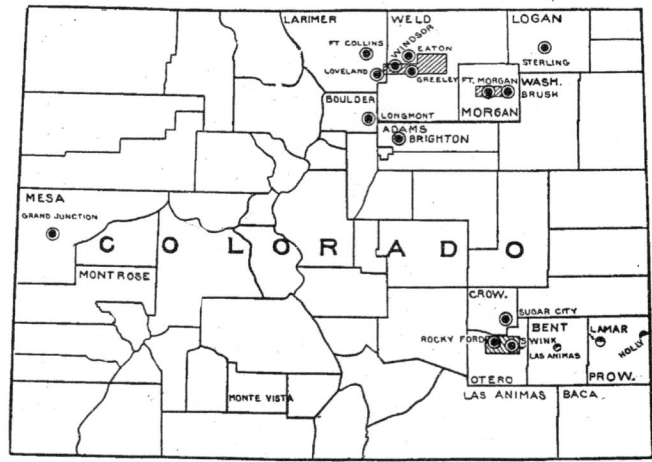

FIG. 1.—Map of Colorado, showing the three districts included in this survey (areas with diagonal lines) in Weld, Morgan, and Otero Counties. The location of each sugar factory operating in 1917 is shown by a black dot within a circle. Each factory idle in 191, is shown by a circle half black and half white. The factory formerly operated at Holly, Prowers County, has been removed.

unimportant except in the Greeley district. Again, cantaloupes and cucumbers are grown commercially only in the Rocky Ford district, while barley is not grown to any great extent there. Although corn is increasing in importance in all the areas, this crop in 1917 was relatively of very little significance. The districts covered in this work are shown on the map (fig. 1).

METHOD USED IN COLLECTING DATA.

The survey method was used in collecting the data presented in this bulletin. In many instances items were taken directly from actual records; in other cases estimates were obtained. Experienced investigators visited the farmers and held personal interviews. Whenever any doubt was entertained as to the accuracy of a record, the data were discarded. The results obtained represent the experience of the better farmers in these districts and therefore show the common methods employed in the production of farm crops.

SOIL TYPES OF THE REGION.

The soils of these districts are, as a rule, deficient in organic matter, but high in available mineral plant food. Commercial fertilizers are not generally used in these regions. Such experimental work as has been done with prepared fertilizers has not proved them profitable for general use. The soil of different parts of these areas varies considerably, but as a rule it is a sandy loam, most of it being well adapted to the growth of such crops as alfalfa, sugar beets, beans, cantaloupes, cucumbers, and small grains. The more sandy or open types of soil are especially adapted to the growing of potatoes.

The Bureau of Soils of the United States Department of Agriculture has made soil surveys of areas in the Greeley and Rocky Ford districts.[1]

Colorado fine sandy loam is the prevailing type of soil of the Greeley district, but the range of soils is from the Colorado sand to Colorado adobe. The Colorado fine sandy loam of the Greeley district consists of a fine sandy loam of approximately 3 feet, underlain by a heavier sandy loam which increases in clay and silt content as the depth increases. The soil is well drained and free from seepage water.

Agricultural methods are primarily the same for the same crop in a given district, but the farmer tilling the soil that is less easily handled must exercise greater care in its preparation and cultivation. These soil variations also affect the selection of crops for the farm and often determine the acreage of a particular crop to be grown. The adobe and heavier soils require that greater care must be taken in the preparation of the seed bed, and consequently they oftentimes show a greater cost for producing the crops.

In the Arkansas Valley 70 per cent of the area surveyed consists of two soil types—the Fresno fine sandy loam and the Maricopa sandy loam. The Fresno sandy loam has a fine silty texture, is yellowish in color, and extends to a depth of 6 feet. This type of soil is especially well adapted to the growth of row-tilled crops and those requiring a good seed bed, as it is a soil that is not inclined to bake or crust and

[1] Holmes, J. G., and Neill, N. P. Soil Survey of the Greeley area, Colorado. U. S. Dept. Agr., Bur. Soils, Field Oper., 1904, p. 951–993, fig. 40. 1905. Lapham, M. H., and party. Soil survey of the lower Arkansas Valley, Colorado. U. S. Dept. Agr., Bur. Soils, Field Oper., 1902, p. 729–776, pl. 46, 53, 3 folding maps. [1903.]

or bake when irrigated or after a hard rain. Most of the
semiarid region are high in mineral fertility, and the probl
tion is in regard to their water absorbing and holding (
water is most often the limiting factor in maximum crop

CLIMATIC CONDITIONS.

A limited rainfall (Table II) of approximately 13 inch
low atmospheric humidity, occasional high winds, and bui
days are the characteristic features of the Colorado clim
conditions cause a rather heavy evaporation of moistu
soil. In order to produce crops, irrigation is practiced
where there is an available supply of water for this pu
principal irrigated sections are located in the valleys a
section of the South Platte River in northern Colorado
Arkansas River in southern Colorado. Rocky Ford was
typical of the southern section and the Greeley and F
districts as typical of the northern section.

TABLE II.—*Average annual rainfall of two sugar-beet districts in nor
and one district in southern Colorado.*

[Depth of rainfall expressed in inches.]

Month.	Greeley.		Fort Morgan.		18
	1888 to 1915 (mean).	1917 a	1892 to 1917 (mean).	1917	(
January	0.30	0.10	0.24	0.45	
February	.46	.18	.44	.22	
March	.86	.40	.75	.25	
April	1.66	....	1.84	.40	
May	2.64	....	2.36	7.14	
June	1.45	....	1.84	1.33	
July	1.83	....	2.48	1.02	
August	.93	....	1.63	2.31	
September	.92	....	.93	1.53	
October	.89	.62	.92	.49	
November	.32	.09	.29	.30	
December	.44	.28	.39	.24	
Total annual precipitation	12.70	....	14.06	15.68	
Altitude—feet	4,639	....	4,338	....	

a Data incomplete for 1917.

Some of the crops studied can be grown without the practice of irrigation in the semiarid climate of Colorado. However, to reach the maximum yield it is necessary to irrigate. There are other crops which can not be grown at a profit except by irrigation. Sugar beets are never grown in this region without irrigation, and cantaloupes and cucumbers are not commercially profitable without it. Beans, potatoes, and small grains are grown on both irrigated and nonirrigated lands at a profit, with the average production per acre much greater on the irrigated areas.

Precipitation and the seasonal distribution of rainfall are much the same for the two valleys. Fortunately, the major portion of the annual rainfall occurs during the growing season. There is a somewhat heavier rainfall in the months of March, April, and May in the South Platte Valley than at Rocky Ford. (See Table II.) This with the slightly increased temperature of the Rocky Ford district accounts partially for the fact that it is customary there to irrigate immediately after or previous to planting some crops. (Fig. 2.)

Fig. 2.—Watering sugar-beet seed for germination, showing an example of row irrigation. The furrows must be well made, and careful attention should be given to the running of the water. The furrows are made as the seed is planted.

The Greeley and Fort Morgan growers do not practice spring irrigation, as there is, as a rule, sufficient precipitation or stored moisture in the soil to germinate the seed and start the crops.

Some rains which fall during July, August, and September do not benefit the crops greatly; in fact, they may do serious damage by forming a heavy crust or by causing the crop to lodge. Many of these rains come in heavy showers, when the run-off is great, and others in light showers which do not penetrate the soil. The average being very low, the evaporation is rapid and excessive. In some years, because the winter rains are light, the fields remain dry and hard and are in such poor condition in the spring that unless irrigation is practiced the seed germinates slowly and unevenly.

The Greeley district is close to the mountains, and the mean annual temperature there is 47° F., as compared with 51° for Fort Morgan. The range between extremes is wide. The nights are cool and the days, as a rule, are warm. The summer temperatures of the Rocky Ford district are somewhat higher than those of the Fort Morgan and Greeley districts. Throughout the entire territory cloudy days are the exception.

High winds, which are a characteristic feature, usually blow with great persistence in the spring, when the fields are without vegetation. Thus, it is a common occurrence for loose soil to be picked up and carried along with each strong current of air. If one of these heavy winds occurs when the plants are small and the soil is dry, much damage may be done to the crop. The seed is sometimes blown out or too deeply covered. Plants are left with their root systems exposed or covered by deposits of dust. At other times the sand carried by the wind cuts the tender plant leaves. Windstorms often damage a young crop to such an extent that it is necessary to reseed it. In some of the longer settled districts this difficulty has been reduced by the growth of windbreaks. These heavy winds accompanied by a low atmospheric humidity often cause the formation of hard crusts on the soil and produce excessive evaporation, which tends to counteract all the beneficial effects of a rain. Cultivation as soon as possible after rainfall is essential for the best results.

SEASONAL DISTRIBUTION OF LABOR.

Before a cropping system can be intelligently established on the farm, it is necessary to study the distribution of labor by months for the various crops in the proposed plan. Certain crops must be planted at the same time, and therefore the land must be prepared at the same time; others must be cultivated simultaneously; while others must be harvested during the same period. In fact, every operation on two or more crops may conflict with others. It is necessary then to plant only as many acres of these crops as can be handled by the available labor.

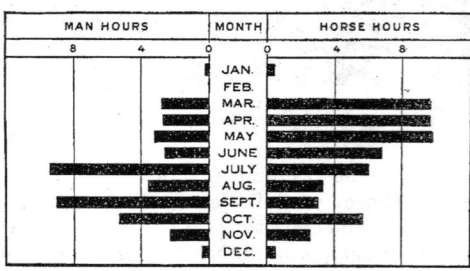

Fig. 3.—Labor distribution by months in growing field beans in the Greeley district of Colorado.

In the diagrams presented (figs. 3 to 8), no crop has been considered for more than one district. Although there is a slight difference in the dates of the various operations in the three districts, the distribution over the year is practically the same. The labor in growing small grains and sugar beets is tabulated for the Fort Morgan district; beans, potatoes, and alfalfa have been worked out under the conditions at Greeley. The cantaloupe and cucumber data pertain to the Rocky Ford district, which is the only area studied where these crops are produced commercially.

The accompanying diagrams showing the seasonal distribution of labor have taken into consideration only the work done in growing the farm crops. No study has been

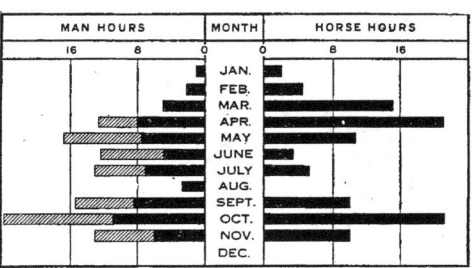

Fig. 4.—Labor distribution by months in growing sugar beets in the Fort Morgan district of Colorado. The lines of hatching represent contract labor.

made of the live-stock enterprises on these farms from the standpoint of labor distribution. Attention has been given to the overhead labor expense, which is a miscellaneous labor charge common to all farms, not definitely connected with any given enterprise, but chargeable to the farm as a whole.

The enterprise survey has been used only to a limited extent as a basis for the study of the seasonal distribution of labor. Such data have usually been obtained by the use of complete labor records of farm operations. The enterprise survey has made available information relating to labor distribution upon a comparatively large number of farms, and the records thus obtained carry suggestions concerning the utilization of labor in growing crops and provide relatively accurate seasonal labor-distribution data for the district specified. Similar methods could be followed in obtaining labor data for the live-stock enterprises of the farm.

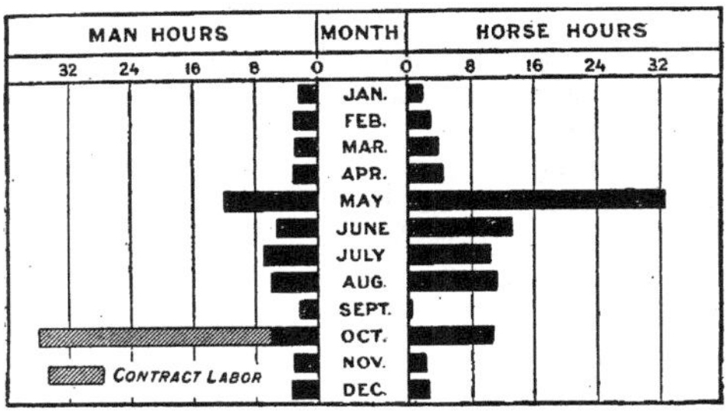

Fig. 5.—Labor distribution by months in growing potatoes in the Greeley district of Colorado.

In regions such as the irrigated-farm areas of Colorado, where there is much competition between certain crops and a variation in

wn by individuals, somewhat greater individual
stribution of crop labor is shown than would be
ιere only one important staple crop is produced
man in this region may have a large portion
to sugar beets, which require much labor duri

harvest sea
October and N
ber, while a ne
may grow wh
most of his far
and have ver
crop labor in
two autumn m
which period
the sugar-bee
vest season. A
may divide hi
acreage betwe

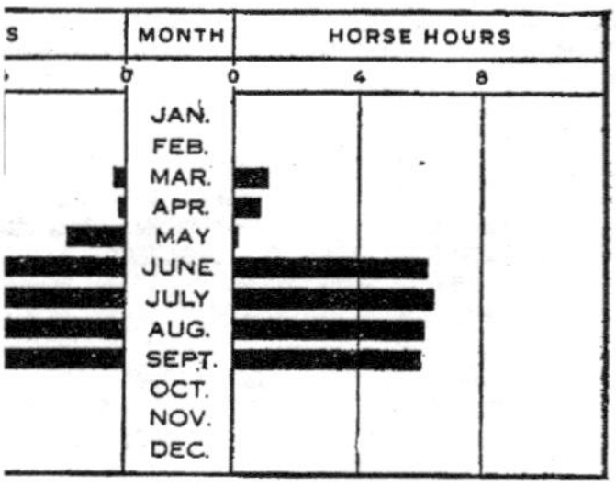

ution by months in growing alfalfa in the Greeley
district of Colorado.

so as to be busy during the entire growing seas(
ime not have the peak load of the labor in gro·
ɔnflict with the peak load of labor for anothei
nay plant two crops that conflict or need atten†
on.   If a farmer plants part of his acreage to p(
to sugar beets, he will not be able to handle s(

either
given
men,
achin-
anted
these
irriga-
·vest
tatoes
ets in
are
ical.
ɔn in

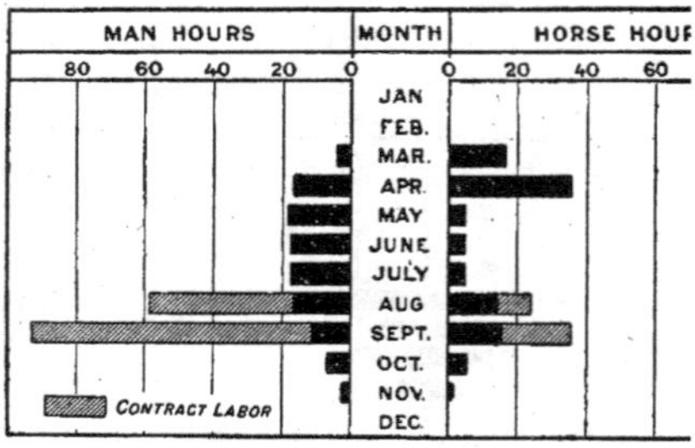

Fig. 7.—Labor distribution by months in growing cantalouɟ
Rocky Ford district of Colorado

ıation of crops is very common.   On a farm wher
sugar beets are grown, the harvest season for
t a later date than on farms growing no potatoes.
act that freezing damages potatoes more than i

each crop on a given farm with a given amount of labor so as to make the most economical use of that labor. From another viewpoint, after the selection of a certain acreage for a definite crop as the one best suited to his soil, the market conditions, and other factors that arise in its selection, the grower should be able to determine with a reasonable degree of accuracy the amount of labor he will need to hire for each month of the year and the number of work animals that will be necessary for the operation of the farm. It is shown that sugar beets require a large

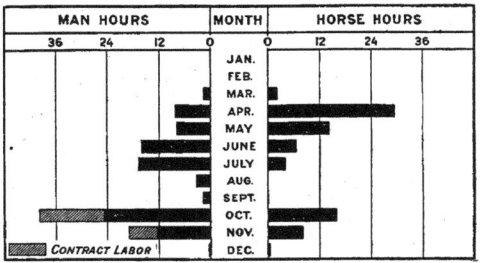

FIG. 8.—Labor distribution by months in growing cucumbers in the Rocky Ford district of Colorado.

amount of contract labor distributed from April to November, with concentration for periods in May, June, September, and October. There are slack periods in which an interchange of labor may take place in connection with other crops on adjacent farms. In fact, this is customary in a region where competing crops are grown. To insure getting labor when needed one should keep the laborer employed on the same farm.

It is also shown by the diagrams that extra man labor is needed for the grain crops at harvest time. These laborers may be used to do the contract work on sugar beets and be employed throughout the growing season, while if the beets were not grown and all the acreage was planted to grain and hay there would be a greater demand for men at grain and hay harvest time. With a limited number of

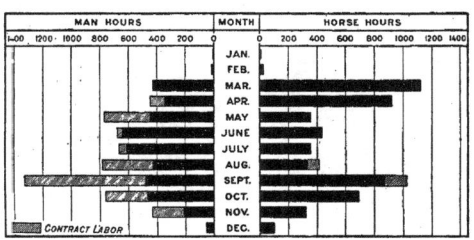

FIG. 9.—Seasonal distribution of labor required to produce 6.16 acres of beans, 20.82 acres of beets, 7.45 acres of cucumbers, 27.28 acres of alfalfa, 2.8 acres of oats, 7.85 acres of cantaloupes, and 2.05 acres of wheat in the Rocky Ford district of Colorado.

helpers in the vicinity, these crops could not be handled so economically as under present conditions, because extra labor is brought in to care for sugar beets primarily, and incidentally these men are employed to help with hay and grain.

11311°—21—Bull. 917——2

Another illustration of the use of farm help is shown when one man and four horses are needed to prepare land for wheat during the month of March and very little work has to be done on wheat in April or May, while for potatoes there is very little work in March or April, but approximately twice as much man and team labor on an acre of potatoes in May as there is on an acre of wheat in March. At the same time the sugar-beet crop requires more labor in April than either the potato or the wheat crop, and the alfalfa crop requires very little labor during March, April, or May.

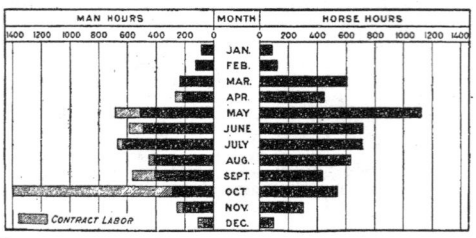

FIG. 10.—Seasonal distribution of labor required to produce 36.25 acres of alfalfa, 4.66 acres of oats, 6 89 acres of beans, 30.25 acres of potatoes, 10.49 acres of beets, 14.06 acres of barley, and 3.39 acres of wheat in the Greeley district of Colorado.

Other diagrams show the average seasonal distribution of crop labor for farms having specified acreages of different crops. These show the season when the farmer must work the most hours each day and hire the most labor.

By intelligent use of these diagrams the amount of labor required by a crop and the months when the labor is expended may be approximated closely, and many items of economic and agronomic importance to the region may be studied.

Figures 3 to 8 show the labor distribution by months on the farm crops produced in three sugar-beet districts of Colorado.

The application of the data on the distribution of labor for each crop is made in planning the cropping system. The

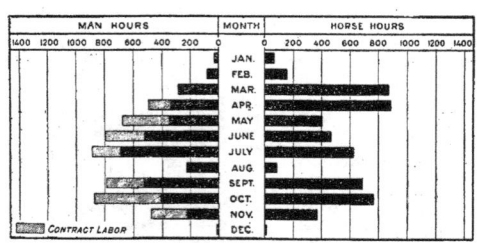

FIG. 11.—Seasonal distribution of labor required to produce 36.41 acres of alfalfa, 9.55 acres of barley, 35.93 of beets, 5.27 acres of oats, and 3.11 acres of wheat in the Fort Morgan district of Colorado.

average acreage per farm devoted to the principal crops in the Greeley district was worked out. Using these acreages and the distribution of labor presented in figures 3 to 8, a diagram was constructed showing the monthly distribution of all the labor used in growing crops on the farm. (Fig. 9.)

To show the seasonal distribution of labor in growing all the çrops of the various regions, the average acreage per farm of each crop grown was taken; also the labor required to produce the crops. From these data diagrams were constructed. (Figs. 10 and 11.)

The diagram for Greeley represents a farm of about 120 acres, the one for Rocky Ford 80 acres, while that for Fort Morgan applies to a farm with an area of about 120 acres.

FARM PRACTICE.

The average number of man and horse hours required to produce the important crops common to these districts has been compiled in Table III. These averages are given to show a comparison of the various practices for the production of the farm crops within a given region rather than a comparison of practices for any given crop common to each of the three districts. Occasional references are found concerning the differences in practice between regions, but the study is mainly devoted to the various crops in the same section.

The farm operations have been grouped under these headings: Manuring, preparation of the seed bed, planting, cultivation, irrigation, harvesting, and marketing. Contract labor is a direct cash outlay and has not been considered in totaling the hours of labor expended in producing the crops. This item has been included in considering the relative cost of the production of crops.

These major groups of farm labor may each contain one or more minor operations, which are enumerated and compared for the individual crops.

TABLE III.—*Distribution of labor per acre required to produce the principal crops grown in the Greeley, Fort Morgan, and Rocky Ford districts of Colorado.*

[Data expressed in hours for man and for horse.]

District and operation.	Crop and area covered by the records.													
	Sugar beets, 5,028 acres.		Potatoes, 1,802 acres.		Beans, 853 acres.		Alfalfa, 1,310 acres.		Oats, 184 acres.		Barley, 742 acres.		Wheat, 160 acres.	
	Man.	Horse.	Man.	Horse.	Man.	Horse.	Man.	Horse.	Man.	Horse.	Man.	Horse.	Man.	Horse.
Greeley district:														
Manuring	6.0	12.0	0.5	1.0	1.1	2.9	0.1	0.4	0.8	2.4	0.9	2.5	0.3	1.2
Preparation of the seed bed	8.3	30.0	6.7	27.9	6.6	24.8	....	....	1.9	7.0	2.5	9.5	3.2	10.7
Planting	1.1	2.1	6.8	7.5	1.2	2.2	....	....	1.0	2.4	1.0	3.1	1.0	3.5
Cultivation	6.5	12.3	11.9	31.2	10.2	15.3	a.4	b1.5	....	....	....	....	....	....
Irrigation	8.5	.2	6.7	.6	5.2	.1	5.8	.5	4.8	1.1	4.7	1.0	5.0	1.0
Harvesting	b5.1	15.5	b2.2	9.1	16.0	10.1	16.0	24.4	6.7	6.2	5.5	5.2	4.7	4.2
Marketing	13.0	32.4	21.9	19.3	1.1	2.1	....	....	.5	1.0	.6	1.0	2.1	3.8
Total	48.5	104.5	56.7	96.6	41.4	57.5	22.3	26.8	15.7	20.1	15.2	22.3	16.3	24.4

a Alfalfa cultivation is practiced by a few growers.
b Contract hand labor on beets and picking potatoes are not included.

TABLE III.—*Distribution of labor per acre required to produce the principal crops grown in the Greeley, Fort Morgan, and Rocky Ford districts of Colorado*—Contd.

District and operation.	Sugar beets, 2,455 acres. Man.	Horse.	Alfalfa, 1,233 acres. Man.	Horse.	Oats, 144 acres. Man.	Horse.	Barley, 262 acres. Man.	Horse.	Wheat, 102 acres. Man.	Horse.
Fort Morgan district:										
Manuring	5.1	10.5	......	......	0.9	2.1	1.1	3.4	1.1	1.9
Preparation of the seed bed	8.4	35.5	......	......	5.7	21.3	4.9	17.6	4.7	16.7
Planting	1.0	2.1	......	......	1.0	3.8	1.0	3.3	1.0	3.9
Cultivation	5.4	11.3	c0.1	c0.4	......	......	......	......	......	......
Irrigation	9.0	1.4	8.2	1.1	5.6	1.4	5.6	1.9	5.9	1.5
Harvesting	c4.1	12.1	18.0	26.8	8.2	9.7	8.8	10.9	10.8	12.9
Marketing	12.3	30.1	......	......	......	......	1.2	2.3	1.7	3.3
Total	45.3	103.0	26.3	28.3	21.4	38.3	22.6	39.4	25.2	40.2

District and operation.	Sugar beets, 2,429 acres. Man.	Horse.	Beans, 179 acres. Man.	Horse.	Cantaloupes, 301 acres. Man.	Horse.	Alfalfa, 915 acres. Man.	Horse.	Oats, 75 acres. Man.	Horse.	Wheat, 82 acres. Man.	Horse.	Cucumber seed, 252 acres. Man.	Horse.
Rocky Ford district:														
Manuring	6.5	12.8	2.6	6.5	0.3	0.5	0.4	1.6	2.6	3.0	4.0	5.3	1.8	2.1
Preparation of the seed bed	10.1	35.5	9.5	33.6	12.2	47.0	......	......	7.0	25.5	6.9	24.6	9.7	37.7
Planting	1.1	2.3	1.3	2.2	4.9	1.8	......	......	1.0	3.1	1.0	3.3	1.0	2.1
Cultivation	9.4	18.2	17.7	12.8	52.1	23.3	......	......	......	......	......	......	33.0	14.7
Irrigation	9.8	1.4	14.8	.2	16.0	.7	7.1	1.1	10.6	1.1	9.1	1.9	11.2	.8
Harvesting	d5.5	18.4	26.3	9.1	(d)	......	17.4	21.8	11.3	10.8	8.8	10.3	37.0	22.9
Marketing	13.6	44.1	1.8	3.6	14.9	28.7	1.0	1.7	.1	.1	2.7	8.0	.8	1.7
Miscellaneous e	......	......	......	......	3.3	3.7	......	......	......	......	......	......	......	......
Total	56.0	132.7	74.0	68.0	103.7	105.7	25.9	26.2	32.6	43.6	32.5	53.4	94.5	82.0

c Contract hand labor on beets is not included.
d Contract hand labor on beets and picking and packing of cantaloupes are not included.
e Miscellaneous includes work upon a building, a packing shed, laying roads, and hauling empty crates from the depot.

PREPARATION OF THE SEED BED.

The preparation of the seed bed embraces numerous distinct operations, beginning with the removal of trash from the land and including disking, plowing, rolling, spike-tooth and spring-tooth harrowing, crowning of alfalfa, scraping, and leveling.

REMOVING TRASH.

Comparatively few farmers practiced removing trash from the land. A few in the Greeley and Fort Morgan districts raked and burned potato vines from the land in preparing it for seed. Some growers at Rocky Ford raked and removed cantaloupe and cucumber vines. In most cases these vines were disked or plowed under. On the potato land the digging of the crop served as a sort of fall plowing, and the next crop was in some cases planted without plowing or disking the land. Usually, the potato vines would interfere so much with harrowing or leveling that it was necessary to remove them. Most farmers preferred to incorporate vegetable matter with the soil rather than to rake it off and burn it. Where trash was to be removed from the land the usual method was to rake it up with a common dump rake and burn it immediately. The total amount of labor expended in this operation is comparatively small.

PLOWING PRACTICE.

The benefits of fall plowing are apparent to those in these regions who grow potatoes or sugar beets, for in harvesting the crop the land is partially plowed. In the spring these fields are very easy to prepare for a seed bed, the winter's freezing and thawing having mellowed and pulverized the soil. The land usually contains moisture stored from the winter and spring rains and snows. With this example and their experience with the few fields that they have been able to get plowed in autumn or winter, most farmers believe there would be an increase in the production of their crops if they could practice more fall plowing. In fact, there is so little available time for fall plowing that only a small percentage of the grain-stubble land is plowed before spring. Some alfalfa is plowed in early winter, but the time of harvesting, especially beets and potatoes, prevents fall plowing. The acreage of these crops is usually large, so that the full season is taken in harvesting, some frost usually being in the ground before the completion of the beet harvest. The winters are seldom sufficiently warm to permit winter plowing, and frost usually remains in the ground until late March or early April. This causes a rush for the preparation of seed beds in the spring, and too often seed is planted in a poorly prepared seed bed.

Only 5 out of 57 men growing small grain at Greeley plowed in preparation for the crop. Table III shows that much of this land had been in potatoes or beets the previous year. Out of 41 men reporting, 13 plowed for grain at Fort Morgan. At Rocky Ford 50 per cent of the men growing grain plowed the land. For beets, potatoes, cucumbers, and cantaloupes nearly all used the plow in preparing the seed bed.

For such crops as sugar beets and potatoes deep plowing is necessary. With beets special care is taken to plow deeply and carefully cover and incorporate all manure and vegetable matter with the soil. Unless deep plowing is practiced for beets the beet roots are likely to be stunted and misshapen, and a low yield results. An impervious subsoil is very detrimental to the yield of a crop of beets, deep plowing tending partially to overcome the ill effects of a close subsoil. The average depth of plowing for beets in northern Colorado was between 8 and 9 inches. Rocky Ford growers reported shallower plowing for beets.

In all three regions 2-way plows are more common than the gang or sulky plows. A 2-way plow is one which has a right-hand and a left-hand plow mounted so that one can be operated at a time. (Fig. 12.) In this way the land is all turned one way by beginning at one

side of a field and plowing back and forth across it. No dead furrows
are made in the field, and this is very important on land that is to be
irrigated. In the Greeley section practically all farmers use the 2-
way plows. These are usually 14 or 16 inch plows, three or four
horses being required to pull them, the depth of plowing and the condition of the soil determining the number needed. A few growers
used 12 to 14 inch gang plows with 4-horse or 5-horse teams. The
gang plow can be operated with less labor per acre for plowing, but it
does not leave the land in as good condition for irrigation as the 2-way
plow. A number of men were found who used sulky plows, but only
a few used the walking type. The 2-way plow is the best for use on
irrigated lands.

Fig. 12—Plowing with a 2-way plow. The use of this implement does away with dead furrows in
the field, which is very important where irrigation is practiced.

Where alfalfa sod is to be broken for planting a crop it is customary
to plow the land twice. The first operation is known as "crowning
the alfalfa" or "scalping the land." The second operation is called
plowing. The crowning of alfalfa is done by plowing the land at an
average depth of about 3 inches, the purpose being to cut the
alfalfa crowns from the taproot of the plant and to have very little
root attached to the crown, so the plow is run only deep enough to prevent its shifting when large roots are encountered. To do this work
the same type of plow is used as in plowing other lands. After crowning the alfalfa it is left to lie a few days or weeks so that the crowns
may dry. Sometimes the land is spike-tooth harrowed, which brings
the crowns to the surface, where they dry more rapidly.

When the crowns have dried, the land is then plowed 6 to 9 inches
deep. This turns the crowns deeply into the ground, and in this
condition they are not likely to sprout and interfere with the sub-

sequent crop. The longer the period between the two plowings the less the number of crowns that will retain sufficient vitality to send up shoots. Where the land is plowed twice there are few plants that do not have the taproot severed. Where alfalfa land is plowed but once there is need of more work in disking and leveling to get the land in condition for a seed bed.

Alfalfa does not leave land in condition to be easily prepared for a seed bed, due to the coarse root system of the plant, but the vegetable matter of these roots contains ingredients very beneficial to the production of most crops. Beet land is left in the best state of tilth for the succeeding crop. Grain crops are often sown after beets with little further preparation of the soil for the seed bed. Grain lands are usually plowed for the succeeding crop, while potato and bean lands are often sown to grains without plowing. Cantaloupe and cucumber lands are usually plowed before planting the next crop.

DISKING.

The disk harrow is used extensively in the preparation of the seed bed for all crops in each of the three districts studied. At Fort Morgan 17 of 41 men growing grain reported the use of the disk and 19 of 66 beet growers used it. At Rocky Ford 8 of 14 bean growers, 10 of 16 cucumber growers, 100 per cent of the cantaloupe growers, 10 of 16 grain growers, and 61 of 109 beet growers used the disk in preparing the seed bed. Rocky Ford growers made a greater use of the disk than those of Fort Morgan or Greeley. At Greeley the disk was displaced by such tools as the spring-tooth harrow. The farmers at Rocky Ford use the disk to pulverize clods and to kill small weeds. There is a greater tendency for the ground to be cloddy at Rocky Ford than at Greeley or Fort Morgan, owing to the distribution of the annual rainfall. Most of the disk users at Rocky Ford plowed before or after disking, while in the northern Colorado district the disk was used more often to take the place of plowing, especially for grain crops and beans planted on potato or beet land. For pulverizing the soil in these three districts the disk is next to the plow in efficiency.

The crew for disking is most commonly one man and four horses, although a greater or lesser number of horses is occasionally used.

SPRING-TOOTH HARROW.

The spring-tooth harrow was used on approximately one-third of the beet land in the Greeley district and on 72 per cent of the grain land. This shows the importance of this implement in this region in the preparation of the seed bed. The Rocky Ford operators do not use the spring-tooth harrow much, and in the Fort Morgan region it is used only to a limited extent. In the Greeley territory it is used in the preparation of the seed bed for all crops. Its most frequent use is in preparing the seed bed for grains. On the row-tilled crops where the land is more often plowed the spring-tooth harrow is less frequently used. A spring-tooth harrow does not do its best work on land that is cloddy or rough, but it is an excellent tool with which to loosen fall-plowed or early spring-plowed lands that have become packed by heavy rains. It also works well in loose mellow fields where some weeds have sprouted. On land which has been planted to summer-tilled crops the spring-tooth harrow displaces the plow in preparing the land for grain.

The spring-tooth harrow of the Greeley region is usually in two sections, each 6 feet in width, and is commonly operated by a crew of one man and four horses. Such a crew will harrow approximately 8 acres in a 10-hour day. The average number of times this operation was performed in the Greeley region was 1.5 for beets, 1.3 for grain, and 1.6 for beans.

The spring-tooth harrow levels the land better than the disk, but does not pack the sod so much. It leaves an excellent surface mulch on the field.

ROLLING.

Smooth rollers are uncommon in the irrigated sections of Colorado, but some men make use of the corrugated roller in preparing the seed bed. Rollers are used for firming the soil after plowing and for connecting the loose surface soil with the moist subsoil. They may also be used for breaking or crushing clods. In the Greeley region rollers are used to firm and smooth the seed bed for shallow-planted seeds. With a firm upper layer of soil the drill plants at a more even depth, and the moisture rises more evenly to the surface. In this section 17 per cent of the farmers used the roller in preparing the beet-seed bed, none used it for grains, and very little use was made of it on bean or potato land.

Fort Morgan operators used the roller to some extent on beet land, but less use was made of it than in the Greeley district. No use was made of it in grain seed-bed preparation. In the Rocky Ford district some use was made of the roller on grain crops by 25 per cent of the growers. One man rolled bean land, 14 of 110 rolled beet land, and 13 of 29 cucumber and cantaloupe growers rolled the seed bed.

The common type of roller was 8 to 9 feet in length and was usually operated by one man and two horses, although sometimes as many as four horses were used. There is considerable variation in the number of acres covered, 12 to 15 being an average day's work. Usually the land is rolled but once.

SPIKE-TOOTH HARROW.

The spike-tooth harrow is used in the preparation of land for all crops. All the Rocky Ford operators except one beet grower and one wheat grower reported the use of this implement in seed-bed preparation. The use of the spike-tooth harrow was reported by 99 per cent of the beet growers in all regions. Fort Morgan grain growers reported its use on 36 of 41 fields. In the Greeley district 31 of 57 grain growers used the spike-tooth harrow, this implement being more used in this region than in any other. Bean and potato growers in Weld County commonly used this type of harrow.

The spike-tooth harrow is used in Colorado for the purpose of leveling the land, pulverizing and packing the surface soil, and destroying small weeds. Where land is plowed, it is customary to harrow the area of land plowed that day. This prevents crusting or the formation of hard clods and excess evaporation of moisture from the soil. After this first harrowing the land is usually gone over at intervals of from 7 to 10 days until the crop is planted. Beet growers went over their ground with the harrow on an average of slightly over 3 times and bean growers 2.6 times. Grain land in Weld County was harrowed with a spike-tooth implement but 1.3 times, in Morgan County 1.5 times, and in Otero County 2.3 times. Cucumber seed beds were similarly treated 3.8 times, and cantaloupe seed beds were gone over 3.9 times.

In nearly every case the harrowing was done with a steel spike-tooth harrow with a steel frame and an adjustable tooth stand. These harrows were of two, three, or four sections and ranged from 9 to 16 feet in length. They were operated by one man and three or four horses, 12 to 15 acres being usually harrowed a day. Accurate data were not obtained as to the number of men who weighted the harrows by riding, although this has much to do with the effectiveness of the operation.

LEVELING.

No operation in the preparation of a seed bed for an irrigated crop is more important than the leveling, but the amount of time put in on any one crop depends upon many factors. Among these one must consider the previous crop and the condition of the land. Another important factor is the accumulative value of previous leveling. If a farmer has been practicing careful and effective methods of handling and leveling his fields for several years, the necessity for this work becomes less each year. A field that is not properly leveled can not be properly irrigated and can not produce its maximum crop.

Leveling is done just before planting, and in the sections studied it is done best with the common box leveler. This implement is usually constructed on the farm of heavy planks set on edge. The length usually is 14 to 18 feet and the width 8 to 10 feet. Four planks are placed on edge, making the box, then one or two cross planks are inserted across the box the narrow way. The leveler takes dirt off all small knolls and ridges and deposits it in depressions. An even surface free from small depressions or knolls is thereby obtained, and even irrigation is made possible. Such a leveler is of further benefit in crushing clods and firming the land.

To properly operate one of these levelers, four horses are necessary. One man and four horses will level from 9 to 15 acres per day. Men with lightly constructed levelers usually find it necessary to go over the land a greater number of times.

Of the beet growers, 98 per cent leveled their land before planting, going over it 1.5 times in the Greeley district, 1.8 times in the Fort Morgan district, and 2.1 times at Rocky Ford. All cantaloupe and cucumber growers reported leveling their land, averaging 2.2 times for each crop. All the grain growers at Rocky Ford reported leveling, going over the land an average of 1.6 times. In the Fort Morgan district 20 per cent of the grain growers did not level their land, the others doing so an average of 1.3 times, while 44 per cent of the grain growers in Weld County did not level the seed bed for grain; those who did went over the land on an average but once. Potato land is furrowed deeply, and there is less necessity of leveling it than for other furrow-irrigated crops.

These figures show that more leveling is done in the preparation of furrow-irrigated crops than with those flood irrigated. In furrow irrigation small depressions or knolls retard the water or cause streams of water in furrows to unite, and there is a necessity for better preparation of the land for these crops.

TOTAL LABOR OF PREPARATION OF THE SEED BED.

The greatest amount of time was occupied in the preparation of beet land for seed. Alfalfa has no charge made for the preparation of the seed bed, for in all cases the crop was sown with grain and the hours of labor were charged to the crop of grain. In most instances no extra work was done on the field that was to have alfalfa sown in the grain.

Approximately the same number of hours were expended per acre in plowing for beets as for potatoes, but the time spent in leveling, rolling, and harrowing was much less for the potato seed bed. The seed bed for beets must be level, firm, moist to the surface, and free from weeds at planting time; otherwise the stand will be poor. The seed bed for potatoes does not need to be as smooth or firm or free from small weeds. Under the head of "Planting" an explanation of this difference in requirements will be given. Bean land requires approximately the same work in preparation as potato land. A somewhat better seed bed is required for beans, as they usually follow potatoes, grain, or beets; but potatoes more often follow alfalfa. The expense of plowing is less for beans than for potatoes, and more time is expended in leveling and firming the seed bed for the bean crop.

Of the grains, oats shows the least work necessary to prepare the seed bed; barley comes second; and wheat requires the greatest amount. Oats is the hardiest grain crop in all three districts.

PLANTING.

The only item of labor included in the planting of a crop is the drilling of seed except in the case of potatoes, which includes the labor of cutting the seed. Where cucumbers and cantaloupes are planted by hand the land is marked with a marker, and this is part of the labor in planting these crops.

For alfalfa there is no labor charge for planting the crop, since most growers use a combined grain drill and alfalfa seeder. Very

FIG. 13.—Ditching potatoes. Deep furrows are made between the potato rows, so that the surface of the water will be lower than the potatoes in the hills.

little, if any, more time is consumed than in planting the grain crop alone. Also, since alfalfa is allowed to grow for several years, the labor of planting would add but little to the labor requirements per ton of hay. Replanting, where practiced, has been included under the planting practice.

Sixty-three per cent of the man labor employed in planting an acre of potatoes is consumed in cutting the seed. The common potato planter of the region requires a 3-horse team. Most of the grain drills are for 3-horse and 4-horse teams, although some use 2-horse grain drills. Two horses are used in planting sugar beets and beans. In planting potatoes it is common to hill the row, and before the plants are up the ridge is harrowed down. This kills all the small weeds and leaves an excellent seed bed at the time that the plants appear. Some farmers ridge the bean rows immediately after planting and harrow down the ridge before the plants come through.

The older types of bean drills have no ridging attachment, but the new types have ridging tools. This method of planting and cultivating potatoes and beans eliminates much of the hand labor of hoeing. It also eliminates the danger of loss of stand from the formation of a crust on the soil. (Figs. 13 and 14.)

Approximately 1 hour of man labor is required to plant an acre of grain, beans, beets, or cucumbers for seed, 6.8 hours for potatoes, and 4.9 hours for cantaloupes. Sugar beets, beans, cantaloupes, and cucumbers require approximately 2 hours of horse labor per acre. Grains average slightly more than 3 horse-hours per acre to plant, while potatoes require the greatest amount of horse labor in planting, 7.5 hours.

In all three sections there is little variation in the method of planting beets or grain. The grain is drilled in rows 8 inches apart, the

FIG. 14.—Harrowing potatoes. When the tubers are planted a deep covering is put on the seed. By harrowing, this covering is removed, leaving the ground free from small weeds when the potato sprouts come through the surface. This practice is followed in bean planting and saves much hand labor in hoeing.

beets in rows usually 20 inches apart, although at Rocky Ford some farmers planted beets 18 inches apart and some men at Fort Morgan and Greeley alternated 16-inch and 24-inch rows. Potatoes are planted in rows 36 to 40 inches apart. Beans are planted in rows 28 to 32 inches apart. Alfalfa is scattered broadcast with a seeder or drilled in rows. Cucumbers are planted in rows 36 to 40 inches apart. Cantaloupes are planted in check-rows or hills 5 to 7 feet apart with four or five plants to the hill. Cucumbers are thinned to approximately 18 inches between plants in the row, beets 10 to 14 inches, beans 2 to 6 inches, and potatoes 18 to 24 inches.

The depth of planting for beet seed is from 1½ to 2 inches; for grains, about 2 inches; cantaloupes and cucumbers, about 2 inches; beans, 2 to 3½ inches; and potatoes, approximately 6 inches.

Crops are planted a few days earlier in the season at Rocky Ford than in the other districts. The dates of planting beet seed at Rocky Ford are from April 1 to June 15, at Fort Morgan from April 10 to June 22, and at Greeley from April 1 to June 20. The greatest amount of planting is done from April 20 to May 10 in each of these districts. As a rule, cantaloupes are planted from April 20 to May 10. Cucumbers for seed are planted from May 1 to June 5, the greater portion about May 25. Potatoes are planted from May 25 to June 10. The planting of winter wheat varies from August 30 to December 1 and of spring wheat from February 28 to April 15. Oats are planted from March 1 to April 15 and barley from March 15 to April 25. As a rule, barley is planted later in the season than other grains. Beans are planted from May 15 to June 10; alfalfa usually in April.

Beet seed is planted at the rate of 15 to 20 pounds per acre; potatoes, 600 to 700 pounds; alfalfa, 10 to 15 pounds; cucumbers (average), 4.5 pounds; and cantaloupes, 3.4 pounds. Beans of the type grown for seed were seeded at approximately 55 pounds, and pinto beans at the rate of 20 to 30 pounds to the acre.

At Greeley the average rate of seeding per acre for wheat was 77 pounds, for oats 75 pounds, and for barley 83 pounds. At Fort Morgan the rate was 59 pounds of wheat, 82 pounds of oats, and 72 pounds of barley. At Rocky Ford the rate was 89 pounds of wheat and 82 pounds of oats.

MANURIAL PRACTICE.

All the crops studied have some labor charge for the application of manure, although to some of the crops no direct application of manure was made. The charge is due to the cumulative value of manure in the soil. The manure value and the labor application cost are charged to the farm crops, according to the place in the rotation that the manure is applied. The schedule is as follows: 50 per cent of the value of the manure and 50 per cent of the work of applying it to the field are charged to the crop receiving the direct benefit, 30 per cent to the following crop, 20 per cent to the crop on the land the third year, no charge being made to crops farther removed from the application of the manure. If manure is applied to the same field for three successive years, the following charge will be made against the crop: 20 per cent of the cost of the first application, 30 per cent of the cost of the second application, and 50 per cent of the immediate application.

In a survey of these regions it was found that 92 per cent of the farmers applied barnyard manure to their crops, 367 growers made reports upon the use of manure, and 310 applied the manure to the beet crop. On 22 farms the manure was applied to potatoes, and on

5 it was applied to grain. These statements show that beet growers consider beets to be the crop most responsive to the application of manure. No use of commercial fertilizer was reported in these districts.

The hours of farm labor charged to manuring show that in each of the three districts studied alfalfa was the farthest removed from the manure application. In the Fort Morgan territory no manure charge was made against alfalfa, as none of the growers visited had seeded alfalfa on land that had been manured during the previous three years. Where alfalfa is put on land which has received a heavy application of manure there is an inclination toward the production of coarse hay. Manure can not well be spread on alfalfa sod, for it can not be properly incorporated into the soil and will be raked up with the hay and injure its quality. However, the principal reason for not manuring alfalfa is the better response of other crops to the manure. Instances are recorded where the average yield of beets on a field has been increased from 50 to 100 per cent with no other apparent factor for the cause of this increased yield than the application of barnyard manure. Manure can be best incorporated immediately and mixed with the soil by putting it on land which is to be devoted to a summer-tilled crop. The tilled crops of these districts are beets, potatoes, beans, cucumbers, and cantaloupes. Cucumbers and cantaloupes did not receive much manure. The men producing these crops alone, as a rule, kept few live stock, and those who grew beets and cucumbers or cantaloupes preferred to put the manure on the beet land.

After breaking out alfalfa, 75 per cent of the farmers in the potato-growing section planted potatoes. On land with so much vegetable matter in the soil from the alfalfa roots and foliage, it would not be advisable to add manure, since it would add an excess of foreign matter to the soil and make it difficult to cultivate. Some growers claim that manure applied directly to the potato crop is likely to cause an excess growth of tops or vine and also to promote disease or increase the number of rough potatoes. Likewise, beans are sometimes inclined to have excess foliage or to be uneven in maturing when heavily manured.

The grain crops do not, as a rule, respond well to a direct application of manure, as they produce a heavy growth of straw under such conditions and the crop is inclined to fall down or lodge.

Different types of soil respond differently when manured, and a crop that on one type of soil would show little benefit from an application of manure might on another type near by show greatly increased yields. However, the rule in these three districts is to put the manure on the beet crop, because the maximum production of beets is on land that has been treated with manure.

There is need of more humus in most soils in these districts. The practice of efficient irrigation requires that the soil have good water-holding capacity, and the climate of the districts is such that the humus rapidly burns out of the soil. Many farms lack a sufficient supply of manure for the land, and few farms use green crops for turning under to supply humus. Some farmers grow sweet clover and turn it under, others turn under considerable foliage when alfalfa sod is broken, but many are inclined to pasture off all alfalfa foliage before plowing the land. Beneficial results were usually reported from the turning under of alfalfa foliage, and the practice is increasing. There is a demand for more care in building up the humus content of the soils of these districts.

Manure is usually hauled to the fields at a time when teams would be idle or when the farm crops are not in need of attention. This hauling is done at all seasons of the year, but least in the late spring and summer months and most in the early spring. More hauling would be done in the winter if it were not for the heavy winds that prevail, causing the manure to drift or dry out on the soil surface. Manure should be spread and disked or plowed under immediately. Where this is not possible it is often placed in small piles over the field and spread with forks at plowing time. Another plan is to place manure in large piles on or near the field and distribute it with spreaders just before plowing. Most farmers used manure spreaders with 3 or 4 horse teams. A number of them had an extra helper to assist in loading the spreader. Where manure was left to be spread until the ground was in condition to be disked or plowed, there was need of the efficient use of the manure-spreading equipment of the farm. The hauling of manure placed in piles was usually done by one man and two horses.

Most of the manure spread was produced on the farms, but in some cases it was hauled from near-by towns and from the sugar-factory feed yards. The greatest quantity was hauled from factory feed yards in the Rocky Ford district. This practice greatly increased the labor required to apply the manure.

The greatest labor expended per acre for applying manure was at Rocky Ford, and the least at Greeley. More tons of manure per acre were applied at Greeley than in either of the other districts; the least at Rocky Ford. In the Greeley district the crews averaged larger and the distance hauled was less than at Rocky Ford. The manuring practice at Fort Morgan more closely resembles that at Greeley than that at Rocky Ford. Beet growers at Greeley manured 49 per cent of the land planted to beets, at Fort Morgan 47 per cent, and at Rocky Ford 41 per cent. Other crops had only a small percentage of the area manured.

CULTIVATION.

The cultivation practice includes all operations, such as breaking crust (fig. 15) before the plants come through the soil, which is e by harrowing or rolling; the cultivating with common types of tivators; furrowing and sledding for irrigation; hoeing; and mis- aneous practices employed to kill the weeds and keep the soil in roper state of tilth. The reason for including sledding and fur- ving for irrigation as parts of the cost of cultivation is that these rations, although primarily performed for irrigation, often take place of regular cultivation.

FIG. 15.—Rolling a sugar-beet field after it has been irrigated to germinate the seed.

Contract hand labor, such as for thinning and hoeing beets and king potatoes, is not included in the hours of labor enumerated in ble III. Since this item is a direct cash outlay, it is considered der the cost of production. Where farmers have done their own nd labor, the labor hours have been reduced to their money equiv nt and charged as a cash item.

On the grain crops no charge has been made for cultivation, al ough a few reports showed that the farmer harrowed the grain er it was planted. This operation is so closely related to the pre ration of the seed bed that it has been charged to the crop unde is heading.

In growing alfalfa 10 farmers renovated the crop. This was ac mplished with alfalfa renovators by 5 of the men, the others usin ks or harrows. Grasshopper poisoning was also included as rt of the labor of cultivating, as it is an operation which has to d th carrying the crop from planting to maturity. The grasshoppe ison used was a mixture of bran, lead arsenate, and sirup. Thi eetened mixture was distributed from a sack around the edges c the fields and along the ditch banks, a horse and buggy sometimes being used to carry the poison. Some crops, such as beets, sometimes have to be sprayed to kill insect pests. (Fig. 16).

Sugar-beet cultivation is well under way before beans or potatoes are sufficiently large to be cultivated. The first cultivation of beets comes before any contract labor has been done. At about the time the plants have four leaves the cultivator is run through the field. At this time the knives are used to cut along close to the row to throw dirt away from the plants. It is advisable to stir the center of the row as deeply as possible with a narrow shovel, thus keeping it from packing and enabling later ditching for irrigation to be more perfectly done. Practically all cultivating and furrowing are done with

FIG. 16.—A type of sprayer used for potatoes and other field crops.

4-row implements requiring 2-horse teams. Beets are cultivated from three to five times, such frequency apparently being essential for a maximum yield. About 8 acres is a normal day's work in cultivating beets. When the plants are small the work is done at a slower rate than later in the season. Furrowing, which is done when the plants are larger, is done at the rate of 9 or 10 acres a day. The methods of furrowing for irrigation at Rocky Ford are somewhat different from those of the two northern districts, where it is not customary to furrow except after the last cultivation. If a second furrowing is practiced it is usually done to make the furrows deeper. At Rocky Ford the first furrowing usually comes soon after planting, a second during the period of cultivation, and a third after cultivation is completed. Sledding is usually done on land that is without a slope.

The cultivation of beans is less exacting than that of beets. The work is often done with beet cultivators adjusted to the width of the bean row and equipped with the heavier types of beet tools. Since the bean plants grow rapidly from the beginning, there is less danger of covering them than in the cultivation of sugar beets. The irrigation furrows between the bean rows are made somewhat deeper than those for beets. The cost of the horse labor required to cultivate beans is somewhat higher than for beets in the Greeley district and less than for beets at Rocky Ford. More hand work is done on beans at Rocky Ford than at Greeley, where beans are often grown without using a hoe. One man and two horses can work approximately 7 acres of beans a day, the crop being cultivated about three times and furrowed twice. A few farmers ditch alternate rows of beans with a potato ditcher and four horses. Others use beet furrowers and ditch each row or alternate rows as preferred. Very little work is done on the beans after the plants begin to bloom. Some beans grown for seed are rogued by the seedsman. (Fig.17).

Fig. 17.—Roguing beans. These beans have been planted for seed, and the seedsman is taking out such plants as are not true to type, an important item in the production of reliable seeds.

The potato crop as studied at Greeley requires more hours of man labor in cultivation than the sugar-beet crop. The horse labor necessary in cultivating potatoes is more than twice that required for beets or beans. Harrowing with a team of three or four horses usually takes the place of the first cultivation of beans. Potatoes are harrowed before they come through the surface of the ground. The cultivation of potatoes is done with the idea of ridging the potato row very high and making a deep furrow between the rows. This requires the use of 3-horse and 4-horse teams, usually the latter.

In growing potatoes it is necessary to ridge the rows. When the crop is irrigated it is advisable to have very deep furrows between the rows, so that the water surface in the furrow is lower than the potatoes growing on the plant roots. (Fig. 18.) Beans and beets do not require as deep furrows for irrigation as potatoes. On account of the large amount of work done by contract labor in hoeing the beet crop, cultivation by the use of farm teams is greatly lessened for this crop. The contract laborers hoe the beets usually three times during the growing season. Since beans and potatoes are usually hoed by day laborers, this labor is included in the hours expended in the cultivation of these crops. The cantaloupe crop requires more horse labor for cultivation than the beet or bean crop, and the hours of man labor are very high. Hand labor is used in thinning and hoeing the crop. In laying back the vines for cultivation and in cultivating and furrowing the field the crew often consists of one man and one horse. After planting the seed, 23 per cent of the cantaloupe growers harrowed or rolled the land. The crop was cultivated from five to seven times and usually hoed (including thinning) three or four times. The irrigation furrows are made three

Fig. 18.—Irrigating potatoes by means of deep furrows.　Only the alternate rows carry water.

or four times and sledded usually three times. It was necessary to lay the vines back twice for furrowing or sledding the furrows. The earlier cultivations are often done with two horses, but later it is necessary to use 1-horse cultivators, furrowers, and sleds, as the vines spread over the field surface. The cultivation of cucumbers is similar to that of cantaloupes, the same types of machinery being used for the two crops. Cucumbers grow more rapidly, and the operations are therefore less in number.

IRRIGATION.

Irrigation includes the time expended in the application of water to the crop and the labor of cleaning, repairing, and making the ditches and laterals. The making of furrows between rows of cultivated crops is considered a part of the labor of cultivation.

In cleaning ditches most of the farmers had to use some horse labor. Ditches or laterals often become filled with trash and dirt, some of it being carried by the heavy spring winds. It is often necessary to use a scraper in cleaning the larger ditches. The greatest amount of horse labor in ditch cleaning is done with a V-drag, which has a long side that scrapes one side of the ditch while the other side smooths the bottom. This sort of drag saves much labor that would otherwise have to be done by hand with a shovel. (Fig. 19.)

Grain crops require another item of horse labor. After the grain is planted it is common to make cross ditches through the field so that irrigation water can get to the crop. These are made at varying intervals throughout the field, depending upon the slope of the land and the type of the soil. They must not be too far apart or too long for the even irrigation of the crop. In flood irrigation, if the field is too long too much water will penetrate the ground near the outlet from the lateral. These laterals in grain fields are made with a plow or common corn lister and are usually smoothed and banked with a V-drag. When harvest time comes they often interfere with

Fig. 19.—The V-ditcher. This implement is used for making new laterals or cleaning and banking of ones. It uses horses to do labor that is often done by men with shovels.

the operation of the binder and are usually partially filled by plowin in the banks. This can often be done by using one horse and makin but one round to each ditch. This practice does not break down o destroy the grain along the ditch bank, as would be done if mor horses were used. This operation is best done after the last irrigatio of the grain and before the ditch banks harden.

In irrigating beans, beets, and potatoes the water can be run greater distance, as it is in a furrow and has more head. There is therefore, often less necessity for temporary ditches through th field. Water can be run on crops by the furrow-irrigation metho two to four times as far as by flood irrigation. (Figs. 20 and 21.

Since alfalfa is a flood-irrigated crop, the ditches made in th nurse crop are usually left unfilled at harvest time or are cleaned wit a V-drag and plow and thereafter each year cleaned out. There i much variation for different farms in cleaning alfalfa ditches, depending upon the type of soil and the slope of the land. Some ditches are inclined to wash clean and deep each year, but others tend to fill up.

Fig. 20.—Irrigating alfalfa by the flooding method. One man can handle a large head of water.

At Greeley and at Fort Morgan the first water of the season is run on the alfalfa. The irrigation practice in these districts is very similar, but at Rocky Ford it is somewhat different. Alfalfa is usually irrigated three or four times at Greeley and at Fort Morgan, the first water being applied about May 20, the second about June 10, and the third about July 1. Where a fourth irrigation is given

Fig. 21.—Irrigating corn. The furrows are deep and a good head of water is used. Corn is a crop of increasing importance in the three districts of Colorado studied.

it is applied about July 25 or in September. This gives two irrigations before the first crop is cut and one soon after the crop is stacked. The fourth irrigation is just after the second or third crop is cut. The time per acre required for irrigation varies greatly with the flow of water, the type of the land, and the number of applications given.   One man will irrigate 6 to 10 acres a day.   This variation holds for all crops.

The grain crops of the northern areas are usually irrigated twice — once about June 1 and again about June 20.   One man will irrigate

FIG. 22.—Irrigating sugar beets. This illustrates the method of letting the water out of the lateral into the furrows between the rows.

from 4 to 10 acres of grain in a day.   In irrigating grain and alfalfa it is customary to let the water run on the crop 24 hours of the day. Some farmers remain continuously in the field attending to the distribution of the water, while others are so situated that the water can be set and allowed to run three to five hours without attention.

FIG. 23.—Irrigating sugar beets. This illustrates the use of canvas checks to turn the water out of the lateral into the furrows between the rows.

Row cultivated crops, such as beets, potatoes, beans, and cantaloupes, may also be irrigated by having a man in continuous care of the water or by making sets and letting the water run a few hours.   This practice depends upon the head of water, slope of the land, type of

soil, and length of rows.   Some men prefer to run the water on row
crops during the hours of daylight and turn it on the alfalfa or grain
crops at night.   (Figs. 22 and 23.)

   The farmers of the Greeley district irrigated their beet crops three
times on an average.   The first irrigation came early in July, the
second late in July or early in August, and the third usually early in
September.   The dates for irrigation at Fort Morgan are similar,
but the average number of irrigations is 2½.   This shows that the
irrigation of grain and alfalfa is practically completed before water
is put on the row crops.   The irrigation of beets is delayed later some
seasons than others.   The water for grain and alfalfa irrigation is
usually obtained direct from the supply in the rivers and streams of

Fig. 24.—Furrowing a field prior to planting cantaloupes.   Seed is planted alongside each row, and water
is run through each furrow to supply moisture for germination.

the region, but for irrigating row crops reservoir water is usually
used, as not much water is flowing in the streams after July 1.   One
man will irrigate 3 to 6 acres of beets per day.

   Potatoes are irrigated like beets, but one man can cover more
acres in a day as a rule, as the furrows are made deeper and the rows
are farther apart.   Water is usually run between each two rows of a
row-tilled crop.   Potato irrigation does not usually begin as early in
the season as that of beets.   The irrigation period for beans was
shorter than for other row crops, being usually begun about the
middle of July and completed soon after August 15.   Beans are
irrigated two or three times.   One man can irrigate 5 to 6 acres of
beans in a day, the average time per acre being 1.4 hours.   Beans
are usually irrigated the first time just prior to the beginning of the
blooming period.

   In irrigating row crops care must be taken to avoid injuring the
plants.   Beans should be irrigated late in the season, lest they make

.ough to shade the ground causes crusting of the soil. Potatc
ould be deeply ditched, so that the water will flow between t
ws, the surface of the stream being lower than the location of t
tatoes in the hill. Care must be taken to avoid an excess of wat
the soil and to prevent heavy crusting or packing. Good subs
ainage is necessary for the successful irrigation of all the cro
udied. At Rocky Ford the climate is somewhat different from th
northern Colorado, and the crops need different care in the practi
irrigation.

FIG. 25.—The cook wagon. This is the boarding house for the thrashing crew.

Alfalfa was irrigated on an average of 3.5 times; oats, 2.6 tim(
heat, 2.7 times; beans, 3.3 times; beets, 4.1 times; cantaloupes, (
mes; and cucumbers, 4.7 times. A man irrigating alfalfa but thi
mes would turn on the water the first time May 1 to 15; next, Ju
to 10; and lastly, June 25 to July 5. If a fourth irrigation is giv
usually comes in September, or after the last crop is harvest(
)me farmers irrigate as often as six times for alfalfa. Grain, bee
id beans are usually irrigated at planting time, so as to furni
oisture for the germination of the seed. Cantaloupe and cucuml
ops are irrigated to germinate the seed. Water to germinate t
ed is applied to row crops by making furrows at the time of plai
g by attaching ditching shovels to the planter. Other irrigatic
e applied by methods similar to those explained for the northe
)lorado regions. In the latter part of May cucumbers are given
:igation to bring up the seed. The other waterings follow
gular intervals up to about August 25.

Cantaloupes are first irrigated when planted, usually in late April or early May. (Fig. 24.) The other irrigations are applied from 12 to 20 days apart until about August 15, when irrigation ceases.

FIG. 26.—Cutting wheat.

To irrigate an acre of the crop at Rocky Ford required for cantaloupes an average of 1.6 hours; cucumbers, 1.8 hours; beans, 2.7 hours; beets, 2 hours; alfalfa, 1.5 hours; wheat, 2.2 hours; and oats, 2.7 hours.

HARVESTING.

In the vicinity of Greeley the labor requirement for the harvesting of grains is less than in the other districts because of the system

FIG. 27.—Thrashing grain.

used in thrashing. However, the cash expense of thrashing at Greeley is greater than at Fort Morgan or at Rocky Ford. At Greeley none of the grain is stacked by the farmer, but is thrashed from the shock. It is not often that much damage is done by rain to the grain in the shock. The thrashing crew consists of an engineer, separator boss, water-wagon man and team, four pitchers, and usually eight men, teams, wagons to haul the shocked grain to the thrasher, and two men to sack the grain and sew the sacks. Usually the thrashing crew is not boarded at the farm house. (Fig. 25.) The farmer has to receive the grain when sacked, pile it back from the machine, and haul it to the bin. Some farmers haul the grain directly from the field to the elevator or shipping point. In these districts the ground is usually dry and firm at harvest time, and cutting the crop is attended with little difficulty. One man and three horses constitute the most common crew, covering 8 to 10 acres per 10-hour day.

Fig. 28.—Cutting beans.

Wheat harvest begins about July 10 at Rocky Ford and extends to July 20, oats being cut from July 15 to 25. At Fort Morgan and Greeley wheat and barley are harvested from July 10 to 25 and oats from July 15 to August 1. Thrashing for grains that are not stacked begins about August 15 in these districts, but for stacked grains no thrashing is done until about September 15. The thrashing of stacked or unshocked grains is usually completed before October 1, as the beet and potato harvest begins about this date, and the cost of getting men and teams for thrashing is then greater; moreover, the farmer does not wish to do thrashing during beet-harvest time. (Figs. 26 and 27.)

The stacking of grain, which may begin a few days after it is cut, is mostly done from August 1 to 15.

Bean harvesting begins about September 1 and continues until October 1. It is done with 2-horse bean cutters. As the beans are cut the plants slide off the end of the knife and to the row center at the side of the machine. On the return across the field another row of plants is thrown in this same row center, so that two rows of beans are together. These plants are usually just matured, and with few dry pods on the plants there is no loss of beans from shelling. (Figs. 28 and 29.)

The beans are not allowed to stand in the windrow, but are bunched with a dump rake or shocked by hand the same day they are cut. The labor is lessened by shocking with a rake, but more beans are lost by shattering than where they are shocked with a fork.

Approximately half the growers thrashed the beans from the field shocks without stacking. The best practice is to stack the beans unless one is able to have them thrashed early in the fall.

FIG. 29.—Shocking beans.

Where beans were stacked it was done in September with wagons and fork or with sleds, slings, and the derrick type of hay-stacking machinery. Some farmers found it necessary to turn the bean shocks before stacking or thrashing, so as to prevent discoloration of the beans. This slightly increased the shattering. Bean thrashing begins about September 1 and may continue into the winter months. The thrashers do not completely clean the beans for market, but the grower has this done at the warehouse. One man and two horses will cut 6 to 7 acres of beans in a day, and one man can shock about 2 acres in a 10-hour day.

Approximately 90 per cent of the horse labor required in the production of the alfalfa crop is used in harvesting, and from 60 to 80 per cent of the man labor.

Three cuttings of alfalfa are usually made during the season. A very small percentage of the growers varied from this practice. The first cutting is made from June 15 to 20 at Greeley, the second from July 18 to August 1, and the third from September 1 to 20. These dates for cutting are approximately the same for the other regions studied.

The crew for mowing was in all cases one man and two horses, cutting from 8 to 10 acres in a 10-hour day. After mowing, it was customary to rake up the hay within a few hours, and not later than 24 hours under normal weather conditions. If hay is left in the swath more than a day the leaves become dry and brittle and break off while it is being raked, causing great loss of feed value. At Fort Morgan and Greeley almost all the farmers used side-delivery rakes, but at Rocky Ford only a few used these implements. The crew was one man and two horses for each type of rake, and by the

FIG. 30.—Bunching alfalfa. After the hay has been raked into windrows by the use of a side-delivery rake it is bunched.

side-delivery method 10 to 16 acres were raked in a day, while the dump rake covered from 12 to 20 acres. After the hay is raked into windrows it is bunched. The Fort Morgan and Greeley farmers did all the bunching with bunching or dump rakes, either of which is operated by one man and two horses. Such a crew can bunch 20 acres or more of alfalfa in a day. At Rocky Ford some growers bunched or shocked the hay with forks, one man handling 4 to 6 acres per day. Only a very few men did not bunch the hay before stacking it.

As a rule, hay is permitted to cure from two to five days in the bunches before stacking, the methods of stacking varying greatly in the different regions and on different farms. A few farmers at Rocky Ford hauled the hay to the stack on wagons. This method is not used by those having large acreages of alfalfa. Push rakes and overshot or side-lift stackers were used by some men in each district. At Fort Morgan most of the growers used overshot stackers and push rakes, the usual crew being four or five men and five or six horses. One man and two horses operated the stacker, with one or two men on the stack. This left two men and four horses on the rakes. At Rocky Ford side-swing stackers were the most common type, the crews being the same as at Fort Morgan. The push rakes automatically load in the field and push the hay upon the stacker without any of the labor of forking. At Greeley the crew most commonly consisted of four to six men and six horses, using a crane stacker with sleds and slings. This equipment consists of two sleds or gates upon which two slings are placed, one at each end of the sled, and on these the hay is pitched in the field and taken to the stack by one man with two horses to each sled.

Fig. 31.—A side-delivery rake. The hay should be raked into windrows soon after it is cut or many leaves will shatter off.

One man stays in the field to help load the sleds. At the stack the slings are lifted by one man and two horses, one or two men being on the stack to handle the hay. Sometimes this crew varies in that three sleds are used and each team is unhitched at the stack to operate the crane, thereby using one man less. (Figs. 30–36.)

The harvesting of the cucumber seed crop consists of throwing the ripe cucumbers into piles by hand, making pits for the storage of the seed before washing, then thrashing, washing, and drying.

The piling of the seed cucumbers in the field is usually done by contract at a specified price per acre, which is put under the cash cost in Table IV of this bulletin. Two men can pile about an acre of cucumbers in a day. This work is done from October 1 to 10. In a few days after piling, the cucumbers are thrashed by special types of machines which remove the seed and some of the pulp from the meaty part of the cucumber and rinds. The seed is hauled to pits and the rinds are dropped in the field near where the piles of cucumbers were.

ed to the pits. In 10 days to 2 weeks the seed is was
e remaining pulp, spread on screens to dry, and t
e washing is done in a sluice box with water from an i
. Three men do this work usually, washing 300 to
ed in a day. Some growers use chemical washers. (F

sting of cantaloupe seed is done in the same manne
ed. Cantaloupe harvesting for market is usually d
by Mexicans, who are paid a given rate per crate. '
king the melons in crates after being sorted and gra
ly done by contract. Melons must be picked regula

alfalfa hay from the field with a wagon. This method is too slow where a large ac
is to be harvested.

field is gone over each day and the marketable c
Where possible, all ripe melons are packed and ship
y are picked. To get the melons from the fields, rc
regular intervals a few rods apart, where the vines b
one side.
ns are hauled to sheds to be packed in crates, which
set up at a contract price. (Figs. 39 and 40.)
to harvest begins the latter part of September an
pleted by the middle of October. In some seasons
harvested later, but there is danger of the frostin
he surface of the ground. Potatoes are harvested by
rs that dig one row at a time and drop the tubers in
nd the implement. Usually the potatoes are clean
rt. A potato digger requires a crew of one man and '

horses, such a crew digging 4 to 5 acres in a 10-hour day. The potatoes are picked up by hand and placed in sacks or are put directly into wagons and hauled from the field to the storage cellar. If they are to be marketed they are hauled from the field to the sorter. The handwork of picking up potatoes is usually done at a contract rate per sack. Before marketing, the potatoes are run over a sorting screen, which takes out all the small ones. All imperfect tubers are picked off the screen. The potatoes are then sacked for market and usually sold in the sack. The crew for sorting potatoes usually consists of three men, one to place the potatoes on the screen and two to sort, sack, and sew the bags. This crew usually works at a contract price per sack. Sorting may be done at harvest time or during the winter or spring. It is done just before the potatoes are marketed.

Fig. 33.—Hauling alfalfa to the stack on a sled. It is easy to pitch hay on a low carrier such as this, and very few leaves shatter off the stems. Hay slings are usually used on these sleds.

Beet harvesting begins October 1 and continues until into November, but all beets should be harvested by November 15, for if left in the ground longer there is danger of loss of the crop by freezing. Beets are harvested by the use of lifters that dig one row at a time. The beets are not completely taken out of the ground, but are lifted a few inches and loosened so that they can be easily pulled up by hand and thrown into piles. The lifters may be operated by two, three, or four horses, depending on the type and condition of the soil. One crew can lift 2 to 3 acres in a day. The piling of the beets by hand is done at a contract price per ton. After piling the beets, the contract laborer removes their tops with a hand knife. The beets are usually hauled direct from the field to market, but a very small number of growers store them in piles in the field and cover them with dirt. Beets when marketed by the usual method must be hauled within a day or two after pulling, to prevent loss of weight by evaporation. The hauling of the beets is considered under "Marketing." The beet and potato harvests come at the same time, and if a man grows a large acreage of one of these crops he can not well grow the other. The harvesting of beets may be delayed later in the season than that of potatoes, as frosting does not injure beets while in the ground. Where both crops are grown, the grower usually completes the potato harvest before beginning with beets. It is not good practice to delay the beet harvest, since bad weather may come which will necessitate additional labor in hauling the crop, and in cold weather the hand-work of topping beets is very tedious. Furthermore, the beet tops have considerable value as stock feed, and if harvested late they may be partly lost on account of being covered with snow.

MARKETING.

Few farms were visited where any labor was performed in marketing hay, almost all being sold by the ton in the stack. Some farmers fed

FIG. 34.—Stacking alfalfa, showing the overshot type of stacker.

it to the stock brought to their farms and received cash for the labor of feeding in addition to the price of the hay. When the hay was hauled to another farm it was paid for at a cash price per ton in the stack.

Oats and barley have a very small average charge for marketing, because the greater portion of the crops was fed on the farms and the grain was delivered by the grower in but few cases.

Wheat was usually hauled to the nearest shipping point, which was often a beet siding or dump where a car was placed to receive the sacked grain. (Fig. 41.)

Beans were hauled to the nearest bean cleaner or elevator in most cases, but were sometimes marketed like wheat.

The marketing of sugar beets consists of loading them on a wagon in the field and hauling them to the nearest beet dump or receiving station, where they are either dumped or shoveled off the wagon. On an average, for the Greeley district the farmer hauled his beets 1.54 miles. Where cars are available and the yards at the factory are of sufficient capacity to receive the beets, they are dumped from

Fig. 35.—Stacking alfalfa hay, showing the side-swing type of stacker.

special-type drop-side wagons so that they go direct into the car. This saves the labor of shoveling. Where the beets are not dumped the company receives them at the loading station and requires the farmer to shovel them into piles on the ground. Beets are delivered as they are harvested.

To market potatoes it is necessary that they be sorted, graded, and sacked. This is done by running them over a screen and picking

Fig. 36.—Stacking alfalfa hay, showing the derrick type of stacker and the use of sleds and slings.

out the damaged tubers, the smaller ones and dirt falling through the screen. A sorting crew usually consists of three men. One puts the potatoes on the sorter or screen, and two men sort them and sew the sacks. This may be done in the field at harvest time or in the potato cellar later, depending upon when the potatoes are sold. Sorting is always done just before the potatoes are marketed. They are hauled and sold in the sacks.

More man labor and less horse labor are required in marketing an acre of potatoes than in marketing an acre of beets.

FIG. 37.—Thrashing cantaloupe seed.

Beets and cantaloupes are the only crops grown that must be marketed as soon as harvested. The other crops are marketed at a time when the field work is less pressing.

COST OF PRODUCTION.

As has been indicated, the prices of materials and the wages for labor were abnormal in 1917. These are factors which may vary

FIG. 38.—Cleaning and drying cantaloupe seed.

appreciably from year to year. Such items as the number of hours of labor, pounds of seed, tons of manure, and pounds of twine remain fairly constant.

Figures on costs are used not to indicate the absolute rates per bushel or per ton in 1917, but to show the comparative cost of producing an acre of wheat and an acre of alfalfa, potatoes, beans, or beets.

FIG. 39.—A cantaloupe field, showing a roadway for hauling the melons.

Where the quantities of materials, labor, etc., are determined, the cost of producing a given crop for any year can be computed by applying the prevailing prices and wages for that period.

Costs are grouped under three headings: Labor, materials, and other costs. "Labor" includes the work performed by men and horses,

FIG. 40.—A cantaloupe packing shed.

whether such employment is paid for by the hour or at a contract rate. "Materials" embraces such items as manure, seed, fertilizer, and water. The item "Other costs" covers the remainder of the cost items, chief of which is the use of the land. Many charges under this group are against the farm as a whole, and the proportion of the

cost applicable to a given crop must be determined by proratir
entire charge among the various enterprises involved.

MAN AND HORSE LABOR RATES.

In figuring the labor cost of producing farm crops a uniforn
per hour for man labor has been used throughout the crop s(
In most sections it is customary to pay higher wages for harve
The average rate per hour during the entire crop year is a littl
for some operations, but high for others.

Horse labor is also figured at a uniform rate per hour for the
crop year.   The average rates for man and horse labor were u;
these three districts, being 30 cents per hour for a man and 20
for a horse.

FIG. 41.—Hauling wheat to market.

LABOR.

Labor is by far the most important factor in the producti
farm crops in the districts studied.   Not only is the variation ·
cost of production to a large extent dependent on the relative
requirement, but the whole farming system is planned from a k
edge of the distribution of labor over the cropping season.
acreage of cultivated crops is limited by the supply of labor tc
care of it during the busy periods.   It is of interest to compa·
labor necessary to grow the various farm crops in the regions st;

Table III shows the hours of labor required per acre to pr
farm crops in the three sugar-beet districts of Colorado consi
in this bulletin.

There are usually three classes of man labor, viz, (1) worl
formed by the operator, (2) work done by hired labor and paid for
by the month or by the day, and (3) work performed by hired lab(
contract rate, such as handwork on sugar beets and picking pot
In computing the cost of production the labor cost of the thirc
mentioned is treated as a cash item, while the labor cost of th

two classes is found by multiplying the number of hours by the labor rate per hour.

Table IV shows the cost of the labor required to produce farm crops in the three sugar-beet districts of Colorado covered in this survey.

Under contract labor the actual amount paid out has been considered rather than the number of hours spent in doing the work. Beans, beets, potatoes, cantaloupes, and cucumbers show some contract labor, while the remaining crops do not.

There is considerable variation in the cost of labor required for the production of farm crops in the districts studied. Cantaloupes show the greatest cost ($125.16 per acre), while beets come second ($53.31 to $58.92), with cucumbers next ($51.55), followed by potatoes ($45.66). The production cost of beans is considerably higher than that of alfalfa and the grains, which show the lowest expenditure per acre for labor.

TABLE IV.—*Labor cost of producing farm crops in three sugar-beet districts of Colorado.*

Crop and district.	Number of records.	Crop area.	Yield per acre.	Distribution of labor costs per acre.			
				Man.	Horse.	Contract.	Total.
Wheat:		*Acres.*	*Bushels.*				
Greeley	9	160	47.4	$4.90	$4.88	....	$9.78
Fort Morgan	7	102	21.3	7.55	8.05	....	15.60
Rocky Ford	6	82	33.6	9.76	10.69	....	20.45
Oats:							
Greeley	15	184.50	61.8	4.71	4.02	....	8.73
Fort Morgan	12	144	37.4	6.41	7.67	....	14.08
Rocky Ford	10	75	54.7	9.78	8.73	....	18.51
Barley:							
Greeley	33	742	53.9	4.56	4.45	....	9.01
Fort Morgan	22	262	46.7	6.77	7.88	....	14.65
Alfalfa:			*Tons.*				
Greeley	36	1,310.50	3.43	6.70	5.36	....	12.06
Fort Morgan	34	1,233	3.36	7.90	5.66	....	13.56
Rocky Ford	25	915	3.13	7.77	5.23	....	13
Beans:			*Bushels.*				
Greeley	35	853.30	24.3	12.44	11.50	....	23.94
Rocky Ford	14	179.50	26.9	17.95	13.60	$4.27	35.82
Beets:			*Tons.*				
Greeley	195	5,028.40	15.57	16.44	20.90	17.26	54.60
Fort Morgan	66	2,455.50	13.65	19.20	20.60	13.51	53.31
Rocky Ford	106	2,428.95	12.99	18.27	26.54	14.11	58.92
Potatoes:			*Sacks.*[1]				
Greeley	44	1,802	140	17.01	19.32	9.33	45.66
Cantaloupes:							
Rocky Ford	13	301	....	34.20	22.10	42.77	99.07
Cucumbers:			*Pounds.*				
Rocky Ford	16	252	477	25.75	16.40	9.40	51.55

[1] Each sack weighing 110 pounds.

MATERIALS.

There are some materials which must be purchased; others are furnished by the farm. Such items as twine, sacks, fertilizer, coal, and irrigation water are in the first group, while manure and seed are usually furnished by the farm. Where materials are purchased, the price paid has been used in the tabulations. Materials furnished by the farm have been figured at the estimated values placed on them by the growers. The cost of materials is shown in Table V.

TABLE V.—*Cost of materials in producing farm crops in three sugar-beet districts of Colorado.*

Crop and district.	Number of records.	Crop area.	Yield per acre.	Seed.	Twine.	Fuel.	Water.	Manure.	Sacks.	Crates.	Labels.	Miscellaneous.	Total.
		Acres.	*Bush.*										
Wheat:													
Greeley	9	160	47.4	$2.20	$0.76	$0.55	$1.34	$0.30					$5.15
Fort Morgan	7	102	21.3	2.06	.73	.51	.98	1.53					5.81
Rocky Ford	6	82	33.6	3.18	.58	.46	.82	.99					6.03
Oats:													
Greeley	15	184.50	61.8	1.59	.65	.44	.83	1.32					4.83
Fort Morgan	12	144	37.4	2.09	.48	.42	1.07	1.54					5.60
Rocky Ford	10	75	54.7	2.08	.51	.39	.87	1.70					5.55
Barley:													
Greeley	33	742	53.9	1.90	.65	.36	1.24	1.42					5.57
Fort Morgan	22	262	46.7	1.83	.61	.62	.91	1.89					5.86
			Tons.										
Alfalfa:													
Greeley	36	1,310.50	3.43	.51			1.21	.26					1.98
Fort Morgan	34	1,233	3.36	.55			1.44						1.99
Rocky Ford	25	915	3.13	.67			.96						1.63
			Bush.										
Beans:													
Greeley	35	853.30	24.3	3.32		.37	1.21	1.16					6.06
Rocky Ford	14	179.50	26.9	5.06	.02	.37	1.05	1.99	$1.58				10.07
			Tons.										
Beets:													
Greeley	195	5,028.40	15.57	1.80			1.36	5.50					8.66
Fort Morgan	66	2,455.50	13.65	2.11			1.15	3.46					6.72
Rocky Ford	106	2,428.95	12.99	2.16			1.49	2.93					6.58
			Sacks.[1]										
Potatoes:													
Greeley	44	1,802	140	31.50	.55		1.36	.87	21.70				55.98
Cantaloupes:													
Rocky Ford	13	301		4.47		.11	1.02	.14		$44.40	$0.78		50.92
			Lbs.										
Cucumbers:													
Rocky Ford	16	252	477	1.03		.50	.96	1.00				$0.84	4.33

[1] Each sack weighing 110 pounds.

Table V shows little variation in the total cost of materials required for the small grains in the three districts studied. Fort Morgan shows a high cost for manure on the wheat crop, while Rocky Ford growers spent the most money for seed wheat. On the other hand, Greeley oat producers had a lower seed cost than the others.

At Rocky Ford the cost of the bean seed was high, and there was a charge for sacks furnished by the growers. At Greeley sacks were used in hauling the beans, but they were returned to the farmer.

In the outlay for materials for the beet crop the difference is due mainly to the higher manure charge in the Greeley district.

Potatoes and cantaloupes cost about the same for materials ($55.98 and $50.92 per acre), while for cucumbers only the small charge of $4.33 per acre for materials was made.

OTHER COSTS.

"Other costs" is taken to include items which can not be considered properly under any of the preceding group headings. Many of these costs are of no less importance than those previously considered. As a matter of fact, the use of land, the largest item in this group, is larger than any other one item except labor.

Most of these costs are chargeable to the farm as a whole and must be prorated among the enterprises involved in order to determine the charge against any one crop.

Table VI gives the remaining items of cost incurred in the production of farm crops in the three sugar-beet districts of Colorado covered by this bulletin.

TABLE VI.—*Other costs in producing farm crops in three sugar-beet districts of Colorado.*

Crop and district.	Number of records.	Crop area.	Yield per acre.	Distribution of costs per acre.					
				Taxes and insurance.	Use of land.	Machinery.	Thrashing.	Overhead.	Total.
Wheat:		*Acres.*	*Bushels.*						
Greeley	9	160	47.4	$1.70	$16.48	$0.69	$6.20	$1.19	$26.26
Fort Morgan	7	102	21.3	1.80	17.25	.95	2.26	1.71	23.97
Rocky Ford	6	82	33.6	1.83	11.80	.67	2.32	2.12	18.74
Oats:									
Greeley	15	184.50	61.8	1.70	19.07	.69	6.30	1.08	28.84
Fort Morgan	12	144	37.4	1.80	12.16	.95	2.84	1.58	19.33
Rocky Ford	10	75	54.7	1.83	12.95	.67	2.59	1.89	19.93
Barley:									
Greeley	33	742	53.9	1.70	16.47	.69	5.94	1.17	25.97
Fort Morgan	22	262	46.7	1.80	15.03	.95	3.56	1.64	22.98
Alfalfa:			*Tons.*						
Greeley	36	1,310.50	3.43	1.70	17.82	.69	....	1.12	21.33
Fort Morgan	34	1,233	3.36	1.80	15.23	.95	....	1.25	19.23
Rocky Ford	25	915	3.13	1.83	14.88	.67	....	1.17	18.55
Beans:			*Bushels.*						
Greeley	35	853.3	24.3	1.70	18.81	2.75	4.18	2.40	29.84
Rocky Ford	14	179.5	26.9	1.83	17.87	2.67	3.93	3.67	29.97
Beets:			*Tons.*						
Greeley	195	5,028.40	15.57	1.70	14.18	2.75	....	5.06	23.69
Fort Morgan	66	2,455.50	13.65	1.80	11.55	3.80	....	4.80	21.95
Rocky Ford	106	2,428.95	12.99	1.83	17.22	2.67	....	5.24	26.96
Potatoes:			*Sacks.*[1]						
Greeley	44	1,802	140	1.70	13.95	2.75	....	8.13	26.53
Cantaloupes:									
Rocky Ford	13	301	....	1.83	13.09	2.67	....	12.00	29.59
Cucumbers:			*Pounds.*						
Rocky Ford	16	252	477	1.83	14.47	2.44	....	4.47	23.21

[1] Each sack weighing 110 pounds.

The charge for taxes and insurance is fairly uniform for all districts. The use of land varied from $11.55 an acre for beet land at Fort Morgan to $19.07 for oat land at Greeley. This item will differ according to the cash rent, the share rent, and the yield per acre. Where cash was paid the exact amount was considered. If a share of the crop was given for the rent, the farm value of that crop was used in the tabulation.

More machinery is needed for cultivated crops than for grains and alfalfa. The use cost of machinery was therefore greater for the former crops than for the latter. At Fort Morgan the highest use cost for machinery ($3.80 per acre for beets) was recorded. The use cost of machinery for grains and alfalfa was also greatest at Fort Morgan. This item in the other districts was fairly uniform.

Thrashing is partly a labor and partly a machinery charge against a crop. The portion of the thrashing labor furnished by the farmer has already been considered under "Labor costs." The charge here is the cash paid to the thrashing crew for thrashing the grain. This charge probably more nearly approaches the contract-labor classification. However, it is considered here as an individual item. The highest cost occurred at Greeley, where the yield was larger and the method of thrashing different. In this area a higher rate per bushel was paid, but more labor was furnished by the thrasher than in the other districts.

The item of overhead, which is based on the amount of labor and materials, varies with these two items. This charge ranged from $1.08 per acre for oats at Greeley to $12 per acre for cantaloupes at Rocky Ford.

The total "Other costs," with the exception of sugar beets, were highest at Greeley. Beans show approximately the same cost at Greeley and at Rocky Ford, while beets show the greatest other cost in the Rocky Ford district. Cantaloupes cost about the same as beans. Potatoes and cucumbers cost about the same as sugar beets for this item.

SUMMARY AND DISTRIBUTION OF COSTS.

When all of the cost groups are added together the sum represents the total cost of production.

A higher percentage of the total cost is shown for labor on cultivated crops than for the other crops with the exception of potatoes, the labor cost for which is 36 per cent of the total cost of production. Where the percentage of labor cost is low the percentage of other costs is high.

Alfalfa had the lowest percentage cost for materials (5 per cent) and potatoes had the highest (43 per cent).

The importance of each group as compared with the total cost of production is readily seen when reduced to a percentage basis.

Table VII shows the distribution of total cost in terms of percentages.

TABLE VII.—*Distribution of costs in producing farm crops in three sugar-beet districts of Colorado.*

Crop and district.	Number of records.	Crop area.	Yield per acre.	Total cost per acre.	Distribution of costs (percentage of total).		
					Labor.	Materials.	Other costs.
Wheat:		*Acres.*	*Bushels.*				
Greeley	9	160	47.4	$41.19	24	12	64
Fort Morgan	7	102	21.3	45.38	34	13	53
Rocky Ford	6	82	33.6	45.22	45	13	42
Oats:							
Greeley	15	184.50	61.8	42.40	21	11	68
Fort Morgan	12	144	37.4	39.01	36	14	50
Rocky Ford	10	75	54.7	43.99	42	13	45
Barley:							
Greeley	33	742	53.9	40.55	22	14	64
Fort Morgan	22	262	46.7	43.49	34	13	53
Alfalfa:			*Tons.*				
Greeley	36	1,310.50	3.43	35.37	34	6	60
Fort Morgan	34	1,233	3.36	34.78	39	6	55
Rocky Ford	25	915	3.13	33.18	39	5	56
Beans:			*Bushels.*				
Greeley	35	853.30	24.3	59.84	40	10	50
Rocky Ford	14	179.50	26.9	75.86	47	13	40
Beets:			*Tons.*				
Greeley	195	5,028.40	15.57	86.95	63	10	27
Fort Morgan	66	2,455.50	13.65	81.98	65	8	27
Rocky Ford	106	2,428.95	12.99	92.46	64	7	29
Potatoes:			*Sacks.*[1]				
Greeley	44	1,802	140	128.17	36	43	21
Cantaloupes:							
Rocky Ford	13	301	....	179.58	55	28	17
Cucumbers:			*Pounds.*				
Rocky Ford	16	252	477	79.09	65	6	29

[1] Each sack weighing 110 pounds.

TABLE VIII.—*Summary of costs in producing farm crops in three sugar-beet districts of Colorado.*

Crop and district.	Number of records.	Crop area.	Yield per acre.	Distribution of costs per acre.			
				Labor.	Materials.	Other costs.	Total.
Wheat:		*Acres.*	*Bushels.*				
Greeley	9	160	47.4	$9.78	$5.15	$26.26	$41.19
Fort Morgan	7	102	21.3	15.60	5.81	23.97	45.38
Rocky Ford	6	82	33.6	20.45	6.03	18.74	45.22
Oats:							
Greeley	15	184.50	61.8	8.73	4.83	28.84	42.40
Fort Morgan	12	144	37.4	14.08	5.60	19.33	39.01
Rocky Ford	10	75	54.7	18.51	5.55	19.93	43.99
Barley:							
Greeley	33	742	53.9	9.01	5.57	25.97	40.55
Fort Morgan	22	262	46.7	14.65	5.86	22.98	43.49
Alfalfa:			*Tons.*				
Greeley	36	1,310.50	3.43	12.06	1.98	21.33	35.37
Fort Morgan	34	1,233	3.36	13.56	1.99	19.23	34.78
Rocky Ford	25	915	3.13	13.00	1.63	18.55	33.18
Beans:			*Bushels.*				
Greeley	35	853.30	24.3	23.94	6.06	29.84	59.84
Rocky Ford	14	179.50	26.9	35.82	10.07	29.97	75.86
Beets:			*Tons.*				
Greeley	195	5,028.40	15.57	54.60	8.66	23.69	86.95
Fort Morgan	66	2,455.50	13.65	53.31	6.72	21.95	81.98
Rocky Ford	106	2,428.95	12.99	58.92	6.58	26.96	92.46
Potatoes:			*Sacks.*[1]				
Greeley	44	1,802	140	45.66	55.98	26.53	128.17
Cantaloupes:							
Rocky Ford	13	301	....	99.07	50.92	29.59	179.58
Cucumbers:			*Pounds.*				
Rocky Ford	16	252	477	51.55	4.33	23.21	79.09

[1] Each sack weighing 110 pounds.

The total cost of labor, materials, and other items in the production of various crops (Table VIII) shows a remarkable uniformity for the three areas studied. On account of the higher cost of labor and materials at Rocky Ford, there is a considerable difference in the acre cost of producing beans.

Wheat, oats, and barley cost about the same per acre. Alfalfa shows the lowest cost ($33.18 per acre at Rocky Ford) and cantaloupes the highest ($179.58). It cost more to produce an acre of potatoes ($128.17) than an acre of beets ($81.98 to.$92.46). Cucumbers cost less per acre of production ($79.09) than sugar beets.

CROP CREDITS.

By crop credits is meant the value of the crop produced. If the crop is all sold off the farm, as was done with the beets, then the receipts and credits are identical. However, if the crop is partly fed on the farm or all fed to farm stock, the receipts do not indicate the total credits, and a farm value for that portion used on the farm must be assigned to the crop.

When this was done, the average crop credits per farm in the districts studied were considerably higher than the corresponding crop receipts in the same districts. The distribution of these credits among the various crops also varies widely. (Table IX.)

TABLE IX.—*Distribution of credits for the principal farm crops in three sugar-beet districts of Colorado.*

District.	Number of records.	Average crop credit per farm.	Total crop credits (per cent).										
			Alfalfa.	Wheat.	Barley.	Oats.	Beans.	Potatoes.	Beets.	Cantaloupes.	Cucumbers.	Corn.	Miscellaneous.
Greeley	53	$10,535	18.7	3.1	8.0	2.1	17.5	35.9	11.5	....	....	1.1	2.1
Fort Morgan	37	6,803	26.4	1.9	6.4	1.9	3.9	8.6	49.0	....	....	1.2	.7
Rocky Ford	40	6,982	19.6	1.9	.....	1.3	9.7	.....	29.0	25.4	10.4	2.1	.6

It will be noticed that while the receipts from alfalfa were approximately 8 per cent of the total, the alfalfa credits ranged from 18.7 to 26.4 per cent of the total crop credits. On the other hand, the percentage of credits for beans, potatoes, beets, and cantaloupes is somewhat lower than the corresponding percentage of crop receipts.

It is of interest to note the distribution of crop receipts from the various farm crops. Some crops are grown primarily for sale, while only the surplus of other crops is to put on the market.

Table X gives the total crop receipts per farm and the percentage of total receipts from each crop; also the yield per acre of the principal farm crops in the three districts under consideration.

. In each district there are three essential cash crops. At Greeley and Fort Morgan these crops are beets, potatoes, and beans. At Rocky Ford the potato crop is displaced by cantaloupes. These three crops bring in more than 75 per cent of all the receipts.

Although the total crop receipts per farm vary-considerably, the percentage derived from the sale of alfalfa is practically the same for each district.

TABLE X.—*Crop receipts per farm and percentage of their distribution and the yield per acre of the principal farm crops in three sugar-beet districts of Colorado.*

Item and district.	Number of records.	Average total crop receipts per farm.	Distribution of total crop receipts (per cent).										
			Alfalfa.	Wheat.	Barley.	Oats.	Beans.	Potatoes.	Beets.	Cantaloupes.	Cucumbers.	Corn.	Miscella- neous.
Crop receipts:													
Greeley	53	$8,118	8.2	3.9	3.1	0.8	21.4	44.8	14.5			0.7	2.6
Fort Morgan	37	4,631	8.1	2.4	4.3	.2	5.4	12.1	67.3				.2
Rocky Ford	40	5,741	8.0	2.0		.2	11.5		34.1	30.7	12.7	.2	.6

Item and crop.	Greeley.	Rocky Ford.	Fort Morgan.	Item and crop.	Greeley	Rocky Ford.	Fort Morgan.
Yield per acre:				Yield per acre:			
Sugar beets....tons..	15.57	12.99	13.65	Alfalfa..........tons..	3.43	3.13	3.36
Beans......bushels..	24.3	26.9		Cantaloupes..dollars..		217	
Oats..........do....	61.8	54.7	37.4	Cucumber seed,			
Wheat.........do....	47.4	33.6	21.3	pounds..........		476.7	
Barley.........do....	53.9		46.7	Potatoes......sacks..	140		

SUMMARY.

(1) The distribution of labor in the three districts in Colorado studied shows that sugar beets have a longer season of labor than any of the other crops, the grains having the shortest seasons.

(2) For the most economical production of crops and the best use of farm labor the farmer should grow a number of crops rather than one. Each farm should have some acreage devoted to the growing of alfalfa, a grain crop, and one or more of the row-tilled crops.

(3) The preparation of the seed bed is very important. Sugar beets require more labor in this respect than any of the other crops. A well-prepared seed bed lessens the labor of cultivation and is essential for obtaining a good stand and yield from all crops.

(4) The labor of planting potatoes is greater than that of any other crop studied.

(5) Manure is considered very valuable. Of the farmers visited, 92 per cent manured some land, and 84.5 per cent of these used the manure on beets.

(6) Grain crops do not respond well to the use of manure, as the straw growth is too great.

(7) Sugar beets require the most labor for cultivation becaus᷾
the handwork necessary in thinning and hoeing.

(8) Cantaloupes require the most labor for irrigating.

(9) Alfalfa shows the lowest cost per acre for production,
cantaloupes the greatest.

(10) Oats, wheat, barley, and alfalfa have approximately
same requirement of horse labor per acre and the three gra
approximately the same requirement of man labor to produce
crop, while alfalfa requires a somewhat greater proportion of ɪ
labor per acre. Beans require approximately twice as much ɪ
and horse labor as alfalfa. Beets and potatoes require more ɪ
labor than beans, because of the greater marketing charge,
they require about double the horse labor necessary to produce
acre of beans, four times the requirement for alfalfa, and five tɪ
the requirement for grain crops.

ADDITIONAL COPIES
OF THIS PUBLICATION MAY BE PROCURED FROM
THE SUPERINTENDENT OF DOCUMENTS
GOVERNMENT PRINTING OFFICE
WASHINGTON, D. C.
AT
20 CENTS PER COPY

UNITED STATES DEPARTMENT OF AGRICULTURE

BULLETIN No. 918

Contribution from the Bureau of Entomology
L. O. HOWARD, Chief, in collaboration with the Federal
Horticultural Board, C. L. MARLATT, Chairman

| Washington, D. C. | PROFESSIONAL PAPER | April 19, 1921 |

REPORT ON INVESTIGATIONS OF THE PINK BOLL-WORM[1] OF COTTON IN MEXICO.

By U. C. LOFTIN, *Entomological Assistant,* K. B. McKINNEY, *Scientific Assistant,* and W. K. HANSON,[2] *Plant Quarantine Inspector.*

CONTENTS.

	Page.		Page.
The Laguna district	1	Dispersal	34
Distribution of the pink bollworm	4	Natural control	38
Life history	5	Repression	47
Seasonal history	19	Summary	56
Feeding habits of larvæ	21	Literature cited	57
Damage caused by the pink bollworm	24	Appendix	58
Food plants	32		

THE LAGUNA DISTRICT.

In 1918 the Federal Horticultural Board deemed it advisable to establish a research station in a locality where there was a sufficient infestation of the pink bollworm to make possible the gathering of detailed information regarding this serious cotton pest. This research station was established in February, 1918, in Ciudad Lerdo, Durango, Mexico, near Torreon. Approximately 95 per cent of the upland cotton produced in the Republic of Mexico is grown in this vicinity, the so-called Laguna district.

[1] *Pectinophora gossypiella* Saunders: Order Lepidoptera, family Gelechiidae.

[2] This report is based on two years' work in the Laguna, conducted by the Federal Horticultural Board under authority given, in the appropriation for the eradication of the pink bollworm, to investigate in Mexico or elsewhere the pink bollworm as a basis for control measures. The experts conducting this investigation were transferred to the Board for this purpose from the Bureau of Entomology and this paper is therefore offered for publication as a joint contribution from these two offices. Provision for the establishment of the laboratory in Mexico and authority for the work was obtained through the courtesy of Senor Pastor Rouíx, Secretary of Agriculture of Mexico. The work was made possible also by the active cooperation and assistance of the cotton planters of the Laguna. Special thanks are extended to the Tlahualilo Company, the Testamentaria de Carlos Gonzales, and to Mr. Lloyd Rone for the use of their plantations for experimental purposes and many other courtesies. This station was established during 1918 under the general field direction of Mr. August Busck and was continued by the authors of this paper under the general direction of the chairman of the Board and Dr. W. D. Hunter.

11696°—21—Bull. 918——1

The Laguna district is an irregularly shaped valley of about 2,000 square miles, almost completely surrounded by mountains. It is situated about 250 miles south of the Rio Grande, on the boundary line of the States of Durango and Coahuila, Mexico. It derives its name from the fact that it was formerly a lake (laguna) serving as an outlet of the Rio Nazas. As recently as 1837 a part of the Tlahualilo property was under water and at present there are considerable areas near San Pedro, Coahuila, which are filled with water when the river is at a flood stage. The soil is a deep alluvial deposit, very rich, and well adapted to the culture of cotton.

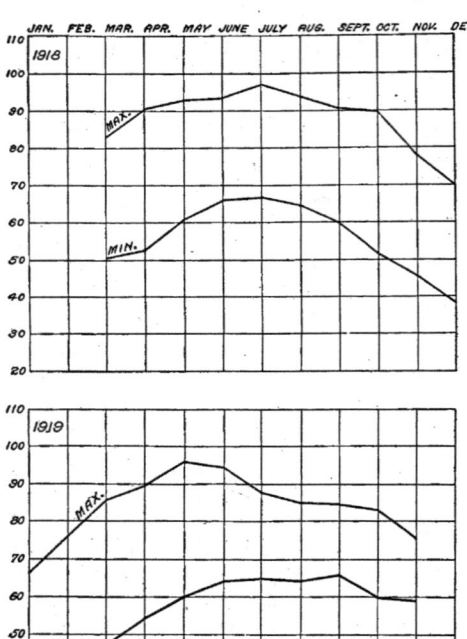

FIG. 1.—Average mean temperature for 1918 and 1919 at Ciudad Lerdo, Durango, Mexico.

CLIMATIC CONDITIONS.

Torreon, the principal city of the Laguna, has an elevation of about 4,000 feet. Generally speaking, this section of the country receives an average of 6 to 8 inches rainfall annually, but in 1919 the precipitation was very close to 15 inches.

In the months of May, June, July, and August temperatures range from 95° to 100° F. during the day down to about 64° (average) at night. In the winter months of December, January, and February the thermometer registers from 69° (average maximum) to as low as 24° F.

Figure 1 gives a graphic record of the thermometer readings taken at the station in Ciudad Lerdo, Durango.

It must be kept in mind that the above charts represent the average of the daily readings for each month and not the extremes which weře reached. The relative humidity is rather high, often reaching the saturation point at night.

From monthly records kept by the Tlahualilo Co., at Tlahualilo, Durango, covering a period of 15 years extending from 1904 to 1918, inclusive, the average rainfall for that region has been 8.07 inches per year.

TABLE I.—*Annual precipitation in inches at Tlahualilo.*

Year.	Precipitation.	Year.	Precipitation.	Year.	Precipitation.
1904	6.09	1909	13.32	1914	11.42
1905	11.31	1910	3.91	1915	4.63
1906	12.09	1911	6.98	1916	4.30
1907	8.71	1912	8.56	1917	3.46
1908	6.43	1913	12.79	1918	7.14

From records taken at the laboratory in Ciudad Lerdo, the following figures are given, covering the years 1918 and 1919, the years during which the observations relating to the pink bollworm in this report were made.

TABLE II.—*Monthly precipitation in inches at Ciudad Lerdo, Durango.*

Month.	Precipitation.	
	1918	1919
January	(1)	1.20
February	(1)	Trace
March	0.35	0.54
April	Trace.	0.00
May	0.02	0.00
June	2.76	1.44
July	Trace.	3.98
August	1.56	5.16
September	0.07	1.75
October	0.09	0.87
November	1.74	0.15
December	0.21	2 0.00
Total	6.80	15.09

1 No record.   2 Record only for Dec. 1-10.

CULTURAL METHODS AND PRODUCTION.

This section is semiarid and depends upon the water from the Rio Nazas and Rio Agua Naval for irrigation. The water usually comes down some time between August and December and is applied at a rate which is equivalent to about 1 meter deep to the fields that are to be planted in the following year. With an occasional rain in June or July or a small amount of water from the river during these months the fall irrigation suffices for the crop. As there is not enough water for all the land, only a small portion is cultivated, and on some plantations a portion of the land regularly lies fallow for several years at a time. Under this system of cultivation the land has to be well prepared and thoroughly cultivated in order to conserve the moisture. The cotton planting begins about February 15 and may continue until June if there are June rains or water in the river. The land is planted as soon as possible after it dries out, as this is necessary to secure germination.

Cotton is the principal crop grown in this section, and while there are small areas devoted to corn, wheat, beans, and alfalfa, most of the planters use their land year after year for cotton and buy the feed for their domestic animals elsewhere. No very reliable data are available on acreage and production in the Laguna, but the annual production varies from 60,000 to 150,000 bales, with an average crop of from 75,000 to 80,000 bales. The yield varies from one-fourth bale to 2 bales per acre, with an average of from one-half to three-fourths of a bale. All of the cotton is of the short-stapled varieties, as it has been found by experience that these give better results than the long-staple or Egyptian varieties.

DISTRIBUTION OF THE PINK BOLLWORM.

The species is widely distributed throughout the cotton-producing world, and according to Gough (*12*)[3] is now known to occur in India, Palestine, Mesopotamia, Ceylon, Burma, Straits Settlements, China, Japan, the Philippine and Hawaiian Islands, East Africa, Zanzibar, Egypt, Sudan, West Africa (Southern Nigeria, Sierra Leone), Brazil, Mexico, and Texas in the United States. It has more recently been found in a limited area in western Louisiana adjoining the infestation in eastern Texas.

INTRODUCTION INTO MEXICO.

The pink bollworm was introduced into Mexico in 1911. During that season two importations of Egyptian seed were made. One consisted of 125 sacks and was planted near Monterey, in the State of Nuevo Leon. The other, consisting of 6 tons, was planted near San Pedro, State of Coahuila, in the Laguna district. From what is known of the abundance of the pink bollworm in Egypt in 1911 it is probable that both shipments of seed were infested and that both of them contributed to the present infestation in Mexico. Cotton culture has not been continued in the vicinity of Monterey, but the crop of Egyptian cotton produced there in 1911 attracted considerable attention and much of the seed was shipped to the Laguna.

At the present time the pink bollworm is generally and uniformly distributed in the Laguna.

PRESENT DISTRIBUTION IN MEXICO.

. Outside of the Laguna district the pink bollworm is known to be established in three localities in Mexico. One of these is at Santa

---

[3] Italic numbers in parentheses refer to "Literature cited," p. 57.

Rosalia, State of Chihuahua, at a point about 200 miles south of El Paso. The other two infestations are located in the northern portion of the State of Coahuila. One of these is at San Carlos, at a point about 15 miles southwest of the town of Jimenez on the Rio Grande, or about 40 miles approximately west of Eagle Pass. At this place infestation has been found in fields in the immediate vicinity of the gin. None of the insects were found in outlying fields. The other infestation in the State of Coahuila is located at Allende. This is about 40 miles from the nearest point on the Rio Grande.

During the season of 1919 inspections were made by agents of the Federal Horticultural Board in the cotton region between Matamoras and Nuevo Laredo. No traces of infestation were found. Likewise the cotton growing in the Imperial Valley in the State of Lower California has been inspected with negative results. Inspection of these regions will be continued, as the insect may at any time become established along the Rio Grande by shipments of seed from the interior of Mexico.

The remarks above refer to infestations in growing cotton. The pest is frequently brought to the border towns of Mexico in cotton seed scattered in freight cars, and living specimens are constantly being found under such conditions by the inspectors of the Federal Horticultural Board.

LIFE HISTORY.

SUMMARY OF LIFE CYCLE.

The moths of the pink bollworm emerge in the early spring and summer from larvæ which have passed the winter in cotton seed or bolls. The eggs are laid soon after emergence on almost any part of the plant. The incubation period is from 3 to 12 days and the larvæ begin feeding in the squares or bolls. During the spring and summer the larval period occupies from 8 to 16 days, but in the fall and winter it is extended over a period of from a few months to two years or more. These two kinds of larvæ, while indistinguishable taxonomically, may be designated short-cycle or "summer" larvæ and long-cycle or "resting" larvæ. Pupation takes place in the soil or trash on the surface of the soil, in the summer stage, and in the ground, seed, or lint in the resting larvæ. The pupal period covers from 6 to 20 days. The average length of the life cycle from egg to egg during the summer is 31 days.

LABORATORY METHODS.

The experiments with the life history of the pink bollworm were all conducted at Ciudad Lerdo, Durango, Mexico. An adobe house was used for a laboratory. The adults were confined in 2-quart fruit jars covered with cheesecloth for oviposition. Branches of cotton plants containing leaves and squares, stuck in tubes of water to keep them fresh, and bolls were provided for oviposition. Pieces of blotting paper dampened with water or sweetened substances were added as food for the moths. The eggs were removed to other jars for hatching and the young larvæ carefully removed to the food. Bolls and squares were used, but the squares were found more satisfactory. The food with the young larvæ was placed in vials plugged with cotton. The pieces of bolls would become discolored, decomposed, and unsuitable for food in one or two days, while a square would remain in good condition several days and the larva could be examined daily with less disturbance.

Wire cages were also used over small potted plants and cotton plants in the experimental plat to check the laboratory results. The pupæ were removed to glass vials with a piece of damp cotton in the bottom to provide the necessary humidity.

Temperature and humidity records were made with maximum and minimum thermometers and recording hygrothermographs placed indoors and outside in a U. S. Weather Bureau instrument shelter.

MOTH.

DESCRIPTION.

The moth with wings spread is about three-fifths of an inch from tip to tip, dark brown in color, with irregular blackish markings on the forewings, the hindwings silvery gray with no distinct markings. The forewings are bluntly pointed, the hindwings acutely pointed, and both heavily fringed posteriorly. When at rest the wings are folded flat over the back.

HABITS.

The moths are very seclusive in their habits during the day. It is exceptionally rare to find one in the fields until after sundown. Just at dusk they can be seen flitting very quickly from plant to plant, and by close examinations with a flashlight at night they can be readily found in a resting position on almost any part of the plant. They are active as late as 12 p. m. No observations were ever made later at night, but it is very likely that they remain active until daybreak. Occasionally they conceal themselves on the plant, but usually they crawl under trash, stones, clods, or even into the loose soil. They are very loath to leave their hiding places during the day, but when disturbed they run with a quick jerky movement or fly a short distance and immediately hide under the nearest object.

In the laboratory the moths emerging from stored cotton would congregate on the window screens at dusk. They would remain quietly till morning and then return to their hiding places. Only rarely would one be seen during the day.

LONGEVITY.

Males and females are produced in about equal proportions and their length of life is about equal. Under favorable laboratory conditions one moth was kept alive for 26 days, but the average length of life of the adult was 14.7 days. There are no indications that moths ever live for long periods of time or pass the winter in this stage.

Whether moths under natural conditions ever take nourishment other than water was never observed, but just as many eggs were deposited in the breeding jars where pure water was used as where sweetened water was substituted. Water is a very essential factor in the longevity of the adult. The average length of life of the moths where no water could be obtained was 7.6 days, compared to 14.7 days when water was supplied daily.

PREOVIPOSITION PERIOD.

Eggs were deposited in captivity from 1 to 6 days after issuance of the moth, with an average of 3.8 days preoviposition period. It is not known how long a period elapses before oviposition begins in nature, but from analogy with other species it is possible that the bulk of the eggs are laid the first night under normal field conditions. The moths were never observed in the act of depositing eggs, either in the fields or in the breeding cages, but from the night-flying habits of the moth it is evident that oviposition takes place at dusk or at night.

FIG. 2.—Egg of *Pectinophora gossypiella*. Highly magnified.

EGG.

DESCRIPTION.

The egg is small, elongate oval, somewhat broader at one end; length from 0.4 to 0.6 mm., breadth 0.2 to 0.3 mm.; shell iridescent, pearly white with greenish tint when first deposited, turning to almost red before hatching; surface finely reticulated with regular longitudinal lines or ridges with irregular cross-connections, resembling the reticulations on the hull of a peanut. (Fig. 2.) The larva can be easily seen inside the shell just prior to hatching.

POSITION ON PLANT.

The eggs are deposited on all parts of the plant, including the bolls and bracts, leaf buds, leaves, stems, and squares. The preference is for some more or less hidden location, such as the base of the boll, between the bracts and bolls, the folds of the small leaf buds, the creases formed by the veins and midribs of the leaves, and the axils of the leaves.

Some heavily infested plants were examined at Lerdo during August and September, 1919, to determine the proportion of eggs deposited on different parts of the plants, the results of which are given in Table III.

TABLE III.—*Location on the cotton plant of the eggs of P. gossypiella.*

Number of plants examined.	Number and location of eggs.							Total number of eggs on plant.
	Leaves.	Stems.	Buds:	Squares.	Bolls.			
					Bracts.	Base.	Tip.	
1......................	7	6	45	1	8	81	0	148
1......................	32	6	107	3	11	108	3	270
1......................	21	36	34	0	74	87	0	253
1......................	94	36	66	2	54	53	1	315
1......................	31	24	37	3	78	49	1	223
1......................	20	16	56	1	93	55	2	243
1......................	22	15	17	3	2	39	0	98
Total(7 plants).	227	139	362	13	320	472	7	1,549
Per cent..............	14.7	9.0	23.4	0.8	20.7	30.5	0.5	....

It is clearly seen that the boll is the most favored place, 51.7 per cent of the entire number of eggs being deposited on the boll and its appendages. The small leaf buds were second with 23.4 per cent, the leaves third with 14.7 per cent, the stems fourth with 9 per cent, and the squares fifth with only 0.8 per cent. It is further seen from this table that the base of the boll is frequently selected, as 30.5 per cent of the eggs were deposited there and only 0.5 per cent were deposited in the sutures at the tip of the boll. The position of the eggs upon the plant is important, for upon it largely depends the fate of the young larvæ. It is essential that the larvæ reach the squares or bolls to feed, as no larvæ were ever found which had developed beyond the second instar on other parts of the plant. It is a mistaken instinct of the moths to oviposit in other parts of the plant, as it is evident that a much larger proportion of the larvæ hatching from eggs laid in close proximity to the food will reach it than of those that have to crawl over the plant exposed to their natural enemies in search of food.

When laid on the leaves, buds, stems, and squares the eggs are usually placed singly or in small groups of from 5 to 10. When laid on the tip of the boll they are placed singly or in small groups in the sutures. In this position the eggs are often flattened or crushed by the growing of the boll. When laid at the base of the boll they are placed between the calyx and the boll or beneath the bracts around the base of the boll, and are usually in masses of from a few to as many as 75 to 100, which are overlapped and flattened out more or less shingle fashion. The flattened appearance in this case is due to the presence of the calyx and not to the natural shape of the egg. In these masses, eggs of all stages of development, as well as shells, are found, showing that they were not all deposited at one time by a single female.

As the female does not deposit eggs readily in captivity, difficulty was experienced in determining exactly how many eggs were deposited by a single female. In our experiment usually from 5 to 20 moths were confined in one cage. Under these conditions it was never known which moths had oviposited and which had not, and while several hundred eggs were often obtained from a cage, it is certain that the maximum number they were capable of laying were never obtained. Often heavy, pregnant females were found dead in the cage and apparently never had deposited any eggs. Upon dissection of gravid females the ovaries were found to contain from 75 to 125 well-developed eggs. Busck (8) places the number at over a hundred and Willcocks (7) says that while small individuals may produce only about 250 eggs, well-developed individuals are capable of laying 400 to 500 eggs or more.

INCUBATION.

All of our records were made under laboratory conditions. Figure 3 shows that the difference between the maximum and the minimum, or the day and night temperatures, for each month amounts only to from 6° to 8° F.

The egg stage, even under these rather constant conditions, varied from 3 to 12 days. The range for the months of April, May, September, and October was from 7

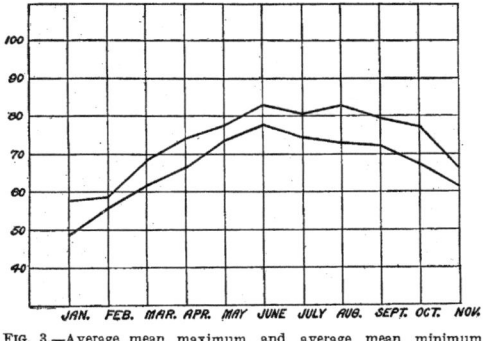

FIG. 3.—Average mean maximum and average mean minimum temperatures for 1919 at Ciudad Lerdo, Durango, Mexico.

to 12 days, and for June, July, and August it was from 3 to 5 days, with an average of 4.6 days for the entire season, the average being taken from 300 records based on thousands of eggs.

HATCHING.

The actual hatching of the egg requires only a very short time. The young larva can be seen moving inside the shell a short time before it actually emerges. An opening is cut in the broad end of the egg and the small larva wriggles out and crawls rapidly away in search of food.

The empty shell is white and soon becomes an almost unrecognizable wrinkled object. It remains on the plant until it decays or is carried away by the wind or other agencies.

LARVA.

NEWLY-HATCHED LARVÆ.

The newly-hatched larvæ are creamy white, with dark-brown head and thoracic shield and long, prominent, dark setæ showing very plainly. They are a little less than 1 mm. in length and gradually taper from the head, having thus a slight wedge-shaped appearance. In this stage the larvæ are very active. Under laboratory conditions they are very restless and crawl rapidly from place to place before entering a square or boll. Many larvæ continue crawling around for 24 hours or more until they become so weakened that they are not able to cut their way into the squares or bolls. It was often observed that most of the larvæ which succeeded in entering the food provided for them did so the day they were hatched. It is not known to what extent this wandering around takes place under natural conditions. Larvæ are found crawling over the plants, but they always seem restless and ill at ease. This probably does not take place normally to any great degree, except in the case of larvæ from eggs laid on other parts of the plant than the squares and bolls.

LARVÆ ENTERING BOLLS.

The larvæ do not seem to have any preference as to where the boll is entered. Sometimes a light netlike web is spun and the entrance is made underneath it. At other times the entrance is made with no protection whatever. The larvæ cut the carpel away, throwing the fragments outside, very little if any being consumed. The time required for the larvæ to enter may vary with the age of the boll, but it usually takes them from 20 to 40 minutes to become completely hidden. If the boll is examined soon after they have entered, the holes are easily located by the surrounding frass, and although minute, can be seen with the naked eye. After 2 or 3 days the frass is blown away by the wind or removed by other agents and the holes close up, leaving only brownish spots which are hard to differentiate from other discolorations on the boll. Then they can only be detected by a trained eye, and the only way to be certain a boll is infested is to examine its interior.

LARVÆ AFTER ENTERING BOLLS.

After the boll has been entered the larvæ become glassy white, soft, and sluggish. They so closely resemble the watery lint at this stage that they would be very easily overlooked, except for their dark heads and thoracic shields, which show as black specks against the lint.

There are three molts, completing four larval instars or stages. The first stage lasts about 2 days; the second and third, 3 to 4 days each; and the fourth, 4 to 5 days,; thus the larval development is completed in an average of 13.3 days in the summer larvæ. The second and third instars resemble the first in general appearance, and it is usually in the fourth or last larval stage that the larvæ change to the characteristic pink color from which the name "pink bollworm" is derived. Sometimes the pink color appears in the third instar, especially if development has been retarded in some way or the larva has been exposed to the air. The coloring first appears as transverse pink lines on the dorsal side of the segments and diffuses and deepens till there is only a small whitish or flesh-colored line left between the segments. The color seems to be more pronounced in the larvæ which reach maturity in the late summer or early autumn and is a very deep pink or dull red. The head and thoracic shield are reddish brown with dark-brown mandibles and anal plate. The ventral side, legs, and prolegs are white to flesh colored, the legs and prolegs with brownish claws and crotches. The full-grown larva is cylindrical and measures about one-half inch in length.

With the fourth stage the larva becomes very active again when disturbed and conceals itself as quickly as possible. A cocoon is spun attached to whatever object the larva is hiding in. The full-grown larva is never content outside a cocoon after it leaves a boll or seed. If it is taken from one cocoon it will immediately make another. How many times this will be repeated was not determined, but a perfectly healthy larva is rarely if ever found outside a cocoon, except when crawling from place to place.

PUPA.

The pupa is whitish, with faint markings of pink when first formed, turning to a mahogany brown as it dries and to a darker brown before emergence. It measures 8 to 10 mm. in length by 2.5 to 3 mm. in width. The surface is covered with a fine velvety pubescence, the posterior end terminating in a short, stout, upwardly pointing, hooklike process.

PUPATION OF SUMMER LARVÆ.

When the summer larvæ have completed their feeding, they cut to the outside of the boll directly through the carpel wall from the last seed attacked and drop to the ground for pupation.

This exit hole through the carpel wall is usually round and clean cut and can be easily recognized as having been cut from the inside of the boll. Plate II, A, gives a comparison of the entrance hole into the boll of the common bollworm, *Chloridea obsoleta* Fab., and the exit hole of the pink bollworm. The entrance holes of the common bollworm are larger, not so clean cut, and surrounded by a raised margin. They are not likely to be confused once both have been seen.

In the case of the summer larvæ, the holes made in the green cotton boll are always for the exit of the larvæ, and not for the issuance of the moth. From an examination in 1919 of over 16,000 green bolls that averaged over 2.5 larvæ per boll, not a single pupa or pupal skin was found. Should a larva cut a hole in a green growing boll for the issuance of the moth, this hole would probably close from proliferation before the pupal stage of 9.3 days is passed.

Occasionally, in mature or dry bolls, as distinguished from green ones, more than a mere exit hole is cut when the larva reaches the carpel wall. The carpel tissues and the adjoining lint are cut away and an elongate pocketlike cavity is made large enough for the larva to become straightened out in its final preparation for pupation. When this is done a light cocoon is spun inside this cavity and a hole cut through the carpel wall to the outside. The last remaining parts of the carpel wall are not cut entirely out leaving an open hole, but the particles are held together and in place by a few fine strands of silk which are easily broken and pushed away when the moth emerges.

The very fact that only a few larvæ pupate in the bolls is conclusive enough that there are other more favorable places for pupation. These places are either on the ground or in the ground. If the moisture conditions are sufficient on the surface, they may spin a cocoon in the trash or on any convenient object, and pupate there; but if it is too dry and the soil is loose they may burrow as deep as 3 inches below the surface, make an earthern cell, line it with a very fine, tough cocoon, and pupate there. During the summer a good many pupæ are probably destroyed by cultivation, but when pupation takes place in the ground, only the exit passage being destroyed and the pupa itself not molested, the moth may be able to escape because of its burrowing power.

Fullaway (3) and Busck (8) found that in Hawaii pupation normally takes place in the boll and only rarely in the soil or other places. Maxwell-Lefroy (2) found that in India pupation occurs in the boll or on the bracts or leaves of the cotton, and in unirrigated black cotton soil might be found in a crack of the dry soil. Willcocks (7, p. 113) says that in Egypt—

Pupation seems most often to take place on the ground under the fallen leaves, or in the fold of a dead leaf or again between two dead leaves, also on old bolls which have dropped or been broken off, and under or attached to small lumps of earth. In fact they may be looked for amongst any shelter of this kind. One situation was noted that seems to be especially favored by the larvæ as a haven to pass the pupal stage, this was furnished by the dead flowers which are of course very numerous below the plants.

In Mexico pupæ were never found on the leaves or bracts under field conditions. When green bolls were picked and left in sacks the emerging larvæ would sometimes hollow out a slight depression and pupate near the base of the boll, or they would pupate between the involucre and boll without making a depression, or spin their cocoons

COTTON BOLLS SHOWING CHARACTERISTIC INJURY BY THE PINK BOLLWORM.

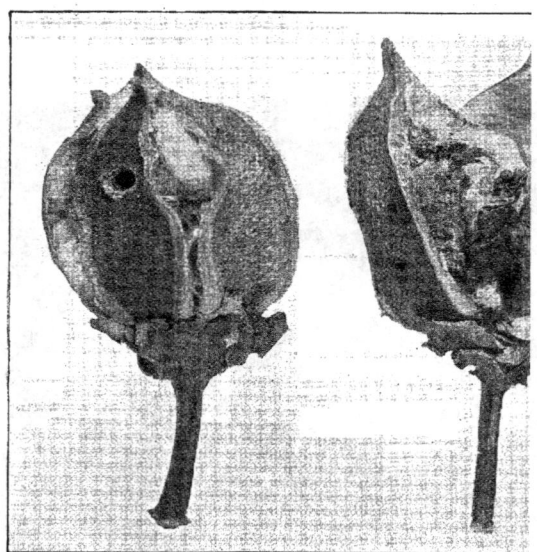

A, On left, entrance hole of *Chloridea obsoleta*.   On right, exit holes of pink b

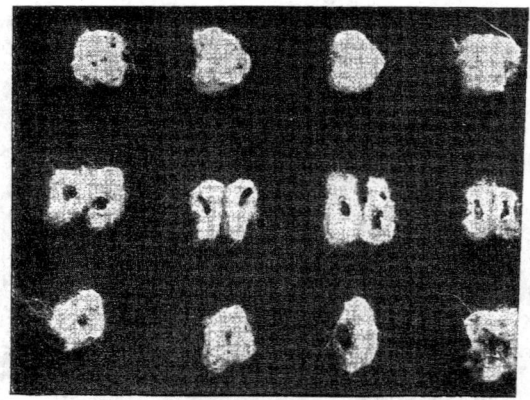

B, Double seed formed by pink bollworm larvae: Above, holes made for is
broken apart to show cavities; below, double seed int

PINK BOLLWORM.

on the sides of the sack. The old flowers under the plants did not seem to be more favored than other bits of rubbish.

The duration of the pupal stage of summer larvæ from 150 records ranges from 6 to 14 days. There is considerable variation among the individual pupæ, some requiring 1 to 2 days more than others which pupated on the same night.

Table IV summarizes over 300 complete records of the various stages of the pink bollworm at Lerdo, Durango, Mexico, during 1918 and 1919.

TABLE IV.—*Duration in days of summer stages of P. gossypiella.*

	Average
Egg stage	4. 6
Larval instars:	
First	2–3
Second	3–4
Third	3–4
Fourth	4–5
Total average	13. 3
Pupal stage	9. 3
Preoviposition period	3. 8
Total period from egg to egg	31. 0

RESTING LARVÆ.

In the preceding part the development of the different summer stages of the pink bollworm has been discussed. There is still another important phase of the life history—the long-cycle or resting larvæ. It is in this stage that the species passes the winter when no food is available or when conditions are adverse in any way. It is also in this stage that the greatest dispersal by man takes place and only in this stage that any known control measures can be used.

Beginning some time in August, when the temperature is still high and there is yet plenty of food available, some of the larvæ upon reaching maturity do not pupate at once, but remain wherever they are as full-fed larvæ. These larvæ are identical in form with those that pupate and can not be distinguished from them. What causes some larvæ to do this and others to pupate as usual when reared under the same conditions is not known, but Willcocks (7) suggests it is probably some instinct inherited from the time when in its original natural habitat there were no food plants available to sustain the species over a long period of time. In November and December, when the temperature is lower and no food is available, all of the larvæ develop this tendency and it is the exception rather than the rule for them to pupate. Thus in the Laguna this resting habit seems to be a combination of estivation and hibernation, for it begins while food is still available and the temperature high. In this section the average frost date is about November 20, and moths emerg-

kes them difficult to separate.

?art of these seeds go through the gin and come out intact
ling double seed is sure evidence of pink-bollworm infestatio
)ften double seeds are formed in seed in different locks, the
:ting cocoon running through the hole made in the partition
is affords good protection for the larva, as it prevents the
m falling to the ground and being exposed to excessive mo
1 other agencies which are more detrimental to the larva o
)und than on the plants.

When the cocoon is spun in the lint or a single seed the lar
a curled-up position and the cocoon is spun tightly arou:
ming a spherical compact mass. Similar cocoons are forn
? ground or attached to any convenient object if larvæ are rer
m seed or lint. The cocoon fits so closely and is so tough t
very difficult to remove without injuring the larva. It is
rd to detect a larva inside a seed, and the only sure way 1
iether the seed contains a larva is to examine the interior.

cks (7) in writing about Egyptian cotton seed, which has a sn
ick coat and is not covered with lint, says the silken-cover(
ince hole can usually be seen with a lens. This, however, do
ld true for short-staple seed.

Few data are available on the number and proportion of
und in the lint and in the single and double seed. Samples (
n were hand-ginned and the number of larvæ in single and (
ed determined, but unfortunately no record was kept of the
r in the lint. It is possible that some of the larvæ counted
igle seeds in the first and second picking samples were in th
it this did not occur in the samples of the third picking. :
i noted that the sample for the third picking is from the 191
id had been stored for some time. At the time of examina
nsiderable part of the larvæ were dead, but this does not aff(
oportion found in the single and double seed, and while the
e not quite comparable, they at least give an idea of the n
larvæ present at different times. The number of larvæ fo
e single and double seed for the different picks are given in T1

TABLE V.—*Number of pink bollworm larvæ found in single and double seed of cotton picked at different dates.*

Weight of sample.	Date picked.	Date examined.	Double seed.			Single seed.		
			Number double seed.	Number of larvæ in double seed.	Per cent of total larvæ in double seed.	Number single seed damaged.	Number of larvæ in single seed.	Per cent of total larvæ in single seed.
First picking:	1919.	1919.						
½ pound..........	Aug. 4	Oct. 10	0	0	0	38	2	100
1 pound..........	Aug. 6	Oct. 8	¹0	0	0	108	1	100
1 pound..........	Sept. 23	Oct. 22	0	0	0	156	3	100
Second picking:								
½ pound..........	Oct. 16	Oct. —	30	29	58	121	21	41
1 pound..........	Nov. 2	Oct. —	²34	30	56.6	467	23	43.4
Third picking:	1918.							
½ pound..........	Dec. 3	Mar. 30	106	95	30	715	250	70
¼ pound..........	Dec. 10	Mar. 20	36	26	33	597	53	67

¹ One pupa in lint, not counted in above.
² Two pupæ in lint, not counted in above.

This table shows that no double seed was found in cotton from the first picking, that 57.3 per cent of the larvæ were found in double seed from the second picking, and that the percentage fell to 31.5 in the third picking. It is probable, however, that occasional double seeds are formed during August and September or in the first picking.

Taking an average of these figures and reducing them to a 1-pound basis, the number of larvæ per bale present in the seed from the different pickings can be calculated. It is thought that no live larvæ pass through the gins in the lint, and that many of the larvæ in the seed are driven out during the cleaning and ginning. It is certain that the large number found in seed when hand-ginned were never found in commercially ginned seed.

TABLE VI.—*Number of pink bollworm larvæ found per pound and the estimated number per bale in cotton from different pickings.*

Weight of sample.	Double seed.				Single seed.				
	Number double seed.	Number larvæ in double seed.	Estimated number of larvæ per bale in double seed.	Per cent of total larvæ in double seed.	Number single seed damaged.	Number larvæ in single seed.	Estimated number of larvæ per bale in single seed.	Per cent of total larvæ in single seed.	Estimated number of larvæ per bale in[1] single and double seed.
First picking:									
1 pound........	0	0	0	0	121	6	9,000	100	9,000
Second picking:									
1 pound........	43	39	58,500	56.5	392	30	45,000	43.5	103,500
Third picking:									
1 pound........	189	161	241,500	28.5	1,749	404	606,000	71.5	847,500

Gough (5), in one of his earlier publications, states that there are two generations of the hibernating larvæ, the older generation consisting of full-fed worms and the younger the winter-feeding brood, which were not full-fed at the time of hibernation and continue developing slowly till about March. In a later publication (*12*) weighings of resting larvæ were made from January to July and it was found that the weight constantly fell from February to July. He concludes that "the fall in weight does not necessarily demand the explanation that the larvæ were fasting, but taken along with the known fact that many hibernating or æstivating larvæ do not feed, it lends considerable weight to the probability of the larvæ not feeding during their resting period."

A very small proportion of the larvæ have not completed their growth when the cotton is picked, and these continue feeding for a while before making their resting cocoon. In some bolls examined November 26, 1918, there was an average of 6.64 fourth-instars and 0.03 third-instars per boll. After the resting cocoon is once spun no feeding takes place. If larvæ are removed from the seeds in which they are resting, other seed will sometimes be hollowed out, but the contents are thrown to the outside and no actual feeding takes place. It sometimes happens that frost does not come in the Laguna till January or February, and it is probable that feeding continues longer than usual in such years.

DURATION OF THE RESTING STAGE.

Larvæ are capable of passing long periods of time in this quiescent stage. Gough (*5*) found in seeds of Indian cotton which had been imported to Egypt larvæ which were over 2 years old. Busck (*8*) in Hawaii compressed cotton seed into small bales and found live larvæ in them for 18 months. Willcocks (*7*) stored a large number of bolls picked in November, 1913, in an outdoor cage, and moths continued emerging till August 28, 1915, a period of nearly 2 years. There were 4.4 per cent of the larvæ in double seed collected in November, 1918, still alive on November 20, 1919, when work at the station was discontinued.

PUPATION OF RESTING LARVÆ.

When the resting stage has been passed in the lint, single seed, or in any place where the larva is curled up in a small, compact cocoon, it is necessary to leave this cocoon and prepare more ample quarters for pupation. In such cases a lighter, more elongate cocoon is usually spun among the fiber or seed, but in some instances in stored seed pupæ are formed without any protection whatever.

When the resting stage has been passed in the double seed the construction of the cocoon between the two seeds makes it elongate enough for the larva to pupate successfully and pupation usually takes place *in situ*. In such cases the emergence hole for the moth is cut just prior to pupation and not when the seeds are first webbed together. Often the end of the pupal shell is seen protruding from the seeds through this opening.

When pupation occurs in old bolls of cotton a favorite method is to make a slight depression in the lint and pupate between the cotton and boll. Where hibernation has been in the fields larvæ may leave the bolls and pupate in the ground. On March 14, 1919, 1½ square yards of soil in the corral at Lerdo, where many bolls were lying around, were examined. Four live larvæ and one dead one, together with one live pupa and several empty pupal cases, were found. All were near the surface, one larva being under a piece of trash and the others an inch or so down. All the larvæ and the live pupa had light cocoons and seemed to have gone into the soil for pupation rather than hibernation. In the case of the old pupal skins it could not be determined whether they came from hibernating larvæ or were left over from the previous summer.

The duration of the pupal stage from 250 resting larvæ ranged from 8 to 26 days, with an average of 10.3 days. This is an average of 1 day more than for the summer larvæ, due to the fact that pupation took place during the colder months. There is considerable individual variation in the length of pupæ formed at the same time, but this occurs in pupæ from summer larvæ as well as from resting larvæ. The pupæ from which male moths emerged required an average of one-half day more than those from which females emerged, the males requiring 10.5 days and the females 10 days.

TIME OF EMERGENCE FROM RESTING LARVÆ.

A few moths may emerge throughout the year in the Laguna. When work was first begun in the early part of February, 1918, freshly formed pupæ were found among seed at the seed warehouses. During the month of March, 1918, there emerged 23.5 per cent of all the moths which emerged during the year from larvæ collected in seed in February and removed to the laboratory. Emergence continued till August, when all of the larvæ had died or emerged, the maximum being reached in May. Pupæ were formed from larvæ collected in the summer and fall of 1918 throughout the fall and into January, 1919, thus completing the cycle of pupation for every month in the year. The pupal period is greatly retarded during the cold months, but this does not prevent emergence on warm days. Table VII shows the monthly emergence of moths from resting larvæ for 1918 and 1919.

11696°—21—Bull. 918——3

TABLE VII.—*The monthly emergence of moths from resting larvæ for 1918 and 1919.*

Months.	1918		1919	
	Number of moths emerged.	Per cent of total emergence.	Number of moths emerged.	Per cent of total emergence during period covered.
March..	3S1	23. 5	1	(¹)
April...	236	14. 6	125	2. 1
May..	525	32. 5	851	14. 3
June..	355	21. 9	1,811	30. 6
July..	105	6. 5	2,302	38. 8
August.......................................	16	1. 0	708	12. 0
September....................................			84	1. 4
October......................................			40	. 7
November....................................			8	. 1
Total...................................	1,618	100. 0	5,930	100. 0

¹ No complete record.

Moths emerging in 1918 were from larvæ collected in seed in February, 1918; those emerging in 1919 were from larvæ collected in bolls during November, 1918. Complete records are not available for December, 1918, or January, February, and March, 1919, due to absence from the laboratory. The percentages of moths emerging each month are based on the total number of moths which emerged and not upon the total number of larvæ. Of the larvæ collected in November, 1918, 4.4 per cent were still alive and had not pupated on November 20, 1919, when the records were discontinued.

A study of Table VII shows that emergence took place much earlier in 1918 than in 1919. During March, 1918, 23.5 per cent of the moths emerged and the maximum of 32.5 per cent was reached in May, while in 1919 only 2.1 per cent emerged in April and the maximum of 38.8 per cent was not reached till July. This seasonal variation depends largely upon the temperature and humidity. The winter of 1917–18 was unusually mild and there was an exceptionally hot period during the first week of March which hastened pupation. It was also found that dampening the seed or lint hastened emergence and a rain followed by warm weather in March or April would no doubt cause large numbers to emerge. As a rule, moths emerging before the first of May would find no suitable places for oviposition and would not be a factor in starting the infestation in the following crop.

ISSUANCE OF MOTH.

The issuance of the moth from the pupal skin requires a very short time. The pupal skin breaks or splits along the dorsal side and the moth works its way out and crawls upon some object in the open so that the wings may develop normally. As soon as the wings have extended to their full length they are raised and held in a vertical position from 5 to 15 minutes to become perfectly dried. Afterward the moth crawls off and hides until dark, if issuance has taken place during the day. What course is followed when issuance takes place at night was never observed.

TIME OF DAY MOTHS EMERGE.

The moths emerge from the pupæ at all hours of the day and night under laboratory conditions, where the temperature and humidity are more or less uniform. From Table VIII it can be seen that between the morning examinations and the afternoon examinations, 421 moths emerged in 134.5 hours, an average of 3.1 moths per hour, and that 348 moths emerged between the afternoon examinations and the morning examinations in 301 hours with an average of 1.1 moths per hour. About three times as many moths emerged during the day as emerged per hour during the night.

TABLE VIII.—*Time of day of emergence of the adult P. gossypiella.*

Date.	Morning examination.		Afternoon examination.		Date.	Morning examination.		Afternoon examination.	
	Time.	Number of adults.	Time.	Number of adults.		Time.	Number of adults.	Time.	Number of adults.
1919.					1919.				
May 22	10.00	(1)	5.25	27	June 4	10.00	(1)	5.30	9
May 23	9.30	16	5.30	5	June 5	10.00	22	6.00	19
May 24	9.30	2	5.30	17	June 6	10.00	25	6.00	20
May 25	10.30	15	5.30	25	June 7	10.00	14	(2)	(2)
May 26	9.30	10	5.00	27	June 8	10.00	(1)	(2)	(2)
May 27	9.30	15	5.30	26	June 9	10.00	(1)	6.00	28
May 28	9.30	17	6.00	13	June 10	10.00	20	5.00	39
May 29	9.30	13	8.30	19	June 11	10.00	26	5.00	27
May 30	9.30	11	6.30	25	June 12	10.00	41	5.00	22
May 31	10.00	46	8.30	16	June 13	9.30	8	(2)	(2)
June 1	10.00	20	6.00	15					
June 2	9.30	14	5.30	42	Total....	....	348	....	421
June 3	10.00	13	(2)	(2)					

1 All removed.   2 No record.

SEASONAL HISTORY.

The data show that moths may emerge at any time during the winter or early spring, and so far as known they may begin breeding if suitable food plants are found. Cotton does not grow as a perennial in this section. Sometimes it is left for the second year to produce a "zoca" crop, but the plants are dormant during the winter and the crop is produced from sprouts sent out from the roots or old stalks. Planting may begin during the first part of February, but usually begins about the middle, depending upon the season. Squares are not formed in any numbers until about the first of May, usually a little earlier on the zoca than on the plant cotton. Hollyhock, another host plant of pink bollworms, may be in bloom earlier than cotton, but it is considered of no economic importance in this connection. Repeated attempts to secure oviposition on young cotton plants during March and April, 1918, were unsuccessful. The first eggs were laid in the breeding jars·on May 5, and the first larva (one of the third instar) was found in cotton in the field on May 15, 1918. The first eggs were deposited on April 9, 1919, and the first larva found in the field on April 28. The general infestation in the fields, however, did not begin till later in 1919 than in 1918.

In general, it may be said that breeding commences in the spring as soon as the squares begin to mature and by the time the first blossoms appear a few larvæ are present. The infestation is extremely light at this season and only by careful search will any larvæ be found. As a rule the bolls are not attacked till they are from one-half to three-fourths grown, though occasionally a larva works down from the blossom to the newly set boll. It is usually about the middle to latter part of July before bolls on plant cotton are sufficiently mature to be attractive to the larvæ. From this date onward the infestation rapidly increases, and in about 10 weeks' time practically every green boll is infested. The cool nights of October and November check the development somewhat, but breeding continues until frost destroys the food plants.

Table IX shows the weekly increase in the percentage of green bolls infested during the 10 weeks during which breeding is most active. It is computed from weekly examinations of samples of green bolls collected on different plantations, an average number of 350 in 1918 and 1,100 in 1919 being used.

TABLE IX.—*The weekly increase in the percentage of green bolls infested with Pectinophora gossypiella.*

Week ending—	Percentage of green bolls infested.		Week ending—	Percentage of green bolls infested.	
	1918.	1919.		1918.	1919.
July 12	1.1		Aug. 30	79.2	20.8
July 19	7.0		Sept. 6	93.0	29.0
July 26	13.6		Sept. 13	97.3	41.0
Aug. 2	20.0		Sept. 20		45.0
Aug. 9	21.0	4.3	Sept. 27		63.0
Aug. 16	42.0	5.0	Oct. 4		83.3
Aug. 23	65.8	10.8	Oct. 11		100.0

From Table IX it is seen that the time of active breeding varies considerably, and that in 1919 it was a month later than in 1918. This depends largely upon the development of the cotton. The same climatic conditions which retard the growth of the cotton also affect the activity of the species, and the relative development of the two is about the same from year to year. It is also clearly shown that there are no distinct broods or generations and that the heavy infestation in the fall is accumulative. If the offspring from moths emerging early in the spring continue breeding throughout the

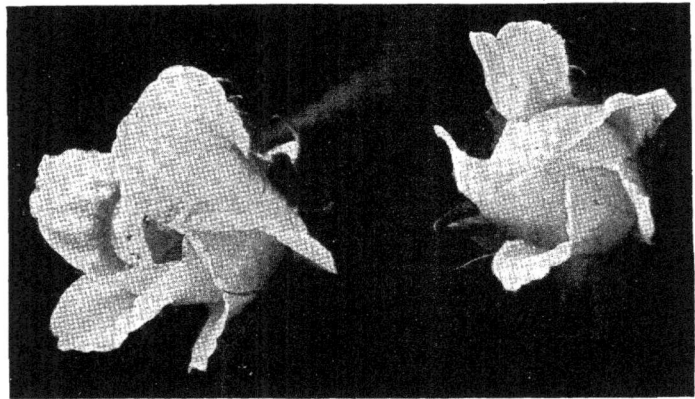

A, Characteristic rosette appearance of cotton flowers infested with the pink bollworm.

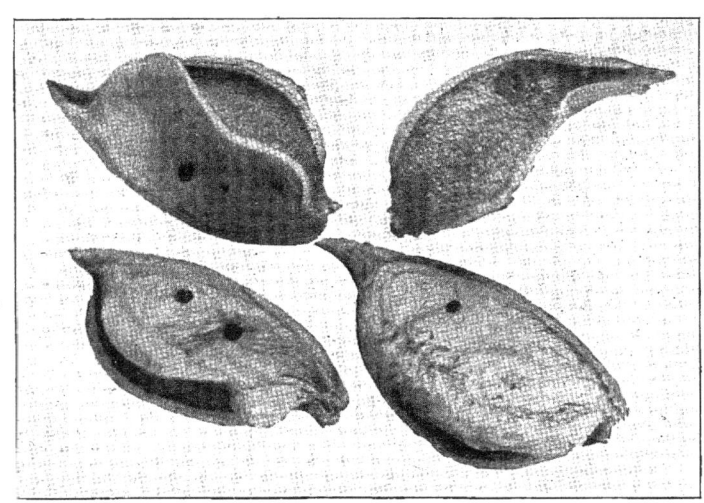

B, Holes cut through partition wall when larva goes from one lock to another. (Hunter.)

PINK BOLLWORM.

season till December and make a complete life cycle every 31 days, there are six generations, but if the moths do not emerge from the resting larvæ until the fall and the first generation goes into the resting stage again, the whole year may be passed in only one generation.

FEEDING HABITS OF LARVÆ.

LARVÆ FEEDING ON LEAVES AND STEMS.

The feeding of the pink bollworm on the leaves of cotton is of no economic importance. It is a forced condition rather than a voluntary one. If the eggs have been deposited a long way from the squares or bolls, the larvæ may feed slightly on the leaves while searching for suitable food. In such cases slight abrasions on the surface of the leaf or minute pinholes through the leaf occur. The larvæ feeding in this manner appear either to die for lack of sufficient nourishment or to be destroyed by other insects. No larvæ older than those of the second instar were ever observed feeding on leaves and only two or three cases of the second instar. No indications of entrance into the bolls by larvæ of the second or later stages were ever observed under field conditions, except where the larvæ had been feeding in blossoms and had worked downward into the newly set bolls. Willcocks (7) records larvæ feeding in the stems of the plants just above the surface of the ground in Egypt, but this class of injury was never seen in the Laguna.

LARVÆ FEEDING IN SQUARES AND FLOWERS.

The young larvæ enter the squares by cutting directly through the undeveloped flower petals and feed on the pollen and fleshy parts of the embryonic flower, usually reaching the third or fourth instar by the time the flower opens. These infested flowers do not open normally, but have a peculiar rosette appearance which is well shown in Plate III, A. The tips of the corolla in infested flowers are webbed together by the larvæ with fine silken threads which prevent their opening wide and exposing the larvæ to the attacks of other insects and the heat of the sun.

These infested flowers are easily distinguishable from normal flowers in walking through fields of upland or short-staple varieties. Even though the percentage of infested flowers was about the same in Egyptian or long-staple cotton the pronounced rosette effect was never seen. The corolla is longer and larger in Egyptian varieties and the threads spun by the larva probably are not sufficiently strong to prevent its opening. When infested flowers are examined the larva is usually found beneath a fine silky web, covered with frass and pollen grains, and feeding upon the anthers. If full-fed when the flower opens it may leave it the first day and drop to the ground for pupation. This is especially apt to occur if the larva is disturbed by other insects, such as the flower beetle, *Euphoria basalis* Gorg. If the larva is not full-fed at the time of opening it may continue feeding inside the flower for two or three days or until after the flower has dropped, or it may work downward from the flower into the newly formed boll. No indication of the larva leaving flowers and going into large bolls was ever observed, and it is exceptionally rare to find more than one larva in a single square or flower. From June 1 till August 10, 1919, a daily record, with a few exceptions, was kept of the flowers opening on a small plot of heavily infested cotton at Ciudad Lerdo. The results are given in Table X.

TABLE X.—*Infestation of cotton blossoms by the pink bollworm.*

Month.	Number of days counted.	Infested.	Non-infested.	Total.	Percentage infested.
June	25	226	8,210	8,436	2.7
July	25	898	12,333	13,231	6.8
August	10	967	2,508	3,475	27.8

On October 3, 50 per cent and on November 10, 90 per cent of the flowers on this same plot were infested. This plot was more heavily infested than is normally the case under field conditions. The infestation is usually highest in June and July, when few large bolls are present on the plants, and decreases during August and September. In October and November, when there are many larvæ present and not so many green bolls, the infestation again increases and the few blossoms appearing at this time are heavily infested. As the feeding in the squares and blossoms is largely on the pollen, the presence of a larva does not necessarily prevent a normal boll from forming. Blossoms were tagged in 1919 and it was found that 40.8 per cent of the noninfested squares and 67.6 per cent of the infested blossoms were shed.

LARVÆ FEEDING IN BOLLS.

That inside the bolls is the most favored feeding place for pink bollworms is shown by the fact that as soon as the bolls are large enough most of the larvæ choose bolls instead of squares or flowers. They attack the boll in all stages of its growth, from the time it is the size of a pea until it begins to open, though most commonly it is not entered until about one-half to three-fourths grown. The larvæ bore into the boll at any point upon its surface soon after hatching and remain in the same boll until ready for pupation. Once the larvæ have entered the boll no definite plan of procedure is followed. They may burrow directly through the carpel and begin feeding on the soft watery lint or they may stop before cutting completely through and burrow for an inch or more in the spongy carpel tissues just beneath the inner wall of the boll. In the latter case they leave brownish, discolored tunnels or burrows resembling the work of young leaf miners. These tunnels, commonly called "railroads," are very characteristic of pink bollworms and when found are sure evidence that a boll is infested. They disappear as the boll grows older and are not noticeable in an open boll.

When the larvæ cut directly through and into the lint sometimes a slightly discolored proliferation resembling a puncture made by a cotton stainer is formed and at other times only a slight discoloration is left. Again, a larva may be found inside a boll and no sign of its entrance place found even when the boll is examined from the inside. The larvæ may tunnel in the carpel tissues or feed in the lint in any direction from the point of entrance and seldom if ever feed on seed until after the first molt. They may burrow between or cut through the fibers of the lint for a considerable distance while feeding on the soft tissues, leaving behind slightly discolored trails through the lint and "railroads" through the immature seed coats; or, on the other hand, they may remain feeding on the lint near the point of entrance.

Second or third instar larvæ are found which seem to have fed exclusively on the lint, but there is always some feeding on the seed before the larvæ become fully mature and second and third instars are frequently found in the seed. The seeds are normally first attacked from the broad end nearer the outer surface of the boll. The contents of the first seed attacked are not eaten completely out before an adjoining seed is attacked. The number of seeds attacked by a single larva varies greatly, due to the age and development of the boll at the time of attack and the behavior of the larva. Cases have been seen where a larva completed its development on as few as two seeds and within a short distance of the place of entrance, while another larva may destroy a whole lock or more. Often a larva will cut through the partition into the adjoining lock instead of going to another seed in the same lock. The hole in the partition is clean cut, round or oval, and is good evidence that a pink bollworm has been in that boll. Plate III, B shows these holes.

When very small bolls are attacked by larvæ working downward from the flowers, they turn brown and usually drop from the plants, but if the bolls are not attacked till about half grown, the presence of larvæ does not cause them to shed. When there are only 2 to 4 larvæ in a boll that is rather far advanced, say three-fourths to full-grown, when attacked, the work may be classed as "clean," but if several larvæ have attacked a boll that has not reached that stage, the entire contents are very likely to be completely broken down into a decayed mass. The presence of larvæ in bolls does not prevent other larvæ from entering, and usually larvæ of all stages are found

in the same boll. During the latter part of the season, wh
infestation is heavy, an average of 6 or 7 larvæ is found per bc
individual bolls may contain many more. One boll was exa
that contained 26 larvæ. The number for all bolls examined th
out the season of .1919 averaged 2.5.

PROLIFERATION OF BOLLS.

The presence of larvæ often causes the bolls to form abı
growth or proliferation. Proliferation is described by Dr.
Hinds (*1*) as:

The development of numerous elementary cells from parts of the bud or bol
are themselves normally the ultimate product of combinations of much mor
specialized cells. The resulting product is thus composed of comparativel
thin-walled cells, which are placed so loosely together that the resulting forn
of a soft texture, and has a granular appearance which may be plainly seen
unaided eye.

Greenish white or discolored brownish opaque swellings are f
on the inner wall of the carpel, the seeds themselves proli
and very little if any lint is formed on them. This spongy n
granular cells develops much more rapidly than lint, thus occ
the space that would have been filled with lint. Badly proli
bolls contain but little lint, and this is matted or felted and
quality, thus greatly increasing the damage done by the pin
worms. Proliferous seeds are not confined to those actually at
by the larvæ. The irritation caused by the presence of the l
a boll or the stimulation from proliferation in seed actually
causes other healthy seed to proliferate. The percentage of pro
bolls increases very rapidly with the advance of the season, v
simultaneous with the increase of the number of bolls attac
the pink bollworm and with the number of larvæ in each bol
Egyptian cotton grown at the laboratory was much more s
ffected by proliferation than were the short-staple varieties

discolor the lint. Just as soon as the bolls are formed they may be attacked by the larvæ working downward from the flower, but usually they are not attacked till one-half to three-fourths grown. The damage to the individual boll is greater the earlier it is attacked. In case the larva enters when the boll is very young, that is, one-half grown or less, the boll is usually completely destroyed. But when a boll is not attacked until it is about half grown an infestation by a larva or even several larvæ does not necessarily prevent the boll from opening and producing some pickable cotton. The cotton from infested bolls is of an inferior grade, the lint usually being short, hard, and kinky. The portion of the boll actually consumed by the larva may be comparatively small, but the damage caused by the feeding habits and presence of larvæ in a boll amounts to a considerable percentage loss to the crop. The irritation produced by the presence of a larva often causes proliferation to take place; and upon entering and leaving the boll the larvæ provide a means for the entrance of air and water, thereby causing decomposition in the green bolls.

RELATION OF AMOUNT OF DAMAGE TO INCREASE OF INFESTATION.

It has been estimated that the natural winter mortality of all insects is about 95 per cent or more. In addition to this, the number of pink bollworms in the cotton fields of the Laguna district is further reduced by the irrigation methods, fall burning of plants, and the grazing of the fields by cattle, goats, etc. It is obvious that at the beginning of the crop the infestation, even where it was general the previous year, would be very light, but as the number of larvæ in the field increases the amount of damage becomes greater.

The pink bollworm attack is not similar to that of other insects like the cotton leafworm, *Alabama argillacea* Hübn., or bollworm, *Chloridea obsoleta* Fab., which practically ruin a crop overnight, but is more of a gradual, built-up attack, starting in the beginning of the crop with practically a negligible infestation and culminating with 100 per cent of the bolls infested with from 4 to 10 larvæ in every boll. Table XI shows the rate of monthly increase of larvæ in several average fields of the Laguna.

TABLE XI.—*Progress of infestation by larvæ of the pink bollworm; number of larvæ per 100 bolls.*

Month.	Plantation.							Average.
	Hormi-guero.	Alvia.	LaCon-cha.	San Isi-dera.	Zaragosa.	Rosas.	Barce-lona.	
August	2.6	15.3	5.0	5.2	32.6	33.6	17.6	15.9
September	103.0	128.7	93.5	62.7	312.0	210.7	188.0	156.0
October	710.0	694.0	585.2	748.0	773.0	807.4	496.6	662.9
November	820.0	790.0	668.0	638.0		864.0	464.0	724.0

The data in the foregoing table were compiled from records kept of weekly examinations made of 100 boll (green) samples taken from different plantations in the Laguna dis rict. The bolls in each sample were taken by walking through the same fields each week and picking the bolls at random.

ESTIMATE OF DAMAGE TO LAGUNA CROP, 1919.

In making an estimate of the damage caused by *P. gossypiella* to the cotton crop of the Laguna for 1919, it was thought best to select certain average fields on average plantations and to keep these particular fields under close surveillance during the entire year.

Through the courtesy of Don Carlos Gonzales y Fariño, of Torreon and of the Tlahualilo Company, Tlahualilo, Durango, certain fields upon their properties were selected. These fields were chosen with the utmost care in order to obtain as nearly as possible an average of all conditions of the Laguna, with respect to factors controlling the amount of damage caused by *P. gossypiella*. Other fields in different parts of the Laguna were examined as often as time would permit for comparison with these fields. Each of these fields was visited regularly (as far as conditions would permit) once a week, and samples of 100 green bolls taken, so that the rate of increase of infestation might be ascertained.

Samples of seed cotton were also taken at the beginning of each pick from each of the experimental fields, to determine the damage caused by the pink bollworm in the different harvesting periods. These samples were ginned in a sample gin separately, accurate weights being kept of the quantity of lint and seed. A sample of lint from each field sample was taken for classification by the Bureau of Markets, United States Department of Agriculture, to determine the discolorations, grades, and spinning qualities of the lint.

A 2-pound sample of seed was taken from each field sample for chemical analysis to determine quality and quantity of oil.

DAMAGE TO SQUARES AND BLOOMS.

The pink bollworms enter the squares just after hatching from the eggs, and continue feeding until they complete the larval stage, notwithstanding the fact that the squares may bloom in the meantime. Larvæ of all stages have been found in the squares, but generally speaking only full-grown larvæ have been observed in the blooms. To ascertain to what extent this floral feeding habit tended to cause damage the following experiment was carried on.

Tags were placed on 343 normal blooms and on 343 infested blooms during June and July. Table XII shows the results.

TABLE XII.—*Results of experiment to determine damage caused by feeding of the pink bollworm in the blooms of cotton.*

Blooms.	Number of tags.	Dropped off.	Set bolls.	Per cent of blooms dropped.
Normal	343	140	203	40.8
Infested	343	232	111	67.6

From the above table it will be seen that 40.8 per cent of the *normal blooms* did not set bolls, but 67.6 per cent of the *infested blooms* did not set bolls, a difference of 26.8 per cent. Granting that under favorable conditions the natural tendency of the plant will be to reset these fruits, it is obvious that 26.8 per cent of the blooms will make bolls at a much later date than they normally would, thereby subjecting them to a far heavier infestation, hence a greater amount of damage. The later maturity of the crop due to shedding of the early squares would also greatly increase the damage by the boll weevil in countries where this insect is present. (See Table XI on "Progress of infestation.")

The rate of monthly increase of the infested blooms in a given field is shown in Table X.

DAMAGE TO BOLLS.

In estimating the damage caused to the mature bolls (Pl. I), pickable as well as nonpickable cotton must be considered. By pickable cotton is meant cotton that is picked, ginned, and marketed from the beginning to the end of the crop; by nonpickable cotton, the bolls or portions of bolls that are left on the plants as unfit for picking, due to damage by the pink bollworm.

PICKABLE COTTON.

To arrive at a conclusion as to the extent the cotton taken from the fields is damaged, a 100-pound sample of seed cotton was taken from each picking in each experimental field. These samples were taken by picking all the open cotton on about every twentieth plant in each row, in this manner obtaining as nearly as possible a composite average sample of the cotton open in the field on that date. After the sample was taken the remaining open cotton was picked in the customary manner, thereby guarding against the possibility of mixing any of the first and second pick cotton in the taking of the later samples.

The samples were stored until the end of the season and then ginned separately, using a small 10-saw sample gin. A gin sample of approximately 2 pounds of lint and a sample of seed weighing about 2 pounds were taken from each of the field samples at the time of ginning.

Loss in the Quality of Lint.

-pound gin samples were sent to the United States Bure:
:ets for examination. Mr. George Livingston, Chief
reported in letter dated April 13, 1920, as follows:

eral way it may be stated that all of the samples were of very poor qualit
as regards length and strength of staple. The results obtained throu
ry commercial classification of cotton were confirmed by individual fit
ists which produced subnormal results. It is commonly considered th
tton should show an average strength for individual fibers of about
t none of the Mexican samples possessed that degree of strength. Seve
ples were so weak that a considerable portion of the fibers broke upon bei
ι the jaws of the testing machine. Such cotton is so weak in staple as to
ɾ unspinnable.

xact degree of the deterioration in the quality of lint me
bove which is due to the pink bollworm can not be definite
ɔut undoubtedly a certain percentage of it is caused by ma
ι of the seed, which arrests the development of the lir
11, p. 265) states:

tion to the actual damage done to the lint and seed of the attacked se
e injury which results to sound seed in attacked bolls. This appears to
ɔf malnutrition, the attacked seed making demands on the supply of t
to such an extent that nearly all the seeds in the boll are deprived o
their nutriment.

Loss in Weight of Seed.

ιe amount of seed destroyed or practically destroyed
piella was found to assume proportions worthy of consid
tice, an attempt was made to ascertain the exact loss
:aused in this manner. From material picked during t
mples of seed cotton were accurately weighed, hand-ginn
seed examined individually and weighed, with the followi

TABLE XIII.—*Loss by weight to seed when hand ginned.*

The damaged seed from the first pick weighed less per seed than from the second pick, and the damage per seed from the first pick was greater than in the second pick. This is probably because the bolls from the first pick were attacked when they were greener and the seeds were attacked when they were more immature than in the other picks. There is no indication that the number of seeds per boll is reduced on account of pink bollworm attack, as pointed out by Gough. Unfortunately, the sample of the third pick is from a different plantation and is not quite comparable with the other samples. It may be pointed out, however, that the average weight of the sound seed in the second and third picks is almost the same and that the loss in the individual attacked seed is greater in the third than in the second pick. This is thought to be because a much larger number of larvæ had prepared to hibernate in the third pick and a hibernating larva needs all the available space, especially in the single seed, and had eaten out the kernels of the seed cleaner to prepare this space. From the data given in Table XIII the loss in weight of the seed in the different picks can be calculated, and this is summarized in Table XIV.

TABLE XIV.—*Summary of table showing the loss in weight of the seed from the different picks due to pink bollworm attack.*

Pick.	Actual weight of seed (grams).	Loss in weight of infested seed (grams).	Corrected weight of seed (grams).	Per cent of loss in infested seed.	Per cent of total seed lost.	Remarks.
First................	261.45	8.42	269.88	3.1	1.24	First pick=40 per cent crop.
Second..............	278.78	13.40	292.18	4.6	1.84	Second pick=40 per cent crop.
Third...............	305.50	72.38	377.88	19.1	3.82	Third pick=20 per cent crop.
Total........	....	....	....	....	6.90	

Table XIV shows a loss of 3.1 per cent in the weight of the seed from the first pick, 4.6 per cent of the second pick, and 19.1 per cent in the third pick. The data secured in 1919 showed that 40 per cent of the crop was harvested in the first pick, 40 per cent in the second, and 20 per cent in the third. The losses in the seed from the different picks when given their proportionate weights with respect to the proportion of the total crop harvested in each pick show that 1.24 per cent of the total seed was lost in the first pick, 1.84 per cent in the second pick, 3.82 per cent in the third pick, or that a total of 6.90 per cent by weight of the seed is lost due to the attacks of the pink bollworm in the pickable cotton.

When the above-mentioned field samples of seed cotton were ginned the seed of the first, second, and third picks were placed in separate piles. Using a 20-liter measure, an equal number of weigh-

ings were made of the seed from each pick to determine the loss in
weight between the seed of the different picks (Table XV).

TABLE XV.—*Weight of even number of containers of cotton seed for each pick.*

Sample No.	First pick.	Second pick.	Third pick.	Sample No.	First pick.	Second pick.	Third pick.
	Kilos.	Kilos.	Kilos.		Kilos.	Kilos.	Kilos.
1...................	10.5	10.5	10.5	8...................	11.1	10.7	10.7
2...................	11.0	10.7	10.6	9...................	10.9	10.9	10.5
3...................	11.1	10.6	10.6	10...................	11.0	10.5	10.6
4...................	11.3	11.0	10.5				
5...................	11.1	10.9	10.6	Total........	110.4	107.5	106.2
6...................	11.2	10.8	10.8	Average............	11.04	10.75	10.62
7...................	11.2	10.9	10.8	Net weight.........	6.24	5.95	5.82

Weight of container, 4.8 kilos: container used=20 liters.

From Table XIV it is shown that there is 3.1 per cent loss in weight
in the seed from the first pick; therefore the weight of one 20-liter
measure (6.24 kilos) would be equal to only 96.9 per cent of the weight
of sound seed, and the corrected weight of a 20-liter measure of sound
seed should be 6.43 kilos.

From these data it is shown that there is a loss of 0.19 kilo in the
seed of the first pick, 0.48 kilo in the second pick, and 0.61 kilo in
the third pick. These losses reduced to a percentage basis would
equal 2.9 per cent of the seed lost in the first pick, 7.4 per cent in the
second pick, and 9.4 per cent of the third. But as 40 per cent of the
crop was harvested in the first pick, 40 per cent in the second pick,
and 20 per cent in the third pick, these figures when given their
weighted values will equal 5.96 per cent of the total seed lost due to
pink-bollworm attack.

This difference of 0.94 per cent between the figures representing
the total loss in the seed when hand-ginned and when commercially
ginned is explained by the fact that part of the damaged seed is
broken in cleaning and ginning the cotton, and passes out with the
cleanings, trash, and even in the lint. It is thought, therefore, that
the figure given for the hand-ginned sample, 6.9 per cent, represents
more nearly the actual loss in the seed of the pickable cotton than does
the figure 5.96 per cent obtained from the commercially ginned
sample.

LOSS IN QUANTITY AND QUALITY OF OIL.

Besides the losses in the weight of the seed, there is also an additional loss in quantity and quality of the oil produced.

Because of the danger of introducing the pink bollworm into the
United States, it was thought advisable not to bring seed out of
Mexico for analysis. Samples were taken from the different field
samples as ginned and given to the chemists of the largest oil mill in
the Laguna district. Owing to the unsettled conditions prevailing
in that section of Mexico during 1920, reports on these samples have
not been received.

Willcox (7) states that there is marked reduction in the quantity of oil produced and that the quality is of an inferior grade.

NONPICKABLE COTTON.

It is in this class that the major portion of the gross damage occurs. As has been previously stated, there is a certain percentage of the cotton damaged to such an extent as to render it unfit for picking. This cotton naturally is left on the plants after the pickings are finished.

An effort has been made to determine the exact portion of the crop that is affected in this manner. By selecting what appeared to be average-sized plants (according to the number of bolls per plant, etc.) in fields of several different average plantations, about 3,000 plants were examined after the cotton had been picked. These plants were examined individually, the total number of bolls on each plant and total number of bolls lost on each plant due to attack of the pink bollworm being recorded. In counting the total number of bolls an empty burr was counted as a boll, and in the calculations has the weight of a perfectly sound boll.

In counting "bolls lost," only bolls or portions of bolls which showed plainly that their damage was caused by the pink bollworm were taken into consideration. Bolls or portions of bolls that showed themselves to be unfit for picking because of conditions other than the pink bollworm, such as those attacked by the common bollworm, *C. obsoleta*, or injured by water, heat, and dryness, were counted as sound bolls (Table XVI).

TABLE XVI.—*Loss to crop in nonpickable cotton caused by the pink bollworm.*

Place.	Total plants.	Total bolls.	Total bolls lost.	Per cent damaged
Hormiguero	248	6,737	1,066	15.82
Alvia	453	14,977	2,618	17.48
La Concha	503	15,117	2,942	19.46
San Isidera	454	20,112	3,768	18.73
Zaragosa	450	10,428	2,544	24.39
Rosas	450	9,282	2,318	24.97
Barcelona	300	6,297	1,325	21.04
Total	2,858	82,950	16,581	141.89
Average				19.98

Table XVI shows that of 82,950 bolls produced by 2,858 plants 16,581 were lost, making a total of 19.98 per cent damage in the nonpickable cotton due directly to the attack of the pink bollworm. The plantations on which these figures are based represent a true average of the entire Laguna. In addition to these plantations, a number of other places were visited in different parts of the Laguna and the amount of damage found ranged from 15 to 25 per cent, with an average of approximately 20 per cent loss due to the pink bollworm, which substantiates the accuracy of the foregoing estimates.

SUMMARY OF DAMAGE BY THE PINK BOLLWORM.[4]

(1) Loss in squares and blooms: 26.8 per cent of the squares and blooms shed.

(2) Loss in pickable cotton:
  Lint: Deterioration in quality.
  Seed: Is reduced 6.9 per cent in weight; quantity and quality of oil also reduced.

(3) Loss in nonpickable cotton: 19.98 per cent of entire crop rendered unpickable.

The damage to the nonpickable cotton and the loss by weight in the seed in the pickable cotton can be reduced to a monetary basis. Assuming lint to be worth 30 cents per pound and seed worth $60 per ton, the value of 500 pounds of lint would be $150 and 1,000 pounds or ½ ton of seed would be worth $30, or a total of $180 per bale. For every bale picked there is 19.98 per cent of the seed and lint left in the field as nonpickable cotton, or, in other words, the amount of cotton actually picked represents only 80.02 per cent of the crop if no pink bollworms were present. Then the value of the crop produced would be $224.90 rather than $180. The loss of 19.98 per cent of the potential crop ($224.90) is equal to $44.93 per bale. In addition to this there is 6.9 per cent loss by weight in the seed of the pickable cotton (which represents the 80.02 per cent of the bale not included in the 19.98 per cent loss or nonpickable cotton), which amounts to $2.07. Therefore the total loss is $47 or 20.89 per cent of the value of the bale.

The calculable loss that can be specifically stated on a definite percentage basis is 20.89 per cent. In addition to this figure there should be added the losses incurred in the shedding of the squares, deterioration in the quantity and quality of the oil in the seed, and the weakening and irregularity of the staple in computing the total damage caused by the pink bollworm.

FOOD PLANTS.

While cotton (*Gossypium* spp.) is by far the most favored food plant, a number of other plants have been recorded as host plants of the pink bollworm. Maxwell-Lefroy (*2*) records a species of Hibiscus and the oily seed of trees (species not given) in India; Fullaway (*3*) reared a single specimen from milo (*Thespesia populnea*) in Hawaii;

---

[4] *Damage during 1920.*—The damage to the Laguna crop by the pink bollworm was unusually severe during 1920. Frost did not come in 1919 till very late and this was followed by a mild winter, which allowed a large percentage of the hibernating larvæ to pass the winter successfully. The fields were examined during the latter part of June, and it was very evident that the infestation in squares and young bolls was heavier than it had been in 1918 or 1919. The cotton was also further advanced and was growing rapidly, with very good prospects for a large crop. About this time there were severe outbreaks of aphids (*Aphis gossypii*), thrips, and rust (*Aecidium gossypii*) which checked the growth of the plants and gave them a setback from which they never recovered. This caused the plants to produce very few bolls, and the infestation by the pink bollworms and the percentage of loss have consequently been very high. Estimates made in November showed that the pink bollworm had injured 31.3 per cent of the crop so badly that it was rendered unfit for picking and that there was 7 or 8 per cent additional loss attributable to the insect by the lowering of the quantity and quality of the pickable cotton, or a total of 38 to 39 per cent loss of the crop.

PLATE IV.

PINK BOLLWORM.

Larvæ feeding in the walls of the pods and seed of okra.

Busck (*8*) bred the pink bollworm from *Gossypium tomentosum* in Hawaii, but did not find it in milo; King (*9*) reports it from hanbuk (*Abutilon* sp.) in Africa; and Gough (*12*) records mallow (*Malva* sp.). Willcocks (*7*) states that the food plants in Egypt are bamia or okra (*Hibiscus esculentus*), teel or hemp (*Hibiscus cannabinus*), and hollyhock (*Althaea rosea*).

A number of malvaceous plants were grown beside heavily infested cotton on the laboratory grounds and several became infested. Okra (*Hibiscus esculentus*) became rather heavily infested in every instance when grown in close proximity to cotton. Table XVII is a complete record of all the seed pods grown on 30 plants at the laboratory during the season of 1919. From August 14 to December 3, 590 seed pods were examined with the following results: 66.7 per cent were infested with live larvæ and pupæ, and the total infestation, including seed pods that were unmistakably infested but in which no larvæ or pupæ were found, was 73.8 per cent. The infested seed pods averaged 2 larvæ, pupæ, and exit holes.

TABLE XVII.—*Seed-pod examination of Okra (H. esculentus).*

Num-ber of pods.	Pods infested.		Infestation.			Num-ber of infested pods without larvæ or pupæ present.	Num-ber of exit holes.	Remarks.
	Num-ber.	Per cent.	Larvæ total.	Num-ber of pupæ.	Pupæ and larvæ.			
38	11	28.9	9	0	9	3	0	Green pods.
33	9	27.2	9	0	9	1	0	Do.
60	36	60.0	48	0	48	1	0	Do.
50	35	70.0	85	0	85	3	0	Do.
100	69	69.0	105	0	105	13	25	Do.
100	79	79.0	106	5	111	13	37	Do.
50	45	90.0	92	4	96	2	13	Dry pods.
84	66	78.5	147	5	152	5	8	Do.
20	12	60.0	37	0	37	1	0	Do.
20	17	85.0	35	0	35	1	1	Do.
35	15	42.8	21	0	21	0	0	Green pods.
590	394	66.7	694	14	708	43	84	

From this one observation it seems that when attacking okra the pink bollworm is more inclined to pupate in the seed pods than in the bolls when cotton is attacked. No plausible explanation can be given as to why this should occur.

The manner of attack and feeding habits in okra are essentially the same as in cotton, but no larvæ were ever found feeding in the flower buds or flowers.

Double seeds or three or four seeds are frequently webbed together in much the same manner as double seed in cotton, though the work is not so clean and particles of frass are usually found attached to them. Plate IV shows full-grown larvæ feeding in okra pods.

One important point to be determined is whether the species is able to sustain and perpetuate itself on okra alone as a food plant. Two large screen cages were constructed over heavily infested okra in the fall of 1918.   The entire plants with the fruits attached were left in the cages during the summer of 1919.   Repeated examainations were made of all fruits formed during 1919 and no infestation ever developed from the hibernating larvæ.   The protection afforded by the okra is not as good as the protection afforded by cotton.   The seed pods crack open on drying and the seeds with the larvæ webbed up in them drop to the ground, the larvæ becoming subject to the detrimental effects of water and attacks of insect enemies.

Under the same conditions hollyhock (*Althaea rosea*), a very common ornamental flower, was found to be subject to the attack of the pink bollworm larvæ, the insects being found in the buds, flowers, and seed pods.

Hibernating cages were also constructed over hollyhock plants and experiments conducted in the same manner as with okra with negative results.   No reinfestation occurred from hibernating larvæ.

The flower buds, flowers, and seed pods of *Hibiscus syriacus* were attacked by the pink bollworm, the manner of attack and feeding habits being the same as in cotton and okra.   The infestation in the flower buds was light, but the seed pods were nearly all infested and some contained several larvæ.

One pink bollworm larva was taken from a seed pod of the Confederate rose (*Hibiscus mutabilis*).

Seeds from 25 species of malvaceous plants were collected in southern Texas and planted in close proximity to cotton at Ciudad Lerdo.   Of this number only the following species grew: *Hibiscus coccineus* Walt., *Hibiscus militaris* Cav., *Hibiscus lasiocarpus* Cav., *Malvastrum americanum* (L.) Terr., *Sida spinosa* L., *Wissadula lozani* (Rose) Fries, and *Kosteletzkya virginica* L.   Some of these have small seed pods and are not well adapted to the feeding habits of the larvæ, but the following species were attacked by pink bollworms.

Only one plant of *Hibiscus coccineus* grew.   It developed 7 seedpods and 5 of these were infested.

Hibiscus militaris was attacked both in the flowers and seed pods. The same rosette appearance takes place in the infested flower as in upland cotton.

Kosteletzkya virginica was also attacked.   The plant is a very profuse bloomer, but the seed pods are rather small to be well adapted for the larvæ, though two full-grown larvæ were found in seed pods.

Malvastrum americanum was infested.   One specimen was taken in a seed pod.

A species of Malva (*Malva parviflora* L. ?) grows rather abundantly along the borders of the fields in the Laguna, but was never found to be infested under natural conditions.   The seed pods are too small to be well adapted for pink bollworms, though larvæ can reach maturity in a single pod.

DISPERSAL.

The most important factor in the dispersal of the species is man. By his transportation of cotton seed and cotton products he has carried the insect from its original home to all parts of the cotton-producing world. Once it is established, local dispersal from one field to another is also by flight, and in some instances the carriage of the larvæ by water is of importance.

CARRIAGE OF LARVÆ IN SEED FOR PLANTING AND OTHER PURPOSES.

The transportation of infested seed by man from place to place is the usual means by which this insect is carried to new localities. It was introduced into Mexico in 1911 with seed for planting; into Brazil in 1911–1913 with seed for planting; and more recently into certain parts of Texas with seed in cotton and seed for milling purposes. From what has already been stated concerning the habits of the pink bollworm, it is evident that seed from an infested field is sure to contain a certain percentage of infestation, and it is known that the resting larvæ can live for at least 2 years in such seed. It is thus seen that the larvæ are admirably adapted for transportation over great distances in this way. Seed, moreover, is often incidentally carried with other products. Railroad cars which have been used for shipping cotton seed are a very dangerous example of this. Seed will usually be found in the cracks and corners and between the walls of the car. Numerous instances of this have been noted, particularly by inspectors at border points, where live pink-bollworm larvæ were taken from cars which had been used for seed in the Laguna district and later used for exportation of other products. Bales of cotton often carry seed and as many as several hundred seeds have been found mixed with the lint and attached to the bagging. Cotton waste and used cotton bagging are other items usually having seed attached to them. Cotton pickers in Mexico often move from plantation to plantation. It is a common practice with them to carry their own picking sacks and among their belongings seed cotton and cotton seed are often found. These and similar practices are common means by which the insect is carried.

FLIGHT AND CARRIAGE OF ADULTS.

While the moth of the pink bollworm is small, it has ample wing power for its size and is capable of quick, darting flight. When disturbed during the day it flies only a short distance and hides under the nearest object. On the other hand, several hundred moths were liberated on top of the house where a light breeze was blowing, in the morning and at dusk. About half of those liberated in the morning flew only a few feet before settling down, while the others flew upward and away as far as the eye could follow them. Those liberated at dusk nearly all flew upward and away till lost to sight. In all cases they flew with the wind and not quartering to it, as some insects do. Up to the present time no conclusive data have

been accumulated along this line, due to the nocturnal hal
moth and the fact that in Mexico it was so generally distrib
no uninfested isolated fields were found.

The average duration of the moth stage in captivity is
days. If the moth flies only a short distance before coming
it would appear certain that it may again proceed for anol
distance. If there were nothing to influence the directi
flight, it might fly in any direction and as likely as not ret
original starting point; but if the direction of the flight is i
by the wind, as it was in our observations, it would fly with
and where there is a prevailing wind from one direction
would be carried in the same general direction farther an
from its starting point and might cover a considerable
before dying. In the eradication work in Texas a 5-1
cotton zone around infested territory is used to prevent
by flight, and it is thought this zone is reasonably safe. T
have seclusive habits, and frequently hide in cracks, crev
dark corners. At the railroad stations in the Laguna c
upon the side tracks within a few yards of the cotton fields
or even weeks at a time while being loaded and unloaded. T
for long periods of time near the fields to unload supplies, :
these stops are made at night, when the moths are flying al
possible that some of the moths might secrete themselves ii
and later be carried to distant points. There is the same dang(
to a lesser degree, in vehicles passing cotton fields along the

CARRIAGE OF LARVÆ BY WATER.

Cotton plants with bolls attached were often seen float
the Rio Nazas when it was at flood stage, and old bolls are ca
distances when fields are overflowed. Some experiments w
at Dr. W. D. Hunter's suggestion to determine how long la
survive exposure to water. Free larvæ with no protection
pupated and produced moths after being in water in tubes for
Larvæ survived for several days after being in water lo
none produced moths. Larvæ in cocoons survived 72 hour
in tubes and free larvæ placed in pill boxes perforated witl
produced one adult after 8 days' submergence in a pitch(
did not survive as long as larvæ. Old bolls picked in Janu
and stored in the laboratory till April, 1919, were subi
water and left floating on the surface of water in a trough
pupated and produced adults after 7 days in both instanc
adults emerged after 11 days in either case.

Several plants containing green bolls heavily infested w
in the river and tied so that they could not float away. W
was enough current in the river to keep the plants float:
end of the string the bolls were all washed away at the en(

that when plants are allowed to float free and move with the current the bolls will remain on the plants longer. When floating in this manner part of the plants are always out of water and, as they revolve more or less, the same bolls will not be submerged all the time and larvæ will survive more than 3 days. To determine how long larvæ would live in green bolls, sample bolls were placed in a trough and examined daily. The bolls floated and larvæ lived for 10 days. On the eleventh day all of the bolls sank to the bottom and were very rotten, and no live larvæ were found in them. The results of these experiments are summarized in Table XVIII.

TABLE XVIII.—*Effect of water on pink bollworm larvæ.*

Condition of exposure.	Number treated.	Time of exposure.	Per cent killed.	Remarks.
		Hours.		
Loose larvæ in tube of water...	5 larvæ................	20	60	1 pupated afterwards.
	7 larvæ................	44	70	2 pupated afterwards.
	20 larvæ and 3 pupæ..	120	100	Larvæ lived several days.
	30 larvæ..............	144	100	
Loose cocoons in tube of water..	10 larvæ..............	48	70	Heavy cocoons; 1 adult emerged.
	20 larvæ..............	72	90	Heavy cocoons.
	.....do...............	96	100	Do.
	10 larvæ..............	120	100	Do.
Double seed in tube of water...	10 double seed (5 larvæ.)	96	100	
	10 double seed (3 larvæ.)	124	66	2 larvæ alive.
Seed and cocoons in pill boxes perforated with needle........ (3 seeds and 2 cocoons in each box. Counted together).	1 box..................	24	0	
	.....do...............	48	0	
	.....do...............	72	40	
	.....do...............	96	0	
	.....do...............	120	50	2 pupated afterwards.
		Days.		
	.....do...............	6.5	40	
	.....do...............	8	60	
	.....do...............	11	100	
	.....do...............	15	100	
	21 boxes..............	17	100	
Bolls floating on water in trough. (Bolls picked in December, 1918, and stored in laboratory. Contained many dead larvæ not included in count.)	20 bolls (29 larvæ).....	7	80	Bolls covered with algæ and rotten.
	20 bolls (12 larvæ).....	11	100	Do.
	20 bolls (56 larvæ).....	14	100	Do.
	20 bolls (17 larvæ).....	17	100	Do.
	120 bolls (273 larvæ)...	18	100	Do.
Bolls submerged in water in trough (same kind of bolls as above).	20 bolls (30 larvæ).....	7	77	2 pupated; bolls covered with algæ and rotten.
	20 bolls (113 larvæ)....	11	100	1 larva lived several days; bolls rotten.
	20 bolls (46 larvæ).....	14	100	Bolls rotten.
	20 bolls (14 larvæ).....	17	100	Do.
	120 bolls (169 larvæ)...	18	100	Do.
		Hours.		
Green bolls submerged in slatted box in river.	10 bolls (37 larvæ).....	48	95	Bolls fermenting and very sticky.
	10 bolls................	72	100	Interior bolls rotten.
	10 bolls................	96	100	Badly rotted.
Plant with green bolls attached floating on surface of river, Sept. 13, 1919.	10 bolls (40 larvæ).....	48	55	Bolls fermenting.
	9 bolls (19 larvæ)......	72	98.4	Interior of bolls rotting.
	7 bolls (11 larvæ)......	96	46	All of live larvæ found in two bolls which were not submerged.
		Days.		
143 green cotton bolls placed in container of water. Water changed daily.	20 bolls (122 larvæ)....	3	7.3	All dead in two badly decayed bolls.
	20 bolls (125 larvæ)....	4	3.1	Decaying.
	20 bolls (133 larvæ)....	5	6.3	Some in bad state of decay.
	20 bolls (107 larvæ)....	6	60.7	Do.
	15 bolls (84 larvæ).....	7	31.5	
	16 bolls (73 larvæ).....	8	38.8	Some bolls rather small and badly decayed.
	10 bolls (61 larvæ).....	9	44.2	Bolls decaying rapidly.
	10 bolls (51 larvæ).....	10	60.7	Some still floating; badly decayed.
	6 bolls (43 larvæ)......	11	100.0	Badly decayed.
	6 bolls (29 larvæ)......	12	100.0	Very rotten.

In general, it may be said that larvæ will live in bolls submerged in water or floating on the surface of the water till the bolls themselves are thoroughly rotten. This may be a week or more, depending upon the condition of the bolls. The old dried bolls and larvæ webbed up in bits of rubbish are particularly likely to carry an infestation a long distance, for they float more readily than green bolls. One of the large plantations was considering dividing their property into zones which would be planted in cotton only every third or fourth year in order to reduce the damage by the pink bollworm, but the danger of reinfestation by irrigation water was considered so great that it was not adopted.

NATURAL CONTROL.

From the data collected in 1918 and 1919, it is concluded that the maximum infestation and the maximum damage to the cotton of the Laguna have been reached by this time, except for slight yearly variations due to climatic conditions which may have some effect on the development of the pink bollworm and its attack on the cotton. It is the belief of the plantation owners that the damage or loss to the crop has remained about the same since 1916, or that the maximum had been reached at the end of five years from the time of introduction.

MORTALITY OF NEWLY-HATCHED LARVÆ.

It has been shown in Table III that 47.1 per cent of the pink bollworm eggs are not deposited on the squares or bolls. The larvæ from these eggs must crawl some distance before reaching food. In this migration they are readily attacked by insect enemies, are exposed to the hot sun, become weakened and exhausted, and eventually may succumb to starvation. It is thought that very few or possibly none of the larvæ from this 47.1 per cent of the eggs ever enter the squares or bolls. Many of the larvæ from the remaining 52.9 per cent of the eggs deposited on suitable parts of the plant never succeed in entering the bolls or squares either. To determine what percentage of the larvæ hatching from eggs deposited on the plants fail to enter the bolls or squares, five plants were examined. These records were carefully made. Every part of the plant was closely examined with a hand lens for eggs and eggshells. The larvæ, pupæ, and exit holes were also carefully counted and the mortality rate calculated from the number of eggshells found on the plants and the total infestation of the plants. The results are given in Table XIX.

TABLE XIX.—*Mortality of larvæ of P. gossypiella.*

Number of plants.	On plant.		Number of larvæ.		Pupæ found.	Exit holes.	Larvæ, pupæ, and exit holes.	Per cent mortality.	Remarks.
	Number of shells.	Number of eggs.	In squares.	In bolls.					
1.....	181	89	3	17	0	7	27	85.1	
1.....	141	111	1	46	0	12	59	58.2	
1.....	190	115	6	84	0	24	114	40.0	
1.....	170	53	0	25	3	13	41	75.9	16 bolls on plant.
1.....	103	143	2	39	0	15	57	44.7	28 bolls on plant.
5.....	785	511	12	211	3	72	298	62.1	

From this table it is seen that the mortality varies from 40 to 85.1 per cent with an average of 62.1 per cent. If it is assumed that none of the larvæ from the 47.1 per cent of the eggs laid on other parts of the plants ever succeed in entering the bolls or squares, this would still leave 15 per cent of the larvæ from eggs laid on the squares and bolls unaccounted for. Since many eggshells had undoubtedly fallen from the plants examined, this percentage of mortality (62.1 per cent) is smaller than what actually occurs.

To determine what percentage of the eggs laid on the bolls are lost, 16 samples of 25 green bolls each were examined, the number of eggs laid on them counted, and the total infestation found (Table XX).

TABLE XX.—*Mortality of pink bollworm larvæ from eggs laid on bolls.*

Number of bolls.	Eggs.			Larvæ.				Exit holes.	Pupæ.	Total infestation.	Per cent of larvæ from eggs laid on bolls recovered in bolls.
	Tip.	Base.	Total.	First.	Second.	Third.	Fourth.				
400..............	61	4,958	5,019	190	347	442	1,005	386	1	2,371	45.8
Average..........	0.15	12.4	12.5	0.47	0.87	1.1	2.5	0.96	....	5.92	....

There were 5,019 eggs and eggshells on the bolls. If larvæ from all these eggs had hatched and all the larvæ gone into the bolls, there would have been an average infestation of 12.5 larvæ per boll, whereas an average of a little less than 6 larvæ was actually found. These examinations were made in October and later examinations showed that the maximum infestation ever reached was an average of 7 per boll.

These figures indicate that about half of the larvæ from eggs laid on the bolls themselves never succeed in entering them. In Table III it was shown that 51.7 per cent of the eggs were laid on the bolls and appendages, and if only half of these successfully enter the bolls this would be equal to 25.8 per cent of the total eggs. This loss of

25 per cent, in addition to the 47.1 per cent laid on other parts of the plants and assumed to be lost, would bring the total mortality of young larvæ up to 72.9 per cent. This figure (72.9 per cent) is thought to approach more closely what actually takes place in the field than that of 62.1 per cent based on the number of empty shells found. This is borne out by laboratory experience where the mortality was 90 per cent or more.

Once the larvæ are inside the bolls there is very little or no mortality during the summer months.

MORTALITY OF HIBERNATING LARVÆ IN THE FIELDS.

There is a very heavy mortality in hibernating larvæ left in the fields during the winter, especially when the fields are irrigated. Examinations of old bolls picked up in the fields showed that about 80 to 90 per cent of the larvæ survived till February, and that the mortality rapidly increased from this date onward. The mortality varies greatly in different samples, but by the end of March it is difficult to find any live larvæ in the scraps picked up on the ground in the fields. There are still live larvæ present, but the old bolls have broken up, scattered, and in cultivated fields are difficult to find. On March 13, 1918, only 3 live larvæ were found from a bushel of old bolls and trash picked up in a lightly infested field at San Pedro. On April 16, 1919, no live larvæ were found in the old bolls left on the ground after cattle had grazed over the fields at Tlahualilo, but about 5 per cent were still alive in the bolls left on the stalks.

To secure more data on this point, two series of experiments were started on November 26, 1918. One experiment was under as nearly normal irrigated field conditions as possible and the other under nonirrigated conditions. The fields in the Laguna are usually irrigated in November, December, or January, when cotton follows cotton, as it does on most plantations. When fields have been lying fallow for a season, the water is applied any time during the year when it is available. About 3 feet of water is placed on the fields and allowed to soak in. This requires from one to several months, depending upon the character of the soil. In the experimental plot irrigation was started on December 2 and continued till December 8, when the motor burned out. Water was again applied on December 23, 1918, and continued daily until January 22, 1919. On account of the small amount of electric current available, the plot could not be filled 3 feet deep, but the daily application of a few inches of water kept the ground thoroughly wet and covered with water at least part of each day.

In each of the series the larvæ were exposed under wire cages in bolls in a single layer on the surface of the ground, in bolls buried 6 to 7 inches deep, and in double seed buried one-fourth inch deep in flowerpots which were set in the soil flush with the surface. Moreover, larvæ removed from all seed and lint were placed in screened boxes and flowerpots and allowed to enter the soil. These were also buried flush with the surface of the ground. A sample of the bolls used was examined at the time and found to contain an average of 6.64 fourth-instar and 0.03 third-instar larvæ per boll. The material was examined at different dates and the results are given in Table XXI.

TABLE XXI.—*The mortality among hibernating Pectinophora gossypiella larvæ under different field conditions.*

Experiment No.	Conditions of exposure.	Examination.					Remarks.
		Date.	Live larvæ.	Dead larvæ.	Live pupæ.	Pupal skins.	
557	300 larvæ removed from seed and lint and buried in wooden box of soil in irrigated plot.	1919. June 11......	0	2	0	0	61 empty dirt cells around side of box.
558A	50 larvæ in flowerpot, same as 557.	May 10.......	0	Several.	0	0	
558C	Same as 558A..........	June 10.......	0	3	0	0	
558B	Same as 558A..........	June 11.......	0	0	0	0	
558D	50 double seeds buried in flowerpot on irrigated plot.	June 11.......	0	0	0	0	Seed well rotted.
560	300 larvæ removed from seed and lint and buried in wooden box of soil in nonirrigated plot.	June 12.......	12	....	3	2	Larvæ webbed up on side of box.
561A	50 larvæ in flowerpot, same as 560.	May 10.......	28	1	1	1	Larvæ in cocoons.
561B	Same as 561A..........	June 11.......	0	7	0	0	
561C	50 double seeds in flowerpot on nonirrigated plot.	June 12.......	6	....	1	3	Seed well rotted.
559A	200 green and dry bolls buried 6 to 7 inches deep on irrigated plot.	Mar. 10 (10 bolls).	0	65	0	0	Bolls rotting badly.
		Apr. 24 (10 bolls).	0	48	0	0	Very rotten and fallen to pieces.
		May 16 (50 bolls).	0	....	0	0	Fallen to pieces.
		June 6 (130 bolls).	0	....	0	10	Bolls so rotten difficult to pick from soil.
559B	200 green and dry bolls left on top of ground on irrigated plot.	Mar. 10 (10 bolls).	39	29	0	0	Bolls in good condition.
		Apr. 24 (10 bolls).	20	36	1	3	Do.
		May 15 (50 bolls).	74	194	2	2	Some of bolls getting rotten, but those which had opened when experiment began still in good condition.
		June 4 (116 bolls).	51	344	6	18	
562A	200 green and dry bolls buried in soil 6 to 7 inches deep on nonirrigated plot.	Mar. 11 (10 bolls).	52	0	0	0	Bolls badly rotted.
		Apr. 24 (10 bolls).	13	13	2	10	Badly rotted and could not separate bolls.
		June 7 (180 bolls).	0	0	0	0	Thoroughly rotten.
562B	200 green and dry bolls left on top of ground on nonirrigated plot.	Mar. 11 (10 bolls).	68	26	0	0	Bolls in very good condition.
		Apr. 24 (10 bolls).	54	28	0	0	Do.
		May 15 (50 bolls).	83	137	0	6	Do.
		June 7 (50 bolls).	152	188	2	11	Do.
		July 25 (25 bolls).	0	100	0	7	Do.
		Aug. 22 (80 bolls).	0	0	0	0	Do.

Table XXI shows that no live larvæ were found during May and June among those removed from seed and lint or in double seed buried in the irrigated plots (Experiments Nos. 557 and 558 A to D), and that 12.8 per cent were alive or had emerged as moths under the same conditions in the nonirrigated plot (Experiments Nos. 560 and 561 A to C). No live larvæ were found in bolls buried in irrigated plots from March 10 (the first examination) until June 6 in Experiment No. 559 A, and none in bolls buried in nonirrigated plot (Experiment No. 562 A) after April 24. The surrounding soil had been irrigated and when the last examination was made on June 7 the soil in the nonirrigated plot was found moist about 3 inches below the surface from water that had seeped in from below. From this experiment 6.2 per cent survived till April 24. There was less mortality in the bolls when left on the surface of the ground than when buried. In the irrigated plot (Experiment No. 559 B) live larvæ were found in bolls left on the surface of the ground at the last examination on June 4, 1919, and 9.7 per cent had survived or previously emerged as moths on this date. On the nonirrigated plot (Experiment No. 562 B) 50 per cent of the larvæ in bolls on the surface were alive on June 7, 1919. At the next examination, on July 25, all of the larvæ were dead.

In all of the experiments, especially the later examinations, many of the larvæ were not recovered because the dead larvæ were so decomposed they were not recognizable. Very few if any escaped, for the buried bolls had close-mesh wire screen over the top and along the sides, extending below the level of the bolls. The earth surrounding the material was carefully sifted and larvæ and pupal skins found here counted with the others. The percentages of mortality for the bolls are based on the number of larvæ found in the samples at the beginning of the experiments. This is not absolutely accurate, because the number of larvæ may vary considerably in individual bolls, but it is the most reliable figure to use inasmuch as the actual number of dead larvæ could not be determined.

It is seen that the mortality increases as the season advances, even where the conditions were most favorable, no live larvæ being found as late as July 25, and that the mortality in all the experiments was greater when the larvæ were buried than when they were left on the surface, and greater when the plots were irrigated than when left dry. These experiments also show that the greatest danger for starting a new infestation from material left in the fields is the old bolls left on the surface of the ground. Over 9 per cent of the larvæ in these bolls on the irrigated plot survived till June 4 and 50 per cent survived in the nonirrigated plot. At this season the cotton will be large enough for oviposition to begin. Under the usual field conditions the irrigated lands will have been cultivated before this date and the mortality increased by breaking up and burying the bolls. On the other hand, the bolls float on water and the wind frequently blows them against the borders on one side of the field, where they are piled up several inches or more deep. This concentration keeps some of the bolls out of the water and affords more protection for the bolls in the interior of the pile against heat and cold. If the fields are not irrigated it means they will not be planted the following year and such fields are usually grazed by goats, cows, and burros, which eat many of the bolls.

Whether or not the results obtained in these experiments during only one winter[5] hold true for what actually takes place in the Laguna it is impossible to say, but they indicate beneficial results from irrigation and burying the bolls. That a very heavy mortality, probably more than 95 per cent, does take place in the fields is shown by field examinations of the bolls and the very light infestation in the early part of the season. There are such enormous numbers of larvæ hibernating in the fields that the crop would be entirely destroyed if the mortality was not very high.

Willcocks (7) in Egypt left bolls out of doors exposed to the sun on the surface of dry ground and ground that was watered periodically (three waterings). He found a very high mortality during April, May, and June, and all the larvæ were dead on June 25. There was a slightly higher mortality among the larvæ in the watered bolls and all the larvæ were dead on April 8, while some survived in the dry bolls till May 3. His figures "most certainly show that the chance of resting-stage pink bollworms surviving in the bolls fully exposed to the sun on the surface of dry sheraki land in May, June, and July is a remote one." He buried another lot of bolls on November 24 in damp soil in boxes. Some of these were kept dry and others wet. Some were stored indoors and others outdoors, though none were in direct sunlight. There was less mortality in the buried bolls than in those left on the surface exposed to the sun, and he says, in speaking of wet conditions, "this does not seem to be materially disadvantageous to the pest." In all of the buried bolls there was a decided emergence of the larvæ to the top of the soil, which began as soon as the bolls were buried (November 24) and continued intermittently in some cases where the bolls were kept dry till the following November. Water hastened this larval emergence when applied in the fall or the following spring, but though the bolls were badly rotted the larvæ were still able to remain in them, and spun up in their almost water-tight cocoons during March, April, and May.

In our experiments in Mexico, larvæ survived better in bolls on the top of the ground than when buried and better when left dry than when irrigated. In Mexico the temperature was never as high

---

[5] These results were substantiated by experiments during the winter of 1919–20.

as it is in Egypt in May and June (107° and 111° F.) and our bolls received some protection from the sun by the screen covering of the irrigated bolls and the cheesecloth covering over the nonirrigated bolls. Furthermore, our bolls were probably kept wetter during the 30 days when they were wet than Willcocks's were, but his were kept wet for a longer time. There was but very little larval emergence in any of our bolls. This is shown by the large numbers of dead larvæ found *in situ* in the earlier examinations, when they were still recognizable, and by the few larvæ or pupal skins found in the surrounding soil. There was more larval emergence from the bolls in the irrigated plots where 12 pupal skins were found in the soil than in the nonirrigated where only 2 or 3 were found. About half of the larvæ recovered in the bolls were in the lint, but no count was kept of this point and it is not known whether there were more than are usually found in lint in the bolls in the fields during the fall or not. In the case of the double seeds in the irrigated plot the following note was made: "Earthen cells were noticed in a few instances, apparently some of the larvæ left the seed." In the double seed on the nonirrigated plot 4 pupal skins were found in the soil.

On March 11, 1919, 100 bolls which were picked on December 7, 1918, and stored in the laboratory till this date were buried 1 to 2 inches deep in a box of soil and wet thoroughly. The box was sprinkled often enough to keep it thoroughly wet for 30 days. On April 11 the contents were carefully examined and 35 live larvæ and 90 dead larvæ were found in the bolls and only 4 larvæ and 2 pupæ in the soil. Willcocks (7) found a very sudden increase in the number of larvæ emerging to the surface in a box of bolls buried in dry soil and watered in the spring.

Unfortunately a sufficiently large sample of bolls for our check was not examined at the beginning of the experiment to determine the mortality until this date, and the check sample examined at the end of the experiment contained more live larvæ than at the beginning. The indications were, however, that the treatment had killed a large number of the larvæ. The bolls were totally rotted and larvæ which were dead at the beginning of the experiment were unrecognizable at the finish.

MORTALITY OF HIBERNATING LARVÆ IN STORED SEED.

The number of larvæ found in the ginned seed is very small compared to the number found in the bolls when the cotton is picked. In the Laguna the seed cotton is passed through cleaners or beaters before it goes to the gins to remove the trash and dirt. This causes most of the larvæ to leave the lint and many are undoubtedly driven from the seed also during the process. Larvæ are thrown out by the thousands with the trash that comes from the later pickings, and in some cases the pile of trash and the sides of surrounding buildings are pink with crawling larvæ. Many of the double seeds are torn apart in the cleaner and gin, though some go through unharmed. It is extremely disappointing to look for larvæ in seed which comes from heavily infested cotton. In such seed in the winter or spring one can rarely collect more than 75 to 100 live larvæ in the course of an eight-hour day. Ten samples of 2,500 seeds each were taken on different occasions during February and March; 1918 and 1919, from seed houses, examined seed by seed, and only 9 live larvæ were found.

For our rearing work larvæ were removed by hand from the bolls and placed in fruit jars with seed to pass the winter. Table XXII shows that the mortality among larvæ removed from bolls in November and stored in the laboratory during the winter of 1918 and 1919 was 22.6 per cent and that 0.4 per cent were still alive November 20, 1919, when the work was discontinued.

Other larvæ were disturbed as little as possible and were left in the double seed where they had prepared to spend the winter. The double seed were picked from the lint by hand and stored in the laboratory under the same conditions as the others. Table XXIII shows that there was 16.2 per cent mortality among larvæ in double seed and that 4.4 per cent were still alive on November 20, 1919.

TABLE XXII.—*Mortality among larvæ removed from bolls and kept in the laboratory in a condition as near to that of stored seed as possible.*

Date collected.	Number entering resting stage.	Number emerged.	Per cent mortality.	Per cent emerged.	Number alive Nov. 20, 1919.
1918.					
Sept. 30.........	83	71	13.2	85.5	2
Nov. 13.........	281	191	31.6	68.0	2
Do.........	256	180	28.9	70.3	2
Do.........	269	153	43.1	56.9	0
Nov. 14.........	260	183	29.7	70.3	0
Nov. 15.........	282	220	22.0	78.0	0
Do.........	309	255	17.5	82.5	0
Do.........	239	201	15.4	84.1	1
Do.........	320	255	19.6	79.6	2
Do.........	299	244	17.7	81.6	2
Do.........	277	211	23.4	76.2	1
Nov. 16.........	260	193	25.0	74.2	2
Do.........	244	192	20.9	77.7	1
Nov. 17.........	265	242	8.6	91.3	1
Nov. 19.........	125	99	20.8	79.2	0
Total.......	3,769	2,890			16
Average.....			22.6	77.0	0.4 per cent.

The moths were removed daily and a record kept for each jar. The percentages used are based on the number of moths emerging and the number of dead and live larvæ found in the jar at the end of the experiment. As these larvæ were carefully removed by hand and stored indoors, the mortality was the minimum that can be expected and is much lower than in seed ginned and handled on a commercial scale. It is difficult to determine the mortality in the seed warehouses, because the dead larvæ are so hard to find, but it is evident to one collecting larvæ that it is much higher in the early spring than in the fall. The mortality was 80 per cent among larvæ thrown out by the cleaners and stored indoors during the winter, and in this sample only the most active larvæ were used.

TABLE XXIII.—*Mortality among larvæ in double seeds removed from lint by hand and stored in jars in the laboratory.*

Date collected.	Number entering resting stage.	Number emerged.	Per cent mortality.	Per cent emerged.	Number alive Nov. 20, 1919.
1918.					
Nov. 15..........	206	182	8.7	88.3	6
Nov. 22..........	190	165	9.4	86.8	7
Nov. 23..........	184	157	8.1	85.3	12
Nov. 22..........	88	76	9.0	86.3	4
Do..........	61	41	22.9	67.2	6
Dec. 25..........	213	119	41.3	55.8	6
1919.					
Jan. 23..........	172	143	11.6	83.1	9
Total......	1,114	883	....	....	50
Average...	....	....	16.2	79.2	4.4 per cent.

MORTALITY OF LARVÆ PLANTED WITH THE SEED.

A screen-wire cage was built so that no infestation could interfere from the outside, and 100 double seeds were planted with sound seed in 30 hills to see what the infestation would be from larvæ planted with the seed alone. No infestation occurred during August, but from September 1 to November 7 the infestation went from 12 per cent to 96 per cent, with an average of 5.6 larvæ per boll on November 7. Thus it is evident that should all the larvæ left in the fields be destroyed either naturally or by artificial means, the infestation arising from the larvæ planted with the seed alone is sufficient to cause a considerable loss (Table XXIV).

TABLE XXIV.—*Infestation of pink bollworm from 100 double seeds planted in a cage.*

Date examined.	Per cent of bolls infested.	Average infestation per boll.			
		Larvæ.	Pupæ.	Exit holes.	Total.
1919.					
Aug. 1..........	0	0	0	0	0
Aug. 6..........	0	0	0	0	0
Aug. 22..........	0	0	0	0	0
Sept. 1..........	12.00	0.12	0	0	0.12
Sept. 30..........	84.00	2.20	0	0.96	3.16
Nov. 7..........	96.00	5.60	0	0	5.60

PARASITES AND PREDATORS.

What part of the mortality in the newly hatched larvæ is due to starvation, exposure to the sun, or falling from the plants, and what to predacious insects, could not be determined, but the toll taken by the nymphs and adults of three species of small undetermined Hemiptera is evidently very high. The attacks on the small pink bollworm larvæ from these predators are so important that daily examinations of all food placed in the breeding cages was absolutely necessary. Often one small nymph would destroy the larvæ from a large number of eggs during the night.

The larvæ of a lace-wing, *Chrysopa rufilabris* Burm., attacks the newly hatched pink bollworm and also the larger larvæ in the flowers.

Only very rarely is a dead larva found inside a boll. The feeding habits within the green boll greatly reduce the chances of attack by parasites and predators during this period. When the exit holes are cut, or the boll begins to open, or when the larvæ are migrating to the ground, they are exposed to these enemies for a short time. This short period of exposure may account for the very few parasites found. Only three species and one specimen of each were found attacking the larvæ. They were the Hymenoptera *Habrobracon* sp., *Parisierola emigrata* Rohwer, and a small dipteron, *Tortriciophaga tortricis* Coquillett. The scarcity of these parasites during the two years proves very conclusively that no relief can be hoped for from this source.

The pupæ of the pink bollworm in Mexico were not attacked by parasites, so far as our observations show.

The small chalcid *Trichogramma minutum* Riley may prove beneficial in parasitizing the eggs of the pink bollworm, but it was not observed attacking the eggs until late in the season, and then only very rarely.

An outbreak of mites, *Pediculoides ventricosus* Newport, occurred on the hibernating larvæ in the laboratory in 1918. Steps were taken immediately to check them by burning all infested material. To what extent these mites occur in the seed houses was not determined.

REPRESSION.

FUMIGATION OF SEED.

From the known instances in which infestations have occurred from larvæ planted in the seed there can be no doubt of the danger of planting infested seed. Several methods of killing the larvæ in the seed have been used in Egypt and other places (*10*), but all fall into three classes: Immersion of the seed in some substance to kill the larvæ, treatment with heat, or fumigation with poisonous gases. Immersion of seed in liquids is obviously out of the question where tons of seed are used for planting on a plantation. In Egypt larvæ can be killed by exposing them to the heat of the sun. Preliminary experiments showed that the temperature in Mexico during the planting season was not high enough to kill the larvæ and that cotton seeds are very poor conductors of heat. Machines (*4, 6*) have been perfected for passing the seed on an endless belt through air heated to 130° F. and houses have (*7*) been constructed for heating a mass of seed sufficiently high to kill the larvæ, but in Mexico fuel is scarce and very expensive, so fumigation with poisonous gases seemed the most economical and practical method to use.

A fumigation chamber of adobe bricks set in mud, the usual type of building in the Laguna, was constructed. The walls of this chamber were about 20 inches thick and were plastered on the inside and outside with cement. The floor was of brick set in mortar. During the fumigation the wooden door was closed and several thicknesses of wall paper plastered over the cracks. The size of the room was 5 by 8 by 10 feet, or 400 cubic feet. Three tons of cotton seed filled it about 5 feet deep. Experiments were made with seed placed in the room in bulk and in sacks. Carbon disulphid and hydrocyanic-acid gas were used.

CARBON DISULPHID.

Live larvæ, pupæ, and adults were placed at different depths in the seed, usually near the top, center, and bottom of the pile. The use of adults was discontinued after the first few experiments on account of the death of all the moths, while in the same experiments the mortality of the larvæ varied a great deal. Pupæ did not seem more difficult to kill than larvæ. Larvæ, and pupæ when they could be obtained, were placed in single, double, and triple pill boxes, at least 60 larvæ and sometimes more being used for each experiment. Larvæ in double and triple boxes were thought to be about as difficult to kill as larvæ webbed up in seed would be. Sometimes the larvæ would spin cocoons in the boxes before they were placed in the house, but such larvæ were killed along with the others. Where only a few larvæ were not killed they were always in the triple boxes on the bottom of the pile.

As only one lot of 3 tons of seed was available, the seeds were taken from the house and left exposed to the sun for several days after each experiment. When the seeds were returned to the house the boxes of larvæ were tied in a muslin bag and placed in position, the disulphid placed in shallow vessels on the top of the seed, and the door sealed.

Considerable difficulty was experienced at first in determining whether larvæ were dead or not. All of the larvæ would appear dead when removed, but they still retained their pink color and some of them would revive and pupate after lying in a comatose state for a week or more. Later all the larvæ were kept until we were absolutely sure whether they were dead or alive. Table XXV is a detailed account of the fumigátions that were made with carbon disulphid.

TABLE XXV.—*Preliminary fumigation experiments with carbon disulphid for P. gossypiella in cotton seed.*

Experiment No.	Dosage.		Length of exposure.	How seed was stored.	Location of larvæ.	Per cent killed in each location.	Total per cent killed.
	Pounds.	Cubic feet.					
			Hours.				
1	1	102	90	In sacks..........	Top sack.................. / Bottom sack..............	100 / 100	100
2	1	161	48	.....do............	Top sack.................. / Bottom sack..............	100 / 100	100
3	1	289	48	.....do............	Top sack.................. / Bottom sack..............	0 / 0	0
4	1	161	23	.....do............	Top sack.................. / Bottom sack..............	12 / 16	14
5	1	161	23	.....do............	Top sack.................. / Bottom sack..............	60 / 26	43
6	1	161	48	In bulk...........	2½ feet deep............. / 4½ feet deep.............	100 / 20	60
7	1	103	48	.....do............	2½ feet deep............. / 4½ feet deep.............	100 / 45	72
8	1	124	48	.....do............	2½ feet deep............. / 4½ feet deep.............	31 / 0	16
9	1	82	48	.....do............	2½ feet deep............. / 4½ feet deep.............	100 / 75	88
[1]10	1	54	24	.....do............	2½ feet deep............. / 4½ feet deep.............	100 / 80	90
11	1	80	42	In bags...........	On top................... / In center................ / On bottom................	100 / 100 / 100	100
13	1	100	1 week.	In bulk 6 feet deep.	On top................... / 2 feet deep.............. / 4 feet deep.............. / 6 feet deep..............	100 / 100 / 84 / 82	91
			Hours.				
19	1	100	48	In bulk 5 feet deep.	18 inches from top.............. / Middle.................. / Bottom.................	100 / 97.5 / 75	94
20	1	80	48	.....do............	Middle.................. / Bottom.................	100 / 100	100
21	1	80	48	.....do............	Middle.................. / Bottom.................	100 / 100	100
22	1	80	48	.....do............	Middle.................. / Bottom.................	100 / 100	100
23	1	80	24	.....do............	Bottom.................	100	100
26	1	80	12	.....do............	Middle.................. / Bottom.................	100 / 90	95
27	1	80	15	.....do............	Middle.................. / Bottom.................	85 / 80	82.5
29	1	85	24	.....do............	Middle.................. / Bottom.................	100 / 100	100
30	1	85	24	.....do............	Middle.................. / Bottom.................	100 / 100	100
31	1	90	24	.....do............	Bottom.................	85	85
32	1	90	24	.....do............	....do..................	60	60

[1] In Experiment No. 10 the larvæ were placed in glass tubes, which were closed with cork stoppers, making them approximately air tight.

In experiments 20, 21, and 22 all larvæ were killed with 1 pound of disulphid to 80 cubic feet in 48 hours. In order to shorten the time, experiments 23, 26, and 27 were made, and all the larvæ were not killed. All of the disulphid had not evaporated at the end of 12 and 15 hours in experiments 26 and 27, but it had evaporated in experiment 23 in 24 hours, and all the larvæ were killed, showing that 24 hours are necessary to evaporate and to secure maximum penetration of 1 pound of disulphid in 80 cubic feet. This was in the summer time, when the temperature inside the house was 75° to 80° F. Experiments 13, 19, 29, and 30 were made to decrease the dosage needed. All larvæ were not killed in experiments 13 and 19, where the dosage was 1 pound disulphid to 100 cubic feet with long exposures, but all were killed in experiments 29 and 30, with 1 pound to 85 cubic feet and a 24-hour exposure.

Table XXVI is a summary of the carbon disulphid experiments. From these experiments it is seen that satisfactory results were obtained by using 1 pound of carbon disulphid to 80 cubic feet for 24 hours or longer when the seeds were not over 5 feet deep.

TABLE XXVI.—*Fumigation of cotton seed with carbon disulphid.*

Experiment No.	Dosage.		Exposure.	Per cent larvæ killed.	How seeds were placed.
	Pounds.	Cubic feet.			
			Hours.		
1	1	102	90	100	Seed in bags.
2	1	161	48	[1]100	Do.
11	1	80	42	100	Do.
20	1	80	42	100	Seed in bulk, 5 feet deep.
21	1	80	48	100	Do.
22	1	80	48	100	Do.
23	1	80	24	100	Do.
29	1	85	24	100	Do.
30	1	85	24	100	Do.
26	1	80	12	95	Do.
19	1	100	48	94	Do.
13	1	100	168	91	Seed in bulk, 6 feet deep.
10	1	54	24	[2]90	Seed in bulk, 5 feet deep.
9	1	82	48	88	Do.
31	1	90	24	85	Do.
27	1	80	15	82.5	Do.
7	1	102	48	80.5	Do.
32	1	90	24	60	Do.
6	1	161	48	51	Seed in bags.
5	1	161	23	37	Do.
8	1	124	48	17	Seed in bulk, 5 feet deep.
4	1	161	23	13.3	Seed in bags.

[1] Record doubtful.   [2] Larvæ in corked vials.

HYDROCYANIC-ACID GAS.

The fumigation of cotton seed with hydrocyanic acid gas proved very unsatisfactory, as the gas is so light that it will not penetrate the seed more than a few inches. In some of the experiments an earthenware crock containing the sulphuric acid was set directly on top of the seed pile and the cyanid lowered by a string from the outside in the usual way. The penetration was so poor that a special generator was designed. A section of 10-inch pipe 14 inches long was fitted with gas-tight caps on both ends and a lead inner pot to hold the acid. The generator was placed outside the house below the floor level and the gas conducted to the inside, where it was allowed to escape in the bottom of the fumigation chamber through perforated pipes. It was hoped that the penetration upward would be greater than downward, but there was very little difference.

Table XXVII is a summary of the experiments with the use of hydrocyanic-acid gas. From these experiments it is seen that it is not practicable to use hydrocyanic-acid gas when the seeds are over 4 inches deep. It could not be recommended even when seed is in ordinary bags, for the center of a bag of cotton seed is more than 4 inches from the surface of the sack exposed.

TABLE XXVII.—*Fumigation of cotton seed with hydrocyanic-acid gas.*

Experiment No.	Position of generator.	Dosage per 100 cubic feet.	Exposure.	Per cent of larvæ killed.	Remarks.
			Hours.		
17	Inside..............	2-2-4	2	100.0	Seed in bulk, 4 inches deep.
24	.....do..............	4-4-8	3	70.0	Seed in bulk, 6 inches deep.
18	.....do..............	2-2-4	2½	62.5	Do.
25	.....do..............	2-2-4	2	60.0	Do.
16	.....do..............	4-4-8	24	47.0	Seed in bulk, 5 feet deep; all not killed 6 inches deep.
15	Outside.............	4-4-8	24	34.0	Seed in bulk, 5 feet deep; none killed 2½ inches deep.
14	.....do..............	2-2-4	24	10.0	Seed in bulk, 4½ feet deep; all not killed 1 foot from floor.
12	Inside..............	2-2-4	48	.6	Seed in bulk, 5 feet deep.

POISONING EXPERIMENTS.

As a possible means of controlling the pink bollworm in the field, poison experiments were conducted in the laboratory with both adults and larvæ. Moths readily drink water in captivity when it is sprayed on the leaves or blotting paper in the breeding jars, and it was thought they might be killed by poisoning the drinking water with an arsenical solution. Repeated trials were made by using a solution of calcium arsenate for the moths to drink. The longevity of these moths was the same as that of those in the check, where pure water was used.

While the laboratory experiments in poisoning the adults were not encouraging, it was thought advisable to try it under field conditions. From the habit of the newly hatched larvæ of crawling over the plants and bolls before they enter, theoretically it seemed possible that a large number of young larvæ might be poisoned.

Average plats were selected at San Isidera, Tlahualilo, and at the laboratory for poisoning the plants. Weekly applications of powdered calcium arsenate were made with hand dusters. These applications were begun about July 15 and continued until the last week in October. The gauges on the machines were opened to their fullest extent and as heavy an application as possible was made each time. (Table XXVIII.)

'eekly examinations of bolls both from the poisoned and
s were made. The average number of larvæ per boll v
itly. These variations, however, occurred in other samp
s where no poison was used and the poisoning did not chec
station. The season of experiments was unfavorable for p
experiments. There was about twice the normal rainfall,
hed the poison from the plants, and, moreover, caused the c
row so rank that it was impossible to get a thorough appli
1 the available labor. Under more favorable conditions it i
e that better results might be obtained.

TRAPS.

Trap Lights.

n the laboratory, where the doors and windows were screene
moths could not escape, they would frequently come to the
lights, resting on the shade or wall near by, but under ou
ditions moths would seldom come to lights. Acetylene anc
lights were suspended repeatedly in front of a white backg
he laboratory cotton plats, where there were thousands of r
the course of 2 or 3 hours not more than 6 to 8 moths
ie to the lights, while at the same time an examination v
hlight would show there were large numbers on the plants
feet away. The few that did come to the lights were prc
s that we disturbed in moving about, and it can not be said
; any attraction whatsoever to the lights.
in electric trap light was also placed within a few feet of the j
h negative results. Another trap light was run all night
secutive nights in an open shed where there were hundreds c
;eeds and only 5 moths were taken. During the same 15

large numbers of moths were emerging from material at the laboratory which had been taken from this same shed a few weeks before, and it is certain that large numbers of moths were emerging in the seed shed while the trap was in operation. Light traps have been recommended as a means of control by several people. Gough (*12*), Willcocks (*7*), Ballou (*11*), and others report catches of thousands of moths per night in light traps. Ballou (*11*) found that most of the moths came to the light in the hour following sunset. Some authors found lights so attractive to the moths that they were used to determine the number of moths emerging from stored material, but in Mexico we found that practically none came to the lights. Busck (*8*) in Hawaii also found that the pink bollworm moths were not attracted to lights.

ATTRACTION TO FRUIT.

Cone-shaped traps of the type used for flies were baited with oranges, bananas, apples, mangoes, guavas, and pineapples and were repeatedly exposed among the cotton plants with absolutely negative results.

RECOMMENDATIONS FOR CONTROL.

Too much can not be said and done in encouraging the destruction of hibernating larvæ. They are the source of infestation for the following year. If 9 per cent or less of the larvæ are able to survive the natural mortality of winter and early spring in irrigated fields, this small percentage, with the larvæ surviving in the seed and other places, produces an infestation the following year that causes approximately 25 per cent gross loss to the Laguna crop. Every hibernating larva killed during the winter or early spring before oviposition begins means the cutting off of many thousand larvæ by the end of the season. The paramount necessity, then, is to reduce the survival of hibernating larvæ to as low a figure as possible.

BURNING OF OLD STALKS AND BOLLS.

Just as soon as possible the stalks should be cut and raked up in piles. Old bolls, sticks, and trash of all descriptions to which larvæ may be attached should be carefully picked up and burned with the the stalks, the main object being to burn everything in the field that contains larvæ or would be likely to afford protection for hibernating larvæ. If possible, the cutting and piling of the stalks should be done while the plants are still green, in this way minimizing the labor and increasing the effectiveness of the operation. Green stalks will retain most of their bolls, which shatter when they are cut dry. Just as soon as the piles lose their green color and become more or less dry they should be burned. Better results can be gained by waiting for this drying to take place rather than by burning the plants while they are yet green. Ordinarily the old stalks are cut and burned in the Laguna when preparing the land for the new crop.   While this is done for purely agricultural reasons to make plowing easier, large numbers of live hibernating larvæ are killed.   On the experimental plot at Lerdo the stalks were cut on the last day of February and examined during March.   At this examination live larvæ at the rate of over 5,000 per acre were found in the bolls attached to the stalks. So many bolls had fallen or were knocked off during the cutting and piling that over half were left on the ground.   A little extra effort in collecting and destroying these is well worth while.   No boll or piece of cotton is so small or negligible that it should not be picked up and burned.

Cutting Stalks and Fall Plowing.

Experiments have shown conclusively that the mortality is greater in hibernating larvæ buried in the soil than in those left on top of the soil and greater in those buried in irrigated soil than in those buried in dry soil.   It has also been found that the most favorable of all places for larvæ to hibernate under field conditions are the old bolls left undisturbed on standing stalks.   During the winter of 1919–20 100 larvæ per 100 bolls successfully passed the winter on old stalks left standing in the fields and were alive on July 12, whereas only 4 larvæ per 100 bolls were found alive on this date in bolls lying on top of the soil.   These facts suggest certain agricultural practices that can be used to good advantage in reducing the number of surviving larvæ.

Ordinarily the old stalks are not left standing in the fields, but on some plantations large acreages which are not to be cultivated the following year are left, and on others where "zoca" is produced the stalks are not cut till late spring or summer.   All fields should be gone over with a stalk-cutter as early as possible, and in many cases the small amounts of cotton which are picked during the winter and spring could profitably be sacrificed in order to do this earlier in the season.   Fall and winter plowing to cover the bolls is recommended whenever it is possible, and water should be applied in years when there is an excess.

Pasturing.

If it is not possible to cut and burn the stalks or plow the field in the above manner, owing to labor shortage, weather conditions, or other causes, it is a very good idea to graze the fields.   Cattle, goats, and burros will eat the majority of the bolls on the stalks.   One important drawback to the grazing plan is that there is a certain amount of infested material tramped into the ground.   In one field near the town of Tlahualilo where the animals had been concentrated, only about one boll per square yard was found on the ground.   In other fields that had been grazed, but not so thoroughly, an average of 5 or 6 bolls per square yard was found.

CLEANING GINS, OIL MILLS, AND SEED WAREHOUSES.

In Mexico, where the infestation grows to be very intensive, thousands of live larvæ have been observed to come from the cleaners with the trash. It is the common practice there merely to collect this trash containing the large number of worms and place it in piles. The "cleanings" should be caught in a receptacle rather than allowed to fall on the ground, because the larvæ will crawl and secrete themselves in cracks, crevices, and rubbish of various kinds. This trash should be either burned or subjected to some treatment insuring the death of the insects contained therein. If the trash does not contain too much dirt to make it unburnable, the best plan is to burn it in the boilers. A very good plan was devised by Mr. T. M. Fairbairn for handling the unburnable material. The end was knocked out of an oil barrel and a small steam line run into the barrel, almost to the bottom. The trash from the cleaners fell into the steaming barrel and all larvæ were quickly killed.

After the season is over the gin plant or oil mill should be thoroughly cleaned. All seed and rubbish should be removed from every nook and crevice of the machinery and buildings and burned. If the structure of the buildings permits they should also be fumigated after cleaning.

It is the usual custom to keep enough seed on the plantations for a second planting in case it is necessary. This seed should be as carefully fumigated as the seed that is planted, and as an additional precaution should be stored in a moth-proof screened room. It was very noticeable that the infestation always began earlier in the season and was heavier in the fields nearest the gins and seed warehouses.

FUMIGATION.

All seed used for planting or kept on the plantation after the first of March should be fumigated. An air-tight room is necessary for a successful fumigation, and it is better to build a special fumigation house at least a hundred yards from the other buildings, so that there will be no danger from fire. Carbon bisulphid is highly inflammable, and no fire should be allowed around the house while fumigation is being done. The ordinary adobe construction is satisfactory, but precautions should be taken to see that plenty of mud is used and all cracks between the adobes well filled. A brick floor set in mortar should be provided and the inside plastered. The plastering not only makes the building more air-tight, but prevents absorption of the gases by the walls. The doors should be of matched wood, and paper should be plastered over the cracks when closed. Seed may be fumigated in sacks or in bulk, but in either case should be packed as little as possible. In no case should the seed to be fumigated be over 5 feet deep. One pound of carbon disulphid should be used for every 80 cubic feet. The entire area of the building should be calculated and not the space occupied by the seed only. As it costs as much to fumigate the air space as it does the seed, it is more economical to make the room only high enough for a person to stand comfortably. The size of the building needed can be calculated from the tons of seed to be fumigated, a ton of seed occupying 85 cubic feet (2½ cubic meters).

All water should be separated from the carbon disulphid and after the seed is in the house the disulphid poured into shallow vessels placed on top of the seed. Not more than a pound should be placed in each vessel, so that it will evaporate quickly. Old gasoline cans cut down to about 3 inches high, or earthenware bowls, make good containers. The vessels should be scattered over the top of the seed pile and the disulphid poured into those farthest from the door first. There is no danger in doing this, but it is more convenient to have a number of half-inch pipes fitted with caps or corks extending through the walls and introduce the disulphid from the outside. As soon as the liquid is poured into the vessels the door should be closed and paper stuck over the cracks with flour paste. The house should be kept closed for at least 24 hours, and longer will do no harm, as continued exposure to the gas does not injure the germination of the seed.

PLANTING EARLY VARIETIES.

From the life history and feeding habits of the pink bollworm it can be readily seen that the later the cotton crop is in maturing the greater will be the amount of loss. Every cultural practice should be used in securing as early maturity as possible of the available cotton varieties.

SUMMARY.

The pink bollworm was introduced into Mexico in 1911 with seed for planting. Five years later it was generally and uniformly distributed throughout the Laguna and had reached its maximum development.

Infestation is started in the spring as soon as squares are formed, by moths emerging from hibernating larvæ, and rapidly increases until practically every boll is infested with several larvæ by fall.

The life cycle is completed in an average of 31 days in the summer, but the larval stage of hibernating or resting larvæ may be extended for 2 years or more.

Dispersal is mainly through the carriage by man of hibernating larvæ in seed, but local dispersion is brought about also by flight and carriage of adults.

The pink bollworm causes approximately 25 per cent gross damage to the Laguna crop by feeding in the bolls and squares. This feeding results in a reduction in the quantity and quality of the lint produced, reduction in the quantity of seed, and lowering of the quantity and quality of the oil content of the seed.

Early cleaning of fields by burning all the old stalks and bolls, cleaning and fumigation of gins, oil mills, and seed warehouses, the fumigation of all seed kept on the plantations, and the early maturity of the crop are recommended as means of control.

LITERATURE CITED.

(1) HINDS, W. E.

    1906. PROLIFERATION AS A FACTOR IN THE NATURAL CONTROL OF THE MEXI-CAN COTTON BOLL WEEVIL. U. S. Dept. Agr., Bur. Ent. Bul. 59. 45 p., 6 pl.

(2) MAXWELL–LEFROY, H.

    1906. INDIAN INSECT PESTS. 318 p., 346 figs., and figs. A–S. Calcutta.

(3) FULLAWAY, D. T.

    1909. INSECTS OF COTTON IN HAWAII. Hawaii Agr. Exp. Sta., Bul. 18. 27 p., 18 figs.

(4) GOUGH, L. H., and STORY, G.

    1914. METHODS FOR THE DESTRUCTION OF THE PINK BOLL WORM (GELECHIA GOSSYPIELLA, SAUND.) IN COTTON SEED. *In* Agr. Jour. Egypt, v. 3, pt. 2, 1913, p. 73–95, 5 pl. Ministry Agr., Cairo.

(5) GOUGH, L. H.

    1916. THE LIFE HISTORY OF GELECHIA GOSSYPIELLA FROM THE TIME OF THE COTTON HARVEST TO THE TIME OF COTTON SOWING. Ministry Agr. Egypt, Tech. and Sci. Serv. Bul. 4 (Ent. Sect.). 16 p.

(6) ———

    1916. NOTE ON A MACHINE TO KILL GELECHIA LARVÆ BY HOT AIR, AND THE EFFECTS OF HEAT ON GELECHIA LARVÆ AND COTTON SEED. Ministry Agr. Egypt, Tech. and Sci. Serv. Bul. 6 (Ent. Sect.). 18 p., 3 pl.

(7) WILLCOCKS, F. C.

    1916. THE INSECT AND RELATED PESTS OF EGYPT. v. 1. The insect and related pests of the cotton plant, pt. I. The pink bollworm. Sultanic Agri. Soc., Cairo. 339 p., 17 figs., 10 pls.

(8) BUSCK, A.

    1917. THE PINK BOLLWORM, PECTINOPHORA GOSSYPIELLA. *In* U. S. Dept. Agr., Jour. Agr. Research, v. 9, no. 10, p. 343–370. 12 pl., 7 figs.

(9) KING, H. H.

    1917. THE WEED HANBUK (ABUTILON SPP.) AND ITS RELATION TO THE COTTON-GROWING INDUSTRY IN THE ANGLO-EGYPTIAN SUDAN. Ent. Bul. 7. 4 p. Khartoum.

(10) STORY, G.

    1917. MACHINES FOR THE TREATMENT OF COTTON SEED AGAINST PINK BOLL-WORM (GELECHIA GOSSYPIELLA SAUND.). Ministry Agr. Egypt, Tech. and Sci. Serv. Bul 14 (Ent. Sec.). 29 p.

(11) BALLOU, H. A.

    1919. COTTON AND THE PINK BOLLWORM IN EGYPT. Pts. I and II. *In* West Indian Bul., v. 17, no. 4, p. 237–292. 9 figs.

(12) GOUGH, L. H.

    1919. ON THE EFFECTS PRODUCED BY THE ATTACKS OF THE PINK BOLLWORM ON THE YIELD OF COTTON SEED AND LINT IN EGYPT. Bul. Ent. Research, v. 9, pt. 4, p. 279–324.

The following generic and specific description is reprinted from "The pink bollworm, *Pectinophora gossypiella*," by August Busck, Journal of Agricultural Research, vol. 9, no. 10, Washington, D. C., June 4, 1917.

HOW TO DISTINGUISH THE PINK BOLLWORM IN THE FIELD.

Definite and final determination of *P. gossypiella* in any stage can be made only by the aid of the microscope; and, unless a collector or inspector is thoroughly familiar with the species, all suspected material should be sent at once to the Bureau of Entomology for determination. Even a fraction of the insect in any of its stages can be recognized under the microscope by the characters given in succeeding sections of this paper.

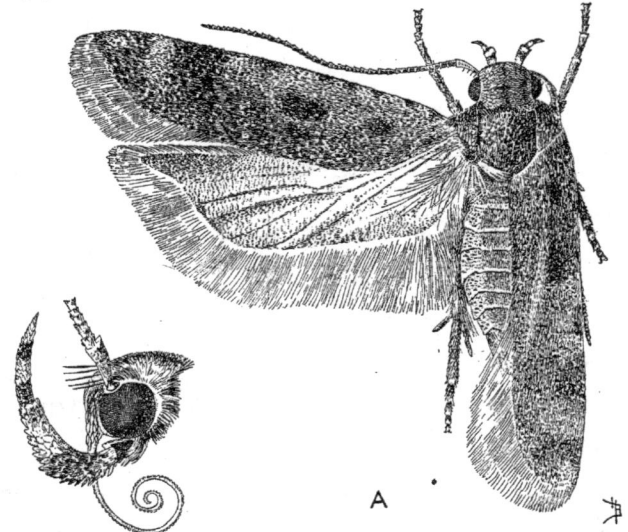

Fig. 4.—Pink bollworm: Adult. (Busck.)

The following essential characters, all of which can be discerned by the aid of a common pocket lens, will enable the practical worker to make a reasonably certain preliminary determination of the insect in all its stages in the field.

If a small dark-brown moth is caught in the cotton field or in a cotton mill or warehouse and is found to have the forewings pointed and the hindwings broad and sinuated below the tip and to possess long curved palpi and long stiff hairs on the first antennal joint, it is reasonably certain that the moth is *P. gossypiella*, the adult of the pink bollworm (fig. 4, *A*).

If, within the cotton boll or associated with stored cottonseed, a small white or pinkish caterpillar with brown head is found and under a hand lens the mandibles are

58

seen to have four teeth (fig. 5, *A–D*) and the crotches on the abdominal prolegs form a partial circle or horsehoe, opening outwards (fig. 5, *H*), the caterpillar will most probably prove to be the pink bollworm.

Again, if, within a cotton boll or otherwise associated with cotton in the field or in the mill, a small lepidopterous pupa is found, which under the lens is found to be entirely covered with a short velvety pubescence and to possess a short, curved, up-turned hook at the posterior end (fig. 6, *A–D*), it may with considerable certainty be determined as a pupa of the pink bollworm.

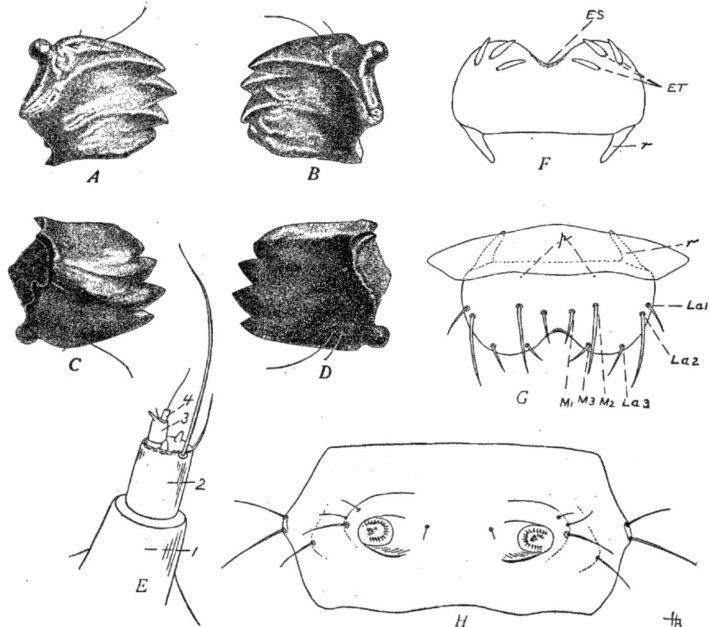

FIG. 5.—Pink bollworm: *A*, Right mandible of larva from underside. *B*, Left mandible from underside. *C*, Right mandible from upper side. *D*, Left mandible from upper side. *E*, Left antenna of larva from underside: *1*, First joint; *2*, second joint; *3*, third joint; *4*, fourth joint. *F*, Epipharynx of larva: *ES*, Epipharyngeal shield; *ET*, epipharyngeal seta; *r*, epipharyngeal rod. *G*, Labrum of larva: *La₁*, Lateral labral seta 1; *La₂*, lateral labral seta 2; *La₃*, lateral labral seta 3; *M₁*, median labral seta 1; *M₂*, median labral seta 2; *M₃*, median labral seta 3; *p*, labral punctures; *r*, epipharyngeal rod. *H*, Underside of third abdominal segment of larva. (Busck.)

GENERIC DESCRIPTION.

Pectinophora, new genus (Gelechiidæ).

Type: *Gelechia gossypiella* Saunders.

MOTH.—Face and head smooth. Labial palpi long, recurved. reaching above vertex; second joint thickened on the underside with slightly furrowed brush, which is evenly attenuated toward apex; terminal joint shorter than second, somewhat thickened with scales in front, compressed, pointed. Maxillary palpi minute, deflected. Tongue long, spiraled, scaled in its entire length. Antennæ serrated and finely ciliated on the underside; basal joint with heavy but sparse (5–6) pecten. Thorax smooth. Forewings (fig. 7, *A*) elongate ovate, pointed, smooth; 12 veins, 7 and 8 stalked to costa, rest separate, 1b furcate at base.[6] Hindwings (fig. 7, *B*) somewhat broader than forewings, trapezoidal; costa deflected from the middle; apex pointed; termen sinuate; 8 veins; 8 connected with cell by an oblique bar; 6 and 7 closely approximate at base; 3 and 4 connate; 5 parallel with 4; frenulum simple in the males, triple in the females.   Male genitalia (fig. 9, *B*), with harpes and uncus well developed; tegumen evenly chitinized.   Posterior tibiæ (fig. 9, *A*) hairy above.

LARVA.—Head (Pl. V and fig. 8) spherical, nearly circular in outline viewed from above, a little wider than long; greatest width a little behind the middle; incision of dorsal hind margin about one-fourth of the diameter of the head; distance between

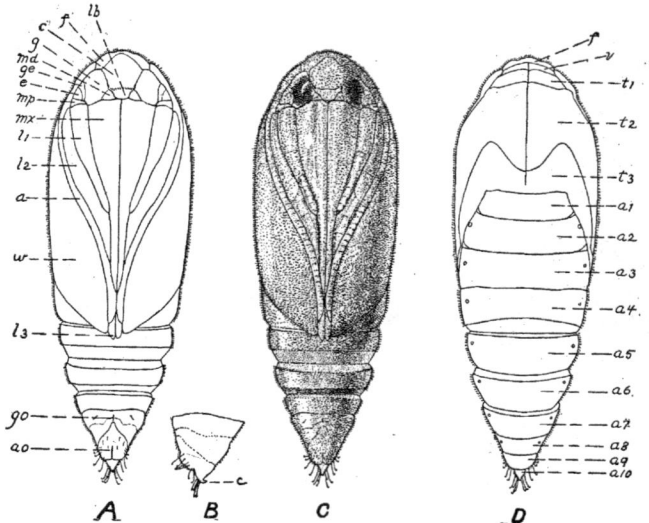

FIG. 6.—Pink bollworm. *A*, Pupa from front: *lb*, Labrum; *f*, front; *c*, clypeus; *g*, gena; *md*, mandibles; *ge*, glaced eye; *e*, eye; *mp*, maxillary palpus; *mx*, maxilla; *l₁*, first thoracic leg; *l₂*, second thoracic leg; *l₃*, third thoracic leg; *a*, antenna; *w*, forewing; *go*, genital opening; *ao*, anal opening. *B*, Tip of pupa from left side: *c*, Cremaster. *C*, Mature pupa, with eyes of the imago visible through pupal skin. *D*, Pupa from back: *f*, Front; *v*, vertex; *t₁*, first thoracic segment; *t₂*, second thoracic segment; *t₃*, third thoracic segment; *a₁*, first abdominal segment; *a₂*, second abdominal segment; *a₃*, third abdominal segment; *a₄*, fourth abdominal segment; *a₅*, fifth abdominal segment; *a₆*, sixth abdominal segment; *a₇*, seventh abdominal segment; *a₈*, eighth abdominal segment; *a₉*, ninth abdominal segment; *a₁₀*, tenth abdominal segment. (Busck.)

dorsal extremities of hind margin about one-half of the width of the head.   Front triangular, reaching beyond the middle; adfrontal sutures somewhat undulating, reaching to the incision of hind margin; adfrontal ridges converging from near the middle, at the point of attachment of tentorial arms, to the longitudinal ridge, which is one-half as long as front.   Projection of the dorsal margin over the ventral is one-half of the diameter of the head.   Triangular plates of hypostoma distinctly separated by a slightly pigmented gula, nearly equilateral, but somewhat elongated and projecting slightly beyond the ventral margin of epicranium.

Ocelli six; i, ii, v, and vi forming a parallelogram; iii and iv on a line between ii and v; v smaller than the rest.[7]   Epistoma with the usual two pairs of setæ (E_1, E_2) well developed.

[6] The European (*Gelechia*) *Pectinophora malvella* Zeller exhibits an amount of variation of the venation in the forewing which is very unusual in this group of insects. Veins 2 and 3 in this species are sometimes coincident or partly coincident at base or at tip; the variations sometimes differing in the two wings of the same insect.   No such variation has been ascertained in *P. gossypiella*, where the venation seems constant, as given above.

[7] This numbering of the eyes differs from that of Fracker in that his numbers 5 and 6 are reversed, so as to make them continuous with the rest. (Fracker, S. B. The Classification of Lepidopterous Larvæ . . . 169 p., 10 pl. Urbana, Ill., 1915. Bibliography, p. 145–146. Illinois Biological Monographs, v. 2, no. 1.)

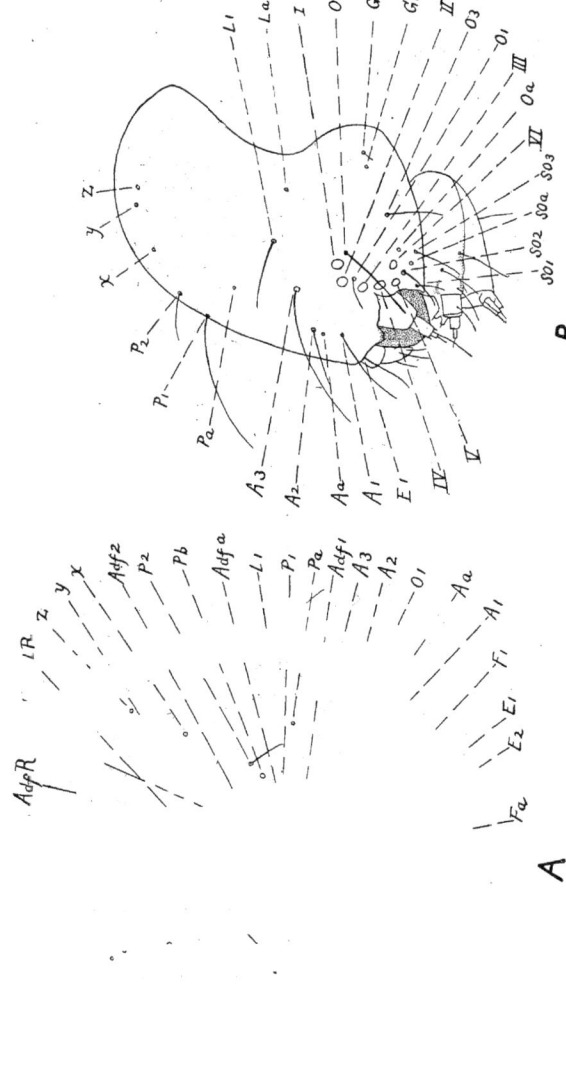

PINK BOLLWORM.

A, Head capsule of larva from front. B, Head capsule of larva from side. AdfR, adfrontal ridge; AdfS, adfrontal suture; LR, longitudinal ridge; E₁, epistomal seta 1; E₂, epistomal seta 2; Fa, frontal puncture; F₁, frontal seta; Adf₁, adfrontal seta 1; Adf₂, adfrontal seta 2; Adfa, adfrontal puncture; A₁, anterior seta 1; A₂, anterior seta 2; A₃, anterior seta 3; Aa, anterior puncture; P₁, posterior seta 1; P₂, posterior seta 2; Pa, posterior puncture a; Pb, posterior puncture b; x, y, and z, ultraposterior punctures; L₁, lateral seta; La, lateral puncture; I, ocellus i; II, ocellus ii; III, ocellus iii; IV, ocellus iv; V, ocellus v; VI, ocellus vi; O₁, ocellar seta 1; O₂, ocellar seta 2; O₃, ocellar seta 3; Oa, ocellar puncture; SO₁, subocellar seta 1; SO₂, subocellar seta 2; SO₃, subocellar seta 3; SOa, subocellar puncture; G₁, genal seta; Ga, genal puncture. (Busck.)

Frontal punctures (Fa) close together, anterior to frontal setæ (F_1); distance between punctures less than distance between puncture (Fa) and setæ (F_1); frontal setæ (F_1) and adfrontal setæ (Adf_1 and Adf_2) nearly equidistant; second adfrontal seta (Adf_2) approximate to but before beginning of longitudinal ridge (LR); adfrontal puncture (Adfa) midway between adfrontal setæ.

Epicranium with normal number of primary setæ, 13, and punctures, 7, and with three small ultraposterior punctures [8] (x, y, and z).[9]

Anterior setæ [10] (A_1, A_2, A_3) in a slightly obtuse angle; A_1 and A_2 closer together than A_2 and A_3; anterior puncture (Aa) between A_1 and A_2. Posterior setæ [11] (P_1, P_2) and posterior punctures (Pa, Pb) near the middle of the head; P_1 on the level with

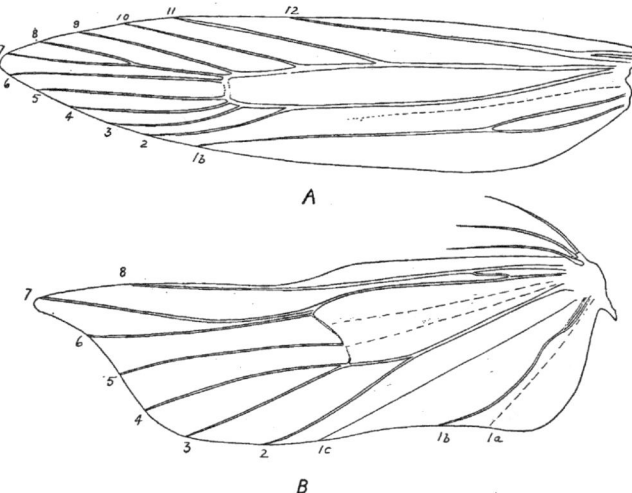

Fig. 7.—Pink bollworm: *A*, Venation of forewing; *B*, venation of hindwing. (Busck.)

adfrontal puncture [12]; P_2 posterior to Adf_2. Pa equidistant from P_1, A_3 and the lateral seta (L_1) remote from the anterior group, nearly on the level with P_1; lateral seta (L_1) remote from A_3, nearly on the level of Pb; lateral puncture (La) posteroventral to the setæ, remote. Of the ocellar setæ (O_1, O_2, O_3),[13] O_1 is equidistant from and lateral to ocelli ii and iii, O_2 is closely approximate and posteroventral to ocellus i; O_3 is directly ventral and remote from O_2, on a line with ocelli v and vi; ocellar puncture (Oa) between O_3 and ocellus vi, approximate to latter. Subocellar setæ (So_1, So_2, So_3) triangularly placed, nearly equidistant; subocellar puncture (Soa) between and equidistant from So_2 and So_3. Genal seta (G_1) and puncture (Ga) both present; puncture anterior to seta.

Labrum (fig. 5, *F*, *G*) with median incision rather deep and evenly rounded. The three lateral setæ (La_1, La_2, La_3) close to edge, La_1 and La_2 closely approximate, La_3 remote; median setæ (M_1, M_2, M_3) in the usual Micro arrangement with M_2 lateral and slightly posterior to M_1; M_3 close to anterior margin on a line with La_3; M_1 and M_2 on a line respectively with La_2 and La_1.

---

[8] The nomenclature of the head setæ has been adopted from Heinrich [Heinrich, Carl. On the taxonomic value of some larval characters in the Lepidoptera. *In* Proc. Ent. Soc. Wash., v. 18, no. 3, p. 154–164, illus. 1916.] with certain minor modifications, noted in the following footnotes and concurred in by Mr. Heinrich.

[9] So-called "secondary punctures" of Heinrich, sometimes bearing minute setæ.

[10] Anterodorsal setæ of Heinrich.

[11] Posterodorsal setæ of Heinrich.

[12] The term "on the level with" is used in these descriptions as the head setæ are seen in frontal projection (Pl. V, *A*); anything above a level is termed "posterior" and anything below is termed "anterior."

[13] Heinrich's numbering reversed.

Epipharyngeal shield (ES) merely a slight chitinization of the edge of the median incision; epipharyngeal setæ narrow plates, triangularly grouped near anterior margin. Epipharyngeal rods not discernible in the labrum proper, only represented by their posterior projections, which are rather well developed.

Mandibles (fig. 5, *A–D*) strong, as broad as long, with four stout, rather short teeth: the three lower ones pointed; the upper blunt; a fifth lower tooth is slightly indicated on the underside; one long and one shorter seta on upper side near lower edge.

Labium and maxillæ normal (fig. 8, *C*).

Antennæ (fig. 5, *E*) four-jointed, with second joint considerably longer than joint 3, longer than broad; the longer seta longer than the entire antenna; papillæ minute, much shorter than third joint.

Three pairs of normal thoracic feet; four pairs of abdominal prolegs with crotches of uniform size in an incomplete circle, opening outwardly (fig. 5, *H*); anal prolegs with a transverse row of uniordinal hooks.

The arrangement of the body setæ is normal, as shown in figure 10, *A, B*. It differs from that of Gelechia in having the three setæ on prespiracular plate of prothorax nearly equidistant, while in Gelechia the posterior seta is farther separated from the two others than they are from each other, and in having the three setæ vii of the proleg-bearing abdominal segments arranged in a triangle, not in a line as in Gelechia.

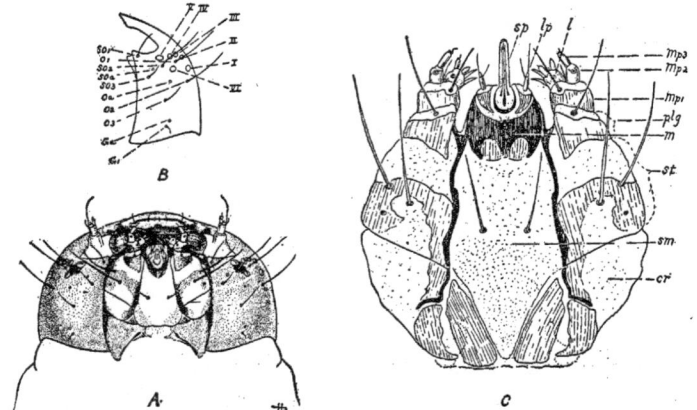

FIG. 8.—Pink bollworm. A, larval head from underside. B, Setæ arrangement of epicranium in figure A: *I*, Ocellus i; *II*, ocellus ii; *III*, ocellus iii; *IV*, ocellus iv; *V*, ocellus v; *VI*, ocellus vi; O_1, ocellar seta 1; O_2, ocellar seta 2; O_3, ocellar seta 3; *Oa*, ocellar puncture; SO_1, subocellar seta 1; SO_2, subocellar seta 2; SO_3, subocellar seta 3; *SOa*, subocellar puncture; G_1, genal seta; *Ga*, genal puncture. C, Labium and maxillæ: *sp*, Spinneret; *lp*, labial palpus; *l*, lacinia and galea; *m*, mentum; *sm*, submentum; *cr*, cardo; *st*, stripes; *plg*, palpiger; mp_1, maxillary palpus, first joint; mp_2, maxillary palpus, second joint; mp_3, maxillary palpus, third joint. (Busck.)

The genus differs further from Gelechia in the possession of an antennal pecten in the moth, and in the arrangement of the setæ of the larval head; Aa is anterior to A_2, not posterior to it as in Gelechia; P_1 and P_2 are posterior, respectively, to Adf_1 and Adf_2, which in Gelechia are nearly opposite to these, and L_1 is posterior to P_1, not on the level with it as in Gelechia.

The most striking larval difference is in the crotches of the abdominal prolegs, which are uniordinal and arranged in an incomplete circle, broken outwardly (fig. 5, *K*). In Gelechia they are biordinal and in a complete circle.

PUPA.—The pupa of *Pectinophora gossypiella* is pubescent, without any long setæ except on last joint, and thus is easily distinguished from the smooth, seta-bearing pupa of Gelechia; cremaster present.

SPECIFIC DESCRIPTION.

MOTH (fig. 4, *A*).—Labial palpi reddish brown; second joint with two diffused black bars exteriorly; terminal joint with two well-defined, broad, black annulations, one at base, the other at apical fourth. Antennæ brown with narrow black annulations;

basal joint with long black pecten. Face and head light reddish brown with some pale iridescent scales. Thorax reddish brown with a sprinkling of black around the collar; patagia somewhat lighter brown, unmottled. Forewings darker brown with a series of small, ill-defined, black spots along the costal edge from base to apical fourth, where there is a larger dash of light ocherous brown; dorsal edge and apical part of wing suffused with darker, blackish brown; the middle of the wing is irregularly sprinkled with blackish scales and contains on the cell an ill-defined, round, blackish spot, sometimes divided into an upper and lower spot; there is also a smaller spot on the base of the cell; the pattern of the wing is rather vague and there is considerable variation in different specimens; in many there is an ill-defined blackish fascia at apical fourth just before the light costal dash, but in other specimens this fascia is not present and the round dorsal spot is dissolved into several smaller spots. Cilia

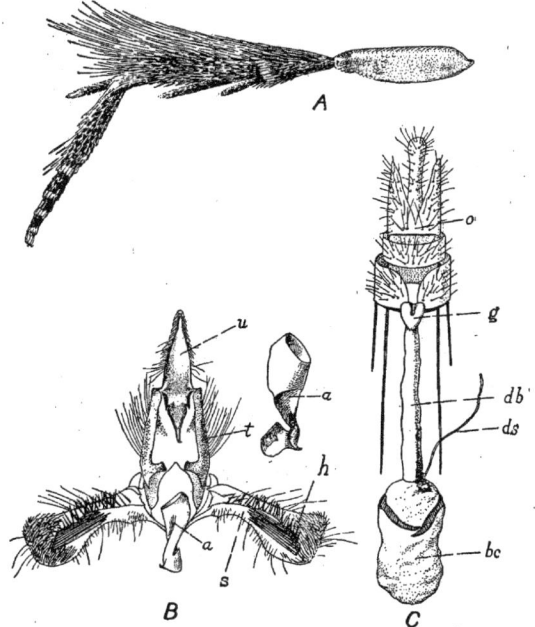

IG. 9.—Pink bollworm: *A*, right hind leg. *B*, genitalia of male: *u*, Uncus; *t*, tegumen; *h*, harp; *a*, ædœagus; *s*, sacculus. *C*, genitalia of female: *o*, Ovipositor; *g*, genital plate with genital opening; *db*, ductus bursæ; *ds*, ductus seminalis; *bc*, bursa copulatrix. (Busck.)

ight ocherous brown, streaked with blackish. Hindwings dark fuscous, somewhat ridescent, lightest toward base; cilia ocherous, terminal and apical parts suffused ith dark fuscous: vein 1c with long, ocherous fuscous hairs on the upper side. bdomen flattened and ocherous above, dark brown laterally with underside suffused ith black and with ocherous scaling at the joints. Legs (fig. 9, *A*) blackish fuscous 'th narrow ocherous annulations at the joints. The abdomen is very similarly aped in the male and in the female and it is exceedingly difficult to distinguish the xes, even in living moths, without dissection or by examination of the frenulum. 1e male genitalia (fig. 9, *B*) are remarkably small in proportion to the size of the ecies: harpes narrow at base, broadening towards tip; tip strongly haired; a uster of long, heavy, straight spines from inner side, well within the tip; sacculus med on its edge with a row of stout spines; uncus moderately long, broad at base, pering to a point, laterally heavily haired; ædœagus short, stout, with a terminal ook. In the female the ovipositor is weakly chitinized, covered with stiff hairs;

genital plate heart shaped; bursa copulatrix with two opposite, strongly chitin hornlike, serrated invaginations (fig. 9, C).

Alar expanse 15 to 20 mm.

FULL-GROWN LARVA.—The full-grown larva (fig. 10, A) is 11 to 13 mm. cylindrical, white, with dorsal side strongly suffused with pink. Head reddish b with blackish brown mandibles and the other trophi yellowish. Thoracic s rather small, divided in the middle, dark brown. [On each side of the thoracic s is a small, slightly depressed, kidney-shaped spot, thinly chitinized and les mented than the rest of the shield. This purely specific character is easy to ob and may be of some assistance as contributory evidence in a preliminary deter tion of the pink bollworm in the field (fig. 11).] Anal plate small, dark b

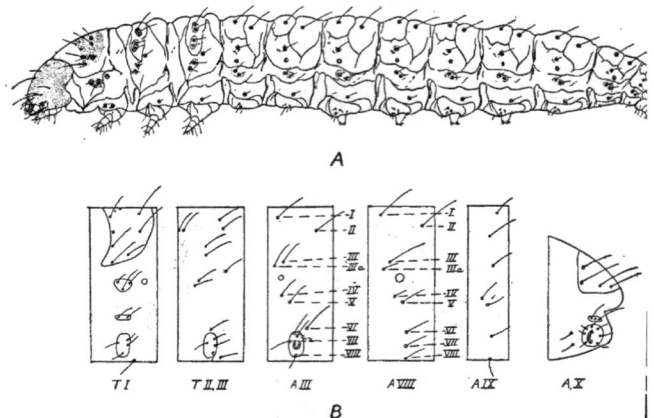

FIG. 10.—Pink bollworm. A, larva. B, schematic chart of arrangement of body setæ of larv first thoracic segment; T II, III, second and third thoracic segments; A III, third abdomir ment; A VIII, eighth abdominal segment; A IX, ninth abdominal segment; A X, tenth abd segment. (Busck.)

Tubercles small, but distinct, yellowish brown, surrounded by deeper pink tha prevalent suffusion and bearing rather short, dark-brown setæ. Crotches of a inal feet 15 to 17.

PUPA.—The pupa (fig. 6, A-D) is 8 to 10 mm. long, rather plump, reddish brown; posterior end pointed and terminating in a short, stout, upwardly turned hooklike cremaster; entire surface finely pubescent; no long setæ, spines or hooks, except on last joint; fronto-clypeal suture distinct and curved sharply upward; clypeus, labrum, pupal eyes and mandibles distinctly indicated; antennæ diverging at their extreme tip and not reaching to the tips of the wings; metathoracic legs reaching slightly beyond the wings to fifth abdominal segment. Spiracles small, normal. Anal opening large, slitlike, surrounded by strong hooked setæ, 5 or 6 on each side; cremaster surrounded with 6 to 8 similar, strong, hooked setæ. Genital opening slitlike, single in both sexes. When mature, the pupa becomes much darker (fig. 6, C); the imago's eyes can be seen prominently under the

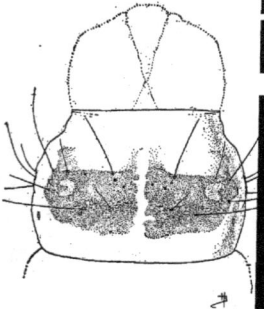

FIG. 11.—Thoracic shield of pink bo larva. (Original.)

UNITED STATES DEPARTMENT OF AGRICULTURE

BULLETIN No. 919

Contribution from the Bureau of Animal Industry
JOHN R. MOHLER, Chief

Washington, D. C. ▼ December 10, 1920

UNIT REQUIREMENTS FOR PRODUCING MILK IN WESTERN WASHINGTON.

By J. B. BAIN, *Dairy Husbandman,* and G. E. BRAUN, *Market Milk Specialist,*
Dairy Division.

CONTENTS.

	Page.		Page.
Character and scope of the work	1	Factors involved in production of milk	10
Methods used in obtaining the data	2	Feed	10
Comparison of winter and summer results	3	Pasture	11
Description of herds	3	Labor	12
Requirements for producing 100 pounds of milk	4	Other costs	13
		Per cent comparison of factors involved in milk production	15
Requirements for keeping a cow one year	6	Average compared with " bulk-line " costs	16
Credit for manure	7	Monthly distribution of factors in milk production	17
Credits for calves	9	Summary	19
Requirements for keeping a bull	9		

CHARACTER AND SCOPE OF THE WORK.

. What does it cost to produce milk? This is a question which has brought increasing concern to each dairyman as the cost of feed has increased and hired men are being attracted to other industries paying higher wages. The United States Department of Agriculture, through the Dairy Division of the Bureau of Animal Industry, began a series of studies in 1915 intended to give the dairymen of the United States information on the cost of producing milk. These studies were made in different sections of the United States. The project with which this bulletin deals was organized in August, 1917, in Skagit County, Wash., about 70 miles north of Seattle.

Other objects of these studies were to separate and analyze various factors to obtain data which would aid in improving general milk-production methods.

The climate and fertility of the soil in this section produce exceptionally good pasturage throughout the larger part of the year. The many herds of black and white cattle grazing over the large expanse of low-lying meadows, together with the numerous windmills dotting the landscape, remind an observer of the description of the Holstein breed in its native country.

At the end of the first year the work was discontinued until January, 1919, because of the war. The value of this work to the dairymen cooperating the first year is reflected in the fact that 15 out of the 17 continued the work for the second year. Two dairymen sold out, and their places were taken by neighboring dairymen during the second year. The data obtained in this study are actual records of facts obtained by regular monthly full-day visits to 15 farms for two years and four other farms for one year.

Most of the milk in this section is sold for condensing purposes and is delivered by motor truck to large milk condenseries. None of the dairies selected were conducted as hobbies or as breeding establishments, but were representative of average dairy conditions found in this section. It is the custom to hire milkers, who milk and take care of 25 or 30 cows per man and give their entire time to the herd. The figures reported show the amounts expended in producing milk under the system of dairy management found.

The dairies were inspected by representatives from the condenseries, and the sanitary conditions were subject to such supervision. The cost of production would have been somewhat different if either higher or lower grades of milk had been produced.

METHODS USED IN OBTAINING THE DATA.

The field agent recorded in detail all available information [1] relative to the dairy business, including the amounts and classes of labor, feeds and bedding used, pasture cost, amount of milk sold and used on the farm, and the current expenses for the month. The data on calves and handling of manure were systematically collected.

By obtaining records on every dairy regularly each month the influence of unusual circumstances at the time of any particular visit was lessened, and by using the records of all the herds for each month average figures could be compiled for each or all of the dairies and representative data for each month, season, and year were thus obtained. Records were obtained the second year as a check on the first year's work and to increase the amount of data available for study.

At the beginning and end of each year an inventory was taken of the dairy buildings, livestock, and equipment used in the care of the herd and its products. On his regular monthly inspection tour the field agent arrived at the first farm of a group in time to observe the first labor operations connected with the evening chores. With

---

[1] Copies of the blanks used can be obtained upon request from the Bureau of Animal Industry, Dairy Division, Washington, D. C.

watch in hand he noted and recorded the,exact. minute each labor operation connected with the dairy was begun and ended. The labor operations during the next morning were recorded in the same manner, to complete the 24-hour period.

The field agent also noted the feeds that were being fed on the day of his visit, recording the kind, quantity, cost, and description of each and comparing them with the quantity recorded by the cow tester in the cow-testing-association books.

The quantity of milk sold and receipts each month were obtained. In addition the whole milk used by the proprietor and his help or fed to calves was measured or weighed and used as a basis for determining the quantity kept on the farm during the month.

Each dairyman kept an itemized account of expenses that were incurred between the monthly visits, and these items were recorded by the field agent. A monthly record was also kept of the purchase or sale of cows, calves, hides, outside bull service, and other miscellaneous information relating to the herd. The condition and method of handling the manure were noted and reported each month.

When all the labor operations about the dairy had been completed for the day at the first farm, the field agent drove to the second farm in time to observe the labor operations connected with the evening chores. This program was followed until Saturday afternoon, when he returned to his headquarters and finished his reports for the week's work. The same program was followed each week in the month, and each farm was visited for a full day every 30 days throughout the two years.

COMPARISON OF WINTER AND SUMMER RESULTS.

Since the winter and summer seasons have a marked influence on the principal factors entering into the cost of producing milk, the results have been computed separately for those periods. The months from November to April, inclusive, represent the winter season and from May to October the summer season. This division of time was based directly on the change in methods of herd management made in November and May.

The various tables found in this bulletin are based upon figures obtained during two years of study, and the weighted average of the two-year records was used whenever it would more accurately express the result. The weighted average was obtained by giving each item a weight in the average according to its relative importance..

DESCRIPTION OF HERDS.

During the first year records were obtained on 17 herds, having an average size of 31.3 cows, with an average annual production of 7,369 pounds of 3.74 per cent milk per cow. During the second year, 18 herds, 15 of which had been in the first year's work, had an average

size of 28.6 cows, and produced an average of 8,323 pounds of
per cent milk per cow. The cows were mostly Holsteins, and
average annual production for both years was 7,833 pounds of
per cent milk. During the first year the pastures were poorer ᵗ
they had been for years, whereas during the second year they ˙
exceptionally good until the last month, when the herds were past
on the second-growth meadows. As a matter of record, many h
grazed on pastures in which the clover stood a foot high—ˌ
enough to be cut for hay. The extreme variation in the conditio
the pastures during the two seasons largely accounts for the incɾ
of 954 pounds of milk per cow during the second year.

For each 100 cows in the herds during the two years, 55 freshⁱ
during the winter six-months period and 42 during the sun
season, while 3 cows did not calve during the year. During the
year the cows dropping calves in winter were dry 1.9 months, ʍ
those cows dropping calves in summer were dry 1.4 months.
corresponding figures for the second year were 2.2 months in wi
and 1.5 months in summer. Nearly one-half of the cows fresheⁱ
dropped their calves during the months from February to ᴵ
inclusive.

REQUIREMENTS FOR PRODUCING 100 POUNDS OF MILK.

The unit requirements for producing 100 pounds of milk du
this investigation are shown in Table 1. In order to secure ɾ
uniform results and to overcome the effect of fluctuating prices, mɵ
values have been eliminated as much as possible. By showing
feeds in terms of pounds and the labor in terms of hours it wiˡ
possible to use these figures for some time to come.

TABLE 1.—*Units required, except cost of management, for producing 100 pɵ
of milk in winter and in summer.*

Item.	Winter.		Two winters.	Summer.		suɪ
	1917–18	1919–20		1917–18[1]	1919	
Feed:						
Purchased concentrates......pounds..	25.8	18.8	22.1	4.3	4.9	
Home-grown grains.............do....	1.1	12.9	7.3	....	1.1	
Total concentrates..................	26.9	31.7	[2] 29.4	4.3	6.0	
Hauling and grinding concentrates....	$0.016	$0.028	$0.022	$0.002	$0.004	
Noncommercial roughage....pounds..	.9	10.2	5.8	....	.2	
Commercial carbohydrate hay..do....	90.1	70.0	79.5	4.4	9.0	
Legume hay.....................do....	3.1	11.7	7.6	.3	.8	
Total dry roughage..................	94.1	91.1	92.9	4.7	10.0	
Silage and other succulent rough- age........................pounds..	156.8	131.1	143.3	42.7	38.2	
Pasture.......................acres..	....	....	....	.027	.02	
Bedding....................pounds..	12.4	5.9	9.0	....	.2	

[1] This season consisted of September, and October, 1917, and May, June, and July, and August,
[2] The summary of the unit requirements by seasons is printed in bold-faced type for convenienɔ
reader.

TABLE 1.—*Units required, except cost of management, for producing 100 pounds of milk in winter and in summer*—Continued.

Item.	Winter.		Two Winters.	Summer.		Two summers.
	1917–18	1919–20		1917–18	1919	
Labor:						
Human................hours..	2.0	1.8	1.9	1.3	1.3	1.3
Horse.....................do....	.01	.01	.01	.01	.02	.015
Other costs:						
Building charges......................	$0.124	$0.130	$0.127	$0.085	$0.092	$0.088
Equipment charges and dairy supplies	.088	.088	.088	.060	.062	.061
Herd charges: Taxes, insurance, veterinary, medicines, disinfectants, and cow-testing associations.............	.043	.034	.038	.029	.024	.026
Interest on cow investment..........	.118	.108	.113	.080	.076	.078
Cost of keeping bull................	.078	.074	.076	.042	.042	.042
Motor-truck charge..................					.001	....
Cash hauling of milk................	.066	.065	.062	.067	.062	.061
Total other costs, except depreciation on cows....................	.517	.499	.504	.363	.359	.356
Depreciation on cows................	.144	.007	.072	.098	.005	.050
Total other costs....................	$0.661	$0.506	$0.576	$0.461	$0.364	$0.406

It will be noted in Table 1 that for producing 100 pounds of milk in the first winter there were required 26.9 pounds of grain, while during the second winter 31.7 pounds were required, an increase of 4.8 pounds. For dry roughage there is a decrease of 3 pounds, and for succulent roughage a decrease of 25.7 pounds per 100 pounds of milk. This increase in grain and decrease in dry and succulent roughages can be accounted for by the fact that two of the herds that were sold out the first year consumed very little grain but a large quantity of roughage.

Since the pastures were of a very excellent quality summer feeding of grain was not followed extensively. Some of the best-producing herds received no grain throughout the summer, which accounts for the low average of 5.2 pounds of grain per 100 pounds of milk during the summer seasons.

While there was a slight advance in prices for both hauling and grinding concentrates during the second year, the increase for these charges per 100 pounds of milk from 16 cents to 28 cents in the winter and from two-tenths of a cent to four-tenths of a cent in the summer of the first and second years, respectively, is due primarily to the increase in the quantity of feeds ground rather than to the advanced rate of hauling and grinding.

The work of collecting milk through this section is thoroughly organized. The milk, shipped in 10-gallon cans, is collected once daily by motor truck. On the return trip the truck brings back the empty cans, which makes it unnecessary to have two sets of cans. As the roads are very good it is not uncommon, in the season of greatest production, for a motor truck and trailer to haul 100 cans. The efficiency

of the truck method of hauling milk is shown by the ·
6.2 cents per 100 pounds of milk in winter and 6.·
pounds of milk in summer. The use of the motor tru·
for the small amount of horse labor.

The cost of keeping a bull includes feed, labor,
expressed in dollars. For closer study a table will be
10 expressing the costs in terms of pounds and hours.

REQUIREMENTS FOR KEEPING A COW ON[

The greater production per cow, in summer, of]
milk, shown in Table 2, is partly due to a larger per·
freshening in the winter and early spring, but more p
the direct result of good pastures. The value of this
cially noticeable when one observes that in winter th
946 pounds of grain to produce 3,217 pounds of milk, v
they required only 241 pounds of grain to produce ·
milk.

TABLE 2.—*Number of cows, average production per cow, and
keeping a cow during each season and for the entire year, e
agement, based on records of the two years' work.*

Item.	Winter.
Number of cows	1,043.1
Average production per cow............pounds..	3,217
Feed:	
Purchased concentrates..........do....	711
Home-grown grains............do....	235
Total concentrates............do....	946
Hauling and grinding concentrates................	$0.72
Noncommercial roughage............pounds..	186
Commercial carbohydrate hay............do....	2,558
Legume hay............do....	246
Total dry roughage............do....	2,990
Silage and other succulent roughage............do....	4,610
Bedding............do....	289
Pasture..................	$1.70 or 0.1 acre.
Labor:	
Human............hours..	60.1
Horse............do....	.29
Other costs:	
Building charges..................	$4.10
Equipment charges and dairy supplies..................	2.34
Herd charges: Taxes, insurance, veterinary, medicines, disin-	
fectants, and cow-testing associations..................	1.22
Interest on cow investment..................	3.62
Cost of keeping bull..................	2.44
Motor-truck charge..................	....
Cash hauling of milk..................	1.98
Total other costs, except depreciation on cows..........	15.70
Depreciation on cows..................	2.30
Total other costs..................	$18.00

The one-tenth of an acre pasture charge shown f·
sents supplementary pasture or pasture on meadow
second-crop meadow and grain stubble in the fall.
are lodged fall pasture furnishes a valuable sour

spring it is a common practice in this dairy section to turn the cows in the meadows for a short time, thereby obtaining a shorter but finer hay crop, which is a decided advantage when hay is inclined to grow tall and coarse.

The small quantity of bedding used was due to the fact that the winters were so mild that the cows were kept in the barn only during January, February, and March, while at least three of the herds received practically no bedding.

The hours of labor expended per cow in summer and in winter did not differ materially. The time required in winter for feeding and for cleaning stables was used in summer for driving the cows to and from pasture; also in summer more time was necessary for milking on account of increased production.

CREDIT FOR MANURE.

On the average dairy farm the commercial value of manure depends upon the use to which it is put. The return in dollars depends upon the increase in the crops raised and in the amount received from the sale of these crops. These facts may reduce or increase the value of manure below or above the market price of the fertilizing constituents contained in it.

The farming land in many parts of western Washington is reclaimed swamp land and the soil is unusually fertile. Dairymen therefore derived very little benefit from the application of manure and did not place a high valuation on it. The credit for the manure, however, which was the same for summer and winter, was based on the market price of the fertilizing constituents contained in it.

The prices per pound of the fertilizing constituents in the manure for the first year were as follows: Nitrogen, $0.25; commercial phosphoric acid, $0.06; and potash, $0.068. The prices during the second year were $0.191 for nitrogen, $0.056 for phosphoric acid, and $0.068 for potash.

Only that manure which was saved or could have been saved under ordinary farm conditions was credited to the cows. In order to determine the amount of manure saved, a monthly record was kept of the time the cows were actually in the stables. This made it possible to figure the weight of manure voided in the barns, for, according to the best authorities, a 1,000-pound cow will produce 13 tons of manure in a year, or 6½ tons for six months. The manure dropped on the pasture was not credited to the herds; if a credit had been given, an offset charge against the pasture for fertilizer would have been necessary.

Many of the stables had holes in the gutters to permit the liquid to escape; therefore a deduction was made wherever necessary to cover this loss. Also a deduction of 25 per cent in the summer and 30 per cent in the winter, or rainy season, was made to cover the loss to the manure while in the yard exposed to the weather.

To determine the fertilizing constituents in the manure the feeds used throughout the winter were classified so that their average composition could be obtained. This was done by referring to standard tables containing the analyses of the various classes of feeds.

Since a cow in the process of digestion utilizes on the average only approximately 25 per cent of the nitrogen, 30 per cent of the phosphorus, and 15 per cent of the potash, it is evident that 75 per cent of the nitrogen, 70 per cent of the phosphorus, and 85 per cent of the potash is available for fertilizers. By knowing the weights of the feeds and their average composition it was possible to determine the approximate amounts of the three fertilizing elements consumed. From these figures deductions were made for that utilized by the cows to obtain the total amounts of the fertilizing elements voided. In figuring the amount of fertilizing constituents saved the same factors were considered that determined the weight of manure credited to cows, namely, the time the cattle were out, making the fertilizer unreclaimable, the amount of liquid lost through holes in the gutters, and the loss in leaching while stored in the yards.

A ton of average manure during the winter was estimated to have the following constituents:

Pounds.
Nitrogen_____ 9. 9
Commercial phosphoric acid_____ 4. 2
Potash _____ 11. 5

No credit was allowed for bedding, as the large acreage of oats and a superabundance of straw from the fertile soil makes the farm price of the straw less than the value of the fertilizing constituents in it. The farm price of the straw is little more than enough to pay for bringing the straw to the barn. It might be hauled directly from the stack to the field instead of the barn, thereby distributing the fertilizing elements on the soil at the same expense.

TABLE 3.—*Manure and fertilizing constituents credited to the herds during the two winters and the two summers.*

Item.	Winter.			Summer.		
	1917–18	1919–20	Average.	1917–18 [1]	1919	Average.
Total manure saved_____tons..	1,128.2	802.3	965.2	179.1	126.8	153.0
Manure per cow_____pounds..	4,200.0	3,200.0	3,800.0	600.0	400.0	600.0
Manure credited per 100 pounds of milk, pounds..	....	....	115	....	....	13

	Winter average.			Summer average.		
	Nitrogen.	Phosphoric acid.	Potash.	Nitrogen.	Phosphoric acid.	Potash.
Fertilizing constituents in manure, pounds..	9,474	4,003	11,134	1,500	634	1,765
Credit per cow_____pounds..	18.2	7.7	21.3	2.9	1.2	3.4

[1] The summer of 1917–18 included the months of September and October, 1917, and May, June, July, and August, 1918.

The low credit per cow for manure is due to the small quantity of manure saved and to the losses incurred in handling it. Since the cost of keeping a bull was charged against the cows under other costs, the bull manure was credited to the herds and included in the credit of 2.1 tons of manure per cow in 1917–18 and 1.6 tons per cow in 1919–20.

CREDIT FOR CALVES.

The seasonal variations in the production of calves show a small increase in the number of calves dropped in winter over the number dropped in summer, but this does not imply that winter dairying was emphasized. A study of the number of calves dropped per month shows that there were more calves born from January to May than during any other corresponding period, which indicates a tendency toward summer dairying.

TABLE 4.—*Total credit for calves produced, by years and by seasons.*

Item.	Credit by years.		Credit by seasons.	
	1917–18	1919–20	Both winters.	Both summers.
Number of calves	514	502	574	442
Total value of calves	$3,399.89	$4,821.11	$4,495.38	$3,725.62
Average value of calves	$6.61	$9.60	$7.83	$8.43
Calves per cow	0.96 of 1 calf.	0.98 of 1 calf.	1.1 calves.	0.84 of 1 calf.
Credit per cow	$6.38	$9.39	$8.61	$7.08
Credit per 100 pounds of milk	0.013 of 1 calf.	0.012 of 1 calf.	0.017 of 1 calf.	0.009 of 1 calf.

The average production of 0.96 of one calf per cow for the first year and 0.98 of one calf for the second year shows a very high average, which ordinarily can not be expected. Their increase in value was wholly due to a rise in the market value of calves.

The greater number of calves were sold for veal when very young. Each calf that was raised was given a value by the farmer, who took into consideration the individual and its breeding. As grade prices were given to the purebred cows, their calves were given a value which corresponded to a grade calf of similar quality. This was done because in these studies the breeding business was separated from the business of producing milk.

REQUIREMENTS FOR KEEPING A BULL.

There is a noticeable difference in both feed and labor requirements for keeping a bull in summer and in winter. On 10 farms the bulls ran on pasture or were tethered out. This accounts for the low feed requirements, other than pasture, and for the low labor requirements for the summer season.

The small quantity of bedding was due to a combination of reasons. In many herds the bulls ran with the cows, and they were kept in the stable only at night during January, February, and March. A

number of the bulls received no bedding at all, and in one instance
where the bull was kept separate his stall was bedded with the refuse
hay from his manger.

TABLE 5.—*Requirements for keeping a bull, by seasons, based on averages
obtained from the equivalent of 34.4 bulls.*

Item.	Winter.	Summer.	Entire year.
Feed:			
Purchased concentrates..................................pounds..	280	166	446
Home-grown grain..do....	129	55	184
Total concentrates....................................do....	409	221	630
Noncommercial roughage..................................do....	339	208	547
Commercial carbohydrate hay..............................do....	3,360	1,790	5,150
Legume hay..do....	193	77	270
Total dry roughage....................................do....	3,892	2,075	5,967
Succulent roughage..do....	1,669	1,400	3,069
Bedding...do....	31	12	43
Pasture...do....	$1.68	$11.88	$13.56
Human labor...hours..	24.0	16.4	40.4
Other costs:			
Interest and insurance on bull investment............................	$10.54	$10.48	$21.02
Bull's share of buildings...	4.06	4.09	8.15
Depreciation...	6.36	6.28	12.64
Total other costs...	20.96	20.85	41.81
Credit for outside bull service.......................................	10.22	10.10	20.32
Total other cost less outside bull service.............................	10.74	10.75	21.49

Table 5 shows an annual depreciation of $12.64 per bull per year.
Most of the bulls were purebred and were purchased when young at
purebred prices. As they grew older their values increased. This
appreciation in value helped to decrease the depreciation on old bulls
sold for beef for less than their purebred value.

A credit for outside bull service of $20.32 per year was due to
service fees obtained from four of the bulls in the association, one of
which was an animal of special merit. However, the large credit
for outside service for this bull was partly offset by the increased
charges for interest, insurance, and depreciation. If both the " other
costs " of keeping the bull and the credit for outside service had been
stricken from the records, the net " other costs " per year for keeping
the other bulls would have averaged $31.69.

FACTORS INVOLVED IN THE PRODUCTION OF MILK.

FEED.

Concentrates is a term applied to grains and to their manufactured
by-products which contain a large amount of nutritious substance in
a relatively small bulk.

Home-grown grains refer to concentrates grown on the farm or in
the locality where fed.

Dry roughage includes various hays and other rough feeds, which
are subdivided into the three following classes:

Noncommercial dry roughage applies to coarse feeds, such as corn stover and velvet-grass hay, for which price quotations are not given in the trade papers. Hay or other dry roughage so foul with weeds or so damaged in curing as not to be readily salable is also classified under this heading.

Leguminous roughage includes alfalfa, clover, cowpea, soy bean, and other commercial legume hays, when pure, or when so slightly mixed with grasses as not materially to affect the protein content.

Commercial carbohydrate roughage refers to all commercial hays except those classified as leguminous roughage.

Succulent roughage consists of mangels, potatoes, silage, and soiling crops.

The quantities of the various feeds used were obtained from actual weights made by the field agent on his regular monthly visit to each farm.

Purchased concentrates were charged at the prices paid, less the value of the sacks in which they were purchased. These sacks were readily salable if not desired for use on the farm and were given the same value for which they could have been sold. The home-grown grains were given the farm price plus such extra charges as hauling and grinding when necessary. When baling or hauling dry roughage was necessary the price for such was deducted from the market value of the feed. If the succulent roughage was salable the farm price was used in determining valuations per ton; however, if it was not salable a price which was commensurate with its value as compared with the value of a marketable product was placed on it.

PASTURE.

In western Washington pasture plays a very important part in milk production. With cool weather throughout most of the summer, plenty of moisture, and a rich soil there is abundant pasture until late in the fall. During the pasture season almost 60 per cent of the milk for the year was produced and at one-third the yearly feed cost.

The charges against pasture consist of interest, taxes, upkeep, and repairs on fences, cutting thistles and weeds, and seeding.

Interest was figured on the unimproved value of the land, which was obtained by deducting from the improved value any increase in worth due to the dairy buildings contributary to it. The rate of interest allowed varied from 6 to 8 per cent. The rate was determined by the per cent the farmer would have to pay if he borrowed money to buy the land.

The amount of the taxes on the whole farm was ascertained from the books of the county authorities; from this the amount incidental to pasture was calculated.

Upkeep and repairs to fences were largely an appro: They were determined by asking the farmers the value an posts, wire, etc., and the labor required to build and keep tl in repair. From these data the annual cost was computed.

Cutting thistles and weeds is a necessary operation on mc pastures; where this was the case the cost for such was inc the pasture charge. A seeding charge was allowed where th takes a regular place in the crop rotation, for in this way th derives some of the benefit from the seeding for meadow.

The annual pasture rent per cow amounted to 1.1 acres, or :

LABOR.

The average labor rate per hour was obtained by dividing t. per month, plus such extra considerations as board, house re and fuel, by the total number of hours available for work.

The hours available for work during the month were de on the monthly visit to each farm. The times work bega morning and when it ceased in the evening were noted, and : period of work was subtracted the time out for meals and re hours per day thus obtained were multiplied by the number ing days in that month, to which were added the hours necessary on Sundays.

TABLE 6.—*Per cent of labor performed and hours per 100 pounds of duced for each class of help.*

Class of labor.	Winter.				Summer.		
	Distribution of work performed.			Labor per 100 pounds of milk.	Distribution of work performed.		
	1917–18	1919–20	Average.	Average.	1917–18	1919	Averaɡ
	Per cent.	Per cent.	Per cent.	Hours.	Per cent.	Per cent.	Per cen
Managers.............	27.5	23.8	25.6	0.48	26.7	27.3	27.
Hired men...........	62.4	66.1	64.2	1.20	60.3	58.1	59.
Total man labor	89.9	89.9	89.8	1.68	87.0	85.4	86.
Women...............	2.5	1.0	1.8	.03	2.9	1.1	2.
Boys.................	7.6	9.1	8.4	.16	10.1	13.5	11.
Total...........	100.0	100.0	100.0	1.87	100.0	100.0	100.

Table 6 shows that 64.2 per cent of the work during the t ters and 59.2 per cent of the work during the two summers · formed by hired men. It is a practice in that part of the especially with the larger dairies, to hire a man and put charge of the dairy. The men who follow this line of work the most part of Scandinavian or Swiss descent. They becc proficient and make excellent dairymen. They follow regula ules for doing their work and develop a wonderful capa milking. During the first year six dairies were handled by these professional milkers, and each man had an average of 32.8 cows in his "string" which he fed and milked alone. During the second year the average "string" consisted of 28.8 cows.

In two of these dairies the milkers were accustomed to be at the barn and ready to start their work at 2 o'clock in the morning. At other farms the time for starting work ranged from 2.30 to 4 o'clock.

The number of cows which a man can care for depends largely upon the quantity of milk they are producing, but usually it ranges between 18 and 30. A specific instance is known where one man milked 42 cows twice daily for a month. The average daily production for a "string" of cows varies from 6 to 10 10-gallon cans in winter and from 10 to 14 10-gallon cans in summer. On one farm one man, for more than a week, milked 22 10-gallon cans full a day.

Milking usually starts between 2 and 4 o'clock in the morning and the same time in the afternoon. Any work which can be done at odd times, such as throwing down feed and mixing grain, is done between noon and milking time in the afternoon. Small dairies, which do not require all of one man's time, are quite often cared for by the owner and his family.

Only a small percentage of the work was performed by women and boys, as shown in Table 6. The women did very little work around the barn, confining their efforts to washing utensils, which was done in the house.

OTHER COSTS.

Other costs include all charges on buildings, equipment, and cattle, such as interest, depreciation, upkeep, and repairs.

TABLE 7.—*Per cent relationship between other costs and capital invested.*

Item.	Buildings.	Equipment.	Cattle.	Total.
Capital invested...............................	$54,647.14	$17,223.89	$108,679.00	$180,550.03
	Per cent.	*Per cent.*	*Per cent.*	*Per cent.*
Interest...............................	7.0	7.4	7.0	....
Depreciation...............................	4.5	19.4	4.4	....
Taxes...............................	1.4	....	} .9	....
Insurance...............................	.2	....		....
Upkeep and repairs...............................	3.1	.9	....	....
Milking-machine repairs...............................	....	.7	....	....
Total...............................	16.2	28.4	12.3	15.4

[1] Per cent of capital invested in the various costs.

BUILDINGS.

At the beginning of the work the buildings and silos were inventoried at their replacement value in normal times. Interest was charged on this value at the rate of 7 per cent. After the first inventory the subsequent values were determined by deducting from the value at the beginning of the year the amount of depreciation during that year. The depreciation per year was based upon the remaining years of usefulness of the buildings. The average depreciation for the two years shows an annual depreciation of 4.5 per cent.

There were no direct taxes on buildings; but, since pasture figures were based on the raw or unimproved value of the land, it was necessary that the dairy should be charged with the taxes due to the improvements caused by the dairy buildings.

Insurance charges were taken from the receipts of the insurance companies.

A monthly account was kept of the money spent for such items as whitewashing, repairs on doors, etc.; but, to determine the amount necessary for painting, roofing, and such expenses which come less frequently, it was necessary to make an estimate on each dairyman's buildings of the amounts required yearly for such purposes. The total cost of upkeep and repairs amounted to 3.1 per cent of the capital value of the buildings.

EQUIPMENT.

The interest charge on equipment was 7.4 per cent of the inventory value of the equipment. Tools and equipment around a dairy barn are usually worn out quite rapidly, which explains the large annual depreciation of 19.4 per cent.

The charge for upkeep and repairs was 0.9 per cent and for milking-machine repairs 0.7 per cent. Supplies, such as gasoline, kerosene, washing powder, etc., amounted to 99 cents per cow per year.

New equipment purchased during the year was added to the first inventory before subtracting the second inventory.

CATTLE.

Milk produced by a purebred cow has no greater value than that produced by a grade cow. Raising purebred cattle is a separate business involving a greater investment and resulting in larger credits for calves. In this investigation the purebred cows were given values of grade cows of corresponding production and purebred calves were likewise given credits as grade calves from dams of corresponding production.

At the beginning and end of the year each cow was given an inventory value. The first value was based on the price at which the owner thought he could replace her. In order to avoid the influence of market conditions her subsequent value remained the same unless her owner thought that she had become a better or poorer cow.

Interest was figured at the rate of 7 per cent upon the investment at the beginning of the year.

To obtain the depreciation on cattle the value of every cow that entered the herd during the year was added to the herd inventory at the beginning of the year; from this result was subtracted the total value of the cows at the end of the year plus the prices received for cows sold during that year.

A depreciation of 4.4 per cent of the capital value of the cattle is shown. This figure would have been considerably higher had it not been for the large number of cows sold the last year for dairy purposes for which the dairymen received a very good price.

Taxes chargeable to the dairy were taken from the county auditor's tax books, and insurance was taken from insurance receipts.

Such items as veterinary fees, medicines, disinfectants, and cow-testing-association dues amounted to $1.45 per cow per year.

PER CENT COMPARISON OF FACTORS INVOLVED IN MILK PRODUCTION.

How did the cost of producing milk in winter compare with the cost in summer? What items were chiefly responsible for the wide variation in the seasons? These questions are answered in the following table:

TABLE 8.—*Per cent of the total costs represented by feed, labor, and other costs, by seasons.*

Item.	Winter.	Summer.	Entire year.
	Per cent.	*Per cent.*	*Per cent.*
Feed and bedding cost	36.6	7.3	43.9
Pasture	.9	11.6	12.5
Feed, bedding, and pasture cost	37.5	18.9	56.4
Labor cost	11.4	12.1	23.5
Other costs, except herd inventory variation	8.7	8.9	17.6
Total cost, except herd inventory variation	57.6	39.9	97.5
Depreciation on herd	1.2	1.3	2.5
Total cost of production	58.8	41.2	100.0

The first two columns show that the wide variation between the winter and the summer costs was due largely to the difference in the cost of feed and pasture. The combined feed, bedding, and pasture cost in winter was 37.5 per cent of the yearly costs, while the cost of these items in summer was 18.9 per cent. The fact that the labor cost in winter was 11.4 per cent and in summer 12.1 per cent shows there was a difference of only 0.7 per cent in this item for the two seasons.

The high prices received for cows sold during the year reduced the depreciation charge, and this item is reported separately, so its effect on the total cost can be seen.

The cost of producing milk in winter was 58.8 per cent of the yearly cost, while the summer cost was 41.2 per cent of it.

AVERAGE COMPARED WITH "BULK-LINE" COSTS.

During the last few years attempts have been made to use the average cost of production as a basis for determining the selling price of milk. Where the average cost basis is recommended it is evident that practically all those producers whose costs are above the average will find the profits reduced if they are so fortunate as not to suffer an actual loss. This will tend to discourage production and reduce the available supply.

In using the bulk-line method for determining a necessary price, only a certain number of the extremely high-cost producers may have costs above this price. The use of this method is illustrated in Table 9.

TABLE 9.—*Net cost, quantity, and per cent of milk produced by each herd, two winters and two summers.*

	Winter 1917–18.				Winter 1919–20.		
Cost per 100 pounds.	Milk produced.			Cost per 100 pounds.	Milk produced.		
	Quantity.	Per cent of total.	Cumulative.		Quantity.	Per cent of total.	Cumulative.
	Pounds.	*Per cent.*	*Per cent.*		*Pounds.*	*Per cent.*	*Per cent.*
$1.91	67,036	4.2	4.2	$2.50	156,032	8.8	8.8
2.26	113,716	7.2	11.4	2.80	113,302	6.4	15.2
2.39	88,736	5.6	17.0	2.88	144,577	8.2	23.4
2.43	60,595	3.8	20.8	2.96	127,348	7.2	30.6
2.56	144,362	9.1	29.8	3.10	66,898	3.8	34.4
2.63	66,956	4.2	34.1	3.11	90,257	5.1	39.5
2.69	195,756	12.3	46.4	3.16	213,169	12.1	51.6
2.80	99,931	6.3	52.7	3.20	92,420	5.2	56.8
2.84	82,857	5.2	57.9	1 3.25			
2.86	131,097	8.2	66.1	3.30	202,567	11.5	68.2
2.89	113,785	7.1	73.3	3.31	56,349	3.2	71.4
1 2.91				3.48	54,677	3.1	74.5
3.02	48,222	3.0	76.3	3.50	62,631	3.6	78.1
3.29	91,896	5.8	82.1	3.60	100,453	5.7	83.8
3.47	112,754	7.1	89.2	3.83	39,680	2.2	86.0
3.59	80,523	5.1	94.2	3.95	113,973	6.4	92.5
3.82	61,283	3.9	98.1	4.01	79,539	4.5	97.0
4.85	30,126	1.9	100.0	4.61	53,581	3.0	100.0
	Summer 1917–18.				Summer 1919.		
$1.06	174,306	7.5	7.5	$1.14	100,428	4.0	4.0
1.24	83,089	3.6	11.0	1.18	210,813	8.4	12.4
1.25	85,339	3.7	14.7	1.30	123,893	4.9	17.4
1.31	92,050	3.9	18.6	1.33	145,812	5.8	23.2
1.33	160,589	6.9	25.5	1.36	89,853	3.6	26.7
1.34	166,339	7.1	32.6	1.39	177,018	7.1	33.8
1.35	132,277	5.7	38.3	1.42	211,960	8.4	42.2
1.38	167,584	7.2	45.5	1.60	89,982	3.6	45.8
1.39	112,097	4.8	50.3	1 1.60			
1.40	213,498	9.1	59.4	1.62	309,716	12.3	58.2
1 1.50				1.64	98,174	3.9	62.1
1.53	63,466	2.7	62.1	1.70	102,351	4.1	66.2
1.57	462,128	19.8	81.9	1.74	89,637	3.6	69.8
1.65	112,066	4.8	86.7	1.77	167,586	6.7	76.4
1.93	136,413	5.8	92.6	1.79	92,741	3.7	80.1
1.95	125,893	5.4	98.0	1.87	132,253	5.3	85.4
3.48	47,846	2.0	100.0	2.03	98,741	3.9	89.3
				2.12	91,808	3.7	93.0
				2.32	175,642	7.0	100.0

1 Average.

In Table 9, for the winter 1917–18, it will be noted that only 73.3 per cent of the milk was produced at $2.89 or less per 100 pounds, which is the first cost below the average cost of $2.91. In many sections this volume of milk would be an inadequate supply. On the other hand, 94.2 per cent of the milk was produced at $3.59 or less per 100 pounds. In order to include 98.1 per cent of the volume of milk, the cost advances to $3.82 per hundred, thus increasing the cost 23 cents per 100 pounds and adding only 3.9 per cent of the volume.

If the price of the milk were placed at $3.47 per 100 pounds, a profit ranging from 18 cents ($3.47 minus $3.29) to $1.56 ($3.47 minus $1.91) per 100 pounds would tend to increase the volume of milk produced by the more efficient dairymen. Similar deductions may be made from the other portions of the table.

MONTHLY DISTRIBUTION OF FACTORS IN MILK PRODUCTION.

A study of Table 10 shows that the per cent of milk produced each season did not vary greatly from year to year; however, there is a noticeable increase for both years in summer production over winter production. During the first year there was 19 per cent more milk produced in summer than in winter, and in the second year 17.4 per cent more was produced. The larger flow of milk in summer can be attributed to better pasture more than to any other cause.

With the exception of the month of November in the first year the feed, pasture, and bedding cost for the winter in both years was decidedly higher than in the summer. The same is true of feed and bedding cost minus the manure credit.

A study of the results of the two years' work shows that the feed costs for the first and second summers were 33.5 per cent and 33.6 per cent, respectively, of the total yearly feed costs. Likewise it is found that the summer production was 59.5 per cent and 58.7 per cent of the total production for the corresponding years.

TABLE 10.—*Monthly distribution of milk prices, milk sold and used, feed cost, and labor required.*

YEAR 1917-1918.

Month and season.	Income per 100 pounds of milk.	Income from milk sold and used.	Milk sold and used.	Feed pasture, and bedding cost.	Feed, pasture, and bedding cost minus manure credit.	Human labor.		Horse labor.	
						Per 100 pounds of milk.	Per cow.	Per 100 pounds of milk.	Per cow.
		Per cent.	*Per cent.*	*Per cent.*	*Per cent.*	*Hours.*	*Hours.*	*Hours.*	*Hours.*
November...........	$2.95	7.4	6.5	7.0	5.7	2.0	9.2	0.002	0.01
December...........	3.01	7.3	6.3	11.3	10.0	2.2	10.0	.008	.04
January............	3.02	7.0	6.0	12.1	10.8	2.2	9.8	.011	.05
February...........	3.01	6.7	5.8	11.6	10.3	2.2	9.2	.014	.06
March.............	2.81	7.8	7.3	12.8	11.4	1.9	10.2	.011	.06
April..............	2.52	8.3	8.6	11.7	10.4	1.5	9.4	.005	.03
Winter........	2.86	44.5	40.5	66.5	58.6	2.0	9.6	.008	.04

TABLE 10.—*Monthly distribution of milk prices, milk sold and used, feed cost, and labor required*—Continued.

YEAR 1917-1918.

Month and season.	Income per 100 pounds of milk.	Income from milk sold and used.	Milk sold and used.	Feed, pasture, and bedding cost.	Feed, pasture, and bedding cost minus manure credit.	Human labor.		Horse labor.	
						Per 100 pounds of milk.	Per cow.	Per 100 pounds of milk.	Per cow.
		Per cent.	*Per cent.*	*Per cent.*	*Per cent.*	*Hours.*	*Hours.*	*Hours.*	*Hours.*
May	$2.21	10.0	11.8	7.5	7.3	1.2	10.6	0.007	0.06
June	2.09	9.4	11.8	4.7	4.5	1.2	10.3	.009	.08
July	2.28	9.1	10.4	5.2	5.0	1.3	10.2	.012	.10
August	2.78	9.4	8.8	5.3	5.1	1.4	9.8	.005	.03
September	2.66	9.1	8.9	4.8	4.6	1.4	9.1	.006	.04
October	2.81	8.5	7.8	6.0	5.8	1.6	9.1	.033	.19
Summer	2.43	55.5	59.5	33.5	32.3	1.3	9.8	.011	.08
Year	2.61	100.0	100.0	100.0	90.9	1.6	9.7	.010	.06

YEAR 1919-1920.

Month and season.	Income per 100 pounds of milk.	Income from milk sold and used.	Milk sold and used.	Feed, pasture, and bedding cost.	Feed, pasture, and bedding cost minus manure credit.	Human labor.		Horse labor.	
						Per 100 pounds of milk.	Per cow.	Per 100 pounds of milk.	Per cow.
November	3.19	7.0	6.3	10.6	9.9	1.9	9.7	.009	.05
December	3.28	7.4	6.5	11.9	11.2	2.0	11.	.004	.02
January	3.65	8.3	6.5	12.0	11.4	2.0	10.	.015	.08
February	3.33	7.0	6.0	11.2	10.5	1.9	9.	.011	.05
March	2.82	7.3	7.4	11.9	11.2	1.7	11.	.012	.07
April	2.47	7.5	8.6	8.8	8.1	1.4	10.	.009	.06
Winter	3.08	44.5	41.3	66.4	62.3	1.8	10.4	.010	.06
May	2.35	9.3	11.4	5.1	5.0	1.1	11.1	.003	.03
June	2.43	9.6	11.3	5.1	5.0	1.2	11.3	.045	.43
July	2.62	9.9	10.8	4.6	4.5	1.3	1.7	.007	.06
August	2.94	9.7	9.4	5.1	5.0	1.4	0.	.022	.17
September	3.04	8.8	8.3	5.7	5.6	1.4	9.0	.019	.13
October	3.12	8.2	7.5	8.0	7.9	1.6	9.5	.003	.02
Summer	2.71	55.5	58.7	33.6	33.0	1.3	10.5	.017	.14
Year	2.86	100.0	100.0	100.0	95.3	1.5	10.5	.014	.10

The number of hours required to care for a cow does not differ materially in summer and winter, but the number of hours required to produce 100 pounds of milk shows a marked increase from November to March, inclusive. This season corresponds quite closely to the months of intensive winter feeding, when the cows are kept in the barns or yards during the nights; it also corresponds to the months in which the smallest volume of milk is produced, and this fact exerts a great influence over the amount of labor required for producing 100 pounds of milk. This is more fully substantiated by the fact that during the months of May, June, and July we find the lowest time requirements for producing 100 pounds of milk because of the higher percentage of milk produced per month.

The small amount of horse labor was due to the use of motor trucks for collecting the milk and hauling it to market.

During the winter horses were used at some farms to haul the milk from the milk house to the road. In summer they were used for driving cows to and from the pasture; however, during July, August, and September, when the horses are hitched to the harvest wagon, they were quite often used to haul milk or to get cans, because this method requires less effort than to carry or cart them. The high figure of 0.43 of an hour per cow for June, 1919, is chiefly due to one man who used a large amount of time cutting and hauling soiling crops.

SUMMARY.

A study of the results presented in this bulletin shows that 56.4 per cent of the total cost of producing milk was due to feed and bedding, 23.5 per cent to labor, 17.6 per cent to other costs, and 2.5 per cent to depreciation (see Table 8).

The requirements for producing 100 pounds of milk during the winter were: Concentrates, 29.4 pounds; hauling and grinding concentrates, $0.022; dry roughage, 92.9 pounds; succulent roughage, 143.3 pounds; bedding, 9 pounds; human labor, 1.9 hours; horse labor, 0.01 of an hour; other costs, $0.576 (see Table 1). Credits for winter production other than milk: Manure, 115 pounds; calves, 0.017 (see Tables 3 and 4). Requirements for producing 100 pounds of milk during the summer were: Concentrates, 5.2 pounds; hauling and grinding concentrates, $0.003; dry roughage, 7.5 pounds; succulent roughage, 40.4 pounds; pasture, 0.025 of an acre; bedding, 0.1 of one pound; human labor, 1.3 hours; horse labor, 0.015 of an hour; other costs, $0.406. Credits for summer production other than milk: Manure, 13 pounds; calves, 0.009.

The following items were provided for keeping the average cow one year: Concentrates, 1,187 pounds; hauling and grinding concentrates, $0.87; dry roughage, 3,336 pounds; succulent roughage, 6,474 pounds; pasture, $23.04 or 1.1 acres; bedding, 295 pounds; human labor, 121 hours; horse labor, 1 hour; other costs, $36.31 (see Table 2). Credits other than milk: Manure, 2.2 tons; calves, 0.97.

To keep a bull one year required 630 pounds of grain, 5,967 pounds of dry roughage, 3,069 pounds of succulent roughage, 43 pounds of bedding, and 40.4 hours of human labor. In addition, $13.56 was expended for pasture and $21.49 for other costs after a credit of $20.32 had been deducted for outside bull service.

During the winter men performed 89.8 per cent of the work and 86.2 per cent during the summer. The remaining labor was performed by women and boys (see Table 6).

Interest, depreciation, taxes, and similar charges against buildings, equipment, and cattle amounted to 15.4 per cent of the capital invested in them (see Table 7).

In the two years 44.5 per cent of each year's income from milk was obtained during the winter. The net feed and bedding cost for the first winter was 58.6 per cent of the net yearly feed and bedding cost, but during the second year the winter net feed and bedding cost was increased to 62.3 per cent (see Table 10).

UNITED STATES DEPARTMENT OF AGRICULTURE

BULLETIN No. 920

Contribution from the Office of Farm Management and Farm Economics.

H. C. TAYLOR, Chief

Washington, D. C.   PROFESSIONAL PAPER   December 30, 1920

FARM PROFITS—FIGURES FROM THE SAME FARMS FOR A SERIES OF YEARS.

Washington County, Ohio, 25 Farms, 1912–1918.
Clinton County, Ind., 100 Farms, 1910 and 1913–1918.
Dane County, Wis., 60 Farms, 1913–1917.

By H. M. Dixon, *Associate Farm Economist*, and H. W. Hawthorne, *Assistant Farm Economist*.

CONTENTS.

	Page.		Page.
Introduction	1	The Indiana area	22
Sources and character of data	3	The Wisconsin area	41
Summary	5	Good management increases profits	55
The Ohio area	7		

INTRODUCTION.

Are many farmers making large profits?

Are there many farmers who are making only a bare living?

How much do farmers make?

Have farmers' profits been greater during the recent years of relatively high prices for farm products than during former years of lower prices?

These are live questions, which concern everyone, farmers and city folk alike, and there are current many widely varying opinions about them. This bulletin, presenting facts as determined by repeated business analysis of groups of farms in three fairly distinct agricultural areas, is designed to throw light on these and other questions that arise in this connection.

While the findings of this study will not justify making flat generalizations as to what the profits of farming are for the country as a whole, they should have weight in the consideration of the general problem, since they represent the results of continuous studies in farm profits covering a longer period of years than any other thus

far completed by the United States Department of Agricultu
the farms studied these results show:

That comparatively few farmers make large profits.

That a considerable number of them are making but a ba:

That most of them make a labor income of less than $500
over and above the things the farm furnishes toward th
living, which, however, constitute an important factor.

That their average return on investment after deducting t
of their own labor was about 3½ per cent prior to 1916 and
per cent for the years 1917–18.

In considering the business status of farming certain c
istics of the farm business should be kept clearly in mind.
first place, farming is an individual business, operated and
largely by individuals who vary widely in knowledge, ambi
desires, and in their standards of living. Moreover, the 1
not merely a laborer. He has money invested, and shoul
interest on his investment and also pay for directing the

Another characteristic of the farm business that should
sidered in a discussion of farm profits is the peculiarly clos
of the home to the business. From an abstract accountir
point it may be possible to separate entirely the farm busir
the home, but in reality it occupies an important place in the
mind in weighing the advantages of farming as compared w
of other lines of business.

Again, the prospect of an increase in the value of land h
factor that has made many farmers content to accept a lov
interest from the actual operation of the farm. As a matte
a number of farmers are not making more than 2 to 3 pei
investment, but in many areas the increase in land values ha
to offset this low return.

NOTE.—Certain terms used in this bulletin are here defined:

Farm capital.—The value at the beginning of the farm year of all real estate, machinery, li
other investment used to carry on the farm business. It includes the value of the farm dwe
of the household furnishings.

Receipts.—The amount received from the sale of crops, the increase from stock, and the
outside labor, rent of buildings, etc. The increase from stock is found by subtracting the sum (
paid for stock purchases and the inventory value at the beginning of the year from the sum (
from stock products, sales of live stock, and the inventory value at the end of the year. If the
or supplies on hand at the end of the year was greater than at the beginning, the difference is
receipt.

Expenses.—The amount of money paid out during the year to carry on the farm business,
the value of the unpaid labor performed by members of the family. If the value of crops or s
end of the year was less than at the beginning, this was considered an expense. Househol
expenses are not included.

Farm income.—The difference between receipts and expenses. It represents the amou
available for the farmer's living above the value of family labor, provided he has no interest to
gages or other debts.

Labor income.—The amount that the farmer has left for his labor after 5 per cent interes
capital is deducted from the farm income. It represents what he has earned as a result of hi
after the earning power of his investment has been deducted. In addition to labor incom
receives a house to live in, fuel (when cut from the farm), garden products, milk, butter, egg
(Note continu

These are factors that can not always be measured in dollars and cents in considering whether the farm business is profitable or not. From a strictly business standpoint, assuming that every business should pay a fair rate of interest on the investment therein and a fair return for the labor expended in its operation, there may be drawn rather definite conclusions relative to the farmer's returns.

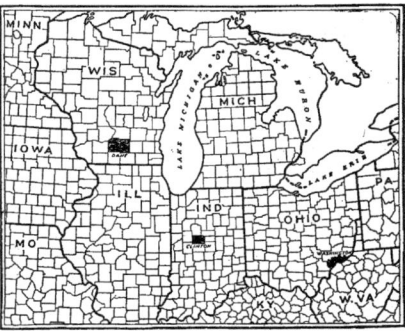

When these are made, however, the compensating factors, such as increase in value of land, the living furnished by the farm, the sentimental appeal of the home site, and the personal desires of the farmer, should be kept in mind.

SOURCES AND CHARACTER OF DATA.

This bulletin presents the data obtained through from five to seven years' continuous analyses of the business of 185 farms in three areas, one each in Ohio, Indiana, and Wisconsin. (See fig. 1.)

FIG. 1.—Map showing the location of the counties in which these studies were made.

The data for the area in Ohio are for 25 farms for seven years, 1912–1918. These farms are located in Palmer township, Washington County—a township typical of the hill land of southern and eastern Ohio. The data for the area in Indiana are for 100 farms for seven years, 1910 and 1913–1918. These farms are located in Forest and Johnson townships, Clinton County—townships typical of crop and live-stock farming in north central Indiana. The data for the area in Wisconsin are for 60 farms for five years, 1913–1917. These farms

as the money earned by his capital. A "minus" labor income means that the farmer received no money returns above food, products, fuel, and house rent for his year's labor, and that he lacked the amount indicated by the minus sign of paying 5 per cent interest on the farm capital.

Per cent return on capital.—The rate returned on the farm capital after the value of the farmer's labor is deducted from the farm income. It represents what the investment earned after all expenses have been deducted and the farmer has received a fair wage for his labor. When the per cent return on the capital is preceded by the minus sign, it means that the farmer did not realize even fair wages for his own labor and management, thus leaving nothing for the earnings on the farm capital.

In computing the return on capital the values of supplies furnished by the farm toward the family living have not been carried in the financial accounts for the reason that if they are carried as a receipt to the farm they likewise must be added as a part of the farmer's own wages. The value given to the farmer's own labor is in addition to what the farm contributes toward his living.

Animal unit.—In order to compare the different classes of animals and to compute the total amount of live stock on these farms all stock has been computed in terms of animal units. In these areas one horse, cow, or steer was counted as one animal unit; two head of young stock (of the above kind) were counted as one animal; 7 sheep, 5 hogs, or 100 chickens were each counted as one animal unit. The number of productive animal units includes all stock except work stock.

are located in Verona and adjoining townships, Dane County—a typical area of the dairying region of southern Wisconsin.[1]

In each area, for the period of the investigation, figures are shown covering the following points:

Distribution of farm area.
Crop yields.
Amount of work stock and of other live stock.
Amount of labor used.
Amount and distribution of farm capital.
Amount and distribution of farm receipts and farm expenses.
Value of the family living direct from the farm.
Amount of the more important products sold and prices received for them.

Farm earnings have been computed as follows:

1. *Farm income.*—The combined earnings for the farm capital and for the farmer's own labor and management, found by deducting the farm expenses from the farm receipts.

2. *Labor income.*—The earnings for the farmer's own labor and management after charging 5 per cent interest for the use of the farm capital. (This is in addition to supplies furnished by the farm toward the family living.) The labor income is found by deducting from the farm income a fair rate of interest on the farm capital.

3. *Per cent return on capital.*—The earnings for the farm capital after allowing for the farmer's own labor and management. This is found by deducting from the farm income a conservative charge for the farmer's own labor and management.

4. *Family income.*—The combined income of the farmer and of his family. This is found by deducting the total expenses (excluding

[1] The authors are greatly indebted to those who cooperated in the study, as the success of conducting these investigations over this period of time is primarily dependent upon the diligent and painstaking efforts of the men performing the field work and the cooperating farmers. The farmers showed increased interest in these studies from year to year. Some began keeping accounts, others kept accounts in more detail than formerly that the data might be more complete. Acknowledgment is hereby tendered to the following named persons for their cooperation in obtaining these data, which should be an aid to farmers in general as well as to others, in a better understanding of the economics of the farm business:

Ohio area.—The Ohio study was conducted each year by Mr. H. W. Hawthorne, assisted at various times by Messrs. E. D. Strait, C. E. Hope, R. D. Jennings, Bruce McKinley, Office of Farm Management; and Mr. S. C. Hartman, of the Ohio Experiment Station. The results of the first five years of this survey were published in U. S. Department of Agriculture Bulletin 716, "A Five-Year Farm Management Survey in Palmer Township, Washington County, Ohio, 1912-1916" (Hawthorne).

Indiana area.—The work in this area was started by Mr. E. H. Thomson for the year 1910, and in addition to the authors, the following investigational force assisted in one or more years of this study: Messrs. H. F. Williams, O. S. Rayner, E. M. McGrew, E. L. Currier, C. Wentsel, W. C. Funk, E. D. Strait, F. H. Shelledy, C. C. Taylor, H. R. Smalley, H. N. Humphrey, J. C. Rundles, T. H. Summers, W. I. Myers, Chas. E. Miller, A. P. Brodell, R. D. Jennings, Office of Farm Management, and W. L. Elser, Lynn Robertson, and W. W. Sylvester, of the Indiana Experiment Station. The results of the first year of this study were published in U. S. Department of Agriculture Bulletin 41 (Thomson and Dixon).

Wisconsin area.—This study was in cooperation with the Wisconsin Experiment Station and was conducted under the supervision of Dr. H. C. Taylor, assisted by Messrs. H. W. Hawthorne, O. A. Juve, S. W. Mendum, C. L. Holmes, J. A. Becker, H. O. Watrud, G. W. Forster, W. I. Myers, and student assistants. The results of this study were published in Wisconsin Experiment Station Bulletin No. 300, "War Prices and Farm Profits" (Taylor and Mendum).

Acknowledgment is also due Miss Mabel G. Darcey and staff of clerical assistants for compilation of these data.

value of family labor and including interest on any indebtedness) from the total farm receipts.

5. *Family living from the farm.*—The value of food products, fuel, and house rent furnished directly by the farm toward the family living. This form of income has been considered in addition to farm income and labor income.

SUMMARY.

The average farm income of 25 farmers in Palmer township, Washington County, Ohio, for the seven years 1912 to 1918 was $610, the labor income $276, and the return on the capital 4.6 per cent.

The average farm income of 100 farmers in Forest and Johnson townships, Clinton County, Ind., for the seven years 1910 and 1913 to 1918 was $1,856, the labor income $558, and the return on the capital 5.7 per cent.

The average farm income of 60 farmers in Verona and adjacent townships, Dane County, Wis., for the five years 1913 to 1917 was $1,293, the labor income $408, and the return on the capital 4.7 per cent.

A considerable part of the farmers' living came directly from the farm. In the Ohio area the value of the items food, fuel, and house rent furnished by the farm was estimated at $359 per farm for the seven-year average, increasing from $300 in 1912 to $494 in 1918; in the Indiana area the value of these items was estimated at $425 per farm, increasing from $356 in 1910 to $620 in 1918; in the Wisconsin area the five-year average value of these items was $391, increasing from $351 in 1913 to $525 in 1917.

Prior to 1916 the price level of farm products was much below that of more recent years. For the years of lower prices the farm earnings in each of these three areas were very low, but with the higher prices of 1916, 1917, and 1918 the returns were more satisfactory.

In the Ohio area the average farm income for the four years 1912 to 1915 was $468; and for the three years 1916 to 1918, $800; the labor income for the former period was $153, and for the latter period $441; the return on the capital from 1912 to 1915 was 2.8 per cent, and from 1916 to 1918, 6.6 per cent.

In the Indiana area the average farm income for the four years 1910 and 1913 to 1915 was $1,407; and for the three years 1916 to 1918, $2,454; the labor incomes for the two periods were $205 and $1,028, respectively; and the return on capital 4.5 per cent and 7.0 per cent.

In the Wisconsin area the average farm income for the three years 1913 to 1915 was $985, and for the two years 1916 and 1917, $1,754; the labor income was $113 for the three-year period and

$850 for the two-year period; the return on capital was 3.2 per cent and 6.8 per cent for the respective periods.

None of the 185 farmers in these three areas made as much as $1,000 labor income every year. Four (2 per cent) made over $500 labor income every year, one each in the Ohio and Indiana areas, and two in the Wisconsin area. Thirty-three farmers (18 per cent) failed to make a $500 labor income in any year of the period, 10 each in the Ohio and Indiana areas and 13 in the Wisconsin area.

Four farmers (2 per cent), after allowance is made for the value of their own time, made over 5 per cent return on their farm capital every year, 1 in the Ohio area, 2 in the Indiana area and 1 in the Wisconsin area; 18 (10 per cent) did not reach 5 per cent return on the farm capital in any one year, 4 in the Ohio area, 5 in the Indiana area and 9 in the Wisconsin area.

Averaging labor income over the several years, 14 per cent of all the farmers failed to make any labor income, and 14 per cent made over $1,000, but most of them made between $1 and $1,000, 84 per cent of the farmers in the Ohio area falling within this range, 70 per cent in the Indiana area, and 72 per cent in the Wisconsin area.

The returns on the farm capital when averaged for the period of years ranged from 2 per cent to 8 per cent on most farms, 52 per cent of the farms in the Ohio area falling within this range, 86 per cent of those in the Indiana area, and 78 per cent of those in the Wisconsin area.

Eighteen farmers (18 per cent) in the Indiana area made over $1,000 labor incomes for the seven-year average, and 7 (12 per cent) in the Wisconsin area for the five-year average. After making a fair allowance for their own wages, 3 farmers (12 per cent) in the Ohio area realized over 8 per cent return on the farm capital for the average of the seven-year period, 10 (10 per cent) in the Indiana area, and 3 (5 per cent) in the Wisconsin area for the five-year period. The greater ability of these farmers, as expressed by the size of their business, their crop yields, their live-stock returns per animal, and the efficient use of labor, won for them the higher returns. While these farmers were getting very good returns, 4 others (16 per cent) in the Ohio area, 12 (12 per cent) in the Indiana area, and 10 (16 per cent) in the Wisconsin area failed to make any labor income. After making due allowance for their own time, 9 (36 per cent) in the Ohio area, 4 (4 per cent) in the Indiana area, and 10 (16 per cent) in the Wisconsin area realized less than 2 per cent return on their farm capital.

Four farmers (16 per cent) in the Ohio area, 32 (32 per cent) in the Indiana area, and 18 (30 per cent) in the Wisconsin area made average labor incomes ranging from $500 to $1,000; and 8 (32 per cent) in the Ohio area, 54 (54 per cent) in the Indiana area, and 25 (42 per cent) in the Wisconsin area realized a return ranging from 5 per cent to 8 per cent on the farm capital.

Many farmers receive low returns for their own labor if the capital represented in the business is allowed a fair rate of interest. Even with a low labor income, the available income of a given farm may be fairly large, if the owner is free from debt. On farms where a relatively large capital is represented the interest on capital may be enough to make the business apparently prosperous.

In figures 6, 12, and 18, the disposition of the farmer's gross income for the three areas is portrayed graphically. Just how much of the income goes for operating expenses, interest on capital, pay for labor performed by members of the farmer's family, the amount left for pay for the farmer's own labor and the value of food, fuel and house rent furnished the farm family may be observed from these charts. The increases in farm earnings for the later years covered by these studies has been more apparent than real, because of the decreased purchasing power of the dollar.

THE OHIO AREA.

The area in Ohio is representative of much of the hill land bordering the Ohio River. The topography grades from rolling to steep and is often rocky. Large unbroken fields are seldom found. The farms are from 4 to 9 miles from railroad points, and the wagon roads are hilly and unimproved. The farmers practice a general or mixed type of farming.

THE FARM BUSINESS.

A summary of the farm business for the 25 farms, over the seven-year period 1912 to 1918, is shown in Table I.

	1912	1913	1914	1915	1916	1917	1918	7-year average.
res per farm	158	156	154	154	156	164	167	158
res in pasture	76	77	79	75	76	80	83	78
res in corn	10	10	10	11	11	12	11	11
res in wheat	9	10	6	10	10	10	11	10
res in hay	20	18	18	18	21	19	21	19
res in other crops	5	4	5	5	4	5	5	4
n per acre...bushels	45	52	41	42	34	43	29	41
eat per acre...do	15	9	18	18	10	15	13	14
y per acre...tons	1.5	1.1	.9	1.1	1.5	1.2	1.2	1.2
ductive animal units	13.5	14.4	15.3	14.9	16.1	17.3	17.2	15.5
Cows...number	2.8	3.1	3.4	3.8	4.3	4.7	4.6	3.8
Ewes...do	18.9	21.5	13.4	14.2	12.6	11.5	14.0	15.2
Brood sows...do	1.0	1.0	1.1	1.1	1.0	1.1	1.0	1.0
Chickens...do	117.0	130.0	131.0	143.0	143.0	143.0	140.0	135.0
Work stock...do	2.6	2.7	2.6	2.8	2.7	2.9	2.8	2.7
Receipts per animal unit	$43	$45	$46	$45	$52	$73	$69	$53
Months of labor	17.4	17.0	17.6	17.1	17.3	17.8	18.0	17.5
rm capital	$6,087	$6,214	$6,422	$6,527	$6,639	$7,163	$7,726	$6,682
Real estate	4,728	4,711	4,735	4,811	4,878	5,247	5,275	4,912
Live stock	781	929	1,029	1,076	1,097	1,228	1,565	1,101
Machinery	295	307	323	326	345	353	364	330
All other	283	267	335	314	319	335	522	339
al estate per acre	30	30	31	31	31	32	32	31
ceipts	$868	$796	$934	$916	$1,112	$1,571	$1,476	$1,096
	Per ct.	Per ct.	Per ct.	Per ct.	Per ct.	Per ct.	Per ct.	Per ct.
Dairy products	3	5	5	7	7	6	6	6
Cattle	16	22	18	21	23	27	25	22
Poultry and eggs	17	20	19	18	18	16	18	18
Sheep and wool	20	12	13	13	12	18	15	15
Hogs	7	13	16	13	13	13	15	13
Crops	26	10	16	20	16	14	13	17
All other	11	18	13	9	11	6	8	9
penses	$412	$375	$423	$430	$456	$547	$757	$486
	Per ct.	Per ct.	Per ct.	Per ct.	Per ct.	Per ct.	Per ct.	Per ct.
Hired labor	12	12	11	10	13	14	11	12
Family labor	21	23	22	21	18	19	18	20
Repairs and depreciation, machinery	7	8	7	7	7	6	5	6
Repairs and depreciation, house	4	5	4	4	3	3	2	3
Repairs and depreciation, other buildings	6	6	6	6	6	6	4	6
Repairs, fences	3	3	3	3	2	2	2	2
Feed purchased	11	6	13	11	14	17	28	16
Seed purchased	5	5	6	6	5	3	4	5
Fertilizer	10	9	10	11	10	10	9	10
Machine work, hired	5	4	3	4	5	2	4	4
Taxes and insurance	12	14	12	13	12	11	9	12
Other	4	5	3	4	5	7	4	4
rm income	$456	$421	$511	$486	$656	$1,024	$719	$610
erest on capital, .5 per cent	304	311	321	327	332	358	386	334
bor income	152	110	190	159	324	666	333	276
erator's labor	288	281	295	290	298	332	347	304
turn on capital...per cent	2.8	2.2	3.4	3.0	5.4	9.7	4.8	4.6
lue of family labor	$86	$85	$92	$90	$82	$105	$133	$96
erest on indebtedness	.19	19	14	12	9	7	5	12
mily income	523	487	589	564	729	1,122	847	694
mily living from farm [1]	300	302	311	317	345	443	494	359
aount sold:								
Cattle...number	3	2	3	3	3	4	3	3
Eggs...dozen	628	648	779	725	696	623	642	677
Wool...pounds	419	405	294	316	335	165	170	301
Hogs...number	5	7	11	11	8	9	9	9
Wheat...bushels	57	15	35	.83	32	55	35	45
ices:								
Cattle...cwt	$5.70	$7.13	$6.97	$7.29	$8.20	$8.32	$10.24	$7.69
Eggs...dozen	.19	.19	.19	.19	.22	.31	.34	.23
Wool...pound	.23	.20	.25	.26	.31	.65	.65	.36
Hogs...cwt	6.52	8.20	8.10	6.60	8.50	12.94	15.87	9.53
Wheat...bushel	.98	.97	1.19	1.15	1.52	2.01	2.02	1.40

Figures obtained from the farmers for 1916 and computed for the other years with aid of index figures own in War Industries Bulletin No. 1.

DISTRIBUTION OF FARM AREA.

The farms averaged 158 acres, approximately one-half of which was used for pasture and one-fourth for growing crops. Of the

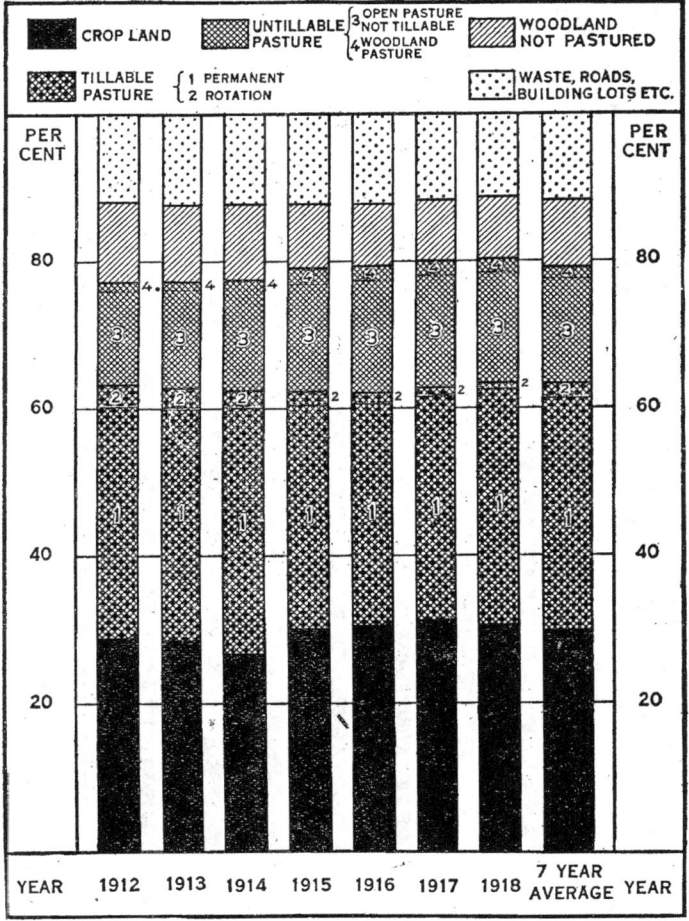

Fig. 2.—Distribution of farm area on 25 farms, Palmer township, Washington County, Ohio, 1912–1918. A large proportion of the farm area is not adapted to cultivation.

crop land, one-fourth was in corn, one-fourth in small grains, mainly wheat, and one-half in hay.

In figure 2 the distribution of the farm area is shown graphically for the average of the 25 farms over the period of study. During the latter years of the study the crop area was slightly increased by reduction of tillable land in pasture. Some of the woodland was also cleared for pasture. Woodland and land taken up by

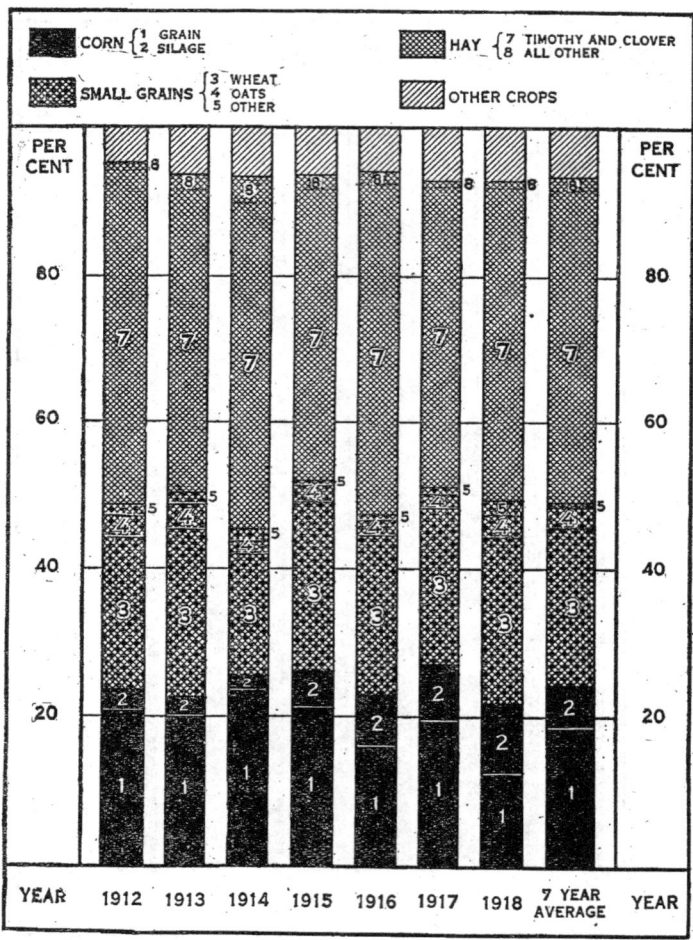

FIG. 3.—Distribution of crop area on 25 farms, Palmer township, Washington County, Ohio, 1912–1918. The years 1915 and 1917 show the largest proportional areas of corn and small grains. In 1918 the poor yield of corn (see Table I) made it necessary to use nearly one-half the crop in filling the silo.

roads, streams, waste, etc., occupies a considerable proportion of the farm area in this section.

Figure 3 shows graphically the average distribution of the crop area. This chart shows the importance of the three crops, corn, wheat, and hay in the organization of these farms, and the variation in the acreage of each over the seven-year period. The use of the silo is being increased in this area. The variation in the proportion of the corn area used for silage was also affected by the yield; 1916 and 1918 were the years of poorest yields and therefore the · years requiring the larger proportion of the corn crop to fill the silo.

CROP YIELDS.

The average yield of corn for the seven-year period was 41 bushels per acre; the lowest average yield for any year was 29 bushels in 1918, and the highest 52 bushels in 1913. The average yield of wheat was 14 bushels per acre, ranging from an average of 9 bushels in 1913 to that of 18 bushels in 1914 and 1915. The average yield of hay was 1.2 tons, being as low as 0.9 ton in 1914 and as high as 1.5 tons in 1912 and 1916. The highest yield of corn was accompanied with the lowest yield of wheat, and an average yield of hay; the lowest yield of corn was accompanied by average yields of wheat and hay. Of the total production, 35 per cent of the wheat was sold, 15 per cent of the hay, 9 per cent of the oats, and 6 per cent of the corn.

LIVE STOCK.

There was an increase in the stock kept on these farms during this period. This increase, representing 3.7 animal units, or over 25 per cent, taken together with rising prices, had much to do with the increase in income. The live stock (exclusive of work horses) when expressed in equivalents of mature cattle, or in what is termed, "a productive animal unit," averaged 15.5 units per farm. This is an average of one head to each 7.9 acres of crops and pasture. The number of cattle increased and that of sheep decreased during the first six years. A small increase in sheep was shown in 1918 over that of 1917· When measured by the amount of feed required, cattle represented 58 per cent of all live stock except work horses, sheep 17 per cent, hogs 10 per cent, and poultry 11 per cent. The number of work horses averaged 2.7 per farm.

LABOR REQUIRED.

It required, on the average, 17.5 months of man labor to operate these farms, of which 12 months represented the farmer's own labor, 3.7 months unpaid family labor, and 1.8 months hired labor. This means that 90 per cent of the labor is performed by the farmer and members of his family, and 10 per cent is hired from the outside. The amount of labor for the various years remained practically constant.

FARM CAPITAL.

The average capital value of these farms was $6,682, of which $4,912, or about three-fourths, was in real estate, $1,101, or 15 per cent, in live stock, $330, or 5 per cent, in machinery, and $339, or 5

per cent, in supplies and operating cash. The value (
sive of buildings, averaged $2,982 per farm, or 45 pe
total farm capital. Real estate averaged $31 per acre

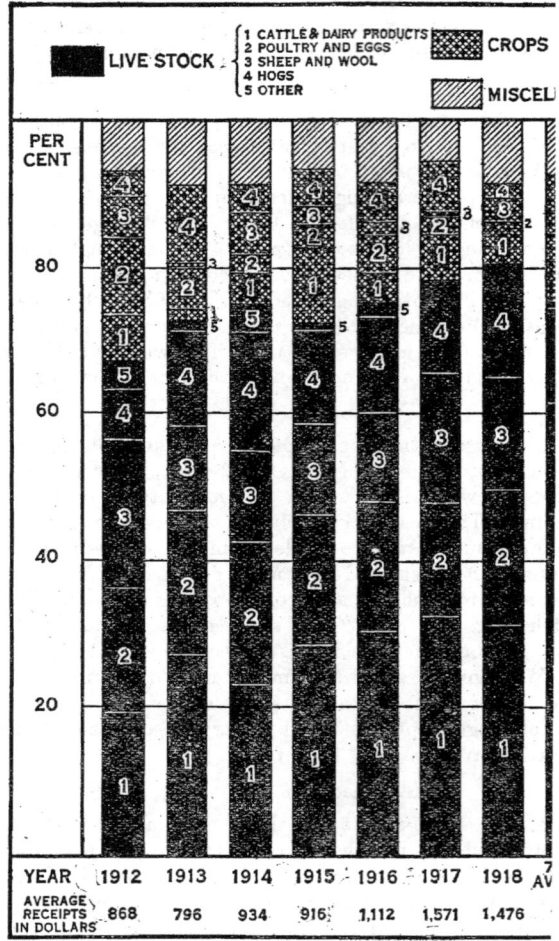

Fig. 4.—Distribution of receipts on 25 farms in Palmer township, Washington Co
Live stock contributed the greatest share of the income in this area. In 1912 crops
of the year's income and in 1918 only 11 per cent.

slight increase during the seven years. It is doubtful
shown covered the cost of additional improvements
farms,

The farm receipts in this area amounted to $1,096 per farm for the seven-year period, ranging from $796 in 1913 to $1,571 in 1917. The slight decrease in 1918 over receipts for 1917 was due to the shortage of crops. There is a large diversity in the sources of income on these farms. The sales of live stock, together with such products as butter, cream, eggs, and wool, amounted to $819 per farm, while the sales of crops amounted to $180 per farm.

Figure 4 shows graphically the average distribution of receipts over the period. Live stock, it will be observed, constituted 67 per cent of the total receipts in 1912, and 78 per cent in 1918. Hogs and cattle show the largest increases and sheep the largest decline. Poultry has maintained practically the same relation to the business as a whole throughout the period. Since these farmers are located a considerable distance from market, many of them have made a practice of using a large share of their wheat crop as poultry feed. The items of greatest variation in receipts on these farms over the periods were wheat and fruit. Apples made a good crop three out of the seven years.

In addition to receipts from live stock, butter, cream, eggs, wool, and farm crops, many of the farmers received some money from the sale of lumber, posts, wood, or shackle poles, for the rent of pasture or farm buildings, for the use of part of the farm equipment, such as the farm machinery or the farm team, and for part of their own labor or time. These have all been considered receipts of the farm business and designated "miscellaneous receipts." They totaled $81 per farm, and made up a little less than one-tenth of the total farm receipts.

All costs in connection with operating the farm business, above those of interest upon capital and the value of the farmer's own labor, are included in the farm expenses. For the seven-year period these averaged $486 per farm, representing 44 per cent, or almost one-half the farm receipts. These expenses include $96 for the value of labor performed by the farm family. The farm expenses for the seven-year period are shown in Table I. The variation for the first five years was small, but the advance for the last two years is quite marked. For one year they were 23 per cent below the seven-year average and for the last year (1918) they were 55 per cent above the average. The expenses have been grouped into 12 classes, namely, hired labor, unpaid family labor, repairs and depreciation of machinery, repairs and depreciation of house, repairs and depreciation of other buildings, repairs to fences, feed purchased, seed purchased, fertilizer, machine work hired, taxes and insurance, and other. The proportion each class represented of the total expenses each year and for the seven-year period is shown graphically in figure 5. While

the cost for the various classes of expenses increased the proportion
remained fairly constant.   The item of feed purchased showed th

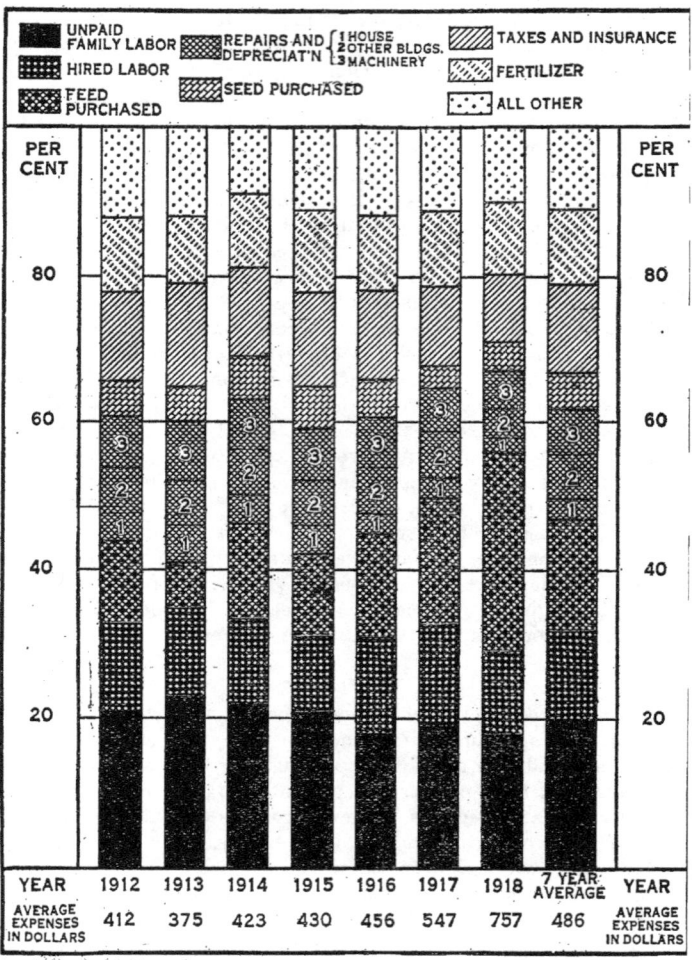

Fig. 5.—Distribution of expenses on 25 farms, Palmer township, Washington County, Ohio. The poo
yield of corn in 1918 made the feed bill a very large item of expense. Most of the items of expense re
tain about the same proportions to the total expense over the period of study.

greatest variation, being directly affected by the production of th
various feed crops raised each year.

The average expenses for the seven-year period were 44 per cen
of the receipts.   When the value of the farmer's own labor an

5 per cent interest on the capital is added to expenses, the total cost is 3 per cent in excess of receipts.

FARM EARNINGS.

From a study of the receipts and expenses it is seen that both showed a marked increase during the period. Comparing the first two years with the last two, it is seen that receipts increased 83 per cent and expenses 66 per cent, thereby leaving a considerable larger farm income for the latter years than for former years, as the farm income represents the difference between receipts and expenses. For the seven-year period the farm income averaged $610 per farm. This was highest in 1917 ($1,024) and lowest in 1913, when it fell to only $421 per farm.

The labor income, which is found by deducting from the farm income 5 per cent interest on the capital, and represents the amount left for the farmer's own labor and management (in addition to farm-furnished products), averaged $276 per farm for the seven-year period. The labor income was less than $200 per farm for each of the first four years; in 1917 it reached $666.

The average value of the farmer's own labor and management was $304, in addition to the supplies furnished by the farm. The value of his labor increased from $281 in 1913 to $347 in 1918. If the value of his labor be deducted from the farm income, the remainder represents the earnings of the capital, which was 4.6 per cent for the seven-year period. The average return varied from 2.2 per cent in 1913 to 9.7 per cent in 1917. It was less than 4 per cent for each of the first four years, and in only one year (1917) did it exceed 6 per cent.

Beginning with 1916 the prices of farm products were on a much higher level than in previous years. The average labor income of the 25 farms in this area for the four years 1912 to 1915 was $153; for the three years 1916 to 1918 it was $441. The return on capital for the earlier period averaged 2.8 per cent and for the later period 6.6 per cent.

The family income, which represents the amount of money available to the family after deducting from the total receipts all farm expenses and interest paid on indebtedness, averaged $694 per farm.

The interest on indebtedness was a small item to the farmers in this area, as only a part of them carried mortgages and most of those reported were small. In 1912, one-third of the farmers had indebtedness varying in amount from $150 to $3,000; in 1918, only one in eight was in debt. During the intervening period the mortgages on five farms were paid off with money made from the farming, and on three others the mortgages were decreased, while the amount was increased in but one case. Indebtedness decreased most rapidly during the years showing greater profits, while in 1913, the year returning least profits, there was no decrease in the indebtedness.

Figure 6 portrays graphically the distribution of the aver[
income on these farms for each year and for the seven-year
The chart shows how much of the gross income is repres

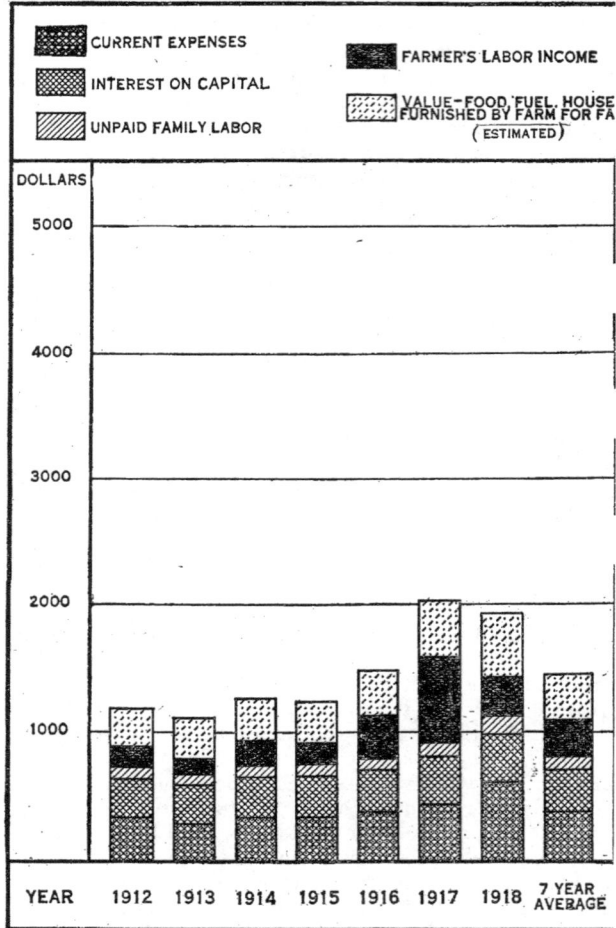

Fig. 6.—Distribution of gross income on 25 farms, Palmer township, Washington County,
with the low price of land in this area ($31 per acre) it will take a long time to pay for a f
profits of the average business. The year 1918 was discouraging, as receipts were below
while expenses had materially increased.

operating expenses, interest on capital, unpaid family lab[
income, and food products, fuel and house rent furnished
farm.

FAMILY LIVING FROM THE FARM.

Farm receipts, farm income, labor income, and value of farmer's labor, as already discussed, do not include the value of the family living from the farm. It is well understood that a very significant proportion of the farmer's family living comes directly from the farm. This may be considered as a form of income additional to that of farm receipts, farm income, or labor income. An estimate of the value of the items food, fuel, and house rent thus furnished in this area was $359 per farm for the seven-year average, having increased from $300 in 1912 to $494 in 1918.

PRODUCTS SOLD AND PRICES RECEIVED.

The amount of farm products produced for sale or for use in increasing the size of the farm business is of value in determining the possibilities of success in various areas. While it is important that a farm be so organized as to contribute liberally toward the farmer's living, a farm can not be considered a profitable business until it is yielding enough products for sale to maintain itself adequately as a business organization. It was not possible to reduce to quantity form all the various products sold from these farms, but in Table I are shown the amounts for the more important sources of income. The number of cattle for the seven-year period averaged 3 head, eggs 677 dozen, wool 301 pounds, hogs 9 head, and wheat 45 bushels. The most cattle were sold in 1917, the most eggs in 1914, the most wool in 1912, the most hogs in 1914–15, and the most wheat in 1915.

The prices also which the farmers received over the seven-year period for these products are shown in Table I. In 1912 the average price received for cattle was $5.70 per hundredweight, in 1916 it had advanced to $8.20, and in 1918 to $10.24. Eggs for the first four years remained at 19 cents per dozen, but in 1918 had advanced to 34 cents. Wool showed a large advance in 1917 and remained at the same price (65 cents per pound) for 1918. In 1913 and 1914 the increased price of hogs brought increased production, but with the drop in price in 1915 the production the following year was decreased. From a study of the production and prices shown in this table it is evident that the increase in profits was due more to increased prices than to increased production.

LABOR INCOME AND RETURN ON CAPITAL OVER THE SEVEN-YEAR PERIOD.

The labor income for each of the 25 farmers is shown for each year in Table II, and the per cent return on the capital in Table III. The farms in each table are arranged beginning with the farm having the highest seven-year average labor income. The labor incomes are also shown graphically in figure 7.

13648°—20—Bull. 920——3

TABLE II.—*Labor income of the 25 farms in Palmer township, Wash.*
Ohio, 1912–1918.

[Arranged according to size of the seven-year average labor income.]

Rank of farms.	7-year average.	1912	1913	1914	1915	1916
1	$824	$559	8776	$661	$603	$70
2	722	236	396	811	389	57
3	618	220	273	−21	397	1,02
4	616	528	282	205	251	63
5	488	247	339	403	303	52
6	474	245	528	464	658	37
7	462	414	−339	−178	609	97
8	459	429	344	622	411	13
9	417	− 20	159	484	108	41
10	386	419	191	228	253	29
11	303	126	− 37	596	−328	44
12	233	105	141	206	93	32
13	224	93	118	253	139	27
14	201	−157	219	102	158	28
15	198	− 11	−116	−166	158	30
16	137	176	−160	− 63	254	6
17	137	10	− 6	155	34	21
18	116	57	186	250	193	8
19	113	− 12	43	108	109	9
20	85	152	34	−116	68	29
21	44	103	−145	−182	−122	5
22	− 2	− 9	83	− 67	− 33	− 1
23	− 8	122	−153	− 40	−211	− 1
24	−161	−131	−189	−170	−202	21
25	−178	−108	−226	−120	−306	−18
Average	276	152	110	190	159	32
Maximum	824	559	776	811	658	1,02
Minimum	−178	−157	−339	−182	−328	−18
Index [1]	100	55	40	67	58	11

[1] Represents the per cent the labor income each year was of the seven-year avera

Following the labor incomes of each farmer over th
period, it is seen that 9 of the 25 farmers made a labor i
year after paying all other expenses (in other words tl
labor incomes each year); 6 farmers had labor incom
the seven years, and so on. One farmer failed to n
income in any of the seven years.

The $1,000 labor income mark was reached only in ₹
year and then by only a few farmers. Not a farmer re
labor income every year. Two farmers had better than
income for two years, and three farmers for one year.

Ten of the 25 farmers did not reach a $500 labor in
year and but 1 had over $500 every year. For the sev₁
age, only 4 farmers exceeded a $500 labor income; tha₁
from $300 to $500; that of 10 others was between ₹
while 4 failed to make 5 per cent on capital, with no ret
own labor outside of the farm-furnished supplies. The f₁
tioned had seven-year average minus labor incomes.

Comparing the labor income returned on these far₁
with the value each farmer placed upon his labor for e₁
found that one-fourth of the farmers got what they c₁

pay for their labor almost every year, and.one-fourth of them about one-half of the years, while the other one-half received reasonable pay for their labor only three years or less of the seven.

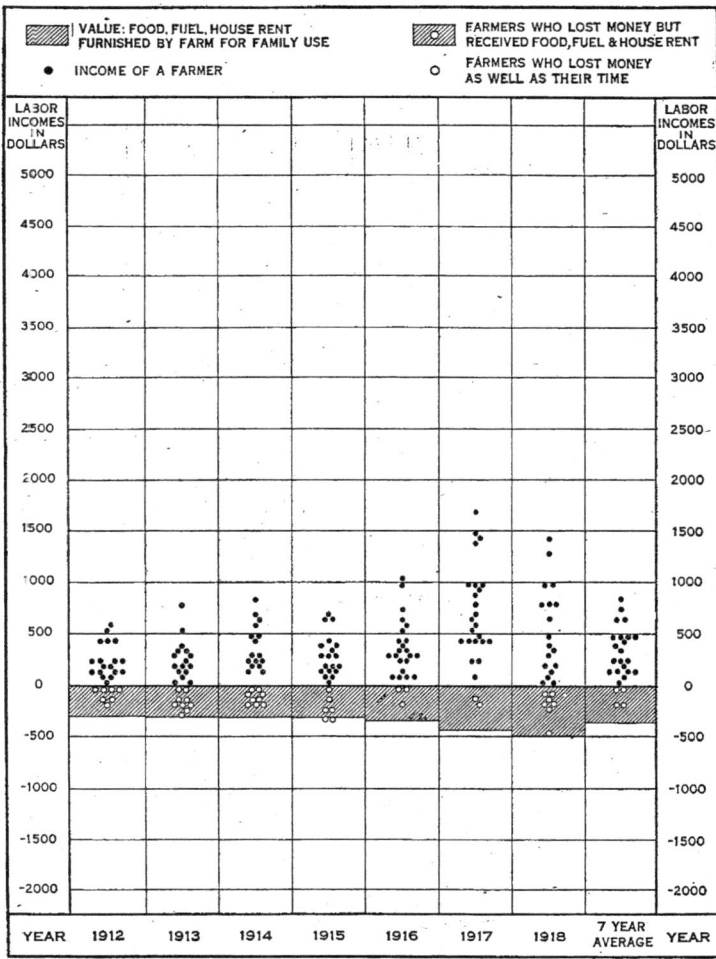

FIG. 7.—The labor incomes of 25 farmers, Palmer township, Washington County, Ohio, 1912–1918. Each dot in this figure represents the labor income of one farmer. The farmers shown in the shaded area of the chart had only the food products, fuel and house rent for their year's labor, and less than 5 per cent on their investment. The white dots below the shaded area represent farmers whose losses were in excess of average value of supplies furnished by the farm for family use. (Fig. 7 is drawn on the same scale as fig. 13 and fig. 19 in order that some comparison of the profits in the three areas may be made.)

In 1912 and 1913, 5 of the 25 farmers made in labor income what they considered their year's labor worth, in addition to food, fuel, and house rent furnished by the farm; in 1914 and 1915, 9; in 1916, 12; in 1917, 19; and in 1918, 11.

TABLE III.—*Per cent return on capital on the 25 farms in Palmer township, Washington County, Ohio, 1912-1918.*

(Ranked according to size of the seven-year average labor income.)

Rank of farms.	7-year average	1912	1913	1914	1915	1916	1917	1918
1	9.3	8.7	9.7	8.4	7.9	7.9	15.3	7.3
2	8.1	4.2	6.1	11.0	6.1	8.2	12.2	8.8
3	7.6	3.9	1.4	1.5	6.1	12.7	17.1	10.9
4	10.5	11.9	4.4	2.0	3.5	14.9	21.9	25.0
5	7.2	4.4	5.5	6.3	5.0	7.6	11.6	10.2
6	7.0	4.3	8.1	7.1	9.6	5.9	6.7	7.7
7	5.5	5.3	.3	1.5	6.5	9.2	7.3	8.2
8	7.4	7.5	5.8	10.9	6.9	2.1	13.7	4.6
9	7.2	1.2	2.3	8.6	3.1	7.5	15.9	11.9
10	6.6	7.9	4.2	3.8	4.3	4.9	15.6	5.6
11	4.9	3.6	2.4	7.2	.6	5.8	12.3	2.7
12	2.7	1.0	1.2	1.7	.5	4.2	8.1	2.3
13	5.7	− 2.7	4.1	8.0	6.0	9.7	10.4	4.5
14	.8	−12.1	2.5	− 1.0	.9	4.6	16.5	−5.7
15	2.6	− 3.2	− 5.7	1.7	1.5	5.2	7.6	11.2
16	− .2	1.2	−10.5	−10.7	5.4	− .4	12.0	1.5
17	.1	− 3.5	− 4.5	.7	−2.9	2.8	9.8	−1.8
18	.6	− 3.5	2.8	5.8	3.9	.2	3.6	−8.5
19	2.3	− 2.3	1.3	2.8	2.9	1.4	10.0	.3
20	−1.4	1.1	− 1.7	− 4.9	− .8	6.1	3.4	−6.8
21	2.6	3.3	− .9	− .5	.3	2.8	7.8	5.4
22	.3	0	2.0	− 1.1	− .5	−1.8	2.4	−2.7
23	−1.4	2.2	− 2.1	− 2.5	−4.8	−1.9	3.4	−4.1
24	− .8	− .6	− 1.3	− .2	− .6	2.8	.3	−5.8
25	−2.9	− .7	− 2.3	− 2.7	−5.2	−2.0	−5.0	−2.7
Average of farms	3.7	1.7	1.4	2.6	2.6	4.8	9.6	3.6
Maximum	10.5	11.9	9.7	11.0	9.6	14.9	21.9	25.0
Minimum	−2.9	−12.1	−10.5	−10.7	−5.2	−2.0	−5.0	− 8.5
Index [1]	100	46	38	70	70	130	259	97

[1] Represents the percentage the returns each year are of the seven-year average (3.7=100).

For the seven-year average shown in Table III only 11 of the 25 farmers made over 5 per cent interest on the farm capital after deducting conservative charges for their own labor and management, and but 3 of these exceeded 8 per cent. Only 1 farmer made better than 5 per cent every year, while 1 failed to make as much as 2 per cent return on the capital in any year.

From Tables II and III and figure 7 it is observed that profits on most farms varied widely from year to year. The uncertainty of the farmers' annual return is partly due to the many conditions over which he has little or no control. Some of the conditions which adversely affected these farms, as well as the Indiana and Wisconsin areas were:

1. Partial crop failures, due to deficient or excessive rainfall; extreme heat or cold; too short growing season; wind or hail storms; plant diseases; insect injuries.

2. Insufficient horse power at critical periods, due to losses of or injuries to work stock.

3. Curtailment of live-stock production, through losses from disease, injury, failure in breeding stock, losses of calves, pigs, or lambs.

4. Lack of sufficient labor at critical periods, due to sickness or accident either to the farmer himself or to members of his family and the difficulty in obtaining hired labor.

FACTORS AFFECTING THE PROFITS OF DIFFERENT FARMS.

While the preceding tables show wide yearly variations in the profits of most farmers, they also show that some farmers made much more money than others over the seven-year period. Some made enough in addition to their living expenses to reduce indebtedness, make improvements, buy more land, or make other investments. Others realized no more than enough to supply the necessaries of life. Table IV shows how each farmer stood with reference to some of the important factors which aided materially in earning larger profits.

TABLE IV.—*The seven-year average labor income, crop area, pasture area, productive animal units, crop yields, live-stock returns and crop acres per man and per horse for each of the 25 farms, Washington County, Ohio, 1912 to 1918.*

Rank of each farm in 7-year average labor income.	7-year average labor income.	Average crop area.	Average acres in pastures.	Average number productive animal units.	Per cent crop yields were of average for all farms.	Per cent live-stock returns per animal were of the average for all farms.	Crop acres per man.	Crop acres per horse.	Per cent of total farm receipts from crops.
1	$824	59	113	32	115	117	30	18	11
2	722	60	83	22	120	128	42	27	15
3	618	58	131	22	102	115	35	14	12
4	616	40	22	11	98	136	28	15	35
5	488	48	78	19	112	119	35	22	12
6	474	47	45	14	117	130	38	17	23
7	462	80	171	33	116	98	35	25	18
8	459	40	57	16	102	100	36	20	12
9	417	36	92	16	111	111	27	18	12
10	386	50	64	10	91	128	36	24	30
11	303	98	173	50	99	77	31	13	8
12	233	40	54	11	96	109	28	14	6
13	224	24	41	9	92	124	19	10	11
14	201	34	16	8	94	98	29	14	13
15	198	24	47	11	97	98	20	10	12
16	137	21	14	5	115	98	17	11	37
17	137	29	59	8	97	75	21	14	25
18	116	38	21	7	86	96	29	12	21
19	113	36	52	8	85	90	29	18	17
20	85	36	84	11	78	74	31	14	23
21	44	46	222	21	85	66	38	23	4
22	− 2	31	53	7	72	68	24	13	8
23	− 8	38	62	13	97	90	30	19	6
24	−161	48	120	10	98	77	36	15	35
25	−178	44	78	10	98	83	31	22	28
Average, all farms....	276	44	78	16	100	100	30	17	17
Average, 5 highest...	654	53	75	21	109	123	34	19	17
Average, 5 lowest....	− 61	41	107	12	90	77	32	18	16

sized business, but not the largest, as measured by crop area
amount of live stock. The crop yields for the seven-year period
15 per cent above the average of all farms. Most of the crops
fed to live stock, which returned more per head than that of
farms of the region. This farm had about the average numb
crop acres per man and per horse. In other words, a comparis
the business of this farm with that of the others shows a much l
business, with better crop yields and higher live-stock returns
the average.

Farm No. 11 had the largest business of all. It had about av
crop yields, but the most of the crops were fed to live stock sh
low returns per head. Had the live-stock returns from this farm
as much per head as from any of the first six farms, it no doubt v
have been at the top in labor income.

Farms 24 and 25 represented the heaviest losers. The si
the business on each of these farms was about the average
measured by crop area, but much below average when measur
amount of live stock. Both farms show poor organization, h
large acreages of pasture with only small amounts of live stock.
live-stock return per head was the factor which so adversely aff
the profits of each farm. The crop yields were also produced
economically than on most of the other farms.

Another interesting comparison in this table is in regard t
range in crop yields, live-stock returns, crop acres per man an
horse. Comparing the crop yields for the average of the seven
period, we find only one man producing crops 20 per cent abov
average of the region; also there are only two producing below 8
cent of the average. In the case of live-stock returns we find a
range; two farms have returns 30 per cent above the average,
two are below 70 per cent of the average. Since both intens
farming and size of farm have a direct bearing upon crop acr
man and per horse, these should always be kept in mind in a stu
the range. The figures do show, however, that in this area bot
man and the horse cover small acreages as compared with
other regions but that the variation in acreage covered withi
region is marked.

THE INDIANA AREA.

The area in Indiana, which is located about 40 miles no1
Indianapolis, is typical of general crop and live-stock farmi
north-central Indiana. The land was originally covered with
hardwood timber, except for a few strips locally known as "pr1
The surface is level to slightly rolling and much of the land is
The main wagon roads are improved, most of them graveled
railroad points are readily accessible the year around. General
ing prevailed, with corn and hogs the leading sources of incom1

THE FARM BUSINESS.

A summary of the farm business for the 100 farms over the seven years, 1910 and 1913 to 1918, is shown in Table V.

TABLE V.—*Summary of the farm business over a period of seven years, 1910 and 1913–1918, Forest and Johnson townships, Clinton County, Ind. (average of 100 farms).*

	1910	1913	1914	1915	1916	1917	1918	7-year average.
Acres per farm	116	124	126	129	130	130	127	126
Acres in pasture	23	27	28	25	28	25	26	26
Acres in corn	37	37	42	43	44	49	41	42
Acres in oats	20	24	25	22	32	27	24	25
Acres in wheat	14	7	11	17	2	2	9	9
Acres in hay	10	17	10	10	12	12	11	12
Acres in other crops	5	6	4	4	3	5	8	5
Corn per acre......bushels	52	55	44	47	48	34	32	45
Oats per acre.........do	47	36	38	53	37	36	52	43
Wheat per acre.........do	20	20	19	19	6	15	27	18
Hay per acre.........tons	1.4	1.5	1.0	1.4	1.4	1.3	1.4	1.3
Productive animal units	18.2	19.2	21.3	21.0	21.1	20.0	20.7	20.2
Brood sows.......number	7.0	6.4	7.1	7.3	6.9	6.4	6.2	7
Work stock..........do	4.8	4.6	4.8	4.9	4.8	4.8	4.5	4.7
Receipts per animal unit	$61	$63	$59	$59	$83	$116	$128	$81
Total labor, months	18.2	18.8	18.9	19.6	19.4	19.6	19.0	19.1
Farm capital	$19,055	$24,936	$25,724	$26,436	$26,599	$27,822	$31,135	$25,958
Real estate	16,977	22,672	23,084	23,728	23,888	24,571	27,720	23,234
Live stock	1,355	1,482	1,709	1,677	1,788	2,084	2,294	1,770
Machinery	286	376	397	406	399	433	459	394
All other	437	406	534	625	524	731	662	560
Real estate per acre	147	182	183	183	184	188	218	183
Receipts	$1,911	$2,261	$2,158	$2,377	$3,004	$3,412	$4,386	$2,787
	Per cent.	Per cent.	Per cent.	Per cent.	Per cent.	Per cent.	Per cent.	Per cent.
Hogs	40	35	40	31	42	53	42	42
Corn	10	15	15	15	20	8	8	13
Oats	12	9	13	15	13	13	14	13
Cattle	8	10	9	9	11	11	13	10
Wheat	11	4	6	12	(1)	1	10	6
Dairy products	2	4	5	4	3	4	4	4
Other	17	23	12	11	11	10	9	12
Expenses	$624	$758	$828	$868	$864	$1,169	$1,408	$931
	Per cent	Per cent.	Per cent.	Per cent.	Per cent.	Per cent.	Per cent.	Per cent.
Hired labor	21	17	18	18	18	15	15	17
Unpaid family labor	8	11	8	9	9	8	8	9
Repairs and depreciation:								
Machinery	8	8	7	7	7	6	6	7
House	4	3	3	3	3	2	2	3
Other buildings	5	4	4	4	4	3	3	3
Repairs, fences	5	5	5	4	5	3	3	4
Feed purchased	11	10	19	15	16	33	25	18
Seed purchased	3	3	2	4	4	3	8	4
Fertilizer	(a)	1	1	1	(a)	(a)	2	1
Machine work hired	6	8	7	6	5	4	6	6
Taxes and insurance	23	22	20	21	22	18	15	20
Other	6	8	6	8	7	5	7	8
Farm Income	$1,287	$1,503	$1,330	$1,509	$2,140	$2,243	$2,978	$1,856
Interest on capital at 5%	953	1,247	1,286	1,322	1,330	1,391	1,557	1,298
Labor Income	334	256	44	187	810	852	1,421	558
Operator's labor	312	325	332	338	349	402	527	369
Return on capital per cent	5.1	4.7	3.9	4.4	6.7	6.6	7.9	5.7
Value of family labor	48	85	70	78	79	89	120	81
Interest on indebtedness	b 47	47	42	49	59	57	55	51
Family income	1,288	1,541	1,358	1,538	2,160	2,275	3,043	1,886
Family living from farm[1]	356	361	368	373	416	551	620	435
Amount sold:								
Hogs..........number	46	47	59	49	53	45	46	49
Corn...........bushels	455	593	482	601	645	274	239	470
Oats..............do	718	630	750	984	976	750	979	824
Wheat............do	238	111	178	302	8	24	220	154
Prices:								
Hogs............cwt	8.16	8.25	8.21	7.04	9.45	15.44	17.39	10.56
Corn......... bushel	.43	.57	.67	.59	.93	1.03	1.41	.80
Oats.............do	.32	.34	.37	.35	.40	.61	.62	.43
Wheat............do	.93	.81	.80	.98	1.40	2.11	2.08	1.30

a Less than 1 per cent.
b No data, but estimated the same as for 1913.
[1] Computed from U. S. Department of Agriculture Bulletin No. 410 and War Industries Bulletin No. 1.

The farms averaged 126 acres, with only 6 per cent of
mproved. Twenty per cent of the land was in pastur

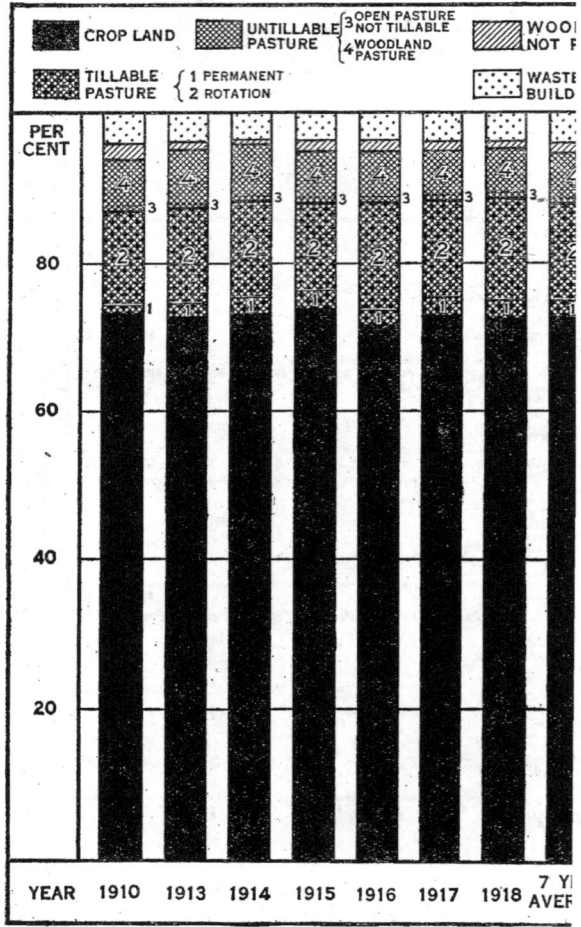

ʹɪɢ. 8.—Distribution of the farm area on 100 farms, Forest and Johnson township
Ind. Nearly 90 per cent of the land in this area may be used for tillage purposes. ʹ1
land area is devoted to crops under the present organization. A large portion of the ᵢ
in the rotation system.

ʹent in crops. Nearly one-half of the crop land was in co:
n small grains, mainly oats,. and the remainder in hay.

In figure 8 is shown graphically the average distribution of the farm area for the 100 farms over the seven-year period. The proportion of the farm area devoted to crops remained practically the same over

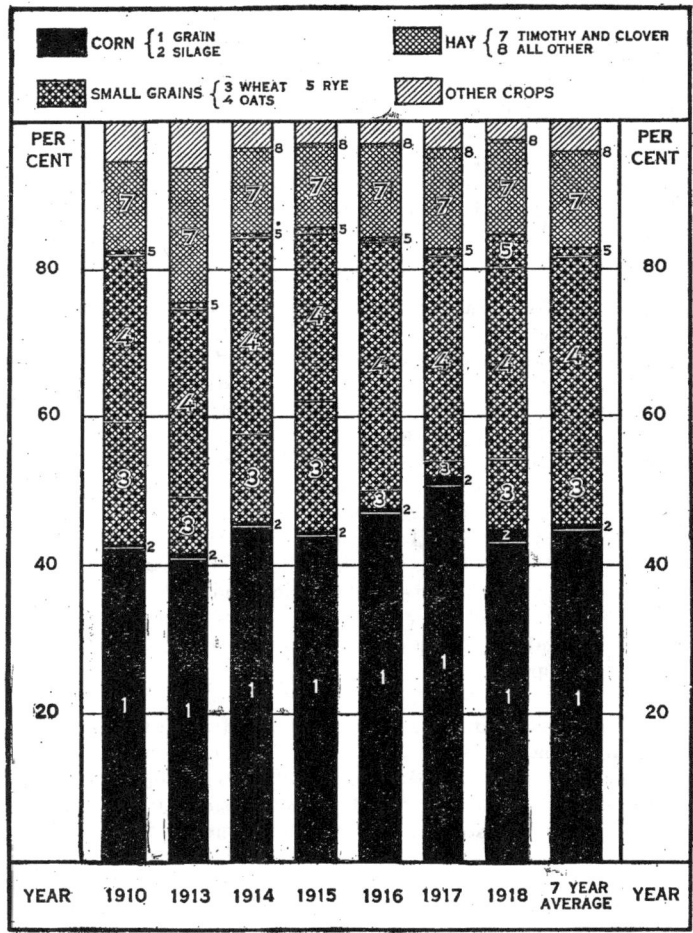

Fig. 9.—Distribution of crop area on 100 farms in Forest and Johnson-townships, Clinton County, Ind. A poor yield in 1917, together with the scarcity of labor, caused a decrease in the corn acreage in 1918. The wheat area shows the widest variation over the period. The area of rye was highest in 1918.

the period. The area of tillable pasture was increased through the improvement of untillable area. Woodland occupies only 1 per cent of the farm area. The acreage taken up by roads, streams, waste, building lots, etc., in this area is a very negligible proportion of th farm area.

Figure 9 shows graphically the average distribution of the crop area Corn and oats occupy the largest acreages, followed by hay an wheat. Comparing the last two years with the first two, the cor acreage was increased 22 per cent and oats 16 per cent, while whea was decreased 48 per cent and hay 15 per cent. Wheat showed th greatest variation in area. In 1916, when wheat was nearly an entir failure, considerable acreages were plowed in the early spring and pu in oats, thereby making the acreage devoted to oats highest in tha year. Because of the unprofitable results in 1916, only a small are was put out the following year and an average of only 9 acres per farr in 1918, when the yield was highest.

CROP YIELDS.

The seven-year average yield of corn was 45 bushels per acre. Th lowest average of any year was 32 bushels and the highest 55 bushel: The two discouraging corn years were 1917 and 1918, and the effect of these were reflected in purchased feeds for these years (shown i Table V and figure 11). The average yield of oats was 43 bushel per acre, the lowest being 36 bushels and the highest 53 bushel: The average yield of wheat was 18 bushels per acre, with a rang of from 6 to 27 bushels. The acreage in wheat varied widely ove the period, with a marked decrease during the later years. Th average yield of hay was 1.3 tons per acre, the lowest 1 ton an the highest 1.5 tons. Oats and hay showed the least variation i yield per acre over the seven-year period and wheat the greatest Twenty-six per cent of the corn, 79 per cent of the oats, 88 per cen of the wheat, and 26 per cent of the hay produced on these farms wer sold as cash crops.

AMOUNT OF LIVE STOCK KEPT.

The number of productive animal units per farm (expressed as th equivalent of mature cattle) averaged 20.2, not counting work horse: This is an average of one head to each 5.9 acres of crops and pastur When measured by the amount of feed required, hogs represented ove one-half of the live stock and cattle about one-third. Brood sow kept averaged 7 per farm, and the number of hogs sold per farm wa 49, or 7 per brood sow. In addition about 4 hogs were slaughtere per farm for home use, so that the average production was 11 pigs pe sow. Work horses averaged 4.7 per farm. Only a small number c cattle were raised, and only a few farms bought feeding cattl Most of the farms produced a small amount of dairy products fc sale. The proportion of the various classes of live stock showe only slight variation over the period. The small increase was i cattle.

LABOR REQUIRED.

An average of 19.1 months of man labor per year was used in the operations of these farms. Twelve months of this was the farmer's own labor and management, 2.8 months unpaid family labor, and 4.3 months hired labor. Thus 77 per cent of the labor in operating these farms was performed by the farm operator and members of his family and 23 per cent was hired.

FARM CAPITAL.

There was a decided increase in the capital value of these farms from 1910 to 1918. Between the period 1910 and 1913 there was a considerable increase in land values. From 1913 to 1917 the increase hardly offset the value of additional improvements put on the farms, but in 1918 there was another marked increase. There were slight increases in the average size of farm and in the amounts and values of live stock and of machinery. The farm capital for the seven-year average was $25,958 per farm. Of this capital $23,234, or 90 per cent, was in real estate; $1,770, or 7 per cent, in live stock; $394, or 1 per cent, in machinery; and $560, or 2 per cent, in supplies and operating cash. The value of land, exclusive of buildings, averaged $21,309 per farm, or 82 per cent of the total farm capital.

RECEIPTS.

While the farm receipts increased from $1,911 per farm in 1910 to $4,386 in 1918, the distribution of the more important items of receipts over the seven-year period shows no marked change in the farm organization in this area. Hogs were the leading source of income, with corn and oats second. The income from wheat varied most, but wheat represented only 6 per cent of the total receipts. Even with the low yields of corn in 1917 and 1918, a number of these farmers maintained the production of hogs by buying more feed than usual, and the higher price of hogs increased their incomes.

Figure 10 shows graphically the average distribution of receipts over the seven-year period. Over the later years of the study the proportion of the receipts from live stock increased and that from crops decreased. This was due in part to the poor yields of the last two years. Comparing the first three years with the last three, the proportion of the total income represented by live stock increased 12 per cent. Corn, in addition to supplying the farm needs, contributed considerable income as a cash crop during most of the years.

EXPENSES.

The distribution of farm expenses is shown in Table V. For the seven-year period these averaged $931 per farm, or 33 per cent of the total receipts. These expenses include $81 for the value of labor performed by the farm family. The expenses were lowest in 1910 ($624),

but for the years 1913, 1914, 1915, and 1916 there were only slight
variations either in amount or proportions. Beginning with the year

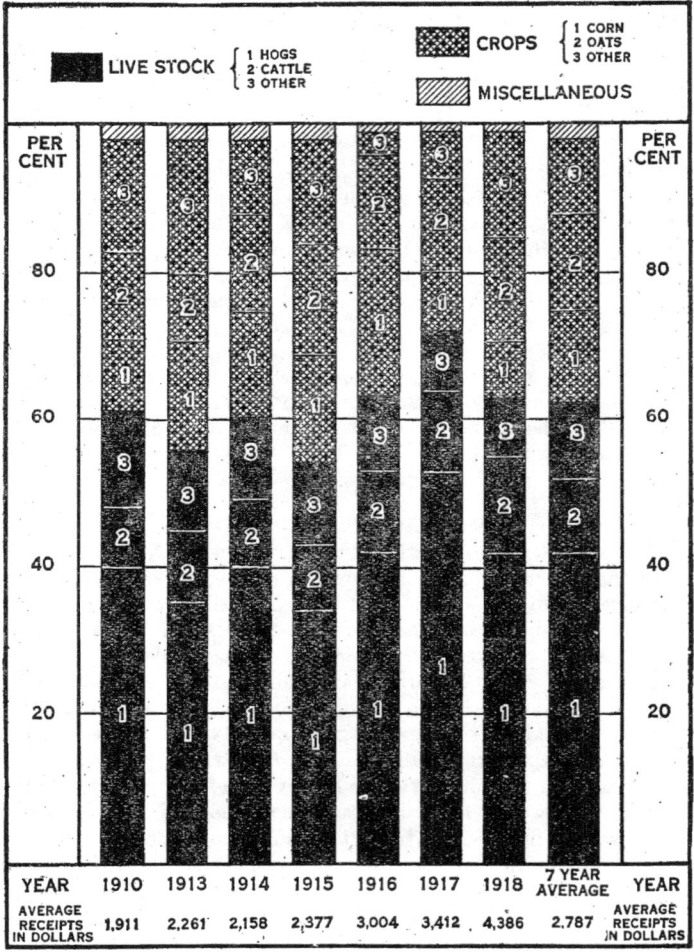

Fig. 10.—Distribution of receipts on 100 farms in Forest and Johnson townships, Clinton County, Ind.
Hogs are the most important live-stock source of receipts, and corn and oats the leading source of crop
receipts. The receipts from wheat varied widely.

1917 the expenses increased rapidly. The items of largest expense
were hired labor, repairs and depreciation on machinery and buildings, taxes and insurance, and feed.

In figure 11 the proportion that each of the more important classes of expense represents of the total expense is shown for each

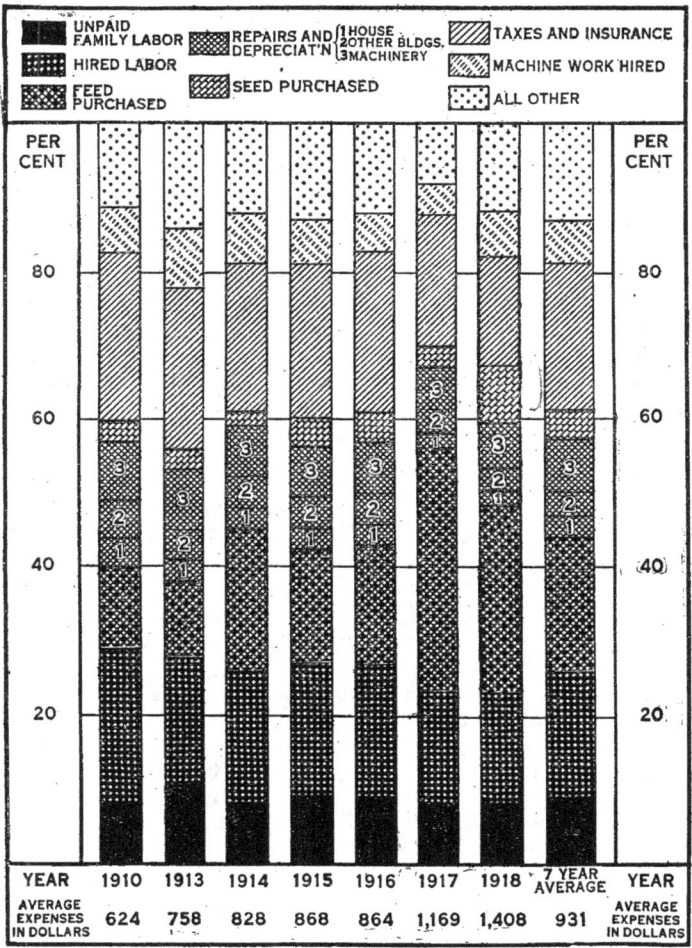

Fig. 11.—Distribution of expenses on 100 farms in Forest and Johnson townships, Clinton County, Ind. The low yield of corn for the years 1917 and 1918 (see Table V) made necessary the purchase of a large amount of feed.

year and as an average for the seven years. For the first two years family labor and hired labor represented 29 per cent of the total, while for the last two years it represented 23 per cent of the total expense. Purchased feeds showed the largest percentage in 1917 and 1918, during which years the proportional expense for hired labor fell off sharply. The expenses for the seven-year average were about one-third of the receipts. When the value of the farmer's labor and 5 per cent interest on the capital are included the total costs equal 93 per cent of the income.   ·

FARM EARNINGS.

The farm income, or the receipts less the expenses, averaged $1,856 per farm for the seven-year period. It was highest in 1918, when it reached almost $3,000, and lowest in 1910, when it was slightly less than $1,300. Comparing the first two years with the last two, the data show that receipts increased 87 per cent and expenses 86 per cent. The seven-year average labor income of the farms in this area was $558, ranging from $44 in 1914 to $1,421 in 1918. The return on the farm capital averaged 5.7 per cent, being as low as 3.9 per cent in 1914 and as high as 7.9 per cent in 1918.

The farm earnings, whether expressed as labor income or as per cent return on capital, were low during the four years of low-price levels, but showed a marked increase during the last three years, when prices were higher. The average labor income of the 100 farms for the four years 1910 and 1913–1915 was $205; for the three years 1916–1918 it was $1,028. The return on capital for the earlier period averaged 4½ per cent and for the latter period 7 per cent.

The family income, which represents the amount of money available to the family after deducting from the total receipts the farm expenses, including interest paid upon indebtedness but exclusive of the value of family labor or the farmer's own labor, averaged $1,886 per farm for the seven-year period, ranging from $1,288 in 1910 to $3,043 in 1918. About one-third of these farms had indebtedness varying from $200 to $12,000 per farm.

Figure 12 shows graphically the distribution of the average gross income on these farms for each year and for the seven-year period. This chart shows how much of the gross income is represented by operating expenses, interest on capital, unpaid family labor, and food products, fuel, and house rent furnished by the farm. Receipts increased materially during the latter part of the period of study, and though expenses also increased the spread between the two became wider, so that the amount left for the farmer's own wages (labor income) grew larger toward the close of the period.

Owing to the capital value of farms in this area being more than in the other areas studied, the item of interest for the seven-year period averaged $1,298 per farm. Because of the size of this item, the available income on many of these farms, if free from debt, may be fairly large, owing to the fact that the interest for the use of capital does not have to be paid out. On many farms where the capital represented in the business is rather large and where the operations are carried on without a large cash outlay, the interest may be of sufficient amount to make the business apparently prosperous even though the farmer's labor income is low.

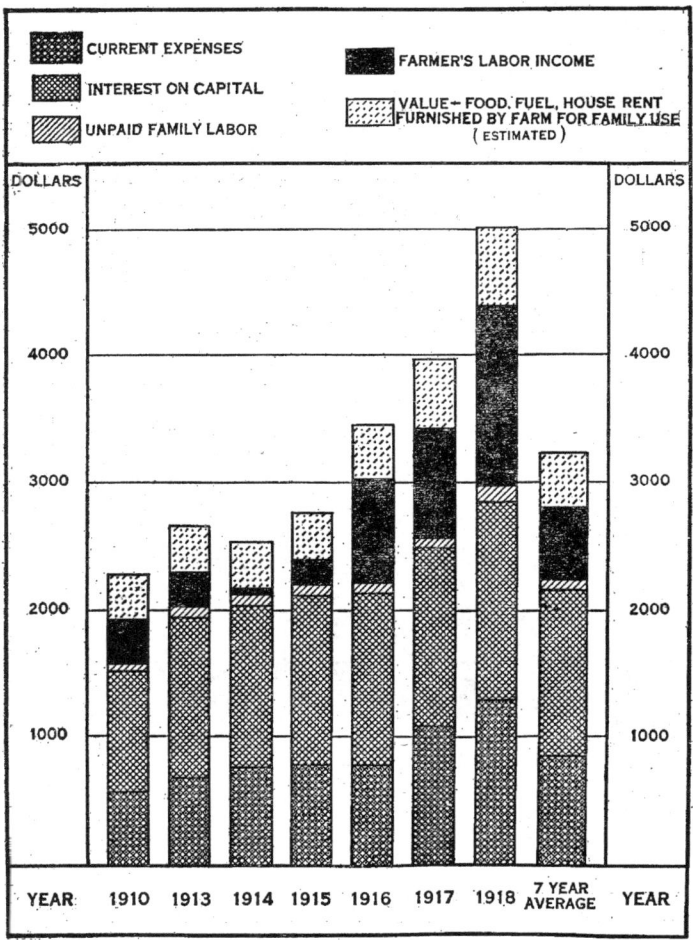

FIG. 12.—Distribution of the gross income on 100 farms in Forest and Johnson townships, Clinton County, Ind. The farmer has money invested and is entitled to a gross income of sufficient size to pay interest upon investment as well as pay for his own labor and supervision. The interest upon investment may enable a farmer to have a considerable income to spend, if free from debt, even though his own wages (labor income) may be very small. For the years 1916, 1917, and 1918 the gross income increased more than expenses, thus giving the farmers a better labor income than in previous years.

FAMILY LIVING FROM FARM.

In addition to the average labor income of $558 made by the far-
mers in this area, they had the use of products from the farm for
family use, in the way of food, fuel, and house rent, estimated to be

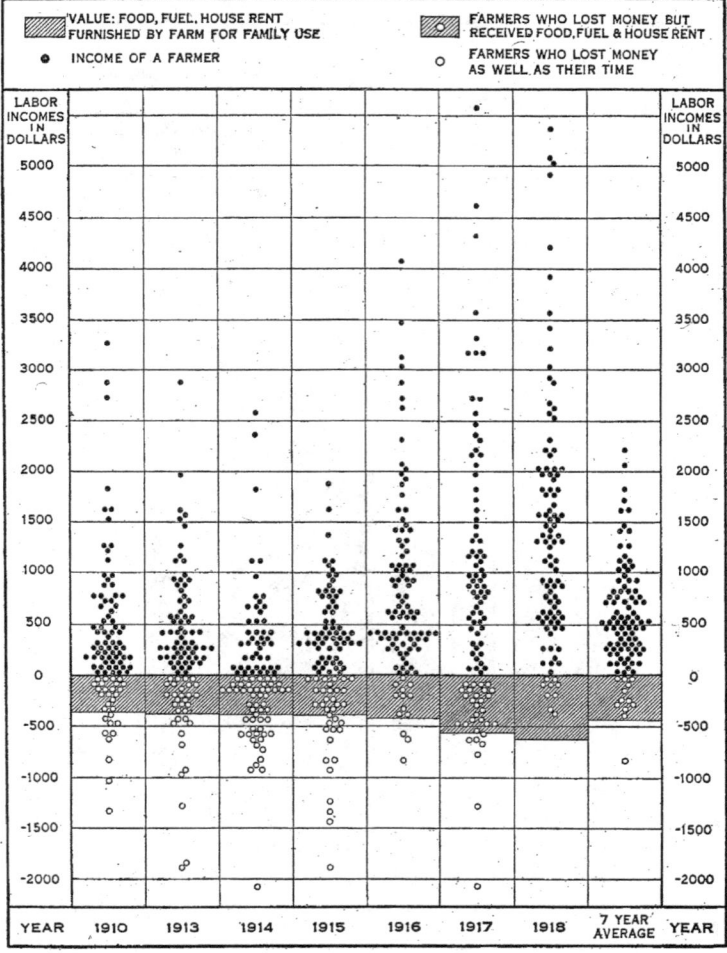

Fig. 13.—The labor incomes of 100 farmers in Forest and Johnson townships, Clinton County, Ind., 1910
and 1913–1918. Each dot represents the labor income of one farmer. The farmers represented in the
shaded area of the chart had only the food products, fuel, and house rent for their year's labor, and less
than 5 per cent interest upon investment. The white dots below the shaded area represent farmers
whose losses were in excess of the average value of supplies furnished by the farm for family use.

worth $435. The value of these items increased from $356 in 1910 to $620 in 1918.

It was not possible to measure quantitatively all the various products sold from these farms, but Table V shows the amounts of the more important sources of income. The number of hogs sold for the seven-year period averaged 49 head, corn 470 bushels, oats 827 bushels and wheat 154 bushels. The most hogs were sold in 1914, the most corn in 1916, the most oats in 1915, and the most wheat in 1915. Hogs and oats showed the least variation and wheat the most.

In 1910, 1913, and 1914, the average price received for hogs was $8.16, $8.25, and $8.21 per hundredweight. In 1915 the price fell to $7.04, but beginning with 1916 the price made a decided advance to the year 1918, when the price averaged $17.39 per hundredweight. Oats showed little advance in 1918 over 1917 and wheat decreased in price slightly. Corn showed the greatest advance in price and wheat and oats the least.

LABOR INCOME AND RETURN ON CAPITAL OF THE 100 INDIANA FARMERS OVER THE SEVEN-YEAR PERIOD.

The labor income and the per cent return on capital for each of the 100 farms are shown for each year and for the average of the seven years in Tables VI and VII. The farms are arranged in order of the seven-year average labor income. The labor incomes are also shown graphically in figure 13.

It will be seen from Table VI that 14 of the 100 had a labor income every year, 32 for six of the seven years, 21 for five of the seven years, 17 for four of the seven years, 6 for three of the seven years, 7 for two of the years, and 3 for only one year.

No one farmer reached the $1,000 labor income mark every year of the period, but several farmers reached $1,000 some of the years. One farmer got over $1,000 labor income six of the seven years, and one-fourth of them about half of the years. Some farmers went above the $1,000 mark for occasional years. Four farmers made over $5,000 for one of the seven years.

Only one of the 100 farmers reached a $3,000 labor income prior to 1916, and he for but one year. Eleven farmers reached $1,000 labor income in 1910, 10 in 1913, 5 in 1914, 7 in 1915, 33 in 1916, 34 in 1917, and 57 in 1918. No one farmer reached $4,000 until 1916, nor $5,000 until 1917. In 1918 three farmers reached the $5,000 mark and two others reached the $4,000 mark.

The seven-year average labor income of 18 farmers exceeded $1,000; that of two of these exceeded $2,000; that of 32 ranged from $500 to $1,000; while that of the other 50 was less than $500. Twelve

TABLE VI.—*Labor incomes of 100 farms in Forest and Johnson townships, Clinton County, Ind., 1910 and 1913-1918.*

(Ranked according to size of the seven-year average labor income.)

Rank of farm.	7-year average.	1910	1913	1914	1915	1916	1917	1918
1	$2,210	$1,252	$510	$2,383	$1,851	$2,042	$2,348	$5,082
2	2,071	58	569	694	833	2,634	4,324	5,385
3	1,812	686	− 343	− 408	543	4,104	3,190	4,915
4	1,704	− 583	1,547	160	803	2,867	4,602	2,535
5	1,620	256	1,965	− 906	762	3,117	3,558	2,590
6	1,606	2,878	− 486	785	479	14	5,560	2,012
7	1,454	687	− 165	778	1,070	3,036	3,188	1,584
8	1,425	3,256	− 58	325	−1,316	2,099	2,091	3,581
9	1,407	1,211	− 296	260	17	431	3,198	5,029
10	1,280	1,618	2,884	− 318	− 826	3,450	−1,294	3,446
11	1,273	499	1,588	424	180	1,922	2,472	1,828
12	1,197	−1,058	550	1,833	− 387	2,706	2,700	2,034
13	1,149	− 348	724	539	657	1,449	812	4,209
14	1,121	1,251	333	− 123	808	1,506	2,246	1,829
15	1,081	1,832	920	655	292	1,271	− 632	3,227
16	1,071	2,702	−1,276	2,578	1,648	− 311	− 508	2,662
17	1,045	480	1,637	1,139	966	423	2,173	499
18	1,009	980	1,169	− 18	1,149	2,308	− 190	1,665
19	972	768	1,472	− 54	− 48	1,777	881	2,010
20	940	300	4	− 122	824	1,865	1,730	1,980
21	901	739	921	316	1,146	1,099	1,620	463
22	901	− 830	20	1,109	949	610	1,549	2,942
23	868	1,531	1,282	− 277	962	1,403	1,228	51
24	843	456	451	644	795	1,072	1,160	1,324
25	840	994	− 423	68	− 204	1,470	966	3,006
26	820	724	101	6	263	1,336	1,800	1,507
27	816	773	151	− 170	356	628	1,995	1,982
28	796	322	1,104	672	− 122	904	886	1,805
29	793	440	759	− 543	413	1,226	1,249	2,010
30	789	170	254	− 148	432	1,005	2,367	1,442
31	767	328	640	354	87	579	1,081	2,303
32	748	− 358	261	27	− 3	911	3,342	1,577
33	720	282	528	532	12	937	1,468	1,306
34	710	− 15	− 190	− 126	− 823	942	2,552	2,627
35	704	− 78	586	− 443	683	1,649	305	2,226
36	700	53	417	399	− 15	1,089	803	2,173
37	656	252	294	− 668	543	1,403	990	1,778
38	647	109	672	358	751	1,616	766	258
39	640	225	550	332	368	1,169	501	1,332
40	596	919	291	− 89	387	655	1,108	904
41	591	512	147	− 273	84	1,971	991	708
42	564	897	898	9	1,024	790	− 775	1,105
43	554	166	90	− 383	317	576	904	2,209
44	549	336	1,104	345	858	434	126	643
45	535	− 79	− 17	− 446	176	404	823	2,882
46	535	421	942	974	17	− 89	− 466	1,947
47	532	152	− 684	− 617	1,365	997	1,321	1,187
48	527	− 129	291	− 133	303	868	870	1,620
49	527	243	39	− 339	405	647	1,161	1,534
50	502	− 598	194	− 900	473	− 176	591	3,933
51	491	193	447	193	328	− 61	569	1,767
52	481	61	149	437	643	616	− 96	1,558
53	473	− 255	859	− 27	442	431	406	1,458
54	467	− 60	112	− 135	484	1,034	− 137	1,974
55	458	54	849	349	626	655	− 275	947
56	457	200	407	51	352	1,021	642	524
57	446	491	− 151	54	− 70	1,319	738	852
58	440	22	978	− 869	− 123	− 566	2,184	1,452
59	400	− 82	279	164	296	267	521	1,354
60	369	17	246	522	738	365	− 100	798
61	368	23	446	66	446	18	1,167	408
62	359	756	287	23	− 326	341	752	681
63	340	197	436	− 121	128	306	934	498
64	338	222	− 77	− 580	116	− 198	1,322	1,557
65	330	116	548	419	12	408	217	588

TABLE VI.—*Labor incomes of 100 farms in Forest and Johnson townships, Clinton County, Ind., 1910 and 1913-1918*—Continued.

Rank of farm.	7-year average.	1910	1913	1914	1915	1916	1917	1918
66	$312	$622	$176	$744	— $261	— $626	$628	$898
67	310	520	262	— 103	— 308	153	250	1,397
68	281	50	404	81	449	— 4	— 413	1,398
69	274	1,641	173	— 337	— 646	34	50	1,003
70	265	— 24	— 62	11	139	798	92	903
71	258	183	330	— 152	— 409	64	678	1,109
72	255	— 303	— 177	— 552	349	439	1,399	631
73	253	533	— 30	— 106	62	279	— 102	1,086
74	249	893	— 23	— 47	— 47	374	— 692	1,282
75	218	404	103	89	384	434	— 57	167
76	213	166	389	210	307	375	— 224	269
77	207	126	198	— 54	306	375	— 69	568
78	166	1,133	57	— 39	— 946	— 847	1,000	806
79	154	— 108	207	48	322	1,092	— 454	— 27
80	143	387	160	185	188	433	— 461	112
81	137	97	284	— 98	66	272	319	20
82	135	— 158	— 342	98	— 25	403	194	772
83	132	406	323	71	— 497	355	— 303	572
84	116	— 123	172	— 19	336	311	459	— 326
85	65	— 186	61	— 125	— 146	571	— 611	888
86	28	— 118	— 129	401	— 114	— 178	— 211	545
87	10	266	— 167	— 588	— 466	146	234	646
88	4	254	— 64	— 403	120	207	92	— 178
89	— 7	— 46	— 927	— 67	— 295	383	— 470	1,300
90	— 20	— 636	707	— 591	— 292	487	457	— 272
91	— 26	— 43	— 217	— 24	— 130	259	41	— 70
92	— 67	— 176	— 469	— 167	— 509	898	— 586	539
93	— 132	— 451	— 248	— 134	— 286	237	— 168	128
94	— 224	13	— 266	— 560	— 533	— 127	— 62	— 30
95	— 244	— 223	245	633	434	716	—2,067	181
96	— 262	—1,341	—1,864	— 514	—1,213	— 373	2,743	729
97	— 270	— 487	— 585	— 814	— 200	80	— 441	555
98	— 312	— 17	— 429	— 748	— 511	66	— 179	— 369
99	— 387	777	— 999	— 272	—1,859	— 374	— 102	123
100	— 802	421	—1,820	—2,065	—1,410	559	— 368	— 88
Average	558	334	256	44	187	810	852	1,421
Maximum	2,210	3,256	2,884	2,578	1,851	4,104	5,550	5,385
Minimum	— 802	—1,341	—1,864	—2,065	—1,859	— 847	—2,067	— 369
Index[1]	100	60	46	8	34	145	153	225

[1] Represents the percentage the labor income each year is of the 7-year average ($558.=100).

of the latter realized no labor income outside of the farm supplies furnished the family, and received less than 5 per cent interest on the capital.

Thirty-two per cent of these farmers realized in labor income every year as much or more than they valued their labor to be worth in addition to the farm-furnished supplies, and 41 per cent about half of the years.

In 1910, 41 of these 100 farmers made in labor income what they considered their labor worth in addition to food, fuel, and house rent; 39 in 1913; 25 in 1914; 43 in 1915; 73 in 1916; 56 in 1917; and 81 in 1918.

From Table VII it will be noted that 60 of the 100 farmers made over 5 per cent interest on capital, after deducting conservative charges for their own labor and management, and that but 10 of these received over 8 per cent. Only 2 farmers made better than 5 per cent every year.

TABLE VII.—*Per cent return on capital on 100 farms in Forest and Johnson townships, Clinton County, Ind., 1910 and 1913–1918.*

(Ranked according to size of 7-year average labor income.)

Rank.	7-year average.	1910	1913	1914	1915	1916	1917	1918
1	8.0	6.8	4.8	8.9	7.7	8.1	7.6	11.8
2	7.6	3.9	5.4	5.7	5.6	9.6	12.6	10.3
3	6.1	5.2	4.2	4.2	5.0	8.5	7.6	8.1
4	8.8	2.2	8.0	4.7	6.4	12.7	17.1	10.6
5	6.7	4.6	7.8	2.9	5.6	9.3	9.6	7.4
6	7.3	11.9	3.8	5.5	5.1	4.6	12.8	7.4
7	8.1	6.5	1.9	6.2	7.0	12.1	14.7	8.6
8	6.6	11.2	4.4	5.1	1.5	7.8	7.6	9.0
9	8.2	11.6	1.3	4.8	3.6	3.6	14.1	18.4
10	6.7	8.4	9.3	3.8	3.3	9.2	2.6	10.4
11	8.6	5.8	10.1	5.3	4.3	11.8	13.9	9.4
12	5.7	1.7	4.9	6.9	4.0	8.0	7.9	6.6
13	6.1	1.8	5.8	4.8	5.2	7.2	5.2	13.0
14	8.1	9.4	5.1	3.3	7.1	9.9	12.6	9.4
15	7.1	10.2	6.6	5.7	4.3	7.4	1.7	13.7
16	5.9	9.0	3.0	7.6	6.4	4.1	3.9	7.4
17	8.3	6.3	11.2	8.8	7.3	5.3	14.0	5.4
18	6.6	7.9	7.1	4.0	6.9	9.6	3.1	7.4
19	7.8	7.8	11.5	2.2	2.3	10.3	6.3	13.9
20	6.3	5.1	4.1	3.6	7.0	9.4	8.5	6.8
21	8.2	6.9	8.3	4.8	8.8	10.2	13.4	4.9
22	7.0	.1	3.6	8.5	7.7	6.3	9.4	13.5
23	6.2	8.6	6.9	3.7	6.2	7.1	6.5	4.1
24	9.9	10.7	9.9	11.6	8.0	9.7	10.1	9.4
25	7.1	8.9	1.6	3.7	2.9	9.8	7.5	15.2
26	7.3	8.1	3.6	3.2	4.5	10.2	12.0	9.7
27	6.5	6.9	4.5	3.4	5.0	6.4	11.0	8.2
28	8.2	5.3	8.8	7.8	.1	10.3	10.0	15.3
29	6.3	5.5	6.4	1.7	5.2	8.1	8.0	9.5
30	7.4	3.1	4.6	2.0	5.4	9.2	17.6	10.1
31	6.4	4.8	6.3	4.4	2.6	5.8	8.3	12.4
32	5.9	2.2	3.1	4.6	3.9	6.5	13.3	7.4
33	8.1	4.9	7.0	7.0	2.4	10.3	13.9	11.1
34	5.4	3.2	2.7	3.0	.3	6.9	11.9	10.0
35	5.9	2.6	6.2	1.0	7.0	9.4	5.0	9.7
36	5.4	2.0	5.4	5.1	3.3	7.3	6.4	8.6
37	6.2	4.7	5.0	−1.2	6.1	11.2	7.6	10.2
38	6.8	3.7	6.8	5.0	7.2	11.9	8.5	4.8
39	7.4	5.4	7.4	4.8	4.3	12.7	5.6	11.8
40	6.2	7.7	5.0	3.5	5.3	6.5	8.2	7.3
41	5.7	6.8	4.3	2.6	4.0	9.4	6.9	6.0
42	5.6	7.3	7.4	3.3	8.0	8.1	−2.4	7.8
43	5.9	4.6	4.1	.8	4.8	6.0	7.7	13.0
44	6.9	6.2	11.2	5.3	8.8	5.9	3.9	7.2
45	5.6	2.2	3.4	1.1	4.4	5.5	7.6	15.2
46	5.8	6.4	7.3	7.5	4.0	3.7	3.1	8.6
47	5.5	4.0	2.7	2.0	9.0	7.7	7.4	5.4
48	6.5	2.3	5.0	3.0	5.0	8.9	8.7	12.5
49	5.1	4.6	3.9	2.9	5.1	5.7	7.0	6.3
50	4.8	2.2	4.6	1.9	5.2	3.7	4.7	11.4
51	5.8	4.8	8.1	4.2	5.1	3.2	5.8	9.6
52	6.0	2.5	4.5	6.4	7.9	8.2	1.6	10.7
53	5.2	.2	8.0	3.3	5.5	5.7	4.6	9.4
54	5.0	.7	4.0	.3	7.0	9.8	2.8	10.7
55	6.0	4.0	8.8	5.3	6.9	7.1	.5	9.4
56	5.4	4.5	5.3	3.7	5.0	8.6	5.9	5.2
57	6.2	6.2	2.2	2.8	2.0	13.7	9.2	7.5
58	5.3	3.6	6.8	1.7	3.8	2.7	10.3	8.0
59	4.8	3.0	4.6	4.1	4.4	4.1	4.6	8.8
60	4.9	3.7	4.7	6.0	6.8	5.1	3.0	5.0
61	5.0	.5	8.8	1.0	7.6	2.3	9.9	5.1
62	5.0	7.8	4.7	3.6	1.4	4.9	6.8	6.1
63	5.2	4.6	5.9	2.2	3.9	5.0	9.8	5.3
64	4.3	4.0	2.5	.6	4.1	2.8	8.5	7.5
65	4.9	3.7	6.9	5.7	3.5	5.1	4.2	5.0

Table VII.—*Per cent return on capital on 100 farms in Forest and Johnson townships, Clinton County, Ind., 1910 and 1913–1918*—Continued.

Rank.	7-year average.	1910	1913	1914	1915	1916	1917	1918
66	5.1	7.9	4.0	7.3	2.9	−.1	6.8	7.4
67	4.7	5.9	4.3	2.2	1.7	4.5	4.9	9.5
68	4.4	2.5	4.4	2.2	6.5	3.3	2.6	9.1
69	4.8	13.5	4.0	1.5	.1	2.9	2.5	7.9
70	5.3	2.4	1.6	2.3	4.1	12.6	1.4	12.5
71	4.2	3.8	5.1	3.0	.4	3.1	6.6	7.2
72	4.4	2.4	3.0	1.6	5.0	5.3	8.3	5.5
73	5.2	5.9	3.5	3.2	3.9	4.7	3.1	12.0
74	5.0	10.0	3.1	3.4	3.4	5.3	.7	8.8
75	4.3	5.2	4.0	4.0	5.1	5.3	3.4	3.2
76	4.4	4.1	7.4	5.1	6.4	7.2	−2.0	2.8
77	4.7	4.1	4.7	1.5	6.1	6.9	1.5	8.2
78	4.5	8.5	4.2	4.0	1.3	1.5	6.6	5.6
79	2.7	−7.0	5.1	3.0	7.9	11.9	−1.4	−.6
80	2.7	4.0	2.0	3.5	3.5	6.7	−3.2	2.7
81	4.0	2.9	6.5	−.8	1.5	6.9	9.4	1.8
82	3.1	.9	−.9	3.0	2.1	5.9	4.1	6.6
83	3.8	7.1	5.8	3.8	−2.2	5.4	.7	6.3
84	3.4	1.7	4.2	3.1	5.2	5.1	4.9	−.4
85	4.4	3.4	4.4	3.7	3.6	5.8	2.3	7.8
86	2.6	1.1	1.7	6.5	2.8	1.0	−.2	5.3
87	3.3	5.2	2.0	−.8	.3	4.4	5.0	7.3
88	3.0	4.7	2.7	.7	3.9	4.3	3.2	1.6
89	3.1	3.5	−1.5	3.0	1.8	5.3	1.5	8.0
90	3.0	.5	6.1	1.7	2.5	6.2	4.6	−.4
91	1.4	2.2	1.9	.7	−.3	4.0	1.6	−.1
92	2.4	2.1	.1	2.1	.4	7.4	−.8	5.2
93	3.2	1.5	2.6	3.2	2.6	4.7	3.2	4.4
94	(a)	2.7	−.5	−3.3	−3.1	.8	1.5	2.0
95	2.6	.9	5.0	.8	5.7	6.4	−2.1	1.3
96	4.1	2.2	2.0	3.8	3.1	4.1	8.1	5.4
97	1.8	−.0	.4	−.8	2.5	3.6	1.2	5.4
98	−.2	3.1	−.3	−4.0	−1.9	3.4	.2	−1.6
99	2.7	6.2	.9	3.0	−1.4	2.8	3.6	4.0
100	2.4	2.9	.2	.2	1.3	5.4	3.3	3.0
Average of farms	5.4	4.9	4.8	3.5	4.2	6.7	6.2	7.7
Maximum	9.9	13.5	11.5	11.6	9.0	13.7	17.6	18.4
Minimum	−.2	−7.0	−1.5	−4.0	−3.1	−.1	−3.2	−1.6
Index [1]	100	91	89	65	78	124	115	143

a Less than one-tenth of 1 per cent.
[1] Represents the percentage the returns each year are of the seven-year average (5.4=100).

FACTORS AFFECTING THE PROFITS OF DIFFERENT FARMS.

Table VIII shows, for each farm, the seven-year average crop area, number of productive animal units, crop yields, live-stock returns per animal, and crop acres per man and per horse, all of which are considered important factors affecting farm profits. The farms are arranged in the table according to the seven-year average labor incomes. A study of this table will show how each farm stood with reference to each of these factors. (An illustration of such study was given for the area in Ohio on p. 22.)

Also certain groups of farms may be studied with reference to these factors, as shown in the lower part of the table. The 10 farms having the highest seven-year average labor incomes averaged 195 acres of crops, as compared with 86 acres for the 10 farms having the lowest seven-year average labor incomes. The highest-labor-income farms had 45 productive animal units per farm, as against 18 for the lowest-labor-income farms. The crop yields of the former farms were 6 per cent above the average of all farms, while those of the latter were 12 per cent below the average. The live-stock returns per animal for the farms with the highest labor incomes were 19 per cent above the average, while those for the farms with lowest labor incomes were 23 per cent below the average. The former group of farms worked 23 crop acres more per man and 7 crop acres more per horse than the latter group. The 10 farms with highest labor incomes averaged $1,659 per farm; but the farms with lowest labor incomes lacked $273 of paying 5 per cent interest on the capital, thus leaving nothing for the farmer's own labor save the food products, fuel, and house rent furnished by the farm.

TABLE VIII.—*The 7-year-average labor income, crop area, pasture area, productive animal units, crop yields, live-stock returns, and crop acres per man and per horse for each of the 100 farms, Clinton County, Ind., 1910 and 1913–1918.*

Rank of each farm in 7-year average labor income.	Average labor income.	Average crop area.	Average acres in pasture.	Average number productive animal units.	Per cent crop yields were of average for all farms.	Per cent live-stock returns per animal were of the average for all farms.	Crop acres per man.	Crop acres per horse.	Per cent of total farm receipts from crops.
1	$2,210	216	19	31	109	118	92	25	48
2	2,071	182	49	43	99	114	84	26	34
3	1,812	344	93	78	112	131	96	30	29
4	1,704	112	53	52	111	110	47	15	17
5	1,620	204	44	52	112	121	72	26	27
6	1,606	249	58	42	104	121	85	44	43
7	1,454	118	30	31	101	111	91	23	24
8	1,425	195	48	66	98	125	56	24	16
9	1,407	84	22	21	118	131	50	17	32
10	1,280	248	28	35	99	106	73	27	49
11	1,273	87	12	15	117	122	55	19	53
12	1,197	234	70	44	101	85	73	20	54
13	1,149	125	44	28	105	126	54	23	30
14	1,121	80	38	31	100	130	58	15	9
15	1,081	109	29	39	101	114	54	20	22
16	1,071	277	53	26	107	104	96	28	69
17	1,045	90	31	26	103	104	71	23	35
18	1,009	121	31	36	102	114	73	23	19
19	972	68	15	18	101	118	60	21	37
20	940	130	27	23	97	104	76	25	41
21	901	75	24	22	115	102	53	22	27
22	901	85	27	22	110	94	65	27	37
23	868	149	53	49	98	122	59	23	17
24	843	64	7	7	100	83	49	18	64
25	840	99	20	20	107	102	65	23	32
26	820	39	19	24	113	140	37	12	4
27	816	118	22	19	95	99	88	19	45
28	796	63	10	8	91	95	54	24	52
29	793	86	49	33	107	137	42	14	9
30	789	58	16	11	118	91	50	22	57
31	767	63	17	18	107	111	54	21	19
32	748	164	37	19	99	85	75	22	57
33	720	47	22	15	108	116	42	16	21
34	710	97	37	29	110	111	45	18	12
35	704	97	24	17	92	110	71	18	39
36	700	87	21	23	109	88	50	22	34
37	656	54	19	23	114	112	40	16	8
38	647	48	15	15	108	141	41	14	21
39	640	37	9	11	93	109	34	13	25
40	596	85	20	20	117	107	49	15	37

TABLE VIII.—*The 7-year-average labor income, crop area, pasture area, productive animal units, crop yields, live-stock returns, and crop acres per man and per horse for each of the 100 farms, Clinton County, Ind., 1910 and 1913–1918*—Continued.

Rank of each farm in 7-year average labor income.	Average labor income.	Average crop area.	Average acres in pasture.	Average number productive animal units.	Per cent crop yields were of average for all farms.	Per cent live-stock returns per animal were of the average for all farms.	Crop acres per man.	Crop acres per horse.	Per cent of total farm receipts from crops.
41	$591	123	13	13	92	85	87	24	61
42	564	82	15	15	91	108	68	27	37
43	554	61	27	23	90	84	46	16	19
44	549	43	13	18	113	121	30	16	6
45	535	69	18	14	85	116	59	22	42
46	535	96	34	32	92	115	53	20	16
47	532	133	10	13	106	133	96	25	53
48	527	60	19	6	116	120	53	35	65
49	527	105	35	30	111	91	46	17	22
50	502	123	50	36	108	124	60	18	23
51	491	64	9	7	107	109	61	24	44
52	481	70	11	3	78	43	69	17	85
53	473	74	17	16	105	88	67	26	33
54	467	61	4	4	88	63	48	21	74
55	458	54	13	10	105	107	32	16	42
56	457	103	7	7	92	89	74	23	71
57	446	62	15	9	102	91	56	16	57
58	440	111	33	27	109	107	57	18	29
59	400	92	22	15	102	101	68	22	37
60	369	78	28	16	81	115	72	18	24
61	368	41	4	5	98	80	38	17	54
62	359	68	29	15	108	83	56	29	48
63	340	58	16	10	100	110	47	15	39
64	338	76	16	12	110	104	52	16	48
65	330	89	24	16	84	111	61	20	29
66	312	67	14	9	105	89	52	29	55
67	310	49	14	10	107	111	37	14	34
68	281	59	14	12	97	106	51	15	29
69	274	62	37	17	95	93	43	16	24
70	265	26	10	6	85	86	24	10	41
71	258	67	11	12	109	94	59	16	37
72	255	101	34	18	100	99	69	23	38
73	253	96	30	15	102	106	64	17	37
74	249	68	26	16	89	96	49	17	29
75	218	75	41	26	99	115	59	14	9
76	213	41	4	4	88	67	38	13	67
77	207	18	14	8	79	98	18	8	10
78	166	102	35	27	96	96	49	13	19
79	154	28	4	5	89	73	23	13	50
80	143	19	6	7	89	68	17	10	41
81	137	15	1	6	111	65	15	6	18
82	135	28	12	12	99	101	27	9	18
83	132	59	9	10	89	70	50	26	50
84	116	65	10	10	90	96	56	20	47
85	65	103	30	18	110	91	49	26	46
86	28	53	17	11	80	84	39	13	37
87	10	57	20	14	104	99	36	15	21
88	4	60	10	6	103	100	53	17	58
89	−7	66	17	19	108	86	44	15	24
90	−20	83	37	25	82	112	54	13	10
91	−26	23	7	5	103	56	23	9	53
92	−67	62	15	12	84	75	53	18	39
93	−132	49	30	17	90	107	38	15	17
94	−224	31	23	9	64	68	27	8	10
95	−244	86	20	6	83	62	68	29	75
96	−262	248	84	42	99	98	93	30	41
97	−270	65	35	13	86	90	43	21	26
98	−312	51	25	9	89	40	33	21	53
99	−387	128	47	30	100	93	60	19	27
100	−802	121	92	37	86	78	84	19	22
Average, all farms	558	93	26	20	100	100	56	20	36
Average, highest 10	1,659	195	44	45	106	119	75	26	32
Average, lowest 10	−273	86	38	18	88	77	52	19	36

Farms may also be grouped with reference to each of the fa shown in the table. If they be grouped with reference to the nu of crop acres, it will be found that of the 20 farms leading in nu of crop acres 15 had labor incomes higher than the average incomes of the 100 farms, and 5 had labor incomes below the ave while of the 20 farms lowest in number of crop acres only fou labor incomes above the average and 16 below the average.

A comparison of the labor incomes of the 20 farms highe amount of live stock (productive animal units) with the lowes shows that 15 of the former group and only 2 of the latter grou labor incomes above the average.

Fourteen of the 20 farms highest in crop yields had labor inc above the average, while each of the 20 farms lowest in crop failed to reach the average labor income of the region.

By selecting the 20 farms with the highest returns from live per animal and the 20 with lowest returns per animal, we find th farms of the former group and only 3 farms of the latter grou labor incomes above the average of that of the 100 farms.

Selecting the 20 farms having the highest number of crop acre man and the 20 farms having the lowest, we find that of the highe fifteen had labor incomes above the average, and of the lowest 2C 3 had labor incomes above the average.

Ten of the 20 farms leading in number of crop acres per hors above the average labor income, while only five of the 20 low crop acres per horse had more than the average labor income.

When making studies of Table VIII it should be kept in that the data shown therein represent a seven-year average for farm, so that the influence of any condition of uncommon occur on a given farm is largely eliminated.

The data in Table VIII also lend themselves to an intere study in range in crop yields, live-stock returns and crop acre man and per horse, since it is based upon an average of seven results. Crop yields did not exceed 18 per cent above the avera any farm, and only three were 20 per cent or more below the ave Live-stock returns show a wider range; the farm with the hi returns was 40 per cent above the average and that with the l 60 per cent below. On the latter farm, however, 53 per of the owner's receipts were from the sale of crops. The fa who receives the greater part of his income from his live will seldom fall below 75 per cent of the average returns i locality when averaged for a period of years, but for any one the variation both in live-stock returns or crop yields may be pronounced. On one farm an average of 96 acres of crops per and 30 per horse were worked and the yields were 12 per cent

. the average. This was a large farm, with 344 acres in crops, and 29 per cent of the total receipts were from crop sales. On another farm only 15 acres per man and 6 acres per horse were worked. This was a very small farm and a part of the operator's time with his team was spent at outside work.

THE WISCONSIN AREA.

The area in Wisconsin is more or less typical of dairying in southern Wisconsin, and is located but a few miles west of Madison. The surface is rolling to hilly and only the main wagon roads are improved.

THE FARM BUSINESS.

A summary of the farm business for the 60 farms over the five-year period 1913 to 1917 is shown in Table IX.

DISTRIBUTION OF THE FARM AREA.

The farms averaged 148 acres, with 51 acres in pasture, 28 acres in corn, 25 acres in oats, and 22 acres in hay. Ninety-two per cent of the crop land was occupied by these three crops.

In figure 14 the distribution of the farm area is shown graphically for the average of the 60 farms over the five-year period. The crop area occupied 54 per cent of the farm area, tillable pasture 19 per cent, untillable pasture 7 per cent, woodland not pastured 9 per cent, and waste, roads, building lots, etc., 6 per cent. There was practically no difference in the distribution for the various years.

Figure 15 shows graphically the average distribution of the crop area. The three leading crops in the organization of these farms are corn, oats, and hay. For four out of the five years the proportion of the crop acreage devoted to these crops was remarkably uniform. In 1916 the corn acreage was short and the hay acreage was increased. The acreage of oats was also increased slightly this year. There was a great variation in the way in which the corn crop had to be utilized in this area. For the years 1913, 1914, 1915, and 1916 the greater share of the crop was harvested for grain. In 1915 and 1917, owing to early frosts, the greater share was cut as fodder corn. The acreage put in the silo increased during the period of study.

CROP YIELDS.

The five-year average yield of corn was 28 bushels per acre, of oats 33 bushels, and of hay 1.7 tons. The yield of corn varied from 19 bushels per acre in 1915 to 36 bushels in 1913. The yield of oats showed less variation than that of corn, ranging from 26 bushels per acre in 1914 to 37 bushels in 1917. Only 2 per cent of the total production of corn was sold, 5 per cent of the oats, and 3 per cent of the hay. Thus practically all the crops grown were fed on the farms and the crop sales were only 3 per cent of the total farm receipts.

TABLE IX.—*Summary of the farm business over a period of five years, 1913–1917, Verona township and adjoining townships, Dane County, Wis. (average of 60 farms).*

	1913	1914	1915	1916	1917	5-year average.
Acres per farm..............................	149	150	146	147	147	148
Acres in pasture...........................	52	52	50	51	51	51
Acres in corn..............................	29	29	29	26	29	28
Acres in oats..............................	25	25	26	27	24	25
Acres in hay..............................	22	22	21	24	23	22
Acres in other crops......................	6	5	4	3	5	6
Corn per acre..................bushels..	36	32	19	34	23	28
Oats per acre......................do....	32	26	35	36	37	33
Hay per acre......................tons..	1.8	1.7	1.6	1.6	1.9	1.7
Productive animal units..................	30.5	30.8	30.1	31.3	30.7	30.7
Brood sows....................number..	7.6	7.6	6.7	6.2	6.6	6.9
Cows.............................do....	15.6	16.3	16.5	17.7	18.6	16.9
Work stock.......................do....	4.6	4.7	4.7	4.8	4.9	4.7
Receipts per animal unit................	60	57	60	76	101	71
Total labor....................months..	22.1	22.9	21.5	22.9	23.0	22.5
Farm capital.............................	$17,307	$17,596	$17,451	$17,803	$18,305	$17,692
Real estate............................	14,762	14,829	14,641	14,847	14,928	14,802
Live stock.............................	1,740	1,918	1,965	2,101	2,359	2,016
Machinery.............................	462	473	480	489	500	481
All other..............................	343	376	365	366	518	393
Real estate per acre.....................	99	99	100	101	101	100
Receipts.................................	1,961	$1,841	$1,858	$2,560	$3,278	$2,300
Sources (per cent).....................						
Dairy products........................	42	45	49	50	53	49
Hogs..................................	33	30	25	27	28	28
Cattle.................................	12	14	17	14	12	14
Poultry...............................	4	4	4	4	3	4
All other..............................	9	7	5	5	4	5
Expenses................................	$882	$906	$917	$1,043	$1,288	$1,007
	Per cent.	Per cent.	Per cent.	Per cent.	Per cent.	Per cent.
Hired labor............................	16	21	18	18	15	18
Unpaid family labor...................	22	20	19	22	21	21
Repairs and depreciation:						
Machinery........................	7	7	7	7	7	7
House............................	4	4	3	3	3	3
Other buildings..................	6	6	7	7	6	6
Repairs, fences........................	3	3	3	2	2	2
Feed purchased.......................	12	10	15	12	17	13
Seed purchased.......................	3	2	2	2	3	3
Fertilizer..............................	(a)	(a)	(a)	(a)	(a)	(a)
Machine work hired..................	4	4	4	5	4	4
Taxes and insurance..................	16	15	15	15	13	15
Other.................................	7	8	7	7	9	8
Farm income............................	$1,079	$935	$941	$1,517	$1,990	$1,293
Interest on capital, 5 per cent..........	865	879	873	891	915	885
Labor income..........................	214	56	68	626	1,075	408
Operator's labor........................	401	429	443	479	575	465
Return on capital, per cent.............	3.9	2.9	2.9	5.8	7.7	4.7
Value of family labor...................	192	185	175	232	276	211
Interest on indebtedness [1].............	115	115	115	115	115	115
Family income.........................	1,156	1,005	1,001	1,634	2,151	1,389
Family living from farm [2].............	351	356	342	388	525	392
Amount sold:						
Milk......................pounds..	67,080	74,165	78,788	81,420	80,910	76,473
Hogs.................................	39.8	35.0	33.8	30.2	33.5	34.5
Calves...............................	8.8	8.4	9.4	9.3	11.9	9.6
Prices:						
Milk...............hundredweight.	1.23	1.12	1.16	1.58	2.16	1.46
Hogs...........................do...	7.36	7.36	6.51	8.72	15.73	9.14
Calves...............................	8.86	8.72	9.77	12.31	13.28	10.59

a Less than one per cent.

[1] Data for "interest on indebtedness" obtained in 1913 and assumed to be the same for the other years.
[2] From U. S. Department of Agriculture Bulletin 410 and index numbers for "cost of living" published by the "Annalist."

AMOUNT OF LIVE STOCK.

The amount of live stock per farm, expressed in terms of mature cattle, was 30.7 head, besides an average of 4.7 work horses. This is an average of one head to each 4.4 acres of crops and pasture. The

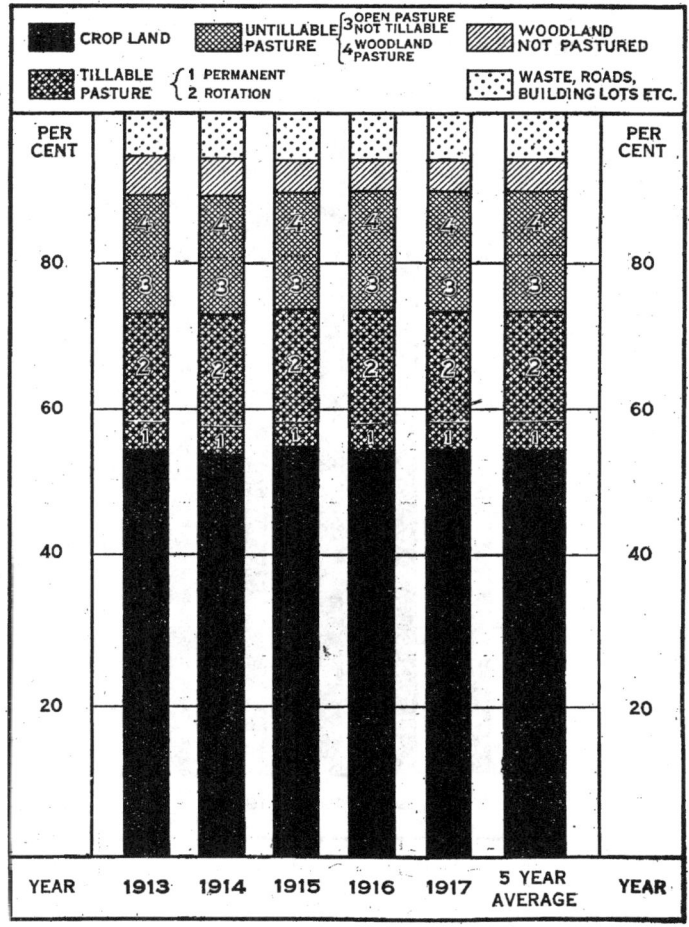

Fig. 14.—Distribution of farm area on 60 farms in Verona township, Dane County, Wis. About three-fourths of the land area on these farms is tillable. The utilization of the farm area for crops and pasture was nearly identical for each year. Most of the pasture and crop areas are used in supporting the dairy herd.

live stock consists mostly of dairy cows and accompanying young
stock. From 1913 there has been a gradual increase in the number

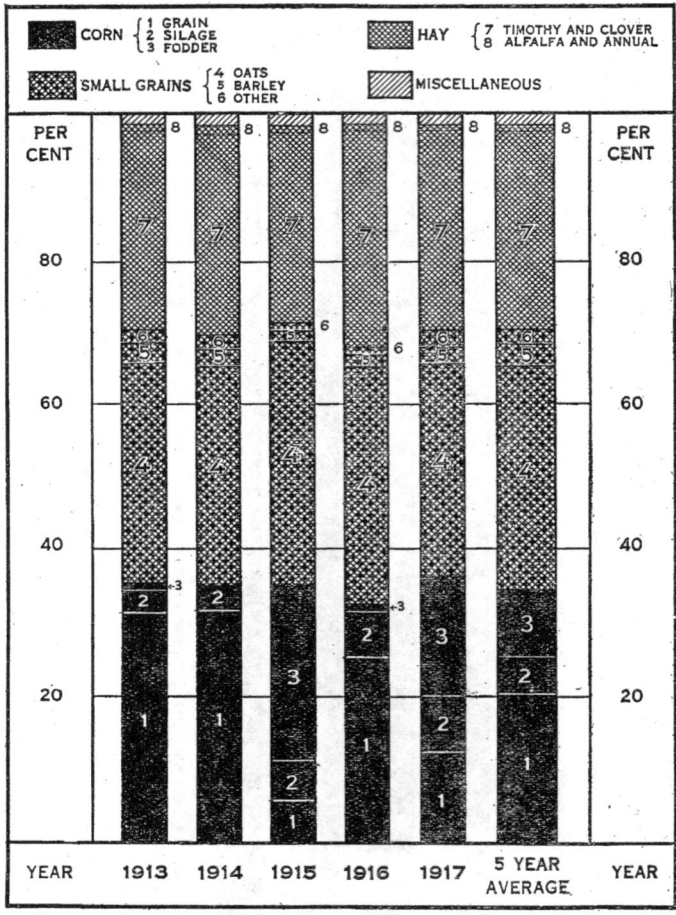

FIG. 15—Distribution of crop area on 60 farms in Verona township, Dane County, Wis. Corn, oats, and
hay are the leading crops. The season has a great influence upon the practices for various years in
handling the corn crop. The years of poorest corn yields were 1915 and 1917.

of cows and some decrease in the number of brood sows. Comparing the first two years with the last two, cows increased 14 per cent
and brood sows decreased 16 per cent.

LABOR REQUIRED.

It required 22.5 months of labor per year to operate these farms, 12 months for the farmer himself, 4.4 months for hired labor, and 6.1 months for family labor. Thus 80 per cent of the work was done by the operator and his family, and 20 per cent hired.

FARM CAPITAL.

The capital value of these farms for the five-year period averaged $17,692; 84 per cent of which was in real estate, 11 per cent in live stock, 3 per cent in machinery, and 2 per cent in supplies and cash. Real estate averaged $100 per acre. The value of land, exclusive of buildings, averaged $12,137 per farm, or 69 per cent of the total farm capital.

RECEIPTS.

The farm receipts in this area (Table IX) averaged $2,300 per farm for the five-year period. They were higher in 1913 ($1,961) than in either 1914 or 1915, due primarily to the decline in the price of milk for these two years. In 1916 the price of milk was advanced, and this together with an increase in the number of cows raised the receipts to $2,560 per farm. In 1917 these same factors aided in increasing the receipts to $3,278 per farm.

Figure 16 shows graphically the average distribution of receipts for each year and for the average of the five-year period. This chart shows the great importance of the live-stock business in the organization of these farms. In 1913 fully 93 per cent of the total income was from live stock, with 4 per cent from crops, while in 1917 live stock represented 96 per cent of the total receipts and crops only 2 per cent. The sale of dairy products heads the list of receipts. In 1913 42 per cent of the income was from this source, and this percentage increased during the period to 53 per cent in 1917. A decrease in the number of hogs for sale was mainly responsible for the decrease in the proportion of receipts from hogs.

EXPENSES.

The expenses connected with operating these farms, above those of interest on capital and the value of the farmer's own labor, averaged $1,007 for the five-year period, increasing from $882 per farm in 1913 to $1,288 in 1917. The largest four items of expense, in order, were family labor, hired labor, taxes and insurance, and feed purchased. These four represented two-thirds of the total expense.

In figure 17 is shown the relation of each of the more important items of expense to the total. The increase in expenses during the period had little effect upon the relative importance of the various items. The poor corn yields in 1915 and 1917 increased the expense for purchased feed these years.

FARM EARNINGS.

The farm income for the five-year period averaged $1,293 p
farm. For two years the average was less than $1,000, and for tl
last two years it exceeded $1,500. The five-year labor incon

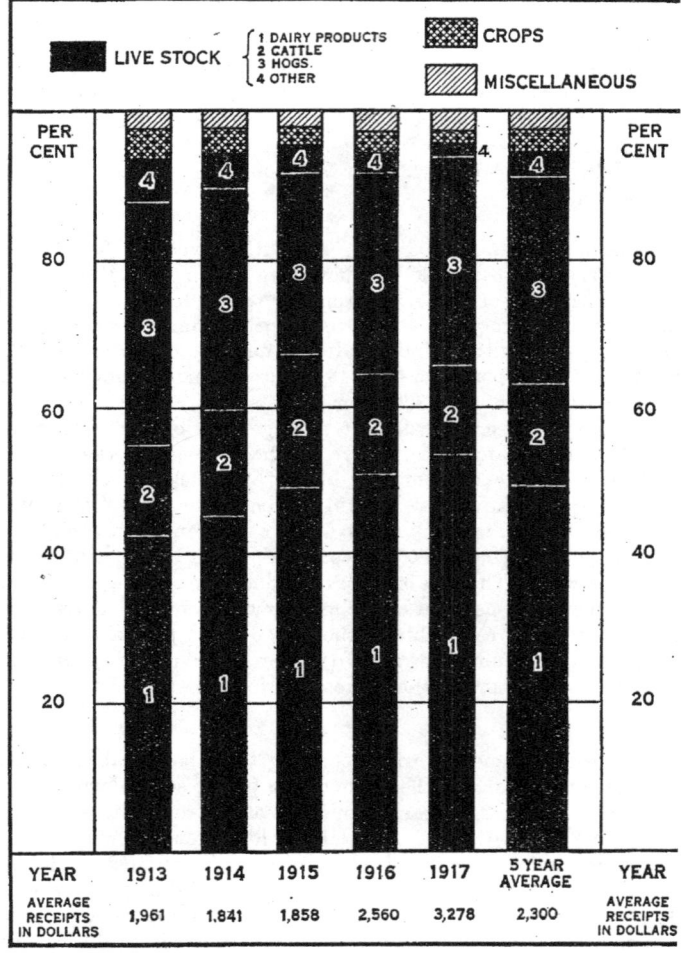

FIG. 16.—Distribution of receipts on 60 farms in Verona and adjoining townships, Dane County, Wis.
1913 live stock returned 93 per cent of the farm receipts, and in 1917 96 per cent. Five-sixths of t
income was from the dairy herd and hogs, the receipts from dairy products showing the greatest g
over the period of study.

averaged $408, ranging from $56·in 1914 to $1,075 in 1917. The return on farm capital averaged 4.7 per cent, ranging from less than 3 per cent in 1914 and 1915, to 7.7 per cent in 1917. Beginning with the year 1916, prices of farm products sold showed a marked

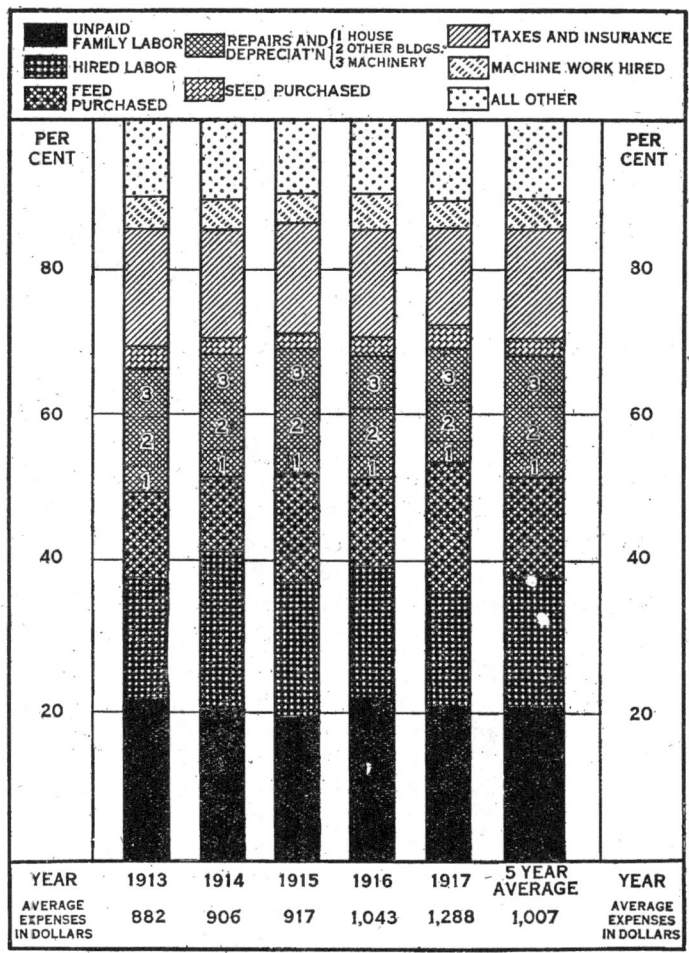

FIG. 17.—Distribution of expenses on 60 farms in Verona and adjoining townships, Dane County, Wis. Family labor is a considerable item on these farms. The poor corn yield in 1915 and 1917 (see Table IX) made an increased feed expense necessary for these years. Expenses increased 46 per cent over the period of study, but the relative importance of the various items made only slight change.

increase, and while the average labor income of the 60 farmers for the three years 1913, 1914, and 1915 was but $113, for the two years 1916 and 1917 it was $850. The return on capital for the earlier period was 3.2 per cent and for the latter period 6.8 per cent.

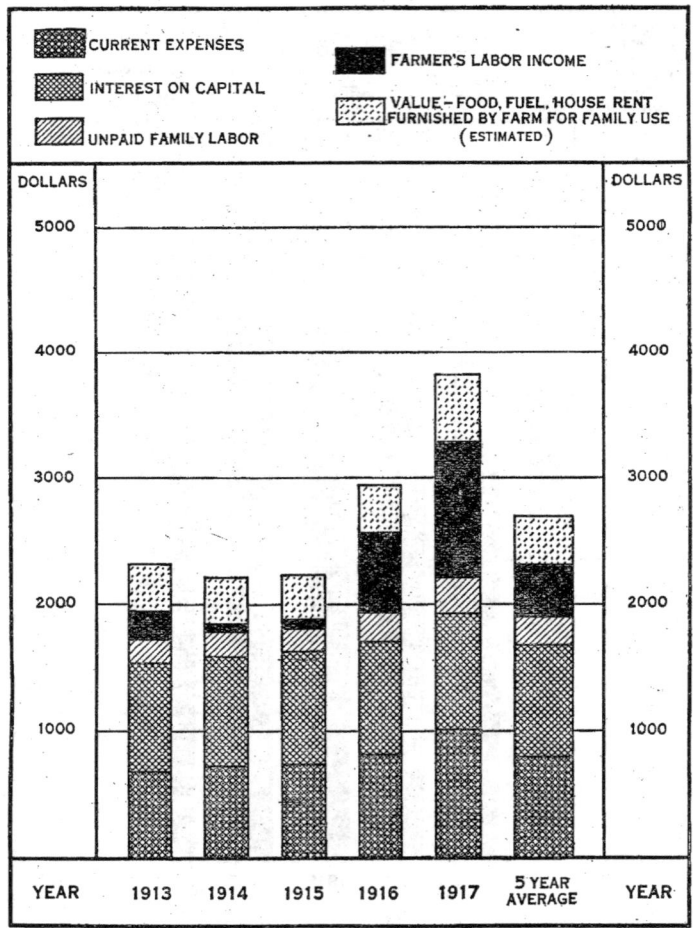

FIG. 18.—Distribution of the gross income on 60 farms in Verona and adjoining townships, Dane County, Wis., 1913-1917. In 1916 and 1917 receipts increased more than expenses, which left the farmer more pay for his own year's wages (labor income) than for former years. This distribution of income shows how farmers may have a considerable income to spend even in years with low labor incomes. If free from debt the interest on investment and value of family labor may give the farm family considerable income to dispose of.

Figure 18 shows graphically the distribution of the average gross income on the 60 farms for each year and for the five-year average. This chart shows how much of the gross income is represented in operating expenses, interest on capital, unpaid family labor, and food products, fuel, and house rent furnished by the farm. As in the case of both the Ohio and Indiana groups, both receipts and expenses increased materially during the last two years, the former more rapidly than the latter, so that the spread between the two became wider, thus increasing the farmer's wages (labor income).

The interest on capital averaged $885 per farm for the five-year period, with no appreciable change over the period. The chart shows how it may be possible for some farmers to have fairly large incomes to dispose of, even though their labor incomes may be small. With the farms that are free from debt the item of interest does not have to be paid out and is therefore available for other purposes.

In Wisconsin Experiment Station Bulletin No. 300, the discussion of receipts, expenses, and profits over the period of study in this area is summed up as follows:

In the years 1914 and 1915 both the gross receipts and farm profits fell below the level of 1913. In 1916, the year prior to our entering the war, farm receipts increased appreciably and were followed by a still greater increase in 1917.

In both of these years the expenses increased, but not so rapidly as the income; hence there was an increasing proportion of the gross income left for the farmer's profits, or labor income.

The study shows that the higher profits of 1916 were due in part to better crops, but more largely to higher prices, and that the relatively high returns in 1917 must be attributed entirely to high prices, because the crops were poorer.

FAMILY LIVING FROM THE FARM.

The estimated value of the family living from the farm in this area amounted to $392, or nearly as much as the labor income. Owing to advances in prices this value increased from $351 in 1913 to $525 in 1917.

PRODUCTS SOLD AND PRICES RECEIVED.

The lower part of Table IX shows the quantity of the more important products sold and the prices received during the period. The amount of milk sold per farm increased from 67,080 pounds in 1913 to 80,910 pounds in 1917. Comparing the first two years with the last two, the average production of milk per cow increased only 50 pounds, which means that the most of this increased production came from increasing the size of the dairy herd. An average of 34.5 hogs were sold per farm and 2.5 produced for family use.

TABLE X.—*Labor incomes of 60 farms in Verona and adjoining townships, Dane County, Wis., 1913-1917.*

(Ranked according to size of the five-year average labor income.)

Rank.	5-year average.	1913	1914	1915	1916	1917
1	$1,337	$865	$1,322	$111	$2,367	$2,018
2	1,164	2,773	— 376	863	484	2,076
3	1,137	869	1,413	517	1,088	1,800
4	1,106	469	942	722	1,326	2,070
5	1,044	596	449	517	1,460	2,197
6	1,010	211	238	57	2,438	2,104
7	1,001	908	515	740	842	2,000
8	997	869	459	370	1,507	1,780
9	874	265	920	67	1,555	1,561
10	869	964	— 159	510	1,233	1,797
11	777	411	677	690	892	1,214
12	773	457	± 200	223	2,101	1,286
13	769	209	155	— 54	1,449	2,085
14	756	— 81	94	772	1,644	1,353
15	731	779	— 680	— 650	1,949	2,255
16	703	516	89	120	1,071	1,719
17	684	1,619	839	88	— 140	1,013
18	642	343	188	524	884	1,273
19	603	514	— 179	— 248	1,174	1,756
20	598	— 50	— 302	270	1,166	1,907
21	565	201	31	97	196	2,298
22	557	777	324	121	262	1,299
23	529	236	21	277	857	1,255
24	524	224	142	250	795	1,210
25	512	112	378	369	561	1,141
26	468	424	— 151	128	567	1,374
27	456	779	247	— 256	587	924
28	441	528	263	185	611	618
29	421	— 27	— 269	310	679	1,411
30	416	7	254	— 87	384	1,522
31	402	266	302	472	274	694
32	367	552	— 55	24	669	647
33	349	283	159	— 56	483	874
34	342	— 714	— 455	368	875	1,634
35	331	— 50	— 72	88	647	1,041
36	313	236	156	— 46	430	790
37	252	69	13	3	490	684
38	246	30	— 117	— 176	102	1,391
39	239	1	365	294	407	858
40	233	— 98	148	162	— 15	968
41	221	417	249	— 49	— 41	53
42	206	196	417	— 227	260	384
43	201	— 17	199	— 102	117	708
44	192	— 201	— 406	— 363	540	1,390
45	182	— 50	— 91	360	286	406
46	175	— 188	220	— 146	194	797
47	137	158	— 149	423	130	122
48	98	— 45	— 115	109	478	64
49	89	± 38	24	— 204	217	197
50	22	— 129	— 457	485	103	109
51	— 20	— 118	— 94	— 340	357	93
52	— 37	— 5	266	— 308	— 152	547
53	— 57	11	— 48	— 258	— 410	420
54	— 100	— 301	330	— 47	102	77
55	— 161	— 531	591	— 687	910	93
56	— 310	— 567	386	— 637	— 443	481
57	— 315	— 275	434	— 423	— 312	131
58	— 347	— 1,584	317	— 927	— 162	1,253
59	— 593	— 490	964	— 455	— 660	— 397
60	— 598	— 747	574	— 866	— 267	534
Average	408	214	56	68	626	1,075
Maximum	1,337	2,773	1,413	863	2,438	2,298
Minimum	— 598	— 1,584	— 964	— 927	— 660	534
Index [1]	100	52	14	17	154	264

[1] Represents the percentage the labor income each year is of the seven-year average ($408=100).

TABLE XI.—*Per cent return on capital on 60 farms in Verona and adjoining townships, Dane County, Wis., 1913–1917.*

(Ranked according to size of the 5-year average labor income).

Rank.	5-year average.	1913	1914	1915	1916	1917
1	7.2	5.9	7.0	4.0	10.3	9.0
2	6.6	12.2	2.0	5.8	4.4	9.0
3	8.6	6.9	8.7	5.1	8.8	13.2
4	8.2	4.9	7.6	6.3	9.8	12.6
5	7.4	6.1	4.7	5.1	9.2	11.7
6	6.8	4.5	4.4	3.7	11.7	10.0
7	8.2	8.4	4.8	6.6	6.9	14.1
8	6.2	6.2	4.4	4.0	8.1	8.1
9	6.1	4.3	7.5	3.1	10.4	5.3
10	6.0	6.5	2.9	5.0	7.1	8.6
11	6.9	5.2	9.0	9.0	10.2	1.4
12	6.9	5.6	2.0	4.2	13.5	9.4
13	6.5	4.1	3.7	2.5	11.0	11.0
14	5.9	2.9	3.7	6.1	9.3	7.6
15	5.5	6.0	1.2	1.3	9.4	9.8
16	6.0	5.6	3.3	3.4	7.6	10.3
17	5.3	8.4	5.9	3.8	3.2	5.3
18	5.3	4.4	3.1	4.9	6.5	7.5
19	5.4	5.3	1.5	1.2	8.4	10.6
20	5.7	2.2	.7	4.1	8.9	12.4
21	6.2	3.7	.9	1.5	2.9	22.0
22	4.8	6.6	4.0	2.8	3.3	7.5
23	5.7	4.0	2.8	4.3	7.7	9.6
24	5.2	2.7	1.0	2.1	8.4	11.8
25	5.0	2.7	4.3	4.1	5.4	8.6
26	5.1	5.1	1.9	3.2	5.6	9.6
27	4.5	6.5	3.6	1.0	4.9	6.6
28	5.8	6.3	4.2	3.6	7.0	8.0
29	4.6	2.7	1.5	4.5	5.8	8.5
30	5.0	2.8	4.2	2.4	5.2	10.4
31	5.0	4.7	4.6	5.3	4.5	5.7
32	3.3	6.5	−1.7	−1.4	7.3	5.6
33	4.0	4.0	3.0	1.5	4.9	6.8
34	3.5	− 1.7	− .2	4.0	6.1	9.4
35	3.7	1.1	.5	2.0	6.2	8.9
36	4.9	4.3	3.4	1.2	5.8	9.6
37	2.0	.4	− .1	−1.3	4.9	6.0
38	3.4	2.8	1.8	1.5	2.7	8.1
39	3.6	2.2	− .2	4.3	4.7	7.4
40	2.5	− .2	1.8	2.0	1.0	7.8
41	3.5	5.6	3.9	.8	.9	6.4
42	3.5	3.8	5.1	1.3	3.6	3.8
43	3.5	2.0	4.3	1.6	2.8	6.6
44	3.4	1.1	− .5	.2	5.9	10.6
45	3.0	1.7	1.4	5.0	3.4	3.5
46	3.8	2.2	4.3	2.5	4.0	5.9
47	.9	2.0	−4.0	6.4	.6	− .6
48	2.7	2.3	1.6	2.3	5.0	2.2
49	.8	.1	.7	−2.4	3.1	2.3
50	1.5	.3	−2.6	5.8	2.7	1.5
51	.6	.1	.3	−2.1	3.8	.9
52	2.1	3.1	1.8	.3	.5	4.6
53	.9	1.6	1.1	− .7	− 1.8	4.5
54	1.0	− .3	− .3	1.7	2.1	1.6
55	2.6	1.5	1.1	.6	6.4	3.4
56	−2.1	− 3.6	−2.6	−4.8	− 3.3	4.0
57	−2.4	− 1.2	−3.0	−3.5	− 2.5	− 1.6
58	2.6	− 1.4	2.8	.9	3.3	7.3
59	−1.1	− .1	−3.2	− .1	− 1.7	− .3
60	.7	.4	.9	− .5	2.1	.6
Average of farms	4.2	3.4	2.4	2.6	5.3	7.2
Maximum	8.6	12.2	9.0	9.0	13.5	22.0
Minimum	−2.4	− 3.6	−4.0	−4.8	− 3.3	− 1.6
Index [1]	100	81	57	62	126	171

[1] Represents the percentage the returns each year are of the seven-year average (4.2=100).

The price received for milk greatly affects the farm returns in
area. As previously pointed out, the decline in the price of
for the years 1914 and 1915 was the largest single factor tendir
decrease the income. Comparing the first two years with the

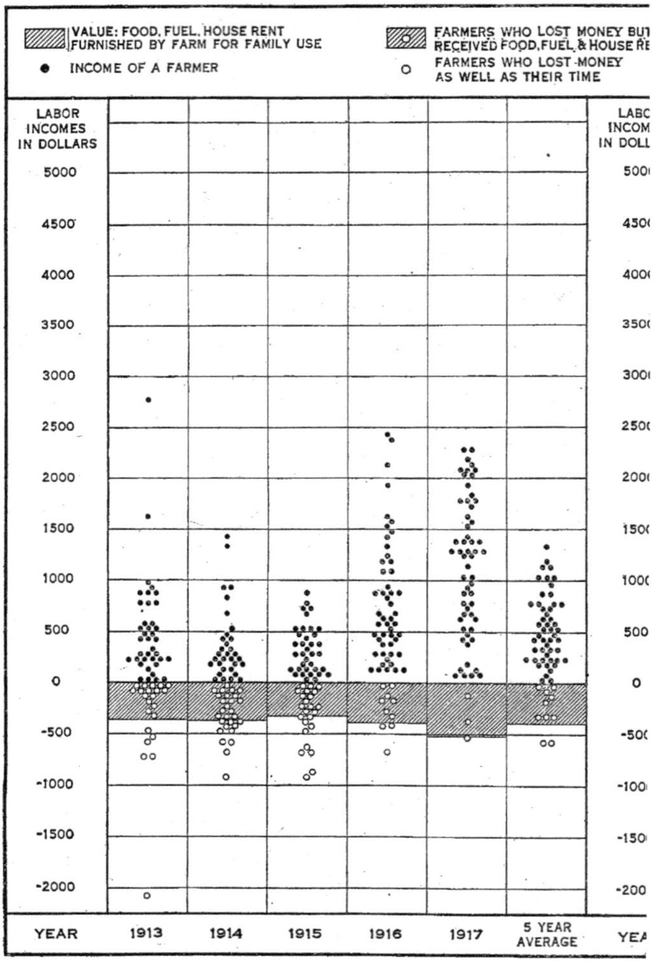

Fig. 19.—The labor incomes of 60 farmers in Verona and adjoining townships, Dane Count;
1913–1917. Each dot represents the labor income of one farmer. The farmers shown in the shad
had only the food products, fuel and house rent, as pay for their own labor, and received a re
capital invested of less than 5 per cent. Those shown below the shaded area had losses in addition

two, milk increased 59 per cent in price and farm receipts increased
.54 per cent.

LABOR INCOME AND RETURN ON CAPITAL OF THE 60 FARMS OVER THE FIVE-YEAR PERIOD.

Tables X and XI show the labor income and return on capital of
each of the 60 farmers over the five-year period 1913–1917, arranged
in order of the five-year average labor income. The labor incomes
are also shown graphically in figure 19.

It will be noted from Table X that nineteen of the 60 farmers made
a labor income each year, 15 for four and 15 for three of the five
years, 5 for two years, and 3 for one year, and that 3 did not make
a labor income in any of the five years.

None of the farmers reached $1,000 labor income every year of the
period. Two farmers had over $1,000 labor income each for three
years; 15 for two years, 16 for one year, and 27 never reached $1,000
labor income.

Two farmers made over $500 labor income every year, while 13
failed to reach $500 any year. In 1913, 1 farmer had over $2,000
labor income; in 1914, 2 farmers each had over $1,000 labor income,
but none had as much as $1,000 labor income in 1915. In 1916, 15
farmers had over $1,000 labor income and 3 of these exceeded $2,000.
In 1917, 33 had over $1,000 labor income, and of these 8 exceeded
$2,000. None of the 60 farmers ever reached the $3,000 mark in
labor income.

For the five-year average, only 7 farmers exceeded $1,000 labor
income, but none reached $2,000; that of 18 farmers ranged from
$500 to $1,000; that of the other 35 was less than $500, and 10 of these
had no labor income.

About one-tenth of these farmers received in labor income each
year as much or more than they valued their labor worth in addition
to farm-furnished supplies, about five-tenths for half of the years,
and four-tenths for less than two of the five years. Seventeen of
these farmers received in labor income what they considered their
labor worth in 1913, 5 in 1914, 9 in 1915, 31 in 1916, and 45 in 1917.

It will be noted from Table XI that 25 of the 60 farmers made over
5 per cent interest on the capital invested, and that but 3 of
these exceeded 8 per cent. Only one farmer made better than 5 per
cent every year, while two failed to make 2 per cent in any year.

FACTORS AFFECTING THE PROFITS OF DIFFERENT FARMS.

Table XII shows for each of the 60 farms the crop area, number
of productive animal units, crop yields, live-stock returns, and the
number of crop acres per man and per horse. This table indicates
the rewards in labor income to those farmers with well-organized and
efficiently operated business, as compared with those inefficiently
managed.

TABLE XII.—*The 5-year average labor income, crop area, pasture area, productive animal units, live-stock returns, and crop acres per man and per horse for each of 60 farms, Dane County, Wis., 1913–1917.*

Rank of each farm in 5-year average labor income.	Average labor income.	Average crop area.	Average acres in pasture.	Average number productive animal units.	Per cent crop yields were of average.	Per cent live-stock returns per animal were of the average.	Crop acres per man.	Crop acres per horse.	Per cent of total farm receipts from crops.
1	$1,337	132	131	66	93	112	56	17	0.4
2	1,164	133	92	59	113	106	51	17	2.1
3	1,137	76	53	42	100	110	30	13	.7
4	1,106	59	31	33	95	118	38	15	.2
5	1,044	85	59	40	111	99	44	18	3.3
6	1,010	125	85	52	108	101	43	21	4.6
7	1,001	64	14	27	110	115	49	17	.3
8	997	148	74	55	100	91	45	23	.5
9	874	97	55	40	98	107	53	16	3.0
10	869	128	92	54	117	110	44	20	.1
11	777	34	40	20	110	103	28	11	.1
12	773	76	94	35	117	104	41	17	.9
13	769	81	42	30	112	107	52	17	.2
14	756	93	32	33	118	125	54	16	.6
15	731	118	96	60	110	87	47	18	.0
16	703	102	79	42	89	101	49	22	.1
17	684	186	114	62	106	96	60	28	8.6
18	642	73	117	37	91	90	47	17	.0
19	603	115	99	36	99	132	52	21	1.1
20	598	47	24	29	127	112	24	12	.0
21	565	45	32	12	88	99	38	11	.9
22	557	79	61	31	103	99	55	13	.3
23	529	83	28	30	84	115	39	19	.0
24	524	51	23	19	80	96	41	24	.1
25	512	66	34	28	109	106	33	16	.0
26	468	96	39	32	81	118	46	19	.8
27	456	79	57	29	90	94	48	14	2.2
28	441	69	29	20	96	131	26	22	8.5
29	421	100	54	30	99	130	51	18	1.6
30	416	59	35	23	125	104	47	18	3.0
31	402	118	87	31	88	92	51	21	13.0
32	367	58	19	14	80	106	50	17	1.3
33	349	68	25	28	94	104	37	17	.0
34	342	99	73	50	109	97	36	15	.0
35	331	52	44	22	87	82	40	13	.0
36	313	42	18	17	97	100	25	13	2.1
37	252	49	28	22	104	72	34	17	3.7
38	246	74	68	35	120	108	37	15	.5
39	239	82	89	28	97	94	43	16	.7
40	233	45	23	16	110	114	36	12	6.1
41	221	63	14	6	86	79	55	14	61.6
42	208	66	48	33	90	92	39	14	.0
43	201	74	39	33	108	101	33	14	.0
44	192	80	70	27	89	94	47	20	.0
45	182	74	32	19	92	86	63	24	9.8
46	175	67	75	33	108	101	44	14	.7
47	137	25	12	10	118	96	21	12	1.0
48	98	55	44	23	106	100	41	13	3.7
49	39	41	29	13	89	89	37	13	.2
50	22	61	26	19	92	90	46	20	12.5
51	− 20	43	28	18	108	92	30	11	.0
52	− 37	71	29	22	128	89	42	22	19.3
53	− 57	62	10	16	93	97	45	21	7.9
54	− 100	84	31	23	80	103	56	21	.2
55	− 161	120	49	51	93	84	42	10	.5
56	− 310	60	13	18	88	89	30	20	.3
57	− 315	37	23	10	110	66	31	15	5.1
58	− 347	148	97	43	99	85	51	20	1.6
59	− 593	92	43	27	75	51	44	23	4.5
60	− 598	136	53	24	84	86	54	27	17.7
Average, all farms	408	81	51	31	100	100	43	24	3
Av., highest 10	1,054	105	69	48	104	107	45	18	2
Average, lowest 10	− 254	85	38	24	96	84	42	19	6

Farmer No. 1, with the highest labor income, had a comparatively large business when measured by crop area or by number of animal units, and while his crop yields were 7 per cent below the average, practically his entire income was from live stock, which returned 12 per cent more per head than the average of the region.

Farmer No. 60, with the lowest labor income, had as large a business as did No. 1, when measured by crop area, but much smaller when measured by number of productive animal units. His crop yields were 16 per cent below the average and his returns per head of live stock 14 per cent below the average of the region.

Only 5 of the 60 farmers had over 10 per cent of their receipts from the sale of crops.

Crop yields for the 5-year average showed a range of from 25 per cent below to 28 per cent above the average, and live stock of from 49 per cent below to 32 per cent above the average. The highest acreage of crops reported per man was 63, and the lowest 21. The highest acreage of crops per horse was 28 and the lowest 10.

GOOD MANAGEMENT INCREASES PROFITS.

The aim of this bulletin has been to show actual economic conditions as they existed in the three areas herein discussed. While the average profits in each area were rather low, and while many farmers made very low profits, yet the well-managed farms gave much larger returns, as pointed out previously. Each farmer is given his place on the labor income charts (figs. 7, 13, and 19) for each year. Figure 19 has been discussed in Wisconsin Experiment Station Bulletin No. 300 as follows. (This discussion has also a general application to the findings for the Ohio and Indiana areas.)

This [chart] shows what skill, energy, and good management can do in the way of winning a good labor income at a time when other farmers are losing money. The fact that under most favorable conditions with respect to prices some farmers win no labor income beyond things furnished the family by the farm, helps one to understand why there may be discontent among the farmers when at the same time many farmers are known to be prospering. It is not to be expected that prices will be high enough to give a labor income to the indolent and inefficient, but it is necessary that the industrious, competent farmers be amply paid for their products if the business of farming is to continue to improve.

In farming, as in other occupations, the prizes are for those who have ability. The wide range in labor income shown in figure 19 and more accurately arrayed in Table X, gives evidence that the man of skill, industry, and judgment can hope to earn a handsome income by operating a farm.

This is the ground for hope that there will ever be those who can climb the ladder to independence. But with this hope for the man at the head of the class goes the gloomy outlook for the man at the foot of the class.

The number of farmers who made a minus labor income in the years 1913, 1914, and 1915 is entirely too great. On the average for the five years one out of every six farmers netted a loss ranging from $20 to $598, omitting what the family received from the farm. This would seem to be too high a percentage of submerged farmers even with war prices in 1916 and 1917 to bring up the average for the five years. Yet it must be admitted that under the same conditions more than half the farmers made labor incomes which, when combined with what the farm furnished the family, put them ·in a position to get ahead financially year after year. The future of American agriculture demands that the road be kept open to the top. A high percentage of the young farmers must be able to save from their earnings 'and buy farms.‚ This requires adequate prices, and while there is no law of human justice which demands that prices be so high that the man without ability and willingness to work successfully under his own guidance shall be made to flourish as the manager of a farm, prices should be high enough to give at least five out of six a labor income. It took the prices of 1916 and 1917 to bring the Verona farmers up to this level and to give them a 5-year average labor income of $408.

From the study of the profits of the farms in the three areas we have seen that the incomes of most farmers were much higher during the last few years than for previous years. In this connection it must be remembered, however, that the increase in income is more apparent than real because of the decreased purchasing power of the dollar.

Whether or not farmers have bettered their conditions through this increased income depends upon the way in which the additional income is used. If the additional money is used in better equipping the farm, providing more conveniences, or, in other words, raising the standard of living on the farm and in the farm home, and a more satisfactory rural social life results, the industry and the rural population have been benefited. On the other hand, if this increased income becomes absorbed in increased land value, it may be of immediate advantage to those selling out of the business but may react upon those who purchase farms by going in debt for them. These purchasers must make interest on the investment, enough for their own wages and management, pay living expenses, and make payments upon the principal. The harm comes when men purchase farms with the idea of paying for them out of the results of their labor and management and at the same time maintaining or improving their standard of living, but later find that they are unable to do this because the land values were not based upon what the land yields.

O

UNITED STATES DEPARTMENT OF AGRICULTURE

BULLETIN No. 921

Contribution from the Bureau of Chemistry
CARL L. ALSBERG, Chief

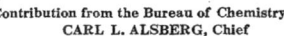

Washington, D. C. ▼ November 9, 1920

SUGAR-CANE JUICE CLARIFICATION FOR SIRUP MANUFACTURE.

By J. K. DALE and C. S. HUDSON.

CONTENTS.

	Page.		Page.
Two methods in general use	1	Vacuum evaporation in making cane	
Disadvantages	2	sirup	12
New method of clarification	2	Use of vegetable decolorizing carbons in connection with infusorial	
Outline of process	2		
Industrial development	2	earth clarification	14
Experimental plant	3	Infusorial earth clarification for	
Operation	3	sugar manufacture	14
Experiments conducted	3	Summary	15
Discussion of results	6		
Economic considerations	7		

TWO METHODS IN GENERAL USE.

Two methods of clarifying sugar-cane juice in the manufacture of cane sirup have been developed and are now in general use in this country. One process, following closely the method of clarification used in the manufacture of direct-consumption sugars and favored principally in the sugar-cane-producing region of southern Louisiana, where sugar also is manufactured, consists essentially in treating the juice, freshly expressed, with fumes of burning sulphur (SO_2) and milk of lime. The juice is heated and the coagulated impurities allowed to settle or removed by settling and skimming, after which the clear liquor is evaporated to sirup in open evaporators or vacuum pans or by a combination of open and vacuum evaporation.

The other and simpler process, used in all cane-sirup-producing regions outside of Louisiana and a small section of Texas, consists in heating the juice and skimming off the scums and coagulated material which rise as the juice becomes hot, forming a thick blanket on the surface. As a rule no chemicals are used in this process, though some sirup makers add a small amount of milk of lime to "make the skimmings rise better." This method requires only the smallest, crudest sort of equipment, but when careful attention is given produces an excellent sirup.

13702°—20

Both of these methods have disadvantages, thereby failing to give entire satisfaction to the sirup manufacturer. The principal disadvantage of the first or Louisiana method is that often the chemicals used in clarification injure the flavor of the sirup, but unless sufficient sulphur dioxid and lime are added to the juice the impurities separate slowly and incompletely. Too much lime makes the sirup very dark and too much sulphur dioxid gives it a metallic taste.

The second and simpler method of clarification is slow and wasteful, and unless very carefully executed the objectionable material is not removed completely. That sirup clarified by these methods is not entirely satisfactory is shown by the fact that it is not sold extensively in many parts of the United States outside of the region where it is made. One of the many reasons for this is that the consuming public of the Northern and Eastern States does not like the flavor of the Louisiana type of cane sirup and objects to the appearance of the sirup made in many parts of the other sirup-producing States.

NEW METHOD OF CLARIFICATION.

The method of clarifying cane juice for sirup manufacture described in this bulletin is the result of experimental work carried out with the object of finding a way to produce a clean sirup that is free from dirt and dregs, and at the same time retains its natural, mild, agreeable flavor.

This process of clarification consists in heating the juice to a temperature just below the boiling point, intimately mixing with it a small amount of infusorial earth (sometimes called kieselguhr or diatomaceous earth), and pumping this mixture of juice and infusorial earth through a filter press. The resulting filtrate is clear and ready for evaporation to sirup. No further skimming or other treatment is necessary. The sirup obtained will be clean, free from dregs, and clearer than sirup clarified by either of the present methods. The color will depend upon the care taken to prevent scorching and caramelization. The flavor will be that of the natural cane juice, since the material added is an inert substance the function of which is to make possible the formation of a porous filter-press cake through which the juice can flow freely, leaving all the scums, dregs, and impurities.

Production of a better sirup in Louisiana and in the other sirup-producing States will follow as a result of the industrial development of this process. A sirup attractive in its appearance and flavor will promote sales and consumption in ever increasing quantities in all parts of the United States.

In the large sirup factories of Louisiana this method of clarification would involve little change or addition to the present equipment. In small steam sirup mills in other parts of the country it would mean the installation of additional equipment, but this outlay of capital would be repaid by the saving in sugar liquor now thrown out or fed to hogs as "skimmings," and also by the improved and more uniform quality of the finished product.

EXPERIMENTAL PLANT.

Before outlining in detail this method of sirup making a description will be given of the experimental plant and equipment used in testing the practicability of clarifying cane juice with infusorial earth. The equipment employed consisted of two tanks fitted with steam coils, each holding slightly over 200 gallons, a duplex $4\frac{1}{2}$ by $2\frac{1}{4}$ by 4 steam pump, and an 18-inch plate and frame filter press having about 80 square feet of filtering area. The two tanks were connected by a header to the intake of the pump with valve arrangement such that the contents of each tank could be pumped separately into the press. This arrangement permitted one tank to be filled with juice and prepared for filtration while the contents of the other were being pumped through the press.

OPERATION.

One tank having been filled with juice, steam was turned into the heating coils and the juice heated to a point just below boiling. The desired amount of infusorial earth was added and mixed thoroughly with the hot juice, after which the mixture of infusorial earth and hot juice was pumped to the filter press. While this tankful of juice was being filtered the second tank was being filled, heated, and treated with infusorial earth so that it immediately followed the first one through the filter press. The process was repeated until filtration became very slow even at a pressure of 40 to 60 pounds, showing that the frames of the filter press had become full. This general procedure was followed in all the experiments.

EXPERIMENTS CONDUCTED.[1]

A more detailed description of some of the experiments follows.

---

[1] The juice used in these experiments was obtained from a sugar mill. The officials of the sugar company also cooperated in the conduct of the work. In most of the experiments the mixed dilute juice was used. The dilution was about 12 per cent, the extraction about 78 per cent, and the average Brix of the dilute juice 13°. In some of the experiments only the crusher juice was used, where the extraction was estimated to be about 40 per cent and the Brix of juice averaged 15°.

EXPERIMENT 1.

Type of juice: Crusher juice, about 40 per cent extraction.
Filtering material: Infusorial earth from Lompoc, Calif.
Amount of filtering material used: 11 pounds to 200 gallons of juice.
Result: 1,065 gallons of juice were filtered with a pressure not exceeding 40
   pounds, forming a very hard, firm press cake.

EXPERIMENT 2.

Type of juice: Crusher juice, about 40 per cent extraction.
Filtering material: Infusorial earth from State of Washington.
Amount of filtering material used: 18 pounds to 200 gallons of juice.
Result: 1,000 gallons of juice filtered rapidly, leaving a firm, well-formed press-
   cake. The filtered juice was bright and clear.

EXPERIMENT 3.

Type of juice: Whole mill dilute juice.
Filtering material: Infusorial earth from Lompoc, Calif.
Amount of filtering material used: 10 pounds to 200 gallons of juice.
Course of filtration:

		Time of filtration.	Pressure.
First	200 gallons	15 minutes.	10 pounds.
Second	200 gallons	15 minutes.	20 pounds.
Third	200 gallons	25 minutes.	30 pounds.
Fourth	200 gallons	40 minutes.	40 pounds.
Fifth	200 gallons	45 minutes.	50 pounds.
Sixth	200 gallons	1 hour 5 minutes.	60 pounds.
	1,200 gallons	3 hours 25 minutes.	

Result: The juice running from the press in this experiment was clear and
   brilliant, free from dirt, dregs, or sediment. It was necessary only to evaporate it to obtain a high-grade sirup. The press cake was very hard with the
   exception of the upper corners, which were a little soft.

EXPERIMENT 4.

Type of juice: Whole mill, dilute juice.
Filtering material: Infusorial earth from Lompoc, Calif.
Amount of filtering material used: 12 pounds to 200 gallons of juice.
Course of filtration:

		Time of filtration.
First	200 gallons	15 minutes.
Second	200 gallons	15 minutes.
Third	200 gallons	15 minutes.
Fourth	200 gallons	30 minutes.
Fifth	200 gallons	45 minutes.
	1,000 gallons.	2 hours.

Maximum pressure, 50 pounds.
Result: During the entire filtration the juice filtered freely and clearly, slow-
   ing up somewhat, however, as the frames became filled. The resulting press
   cake was very firm, each frame being completely filled.

EXPERIMENT 5.

Filtering mater'al: From Lompoc, Calif.
Amount of filtering material used: 11 pounds to 200 gallons of juice.
Result: 1,150 gallons were filtered. The total time of filtration was between 3 and 4 hours, the pressure never rising above 50 pounds. A firm press cake was formed, completely filling the frames.

EXPERIMENT 6.

Filtering material: Infusorial earth from State of Washington.
Amount of filtering material used: 11 pounds to 200 gallons of juice.
Result: 800 gallons ran through rapidly and clearly with a pressure of not over 40 pounds. On attempting to filter more, the pressure ran up rapidly. The press cake was firm, but the frames were filled only three-fourths of the way to the top.

An outline of these experiments is given in Tables 1 and 2.

TABLE 1.—*Filtration of sugar-cane juice with infusorial earth.*

WHOLE MILL JUICE.

Experiment No.	Juice filtered.	Source of infusorial earth.	Amount used.	Maximum pressure.	Time of filtration.	Remarks.
	Gallons.		*Pounds.*	*Pounds.*		
3	1,000	Lompoc, Calif..	60	60	....	Firm press cake formed; clear filtrate.
5	1,200	.....do..........	60	60	3 hours, 25 minutes.	Very firm press cake formed; clear filtrate.
8	1,000	.....do..........	60	50	2 hours......	Very firm press cake; filtration rapid and smooth.
9	1,100	.....do..........	70	50	....	Press cake slightly soft at top.
10	1,200	.....do..........	72	60	....	Very hard press cake; filtration very slow toward the end.
12	1,000	.....do..........	60	40	....	Filtration rapid; filtrate clear and cake firm.
15	1,100	.....do..........	60	60	3 hours, 14 minutes.	Good filtration in all respects.
21	1,100	.....do..........	64	50	4 hours, 15 minutes.	Press cake very firm; filtrate clear.
22	1,150	.....do..........	64	50	....	Filtration satisfactory in all respects.
24	800	State of Washington.	44	High.	....	Frames filled two-thirds with hard press cake; tops of cloths coated with slimy material.

CRUSHER JUICE.

	1,350	Lompoc, Calif..	56	40	....	Firm press cake; clear filtrate.
	1,000	State of Washington.	92	50	....	Very firm press cake; clear filtrate.
	1,000	Lompoc, Calif..	55	....	....	Satisfactory filtration in all respects.
	1,065	.....do..........	58	....	....	Do.
	500	Maryland......	40	High.	....	Unsatisfactory.

TABLE 2.—*Washing of infusorial earth press cake.*

Experiment No.	Weight of press cake.	Sucrose in press cake.	Amount of wash water.	Sucrose in washed cake.	Remarks.
	Pounds.	*Per cent.*	*Gallons.*	*Per cent.*	
....	252	6.4	....	....	These experiments in washing press cake followed filtration experiments of same number as described in Table 1.
....	....	....	200	0.0	
....	252	6.2	50	1.2	
1.................	....	....	25	4.0	
5.................	300	6.5	100	.8	
2.................	....	....	80	1.0	

DISCUSSION OF RESULTS.

These results show that raw cane juice, without the addition of lime, sulphur dioxid, or other chemicals, can be rapidly filtered in an ordinary plate and frame filter press when sufficient infusorial earth of a good grade is added to the heated juice. It is very desirable, however, that the infusorial earth be of very low specific gravity and also of fine mesh. The best results were obtained with commercial grades of infusorial earth obtained from California, Oregon, and Washington. It is also desirable that the infusorial earth be dry and free from lumps and trash. For successful filtration the infusorial earth must be mixed thoroughly with the juice. If it is wet and lumpy it does not mix well, and if it is trashy there is always trouble with the pump valves becoming clogged. However, with a good, clean, dry grade of infusorial earth, such as is at present on the market, no trouble whatever was experienced in obtaining a steady filtration, a firm press cake with each frame entirely filled, and a filtered liquor bright and clear.

Most of these experiments were made by adding a weighed quantity of infusorial earth to 200 gallons of juice. Based upon a 78 per cent extraction obtained by the mill, a dilution of approximately 14 per cent, and the average final Brix of the dilute juice, which was 13°, this volume of juice is almost exactly the amount obtained from 1 ton of cane. With a good quality of infusorial earth 10 pounds to the ton of cane gave a satisfactory filtration. With less than this amount the filtration was slow and there was danger of a slimy, almost impervious, coating forming on the cloths which would retard the rate of filtration.

With 10 pounds of infusorial earth per ton, 1,200 gallons of juice, or that from 6 tons of cane, could be put through the 18-inch 18-frame filter press in about three and one-half hours. Using 12 pounds of this earth to 1 ton of cane, a much more rapid filtration resulted, the juice from 5 to 5½ tons of cane filtering in two to three hours. With 11 pounds of high-grade infusorial earth per ton, satisfactory results were also obtained, the juice from 5 to 6 tons of cane filtering in about four hours. No trouble at all was experienced in obtaining a steady, clear filtration and a firm press cake. It is not well, however, to try to put through the press a larger quantity of juice than will filter readily under moderate pressure. In the press available for these experiments, using 11 pounds of infusorial earth per ton of cane, it was found best not to try to force through more than the amount of juice from 5½ tons of cane. This amount, filtered in about four hours with a pressure not exceeding 40 to 50 pounds, made a hard and firm cake throughout the entire frame. This press cake could be washed easily and thoroughly and peeled readily from the press cloths, leaving them clean and in good condition for another filtration.

By this method of clarification a clean, clear, bright juice was obtained. Only the insoluble material in the original juice or that flocculated by heat was removed, that is, the material which the simple process of straining and skimming attempts to remove and does less thoroughly. After filtration by this method, it was necessary only to evaporate the resulting clear juice to sirup. As no further "skimmings" appeared the full heating capacity of the evaporators could be employed and evaporation was conducted as rapidly as the type of evaporator in use permitted.

The resulting sirup was not absolutely clear, owing to the separation during concentration of material which was soluble in the thin juice, but insoluble in the more concentrated sirup. However, this material formed only a slight cloud in the sirup, which is not objectionable. All the dregs and dirty-looking material which unfortunately are so characteristic of the usual run of cane sirup were removed by the filtration process, making the final sirup clean and pleasing to the eye. The color of the sirup made by this process was much better than that of the average unbleached cane sirup, as no particles of bagasse or other trash were present to stick to the coils or sides of the evaporators and cause discoloration by burning. Also the juice could be cooked to sirup more rapidly, allowing the man in charge to give his whole attention to the evaporation without having to worry about skimming or to take care lest "the skimmings boil in."

After this method of clarifying, the juice is in good condition to be evaporated under diminished pressure in one of the various types of vacuum evaporators, for it is clean and no additional scum forms as the evaporation proceeds.

ECONOMIC CONSIDERATIONS.

A description of a new method or process of manufacture would not be complete if it did not give an estimate of its practicability, convenience, cost, and advantages in comparison with the processes in general use at the present time. For purposes of comparison the prevailing methods of making sirup may be classified into three groups:

1. The method used by the individual farmer who raises only a few acres of cane and makes this cane into sirup by his own labor and that of his hired help. His equipment consists usually of a comparatively small mill, operated either by horsepower or by a gasoline engine. The juice is evaporated in a kettle, home-made vat, or baffle-plate evaporator placed directly over a wood fire. The daily production is seldom over 300 gallons and is often less than 100 gallons.

2. The method employed by the owners of small steam factories regions outside of Louisiana. A number of these factories, scat-red throughout the entire Gulf coastal region from Texas to orida, operate by the general method which the individual farmer ploys with his small equipment, but use steam power and steam-ated coils for evaporating the juice to sirup. They vary in ca-city from a few hundred to several thousand gallons per day.

3. The method employed in Louisiana for making sirup. Here, o, the power is furnished by steam and evaporation is effected by am-heated coils, but this method differs from the others in that ne and the fumes of burning sulphur are added to the juice to fect clarification, and, in addition to skimming the heated juice, ttling tanks are provided in which the material is allowed to settle it. The capacities of the Louisiana sirup factories are usually uch larger than those of the factories in the other States of our rup-producing area.

Since the farmers employing the first method of sirup making erate on a very small scale and with simple equipment, it is hardly robable that the method of clarification described in this bulletin ill be practicable for them. For this reason a comparison will be ade between this method and the other two methods, where the rup making is conducted on a factory or semi-factory scale.

For comparison we will consider a plant of 50 tons daily (24 ours) capacity, operating by the simple method of clarification in-olving skimming only. A plant of this type usually has a vat tted with steam coils into which the juice runs direct from the mill. [ere the juice is heated until the thick blanket of scum which rises egins to crack. The heat is then turned off and this blanket of um is removed by skimming. From this clarifying vat the juice run directly to one or more evaporators, where it is immediately oked to sirup, additional scum being removed during the evapora-on. The changes and additions to such a plant for the purpose of sing infusorial earth clarification would be appreciable, namely—

(a) Filter presses totaling about 200 square feet in filtering area. t is estimated from experimental results obtained with the 18-inch lter press that 200 square feet of filtering area will handle the ice from 50 tons of cane in 24 hours. In actual experiment, using 1 pounds of infusorial earth to 1 ton of cane, the juice from 6 tons as handled in 4 hours. Suppose, for good measure, that 6 hours ere required for handling 6 tons with 80 square feet of filtering rea, then in 24 hours with 80 square feet, 24 tons could be handled, nd by doubling the filtering area, or with 160 square feet, 48 tons ould be handled. To make the estimate liberal an additional 40 square feet filtering area is added. Thus there appears to be no reason why the juice from 50 tons could not be filtered easily with 200 square feet filtering area in 24 hours, including all time necessary for cleaning and dressing the presses whenever necessary. In this connection it is suggested that two 100-square-feet presses would give more satisfaction than one press of 200 square feet filtering area.

(*b*) A pump with a capacity of at least 500 gallons per hour. A 6 by 4 by 6 duplex steam-piston pump would be satisfactory.

(*c*) Two or more vats of several hundred gallons capacity, each fitted with steam coils to keep the juice hot while being filtered, to serve as vats for mixing the infusorial earth with the juice, and in case no method of preheating the juice is employed, to serve also as the original juice-heating vats. While not essential, a tubular juice heater for heating the juice before it goes to the infusorial-earth-mixing tanks would be convenient, economical, and a great time saver. If a juice heater were employed the tanks mentioned above would be needed only for mixing the proper amount of infusorial earth with the juice and for keeping the juice hot while the filtration was in progress. In addition to this equipment there would, of course, be necessary a certain, though not large, amount of pipe, fittings, valves, connections, etc.

No changes would be necessary in either the grinding or the evaporating equipment, though very high extraction could be employed and a good sirup still produced by this method of clarification, whereas it is generally believed that it is impossible to make a high-grade sirup by the ordinary method of clarification when very high extraction is obtained. This method of clarification also opens up the way to the use of a less expensive method of evaporation, namely, evaporation under diminished pressure in a vacuum pan, which is impossible when skimming alone is depended upon to effect clarification.

An estimate of the cost of the above apparatus, necessary for clarification with infusorial earth, is rather difficult to give, owing to the rapid fluctuation in prices of machinery at this time. However, the cost of filter presses, pumps, and tanks as obtained from leading dealers at this time, July, 1920, is given here so that an idea at least may be obtained as to the cost of installing a filter press with its accessories.

Filter presses, 200 square feet total filtering area	$900
Pump for filter press	150
Freight, pipe, valves, etc	150
Two 400-gallon tanks, with coils	500
Total	1,700

The increased cost of operating the clarifying department of a sirup factory of 50 tons daily capacity, using infusorial earth and the above equipment, in comparison with the skimming method, may be estimated as follows:

> Cost of infusorial earth delivered, 11 pounds per ton of cane,
>   or 550 pounds, at 2 cents per pound_____ $11
> Extra labor—one man each shift, at $2.50_____ 5
>   16 [2]

The total increased cost per ton, assuming an operating period of 60 days, or a total tonnage ground of 3,000 tons, can be estimated as follows:

		Cents.
Interest on investment, at 6 per cent_____	$102÷3,000=	3.4
Depreciation, 10 per cent of investment_____	170÷3,000=	5.6
Filter cloths_____	80÷3,000=	2.6
Infusorial earth and extra operating expenses, as per above_____		32.0
Total, per ton_____		43.6

It is necessary now to show what financial advantages result from making sirup by this infusorial earth and filter press method to offset this apparent appreciable increase in cost. The outstanding feature is that no skimmings are obtained. Ordinarily, in a factory of this capacity, from 2,000 to 4,000 pounds of skimmings per day will be thrown away or fed to the hogs. These skimmings, with an average sugar content of 10 per cent, show a loss of 200 to 400 pounds of sugar. Figuring 8 pounds of sugar to the gallon of sirup, in grinding 50 tons of cane, from 25 to 50 gallons of sirup are lost.

In the above experiments on filtering the whole juice with infusorial earth, the resulting press cake from 6 tons of cane averaged 275 pounds weight with a sugar content of 6 per cent. From 50 tons of cane about 2,291 pounds of press cake would be obtained, which with 6 per cent sugar would give 137 pounds of sugar lost, or only 17 gallons of sirup per 50 tons. However, this loss can be reduced further. The press cake that is formed is very porous and is washed easily. Twenty gallons of water per ton of cane will easily reduce the sugar content of the press cake to 1 per cent, in which case the loss on 50 tons would be about 23 pounds of sugar, or about 3 gallons of sirup.

If a value of $1 per gallon is assumed for sirup, the saving in items of dollars and cents on 50 tons of cane can be calculated as follows:

> Loss by skimming process, 25 to 50 gallons of sirup, or $25 to $50.
> Loss in the infusorial earth clarification process when the cake is not washed, 17 gallons of sirup, or $17.

---

[2] Or 32 cents per ton.

Loss in the infusorial earth process when the cake is washed, 3 gallons of sirup, or $3.

A fair estimate is that 25 gallons of sirup would be saved on an average per 50 tons of cane. At $1 per gallon this would be a saving of 50 cents per ton. Thus the increased cost of this process is well offset by the reduction in the amount of sugar lost and in the corresponding increase in the yield of sirup.

It remains to compare this method of clarification for sirup making with that in general use in Louisiana. Here the changes required for the introduction of this process would not be so great as in the other sirup-making regions with which the comparison has been made. In Louisiana the filter press is an indispensable part of the factory equipment, being in general use throughout the sugar-and sirup-producing section of the State. As practically all of the sugar factories and many of the sirup factories are fully equipped with presses, little or no change would be necessary in altering the equipment for infusorial earth clarification. Eighty square feet of filter press area per ton-hour is sufficient for filtering the whole cane juice with infusorial earth. The cost of manufacturing sirup by this new process would be practically the same as that of the lime and sulphur process, since fuel and labor costs would be about the same. The cost of the clarifying materials would be somewhat more in the infusorial earth method, as shown below:

	Cents.
Infusorial earth, 11 pounds per ton, at 2 cents	22. 0
Against—	
Lime, 2½ pounds per ton, at 1 cent	2. 5
Sulphur, 1.4 pounds per ton, at 4½ cents	6. 3
Total	8. 8

As shown above, the cost of the clarifying materials is somewhat greater, but this is more than offset by the smaller amount of sucrose lost in the process of manufacture owing to the ease and thoroughness with which the press cake can be washed. Another advantage is that there is no need for settling tanks, skimming tanks, bag filters, or other clarifying equipment in addition to the filter presses, since the juice as it comes from the presses is ready for immediate evaporation to sirup without further treatment.

The only loss of sugar in a well-managed sirup or sugar house in Louisiana after the juice has been extracted from the cane is in the filter-press mud. Here it is figured that 36 pounds of press cake of an average sugar content of 6 per cent are produced per ton of cane, i. e., a loss of 2.16 pounds of sugar, or 0.27 gallon of sirup. Figured on a basis of $1 per gallon for sirup, this is a loss of 27 cents per ton.

In infusorial earth filtration about 45 pounds of press cake were obtained per ton. Considering the ease and rapidity with which this cake can be washed, there seems to be no reason why the sugar content should not be reduced easily to less than 1 per cent. The loss then would amount to about 0.45 pound of sugar or about 0.06 gallon of sirup per ton. On the basis of $1 sirup, this would be a loss of only 6 cents per ton. The difference in the losses, 21 cents per ton, would more than pay for the difference in the cost of the clarifying materials. However, the principal advantage would be in the improved flavor of the resulting sirup, which when properly evaporated compared favorably in color with the leading brands of Louisiana cane sirup on the market. The flavor was, in the opinion of the writer and others, milder and more agreeable, lacking the somewhat tart and metallic flavor of the usual Louisiana type of sirup.

The manufacture of sirup by the clarification method just described requires a larger outlay of capital and somewhat larger operating cost than when the manufacture is by the simple process of skimming and evaporation in open evaporators. The advantages are that a cleaner and better product can be obtained, the capacity of the evaporators can be increased—for it is not necessary to retard the evaporation as is at present the case to permit of proper skimming—the yield of sirup can be somewhat increased owing to the fact that all the scums and dregs are obtained in a hard, compact mass instead of in a thin mush containing a large amount of juice, and finally that the quality of the resulting sirup will be more uniform and will depend less upon the individual sirup maker and the care taken in skimming.

VACUUM EVAPORATION IN MAKING CANE SIRUP.

Though no exact information is available on the subject, it seems to be the general opinion that open evaporation is necessary in order to produce the finest-flavored cane sirup, some maintaining that the best flavor or aroma can be obtained only by cooking the juice in open evaporators. Some assert that sirups made in multiple-effect evaporators and vacuum pans are darker than those produced by rapid evaporation with live steam in open vats, while others state that a very high grade of sirup can be obtained, even though the evaporation is conducted mainly in vacuo, provided at some stage of evaporation it is boiled a few minutes in an open vat or brush pan. For the larger factories it is undoubtedly true that from an economic standpoint it is desirable to carry out as much of the evaporation as possible in multiple effects or vacuum pans, since evaporation can then be effected largely by exhaust steam. Even when it is necessary to use live steam the fuel consumption is not so great as in the case of open evaporation.

By employing the method of clarification with infusorial earth as described above the practicability of vacuum evaporation for sirup manufacture is increased largely. This condition is just a little different from any at present existing. In the regions where sirup is made without the use of sulphur or lime, owing to the necessity of almost continuous skimming, all factories employ open vats or pans for evaporation. In Louisiana and parts of Texas, where large amounts of sirup are made in vacuum pans, the juice is clarified with lime and sulphur dioxid. Using this infusorial earth clarification method, the juice is ready to go to the evaporators after coming from the filter presses without further treatment. The juice is clean and clear, no further scums appear during evaporation, and no coagulation or sedimentation takes place as the juice becomes more and more concentrated.

In connection with this work on clarification a small vacuum pan was installed. The filter-pressed juice was taken directly into the pan and evaporated to sirup, the pan being charged continuously until its capacity was reached. The sirup thus produced was of a light color, comparing very favorably in this respect with the highest grade of Louisiana sirups. The flavor, which, after all, is the principal quality to be considered, was excellent. It was quite mild, yet possessed the pleasant aroma and flavor characteristic of good cane sirup and was free from the peculiar after-effect that the highly sulphured sirup of Louisiana often leaves in the throat. In the author's opinion the flavor had lost nothing by the vacuum evaporation, though it may have been somewhat milder than that of the ordinary run of sirups, a characteristic that is decidedly desirable if a large market is to be developed for cane sirup in our Northern and Eastern States.

It is claimed by many that sirups made by the ordinary method of clarification with lime and sulphur are darkened by evaporation in the multiple effects and pans and that vigorous open evaporation makes a lighter sirup. This was not found to be the case with sirups·clarified by infusorial earth filtration, but rather a lighter sirup was produced in the vacuum pan than in the open evaporators. No darkening of the sirup in the vacuum pan in excess of that produced by open evaporation was observed. In fact, the sirup made by vacuum evaporation was in general much lighter in color than that made entirely in open evaporators.

USE OF VEGETABLE DECOLORIZING CARBONS IN CONNECTION WITH INFUSORIAL EARTH CLARIFICATION.

Much interest is being taken at present in the use of decolorizing carbons of high efficiency in the manufacture of sirup and sugar. Those which have been produced up to the time of this writing are expensive and for economy must be used over and over again and then reclaimed when their decolorizing power begins to diminish appreciably. Therefore, it is essential for efficiency and economy that the juice or liquor which the carbon is used to decolorize should be as clean as possible, that is, with no dregs, dirt, or slime to clog up prematurely the pores of the carbon. Filtration of the juices with the aid of infusorial earth leaves them in an ideal condition for treatment by the decolorizing carbons.

Preliminary experiments with these carbons showed that a fine sirup could be produced by this method. The juice after being filtered with infusorial earth was thoroughly mixed with an amount of an active decolorizing carbon, figured as 1 per cent on the solids in the juice. After it had been repumped through a plate and frame filter press to remove the carbon, it was lighter in color and clearer than the best grades of Louisiana sirup. Though much of its characteristic so-called cane flavor was lost, that retained was very mild and pleasing and should win favor in those regions where sweetness rather than strongly marked flavors is the quality principally desired.

The end of the grinding season prevented more extensive experiments and tests on this subject.

INFUSORIAL EARTH CLARIFICATION FOR SUGAR MANUFACTURE.

A preliminary clarification of the sugar-cane juice by filtration of the whole juice with infusorial earth is a subject that should be considered by those interested in the production of white sugars on the plantations. Naturally, the cleaner the juice going to the effects and pans the better the final quality of the sugar will be.

In crushing and grinding the sugar cane a great deal of very finely divided particles of bagasse and other material becomes incorporated with the juice. By the ordinary process of sulphuring, liming, and settling much of this finer material is left in the juice as a fine suspension. This material must have some deleterious effect upon both the yield and quality of the final sugar. The precipitate formed by sulphuring and liming the juices settles rapidly and completely, so

if a juice already perfectly clean and clear could be delivered to the
sulphur tower and liming tanks an exceptionally pure and brilliant
juice should be obtained subsequently from the settlers. No experiments have been made on this subject, but in view of the unusually
clear liquors that can be obtained by merely filtering the whole cane
juice with infusorial earth it seems reasonable to suppose that such
a liquor would have advantages in the manufacture of sugar as well
as table sirup.

SUMMARY.

Sugar-cane juice with the addition of infusorial earth can be
filtered rapidly, while hot, through a plate and frame filter press.
The resulting filtered liquor will be very clean and clear.

This filtered juice can be evaporated to sirup without further
treatment. No skimming is necessary, nor is it necessary to add
lime and sulphur dioxid.

The juice can be evaporated either in an open evaporator or under
diminished pressure in a vacuum pan. The sirup made by vacuum
evaporation is lighter in color and milder in flavor than that made
by evaporation in open evaporators. A very fine flavored sirup can
be made by evaporating the juice previously clarified by filtration
with infusorial earth in a vacuum pan to 30° Baumé and then finishing in an open pan or vat.

Infusorial earth clarification of cane juice followed by treatment
with an active decolorizing carbon produces a sirup very light in
color and with little characteristic flavor.

After filtering the juice with infusorial earth the resulting press
cake can be rapidly and thoroughly washed free from sugar, thus
insuring a minimum loss of sucrose in the factory and a proportionately larger yield of sirup.

Regardless of whether low extraction or high extraction is obtained at the mills, an excellent sirup can be made by clarifying the
juice by the method described, which is feasible in any factory
using steam as the source of power.

Filtration of the entire mill juice with the aid of infusorial earth
before chemical treatment has possibilities of producing for the
sugar industry a purer liquor, hence a better yield and better quality
of sugar.

An excellent quality of sirup is made from juice clarified by filtration with infusorial earth. This sirup has a milder flavor than
the present Louisiana type and is lighter in color and cleaner than
the Georgia type of sirup.

UNITED STATES DEPARTMENT OF AGRICULTURE

BULLETIN No. 922

Contribution from the Bureau of Entomology
L. O. HOWARD, Chief

Washington, D. C.   PROFESSIONAL PAPER   December 21, 1920

CLOVER-LEAF WEEVIL.

By

D. G. TOWER and F. A. FENTON,

Cereal and Forage Crop Insect Investigations.

CONTENTS.

	Page.		Page.
Introductory	1	Life history	6
Distribution	1	Life cycle	6
Description	2	Copulation	11
Adult	2	Oviposition	11
Egg	3	Habits	12
Larva		Feeding experiments	12
Cocoon		Natural enemies	16
Pupa	3	Control	18
Food plants and injury	6	Literature cited	18

INTRODUCTORY.

The clover-leaf weevil, *Hypera punctata* Fab. (fig. 1), ranks as one of the important clover pests. Although it is usually unnoticed, it annually exacts its toll of the crop. It seldom devastates entire fields, however, because the larvæ are ordinarily checked by an ever-present fungous disease which spreads rapidly and reduces their numbers to a negligible quantity in a remarkably short time.

DISTRIBUTION.

This insect was introduced accidentally into this country from Europe, where it is well known. It also occurs in northern Asia and probably in central Asia and China. So far as known it is the only species of Hypera that has reached this country, the genus being indigenous to the eastern hemisphere.

The first record of *Hypera punctata* occurring as a pest in the United States was in 1881 when a severe outbreak occurred at Barrington, N. Y. A single specimen taken about 1850–1855 in Canada by the Geological Survey and identified by Dr. LeConte in 1876 shows that this species had been in America for some time before becoming noticeable or seriously injurious.

FIG. 1.—Adults of the clover-leaf weevil feeding.

ish
405-

]
the
of
Ka
Ma
Mi:
Ne
shi
Or
Te
Ut:
ing

T
tak
froi
404
by
clo:

A
to 1
mm

Stout, black or brownish black. Clothed with blackish brc
brown or gray scales which are short broad and emarginate aj
erect bristles, edge of elytra yellow brown or at least paler tb

Head clothed with short metallic yellowish scales; *front* no
eye, densely clothed with dark yellow hairs or scales which
of the beak; *eyes* elongate oval, narrowed beneath, rather p
two-thirds the length of the prothorax, and one-half thicker at
beneath on the sides and near the tip polished and densely
impression on dorsal surface above the antennal groove; a

---

[1] Reference is made by number (italic) to " Literature Cit

deep, punctured; *antennæ* reddish-black, scape reaching to middle of eyes, not as long as funicle, not greatly enlarged at tip; first joint of funicle distinctly longer than second, enlarged at the apex so that it is about one-half as thick as long, second joint equal to three and four united, joints three to seven regularly shorter and broader, seven as wide as long, club elongate-oval, pointed at the tip, antennæ with many fine hairs, those on club very fine and dense. Mandibles polished, dull red, not emarginate at tip, maxillæ and all the palpi pale brownish-red.

Prothorax broader than long, broader in female than in male, in the female broadly widened in front of the middle, in the male converging more behind than in female; sides broadly impressed, only slightly swollen; dorsum densely rather coarsely punctured, densely clothed with scales and with many slender pointed hairs; usually with a narrow pale median dorsal line bordered with wide dark, almost black in some, bands of scales which reach to the sides; sides and beneath with dark yellow scales, generally with a dark spot on sides behind and an indistinct dark line running from this spot toward the front.

Scutellum extremely small, narrowly triangular, clothed with pale scales.

Elytra very broad, at tip broadly rounded, sides especially in the male nearly parallel, humeri prominent and clothed with darker scales. Suture and alternate interspaces more strongly elevated than others, deeply striately punctured, striæ without setæ; each interspace with a single row of black setæ pointing backward and partially decumbent, more erect behind; tip of elytra and often the sides with some short white hairs. The coloration of the scales varies from solid gray to black, through various shades of brown yellows. Some speci-

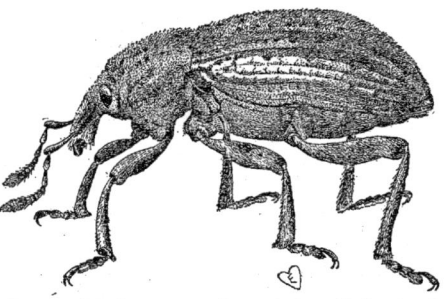

FIG. 2.—Adult clover-leaf weevil, lateral view. Much enlarged.

mens are tessellated with brownish-yellow and black, the tessellation usually on the more elevated interspaces.

In the male the outer interspaces have paler scales even in the darkest specimens, in the female this pale coloration is sometimes, but rarely, entirely absent.

Venter with lighter colored scales and many light hairs; front coxæ slightly separated, mesosternal process between middle coxæ broad perpendicular, triangular at tip; intercoxal process of first abdominal segment very broad, coxæ separated by more than their width. First segment in male impressed, emarginate posteriorly. Stem of male genitalia nearly or quite as broad as long.

Legs short, stout, especially the femora; black, tarsi often ferruginous, claws long curved, red and darker at tips; front tibiæ and hind femora distinctly curved, front tibiæ more so in male; legs usually clothed with lighter scales and hairs than the body, femora scaled, tibiæ and tarsi sparsely haired; middle tibiæ with a distinct apical hook.

Egg [fig. 3]: Elongate oval, 1.1 mm. to 1.2 mm. long, 0.5 to 0.6 mm. broad, very regularly hexagonally sculptured * * *. [Watery yellow when laid, with a smooth shining shell, the yellow color deepening with age to pale olive green and finally turning to a dull black.]

Larvæ [2] (Descriptions from Riley, Folsom, and observations by the author). *First stage:* 1.5 to 2 mm. long, narrow, thickest at middle, tapering toward both ends;

---

[2] The head widths for the different larval instars are quite constant and the averages will be found in Table I.

head brown, blackish-brown or black, with many fine transverse lines on the face; eyes very small, circular, projecting; mandibles terminating in two large sharp teeth, more or less separated, the lower one again divided into two or three parts; palpi pale yellow, mandibles brown or dark brown; dorsum of first thoracic segment with a rectangular dark band interrupted by a paler dorsal line which is the continuation of the stem of an inverted Y on the face, this dorsal band becomes wider on the abdominal segments and extends to the tip of anal segment. Hairs on the tubercles clavate as in several other species. [The color varies from the usual pale green to a bluish green or yellow when hatched. Yellow larvæ may retain this color throughout development.]

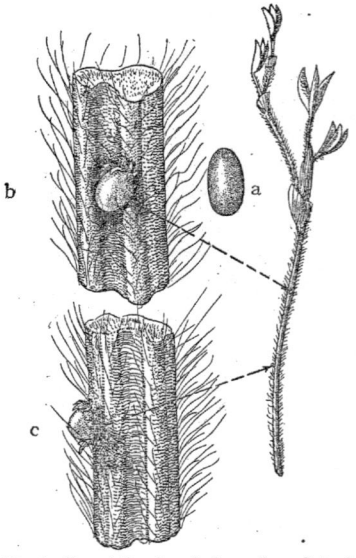

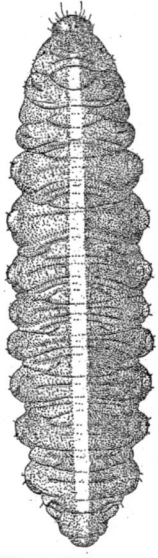

FIG. 3.—Egg of the clover-leaf weevil: a, Lateral view; b, egg inserted into stem of clover plant; c, lateral view of b. Much enlarged.

FIG. 4.—Full - grown larva of the clover-leaf weevil, dorsal view. Much enlarged.

Second stage: Color greener, head dark brown, front and sides of rectangular plate on first thoracic segment dark, the remainder greenish; dorsal median line with a fine dark border, darker than the remainder of the larva. Side line below spiracles indistinct. Length 4–4.5 mm., width 2 mm.

Third stage: Black lines on each side of dorsal line very distinct [head brown or yellowish brown], eyes densely black, antennæ darker. Color of larvæ (Folsom) may be blue green [yellow, or with a pinkish tinge]. Usual color pale green. Length 5 to 7 mm., width 2.5 to 3 mm. in the middle.

Fourth stage [fig. 4]: Dorsal line very white or pinkish, bordered by rose color, usually rather pale but sometimes rosy-black, the outer borders of this coloration are black and form distinct lines, interrupted on the margin of each segment [head brown or yellowish brown]; larva much darker green [or still may retain its yellow, blue green, or pink color]; lines below the spiracles dark both showing a tendency to be brown or blackish [posterior segments yellowish]; the surface of the body much rougher in this stage than in others, the triangular points of the cuticle standing out prominently; tubercles [fig. 5] on thoracic segments below very strong and the hairs more prominent than in earlier stages. Length 8 to 14 mm.

Cocoon [fig. 6]; * * * Oval, 9–10 mm. long and 6.5 to 7 mm. wide. [A fine network of coarse threads which are light straw color when spun and brown after aging.]

Pupa: When first formed with yellow-green head [lighter colored antennæ, legs and wing-pads] * * *. Abdomen dark green with a distinct pale dorsal line that extends onto prothorax * * *. Frontal row of hairs rather distant from margin; central pairs close together, three following pairs form a curved line ending near the posterior outer edge; a few hairs on remainder of thorax; transverse rows of blunt setæ on each dorsal abdominal segment;

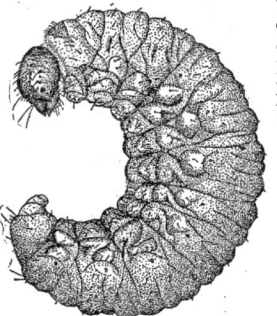

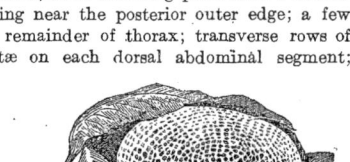

Fig. 5.—Full-grown larva of the clover-leaf weevil, lateral view. Much enlarged.

Fig. 6.—Cocoon of the clover-leaf weevil surrounded by leaves of clover plant. Enlarged.

hairs on beak rather short and thin; those on anal segment moderately long, stout and dark. [The pigmentation of the eyes, mandibles, and leg joints occurs at later dates in order named.] Length 5.5–7 mm. Width 3.5–4.5 mm.

The measurements of the larva are given in tabular form, as follows:

TABLE I.—*Larval measurements (mm.) of Hypera punctata.*

Number of specimens averaged.	First instar.				Second instar.			
	Width of head.	Length of body.			Width of head.	Length of body.		
		Minimum.	Maximum.	Average.		Minimum.	Maximum.	Average.
24	0.2	1.9	3.4	2.7				
20					0.55	1.8	5.9	3.8

Number of specimens averaged.	Third instar.				Fourth instar.			
	Width of head.	Length of body.			Width of head.	Length of body.		
		Minimum.	Maximum.	Average.		Minimum.	Maximum.	Average.
18	0.8	3.8	9.5	6.3				
19					1.2	5.1	13.1	9.3

FOOD PLANTS AND INJURY.

The food plants in Europe are listed as Trifolium (clover) and *Medicago sativa* (lucerne, alfalfa). In this country all kinds of clovers, including *Trifolium pratense, T. incarnatum, ·T. hybridum*, and *T. repens* are eaten, as well as alfalfa and sweet clover (*Melilotus alba*). Webster reported white clover being eaten in preference to red in Ohio, but other observers, including the present writers, have noted that red clover and alfalfa are more often chosen. Both larvæ and adults will feed on beans, and the adults have been observed eating timothy, burdock, soy bean, and the flowers of goldenrod. W. H. Larrimer observed beetles feeding on corn foliage at McFarland, Kans., August 10, 1915.

In Europe this species has several times been reported as injurious locally, but only for short periods. The earliest record I have found is Villa's statement at the time of the outbreak in the region of Lombardy in 1868 when he says that Moretti in a revised edition of Gene's publication in 1853 reports this species as injuring clover and believes that this referred to a previous serious injury about 1834–35. * * * In 1868 the species caused serious damage in Northern Italy so that a commission was appointed to investigate the matter and published several papers giving recommendations. Targione-Tozzetti in 1879 notes a severe outbreak in the region around Florence. It was again injurious in the region of Florence in 1902–3. (Tittis 7, *p. 408.*)

The first record of the destructive work of this species in America occurred at Barrington, Yates County, N. Y., in 1881 and 1882, but since that time it has been controlled largely by an epidemic fungous disease. The clover-leaf weevil has spread rapidly over the country, and outbreaks have occurred repeatedly, but usually have been checked before serious damage was done. The most notable of these late outbreaks occurred in Michigan and persisted for a year or two before the fungus succeeded in checking the insect. In this connection Pettit (*5, p. 46*) records that cattle pastured on clover at the time the larvæ were being destroyed by this fungous disease were made seriously ill, and so many complaints were received in Michigan that it was advised that cattle be kept out of clover pastures until the bodies of the dead larvæ had dropped to the ground.

LIFE HISTORY.
LIFE CYCLE.

The life history of this species was first studied in the United States by Riley (*6, p. 171–179*) in 1882, and Folsom's paper on clover insects in 1909 (*3, p. 155–164*) gives much additional information. Numerous other writers have added notes on the distribution, habits, and life history, and these have been drawn on by the authors. The life cycle is one year according to observations made by the present writers, which agrees with the results obtained by Folsom. Briefly, the life cycle is as follows:

The eggs are laid in or on different parts of the clover or alfalfa plant, more often in a puncture on the stem or leaf sheath or on the outside of these parts in the fall of the year between September 8. and November 29. The eggs laid previous to October 25 hatch the same fall, and hibernate as first, second, and third instar larvæ while those laid after October 25 usually remain over winter as eggs, and, except in the case of eggs laid quite late, hatch the following March. The larvæ feed on the foliage of their hosts and become full grown by the last of May, when they spin cocoons at or just below the surface of the soil, pupating therein and issuing as adult beetles in June or July. The beetles feed on foliage of clover intermittently until September when they mate, and soon thereafter egg laying begins.

Since the period of oviposition extends over a number of weeks and, furthermore, eggs laid late in the season do not hatch until spring,

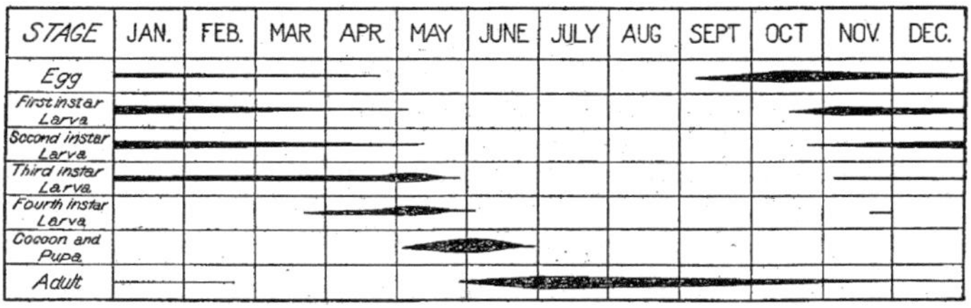

STAGE	JAN.	FEB.	MAR	APR.	MAY	JUNE	JULY	AUG	SEPT	OCT	NOV.	DEC.
Egg												
First instar Larva												
Second instar Larva												
Third instar Larva												
Fourth instar Larva												
Cocoon and Pupa												
Adult												

Fig. 7.—Diagram illustrating life history of the clover-leaf weevil and indicating the abundance of the different stages during the season in the latitude of La Fayette, Ind.

the various stages greatly overlap. The accompanying diagram (fig. 7) illustrates graphically the life cycle of *Hypera punctata.*

The experiments made by the authors were not started until September 8, 1915, but some of the beetles collected September 1 had oviposited previous to September 8.

The eggs are laid in the fall during September, October, and the first two weeks in November, although oviposition was observed as late as November 29 in 1915. Females laid during periods of 64 to 68 days and individuals laid the following numbers of eggs: 74, 83, 108, 162, 166, 176, 181, 196, 287. Following the last oviposition the females lived from 1 to 16 days, and all the males and females used in the experiments in the fall of 1915 and kept out of doors under normal conditions were dead by February 18, 1916.

The beetles laid consistently between September 8 and November 15, there being a marked increase in the numbers laid between October 15 and November 15. After November 15 the laying records were scattered. It was noticeable that none of the eggs laid after October 21 hatched previous to March 1, 1916, except in one case when eggs laid October 25 hatched during a period of

eggs may retain their yellow color through the
being arrested. Early in the fall the eggs that
sculptured in a day or two, but later on the
these changes may be lengthened to weeks or r
ticeable change in the egg is the rapid pigme
the embryo which appears beneath the shell as
spot. In the early fall the egg hatches in from
change, although later such eggs may go thr
condition or may hatch during some of the m

During the fall of 1915 the shortest egg pe
eggs being laid September 10, and the longes
overwintering eggs, was 46 days, the eggs i
October 21. The average of the records of 5
September 8 and October 21 was 25.8 days.

Just previous to hatching the embryos are
and can be seen moving around. They emer
round hole large enough for the larva to pass
one end of the egg. The eggshells are never e
they have emerged. The larvæ will comme
placed on clover leaves, but may live a long ti
the case of those hatching during the winte
larval stages is very variable in the fall, for
during adverse weather and resumed in mil
secured for the first stage was 13 to 14 days
12 to 14 days, and for the third stage 10 days.
were obtained in these experiments during the
sent the larvæ into hibernation. Table II sun
the different stages and larval instars as ob
Ind., in the spring and early summer.

Numerous larvæ were collected on differ
winter to determine the ages of the wintering
of such collections are given in tabular fo:
adults were found by the authors but Folsom
nating adults collected in the spring were muc
to lay eggs. He suggests the possibility of
beetles farther south which hibernate and

and observations made by different members of the Bureau of Entomology would indicate that ovipositing beetles in the latitude south of southern Indiana are capable of laying fertile eggs in the spring and that two broods sometimes, if nor ordinarily, occur annually.

The larvæ have often been observed feeding during the mild days of winter on the small leaves at the crown of the clover plant. In the early spring the larvæ commence to feed as soon as the clover starts its growth, but feeding and growth are intermittent, due to climatic changes, so that larvæ of all stages may be found during April and May. Larvæ in the first three instars are most numerous in April, but beginning with May there is a gradual falling off in numbers of larvæ in the first two instars, those in the third and fourth predominating. By the end of May few active larvæ remain and by June 20 practically all have completed their growth and spun their pupal cocoon. Tables II and III give the number of days passed in different stages and the dates of their occurrence in the field.

TABLE II.—*Hypera punctata: Length of larval and pupal periods.*

Stage.	Number of examples.	Minimum.	Maximum.	Average.
		Days.	*Days.*	*Days.*
Larva....{ First instar......................................	6	17	20	18¾
Second instar.....................................	19	4	15	10
Third instar......................................	23	4	13	8½
Fourth instar.....................................	32	8	21	14½
Spinning cocoon..................................	57	1	2	1+
Prepupa..	44	1	10	4
Pupa...	53	5	16	11⁷⁄₁₀
Length of time remaining in cocoon after adult..............	56	1	5	2⅜

TABLE III.—*Hypera punctata: Stages occurring in field at different dates.*

Date collected.	First stage.	Second stage.	Third stage.	Fourth stage.	Prepupa.	Pupa.
1915.						
Oct. 14...	2					
Oct. 19...	2	3				
Oct. 20...	1					
Oct. 21...	1	3				
Oct. 22...	1	1				
Oct. 27...	18	2				
Nov. 4..	19	19	2	1		
Nov. 23...	18	45	14	1		
Dec. 13...	32	34	13			
1916.						
Jan. 3..	6	7	1			
Jan. 28...	33	28	5			
Mar. 25...		3	4			
Mar. 31...	1	6	4	1		
Apr. 3..		6	4	1		
Apr. 5..	2	4	2	2		
Apr. 10...		3	2			
Apr. 15...	10	15	12	4		
Apr. 18...		4	1			
Apr. 20...	3	2	1			
Apr. 27...	2	5	9	6		
May 5..	2	11	14	14		
May 8..			9	9	3	
May 18...			10	10	1	
May 25...				2	1	1
May 26...				4		

The cocoon (fig. 6) is spun in an oval cell made by the larva in the soil just beneath the surface or among the stems and rubbish at the base of the clover plant. This cell is formed by the larva turning around and around with its body in the characteristic curved position and is smoothed with its head. The spinning is done by the mouth but the bulk of the spinning material is drawn from the anus and every few minutes during the construction of the cocoon the larva reaches back to the anus for a fresh supply. Knab (4) shows by his dissections of these larvæ that there is an enormous development of the malpighian tubes and reasonably supposes that the bulk of the spinning material primarily arises in these tubes and is drawn from the anus by the larva. He further observes that the necessarily smaller amount of silk produced by the silk glands which open into the mouth may be used in waterproofing the other materials, for he has noticed the larva passing its mouth along the threads after they have been drawn out and put in place.

The cocoon is spun in from 1 to 2 days and the larva pupates within four days after the cocoon is completed. In one instance at La Fayette, during excessively hot weather, a larva pupated within a day after completing the cocoon, and in another instance under adverse conditions this prepupal period extended over 10 days. The newly formed pupa is pale green but later changes to yellow and finally to a brownish color.

The beetle issues 5 to 16 days after pupation, the average pupal period, according to our observations, being 11 days. The adult is at first soft and pale green, the wings protruding beyond the elytra, the pupal and larval skins remaining as a small shriveled pellet at an end of the cocoon. The elytra gradually become silver, iridescent, and pale green through which the maculations are faintly visible, the ventral surface of the abdomen is pale green, the lower part of the head reddish brown, the prothorax tan colored. The wings are soon withdrawn beneath the elytra and within 24 hours the insect has become mature, after which the beetle issues by eating an irregular hole in the cocoon. The first beetles issuing at La Fayette in 1916 emerged on May 26 and the last June 26, although other observers in the same latitude give the period of greatest emergence as the last week in June, the period of emergence extending from May 9 to July 15.

After emergence the beetles feed during the night and conceal themselves during the day under rubbish or in cracks in the ground. They feed steadily for about two weeks, after which they become semidormant and remain inactive until about the first of September, whereupon they become sexually active.

COPULATION.

As stated, the beetles resume activity the last of August or the first of September. The record of copulation for one pair reads September 15, October 4, 8, 14, 17, 27, and November 7, the female of this pair laying 196 eggs between September 25 and November 27. As these beetles were examined but once or twice each day probably only a few of the copulations were observed. Mating probably takes place normally during the day, for beetles in copula have been collected in the field only at this time.

OVIPOSITION.

The records of other writers give as places of oviposition the ground, base of plant, stems, and the inside of dead stems. Careful search was made in the field for eggs during the laying season, but only three were found, these being placed singly on dead stems. In the breeding cages the beetles rarely laid on the ground but in or on some portion of the plant. When fed alfalfa they laid the eggs singly in punctures in the stem. (Fig. 3.) Sometimes it seemed impossible for the beetle to make punctures enough to contain all the eggs she wished to lay, so she would fasten several in a mass on the stem by means of a rapidly drying secretion. When fed clover the females practically always laid inside the petiole or the leaf sheath; and if these were not present and only stems provided, the eggs were laid as in alfalfa. In laying the eggs in the petioles the female usually cut a hole with her mandibles just large enough to admit one egg at a time, through the side of the petiole, but in the case of an old matured petiole a cavity would be made into which the ovipositor could be thrust and from 1 to 23 eggs laid, part of which would be pushed up and part down the stem. Measurements showed that the eggs were sometimes pushed in the petiole as far as $3\frac{1}{2}$ mm. above and 6 mm. below the puncture. Unless the last egg was left in the opening, as infrequently occurred, the opening practically healed before the eggs hatched. In case the petiole was solid, the inside would be eaten out and the eggs laid as before. It was noticeable that petioles and their leaves never appeared to be injured when eggs were laid in them. The eggs were also readily laid in the sheath at the base of the petiole, a tiny hole being cut through its side and a mass of eggs deposited within, as many as 33 eggs being laid by one female at one time in this way. In all the experiments the largest number of eggs laid by one female at one time was 34, 18 to 25 being common. The eggs are usually laid at night but some were recorded between 8 and 9 a. m., and it was noticeable that there was a marked tendency to lay during the day in the fall when the nights were very cold.

HABITS.

The young larvæ feed during the day, largely on the underside of the leaves, eating small holes in them. Whether they feed from the underside because it is more protected or because there are more epidermal hairs for them to cling to is not known. After the third molt they eat patches from the edges of the leaves, feeding only at night, and dropping to the ground when disturbed, curling themselves tightly end to end. During the day they lie coiled at the base of the plant, hiding under dead leaves and other débris.

The larvæ are legless but are supplied with pairs of muscular fleshy tubercles on the ventrum of the segments and these are used in grasping epidermal hairs, edges of leaves, etc. The young larvæ move about by grasping the epidermal hairs with their mouths, the folds between segments, and the transverse folds. Older larvæ ascend petioles spirally, using the muscular abdomen as a means of locomotion, and with each successive advance securing a new hold with the mouth and forepart of the body. As this is repeated, the larvæ move around and around the stem with a spiral motion.

When handled, the larvæ will often emit a greenish saliva, which appears to be for defensive purposes, and in addition may pass their blackish semiliquid waste.

The young larva molts by first coiling itself about a bunch of epidermal hairs and then crawling out of the larval skin, which opens in the head region, leaving the empty skin coiled around the hairs. The larvæ have never been observed to eat the cast skins.

The adult, after casting off the pupal skin, which shrivels to a small pellet at one end of the cocoon with the last larval skin, soon eats its way out and feeds during the summer, ragging the clover leaves and sometimes eating the plants to the ground. During the day they usually hide under rubbish or in cracks in the ground but have been observed to feed, and many have been collected by sweeping the tops of clover plants at this time.

FEEDING EXPERIMENTS.

Feeding experiments were conducted at La Fayette, Ind., to determine the amounts of clover foliage eaten by *Hypera punctata* at different seasons and during the larval and adult stages (Table IV). The amount of food eaten by individual larvæ averages 3.09 square inches of red clover foliage from 25 examples studied, and of this amount 2.48 square inches, or approximately 80 per cent, is consumed during the last instar. Comparatively small amounts of leaf tissue are eaten during the first three instars—0.019 square inch being eaten during the first, 0.087 in the second, and 0.504 in the third instar (Table V and fig. 8).

As has already been noted, the beetles begin to feed immediately upon issuing in May and June and continue for a period of about two weeks. They then become dormant and do not resume feeding until early in September, coincident with the beginning of sexual activity. During the early period of feeding the foliage is the principal part of the clover plant eaten, but in late fall the beetles, and especially the females, show an increasing tendency to feed upon the stems and petioles.

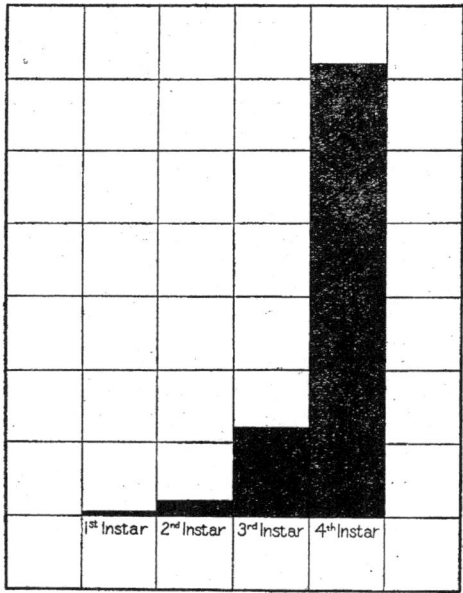

Fig. 8.—Diagram showing average comparative amounts of clover foliage consumed by larvæ of the clover-leaf weevil in their different instars.

The life of the adult, therefore, is divided into two distinct feeding periods, separated by one of inactivity during the months of July and August. During the first active feeding period enough nourishment is taken to tide the insect over midsummer when but little food is available. Beetles deprived of foliage immediately after emergence from the cocoon die within a few days. According to experiments made by the writers, the average amount of clover foliage eaten by individual beetles prior to the inactive summer period, during what might appropriately be termed the predormant period, is 3.28 square inches, which is consumed in an average of 23.5 days. Beetles issuing late in May become dormant late in June, while those emerging from the middle to the end of June do not stop feeding until early in July. The amount of foliage eaten during the postdormant period, that is, after the summer inactive period, is 1.48 square inches and extends over an average of 82 days, that is, not one-tenth as much per day as is eaten in the predormant stage (Table VI and fig. 9).

The amount of food consumed by the individual beetle during its entire adult stage averages 4.76 square inches, 0.045 of an inch per day during the feeding periods. The feeding by the beetles is therefore so slow and gradual that they seldom do an appreciable amount of injury except when in unusual numbers. On the other hand, the larva needs approximately 2 square inches less of foliage for its development than is eaten by the adult, but of the 3.09 square inches of leaf eaten by each larva, 2.48 inches are consumed during the last instar, which occupies a period of 10 days or less, and the large amount of foliage taken in so short a period greatly increases the liability of injury.

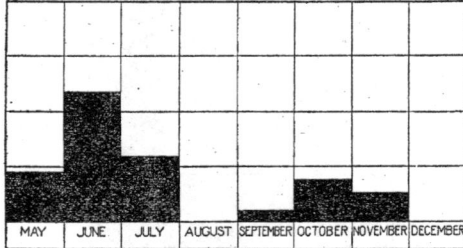

Fig. 9.—Diagram showing the comparative amounts of clover foliage eaten by adult beetles of the clover-leaf weevil during the different months of the season.[1]

Tables IV, V, and VI give the amounts of clover foliage eaten by adults and larvæ.

TABLE IV.—*Average amounts of clover foliage eaten by adult and larva of Hypera punctata.*

Stage.	Average amount food eaten.	Average length feeding period.	Average per day.
	Inches.	Days.	
Predormant beetle	3.28	23.5	0.139
Postdormant beetle	[1].74	82.0	.009
Larva 1st instar	.019	18.6	.001
Larva 2d instar	.084	10.0	.008
Larva 3d instar	.504	8.5	.059
Larva 4th instar	2.480	14.0	.177
Total—larva	3.087	51.1	.06
Total—beetle	4.02	105.5	.038

[1] The beetle consumes at least an equal amount of stem during this period and this could not be measured.

[1] As recorded in Table IV, at least an equal amount of stem is eaten in the fall in addition to the foliage, and due consideration is taken of this fact.

TABLE V.—*Amount (inches) of clover foliage eaten by larvæ of Hypera punctata.*

Cage No.	First instar.	Second instar.	Third instar.	Fourth instar.	Total.
Laf. D454:					
ba	0.0025	0.08	0.66	2.14	3.1425
bb	.005	.1	.2525	2.4121	2.7696
bc	.005	.055	.195	2.415	2.67
bd	.0025	.005	.62436	2.80952	3.4414
bf	.0025	.03	.37		
bg	.015	.06	1.23868	2.668	3.9817
bh	.01	.11	.54	2.90332	3.5633
bi	.0275	.08	.2975	2.61	3.015
bk	.005	.05	.80428	2.27668	3.29
bl	.03				
bm	.005				
bn		.1025	.88375	2.70375	
bo	.025	.1025			
bq	.03	.18			
br	.025	.12	.47748	2.85104	3.4735
bs	.03	.396	1.0034	1.11412	2.5435
bt	.02	.035			
bu	.04	.09	.77892	3.05864	3.96756
bv	.01	.055	.905	1.945	2.915
bw	.0125	.025			
bx	.04	.1	.5125	2.7475	3.395
baa		.025	.7825	1.8175	
bab	.0125	.1925	.763		
bac	.0275	.04	.7725		
bad	.025	.035	.495	2.4325	2.98
baf	.0825				
bag	.065	.1	.4428	1.94452	2.5524
bah		.0375	.2825	1.465	
bai	.025				
baj	.0225	.025			
bak	.0125				
bal	.03				
bam	.01				
ban	.0075				
bao	.01				
bap	.014	.035	.3475	1.6125	2.009
baq	.03	.04844	.56052	2.40124	3.0401
bar	.045	.07612	.3806	2.23516	2.7369
bas	.01	.0525	.07275	1.9425	2.0778
bat	.02	.1			
bau	.0175	.055	.5875	2.2475	2.9075
bav	.008	.04	.465	3.205	3.718
baw	.01	.145	.3125		
bay	.01	.03			
baz	.02	.05536	.63664	2.66892	3.3809
ca	.02	.08304	.346	2.87872	3.3277
cb	.01	.1221	.3375	1.845	2.3146
cj	.02	.025			
ck	.0025	.0675	.51	2.11	2.69
cl	.0325	.0375			
cm		.0775	.225		
cn		.0625	.825	2.7025	
cp			.4675	3.0625	
cq		.02	.22		
cr		.08	.68508	3.3908	
cs		.0525	.66	3.7925	
ct		.242			
cu		.0375	.8875	3.4425	
cam			.455		
Average	.019	.0874	.50401	2.48035	3.09076

TABLE VI.—*Amounts (inches) of clover foliage eaten by beetles of Hypera punctata.*

DURING PREDORMANT PERIOD.

Cage No.	Number of beetles per cage.	Date of emergence.	Date stopped feeding.	Total feeding period	Amount of foliage eaten during—				Sex.
					May.	June.	July.	Total.	
				Days					
D363a	1	May 25	June 20	26	1.36	1.08	....	2.44	♂
D363b	1	May 26	June 14	19	1.19	2.46	....	3.65	♂
D363g	1	May 28	June 20	23	.25	3.13	....	3.38	♀
D363n	1	June 3	June 27	24	....	4.9	....	4.9	♀
D363s	1	June 4	June 30	26	....	5 61	....	5.61	♀
D363t	1	..do..	..do..	26	....	4.39	....	4.39	♀
D363aa	1	June 13	July 5	23	....	3.07	0.93	4.00	♀
D363ad	1	June 15	July 8	24	....	3.56	.84	4.4	♀
D363ag	1	June 17	July 7	21	....	2.51	.52	3.03	♀
D568a	2	June 27	July 10	24	....	1.06	2.19	3.25	♂♀
D568c	2	...do....	July 8	22	....	2.39	2.6	4.99	♂♀
D568d	2	...do....	July 10	24	....	1.46	3.73	5.19	♂♀
Total average per beetle	....	....	....	23.5	.93	2.37	1.2	3.28	

DURING REPRODUCTIVE PERIOD.

Cage No.	Number of beetles per cage.	Amount of foliage eaten during—				Total period.	Sex.
		September.	October.	November.	December.		
D363a	2	0.152	0.792	0.498	0.149	1.591	♂♀
D363b	3	....	.754	.228	.032	1.014	♂♀♀
D363g	2	.104	1.240	.430	.232	2.006	♂♀
D363n	2	.080	.922	.283	.155	1.440	♂♀
D363s	2	.045	.640	.459	.346	1.490	♂♀
D363t	2	.436	.818	.440	.280	1.974	♂♀
D363aa	2	.249	.461	.503	.195	1.408	♂♀
D363ad	2	.285	1.221	....	....	1.506	♂♀
D363ag	2	....	.806	.505	.138	1.449	♂♀
D454e	2	....	.844	1.341	.690	2.875	♂♀
D454h	3	....	.376	.563	.136	1.075	♀♀♀
Total average per beetle	....	.0965	.369	.239	.011	.7155	

NATURAL ENEMIES.

The most important check on the abundance of *Hypera punctata* is the fungous disease *Empusa sphaerosperma* Fres., which kills the larvæ in vast numbers during the months of April and May and again in October and November. This disease is epidemic, and contagion so rapid and thorough that in from two to four weeks it is almost impossible to find living individuals where previously there were thousands.

The sick larvæ of all ages crawl up the herbage during the night, and instead of again concealing themselves near the ground on the approach of light, as the healthy ones do, ascend as high as possible, and if on grass, coil themselves in a horizontal position about the apex of the blade, or if on other objects, take a position as nearly similar as the shape of the object permits. If disturbed before the middle of the forenoon the majority are still able to crawl, although sluggishly; by noon most of them are quite dead, but unchanged in appearance. . . . Late in the afternoon, the body has changed from the normal yellowish or pea green and smooth appearance to velvety gray. The next morning there is only a small, blackened and shriveled mass remaining, while the surrounding foliage is powdered with a whitish, clinging dust, composed of the spores of the fungus. (J. C. Arthur (*1, p. 285–289*).)

The fungus mycelia ramify through the body of the larva, absorb the body fluids, but do not penetrate the tracheal or alimentary tract. A portion of the mycelium pushes out through the ventral side of the larva and forms rhizoids attaching the larva securely to its support. Other mycelial threads push out from other portions of the body and form a gray velvety coating over the body of the larva. On the tip of some of these branches is formed a spore which is projected forcibly into the air to infect other larvæ with which it may come in contact. These are the temporary spores and germinate at once to infect new hosts. Resting spores are also formed and these develop in the body of the larva and are capable of retaining their virility for a longer time.

This disease is well distributed in the United States and attacks numerous other insects, among them the common cabbage worm (*Pontia rapae* L.), mosquitos, flies, ichneumon wasps, and certain leafhoppers.

According to Riley the larva of a small beetle (*Collops quadrimaculatus* Fab.) feeds on the eggs of the clover-leaf weevil and one of the tiger-beetles (*Cicindela repanda* Dej.) probably preys on the larvæ. In Europe several larval parasites are known but none have been recorded from this country. H. L. Parker, of the Bureau of Entomology, collected a clover-leaf weevil larva at Hagerstown, Md., April 30, 1915, bearing a tachinid egg, but the adult was not reared therefrom.

Poultry, especially turkeys and chickens, are fond of the larvæ and beetles, and if given the opportunity will consume large numbers.

Birds are valuable and important natural checks on this insect and according to the Bureau of Biological Survey (*2, p. 7*),

The common or large clover-leaf weevil is the prey of 25 species of birds. The nighthawk, crow, red-headed woodpecker, purple martin, and crow blackbird have the best records for the destruction of adults, and the Savannah and vesper sparrows of the larvæ.

In literature we find the following birds listed as feeding on *Hypera punctata:*

American crow	*Corvus brachyrhynchos.*
Bobolink	*Dolichonyx oryzivorus.*
Bobwhite	*Colinus virginianus.*
Catbird	*Dumetella carolinensis.*
Crow blackbird	*Quiscalus quiscula.*
Flicker	*Colaptes auratus.*
Horned lark	*Otocoris alpestris flava.*
Kingbird	*Tyrannus tyrannus.*
Meadowlark	*Sturnella magna.*
Nighthawk	*Chordeiles virginianus.*
Purple martin	*Progne subis.*
Red-headed woodpecker	*Melanerpes erythrocephalus.*
Robin	*Planesticus migratorius.*
Sparrows:	
English	*Passer domesticus.*
Savannah	*Passerculus sandwichensis savanna.*
Vesper	*Poœcetes gramineus.*
Wood pewee	*Contopus virens.*

Toads and frogs sometimes prey upon the weevils. Mr. T. S. Wilson, of the Bureau of Entomology, found one adult in a toad's stomach at Wellington, Kans., July 12, 1915, and Mr. H. L. Parker found 11 adults and one pupa of *Hypera punctata* in the stomachs of four frogs (*Rana* sp.) collected at Bridgeport, N. Y., December 6, 1915, out of 14 examined.

CONTROL.

The outbreaks of this insect are eventually suppressed by the fungous disease mentioned and, except in rare cases, before serious damage is done. Often what promises to be a serious attack is wiped out by the disease just as it seems to appear most threatening, or, as was the case in 1917, the weather conditions may enable the clover to make a rank growth and overcome injury by the larvæ, even though they may be present in enormous numbers.

Usually the need of remedial precautions does not become apparent until too late to apply practical measures. The insect does not ordinarily become abundant in a clover field until the second season, and in localities where it is known to occur in occasional or frequent abundance it is a good practice to pasture lightly all first-year clover in the fall or to clip it back in spring and further to hinder the increase of this insect in the locality by thoroughly plowing under the second year crop in the fall.

Other measures, such as burning clover fields in winter, rolling, dragging, and flooding, have been advised, but the practical value of these measures has not been proved; and clipping and plowing under clover at the end of the second season, in themselves valuable in the control of other clover insects as well as being good farm practices, seem all that is necessary, as a rule, for prevention of injury

LITERATURE CITED.

(1) ARTHUR, J. C.
    1886. REPORT OF THE BOTANIST. *In* 4th Ann. Rept. N. Y. Agr. Exp. Sta.
        (Geneva), 1885, p. 268–292.
(2) BEAL, F. E. L., McATEE, W. L., and KALMBACH, E. R.
    1916. COMMON BIRDS OF SOUTHEASTERN UNITED STATES IN RELATION TO AGRI-
        CULTURE. U. S. Dept. Agr., Farmers' Bul. 755. 44 p., 22 figs.
(3) FOLSOM, J. W.
    1909. THE INSECT PESTS OF CLOVER AND ALFALFA. Univ. Ill. Agr. Exp. Sta.,
        Bul. 134, p. 113–197, 2 pl., 34 figs.
(4) KNAB, F.
    1915. THE SECRETIONS EMPLOYED BY RHYNCHOPHOROUS LARVÆ IN COCOON-
        MAKING. *In* Proc. Ent. Soc. Wash., v. 17, no. 3, p. 154–158.
(5) PETTIT, R. H.
    1910. INSECTS OF FIELD CROPS. Mich. Agr. Coll. Exp. Sta., Div. Ent., Bul.
        258, p. 36–84.
(6) RILEY, C. V.
    1882. REPORT OF THE ENTOMOLOGIST. *In* Rept. U. S. Dept. Agr. 1881–1882,
        p. 61–214 ([167] p.).
(7) TITUS, E. G.
    1911. HYPERA AND PHYTONOMUS IN AMERICA. *In* Ann. Ent. Soc. Amer.,
        v. 4, no. 4, p. 383–474, pl. xxiv–xxxiv, 11 maps.
        Bibliography, *Hypera punctata:* Pages 396–401.

UNITED STATES DEPARTMENT OF AGRICULTURE

BULLETIN No. 923

Contribution from the Bureau of Animal Industry
JOHN R. MOHLER, Chief

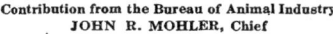

Washington, D. C.   ▼   February 21, 1921

UNIT REQUIREMENTS FOR PRODUCING MARKET MILK IN VERMONT.

By J. B. Bain, Dairy Husbandman; R. J. Posson, Market Milk Specialist; and Ralph P. Hotis, Assistant Market Milk Specialist, Dairy Division.

CONTENTS.

	Page.			Page.
Character and scope of the work	1		Factors involved, etc.—Continued.	
Methods used in obtaining the data	2		Feed	9
Winter and summer feeding	3		Pasture	10
Description of the herds	3		Labor	10
Requirements for producing 100 pounds of milk	4		Other costs	11
Requirements for keeping a cow one year	5		Per cent comparisons of factors involved	13
Credit for calves and manure	7		Determination of the bulk line of production	14
Requirements for keeping a bull	8		Monthly distribution of factors in milk production	14
Factors involved in the production of milk	9		Summary	17

CHARACTER AND SCOPE OF THE WORK.

To determine the requirements of milk production and to obtain data which would aid in improving milk-production methods, the United States Department of Agriculture, through the Dairy Division, Bureau of Animal Industry, began a series of studies in 1915. These studies were made in detail on practical dairy farms in various market. milk centers of the United States, and the project with which this bulletin deals was undertaken in a market milk section of Vermont.

The work of this project, which was located in Addison County, was begun on all but three of the herds in November and December, 1916, and on these three in March, 1917. Although the records of the last three herds were not completed until March, 1919, they are included and reported with the records of the herds completed in December, 1918.

15786—21——1

The project was located in this section b
produced was market milk. The milk fron
to central receiving stations for shipment t
the equipment and methods used in the p
of the milk were subject to the supervisio1
from the city, who visited the dairies regular
show the relation of the various factors use
the section studied and probably approxim
similar sections, but they do not apply to da
other conditions and management prevail.
represented typical conditions in the sectic
operation of members of cow-testing associat

The quantities of feed and labor are expres
instead of money cost, so that current prices 1

METHODS USED IN OBTAINING

The figures are actual records obtained 1
hour visits to 17 farms during the first year [1]
second year. The record work was continue
11 of the 17 farms visited the first year.

The field agents of the department record
information relative to the dairy business, in
classes of labor, feeds, bedding, pasture cost,
used on the farm, and current expenses for th
on calves and first-hand information on meth
were systematically collected.

By obtaining records [2] on every dairy regu
fluence of unusual circumstances at the tim
was lessened, and by using the records of all t
complete data for each month, season, and ye
were obtained for two entire years in order t
the other in the same section and to increase
study.

At the beginning and end of each year th
ventory of the dairy buildings, livestock, an
care of the herd and its products. On his re
tour he arrived at the first farm of a group i1
labor operations connected with the evening
hand he noted and recorded the minute each l
with the dairy was begun and ended. The
the next day were recorded in the same mann

[1] Howard B. Cannon carried on the field work during
taken over by Ralph P. Hotis.
[2] Copies of the blanks and description of the methods 1
tion to the Dairy Division, Bureau of Animal Industry.

The field agent also verified the records of feeds that were being fed on the inspection day, recording the kind, quantity, cost, and description of each, and compared them with the quantities recorded by the cow tester in the cow-testing-association books.

The quantity of milk sold and receipts each month were obtained, and the whole milk used by the proprietor and his help or fed to calves which were being raised was measured or weighed and used as a basis for determining the amount kept on the farm during the month.

Each dairyman kept an itemized account of expenses which were incurred between the monthly visits, and these items were recorded by the field agent. A monthly record was also kept of the purchase or sale of cows, calves, and hides. Outside bull service and other miscellaneous information relating to the herd were recorded. The field agent also noted the condition and methods of handling the manure and reported it each month.

When all the labor operations about the dairy had been completed for the day at the first farm, the field agent drove to the next farm in time to observe the labor operations connected with the evening chores. This program was followed each day until Saturday afternoon, when he returned to his official headquarters and finished his reports for the week's work. The same program was followed each week, so that each farm under observation was visited for a working day every 30 days throughout the two years.

WINTER AND SUMMER FEEDING.

Since the winter and summer seasons have a marked influence on the principal factors entering into the cost of producing milk, the results have been computed separately for those periods. The months from November to April, inclusive, represent the winter season, and from May to October the summer season.

The various tables found in this bulletin are based upon figures obtained during the two years of the study, and the weighted average of the two-year records was used whenever it would more accurately express the result. The weighted average was obtained by giving each item a different weight in the average according to its relative importance.

DESCRIPTION OF THE HERDS.

The principal dairy breeds were well represented by grade and purebred animals, but the Holsteins were most numerous. During the first year records were obtained on 17 herds having an average size of 26.1 cows, with an average annual production, per cow, of 5,415 pounds of milk, testing 4.0 per cent butterfat. Eighteen herds were studied during the second year. These herds had an average

ιg was practiced to so great an extent as the number of
ng at that time would seem to indicate, for most of
shened in the latter part of the winter and were really
ς."

ΛΕΝΤS FOR PRODUCING 100 POUNDS OF MILK.

e of milk is generally based on 100-pound quantities,
nts for milk production were based on this unit. The
·en in Table 1 and the credit for calves and manure in

*requirements, except charge for management, for producing 100
pounds of milk in winter and in summer.*

m.	Winter.		Average of two winters.	Summer.		Average of two summers.
	1916–17	1917–18		1917	1918	
trates......pounds..	29.0	30.2	29.6	7.2	9.2	8.1
ns...........do....	3.2	3.8	3.5	.5	.6	.6
tes...........do....	32.2	34.0	33.1	7.7	9.8	8.7
ɔughage.......do....	1.1	1.2	1.2	3.4	.5	2.1
ιage:						
ay............do....	108.7	121.4	114.7	10.4	18.2	13.9
..............do....	18.2	9.4	14.0	2.9	2.6	2.7
ghage.........do....	128.0	132.0	129.9	16.7	21.3	18.7
succulent roughage ....pounds..	193.2	189.2	191.3	19.9	37.4	27.8
.............acres..	....	....	....	.09	.11	.10
............pounds..	10.0	12.5	11.2	....	....	....
ding concentrates ....dollars..	....	....	0.020	....	....	0.005
.............hours..	2.7	2.7	2.7	1.9	2.1	2.0
..............do....	.6	.5	.6	.4	.3	.4
............dollars..	0.177	0.174	0.176	0.128	0.140	0.133
ɪs and dairy supplies ....dollars..	.077	.097	.087	.056	.078	.066
ɪes............do....	....	.003	.002	.005	.017	.010

TABLE 1.—*Unit requirements, except charge for management, etc.*—Continued.

Item.	Winter.		Average of two winters.	Summer.		Average of two summers.
	1916-17	1917-18		1917	1918	
Other costs—Continued.						
Herd charges—						
Taxes, insurance, veterinary, medicine, disinfectants, and cow-testing associations.dollars..	.048	.066	.056	.035	.053	.043
Interest on cow investment.....do....	.098	.118	.107	.071	.095	.082
Cost of keeping bull..............do....	.033	.063	.048	.018	.046	.031
Total of other costs except appreciation and depreciation on cows....................dollars..	.433	.521	.476	.313	.429	.365
Depreciation on cows...........do....		.166	.079		.133	.060
Appreciation on cows...........do....						
Total of other costs ....dollars..	.433	.687	**.555**	.313	·562	**.425**

NOTE.—The summaries of the unit requirements are printed in bold-faced type for convenient reference.

TABLE 2.—*Credit for calves and manure for each 100 pounds of milk produced.*

Item.	Winter.		Average of two winters.	Summer.		Average of two summers.
	1916–17	1917–18		1917	1918	
Credit for calves.................number..	0.024	0.026	0.025	0.009	0.009	0.009
Credit for manure.................pounds..	370	394	382	46	68	56

REQUIREMENTS FOR KEEPING A COW ONE YEAR.

The requirements for keeping a cow for one year are shown in Table 3. It will be noted that there was a wide variation between the quantities of purchased and home-grown concentrates fed. Most of the dry roughage fed consisted of salable hay. Of course, the difference between the quantities of feed used in winter and in summer was due to the large amount of pasture grazed during the summer.

TABLE 3.—*Number of cows, average production, and requirements for keeping a cow, except charge for management, based on the records obtained for the two years, 1916–17 and 1917–18.*

Item.	Winter.	Summer.	Entire year.
Number of cows.............. ....average..	819.2	874.6	847.0
Average production.. ....pounds..	2,353	2,899	5,252
Feed:			
Purchased concentrates.... ....do....	696	235	931
Home-grown grains.. ....do....	83	16	99
Total concentrates.. ....do....	779	251	1,030
Noncommercial roughage...............................do....	27	61	88
Commercial carbohydrate hay.........................do....	2,700	403	3,103
Commercial legume hay..................................do....	330	79	409
Total dry roughage.....................................do....	3,057	543	3,600

Table 3.—*Number of cows, average production, etc.*—Continued.

Item.	Winter.	Summer.	Entir year.
Feed—Continued.			
Silage and other succulent roughage..................pounds..	4,502	805	5,
Pasture...acres..	....	3.0	
Bedding [1]..pounds..	263	....	
Hauling and grinding concentrates.........................dollars..	0.47	0.14	(
Labor:			
Human labor...hours..	64.2	58.8	1
Horse labor..do....	13.7	10.4	
Other costs:			
Building charges..dollars..	4.13	3.87	
Equipment charges and dairy supplies....................do....	2.04	1.91	
Motor truck charge.......................................do....	.04	.30	
Herd charges—			
Taxes, insurance, veterinary, medicine, disinfectants, and cow-testing association.........................dollars..	1.33	1.24	
Interest on cow investment............................do....	2.52	2.37	
Cost of keeping bull...................................do....	1.12	.89	
Total of other costs, except depreciation and appreciation on cows..................................dollars..	11.18	10.58	2
Depreciation on cows......................................do....	1.86	1.74	
Appreciation on cows......................................do....	....	....	
Total other costs ....do....	13.04	12.32	2

[1] The small amount of bedding used was partly due to the use of refuse hay and other roughage lef the mangers.

The fact that almost as much labor was required to care for a c in the summer as in the winter probably was due to the lower p portion of dry cows and a higher production in the summer, whi made it necessary to use more labor for milking.

Table 4.—*Cost of keeping a cow and per cent increase of the cost for the sec year over the first.*

Item.	1916–17	1917–18	Increa in cost secon year ov first ye
			Per ce
Feed, pasture, and bedding...	$50.24	$65.74	
Labor...	20.73	23.47	
Other costs except depreciation or appreciation on livestock........	19.67	24.04	
Appreciation on livestock...	....	....	
Depreciation on livestock...	....	7.56	
Yearly cost per cow...	90.64	120.81	
Credit for calves and manure.......................................	22.32	26.68	

An increase in the market price for cows increased the invent so much at the end of the first year that it just balanced the dep ciation on the herd. There was an increase in prices during second year also, but the losses from tuberculosis in a number the herds were large enough to overbalance the increase in mar values and result in a net depreciation of $7.56 per cow.

CREDIT FOR CALVES AND MANURE.

CALVES.

Most of the heifer calves were raised or sold to neighbors for raising. The grade bull calves were usually vealed, and the whole milk sucked from the cows was credited to the herd by crediting the selling price of the calves and not the birth value.

TABLE 5.—*Credit for calves produced, by years and seasons.*

Item.	Year.		Seasons.	
	1916–17	1917–18	Two winters.	Two summers.
Number of calves	374	341	481	234
Total value of calves.........dollars..	2,275.05	2,647.37	3,160.99	1,761.43
Average value of calves.........do....	6.08	7.76	6.57	7.53
Calves per cow	0.84	0.85	0.58	0.27
Credit per cow.........dollars..	5.13	6.56	3.86	2.01

Since the purebred cows were given the same value as grade cows of like producing ability, the purebred bull calves were credited to the herds at what they would have been worth when 4 days old to fatten for veal and the purebred heifer calves at the value of grade heifer calves.

MANURE.

The credit for manure was figured after taking the following factors into consideration: Fertilizing constituents in the feeds;[3] quantities of nitrogen, phosphoric acid, and potash not utilized in the bodies of the cows but voided in the manure; the per cent of the total manure dropped in the barn; the per cent of manure saved in the storing and handling; the nitrogen, phosphoric acid, and potash contained in the bedding; and the value of these fertilizing constituents saved in the manure and bedding, all being figured at wholesale prices for commercial fertilizer.

TABLE 6.—*Credit for manure and fertilizing constituents, by seasons.*

Item.	Winter.	Summer.
Manure and bedding saved:	*Tons.*	*Tons.*
First year	1,862.7	327.9
Second year	1,815.4	384.4
Average per cow	4.5	0.8

[3] Obtained from " Feeds and Feeding," by Henry and Morrison.

Item.	Winter.			Summer.		
	Nitrogen.	Phos-phoric acid.	Potash.	Nitrogen.	Phos-phoric acid.	Pota:
	Pounds.	*Pounds.*	*Pounds.*	*Pounds.*	*Pounds.*	*Poun*
Manure	39,470	13,005	42,102	7,587	2,525	8,
Bedding	1,145	397	2,854			
Total fertilizing constituents	40,615	13,402	44,956	7,587	2,525	8,
Credit per cow	49.6	16.4	54.9	8.7	2.9	

The average credit allowed for manure and bedding each year i cludes the manure from the bulls, and represents what was or cou easily have been saved under local conditions. Since the total cost keeping bulls is charged against the cows, the bull manure is includ as a direct credit to the herd, and the combined credit was estimat to be 5.3 tons per cow.

The fertilizing constituents in 1 ton of average manure and be ding from the cows during the winter were estimated to be as follow

Poun
per t
Nitrogen -- 1(
Commercial phosphoric acid--------------------------------- £
Potash--- 11

Without bedding, 1 ton of average winter manure was estimated contain:

Poun
per t
Nitrogen--- 1(
Commercial phosphoric acid--------------------------------- £
Potash--- 1]

The fertilizing constituents in the manure and bedding were valu at the following prices a pound during the first year: Nitrogen, cents; commercial phosphoric acid, 6 cents; and potash, 7 cents; a: during the second year: Nitrogen, 25 cents; phosphoric acid, 6 cent and potash, 7 cents.

On the average dairy farm the commercial value of manure c pends upon the use to which it is put. The return in dollars depen upon the increase in the crops raised and the amount received fro the sale of these crops. These facts may reduce or increase the val of manure below or above the market price of the fertilizing constit ents contained in it.

REQUIREMENTS FOR KEEPING A BULL.

The record on one bull for one month, called a bull month, w taken as a working unit. The bulls on about three-fourths of t farms were kept in the barn in the summer. This accounts for t comparatively large amount of labor and feed required during the summer.

TABLE 7.—*Requirements for keeping a bull, based on averages obtained from the equivalent of 27.1 bulls.*

Item.	Average of two winters.	Average of two summers.	Average for year.
Feed:			
Purchased concentrates....................pounds..	162	104	266
Home-grown grains.........................do....	57	13	70
Total concentrates......................do....	219	117	336
Dry roughage:			
Noncommercial.............................do....	56	68	124
Commercial carbohydrate hay...............do....	2,894	2,717	5,611
Commercial legume hay.....................do....	765	234	999
Total dry roughage.....................do....	3,715	3,019	6,734
Silage and other succulent roughage.......do....	1,819	577	2,396
Bedding..................................do....	269	....	269
Pasture.................................dollars..	....	1.92	1.92
Human labor..............................hours..	22.3	15.4	37.7
Other costs:			
Interest on bull investment..............dollars..	3.06	3.55	6.61
Bull's share of buildings.................do.....	4.13	3.47	7.60
Total of other costs....................do....	7.19	7.02	14.21
Appreciation on bull....................do....	1.09	.99	2.08
Total of other costs less appreciation....do....	6.10	6.03	12.13

The appreciation was due to the fact that in the first inventory the value of the bulls was placed at $125 a head. While in the herd they increased in size and thus increased their selling price when sold for beef.

FACTORS INVOLVED IN THE PRODUCTION OF MILK.

FEED.

The cost of hauling purchased concentrates varied from 50 cents to $1.50 a ton and the grinding charges ranged from 6 cents to 12 cents for each 100 pounds of grain. The quantities of the different kinds of feed were obtained from actual weights made by the cow tester during one full day of each month. The quantities were also checked frequently by the field agent.

Concentrates is a term applied to grains and to manufactured by-products suitable for feeding. The concentrates are low in fiber and contain a large amount of nutritive material in a relatively small bulk.

Home-grown grains consist of concentrates commonly grown on the farm or in the locality where fed.

Noncommercial dry roughage applies to corn stover, corn fodder, and other dry, coarse feeds for which price quotations are not given in the trade papers. The term is also applied to hay so foul with weeds or so damaged in curing as not to be readily salable.

15786°—21——2

Leguminous roughage includes alfalfa, clover, cowpea, soy bean, and other legume hays when pure, or when so slightly mixed with grasses as not materially to affect the protein content.

Commercial carbohydrate roughage includes all commercial hays except those classified as leguminous roughage.

PASTURE.

The pasture cost included the interest on the value of the land, the general cost of maintaining the fences, and such other items as seeding, cutting weeds, and repair and maintenance of watering troughs. The value of the land was obtained by subtracting the value of the improvements from the total value of the farm. The cost of pasture was distributed over the six summer months on a percentage basis. The per cent allowed for each month on each farm was estimated as nearly as possible in proportion to the condition of the pasture and the quantity of feed the herd received from the grass each month. The average from the various farms gave the following per cents of pasturage for the summer months: May, 15 per cent; June, 22 per cent; July, 18 per cent; August, 16 per cent; September, 15 per cent; October, 14 per cent.

LABOR.

The hours of labor were obtained by actually timing the various labor operations performed about the dairy during one entire day each month; this time was multiplied by the number of working days in that month plus the hours of work done on Sundays.

TABLE 8.—*Per cent of labor performed and hours per 100 pounds of milk for each class of help.*

WINTER.

	Distribution of work performed.			Labor per 100 pounds milk.		
	1916–17	1917–18	Average.	1916–17	1917–18	Average.
	Per cent.	Per cent.	Per cent.	Hours.	Hours.	Hours.
Managers...........................	41.7	41.7	41.7	1.1	1.1	1.1
Hired men...........................	50.3	43.6	47.0	1.4	1.2	1.3
Total man labor...................	92.0	85.3	88.7	2.5	2.3	2.4
Women..............................	3.2	3.8	3.5	.1	.1	.1
Boys and girls......................	4.8	10.9	7.8	.1	.3	.2
Total...........................	100.0	100.0	100.0	2.7	2.7	2.7

SUMMER.

Managers...........................	40.2	37.9	39.1	0.8	0.8	0.8
Hired men...........................	44.1	40.8	42.4	.8	.9	.8
Total man labor...................	84.3	78.7	81.5	1.6	1.7	1.6
Women..............................	5.4	4.3	4.9	.1	.1	.1
Boys and girls......................	10.3	17.0	13.6	.2	.3	.3
Total...........................	100.0	100.0	100.0	1.9	2.1	2.0

TABLE 9.—*Human labor required for producing, handling, and hauling 100 pounds of milk to the shipping platform.*

Kind of work.	Winter.						Average of 2 winters.		Summer.						Average of 2 summers.	
	1916–17		1917–18						1917		1918					
	Hours.	Per cent.	Hours.	Per cent.			Hours.	Per cent.	Hours.	Per cent.	Hours.	Per cent.			Hours.	Per cent.
Production.....	2.2	81.0	2.1	78.7			2.2	79.9	1.5	77.8	1.6	77.3			1.6	77.6
Handling......	.2	6.8	.2	8.2			.2	7.4	.2	8.9	.2	10.0			.2	9.4
Hauling........	.3	12.2	.4	13.1			.3	12.7	.2	13.3	.3	12.7			.2	13.0
Total.......	2.7	100.0	2.7	100.0			2.7	100.0	1.9	100.0	2.1	100.0			2.0	100.0

OTHER COSTS.

The " other costs " charged against the production of milk did not include the interest, taxes, and similar items against the entire farming enterprise, but covered only the dairy's share of the buildings and equipment.

BUILDINGS.

Interest was figured at the customary rate of 5 per cent on improved real estate on the inventory value taken at the beginning of the year. The annual depreciation charge was obtained by dividing the first inventory by the number of years it was estimated the buildings would remain in a usable condition. The annual cost of painting and repairs was computed. Slate roofs, because of their long life and durability, made the depreciation lower on many of the buildings. Taxes and insurance premiums were obtained by examining the individual tax records and insurance premium receipts. Annual repairs were included in the general charge against the buildings. The expense for buildings charged against the dairy was in proportion to the space used for it. The total amount of these charges amounted to 9.5 per cent of the inventory value of the portion of the buildings used by the herd.

EQUIPMENT.

An inventory was taken at the beginning and end of each year. Six per cent interest was charged on the first inventory value. The difference between the first inventory plus equipment purchased and the inventory taken at the end of the year plus equipment sold constituted the depreciation. A record of all repairs on equipment was kept by the dairyman and given to the field agent each month. The total of these charges amounted to 26.3 per cent of the inventory value of the equipment. Miscellaneous supplies, such as strainer cloths, washing powder, brushes, gasoline, and oil for running machines, amounted to 70 cents per cow per year.

HERD.

Each cow and bull was inventoried at the beginning of eac
at the market value, and to this inventory was added the v:
animals entering the herd during the year.   Interest was fig
6 per cent.   Each grade cow purchased or sold was recorded
price paid.

As the requirements for producing milk by a purebred cow
same as by a grade cow of equal productive capacity, it becoi
parent that her greater value is due to the value of her of
and not the value of her milk.   Since the purpose of the bullet
deal with the requirements for producing milk, raising pu
must be considered as a separate business.   In order to avoid th
ence of the purebred business upon the requirements for pro
milk, purebred cows have been given the same value as grade (
the same productive capacity and purebred calves have beei
corresponding grade values.

Death losses were taken care of in the difference in inve:
At the end of the year the inventory value of each animal in tl
took into consideration any increase or decrease in value over t
inventory.   To the second inventory was added the value c
or hides sold during the year.   The difference between these a
constituted the depreciation or appreciation.   During the fir
there was no change in the value of the average cow, but
the second year the removal of animals with tuberculosis k
a heavy depreciation charge which probably had been acct
ing during past years.   Undoubtedly it was much larger i
would have been if the herds'had been tested regularly for t
losis.

The taxes were obtained directly from the township recor
where insurance was carried the amount of the premiums v
tained from the receipts.   The total of all costs against the
amounted to 11.4 per cent of the inventory value taken at the
ning of each year.

MOTOR-TRUCK CHARGES.

On some of the farms the milk was hauled by motor trucks during a part of the year, and the charge was based directly upon the cost of keeping and operating the truck.

TABLE 10.—*Per cent relationship between the other costs and the capital invested for all herds.*

Item.	Buildings.	Equipment.	Herds.	Total investment.
Capital invested	$71,028.50	$10,461.37	$69,048.00	$150,537.87
Capital invested, per cow	83.86	12.35	81 52	177.73
	Per cent.	*Per cent.*	*Per cent.*	
Interest	4.8	6.0	6.0	
Depreciation	2.6	17.8	4.4	
Taxes	.9		} 1.0	
Insurance	.3			
Upkeep and repairs	.9	.8		
Milking-machine repairs		1.7		
Total of other costs	9.5	26.3	11.4	11.5

The figures at the foot of each of the four columns show the per cent relationship of the cost to the capital invested as recorded at the heads of the columns.

PER CENT COMPARISONS OF FACTORS INVOLVED IN COST OF MILK PRODUCTION.

There was a noticeable difference in the cost of producing milk in winter and in summer. The following table shows that the cost of the feed was the chief cause of this difference.

TABLE 11.—*Per cent of the 2-year cost of milk production represented by feed, labor, and overhead and other costs.*

Cost item.	Average of 2 winters.	Average of 2 summers.	Average of 2 years.
	Per cent.	*Per cent.*	*Per cent.*
Feed and bedding	39.0	10.4	49.4
Pasture		5.5	5.5
Labor	10.8	10.2	21.0
Other costs except herd inventory variations	10.3	10.4	20.7
Total cost except herd inventory variations	60.1	36.5	96.6
Herd depreciation	1.7	1.7	3.4
Total cost of production	61.8	38.2	100.0
Credits:			
Calves	3.5	2.0	5.5
Manure	14.9	2.8	17.7
Total for calves and manure	18.4	4.8	23.2

The cost of feed, bedding, and pasture in winter was 39 per cent of the yearly cost, while in summer it amounted to 15.9 per cent of the yearly cost. It is also interesting to note that the labor cost and other costs except the herd inventory variations were practically the same in winter and in summer, and also equal to each other, being slightly more than 10 per cent in each season for each of the two items. The average yearly cost is shown in the last column.

The percentages obtained show the relationship which existed between the various factors under the system of dairy management

practiced in this section where many cows freshened in the
and where a large amount of good pasture furnished an abu
of feed for "summer dairying." Although they may appro
the relationship found in near-by sections, they can not be ap]
all sections of the United States.

DETERMINATION OF THE BULK LINE OF PRODUCTIO

When it is required to fix a price to represent the cost of]
ing milk for any section or group of dairymen, it is evident
the actual average cost is used for this purpose then one-half
milk is produced at a cost greater than the sum fixed. There
the price of milk is based on the average cost of production it
tend to discourage production and decrease the supply. (
other hand, the least economical producers should have littl
ence in determining the cost of production for any group of
men.

There is a line on the scale of costs, however, below wh
greater quantity of the milk is produced. This line, called tl
line, is placed where it will usually include from 80 to 90 p
of the volume of milk produced. It is aimed to cover the
producing all milk except that produced at extremely high co

Some of the factors to take into consideration in locating tl
line are illustrated in figures 1 and 2. Attention is called
fact that the higher the cost the less the volume of milk pr
The horizontal lines which indicate volume of milk are long
middle of the group and the vertical lines are short, but as t
of production increases the vertical lines rapidly increase in le

As regards the placing of the bulk line in connection w
volume of milk produced in the present investigation, the l
the summer of 1917 might have been located in figure 1 at th
A, or possibly at C, but hardly at E, because the rapid incr
cost, as shown by the length of the line CD, is not compensa
by the extra volume of milk (line DE) produced at the hig
Similarly the line for the summer of 1918 would not be placed
than F. The bulk line for the winter production of 1916–17
might be placed at either A or B, and that for the winter of 1
at C.

MONTHLY DISTRIBUTION OF FACTORS IN MILK PRODU

The lower net feed cost for November as compared with Oct
Table 14 is due to the larger credit for the amount of manure
in the barn. The gross feed and bedding cost is a more a
index of the relationship of the cost of feed in Octob
November.

It will be noted that during the first year the income fro
during each season corresponded very closely to the volume (

produced. In each year, however, there was no correlation between the seasonal production of milk and the gross cost of feed required

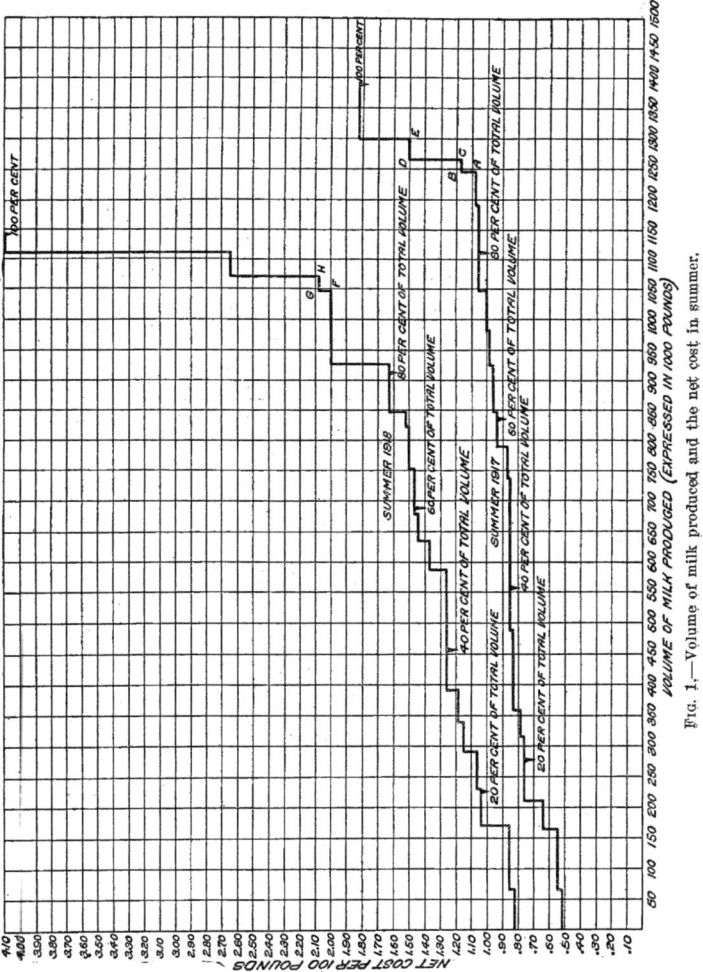

FIG. 1.—Volume of milk produced and the net cost in summer,

to produce it. There was no correlation between the feed cost and the income from milk, although the per cent of income from milk during the second season more nearly corresponds to that of the

gross feed cost of producing it than during the first winter. . This
was due to a higher price paid for milk during the second winter.

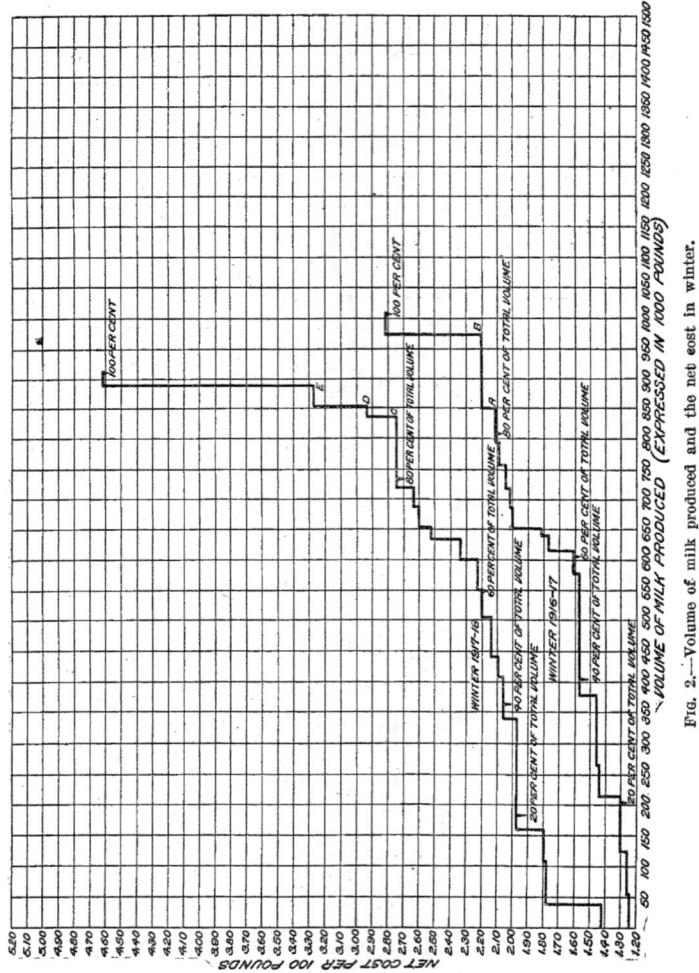

Fig. 2.—Volume of milk produced and the net cost in winter.

It will be noted that the gross winter feed and bedding cost was
71.9 per cent and 72.4 per. cent, respectively, of the first and second
year's gross feed, pasture, and bedding cost, while the per cent of the

year's milk production for the same season was 42 and 44.5, respectively. Subtracting the credit for manure and bedding from the cost of feed, pasture, and bedding in winter produced a closer correlation to the price received for winter milk. However, this did not prove to be equally true for the summer season.

TABLE 12.—*Distribution, by months, of milk prices, milk sold and used, feed cost, and labor required for two years.*

Months and seasons.	Price received per 100 pounds of milk.	Year's income from milk sold and used.	Year's milk sold and used.	Year's feed, pasture, and bedding cost.	Feed, pasture, and bedding cost minus manure and bedding credit.	Human labor.		Horse labor.	
						Per 100 pounds milk.	Per cow.	Per 100 pounds milk.	Per cow.
		Per cent.	*Per cent.*	*Per cent.*	*Per cent.*	*Hours.*	*Hours.*	*Hours.*	*Hours.*
1916–17.									
May	$2.20	10.1	11.5	10.3	9.5	1.8	10.9	0.3	1.8
June	2.11	11.0	13.2	2.4	1.6	1.5	10.5	.3	2.0
July	2.30	10.5	11.4	2.2	1.3	1.8	10.9	.3	1.9
August	2.79	9.4	8.5	2.8	1.9	2.2	9.7	.4	1.7
September	2.83	8.3	7.4	3.8	2.9	2.2	8.6	.5	1.8
October	3.40	8.1	6.0	6.6	5.8	2.5	8.0	.6	1.9
Summer	2.49	57.4	58.0	28.1	23.0	1.9	9.8	.4	1.9
November	3.08	6.7	5.5	9.7	4.9	2.9	8.6	.6	1.9
December	2.74	6.4	5.9	11.8	7.0	3.0	10.0	.5	1.7
January	2.61	6.2	5.9	10.9	6.0	3.4	11.8	1.0	3.4
February	2.52	6.4	6.4	12.2	7.4	2.7	9.7	.7	2.6
March	2.38	8.0	8.4	13.4	8.5	2.4	11.1	.6	2.6
April	2.26	8.9	9.9	13.9	9.0	2.3	12.2	.5	2.4
Winter	2.55	42.6	42.0	71.9	42.8	2.7	10.6	.6	2.4
Entire year		100.0	100.0	100.0	65.8				
1917–18.									
May	2.62	11.2	12.8	4.6	3.7	1.8	11.2	.3	1.9
June	1.96	8.4	12.7	3.3	2.4	1.7	10.7	.3	1.7
July	2.40	8.5	10.6	3.0	2.1	2.0	10.3	.4	1.9
August	2.91	7.6	7.8	2.9	2.0	2.4	9.2	.4	1.4
September	3.19	6.7	6.3	5.0	4.1	2.7	8.4	.4	1.2
October	3.86	6.9	5.3	8.8	7.9	3.4	9.0	.5	1.2
Summer	2.65	49.3	55.5	27.6	22.2	2.1	9.8	.3	1.6
November	3.93	6.9	5.2	10.9	6.6	3.3	8.4	.6	1.5
December	3.84	8.3	6.4	11.9	7.5	3.1	10.4	.6	2.1
January	3.55	8.4	7.1	11.7	7.3	3.1	11.8	.8	2.9
February	3.38	7.8	6.8	11.3	6.9	2.6	10.2	.4	1.6
March	3.43	9.9	8.6	12.3	8.0	2.5	12.2	.4	2.1
April	2.70	9.4	10.4	14.3	9.9	2.2	12.1	.4	2.3
Winter	3.39	50.7	44.5	72.4	46.2	2.7	10.8	.5	2.1
Entire year		100.0	100.0	100.0	68.4				

SUMMARY.

The figures reported in this study were obtained from typical farms in a market milk section of Vermont. Although they show the requirements for producing milk in that section and may approximate the requirements in similar sections, they do not apply to dairy sections where other conditions and methods of management prevail.

The unit requirements for producing 100 pounds of milk in winter were: Concentrates, 33.1 pounds; hauling and grinding concentrates, 2 cents; dry roughage, 129.9 pounds; silage and other succulent roughage, 191.3 pounds; bedding, 11.2 pounds; human labor, 2.7 hours; horse labor, 0.6 hour; other costs, 55.5 cents. The credits other than milk were 0.025 of one calf and 382 pounds of manure. (Tables 1 and 2.)

In summer the unit requirements were: Concentrates, 8.7 pounds; hauling and grinding concentrates, 0.5 cent; dry roughage, 18.7 pounds; silage and other succulent roughage, 27.8 pounds; pasture, 0.1 acre; human labor, 2 hours; horse labor, 0.4 hour; other costs, 42.5 cents. The credits other than milk were 0.009 of one calf and 56 pounds of manure.

The unit requirements for keeping a cow one year were as follows: Concentrates, 1,030 pounds; hauling and grinding concentrates, 61 cents; dry roughage, 3,600 pounds; silage and other succulent roughage, 5,307 pounds; bedding, 263 pounds; pasture, 3 acres; human labor, 123 hours; horse labor, 24.1 hours; other costs, $25.36 without charge for management. Credits other than milk; 0.85 of one calf; 5.3 tons manure. (Table 3.)

The tabulation of the figures obtained for the expenses of the herd and for the herd's share of the buildings and equipment showed that the annual expense for the buildings amounted to 9.5 per cent of the inventory value of the buildings. The charges on equipment were 26.3 per cent of the inventory value of the equipment; and the herd charges amounted to 11.4 per cent of the inventory value of the herd. The total of the charges against buildings, equipment, and livestock amounted to 11.5 per cent of the capital invested in them.

The percentages of the total cost represented by the various cost and credit factors, except charge for management, were as follows: Feed, pasture, and bedding, 54.9 per cent; labor, 21 per cent; other costs, 24.1 per cent; credit for calves and manure, 23.2 per cent of the cost. (Table 11.)

The men performed 88.7 per cent and 81.5 per cent of the work in the winter and summer periods, respectively. The remainder of the work was done by women or by boys and girls. (Table 8.)

In the winter periods the dairymen received much less for their milk than the gross feed and bedding costs of producing it; there was a reversal of this situation during the summer. (Table 12.)

UNITED STATES DEPARTMENT OF AGRICULTURE

BULLETIN No. 924

Contribution from the Bureau of Plant Industry
WM. A. TAYLOR, Chief

Washington, D. C.   PROFESSIONAL PAPER   January 26, 1921.

TEAR-STAIN OF CITRUS FRUITS.

By JOHN R. WINSTON,

Pathologist, Office of Fruit-Disease Investigations.

CONTENTS.

	Page.		Page.
Description of the disease	1	Inoculation experiments	9
Review of the literature	2	Conclusions	11
Spraying experiments	3	Summary	11
Cultural work	5	Literature cited	12
Histological examination	9		

DESCRIPTION OF THE DISEASE.

Florida citrus fruits are subject to two distinct types of tear-streaking, namely, wither-tip tear-stain and melanose tear-streak. The former has been attributed to *Colletotrichum gloeosporioides* Penz., while the latter, which will not be discussed in this bulletin, is doubtless due to a peculiar distribution of the spores of the causal organism (*Phomopsis citri* Fawcett) in trickling waters.

Wither-tip tear-stain is a smooth, more or less brownish discoloration of the surface which occurs typically in fingerlike patterns about one-fourth of an inch in width, extending longitudinally toward the stylar or blossom end of the fruit. (Pl. I.) These streaks may or may not be confined to one side of the fruit, and frequently they appear to arise in areas russeted by rust mites (*Eriophyes oleiveros* Ashmead). The streaks are usually few in number, seldom more than six or eight; occasionally two or more merge and form a rather wide discoloration, in which event the injury is generally attributed to rust mites. (Pl. II, fig. 1.)

Wither-tip tear-stain as it occurs in Florida is one of the minor diseases of citrus fruits, and for that reason it has received little attention from investigators. Its effects are principally observed on the round orange and grapefruit, more noticeably and frequently on the latter and to a less extent upon other economic species of citrus.

15580°—21—Bull. 924

The economic importánée of this blemish is chiefly financial loss which the grower sustains as a result of t market value of the affected fruit, which is rendered un unattractive. However, tear-stained fruit seems to po and keeping qualities essentially equal to fruit which i these markings.

REVIEW OF THE LITERATURE.

A careful survey of the literature reveals the fact that has been published on the subject. The cause of tea investigated and first reported on by Rolfs (7),[1] who is follows:

This peculiar form of russeting manifests itself by streaks running from the side that hangs uppermost to the point which is nearest the cause of this peculiar form of russeting is that somewhere above the occurs which has been infested by the fungus [2] and which contains spores. Whenever sufficient rain or dew occurs to cause a dripping fro infected twig on to the fruit, the disseminating spores are liberated and carried with the rain or dew over the epidermis of the fruit. Many are left along in different places, and these produce sufficient irritatic dermis to cause russeting along in streaks; hence we have the peculia staining or tear streaks.

Again in 1911 Rolfs (8) discussed the subject as follows

Russeting and tear streaking can nearly always be traced back for th to a small dead spur or sprig. The fungus [2] lives in the dead spur or s from rains and moisture following heavy dews collect in drops on the spurs and the drops when they fall carry with them numerous fungous sp spores come in contact with the epidermis of the fruits and germin minute lesions on the epidermis, too small for complete infection and th of anthracnose.

This explanation as presented by Rolfs, to the effect *letotrichum gloeosporioides* is the responsible agent, seem been accepted by several investigators at various time them Fawcett (2–5), Stevens (9), Stevenson (10), and Ma

On the other hand, Earle and Rogers (1) recognized i of Pines two types of russeting or tear staining said to distinguishable, the one attributed to rust mites and thought to be caused by a fungus. In discussing withe make the following statement:

One of the serious troubles attributed to the wither-tip fungus in Fl water washing down from infected twigs will cause the serious discolor fruit known as tear streaking. The discoloration is often confused with the rust mite, though it is easily distinguished. It frequently occurs I be always traced to some dead twig, but we are still uncertain whether it secretions of the wither-tip fungus or the Diplodia.

---

[1] The serial numbers in parentheses refer to "Literature cited" at the end of this t
[2] *Colletotrichum gloeosporioides*, mentioned in the context.

The publications cited contain practically all the more important references to wither-tip tear-stain in Florida or near-by sections where the round orange and grapefruit are grown in large quantities, and no presentation of actual experimental data is made therein on which the fungus theory regarding the cause of tear-stain is based. However, it can not be denied that this theory, first stated by Rolfs, is so plausible that it has been accepted readily without the support of published experimental data. It was not until results very strikingly inconsistent with this theory appeared in experimental spraying tests that its validity was questioned, and this has led to a thorough investigation of the causation of the type of injury commonly known in Florida as "wither-tip tear-stain." The evidence presented in this bulletin indicates that *Colletotrichum gloeosporioides* is not responsible for tear staining in Florida. If this fungus ever produces such an effect, it must be extremely rare in that section.

SPRAYING EXPERIMENTS.

During the season of 1917, in connection with spraying experiments which were conducted in a bearing grapefruit grove for the control of citrus scab, it was observed that tear staining was almost entirely absent from those plats that received several applications of lime-sulphur solution, though it was quite prevalent where Bordeaux mixture had been applied during the scab-spraying season. Since this first observation, many similar manifestations of the lack of control of tear-stain by copper sprays have appeared in the experimental plats. Such a failure has been proportional to the severity of rust-mite attack.

Ordinarily the scab-spraying season in Florida begins in February when the spring growth starts and extends over a period of two or three months. It is followed rather closely by the period of very severe attack by rust mites. The latter are usually most abundant during May and June and are readily controlled by two or three applications of lime-sulphur solution diluted 1 to 66. With this explanation the data in Table I can be readily interpreted.

In general, the results of this spraying experiment show (1) that tear-stain was controlled on plats 3 and 5, which received applications of lime-sulphur solution shortly before the period of maximum abundance of rust mites; (2) that tear-stain was materially reduced on plat 4, which received applications of lime-sulphur solution considerably in advance of the period of maximum numbers of rust mites; (3) that tear-stain was not reduced on plats 1 and 2, which received spray applications of copper mixtures. Assuming that tear-stain is caused by a species of Colletotrichum or other fungus, it would be reasonable to expect that plats 1 and 2 would show at least as good control as plat 4. The fact that control of tear-stain was so closely associated with rust-mite control is strong evidence that rust mites might be largely concerned in the causation of the condition that is generally recognized as wither-tip tear-stain.

TABLE I.—*Effect of various sprays on the control of tear-stain on grapefruit.*

Date.	Plat designation and spray application.					
	No. 1, Bordeaux mixture.	No. 2, Burgundy mixture.	No. 3, Bordeaux mixture.	No. 4, lime-sulphur.	No. 5, lime-sulphur.	No. 6.
1917.						
Jan. 29	3–4–50	3–3½–50	3–4–50	1–40	1–40	Not sprayed.
Mar. 23	3–4–50	3–3½–50	3–4–50	1–40	1–40	Do.
Apr. 7	3–4–50	3–3½–50	3–4–50	1–40	1–40	Do.
May 2 and 22	3–4–50	3–3½–50	Lime-sulphur, 1–40.	Not sprayed.	1–40	Do.
June	Not sprayed.	Not sprayed.	Lime-sulphur, 1–66.	.....do....	1–66	Lime-sulphur, 1–66.
1918.						
February (final count of 1,000 fruits), tear-stained, per cent.	70.39a	38.2	1.3	7.5	1.25	25.9.

a The excessive number of tear-stained fruits on the plat sprayed with Bordeaux mixture may be explained by the fact, quite frequently noted, that rust mites become unusually abundant on trees sprayed with that material. The injury did not resemble Bordeaux russet, but was similar in every respect to the tear staining on plat 6.

A part of a grove of grapefruit was sprayed experimentally in June, 1919, using 3–4–50 Bordeaux mixture for plat 1 and 1–66 lime-sulphur solution for plat 2. Plat 3 was an unsprayed check. This grove had not been sprayed previously that season. At the end of July the fruit in plat 2 was free from tear staining, but numerous tear-stained specimens were observed in plats 1 and 3. The fruit on these plats ripened and was harvested in February, 1920, with no increase of tear-stain over that observed in July, 1919. This indicates that one application of weak lime-sulphur solution applied at a time suitable for rust-mite control in that grove was equally effective for the control of tear-stain, while the standard strength of Bordeaux mixture applied at the same time did not reduce this blemish. (Pl. II, fig. 2.)

Other experimental data obtained during the past four years show without exception similar results.

The conclusion of Yothers (11), based on numerous extensive experiments to control rust mites in various parts of Florida, is that bright fruit—i. e., fruit free from rust-mite injury—is invariably free from tear-stain as well. (Pl. II, fig. 1.)

Growers generally throughout the Florida citrus belt have accomplished commercial control of tear-stain whenever they have controlled rust mites by following the spraying schedules established for these pests.

Definite observations in commercial groves show clearly the following facts: (1) Where rust mites are naturally absent tear-stain is not observed; (2) where rust mites occur and are successfully controlled tear-stain is also controlled; (3) where rust mites are

PLATE I.

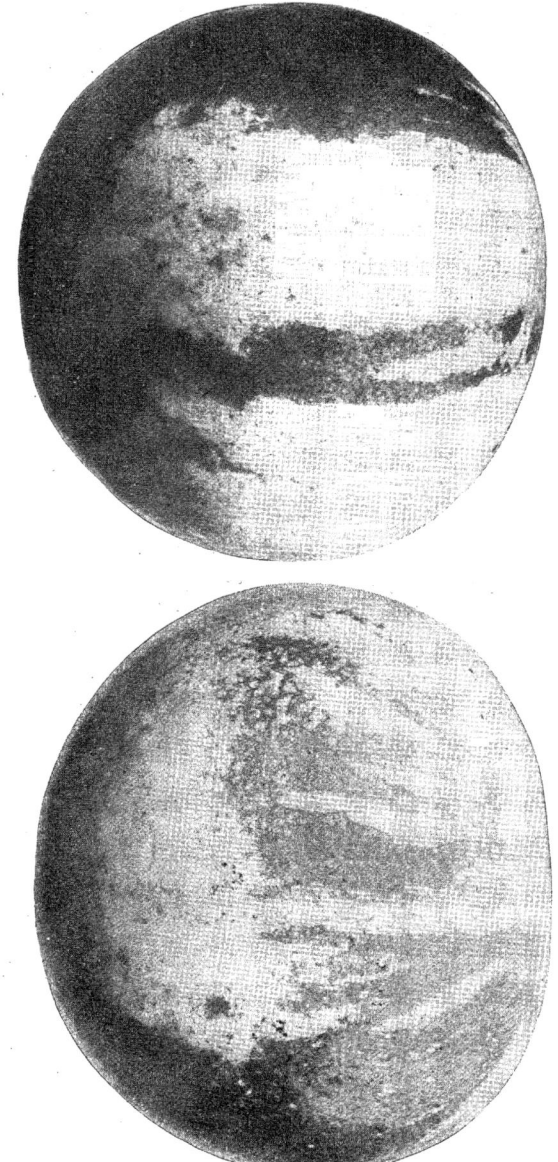

GRAPEFRUITS SHOWING THE RESULTS OF INFESTATION BY RUST MITES.

These grapefruits show the variant forms in which tear-stain appears. At the left is an example of what may be termed "multiple tear-stain," while at the right is shown a fruit illustrating a form more distinctly marked. These variant types of injury are frequently observed. One side of the fruit may be severely russeted while the other side is bright or tear stained.

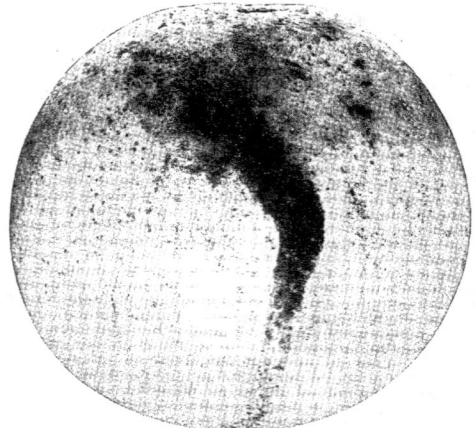

FIG. I.—DAMAGE TO GRAPEFRUIT BY RUST MITES.

Dark tear stains are found frequently on areas more or less russeted by rust mites, especially where the applications of rust-mite sprays were delayed. For all practical purposes, both tear-stain and russeting are absent from fruit kept free from rust mites. Note the zone of faint russet.

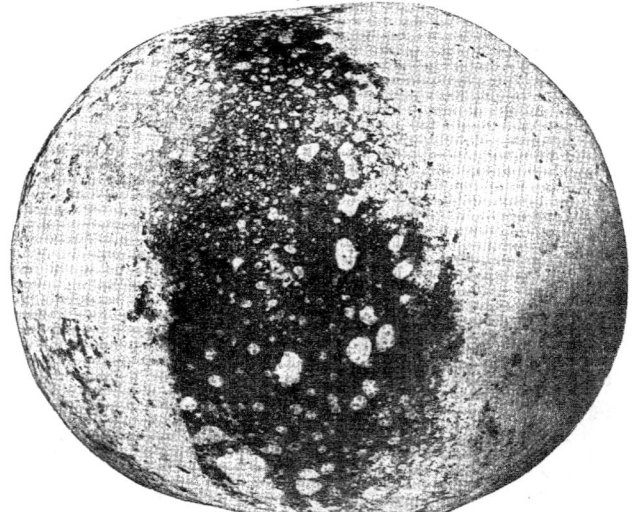

FIG. 2.—THE WORK OF RUST MITES ON GRAPEFRUIT SPRAYED IN JUNE WITH BORDEAUX MIXTURE.

In the zone of rust-mite activity injury is confined to the area not covered with spray. Near-by grapefruit trees sprayed on the same date with lime-sulphur solution (1-66) matured fruit entirely free from russeting or tear-stain.

present and are not controlled tear-stain occurs and usually varies proportionately with the severity of the rust-mite attack; (4) rust-mite russet and wither-tip tear-stain develop simultaneously.

Usually in Florida a small proportion of late citrus blooms occur in June. Fruits from such blooms develop after the normal rust-mite period and almost invariably ripen free from tear staining unless rust mites happen to become abundant during the following winter or early-spring months.

CULTURAL WORK.

Fungi are admittedly capable of producing tear-streak patterns on the host; for example, *Phomopsis citri* is known definitely to produce melanose injury in distinct tear streaks on various citrus fruits. Consequently a careful study was made to determine the frequency of the occurrence of *Colletotrichum gloeosporioides* or other fungi in typical wither-tip tear-stain areas.

In preliminary tests made during the fall of 1918 oranges and grapefruit were selected that showed typical wither-tip tear-stain, as well as fruit affected with rust-mite russet which shaded off into tear-stain. Usually 30 cultures were made from each fruit, 10 each from areas selected as follows: (1) Typical rust-mite russet, (2) typical tear-stained streaks or slightly discolored areas on fruits showing no streaking, and (3) normal areas not discolored. The fruits were washed 1 minute in 1–1,000 mercuric-chlorid solution and afterwards thoroughly rinsed in sterile water. Bits of tissue were then removed with flamed instruments to sterile Petri dishes and covered with melted corn-meal agar. These cultures were allowed to grow five days at room temperature. The results of this preliminary culture test are found in Table II, the percentages being based on the number of the bits of tissue used in each test.

TABLE II.—*Culture tests for the isolation of Colletotrichum gloeosporioides* [1] *from normal and affected parts of orange and grapefruit rind.*

Series.	Number of fruits.	Bits of tissue cultured.	Colletotrichum gloeosporioides.	Miscellaneous organisms.	No growth.
A. Russeted	17	170	38.2	18.8	43.0
B. Tear stained	16	160	21.1	19.3	59.6
C. Normal	19	190	6.2	15.7	78.1

[1] The use of the name *Colletotrichum gloeosporioides* in the culture data of this publication merely follows established custom and is without prejudice as to the proper designation of the organism. Any Colletotrichum showing characteristic growth on corn-meal agar was recorded as this species.

It thus appears that *Colletotrichum gloeosporioides* is recovered in rather low percentage from tear-streaked areas, that it is present to some extent in normal as well as badly russeted areas, and that the frequency of occurrence varies directly with the degree of injury.

TABLE III.—*Isolation of Colletotrichum gloeosporioides, a saprophytic type of Cladosporium, and miscellaneous fungi and bacteria from orange and grapefruit rind having various degrees of russeting and tear staining.*

Lot and number of fruits in group (96 fruits in all).	Variety.	Remarks.	Not disinfected.[1]									Disinfected.[1]								
			Series A, russet.			Series B, tear-stain.			Series C, bright.			Series A, russet.			Series B, tear-stain.			Series C, bright.		
			C.g.	Clad.	Misc.	C.g.	Clad.	Misc.	C.g.	Clad.	Misc.	C.g.	Clad.	Misc.	C.g.	Clad.	Misc.	C.g.	Clad.	Misc.
Lot A, 4 fruits.	Grapefruit.	Average tear stains.				31	23	17							5	4.2	3.7			
Do.	do.	Average bright fruit.							17	12	19							4.5	4.7	11
Do.	Orange.	do.							5.5	11	11							6	1.7	1
Lot A, 3 fruits.	do.	Average russet fruit.	12	13	139							3.6	4.3	3						
Lot A, 2 fruits.	do.	Average tear-stained fruit.				14	20	113	7	5	17				6.5	6.5	13	3	2	.5
Lot B, 3 fruits.	Grapefruit.	Dark-colored tear stains.				38	29	89	22	18	36				27	7.3	3.3	6.6	2.3	3.6
Do.	do.	Medium-colored tear stains.				36	14	32	22	16	24				28	14	4	5.8	1.6	1.3
Do.	do.	Faint tear stains.				31	29	200	14	8.6	69				28	13	6	5.6	5	5
Lot B, 2 fruits.	do.	Typical rust-mite russet, with accompanying tear streaks.	37	32	120							13[2]	5	4.5						
Do.	do.	Very dark russeted area.	47	26	45							17	7.5	3.5						
Lot B, 4 fruits.	do.	Typical rust-mite russet[2].	33	15	20							9.5	6.7	4.7						
Lot C, 2 fruits.	do.	Medium tear stains on one side only; other side bright.				43	20	28	24	25	25				5.5	1	1.5	2.5	3	1.5
Lot D, 4 fruits.	do.	Tear stains on one side only.				46	38	200							23	10	5			
Do.	do.	Russeted on one side only.	40	17	200							7.5	3	3.5						
Lot F, 4 fruits.	do.	Medium-colored tear stains; one side bright.				27	16	33	7.7	7.7	23				.5	.5	1	5.7	6.2	3.7
Do.	do.	Medium rust-mite russet.	42	42	51				21	9.2	92	2.7	1.2	1.7				2.5	0	.8
Lot G, 2 fruits.	do.	Fruits entirely russeted.	36	16	36							35	7.5	2						
Lot H, 4 fruits.	Orange.	Black (severe) rust-mite russet.	1	2.3	38							1.2	.5	3.2						
Do.	Grapefruit.	Dark (severe) rust-mite russet.	38	33	72							20.8	4.7	5						
Do.	do.	do.	37	28	47							24	8.5	5						
Lot H, 2 fruits.	do.	Free from visible blemishes.							36	26	50							24	17	2
Lot I, 4 fruits.	Orange.	Medium russets.	47	17	33							4	1	.5						
Lot J, 4 fruits.	do.	Severe rust-mite russet.	20	11	20							1.7	.3	.3						
Lot K, 4 fruits.	Grapefruit.	Free from visible blemishes.							14	10	22							17	8.3	7.7
Lot L, 2 fruits.	do.	Medium rust-mite russet.	34	28	128							20	11	4.3						
Do.	do.	Free from visible blemishes.							19	22	18							.5	.5	1
Do.	do.	Medium rust-mite russet.	46	29	20							32	13	30						
Lot M, 2 fruits.	do.	Free from visible blemishes.							0	1.5	16							0	0	.5
Do.	do.	Dark tear stains.				5.5	1.5	13							19	4.5	1			
Do.	do.	Medium rust-mite russet.	8	.5	39							30	20	38						
Lot N, 2 fruits.	do.	Medium-dark tear stains on part of fruit.				58	28	99							15	5	3.5	12	4.2	3
Lot O, 4 fruits.	do.	Medium tear stains.				42	21	78	39	35	77				28	9.5	7.2	20	3.5	3.2
Average for all lots.			32	20	65	34	22	40	19	16	35	15	6.2	7.6	17	6.8	4.4	7.7	4	3

[1] Symbols: C. g. = *Colletotrichum gloeosporioides*, Clad. = *Cladosporium*, Misc. = Miscellaneous.

[2] No streaking.

In the fall of 1919 a more extensive test was conducted. Fifteen lots of fruit were involved. Five of these lots were selected by the writer, and the remaining ten lots were selected in various parts of Florida by persons specially chosen for their competence to select typical rust-mite injury and typical wither-tip tear-stain. Each of these lots was sorted into several groups of one to four fruits each according to the variety of fruit, the particular type of effect, and the intensity of it. For a comparative study, cultures were made from fruits in the same lot that were free from blemishes or from unblemished areas on the russeted or tear-stained fruits. One hundred bits of tissue, approximately 1 square millimeter in surface area, were cultured from each test area of each fruit, using 10 Petri dishes, each with 10 bits of tissue. The results when reduced to a percentage basis, as in Table III, also represent the average numbers of occurrence per fruit. Corn-meal agar was used as a culture medium and the plates were held six days at room temperature. Counts were made of the common saprophytic type of Cladosporium as well as of Colletotrichum colonies. Bacteria and fungi other than these were reckoned as miscellaneous. Two parallel series were made, one for undisinfected tissue and one from similar areas on the same fruits washed with a disinfectant. Bichlorid of mercury solution (1 to 1,000) was used for 1 minute with subsequent rinsing on all disinfected lots except K, L, and M; on these three lots undiluted fresh hydrogen peroxid was used without rinsing. Table III gives the results, with fractions omitted for the higher percentages.

Table III shows that *Colletotrichum gloeosporioides* is practically universally distributed on citrus-fruit surfaces and that it escapes to a considerable degree the surface disinfection process ordinarily practiced in culture work. It is present about equally on the average in tear-stained and russeted areas. The amount varies in different lots of fruits, but seems to be more abundant where the visible effects are most pronounced. A saprophytic type of Cladosporium is isolated with the same constancy as *Colletotrichum gloeosporioides*, but with less frequency. These extensive culture tests show, therefore, that it would be about as reasonable to ascribe the blemishes to one of these organisms as to the other, if constancy of isolation from lesions is to be the deciding consideration. However, neither fungus reaches a frequency of occurrence high enough to justify holding it to be the causative organism on this evidence alone.

Certain fruits having the melanose type of tear-streak were selected, and cultures were made from these in the manner already described, comparative tests being made from unblemished areas, from melanose tear-streak, and from diffused melanose areas; and cultures from the surface blemish known as "shark skin" were also made. The results are given in Table IV.

Table IV.—*Isolation of Colletotrichum gloeosporioides, C laneous organisms from orange and grapefruit rind aff "shark skin."*

Lot and number of fruits in group	Variety.	Remarks.	Series A, diffused patches.			
			Colletotrichum gloeosporioides.	Cladosporium.	Miscellaneous.	Colletotrichum
Not disinfected:						
Lot E, 4 fruits.	Grapefruit.	Melanose tear streaks.				
Do...	.....do.....	Bright area on melanose fruits.				
Lot G, 2 fruits.	.....do.....	Melanose tear streaks.				
Lot L, 2 fruits.	.....do.....	.....do.................				
Lot N, 1 fruit.	.....do.....	Mud-caked melanose.	32	19	67	
Lot J, 4 fruits.	Orange....	Decided "shark skin"	31	17	49	
Lot K, 4 fruits.	Grapefruit.	.....do................	25	15	11	
Disinfected:						
Lot E, 4 fruits.	.....do.....	Melanose tear streaks.				
Do...	.....do.....	Bright area on melanose fruits.				
Lot G, 2 fruits.	.....do.....	Melanose tear streaks.				
Lot L, 2 fruits.	.....do.....	.....do................				
Lot N, 1 fruit.	.....do.....	Mud-caked melanose.	8.5	2	1	
Lot J, 4 fruits.	Orange....	Decided "shark skin"	0	1	1	
Lot K, 4 fruits.	Grapefruit.	.....do................	19	0.7	3.5	

It appears from Table IV that *Colletotricl* recovered with about the same frequency as i thus indicating that no positive conclusion a tear-stain can be reasonably based on isolatior

All the cultural work shows that *Colletot* has an isolation percentage from tear-stained for it to be the active pathogen and that th to some extent on normal as well as badly r quency varying with the degree of injury.

, The fungi in various types of miscellaneous were examined by similar cultural methods. spray-burn scars, hail bruises, thorn scratche lesions. The fungous flora was very similar tear-stained and russeted areas. Colonies o dominated, the saprophytic Cladosporium ra onies of bacteria and various other fungi occurr

HISTOLOGICAL EXAMINATION.

To the unaided eye, rust-mite russet with its several patterns and the so-called wither-tip russet or tear-stain intergrade imperceptibly. Ordinarily the grower calls the streak tear-stain and the solid area rust-mite russet.

It was deemed important to make careful microscopic examinations to determine whether distinctive features exist in the rind tissue of the affected parts. Fruits were examined showing typical patterns of rust-mite russet as well as those showing several degrees of the so-called wither-tip tear-stain. Under the microscope there appears to be no material difference between these types of injury. The examination of the injured parts in both instances indicates that the cuticle and epidermal cells appear to be punctured, and beneath, depending upon the degree of russeting, one to three layers of cells, together with their contents, are of a rusty brown color. Quite frequently mycelial threads and spores of fungi are found adhering to the affected parts. These fungi prove to be the types commonly found on citrus, such as species of Colletotrichum and Cladosporium.

The histological examinations have not revealed any feature that would serve to distinguish between the rust-mite russet and the so-called wither-tip tear-stain.

The presence of punctures in the epidermal cells of the tear-stained areas would strongly suggest the work of sucking parasites rather than that of parasitic fungi. This suggestion is further substantiated by the following observation: In July, 1919, by the aid of a hand lens, numerous tear-stained immature grapefruits were examined while still hanging on the tree in an unsprayed grove near Orlando, Fla. The rust mites and their castings were more or less generally distributed over the fruits, but were present in especially large numbers over the tear-stained areas. This condition was very noticeable early in July. By August 2 such a marked segregation of mites in streaks was not particularly evident, and the mites themselves, as well as their castings, were nowhere present in very large numbers, but the tear stains, presumably caused by rust mites, were quite evident.

INOCULATION EXPERIMENTS.

An inoculation experiment was conducted the last week in June, 1919, on immature grapefruits which were about 2 inches in diameter and so far as could be determined free from blemishes. Fifty fruits were used in this experiment. The inoculum was derived in part from dead sweet-orange twigs which had been held in moist chambers and on which developed a copious growth of the wither-tip fungus and in part from pure cultures of *Colletotrichum gloeosporioides*,

d been isolated from an injured grapefruit leaf.
re washed off the twigs and mixed with those from
bes. This wash water, which was clouded with fresh vi;
is used in saturating wads of absorbent cotton, whicl
placed on the fruit. The inoculated fruit was cove
or three layers of waxed paper for 48 hours. At
. of this time the paper and wet cotton were removed
eft unprotected. To serve the purpose of a control, oí
e similarly treated, except that the cotton was we
e water. These inoculations gave negative results.
inoculation tests were made during the fall of 1919, u;
m a mixture of a number of strains of *Colletotrichum gl*
isolated from typical tear stains on grapefruit and f
efruit twigs, as follows:

r 20, 1919, on almost fully grown grapefruit; on October 27, on grape
t yellowing; on November 7, on grapefruit approximately one-half col
r 15, on grapefruit almost fully colored; and on December 3, on m;
This test was repeated during the late spring, summer, and fall of
inoculum from the same strains of *Colletotrichum gloeosporioides.* Ir
made on May 15, on grapefruit averaging 1 inch in diameter; on Ma
t averaging 1¼ inches in diameter; on June 15, on grapefruit aver;
. diameter; on June 30, on grapefruit averaging $2\frac{7}{16}$ inches in diam
on grapefruit averaging 2½ inches in diameter; on July 30, on grape
inches in diameter; and on November 1 and 6, on grapefruit just
olor.

ults of all these tests were negative. Not the sligh
of tear-stain in any of the fruits inoculated during l
letected as late as February, 1920, when the crop was
The fruit inoculated during 1920 was free from tear-s
l observations were made in November.
itions were made to determine the frequency of associa
ain with dead twigs that might harbor Colletotrichun
ri. Unsprayed groves with more than the average pro
ead wood present were examined carefully during the l
i. Among the properties inspected in Florida 4 are in
0 in Polk County, 2 in Hillsboro County, 3 in Pine
i in Osceola County, 10 in Orange County, 2 in Vol
in Brevard County, 3 in St. Lucie County, and 4 in L
The data obtained indicate that dead twigs, spurs, etc.,
nediately over not more than 10 per cent of the tear-stai
that in damp, densely shaded, low-hammock proper
es have an unusually large number of dead twigs and wl
ental factors would appear to be especially favorable for
ent of fungi, tear-stained fruits are very seldom found.
hand, tear-stain is most abundant in higher and drier
here light and moisture favor the greatest rust-i
ent.

CONCLUSIONS.

While the foregoing evidence is to the effect that tear staining of Florida citrus fruits is caused by rust mites rather than by the fungus *Colletotrichum gloeosporioides*, as claimed by Rolfs, it must be admitted that the writer may not have seen all types of this injury. However, if a special type of tear staining caused by this fungus occurs in Florida it must have been exceedingly rare during the past four years to have escaped detection by the writer. The experimental and observational data on the control of what has been regarded as wither-tip tear-stain by investigators and Florida growers seems to be definite enough to warrant the conclusion that practically all of the so-called wither-tip tear-stain in Florida is caused by rust mites and can be readily controlled by controlling these pests.

SUMMARY.

(1) Pure cultures from typically tear-stained fruit show that *Colletotrichum gloeosporoides* is not confined characteristically to the tear streaks, but is even more prevalent on the larger russeted areas and is almost invariably found on normally colored areas.

(2) Inoculations on grapefruit in various stages of development with cultures of the fungus *Colletotrichum gloeosporioides* failed to produce tear streaks or other positive reaction.

(3) Dead wood that might harbor *Colletotrichum gloeosporioides* was found associated with not more than 10 per cent of the affected fruit.

(4) It is impossible to distinguish by histological methods between the ordinary rust-mite russet and so-called wither-tip tear-stain.

(5) Rust mites were found very abundant in recently developed tear-streak patterns on grapefruit.

(6) Spring-bloom fruit on unsprayed trees usually becomes seriously tear stained; June-bloom fruit on such trees usually ripens free from these markings.

(7) Copper sprays applied in the spring and not followed by rust-mite applications of sulphur sprays tend to increase tear staining, but when followed by rust-mite applications no appreciable amount of tear staining develops.

(8) When sulphur sprays are applied during the early spring, which is usually too early for the best rust-mite control, and are not followed by the regular rust-mite application tear staining is greatly reduced.

(9) When only the rust-mite applications are made, tear staining is practically eliminated.

(10) The same local and seasonal conditions of moisture and light that favor rust-mite injury also favor tear-stain.

(11) Practically all of the so-called wither-tip tear-stain in Florida is associated with rust mites and can be readily controlled by controlling these mites.

LITERATURE CITED.

(1) EARLE, F. S., and ROGERS, J. M.
　　　1915. Citrus pests and diseases at San Pedro in 1915. *In* San Pedro Citrus
　　　　　Path. Lab., 1st Ann. Rpt., 1915, p. 5–41, 19 fig.

　　FAWCETT, H. S.
(2)　　1910. Summer pruning for wither-tip. Fla. Agr. Exp. Sta. Press Bul. 151,
　　　　　2 p.

(3)　　1912. Report of plant pathologist. *In* Fla. Agr. Exp. Sta. Rpt. [1910]/11,
　　　　　p. lviii–lxvii.

(4)　　1914. Citrus diseases. *In* 8th Ann. Rpt., Cuban Nat. Hort. Soc., 1914,
　　　　　p. 21–30.

(5)　　1915. Citrus diseases of Florida and Cuba compared with those of California.
　　　　　Calif. Agr. Exp. Sta. Bul. 262, p. 149–210, 24 fig.

　　MATZ, JULIUS.
　　　1919. Citrus spots and blemishes. Porto Rico Dept. Agr. and Labor, Insular
　　　　　Exp. Sta. Circ. 16, 8 p., 3 col. pl.

　　ROLFS, P. H.
(7)　　1905. Report of committee on diseases of Citrus. *In* Proc. 18th Ann. Meet-
　　　　　ing Fla. State Hort. Soc., 1905, p. 29–32.

(8)　　1911. Russeting and tear streaking caused by wither-tip fungus. *In* Fla.
　　　　　Agr. Exp. Sta. Bul. 108, p. 30–32, fig. 12–13.

(9) STEVENS, H. E.
　　　1918. Florida citrus diseases. Fla Agr. Exp. Sta. Bul. 150, p. 13–110,
　　　　　fig. 7–54.

(10) STEVENSON, J. A.
　　　1918. Citrus diseases of Porto Rico. *In* Jour. Dept. Agr., Porto Rico, v. 2,
　　　　　no. 2, p. 43–123, 23 fig.

(11) YOTHERS, W. W.
　　　1918. Spraying for the control of insects and mites attacking citrus trees in
　　　　　Florida. U. S. Dept. Agr., Farmers' Bul. 933, 38 p., 24 fig.

○

UNITED STATES DEPARTMENT OF AGRICULTURE

BULLETIN No. 925

Contribution from the Bureau of Plant Industry
WM. A. TAYLOR, Chief

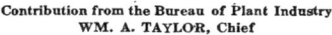

Washington, D. C.   PROFESSIONAL PAPER   February 18, 1921

A BRACHYTIC VARIATION IN MAIZE.

By J. H. KEMPTON, *Assistant in Crop Acclimatization.*

CONTENTS.

	Page.		Page.
Definition of brachysm	1	Inheritance of brachysm in hybrids	
Review of the literature	2	with commercial varieties	14
Origin and description of the variation	2	Brachytic × Boone	14
		Teratological variations	19
Inheritance of other brachytic variations	6	Ears ending in staminate spikes	20
Morphological significance	8	Brachytic × Hopi	23
Associated changes	9	Conclusions	26
Agricultural advantages	11	Literature cited	28

DEFINITION OF BRACHYSM.

Practically all the organs of maize are subject to profound modification, with heritable variations the rule rather than the exception. Many of these variations are undesirable abnormalities, and a knowledge of their origin and inheritance is of practical importance chiefly as an aid to their elimination. Among the many variations, however, one has appeared which gives promise of becoming of agricultural value, since it possesses several highly desirable features advantageous for dry-land and irrigated conditions.

This variation consists of a shortening of the internodes without a corresponding reduction in their number or in the number and size of other organs. (Pl. I.) Variations of this nature are found in many agricultural plants, as, for example, the "bush" varieties of peas, beans, squashes, and tomatoes, and are popularly known as dwarfs. The distinction between this type of dwarfing and that in which many if not all of the organs have suffered a reduction in size has been pointed out by Cook (4),[1] who studied similar variations in cotton and suggested the term brachysm for that type which involves a shortening of the internodes only.

---

[1] Serial numbers in parentheses refer to " Literature cited " at the end of the bulletin.

16071—21——1

three progenies grown from self-pollinated ears. Two of thes(
progenies were closely related, but the third had an entirely differen
ancestry. A third independent origin of this anther-ear dwarf wa
reported by Montgomery (14), who received the seed ear from C. F
Hartley.

A fourth independent origin of this same peculiar variation i
reported by East and Hays (5), who found it in a commercial strai)
of the Stowell's Evergreen variety of sweet corn. While the dwar
found by Emerson and that of East and Hays have not been com
pared by crossing, there can be little doubt that the three variation
involve a similar genetic change.

Emerson (7) also records the origin and inheritance of still anothe
type of dwarf which, in addition to reduced stature, produces mos
of the seeds in the terminal inflorescence. This variation has bee)
designated "tassel ear."

Hartley (9) records the origin of a brachytic dwarf, the leaves o
which were shorter and broader than those of the parental variet)
When the dwarf plants were crossed among themselves they wer
found to breed true.

Gernert (8) found a dwarf plant in a plat of Leaming Yello\
Dent. The plant was less than one-third the height of normal plant
of the parental variety, but produced as many nodes. The leave
were as long as those of the variety mentioned, which would seem t
establish it as a true case of brachysm. The plant produced no ea)
but was used as the male parent in crosses with plants of norma
stature. There was no report on the progeny of these crosses.

In addition to the brachytic variation to be discussed later, othe
brachytic plants have appeared in two instances in our breedin,
block, but, contrary to the usual behavior, the brachysm in thes
cases did not behave as a simple Mendelian character. The inherit
ance of these variations is considered briefly on pages 6-7

ORIGIN AND DESCRIPTION OF THE VARIATION.

The brachytic strain of maize under consideration arose in
hybrid between the Algerian pop-corn and the Chinese waxy varie

ties (No. Dh 416). The second generation, in which the brachytic plants appeared, was the result of self-pollinating a first-generation plant which was being grown for seed characters (10). Approximately one-quarter of the plants were brachytic, the actual numbers being 5 brachytic and 21 normal (11).

The appearance of brachytic plants in the second generation of this hybrid may be explained by assuming that the Chinese parent was heterozygous for brachysm. The reasons for this assumption will appear later. On this hypothesis one-half of the F_1 plants when self-pollinated should give progenies having one-quarter of the plants brachytic, and if the Chinese parent had been self-pollinated, one-quarter of its progeny also should be brachytic. The Chinese plant, unfortunately, was not self-pollinated, so that the possibility of its having been heterozygous for brachytic culms can not be tested directly. However, many hundred progenies and several large bulk plantings of this waxy variety have been grown without brachytic plants having been found. It would seem, therefore, not unreasonable to conclude that this variation is the result of a relatively recent genetic change and is not the result of bringing into expression a recessive variation which has been masked by the dominance of normal culms.

The brachytic plants might also be accounted for by assuming that a single gamete of the Chinese parent mutated and was fertilized by a normal gamete of the Algerian variety, but since only three second generation progenies of the hybrid Dh 416 have been grown, there is a possibility that more than one gamete of the Chinese parent of this hybrid had mutated.

One of the brachytic plants was self-pollinated and the resulting progeny were all brachytic. At the present time 16 progenies, derived from self-pollination or crosses between sister brachytic plants, have been grown. These progenies without exception have produced nothing but brachytic plants.

In addition to these 16 progenies several crosses have been made between plants of normal stature and brachytic plants. The first generations of such crosses were all as tall as or taller than the normal parent, while the second generations show a segregation into normal and brachytic plants closely approximating the Mendelian 3 to 1 ratio.

Both parents of the hybrid from which the brachytic plants arose may be considered of the pop-corn type and bear several small ears. The brachytic plants are in no sense inferior to their parents in leaf area or yield of grain. A comparison of normal and brachytic progenies is shown in Table I. These progenies were grown from self-pollinated ears of sister plants.

Table I.—*Measurements of maize plants of two sister progenies, one of which was brachytic and the other normal in stature.*

Plant character.	Brachytic.	Normal.
Height of plant...decimeters..	8.66±0.10	14.40±0.24
Number of leaves:		
Above the upper ear...	3.20±0.08	3.37±0.09
Total...	22.90±0.19	20.80±0.27
Number of branches in the tassel...	15.30±0.64	25.90±1.01
Ear length:		
Upper ear...centimeters..	14.20±0.27	16.40±0.23
Total...do....	27.60±0.98	28.10±0.71
Number of rows on upper ear...	16.30±0.26	21.20±0.30
Diameter of stalk...$\frac{1}{10}$-inch..	20.50±0.35	12.40±0.21
Fourth leaf from top:		
Length...centimeters..	62.60±6.20	64.40±8.90
Width...do....	9.20±1.40	12.30±1.50

The range in height of the brachytic plants was from 6 to 10 decimeters with a coefficient of variability of 10.1±0.81. Nine hand-pollinated ears were obtained from these brachytic plants, from which progenies were grown the following season (Table II). In five cases colored and white seeds were planted separately, making 14 progeny rows. Since no differences were found between the plants grown from seed of the two colors, they may be considered as single populations. The progenies from seeds of different colors of the same ear are grouped together in the table. In each pair the progeny grown from white seeds appears first. The differences in height between the progenies were for the most part insignificant, and while the measurements are given separately in Table II, it would seem not unfair to consider them as a single population. The number of individuals is then 286 with a mean height of 8.81±0.046. The range in height is from 5 to 13 decimeters with a coefficient of variability of 13.1±0.37.

The progenies differed somewhat in appearance, some having stiff erect leaves while in others the leaves were long and drooping, like those of the plant shown in Plate I. They differed also in productivity, the best-yielding progeny exceeding the poorest by more than 100 per cent. The diversity among the progenies, however, was no greater than is ordinarily found among sister progenies of normal stature.

All but one progeny had about 25 per cent of the plants with aborted male inflorescences (Pl. III). The degree of abortion varied from plants having a few of the branches aborted at the tips or perhaps several short naked branches to those which aborted all the tassel branches or bore only undeveloped spikelets. The progenies also varied in the percentage of affected plants, but for the 274 plants involved 27±1.81 per cent showed this abnormal behavior.

The abortion of the male inflorescence did not affect the female inflorescence, and the yield of such plants was as great as that of unaffected plants. The fact that one progeny was free from this undesirable characteristic affords evidence that it is inherited and that strains free from this defect can be grown.

TABLE II.—*Measurements of maize plants of 14 brachytic progenies directly descended from the original·variation.*

Designation of the progeny.	Height (dm.).	Length (cm.).		Number of nodes above the ear.	Total number of leaves.	Longest leaf (cm.).	
		Longest tassel branch.	Ear stalk.			Length.	Width.
Dh 416 L2 L1......	8.7±0.16	15.4±0.72	....	3.1±0.03	19.4±0.21	66.4±0.88	5.8±0.02
Dh 416 L2 L1 L3–3..	8.3±0.23	14.0±1.13	....	4.1±0.06	21.5±0.49	71.1±2.2	7.0±0.15
Dh 416 L2 L1 L3–4..	7.5±0.31	12.3±1.99	....	4.0±0.17	22.7±0.50	71.2±1.89	7.5±0.32
Dh 416 L2 L1 L4–3..	9.6±0.28	15.7±2.35	....	2.1±0.04	20.9±0.30	74.8±1.53	7.8±0.33
Dh 416 L2 L1 L4–4..	9.2±0.23	15.7±0.93	....	1.9±0.04	20.9±0.18	72.9±0.82	7.0±0.17
Dh 416 L2 L1 L5...	9.2±0.17	18.8±0.72	5.8±0.16	2.1±0.06	20.6±0.40	67.8±1.26	7.5±0.17
Dh 416 L2 L1 L6–3..	8.7±0.11	18.8±0.55	10.0±0.28	3.5±0.13	21.4±0.15	69.5±0.74	8.2±0.15
Dh 416 L2 L1 L6–4..	8.1±0.15	17.2±0.79	10.0±0.24	3.6±0.11	....	69.8±0.68	8.7±0.08
Dh 416 L2 L1 L7...	8.0±0.14	17.8±0.59	7.9±0.21	2.7±0.07	....	75.4±0.59	7.6±0.03
Dh 416 L2 L1 L9–3..	8.9±0.18	15.8±1.56	10.9±0.62	3.7±0.12	....	73.5±1.44	7.8±0.17
Dh 416 L2 L1 L9–4..	8.7±0.27	19.3±1.18	10.2±0.34	3.8±0.12	....	74.2±0.61	7.7±0.13
Dh 416 L2 L1 L8...	9.0±0.17	18.6±0.76	8.6±0.34	3.1±0.08	....	71.1±0.86	8.4±0.16
Dh 416 L2 L1 L11–3	9.6±0.09	22.7±0.54	9.4±0.26	3.1±0.08	....	70.7±0.52	8.1±0.11
Dh 416 L2 L1 L11–4	9.2±0.12	17.7±0.75	8.9±0.31	3.0±0.14	....	68.5±0.79	7.6±0.13

Designation of the progeny.	Length (cm.).		Number of tassel branches.	Length of ear (cm.).		Number of rows.	Diameter of stalk (1/16 inch).
	Branching space of tassel.	Central spike.		Upper.	Total.		
Dh 416 L2 L1......	4.0±0.26	19.9±0.71	13.3±0.58	11.5±0.23	12.3±0.34	15.5±0.17	....
Dh 416 L2 L1 L3–3..	3.5±0.17	19.4±1.77	15.0±0.86	12.3±0.34	22.0±0.51	16.3±0.16	....
Dh 416 L2 L1 L3–4..	2.7±0.60	17.0±1.86	12.4±0.68	11.5±0.44	18.5±1.64	16.0±0.25	....
Dh 416 L2 L1 L4–3..	2.4±0.25	21.9±2.35	15.3±1.59	10.3±0.63	27.7±0.96	16.0±0.20	....
Dh 416 L2 L1 L4–4..	3.3±0.19	24.5±1.08	14.0±0.64	9.2±0.30	18.6±0.59	14.7±0.18	....
Dh 416 L2 L1 L5...	3.2±0.16	28.3±0.69	10.5±0.59	10.1±0.30	18.7±0.75	14.9±0.23	16.2±0.44
Dh 416 L2 L1 L6–3..	2.9±0.08	26.2±0.70	13.5±0.36	10.7±0.21	18.3±0.78	16.8±0.23	16.2±0.24
Dh 416 L2 L1 L6–4..	3.3±0.19	24.7±1.1	14.3±0.31	10.4±0.18	20.5±0.59	17.3±0.24	17.3±0.21
Dh 416 L2 L1 L7...	4.3±0.24	25.5±0.94	14.5±0.46	11.8±0.27	23.1±0.75	15.3±0.21	18.0±0.34
Dh 416 L2 L1 L9–3..	3.9±0.42	21.8±2.32	13.9±0.84	12.8±0.34	25.5±1.05	16.5±0.21	18.1±0.29
Dh 416 L2 L1 L9–4..	4.4±0.31	27.5±1.26	14.3±0.47	13.5±0.24	23.6±0.81	15.9±0.15	15.9±0.22
Dh 416 L2 L1 L8...	4.3±0.45	26.5±0.80	16.3±0.55	12.9±0.26	27.6±0.82	15.8±0.10	17.9±0.23
Dh 416 L2 L1 L11–3..	6.4±0.37	31.3±0.41	16.4±0.36	12.4±0.39	26.4±0.83	16.5±0.13	18.3±0.22
Dh 416 L2 L1 L11–4.	4.4±0.24	25.5±1.51	14.2±0.46	11.7±0.40	21.1±1.00	16.8±0.22	17.6±0.31

Designation of the progeny.	Height of ear from ground (dm.).	Number of nodes.		Length of the longest leaf sheath (cm.).	Number above the longest—		Length of internode (cm.).	
		Without roots.	With roots.		Leaf sheath.	Internode.	Longest.	Uppermost.
Dh 416 L2 L1......	4.3±0.10	....	....	....	....	....	....	....
Dh 416 L2 L1 L3–3..	3.3±0.11	....	....	....	....	....	....	....
Dh 416 L2 L1 L3–4..	3.5±0.19	....	....	....	....	....	....	....
Dh 416 L2 L1 L4–3..	4.9±0.10	....	....	....	....	....	....	....
Dh 416 L2 L1L4–4..	4.5±0.10	....	....	....	....	....	....	....
Dh 416 L2 L1 L5...	4.0±0.07	12.3±0.26	8.4±0.18	21.1±0.18	10.2±0.20	7.4±0.19	4.2±0.10	7.3±0.21
Dh 416 L2 L1 L6–3..	3.6±0.08	12.8±0.09	7.8±0.16	19.5±0.16	10.8±0.14	8.5±0.21	3.9±0.09	7.5±0.22
Dh 416 L2 L1 L6–4..	3.7±0.07	13.6±0.12	....	19.6±0.16	11.8±0.13	9.4±0.29	3.6±0.09	6.6±0.21
Dh 416 L2 L1 L7...	3.1±0.04	12.7±0.22	....	19.4±0.14	10.3±0.17	7.5±0.30	3.5±0.12	7.7±0.18
Dh 416 L2 L1 L9–3..	4.5±0.14	13.7±0.15	....	21.2±0.45	11.7±0.25	7.8±0.38	5.8±0.20	....
Dh 416 L2 L1 L9–4..	4.1±0.05	12.7±0.10	....	21.2±0.16	11.0±0.14	9.0±0.15	5.6±0.15	....
Dh 416 L2 L1 L8....	3.9±0.03	13.2±0.18	....	19.9±0.22	11.4±0.20	7.9±0.26	4.0±0.08	....
Dh 416 L2 L1 L11–3..	3.5±0.10	13.9±0.09	....	20.0±0.13	12.6±0.17	9.4±0.32	4.3±0.08	....
Dh 416 L2 L1 L11–4.	3.8±0.05	13.4±0.21	....	19.6±0.22	11.9±0.19	8.8±0.31	4.5±0.14	8.5±0.29

Brachytic plants are of two general types with respect to the shape of the internodes. The most common type has internodes of the familiar cylindrical form. A longitudinal section through the long axis of the other type of internode is almost triangular, the internode being in the shape of an obliquely truncated cylinder. This form of internode is due to the position of the node, which in these cases instead of being horizontal and at right angles to the main axis is borne obliquely (Pl. IV). This character of the node does not always extend throughout the entire plant, the upper nodes tending to assume the horizontal position. A tendency toward such a difference in the position of the nodes probably exists also in plants of normal stature, but has escaped detection until accentu-ated by brachysm. The alteration in the position of the node seems to be unaccompanied by other changes, and whether it will be inherited remains to be seen. The buds are borne in the leaf axils on the long side of the internodes and seem to be entirely normal.

The internodes of brachytic plants differ also in the shape of the sides, which in some cases are convex and in others concave. This difference seems irrespective of the length of the internode in brachytic plants, although in normal plants short internodes are frequently convex, indicating a partial compensation in girth for the loss of height.

INHERITANCE OF OTHER BRACHYTIC VARIATIONS.

In one other instance brachytic plants have appeared in the progeny of a hybrid of which one of the parents was Chinese (Pl. V). In all probability the brachytic characteristic in both these cases is derived from the Chinese parent, since this variety produces a rather large number of nodes for the height of the plant. The usual number is about 19, with an average height of 135 cm. as compared with the well-known Boone County White variety, which produces about 20 nodes, with an average height of 240 cm., indicating an internode length of about 12 cm. for Boone and 7 cm. for the Chinese.

The hybrid in question was between a white dent variety from Kansas and Chinese, grown from original seed. The first generation was of normal stature, and no evidences of brachysm appeared in numerous progenies until the fourth generation. In the fourth generation, however, two brachytic plants were found in a progeny of only 20 individuals. One of these plants was self-pollinated, and its progeny offers a striking contrast to those derived from the Chinese-Algerian hybrid. Only 10 plants were grown from this self-pollinated ear and 9 of them were of normal stature, the other being brachytic. This latter plant has been self-pollinated, but a progeny has not yet been grown. The pedigree of this hybrid is shown in figure 1.

A brachytic plant appeared also in a progeny of the Esperanza variety of *Zea hirta* (Pl. VI). This plant was not self-pollinated, but was crossed with a normal plant of the Chinese waxy variety.

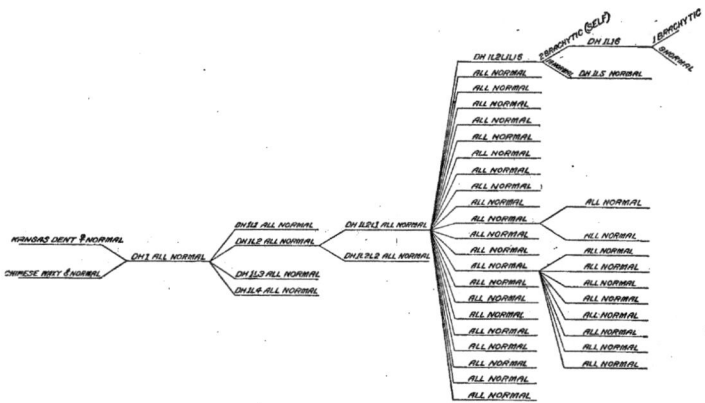

FIG. 1.—Pedigree chart of a brachytic strain which does not breed true. None of the progenies shown in this chart were the result of self-pollination except Dh1L16, the progeny of a brachytic plant.

The hybrid has been designated Mh 17 by Collins (1). The first-generation plants were all much taller than either parent. Three plants were hand-pollinated, but not selfed. The second-generation progeny of these plants gave no evidence of brachysm, as is shown by the frequency distribution for plant height (fig. 2). The modal height of the second-generation plants was 190, which is the average height of normal Esperanza plants. The brachytic Esperanza parent of this hybrid was 105 cm., while the Chinese parent was but 167 cm. high. Succeeding generations have continued normal in stature, although progenies differing widely in height have been isolated. It is hoped that crosses between some of these progenies and true-breeding brachytic strains will explain the complete disappearance of this variation in the Mh 17 hybrid.

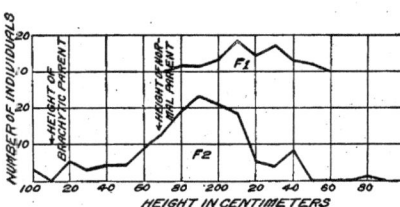

FIG. 2.—Frequency distributions of height of plant of the first and second generation hybrid between the brachytic Esperanza plant shown in Plate VI and a Chinese waxy plant of normal stature.

MORPHOLOGICAL SIGNIFICANCE.

The recurrence of brachysm in maize is perhaps to be understood from the normal presence of this characteristic in both staminate and pistillate inflorescences. In cotton it appears as a lack of differentiation between the floral parts and the internodes of the fruiting branches, and not only are the internodes reduced but the floral bracts are modified, becoming leaflike while the leaves become bractlike (4). In maize, however, there is no indication of changes on the main culm other than the shortened internodes, and the leaves are normal.

The most striking example of brachysm in maize is the normal pistillate inflorescence. Here a lateral branch has suffered so extensive a reduction in the length of the internodes that even the lower leaf sheaths of the branch inclose the terminal inflorescence. In this respect the brachysm of the pistillate inflorescence resembles that found in cotton, since the leaf blades have become much reduced or more frequently lost and only the sheath remains. This is an approach to the floral condition where the glumes of the spikelets are homologous with the leaf sheaths, and in this respect the brachysm may be said to represent an intermediate condition between floral and vegetative parts belonging to that class of variations designated by Cook (4) as metaphanic. This brachytic tendency is usually confined to the branches from the upper nodes, while those produced at nodes near but not necessarily below the surface of the ground have internodes of normal length. In some tropical varieties of maize the brachytic specialization of the upper branches has been lost, and the result is a grotesque plant with one or two ears borne at the ends of enormously lengthened ear stalks which frequently exceed the main culm in height (Pl. VII).

When accidents force into growth the branches below the ear, which ordinarily remain dormant, they increase in length, or, in other words, reduce in specialization, progressing toward the base of the plant. The place where these branches change from having pistillate to staminate terminal inflorescences is usually marked by a more complete abortion of the buds, leaving an unbranched section of two or three internodes. Thus the brachysm of the lateral branches is an excellent illustration of a graded specialization, indicating gradual development, but, although there are all stages of branch brachysm on an individual plant, the advanced stages, as found on ear stalks, are little affected by environment.

Euchlaena, the nearest relative of maize, has no such specialization, and, although all of the nodes except the uppermost produce a branch, the apices of these branches are usually about the same height from the ground. This results from the fact that in progressing toward the apex of the plant each succeeding branch has one less node than the

A BRACHYTIC CORN PLANT COMPARED WITH A PLANT OF NORMAL STATURE.

The brachytic plant produced two leaves more than the normal plant.

A BRACHYTIC CORN PLANT COMPARED WITH A PLANT OF THE DWARF VARIATION FOUND BY R. A. EMERSON.

Anthers are always found interspersed among the seeds on the ears of the Emerson dwarf, and because of this fact it has been designated "anther ear."

TWO SISTER BRACHYTIC CORN PLANTS FROM THE SAME PROGENY ROW, SHOWING
AN EXTREME EXAMPLE OF ABORTED TASSEL.

The plant with the aborted tassel bore ears which were broken off in dissecting.

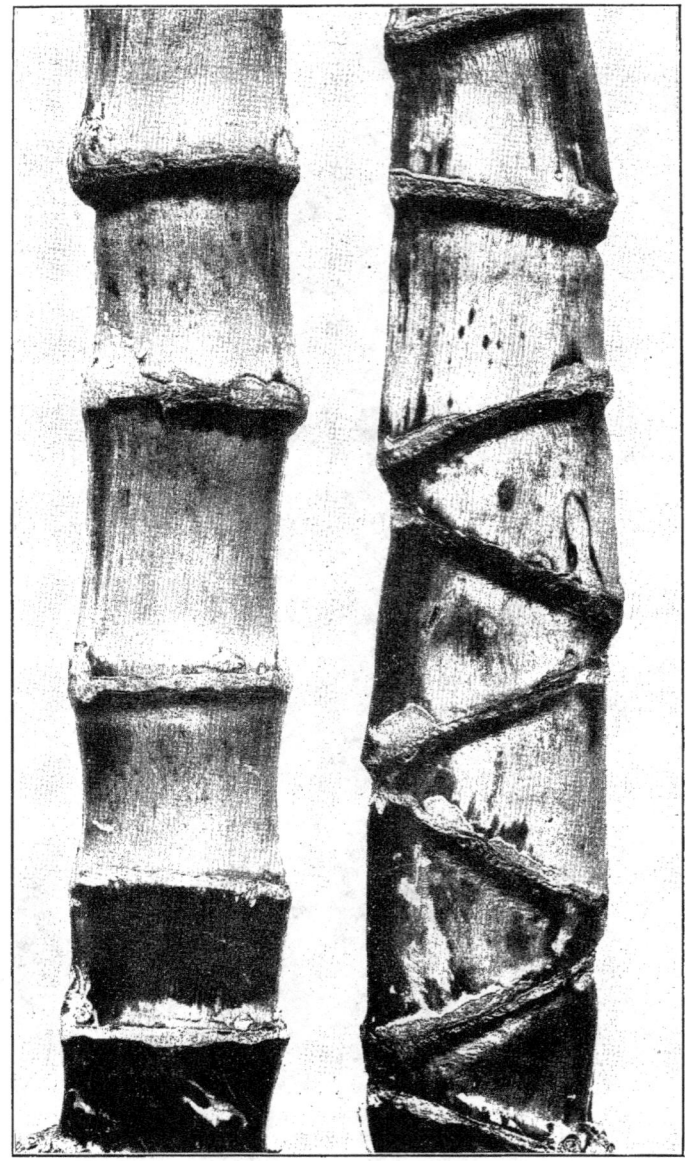

TWO TYPES OF BRACHYTIC CULMS.

The buds are borne on the node at the long side of the internode.   (Natural size.)

A BRACHYTIC CORN PLANT WHICH APPEARED IN THE FOURTH GENERATION OF A HYBRID BETWEEN THE CHINESE-WAXY MAIZE AND A VARIETY OF WHITE DENT CORN FROM KANSAS.

When this plant was self-pollinated it did not breed true, but its progeny included a few brachytic plants.

A BRACHYTIC CORN PLANT FOUND IN A STRAIN OF THE ESPERANZA VARIETY
OF ZEA HIRTA.

Progenies of this plant failed to show any evidences of brachysm.   This plant is 105 centimeters tall.

A MAIZE PLANT WHICH HAS LOST THE BRACHYTIC SPECIALIZATION OF THE EAR
STALK.

This plant was grown at Chula Vista, Calif., from seed obtained in Bolivia.

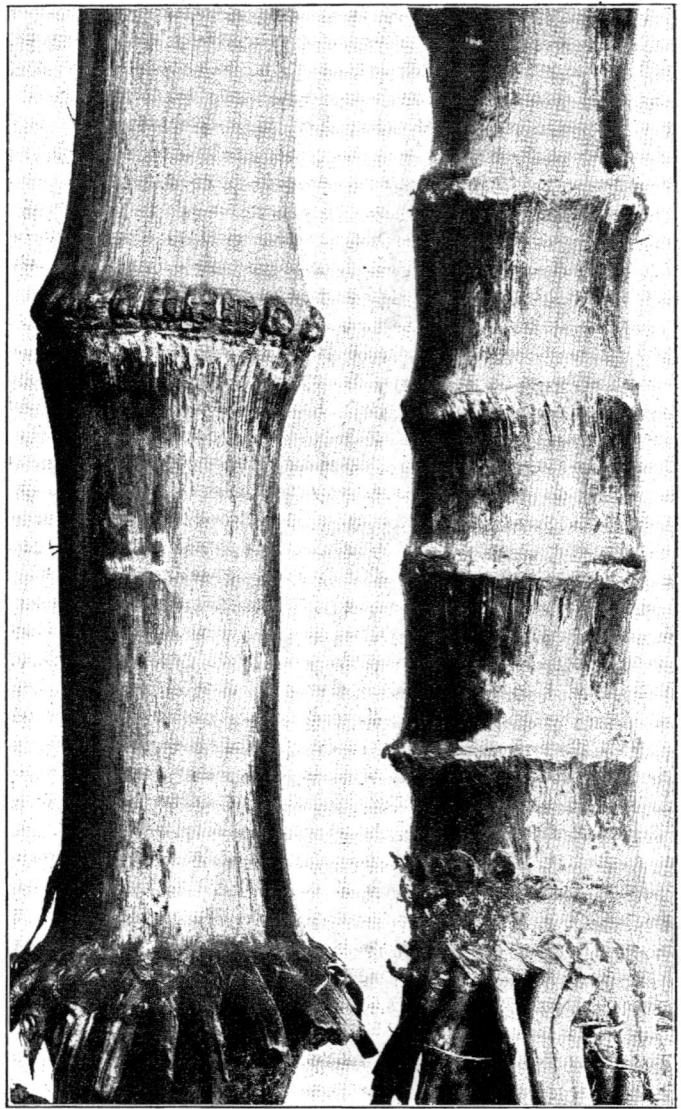

BASAL SECTIONS OF NORMAL AND BRACHYTIC STALKS OF MAIZE, SHOWING
THE NODES JUST ABOVE THE SURFACE OF THE GROUND.

This illustrates the increase in root-producing nodes which could be obtained on the brachytic plants
by a cultural method which would cover this section of the stalk with soil.   (Natural size.)

branch immediately below until the uppermost branch, borne in the axis of the second leaf from the top, has but two nodes. Thus each branch has one more internode than has the portion of the main culm, which is immediately above it. Contrary to Montgomery (13), this does not hold true for maize, but the relation may have been modified through brachysm. There is some evidence to show that the total number of nodes is increased when the main culm is brachytic, and if this fact held true for lateral branches it would account for the difference between maize and teosinte in this respect. When the ear stalk is lengthened, as in the tropical varieties previously mentioned, it becomes possible to ascertain the number of nodes with accuracy. In these cases it has been found that there are 15 or more nodes, while only 5 or 6 nodes of the main stalk are above the ear-bearing branch.

Although the pistillate inflorescence of maize affords the most striking example, there are indications of brachysm in the formation of the male inflorescence. If it is assumed that the internodes of the main axis are shortened and the terminal spike is formed through a reduction of lateral branches, this would constitute a still further stage of brachysm.

Brachysm of the main culm might be considered an example of homoeosis (12), but on this hypothesis it is difficult to understand the absence of any tendency for the brachysm of the upper branches to become transferred to lower ones, a step much more direct than that involved in transferring this characteristic to the main culm. There is, however, some support for this view in that several of the brachytic plants developed pistillate flowers in the otherwise unaltered staminate inflorescence, and although none of these pistillate flowers developed seed this fact suggests that an association exists, however slight, between bracytic internodes and the development of female flowers.

ASSOCIATED CHANGES.

Mutations in most organisms are not confined to single characters, but alter the expression of many and frequently unrelated parts. Usually a particular character is changed greatly, serving to divert attention from minor changes in other characters. Careful examination of many characters of an individual which has mutated obviously in a single one often reveals the presence of the other changes.

With the intention of determining whether other characters than internode length had undergone alteration in the original brachytic plants, careful measurements were made of other organs. Only two other changes were observed. The ears were flattened somewhat, doubtless due to the mechanical pressure of the large number of leaf sheaths. Such an alteration can not be considered as mutative, since it is an indirect manifestation of the brachytic condition. The other

16071°—21——2

reflected in the main culm.

This further shortening of the ear stalk on brachytic plants indicates that the brachytic stalks of normal ears are the result of a genetic change separate from that which caused brachytic internodes on the main culm.

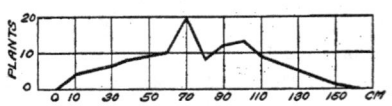

Fig. 3.—Frequency distribution for the length of the third branch in an F_2 of Tom Thumb pop corn × Florida teosinte.

Support for this latter contention is derived from a hybrid between Florida teosinte and Tom Thumb pop corn (3). If the ear stalk is an example of brachysm similar to that of the main stalk, the second generation of the hybrid between teosinte and maize should give the same evidence of segregation of this character as is found with the internodes of the main culm when plants with brachytic culms are crossed with those of normal stature.

With the second-generation plants, the third branch from the top on the main culm is assumed to be homologous with the ear stalk of normal maize, since it is borne at approximately the same node as the ear of maize. The frequency distribution for the length of this branch on second-generation plants of the Tom Thumb × Florida hybrid is shown in figure 3.

It is apparent that there is no bimodality in the distribution of branch lengths, and it must be concluded that the brachysm of the ear stalk of normal maize does not behave as a simple Mendelian character in crosses with teosinte.

Slight evidence for the discontinuous nature of the brachysm of ear stalks is to be found in the second generation of a cross between Boone County White and the brachytic strain. The frequency distributions for the length of the ear stalk on brachytic plants directly descended from the original variation and on the first and second generation plants of the brachytic-Boone cross are shown in figure 4. While the brachytic plants had shorter ear stalks than normal plants, the frequency distribution for this character on the normal segregates of the second generation of the hybrid suggests a bimodality that is most easily explained by assuming an independent inheritance of the ear-stalk character. Too much confidence must not be placed in results of this sort, as it is obvious that at least one other factor besides length of internode is involved in the length of the ear stalk. This factor is the number of nodes. The actual number of nodes can not be determined with accuracy, and an estimate is likely to give very misleading results.

Further evidence for the independent inheritance of the brachysm of ear stalks and that of the culm is to be found in an analysis of the correlations of these characters.

In the normal plants of the second generation of the brachytic-Boone hybrid there was a correlation of 0.295 ± 0.06 between the length of the longest internode on the main culm and the length of the ear stalk. This correlation is reversed in the brachytic plants of the same hybrid, but the coefficient of 0.09 ± 0.09 is not a significant deviation from no correlation. These low correlations indicate an

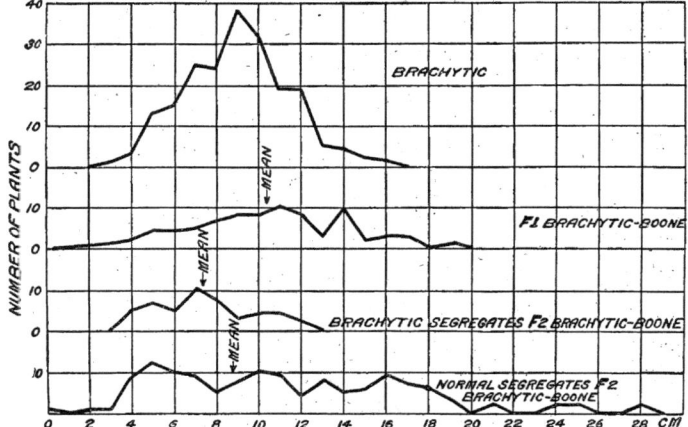

Fig. 4.—Frequency distribution of length of ear stalk on brachytic, brachytic × Boone F₁, and brachytic and normal plants segregated in the F₂ of brachytic × Boone.

almost complete independence of the factors which affect the internode length of the culm and those which affect the ear stalk.

AGRICULTURAL ADVANTAGES.

Brachysm in maize produces a form of plant which seems admirably adapted to meet the unusual requirements of dry land and irrigated regions. The chief obstacles to the utilization of such variations lies in the numerous defects which commonly accompany them (Cook, 4), but the present brachytic strain is relatively free from undesirable corollaries.

The striking characteristics of this brachytic type of plant are its reduced height and sturdy erectness. There are many situations in

comes very soft when wet.

·While it may not be worth while to consi
brachytic varieties for the ordinary varieties
latter do well, there are many situations in w
of the maize plant and its tendency to lodge
down in drying winds place it at a decided d
situations it would seem to be worth while
which this brachytic character is combined
adapted to the region.

In addition to these two very obvious adva
which might be fully as important in certa
This latter advantage lies in the fact that be
internodes more nodes are in contact with the

With the exception of the Navajo or Hopi
which appear at germination serve only to es
ling. Subsequent growth and development
produced from nodes. In most varieties of m
mon cultural methods, from four to eight n
with the ground and produce roots. The upp
duces roots is usually somewhat above the s
this node in the Boone County White variety
roots is about 20. The young roots are cover
parent gelatinous substance which affords p
atmosphere and permits them to reach the soil
10 cm. Maize plants are capable of produci
every node below the ear and possibly even a
these nodes are brought in contact with the g1
abnormally moist. Some tropical varieties h
roots at 15 nodes above the surface of the grou
attained a length of 8 or 10 cm. before final
specialized commercial varieties have not lost
roots from the upper nodes, and within 24 h
plants will be found to have started roots fron
contact with the ground.

In brachytic plants the reduction in the le
results in more nodes coming in contact with
creasing the production of roots. If it were fo
root-producing nodes could be increased as m
the common dent varieties by a proper syste
greater increases are possible by listing, a pr

graphically shown in Plate VIII. In addition to the increase in
the number of roots due directly to the shortened internodes, there
is a further increase of about 15 per cent, due to the fact that the
reduced height is accompanied by an increase in the diameter of
the culm, thus increasing the periphery of the nodes from which the
roots arise.

This increased root system obtained under ordinary conditions of
flat surface tillage is of no mean advantage. In irrigated regions
where the flooding system is practiced or even under most furrow
systems the taller varieties of maize lodge badly following an irrigation, especially if there is a moderate wind. The brachytic plants
are thoroughly anchored and by reason of their greatly reduced
height would be able to withstand such conditions and remain erect.

In addition to the increased root system, brachytic plants offer another character that may be of advantage for dry-land culture. The
reduction in internode length brings the leaves close together, thus
effecting a partial shade at the time when the sun is at its height. In
this manner transpiration may be reduced at the critical period, and
if this reduction is appreciable it should result in a lower water requirement for brachytic plants. The feature of partial shade may be
desirable also for irrigated regions where, during the bright days of
summer, the plants frequently are unable to obtain water from the
soil with sufficient rapidity to supply the heavy demands of midday
transpiration, even though the soil is thoroughly wet.

It remains to be determined just how far farm practice can be made
to comply with the requirements of harvesting such a crop. Where
the practice of hogging off is followed, the brachytic plants are ideal,
since the ears are brought within easy reach of the animals and little
waste should occur.

As a general rule, the commercial varieties of corn are taller than is
necessary to satisfy the physiological requirements for yield of grain.
This increased height is due almost entirely to the elongation of the
internodes and not to an increase in the number of nodes. An increase
in the height of the culm would seem to be a disadvantage unless it is
the result of an increase in the number of nodes, as otherwise no additional leaf area results. The brachytic variation affords a means of
reducing the stature, with no corresponding reduction in leaf area.

There is, of course, a physiological limit to the production of grain
upon small plants, beyond which it is impossible to proceed. This
limit is obviously dependent upon the leaf area available for purposes of photosynthesis. The reduction in internode length does not
reduce the number of nodes, nor is it accompanied by a reduction
in the size of the leaves, and the total leaf area therefore remains the
same. The leaves, however, are brought closer together, and possibly

the area available for photosynthesis has been reduced somewhat. The degree of this reduction is yet to be determined, but with the exception of this reduction which, under certain conditions, may be beneficial, there should be no other physiological difficulties in combining high productivity with brachytic stature.

Genetically, however, more difficulties are to be expected. Yield of grain, like most quantitative characters, is one of those relatively unstable characters difficult to recover from hybrids involving small-eared varieties. If only 10 factors are involved in maximum grain production, all 10 of these would be expected to occur in homozygous combination with brachytic culms in an F_2 hybrid only once in 4,195,304 plants. To be reasonably certain of securing the combination in an F_2 hybrid, at least 12,585,912 plants should be grown. It is, however, an unfortunate fact that probably many more than 10 factors are involved. The form of the inflorescence alone can be resolved into several component parts, such as length, diameter, number of seeds, size of seeds, number of rows, volume, and weight of seeds, all of which are known to be inherited separately, and even these subdivisions are far from being simple characters.

With the several advantages, the commercial value of the brachytic variation depends upon the success with which the shortened internodes may be combined with the grain production of the standard dent varieties. It is not unlikely that if such a combination were effected the value of the strain would be appreciated in areas outside the regions of extreme climatic conditions. The brachytic character is one which reappears in the perjugate generation of hybrids, and the possibility of combining the dwarf stature with the high productivity of commercial varieties will be considered.

INHERITANCE OF BRACHYSM IN HYBRIDS WITH COMMERCIAL VARIETIES.

BRACHYTIC × BOONE.

In an effort to combine the brachytic character of the culm with the high productivity of commercial varieties, several crosses have been made. Two crosses were made with the Boone County White variety, and a few first-generation plants of each cross were grown in the greenhouse and self-pollinated. Three ears resulted, and a progeny of each of these, as well as a large population of the first generation, was grown in the field at Lanham, Md. The first-generation plants grown in the field were fully as large as the Boone parent and remarkably uniform. A number of characters were measured, as shown in Table III.

The three second-generation progenies segregated into normal and brachytic plants, with well-defined classes closely approximating the 3 to 1 monohybrid ratio. The actual number was 234 normal and 74 brachytic, the percentage of the recessive class being 24.0 ± 1.7. The measurements of these second-generation plants also are given in Table III.

TABLE III.—*Measurements of maize plants of the first and second generations of the brachytic × Boone hybrid.*

[The ears had dark and pale colored seeds, and the number 11 following the progeny designation indicates that the color of the seed planted was dilute. Figures in the last two columns in black-face type indicate the characters in which the brachytic plants exceeded the plants of normal stature.]

Character.	First generation.				Second generation.			
	Dh 435.	Dh 435–11.	Dh 436.	Dh 436–11.	Normal.	Brachytic.	Difference.	Difference ÷ probable error.
Height of plant, decimeters............	27.2±0.25	26.8±0.36	26.0±0.22	26.1±0.37	29.7±0.19	10.4±0.12	19.3±0.17	114.0
Height of upper ear from the ground..decimeters..	13.0±0.25	12.4±0.28	12.3±0.19	11.7±0.26	12.0±0.12	3.9±0.06	8.1±0.13	62.2
Length of branching space....centimeters..	19.5±0.27	19.0±0.37	18.2±0.34	17.1±0.54	15.1±0.16	12.2±0.22	2.9±0.27	10.7
Length of central spike, centimeters............	32.0±0.67	30.0±0.50	30.7±0.61	32.7±0.71	30.0±0.28	30.7±0.56	0.7±0.63	1.1
Length of longest tassel branch....centimeters..	29.1±0.50	27.0±0.46	27.7±0.51	28.2±0.40	24.3±0.43	24.4±0.29	0.1±0.48	.2
Number of tassel branches..	37.8±1.24	34.0±1.21	29.3±1.33	24.2±1.34	31.7±0.46	36.4±0.72	**4.7±0.77**	6.7
Longest leaf: Length..centimeters..	103.5±0.57	91.5±1.24	86.5±0.87	85.8±1.28	95.2±0.42	90.2±0.62	5.0±0.75	6.7
Width........do....	9.9±0.15	9.1±0.15	8.7±0.12	8.9±0.12	8.9±0.06	8.9±0.07	0.0±0.09	0
Length of longest internode..,....centimeters..	16.8±0.34	18.2±0.13	17.8±0.29	17.5±0.16	16.8±0.12	5.4±0.12	11.4±0.17	67.0
Number of internodes above longest..........	9.9±0.29	7.7±0.18	7.4±0.21	7.3±0.15	7.5±0.09	7.1±0.18	0.4±0.20	2.0
Diameter of stalk, 1⁄16 inch..	16.9±0.29	13.8±0.39	13.1±0.18	13.1±0.31	14.2±0.12	16.0±0.23	**1.8±0.26**	6.95
Number of ears............					1.25±0.02	1.5±0.05	**0.25±0.05**	4.6
Ear length: Upper ear, centimeters............	23.2±0.53	21.4±0.55	18.8±0.41	20.2±0.38	16.2±0.20	14.0±0.21	0.22±0.09	.76
Total..centimeters..	26.8±1.25	22.2±0.54	22.2±0.90	24.3±0.94	20.7±0.40	20.6±0.57	0.1±0.7	.1
Number of rows on upper ear..............	18.2±0.11	16.6±0.24	17.7±0.11	16.2±0.11	18.2±0.12	17.0±0.13	1.2±0.17	7.13
Length of staminate spike on upper ear, centimeters............					5.5±0.30	4.8±0.46	0.7±0.65	1.3
Number of leaves: Above the upper ear..	5.7±0.09	5.2±0.08	5.0±0.06	5.0±0.08	4.9±0.03	4.8±0.04	0.1±0.05	2.0
Total...............	22.3±0.20	20.3±0.25	21.0±0.21	21.9±0.75	21.7±0.09	22.3±0.12	**0.6±0.15**	4.0
Number of nodes: With roots..........	7.5±0.14				7.3±0.07	8.5±0.05	**1.2±0.08**	15.5
Without roots........	14.7±0.25	14.4±0.22	14.1±0.14	13.6±0.17				
Length of longest leaf sheath....centimeters..	23.6±0.29	22.6±0.25	20.9±0.20	20.0±0.43	22.7±0.13	22.4±0.19	0.3±0.2	1.5
Number of leaf sheaths above longest..........	13.0±0.27	12.4±0.42	12.0±0.27	11.4±0.24	11.3±0.09	11.6±0.14	0.3±0.16	1.8
Length of upper ear stalk....centimeters..	12.7±0.46	10.2±0.56	9.6±0.40	9.5±0.70	8.7±0.23	7.4±0.23	1.3±0.31	4.2

While no difficulty was encountered in classifying the plants as to stature, a closer examination showed that several plants, classed as normal, in reality had one or more shortened internodes. The actual number was 14 plants with one or two shortened internodes in a population of 130 otherwise normal plants. These brachytic internodes were located either near the base or near the top of the plant. (Pls. IX and X.) Such plants may be heterozygous for the brachytic character with a partial failure of dominance or they may be considered as instances where the segregation has been incomplete.

In either event the well-defined difference between these brachytic internodes and the adjoining normal nodes emphasizes the individuality of the node and internode as a metamer. If these cases are looked upon as partial failures of dominance, it is significant that instead of a general shortening of internode length throughout the entire plant single internodes only are affected and become abruptly and decidedly shorter than their mates. This fact indicates that no general lengthening of the internodes is to be expected as the result of contamination by repeated "back crosses" on plants of normal stature.

These cases would seem to offer some support for the hypothesis of somatic segregation or perhaps bud variation. If such an explanation is adopted, a question arises whether an ear borne on a node subtended by a brachytic internode would behave in heredity as a true brachytic. No such cases have arisen as yet, and there would be some difficulty in distinguishing them unless the brachysm was pronounced, as in the case shown in Plates IX and X.

The internode borne on the same node with the ear is almost invariably shorter than the internodes immediately above and below, so that to be detected brachysm of the internode at this point must of necessity be pronounced.

Although an ear borne on a brachytic internode might be germinally brachytic, it of necessity must be fertilized by male gametes from an inflorescence produced from a normal node. The resulting seeds, therefore, would give rise either to plants of normal stature only, or, if the parental plant had been heterozygous for brachysm, one-half of the progeny could be brachytic. The point is of interest in connection with the sudden appearance of brachysm in the two Chinese hybrids.

The brachytic segregates in the F_2 of Boone-brachytic hybrids had a mean height in decimeters of 10.42 ± 0.112, with a coefficient of variability of 14.3 ± 0.79 and a range of 7 to 15 decimeters. The coefficient of variability of the brachytic segregates compared with that of the 14 brachytic progenies shows that there was no significant increase in variation in the segregates, the increase being only 1.2 ± 0.87. A somewhat larger increase is obtained if the coefficient of variability of the brachytic segregates is compared with that of the brachytic progeny grown in 1918; the difference then becomes 4.2 ± 1.13, or 3.7 times the probable error, but since these progenies were not grown the same year the propriety of comparing their variability is questionable. While the average height of the brachytic segregates was greater than that of brachytic plants directly descended from the original variety, the difference of 1.61 ± 0.87 is

TWO BRACHYTIC INTERNODES ON A CORN PLANT THE OTHER INTERNODES OF
WHICH WERE OF NORMAL LENGTH.

This plant was found in the second generation of the brachytic-Boone hybrid.   (Natural size.)

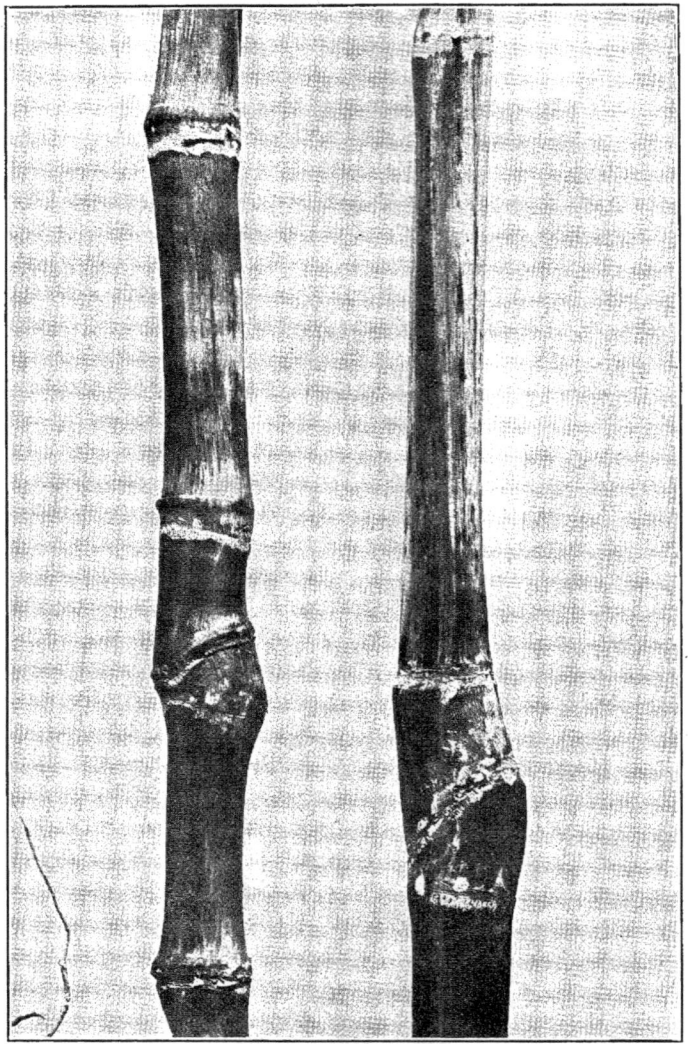

TWO CULMS OF MAIZE, EACH SHOWING TWO BRACHYTIC INTERNODES, THE OTHER
INTERNODES BEING OF NORMAL LENGTH.

These plants were segregated in the second generation of the brachytic-Boone hybrids. The portion
shown at the left is from the base of the plant. (About one-half natural size.)

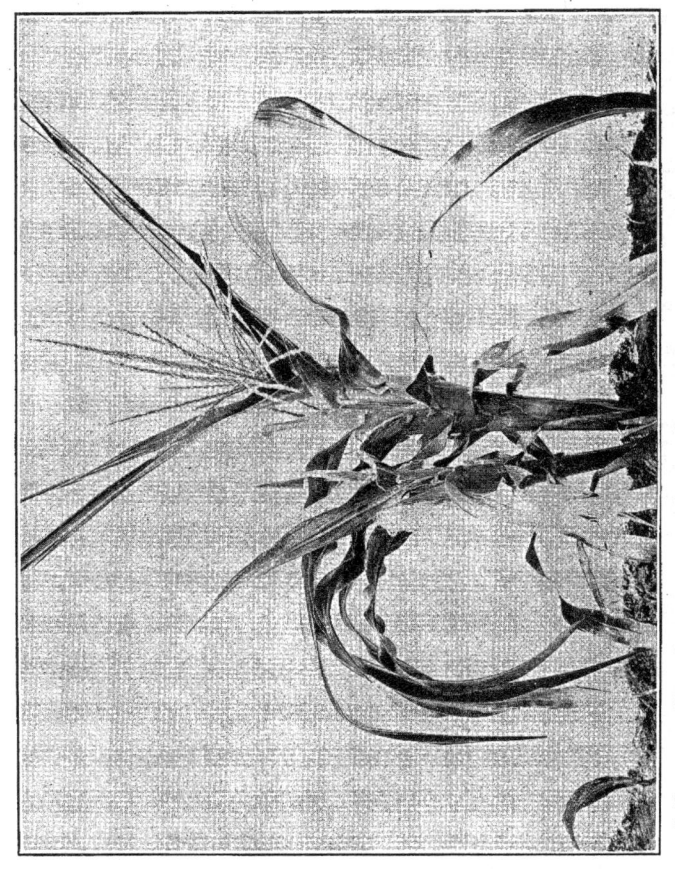

A BRACHYTIC CORN PLANT FROM THE SECOND GENERATION OF THE BRACHYTIC-BOONE HYBRID.

This plant produced the longest leaves of any brachytic plant. In length of leaf it exceeded the average of the normal plants and is among the 30 plants which produced the longest leaves in any of the progenies.

THE SAME CORN PLANT SHOWN IN PLATE XI WITH THE LEAVES AND HUSKS
REMOVED TO SHOW THE CHARACTER OF THE INTERNODES.

Note the brachytic tiller.

AN "ADHERENT" VARIATION OF MAIZE WHICH APPEARED IN THE SECOND
GENERATION OF THE BRACHYTIC-BOONE HYBRID.

The upper leaves of such plants adhere as if glued, and the branches of the tassel are compacted into
a hardened mass. This variation has been found on plants of normal stature only.

UPPER SECTION OF AN ADHERENT CORN PLANT.

The tassel, the silks of the upper ear, and the contortions of the culm are shown.
(Nearly natural size.)

EARS OF CORN SHOWING TWO EXTREMES IN THE EXPRESSION OF THE STAMINATE
SPIKE CHARACTER IN THE FIRST GENERATION OF THE BRACHYTIC-BOONE
HYBRID.

Note the few staminate spikelets about 6 centimeters from the tip on the ear at the right. (Slightly
reduced.)

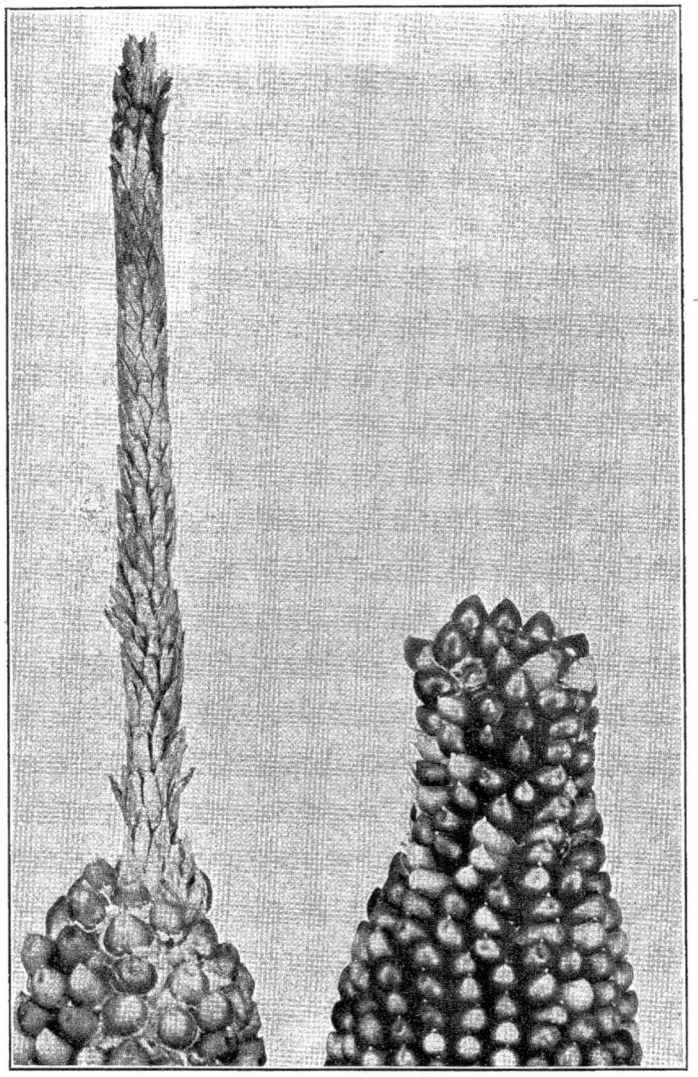

TIPS OF EARS OF CORN SHOWING THE EXTREMES IN THE EXPRESSION OF THE
STAMINATE SPIKE CHARACTER.

These ears are from the second generation of the brachytic-Boone hybrid. (Nearly natural size.)

not significant. The frequency distribution for height of plant is shown in figure 5.

In yield, as measured by the total ear length, neither the normal nor the brachytic F_2 plants equaled the first generation, but individual plants were obtained which yielded fully as well as the best

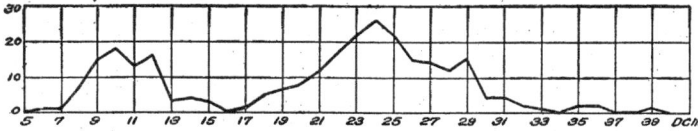

FIG. 5.—Frequency distribution of height of plant in brachytic × Boone, second generation.

of the F_1. With a sharp segregation into normal and brachytic plants and a failure to increase the variability of height in the segregated brachytic plants, the procedure to be followed in securing the desired combination of brachytic stature with high yield becomes greatly simplified and eventual success becomes more certain. It is necessary only to back cross the best yielding of the segregated brachytic plants upon the high-yielding commercial varieties and repeat the procedure until the desired combination is obtained.

While the mean length of ear of the brachytic segregates in the second generation of the brachytic-Boone hybrids is little, if any, greater than that of the 14 brachytic progenies, several plants were

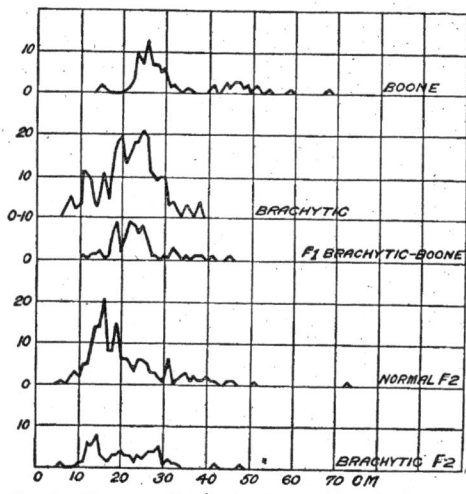

FIG. 6.—Frequency distribution for total length of ears on Boone, brachytic, Boone × brachytic F_1, and the normal and brachytic plants segregated in the brachytic × Boone F_2.

obtained which greatly exceeded in length of ear the directly descended brachytic plants (Pls. XI and XII). The frequency distributions for ear length are shown in figure 6.

The normal plants of the second generation exceed the brachytic plants not only in stature but also in the length of the longest leaf, in the number of rows on the upper ear, and in the length of the ear stalk. The brachytic plants, on the other hand, exceed the plants of normal stature in the number of branches in the tassel, the diameter of the culm, the total number of leaves, and the number of nodes that produce roots. The frequency distributions for the total number of nodes for the Boone, brachytic, and first and second generation hybrids are shown in figure 7.

The reduced length of the branching axis of the tassel of the brachytic plants clearly indicates that brachysm includes the termi-

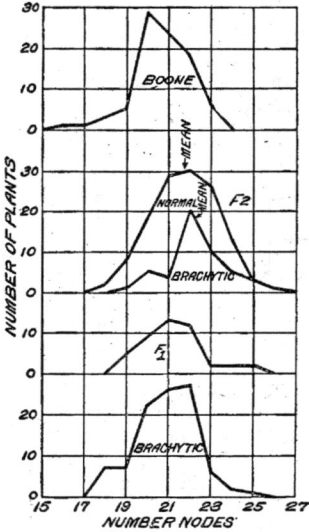

FIG. 7.—Frequency distribution for total number of nodes in .Boone, brachytic, Boone × brachytic F₁, and the normal and brachytic segregates in the F₂ of brachytic × Boone.

nal inflorescence. Although the length of the rachis from which branches arise is reduced, the total number of branches is increased. This increase is comparable to the increase in the number of nodes on the culm, which is coincident with reduced stature.

The abortion of the terminal inflorescence discussed on page 4 did not appear in the progeny of the . brachytic-Boone hybrid. As the evidence available thus far for this character indicates a Mendelian behavior, it would seem that the brachytic-Boone combination will be free from this defect.

It is an interesting fact that, although the longest internodes on brachytic plants are less than one-third the length of the longest internodes on normal plants, the length of the longest leaf sheath is not reduced on the brachytic plants, nor is the position of the sheath altered.

There is a correlation of 0.434±0.047 between the length of the leaf sheath and the length of the internode on normal plants, indicating a definite tendency for the sheaths to cover the internodes. Curiously enough, however, the longest leaf sheath does not inclose the longest internode, but on the contrary is produced, on the average, four internodes below the longest internode. That the correlation is no closer than 0.434 is not surprising, since the length of internodes on plants of normal stature is so largely determined by environmental conditions and may be altered at a comparatively late date, while the dimensions of the sheath are relatively constant.

While there is a definite relation between the length of internodes and sheaths on normal plants, this relationship is not found on brachytic plants. On these plants the coefficient of correlation between these characteristics is but 0.036 ± 0.097, indicating complete independence in the size of these two organs.

Since the length of the longest sheath has the same range and variability in both brachytic and normal plants, the absence of a correlation with length of internode on the brachytic plants indicates that the variability in internode length on these plants is due to environmental rather than inherited differences.

TERATOLOGICAL VARIATIONS.

Although brachysm is commonly accompanied by other abnormal manifestations, only two teratological forms have been observed in the progenies of brachytic-normal maize hybrids. One of these abnormalities is ears which end in staminate spikes. This abnormality has been observed frequently in strains not involving brachysm and therefore may be considered as having appeared incidentally in these hybrid progenies, with no direct relation to the brachysm of the culm.

The other variation is entirely new in our experience, and while there is no evidence to indicate that it is caused by brachysm it seems desirable to record briefly the more general features of its inheritance. In this variation the leaves adhere to one another as if glued (Pl. XIII). With many plants the upper leaves are affected most severely, but the seedling leaves also are subject to the abnormality.

Seedlings in which this peculiarity is pronounced fail to develop, and even those plants which exhibit the character in a minor degree produce but little seed. When the variation makes its appearance relatively late in the life of the plant the upper leaves adhere so firmly that the culm is forced into many contortions in attempting to elongate. In some instances the ear-bearing node is involved, in which case the ear also is contorted. The branches of the tassel are compacted into a solid structure which in expanding bursts through the confining blades and sheaths (Pl. XIV). The spikelets are adversely affected and become shortened and twisted. In view of the nature of this variation it has been designated "adherence."

The variation appeared in two second-generation progenies of the brachytic-Boone hybrid, but in none of the other progenies involving brachytic. In these two progenies the percentage of total plants that were adherent was 19.1 ± 1.85. The adherent variation was, however, confined to plants of normal stature, and the percentage of adherent among the nonbrachytic plants was 23.9 ± 2.1. The nature of the abnormality was such that the stature of the adherent plants was reduced, but there can be no question that the variation appeared only on plants genetically of normal stature. This is well demon-

cult to differentiate from the rachis of the tass
always well below the ear, and hence below the ‸
adherent plants.

If the adherent variation is considered as bei
factor, completely coupled or linked with norm:
adherent plants should be 25 per cent of the total.
percentage is 19 ± 1.85. While this deviation seer
of the variation is such that many of the plants
in the seedling stage and doubtless escape notic
of adherent plants necessitates the assumption th
recessive to the normal condition, and if the a
perfect linkage with normal stature is correct,

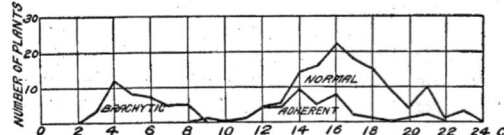

FIG. 8.—Frequency distribution of the length of the longest iı
ternode on brachytic, adherent, and normal plants from tɧ
second generation of brachytic × Boone.

spect to both characters, and in the second gene
be three classes of plants in the proportion of on
and adherent, two normal in stature and nor
brachytic and nonadherent. The Boone plant
with brachytic must have been heterozygous for ɛ
wise it would have exhibited this character. T
enies of one-half of the F_1 plants should have
plants adherent. As yet only three progenies ha
two have exhibited the variation, but 30 additioı
ears remain to be tested.

EARS ENDING IN STAMINATE SPIKES

The staminate spike variation was found not
brachytic hybrid but also in some of the othe
hybrids. The ears in this variation terminate in
ing several rows of paired staminate spikelets. ꓔ
of these staminate spikelets, in the cases where
mined with reasonable accuracy, is usually less ꜜ
rows of seeds upon the ear.

The character is extremely variable in expressi
second generation of the Boone-brachytic hybri

ears were found with staminate spikes ranging from 15 cm. in length to those with just a few scattered spikelets near the tip or with only a disorganized area where spikelets failed to develop, leaving a bent and deformed ear. The range of variation in the Boone-brachytic hybrids is shown in Plates XV and XVI.

The variation is one which is found frequently in maize in several forms. The nature of its inheritance has not been reported, but that it is heritable seems certain.

While neither the Boone nor the brachytic parent plants produced ears with staminate spikes, many plants of the first generation produced such ears. The exact ratio in the F_1 was 17 with staminate tips to 63 normal. This is a very close approximation to a Mendelian monohybrid ratio, where the variation is recessive to the normal form of the ear. To secure such a ratio in an F_1, it may be assumed that both parents were heterozygous for the character involved. The same result would be obtained if normal ear form were the result of two dominant independent factors with the brachytic parent heterozygous for both of these factors and the Boone parent homozygous for one dominant factor and heterozygous for the other. On this latter hypothesis the progeny of the self-pollinated brachytic parent would have 43.75 per cent of the plants bearing ears terminating in staminate spikes, while the self-pollinated Boone parent would give 25 per cent of the progeny with such ears.

Of the nine hand-pollinated ears obtained from brachytic plants, six were the result of self-pollination, the other three representing crosses between sister plants. Only one progeny grown from these nine ears exhibited the staminate spike character. This progeny was from a self-pollinated ear. Ears were produced by 36 plants, 20 of which had staminate spikes that ranged in length from 2 to 12 cm. The average length was 6.55±0.52 cm. The percentage of plants having staminate spikes (55.5±5.6) is very close to that for a Mendelian dihybrid, where the character is the result of the combination of two dominant factors and the parent plant is heterozygous for both of them. As in all the second-generation progenies in which this character reappeared it behaved as a recessive character, the percentage of 55.5 may be considered a chance departure from 43.75. With the small number involved (only 36), the deviation of 11.75 per cent above the 43.75 is less than three times the probable error.

If the above explanation is correct, self-pollinated F_1 plants should give the following progenies: One all normal, three with 25 per cent of the plants with staminate spikes, two with 43.75 per cent of the plants with staminate spikes, and two with all the plants with staminate spikes. The last two, of course, would be recognized in the first generation, since they would result from self-pollinating plants exhibiting the variation.

If the hypothesis is correct that both the Boone and the brachytic parents were heterozygous for the variation, three classes of progeny should be obtained from self-pollinated F_1 plants, one class producing nothing but normal-eared plants, one with 25 per cent of the plants with staminate-spiked ears, and one with all the plants having ears with staminate spikes. The ratio in which these progenies should appear would be the familiar $1 : 2 : 1$.

As in the other hypothesis, the F_2 progenies which would have all the plants exhibiting the variation would be recognized in the F_1, since they would show the variation in that generation. Since only three self-pollinated progenies have been grown thus far, it is not possible to test crucially the two hypotheses. The F_1 progenies which furnished seed for the second generation were grown in the greenhouse. The ears produced by these plants gave no indication of staminate spikes, and it was only in the larger planting in the field that the variation appeared in the first-generation plants.

The three second-generation Boone-brachytic progenies were fairly consistent with respect to the percentage of plants that produced the variation, all three closely approximating 25 per cent with staminate tips. The variation obviously is detrimental, since the ears affected are reduced in length. Although the staminate spike is not developed entirely at the expense of the pistillate portion, the evidence from the Boone-brachytic hybrid indicates that the length of the ear is reduced about one-half the length of the staminate spike.

It is of practical interest, therefore, to determine whether this undesirable variation is associated with stature. In this respect the three Boone-brachytic progenies differ somewhat. All three progenies show that the gene, or at least one of the genes for staminate spikes, is located in the same chromosome with the gene for stature. In the present hybrid, staminate spikes are associated with normal stature, so that the improvement in yield of the brachytic variation is not threatened in these cases. It must not be overlooked, however, that by suitable crosses these correlations could be reversed, thereby increasing the percentage of brachytic plants with the undesirable staminate spike variation.

The three progenies exhibit varying degrees of closeness of the relationship of stature to staminate spikes on the ear, with an average correlation of 0.37 ± 0.112. Such a correlation coefficient indicates a rather loose linkage, but it is apparent that in some progenies this relationship might be very much closer. That such cases may be expected is shown by the F_2 of the brachytic-Hopi hybrid where the brachytic plants appeared in combination with the staminate spike character in half the cases. In this particular cross also the spikes were unusually well developed. (See Table IV.)

BRACHYTIC × HOPI.

The Hopi variety, in common with other varieties grown by the Indians of the Southwestern States, possesses the long mesocotyl, which permits deep planting. An attempt was made by crossing brachytic and Hopi to combine the brachytic stature with the deep-planting adaptation. The strain of Hopi used in this cross was particularly vigorous, with plants fully as tall as those of the Boone variety.

The first generation was a complete surprise and was practically worthless. The plants were tall but differed from all the other first-generation hybrids of which brachytic was one parent in that they were weak and soon lodged. The ears were small and the yield poor.

TABLE IV.—*Distribution of plants with respect to the staminate spike characters in the brachytic × Boone and brachytic × Hopi hybrids of maize, including plants of the first and second generations,*

Progeny designation.	Normal stature.		Brachytic stature.		Total.	Percentage.		Coefficient of association.[1]
	Normal ears.	Ears with ♂ spikes.	Normal ears.	Ears with ♂ spikes.		Brachytic.	Staminate spikes.	
Brachytic × Boone:								
Dh 436 W 2 L19, F₂	39	21	16	7	83	27.7	33.8	0.10±0.20
Dh 435 W 1 L19, F₂	51	20	27	5	103	31.0	24.3	.45±0.17
Dh 436 W 1 L19, F₂	48	18	18	0	84	21.4	21.4	1.0 ±0
Total	138	59	61	12	270	27.0	26.3	.37±0.112
Dh 436 F₁	63	17			80		21.3	
Brachytic × Hopi:								
Dh 438 W 1 L19, F₂	71	3	11	10	95	23.2	13.7	.91±0.04
Dh 438 F₁	20	2			22		9.1	

[1] The correlations are between normal stature and staminate spikes with the exception of the last one, which is a correlation between brachytic stature and staminate spikes.

The second generation was little better, and no good plants were found. The brachytic plants especially were poor, one-half of the plants having ears which terminated in the staminate spikes found in the brachytic-Boone hybrids and described on pages 20–22. In the Hopi hybrid, however, the staminate spikes were much longer in proportion to the length of the pistillate part. The magnitude of this difference between the pistillate and staminate parts is shown in Table V. In the other hybrids the staminate spikes on the ears of brachytic plants were no longer than those borne on sister plants of normal stature. The ears with staminate spikes in the Hopi hybrid contrasted sharply with the normal ears, and no gradations were found. In this respect they differed from the Boone hybrids, where

Character.	Dh 438F₁.	Dh 438F₂.		D
		Normal.	Brachytic.	
Height of plant...................decimeters..	25. 9±0. 28	23. 1 ±0. 28	10. 2 ±0. 23	1!
Length of longest tassel branch........centimeters..	28. 8±0. 62	12. 2 ±0. 14	5. 1 ±0. 25	
Length of branching space.....................do....	14. 7±0. 33	12. 5 ±0. 27	10. 4 ±0. 35	
Length of central spike........................do....	32. 6±0. 60	29. 1 ±0. 35	31. 3 ±0. 87	
Number of leaves:				
Above the upper ear.........................	4. 1±0. 07	23. 0 ±0. 40	22. 7 ±0. 56	
Total......	19. 4±0. 17	28. 9 ±0. 70	22. 1 ±1. 10	
Longest leaf:				
Length................................centimeters..	90. 5±1. 15	94. 6 ±0. 72	91. 5 ±0. 87	
Width...............................do....	8. 7±0. 14	8. 6 ±0. 09	8. 7 ±0. 16	
Number of tassel branches.........................	29. 8±0. 98	3. 79±0. 05	1. 50±0. 31	
Ear length:				
Upper ear....................centimeters..	19. 9±0. 47	16. 9 ±0. 31	10. 1 ±0. 67	
Total a.............................do....	21. 9±0. 78	20. 0 ±0. 53	21. 7 ±1. 2	
Number of rows on upper ear.......................	18. 8±0. 22	16. 6 ±0. 20	15. 2 ±0. 39	
Length of staminate spike.............centimeters..	....	b 2. 3	12. 3 ±1. 5	1

a The total ear length includes only the length of the pistillate portion on those ears which staminate spikes.
b Only three plants.

The brachytic plants of the Hopi hybrid also differed fro brachytic segregates of other hybrids in that the ears were bo the axils of the uppermost leaves, or in extreme cases appeared lowest branches of the terminal inflorescences. This tende have ears at the base of the tassel is one which has been ob often in plants of the Chinese waxy variety and also in hybr volving this type. (Pl. XVII.) Its appearance, therefore, brachytic-Hopi hybrid is not to be attributed to the same ς change which caused the reduction in length of internode culm, although its expression in this hybrid was confined to bra plants.

Like most variations in maize, this tendency is inherited. plants were grown from a self-pollinated ear of a Chinese which had produced ears at the base of the tassel. All seven o plants showed evidence of this trait. On three of these plai only symptom was a cluster of bracts at the base of the tasse plant, in addition to these bracts, had scattered pistillate spike the lower tassel branches; another plant similar to the pare veloped an ear at the base of the tassel; while the two rem plants both had ears borne in the normal position, but terminat staminate spikes.

The character is expressed in a variety of forms, sometim pearing simply as a group of pistillate spikelets at the base otherwise normal staminate branch, and at other times well-f ears with regular rows and not much smaller than those borne

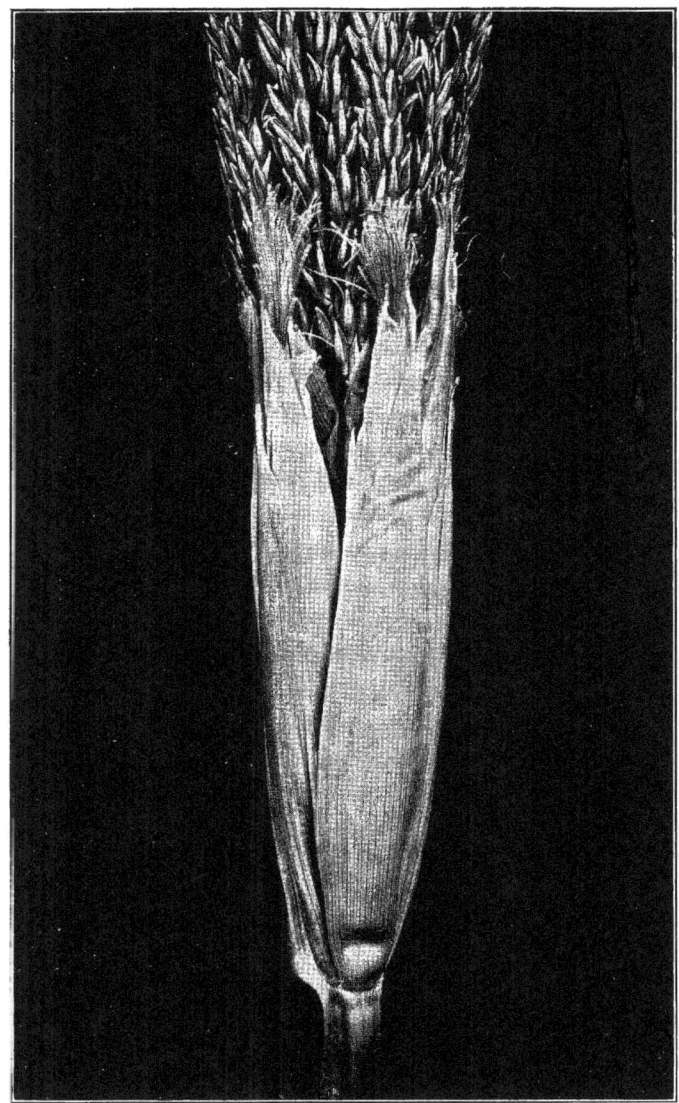

BASAL SECTION OF A TASSEL OF CHINESE WAXY MAIZE, SHOWING CLUSTER OF EARS.

(Natural size.)

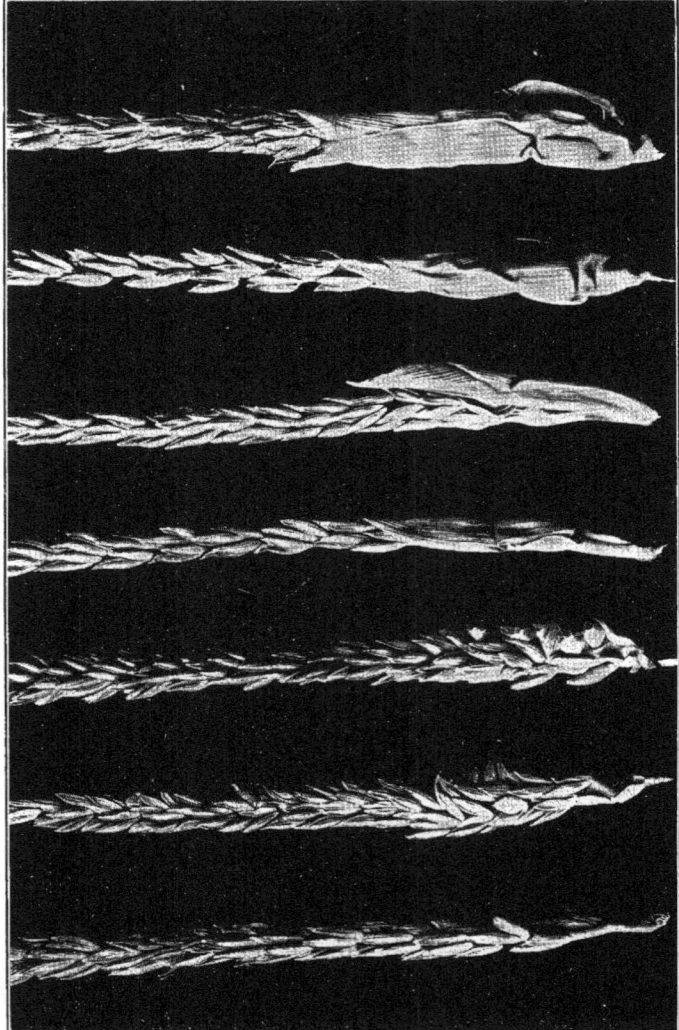

BRANCHES FROM THE TASSEL OF CHINESE MAIZE SHOWN IN PLATE XVII.

These branches show the transition from staminate to pistillate spikelets, the more advanced stages of which are shown in Plate XIX.   (Natural size.)

PLATE XIX.

EARS FROM THE TASSEL OF CHINESE MAIZE SHOWN IN PLATE XVII.

The bracts have been removed to show the gradations from pistillate to staminate branches. (Natural size.)

usual position are found. The intermediate stages between these well-formed ears and branches which have only a few pistillate flowers at the base closely resemble the ears that terminate in staminate spikes.

The pistillate branches, or ears, are clustered around the base of the tassel, the internodes being so short as to be indistinguishable from one another. (See Pl. XVII.) The transformation from male branches to ears is accomplished by a shortening of the rachis which is first noticeable at the base of the branch. In the advanced stages this shortening results in a crowding of the spikelets, which frequently is augmented further by a zigzagging of the rachis. In these cases there often is evidence of twisting. The spikelets in the early stages of the transformation of the branches are little altered, but with the added shortening of the rachis the glumes become reduced in length and gradually assume the characteristics of glumes on normal ears (Pls. XVIII and XIX).

While the tendency to have ears clustered at the base of the tassel is found on plants with normal internodes as well as on brachytic plants, the nature of the transformation from staminate to pistillate branches strongly suggests brachysm. Thus, there is an abrupt shortening of the main axis at the point where the branching occurs and also a marked shortening of the rachis of the branches, accompanied by a development of pistillate flowers. These changes are essentially those which took place in the development of the normal ear and are similar to those indicated in the brachytic plants of the Chinese-Algeria hybrid.

Taken in connection with the fact that half the brachytic plants of the Hopi-brachytic hybrid produced ears terminating in staminate spikes and that the brachytic plants had but few nodes above the ears, the close resemblance of tassel ears to ears in the normal position with staminate spikes suggests a possible origin of these staminate spikes.

Viewed in this light, the ear of maize may have developed not from a central spike of the terminal inflorescence of a lateral branch but from the transformation of the lower staminate branch of the terminal panicle into a pistillate branch. If this hypothesis is adopted, the sterile nodes which intervene between the pistillate and staminate inflorescences are not so difficult to explain and become with the ear a part of the terminal inflorescence.

The lower branches of the tassel occasionally develop into replicas of normal plants and even more frequently are subtended by bracts. These lower branches are relatively unstable, being the first to develop pistillate flowers, and the number of rows of spikelets often exceeds four. This increase in the number of rows may arise through the reduction of secondary branches or perhaps from a zigzagging of the rachis and subsequent twisting of the saddlebacks, as suggested by Collins (2).

The occurrence of ears at the base of the tassel and their restriction to brachytic plants suggests a relationship between these plants and the tassel-ear variation (6). Although the resemblance is not marked, the variation is in much the same direction, and seems to emphasize the association of brachysm with the development of pistillate flowers. Economically the combination of brachytic with Hopi has been a complete failure, and demonstrates the impracticability of predicting the value of a hybrid from the characteristics of the parents.

CONCLUSIONS.

Heritable variations occur frequently in maize. Few of these variations are of economic value and most of them are undesirable. One of the most frequent variations is a marked reduction in stature. A reduction in stature which affects only the length of the internodes while the other organs remain unaltered in size or number is known as brachysm. Such variations have appeared not only in maize but also in cotton, beans, peas, squashes, oats, wheat, and tomatoes, where some of them have been utilized by breeders to establish "bush" strains.

While brachytic maize plants are not of value directly for "bush" qualities, the reduction in stature produces a plant which seems admirably adapted to dry-land and irrigation culture.

The shortening of the internodes places more nodes in contact with the ground and thereby increases the number of primary roots. The plants in consequence of the short stature and highly developed root system are exceptionally sturdy, while the leaves are brought close together, thus effecting a partial shade.

The yield of the brachytic variation as compared with the varieties of the corn belt is low, but the reduced stature, sturdy erectness, and increased root development offer advantages for extreme conditions which may outweigh consideration of yield. Hybrids have been made with high-yielding strains in an effort to improve the yield of the brachytic plants, and a successful combination seems assured. Brachytic stature apparently reappears uncontaminated in the perjugate generations of hybrids with varieties of normal stature. This fact makes it possible to obtain rapidly the desired combination of yield and stature by repeatedly "back crossing" the high-yielding brachytic plants on high-yielding normal plants.

Only two teratological forms have appeared in the hybrids between brachytic and normal plants. One of these variations has not been observed previously, while the other is relatively common in many nonbrachytic strains.

The new variation appeared in the perjugate generation of the brachytic-Boone hybrid. This variation has been designated " adherence." It seems to be completely associated with normal stature and therefore offers no obstacle to securing the combination of high yield and short stature.

The other variation has appeared in several hybrids with brachytic. In this variation the ears terminate in staminate spikes. These spikes, to a certain extent, develop at the expense of the pistillate portion and therefore are undesirable. This variation also appears to be associated with stature, indicating that the genes for these characters are located in the same chromosome. The amount of crossing over, however, is relatively large, so that no difficulties are expected in obtaining brachytic plants of high yield free from this defect.

The close relation of ears terminating in staminate spikes to ears borne as basal branches of the terminal inflorescence is indicated in a hybrid between brachytic and Hopi. The evidence from this hybrid suggests that the ear of maize may have developed from the basal branches of the terminal panicle rather than from the central spike of the terminal inflorescence of a lateral branch of the main culm.

LITERATURE CITED.

Collins, G. N.
(1)   1916. Correlated characters in maize breeding. *In* Jour. Agr. Research,
        v. 6, No. 12, pp. 435–453, pl. 55–63. Literature cited, pp. 452–453.

(2)   1919. Structure of the maize ear as indicated in Zea-Euchlaena hybrids.
        In Jour. Agr. Research, v. 17, No. 3, pp. 127–135, pl. 16–18.

(3) —— and Kempton, J. H.
        1920. A teosinte-maize hybrid. *In* Jour. Agr. Research, v. 19, No. 1, pp.
        1–38, pl. 1–7.

(4) Cook, O. F.
        1915. Brachysm, a hereditary deformity of cotton and other plants. *In*
        Jour. Agr. Research, v. 3, No. 5, pp. 387–400, pl. 53–62.

(5) East, E. M., and Hayes, H. K.
        1911. Inheritance in maize. Conn. Agr. Exp. Sta. Bull. 167, 142 p.,
        25 pl. Literature cited, pp. 138–142.

Emerson, R. A.
(6)   1912. The inheritance of certain "abnormalities" in maize. *In* Ann.
        Rpt. Amer. Breeders' Assoc., v. 8, pp. 385–399, 7 fig.

(7)   1920. Heritable characters of maize. II. Pistillate-flowered maize
        plants. *In* Jour. Heredity, v. 11, No. 2, pp. 65–76, illus.

(8) Gernert, Walter Byron.
        1912. The Analysis of Characters in Corn and Their Behavior in Trans-
        mission. 58 p., illus. References, pp. 56–58.

(9) Hartley, C. P.
        1903. Improvement of corn by selection. U. S. Dept. Agr. Yearbook,
        1902, pp. 539–552, pl. 71–77.

(10) Kempton, J. H.
        1919. Inheritance of spotted aleurone color in hybrids of Chinese maize.
        In Genetics, v. 4, No. 3, pp. 261–274. Literature cited, p. 274.

(11)   1920. Heritable characters in maize. III. Brachytic culms. *In* Jour.
        Heredity, v. 11, No. 3, pp. 111–115, fig. 10–12.

(12) Leavitt, Robert Greenleaf.
        1909. A vegetative mutant, and the principle of homoeosis in plants.
        In Bot. Gaz., v. 47, No. 1, pp. 30–68, 19 fig.

Montgomery, E. G.
(13)   1906. What is an ear of corn? *In* Pop. Sci. Monthly, v. 68, No. 1, pp.
        55–62, fig. 1–14.

(14)   1911. Perfect flowers in maize. *In* Pop. Sci. Monthly, v. 79, No. 4,
        pp. 346–349, 6 fig.

28

UNITED STATES DEPARTMENT OF AGRICULTURE
BULLETIN No. 903
Contribution from the Bureau of Entomology
L. O. HOWARD, Chief

| Washington, D. C. | PROFESSIONAL PAPER | April 22, 1921 |

THE
GRAPE PHYLLOXERA IN CALIFORNIA

By

W. M. DAVIDSON, Scientific Assistant, and
R. L. NOUGARET, Entomological Assistant,
Deciduous Fruit Insect Investigations

CONTENTS

	Page		Page
California History	1	The Nymph and Winged Form	73
Accidental and Natural Spread	7	Nymphicals or Intermediate Forms	82
Distribution of Phylloxera in California	11	The Sexual Forms	90
Vineyard Destruction	15	The Gallicole and its Relation to Cali-	
Nomenclature and Synonymy of the		fornia Conditions	95
Grape Phylloxera	26	Effects of Water and Heat on Phylloxera	98
Biology of the Grape Phylloxera in Cali-		Diffusion of Phylloxera	100
fornia	27	Summary	122
The Radicicole	44	Literature Cited	127

WASHINGTON
GOVERNMENT PRINTING OFFICE
1921

UNITED STATES DEPARTMENT OF AGRICULTURE

BULLETIN No. 905

Contribution from the Bureau of Animal Industry
JOHN R. MOHLER, Chief

Washington, D. C. ▼ December 8, 1920

PRINCIPLES OF LIVESTOCK BREEDING

By

SEWALL WRIGHT, Animal Husbandry-Division

CONTENTS

	Page		Page
Evolution of Animal Breeding	1	Mendelian Heredity in Livestock	30
Reproduction	2	Heredity of Form and Function in Livestock	34
The Reproductive Cells in Relation to Heredity	11	The System of Breeding	42
Details of Hereditary Transmission	15	Methods of Selection	47
The Determination of Sex	23	The Value of Purebreds	54

WASHINGTON
GOVERNMENT PRINTING OFFICE
1920

UNITED STATES DEPARTMENT OF AGRICULTURE
BULLETIN No. 906

Contribution from the Bureau of Public Roads
THOMAS H. MACDONALD, Chief

Washington, D. C.   March 23, 1921

THE USE OF CONCRETE PIPE IN IRRIGATION

By

F. W. STANLEY, Senior Irrigation Engineer, with Introductory
Paragraphs by SAMUEL FORTIER, Chief of
Irrigation Division

CONTENTS

	Page		Page
Introduction	1	Laying Concrete Pipe	13
The Use of Pipe in Irrigation	2	Causes of Failure in Concrete Pipe	15
Incasing Old Pipes of Metal and Wood with Concrete	4	Pipe Systems for Irrigation	23
Concrete Pipe	4	Settling Basins and Screens	27
Reinforced Concrete Pipe	6	Air Vents	29
Manufacture of Plain Concrete Pipe	8	Relief Stands	30
Quality of Concrete Pipe	9	Measuring Devices for Pipe Irrigation Systems	31
Cost of Unreinforced Pipe	12	Distributing Hydrants	44

WASHINGTON
GOVERNMENT PRINTING OFFICE
1921

UNITED STATES DEPARTMENT OF AGRICULTURE

BULLETIN No. 907

Contribution from the Bureau of Entomology
L. O. HOWARD, Chief

Washington, D. C.   PROFESSIONAL PAPER   October 20, 1920

FUMIGATION OF CITRUS PLANTS WITH HYDROCYANIC ACID: CONDITIONS INFLUENCING INJURY

By

R. S. WOGLUM, Entomologist, Tropical and Subtropical Fruit Insect Investigations

CONTENTS

	Page
Introduction	1
The Effect of Hydrocyanic Acid on Plants	2
Details of Experiments	3
The Effect on Plant Injury of Temperature, Light, and Moisture before Fumigation	4
The Effect on Plant Injury of Temperature, Light, and Moisture after Fumigation	10
The Effect on Plant Injury of Temperature, Light, and Moisture during Fumigation	22
General Discussion of Factors which Influence Fumigation Injury	27
The Concentration of the Gas	28
The Length of Exposure	29
The Physiological Condition of the Plant	30
Atmospheric and Light Conditions	33
Summary	41
Literature Cited	42

WASHINGTON
GOVERNMENT PRINTING OFFICE
1920

UNITED STATES DEPARTMENT OF AGRICULTURE

BULLETIN No. 908

Contribution from the Bureau of Chemistry
CARL L. ALSBERG, Chief

Washington, D. C.　　PROFESSIONAL PAPER　　January 18, 1921

THE MAINE SARDINE INDUSTRY

By

F. C. WEBER

Chemist in Charge

With the collaboration of H. W. HOUGHTON and J. B. WILSON
Assistant Chemists, Animal Physiological Chemical Laboratory

CONTENTS

	Page
Introduction:	
The Sardine	1
The Maine Sardine Industry	3
The Maine Sardine	4
Food Value of the Canned Sardine	5
Purpose of Investigation	6
Methods Employed in Packing Sardines	6
Experimental Work:	
Methods of Analysis	12
Composition of the Sea Herring	15
Food of the Sea Herring	17
Swells	20
Transportation of the Fish	26
Pickling and Salting the Fish	34
Flaking the Fish	50
Drying the Fish	51

	Page
Experimental Work—Continued.,	
Packing the Fish	58
Adding the Oil	60
Processing the Sardines	69
Storing the Sardines	70
Decomposition of the Fish	86
Grading the Fish	93
Standardization of the Sardine Pack	96
Sanitary Precautions in Packing Sardines	98
Waste in Packing Sardines:	
Elimination of Unnecessary Waste	102
Utilization of Unavoidable Waste	109
Economic Considerations	115
Summary	121
Bibliography	125

WASHINGTON
GOVERNMENT PRINTING OFFICE
1921

UNITED STATES DEPARTMENT OF AGRICULTURE
BULLETIN No. 909

Contribution from the Forest Service
WILLIAM B. GREELEY, Forester

Washington, D. C.   PROFESSIONAL PAPER   January 17, 1921

UTILIZATION OF BLACK WALNUT

By

WARREN D. BRUSH, Scientific Assistant

CONTENTS

	Page
Introduction	1
Properties of the Wood	2
Insect and Fungus Attack	6
Supply	7
Demand	21
Utilization by Industries	22
Export	74
War-time Utilization	76
Summary of General Market Conditions	79
Marketing Walnut Timber	80
Summary and Conclusions	85
Appendix: Detailed List of Uses	88

WASHINGTON
GOVERNMENT PRINTING OFFICE
1921

EXPERIENCE OF EASTERN FARMERS WITH MOTOR TRUCKS

AN ANALYSIS OF 753 REPORTS FROM FARMER TRUCK-OWNERS

By

H. R. TOLLEY, Scientific Assistant, and L. M. CHURCH,
Assistant in Farm Accounting

CONTENTS

	Page
Summary	1
Method of Study	3
Location of Farms and Types of Farming	3
Distance to Market	4
Size of Truck	6
Age of Trucks	7
Are These Trucks Profitable Investments?	7
The Best Size	7
Advantages and Disadvantages	9
Road Hauling with Trucks	10
Road Hauling for Which Trucks are Not Used	13
Hauling on the Farm with Trucks	15
Custom Hauling	17

	Page
Effect of Different Kinds of Roads on Use of Trucks	17
Change of Market	19
Annual Use of Trucks	21
Life and Depreciation of Trucks	23
Repairs	24
Gasoline and Oil	26
Tires	27
Reliability	29
Cost of Operation	32
Cost of Hauling with Trucks	33
Saving of Hired Help	34
Displacement of Horses	35
Farms on Which Tractors are Owned	36

WASHINGTON
GOVERNMENT PRINTING OFFICE
1920

UNITED STATES DEPARTMENT OF AGRICULTURE

BULLETIN No. 911

Contribution from the Bureau of Entomology
L. O. HOWARD, Chief

Washington, D. C.　　　PROFESSIONAL PAPER　　　December 13, 1920

LIFE HISTORY OF THE GRAPE-BERRY MOTH IN NORTHERN OHIO

By

H. G. INGERSON

Scientific Assistant, Deciduous Fruit Insect Investigations

CONTENTS

	Page		Page
Method of Conducting Rearing Work	1	Seasonal-history Studies, 1917	7
Weather Conditions in 1916, 1917, and		Seasonal-history studies, 1918	24
1918	2	Miscellaneous Records	32
Seasonal-history Studies, 1916	2	Summary	37

WASHINGTON
GOVERNMENT PRINTING OFFICE
1920

UNITED STATES DEPARTMENT OF AGRICULTURE
BULLETIN No. 917

Joint Contribution from the Bureau of Plant Industry
WM. A. TAYLOR, Chief
and the
Office of Farm Management and Farm Economics
H. C. TAYLOR, Chief

Washington, D. C. ▼ March 11, 1921

FARM PRACTICE IN GROWING FIELD CROPS IN THREE SUGAR-BEET DISTRICTS OF COLORADO

By

SAMUEL B. NUCKOLS, Agriculturist, Office of Sugar-Plant Investigations, Bureau of Plant Industry, and
THOMAS H. SUMMERS, formerly Scientific Assistant, Office of Farm Management and Farm Economics

CONTENTS

	Page		Page
The Districts Studied	1	Manurial Practice	21
Method Used in Collecting Data	3	Cultivation	24
Soil Types of the Region	3	Irrigation	27
Climatic Conditions	4	Harvesting	33
Seasonal Distribution of Labor	6	Marketing	40
Farm Practice	11	Cost of Production	42
Preparation of the Seed Bed	12	Summary	51
Planting	19		

WASHINGTON
GOVERNMENT PRINTING OFFICE
1921

UNITED STATES DEPARTMENT OF AGRICULTURE
BULLETIN No. 918

Contribution from the Bureau of Entomology, L. O. HOWARD, Chief
in collaboration with the Federal Horticultural Board
C. L. MARLATT, Chairman

| Washington, D. C. | PROFESSIONAL PAPER | April 19, 1921 |

REPORT ON INVESTIGATIONS OF THE PINK BOLLWORM OF COTTON IN MEXICO

By

U. C. LOFTIN, Entomological Assistant, K. B. McKINNEY, Scientific Assistant, and W. K. HANSON, Plant Quarantine Inspector

CONTENTS

	Page			Page
The Laguna District	1	Dispersal		34
Distribution of the Pink Bollworm	4	Natural Control		38
Life History	5	Repression		47
Seasonal History	19	Summary		56
Feeding Habits of Larvæ	21	Literature Cited		57
Damage Caused by the Pink Bollworm	24	Appendix		58
Food Plants	32			

WASHINGTON
GOVERNMENT PRINTING OFFICE
1921

H. M. DIXON, Associate Farm Economist, and
H. W. HAWTHORNE, Assistant Farm Economist

CONTENTS

	Page		Page
Introduction	1	The Indiana Area	22
Sources and Character of Data	3	The Wisconsin Area	41
Summary	5	Good Management Increases Profits	55
The Ohio Area	7		

·UNITED STATES DEPARTMENT OF AGRICULTURE
BULLETIN No. 925

Contribution from the Bureau of Plant Industry
WM. A. TAYLOR, Chief

Washington, D. C.   PROFESSIONAL PAPER   February 18, 1921

A BRACHYTIC VARIATION IN MAIZE

By

J. H. KEMPTON
Assistant in Crop Acclimatization

CONTENTS

	Page
Definition of Brachysm	1
Review of the Literature	2
Origin and Description of the Variation	2
Inheritance of Other Brachytic Variations	6
Morphological Significance	8
Associated Changes	9
Agricultural Advantages	11
Inheritance of Brachysm in Hybrids with Commercial Varieties	14
Conclusions	26
Literature Cited	28

WASHINGTON
GOVERNMENT PRINTING OFFICE
1921

CPSIA information can be obtained
at www.ICGtesting.com
Printed in the USA
BVHW072140231118
533618BV00054B/576/P